WOODROW WILSON

WOODROW WILSON

From the portrait by Seymour Thomas hanging in the office of the Governor
of New Jersey

ARTHUR WALWORTH

WOODROW WILSON

Third Edition

W · W · NORTON & COMPANY · INC · NEW YORK

To Betsy Ross,

and a little "Miss Ellie Lou"

Library of Congress Cataloging in Publication Data
Walworth, Arthur Clarence, 1903– .
  Woodrow Wilson.
  Bibliography: p.
  Includes index.
    1. Wilson, Woodrow, Pres. U. S., 1856–1924.
  2. Presidents—United States—Biography. 3. United
States—Politics and government—1913–1921.
E767.W34 1978   973.91′3′0924 [B]   78–8706

ISBN 0-393-07533-8
ISBN 0-393-09012-4 pbk.

1 2 3 4 5 6 7 8 9 0

ACKNOWLEDGMENT

SINCE THE DAY, some thirty years ago, when Professor Arthur M. Schlesinger, Sr., spoke of the need for a biography of Woodrow Wilson suitable for his students, I have sought the aid of many men in the writing of one that would serve that purpose and interest other readers as well. The response has been generous and stimulating.

Professor Allan Nevins gave advice and encouragement at a time when the drawing together of the threads of research seemed a task almost insuperable. Stewart Mitchell, Director of the Massachusetts Historical Society, read the manuscript and offered constructive criticism. Certain chapters have been read and criticized by Helen Woodrow Bones, Louis Brownlow, Homer S. Cummings, Marjorie Brown King, Eleanor Wilson McAdoo, Bliss Perry, Sir William Wiseman, Professor Harvey Wish, and Robert W. Woolley.

My debt to President Emeritus Charles Seymour, who many years ago quickened my interest in history by his lectures, has been compounded by the patient and stimulating criticism that he has given freely.

The Woodrow Wilson Foundation has made it possible for me to extend my research and to have necessary secretarial assistance. Mrs. Julie d'Estournelles, Executive Director of the Foundation, has been most helpful in introducing me to the books and pamphlets collected by that organization.

My obligations to those who assisted me in the various libraries in which I have delved are too numerous to detail. The constant solicitude of Mrs. Zara Powers of the Yale University Library and of Laura E. Turnbull, Dr. Henry L. Savage, Alexander P. Clark, and Julie Hudson of the Princeton University Library was invaluable in exploring the large collections relating to Wilson in those institutions. As to Ray Stannard Baker and to many other writers, Katharine E. Brand has given help far beyond the call of duty. I am indeed fortunate to have had her guidance in approaching the vast collections in the Library of Congress, and particularly the Ray Stannard Baker Papers and the Wilson Collection itself, to which Mrs. Woodrow Wilson kindly granted access.

For sharing with me their recollections of Wilson and his family, in an interview or by letter, or both, I am indebted to the following: Margaret Calloway (Mrs. B. Palmer) Axson, B. Palmer Axson, Jr., Bernard M. Baruch, Julian B. Beaty, Helen Woodrow Bones, Edward W. Bradford, Thomas W. Brahany, Edward M. Brown, Louis Brownlow, Charles Bryant, Vincent Burns, William C. Bullitt, Robert C. Clothier, Edward Capps, Viscount Cecil of Chelwood, Gilbert F. Close, Edwin G. Conklin, Edward S. Corwin, Jack Randall Crawford, Homer Cummings, Jonathan Daniels, Joseph E. Davies, John W. Davis, Cleveland E. Dodge, George Dunlop, Will Durner, Luther P. Eisenhart, Captain Fred J. Elder, Margaret Axson Elliott, Virginia McMaster Foard, Raymond B. Fosdick, Arthur Hugh Frazier, Millard Gamble, Lawrence H. Gipson, Joseph C. Grew, Mrs. Charles S. Hamlin, Lord Hankey, Mrs. Will Harbin, Mrs. George McLean Harper, Mrs. J. Borden Harriman, Edith Benham Helm, Herbert C. Hoover, James Hoover, Stanley K. Hornbeck, Margaret Flinn Howe, Florence Hoyt, Wade C. Hoyt, Andrew C. Imbrie, Warren Johnson, Hugh McNair Kahler, Albert Galloway Keller, George Dwight Kellogg, Benjamin King, Marjorie Brown King, Katharine Woodrow Kirkland, V. K. Wellington Koo, Arthur Krock, David Lawrence, Margaret Lawton, Walter L. Lingle, Philena Fine Locke, Breckinridge Long, Eleanor Wilson McAdoo, Francis C. MacDonald, Alice Wilson McElroy, Charles H. McIlwain, Fitz Hugh McMaster, Colonel George McMaster, David Magie, Charles D. Mahaffie, A. Howard Meneely, John Moody, T. H. Vail Motter, Mr. and Mrs. Charles G. Osgood, Frederick Palmer, Bliss Perry, Lewis Perry, William Phillips, William E. Rappard, Edith Gittings Reid, Henrietta Ricketts, Ross Rollins, Hallie Alexander Rounseville, Henry L. Savage, Francis B. Sayre, Beth Hibben Scoon, Robert Scoon, Ellery Sedgwick, Lucy Marshall Smith, Charles Seymour, Charles Skillman, Frances Snell, Arthur Sweetser, Charles L. Swem, Herbert Bayard Swope, Huston Thompson, F. M. Tibbott, Mr. and Mrs. Randolph F. Tucker, Charles Warren, Thomas J. Wertenbaker, Fitz William McMaster Woodrow, James Woodrow, Thomas R. Woodrow, Mr. and Mrs. Thomas Woodward, Robert W. Woolley, Florence Young. Many of the above have generously permitted me to read pertinent manuscripts that are in their possession.

Mrs. Woodrow Wilson has granted permission to quote from certain unpublished letters of her husband, and Mrs. Eleanor Wilson McAdoo has allowed me to draw upon letters of her mother. I owe a debt, too, to Jonathan Daniels for unpublished passages from the diary of his father; to Charles Seymour, Curator of the House Collection at the Yale University Library, for unpublished quotations from the diary of Colonel House; to Henry Cabot Lodge for permission to quote from unpublished letters written by his grandfather to John T. Morse, Jr.; to Joseph C. Hostetter for a quotation from a letter of Newton D. Baker; to Martha Dodd Stern for permission to use the papers of her father, William E. Dodd, and to quote from them; and to Charles P. Taft for permission to quote from a letter of his father.

QUOTATIONS OF THE FOLLOWING WORKS HAVE BEEN PRINTED WITH THE PERMISSION OF THEIR PUBLISHERS:

Woodrow Wilson, by Ray Stannard Baker; *Eight Years with Wilson's Cabinet*, by David F. Houston; and *Unfinished Business*, by Stephen Bonsal, all copyright by Doubleday and Company.

The Intimate Papers of Colonel House, arranged as a narrative by Charles Seymour; and *Crowded Years*, by William G. McAdoo, both copyright by Houghton Mifflin Company.

My Memoir, by Edith Bolling Wilson, copyright 1938, 1939 by The Bobbs-Merrill Company; *Memoirs*, Vol. I, by Herbert C. Hoover, copyright by The Macmillan Company; *Woodrow Wilson*, by Edith G. Reid, copyright by the Oxford University Press; *Rebel at Large*, by George Creel, copyright by G. P. Putnam's Sons; *American Chronicle*, by Ray Stannard Baker, copyright by Charles Scribner's Sons; *The Wilson Era*, by Josephus Daniels, copyright by the University of North Carolina Press; *Brandeis, A Free Man's Life*, by Alpheus Mason, copyright by The Viking Press; *Letters of Theodore Roosevelt*, edited by Elting Morison, published by the Harvard University Press.

Permission has been given by Brandt and Brandt to quote from *The Letters of Franklin K. Lane* and by Charles P. Taft to quote from Pringle's *William Howard Taft*.

FOREWORD TO THE THIRD EDITION

MORE THAN FIFTY YEARS have now passed since Woodrow Wilson died in his house on S Street while citizens knelt in reverence on the walks outside. During this span of time the clouds of prejudice have somewhat receded, and the contemporary and post-mortem commentaries on his life have fallen into their niches in the grand historical edifice that is a-building. At the same time the light of documentation has grown stronger.

In view of the limitations of the point of view of both friends and foes of this man who loved and scorned strenuously, their testimony cannot be accepted uncritically. The task of evaluating it is made the more difficult by the varied and often contradictory aspects of Wilson.

It is possible that the ultimate historical image of the man will not differ greatly from the picture of himself that he gave to his intimates. Accustomed to brood introspectively in his youth, he heeded the injunction: "Know thyself." He spoke often about the war between his Scottish blood and his Irish blood. We learn from his own words of his "one-track mind," his dependence upon the grace of God and the graciousness of ladies, his affinity with life in the South, and his concept of his duty as a "leader of men."

Writing as an undergraduate to his father, he confessed himself "a queer fellow" and analyzed himself with an objectivity and clarity rare in one so young. His love letters are filled with frank revelations of self, and he was accustomed to confess his thoughts to sympathetic lady friends. This habit did not escape his self-scrutiny.

Biographers of Wilson are fortunate in having a huge store of personal letters in which he revealed his great heart and high spirits as well as the concerns of his mind. Although not all of this correspondence was available when this biography was written, the writer was able to see typical examples of each file. In 1962 Eleanor Wilson Mc-Adoo published, in a volume entitled *The Priceless Gift,* selections from letters exchanged between Woodrow and Ellen Axson Wilson. In 1963, after the death of Edith Bolling Wilson, another large collection of intimate family letters was found in the Washington home of the Wilsons. Still other fugitive manuscripts have been captured by the editors of *The Papers of Woodrow Wilson,* and some of these appear or will appear in the volumes of this comprehensive series (see page 426 of Volume II).

In 1977 the Library of Congress released a file that is of vital importance to historians as well as to biographers. It consists of hundreds of letters that passed between Wilson and Edith Bolling Galt before their marriage in 1915, as well as several written later on the few occasions when they were separated. Under the terms of Mrs. Wilson's gift, the text of letters written by her husband is to be printed first in *The Papers of Woodrow Wilson.* Excerpts from the letters of Mrs. Wilson will be found in this biography.

The correspondence of 1915 illuminates the depths of their understanding as well as the extraordinary vitality of Wilson. The letters throw light on his official business and his relationships with Ambassador Bernstorff and Secretary of State Bryan during the days of the crisis precipitated by the sinking of the *Lusitania.* Of first importance is the revelation of the opinion that Edith Galt Wilson formed of Colonel House at the very beginning of their acquaintance—an opinion that was impulsive and superficial and that Wilson refused to accept until, at the Paris Peace Conference in 1919, worn down by the cares of state and by severe illness, and distressed by indiscretions of House and his family, he finally capitulated.

With the Wilson–Galt letters before me I have rewritten Chapter XXV. It is my hope that this revision and a few minor changes will make this volume, which does not pretend to serve as definitive history, more satisfactory as a biography of a great but flawed prophet.

ARTHUR WALWORTH

New Haven, 1978

CONTENTS

BOOK ONE: *American Prophet*

I	A Boy Finds God Amidst Civil Strife	1
II	A Student Commands His Own Development	18
III	Amateur in Life	29
IV	Noticeable Man	45
V	Family Man	70
VI	University Pastor	84
VII	Voice in the Wilderness	98
VIII	Principles, Not Men	116
IX	From Campus to Political Arena	140
X	Fall of an Old Regime	162
XI	"Prime Minister" of New Jersey	181
XII	Candidate for the Presidency	200
XIII	Choice of The Democracy	222
XIV	Winning the Presidency	235
XV	Time to Think	254
XVI	At Home in the White House	262
XVII	Revolution in a Democracy	287
XVIII	Banking and Currency Reform	300
XIX	Clarifying the Antitrust Laws	322
XX	Moral Frontiers Abroad	342
XXI	Philistines in Mexico	358
XXII	A Foreign Policy Takes Shape	377
XXIII	In the Valley of the Shadow	393

XXIV Carrying on Alone   408

XXV A Lonely Man Finds a Comrade   426

Book Two: *World Prophet*

I The War Strikes Home   1

II The Prophet Hears the Voice of the Lord   25

III Keeping His Powder Dry   41

IV Caught in the Web of War   67

V Leading a United People into Conflict   86

VI Call of Arms   101

VII "We Are No Longer Provincials"   123

VIII The War of Ideas and Words   137

IX "Force without Stint or Limit . . . Righteous and Triumphant"   157

X Building for a Wilsonian Peace   176

XI Party Battles   199

XII The New World Comes Back to Redeem the Old   216

XIII Making a Covenant for the Twentieth Century   236

XIV The New World Grows Old   261

XV Revelation and Revolution   282

XVI The Peace Is Signed   306

XVII Challenge to America   333

XVIII Last Appeal to the People   355

XIX Pulling Down the Temple   374

XX Latter Days   395

XXI Reconciliation   410

A Note on Sources   423

Index   427

Book One

AMERICAN PROPHET

CHAPTER I

A Boy Finds God Amidst Civil Strife

During the year 1856 the political atmosphere of Europe was cleared, temporarily. The swords of national ambition that had let blood in the Crimea were returned to their scabbards at the Congress of Paris.

In the Hall of Clocks at Versailles a group of diplomats of the old school, dignified by high collars, black stocks, and side whiskers, faced one another around a velvet-topped table and invoked the principle of legitimacy—"*long live the* status quo." Undercover, the old game of power politics went on. Lobbyists, male and female, plied their trade. Intrigue was carried into the theater, the drawing room, even into the boudoir. Finally, after a month of plot and counterplot, one of the delegates at Versailles remarked: "Everybody is on edge. It is time to sign." And so a feather was plucked from a black eagle in the Jardin des Plantes, and a quill from it was used in signing a few of the twenty-eight documents of peace. A hundred and one guns boomed from the Hôtel des Invalides, and Europe was at peace!

It was a compact between haughty nations that held themselves above the moral standards that rule ethical individuals; and it brought to Europe a fragile truce that was destined to last but three years. To be sure, tenuous provision was made for containment of Russian expansionism and four "maxims" were set forth to strengthen the rights of neutrals on the high seas in time of war. These measures marked some progress toward the rule of national appetites by law, and within a year more than forty nations approved the Declaration of Paris. But the young United States stood out for complete freedom of the seas, contending that the maxims did not go far enough, that all innocent private property should be immune on the oceans of the world.

Europe's political resources had been running out. The years 1830 and 1848 had been darkened by barricades and bloodshed, and now the Continent was to sink into the morass of the hundred-year feud between France and Germany. In the mills, workers were ground fine on the wheels that were turning for the glory of Empire—or because of it. On the land, peasants bowed to the czar's manifesto: "Listen, ye heathen, and submit, for with us is God." Men lost faith in Europe and put their trust in the New World across the Atlantic. They saved and borrowed, sold some of their possessions, stowed some about their persons, and set their faces toward the west. Millions of them went, in the eighteen-fifties.

Among those who migrated in large numbers were the Scotch-Irish. Another wave of these restless folk had reached the American shore early in the eighteenth century and had broken into the Shenandoah Valley in the colony of Virginia. There they had laid off the town of Staunton as the seat of a territory that stretched from Pennsylvania to the Carolinas—a fertile, cloud-kissed region that George Washington called "the garden of America."

In 1856, Staunton was a town of some three thousand souls, most of whom had Scotch-Irish blood. It was a community always astir, a market for the farms of Augusta County. The inhabitants were vigorous folk, taking a lavish yield from the well-watered grasslands and fashioning articles from the coal and iron that the region provided. Public life in this county seat revolved about the courthouse, the schools, and the several churches: Catholic, Baptist, Lutheran, Methodist, and oldest and most aristocratic of all, Episcopalian, in which the legislature of Virginia had taken refuge during the darkest hours of the American Revolution. The intellectual tone of the town, however, was set by the Presbyterians, who worshiped on a hillside, in a brick church with a Grecian façade.

Next door was the Augusta Female Seminary, which was preparing to take in boarding pupils in dormitories then abuilding. A school of high repute in the Presbyterian denomination, the seminary had been directed for the past year by one of its trustees, a young Scotch-Irishman named Joseph Ruggles Wilson. He was a hearty man whom his girls thought "not very strict—you could go walking without a teacher"; but he clung to the traditions of the school, training the young ladies to be homebodies rather than social butterflies, to cook well and lead charitable enterprises rather than to dance cotillions.

Dr. Joseph Wilson served also as pastor of the Presbyterian church and lived in its manse. This residence, built only ten years earlier, stood on a spacious corner lot, on a slope facing the kirk and the school. There, behind a shielding fence, the preacher's wife and two daughters dwelt in sanctuary, removed from the bustle of trade and traffic. The square brick house was painted white and had wide, pillared porches and large chimneys. Writing his sermons on a veranda at the back of the manse,

Joseph Wilson could look out over his wife's garden, over the roofs and chimneys of the town.

In the ground-floor chamber of the Wilson manse, near midnight on the third day after the Christmas of 1856, Jeanie Wilson gave to her Joseph his first son. They named him Thomas Woodrow,[1] after his maternal grandfather.

The baby was put into a well-fashioned crib and was cared for and fed by free Negroes who cooked in the cellar over an open fire, baked in a brick oven, and drew water from a well. Before the child was a month old, arctic winds swept down upon Staunton and drove snow through the cracks of less substantial houses. The town was cut off from the world for ten days. But in his snug home the infant was safe and warm, and grew larger and fatter than his sisters had been. In four months Jeanie Wilson was writing to her father that she had a baby whom everyone called "beautiful," and that he was "just as good as he can be," that Joseph's congregation was growing and there was "no desirable thing" that God had not done for her.

Her husband and children were life itself to Jeanie Wilson. From under wide brows her eyes looked out luminously, understanding and sympathizing with all that was good. Pursuing the ways of her Scottish ancestors and respecting Southern traditions of gentility, she kept her distance from worldly folk. She was not a "joiner" of church societies, was not content to let the Lord provide, but insisted on looking out for even the smallest needs of her dear ones. Her resentment against defamers of her clan was as fierce as a storm in the Highlands, and her self-respect as strong as her fealty. She was content to leave the foreign relations of the family in the hands of her aggressive husband.

Dr. Joseph Wilson liked to cut a figure in his little world. Squarely built, and not so tall as his son grew to be, he transfixed his hearers with fiery brown eyes and a long, straight nose that flexed at the tip. Side and chin whiskers and a heavy shock of hair framed his commanding face. He talked rather too much, and punned habitually. Once a parishioner, noticing dust or dandruff on his coat collar, remarked that his horse was better cared for than its owner, and the preacher retorted: "Yes. The reason is that I keep my horse and I am kept by my congregation." Occasionally his wit lashed unkindly at men whose intentions were better than their performances. As a young teacher he had once

---

[1] Through boyhood and college days, Woodrow Wilson signed his name "Thomas W. Wilson" and was called "Tommie." His mother was born "Janet" but came to be called "Jessie," and by her family "Jeanie."

felled an impertinent student with his fist. He was never a man to be ignored. Compelling in the pulpit and courtly in the parlor, he constrained men of the world to heed him; and his yielding little wife, too refined to laugh heartily at his boisterous jokes, listened well and managed a smile when courtesy required it.

Growing up under the eyes of this masterful man and dutiful lady, Tommie absorbed so much of domestic virtue that when he himself became a parent he was moved to bless God for his "noble, strong, and saintly mother" and for his "incomparable father."

The marriage of Joseph Wilson and Jeanie Woodrow had grown out of love at first sight and had been confirmed by the bonds of Scotch-Presbyterian faith. They were well fortified by inheritance to bear the chafe of life. For generations both Woodrows and Wilsons had made their own way among men, fighting not with money or swords but with words and the Word. Though quick to move about, they had clung tenaciously to moralities from which their words and acts sprang. Joseph's parents had come to America in 1807 from County Down in the North of Ireland, whither their ancestors had migrated from Scotland. They were a high-spirited couple—James Wilson a handsome, rollicking lad of twenty, and Anne Adams a homely, determined, humorless lass of sixteen; and they came to the New World not in pursuit of any cause or faith but simply to get on in the world.

Always restless, Grandfather James Wilson moved repeatedly westward: first across the Atlantic to Philadelphia—where he became a printer and an associate of William Duane, publisher of the rabidly Jeffersonian *Aurora*—then to Pittsburgh, into Ohio at Lisbon, and finally to Steubenville, where in 1815 he took charge of the *Western Herald and Gazette*. Under the masthead was printed: "Principles, not men." He was consistently antislavery and protariff.

Elected to the Ohio legislature, James Wilson held himself duty bound to vote as his constituents wished; but when proposed as a candidate for governor he was unacceptable because, it was said, his bold words marked him as "a conspicuous politician, one heretofore marked for assault and vilification." An opponent referred to him, in a private letter, as "Paddy Wilson." The editor spent his fervor in castigating his adversaries rather than in praise of the Lord: the non-Jefferson newspapers were scorned as "anything or nothing, some singing lullabies and others up for sale." He feared no power on heaven or earth except perhaps his wife, who induced him merely to attend the church to which she gave zealous allegiance.

Though not a lawyer, the editor was made an associate judge of the

Court of Common Pleas. Judge Wilson pioneered in many a local enterprise, becoming president of a turnpike company, taking part in promoting the building of the first bridge over the Ohio River, serving as a director of a bank, dabbling in real estate, and finally undertaking the building of a great house for his family of ten children. In the midst of this operation, however, he was seized by a fatal attack of cholera. His grandson Tommie never saw him; nor is there evidence that he ever knew churchgoing Grandmother Wilson, who capably managed her husband's business in his absences and had an intense moral pride that made her shut her heart implacably against a daughter who eloped.

From his mothers's clan, the Wodrows, Tommie Wilson received a faith no less compelling, though more gently manifested. The Wodrows had been distinguished for scholarship for three centuries. In Scotland many of the family were theologians or elders of the Presbyterian Church. For six generations at least one of them had been a minister. Some were writers, one was a famous editor, and almost all were jealous of their thoughts. The men were eloquent and gentlemanly; the women, soft-spoken and very feminine. Yet all had a sinewy moral rectitude, were afire with passion for Absolute Truth, and were zealous in propagating it as they conceived it. They were a stock hard as blackthorn, and sometimes as prickly.

Thomas Woodrow,[2] Tommie Wilson's grandfather, was disciplined rigidly in the classics and the theology of the kirk and went forth to proclaim the gospel in the Orkney Islands. Later he accepted a call to the pulpit of the Independent Church at Carlisle, England, and in doing so became the first of his line to move out of Scotland for four hundred years. With him he took a bride, Marion Williamson, whose ancestors were Highlanders; and she bore him eight children, Jeanie arriving in 1826.

In November of 1835, after a long pastorate at Carlisle, all the Thomas Woodrows sailed for America. Two months after setting out from Liverpool they landed at New York; but the mother was so shaken by the stormy voyage and by the severity of the American winter that she died five weeks later. Fortunately, however, her sister Isabella had accompanied the family and assumed the duties of a mother.[3]

[2] When Thomas Wodrow left Scotland, he changed the spelling of his name to "Woodrow" to conform with English pronunciation.

[3] Later Thomas Woodrow married her and had four more children. Jeanie lived in Chillicothe with her brother Thomas and her sister Marion at the time of her betrothal to Joseph Wilson; and these three formed strong bonds of fraternal devotion.

After a short term of missionary work in Canada, Dr. Woodrow went to Ohio and served as pastor of several churches, striving to maintain Glasgow standards of learning among Philistines. This short, dynamic preacher spoke with a burr that broadened with rising enthusiasm. He was a rock of conservatism, scholarly, most fervent in prayer. He went straight to the pith of the gospel; and his action, like his speech, was direct and vigorous. He instructed his children and grandchildren and encouraged them to converse well at table. He found recreation in solving mathematical puzzles; and the harder they were the more fun he had.

Woodrow Wilson was often to acknowledge the two strains that ran in his veins: that of the Woodrows—pure Scottish, scholarly, tenacious, gentle, modest; and that of the Wilsons—Scotch-Irish, boisterous and mercurial, loving drama, applause, and exaggeration. From both he inherited a capacity for ferocious devotion to his kin and to a Scotch-Presbyterian God.

It was of the pure Scottish blood of the Woodrows that Tommie was to become most proud. But feeling that there was a streak of Irish in his Wilson ancestry, he gave it free play when he wished to escape from his strait-jacket conscience. In his forty-fourth year, speaking with Hibernian extravagance, he was to prophesy before a gathering of proud Yankees that Scotch-Irish memorialists one day would record "how every line of strength in the history of the world is a line coloured by Scotch-Irish blood."

In the year of Woodrow Wilson's birth, while European statesmen were meeting at Versailles to patch the flimsy fabric of international law, Americans were agitating the causes of peace and justice. In the vestry of Dr. Wilson's church at Staunton one could hear excited whisperings about John Brown and "bleeding Kansas." Men lingered on the church steps to ask one another whether the issue of slavery could be settled without more bloodshed. Peace-loving folk were citing Charles Sumner's declaration of war against war: "Can there be any peace that is not honorable, any war that is not dishonorable?" And possibly some brother, deep in dissenting thought, was quoting a political essay of that year written by Parke Godwin: ". . . there can be no finality in politics, except in the establishment of justice and truth."

When the Civil War began, Tommie Wilson's father was preaching in the First Presbyterian Church of Augusta. Though born and bred in the North and the son of an abolitionist, Dr. Wilson accepted the political views of his parishioners; and when in 1861 the Presbyterian Church divided on the issues of the war and split into two factions, the Southern branch held its first General Assembly in the church at Augusta. Joseph Wilson became clerk of his sect—a position that he was to hold for thirty-seven years. Moreover, he served as a chaplain in the Confederate Army, and one Sabbath morning when a battle was impending, he sent his flock scurrying to the local ammunition factories to roll cartridges. Dr. Wilson kept slaves and had created a Sunday school for Negroes, but he did not venture to defend or to indict the institution of slavery. However, the North's denial of the right to secede grated on his independent spirit.

During the hostilities the Woodrows and the Wilsons were each a clan divided. Children of the frontier and the kirk rather than of North or South, their roots not fixed in any region, they went along with the political sympathies of their neighbors. But during the strife Joseph Wilson and his wife grew lonely for their clans, and in 1866 the tide of blood affection that had been dammed up for four years flowed freely once more. The pastor in Georgia wrote to his father-in-law in Ohio: ". . . my people will be greatly pleased to have you occupy my pulpit, even if you have voted the radical ticket! . . . I feel sure that you are mistaken with reference to some important points of existing differences between the two sections. But you, at least, are thoroughly honest in your convictions, and I honor you none the less for your expression of them. We can, as Christians, talk over these matters when we shall meet . . ."

With his own brothers and sisters in the North, however, Dr. Wilson found reconciliation more difficult. When he traveled to Ohio in 1866 for a gathering of the clan, the brothers, some of whom had fought for the North, fell to bickering about political principles. Though Tommie Wilson had some fifty first cousins, he became intimate with only a chosen few of his relatives, almost all on the Woodrow side.

Only a few of the war's events took root in the boy's memory. At the age of three, standing at the door of the manse in Augusta, he heard a strident voice yell: "Mr. Lincoln's elected. There'll be *war*!" Toddling into his father's study, he asked: "What is war?" That was the first occurrence in his life that he could remember; and another experience of the war years—that of standing beside General Lee and looking up into his face—was one that Tommie Wilson was to treasure all his life.

Dr. Wilson's church was used as a hospital for Confederate soldiers and, standing on the sidewalk, Tommie peered anxiously toward prisoners who were fenced within the churchyard. But the manse was a sheltered home, though the Wilsons ate unsalted cow-pea soup and plug tobacco was hoarded in the attic, and a little gold. The suffering of the family was not so great that they could not remember those whose needs were more dire: one Sunday during the war the doctor took up a collection to support missions in China.

The years of Reconstruction left their mark on Tommie. Jefferson Davis marched past the lad under guard of federal troops. The enemy occupied Dr. Wilson's church and the town was overrun with human derelicts. Glum prisoners, groaning casuals, Negroes on the loose, and marauding Yankees haunted Tommie up to the beginning of adolescence. What he observed at Augusta and in summers spent in Staunton —the efforts of his family and other good folk to preserve whatever was left of the virtues of their life—ground into the boy's marrow a sympathy that was never to leave him. He was able to say later that the only place in the country, the only place in the world where nothing had to be explained to him was the South.

In the manse at Augusta the Wilsons [4] had time and means for the good life. The children learned neither to crave nor to scorn money, but to ignore the pursuit of it. The minister of the First Presbyterian —the most active if not the most aristocratic of Augusta's churches— was a man of mark and substance. Yet, in spite of the duties of his office, time was reserved for occasions that were sacred to the family alone: daily prayers, with everyone kneeling; hymn singing, at dusk on Sundays and at other times; and long readings of fiction, especially of Dickens and Scott. The doctor would recline on the floor, his back against an upturned chair, while his wife sat erect and knitted and Tommie, lying flat on his back, was carried away by his father's voice and infectious laughter.

To his son, Joseph Wilson was preceptor, confessor, playmate. Dr. Wilson's mind worked with precision and to his son his expression seemed Godlike. In conversation he did not hesitate to pause in the middle of a sentence to conjure up *le mot juste*; and the boy marveled

---

[4] In 1856, the year of Thomas Woodrow Wilson's birth in Staunton, his sister Marion was six years of age and Annie Josephine Wilson was two. Another boy was born in 1866. He was called Joseph R. Wilson—not Joseph Ruggles Wilson, a name that the father reserved for himself alone. Marion married the Rev. Ross Kennedy, a Presbyterian minister in Arkansas. Annie married George Howe, M.D., of Columbia, S.C. Joseph R. became a political writer in Tennessee and editor of the Nashville *Banner*.

at his skill in producing it. Often during meals the table was piled high with intellectual fare—books that had been fetched to elucidate topics that were under discussion, reference works such as *Inquire Within, or Over Thirty-Seven Hundred Facts Worth Knowing*. From his father Tommie took many a drubbing at chess and a few at billiards. They did not play cards, however. In the manse a rigid line was drawn between tests of skill and games of chance.

Neither Tommie's father nor his mother, who resented having been forced to study Latin in her sixth year, hurried the formal schooling of their boy. Though he early learned many of the secrets of good talk and could join in the family's singing, he could not read with ease until he was eleven. He confessed to being lazy, intellectually. When finally he went to Professor Derry's "select classical school" to study Latin, history, writing, and bookkeeping, his work was below average, his attitude indifferent.

Yet the preacher thought his son's brain a gem worth polishing. Tommie learned more from him than most boys learn at school in their earliest years. Dr. Wilson devoted Sunday afternoon, in particular, to the cultivation of Tommie's mind; and at that time they talked like master and scholar of classical times, the father giving the boy, in digestible doses, what he had learned of the world, of literature, the sciences, and theology—imparting it all with humor and fancy. Then, on Mondays, the two usually went on an excursion into the shops of the city or into the neighboring country. Often these forays took in a cotton gin, or a mill, or the factories that made ammunition for the Confederacy. Tommie was told how corn was grown and ground, learned how power was generated and how it worked, and saw sooty-faced men who labored beside furnaces and darting sheets of flame.

After returning home the boy was quizzed about what he had seen and what he had been told. "Do you thoroughly understand?" he was asked; and when he replied "Oh, yes," he was told to put his ideas in writing. Then the father would pounce upon the paper that was handed to him: "What did you mean by that; did you mean such and such a thing?" And when Tommie said "Yes," his preceptor went on: "Well, you did not say it, so suppose you try again and see if you can say exactly what you mean, and if not we'll have another go at it." The boy was sent to the dictionary to get precise definitions, and he was coached in oral expression. "Learn to think on your feet," his father ordered. "Make your mind like a needle, of one eye and a single point. Shoot your words straight at the target. Don't mumble and fumble."

The boy was quizzed mercilessly on the books that he read, and father
and son together tried to improve upon the writings of Charles Lamb
and Daniel Webster. They played with words, and scored by speaking
in a novel or striking way.

There were readings, too, in the big leather-bound Bible. The doctor
penciled notes in the margins that interpreted the text in the language
of the day. His religion had no cant and was suffused with a love of
mankind that often overflowed sectarian bounds.

Young Tommie was exposed to the best that Augusta offered in religious education. In the Sunday school, of which Uncle James Bones
was superintendent, the boy memorized the Shorter Catechism. To his
roving mind this was as painful as formal schooling, and he did not
remember the words permanently.

Yet Tommie was a child of the kirk and it was always with him.
Often he rode in his father's buggy when the preacher made parish
calls. His favorite playground was the shady churchyard, inside a picket
fence that had been made by the hands of slaves. From the window of
his bedroom he could see the solitary white spire, pointing confidently
above the dark hackberry grove to the one true way. Even as he lay in
bed on summer evenings the strains of the organ soothed him. Music
affected his emotions: he would sometimes weep at the communion
service when moving hymns were sung.

While taking part in the daily events about him the lad sometimes
gave the impression that he was absorbed in something beyond the ken
of his fellows. Particularly at Sunday services he seemed to indulge in
the long, long thoughts of youth. Sitting in the family pew, four from
the front, his little legs dangling, his earnest face elevated toward the
pulpit so that the sharpness of his nose and chin impressed those who
sat near, Tommie's pride of kin swelled as his father mastered adult
minds, summoned doubters to acknowledge Christ as their Savior, or
charged the elders to take heed unto themselves and to *all* the flock.
If his father hesitated for a word, Tommie would silently supply one;
and if his word came forth from the pulpit, a thrill ran along his spine.
He noted the doctor's rare mistakes and brought them up for discussion
in the privacy of the manse, where father and son could laugh together
over each other's errors.

It was inevitable that a young lad who was spoken of as "Dr. Wilson's son" should feel that he was predestined to lead others. But how
could a slip of a lad who was always minimized by the diminutive
"Tommie" and never called "Tom," who was freckle-faced, wore

glasses, had a head that was awkwardly large at the back, and a finger that had been jammed out of shape—how could such a boy be a leader of playmates whose families were as distinguished as his own?

Before he was ten years old Tommie played much with girls. His mother would tell stories to the children, often from *The Talisman,* and with quiet determination Tommie would manage dramatizations. During the war years there were no toys or properties except those made at home. Broomsticks became Arab steeds, banners were made from scraps of yellow homespun daubed with charcoal, and coats of mail were fashioned out of skeletons of carpets that had been raveled of their wool for soldiers' mufflers. A euonymus bush was a medieval castle from which Christian maidens were boldly rescued. The boy's motive was usually succor, never revenge or ambition.

Sometimes Mrs. Wilson traveled north in the summer. Then the lad, seated firmly on his father's big horse, would ride out to the country to visit his aunt Marion Woodrow Bones. Her daughter Jessie was a tomboy and had an imagination equal to that of her cousin Tommie. Together they read Cooper's Indian tales and conspired in crime. Staining their skins with pokeberry juice, feathering their heads, and arming themselves with bows and arrows, they went deep into the pine woods and stalked pickaninnies, terrifying them with war whoops and whirling tomahawks. Jessie offered herself for scalping and burning by the big-chief cousin whom she idolized. Once she impersonated a squirrel up a tree, and that time Tommie made the mistake of hitting her with an arrow. She fell in a limp heap, unconscious but not seriously hurt; and he carried her to the house, remorsefully bawling, "I killed her! It's no accident. I'm a murderer!" The Woodrow conscience already had fastened itself upon him.

When he outgrew the company of girls Tommie took part in the normal pursuits of boyhood; and everything that he did, except studying, he did with intensity. There were ball games, bull-in-the-pen at recess, rides on bobtail streetcars, rooster fights, and games of hide-and-seek among the bales of cotton in a warehouse near school. One day he ran away to the circus, and on the way back he took the precaution of padding himself with cotton against the wrath of his teacher.

In these pursuits Tommie was just one of a gang, and his frustrations showed themselves in occasional moods and fits of temper that kept him from running constantly with his playmates. When the talk and play became too rough, he would withdraw shyly into the protection of his father and mother. But the instinct for leadership would not be downed; and finally the boy hit upon his *metier*. Though he could not excel physically, he found that, thanks to his father's coaching, he could talk better than the other boys.

In the Wilson back yard, only a few rods from the slave quarters, stood a little stable that had a hay loft. Up there, instead of tumbling and frolicking, Tommie organized a gang of boys into the "Lightfoot Club." Under a red picture of His Satanic Majesty torn from an advertisement, the minister's son prepared the constitution of the body, presided over the meetings, and insisted on the niceties of parliamentary procedure. His chums noted that he was deliberate in his speech and measured in his movements, and they listened to him even though he belonged only to the second baseball team. Thus he came to feel the thrill of mastering men with words.

Finally, in the autumn of 1870, the boyhood days in Augusta came to an end. Dr. Wilson resigned his pastorate and became a professor in the theological seminary at Columbia, the capital of South Carolina; and the Wilsons moved to a city that, only five years before, had been reduced to ruin by Sherman's troops. Indeed, the government of South Carolina was still in the hands of carpetbaggers and scalawags.

During the years in Columbia the boy found his God and learned to hate war and all its works. There he fell under the tradition of Henry Timrod, the poet and prophet who throughout the war had tried to keep alive a vision of universal peace but, dying in ravaged Columbia in 1867, had seen only "beggary, starvation, death, bitter grief, utter want of hope." Two-thirds of the buildings had been burned, leaving a wilderness of crumbling walls, naked chimneys, and unroofed pillars. The luxurious shade trees of what had been called the most beautiful of state capitals were reduced to charred trunks. In desolated gardens the fountains were dry, the basins cracked. Banks and insurance companies were insolvent. The most respected citizens were barred from public office; in the college, the professors were unpaid and the student body had shrunk from two hundred fifty to thirteen; the theological seminary was holding chapel services in a made-over stable, its faculty barely able to meet the needs of life. Freed Negroes had trailed Sherman's soldiers into the city, and many of them thought that "freedom" gave license to loaf, to thieve, and to rape. Even by 1870, Main Street had been only half rebuilt with shacks of frontier style.

In ravaged Columbia, where Uncle James Woodrow was a neighbor and joined with Dr. Wilson and other pillars of the church in efforts to restore political order, Master Tommie found inspiration for an ambition to serve his fellow men. He absorbed much of the theology of his elders from lectures by his father that he chose to attend, from visits to the house of his favorite Uncle James, and from his white-bearded, rosy-cheeked Grandfather Woodrow, who read the Bible in Greek and in Hebrew on his way to breakfast, sang old Scottish ballads in a treble voice, pipe in his mouth and a toddy at his fingertips, and until his death in 1877 never let his grandson forget the answer to the question in the catechism: "What is the chief end of man?"

In such an environment, with the outer world of the unsaved in chaos, the boy inclined toward a relationship with God that would build the confidence and purpose that his elders showed. When he was sixteen his religious awakening was quickened by the leadership of a young zealot named Francis J. Brooke, who held prayer meetings in the little stable-chapel where the faithful sat on wooden benches and faced pictures of the saints. Finally, on July 5, 1873, the boy who had once led the Lightfoot Club under the picture of His Satanic Majesty made his confession and applied for membership in the church. And so the native Scottish fiber of the boy was encased within the steel of Calvinist faith. From this day hence he prayed on his knees at his bedside every night.

The Shorter Catechism taught that every man was a distinct moral agent, responsible not to other men but through his own conscience to his Lord and Maker. The compulsion of others, a Presbyterian Scot might escape; but the dictates of his own conscience, never! Man was a lonely soul confronted by the Source of all souls, and he must study deeply so that he might surely know the truth.

The immediate effect of the boy's allegiance to a divine power was improvement in his studies. At his "select school" he struck the son of the master as extremely dignified, not like the other boys, and yet popular and helpful to his younger mates. He showed little interest in natural science. Now that his strong will was reinforced by belief in divine sanction, the lad more than ever let his creative impulses work in their own channels. In the gropings of adolescence he strained the understanding of even his loving family, as his mind sprouted in directions of his own choosing. He had a queer way of going off by himself, sometimes down to see the railroad trains come and go early in the morning. In the lovely building of the theological seminary that housed the library, he tucked himself away in an alcove with favorite books. Especially he steeped himself in the romances of Marryat and Cooper. In his imagination he roved the seas, pursued pirates into uncharted lairs, and delivered their captives. These campaigns were not the whim of an hour or a day, but lasted for weeks and months. The young commander knew every type of sailing ship, its sails, spars, sheets, and shrouds; and he sketched vessels by the hundreds. He filled a scrapbook with news clippings about yacht races, with pictures of famous steam frigates and hydraulic docks, with news of college rowing regattas. Reciting Shakespeare, he showed dramatic talent that made his mother predict that he would be an orator. Save for his attachment to kirk and kin, he was very much alone—a leader without a "gang." There were, to be sure, tentative gropings that later were magnified in his memory into "scrapes" and "love adventures." But in the main his kin absorbed his affections. In the summers, during his teens, the Wilsons joined the families of Uncle Thomas Woodrow and Aunt Marion Woodrow Bones; and the cousins played together in the intimacy of clan affection.

The boy was finding a goal more practical than the capture of imaginary pirates in dream ships. In his copy of one of Cooper's novels he left a slip of paper on which he had practiced signing first his father's name and then his own in a script distinguished by boldness and flourish—such signatures as might be attached to documents of state by great men. One day Cousin Jessie Bones came upon him studying under an unfamiliar portrait and asked who the old man in the picture was; and the lad's face lighted up as he replied: "That is the greatest statesman who ever lived, Gladstone, and when I grow to be a man I mean to be a great statesman too." Thomas Woodrow Wilson was finding his models and his heroes in Britain—the land from which his grandparents had migrated, the nation that had befriended the Confederacy and to which the old aristocracy still looked for their culture and their styles.

Materially, his family fared better than others of their station in the South. In addition to his post in the theological seminary, Dr. Wilson filled the pulpit of the First Presbyterian Church; and his wife had received a legacy. They bought a lot and Mrs. Wilson drew up plans for a new house and planted magnolia trees in the front yard. In 1872 the family moved in, and they were established in comfort when Tommie left Columbia with Brooke, in the autumn of 1873, for the rigorous life that then prevailed at Davidson College. It was understood that he, like his friend, would prepare himself for the ministry.

The wrench of the boy's first separation from his home was painful. "I remember how I clung to her," he wrote of his mother many years later, "(a laughed-at 'mamma's boy') till I was a great big fellow."[5] In his teens, as in later years, he exchanged the most affectionate of let-

[5] W. W. to Ellen Axson Wilson, April 19, 1888; Ray Stannard Baker, *Woodrow Wilson: Life and Letters* (hereinafter referred to as Baker) vol. 1, p. 35. Letters of Jeanie Wilson of May 20 and 26, 1874, addressed to "my darling boy," reveal a mother's concern for the health of her son. Wilson pa., Ac. 12,764, boxes 2, 3.

ters with his parents, worded with precision and penned impeccably. And when father and son met after a separation, they always kissed. In the unremitting battle that the clan felt they were waging with chilling grievance and sin, the warmth of family affection was all the more cherished.

Davidson College, a struggling Presbyterian institution of which Dr. Wilson was a trustee, stood on the plank road north of Charlotte. Its sponsors aimed to bring the benefits of education within reach of impecunious students and to prepare them for the ministry. Life on that campus challenged a boy's body as well as his mind; and Tommie Wilson, entering very young and ill-prepared in mathematics, required all his new-found resolution to stick it out. He subsisted on a boarding-house diet in a region that had not recovered from the war. He made his bed, filled his own oil lamp, hauled water from the well, served on a Stove Committee that fetched wood and pine knots to heat the hall, and learned to dress in the cold in record time so that he might dart into the chapel before the door was closed. The months at Davidson gave solid food to his quickening power to understand and to reason, and he saw men cheerfully endure physical hardship to get intellectual light.

The high emotional intensity that had gone into the lad's religious experience in Columbia made his mind vibrate too fast, and poor diet and lack of exercise began to tell on him. Moreover, he was given to morbid introspection, to self-reproach for having spent so few years "in the fear of God" and so many "in the service of the Devil." He resolved, in writing, to try to serve the Lord thenceforth, to seek perfection in character. In the spring of 1874 illness caused several absences from class; and in May the boy withdrew and returned to his kin, his body exhausted by nervous indigestion. For a year and a half he remained at home. Asked why he left college, he said that he liked it but wanted "to get closer to where they are doing things."

During the year 1874, Tommie accompanied Dr. Wilson to a new pastorate at Wilmington, North Carolina. There the intimacy of father and son was renewed. The lad was tutored in Greek and in other studies and read much in books and magazines, especially the *Edinburgh Review* and the *Nation,* and from these journals he derived a philosophy of Manchester liberalism. He read proof for the preacher; and the doctor set him to editing and auditing the reports that came to him, as stated clerk of the denomination, from county presbyteries. When the boy raised philosophical doubts, the doctor dispelled them by saying: "My son, don't you worry about these doctrinal problems.

Ask yourself this question: Do I love and want to serve the Lord Jesus
Christ? If you can answer that in the affirmative, you need not worry."[6]

At Wilmington, Tommie was as restless as ever; but now, in his maturing young manhood, he did not seek escape at the circus or in day-
dreams in a library, but instead thought of running off to sea. He talked
much about it and puttered around the docks, once hurting himself by
falling into the hold of a vessel. During the Civil War many a blockade
runner had nested in the Cape Fear River, and tales of derring-do
gripped the lad's imagination. Even in his play he was thinking of his
British heroes, of foreign ships that had aided the Confederacy.

Overgrown and gangling, more than ever drawing apart from the
life around him, the lad seemed to the Negro butler to be "an old
young man who tried to explain the reason of things." He did his best
to cultivate manners worthy of a great preacher's son, took his mother
on his arm to church, cared for her devotedly during an illness, and
conscientiously took as much notice of the young ladies as fine breeding demanded. There were no girls in Wilmington with whom Tommie could converse with satisfaction. He had no young friend to share
good talk save one, John D. Bellamy, later a member of Congress.

The lad was already well launched upon the course that he was to follow all his life and to which he was to devote the intense mental energy
that he had inherited, the understanding that had come to him as he
watched economics and politics operate in their most elementary forms
during Reconstruction, and the driving passion for truth and for service
that his religion instilled. The restless blood of pioneers, the agony and
the gentility of the South, the yeast of Scottish Calvinism—all these
forces were churning within him when he started north in the fall of
1875 to the College of New Jersey at Princeton.

[6] During Wilson's year at Davidson a controversy developed among the religious leaders at
Columbia that became bitter and drew out some of his father's worst qualities. Dr. Wilson had
never been one to overrate the intelligence of his parishioners or to undervalue his own worth.

At Columbia his congregation decided to employ a pastor, in addition to their preacher, to
perform the pastoral duties in which Dr. Wilson had not given the comfort and satisfaction that
his flock craved. This action so infuriated the doctor and his friends that they tried to retaliate
by requiring their students to attend chapel services in the seminary instead of going to the
First Presbyterian Church. Thirteen students asserted that this was an interference with their
religious liberty, carried their case to the Presbyterian General Assembly, and were sustained. As
a result, Dr. Wilson and an associate resigned, attendance at the seminary was cut in half, and
the institution barely kept alive until, in the next decade, another bitter controversy, of which
Tommie's Uncle James Woodrow was the center, compelled it to close. (See p. 59.)

Dr. Wilson, still highly esteemed as a preacher, was called to Wilmington in 1874, and there
enjoyed the longest pastorate that the church had had up to that time. See S. L. Morris, *An
Autobiography*, p. 5. On Oct. 21, 1882 Dr. Wilson wrote thus to his son: "My work here in
Wilmington seems to be done, and I think I see evidences amongst the people that some of them
think so too. Yet I never preached so well. . . . The fault they find with me is as to visiting.
They want a gad-about gossip." Wilson pa., Ac. 12,764, box 7.

CHAPTER II

A Student Commands His Own Development

IN THE EIGHTEEN-SEVENTIES the college at Princeton was gradually regaining the reputation that it had held before the Civil War as an ideal school for young gentlemen of the South. Moreover, it was still known as an institution where upcountry youth learned "to preach, to reform, and to lead." Into this tradition young Wilson, a son of the South and a grandson of the middle frontier, fitted well, and as the son of a Presbyterian pastor he was entitled to free tuition. His father had studied at the theological seminary in Princeton; but when Tommie arrived on the college campus he was too shy to present a letter that Dr. Wilson had written to President McCosh.

James McCosh was an educator of whom the Wilsons could approve heartily. Born on the banks of the River Doon, he boasted that he had *talked* with men who "dr-runk whiskey with Bur-rns." In his mature years he had won renown as a religious reformer, and when he had arrived at Princeton in 1868 he had dared to attack the brutalities of hazing and the societies that had operated in secret, had encouraged sport for sport's sake, and had gone himself to the college games. The boys loved him as much as they feared his righteous wrath and laughed at his burr and his extravagances. He insisted that college students should be treated as growing mortals and not as disembodied intellects and that teachers were, properly, *in loco parentis* and responsible for developing men of character. Every Sunday afternoon he lectured on religious subjects, and once a week he heard students recite.

To make up for inadequate preparation, Tommie's energy at first went mainly into his studies; but in June he was not among the twenty honor students of his class. In sophomore year, however, his mind came into its own, and at the end of his college course he stood among those who for the four years had maintained an average of 90 per cent. The boy gained confidence, and wrote to his father that he had discovered he had a mind. He took notes in the neat shorthand that he had mastered, by correspondence course, as a means of saving time; but he did not rely greatly on his teachers, who were not men of marked genius. His grades in the humanities were consistently higher than those in science and mathematics.

Dr. Wilson continued to coach his son in oratory. "Study manner, dearest Tommy, as much as matter," one of his letters advised. A speech's sentences "ought to resemble bullets—that is, be compact and rapid, and prepared to make clean holes." Writing to console Tommie after a defeat in an oratorical contest, the father encouraged him to take a long view. "Dismiss ambition," he advised, "—and replace it with hard industry, which shall have little or no regard to *present* triumphs . . . *I* know you. You are capable of much hard mental work, and of much endurance under disappointment. You are manly. You are true. You are aspiring. You are most lovable every way and deserving of confidence. But as yet you despise somewhat the beaten track which all scholars and orators (almost) have had to travel—the track of partial study in mathematics, in languages, in science, in philosophy. Dearest boy, can you hope to jump into eminency all at once?"

The young man was well aware of his limitations. Thomas Wilson, he confessed to his father, was "a queer fellow. He is entirely free from anything like his father's clear-sightedness and altogether his mind seems to be remarkably bright and empty. You could easily distinguish him in a crowd by his long nose, open mouth, and consequential manner. He is noted in college as a man who can make a remarkably good show with little or no material. But, after all, he is a good enough sort of fellow and what he lacks in solidity he makes up in good intentions and spasmodic endeavors. He has a few queer ideas of his own and very few of them are his own. He writes sometimes but his style lacks clearness and his choice of words is far from good. Ideas are scarce in his compositions and what few there are go limping about in a cloud of wordy expressions and under a heavy weight of lost nouns and adjectives. Ideas are to his writings what oases are to the desert, except that his ideas are very seldom distinguishable from the waste which surrounds them. . . . From what I have seen of him he is apt to allow himself to sympathise almost too heartily with everything that is afloat and, consequently, subjects his nervous system to frequent severe and, sometimes, rather unnecessary strains."

When a letter from son to father lamented a decline in his grades Joseph Wilson wrote to comfort him: "We share your surprise and your indignation in view of the extraordinary 'report.' Be assured, though, that we accept your report rather than that of the faculty. . . . One reason for their grading you as far down as they dared is that you have never taken pains to 'cringe the pliant knee.'"[1]

---

[1] Letters in Wilson pa., Ac. 21,764, boxes 2, 3, 37.

Wilson did not work for credit alone, though after junior year he lamented that he had dropped from twentieth to thirty-seventh place in the class and had fallen into the seventies in physics because of "the injustice of old ———." He was using the college library freely and made the most of Dr. McCosh's elective system, driving himself to develop a persuasive style of expression and to learn all that he could about the history and theory of government and the lives of statesmen. It was in the realm of government rather than in that of theology that this Wilson was finding causes to love and for which to fight.

"Principles, not men," had been the motto of Grandfather Wilson; and yet Tommie even in his teens seemed aware that in order to advocate causes effectively he would do well to study the lives of great men of principle. He saw that progress depended on leadership; he began to note the ways in which political leaders had used levers of power; and he cultivated the spontaneous style of oratory that was in vogue in the House of Commons rather than the set form in which American declamation of the day was strait-jacketed.[1a] He was delighted to find that at Princeton there were some who took him seriously.

Not content to mouth the great truths of democratic government, he took the lead in putting them into action. He did not compete on the college debating team; and, though he joined the old Whig Society that James Madison had founded and took part in discussions of business and constitutional matters, he was fined more than once for nonperformance when it was his turn to write an essay. He was more interested in organizing a Liberal Debating Club that experimented with the British parliamentary system under a constitution drafted by "Secretary of State" Wilson. Subjects of vast scope were attacked: such as "Resolved, that morality does not keep pace with civilization." Questions were raised from the floor and if the prime minister could not defend his policies successfully his "party" was turned out. Though this club was Tommie's first love at Princeton and gave him experience in leadership, he did not scorn the disciplines that could be found in other activities.[2]

[1a] Wilson talked much of Edmund Burke and spoke of "our kinship with England"; and in a "private" diary he noted particularly two phrases in Morley's life of Burke: "In studying the problems which confront us in matters of government we must have regard 'not merely to forms of government and law' but more especially to 'whole groups of social facts which give to law and government the spirit that makes them workable.'"

[2] Wilson served as managing editor of the *Princetonian*—a position that required him to keep well posted on the affairs of the college and to guide and stimulate the reporters and the other editors. Moreover, he wrote editorials on many phases of college life: sportsmanship, discipline, the instrumental club, and the need of funds for adequate buildings. Though not an

In commanding his own development, Wilson refused to be diverted from ultimate goals by the lure of immediate gain. "We wish the training," he wrote in the *Princetonian*, ". . . and the prizes are of secondary importance." Urged to submit a literary essay in competition for a prize that many thought he could win easily, Tommie refused to do the necessary studying because the subject did not fit into his chosen path. Again, when the luck of the draw ordained that he debate in favor of a protective tariff, Wilson refused, for he did not believe in a tariff for protection. Already he was focusing his oratorical powers on causes that his conscience could approve. To him debate was not an opportunity to show off, but a means of arriving at truth and educating men who were less discerning.

In the presence of boys with whom he was not intimate, Tommie carried himself with the easy, affable air of a Southern gentleman, refusing smokes and drinks without offensiveness, telling clean jokes without prudery and without making a clown of himself. He could jest about his personal ambitions without weakening them. Sometimes he told his intimates that he would argue out a point when he met them "in the Senate"; and he left in one of his books a card on which he had scrawled "Thomas Woodrow Wilson, Senator from Virginia." He could not be baited into emotional outbursts about the miseries of the South, though he stood ready to debate rationally with those who were keen to get at the truth about the Civil War and Reconstruction.

Formal, perfunctory expressions of religion did not appeal to Tommie. One evening when a professorial knock on the door surprised him in a forbidden game of euchre, his opponent swept the cards under the table, went to the door, and, glancing back before opening it, saw Tommie roguishly reading the Bible with a mien of mock innocence. It was as if he were saying, in derision of Puritan cant: "See, what a good boy am I! I read the Bible, and so wouldn't *think* of playing cards."

At social functions he was self-conscious. Once, entering a long, elegant drawing room, he slipped on a small rug, skated over a glossy floor, arms thrown out for balance, and stopped just short of an imposing hostess. The memory of his misery plagued him for years.

Living in stylish Witherspoon Hall, where the boys decorated their rooms with bits of lace, bonbons, locks of hair, and tintypes, Tommie

---

athlete of varsity caliber (as a senior he weighed only a hundred and fifty-six pounds and stood 5 feet 11 inches), Wilson commanded the respect of his heavier-muscled friends and was chosen president of the baseball association and secretary of the college football organization.

fell in with Princeton traditions. Yet he kept his distance, and went with a crowd only when it was going his way. Those who knew the lad best could perceive at times that dissenting blood was skirling beneath his pleasing manners. Sometimes he had difficulty in controlling his temper; and for all his gentleness and gaiety he could turn stubborn quickly on a matter of principle. He was happiest in a small circle in which he was the leader in good-fellowship, using his voice to sing with the "gang" in his dormitory rather than in the formal concerts of the Glee Club. With a few intimates he forged friendships that were founded as much on mutual delight in eating, singing, storytelling, and theatergoing as on a sharing of deeper interests. His intimates looked to him to take the initiative in correspondence. "I suppose," he wrote to one of them, "that they think my writing powers—my gift of gab—unlimited."

The parting from his classmates after graduation, he told one, "most emphatically and literally struck in." Perhaps he sensed the fact that never again would he find the essence of human friendship so purely distilled. The Princeton friends became even dearer in later years, as Wilson placed less and less confidence in his associates. He never forgot a solemn covenant that he had made with his classmate Charles Talcott, to acquire knowledge so that they might have power, to drill themselves in the art of persuasion so that they could enlist others in their purposes.

At Princeton the gangling lad had become a man. He might have been as well taught at other colleges: but what he himself had created on the New Jersey campus—the Liberal Debating Club, political essays, and the spirit of comradeship—he could later recollect in no other setting. He was to look back on his undergraduate years as the most satisfying of his life.

As Tommie Wilson was setting his future course by stars that were both high and permanent, the way that he was to travel was magnified by a foreign glass. At Princeton he happened to read bound volumes of the *Gentleman's Magazine* of London, which was at that time publishing reports of proceedings in the British Parliament. To less receptive eyes the articles were not epoch-making. But they thrilled the lad who already had been worshiping the great parliamentarians, the leaders of the nation that had befriended and trusted the South. The young man's own powers were challenged and brought into play. With the reports from London to inspire him, he could suck the last drop of meaning in his readings in Bagehot and Macaulay, Burke and Bright, and

Green's *Short History of England.* From the last, particularly, he gained a deep reverence for Anglo-Saxon institutions, and he was stirred to envision the writing of the story of the continuance and modification of those institutions in America. Books that he used were annotated to the very edges of the pages.

At Princeton, the writings of Tommie Wilson brought him greater fame than his speeches. He contributed two significant essays to the *Nassau Literary Magazine.* One, on Bismarck, was written in his sophomore year; the other, on Pitt, won a prize in his senior year, though Wilson confessed to his bosom friend, "Bobby" Bridges [3] that he thought it a "rather lame affair." He was swept along in the Iron Chancellor's ambition and carried away by the intense earnestness of the English statesman. Though in his essays he showed mature judgment in anlyzing the talents of his heroes and in describing the national atmospheres in which they worked, and though he recognized their failings, his youthful generosity condoned them. He insisted that his readers keep in view the long-range purposes of the statesmen, the devotion with which they pursued them, and the successes that they achieved. Like these heroes, ideal political leaders should be "men of independent conviction, full of self-trust, and themselves the spirit of their country's institutions." Such were the qualities that young Wilson worshiped. In contrast, congressmen of his own country seemed petty and weak. The legislative body that had inflicted the horrors of Reconstruction on the South found no indulgence in the mind of this Southerner.

It was a London critic, Walter Bagehot, who gave the young Anglophile a model for his criticism of American political institutions. A banker, member of Lloyd's, and editor of the *Economist,* Bagehot delighted in paradox and surprise, in re-examining old concepts of political economy in the light of new ideas and the actual conditions of his day. Years later Wilson looked up to him as "my master, Bagehot—the most vivacious, the most racily real, of writers on life—whether the life be political, social, or separately intellectual." Bagehot's essays on the English Constitution set Wilson to analyzing his own nation's Congress in similar terms, and the Englishman's frankness gave the young American courage to speak his mind.

In his senior year at Princeton, Wilson developed his ideas in a maga-

---

[3] Of Bridges, Wilson wrote that this "dear, genuine old Scot" was his *"best* friend in the world," if he had any. "None of Bob is on the surface, but the deeper you dig the finer the ore." W.W. to Ellen Axson, Nov. 20, 1884. After a journalistic career, Bridges became editor of *Scribner's Magazine.*

zine article on "Cabinet Government in the United States." To the young critic the cardinal fact was that frank and open debate is the essential function of a popular representative body. "Congress," he asserted, "is a deliberative body in which there is little real deliberation; a legislature which legislates with no real discussion of its business. Our Government is practically carried on by irresponsible committees. . . . There could be no more despotic authority wielded under the forms of free government than our national Congress now exercises."

Wilson wished Cabinet members to have seats in Congress, the right to initiate legislation, and some part of the privileges of the standing committees. By such a move, the writer argued, the President's power would be enlarged and the balance intended by the framers of the Constitution would be restored.

The article was accepted by the *International Review,* of which one Henry Cabot Lodge was a junior editor. This was by far the greatest triumph of Wilson's university days. He had stepped out beyond his classmates and had become a man among men. The independence and sureness of his thought were acclaimed as rare in an undergraduate. To the ideals that he set forth in this paper—insistence on open and candid transaction of public affairs and upon responsible executive leadership —he was to cling with all the tenacity of his Scotch-Presbyterian blood.

It was the dream of Tommie's family that he would add one more devoted life to the line of Woodrows and Wilsons who had served the church; but in spite of the young man's reverence of God and his love for his kin, his course already was set in a different direction when he was graduated from college. Educated young gentlemen of the South were expected to enter a profession; but the higher statesmanship to which Wilson aspired and to which he hoped to give professional dignity was a calling wtihout a well-defined course of training, a vocation toward which boys born in log cabins and bred in camp meetings and in frontier rough-and-tumble started with some advantage over sons of the manse. And so, instead of taking the easy way that led through theological school into an assured but circumscribed career, Wilson chose to study for the law—a profession that he heartily disliked in its commercial applications but that, as "a branch of political science," might contribute to his preparation for what he conceived to be his larger work. He would filter his enthusiasm for his profession, he said, "through the dry dust of law."

There was only one law school suitable for a Southern gentleman who aspired to statesmanship, and that was at Thomas Jefferson's University of Virginia. There Wilson fell under the charm of the tradition and the beauty of the campus of Charlottesville. But actually Woodrow Wilson was not cast of Virginia clay. Fundamentally he was of harder substance—the moral granite of Scotland and the rough-hewn timber of frontier press and pulpit. Not moved even to walk out to Monticello, Tommie considered himself "somewhat of a federalist" who was intensely concerned for national unity. Though he would gladly learn from his elders *how* to think and to talk, no one, not even his dearest relatives, could dictate *what* the young man thought.

In Virginia's Department of Law young Wilson worked under Dr. John B. Minor, whom he regarded as, next to his father, his greatest teacher—"I can say with perfect sincerity that I cannot conceive of a better," he wrote to Bridges. An aristocrat of impressive presence, a stern Socrates in the classroom, Minor disciplined the minds of his pupils unmercifully. To Wilson the knowledge that he was forced to digest was "as monotonous as . . . Hash." However, he prided himself upon "swallowing the vast mass of its technicalities with as good a grace and as straight a face as an offended palate will allow." Actually, he did succeed in mastering the trifling points of procedure, the precedents, and the language of the law; and he acquitted himself so well that in the second year he was honored by being chosen judge of the university's "moot court."

At the same time this law student managed to read many volumes of orations, history, biography, and poetry. In one month he drew out Wirt's *Henry,* Jebb's *Attic Orators,* and Stubbs' *Constitutional History of England.* The next month he held out Shelley's poems so long that he was fined 50 cents. "Passion is the pith of eloquence," he had written in his essay on Pitt, but "imagination must be present to give it wings and a graceful flight."

Because of the distinction of his family and the quality of his published article on Cabinet government, Wilson was a marked man when he came to Charlottesville. At Virginia there were two competing debating societies, the Washingtonian and the Jeffersonian. Wilson joined the "Old Jeff," four days later was chosen its secretary, and eventually became president. Here he could indulge freely in debate. Immediately he attracted his fellows by suggesting lively subjects for argument, fresh themes that were of current concern to the man in the street, issues that were being aired in the press, topics on which he had thought much himself. According to the *Magazine,* a new constitution adopted by the

Old Jeff reflected "great credit in every respect on its framers, Messrs. T. W. Wilson, etc."

In March of 1880, Wilson delivered an oration on John Bright that commanded more than local attention. So famous had the orator become that both outsiders and ladies of the university asked to be admitted and people were standing in the aisles before the challenging opening sentence came forth. The *Magazine,* which later published the speech in full, reported that "he was listened to with much attention; even the ladies who find it so difficult to restrain their natural and charming propensity to chin-music were unusually quiet." Their enthusiasm was not wasted on the speaker; one of the professors felt that he never knew a man who more keenly relished applause.

The oration on Bright revealed a growth of perception into the realities of politics: "Tolerance is an admirable intellectual gift; but it is of little worth in politics. Politics is a war of causes; a joust of principles." This young man who had heard his elders stake their positions on theological principles could understand political conflict. Taking his hero's message to heart, before his audience of Southerners, Wilson justified John Bright's opposition to recognition of the Confederacy. "I yield to no one precedence in love for the South," he said. "But *because* I love the South, I rejoice in the failure of the Confederacy. Suppose that secession had been accomplished? Conceive of this Union as divided into two separate and independent sovereignties! . . . Even the damnable cruelty and folly of reconstruction was to be preferred to helpless independence."

These words were a challenge to the intellects of this Southern audience. Perhaps their minds would not have been able to triumph over their emotions had the argument been presented less persuasively. The speaker had learned to conquer the nervous tension that oppressed him when he rose to speak. He was thin, his complexion was not clear, and his searching blue eyes looked out from under heavy, dark hair. He loved the Anglo-Saxon tongue and rarely used a word of other derivation.

The spring of 1880 was a busy time for Wilson. The very next month after his speech on Bright he was represented in the university magazine by a powerful article on Gladstone. In this essay there appeared the concept, so strong in Scots, that required in great men a moral or romantic quality that elevates them above worldly standards of success. The mainspring of the statesman's mental processes was seen in his intuitive concept of Right and Wrong. Wilson found in his hero "a keen poetical sensibility, such a sympathy as makes a knowledge of men an intuition instead of an experience," a sort of power that enables statesmen to put themselves in the place of the nation over which they are set. He made it clear that, once Gladstone was given responsibility, his abstract theories broke down at once and completely.

In a university debate Wilson was one of two men chosen to support the negative of the question: "Is the Roman Catholic element in the United States a menace to American institutions?" To accommodate those who wished to hear the debate, it was transferred to a larger hall. The contest was an annual event for which two medals were awarded by the judges: one, considered the first prize, to the best debater; the other, in effect the second prize, to the best orator. Many of the audience disagreed with the decision, and Wilson was disappointed in failing to win what was commonly regarded as the first prize. He felt that he had made no pretense of oratory and was the best debater or nothing. Moreover, salt was rubbed into the wound when an essay by William Cabell Bruce won a medal, and Wilson's efforts on Bright and Gladstone received only honorable mention. Showing some of the pettiness of spirit that his father had displayed when his parishioners had appointed an assistant pastor without his consent, the young man set his own prejudiced opinion against that of the judges and was disinclined to accept the orator's medal that was offered as second prize. Finally, however, he overcame his grievance and allowed himself to be persuaded by friends to take the proffered prize at Commencement, which was to him a time "of dancing and monotony." His speech of acceptance was praised by the university magazine as "one of the clearest, soundest, most logical, and thoroughly sensible addresses ever pronounced here at the University by a man so young."

Thus Wilson turned defeat into a triumph: and, more important, he curbed the tendency to feud that ran so strongly in his blood. In August he wrote humbly to Bridges, declaring himself "fortunate" to have won the orator's medal and "not a good speaker yet by any means," though more competent than he had been at Princeton. And in a subsequent letter he wrote: "I know you will not mistake candid confidence for brag." [4] To Bridges, of whose "intellectual sympathy" he felt sure, he

---

[4] W.W. to Bridges, Feb. 25 and Aug. 22, 1880, and Jan. 1, 1881. Conscious of his progress toward his goal of statesmanship, Wilson gladly accepted a suggestion from his mother that he write his name "T. Woodrow Wilson" so that all his inheritance would be displayed; and later he dropped the "T" as superfluous. W.W. to Bridges, Aug. 22, 1881. "You see I am gradually cutting my name down to portable size," he jested in a postscript to Bridges. W.W. to Bridges, April 1, 1882.

could confess shortcomings that his pride would not allow him to discuss with strangers.

In song as in debate, his voice was smooth and strong and contributed much to the choir and to Sunday evening singing at Dr. Minor's home. Sometimes rambles of the Glee Club led at night to the windows of ladies whence, amidst tittering, flowers and cards of thanks were thrown to the troubadours.

Wilson was courteous and affable to all, though sometimes his wit, to raise a laugh, spared neither himself nor others. Within a month of his arrival in Charlottesville he was initiated into a secret society that had no "house" in which to meet. He had a few intimates who were honored and charmed by his company. He would dramatize by ludicrous twists of his face and preferred the slapstick of vaudeville to the delicate humor of comedy. The bleakness of the dormitory often was relieved by elaborate pranks, and no one could put mock pomp into a college parade so well as Tommie Wilson; but he missed his Witherspoon gang and wrote nostalgic letters to them. As in earlier years, Wilson took one friend more closely to his heart than all others at Charlottesville. His new chum was Heath Dabney. These comrades vied in expressing the mock contempt that young men often use to veil strong fraternal feeling. Wilson's choice epithet for Dabney was "thou very ass"; Dabney's for Wilson, "illimitable idiot." They corresponded almost up to Wilson's death.

In the early winter of his second year in Charlottesville, Wilson overreached the limit of his energy. In addition to the prescribed work he had been riding his own hobby hard.

A spirit so ambitious chafed bitterly under frailties that afflicted the flesh. "How can a man with a weak body ever arrive anywhere?" he asked gloomily, apparently not realizing that he had been putting out energy at a suicidal rate. For heat he had only a fireplace that burned soft coal. Though he had tried to diet strictly and had exercised regularly, he complained that he was "exceedingly ill fed" and troubled with indigestion. He suffered from catarrh and his complexion gave evidence of dyspepsia. He was stricken with a cold that left him unfit for study at examination time, and in January his father advised him to come home. He was paying again, as at Davidson College, for the boyhood hours spent in the library instead of on the playing field.

The break with the campus was made hurriedly, but with honor. The *Magazine* broke precedent to print a laudatory paragraph about the departing genius. To Wilson, studying law at home in Wilmington, the associations of Princeton and Charlottesville were cheering rays in his solitude. He corresponded with Dabney and begged for news of the campus and the fellows of the Old Jeff. Some of his memories, however, were not kindly. He had only scorn for classmates who were slovenly in appearance or affected in manner, though he himself was cultivating side whiskers that he had described to Bridges as "quite *distingué* compared with which yours—much bragged of, of you—were but as a fleeting shadow!"

Again, as after his withdrawal from Davidson College on account of illness, Wilson lingered for a year and a half at the family hearth. Dutifully he went on church picnics, though he thought them too promiscuous. He confided to his favorite cousin, Harriet Woodrow, that one was never sure of having a nice time "because one could never be sure of being able to pick one's company for the day." He shrank from religious orgies, and thought of camp meetings as "flirting made easy." Young men and women could hardly be blamed, he thought, for yielding to a temptation that everything conspired to make irresistible. He knew well enough, he once confessed to Bridges, that he could pretty safely predict his own course under such circumstances.

With only church and family duties, musicales at which he played a violin and his mother strummed a guitar, swimming parties, and rides on a little mare, life would have seemed empty for one who aspired to so much had Wilson not read constantly and persisted daily in grinding at the law and in exercises in elocution. Finally he made his delivery so eloquent that he could imagine that the empty pews in his father's church smiled when he addressed them. Reading omnivorously in Cicero, Trollope, Trevelyan's *Fox,* and the English Men of Letters series, he reacted with strong emotion, favorably to the classics and scathingly to stupid writing.

There seemed to be no question in any mind that the young man would be capable of completing his studies under his own direction. That autumn he was ready to be tested for the bar. It surprised no one that he made one of the best records ever to come under the eyes of the examining judge.

CHAPTER III

Amateur in Life

At the university of virginia Wilson's yearning for a mate became violent. From his room in West Range, in the fall of 1880, he could look through the portico to the Blue Ridge and dream of fair maids in an idyllic valley beyond the setting sun; and sometimes the stirrings of his blood moved him to journey over those hills to Staunton to visit the Augusta Female Seminary, of which his father had once acted as principal. At one time five of his cousins were at school there. He seemed interested mostly in his own kin, perhaps fearing to look outside the clan for the warm genius in homebuilding that his relatives had shown. Thinking himself in love with Cousin Harriet Woodrow, a handsome girl of many talents, he applauded her loudly when she played the piano in a concert; but when he went to a party with her he stood awkwardly with his back to a wall, looking wistfully at fun in which he was too shy to mingle, until the embarrassed Harriet had to beg her friends to be kind to him. The ardor of his attention provoked idle gossip that annoyed the girl; and when he heard of this it pained him and he apologized to her.

However, Tommie made opportunities to see Harriet at the home of their cousins, gave her a volume of Longfellow's poems that appealed to him because it was handsomely bound, and inscribed it "with the warmest love of Cousin Tommie." He took long walks with her over mountain roads, reciting from the lawbook that Blackstone had written for the gentlemen of England, and vowing that he was going to settle down in the practice of law and make money to support a wife. He wrote often to Harriet, addressing her as "My Sweet Rosalind." Remarking that his notes were a "labor of love," he asserted that ladies are the only natural writers of letters; but after they had exchanged a few notes filled with amiable gossip and nonsense, he confessed that thoughts slipped more easily from his pen than from his tongue. Warning the girl against insincere suitors, he commiserated with her on having a music teacher who did not respect the Sabbath and, a little jealous, suggested that such a man was not worthy of her respect. As for himself, he feared that the girls of Wilmington, who had heretofore thought

29

him very sedate, might be surprised to find him a real "ladies' man"!

In the summer of 1881 he went to Chillicothe to make his proposal at the home of Thomas Woodrow, the girl's father and the uncle who had cared for his mother before her marriage. There was much picnicking and whist, and the cousins sang duets. Even in reproving his younger relatives, Cousin Woodrow endeared himself to them, and to one he seemed "the cleanest man ever known." But he did not enjoy the parties, and in the middle of a dance he took Harriet aside and said that he could not live without her and they must marry right away.

While courting in Chillicothe, Wilson tried to get on with his legal career by reading law in the office of a half uncle. But he was obviously a misfit. He had brilliant talents, worked hard, and could state the terms of a contract precisely; but the clients were not drawn to him, and so his uncle advised him to give up the law and go into teaching.[1]

Wilson quit the office in a huff and told Harriet that if she rejected him he would renounce the law and "do teaching." One night he wrote a final appeal to her, begging her to reconsider the dismissal that she had given him that evening, complaining that he could not sleep, grasping for one faint hope to save him from the terror of despair. But, though Harriet was fond of him, she did not love him. To spare his feelings she told him that it would not be right for them to marry because they were first cousins; but when he insisted that their parents approved, she had to tell him that she did not love him as he wished. At that, he left the house abruptly and went to a hotel. There he wrote a last desperate plea, on a torn bit of yellow paper, explaining that the strain had been so intense that he could no longer trust himself to leave the subject alone in the girl's presence and so had gone away to spare her feelings. The next morning she received him and assured him that she loved him as dearly as ever, as a cousin. But he refused the invitation of the Woodrows to continue the visit and retired to Wilmington, whence he wrote to implore his love to send a photograph posed just as he liked to remember her. Though she assented to this, and broke off their correspondence in order to help him forget, his burning heart was unappeased and his confidence in his legal career was shaken.[1a]

[1] Letter and statement from Henry T. Bannon of Portsmouth, Ohio, in the Alderman Library, University of Virginia. The half uncle was Henry Woodrow, son of the elder Thomas Woodrow by his second wife, Isabella.

[1a] Dr. Joseph Wilson, visiting the Woodrows in Chillicothe, wrote thus to his son on Aug. 28, 1882: "I honestly and firmly believe that the marriage that you desired would have made you happy only for a very little while. . . . I admire your unselfishness in still loving where you cannot secure . . . all the family, including H, speak of you in terms of most flattering admiration." Wilson pa., Ac. 12,764, box 7.

Not until the next spring was he able to write of the affair to so close a friend as Bridges and to assert that he had refused to be "unmanned even by a disappointment such as this"; and even then he could not confess that Harriet had not desired him, and preferred to hide his wound under the excuse that she had given.

Finally the young man's spirits rose and impelled him to face the world alone. To a young attorney who hoped to swim in the main current, Atlanta seemed the best place to make the plunge. There the wheels of industry were beginning to turn more rapidly and a thriving commerce promised work for the legal profession. Moreover—perhaps more important, in Wilson's view—the city was the capital of a "thrifty" state, the center of Georgia's cultural life, and the home of such progressive leaders as Henry W. Grady of the Atlanta *Constitution*. He wished to begin work in a large city where there was at least opportunity for great things to be accomplished, whether he was equal to their accomplishment or not.

The move to Atlanta was discussed throughly in family councils; for Dr. Wilson, justly estimating his son's quality, was concerned that each step should lead toward a great career. Once the decision was made, the young lawyer's parents supported him with both love and money. His mother made shirts for him; and when she learned that her boy had found a partner of good Virginia stock and irreproachable character, she wrote that that was the thing she was "most glad of."

Wilson thought his associate, Edward Renick, a lovely being, and found in him a mind kindred in scholarly pursuits. As a business partner, however, he was as ineffectual as charming. In Atlanta there was a lawyer for every two hundred seventy of the population, and newcomers could hope to attract customers only by aggressive tactics. Unfortunately, Renick and Wilson were more interested in discussing ways and means of reconstructing the world, in reading together in the *Aeneid,* and in going to the theater. Wilson watched the Georgia legislators in action and thought them crude and bumbling. He sputtered when they refused to vote adequate support to the schools of the state and, taking the easiest course politically, shirked their responsibility and begged aid from Washington. But the partners built no law practice, and Wilson's only important client was his mother. Nevertheless, his political education was advanced in Atlanta when Dr. Wilson made his son an aide and gave him a seat on the platform at the General Assembly of the Southern Presbyterian Church, of which the doctor was then moderator. There young Wilson could learn to catch the sense of a meeting of free souls, could witness the calling together of a congregation of elders for discussion of church polity.

While more aggressive attorneys slapped backs and pumped hands in courthouse corridors, joined clubs, and celebrated Christmas Day by going on what Wilson called a "universal drunk," the son of the manse practiced elocution in his office and lived quietly at a boardinghouse where he was known as "the professor" and where, he said, his landlady's pretty niece helped him "nobly to while away" the time. Actually, Wilson was gradually swinging into his lifework—the thing that he wanted to do above everything else. Through Robert Bridges, who acted as his literary agent in New York, he sold an article on convict labor to the *Evening Post*. He was less anxious than he had been to get his work published, more content with his own view of it, and ready to wait until no one would be responsible for what he wrote but himself. He wanted reputation, not quick money, he informed Bridges. "I want a *start*, and am willing to make it on any terms within my reach." He so loved to write, he said, that he sometimes imagined that he would be "happy and useful" on the staff of some such paper as the *Nation*. Though he could easily bear rejection of articles that he wrote for his own pleasure, he considered it a "dismal failure" when Bridges failed to place a piece [2] in which he rehashed the arguments for parliamentary reform that he had presented in "Cabinet Government."

However, Wilson did not allow himself to grieve long over the rebuff of the editors. Actually, as his business became a liability, his avocation was opening paths to a career. In the fields of letters and government he was making valuable friends and a reputation that carried beyond Georgia. He kept up his study of elocution, for it was by oratory that governments had been made and unmade in Parliament and he must keep his weapon sharp for his day of opportunity.

In September of 1882 he had his first chance to influence national legislation. One day an energetic young reporter came into the little law office on the second floor back. Renick introduced him as an old friend, Walter Hines Page of the New York *World*. A Democrat and fellow Southerner, Page had come to town with federal commissioners who were to hold a hearing at Atlanta on the tariff. Convinced that the public good was not served by protection, he had been traveling about with the officials; and in Wilson's view he had been destroying

---

[2] This article finally appeared in January, 1884, in the *Overland Monthly,* under the title, "Committee or Cabinet Government." See *The Public Papers of Woodrow Wilson*, edited by Ray Stannard Baker and William E. Dodd, Vol. I, 95. This is a work designated hereafter as *P.P.*

their reputation and overthrowing their adventitious dignity by smart ridicule.

Page was impressed quickly by the earnestness with which Wilson set forth his views on the tariff, and he persuaded the young lawyer to address the commission, promising that, though Wilson could not expect to impress the commissioners, his speech would be printed in the *World* and included in the report to Congress. And so, when other young attorneys were serving commercial interests that would pay them spot cash, Wilson appeared at the hearing to speak gratuitously for the common welfare. To him, the six commissioners who sat smugly around the table in the breakfast room of a hotel, surrounded by local dignitaries and the press, were incompetents.

Though he was annoyed by the sneers of prejudiced partisans and tripped on a point of fact by the commissioners, he pleaded the cause of peace and international trade so eloquently that the local congressmen remarked that he knew "what to say and how to say it."

The protectionist "advocates a system which prepares for war," he argued, "while it has not any consideration for the requirements of the country in time of peace. I ask, is it worth while during fifty years of peace to provide by taxation for one year of war?" Quoting Gladstone and referring to Mill, he maintained that "manufacturers are made better manufacturers whenever they are thrown upon their own resources and left to the natural competition of trade rather than when they are told, 'You shall be held in the lap of the government, and you need not stand upon your feet.'" Asked whether he advocated the repeal of all tariff laws, he replied: "Of all protective tariff laws."

That very night, with Page still present, Wilson called a few disciples together in the humble little law office to discuss the issue of the day, and in a few months this group had become a branch of the Free Trade Club of New York. They became a miniature House of Commons, in which almost all the talking was done by Wilson. Quite serious and very self-conscious, the youth was casting himself in a traditional role —half Southern rebel, half English Parliamentarian—as he set forth the standard arguments of the cotton-planting aristocracy.

When Wilson qualified for the federal courts, in March of 1883, he could pay only half the fee of ten dollars. For a year his father staked him, with no more complaint than the casual remark that Tom "didn't seem to be earning his salt." The young man who had told manufacturers that they should stand on their own feet, and who had sometimes been critical of indolent Southern gentlemen, was himself dependent still upon his family. This shamed him to the marrow; and yet he was not willing to sell himself to the prosecution of causes that to his Presbyterian conscience were immoral and, to his exacting mind, insignificant. To him the philosophical study of the law was a very different matter from its "scheming and haggling practice." Describing himself as "buried in humdrum life down here in slow, ignorant, uninteresting Georgia," he complained: "hereabouts culture is very little esteemed."

Early in the spring of 1883, flaunting side burns and a newly grown mustache, Woodrow Wilson set out from Atlanta. As his mother's attorney, he went to the town of Rome to confer with his uncle James Bones about the management of lands in Nebraska in which Mrs. Wilson and her sister Mrs. Bones, now deceased, had holdings.

There was an old friend in Rome of whose presence the visitor was unaware. At the age of seven he had insisted on holding in his arms a dimpled baby daughter of a friend of his father. A family tradition recorded that he had fallen very much in love with the child[3]. As Woodrow walked along a street in Rome on an April day, that very girl looked down on him from the porch of a friend's house, marked the confident bearing, the clean, sharp features, the wide, sensitive mouth, and asked: "Who is that fine-looking man?"

He did not see her then; but on the first Sunday of the month[4] he went with his cousins to the Presbyterian church, of which the girl's father was minister. There he saw, under a black crêpe veil, what he was later to remember as "a bright, pretty face" with "splendid, mischievous, laughing eyes." After the service he made up his mind to seek an introduction.

The Reverend Samuel Axson, son of an eminent Presbyterian minister in Savannah, had begun his career under the eyes of Dr. Joseph Wilson at Augusta. Mourning for a wife who had died in childbirth, he leaned heavily on his eldest child. She often called on sick parishioners in her father's stead, her arms filled with flowers from a garden that she tended. Intent on carrying out her dead mother's charge to care for her father, she undertook also to rear two young brothers.

When Woodrow Wilson called on Monday at the parsonage and asked pointedly about Ellen's health, the minister summoned his daughter to the parlor and gave the young man an opportunity to exhibit his conversational charm. Cousin Jessie arranged for him to meet "Miss Ellie Lou" at tea on Wednesday, and afterward he escorted

[3] W.W. to Ellen Axson, July 30, 1883, Wilson pa., Ac. 12,764, box 8, L.C.
[4] E.A. to W.W., April 7, 1884, source cited, box 10.

her home. "I remember leaving you that afternoon with a feeling that I had found a new and altogether delightful sort of companion," he wrote to her later. He knew now that her friends had good reason for considering her one of the rarest and most beautiful girls that ever lived in Rome. The next day he left for Atlanta with great reluctance.

His prospects for making a living there were bleak. His father, who at first had advised him "to stick to the law and its prospects be they ever so depressing or disgusting," had written later that he would not object if Woodrow went into teaching. He had written to President McCosh and two other educators about his son's qualifications. Jeanie Wilson had sought the counsel of her brother, James Woodrow; and he, noting a tendency among colleges to choose professors who were trained in Baltimore at the Johns Hopkins University, advised that it might be well for his nephew to apply for a fellowship and, in accord with a suggestion that James Woodrow received from his friend Gildersleeve of the Hopkins faculty, to enroll as a graduate student.[5] Having few qualifications for the fellowship that was immediately available, Wilson resolved to go to Baltimore in the autumn, attend the university lectures, and pursue his own creative work in the library. He hoped that this might lead to a subsidy in the future.

Wilson still carried in his mind's eye the prospect that since boyhood had been most precious to him. The goal of political leadership lured him; but he realized that without an independent income he could be at best an "outside" power in politics, "a speaker and writer of the highest authority on political subjects." What he needed, he wrote Dabney, was a profession that offered moderate support, favorable conditions for work, and considerable leisure. "What better can I be, therefore, than a professor, a lecturer upon subjects whose study delights me?"

Though he had no natural bent toward science or mathematics, he could not ignore the value of the scientific disciplines that were currently being applied to graduate studies in his chosen field of politics. Before the 1870's this subject had been taught scarcely at all in American colleges. At Princeton most of Wilson's study in economics and politics had been carried on in an atmosphere dominated by reverence for the *status quo;* but in the oasis that had opened in 1876 at the Johns Hopkins he might expect to drink deeply of strong elixirs.

[5] J. R. Wilson to W.W., Feb. 13, Jeanie Wilson to W.W., Feb. 26, James Woodrow to Jeanie Wilson, Mar. 14, 1883. President McCosh wrote to Joseph R. Wilson on April 18 to ask to be informed as to the outcome of Woodrow's "present application." Wilson pa., Ac. 12,764, box 8.

His father volunteered to pay the expenses from the family's savings, but Wilson's visit to Rome had made him reluctant to postpone the day when he would be self-supporting. He could not ask any girl to marry him now. But he was sure that he loved Ellen Axson and he wanted to find the courage to tell her so. If he could be sure of her love, he might overcome his aversion to the law and strive to succeed in its practice. He responded eagerly, therefore, when Uncle James Bones asked him to come again to Rome.

He knew that he must woo with patience and tact. Miss Ellie Lou was shy, and felt that her family responsibilities made her unavailable for matrimony. He decided to court her with the formality that was expected of southern gentlemen, and especially of the sons of clergymen. Two hours after reaching Rome he sent a formal note from Cousin Jessie's home, asking whether he might escort Ellen to a concert;[6] and he was not surprised when he received a cool but cordial reply that pleaded "a previous engagement." He found encouragement in her signature: "sincerely your friend."

Four days later he made another advance, hiring a horse and buggy for the afternoon and inviting Ellen to ride with him. This time she accepted. They drove through apple orchards, he talking in a stilted way, she listening quietly and agreeably. Uncle James Bones prolonged his nephew's opportunity by artfully extending their conferences; and in the days that followed Woodrow called on Ellen, took her to a concert and a prayer meeting, and squired her to a picnic. Accepting, she addressed him as "Mr. Woodrow." This, coming from so reserved a young lady, took his breath away. Thus encouraged, he led her along the bank of a river and up on a jutting rock that commanded a pretty view, and confided to her the needs of his heart, the uncertainty of his prospects, and the narrowness of his means. In an effort to elicit an expression of her feelings, he confessed his disinclination to ask any woman whom he could love to make the sacrifice of marrying him. Her comment, as he described it later, "was very brief and non-committal, though not altogether uncomforting." She went so far as to suggest that such a marriage "might . . . be less burdensome than the common fate of marriageable damsels who might expect to keep house for some humdrum tradesman. . . ."

A girl of twenty-three who had had beaux since she was sixteen, Ellen was not so unladylike as to reveal her feelings until a man proposed. But once, when Woodrow gave her some verses as they

[6] W.W. to Miss Axson, "Thursday afternoon," Wilson pa., Ac. 12,764, box 37.

rode home from a picnic, she could not control her blushes. He dared not tell of his love, and risk a rejection that would forever doom him, but he did ask, and receive, her permission to correspond.[7]

He went from Rome to Wilmington, to spend the summer with his parents; and on July Fourth he wrote a long, rambling letter to Ellen about his journey.[8] In August he accompanied his mother to the resort of Arden, in the mountains of North Carolina. On September 1 he sent a letter to Ellen, who was visiting friends in the nearby village of Morganton, to ask her to write to him. This she did twice within the next fortnight. In one of these letters she wrote: "you are quite welcome to call me anything you wish except Ellie Lou." Explaining that only her father used this and that she had a "decided dislike" for all compound names, she suggested five alternatives. From these he later chose "Eileen."

She expressed sincere interest in his plans, and justified her curiosity by professing friendship. ". . . of course I 'believe in you'—there is no reason why I shouldn't!" But on September 12 she had to send bad news. Two cards had just come from her father, telling her that he was ill and wanted her to come home immediately. "I hope . . . it is not very serious," she wrote. ". . . I am extremely sorry that I shall miss seeing you."[9] She was also a little relieved, because it would not be necessary to confront her suitor and withstand a proposal that she felt duty-bound to reject.[10]

At this juncture a kind Providence intervened. Wilson, unhappy about the financial sacrifice that his parents insisted on making, set out for Baltimore, and on the way he stopped at Asheville to do a church errand for his father. Looking from the street at a hotel, he caught a glimpse of a girl's head as it receded from a window. The hair was coiled in a way strangely familiar. Bounding up the steps, he hurried to Ellen and in a public room, his judgment shaken by the suddenness of their meeting, made his profession of undying love. When she saw

[7] McAdoo, *The Priceless Gift,* pp. 8–10; letters, Jeanie Wilson to W.W., June 7, 12, 21, 1883, Wilson pa., Ac. 12,764, box 8.

[8] The letter is in the Wilson pa., Ac. 12,764, box 8.

[9] W.W. to E. A., Sept. 1, E.A. to W.W., Sept. 4, 8, 12, 1883, Wilson pa., Ac. 12,764, boxes 8, 9, 37. At some time during the summer of 1883 Ellen Axson visited Mrs. Wilson at Arden Park. "I could discern that she cared for you when she was here," Jeanie Wilson wrote to her son on Sept. 19, 1883. Wilson pa., file 2.

[10] Hallie Alexander Rounseville to the writer. Ellen Axson wrote thus to Wilson on Sept. 21, 1883, in regard to the proposal that he made on September 16 at Asheville: ". . . it is not strange that I should have been bewildered to find things had ended so differently from what I intended when you began to speak. For I was resolved that I would not let you do anything so foolish—certainly not for a long, long time, not before you had well considered." Wilson pa., Ac. 12,764, box 9.

him, she confessed five days later, her heart gave "a great suffocating throb" and "a wild desire to escape" possessed her. He explained that a bachelor was actually what Bagehot had called him—"an amateur in life"—and he assured her that he would help to care for her father and brothers. Then he drew out her love by asserting that further uncertainty would interfere with his work and spoil his year at the Hopkins. ("I could not bear to think of that," she told him afterward. She yielded, she said, "only because there was *no* 'tomorrow.' You were going away and that is the secret of it all . . . I had no smallest idea how much I loved you until I found how wretched I was made at the thought of your leaving . . .") He held her in his arms and kissed her, still calling her "Miss Ellie." When he asked for her ring as a token of their troth, she willingly gave it. Then they went the separate ways to which duty called.[11]

Returning to her family, Ellen told her brother that she was betrothed to "the greatest man in the world and the best." Going to Baltimore, Woodrow said a cavalier farewell to bachelorhood in a letter to Dabney: "I've fallen in love and *become engaged*. Yes, it's so. I'm bagged! . . . Of course it goes without saying that I am the most complacently happy man in the 'Yewnighted States.' "

During the long engagement that followed, almost two years in length, the lovers reached an understanding that grew in depth and in intensity of feeling. They poured out everything that was in their hearts and minds. Sure of her love, he made her the keeper of his secrets and the sharer of his aspirations. She responded quickly and deftly to all his moods. She wrote at one time that she was "quite awfully proud" of him, of his "various gifts and the high, pure, and noble purposes to which they are dedicated." And on another occasion: "I can afford to be saucy, can't I, since you are sure to understand."[12]

A little later he assured her that he would rather be loved by her than be famous, and that every time he received a letter telling of her love he felt that it would be easy to become famous. "We'll *make* the love story as we live on for and with each other," he wrote, "and we can make it different from all other stories by making it

---

[11] This paragraph is based on *The Priceless Gift,* pp. 11–12, amended by new evidence found in letters, E.A. to W.W., May 20, 1885 and Sept. 21, and W.W. to E.A., Sept. 18, 1883, Wilson pa., Ac. 12,764, box 9. In his letter Wilson described the encounter at Asheville thus: ". . . the formal, embarrassed, almost stiff, declaration in the public hall-way, the sweet, hesitating acceptance, the constraint of surroundings, and the hateful publicity."

Writing to Samuel Axson on Sept. 19 to ask for his daughter's hand, Wilson explained: The "engagement must necessarily be prolonged. . . . our almost providential meeting in Asheville upset my judgment." Reporting the writing of this letter to his fiancée on September 21, he commented: "I believe I never did harder work."

[12] E.A. to W.W., Nov. 5, 1883, Feb. 11, 1884, Ac. 12,764, boxes 9, 10.

happy . . ." After they had been engaged for more than a year he shared with her a foreboding of martyrdom: "What fools those very perspicacious people have been who have judged me by my cold exterior and have imagined my feelings as temperate as my reason. They would be surprised and shocked, doubtless, to see me offer up my life for that which I believe or for her whom I love! It would be *so* hard to believe that they were mistaken!"[13]

Ellen found the needs of her father very confining. He suffered from insomnia and fell into what she called "sulks." At times he required her presence constantly. He was seized occasionally by paroxysms, and finally was committed to a state asylum. Ellen went to dwell with her grandfather—"the great Axson"—who seemed to her to "live above all the storms of this world," and her grandmother, who had a firm conviction that "men were made to be taken care of" and who worried about health almost as much as her tormented son. Wilson traveled to Savannah to visit her in January at the Presbyterian manse.

Samuel Axson's seizures became frequent and more violent, and on May 28 he died. His daughter grieved deeply.[14] Wilson, who protested that his heart was "nearly starved" during the days when her father gave her no time to write, tried to strengthen her faith in immortality. He went to Rome immediately and stayed there for two weeks.

The passing of Samuel Axson gave his daughter freedom to marry. But Wilson's impecuniousness remained an impediment. His work at the Hopkins won him a scholarship for a second year there, but in his impatience to live with his beloved he thought of taking a teaching position that would bring him a salary. His impulse to earn money increased when he learned she had applied for a position as teacher of art in Augusta, in order to assist her grandparents in supporting her family. But she held him steady in the long course. "I am *so* glad, so *very* glad and *proud,* my darling that you have taken the scholarship. . . . What a *splendid* man you are, to be sure! What an 'extra-special man' . . . I am struck dumb with awe . . . My darling, are you *very sure* that you are wise to think of going elsewhere next year? . . . I am *so* anxious that you should decide on that course which would be wisest 'in the long run.' And especially that you should be unbiased in your decision by any considerations in which *I* am involved." She had "a positive offer of a place as art teacher," and must decide in a few days.[15]

The decision was made for them when word came that the position

13 W.W. to E.A., August 23, 1884, Wilson pa., Ac. 12,764, box 11.
14 E.A. to W.W., Oct. 23, 1883, Feb. 4, 18, April 23, May 1, 6, 8, 9, 12, Wilson pa., Ac. 12,764, boxes 10, 11. June 2, 1884, Samuel Axson to E.A., Feb. 16, 1884.
15 E.A. to W.W., June 2, 1884, Wilson pa., Ac. 12,764, box 11.

that Wilson hoped to fill in a university in Arkansas was not to be available that year, and a little later Ellen learned that her father had left enough resources so that she would not have to earn a living. Deeply disappointed because he would have to live alone for another year, he agreed to return to the Hopkins to take part in what he called "the greatest Educational Show on Earth."

In the summer of 1884, overcoming the opposition of conventional Grandmother Axson with the help of Woodrow's tactful mother,[16] they spent weeks together at the home of the Wilsons at Wilmington. In the autumn he escorted her to New York, where she was to study at the Art Students' League. They stopped at Washington, and boarding a trolley car went uptown so that Ellen might see the White House. When he went away to his boarding house in Baltimore, she threw herself on her bed and wept. She wrote to him daily about her art work and new friends, and occasionally he visited New York. She sought his advice about a very young admirer from Boston who, she said, was her "devoted champion in a strictly platonic sense" and "of the greatest service." Confessing that earlier efforts to establish platonic relations with her beaux "were not brilliant successes," she remarked that "those were Southern boys,—and it is different with the cool-headed New Englanders." She thought that in this case she could enjoy a man's friendship without stirring his emotions too deeply.

A few months earlier, when Wilson had heard that a friend accused his beloved of flirting, it had vexed him. ". . . when I cease to trust you," he asserted, "I will go and hang myself; and when I cease to resent any jokes which affect our love for each other, I shall have ceased to be my natural self." He took alarm at her new friendship in New York,[17] and his warnings were justified when Ellen failed in efforts to "let down" her Yankee admirer gently and was forced to meet an embarrassing emotional outburst with a firm rejection. Reminding his fiancée at this time that the intellectual life was "a fearfully solitary one," Wilson wrote: "I have the uncomfortable feeling that I am carrying a volcano about with me. My salvation is in being loved. . . . There surely never lived a man with whom love was a more critical matter than it is with me!"

Always understanding, always giving her man the benefit of any doubts that arose, Ellen shared Woodrow's deepest allegiance only with his God. He joked often about "orthodoxy," for nothing so much

[16] Correspondence between Mrs. I. S. K. Axson and Jeanie Wilson, Wilson pa., Ac. 12,764, box 11; McAdoo, *The Priceless Gift*, pp. 69–74.

[17] W.W. to E.A., Dec. 18, 22, 1884, Wilson pa., Ac. 12,764, box 12.

irked this spirited practitioner of religion as the cant of fundamentalists. To him and to Ellen, hell was only a state of mind. Wilson's belief
in the God of his fathers inspired his acts and gave him strength and
comfort. When Ellen, who read deeply in philosophy, was beset with
doubts, Woodrow brought his rugged faith to her support.

At the beginning of 1885 Wilson found that he had achieved a
degree of fame unusual to one so young. His first book, *Congressional
Government,* in which he analyzed and criticized the work of Congressional committees, received appreciative reviews from critics of
distinction. The author had flattering invitations to write and to speak.
Lacking confidence to believe that he could ever enter into "active
affairs" of government, he aspired to be an alert and independent critic.
"Under the existing conditions of our public life . . ." he explained
to Ellen, "I *prefer* outside influence, not only because its ways are more
congenial, but because its *power* is greater. The only difficulty will be
in avoiding the danger peculiar to a professor's position, the danger of
being accounted a *doctrinaire.*" And Ellen agreed that "politics is a
terrible business," intolerable to a man like her fiancé, and requiring
"the hide of a rhinoceros." But she refused to let him give up, "except
for the present," what she called his "birthright" of political leadership.[18]

In January they began to consider setting a date for their wedding,
and Ellen wrote: "If you wish, you may come to me in June, my love."
They decided upon the twenty-fourth of the month, and as the
time approached their expressions of devotion became more unreserved.
In May he wrote: ". . . you have taken to talking, all your letters
through, about your love, about *our* love, and as I read I can't for the
life of me tell whether I am sitting still or standing on my head!"

She urged him to go to his Princeton reunion just before the wedding, lest his classmates be disappointed. Shrinking from the "display"
of a church ceremony, she chose to be married in the parlor of the
manse of her grandfather's church in Savannah.[19]

At last united, they passed a long honeymoon in a vine-covered
cottage of the Arden Park Hotel, finding the completeness of soul that
they had celebrated in their correspondence. There, in the hills of
North Carolina, he sang and they walked and read much together, and
Woodrow Wilson's confidence in his destiny was given an impulse
that his Presbyterian God had not been able to supply.

[18] E.A. to W.W., Feb. 26, Mar. 2, W.W. to E.A., Mar. 3, 1885, Wilson pa., Ac. 12,764
box 14.
[19] E.A. to W.W., Jan. 14, Feb. 16, 26, Mar. 2, 4, 6, 9, 11, May 25, June 6, W.W. to
E.A., Mar. 5, 15, May 22, 1885, Wilson pa., Ac. 12,764, boxes 14–16.

CHAPTER IV

NOTICEABLE MAN

INSPIRED BY THE LOVE of Ellen Axson, Wilson did original work of great distinction at the Johns Hopkins. But his spirit chafed against the yoke of research and rebelled against the quality of the teaching in the Historical Seminary, where he sat with young men who were to set the pace of American scholarship. Herbert B. Adams, cloaked in the authority of a Ph.D. degree from Heidelberg, presided and deftly led the scholars into what he called "institutional history." Adams was reminded of a race horse as he watched Wilson's strong face, saw a nostril quiver or the head toss back in revolt against academic bridles.[1a] He gave the young colt his head when Wilson asked to be relieved of research so that he might devote all his energy to study of the working of government in his own day.

Wilson plunged furiously into the writing of a book on the functioning of the American Congress. When his fellow-scholars praised chapters that he read to them, he dared to send a sample to Houghton Mifflin & Company. Encouraged to submit a complete manuscript, he worked at home in Wilmington in the summer of 1884, maintaining the "free spirit of courageous, light hearted work" on which he prided himself. He enjoyed the stimulus of his father's mind. "The life he stirs up in my brain," he wrote to Ellen, "is worth a whole year's course at the Hopkins."[1b]

In the autumn the finished manuscript went to the publisher and the author held his breath. Finally he reported to Ellen: "They have actually offered me as good terms as if I were already a well-known writer! The success is of such proportions as almost to take my breath away—it has distanced by biggest hopes." *Congressional Government* won favorable attention from competent reviewers and was acceptable

---

1a When Professor Ely asked Wilson to participate in the writing of a history of political economy in the United States, Woodrow wrote in despair to Ellen: "Alas! Alas! Think of the trash I shall have to read. . . . For I can't refuse. I came here to advertise myself for a position (as well as to learn what I could) and the best way to do that is to please the professors and get them to push me! . . . I hate this thing of serving other men; but it's politic; and the service is honorable." W.W. to E.A., Feb. 19, 1884, Wilson pa., Ac. 12,764, box 10.

1b W.W. to E.A., Aug. 16, 1884, Wilson pa., Ac. 12,764, box 11.

to Dr. Adams as a thesis for a doctor's degree. This success was sobering. "So far from feeling any elation," he wrote to Ellen, "I feel more and more a deep sense of personal responsibility. I have—almost unwittingly—taken the lead in a very great work. My book succeeds because I *have* taken the lead; and now, the opening having been made, I must come up to my opportunities and be worthy of them. That is enough to sober—as well as enough to inspire—anyone!"[1c]

Wilson balked, however, at the discipline required to prepare for an examination for a doctor's degree. Both physical and mental health, he explained to Ellen on November 8, 1884, "would be jeoparded by a forced march through fourteen thousand pages of dry reading." But, he went on, "it is probable that I would fetch a bigger price with a Ph.D. label on me than I can fetch without. It's a choice, apparently, between pecuniary profit and mental advantage. . . ." Though his father and mother thought that he should not put his health in hazard, he hoped to take the degree for Ellen; but she confessed she was "*immensely* relieved" when she heard of his decision, though she thought it "a great pity" to forfeit the degree.[1d]

To earn money for immediate needs Wilson acted as correspondent

[1c] W.W. to E.A., Mar. 14, 1885, Wilson pa., Ac. 12,764, box 14. Gamaliel Bradford, whose earlier articles in *The Nation* (see Arthur S. Link, *Wilson: Road to the White House*, pp. 15–19) set forth many of the ideas developed by Wilson, praised the book, asserting that "in a resolute advocacy of such a proposition lies the broadest and most open road to the Presidency." *Nation*, No. 1024 (Feb. 12, 1885), pp. 142,143. However, the true importance of both the work and the author was to dawn slowly upon the nation. In 1892 the book was awarded the John Marshall Prize at the Johns Hopkins. James Bryce was influenced by it and quoted from it in *The American Commonwealth*. It has been translated into several foreign languages and printed thirty times in the United States—the last time in 1956, with an introduction by Walter Lippmann.

The first review to reach Wilson came from Walter Hines Page, who, buggy-riding in North Carolina with Josephus Daniels, prophesied greatness for the author. But the response that most touched his heart came from his father, to whom the book was dedicated. "The 'dedication' took me by surprise," the old man wrote, "and never have I felt such a blow of love. Shall I confess it!—I wept and sobbed in the stir of the glad pain." Joseph Ruggles Wilson to W.W., Jan. 30, 1885. For the dissenting minority of reviewers Wilson had only scorn. He referred disapprovingly to "a sneering review in a small local sheet of no circulation." Of Bradford's review he wrote to Ellen: ". . . he misjudges my purpose altogether." Letter of Feb. 15, 1885, Wilson pa. Ac. 12,764, box 13. But after talking with this critic he wrote ecstatically to Ellen of Bradford's "sympathy and power to stimulate thought." McAdoo, *The Priceless Gift*, pp. 116, 133–4.

An unfavorable review in the *New York Times* was denounced by Ellen as "a yea-nay article. Not one *positive* or straightforward word in it; I daresay the poor creature is simply a fool . . ." E.A. to W.W., Mar. 17, 1885, Wilson pa., Ac. 12,764, box 14.

[1d] W.W. to E.A., Jan. 18, E.A. to W.W., Feb. 18, 21, 1885, Wilson pa., Ac. 12,764, box 13. Wilson's courses in his first year at the Johns Hopkins were the usual formal ones: International Law, Advanced Political Economy, English, Constitutional History, and Sources of American Colonial History; in the second year he studied Modern Constitutions, Public Finance, Commerce, Administration, and History of Politics.

for the New York *Evening Post* and lectured in outlying towns. He sang regularly with the Glee Club.

He had a select circle of friends, and to them he gave his heart. But he ignored men whom he found dull, pompous, or vulgar. He liked to dodge crowds and sit aside with friends for quiet chats. In a tête-à-tête he said: "No man would, on account of my Scotch physiognomy, ever familiarly slap me on the back in a hail-fellow-well-met way . . . I should just hate it; I should be most uncomfortable; I could not conceivably slap him back, and what a prig I should feel because I couldn't."

Strangers who tried to be too familiar were rebuffed by shy distrust. To anyone suspected of sycophancy Wilson presented a hard and insulating shell. At formal Baltimore parties he protected his oversensitive feelings with a mask of diffidence. Even that, however, was distinguished. "How does he manage that bed-side manner and make his dress clothes look like a preacher's?" people asked. "He's terribly clever but he is provincial." Jokingly they warned him not to become a "Hopkins genius"—a grind who could not mix in the society of the city. They valued the traditions of Southern gentility and culture far above efficiency in scholarship. Some of Wilson's friends felt sorry because a gentleman of his background was forced to yield to eccentric men of no social standing who had been given places on the Hopkins faculty. They tried to draw him out, asking, "How do you like the Hopkins?" Hesitating, he answered that it lacked the cultural atmosphere of the University of Virginia, but that it was sponsoring splendid research and was a wonderful place in its way. "Unfortunately," he added, "I like my own way too much for my own and other people's comfort."

Draw him out on the theme of his deepest intellectual loves, and to his intimates he would expose his soul. When national politics came under discussion, he threw back his head as if to get the highest perspective possible. Then he would talk very precisely, every trace of diffidence gone, appraising the presidents from Washington to Cleveland ("Washington gave America her liberty; Lincoln's gift was the heart"). Answering those who told him that he was cut out to be an English rather than an American statesman, he would argue: "Would you pigeon-hole a man as an alien because he imports some of his fuel from outside? . . . I think there are few things so poor and cheap as prejudice—and so pernicious." He loved to voice his deep faith in democracy, and proclaimed that the old order of Baltimore society was giving way to an age of vigorous individualism. Then he would drop from his eagle's view and his far-ranging judgments and fall into the rut of the general talk with a little whimsical turn of phrase.

Late in 1884, when he was almost half through his second year at the Hopkins, Wilson was introduced to the dean of a new Quaker college for women that was to open the next fall at Bryn Mawr, Pennsylvania. Martha Carey Thomas had returned from graduate study in Europe converted to the worship of facts and reason. With an inflexibility of purpose that to Southern gentlefolk seemed brazen, she resolved to exalt American girls to the level of masculine scholarship.

Wilson was interested in the new venture in spite of himself. He could pay only lip service to German scholasticism, and neither he nor Ellen was devoted to the ideal of higher education for women. He preferred not to teach girls, and not to work under a woman no older than himself and positive in her opinions.[1e] But he thought the higher education of women "certain to come in America" and wanted "to get into a chair somewhere and get into permanent harness," and Bryn Mawr offered certain advantages: leisure for private study; proximity to the Johns Hopkins, where he hoped to give a course of lectures; and an opportunity to get experience before seeking a more conspicuous and more demanding place. When after some preliminary negotiations the trustees offered a two-year contract at an annual salary of $1500, Dr. Wilson advised his son that the proposition was "worth a fair trial," that perhaps there was need of "the discipline of such narrowness" to enable the young man to show the stuff of which he was made. Ellen, however, feared that the salary would not be enough to care for them and for one or both of her brothers, and she suggested that they put off their marriage for another year. But Woodrow persuaded her that there would be "nothing imprudent" in the venture, and sent his acceptance to President Rhoads.[1f]

The couple therefore went to live in the autumn of 1885 in the little

---

[1e] ". . . it seems to me that it is rather beneath *you* to teach in a 'female college' . . . a vile phrase," Ellen wrote on Nov. 28, 1884. Wilson pa., Ac. 12,764, box 13. He assured her that he would not be under the dean, but under Dr. Rhoads, the president. McAdoo, *The Priceless Gift*, pp. 97, 99.

[1f] McAdoo, *The Priceless Gift*, pp. 100-1, 108-12, Joseph R. Wilson to W.W., Dec. 2, 1884, Jan. 15, 1885, E.A. to W.W., Nov. 28, Dec. 1, 1884, W.W. to E.A., Dec. 3, 1884, Jan. 18, 1885, J. E. Rhoads to W.W., Jan. 10, 1885. With the last letter was enclosed a copy of Wilson's two-year agreement. On Feb. 27, 1885 Rhoads wrote that he felt sure, though he could not "write with any certainty," that the trustees would wish to make Wilson an Associate Professor "with corresponding salary" upon the expiration of the present agreement, if not before. Letters in Wilson pa., Ac. 12,764, box 13.

rural village ten miles northwest of Philadelphia. There were only forty-two students and two buildings that first year. Twice during his residence at Bryn Mawr his wife went to visit an aunt in Georgia, and each time she returned with a baby girl. "Woodrow's little annuals," old Joseph Wilson called them. The young father confessed that he was, at first, "a little disappointed" that the child was not a boy.

Wilson eschewed social life, stayed at home to tend the garden, pump the water, and protect his precious wife. Once, when a maniac was thought to be prowling in the woods outside, the laird went out and fired his pistol. "You are, and always will be," he wrote to his wife after three years of matrimony, "to me at once sweetheart, bride, wife, life-companion, my children's mother—everything in one . . . it is *you* who keeps me young, not myself. . . . Old age of heart will never touch me. . . ."[1g]

Taking into her family her eleven-year-old brother and a cousin who wanted to attend Bryn Mawr but needed financial help, Ellen swept, cleaned, darned, cooked, and cared for her babies until, with the help of income from her father's small estate, they managed to hire a cook. She found time too to listen to paragraphs that her husband read to her to make sure that they were clear.

In the spring of 1886 Wilson, now fully aware of the importance of an advanced degree to his career, wrote to Adams that he had "all along coveted such recognition as a Ph.D. from the Hopkins would give." Explaining that he needed the degree *now*, that he "always cut a sorry figure" in examinations "from sheer perversity of natural disposition," that he was a nervous fellow who could not for the life of him "pull in ordinary harness," Wilson persuaded Adams and Ely to make his "a case of special arrangement."[1h] The degree granted, he wrote to Ellen: "Hurrah—a thousand times hurrah—*I'm through, I'm through*—the degree is actually secured! Oh, the relief of it! I won the degree *for you*."

At Bryn Mawr, Wilson got up courses in ancient and medieval history as well as in constitutional law, often composing lectures during afternoon walks over the rolling countryside. Yet his work was not satisfying. Only by "very constant and stringent school-

---

[1g] Letters, W.W. to E.A., April 17, 20, 29, 1886, Wilson pa., Ac. 12,764, box 17; McAdoo, *The Priceless Gift*, pp. 156, 169.

[1h] On April 7, 1886 Dr. Adams wrote to Wilson to propose a special plan: written examinations in five subjects, and an oral examination before the board. An interview took the place of a formal oral examination. Correspondence in the Johns Hopkins University Library; H. B. Adams to W.W., Wilson pa., Ac. 12,764, box 17.

ing" he said, could he endure academic methods. The business of teaching women threw him into an inescapable dilemma. The girls, their most ladylike instincts evoked by their courteous, gallant professor, wrote down even his jokes in their notebooks, and in the examinations they faithfully handed back what he had given. Though he allowed time for the asking of questions, he did not succeed in drawing out intelligent discussion. The thinking, and most of the talking, was done by the professor. In permitting this he showed himself an inexpert teacher, according to the tenets of Dean Thomas; but had he encouraged his girls to raise their voices in masculine argument he would have been no gentleman, according to the tradition of his family.

As he began his third year at Bryn Mawr his perplexity flamed into rebellion and he protested to his wife: "I'm *tired* carrying female Fellows on my shoulders! . . . When I think of you, my little wife, I love this 'College for Women,' because *you* are a woman; but when I think only of myself, I hate the place very cordially . . ." He brooded over his lot, worried about his health, and wondered how he could earn a living by teaching undergraduates and at the same time keep his literary fancy free.

He felt again the urge to strike out for himself in a statesman's career. This, he had written to his Ellen before their marriage, was his "heart's primary ambition" and his "mind's deepest secret." Doubting that he had ability enough to indulge this desire, and still allured by what he called "the stir of the world," he hoped in 1887 that he might find "a seat on the inside of the government—a seat high enough to command views of the system." The offer of a federal position, whether he accepted it or not, seemed a good asset in getting ahead in his profession. Going to Washington to call on Renick, formerly his partner at Atlanta and now an official in the Treasury, he paid his first visit to Congress and interviewed chiefs of bureaus. But it was suggested to him that, much as a government post might benefit Woodrow Wilson, the country could be better served by men drilled in the service; and he quickly saw the justice of that argument.

But his aspiration toward political leadership kept surging up. He wrote to Talcott of "special work in administration"[1i] that he wanted to do eventually, and suggested to this Princeton classmate that they renew their covenant of college days and form a "committee of correspondence" composed of a half dozen vigilantes. He wanted, he said,

[1i] While at Bryn Mawr Wilson wrote "The Study of Administration," an essay that was published in the *Political Science Quarterly* in June of 1887.

to meet "men who have direct touch with the world," so that he might study *affairs* rather than doctrine. "What I go in for," he wrote to Professor Adams, "is the *life,* not the texts, of constitutions, the practice not the laws of administration."

He reviewed Bryce's *American Commonwealth,* criticizing the author's reliance on description, his scanting of the historical experience that testifies that "for a body of English people *the fundamental principles of the law are at any given time substantially what they are then thought to be."* He himself undertook to supply what he found lacking in Bryce, showing in an essay how America's government had changed under the spur of a world-wide "drift toward democracy" and under the pressures that resulted from immigration and the industrial revolution. American democracy is "a stage of development," he wrote. "Its process is experience, its basis old wont, its meaning national organic unity and effectual life. It came, like manhood, as the fruit of youth. Immature peoples cannot have it, and the maturity to which it is vouchsafed is the maturity of freedom and self-control . . ." [2]

Though he still paid tribute to Bagehot and to Burke, who, combined with Montesquieu, represented for him all that had force in political thought, the ardor of Wilson's worship of parliamentary heroes had cooled somewhat since his undergraduate days. The boyish feeling that he had long cherished, he confided to his Ellen in 1889, was giving way to another feeling—"that I need no longer hesitate (as I have so long and sensitively done) to assert myself and my opinions in the presence of and against the . . . opinions of old men, 'my elders.'" An admirer at Baltimore had interrupted him once to ask: "Do you never think yourself wrong?" And he had answered: "Not in matters where I have qualified myself to speak."

On his thirty-third birthday, in 1889, he wrote in his journal: "I have great confidence in progress; I feel the movement that is in affairs and am conscious of a persistent push behind the present order." Why, he asked himself, might not his age write through him its political autobiography?

Wilson's passion for leadership expressed itself in 1890 in a Commencement address entitled "Leaders of Men," delivered at the University of Tennessee. Denied satisfaction of his impulse to lead men in political action, he tried to resolve "the perennial misunderstanding between the men who write and the men who act." He explained "the

---

[2] *P.P.,* I, 176–77. For illustration of the way in which Wilson refined his writing when he repeated, cf. *Woodrow Wilson, An Old Master and Other Political Essays,* pp. 116–17.

well-nigh universal repugnance felt by literary men towards democracy." The leader that he aspired to be—and must wait decades to become—would be a thinking man in action.[3]

All the while, as he wrote in this vein, the instructor stayed close to his home and his college girls, conceiving a gargantuan feat of scholarship. He proposed, he wrote to editor Horace Scudder, to apply the inductive method to the study of democratic government, and especially to its genesis and development in the United States. "The true philosophy of government," he asserted, "can be extracted only from the true history of government." Aristotle, he pointed out, had studied politics in that manner but did not go beyond the outward differences of institutions; Wilson would "press on beyond logical distinctions to discover the spiritual oneness of government, the life that lives within it." For years this grandiose dream haunted him. Allusions to it appear in his jottings, and his family spoke longingly of the day "when father comes to the writing of the p. o. p."—The Philosophy of Politics. Appraising a tentative draft of a chapter or two, he wrote: "I should burn it up, and have it *all* to write over again. It isn't so bad, I suppose, *absolutely* —but *comparatively*—compared with what I would have it—it is *all wretched*. If the public should think otherwise, I shall write the public down an ass."[3a]

Instead of pursuing his soul-satisfying goal, the professor accepted a commission to write a college textbook to be called *The State*—"a fact book," he called it, " a plebian among books . . . vulgar-looking." It was necessary to consult sources in German, which he could not read at sight. He had hesitated to speak foreign tongues for fear that the purity of his English might be tainted; but now he wanted to go to Berlin. Unwilling to follow his father's advice that he accept his wife's generous proposal that he go alone, he wanted to take his family. But this was too costly; and so he and Ellen attacked German texts together, one using the dictionary, the other writing down translations. When it was done, though he recognized that the discipline was "serviceable," he resolved thereafter "to be an *author*—never more a book-maker."[4]

Yet here the germs of a league of nations appeared. International law, Wilson wrote, *"ought* to govern nations in their dealings with each

[3] *See* T. H. Vail Motter (ed.), *Leaders of Men*. Wilson delivered his address on this theme four times in the nineties, but did not publish it. Motter has suggested that his diary, under date of Jan. 17, 1897, explains his desire for privacy. Though "a living and effectual utterance of himself might validate him," Wilson wrote, it was "an unnecessary risk—a hazardous exposure of his workshop and materials." *Leaders of Men*, p. 11.

[3a] W.W. to E.A.W., Aug. 16, 1886, Wilson pa., Ac. 12,764, box 17.

[4] J. R. Wilson to W. W., Nov. 15, 1887, Wilson pa., Ac. 12,764, box 19; McAdoo, *The Priceless Gift*, p. 169.

other," but lacked "forceful sanction." And it was while he was working on *The State* that he wrote in a magazine article: "There is a tendency—is there not?—a tendency as yet dim, but already steadily impulsive and clearly destined to prevail, towards, first the confederation of parts of empires like the British, and finally of great states themselves. Instead of centralization of power, there is to be wide union with tolerated divisions of prerogative. This is a tendency towards the American type—of governments joined with governments for the pursuit of common purposes, in honorary equality and honorable subordination."

Old Joseph Wilson had proclaimed an ecumenical gospel; and, nourished on it, Woodrow Wilson's mind easily envisioned the political union of mankind under the ideal of peace and justice. He did not, however, expect to reach Utopia overnight. "In government, as in virtue," he explained, "the hardest of hard things is to make progress."

At the same time, in his early political writing, Wilson warned against revolution as a means of political progress, explaining that violence was always followed by reaction. In the last chapter of *The State* he came to grips with the problem of reconciling a liberal philosophy of politics with contemporary social conditions. The state must perform certain functions that were obviously "necessary," he wrote; but "optional" functions might well be left to private agencies. Just what powers should be exercised by government, and how far, must be determined by experience and the demands of the times.

In 1888 little Wesleyan College asked Wilson to join its faculty at a salary higher than that paid at Bryn Mawr. Failing to persuade his present employers to "very much increase" his income and protesting that he could not live on what he received, he claimed, after consulting legal counsel, that Bryn Mawr had invalidated his three-year contract by failing to honor one of its clauses. The trustees of the college refused to annul the contract, but acquiesced when Wilson decided to leave and submitted a seven-page brief in justification of his position.[5] He accepted the post offered at Middletown, Connecticut, realizing that he had "for a long time been hungry for a class of *men*."

---

[5] Wilson's contract with Bryn Mawr provided that he should have an assistant "as soon as practicable." He understood orally from President Rhoads that this meant "financially practical." Rhoads admitted that an assistant could be financed but thought one unnecessary for the year 1887–8. Rhoads to W.W., Sept. 8, W.W., to E.A.W. Oct. 2, 1887, W.W. to Rhoads, June 7, and typed brief, "To the President and the Board of Trustees of Bryn Mawr College," Rhoads to W.W., June 27, July 6, 1888, Wilson pa., Ac. 12,764, boxes 21, 23.

At Wesleyan, Wilson instructed all seniors and juniors in political economy and the Constitution of the United States, and gave optional courses in the history of England, of France, of the United States, and of "institutions."

In observing the machinations of student cliques and secret societies, he received an education in the ways of boss politics; and a fight that he waged to place the ablest men on the athletic teams, without consideration of social status, presaged larger battles to come. He made a lifelong friend of his pastor, nicknamed his colleagues and called them "a faculty with less dead wood" than any similar body of his acquaintance. They laughed at his endless repertoire of stories, thought him a good fellow who put on no airs.

Absences from home brought tears at parting. On his "sprees," the professor kept a careful account of his expenses and wrote loving letters to his wife, assuring her that without her he could not have discovered his "whole self," that she made him the man that he was, and at the same time detailing his many and catholic activities: a trip on a coastwise steamer; a visit to Robert Bridges in his office at Scribner's; nights at the theater, once to hear Sothern, later to see *Bootle's Baby*; a boat ride and concert at Coney Island; a day at Seabright, and another at a professional baseball game. Freed from the work in which his conscience drove him, he could have been a famous sybarite. He liked to see his fellow Americans diverted by innocent amusement as much as he delighted in seeing them energized by a positive faith. Although four years previously he had criticized an eloquent, demagogic harangue by Henry Ward Beecher as "shallow" and "noisy," it did not offend his religion or his intelligence to see Dwight L. Moody practice personal evangelism in a barbershop in Middletown.

Another man might have settled into lifelong enjoyment of academic serenity and the easy and companionable society of Middletown; and a humorless man might have reveled in the adulation that his lectures evoked. But the life of a "lion" could not satisfy the urges of his blood. Woodrow Wilson was still looking toward the intellectual horizon, toward new fields to be cultivated by his mind. He could hardly hope that his passion for good government among free men could be requited in teaching history in a small college. What he craved was a chair in public law at his own College of New Jersey. From such a pulpit he would be able to advise and criticize the nation's statesmen.

Fortunately he had in Robert Bridges a loyal and ardent campaign manager. This chum and classmate had introduced him to Francis L. Patton, who succeeded Dr. McCosh in the presidency of the College of New Jersey. Impressed by a reading of *Congressional Government,* Patton suggested that Wilson fill a vacant chair in political economy for a year, until a professorship of public law could be created for him.

Bridges urged him to acceptance, saying that Professor Sloane had been overburdened by carrying the teaching in political economy and was anxious to be relieved of it, that his influence with the trustees was very great. "Speaking confidentially, and with some guile," Bridges wrote, "I believe that he is a good man to conciliate . . . you could sail along beautifully together, notwithstanding radical differences in your historical points of view."

For the sake of his loved ones, Wilson had sometimes swallowed his pride and played the worldly game of getting ahead from which he had revolted as a bachelor at Atlanta. In 1886 he had at first refused to go to a dinner of Princeton alumni in New York because his conscience would not let him spend time or money for pleasure; but when they had asked him to speak he had accepted, hoping to identify himself with Princeton. Wilson's speech had been far too long and too serious for the taste of banqueting alumni, and he feared that it had hurt his chances for a Princeton professorship. He caused the idea of endowing a chair at the College of New Jersey to be insinuated into the mind of a philanthropist, hoping that he might occupy it himself. And now he wrote to Professor Sloane and was informed, very cordially, that there was no immediate prospect of a division of labor in his department.

Declining to consider a call to Williams College, Wilson decided to wait for a chair of public law. Meanwhile, Bridges warned that "the Philistines" at Princeton were "whispering behind their hands." This faithful friend campaigned for Wilson among the trustees of the college, bringing pressure on one opponent who disliked Wilson's position on the tariff, on another who complained that he was a Southerner and would "make trouble," and on several who feared that his learning was too deep to permit him to interest the boys! [6]

Finally, in February, 1890, word came of his election to a professorship of jurisprudence and political economy. Thereupon the authorities at Wesleyan let it be known that they would grant almost any request to induce the brilliant lecturer not to move. Old loyalties as well as the needs of the family pulled toward Princeton, however; and after doing everything in his power to get a strong man to take over at Wesleyan, the professor packed up his household and moved. "I find," he wrote

---

[6] Wilson had feared rather that the authorities at Princeton would not think him learned enough. The *Nation*, in reviewing one of his books, had classed him with those who "impose only on the vulgar." And in submitting a light essay to *Scribner's Magazine*, Wilson had signed it with a *nom de plume*, explaining that it was whimsical and contained half-playful opinions that university trustees might think *infra dig*.

to his father, "that everybody regards my election to Princeton as a sort of crowning success."[7]

In his new post, in the nineties, Wilson still found time to write. He evaluated the heroes of American history in an essay called "A Calendar of Great Americans." In this work he showed that he had so developed his critical faculties that he could no longer give himself wholly to emulation of any hero. "I can find no man in history I should care to be like. I want to be myself," he said to his Ellen.[8]

Fresh and far-ranging as were Wilson's writings on politics during the eighties and nineties, they were criticized by scholars who found his thought hazy and out of focus, his sentences overrhetorical. By exercising the love of words that his father had instilled in him as a boy, Wilson built a vocabulary of some 62,000 words. But he had no smugness about his style. Though he confessed to his Ellen that he was immensely pleased that his writing should have been considered good, he was forever reaching out for the moon, complaining that his sentences were "stiff, dry, mechanical, monotonous," that the effect was altogether "too staccato."

It occurred to him that by writing on lighter, more literary themes he might loosen and vary his style. Though he had been unsuccessful in selling short stories, he had not given up his ambition to write literature; and in his view the poets of the race came nearer than the scholars to the eternal verities of politics and economics. He was quite aware,

[7] W.W. to Joseph Ruggles Wilson, March 20, 1890. Writing to Bridges, Wilson explained that there was but one argument for Princeton: "namely, that it is Princeton—a big institution of the first class, with superior facilities for work, with the best class of students, and affording a member of its faculty a certain academic standing." Patton hesitated to agree that Wilson should go on with his lectures at the Johns Hopkins, and Wilson thought him "afraid of the Trustees and the faculty—of jealousy on their part—for Princeton, for themselves." The young professor was inclined to make an ultimatum either of the continuation of the Hopkins lectures or of a greater salary, and preferably the former, for he felt that he derived much more than money from his continuing association with the Hopkins. He asked the advice of Bridges, on whom he depended, he said, in closest friendship and completest trust. W.W. to Bridges, Feb. 13, 1890.

[8] As his confidence in his own powers grew he ventured to criticize a book by John W. Burgess of the Columbia Law School, the teacher of Theodore Roosevelt and probably at that time America's most influential student of government. Burgess seemed to write in the language of natural science, not in that of literature and political fact, to apply the theory of the survival of the fittest too patly to politics, and to believe that the Teuton dominated the world by his superior political genius.

The true nature of government, Wilson had insisted in *The State*, is "hidden in the nature of Society," which is "compounded of the common habit, an evolution of experience, an interlaced growth of tenuous relationships, a compact, living, organic whole . . ."

Referring to "social organisms" and characterizing the evolution of political institutions as "scarcely less orderly and coherent than that of the physical world," Wilson occasionally fell into the phrasing of popular interpretations of social Darwinism, but he felt that the social Darwinists attached too little importance to the human will. Such understanding as he had of Spencer probably came indirectly, through Bagehot.

he had written to Miss Ellie Lou, that at his birth "no poet was born" and had asked her whether it was not a legitimate ambition "to wish to write something (!) that will freshen the energies of tired people and make the sad laugh and take heart again: some comedy full of pure humor and peopled with characters whose lives are in order, who live up to the moral that life, even with the pleasures of vice left out, is worth living; lay sermons full of laughter and a loving God: a fiction that may be suffered to live, if only because it has real people in it and no sham enthusiasm?" He could wish, he said, to be "the favoured correspondent of children, as well as a counsellor of the powers of the earth." [9]

He composed essays [10] that were designed not to please editors or scholars, but only himself and the bosom friends to whom he dedicated them. With one of these, brother-in-law Stockton Axson, he bicycled from Princeton out into the country; and sitting on an old stone bridge he threw out a challenge: "We who know literature by sight have the responsibility of carrying on a war with those to whom the so-called 'scholarship' is everything." Even in the writing that he had undertaken for relaxation and diversion problems of style began to haunt him. If only he might equal the "quick stroke, intermittent sparkle, and jet-like play" that he so admired in Walter Bagehot! Fond of epigram, he shuddered at the cheap, the smart-aleck, the sentimental. He would not admit to his writing the offhand gleams of farce that shone in his intimate talk. He fretted, corresponded with friends, picked to pieces some of his books.

It was clear, in the mid-nineties, that Woodrow Wilson would not make an indelible mark on the world by impressing scholars with political treatises or his intimates with belles-lettres. As an essayist and textbook writer he was competent; but his editor had complained that he wrote as if there were "an audience before some of his sentences." When the audience came alive, however, and the prophet could address it directly, he showed himself to be superb.

Ever since he had sat as a boy in his father's churches and been thrilled by what came from the preacher's lips, Woodrow Wilson had been excited by the spoken word. His command of it had given him his

9 W.W. to Ellen Axson, Oct. 30, 1883, unpublished letter printed by permission of Eleanor W. McAdoo and Edith Bolling Wilson.

10 Among the random literary essays were such autobiographical papers as "The Author Himself," "On an Author's Choice of Company," and "When a Man Comes to Himself." After publication in magazines, some of the pieces were collected and bound in volumes that were given such titles as *Mere Literature* and *On Being Human*.

greatest triumphs at college and law school, and at the Hopkins he said of oratory: "It sets my mind—all my faculties—aglow . . . I *feel* a sort of transformation—and it's hard to go to sleep afterward." Like his ancestors who had expounded the Word, he felt "absolute joy in facing and conquering a hostile audience . . . or thawing out a cold one." And when his chosen medium—the spoken word—was applied to his favorite of all subjects—politics—Woodrow Wilson reached his greatest heights.[11]

Haunted by the memory of mediocre teaching to which he himself had been exposed, Wilson resolved never to be dull. Good oratory, he once explained to Ellen, "does not generally come into the lectures of college professors; but it should. Oratory is not declamation, not swelling tones and excited delivery, but the art of persuasion, the art of putting things so as to appeal irresistibly to an audience . . . Perfunctory lecturing is of no service in the world. It's a nuisance."

And so Wilson lectured at Princeton with a persuasiveness that he had labored for years to perfect. In the chapel—the largest classroom on the campus—he spoke on public law: "its historical derivation, its practical sanctions, its typical outward forms, its evidence as to the state and as to the character and scope of political sovereignty." This was his heart's blood, the subject on which he felt that he had qualified himself to speak as an oracle. So completely did he master both subject and pupils that he drew classes that increased from about 150 in 1890 to 305 in 1902.

Looking down on his students, he stood squarely on his long legs, his short body slanting forward a bit and his fingertips barely touching the top of the desk before him. Above a turnover collar and black string tie, his features stood forth in all their Scotch-Irish bluntness: jutting jaw, big upper lip over a strong mouth, large ears that fitted close below a long and narrow cranium. Black straight hair thatched his head and eaved down in short side whiskers. His Adam's apple and the tip of his

---

[11] At the Johns Hopkins, Wilson had taken it upon himself to reform the constitution of the Literary Society as well as to improve its oratory. "It is characteristic of my whole self," he had confessed to Miss Ellie Lou, "that I take so much pleasure in these proceedings . . . I have a sense of power in dealing with men collectively which I do not feel always in dealing with them singly . . . One feels no sacrifice of pride necessary in courting the favour of an assembly of men such as he would have to make in seeking to please one man."

At Wesleyan, Wilson had encouraged the boys to transform the old college debating society into a new "Wesleyan House of Commons," where causes were argued from conviction rather than by assignment. He felt, however, that the House was "kept moribund by the vitality of fraternities," and the tendency toward too rapid changes of ministry was as pronounced as in France. At Princeton, the professor urged students to join one of the debating societies even if they must slight the work of his course.

nose flexed vertically, and he moved his arm first up, with palm pressing upward, then down, with fingers drooping. Now his full, mobile lips would flash out a smile, baring teeth that were patched; and later his jutting jaw would snap with finality on the end of a period of graceful phrases.

On the stroke of the classroom bell this imposing figure said "Good morning, gentlemen," and the boys came under the spell of his luminous eyes. From his lecture notes, typed out and underlined in red for emphasis, he would read a series of statements, sometimes emphasizing their sequence by curling his fingers in his palm and then gracefully opening them one at a time, the forefinger first. The most important points were stated twice, and after the repetition the lecturer stopped while pencils flew. Telling the boys to put their notebooks aside, he would compel their attention by a barrage of wit, characterization, and word pictures. He used current news stories to illustrate points of law, and when he dramatized a town meeting, boys felt that they were seeing the real thing. He was at his best in depicting scenes in the age-long battle for free government. Valuing the moral lessons of history above scholarly analysis of the facts, Wilson once said to an instructor in the classics: "I should be quite content if the students entered Princeton knowing only those parts of Roman history that are not *so*!" [12] His class did not forget their professor's account of the signing of the Covenant on a Sunday in 1638, by rugged Scots, on a flat tombstone in Greyfriars' Churchyard. Sometimes they interrupted him with cheers, and many were moved to pursue into the library those paths of which he gave alluring glimpses. His language, the light in his eyes, the pleasing clarity and fullness of his voice—these made converts. Like his preaching father, he engendered courage, hope, faith—along with knowledge and understanding.

Wilson suffered torture from the strict standards of expression that his conscience forced upon him. In talking with students he sometimes used vivid slang phrases, but it was done with a wrinkling of his nose; and the crudeness of the language of his boys made him writhe. After helping to coach the debating team he feared to go to the debates, flinching at the thought of the pain that would strike him if his boys spoke ineffectively.

To many students Wilson was unique among professors as a personification of the majesty and power of ideas. To save time he rode a bicycle to class, in tall hat and striped trousers. His coattails flew out

12 George Dwight Kellogg to the writer.

and he pedaled at a precise pace, neither too fast nor too slow. Once a student, trying out one of the first motorcycles to burst upon the quiet village, came on Wilson bicycling outside the town and offered him a tow. The professor caught the rope that was thrown to him and put it over his handlebars; but, after being pulled to the edge of the village, he signaled the boy to stop, suggesting that it would not be appropriate for him to be seen crossing the campus at a breakneck pace behind a machine that conservatives then regarded as an invention of the devil.

When his boys came to him seeking a good subject for debate or suggestions for independent reading, or help in tutoring obtuse football players, or merely aid in getting out of a scrape, "Tommie" Wilson was their man. He was secretary of the board of football directors, and a delegate to the Intercollegiate Football Association; one autumn he drove the eleven through practice, giving more of inspiration than of useful instruction; and as long as he was at Princeton he kept an eye on the team and spoke in sympathy to boys who were injured. He served as class officer for the seniors and for five years as a member of one of the strictest discipline committees in the history of Princeton. In his course in public law, the first year, he gave few A's and one boy in thirteen flunked. Students thought his standards severe but knew him to be everlastingly fair. Year after year they voted him the most popular of professors. Almost everyone wanted to "take Wilson," and promising students came to Princeton just for that purpose. Very soon he became an institution.

In everything that the young professor did, he had an eye for morale and lifted the spirits of those about him. Breathing fresh air into the college's little parliament—its faculty meeting—he soon skirmished with President Patton. In 1893 the undergraduates petitioned that they be put on their honor as gentlemen and not patrolled as presumptive cheaters. Wilson, who had seen the honor system operate with success at the University of Virginia, supported the plea. President Patton, however, foreign born and less sympathetic than the Southern-bred professor with the code of honor of American lads of good breeding, took the floor and opposed the proposal with ridicule that hurt. White-hot with anger, Wilson kept his poise and pressed his arguments so eloquently that he carried the faculty with him. The honor system went into effect, to the joy of the undergraduates. From that time on, whenever "Tommie" Wilson spoke in faculty meeting there was a quickening of interest.

In the eighteen-nineties Wilson was much sought after as a lecturer and did his best to satisfy the popular craving for culture. He developed powers that could lead to greatness, though his talks seemed to some critics a bit too facile, too formally set in the lyceum style of the day. A fellow professor, turning away from a speech in which Grover Cleveland had banged home a truth with a trip-hammer sentence, remarked that that was "just the weapon for a President," and then went on to say: "You know, you don't want to have a President of the United States write with as fine a style as Woodrow Wilson." To reach prophetic stature the professor needed to be fired by the challenge of large issues and great occasions. He himself knew this, and wrote: "Style is an instrument, and is made imperishable only by embodiment in some great use."

Editors were commenting on the speeches of Woodrow Wilson and academic honors began to come to him. Old Joseph Wilson wrote from his theological school in Tennessee: "I am beginning to be known as the father of my son . . . You are preaching a gospel of order, and thus of safety, in the department of political morals and conduct, such as has not heretofore been heralded . . ."

It was in the field of education, however, rather than in politics that the first occasion arose to bring Wilson the orator into national prominence. When he began to apply his forensic power to the exaltation of American education, the colleges were growing fast and their presidents had great influence over national affairs. Students were coming in larger numbers from the homes of traders and manufacturers, and these boys and their parents often rebelled against clerical scholasticism. Graduate schools, professional schools—even technical schools—were springing up. Philosophy was being freed from theological bonds, and rhetoric and belles-lettres began to lose devotees. It was becoming clear that colleges that would remain in business would have to give their boys more freedom in choosing their work and more courses from which to select. Wilson was aware, too, as he returned to the campus in 1890, that the alumni were becoming the most important patrons, and thus the university was coming more and more to transmit its essential qualities.

Wilson found many changes at Princeton. McCosh had reformed the curriculum and had raised funds for several buildings, cannily making the most of the paradox that no university can be prosperous that is not on the verge of bankruptcy. Princeton was still under the spell of his personality, and buildings continued to sprout from seed that he had planted. The emphasis on science that marked the age was facilitated by improved laboratories and a new observatory. McCosh had boldly accepted the teaching of emancipated science, declaring that "when a scientific theory is brought before us, our first inquiry is not whether it is consistent with religion, but whether it is true." A course was offered on Harmony of Science and Religion.

In his championing of a rational view of science McCosh was a man after the heart of James Woodrow. A few years before Wilson came to teach at Princeton, this revered uncle had shaken Southern Presbyterianism to its foundations in an Olympian controversy. Unlike McCosh, whose magnetism could allay the resentment of even the stuffiest theologians, James Woodrow was not personally popular among all his Presbyterian brethren. A careful and calm thinker, he had exercised his brilliant mind in many fields, having taken a degree in science at Heidelberg, *summa cum laude,* superintended a Confederate laboratory for the making of medicines, promoted businesses, and printed religious journals and state papers. Delegating nothing, unlocking his own office, and keeping his own books, he was too busy to cultivate friendships.

James Woodrow respected nothing so much as truth, and finally insisted on telling his students in the Columbia Theological Seminary that the Darwinian hypothesis was "probably true." Some of his colleagues protested, and a schism developed in the faculty. Without giving Woodrow a chance to answer his inquisitors, the trustees elected another man to fill his chair. Though he cared nothing for his position —he had many other interests—James Woodrow saw and seized the opportunity to educate the brethren. He engaged in a battle that dragged on for three years, was threshed out in state synods, in the Augusta Presbytery, and finally, in 1888, in the General Assembly of the Southern Presbyterian Church.[13]

Woodrow Wilson was there at the trial before the General Assembly at Baltimore, sitting on the edge of his chair and all but cheering as James Woodrow's stilettos of dialectic, aimed without regard for tact or expediency, made his defamers writhe and his friendly advisers mutter: "*Why* did he have to say *that?* We told him *not* to say *that.*"[14] People who were acquainted with both nephew and uncle saw simi-

[13] In most of the trials and hearings, Woodrow was not upheld. He was separated from the seminary and, as in the case of Joseph Wilson's controversy in 1873, the institution was shaken to its foundations. (Cf. p. 16 n.) In this case it had to close temporarily. Professor Woodrow held the respect of his denomination, however, and later served as president of South Carolina College and moderator of the Synod of South Carolina.

[14] Edith Gittings Reid, who was present at the hearing with Dr. Thornton Whaling, to the writer. Also an article quoting Whaling, Louisville *Courier-Journal,* July 19, 1925.

larities in their characters—mental vigor, purposefulness, complete devotion to kith and kin, and capacity for protecting their inmost thought from both irrelevance and irreverence. To the idealistic nephew his dissenting uncle was a martyr.

Unlike McCosh and the Woodrows, President Patton found it hard to reconcile his Calvinist theology with the worldly impulses that were pressing the colleges; and he was particularly fearful of economic theories that might be regarded by some of the brethren as heresies. Nevertheless Professor Wilson, who thought utilitarian economics arid and too much complicated by mathematical calculation,[15], gave a course in political economy during his first year at Princeton in which he managed to explain current theories of socialism and Henry George's single-tax proposal. At first, boys from conservative families thought their professor a "radical"; but soon they realized that he was doing his duty as a competent teacher. He compiled notes for an elective course in socialism in 1890, but it was not given. When he suggested that his assistant teach sociology, Patton's religious scruples were touched and he ruled that, if work in a new field must be provided, public finance would be a safer subject. Much as Patton's brilliant preaching was admired by Wilson, he thought the president suffering from "paralysis of the will."

Wilson was given an opportunity in 1893 to present his own convictions regarding education when he was asked to speak at the World's Fair at Chicago, before the International Congress of Education. His subject was specific and limiting. However, he injected life into his talk by taking the point of view of the average citizen rather than that of the expert. Speaking for "the self-interest of the community," this scholar who had himself rebelled against a formal doctoral examination now criticized the selfishness of students who wished to get professional degrees quickly so that they might turn them into cash. He struck out at overspecialization—"that partial knowledge which is the most dangerous form of ignorance"—and argued that professional men should get a liberal education along with their technical training. Many of his ideas came forth again the next year in other addresses, and he was recognized far and wide as a spokesman for the adjustment of education to the needs of the age.

[15] In "Of the Study of Politics," which appeared in the *New Princeton Review* of March, 1887, Wilson showed a distrust of economic generalizations that reflected his devotion to Bagehot, the "literary politician" of London. Wilson set down the new-school economists as "doctrinaire" and called their so-called picture of life a mere "theorem of trade." He objected that they deliberately stripped man of all motives save self-interest.

In the autumn of 1896 came an occasion that brought the "notice-able man" to the platform at Princeton before august scholars and statesmen. His "primary" ambition was stirred, and his deep affection for Princeton called forth every volt of oratorical power that he could generate. The Old College of New Jersey had awakened to the new voices, and on the hundred fiftieth anniversary of its founding was to become Princeton University. Woodrow Wilson, the favorite lecturer of the undergraduates, was invited to be the orator of the day. This was the great opportunity for which he had been preparing since boyhood. He must not fail.

After a summer of travel in Europe, his ideas finally took shape. On Nassau Street, one day, his bicycle overtook a colleague's buggy and he shouted: "I've decided on my opening sentence. That means the battle is won." The first magic words had sprouted, the phrases were in blossom, the whole had been pruned into noble prose: "Princeton pauses to look back upon her past, not as an old man grown reminiscent, but as a prudent man still in his youth and lusty prime and at the threshold of new tasks, who would remind himself of his origin and lineage, recall the pledges of his youth, and assess as at a turning in his life the duties of his station."

The title of Wilson's address—"Princeton in the Nation's Service"—made it apparent that he was resolved to strike at issues that were fundamental and general in American colleges. "It has never been natural, it has seldom been possible," he said, "in this country for learning to seek a place apart and hold aloof from affairs." The Presbyterian ministers who founded Princeton, he pointed out, acted as if under obligation to society rather than to the church. Religion, conceive it but liberally enough, is the true salt wherewith to keep both duty and learning sweet against the taint of time and change; and it is a noble thing to have conceived it thus liberally, as Princeton's founders did . . . Duty with them was a practical thing, concerned with righteousness in this world, as well as with salvation in the next."

Having looked to the past to see what gave the place its spirit and its air of duty, Wilson talked of "progress": "There is nothing so conservative of life as growth; when that stops, decay sets in and the end comes on apace. Progress is life, for the body politic as for the body natural. To stand still is to court death."

With this assertion, however, went a warning: "Not all change is progress, not all growth is the manifestation of life." He was much mistaken, he went on, if the scientific spirit of the age was not doing a great disservice. For the achievements of science Wilson had only praise, but he objected to the projection of the scientific spirit into other fields of thought: "It has made the legislator confident that he can create, and the philosopher sure that God cannot. Past experience is discredited and the laws of matter are supposed to apply to spirit and the make-up of society." He suspected science of having enhanced passions by making wealth "so quick to come, so fickle to stay."

"Can anyone wonder, then," he went on, "that I ask for the old drill, the old memory of times gone by, the old schooling in precedent and tradition, the old keeping of faith with the past, as a preparation for leadership in days of social change? . . . Of course, when all is said, it is not learning but the spirit of service that will give a college place in the public annals of the nation. . . . We dare not keep aloof and closet ourselves while a nation comes to its maturity. The days of glad expansion are gone, our life grows tense and difficult; our resource for the future lies in careful thought, providence, and a wise economy; and the school must be the nation." He had read a draft of his speech to Ellen Wilson and she had asked for a Miltonian touch, and so he had conjured up an exalted dream of a scholar's paradise. And then, at the very end, he asked a question: "Who shall show us the way to this place?"

The applause left little doubt about the answer. Princeton, in the person of Woodrow Wilson, had an hour of triumph before the nation and the world. At last the full power of the whole man had come forth in dazzling brilliance. There was a blissful truce in the intermittent war between his conscience and his impulses. It healed his strained nerves to hear the cheering that interrupted the oration time and again and to have his hand wrung by Princetonians who were in a frenzy of pride because one of their number, a homebred, had so moved a gathering so distinguished. Editors quoted and commented, and a magazine published the address in full. Commanding the respect of both scholar and Philistine, the prophet had won eminence in his own land.

But still his striving for style did not slacken. "After forty years," a friend said, "your style is yourself—as much as the shape of your hands. You couldn't, you shouldn't try to change it." His laugh was a little wistful as he said: "You are thinking of a man who has arrived; I, of one imprisoned in a task." [16]

[16] Reid, *op. cit.*, 81–82.

Wilson's triumph at Princeton's Sesquicentennial gave his name luster in the eyes of the trustees. One of them wrote to him that there was no honor too high for him in the future so far as Princeton was concerned; and several alumni, to hold him for five years, volunteered to pay him $2,400 annually in addition to his salary.

The new age was demanding strong men who would apply business efficiency to matters that could not be allowed to drift at the mercy of sentiment and theological conviction; but at the same time the new type of leader must be a man whose academic record would command the respect of teachers. For the next few years, when an important university post became vacant, eyes usually turned toward the professor at Princeton. The University of Virginia, feeling that an administrator was needed to preside over its faculty, wooed its prominent alumnus; but Wilson feared that by accepting he would end his literary career and hurt beloved Princeton.

If a call came from his own institution, his answer might be different. However, he gave no evidence that such a possibility was prominent in his thoughts at the turn of the century and seemed rather to withdraw from administrative affairs and to wrap himself in literary work and to retire into a world of historical truth. Writing was the escape most accessible to him, and it gave opportunity to commune with his permanent gods, think in terms of "the chief end of man," political principles, the common good; and he could continue to go his own way without giving offense to others. His wife, seeing that both his soul's longings and practical necessity would be served, cheered him on and criticized his work. "I shall write for you," he told her. "We must be partners in this . . . else I shall grow cold to the marrow, and write without blood or life."

During the years near the turn of the century, Wilson was still exercising his style in literary essays; but his major effort in this period went into two works in history that were written for the general reader. He had already made his mark as a historian in a small book entitled *Division and Reunion,* which treated the political history of the United States between 1828 and 1889. In it he had shown himself able to write objectively about Civil War and Reconstruction. This was the more remarkable because he was in Georgia, body and soul, during the summers when he was composing the book. He still loved the old South of tradition. "Bless the old section," he wrote to Dabney, "as it was before the 'money Devil' entered into it!" But he did his scholarly duty and judged the South to have been legally right, but historically wrong. Northern critics marveled that this Southern historian had stood so apart from his background, and *Division and Reunion,* ably edited by Professor Albert Bushnell Hart of Harvard, was accepted as his best work in history.

The author was pleased when a note came from Professor Frederick J. Turner of Wisconsin, proclaiming that the book had "vitality—a flesh and blood form."[17] Wilson had lectured to Turner at the Johns Hopkins and they had boarded at the same house. They talked and corresponded much, and Turner had thrilled his friend by reading aloud to him his revolutionary paper on "The Significance of the Frontier in American History." Wilson already had revolted against the concept that viewed American development as a projection of New England across the continent. "The typical Americans," he asserted, "have all been Western men, with the exception of Washington."

Unfortunately for Wilson's reputation as a historian, this "exception" diverted him from his deeper purposes. He wrote, for book and serial publication in 1897, what passed as a biography of George Washington. Actually it was a long essay on American history of the eighteenth century, with the hero strutting on and off the scene, on stilts. Old Joseph Wilson perceived that his son's love of the picturesque and the dramatic had got out of hand. "Woodrow," he remarked, "I'm glad you let Washington do his own dying." Unlike the boyish author who had flared up at those who had scoffed at his first book, the professional writer of *George Washington* not only accepted criticism meekly but added some of his own. "What *am* I to do without you to read this stuff to!" he wrote to his wife as he worked alone at Baltimore. ". . . It will actually have to be *sent off* without being read to you; and the thought disconcerts me."

Wilson wished to undertake profitable historical writing that would be significant. He had informed his friend Bridges, in an effort to interest Scribner's in a popular history of the United States, that he would be "quite as slow as may be decent" in coming to terms with a publisher. At the turn of the century he felt that he had been too

---

[17] F. J. Turner to W. W., Dec. 24, 1894, Wilson pa. Wilson did his best to have Professor Turner of Wisconsin invited to Princeton. A letter written by Secretary John A. Stewart of the Princeton trustees explained that while the board thought that Turner's "religious influence" on the campus would be unexceptionable, it would be inexpedient to allow orthodox Presbyterian contributors to witness the appointment of a Unitarian. W.W. to E.A., Feb. 2, 16, 1897, Wilson pa., Ac. 12,764, box 32. Wilson wrote to Turner on Dec. 12, 1896: "A plague on boards of trustees! . . . Our president daunts us by having no will or policy at all." *See* W. R. Jacobs, "Wilson's First Battle at Princeton," *Harvard Library Bulletin,* Winter, 1954, pp. 74–87.

sentimental in his literary business; and when George Harvey of Harper's offered $12,000 for a history of the United States in twelve installments, author and publisher came to terms for the most extensive of Wilson's published works—*A History of the American People*.[18]

Actually, the feverish wooing of style served only to water the historical sense of the work to a thinness that, to the taste of professional historians, approached insipidity. "A *tour de force* of fine writing," one of his colleagues called it. The author himself was not fond of his longest work. To a friend who asked about the reception of the book he wrote: "I have reason to believe that it is growing in popularity and will prove a useful work. Walking along the street last week I saw a faker at the corner selling patent medicine. He was standing on a box marked 'Wilson's *History of the American People*.' If all the fakers in the country buy this book I ought to be satisfied. Don't you think so?" Realizing that John Fiske was using a surer and a lighter touch in making literature of history, the professor said with a rueful smile: "I wish he would keep out of my bailiwick."

Yet there were in his historical writings certain political themes that were sacred. Still mindful of James Bryce's slighting of history in his description of the American commonwealth, Wilson had an eye for the forces that had given vitality to America's exercise of democracy. In his view the life of the frontier was such a force. He could see here a connecting link between the stirrings of democracy in the Old World that he had studied and written about and the moving, vital spirit of political adjustment that was to him the hope and salvation of America.

Complaining that scholars were parching their story in a desert of footnotes, Wilson conceived of the history of nations as spiritual, not material, a thing not of institutions but of the heart and the imagination. "I love history" he wrote to Turner, "and think that there are few things so directly rewarding and worthwhile for their own sakes as to

[18] "I am corrupted," Wilson wrote to his Hopkins classmate, Franklin Jameson. ". . . it is a piece of work I meant to do anyway,—and I alter the quality not a bit,—nor dilute the stuff, neither,—to suit the medium." Writing to Turner about the difficulty of weaving the story of the American colonies into historical narrative, Wilson said: "I pray it may grow easier or it will kill me. And yet it would be a most pleasant death. The ardour of the struggle is inspiriting. There is a pleasure in the very pain,—as when one bites on an aching tooth." W.W. to Turner, Dec. 27, 1894, in Jacobs, *op. cit.*, pp. 74–87.

Lay readers bought Wilson's *History* by the thousands, from agents who came into their homes and offices. Published in *Harper's Magazine* in 1901 and in five volumes in 1902, the work went through many editions and was translated into several foreign languages. Within two years of publication, the author was rewarded by royalties larger than any theretofore received in the same time for any work of nonfiction of a similar number of words. In 1900, Wilson's "extra earnings" from writings and lecturing amounted to more than $7,000. It was still a source of regret, however, that he lacked means to give his little Nellie a pony.

scan the history of one's own country with a careful eye, and write of it with the all absorbing desire to get its cream and spirit out." These were not the concerns of a historian's historian; and yet Wilson was accepted into the brotherhood of the American Historical Association. At a meeting of that organization he fell into an acrimonious discussion with Henry Cabot Lodge,[19] a Harvard-trained scholar who saw history from a New England bias and had written a biography of George Washington that was scarcely more scholarly than Wilson's.

Meanwhile, as Professor Wilson devoted himself to profitable writing in history, the drums of revolt were beating more insistently on the Princeton campus. Dissatisfaction with Patton's administration mounted. He was criticized, during the summer of 1899, by malcontents who gathered on the porch of Professor Andrew West. The alumni, now more numerous and better organized than ever, doubted that the president shared their sentimental devotion to the college. They grew impatient with his inertia. Patton went to football games only from a sense of duty, while Wilson went as a "rooter" for Princeton, swinging along in step with the band, sitting in the stands with his cane between his knees, thumping it and cheering in a loud staccato when his "Tigers" scored. Men like Wilson and Professor Henry B. Fine took up the intellectual leadership that Patton shirked.

Finally, in 1902, one of the trustees wrote to the president to ask for his resignation "in order to make way for urgent needs in the matter of university reform." Patton, weary and content to withdraw into his own studies, gave in. He resented criticism of his administration by trustees who had made Professor Andrew West dean of graduate students. And now, to prevent the choice of West as his successor, he suddenly recommended the university's greatest orator, the idol of the undergraduates, the favorite of the younger alumni and the Western men, but a man with little executive experience—Woodrow Wilson.

Twenty-four of the twenty-eight trustees of the university—ex-President Grover Cleveland was among them for the first time—met with Patton on June 9, 1902, accepted the president's resignation, and appointed a committee on the choice of a successor. That very afternoon the committee reported that they had agreed with the president on the name of Wilson. Suspending a section of the bylaws that would have delayed the final balloting, a unanimous vote was cast for the popular

---

[19] Edward Channing to Stewart Mitchell to the writer. For criticism of Lodge's *George Washington, see* John A. Garraty, *Henry Cabot Lodge,* pp. 57–59. Writing to Howard Pyle, illustrator of his own *George Washington,* Wilson referred to Lodge's life of Washington as the "latest authoritative biography," but a "secondary authority." W.W. to Pyle, Jan. 12, 1896.

professor, and three trustees of the Class of '79 went immediately to notify their classmate.

Though not surprised, the house of Wilson was overwhelmed by the speed and unanimity of the action. Ellen Wilson had noted that her husband had "a great taste for administration" and had been successful as chairman of important committees, but she wrote now to a friend: "It is enough to frighten a man to be so loved and believed in." Sheafs of congratulatory messages came in. Old Joseph Wilson, lying in his son's home on his deathbed, sent for his three granddaughters and, peering from deep-set eyes that had softened almost to tears, said solemnly: "Never forget what I tell you. Your father is the greatest man I have ever known . . . This is just the beginning of a very great career." [20]

In facing up to his responsibility Wilson was both humble and confident. "Definite, tangible tasks," he thought, would take "the flutter and restlessness" from his spirits. He might have doubted whether he was the man for the job had he not been for a long time intimately acquainted with the life of the university. If he had needed chastening he would have found it in a message from his old chum Dabney: "Who could have guessed that an Illimitable Idiot would ever be selected as the President of a great university?"

There was criticism of the haste with which the new leader had been chosen, and it was noted that Wilson was the first president of Princeton without formal theological training. But the tradition of his family guaranteed that he would not depart from the spirit of the old religion, and there was no doubt that he belonged to the campus in mind and body and soul. He was thrilled when the applause of reunioning alumni assured him that the Princeton family loved him. But with his exaltation he felt a twinge of renunciation. "No doubt I shall have to give up writing for the next three or four years," he wrote, "and that is a heartbreaking thing for a fellow who has not yet written the particular thing for which he has been training all his life."

Near the end of October, crowds poured into the little village for the inauguration. Orange-and-black banners floated against red and yellow leaves and the slanting sun struck everything into gold. Scores of educational dignitaries of America and Europe fell into line. The great of the nation were there—Grover Cleveland and Theodore Roosevelt,

[20] Eleanor Wilson McAdoo, *The Woodrow Wilsons*, pp. 59–60. The year before, at Wilmington, the preacher had told his Negro servant, David Bryant, that someday "Mr. Tommie" would be a candidate for the Presidency of the United States and made the Negro promise to cast a vote as his proxy.

J. P. Morgan and Mark Twain, George Harvey and Walter Hines Page. Lawrence Lowell of Harvard was a house guest of the Wilsons'. Booker T. Washington came, and at the dinner following the ceremonies made what Wilson thought was the best speech of the occasion.

To Woodrow Wilson the inaugural address was as vital as the first speech of a prime minister to a parliament. In "Princeton in the Nation's Service," at the Sesquicentennial, he had talked of the institution's great past and had set a spiritual tone for its future. Now, however, he must come to grips with immediate issues.

In meeting the rising demand for technical and professional education, he explained, universities had so spread and diversified the scheme of knowledge that it had lost coherence. Of the two supreme tasks of a great university—"the production of a great body of informed and thoughtful men and the production of a small body of trained scholars and investigators"—Wilson was concerned chiefly with the former. The new president could not be satisfied with anything less than "a full liberation of the faculties" of the undergraduates; and yet he felt that in the organization of a university, as in a political democracy, there must be discipline and system before there could be effective freedom. He would pick up the "threads of system" that had been dropped, would knit them together in a comprehensive course of study that the undergraduates and his preceptors would plan together.

The prophet reminded his audience that he had charge "not of men's fortunes, but of their spirits." The final synthesis of learning is in philosophy, he said, and he held the philosophy of conduct dear. He advocated the "energy of a positive faith," insisting that "we are not put into this world to sit and know; we are put into it to act." The new generation "must be supplied with men who care more for principles than for money, for the right adjustments of life than for the gross accumulations of profit . . . We are here not merely to release the faculties of men for their own use, but also to quicken their social understanding, instruct their consciences, and give them the catholic vision of those who know their just relations to their fellow men."

If the Sesquicentennial address had been a Gospel, this was The Acts. Those who heeded it knew that the days of drift were over. Afterward the orator's friends crowded around him, cheering incessantly. He appealed to them for understanding and confidence: "I ask that you will look upon me not as a man to do something apart, but as a man who asks the privilege of leading you and being believed in by you while he tries to do the things in which he knows you believe." The still-youthful executive yearned to be loved and trusted as passionately as he insisted on crusading for what he thought right; and in the two passions—the bonhomie and the Covenanter's devotion to Truth—was potential enough to tear the man asunder when the currents crossed.

Some among the alumni may not have been converted, some may not even have understood, but they could not fail to note that "people said" that their man Wilson was a great leader. They were convinced that he would keep school faithfully and that the boys would like him, and surely this Scot would use money thriftily. As for his "principles," they were, to some of the Princeton family, just good talk. "Very beautiful speech of Wilson's, very noble," remarked a visiting journalist, "but over the heads of two trustees who sat in front of me."

It was over the head, also, of William J. Thompson, "Duke" of the Gloucester race track, a little Democratic politician who sat in the audience and was overwhelmed by the power of the speaker. Perceiving only that this orator would make a "great candidate," he boasted: "Why, I could twiddle that man right around my fingers. . . . I know the boys who can reach him."

CHAPTER V

Family Man

THE NOTICEABLE MAN was now president of a great university. The independent critic, the rollicking chum, the heady lover, the wooer of the Muses—all these fell now under the pressure of pastoral responsibility. The eloquent prophecy that had stirred the Princeton constituency would have to be tempered by tact and patience; for as the servant-leader of an academic community he must concern himself not only with principles but with men of many kinds—those whom he had to love as well as those whom he liked to love.

Soon after coming to Princeton to teach, Wilson had written to his father: "My mind cannot give me gratification. I know it too well and it is a poor thing. I have to rely on my heart as the sole source of contentment and happiness, and that craves, oh, so fiercely, the companionship of those I love." In the early nineties, in a house that the Wilsons rented on Library Place, there had been time to revel in the love of kin and the comradeship of friends. In the absence of shows, automobiles, and country clubs, the college faculty found their recreation in good conversation. And they talked brilliantly: Harry Fine, blunt and hearty, an unwavering disciple of Wilson's educational principles; Jack Hibben, whom the students toasted as "the whitest man in all the fac"; George Harper, authority on beloved Wordsworth; charming Bliss Perry; quizzical Winthrop Daniels; witty President Patton. There were guests, too, from the outside world; Humphry Ward, Walter Hines Page, and Mark Twain. Ellen Wilson arranged that brilliant men and women should come into their drawing room.

When there was occasion to meet strangers, however, Wilson often turned shy and made excuses. Ellen would have to coax him; but, once introduced, he enjoyed himself and dominated the talk. After telling a story he did not chuckle, but fixed a challenging eye on his hearers until they laughed. People who saw Wilson in repose often thought him homely; but once his countenance burst into conversation, they watched his mouth in awe at the precision of the words that came from it. In familiar conversation he was not didactic, and he was utterly candid.

In one breath he could be witty, ridiculous, profound. He could listen well, too, to talk worthy of his mettle. Emotional reactions showed in his face, and usually he could respond with an anecdote or comment that was pat. When his mind worked at its highest pitch, he dazzled even those who knew him best.

His powers of talk ran riot in the presence of ladies whom he thought "charming and conversable"; and it often happened that he thought the more charming the more conversable. ". . . you know how seldom a woman who is not pretty attracts me," he wrote to his wife in 1898. "Perhaps a southern woman manages it by dint of grace and sweetness." When he discovered feminine charm he wrote to Ellen about it with the ardor of a prospector striking gold. Of one of his discoveries he wrote: "while she delights me, you enslave me."

In the company of vigorous men, however, he was ill at ease. After a stag party in the country he confessed to Ellen that he felt "sadly out of sport, being unable to play golf or to fish with flies." Regretting that he appeared "a mere book-man—a mere theorist in life—a mere man of letters," he artfully pretended to drink punch in response to toasts in order "not to dampen the jovial spirit of the occasion!"[1]

Feeling that she was not by nature "gamesome," Ellen Wilson encouraged and shared her husband's friendships with brilliant ladies. And his gallant adventures served only to raise the pedestal on which he kept his Ellen enthroned. They kept their covenant, made before their marriage, to be quite open with each other in everything. All their treasures were held in common—books, money, pleasures, and friends, both men and women. Their opinions often differed, but even their closest relatives never heard them quarrel. His letters courted her constantly. Sometimes she would read them to her daughters, occasionally skipping a page or two, saying with a smile, "This part is sacred."

As the strain of Wilson's duties became heavier and began to tell on his health, his wife watched over him, realizing, as she said to a friend, that "a woman's place is to keep one little spot in the world quiet."

In her home she created an atmosphere in which a man could transmute his love into literary achievement. Beaming warmly on the family teasing that eddied around her, she did not allow her husband's impatience with stupidity to get out of hand. When Wilson, in the privacy of the family, blurted out an opinion that was hasty or unkind, his wife would say: "Oh, Woodrow, you don't mean that." And the professor would reply: "Madam, I ventured to think that I meant that until I was

[1] Letters, W.W. to E.A.W., June 6, Sept. 11, 12, 1898, Wilson pa., Ac. 12,764, box 35; McAdoo, *The Priceless Gift*, p. 189.

corrected." Ellen Wilson could be intense in argument, but never showed bad temper except when she thought her husband unfairly attacked or imposed upon.

She had books before her as she dressed in the morning, and she read aloud at night. One moment she would soar with the poets into a realm in which she could best release her husband from his implacable conscience. Or, alone, she would burrow into a deep work in history or philosophy and lose herself in it until some of her family came in and made a game of catching her attention with signs, whispers, clearings of the throat, and finally, voices. Then she would be all sympathetic eagerness, keen to listen and advise.

Under masses of coppery hair and bangs that hid a forehead that she thought too high, her brown eyes shone with varied lights, now tender in sympathy, now bright with laughter. Before going out to parties she sometimes crushed rose leaves and applied them to her cheeks with a rabbit's foot that she kept hidden in a drawer for shame at such stooping to artifice.

Life in the household moved with a smooth rhythm. Fresh flowers were kept in their bedroom. Nothing was out of place: not so much as one stocking was allowed to lie on the floor. Ellen Wilson made dresses for herself and her girls and one year took pride in spending less for clothes than her husband spent for books. She trained two white servants, who stood loyally by her for decades. Drawling softly, she imparted to the cook the secrets of the Southern dishes that her husband relished. Sitting at lunch with him after a morning of proofreading, they would make a game of their labors. "I dare not have the blues!" she wrote to a girlhood friend. "If I am just a little sky blue he immediately becomes blue-black!"

In this serene home Wilson achieved an output that would have been creditable even for a man who did nothing but write. Though at first without secretarial help, he responded to appeals from dozens of relatives and personal friends, whether they wanted advice, criticism, money, or sympathy. He initiated projects in correspondence, too— sometimes more than he could carry through. Even with the aid of shorthand, the mechanical labor of writing became so great at one time that he suffered severely from neuritis, or "writer's cramp," and lost the use of his right hand for months. For a while he depended on his wife to write letters for him; but soon he had driven himself to learn to write clearly with his left hand. And by massage, rest, and regular exercises his ailing right hand was restored to usefulness.

His driving conscience worked his mind as hard as his muscles. When his train of expression came to an unbridged chasm he did not boggle. Keeping his thoughts straight on the course, he sat rigid over his typewriter, conjuring up a trestle of words. When the *mot juste* eluded him, he forced himself to sit with his fingers on the keys and make the right word come. He had no doubt that the word that came was the right one. "A Yankee always thinks that he is right, a Scotch-Irishman *knows* that he is right," he liked to quote. His discipline and concentration increased with the years and permitted him to plow through work with a smoothness that concealed the worry that it cost him. But as he neared the end of his longest book his mind became so jaded that one afternoon, going upstairs to dress for dinner, he absent-mindedly undressed and climbed into bed. Ellen Wilson made a joke of it, and yet worried about him and persuaded him to bicycle in England the next summer.

In the nineties he traveled far in America, making lecture trips to Chicago, to Massachusetts, and to Colorado. Early in 1896 he spent a month at Baltimore, lecturing and laboriously composing his biography of George Washington, undergoing treatment for ailing digestion and what he described as a "derangement of the bowels," pining for Ellen and writing daily to tell her of his love. The following summer, yielding to her insistence, he made his first trip abroad. He went alone, seeing the things that appealed to him most, writing frankly and freshly to his Ellen of his enthusiasms and impressions. To her he sent grass from the grave of Adam Smith, a leaf from the burial place of Walter Bagehot, to be pressed and kept for him. The colleges of Cambridge struck him as "beyond measure attractive," and a mere glance at Oxford was "enough to take one's heart by storm." From his visits to the universities he drew inspiration for his later work at Princeton. ". . . and yet," he asserted, "I have not seen a prettier dwelling than ours in England!"

Mostly he occupied his time with pilgrimages to literary shrines—the cottage in which Burns was born, the Shakespeare country, the plain church and simple tablet beside which Burke lay, and most exhilarating of all, the Lake Country and Wordsworthian shrines. Of all landscapes that he saw, the River Wye won his heart most completely; and sitting on a grassy bank near Tintern Abbey he was filled with exalted emotion as he quoted from Wordsworth. At London he looked up James Bryce, invited him to lecture at Princeton.

In February of 1898 the professor's latent political ambition impelled him to pass a fortnight in Washington, which he found an "unnatural place," a city that was "nothing but the seat of the national government, —and of an idle society of rich people." It would be far more wholesome, he thought, if the capital were "one of the great cities, with an independent life of its own,—out of which the representatives of noncommercial communities might take the instruction they so sadly lack, and can't get in Washington." To Ellen he wrote: "There are a number of people here upon whom I really *ought* to call, despite my shyness and disinclination . . . I am too proud to *seek* acquaintance even with men who, I feel sure, would like to know me." He visited for ten minutes with the Speaker of the House and learned that that official had read *Congressional Government* with astonishment that an outsider had been able to grasp the features of "government by helterskelter." Afterward Wilson described the Speaker to Ellen as "agreeable . . . even attractive, frank, sensible, and interesting."[1a]

In 1899 Wilson went off again at his wife's insistence to England, this time with Stockton Axson, Ellen's brother. They went over much of the same ground as in 1896 but passed more time in the Burns country. His conscience hurt him because he feared that he was not tired enough to justify the expense and pain of separation. "Here I am simply spending money and pining for you!" he wrote to his Ellen.

He came home revived; and it sustained his lifted spirits to feel once more the love of his "three little thoroughbreds" and their incomparable mother. It was good to sit again at his own hearth in the evening, with his Ellen beside him, embroidering and mending while she helped her daughters with their lessons. And in the daytime he would come upon her making paper dolls and teaching the girls how to color them, or tucked away in her own room painting a portrait of a daughter.

The Wilsons tried to give their children serenity of soul, as well as knowledge and grace. On the Sabbath their household was slowed down. No games were permitted, and only readings that built character. The Wilsons did not send their daughters along the easy and conventional path to Sunday school. Feeling that most teachers in church schools were not trained to give a true view of religion, Ellen Wilson gave Bible lessons to her daughters in her own room. Mostly, the parents taught by example, making virtue attractive and good manners and morals habitual. "I feel daily more and more bent," Wilson once wrote to his father, "toward creating in my own children that combined respect and tender devotion for their father that you gave

[1a] Letters, W.W. to E.A.W., Feb., 1898, Wilson pa., Ac. 12,764, box 34.

your children for you. Oh, how happy I should be, if I could make them think of me as I think of you!" Though sobered by paternity, Wilson felt "a great deal of the boy revived" in him by the companionship of his little ones.

In the few instances in which moral suasion was not enough, Ellen Wilson spanked. Her face grew pink, and she was as likely as the child to shed tears; but she did not bother her husband with accounts of this unpleasantness. To the girls their father was all tenderness, gaiety, and play. He had a way with children. First he would listen solemnly to whatever childish concept they might express, then he would use his mobile face and dramatic talent to amuse them, perhaps blowing his cheeks into balloons to be patted by childish fingers, or pulling out loose flesh on his face and snapping it, or letting his chin sag lower, notch by notch. His hands seemed to his children to have life of their own. He could make his fingers creep like animals on the arm of his chair, or slapping his knees he could do the galloping horse—slappety-slap, slappety-slap, growing louder and then fading gradually as if in the distance. A little playmate of his sister-in-law called him "a regular guy."

Insisting that the girls be punctual at meals, he came to breakfast at eight o'clock sharp. Before eating he said a formal blessing, slowly and reverently; but grace was not offered at the end of meals, as in the homes of some church folk of that day. Instead, after breakfast and lunch, the children were dismissed by delicious nonsense, jingled in singsong: "Now, chickens, run upstairs, wash your face and hands, brush your teeth and put your bibs away before I count three—or I'll tickle, pinch, and spank-doodle you."

In the evening, after the "now-I-lay-mes" were said, the father read Uncle Remus or sat by the nursery fire and sang "Sweet and Low," "Watchman, Tell Us of the Night," and lilting rhymes of nonsense. Once, when Nellie had scarlet fever, Wilson relieved his wife in keeping vigil, building with the child's blocks in favorite Norman designs. He fed the little one and slept beside her, wrote letters for her and sent them to her sisters in a basket that traveled on a pulley that he had rigged. Visiting the sickroom of his little sister-in-law when she was shaken by malarial fever, he cheered her by telling of a victim of chills who shivered so hard that when he drank milk it turned to butter. And as he told the story his supple body shuddered, acting it out.

For economy, the furnace was kept low. Wilson himself stoked it, taking aim as carefully as when he tried to play golf on a rough course that colleagues had laid out back of his house. He enjoyed working in the garden, sometimes mowed the lawn, and polished his shoes; and one night when a guest left his boots outside the door, Wilson polished those too. Each year he and his Ellen budgeted his salary.

As the children grew and relatives joined the household, more space was needed. And so the Wilsons decided to build a new house, to stand on a lot next to the one in which they were living. There were trees ready grown for the family to worship: pines and oaks, a large sycamore, and in the rear a radiant copper beech, with huge limbs spaced just right for climbing, and beneath them a sun-speckled fairyland for children's play. The beech was the chief reason, Ellen Wilson told her friends, for building on this lot.

Wishing to temper dignity with grace, the Wilsons chose the half-stone, half-stucco style of the English Norman country home, with trimmings of stained wood. They spént hours in discussing the line of the roof. Woodrow drew the plans and Ellen made a clay model; and when the architects' bids ran $2,000 above their resources, he resolved to lecture for the University Extension Society to make up the difference. For a hedge they decided on privet, for quick growth. Their children were offered a nickel for every basket of weeds that they pulled from the lawn. Flowers and shrubs were planted copiously, and ivy to creep on the walls. After a year of building, Ellen Wilson supervised the moving in; and her husband came home one night to find everything installed in the new house: furniture, pictures, maids, children, canary, and Puffins the cat.

On the first floor back was a spot sacred to Wilson alone—his study. Here were hung likenesses of the professor's favorite gods: over the mantel his father; and elesewhere crayon enlargements that Ellen Wilson had made of Washington, Webster, Gladstone, Bagehot, and Burke. These were the only ornaments of the room. It had the air of a place of business. The drawers of the desk were labeled in neat script, and there were metal filing cases and a revolving bookcase. Two of the walls were lined to the ceiling with books. They were accumulating rapidly. Ponderous tomes were arriving for a study of the German legal system. When students came to his office he put them at ease with courtesy and good humor, and insisted that they call him not *Dr.* or *Professor*, but *Mr.* Wilson. Once convinced of the good faith of those who came to him, he would talk to them like a father. When a boy whom he tried to help failed to confide in him, he was distressed; but he could be brusque with those bent merely on ingratiating themselves.

In his composition, as in his professional appointments, the professor was a clock of regularity. He never left his desk in disorder, but wiped his pen, put it in place, closed the inkwell, tidied his papers, covered his typewriter, and returned the books that he had been using to their places on the shelves. From a window seat he could look out into the garden and watch his children at play under the glorious copper beech. When they came to the window or to his door, he was not too preoccupied to give a quick, loving glance. He never demanded absolute quiet in the house while he worked; but when quarreling broke out he would call the girls into his study, ask them what the trouble was, and explain gently the rights and wrongs of the case. Once, when the little Wilsons and Clevelands fought with neighbors of Republican heritage, he said: "You must never quarrel about religion or politics. Both are very private, and you will never change anyone's mind."[1b] When the children tried to divide the world among themselves, he arranged straws for them to draw.

When the roll top of their father's desk slammed, the lock clicked and the youngsters heard a soft whistle and a jingling of keys. They knew then that their choicest playfellow might join them for merrymaking. They voted their father "the world's greatest orator" and thought him capable of being president of the United States or of anything else. But sometimes, when the problems of composition seemed insuperable, Woodrow Wilson threatened to give himself to the writing of stories for children. Once, attacking hypocrisy in education, he said: "We must believe the things we tell the children."

Growing older, the Wilson girls sat up evenings with the family in the central living room, where their father would prance and jig with them. Or he might take off a drunk, or a stuffy, monocled Englishman. He could tell stories in dialect—Scottish, Irish, and Negro. Dressing up for a charade, he would put on a lady's hat and a feather boa, wrap himself in a long velvet curtain, hold one hand high for a "social" handshake, and gush in high falsetto in burlesque of a grand dame. Sometimes it would be the "heavy villain" of melodrama, or a Fourth of July orator who gestured with his legs instead of his arms. Or he would take up the Ouija board, ask it the name of the latest beau of one of the girls, and regard her dismay with a chuckle as the name of the most outlandish campus character was spelled out.[2] Often his clear tenor would pour out "The Kerry Dance" or "The Duke of Plaza-Toro," a

---

[1b] Eleanor Wilson McAdoo to the writer, March 10, 1952.
[2] F. C. MacDonald and Eleanor Wilson McAdoo to the writer.

Scottish ballad or an old hymn of the kirk. He liked quaint sayings such as "Good Lord deliver us from witches and war-locks and from things that say woo-oo in the night."

On New Year's Eve, in Scottish fashion, the clan gathered in the dining room, drank a toast, sang "Auld Lang Syne," standing each with one foot on a chair and the other on the table, and then ran to open the front door so that the old year might go and the new year enter. On one of these occasions the president of Princeton threw his family into fits of laughter by mimicking the classic figures that stood in the hall—a proud Roman emperor and Apollo with finger coyly poised. Sometimes he feared the very momentum of his own spirits, once confessing that he "dared not let himself go because he did not know where to stop." [3]

He was as clever in conjuring up rhymes to fit occasions as was his wife in quoting serious verse that was apropos. Often he called his memory the "silliest" in the world, for he never forgot a nonsense rhyme and didn't know one piece of fine poetry by heart. Yet he loved to read and to hear his Ellen read the English poets. Wordsworth was his favorite: he himself aspired to be "the happy warrior"; his Ellen was to him "a phantom of delight." When *A Shropshire Lad* was read to him, Wilson was repelled, asked whether it was *all* about wanting to die, and turned to Henry V—"something with good red blood in it."

Often relatives joined in the fellowship of the home on Library Place. They came to make visits in the Southern tradition—to stay for weeks, months, sometimes years—and the Wilsons were not hurried or flurried. Ever since their marriage they had planned for the education of kinfolk who had less of the world's goods. Wilson threw gentle, fatherly protection over all the clan. He would draw out confidences from each one and he taught them that selfishness was very nearly the deadliest of sins and the root of most crime. It was assumed in the household that one tested one's conduct by asking whether it would be possible to "sleep happily with one's self." But Wilson would not allow holier-than-thou criticism of even the black sheep of the clan. "After all," he would say, "he is your own flesh and blood." [4]

To her orphaned brothers and little sister, Ellen Wilson was a mother. Stockton Axson had lived in her home as an undergraduate at Wesleyan; and joining the family at Princeton, he became Wilson's dearest

3 Helen Woodrow Bones to Baker. R. S. Baker Papers. Also Miss Bones to the writer, at the Biltmore Hotel, Asheville, N.C., April 5, 1948.
4 Helen W. Bones to the writer, April 5, 1948.

comrade. Together they would bandy wit and bookish fun for hours on end. Axson was pure-bred Southerner, of a nature milder than that of Wilson; and in the nineties he fitted easily into the gaiety of the Wilson household, helped to keep its spirits and ideals high.[5]

In the attic of the home on Library Place young Edward Axson, an undergraduate specializing in science, carried on experiments in a world of instruments and odors far removed from the child play and literary talk that went on below. Wilson helped the lad to overcome a habit of stuttering; and Edward fixed the household gadgets when they broke. This brother-in-law and his classmate George Howe, Wilson's nephew, stood in Wilson's eyes in the place of sons.

At the turn of the century the household was primarily one of men. Dominating them all with his masculine vigor was Joseph Wilson, who was made to feel at home in the house on Library Place. The doctor was still a doughty contender. When his theological school was in danger of losing the support of the synod, the old warrior informed his son that he "met the Kentucky men throughout a four hours' debate. The upshot was that we routed them, horse, foot and dragoon . . . I made a good speech—the papers saying that Tennessee ought to be proud of me, etc., etc.,—you know the sort of nonsense . . . We have to become men of the world sometimes in order to keep from being men of the monastery. The stilts of study are not good for *constant* use." Dr. Wilson's dislike for narrow theology grew with advancing age.

Often during the nineties the father wrote letters of extravagant affection, speaking frankly of his parental pride and of his concern for Woodrow Wilson's brother and sisters. The oldest, Marion Wilson Kennedy, died in Arkansas in 1890, and the Wilsons took thought for the care of her four orphaned children. But the blow that touched the Wilsons most was the death of their brother-in-law and old friend, Dr. George Howe. "Oh, for some great heart-word to tell you what we suffer . . ." Wilson wrote to his sister Annie in sympathy. For years the Woodrow Wilsons had depended on Dr. Howe for medical advice, by correspondence. It was a close-knit family, the members sometimes lending money to one another without interest, and after Dr. Howe's death the care of his wife and children fell to some extent on the already strained treasury of the Wilsons. "We are one," the old doctor used to write, quoting Scripture. But when the preacher learned of

[5] In one of the two books that Woodrow Wilson did not dedicate to his wife is this tribute: "To Stockton Axson; By every gift of mind a critic and lover of letters, by every gift of heart a friend: This little volume is affectionately dedicated." Dedication of *Mere Literature*.

brother-in-law James Woodrow's controversy with the fundamentalists, he wrote to his son: "I regret this exceedingly. . . . What asses Presbyterians are capable of becoming—whose ears extend to all the earth."

Joseph Wilson's vanity was puffed by the fact that he was the only man who could dictate to his prominent son. To young lady relatives from the South, the old man was sometimes an irascible bear. The fiancée of one of his grandsons baited him with: "Now that I have met you at last, I see where your grandson got his good looks." And the old man trumpeted, "He did not! I still have my good looks!"[6] In his seventies he took a fancy to a widow to whose religious journal he contributed, and wrote more than a hundred letters filled with religious admonition and mawkishness.

Woodrow Wilson would endure teasing from his father with filial patience. But he did not like to have the preacher at his lectures. Once, when the old man crouched in a rear seat as if to escape detection, his son felt like a boy who would have to answer to him afterward for everything said.

Often, after lunch, the men of the family would sit on the porch and talk. Stockton Axson noticed a resemblance to Emerson but found no sympathy for transcendentalism in the mind of Woodrow Wilson. The old doctor's leonine head was fuller of knowledge than Woodrow's, but less subtle in interpretation, less energetic in concentration, less skillful in application. Once, reading one of his son's manuscripts, he was moved to kiss him tearfully and lament: "Oh, Woodrow, I wish, with that genius of yours, you had become a preacher." Though a better debater than the doctor, the son would not push points home in conversation. Sure that his father was by far the abler man, he used to scold him for not publishing anything.

In 1901 the old preacher had an attack of "rigor" at Wilmington. His son gave up a projected trip to Europe and brought him to Princeton, where he lingered for almost two years. As his arteries hardened, he grew childish and querulous, was put out when his boy went on lecture trips without saying goodbye to him, felt better when favorable reports of a Wilson speech came in. Finally, at the end of 1902, Ellen Wilson was writing to a friend: ". . . he had to be attended to exactly like a baby . . . He seems to suffer constantly and when coming out of his stupors moans and cries—even screams—for hours . . . I am very glad that Woodrow is out of the house and out of town so much about his business that he sees very little of it . . ." When his son could be at

6 Mrs. Margaret Flinn Howe to the writer, at Columbia, S.C.

his bedside he comforted the old man by singing to him—"Crown Him with Many Crowns" and other favorites.

Finally the end came, in January of 1903. Jack Hibben was at the bedside, and seeing the bed start to give way beneath the weight of the agonized figure, he quickly crawled under and held it up, remaining there until there was no life to support.[7]

Woodrow Wilson, stony-faced and inconsolable, picked Princeton ivy from the vine of the Class of '79 and put it on the old man's casket, went down to Columbia for the funeral, and begged his sister to make the slip grow over their father's grave in the churchyard.[8] For a few hours he could feel that he had fallen again into the slow-paced Southern life that seemed to him the most natural of all. He himself composed a long epitaph for his father's stone, and in a pocket notebook treasured these lines:

> Enough to know
> What e'er he feared, he never feared a foe.[9]

Bereft of his most devoted friend and teacher, Wilson returned to Princeton feeling that he was now on the firing line, with no older generation ahead of him. He gave thanks that he still had all that was best of long association with the departed saint, as "spiritual capital" to live upon.

On the first day of 1904 he was attacked by neuralgia, and sat with his wife before the study fire and discussed ways of getting rest. He was solicitous, too, for her health under the burdens that she assumed as Princeton's first lady. Sometimes he restored his own powers by giving himself the pleasure of strengthening hers. In the summer of 1903 they traveled together in France and Italy; and in 1904 he sent her abroad with a daughter while he took responsibility for the household.

Soon after her return she was thrown into the deepest sorrow of her life. Brother Edward Axson was drowned, with his wife and baby, while ferrying across a swollen river in the South. Ellen Wilson was inconsolable for weeks, and was sent by her husband to recuperate in the quiet town of Lyme, Connecticut. Woodrow Wilson went himself to the bedside of ailing Stockton Axson, remarking as he related the tragedy that dear Jack Hibben was standing by and watching over the family in its grief.

[7] Professor and Mrs. Robert Scoon to the writer, letter of June 15, 1950, and enclosure.
[8] Mrs. Margaret Flinn Howe to the writer.
[9] Clipping from a poem by Hugh MacNaughten, found in W.W.'s pocket notebook for 1902-3.

Margaret Axson was stunned by the blow. But Woodrow Wilson took her into his study, spoke of Edward as they had known him in his sweet, mischievous boyhood, of the growth of his finely disciplined mind and high character. "He had all the virtues I could have wished for a son of my own," he said, "even the virtue of not being too good." And the impressionable girl forgot the horror of the drowning. Suddenly she had him back again, her brother, as she would always remember him. "Thank you," she said, looking up into the clear eyes of a brother-in-law who always understood.

The household revolved around Woodrow Wilson, and especially around his voice, which played chords on the keyboard of human emotion. Given a family of daughters, he strove to make himself agreeable to girls. If he would have preferred boys, he never allowed those nearest him to suspect it. Of the peccadilloes of his young kinsfolk he could disapprove sternly, but he could tease them out of their bad habits without, like his father, inflicting pain. His regard for the feelings of others was immense. Even when his quick, precise mind was irritated by dullness or repetition, he tried to conceal his impatience, though to his immediate family he would often complain: "I can't understand why people tell me the same thing over and over—I'm really not a fool." He did not lose his temper over petty personal hurts. But let one of his sacred causes be attacked unfairly or untruthfully, and his face would turn white and his quiet, sharp words would fairly bite. In one of their family evenings together, someone asked for the one word that would describe the most admirable human quality, and Woodrow Wilson said: "Loyalty." Within the circle of intimates there was fealty fierce and stout. They would cut their bones for each other and for their mutual causes.

They needed all their morale, now that the master of the house had become president of Princeton. As a concession to college tradition, they had to move to a campus residence from the sweet home in which they had lived so blithely on Library Place. They were now public personages immured in an architectural monstrosity called Prospect. Ellen Wilson, however, was equal to the challenge. Removing affectations that were *fin de siècle*, she restored the main rooms to good taste. In place of the old Victorian garden that had been heavy with coleus and canna, she planned a wistaria-draped pergola at the end of a walk lined with rhododendrons and cedars and, beyond, a garden like one that she had seen in Italy, with marble seats and sundial. In the presence of the family, Woodrow and Ellen Wilson did not flinch under their new responsibilities. But one night the girls overheard their mother crying and her husband saying, very tenderly: "I should never have brought you here, darling. We were so happy in our own home."

The atmosphere of Prospect, however, was not uncongenial to Woodrow Wilson. Sitting at the long flat desk in the same study that McCosh had occupied, he enjoyed conjuring up recollections of old "Jimmy" opposite him. But his holy of holies was the room high in Prospect's square tower. There, with windows on all sides, he got perspective and did most of his vital writing. When he retired to that eyrie he was "out" to visitors.

In their own home the Wilsons had been able to choose their guests; but at Prospect much of their entertaining was in the name of the college. Though the president tried to select Sunday preachers of wit and eloquence, irrespective of creed, he sometimes felt like saying from his seat behind the pulpit: "Oh, let's quit and sing a hymn!" [10] But on Saturday nights the dull ministers had to be cared for at Prospect with the same warmth that was lavished on the inspired. The Wilsons hated to say polite nothings to guests to whom they could not give their hearts. Ellen Wilson feared to profane the spirit of true hospitality by entertaining the wealthy friends of the university. She did her duty, however, and in one winter had sixty-five dinner parties. Wine was served, cigars were passed, and the men were expected to smoke as they wished. Once, when the women retired to take coffee before a log fire in the living room, Beatrice Webb remained with the men to smoke, and even Ellen Wilson lost her composure.

Thus the cloud of responsibility descended to brood over the idyllic home, and along with it thunderbolts of illness and death. Joseph Wilson and Edward Axson had been snatched away, and Stockton Axson had an attack of melancholia that lasted for six months. In the two years after the inauguration, Prospect became a household of women. A man surrounded by adoring ladies had to make a success of his life, he told them; for they wouldn't let him fail.

[10] Benjamin Chambers, typescript, in the possession of Cleveland E. Dodge, p. 42.

CHAPTER VI

University Pastor

When woodrow wilson entered the presidency of Princeton, in the autumn of 1902, he could feel sure of his pre-eminence in the service of the university. One of the professors who had opposed Patton wrote to the new leader to assure him that he was the one under whom they wished to serve, that they would stand by him until things were "right." But in his hour of ascendancy Wilson turned to Bliss Perry with a grim and knowing smile and said: "If West begins to intrigue against me as he did against Patton, we must see who is master!"

Andrew Fleming West, a graduate of the Class of '74, had not been content to remain merely an able professor of the classics at Princeton. He had larger ambitions and had worked hard for their realization. But in the nineties it had been plain that his ideals and Wilson's were not compatible. In a soft, mellow voice West lulled his boys with the verse of Horace. Somewhat casual about attendance at classes, he had come to depend more on wit and social charm than on intellectual effort to maintain his place in the Princeton community. His home saddened by the chronic illness of his wife, he found pleasure in the company of cultivated men; and as a charming diner-out, and a greeter adept at making returning alumni feel at home, he appeared to be striking up friendships with men from whom he might hope to get financial support for his educational ambitions. While Woodrow Wilson, who rarely praised and never jollied anyone designingly, was wearing himself thin over his typewriter and in public speaking, ruddy-cheeked Andrew West was expanding his huge frame and genial spirit in good living and in deeds of personal kindness to his friends and colleagues.[1] He was in his element in New York's Gin Mill Club,

[1] West took an active part, too, in Princeton's administration and publicity. As secretary of the Committee on the Schedule, he had labored to make the old College of New Jersey into a university. He it was who had organized and promoted the Susquicentennial celebration; and under his aegis was published a lavish and pompous memorial tome. West had observed the fine points of academic protocol at English universities and was restless to import them to Princeton. He had taught Latin in a high school and in 1883 had received a Ph.D. degree at Princeton and had become a professor of the classics there. He had produced no considerable scholarly work of depth.

which Professor Sloane frequented and to which Trustee Moses Taylor Pyne once undertook, unsuccessfully, to introduce Woodrow Wilson.[2]

Having been made dean of graduate students, responsible to a committee of trustees, West continued to hold that position in Wilson's presidency, and in university councils he championed the causes of the graduate school and the classics.[3] He argued that Greek must remain compulsory, even though as a result Princeton might lose boys of great promise in other fields. Wilson, thinking his spirit too close, noted in his diary one day: "Interview with West, in wh. he showed the most stubborn prejudice about introducing a Unitarian into the Faculty."

In the absence of endowment, Dean West found that if he was to house his graduate students well he must find patrons; and among those from whom he hoped for support was President Grover Cleveland. In November of 1896, looking forward to escape from the responsibilities of the White House, Cleveland had written to West "a little bit confidentially" that he wanted a house at Princeton with some ground about it, and a pleasant social life. The mansion that West found for him was named "Westland," and as the years went by West did his best to make the Clevelands feel at home in Princeton society. He hunted and fished with the ex-President, was invited in for "potluck" and to play billiards, and wrote of the joy that he derived from their friendship. Cleveland amused himself with the nominal duties of a Princeton trustee, cherishing a patriotic hope that a graduate school might be established at the university that would make it unnecessary for American boys to go to Europe for advanced study. The prestige of his name was great, his knowledge of the business that education was becoming, dangerously sketchy.

If West felt disappointment when another was elected to lead the university for which he had labored so long, he concealed it well. He was sent abroad by the trustees to study graduate education. His attitude toward the new president was punctiliously correct; and Wilson reciprocated by acknowledging that the Tudor Gothic style of archi-

---

[2] President Nicholas Murray Butler of Columbia University explained, in an understatement, that Wilson "was not the sort of person to adjust himself to the atmosphere which this group had created." After Pyne took him to the annual Christmas luncheon of the Gin Mill Club, he was not asked again. Butler, *Across the Busy Years,* II, 418.

[3] West not only was responsible to the trustees' committee on graduate work, but was expected to report to the faculty annually. Moreover, he was as much responsible to the president as any other professor.

Wilson himself valued the study of Greek highly, but thought it impractical to insist on it. "The man who talks Greek," he wrote, "puts himself—is not driven—through the process that produced the modern mind." *See* Charles Osgood, "Woodrow Wilson," in *The Lives of Eighteen from Princeton,* p. 288.

tecture that had been advocated by West had added a thousand years to the history of the university.

In the autumn of 1902, with his God-given assurance reinforced by a mandate from a united constituency and conscious that the educators of the nation were looking toward Princeton for portents of the future, Woodrow Wilson was ready to move forward rapidly on lines that he and some of his colleagues already had projected and to try to sweep West along with the rest in devotion to the larger interests of the university. Declining an invitation to address an association of historians, he explained that he had ceased to be a historian and had become involved in a business so absorbing that he must devote himself wholly to the learning of it. He conceived that he was preparing history for future generations. He seemed to be straining ferociously at the bonds of health, impetuous to make Princeton "the perfect place of learning." Stockton Axson had sensed the change in the late nineties, had heard his brother-in-law cry out: "I am so tired of a merely talking profession! I want to *do* something!"

The new president conducted faculty meetings with courtly dignity, spoke briefly, kept discussion pointed toward constructive ends. He liked to get quickly to the pith of every matter that he took up. His diary records: "Day of routine. Kept in my office till quarter of 5 on business that might have been finished before 3 if academic men were only prompt in movement and brief in statements!" When discussion strayed, he would drop a tactful hint by apologizing politely for having a one-track mind. Very soon he reconstituted the faculty committees, except that on the graduate school, which was headed by Dean West.

Determined to be gentle as well as just, he schooled himself in patience. When deadwood had to be pruned from the faculty or the student body—or, for that matter, from the board of trustees—he talked frankly, man to man, with as much regard for humane feeling as for the dictates of duty. A face-to-face talk was better than a letter, he believed. To a mother who was to be operated on and feared that she would die of shock if her boy, a cheater, was expelled from college, Wilson said: "Madam, you force me to say a hard thing, but if I had to choose between your life or my life or anybody's life and the good of this college, I should choose the good of the college." And then he went to luncheon, white and unable to eat.

Students were expected to be gentlemen. They could drink, but drunkenness was taboo; and dishonesty was cause for dismissal. The president did not allow smoking in classes and insisted on a careful record of attendance. Daily chapel was retained, he said, because it was one of the oldest customs and had been productive of good. And yet he knew that religion could not be "handled" like learning. "It is a matter of individual conviction," he wrote in the Introduction of a *Handbook of Princeton*, "and its source is the heart. Its life and vigour must lie, not in official recognition or fosterage, but in the temper and character of the undergraduates themselves."

He frowned upon hazing: once, coming suddenly upon a group of sophomores who were forcing a freshman to grovel and pick up twigs with his teeth, he said icily: "Isn't that a fine occupation for a gentleman?"[4] Yet sometimes, looking back on the rough-housing of his own college days, he wondered whether the boys were not now too docile, whether their spirits were high enough to lift them to great lives. The lads were quick to sense the new vigor of the place. "Square and loyal, firm and true," they sang of their "Tommie" Wilson, "a man we honor through and through."

As the standards of scholarship rose, boys dropped out by the scores and fewer candidates for admission were accepted. The class admitted in 1902 under the lax standards of the old regime, lost one-fourth of its members in a year; and by 1904 the entering class was smaller by one-eighth. The boys jested grimly about the high rate of mortality. Though Wilson well understood that the undergraduate's love was "for sport and good comradeship and the things that give zest to the common life of the campus," yet he insisted that "the ordinary undergraduate" was being educated, knew it, and had a certain strong, even if unconscious, respect for the thing that was happening to him. He refused petitions for the introduction of "cinch" courses and encouraged boys to develop their minds by study in fields unfamiliar and difficult. Taking the longer view, Wilson knew that Princeton was acquiring prestige that would be priceless in the educational market place. But alumni who set more store by quantity than by quality were disturbed by the decline in enrollment.

Conceiving progress to be something "to be compounded out of common counsel," Wilson thought it his duty to canvass the best minds that he could call on, listen carefully, arrive at the most valid policy that he could conceive, and then act accordingly. This procedure was as sacred to him as his religion. He would follow it honestly, let emotions and sentiments suffer as they might. He could battle with strong men on this ground and come out of his differences without hurt

[4] Edward W. Bradford to the writer, Sept. 2, 1956.

feelings. Henry B. Fine, who seemed to Ellen Wilson like "Aaron upholding the arm of Moses," and who, whether traveling abroad or working at Princeton, appeared never to let up in his drive to strengthen his chief's efforts for a renaissance of intellect, argued and disputed often with Wilson, gave advice more often than he received it, and yet remained a friend. In his writings on political science Wilson had stressed the importance of viability; and now as a responsible executive he showed himself ready to meet the minds of others and arrive at compromises that did not profane his basic principles.

Swiftly and surely, Wilson guided the sentiment of the faculty in revising the course of study and setting up a departmental organization that the trustees authorized. The demands of the age had brought in many new and uncoordinated courses, and both faculty and students had regretted Patton's failure to reorganize the curriculum. The problem was intricate, raveled as it was with men's ambitions and jealousies.[5]

It was necessary to redefine jurisdictions, do away with duplication and overlapping, weigh the time allotted to the various subjects. Building on a plan for curriculum revision that had been formulated by a faculty committee under Dean West's chairmanship and submitted unsuccessfully to Patton, Wilson met weekly with a group of his colleagues. Minor questions were referred to subcommittees. During the negotiations he once showed irascibility toward a weak, unoffending professor and thereby provoked a flare-up of feeling; but on the whole, the task was done to the satisfaction of the campus family. ". . . we began," he told Ellen Wilson, "a group of individuals and ended a *body* agreed in common counsel,—except for a final, purely temperamental 'kick' by ——— who will quietly get over it."

When the committee's report was presented to the entire faculty— Wilson's "House of Commons"—the president took the floor, with Dean Fine temporarily in the chair, and debated the new measure; and in a few days he was able to report to his wife: "It took only four meetings to put it through all its stages . . . Everyone seemed to accept the *principle* of the report and all the main features of the scheme at once and without cavil; and the final adoption was characterized by real cordiality. All of which makes me very happy. It is not, as it stands now, exactly the scheme I at the outset proposed, but it is much better."

[5] Harvard, under Eliot, had given boys almost unlimited choice of studies, with the faculty absolving themselves of responsibility. Yale, after Hadley became president in 1899, had broken away from an overrigid regimen: all absolute requirements were abolished, Greek was no longer essential for entrance, and the course was revised in such a way as to give some freedom of choice within limits that guaranteed reasonable breadth, continuity, and concentration.

It was one of Woodrow Wilson's major parliamentary achievements, conceived in the spirit of the times and prosecuted with a balance of persistence and tact that promised much for his future as an administrator.[6]

Having settled what was to be taught in the university, Wilson turned next to put vigor into the teaching and to prevent the stuffing of knowledge into heads that were made receptive only by fear of examinations. Wilson's own tests often called on boys for more than categorical answers. Some of his colleagues thought his examinations too lax; but one of his students once protested, much to his professor's delight: "This question is unfair. It requires thought." Wilson aspired, as he told alumni, "to transform thoughtless boys performing tasks into thinking men."

To achieve his ideal, the new president of Princeton had a plan ready —a concept that he had been turning over in his mind for twelve years or more and that grew out of observation of tutorial work at Oxford and Cambridge and out of discussions of tutorial teaching that had arisen among his colleagues.[7] It seemed clear that, if Princeton was to fill men with enthusiasm for study, inspire them to independent reading and investigation, and wean them from the pap of textbooks and formal lectures, it would be necessary to infuse new blood into the faculty— young instructors on fire with love of scholarship, men who were gentlemen and good comrades. Such tutors, Wilson felt, could live in the dormitories, meet the boys in their own studies or in small classrooms,

[6] On Feb. 3, 1915, addressing the United States Chamber of Commerce on "Cooperation in the Business of Government," Wilson referred to the reorganization of the Princeton course of study as one of his "happiest experiences" in "common counsel."

The new course of study retained the classics as the basis of work in the humanities, but allowed candidates for the degree of B.S. to substitute a modern language for Greek. The number of courses was reduced and, in general, the time given to each was extended. The work of the first year was prescribed for all boys; in the second year some freedom of choice was allowed among studies that were fundamental to the work to be taken later; and in the upper years there was to be wide choice within a scheme of related subjects, and at the same time an insistence that the student should round out his understanding by electing at least some work outside his particular field of concentration. Formal departments of study, with responsible chairmen, were set up; and the faculties of the college and the Green School of Science were combined and the separate budgets were abandoned.

The president was able to say to the trustees, in the fall of 1904, that the system was "cordially received even by that arch-conservative, the undergraduate himself."

[7] Wilson's ideal of preceptorial work doubtless was inspired in part, at least, by the concept of university education presented in an article by Walter Bagehot. "In youth," Wilson's hero wrote, "the real plastic energy is not in tutors or lectures or in books 'got up' but . . . in books that all read because all like; in what all talk of because all are interested; in the argumentative walk or disputatious lounge; in the impact of young thought upon young thought, of fresh thought on fresh thought, of hot thought on hot thought; in mirth and refutation, in ridicule and laughter . . . Quoted by Wilson in "A Wit and a Seer," *Atlantic Monthly,* October, 1898, pp. 527–40.

and walk and talk informally with groups of lads. Keep these preceptors not more than five years, Wilson cautioned, and avoid the error of English universities that allowed dons to go to seed in tutorial service.

More than the reform of the course of study, Wilson considered this project his own; and he did not discuss it with his colleagues in faculty meeting. But his eloquence and enthusiasm won alumni, faculty, and trustees to the scheme; and he pressed on even though the students seemed apathetic and some professors wondered whether the fifty recruits that Wilson desired could be absorbed quickly and peacefully into the teaching ranks and given the promotions that they would want.

The most serious question was that of funds. Even before his inauguration Wilson had asked his trustees for more than six million dollars[8] to finance several projects. He was eager to handle affairs in a manner that would be thought businesslike. The institution was "insufficiently capitalized for its business," he had told the trustees in his first report. ". . . our staff is overworked and underpaid, the University lacks necessary equipment in almost every department . . . We are not doing honestly what we advertise in our catalogue." He threatened, if millions were not forthcoming, to "earnestly advocate a sufficient curtailment of . . . present work to put it on a business-like basis of efficiency." In presenting his program to a gathering of New York alumni in December, 1902, he mentioned the cost of a preceptorial system and the audience whistled. Undaunted, he struck back: "I hope you will get your whistling over, because you will have to get used to this, and you may thank your stars I did not say four millions and a quarter, because we are *going* to get it. I suspect there are gentlemen in this room who are going to give me two millions and a quarter to get rid of me." There was not another university in the world, he boasted, that "could transmute twelve millions and a half into so much red blood."

[8] Two and one-quarter millions for a preceptorial system of teaching, one million for a school of science, and two and three-quarter millions for buildings and increases for teachers. Also, as future objectives, Wilson requested three millions for a graduate school and almost two and one-half millions for a school of jurisprudence, a school of electrical engineering, and a museum of natural history. For an institution that in 1902 had productive resources totaling less than four millions, this was a tremendous sum. When Wilson became president, it had already become traditional for the university to roll up annual deficits that were met by emergency gifts from alumni. These deficits grew from about $30,000 in 1901 to about $145,000 in 1906, as the faculty increased from 112 to 174 men; but the special gifts increased even more, so that each year between 1905 and 1910 the deficit was overcome. Actually, by constantly pressing for new developments, Wilson was increasing the annual income of the university, as well as its endowment.

In his crabbed shorthand the president drafted letters asking gifts from wealthy philanthropists. He could deliver bold and eloquent appeals to masses of men; but confronting a prospective donor, the thin skin of his conscience would be pierced and he would lose assurance, feeling himself something of a beggar. There was not enough brass in his make-up to enforce his threats to the New York alumni. He was not facile, as McCosh had been, in showing "the menagerie" to anyone who had money to give. He and Mrs. Wilson could not bring themselves easily to entertain philanthropists in the hope of extracting gifts. A committee of the trustees, however, worked with the president to secure contributions of moderate size so that the preceptorial plan, though not endowed, was assured of support for a few years at least; and in June of 1905 it was formally approved by the board.

When it came to recruiting the preceptors, Wilson's genius shone at its brightest. As a professor he had attracted talented teachers, and by 1902 the one-man department of jurisprudence had grown to a six-man department of history, economics, and politics. Now, faced with the task of finding fifty exceptional teachers within a few months, he put the problem before his department heads, helped them to sift the records of hundreds of applicants, sought opinions on the worth of the candidates, talked with each of them, touched them with his fervor for the new work at Princeton. The importance of the whole system lay in the characters of the men obtained, he explained. Like McCosh, he asked first about each candidate: "Is he alive?"

Vigorous young teachers flocked to him, convinced that here was a leader who knew his business and sympathized with their impatience with conditions that they had found restrictive elsewhere. Wilson in turn took the preceptors to his heart, gave generously of counsel and inspiration to those who needed it, often concluding his advice with a friendly "Don't you think so?" To the youngest, most inexperienced, he would say a fatherly word of reassurance, invite them to come to him at any time for aid. In his study they found their god to be a very human man. He urged his young protégés to informality, breadth of view, and at the same time, accuracy. Conscious of the power of nomenclature, Wilson insisted that meetings of preceptors with students should be called "conferences," not "classes." Preceptors were to find out not what the boys knew but what they did not know, so that they might be guided to sources of enlightenment. Excoriating the use of syllabi, he insisted that students were not to be spoon-fed, but urged to independent investigation; and the boys were to be examined on what they read rather than on what they were told in the classroom. He himself met with a small preceptorial group.

In his zeal for perfection the president let it be known that he thought competition the life of teaching, as of trade. Catching a bored student in the act of skipping class by way of a window and fire escape, he merely asked: "Who is the lecturer? He must be very nearsighted. Was it very dull?" He would have liked to make attendance at some lectures optional, so that each professor would have to hold his boys by sheer ability. Preceptors who married wealthy wives and seemed to lose enthusiasm for their teaching sometimes became the object of cutting remarks at the Wilson dinner table, where personal likes and dislikes were aired frankly.

There were features of the preceptorial plan that in practice had to be changed or dropped. Scarcity of funds made it impossible, sometimes, to attract competent men to replace those who were not content to delay their advancement by remaining in preceptorial service. However, in introducing the conference method of teaching and a corps of able young instructors Wilson contributed new vitality to Princeton and to American education. The drawing force of his personality called forth such a flowering of teaching genius as neither money nor pure reason could duplicate. In the spring of 1906 he could say to alumni with confidence that his words were substantiated by good works, that he was "covetous for Princeton of all the glory that there is, and the chief glory of a university is always intellectural glory."

In groups of five or six that met once a week, sometimes in a preceptor's room or home, boys learned to talk naturally and wittily about books, plays, public questions, personalities, and the Jersey countryside through which they often walked. Bonds of intellectual comradeship were formed that lasted for decades. Students began to make more use of the library, mischief decreased, scholarship improved, and soon graduates of Princeton were carrying off high honors in professional schools elsewhere. Many of the older professors responded to the challenge, shared in the new spirit of fellowship, rewrote their lectures, gave more attention to individual boys. "We are all preceptors," the president was able to say when his experiment was scarcely a year old. There was an air of renaissance on the campus, and pride in a rising aristocracy of brains. The seniors caught the spirit of informality, sang:

> Here's to those preceptor guys,
> Fifty stiffs to make us wise.

In the first three years of his presidency, in addition to outside addresses, efforts to raise funds, the working out of the new course of study and the preceptorial plan, and a guiding interest in his own department, Wilson found time to strengthen the university in other respects. His attitude toward science, which in earlier years had been based largely on his experience in an elementary course that was taught by lectures and table demonstrations, had been broadened by talks with Fine and other colleagues. In his inaugural address he had not repeated the misgivings about the influence of scientific method on education that he had expressed in 1896. In fact, he had proclaimed that science opened a new world of learning, as great as the old.

The trustees' committee on buildings and grounds, which was created to put the administration of the university's property on a businesslike basis, had the active assistance of the president. Determined that there should be coherence in the physical development of the university, that donors should not prescribe diverse and conflicting styles of architecture nor place their buildings in helter-skelter pattern nor construct laboratories that looked like factories, Wilson laid down the law. He insisted on the appointment of Ralph Adams Cram to coordinate Princeton's landscape, architecture, and building material, explaining that he had not the next decade merely but the next fifty years in view.

When it was made clear that it would be economical to concentrate the business of all departments under one manager, he quickly brought to the trustees a resolution providing for a "financial secretary." The president himself found time to attend to irritating little flaws in the operation of buildings. In a notebook he recorded the presence of rats in a cellar. He had a little time even for pastoral care of the university community: when Grover Cleveland's daughter died, he carried a note of sympathy to the house, where the butler took it through a crack in the door. He remembered to write, each year, an affectionate letter to the Hibbens on the anniversary of their marriage; and one night, when Jennie Hibben telephoned that her husband was away and there was a burglar in the house, Wilson rushed out to the rescue while his family called after him: "*Must* you go?"

He was the only man at Prospect now. In the spacious dining room, where sun flooded a long window filled with greenery, at a table decorated with flowers in season, the president presided over a court of ladies. "I am submerged in petticoats," he would say in jest. The girls would joke with him, but none of their soft voices rose strenuously against his will; and the more paternal he became the more he bristled toward the outside world in defense of the family's snug and blissful security.

To protect his wife's garden and the privacy of his girls, the president had an iron fence built. It offended students, who now had to walk around instead of across a corner of the lot. Alumni thought it marred the beauty of the campus. Students paraded in indignation, carrying derisive placards; and one night the structure was toppled into a trench dug for it, and buried so that only its spiked top protruded. The next morning Wilson was on the scene early, and his eyes were a steely blue-gray as he struck at the spikes with his cane. The fence was rebuilt, and the next June it was guarded by college proctors.

Gone now were the days when Edward Axson's practical mind balanced the Wilson household, the hours of philosophical contemplation with Stockton Axson and old Joseph Wilson, the afternoons passed at the Faculty Club at billiards or in chat with fellow professors. Instead of going to the barbershop and catching the drift of village gossip, he now stropped his razor and shaved himself, to save time. Then, too, to conserve his energy he felt that he must post afternoon office hours—an innovation that discouraged casual and informal calls from friends. Even the two-mile walks that had taken the place of bicycling were usually made alone, exactly at five o'clock. He was drawing apart from the actual conditions of life that he had commended so warmly to the attention of men who would lead a people. And in drawing apart from individuals he was depending more and more on intuitive insight to tell him what motives and ideas ruled the minds of Princeton men.

One Christmas, Ellen Wilson had a billiard table installed in the east wing of Prospect, hoping that men would come in to play; but when they did, usually they leaned on their cues and talked, and soon the seamstress was using the table for the cutting of dance frocks for the girls. And so, gradually, as the duties of office exacted more and more of the president's energy and the transcendence of his mission for Princeton possessed him, there developed a legend that he was cold and inaccessible.

Immediately after his inauguration in 1902, Wilson had expressed the hope that he might not lose direct contact with undergraduates in the classroom. He continued to lecture regularly all through his presidency. He expected his audience to take him seriously, even on the morning of the football game with Yale. His humor was often gay. He jested about his pince-nez, remarking that he thought of wearing them on the end of his nose so that he could see his words before they came out. He was still calculating the effect of every word, digressing now and then from his subject to try out bits of homely wisdom that he later used in public speeches. Sometimes, before the bell gave the signal for the lecture to begin, he sat at his desk concealed behind the morning newspapers. When he had said all that he planned to say, he did not extemporize until the bell announced the end of the period. He would leave the room quickly by a side door, unless boys came to his desk with worth-while questions. But on the days when he continued to talk after the last bell, and students rushed pell-mell from neighboring classrooms, Wilson's boys would sit quiet and hear him out.

There were occasions when the lowliest of undergraduates could draw close to their godlike master. Sometimes a winning debating team was invited to dine at Prospect; and he spoke informally in the halls of the debating societies and attended dress rehearsals of college shows. Occasionally Ellen Wilson would entertain and invite girls to help her, but the president proved a greater attraction and the students would drift into the library to hear him tell stories. The boys found out their "Tommie," too, after athletic victories. They would snake-dance up to his porch and call him out. He had only to speak quietly to still the uproar. Then, raising his voice in boyish glee at the triumph, he would send them off howling like a jungle pack.

One spring it was announced that the president was to speak informally to the campus religious society and the traditional singing on the steps was postponed to give everyone a chance to hear him. Standing halfway up the aisle, he confided in the earnest young disciples, told them how his own father had helped him, in his youth, to understand things that his mind could not then grasp. Speaking of the Bible as "the book that best sums up the human spirit," he proclaimed the way of Christ the hardest of paths, and as proof of the vitality of Christianity he cited "the great amount of modern preaching it survives." [9] Good character was to him a by-product that came not from seeking, but from doing right at every turn, from sticking to a job, day in and day out.

Invitations to speak outside Princeton were received at the rate of three a day. Many came from former students, in behalf of alumni clubs. It gave the president joy to drop his cares and renew old associations. With the old grads he could revel in the spirit of comradeship from which health and conscience separated him on the campus. Often he would surprise them by calling them by name and asking about

9 Chambers MS.

their Princeton relatives. After he had dined and addressed them he would jump down from the platform and join vigorously in their lockstep "pee-rades."

His moral sense was often offended as he saw alumni lounging and drinking in their clubs and airing irresponsible views on the nation's institutions. But when he was impelled to suggest reproof he spoke with sly wit. Chatting once with two of his old boys in a Washington club, he saw youngsters take a nearby table and drink excessively. One of his companions asked the other: "Are those habitués of your club?" And Wilson cut in quickly with: "No. They must be sons-of-habitués." [10]

Though Wilson had set aside both literary and political ambitions, his health was strained by the intensity of his efforts in the classroom and on public platforms. Even during his first year in the presidency he had felt so pressed by responsibility that sometimes when he went home at night he seemed to meet himself coming back in the morning. He could afford only part-time secretarial help from students, and handled his own mail and did much of his own typing.

With his Ellen's help he had disciplined himself in diet, in work, and in relaxation; and when opportunity to sleep came, he could drop his cares and doze off quickly. The family spent much of the long summer vacations out of doors, on the Maine coast in 1902 and later at Muskoka Lake in Canada, where Wilson taught his children how to paddle a canoe and cooked their food over open fires, and during a squall on the lake felt intimations of mortality so keenly that he made a will soon afterward. Early in 1905 he was operated on for a rupture that had resulted from portaging a canoe; and during his recovery he was stricken with phlebitis. After five weeks in the hospital, he was taken to Florida by his anxious wife. When they returned she was thinner and paler than he.

The next year was critical for Wilson's health and fortunes. He could have rested on his record, secure in the knowledge that by reforms already accomplished he had raised the standing of Princeton among American universities. He could have safeguarded his health, relaxed into tweedy geniality, and let his able and loyal lieutenants carry on. But he conceived that he was a responsible minister, elected on a reform platform and given authority to execute the wishes of his constituency. He had been reminded by illness that life was short, and there was much to be done. Princeton must rise to the top, and serve the nation.

[10] George Dunlop, Princeton '92, and one of Wilson's companions on this occasion, to the writer.

Determined that the good fight should go on, he stepped up the tempo of his speechmaking. In 1905–6 he made a dozen powerful addresses. Speaking to the Western alumni at Cleveland, he began in a light, facile vein, saying: "About this table I recognize the faces of some who were ingenious in resisting the processes of learning—and if they have applied as much ingenuity to their business as they did then to their pleasure, I congratulate them upon their success." And then gradually and artfully he warmed to his subject: the new teaching at Princeton.

The ideals that we talk about, the ideals that we try to translate into definite programmes of study, are not things which we can take or leave as we please, unless you believe that we can take or leave life itself as we please . . . If there remain any little band of men keeping the true university spirit alive, that band will, after a while, seem to be all that there is of a great nation, so far as the historian is concerned . . . And so, our ambitions for a university which retains this spirit are not hopes so much as a definite confidence that certain things must come to pass. The best thing, to my thought, about what we call the Princeton spirit is the manliness and the unselfishness and the truthfulness that there is in it . . .

Eleven times the short speech was interrupted by cheering, and at the end the applause was thunderous and prolonged. The Western alumni loved, respected, trusted their "Tommie" Wilson.

CHAPTER VII

VOICE IN THE WILDERNESS

ON A MAY MORNING in 1906, Woodrow Wilson awoke and found that he could not see out of his left eye. For some time his left shoulder and leg had been racked by neuritic pains, and his right hand had been affected again. Apprehensive, his wife took him to two specialists. Having watched Joseph Wilson die only four years before, she was terrified by the verdict. "It is hardening of the arteries," she wrote to a friend, "due to prolonged high pressure on brain and nerves. He has lived too tensely . . . Of course, it is an awful thing—dying by inches, —and incurable. But Woodrow's condition has been discovered in the very early stages and they think it has already been 'arrested.'" He would have to meet not only the physical danger of the hardening of his arteries,[1] but also the psychic ravages of fear—dread that he might not live long enough to make Princeton "the perfect place of learning," that he might suffer the excruciating agonies of his father.

The prospect of physical suffering seems not to have shaken Wilson's confidence. "I have never *felt* as if there were anything the matter with me, except the eye," he wrote to his sister. He accepted the doctor's diagnosis calmly and prepared to carry out the prescription of three months of rest. Dean Fine was made acting president of Princeton, and Hibben acting dean.

For refreshment after mental strain, Wilson always had leaned heavily on friends. Now, when forced to leave the campus in search of health, he was reminded how much his friends loved him. Messages of good-will came from trustees, alumni, associates. "Dear love and good-bye," Jennie Hibben wrote, "and try to be careful of yourself through this trying week. How lovely and good you are to us! Ever devotedly yours." Andrew West wrote to wish the president a summer "in every way delightful" and closed his letter with "ever sincerely yours."

Wilson's family took him to the English Lake Country, the pastoral

[1] Fifty-year arteries do not go back to an earlier condition. Modern doctors realize, better than did those of 1906, that vascular occlusions may be followed by sleeplessness, moods of emotional uplift and depression, nervous breakdown, spastic indigestion, even moral relaxations. Dr. Robert Monroe to the writer. *See* Dr. Walter C. Alvarez, "Cerebral Arteriosclerosis," in *Geriatics,* I (May–June, 1946) 189–216. The vision of Wilson's left eye was permanently impaired. McAdoo, *The Priceless Gift,* p. 243.

realm in which his mind often had sought release. At Rydal he communed not only with natural beauty but with a friendly artist who was seeking to interpret it. Stopping once on a bridge and looking down into the Rothay River, he heard an unfamiliar voice ask: "Is this President Wilson?" The words came from a sensitive face that was topped by tousled gray hair. "My name is Yates." the stranger went on. "We live near here. We are poor but, thank God, not respectable." Wilson needed to look at such a man but once, to love him. An idyllic friendship began there, between Fred Yates the artist and his wife and daughter and the Wilsons. The two families talked, read, and sang together. The sillier the songs the more relaxation Wilson found in them.

As sight came back in his eye he became restless to go on with his mission at Princeton. He consulted a wise old doctor in Edinburgh and was advised that, if everyone stopped work because of such a condition as his, a good many of the world's tasks would remain unfinished. It seemed a mistake for a man of his temperament to be kept away from his duties while the university was in session; and so he was allowed to return to the campus in the autumn and to work moderately. His left eye never recovered fully, in spite of his assurance to his wife that he would train it to behave. His hand still bothered him, but a pen with a large handle was made to relieve the pain of writing. After meals a bottle of whisky was set beside him and he measured out a medicinal dose, then apologized roguishly to his family for not sharing his liquor with them. By pruning his engagement calendar, systematizing his work, and insisting on ample sleep, he was able to take up his task again.

The accumulation of business was so great that he wrote in November: "I did not take a long breath for two weeks." After three months of overwork, however, he kept a promise that he had given the doctors and made the first of several trips to Bermuda. "I love my work too much," he said, "to be willing to run the risk of rendering myself unfit for it!" He begged his Ellen to go with him, but she said that she must stay in her home "like the fixtures."

In Bermuda, Wilson wrote lectures and preached in a local church on the text: "The letter killeth, the spirit giveth life." But to restore his own spirits he craved human comradeship. Fortunately, he found escape in a blithe friendship with Mary Allen Hulbert Peck. The first husband of this lady had been killed in an accident and she was estranged from her second, Thomas D. Peck, a manufacturer of Pittsfield, Massachusetts. She dwelt unconventionally in an Eden of sunlight and fancy, without stripping the boughs that hung well laden all around her. She was at home in cosmopolitan society, could fence nimbly with both swords and words, and knew how to listen to men who talked well.

He met Mary Allen Peck at a dinner party, and she diverted him, rallied his spirit of gallantry. In her the frustrated poet found the mind that he most desired to see in woman—a wit that stirred him without irritating, amused and yet subtly instructed. In him she at once saw a Christlike quality, a serene radiance that reminded her of Phillips Brooks. He rang true, and promised intellectual stimulation. She arranged a party for him at her home; and he held the men spellbound with good after-dinner talk, so that the ladies were left long alone. Then there was music and general chat, and the guests went home under a deep violet sky.

He loved to walk on the shore road with Mary Peck and read to her from the *Oxford Book of Verse*. But being a man who did not smoke, drink, or dance, he was inevitably a looker-on, and held her scarf when she joined the dancers in the ballroom of the Hamilton Hotel. Gossip linked Mary Peck and the governor in matrimony; and Woodrow Wilson protested in jest that he resented such talk, though she brushed it aside as "the inevitable tattle." Other women, protesting the best of intentions and showing the worst of motives, asked Wilson about her with a particularity and persistence that made him boil. But he could laugh uproariously when his fondness for Mary Peck led him into situations that set malicious tongues awagging. One Sunday morning, as they returned from a walk to the South Shore, the congregation was coming out of the church in which Wilson had preached.

"This is terrible!" he said in mock horror, as he doffed his cap to the worshipers. "Last week, dressed in solemn black, I stood up before that congregation and admonished them about their Christian duty—and here I am today standing, just like an undergrad, under a tree with a pretty girl."

And when she laughed he went on: "Worse, distinctly worse. Caught laughing with a pretty girl on the holy Sabbath-day. Here goes my last shred of reputation."

In Bermuda, Wilson loved the company of Mark Twain, too, and would spend mornings with him over croquet, or a game of miniature golf of their own invention. Though the humorist and his friend H. H. Rogers cut capers and clowned together, they put on party manners when the president of Princeton approached. This made it hard for him to lose his dignity in the carefree, boyish play of which he seemed never to have had enough. He could not cut loose from his position. Even when he visited the aquarium he was driven up on his professional stilts by an attendant who insisted on exhibiting his scientific knowledge.

He liked to watch people in Bermuda, especially the sleepy drivers of the leisurely carriages, and he contemplated with horror the coming of automobiles. To prevent such a desecration of paradise, he drafted a petition to the island legislature.[2] He never bought an automobile for himself. They were to some men, he thought, a symbol of the "arrogance of wealth."

The simplicity of life in the Lake Country and in Bermuda accentuated, by contrast, new ways of life at Princeton that seemed to Wilson to divert his undergraduates from "the chief end of man." Returning from vacations, he felt that he was moving from idyllic reality to masquerade.

Once there had been a social line drawn down the middle of Princeton's main street. In the early years the teachers of the college had been consigned by the estate owners to the side that was inhabited by shopkeepers and workmen; but gradually the aristocracy of wealth had merged with that of intellect to form a "gown" society with interests remote from the town of Princeton. The rift widened with the coming of wealth from the cities. A very few local patrons of the college, including trustees, lived on a scale that seemed to poor professors to be palatial; and yet some of the academic men tried to keep pace with their affluent neighbors. In a few country places millionaires extolled the virtues of the simple life. Only one thing was lacking in these twentieth-century affectations of the Sabine Farm. Where was Horace? The patrons found him in the person of "Andy" West—a comrade hearty, jovial, kindly, able to deliver Latin inscriptions to order.

The Wilsons themselves were astraddle the social line. Ellen Wilson was a descendant of Nathaniel Fitz-Randolph, who had given acres of land to the infant College of New Jersey; but by joining the lesser of the village's two Presbyterian churches[3] she and her husband had put themselves on friendly terms with the villagers. Once Wilson stopped

[2] Hudson Strode, *The Story of Bermuda*, p. 147. The petition said in part: "It would, in our opinion, be a fatal error to attract to Bermuda the extravagant and sporting set who have made so many other places entirely intolerable to persons of taste and cultivation."

[3] The family had joined the smaller church because they thought it in need of help and Wilson served as an elder. He encouraged the merging of the two churches, but when his congregation refused to do this, the Wilsons thought them shortsighted and went over to the larger First Church. Eleanor Wilson McAdoo to the writer, March 10, 1952.

on a street corner, hat in hand, to answer a random question from an old Negress. To watch the annual sleigh race he would stand on the curb, and after the sleighs had swished by he would linger to chat with other spectators. Moreover, he encouraged worthy young men of the village who were entering politics; and once he took a hand in ridding the town of a "bucket shop."

Black sweaters and corduroy pants, once worn proudly as emblems of democracy, were giving way to tweeds. President Wilson complained, in his first statement to the trustees, that Princeton was in danger of being regarded, "to her great detriment and discredit," as one of the most expensive places for students to live. He felt that too many boys came to college to get social sophistication, and frittered away time in dilettantism and campus politics. Dean West pleaded that boys be admitted by certificate from a favored private school, while valedictorians from public schools had to prove themselves. Moreover, and probably most distressing of all to an old Princetonian like "Tommie" Wilson, the debating societies that had been so dear to him had lost their glamour and were no longer self-supporting. The students now threw their social energies into "heeling" for election to one of the eating clubs where talk was more informal and far less exalted, and members were tempted to spend their evenings playing billiards or sprawled before an open fire reading popular journals.

After the abolition of secret societies at Princeton in the presidency of McCosh, clubs had grown up to satisfy the natural desire of students to eat with a congenial crowd. Wilson himself, as an undergraduate, had belonged to "The Alligators." Twenty-five years later, however, these simple organizations were so rooted in tradition and so heavily endowed that Wilson spoke publicly, in 1906, of their dangers. The influence of the clubs on the extracurricular life of the university was in many ways admirable; unlike the abolished fraternities, they were not secret and they countenanced no dangerous hazing. Moreover, their members continued to reside in the college dormitories. They were rallying grounds of alumni loyalty to the college, and the president of the university appreciated their virtues as much as he deplored their tendency to separate undergraduates one from another and from intellectual pursuits.

As early as 1897, Wilson had told Stockton Axson that if he were president of Princeton he would reorganize the social life so that clubs would not cut off freshmen from contact with older students. And in 1905 he had developed this last thought further. "The most influential

Seniors," he wrote, "govern their own class and the University in all matters of opinion and of undergraduate action . . . They lead because they have been found to be the men who can do things best . . . 'Leading citizens' are everywhere selected in the same way . . . The university authorities consult the leading Seniors as a matter of course upon every new or critical matter in which opinion plays a part and in which undergraduate life is involved . . . Such comradeship in affairs . . . breeds democracy inevitably. Democracy, the absence of social distinctions, the treatment of every man according to his merits, his most serviceable qualities and most likeable traits, is of the essence of such a place, its most cherished characteristic." [4]

For ten years there had been talk of reform in the club system at Princeton, and other colleges were facing the same problem; but nothing was being done. In Wilson's view the situation had grown critical since his inauguration, as new and more palatial clubhouses had appeared on Prospect Avenue. Another two years of such growth and, he feared, the university might be only an antiquarian and artistic background for club life. But not until the preceptorial system was in action was he ready to crusade for the social regeneration of Princeton. Surely if any university president in America could force action, Woodrow Wilson—a great orator, a magnetic leader, a man with the credential of uninterrupted success—might hope to prevail. And if his morale needed any spur, it was perhaps found in a reminder from a relative that the crest of the Woodrows bore a bull's head with the motto: *Audaci favit fortuna.*

In December of 1906 he gave to the trustees a clear outline of a constructive plan—"heretical in character," he told them quite frankly but "the fruit of very mature consideration." He alluded to the elaboration of club life and "the decline of the old democratic spirit of the place." Describing unhealthful trends, complaining that, under the current system of electioneering, comrades were chosen in social groups rather than as individuals, he expressed willingness to preserve the better values of the clubs. Cautioning that it would be unwise as yet to discuss the matter publicly, he nevertheless set forth his conviction that it was time for action.

Wilson wished to make the undergraduates live together, not in clubs but in colleges. "I propose," he said, "that we divide the University into

---

[4] John Rogers Williams, *The Handbook of Princeton*, p. xvi. In Wilson's notebook for 1907 is this line: "Plans: A conference of Seniors at the beginning of each academic year, to talk of the self-government of the university."

colleges and that the strong upperclass clubs themselves become colleges under the guidance of the University. By a college I mean not merely a group of dormitories, but an eating hall as well with all its necessary appointments where all the residents of the college shall take their meals together. I would have over each college a master and two or three resident preceptors, and I would have these resident members of the faculty take their meals in hall with the undergraduates. But I would suggest that the undergraduates of each college be given a large share of the self-government . . . Each college would thus form a unit in itself, and largely a self-governing unit." [5] The question of expense was, Wilson then thought, a minor one. "The changes necessary to effect the transition," he said, "would be, in form at any rate, very slight."

The reaction of the board was sympathetic, though some thought the proposal "just one of Woodrow's pipe dreams." A seven-man Committee on Social Coordination was appointed, with Wilson as chairman, to study the matter and report six months later, in June.

Less than a week after the presentation of the plan to the trustees, the first whisper of opposition came to Wilson's ears; and it did not come, strangely enough, from the student or alumni members of the clubs. Grover Cleveland, who in 1904 had become chairman of the trustees' committee on the graduate school, complained to a colleague that the realization of Wilson's plan might postpone the day when Dean Andrew West would have new buildings for his graduate college.

Only a few months earlier, West reported that he had been called to the presidency of the Massachusetts Institute of Technology, at an increase in salary. As his terms for remaining at Princeton he had asked "the cordial and unanimous assurances of the President and Trustees that a renewed and determined effort will be made to secure the Graduate College." He had felt that his work for Princeton was unappreciated and accused Wilson of personal unfriendliness. "The trouble . . ." he had complained to the president, "is that I have not hit it off with you." He did not wish to leave Princeton, however, and could be sent away only if the president denounced him before the trustees. Some of Wilson's warmest supporters on the board thought that the

[5] Some of the concepts presented by Wilson had been set forth by Charles Francis Adams in June of 1906 in an address delivered before the Phi Beta Kappa Society at Columbia University on "Some Modern College Tendencies." And, more specifically, in a footnote added by Adams when his paper was printed in a book, *Three Phi Beta Kappa Addresses,* in 1907. In the footnote Adams quoted from Wilson's "Annual Report for 1906" on Princeton's experience with the preceptorial system. In a faculty meeting Wilson alluded to Adams's view.

time had come to make it clear to West what his responsibilties were to the whole university and its president. By a nod of his head Wilson could have separated the dean from Princeton or put him firmly under the president's control.

But Wilson leaned back. Distrusting the dean's capacity for putting Princeton's best interests before his own and yet recognizing West's value to the university, disliking to feud, putting his emphasis on constructive principles, and rising above the temptation to petty recriminations that West's reproaches had put before him, Wilson wrote a resolution urging the dean to remain. "The board," it said, "has particularly counted upon him to put into operation the Graduate College which he conceived and for which it has planned . . . It begs to assure him that he cannot be spared." West took this as a promise that he was to have virtually a free hand in directing graduate affairs.

However, sympathetic as he was to the development of graduate work, Wilson persisted in giving priority to the plan that would affect the larger number and thought it "small-minded" of West to let his desire for a residential college for a few graduate scholars stand in the way of the building of quadrangles that would benefit hundreds of undergraduates. It seemed to the president that the two projects might well go along side by side. Grover Cleveland, however, with whom West had become ever more intimate, could not be convinced of this; and West, who four years earlier had acquiesced in the placing of major emphasis on undergraduate work, had been so emboldened by the offer from Massachusetts that from now on he was to press implacably for the realization of his own vision.

In the early months of 1907 the president's proposal of residential quadrangles for undergraduates—familiarly called the "quad plan"— was the talk of the campus. There was general agreement on the need for reform, and some of the trustees went further than their leader in condemnation of the *status quo*. From many Princetonians, however, the reaction was not wholly positive.[6]

[6] President Emeritus Patton, who had become president of the Princeton Theological Seminary and to whom Wilson had shown scant courtesy, spoke in general terms about arrogant assumption of omniscience by university administrators. Senior members of the faculty were not pleased by their president's failure to take them into his confidence. Dean Fine, loyal to his chief and believing in his purposes, expressed himself in favor, yet was heard to remark: "We dearly love Woodrow. but he does drive too fast!" Hibben, too kind to dampen the ardor of his friend's virtuous intent, admitted the evils but was noncommittal about the remedy. Professor Henry Van Dyke, whom some had considered a candidate for the presidency of the university in 1902, differed with Wilson on principle, felt that through the natural foregathering of boys of similar interests, the proposed quandrangles would become stereotypes, like English "colleges." This opponent expressed gentlemanly regret at the president's haste and complained to alumni that proposals for greater deliberation "were rejected by authority." Van Dyke offered to resign; but Wilson and the faculty, respecting his opposition as sincere, persuaded him not to leave.

Wilson rethought and revised his purposes and drafted a new statement. His committee of trustees discussed it and gave it general approval; and on June 10 he read it to the entire board in a solemn session. To that company of able men who both loved and trusted him, he said: "I have never had occasion, I probably never shall have occasion, to lay a more important matter before you than the proposals contained in this report." He pleaded for his plan, not primarily as a means of reforming the club system but rather as an indispensable part of his effort "to give the University a vital, spontaneous intellectual life." Reviewing what had been accomplished already—an achievement in which Princeton men took pride—he went on to explain in what ways the social clubs were, in all innocence, stifling the intellectual life of the boys. Without entering into controversial detail, he elaborated somewhat on the bare description of the proposed residential colleges that he had given six months before. The report ended with a recommendation that "the President of the University be authorized to take such steps as may seem wisest for maturing this general plan, and for seeking the cooperation and counsel of the upper-class clubs in its elaboration . . ."

Wilson had contemplated asking the trustees for authorization "to take such steps as may seem wisest for maturing *and executing*" the quad plan; but he omitted the last two words when one of his close friends on the board advised him to do so in order to give the trustees the privilege of further consideration.

The confidence that he placed in his board proved, at the June, 1907, meeting, to be justified. Only one trustee, wishing more time for deliberation, voted against the adoption of the report. The president was authorized to "mature" his ideas.

Allowing his ardor to outrun the letter of the law, Wilson jumped to the conclusion that future debate would turn "not upon the facts, but only upon the means and methods of organization." He said: "We have a body of Alumni for whom the interests of the University as a whole, as they may be made to see those interests at any moment of action, take precedence of every other consideration, give free and wholesome vigour to the life of the University . . ."

The idealism of college youth responded to this. But Wilson had also to deal with businessmen who loved their clubs and honored tradition and property as well as scholarship. His report to the trustees was printed during Commencement Week, and reinforced by spirited addresses from the president. But Wilson had not taken pains to talk with the editor of the *Alumni Weekly* and other leaders of the younger graduates, to win them man by man to support his grand design. Instead, he caused an explanation of his plans to be read at the annual banquets of the clubs. Thus many of the alumni in reunion, having heard only rumors, first drew the full import of the new plan from the cold phrases of a formal article at the very time when they were reveling in the pleasures that their clubs afforded. Would they follow their president in devotion to Princeton's intellectual glory?

There were some indications that some men would not, and sensing this, Wilson showed the determination with which men of his clan had been accustomed to meet opposition: ". . . now there is a great deal of wild talk," he wrote to one of the most steadfast trustees, "and amidst the wild talk scores of particulars come to life which show that the situation is even worse than I had supposed, and that the remedy is absolutely imperative."

Soon the discussion had become a dispute, the dispute a bitter feud that ramified through all the Princeton community. Students, professors, families of professors, resident alumni—all took sides; and waves of gossip and recrimination slapped about in that little social sea. As argument fell from educational principles to personalities, the president was cursed as a confiscator of property, a spoilsport, a prig, a tyrant, a fool; defenders of the clubs were called tories, plutocrats, dissolutes.

Wilson felt that without residential colleges of some sort his preceptorial system could not come to full bloom. "The fight is on," he wrote on the first of July, "and I regard it, not as a fight for the development, but as a fight for the restoration of Princeton. My heart is in it more than it has been in anything else, because it is a scheme of salvation." He would fight, as his ancestors had fought, for the truth. He felt that he was engaged in nothing less than the most critical work of his whole administration, the work upon which its whole vitality and success depended. Wilson's will, like his arteries, was hardening, and was driving full speed ahead, with little regard for obstacles.[7] The president considered that he had convenanted with the trustees, and they with him, to go forward. There seemed to be no valid reason for hesitation.

Dean West burst into righteous indignation and addressed to the

[7] Wilson's purpose was strengthened by moral support from educators in other universities. To a new trustee who was a leader among the younger alumni he wrote: "As for myself, I feel that we are here debating, not only a plan, but an opportunity to solve a question common to all the colleges and obtain a leadership which it will not be within our choice to get again within our lifetime." W.W. to Andrew C. Imbrie, July 29, 1907.

president an accusation of disregard for the interests of the graduate work. But, patiently reproving the dean for lack of faith in his character and without retreating from his understanding that the board had approved his plan in essence, Wilson bade the doubters among his colleagues to wait until autumn, when opportunity would come to debate the plan. So certain had he been of his hold upon the confidence of his faculty that he had never discussed his quad plan with them; and now he had to explain that he had gone to the trustees first because the matter involved many elements that lay within the province of the board alone.

Unconvinced, West continued to encourage opposition among his friends; and he and the Clevelands brought their arguments to bear even upon trusted Jack and Jennie Hibben.

During the summer the trustees were bombarded with protests from alumni. They were responsible for the financial accountability of the university, and the deficits that had to be made up by emergency gifts had grown annually larger. How, they wondered, were they to get support for expensive new quadrangles? On this question there was a division of opinion. Some were convinced that patrons would not give willingly to a university that was overshadowed by private clubs. On the other hand, among the protesting club men were many large givers who seemed determined to donate neither buildings nor money to the proposed quandrangles. Wilson himself persisted in hoping that the clubs might be absorbed rather than abolished. If only the jumpy economic nerve of his trustees could be soothed, the protests of the opposition would subside, he felt sure.

During the summer he sought sanctuary in the Adirondacks. His imagination had been caught often by hill-rimmed security; though he seldom perused novels, he had read *Lorna Doone* over and over. Now, while the prophet guarded his vision behind Doone Gate, within a valley in his mind, disaffected alumni agitated the plains and clouds of dust arose. The quadrangles would end "class spirit," they were saying: on the contrary, said their leader, "nothing is more damaging to the homogeneity and spirit of the classes than what is going on." To the cry that "no one should make a gentleman associate with a 'mucker,'" Wilson repeated that the primary object of his reform was not social but intellectual. More than once he wrote: "I should be very much distressed to have the plan regarded as an attack on the clubs." The president gave much of his vacation to answering, as fully and persuasively as only he could do it, many letters of query that came to him. Meanwhile Hibben was yielding to the counsel of West and the protest of clubmen. "Woodrow does not know the trustees as I do," he warned. "Some will not stay hitched. He is going to split the college."

If anyone could influence Wilson in the name of friendship, Hibben was the man. Partly from shyness, partly from fastidiousness in choosing friends, Wilson had seldom indulged his passion for genuine friendship. But the Hibbens had made themselves utterly agreeable and the president had dared to admit them to the bosom intimacy that a Scot reserves for a very few. "What I really wanted to say to you today stuck in my throat through dryness," he had written one day to Hibben. In his own mind, and without Hibben's consent, he had bound this dear friend by a clannish covenant of allegiance. Now he felt that this disciple must be held loyal. And so Wilson wrote to assure him that not the least shadow had darkened their perfect understanding, that he still valued Hibben's advice on the quad plan, and that it had disposed him to look for opportunities of concession. But never could he yield his dearest principle, he explained: the club system must give way to an organization absolutely controlled, not negatively but constructively and administratively, by the authorities of the university. Not to insist on that, the president thought, would be to temporize with evil.

Hibben was summering in Greensboro, Vermont, where he was in correspondence with members of the opposition. He knew the strength and determination of West and the Van Dykes, of Cleveland and the Morgans. And so he went up to the prophet's retreat in the mountains to plead expediency, to try, as he put it, "to save Woodrow from himself."

No approach could have insulted Wilson more. It pained him that his bosom friend understood him so poorly as to imagine that he could surrender educational principles so essential. He had prepared his soul for martyrdom, if need be. Though there was no irreparable break then and there, the family saw their man's face turn white with anger at what he regarded as the defection of a weak disciple. "Jack keeps driving into my ears—delay," he said, "but the one thing to do is to go ahead and fight. The trustees have spoken . . . There are men on that board who will stand pat till the skies fall."

Determined to go on through what he called, optimistically, a "dust cloud," Wilson came down from the Adirondacks in the fall of 1907 with will unshaken. He was now ready to do battle at close grips. During the summer his undergraduates had been influenced by the talk of clubmen among the alumni. He must bring them back to "things of the mind" and "discipline of the spirit." At the annual dinner of the college newspaper he rose with eyes steely and jaws jutting. The applause was light and chilling, and he began low and clear: "It is my lonely privilege, in gatherings of educated men, to be the only person who speaks of education." Opposition had sharpened all his latent pride and put it on the tip of his tongue. His family had never heard him speak in this tone before. To his opponents the effect was one of arrogance, while his friends saw the "independent conviction" and "self-trust" that "Tommie" Wilson in his student days had thought essential to a political leader. Ten minutes later, after he had scorched his defamers and condemned their unresponsiveness to the intellectual glory that might be Princeton's, his boys were on their feet, climbing tables, cheering. When asked why they applauded a speech with which many of them did not agree, a student replied: "They know a man when they see one." Even Dean West's son was moved to remark: "Sometimes I wish that I were on the other side." [8]

The speaker sat down, grim and silent. Walking home across the campus, he muttered, "Damn their eyes! Damn their eyes!" It seemed to him that they were growing to resemble their fathers, praising him when he talked about democracy but refusing to follow him in democratic action when their "interests" were touched.

In September the faculty threw itself into the fray in earnest. The young preceptors supported their president almost to a man. Factions formed among the older professors, however, and met to discuss plans of action. The opposition met at West's house, which once had been the center of opposition to President Patton; the loyalists, at Dean Fine's.

Finally the time came for the faculty to debate the quad plan in Princeton's House of Commons. Tense and worried, Wilson's colleagues filed in to the vaulted room in historic Nassau Hall, where in three formal meetings the issue was joined and the arguments aired. In the first session Henry Van Dyke made a motion that was designed to sidetrack Wilson's proposal for further study of the quad plan. When Hibben seconded the motion, Wilson turned pale. Controlling his voice with difficulty, the president asked: "Do I understand Professor Hibben seconds the motion?"

"I do, Mr. President."

The silence was sepulchral. Woodrow Wilson, who could be easily hurt by a close friend, suffered a martyr's agony.

8 Francis C. MacDonald, who sat next to Randolph West, to the writer.

Then West led a sniping attack, suggesting that Wilson's quads would resemble the "quod" (jail) at Princetown, England, and would curtail liberty by making students come in early of evenings. And Wilson in an extravagance of enthusiasm retorted: "Certainly not. We'll have ladders at every window!" [9] The debate took on a tone more common to political bodies than to convocations of scholars.

In the second meeting of the faculty a vote on the Van Dyke resolution gave Wilson a majority of twenty-nine to twenty-two of the old faculty and the support of all but one of the preceptors.

In the third meeting, in a speech that friend and enemy alike hailed as superb, the president again set forth his educational principles. Quoting statistics, he said that the records showed that the clubmen were not taking their share of academic honors. No vote was taken, but at the end of the discussion that followed it was evident that the "prime minister" had held his House of Commons in line and would go with their support to the House of Lords—the board of trustees. [10]

When the trustees met on October 17 their interest in the quad plan had been dampened by the waves of criticism that had come from students and from alumni, more than half of whom opposed the president's project. The influence of the secular alumni had now grown to such strength that it dared to challenge the administration on a point of educational policy. In the face of threats of withdrawal of financial support and in the absence of funds for new buildings, the trustees felt themselves powerless. Convinced that the day was lost, Wilson yielded to the advice of his supporters and announced that his Committee on Social Coordination had no report. A resolution offered by Chairman Pyne proposed that the action taken in June be reconsidered, that the president be requested to withdraw the plan, and that the committee be discharged; but to recognize the rectitude of Wilson's conscience and his right to free speech, the trustees stated that they had "no wish to hinder him in any way in his purpose to endeavor to convince the members of the Board and Princeton men that this plan is the true solution." Moreover, Grover Cleveland proposed that the trustees resolve that *something* be done about the problem of the clubs.

The man who had forced the plan into the consciousness of the

[9] F. C. MacDonald to the writer.
[10] V. L. Collins recorded that West told him, on April 14, 1930, that Wilson arranged to have his quad plan tabled without approval at the third faculty meeting (Oct. 17) because Pyne had warned him that the trustees would request his resignation if a faculty vote were taken. *See* Collins's notes in a copy of Baker's *Woodrow Wilson: Life and Letters*, Vol. II, in the Princeton University Library. Collins attended the meetings as secretary of the faculty.

nation felt that he got nothing out of the transaction except complete defeat and mortification. For the first time his family saw his high spirits yield to the discouragement of disillusion. The Hibbens called at Prospect to cheer him, as they had done so many times before; but Wilson treated them so discourteously that he was moved the next day to write in repentance, begging to be forgiven for what he called boorish behavior. When a "black mood" settled on him, he explained, he seemed to forget that he was bred a gentleman. Despite the apology, however, the old familiar relationship was never resumed.

The president told his faculty that the trustees plainly could not support him further in the only matters in which he felt that he could lead and be of service. He thought of resigning, but refrained, he said, because he saw that he did not have the right to place the university in danger of going to pieces.[11]

Wilson was not willing to offer up Princeton on the altar of Absolute Truth. He loved his own *alma mater* too much. He must have marked the similarity of his fight to that of Uncle James Woodrow, whom the trustees of the Columbia Theological Seminary had supported until the financial secretary had expressed fear of the effect of the new ideas on unenlightened contributors. Dear, gentle, crusading uncle, who had just entered eternal peace—the last of the great saints of the older generation—"a man made to love (in the quiet, self-contained Scottish fashion, but very, very deeply, none the less)"! In a wilderness of secularity the prophet at Princeton was now very much alone.

The faith that was bred in Woodrow Wilson and that had survived Civil War and Reconstruction was not shaken. Within a week of the fateful meeting of the trustees, pitching his voice above the whispers of expediency, he preached to his boys on "the importance of single-mindedness," on "principles held with steadfastness," using as his text: "He that observeth the wind shall not sow; he that regardeth the clouds shall not reap."

The press was dramatizing the controversy at Princeton as a battle for social democracy that had national import. Loyal trustees were goading their leader with fighting letters, suggesting that from now on the battle must be frankly one of democracy against special privilege. A theologian trustee assured Wilson that the controversy was "being taken most seriously by the great public who are interested in the matter far more deeply than the smart set of the Clubs or the scared set of

11 A year later Pyne assured Wilson that he was still "Princeton's best asset," that he was needed "more than ever" to help to "clean up the finances."

the Board at present realize." Later the president was urged to make clear "the money spirit of the opposition."

Wilson caught his breath quickly and took the warpath. In November he wrote to a loyal trustee: "If we can bring our Princeton constituency to see the necessity of the reform, it is clearly our duty to do so, no matter how long it takes or how hard the task may prove.'

Soon he was showing that he had the stuff of which political campaigners were made. His pluck in fighting on alone when hope seemed dim was endearing him to millions of Americans. In Tennessee, in Maryland, in Indiana, he spoke hotly in rebellion against educational ineffectiveness, keeping his argument on professional grounds. When an honest opponent of the quad plan was proposed as a candidate for the board of trustees, he called the suggestion "excellent."

In January he escaped for a few weeks to Bermuda, spraining his knee on the rough voyage and, once ashore, allowing Mary Allen Peck and her mother to coddle and humor him into gayer spirits. The vitality and ingenuity of his words claimed Mrs. Peck's affection; but he was no Lothario, and he knew it. "Women would not look at me twice, dear lady," he told her, "if they did not think I was something in particular and did not find I had a store of amusing stories." To his wife he wrote: "Of course I am seeing a great deal of Mrs. Peck. She is fine and dear. But I am remembering your injunction." [11a]

In Bermuda, Wilson was able to jest about the defeat that had cut so deep. "I didn't get the quads," he said, "but I got the wrangles." [12] He always came back from the island, he wrote, "more sane about everything." [13] Returning in the winter of 1908 with nerves rested, he was determined "to make the issue clear without making it exasperating." He appealed to the alumni and, lifting the issue to a national level, warned: "The particular threat that seems to me most alarming to our life at the present moment is that we are beginning to think in classes." He continued to make it clear to his audiences that, as he said in a speech at Chicago, he was "a good fighter," that "on the whole" he "would rather fight than not . . ." And he was finding that the more belligerent were his words the more hearty was the applause of the Western alumni. [14]

[11a] *The Papers of W.W., 17,* 612.

[12] To Mrs. Borden Harriman. Mrs. Harriman to the writer, Feb. 22, 1951.

[13] W.W. to O. G. Villard, Jan. 26, 1908, Villard Papers (Houghton Library, Harvard University, Cambridge, Mass.).

[14] Wilson got a sympathetic response, too, from the undergraduate club members, when he could talk to them in their houses. Invited in the spring of 1909 to the Cottage Club, he listened

A committee of friendly trustees investigated the clubs and in April presented their findings to the board. The report recognized evils in the system but at the same time undermined Wilson's position by remarking that club life did not seem to discourage study in itself or to lower academic standards. Choking with frustration, Wilson confessed to Stockton Axson what he had been too diplomatic to say in his public utterances. At last he was accepting the issue that had been drawn first by one of the clubmen and later by the press of the nation and by friendly trustees. "I'll never win," he admittted grimly. "What I am opposing is privilege. They would let me do anything in educational reform, but here I am attacking their social privileges."

To be sure, there had been formal honors aplenty from those who had ears to hear a prophet. He had been elected to the American Academy of Arts and Letters, had been made a member of the board of the Carnegie Foundation, had been awarded his ninth honorary degree, and had received more invitations than ever to speak to distinguished audiences. Moreover, Lawrence Lowell, soon to assume the presidency of Harvard, had come to his support in a speech at the Princeton Commencement. "Your President," he said, "is one of the men who have grappled with the problem as it exists today, the problem of the college, of the undergraduate department. He has begun solutions which are an example and encouragement to every college in the United States."

But the gentle Scottish soul beneath the crusading armor longed for peace and friendship, and his ideal comradeship with Hibben had been broken. His beloved undergraduates had disappointed him. He had lost his adored Uncle James Woodrow. However, there were resources in his religion that fortified him in his personal grief. He spoke of them in his Baccalaureate to the class of 1907: "To one deep fountain of revelation and renewal few of you, I take it for granted, have had access yet,—I mean the fountain of sorrow, a fountain sweet or bitter according as it is drunk in submission or in rebellion, in love or in resentment and deep dismay. I will not tell you of those waters; if you have not tasted them it would be futile,—and some of you will understand without word of mine. I can only beg that when they are put to your lips,

---

to a brilliant attack on his quad plan, delivered in Biblical parable by President Emeritus Patton and responded extemporaneously in the same style, carried the boys with him, and sat around and entertained them until midnight.

Walking by the Cottage Club one day, Wilson said to Julian Beaty, his student secretary: "I think they ought to change its name to Castle." Then he added: "Perhaps I shouldn't say that, as I think I am an honorary member." J. Beaty to R. S. Baker, July 2, 1926. Confirmed by Beaty to the writer.

as they must be, you will drink of them as those who seek renewal and know how to make of sadness a mood of enlightenment and of hope."

The prophet could face up to his personal losses and accept them if only his cause prospered. But it was not easy to reconcile himself to the fact that he had failed to give effect to what he regarded as the will of God for Princeton. He had not provided the tactful planning and the liaison with men of wealth and influence that were required for the realization of a sound but revolutionary educational ideal. One of his careless remarks—trenchant and indiscreet—had leaked into circulation: "After all, what does Grover Cleveland know about a university?"[15] And Cleveland had retaliated by writing to a friend[16] that the president of Princeton was without a vestige of professional honesty.

[15] Bliss Perry to the writer.

[16] Prentiss Bailey, editor of the Utica *Observer*. See O. G. Villard, *Fighting Years,* p. 228 n. The extent of Cleveland's commitment to West's cause is revealed in a letter of Mar. 23, 1907, from Cleveland to West: ". . . I have never been enlisted in a cause which has given me more satisfaction or a better feeling of usefulness." Graduate School papers, Princeton University Library.

CHAPTER VIII

PRINCIPLES, NOT MEN

WITH WILSON'S PLAN for undergraduate quadrangles decently buried, the trustees could give closer attention to constructing the graduate college for which Dean West had been pressing.[1]

In 1902, after studying graduate work in European universities, West drew up a formal plan for a graduate college that would be so placed that the undergraduates would pass by in their daily walks. This was a scheme close to the heart of Wilson. In his first report to the board, on October 21, 1902, he asked for three million dollars for endowment of a graduate establishment. He told the trustees what he later wrote in a preface for a pamphlet in which West's plan was printed: that the project was one by which "a group of graduate students are most apt to stimulate and set the pace for the whole university." And in his inaugural address Wilson had been even more explicit. The graduate college would be built, he said, "not apart, but as nearly as may be at the very heart, the geographical heart, of the university; and its comradeship shall be for young men and old, for the novice as well as for the graduate." During his years at the Johns Hopkins Graduate School, as student and as lecturer, Wilson had seen the advantage that came to both undergraduates and graduate students from close association outside the classroom. The younger men caught something of the serious intent of the professional scholar, and the graduates were saved from scornful misunderstanding of the men they were preparing to teach.

The board of trustees had not formally adopted the proposals made in West's pamphlet and approved by Wilson. The president's drive for funds for the preceptorial system, which West supported heartily, had made it impossible for the dean to make rapid headway until, in 1905— the year after Grover Cleveland became chairman of the trustees' committee on the graduate school—West finally accumulated resources

---

[1] The trustees, acting upon a faculty report signed by Wilson in 1896, recognized a graduate residence as "of the first importance for the organization and development of the graduate work." Memorial to the trustees, Dec. 10, 1896, from a faculty committee appointed by Patton and including Wilson but not West. On March 6, 1896 Patton wrote to Isaac C. Wyman, a Boston alumnus, of Princeton's need for a million dollars to "erect buildings" and endow a "graduate college." Letters in the Graduate School pa., Princeton University Library.

enough to take over an old estate that he named "Merwick." There, about a half mile from the campus, he installed a few of his scholars. But when he asked that the drive for funds for the tutorial program be supplemented by "a determined and unremitting effort in behalf of the graduate college," the trustees merely encouraged him to campaign on his own. The dean did as suggested; and early in 1906 a wealthy Princeton lady, Mrs. Swann, left a bequest to the university to further the dean's purpose. Wilson expressed delight over the gift, and on December 13 expressed his pleasure over the work at Merwick and the fact that the college to be built would enlarge the community life of the graduate students.

In the spring of 1908, at the very session of the trustees at which Wilson's quad plan was dealt its death blow, it was voted to accept Ralph Adams Cram's recommendation that the Swann bequest should be used for the construction of a graduate college at the heart of the campus. This was an endorsement of Wilson's views, contrary to the desire of West and Cleveland that the new unit be placed off campus, preferably at Merwick.

There the issue rested in the summer of 1908, when Wilson sought relaxation by traveling in England. When trustees offered to pay the expenses of the trip, he declined, saying to his wife: "I may have to oppose some of these men upon the vital educational policies of Princeton, and I should be trussed up if I accepted such favours from them."

On the byways of Scotland and at Carlyle's birthplace, Wilson found his appetite for life reviving, though his afflicted eye and his pen hand still bothered him. From abroad he could look with magnanimity on Grover Cleveland, who died in June. "I do not think," he commented in a letter to his wife, "that my knowledge of how he failed and disappointed us during the past few years, and particularly since he allowed himself to be made West's tool, will long obscure my admiration for his great qualities and his singularly fine career."

When he reached the Lake Country, his old friend Mrs. Yates threw a hospitable arm about him and he looked up to a Wordsworthian hill that rose before him "like some great nourishing breast." At Carnegie's Skibo Castle he met a fascinating assortment of fellow guests and enjoyed talk with Burke's biographer, John Morley, whom he thought an "old goose" for accepting removal to the House of Lords from the House of Commons. He found his hostess "*very* sweet and true," but in writing to Ellen he reserved "for the modulations of the voice" many things "not suitable to be written down"—his opinion of his host in particular. And yet, for dear Princeton's sake, he had to be civil to the philanthropist.

Returning to the campus in the autumn of 1908, his vigor completely restored, Wilson found that the problems of social life were becoming more acute. He revealed his discomfiture and restlessness to Frank A. Vanderlip, a banker who, he hoped, might secure a large gift from Carnegie that would make the quad plan practicable. "I must get the money . . ." he wrote. "If I cannot do this, I must turn to something else than mere college administration—forced not by my colleagues but by my mind and convictions, to the impossibility of continuing at things I do not believe in . . ."

Several of the trustees had come to see what a few had commented on in 1906—the folly of allowing Dean West to remain at Princeton and carry on graduate work without an exact understanding of his accountability to the president and the faculty. In the spring of 1909, at the urging of new professors whom Wilson had attracted to Princeton, the trustees decided to correct this situation by lodging control of graduate studies in a six-man faculty committee of which Dean West was made a member. To his associates on this body, West seemed stubborn in his prejudices—a man who ruled by exceptions.[2] Fireplaces and private baths, they said, could not be afforded by many of the scholars who were qualified for admittance. In fact, they felt that graduate students of serious purpose would be repelled by any scheme that laid emphasis on considerations other than scholarship.

Wilson doubted that this committee would bring lasting peace. Appreciative of the refinements of culture and realizing that they were "too hard to find in America," he had warned that "culture is a word it is easy to drawl and make too mawkish distinctions about." He feared that Andrew West was making a fool of himself. In the ideal graduate college, Wilson said, "a certain simplicity of life still of necessity prevails. The studious pursuits of such schools are of necessity so important, so engrossing, so directly related to the practical success of the men who have sought the place out for preparation that little else is heeded." Such luxuries as West recommended might make of the graduate college merely another club where the minds of the scholars

[2] The newcomers, like Dean Fine who became the leader of the majority group of the new committee, had had more experience than West in the ways of graduate study both abroad and in America. One of them, for example, Edward Capps, had taken the degree of Ph.D. at the Yale Graduate School, had done graduate work in Germany and at Athens, and had taught graduate students at the University of Chicago and at Yale. A majority of the new committee did not take kindly to certain luxuries in the elaborate plans that West presented.

would become as soft as the cushions on which they would sit, and Princeton would fall far short of the standard of graduate study that Wilson had himself known. Moreover, the undergraduate work needed funds so badly that it seemed wasteful, from the point of view of the entire university, to supply unnecessary luxuries to graduate scholars. West, who understood that his leadership had been endorsed in 1906 when he had been urged not to go to M.I.T., asked Wilson why control of graduate education had been given to the new faculty committee; and Wilson replied: "I wish to say to the Dean somewhat grimly that he must be digested in the processes of the university."

When an opportunity came to fight back, West seized it and chose his weapon shrewdly. William Cooper Procter, a former student and a wealthy manufacturer of soap, offered a half-million dollars toward the fulfillment of West's dreams, provided that his gift was matched by others totaling the same amount. Examining the site near Prospect that Cram had recommended for use of the Swann bequest, Procter pronounced it unsuitable and said that his offer was made on the understanding that some location be chosen that would be satisfactory to him. This meant, everyone knew, that the site must be acceptable to Andrew West.

Promoters of Princeton were thrilled by the prospect of a further addition to what the college newspaper had headlined as the "unprecedented material growth of the university." But there were hard, cold reasons why Woodrow Wilson felt that he could not accept the Procter offer.[3] Moreover, he had been emotionally prejudiced against it by disturbing gossip, rumors that gifts were being solicited for Princeton behind the president's back. Wilson had protested that "all of this movement of groups in entire independence of each other" made him very uneasy and rendered "proper government of the University impossible." He was not reassured when Procter addressed his proposal not to the trustees or the president, but to Dean West, who had been authorized to negotiate with the donor as a representative of the trustees' committee on graduate work.

The balance of power at that juncture lay in the hands of Moses Taylor Pyne, who had succeeded Cleveland as chairman of the trustees' committee on the graduate school. A kindly, disinterested man who hated discord, he could be depended on to base his opinions on an hon-

---

[3] Wilson believed that the legal terms of the earlier bequest of Mrs. Swann would prevent its use with the Procter gift for a plant off-campus; and he accepted the condition attached to the Swann contribution the more readily because it coincided with his educational plan.

est devotion to the interests of Princeton University as he conceived them.

This genial philanthropist was at first neutral in the controversy over the location of the graduate college; but when Procter, who preferred to build at Merwick, agreed to compromise on the golf links as a site, Pyne supported that proposal and with West[4] campaigned actively for a vote of the board that would satisfy the desire of the alumni for acceptance of the proffered money on any terms that would seem reasonable to laymen.

Wilson told a friendly trustee that he felt the pressure and embarrassment of his position keenly; but he reined his temper well. He resented the presumption of a benefactor in dictating the use of a gift. And yet, realizing that his accountability to trustees and alumni forbade the refusal of a half-million dollars without a determined effort to find a way to use it effectively, aware that any strong stand on his part would merely add power to the cry of "dictator" that his enemies had been raising, Wilson pleaded with Procter. But the West faction would not consider the campus as a site for the new college, though they could give no convincing educational argument for their dissent; and the clamor of the alumni was becoming more insistent.

That summer Wilson tucked himself away in the quiet town of old Lyme, Connecticut, and tried to fortify his spiritual resources. Free from the whirl of university politics, covenanting only to obey the law of inertia, he meditated on the philosophy that always had guided him. He felt young again, his thoughts reverted to his childhood, and he consoled himself in the knowledge that in his own mind he was as independent as when he was a dreaming boy. He was beginning to remind his daughters, now, that there were some people who could not be trusted.

After two summer months spent in comparative idleness and in small and chivalrous attentions to his loved ones, he was chafing again for contact with affairs that were hard and essential. Work appealed to him as an end in itself, and the most wholesome and satisfactory thing in an uncertain world. It was never straightforward, independent work that harassed him at Princeton, but rather the tiresomeness of sophomoric young fools, the long-windedness of professorial old ones, the pathetic delusions of doting parents, the empty and injudicious

4 As in the case of his relations with Cleveland, West had not been backward about cultivating a friendship with Pyne. On Pyne's birthday in 1907, West had presented an original poem, luxuriously printed and bound, and inscribed with a Greek phrase meaning "Keep young, dear soul."

minds of young alumni, the officious pomp of certain trustees, the importunities of vain patrons. And these crosses were never so hard to bear as when they interfered with constructive work designed to quicken the intellectual life of the university.

In the fall of 1909, when he had an opportunity to speak to young ministers at Chicago, Wilson seized upon the occasion to put backbone into individuals, including himself. In directing his sermons at his own needs, he said, he hoped also to help others who were like him. "The great danger of our day," he warned, ". . . is that men will compound their conscientious scruples on the ground that they are not free to move independently . . . For they say, 'The penalty will be that we shall be absolutely crushed.' The organization must dictate to us, if we be members of a corporation; if we be members of a union, the union; if we be members of a society of whatever kind, the programme of the society must dominate us . . . Every turning point in the history of mankind has been pivoted upon the choice of an individual, when some spirit that would not be dominated stood stiff in its independence and said: 'I go this way. Let any man go another way who pleases' . . ."

In a magazine article he tried to answer the question: "What is a College for?" It is "for the use of the nation," he reiterated, "not for the satisfaction of those who administer it or for the carrying out of their private views." He remarked upon the increasing number of rich students, feared that their wealth would remove all incentive to work and they would be "foredoomed to obscurity." In the colleges of the day, he complained, "the side shows are so numerous, so diverting—so important, if you will—that they have swallowed up the circus, and those who perform in the main tent must often whistle for their audiences, discouraged and humiliated." Do not cast out the side shows, he advised, but they must be subordinated.

In October the majority of the faculty committee on the graduate school presented a report to the trustees—not published until February, 1910—in which they argued that the separation of the graduate residence from the campus would impair efficiency both in administration and in student work. Further, they pointed out that "the untoward effect of the isolation of particular schools has been witnessed at Columbia, at Pennsylvania, at the Johns Hopkins, and elsewhere; and early mistakes in location have been remedied, where possible, at great expense." However, Hibben joined with West in signing a minority report that recommended an off-campus site, justifying this position by the success of the graduate residence at Merwick.

When finally the Hibbens stood openly with West on graduate policy, the Wilsons believed that their friends were not only disloyal but ambitious, as well, for the presidency of Princeton. Ellen Wilson, who had observed Jennie Hibben's preference for the company of Mrs. Cleveland, now let it be known that there would be no forgiveness. The door was closed.

As for West, Wilson had concluded that it was impossible to deal directly with him. To a proposal that the dean sent through Professor Daniels, the president replied: ". . . the method he is using is entirely illegal . . . The letter . . . fills me with amazement." Wilson asked Daniels to report this reaction to West, in order to avoid the delivery of a reprimand in faculty meeting. Personal recrimination made him ill; moreover, it would merely strengthen West's feeling that he was persecuted. It was better, he felt, to preach general principles and to encourage the faculty committee to argue the case on its merits.

In the eyes of many lay alumni, however, the refinements of educational policy were blurred. They could see only folly in rejecting a half-million dollars in deference to ideals that were to them both nebulous and pious; and some businessmen took the attitude that if West made the sale to Procter he should have the credit. So, in October of 1909, the board of trustees, faced with a large deficit for the preceding year, noting that Wilson had made no successful effort to secure funds for the graduate college, sensitive to alumni opinion, and confident that another half million could be raised to match Procter's offer, voted to overrule the majority report of the faculty committee, to accept the gift, and to build the new unit on the golf links almost a mile from the university library, provided that the earlier Swann bequest could be used legally on that site.

Wilson's close friends, now a minority of the trustees, ridiculed the decision. They laughed at the haste with which certain educators and clergymen on the board clutched at the half-million dollars, regardless of the merits of the proposition. Wilson himself was stunned. He was now losing a battle that, before the appearance of Procter's money, had been won. He could only conclude that the trustees had acted as they did, not because they trusted West—whom he now considered an archintriguer—but because money had talked more convincingly than their president. Wrath rioted in his veins and muddled his thinking. Disheartened and disgusted, he feared that his sharp tongue would betray his scorn and that a careless word might irreparably damage the institution that he loved and for which he was responsible. His impulse was to resign and let his antagonists explain their case to the country as best they could. But he told himself that it would not be sporting to quit while there was any chance of winning.

A few weeks later, driven by concern for Princeton's harmony, he forced himself to suggest a compromise, to carry out a precept that he had given his students: "There can be no compromise in individual morality; but there *has* to be a compromise, an average, in social morality. There is indeed an element of morality in the very fact of compromise on *social* undertakings." [5] On December 31, Wilson suggested to Pyne, unofficially and tentatively, that the Swann bequest be used to build a residential college for graduate students on the campus and the Procter gift be used for graduate instruction on the golf links site. This personal suggestion, a makeshift, seemed to Pyne "a ridiculous solution of the question" and "not worth considering."

And so, at the end of 1909, Wilson was in deepest gloom. In October the University of Minnesota had tried to lure him to its presidency and he still had that offer under consideration when he made a last effort, on December 22, to convert Procter to the compromise proposal that Pyne had rejected. He was desperately worried, he said, for he felt that as prime minister of Princeton he was assuming all the responsibility that Procter suggested should belong to the trustees. When the philanthropist said, "You had better change your board of trustees," Wilson replied, "No, I think they had better change their president." Failing in his effort to compromise, learning that Procter and West were determined to dictate the disposal not only of the Procter gift but of the matching half million and—illegally, he thought—of the Swann bequest as well, Wilson saw no further hope of serving Princeton. Sitting down in the railroad station at Jersey City, he penciled this sentence to Pyne: "The acceptance of this gift has taken the guidance of the University out of my hands entirely—and I seem to have come to the end." He had failed to command the confidence of the constituency on the quad plan, and now on his policy for the graduate college.

When Pyne, alarmed at the loss of educational prestige that the university would suffer, replied that he hoped that the president's note from Jersey City did not "represent . . . well considered conclusions" and that it would be withdrawn, Wilson sat down at his desk on Christmas Day and unburdened himself. The board's acceptance of the Procter offer, Wilson wrote to Pyne, reversed the policy of the faculty and

[5] Raymond Fosdick's address, "Personal Recollections of W.W.," given at the University of Chicago, Jan. 30, 1956.

the leading concept of his whole administration in an educational matter of fundamental importance. "I am not willing to be drawn further into the toils. I cannot accede to the acceptance of gifts upon terms which take the educational policy of the University out of the hands of the Trustees and Faculty and permit it to be determined by those who give money . . . I cannot consent, if the gift is deliberately accepted on such terms, to remain responsible for the direction of the affairs of the University or for the development of her educational policy."

Reviewing the history of the controversy, Wilson reminded Pyne that "West's first idea" contemplated a graduate college that lay in every sense at the heart of things, and that modification of his purpose[6] had played no small part in depriving him of the confidence of his academic colleagues. "He has now lost their confidence completely," Wilson wrote, "and nothing administered by him in accordance with his present ideas can succeed."

His passionate concern for academic freedom led Wilson to add to his denunciation of Dean West a fateful sentence: "Indeed, nothing administered by him can now succeed." Wilson all but accused his ambitious colleague of trying to buy position and preferment. A few days later he wrote to a friendly trustee: "We now know, indeed, that Mr. Procter's gift is made to put West in the saddle, but we cannot make that a matter of public discussion." To do so, he said, would "make it appear a personal matter, which the friends of the University would certainly misinterpret greatly to our discredit." When he was asked, later, what sort of fellow West was, he said merely: "A little difficult. I suspect he thinks I am too." Discussing the dean's educational policies, however, he flared into incandescence.

The absolute necessity of the moment, Wilson thought, was that his friends should find money with which to buy freedom.[7] Pyne confessed that he was "torn almost in two." Finally, in a last-minute effort at reconciliation, Procter was persuaded to accept the compromise that

[6] It was indeed true that West had modified his views and purposes, chiefly in the direction of luxury and concentration of executive power in his own hands. For Wilson's considered opinion of West's policies, see the statement that Wilson drew up in 1912 and that is printed in Baker, II, 358–60. In this statement Wilson asserted that he had opposed West's plan "in the essential particular of its site and consequent spirit and character, and sought by every possible suggestion to bring it back to what it had been originally intended to be."

[7] Professor Harper thought that the issue before the board was boiling down to this: "which can Princeton least afford to lose, Professor West and $500,000, or Woodrow Wilson and an honorable rank among American universities?" The faculty, Harper thought, would decide in favor of President Wilson by a vote of four to one. George McLean Harper to Wilson Farrand, Feb. 3, 1910, Farrand Papers (Princeton University Library).

had been proposed on December 22 by Wilson, personally and unofficially and with no confidence that it was a proper solution—a compromise that Pyne had thought not worthy of consideration.

This about-face was reported in meetings of the graduate-school committee and the full board of trustees in January. Thrown into confusion by the sudden blurring of the issue that he had drawn so clearly, surrendering to the temptation of friends who had advised him to denounce West publicly, Wilson made an extravagant statement that later was to be regretted. Dean West's ideas and ideals, he said, were not those of Princeton. Upsetting with a short, careless phrase all the professional argument on the question of site that had been built up over a period of years, the president contended that *his* faculty could make the graduate school a success "anywhere in Mercer County." He had been startled into letting down the shield of conviction and opening himself to attack as a feuding dictator.

His friends understood and applauded.[8] The opposition, however, had embarrassing questions to ask. Why, they queried, had the president for so long made the site the main issue? Unable or unwilling to comprehend the forbearance that executive responsibility had forced on him, they thought that he had been insincere in insisting on location as the basic issue, that in reality he had been acting all along out of spite against West.[9] And their wavering confidence was further shaken by a characteristic lapse of memory on the part of the president. Attempting to dramatize the issue, Wilson held up before the trustees a copy of West's original printed report, *Proposed Graduate College of Princeton University*, and exclaimed: "The fundamental difficulty with Mr. Procter's offer is that it is specifically intended to carry out the ideals of that book. A graduate school based on these ideals cannot succeed." In impulsively seizing on this publication as an objectification of all that West stood for, Wilson forgot, in his flurry of emotion, that when it was printed, in 1903, West had not expressed either his present views on the site of the graduate college or the desire for dictation of policy and personnel that now seemed so outrageous. Actually, except

[8] A majority of the faculty committee on the graduate school gave the trustees a statement buttressing the president's disapproval of the dean's plans, asserting: ". . . we cannot attract strong men by adherence to dilettante ideals." Baker, II, 324.

[9] The truth is that Wilson liked neither West nor his ideas and thoroughly distrusted his motives. As a responsible executive, however, his only effective course of action was to argue on an ideological plane. There is no evidence to show why the president at first chose to stress the question of site above the educational considerations that were raised by the majority of the faculty committee on the graduate school: perhaps because, being a more concrete matter, it could be grasped more easily by the minds of laymen; but more likely, because it was Procter's attempt to dictate the site that raised the essential question of academic freedom.

for a tendency toward unproductive luxury, most of what West had written in 1902 could still be approved by Wilson in 1910. In fact, *he himself had written a preface commending the very work that he was now damning!* [10]

West's supporters saw the inconsistency and exploited it. One of them asked why Wilson had praised West's report in his preface if it was so unacceptable. Completely confounded, the president could only mumble an unconvincing and very damaging remark to the effect that he had not really seen West's pamphlet when he wrote the preface.

Wilson had assured his students that a man of simple truthfulness had no need to worry about petty details, that only liars had to remember everything carefully to avoid incriminating themselves by inconsistencies.[11] His own memory, so notoriously defective that he had been known to repeat an anecdote to the very man who had told it to him the day before, did not come to his rescue and remind him, in this atmosphere of cross-examination, that most of the anathema had crept into West's doctrine during the eight years since his pamphlet was printed. As a trial lawyer Wilson was not, had never been, convincing. He had not yet learned that an executive must keep up his guard even when among those whom he counted as friends. Before he could be a great parliamentarian he would have to learn to put less trust in the confidence of his associates in his good intentions.[12]

As a result of the give-and-take of the January meeting, and in spite of a conciliatory note from the president, Pyne lost all confidence in Wilson's integrity and in his executive ability, and from that time on opposed him at every turn. He could explain the president's contradictory statements only on the ground either that he was mentally unbalanced or that he was suffering from extreme jealousy. He tried to conspire with Procter to force the resignation of Wilson, and a trustee warned the president that things would be done purposely to goad him into a position where he would want to resign. Pyne haunted Wilson's

[10] *See* p. 116 above.

[11] Chambers MS, p. 28.

[12] Wilson's confusion was further confounded in a bristling skirmish over the reasons for his change of opinion regarding the compromise plan that Procter had first refused but later accepted. It came out that Wilson had presented the makeshift plan to Pyne with assurance that it had the "hearty concurrence" of his faculty colleagues, and that actually the proposal had so offended them that some of them had since persuaded the president that it was unwise. (The phrase "hearty concurrence" was but another instance of the prophet's tendency to project his own ideas into other men's minds without their leave.)

Wilson was utterly unable to defend himself against the sudden and unforeseen attack on his integrity. "I was so . . . angered at the evident trick that had been played upon us," he wrote afterward, "that I did not feel at all sure that I had acted with self-control and propriety . . ." W.W. to Henry B. Thompson, Jan. 17, 1910, in Baker, II, 322.

dreams as a man incalculable, almost irresponsible, prowling deviously in the underbrush while the president, like a treed cat, held himself poised to jump in any direction.

Despite the crosscurrents in the January session of the board, the tide of opinion was still flowing toward the president. He was empowered to appoint a special committee of five trustees which was to report at the next meeting. While this body was at work, Procter, seeing that his offer was about to be declined, withdrew it.[13] In February the special committee gave to the full board a unanimous report opposing an off-campus site for the graduate college.

All the meetings, reports, and letters had been hedged about by secrecy and an air of high tension. Trustees had conferred excitedly in twos and threes. Little groups of rumormongers had whispered and agitated in Eastern cities; but there were no public blasts until, in January, distorted and sensational stories began to appear in New York newspapers. On February 3 the lid blew off completely. H. B. Brougham, editor of the *New York Times*, had learned about the controversy, had composed an editorial supporting Wilson, and, just before publishing it, asked him for confirmation; and he, pressed for time, again lowered the guard of executive responsibility for a moment and sent to the editor what he considered to be a "perfectly candid and confidential statement of the whole matter." Procter, Wilson wrote, had insisted on certain ideas that a majority of the faculty thought demoralizing. Following his wishes would result in fastening on graduate students "the same artificial and unsound social standards" that already dominated the life of undergraduates. There was no obscuring the fact, he asserted, that the issue was now joined between a college life into which all the bad elements of social ambition and unrest intrude themselves and a life ordered upon a simpler plan under the domination of real university influences and on a basis of genuine democracy.

The editor of the *Times* fell hungrily upon Wilson's words, disregarding their "confidential" nature. Appropriating a few and paraphrasing others, he prefaced the whole with nation-shaking rhetoric: "At Princeton, the scene of a battle fought a century and a third ago

---

[13] Replying to a letter from the Committee of Five asking him to define the conditions of his gift, Procter withdrew his offer and explained that he had acted under the belief that Dean West's pamphlet of 1902 "bore the authority of the university." He had perhaps been misled by West's statement therein to the effect that "the proposal" had been "adopted by the Board of Trustees, after full consideration." Actually, the trustees had not formally adopted West's proposal of 1902 but had merely approved, in 1896, a proposal made by the faculty "to establish a graduate school at Princeton." *See* the Minutes of the Princeton Trustees' Meeting, Feb. 10, 1910, Report of the Special Committee of Five.

for the establishment of the American democracy, is in progress today a struggle not less significant for the future of American youth and of Government in the United States . . . The Nation is roused against special privilege. Sheltered by a great political party, it has obtained control of our commerce and our industries. Now its exclusive and benumbing touch is upon those institutions which should stand pre-eminently for life, earnest endeavor, and broad enlightenment."

The question to be settled, the *Times* editorial asserted on February 3, was whether Princeton and other endowed universities were to "bend and degrade" their energies "into fostering mutually exclusive social cliques, stolid groups of wealth and fashion, devoted to non-essentials and the smatterings of culture . . . All the college Presidents have cried out against this stultifying influence, and none more earnestly than President Woodrow Wilson of Princeton."

The prestige that came to Wilson's name from this editorial and from subsequent discussions in the press was a valuable asset to a man who had always aspired to serve the nation; but the words of the *Times* fell into the camp of the enemy like sparks of dry powder. Pyne and his friends sent a refutation of the charges to the *Times* for publication and tried to smoke out Wilson's attitude toward the editorial, calling on him to reject it as "unquestionably false." Paul Van Dyke called on the president and denounced it as a slander on Grover Cleveland.

Wilson replied that Cleveland, lacking experience in education, had been misled by West, as he himself had been for a time. The president maintained that, though the color of the editorial was much exaggerated, it was founded in truth. Though the men supporting West were not consciously trying to foster "stolid groups of wealth," that would be the effect of their plans, Wilson said. Actually, as he wrote Brougham a few days later, he believed "every word" of the editorial to be true. Pyne, his "life-long friend," had been misled, he asserted.

Further publicity was given to the controversy in February when two key reports were published in the *Princeton Alumni Weekly* on February 16.[14] The arguments were now in the open, to be bandied about by anyone who might care to strike.

Two days before the committee reports became public, Wilson broke away for a short trip to Bermuda. It gave him "an unspeakable sense of

---

[14] The reports published were that of the special Committee of Five of the trustees and that of the majority of the faculty committee on the graduate school, which had been presented to the trustees in the preceding autumn.

relief," he wrote to Dodge before he sailed, to have been made free, by the withdrawal of Procter's offer, "to govern the University as our judgments and consciences dictate! . . . I know what is coming; but nothing can put me from the presidency now except some adverse *action* of the Board itself. The heavier the storm, the tighter I will sit. But he confessed to Ellen that he was ashamed to find himself "very deeply affected" nervously by the abuse heaped upon him.

His spirits rose at the arrival of messages of support from alumni, especially from the Western men. Soon his jangling nerves were quieted and he could write to his Ellen: "We have no compromises to look back on, the record of our conscience is clear in this whole trying business. We can be happy, therefore, no matter what may come of it all. It would be rather jolly, after all, to start out on life anew together, to make a new career, would it not? Experience deepens with us . . . and with experience love, and I thank God with all my heart!"

Returning from Bermuda, the president found Mrs. Wilson uneasy, and feeling as if the whole air about her was poisoned. He was reassured, however, by letters of encouragement from A. Lawrence Lowell and from President David Starr Jordan of Stanford University. To his old friend Hiram Woods he outlined his policy for meeting personal attacks: "The other side is not in a temper to receive any statement from me. Their attack is personal and not on its merits . . . To state the interior of this business would be to discredit a number of men of whom the alumni at present have a high opinion. I think it would do the University more harm than good to do such a thing, because it would add bitterness untold to the controversy. It is much better that I should take the brunt of it than to do that."

What Wilson called the "little Princeton party" was most vociferous in the Eastern cities. There alumni were proposing as a new trustee a man who would strengthen their cause. To hold his majority in Princeton's "House of Lords" the president felt that he must make an appeal to the country, and so he took the stump at five Princeton alumni meetings. His argument was rational, conciliatory, soothing.

In New York at the Princeton Club he confronted the Philistines face to face, coming down off the "stilts of study" as his father had taught him that a real man must do. To a suggestion that he might wish to dine in private before his address, he replied that he would not like to appear to avoid his antagonists. Because there had been occasions on which reporters had attributed to Wilson certain words that he disavowed, responsible stenographers were brought to this dinner to record every word spoken. The speaker was received by cold and formal applause for the "president of Princeton," instead of the usual "tiger" for Wilson.

Talking to these businessmen about the "business of a university," he reminded them that "just when all the academic world was waiting for somebody to take the initiative . . . Princeton had the audacity to step forward and take it." Undergraduate work had made great strides but the graduate studies had lagged, he said: while the graduate enrollment at Yale had more than quintupled, Princeton's had increased very slowly up until 1909. And why? "The graduate school of Princeton University was, by the bylaws of the Board of Trustees, kept during most of those years in the hands of a single officer . . . The energy and enthusiasm of the faculty was not behind the enterprise." Now that a committee of the faculty had been given control of the graduate school, he pointed out, the number of students had doubled within a year. In one of the oversimplifications to which Wilson's oratory was prone, he said that Princeton must decide whether to take Procter's money "at the risk of having no graduate students, or get the graduate students at the risk of having no money."

He went on with mounting fervor: "Divorce the universities of this country from their teaching enthusiasm, divorce them from their undergraduate energies, and you will have a thing which is not only un-American but utterly unserviceable to the country." And in a final grand hyperbole: "There is nothing private in America. Everything is public; everything belongs to the united energy of the nation . . . We must not be afraid of publicity."

To his sophisticated audience this sounded like the "political talk" of William Jennings Bryan and his cohorts. Not since Wilson made his first immature speech to New York alumni, more than twenty years before, had an audience received him so coldly. He talked more than an hour and made few converts; but this time, at least, they heard him through.

At St. Louis, Western graduates rallied to cheer him as he reviewed and defended his policy. Suggesting that the faculty be trusted to settle the difficulties, he asserted: "If they should vote against my judgment, I should yield my own judgment, not because they outvoted me but because I should feel that I was wrong if they did not agree with me."

But the faculty were not permitted to vote. As Wilson feared, at their April meeting the trustees postponed reference of graduate school issues to the faculty and favored a new plan for persuading Procter to renew his offer. When one vote on which he had counted swung the decision against him, as a trustee argued that to consult the faculty at so late a date would be merely to add to the confusion, Wilson plainly showed his resentment.

The prophet's cup of bitterness was full. Worried about his health, he went to his physician for his annual checkup and was reassured. "Wilson, there is just one thing," the doctor said to him. "Keep your enemies fighting you." He thrived on a fight, once the issue was clearly drawn and the battle fairly joined. But now he was caught in a tragic conflict of responsibilities. He must provide for his precious family; yet without the approval of his own conscience and the respect of his colleagues, his spirit would starve. "Members of Congress and ministers of the Gospel should not marry," he once remarked, "so that they would be free always to fight for what is right." [15]

Twenty-five years earlier he had said of one of the antagonists of his Uncle James Woodrow: "I hope that the Seminary *will* die, and die soon, if such pestiferous fellows as he are to be put into its hitherto honored chairs." And now Woodrow Wilson was tempted to let Princeton go with Dean West to perdition. Yet he loved the college that he had known in the seventies and in the nineties, still treasured the loyalty of his "little band of university men" in whom he saw the spirit of truth persisting and who would go through hell-fire with him, still looked with fatherly affection on the boys whom he was leading. If he were to follow his impulse to apply his talents to the service of state or nation, what *would* become of the university that was so dear to him?

Torn by these conflicting emotions, Woodrow Wilson went in mid-April to Pittsburgh to address a gathering of alumni. The speech that he made there proved to be the crossing of the Rubicon in a march to the nation's capital.

In speaking to alumni at Pittsburgh, the president of Princeton was returning to the battleground of the grandfather he had never seen, the Jeffersonian editor who set up the first mechanized printing press in the city and who never sidestepped a verbal fight. In what he said to his twentieth-century constituency there were echoes of the spirit of the Scotch-Irish "movers" of frontier days.

There was still wilderness left in America, to be sure, in the year 1910. Men with wandering feet could roam at will. But the best land had been

[15] Chambers MS, pp. 21, 53.

taken, and the rainbow of vast opportunity was ceasing to shine in men's imaginations. Turner had relegated the frontier to history, and Woodrow Wilson said in 1895: "The westward march has stopped, upon the final slopes of the Pacific, and now the plot thickens . . . The stage of America grows crowded like the stage of Europe. The life of the new world grows as complex as the life of the old."

As a young man Wilson had sensed the great challenge of the industrial age to human intelligence. "Civilization," he had written to Bobby Bridges in 1881, " has taken to itself steel wings which never tire and steam lungs which are never exhausted and voices electric and telephonic which disregard distance, and man must be smart indeed to escape her influence. "Writing a decade later as a historian surveying the state of the nation, he had observed in *Division and Reunion*: "Individual fortunes came almost suddenly into existence such as . . . the world had seldom seen since the ancient days of Eastern luxury or Roman plunder. Self-indulgence and fashion displayed and disported themselves as never before in the sober republic." But at the same time the Princeton professor sensed that "the nation felt itself big and healthy enough to tolerate even folly for the sake of freedom . . . the new troubles bred new thinkers, and the intellectual life of the nation was but the more deeply stirred."

In the new age of machinery, financial powers had grown up that were beyond the experience of the Woodrows and the Wilsons. The capitalists of the day led a precarious life, subject alike to the strain on moral fiber that comes with great riches and to the threat of bankruptcy in periods of panic. Some became sensitive, even supersensitive, to actions and words that might upset the very delicate balance in which the new machine economy hung. They were, they thought, America's indispensable men. They were making the nation's economy viable, just as Wilson was aspiring to give viability to education. They fed the goose that laid the golden eggs that fed the government. They maintained churches, schools, charities. The material blessings of the new Princeton that Wilson had created were made possible by their wisdom and beneficence. Who would finance and direct industrial growth so that it would be efficient and productive if they did not? Certainly not the government, they thought, with its councils responsive to inexpert and unstable opinions.

As the machines became more complicated and the financing of them more complex, the directors of industry were drawn into deeper and more absorbing study. They seemed willing to leave political matters to agents of slight intellect and weak conscience. Soon they were far beyond the boundary of Wilson's economic background; and he, in turn, had a perspective on American society and government that far outspanned that of financial managers.

To anyone except a man blinded by self-interest, the depredations of the financial leviathans were as obvious as the blessings that they conferred. Some trustees and managers had proved themselves faithless: some had brazenly bought the favor of public officials. Corporation lawyers of a type that had sickened Wilson at Atlanta were in evidence. Any alert layman could not help but be aware of lobbies that were trying to divert the minds of legislators from the common welfare to biased interest; any Presbyterian elder who took responsibility for his fellow man must lament the amassing of squalor that came with the sequestering of wealth. What would be the end of it all? Would the sons of the free men who had come over in the nineteeth century, along with the Latins and Slavs of later migrations, be caught now in a twentieth-century treadmill?

The "children of Israel"—the God-fearing, hard-working marrow of America—were crying out for a prophet, a responsible leader, someone who could tell them what it all meant, who could either justify or curb the vast power that sheer money had gained. Their hope for a revival of the old, rosy spirit of the frontier lay in the appearance of a political messiah—a prophet who would utter wisdom and give justice.

Curiously enough, their leader arrived quite by accident.

When he went to Pittsburgh in April of 1910 to speak to some of his Princeton family, Woodrow Wilson was moody. His nerves were on edge and he was wearied by lavish entertaining—a sightseeing tour of the city and dinner at a fashionable club. The Princeton trustees had just refused to refer the question of the graduate college to the faculty of the university. A bitterness was writhing in the president, such an acridity as he had felt toward Atlanta when he left that city after failing in the practice of law. With his personal resentment was mingled another sentiment—a deep sympathy for able, honest men to whom fate had been unkind. He had no sympathy for idlers, whether rich or poor. He was interested in the preserving of opportunity—such opportunity as the old frontier had presented—for a man to make good on his own.

As a teacher, Wilson had been an employee of what the Western democracy was calling "the money power." He had borne himself in public as a patrician, a charming and witty littérateur, a respectable

son of an honored clergyman. To workmen on the Princeton campus
he had seemed an archaristocrat striding about in formal dress, wearing
a silk hat. They did not know that at home he danced jigs wearing the
hat cocked on the side of his head. They did not know that when he
watched them work on a new dormitory he wished that he could handle ideas as precisely as they laid stones. Nor were they aware that he
had often ridden through a slum area of the village, his head so bowed
in meditation over the manifestations of poverty that he had to be reminded that he was breaking an ordinance by riding on the sidewalk.
The accumulation of money had never obsessed him. He had angered
a colleague by arguing that men had no natural right to store up the
world's goods without limit and without regard to the rights of other
men. He expected only to be made comfortable in return for services
gladly given. His old father had taught him what was written in the
family Bible: "No station or wealth can buy heaven."

In the Johns Hopkins Graduate School, under the teaching of
Richard T. Ely, Wilson had begun to question conventional theories of
economics and during the following decade he had watched the clouds
of social pressures massing on the political horizon. He could not escape
from Bagehot's maxim: "The public good is not to be achieved by
following the rules of private good."[16] Either Wilson's political conviction or his economic beliefs had to yield; and since he thought himself "born a politician," his preference for laissez-faire economics inevitably had to give ground. The yielding, however, was slow and
uncertain, and took the form of "exceptions."

Wilson had come to regard the partisan drives of economic groups
as forces not to be ignored, and as challenges to the flexibility of the
national polity. He had insisted that it was within the province of the

[16] Walter Bagehot, *Physics and Politics,* 1948 edition, Introduction by Jacques Barzun, p. xiv.
Wilson's sense of moral responsibility prevented him from asserting cynically, as had Bagehot,
that men in the mass were ruled by "the weakness of their imaginations," that governments
needed symbols "to impose on their quiescent imaginations what would otherwise not be there."
Ibid., Introduction, p. xvi. Professor Wilson preferred to stress the glory of the shepherd rather
than the abjectness of the herd. In John B. Clark's *Philosophy of Wealth* he found aid in reconciling Christian principles with economic realities. "The book . . ." he wrote to Clark, "has
fertilized my own thought . . . besides refreshing me with its original views and methods it has
cheered me not a little by its spirit,—its moderation and its Christianity." W.W. to Clark,
Aug. 26, 1887, Princeton University Library.

In *Congressional Government* (p. 296) he had quoted from William Graham Sumner's
Andrew Jackson: "The modern industrial organization . . . is largely regulated by legislation.
Capital is the breath of life to this organization, and every day, as the organization becomes
more complex and delicate, the folly of assailing capital or credit becomes greater. At the same
time it is evident that the task of the legislator to embrace in his view the whole system, to
adjust his rules so that the play of civil institutions shall not alter the play of economic forces,
requires more training and more acumen."

social scientist "to study wealth from the social, as well as the political point of view." Yet he feared that socialism would hasten the centralized and corruptible kind of government that good men were seeking to escape.

In the spring of 1908, frustrated by the opposition of financial supporters of Princeton, he allowed himself to make intemperate generalizations. Addressing the National Democratic Club at New York, he inveighed against wealth made through speculation.

"Predatory wealth," he said, was to be found "in stock markets, not in the administrative offices of great corporations where real business is conducted, real commodities made or exchanged." During the presidential campaign in the autumn he declared to the American Bankers' Association that legitimate undertakings had been "pushed to illegitimate lengths," that men feared their new, impersonal ruler and were "jealous of its domination." And again, in January of 1910, he told bankers assembled in the Waldorf-Astoria Hotel that they had allowed their minds to narrow and took no interest in the small businessman. "You don't know the country or what is going on in it and the country doesn't trust you," he charged. "You are not interested in the development of the country, but in what has been developed." At the head table J. P. Morgan puffed at his cigar and looked glum. Could this, he must have wondered, be the same man whom he had heard speak so conservatively at the inauguration at Princeton in 1902? When the banker told Wilson that the aspersions hurt him personally, the speaker replied that he was talking of principles, not of individuals, and expressed surprise that Mr. Morgan should think of himself as the nation's banking system.

It had been thirteen years now since Wilson had said to the Virginia Bar Association: "This is not a day of revolution, but it is a day of change, and of such change as may breed revolution, should we fail to guide and moderate it." In those years the tocsin had grown louder —it was always ringing distantly in the ears of the president of Princeton. Unfamiliarity with the workings of finance combined with disgust at its abuses to breed mistrust in the mind of the prophet. His Scottish imagination saw bogies in the mist, witches on Wall Street. He had his revelation.

When he thought that he saw financiers fail to encourage healthy business activity, Wilson could assuage his conscience with the belief that such things were of no direct concern to a professor of political science. He had even been able to bear political abuses with only intellectual distress and protest. But when he conceived that the power of money was dominating and corrupting churches, courts, and even universities, that was too much for a good Presbyterian and a good American to abide. The money-changers were invading the temple, and the prophet's temper came to the boiling point in April, 1910, at Pittsburgh.

Surfeited with entertainment and sightseeing, and suffering from one of his black moods of dejection and world-weariness, Wilson was taken by his hosts to the big reunion tent that had been erected in the dining room of the Hotel Schenley and decorated with fluttering orange-and-black banners. An orchestra played, a quartet sang "Going Back to Nassau Hall," favorite alumni were called on for their stock stories; and as a grand climax, the waiters trotted in bearing ices decorated by a papier-mâché tiger, recumbent under a paper coconut tree, its eyes illuminated. The prophet took it all in, listened while an ardent purveyor of homely epigrams, cigar atilt and jaws snapping, said: "I am not going to refer to *that little matter*. But I am satisfied that we will get that five hundred thousand back—some way." And then the toastmaster introduced the guest of honor—"the true type of American statesman" who "has loved truth for truth's sake, and for truth's sake alone."

The prophet could no longer contain himself. Over the gaudy scene he vented his feelings in clouds of fire, relaxing the strict discipline under which he usually ruled his emotions. He had taught many of those to whom he spoke, and so felt that he was talking within a family that would chant a filial "Amen!"

Andrew Jackson, when his Scotch-Irish dander was up, had so choked on his rage that he could not articulate. When he had wanted to speak up for his immigrants and backwoodsmen—whom Wilson once described as a "roughened race . . . delicate in nothing but the touch of the trigger"—he could only stand in the Senate and froth and splutter. But now they had an eloquent champion, those descendants of the old frontier, of the James Wilsons and the Thomas Woodrows. The ire of this leader burned like dry ice. He would not just splutter. He might be weary, he might be despondent, he might be furious; but so well had his weapon been forged and tempered that he could wield it eloquently. When his prophetic fire was unloosed, it burned quickly through the artifices by which he had decorated his talk in the academic world—courtesy, tact, humor, literary polish—all these fine furbelows were consumed in the oxygen of frontier air.

Gusts often had blown through great spaces in this prophet's soaring imagination. Sometimes they were steady tradewinds, driving away mist and cloud and leaving the purest of airs. But not now. His own nature, as he had said of Henry Clay's, "was of the West, blown through with quick winds of ardor and aggression, a bit reckless and defiant; but his art was of the East, ready with soft and placating phrases, reminiscent of old and reverenced ideals, thoughtful of compromise and accommodation." The manners of the Old South could make a polished man of letters; they were not enough to make a great political leader of all the United States. The "ardor and aggression" must be there.

Though Wilson was not consciously trying to make political capital out of his position at Princeton, any doubts about the sureness of the political appeal of the man's ideas could hardly have survived his speech at Pittsburgh. Blurting out convictions that had been pent within him for months because of the confidential nature of the proceedings at the university, he addressed himself to the nation over the heads of the alumni and trustees. "The people are tired of pretense," he declared, "and I ask you, as Princeton men, to heed what is going on." In the private universities, he asserted, "we look for the support of the wealthy and neglect our opportunities to serve the people." State universities, however, were honestly striving to serve "the people," were "sensitive to the movements of general opinion, to the opinion of the unknown men who can vote." From "the great mass of the unknown," he reminded his hearers, came the strength of America. "Most of the masters of endeavor in this country have not come through the channels of universities, but from the great rough-and-ready workers of the world." With a vast metaphor he reached out to embrace the virile manhood of the nation:

The great voice of America . . . comes in a murmur from the hills and woods and the farms and factories and the mills, rolling on and gaining volume until it comes to us from the homes of common men. Do these murmurs echo in the corridors of the universities? I have not heard them.

Lincoln's value to his country would have been impaired by education in a private university, Wilson said.

Finally he worked himself up to a spasm of zeal. "I have dedicated every power that there is in me," he said, "to bring the colleges that I have anything to do with to an absolutely democratic regeneration in spirit." He vowed to follow this ambition until the colleges were imbued with "the same thought, the same sympathy that pulses through the whole great body politic . . . Will America tolerate the idea of having graduate students set apart? America will tolerate nothing except unpatronized endeavor. Seclude a man, separate him from the rough-and-tumble of college life, from all the contacts of every sort and condition of men, and you have done a thing which America will brand with contemptuous disapproval."

And then he pressed his attack into the fields of religion and government. "I trust that I may be thought among the last to blame the churches, yet I feel it my duty to say that they—at least the Protestant churches—are serving the classes and not the masses of the people. They have more regard for pew rents than for men's souls. They are depressing the level of Christian endeavor . . . The American people will tolerate nothing that savours of exclusiveness. Their political parties are going to pieces." He had at last let himself go and, as he had feared, he did not know where to stop. "What we cry out against," he charged, "is that a handful of conspicuous men have thrust cruel hands among the heartstrings of the masses of men upon whose blood and energy they are subsisting." His long-suffering patience was gone. Fearing that the day of opportunity for peaceful change was slipping away, he ended his speech by predicting that "if she loses her self-possession, America will stagger like France through fields of blood before she again finds peace and prosperity under the leadership of men who know her needs."

"Disaster Forecast by Wilson—Denounces Churches—Talks about Blood!" So screamed a headline the next morning, and the explosion at Pittsburgh reverberated through the press of the nation. The opposition at Princeton was furious and had "that Pittsburgh speech" printed for all who would read it. Impartial editors thought that Wilson had been rash and intemperate, and the speaker himself, when he read snatches of the address in cold print, felt that he had blundered. He had failed to heed the counsel of Bagehot, who had noted that Anglo-Saxons fear nothing so much as bloody revolution and have therefore an inexhaustible capacity for tolerating mediocrity in the name of moderation. After the event Wilson realized that, as a responsible administrator whose duty it was to make men of diverse opinions work constructively and in harmony, he should not have aired his personal feelings so freely. In his "deep excitement" over an adverse vote of the Princeton trustees just two day before, he explained, he "did not stop to think how it would sound in the newspapers." He should have done so, he said. In a manuscript of his Pittsburgh talk that he corrected for publication, the incendiary final sentence was omitted. To the New York *Evening Post* he complained that reports of his speech had, by piecemeal quotation, conveyed an entirely false impression. And a few days later he refused to write an article on college fraternities, "in order not to complicate an already complicated situation."

In the next important address before Princeton graduates, Wilson's instinct for responsible leadership reasserted itself. In preparing a talk for Chicago alumni, he again assumed the yokes of charity and humility; and the message that he gave was less menacing, more challenging to constructive action, more closely confined to Princeton affairs.

It was too late, however, to retract what had been said at Pittsburgh or to rub out the mark that the news reports had made on the public consciousness. In unmasking deep personal feelings the speaker had touched sensitive chords in millions of his fellows who identified themselves with the "masses of men upon whose blood and energy" a "handful of conspicuous men" were "subsisting." Woodrow Wilson had played—by ear—the music that lures votes. The destiny that he had wooed was claiming the boy who had worshiped Gladstone's picture and prepared himself to lead a people.

In the black mood into which he had fallen at Pittsburgh, Wilson had despaired of spiritual regeneration either in education or in politics. He had complained to his host that his life had been a failure, that in taking the moral position to which his conscience drove him he was throwing away all opportunity of realizing his educational ideals. Moreover, he was not blind to economic consequences: outside of his salary, he said, he had little means for the support of his large family. "But what can I do?" he asked Woods. "I must follow what I think is right." He had long since committed his life into the hands of the God of truth and service. Like his uncle under the attack of theologians, like the Scottish prophets who came before him, he could only speak out. Had he kept silent his career might have ended, and with it the spiritual force that he personified.

As an academic executive, Wilson had failed. But in failure he had learned lessons invaluable to an administrator. He had held the confidence of precious friends and of most of the Princeton faculty. He had retained his youthful vision of political leadership and his faith in the American people and in the great principles that he loved to proclaim. He had reason to believe that the people of New Jersey wanted his leadership. But anyone who might try to purchase Woodrow Wilson's assets for advantage to person or party would do so at his own risk. Let the buyer beware!

CHAPTER IX

From Campus to Political Arena

Negotiations at princeton dragged on into the month of May. Trustees arranged a compromise that was acceptable to the moderate men of both factions; but neither of the principals would yield. The proposal was nothing new, Wilson thought, and to accept it was to forgo his fundamental judgment in the whole matter of education. When one of the friendly trustees tempted the president to resign in June, arguing that in this way he could at once confound his enemies and enhance his political position before the country, Wilson was unmoved. He would not be vindictive, and he would not make capital for himself at Princeton's expense. He would not resign in petulance, nor would he recant.

Andrew West, meanwhile, had been busily seeking financial support for his concept of a graduate college. A millionaire alumnus named Isaac C. Wyman had signed a will that left his fortune in the hands of two executors, one of whom was West. Wilson, reluctant fund-raiser that he was, had written a polite letter to the prospective donor and had tried unsuccessfully to see him in Boston and to invite him to the inauguration in 1902. West took pains to visit Wyman in Salem, to invite him to ride at the head of an alumni parade, and to entertain his agent.[1]

Suddenly death took old Mr. Wyman, and in taking him solved the problem of the graduate college.

On May 22, near midnight, the president of Princeton was awakened by a phone call. It was a telegram from West, reporting the filing of the Wyman will and a bequest amounting to "at least two million and maybe more." Mrs. Wilson heard enough to catch the import of the message and leaned back in her chair, close to tears. As her husband put down the receiver, he was grim. He could "lick a half-million," but this was too much. The bequest was to finance a graduate college at Princeton that was to be controlled by the board of trustees.

Wilson could take some satisfaction in the thought that the new gift was large enough so that a separate faculty of outstanding ability

[1] McAdoo, *The Priceless Gift*, pp. 227–8. The personal nature of West's relationship with Wyman's agent, John M. Raymond, is revealed in a letter, Raymond to West, June 4, 1909. Reporting that Wyman was giving "great consideration" to making a gift to Princeton, Raymond wrote: "I speak thus frankly to you alone." Graduate School pa., Princeton University Library.

could be attracted to the graduate college. He was now ready, he said, to entertain a renewal of Procter's offer for a building on the site chosen by the donor, provided there was no restriction on the policies and management of graduate work. As he saw it, he must either yield in the matter of the site and remain in control of the administration and stand by his friends on the faculty and the board, or else retire. To quit immediately would be to risk the demoralization of Princeton, he felt. What the future would bring was still an open question. West's prestige was now tremendous. President Butler of Columbia sent him "hearty congratulations"; and Moses Taylor Pyne, to whom West wrote gleefully of his triumph in a letter signed "Little Willie," assured the dean that he had "made good in every sense of the word." Recognizing West's great power under Wyman's will, Wilson realized that the dean must be handled most wisely and diplomatically, and he was not at all sure that he had a strong enough stomach for it.

Early in June, encouraged by the acceptance of the Wyman bequest, Procter renewed his offer of a half-million dollars and it was accepted by the board. At Commencement it was apparent that, though the alumni elected a trustee favorable to Wilson, a majority of the board had lost confidence in their president's usefulness to Princeton. Some thought that in his public speeches he had maligned the university and ruthlessly stepped upon it in a climb to high political office.

Commencement Week, 1910, was one of Woodrow Wilson's finest hours. He played out the game, making no public show of pique or petulance when the alumni celebrated the Wyman gift and toasted its procurer. Though his wife suffered a social snub, Wilson made a felicitous speech of presentation when Pyne was given a silver cup in recognition of twenty-five years of service to Princeton. West gave a dinner to celebrate the bequest, inviting none of Wilson's supporters; and the president, attending, tried to ignore the pall of conspiracy that he felt in the very air.

Addressing the Class of 1910, at the close of his Baccalaureate Sermon the president warmed their hearts at the altar of loyal sentiment.

The atmosphere was one of "farewell" rather than of "au revoir." His boys were loath to let him leave, and revised their old faculty song to let "Tommie" knew how they felt about his going into politics:

> Here's to Wilson, king of men,
> He rules this place with 1910.
> We have no fear he'll leave this town
> To try for anybody's crown!

And then they told off West and his millions:

> Here's to Andy eight-million West,
> Sixty-three inches around the vest,
> To get him Boston tried her best,
> He winked his eye—you know the rest.

After the valedictory they cheered their president again and again and again, until tears streamed down his face. The alumni, too, warmly applauded his speech at their luncheon; and his supporters on the board told him that he was free to go or stay, as he pleased, though he was reminded that he was "the soul of the fight." Thinking his friends the finest in the world, he resolved not to disappoint them in character even if he should disappoint them in ability. He preferred to fall fighting, rather than seem to run away from the university. One Saturday afternoon, when politicians were coming to Prospect to press him to become a candidate for the governorship, he packed his bag for a trip to New York and said: "Ellen, I don't want to be away over the weekend. But I don't want to meet those men."[1a]

However, certain politicians were becoming persistent in efforts to "reach" the patrician-Democrat at Princeton and use him to restore the fortunes of a party that had been out of power so long that its leaders found it difficult to raise campaign funds. A tide of public protest was rising in New Jersey; and the bosses of the old regime, lacking a will to meet demands for reform, saw in Wilson a man who might appease insurgents by his prestige and his words.

Muckraking journalists had given New Jersey a reputation as a sanctuary for corporations. Citizens had begun to understand how public service companies, by financing a few bosses in each party, were buying influence over the legislature, and how the bosses in turn were controlling elections by nominating the candidates and buying votes in return for jobs and other benefits. With perfect understanding of each other's method's, politicians of both parties had been playing exciting games with the public trust. Already many voices had been raised in protest. Everett Colby had risen in a one-man revolt and had whipped the candidate of the Republican machine to win a seat in the state Senate, where he rallied a group of insurgents who were devoted to what they called the "New Idea." In Jersey City, Mayor Mark M. Fagan had employed a progressive adviser named George L. Record to help him reform the municipal government. A persuasive speaker, Record

---

[1a] James Woodrow, who was present, to the writer.

had swung from the Democratic to the Republican party in protest against Byran's silver policy, had accepted Henry George's condemnation of monopolies based on special privileges, read Emerson, covered his walls with pictures of Lincoln, and let it be known that he "didn't give a damn about being personally popular." It was "these ideas" that were important, he insisted. Record and other progressives had achieved the enactment of a state civil service reform law and tentative measures for direct primaries and control of corporations.

To compete with the leadership that had been given to Republicans by progressives and liberal thinkers, Democratic bosses had been angling for Wilson for several years. Impressed by his inaugural address at Princeton, "Planked-Shad" Thompson had commended him to James Smith, Jr., boss of Essex County. A wealthy banker and publisher, Smith had served in the United States Senate and had made himself obnoxious to Wilson by opposing Cleveland's efforts at tariff reform for reasons that seemed to reflect an undue concern for sugar interests. He was known as "Sugar Jim." Portly and well dressed, a man of magnetism, he was an utter realist, so sardonic that he could say to a fly-fisherman, with the irony of mock innocence: "You not only *kill* your fish. You deceive them as well." [2] Smith's "fish" voted as he told them to vote, with not too close scrutiny of the reasons. And when he delivered his catch, he held that he was delivering marketable goods.

This cynic, observing that his party had been out of power so long that corporations no longer "came across" with campaign funds,[3] saw at once that Wilson could be useful in ending the famine. But he doubted that the time was ripe. After all, the educator was not a native son and his religion was not congenial to the rank and file of the party. Moreover, no one knew Wilson's exact feelings toward corporations, unions, and the liquor interests. Nevertheless, Smith insisted that, if the Democrats were ever to elect another governor of the state, it would have to be a man like the president of Princeton; and he had passed the word along to George Brinton McClellan Harvey, president of the reorganized firm of Harper's and publisher of Wilson's successful *History of the American People.*

Harvey had been conspicuous at the inauguration at Princeton—"fascinatingly ugly," one observer had thought him, a man arrogant, with defiant inferiority, carrying upon a scrawny neck a death's-head whose eye sockets were dark as inkwells and whose thin tight lips smiled

[2] John Pursel, who heard Smith say this, to the writer.
[3] John Moody, *The Long Road Home,* pp. 106-7.

superciliously.[4] Reading everything that Wilson had written, Harvey became convinced that this man was of sufficent stature to take the leadership of the Democratic party away from William Jennings Byran and to rehabilitate it on sound principles. In the winter of 1905–6, when the popular president of Princeton was stepping out of academic bounds often to exhort the public to serve the nation, Harvey gave a dinner in honor of his hero at the Lotos Club in New York and spoke with a sense "almost of rapture" of the possibility of voting for Woodrow Wilson for the Presidency of the United States; and the next month the publisher set forth in *Harper's Weekly* thirteen qualifications of his candidate. Though Wilson was not convinced, and spoke modestly of "other wires taller than mine which will attract the lightning," the response in the press and through the mails showed isolated ripples of interest that might one day merge in a booming wave. From that time Wilson's name was bandied about freely by men who aspired to manage Democratic policy.

In 1906, Wilson was appointed to his first public office—membership on the New Jersey Commission on Uniform State Laws; and in the autumn it was rumored that he might be the Democratic candidate when the New Jersey legislature chose a United States senator in 1907. It was not expected that a Democrat could win a Senate seat; but Harvey calculated that the publicity of the campaign would redound to the credit of his man on the national scene.

Wilson was at first cold to the idea, telling reporters that his first duty was to Princeton. Yet when it became sure that the Republicans would win the election, Wilson fell in with Harvey's suggestion. The honor, even though an empty one, beguiled the educator.

Meanwhile, young Democrats in New Jersey were rebelling against Smith and the other bosses whom Harvey had enlisted in support of his candidate for the Senate. The reformers proposed the name of Edwin A. Stevens, of the Princeton class of 1879. Wilson told this

---

[4] *See* George Watt, *Is the Liar In?*, pp. 285–91. A Vermonter who had made good as a political reporter in New Jersey, Harvey had become banking commissioner in that state and an honorary "colonel" on the staff of the governor. As editor of the New Jersey edition of the New York *World*, he had aided Smith to reach the Senate in 1892.

In undertaking to promote Wilson for the Presidency of the United States and thus enhance his value as an author to the house of Harper's, Harvey was perhaps encouraged by a letter from "An Old-fashioned Democrat," printed in the Indianapolis *News* on May 5, 1902, endorsing Wilson for the Presidency. Moreover, in June of 1902, Dwight L. Moody introduced Wilson at a student conference at Northfield as a man who might someday be president of the United States. Allan Lightner, who heard Moody, to the writer, Sept. 30, 1955. Even as early as 1901 and 1902, Princeton students saw in Professor Wilson a future candidate for the Presidency of the nation.

classmate that he would not run in opposition, but refused to state this publicly for fear of intervening in what seemed to be mere "factional differences." [5] The president of Princeton was not yet sure of himself in the political arena, not quite ready to joust with professional campaigners.

Wilson was thrilled to feel that he would not be forever a mere "outside force" in government. He had never entirely given up his "primary ambition" to be a statesman; and in 1902, the year in which he assumed the Princeton presidency, he confided to his friend Turner that he had been "born a politician" and asked a classmate what his duty to Princeton would be if he were called to lead a political constituency.[6] But now that his opportunity was at hand, his first glow of delight was followed by reaction in his spirits. Realizing his ignorance of the ways of practical politics, he became worried and suspicious. He had welcomed the intercession of Robert Bridges in behalf of his appointment to the Princeton faculty, for he had felt that his classmate acted out of pure friendship. But Harvey might have other motives in promoting his name. Whether this publisher believed in Wilson's power to serve the nation or was gambling on large future returns, the "literary politician" could not be sure. Though inexperienced, he was naturally canny enough to have misgivings. He feared that the trial balloon might burst in his face and make him ridiculous. "This linking of my name with political office," he told Stockton Axson, "is doing no good to either Princeton or me." When Harvey began to sound out the conservative leaders of the Democratic party,[7] Wilson became so embarrassed that he asked his sponsor to desist.

[5] Finally Stevens peeled the eyes of the novice, made him see that the bosses were using the name of the president of Princeton to delude earnest reformers. Wilson, believing in the honesty of Stevens and still conscious of his own inexperience in such matters, wrote to Harvey, thanked him politely for his support, said that it was not possible in good faith to oppose Stevens, and asked advice on the "most courteous and convenient way" to withdraw. And Harvey told his protégé how to extricate himself from the muddle without giving offense to anyone and without strengthening the cause of the reformers. Wilson fell in with the prescribed formula and failed to support Stevens.

[6] Stephen Wise, *Challenging Years*, p. 161. There had never been a time, Wilson said to Rabbi Stephen Wise years later, when he was not preparing himself for the White House. Eleanor Wilson McAdoo feels that this statement was made in jest, and states that her father's intimate letters to her mother indicate that when he took the presidency of Princeton it was with the expectation of devoting the rest of his life to that charge. E. W. McAdoo to the writer, March 10, 1952. It is clear that in 1899 Wilson's interest in an active political life was keen. In that year he kept a book of "Notes on Statesmanship" and spoke to Grover Cleveland of his desire to find practical ways in which men of conscience could influence the machinery of political parties. And it was at about this time that he complained to Stockton Axson of popular superstitions about the incompetence of academic men as public officials.

[7] Harvey's trial balloons were kept aloft by support from conservative idealists, particularly those from the South. Wilson "would not stir up discontent; he has no fortune; he does not

Eloquent as Professor Wilson had been in virtuous generalities, his public utterances on political issues of the day, like those on economic problems, had become cautious; and when he had lectured to classes on current politics, he had the doors closed and had asked that he be not quoted outside the campus. He had been content for the most part to teach the energizing principles of jurisprudence and the origin of law in public opinion. He thought that education could be only "minor statesmanship," and yet continued to preach to his university constituency about their patriotic responsibilities. He accepted the political party as an American institution, but took a lofty view and distrusted both Democrats and Republicans.

When a friend asked him why he didn't "get out and tell the world," he replied: "Simply because I cannot afford to. Sometimes I feel strongly tempted to do so, and perhaps the time will come when I can take a hand in political business." [8] On a Bermuda beach, in 1908, he discussed his future with Mary Allen Peck. "My friends tell me," he said, "that if I will enter the contest and can be nominated and elected Governor of New Jersey, I stand a very good chance of being the next President of the United States. Shall I, or shall I not, accept the opportunity they offer? . . . The life of the next Democratic President will be hell and it would probably kill me." When the lady encouraged him, he stood with hat off and said: "Very well, so be it!"

To beat Bryan, he confided, a man must personify a cause and not be content to offer himself as a candidate ready to listen to anything expedient.[9] But in giving himself unreservedly to a principle, a man opened himself to attack as an ambitious dictator. There was the rub. Let some other fellow run the risk, Wilson was thinking. He would be glad to help, but not to take the chief onus. Perhaps, though, if the

---

speak the language of Utopia or riot," wrote Walter Hines Page in 1907. ". . . he is a Democrat of the best traditions. What if a political miracle should happen and the long-lost old party should find itself by nominating such a man?" Three reactionary Democrats invited Wilson to dine with them at Delmonico's in New York; and afterward, when one of them tried to draw out his thoughts on politics, he responded with a draft of a "Credo" in which he denounced labor unions as threats to individual liberty and expressed faith in the Constitution and the provisions of civil and criminal law as adequate safeguards of morality in the operation of those corporations that had become necessary to the efficient conduct of business. It seemed to Harvey and his friends that Wilson was an innocuous moralist who might appeal to voters sated with Bryan and alarmed by Roosevelt.

[8] Patterson, *op. cit.,* p. 38.

[9] In the revealing talk that he delivered four times during the eighteen-nineties—"Leaders of Men"—Wilson had asserted that "the dynamics of leadership lie in persuasion." Great leaders must have insight of the heart rather than of the intellect. "By methods which would infallibly alienate individuals they master multitudes, and *that* is their indisputable title to be named 'leaders of men.' "

Princeton trustees did not awaken to their responsibilities toward the university's intellectual life, he might retire from the presidency in two years and become free to be a martyr to the rehabilitation of the Democratic party. It occurred to him that he might lead in a movement of reform and that, after the fire of the opponents had been irrevocably centered upon his own head, he could withdraw in favor of another man. He was fancying himself as a campaigner born and bred, and saw in the rough and manly cudgeling of political warfare a welcome relief to bouts fought with innuendo-tipped swords on a confining university floor. First, however, he must find a worthy cause that could overwhelm his fear of showing personal egotism. His old father had jotted on the margin of his Bible, beside a verse in *John*: "No preacher has any light of his own to show—but he is a witness only to the *heavenly light* —a light-bearer." Woodrow Wilson had been carrying a torch too bright for the eyes of Princeton alumni; but he was groping, at the end of 1908, for a torch that a political following would heed and steer by. He had not forgotten what he had written in one of his essays: "Politics is a war of causes, a joust of principles."

During the next two years Wilson remained the figure that he had described in *Mere Literature*—"a man with an imagination which, though it stands aloof, is yet quick to conceive the very things in the thick of which the politician struggles." Refusing to let his name be considered at the Democratic convention in the summer of 1908, he nevertheless continued to proclaim a political gospel.[10]

Observation of President Theodore Roosevelt's strong grasp on national affairs was confirming Wilson's faith in the opportunity of the chief executive as a leader in reform; and Roosevelt's sympathy for progressive causes helped to convince him that statesmen must heed the new voices of the times. Nevertheless, when Roosevelt succeeded

---

[10] In a series of lectures at Columbia University, published in 1908 under the title *Constitutional Government in the United States,* Wilson coldly analyzed American politics and showed a deeper understanding of the machinery of Congress than he had possessed when he wrote *Congressional Government.* He now referred to the iniquities of "special interests," lobbies and newspapers, declared that "our very constitutional principle has fallen into dangerous disrepair" because of the advantage in prolonged litigation that was given to certain men by the very fact of their wealth; but he conceived of the Senate as relatively free from corrupting influences and in truth "the choice of the people." His lectures at Columbia set forth two concepts that were to guide him when he came to take a responsible part in government: first, a faith in state governments as potentially "real organs of popular opinion"; second, emphasis on presidential, rather than Cabinet, leadership in the federal government. His lectures, moreover, held out the American system as a faith for other peoples to embrace. The relation of the states with the federal union, he thought, might yet give the entire world a model of federation and constitutional liberty.

As president of Princeton Wilson wrote comparatively little and sometimes spoke disparagingly of his earlier output, calling it a symptom of "literary afflatus."

McKinley, the Princeton professor had remarked privately: "What will happen to the country—with that mountebank as president?" Wilson had not been greatly impressed when Roosevelt praised a speech of his and invited him to spend a night at the White House. In 1905 he considered the President of the nation "not quite a statesman," incapable of analyzing fundamental social problems or leading Congress in solving them; and at a meeting of the Princeton faculty he raked TR's record fore and aft.

When Roosevelt came to Princeton for a football game he was entertained by the Wilsons in the charming tradition of the South. But his manners were those of the jungle. His voice boomed above all other sounds. At dinner he had eyes only for colorful Margaret Axson, slam-banged the table, and shouted teasing remarks about "the gray-haired old grandfather" on her left and "the rich bachelor" on her right until she was moved to wish that, if that was the way presidents behaved, she might never meet another. Afterward she asked her brother-in-law: "Woodrow, who on earth would ever want to be president?" And he replied, half in jest: "I should; I know a whale of a lot about the Constitution of this country and I'd rather like to watch the wheels go round."

Though Wilson's mind accepted the strengthening of the Presidency as a historical fact, his conscience was troubled by the threat posed to constitutional processes. He protested against efforts being made in Congress to carry the implications of federal powers "beyond the utmost boundaries of reasonable and honest inference." Moreover, he inveighed against the "passion for regulative legislation" that the Roosevelt administration had shown. He predicted that, even should regulation by government come, it would "sooner or later be completely discredited by experience." He distrusted rule by the discretion of individual officeholders as a substitute for a rule of law. The shifting of responsibility from corporations to government bureaus, from courts to commissions, he looked on with suspicion. Appealing to "the old Jeffersonian principle: as little government as possible," he recalled that the United States was built on a belief that free men had a much more trustworthy capacity for taking care of themselves than any government had ever shown or was ever likely to show in taking care of them. "What we need," he said in the spring of 1907, "is not a square deal, but no deal at all—an old-fashioned equality and harmony of conditions—a purged business and a purged law." He called not for more law but rather for honest enforcement of existing laws.

Being suspicious of the ultimate effects of measures that were being proposed by hotheaded and shortsighted reformers, it was natural for the prophet to fall back on Scripture and Thomas Jefferson, and preach a "new morality." He talked on such themes as "True Patriotism," "Ideals of Public Life," and "Law or Personal Power." Corporations could not be attacked effectively, but their directors could. By speaking for the common good and recommending a morality that would serve it, Wilson identified himself more and more with the interests of government. Government, he explained, had had to step in to restrain those who were abusive of the very privileges that the government itself had guaranteed.

As Wilson perceived in the opposition at Princeton the same repressive spirit that he saw in the nation at large, his impatience grew. What was needed, he thought, was an intellect to champion social justice, a leader to show the people where their own best interests lay. He said in February of 1909: "We have heat enough; what we want is light. Anybody can stir up emotions, but who is master of men enough to take the saddle and guide those awakened emotions?" Wilson was still exuding sweetness and light, in 1909, but a fire was smoldering.

Thus, in the years 1908 and 1909, the prophet's utterances on social and economic problems gained in boldness, in frankness, in power of expression.[11] Gradually he had been setting up ideals of political administration that only Woodrow Wilson himself could be trusted to execute. His impulses had not crystallized in consistent specifications of policy, but he stood by the generalizations set forth in 1888 in *The State*, believing still that the sovereign people should allow their government to assume only "necessary" powers. In this and in his philosophy of slow, reasoned change, in his preaching of a "new morality," in his

[11] Wilson's mind had long dwelt on the difficulties of capital-labor relations. A year after his father urged him to consider whether it was necessary "to write 'versus'" between the two terms and suggested adjustments through "boards of arbitration authorized by law," Wilson informed John B. Clark that he sympathized with labor leaders who found "all the necessary stimulations of hope . . . in the slow processes of conservative endeavor." J. R. Wilson to W.W., Feb. 27, 1886, Wilson pa., Ac. 12,764, box 17; W.W. to John B. Clark, Aug. 26, 1887, Princeton University Library.

In 1909, Wilson carried his championing of individual freedom and efficiency into discussion of labor problems. He avowed himself "a fierce partisan of the open shop and of everything that makes for individual liberty," and warned his graduating class at Princeton that the labor of America was "rapidly becoming unprofitable under its present regulation by those who have determined to reduce it to a minimum." Yet he could sympathize with workmen in their struggle with industrial monopolies. He was nostalgic still for the sort of employer that Heath Dabney's grandfather had been—the "chivalrous gentleman" of humane and noble outlook. Both corporations and unions were thought beneficial to society only in so far as their managers respected the welfare of their whole industries and of the nation. Wilson's generalizations regarding the labor movement drew strong protests from labor leaders.

pleading for the common good against the pressures of special interests —in these large and general thoughts he offered a program of definite and enduring principle.

Wilson's doctrine appealed to the bedrock Americanism of free men who were as doubtful of the benefits of revolution as they were suspicious of large organizations that promoted selfish economic causes. The nation's middle class, then growing rapidly, was skeptical of "rackets"—whether of capital, of labor, or of government bureaucracy. The president of Princeton, as his educational views diverged more and more from those of alumni and trustees, was falling into sympathy with the instinctive sense of fair play and the almost superstitious fears and prejudices of citizens who were being hurt by large corporations that used competition to kill rather than to stimulate and took advantage of tariff rates and a monopoly position to lift prices outrageously. Small businessmen, church folk, and professional people sensed the man's passion for service of the right, his utter sincerity of purpose; and they were not greatly disturbed by his exaggerations and inaccuracies.

In January of 1910, Wilson addressed a gathering of reformers. Like the ideal orator whom he had envisioned, he himself showed power to "make men drunk with this spirit of self-sacrifice." The liberals thought him "a great leader of progressive impulse and thought," but "politically impossible." Ray Stannard Baker, who had exposed railroad malpractice and had written frankly of the plight of labor, was so captivated by what he recognized as "the finest mind in American life" that he went to Princeton to interview the prophet; and his questions were met squarely by practical, well-reasoned explanations and without regard to the concentration of political power and the winning of sectional votes.

In 1910, moreover, the prophet was speaking out boldly in party councils. Early in March, when Villard of the New York *Evening Post* quizzed him about his political aspirations, Wilson said that, though nothing was decided, his mind was leaning toward the governorship of New Jersey. Democratic leaders who felt that Princeton's president should "make the sacrifice" and accept the nomination for governor organized a dinner at Elizabeth; and though their hero refused to have his candidacy proclaimed, he could not keep the audience from shouting "Our next governor!" In his speech he aligned the Republican party with the vested interests, described the Democrats as the party of profound and abiding confidence in the people. In this he spoke like the young Wilson whose blood had danced when the Irish cause was advanced in Parliament or when Gladstone won an election. Once during his early academic years he had written to his wife: "It is singular, considering the judicial frame of mind I *try* to cultivate, what a partisan I am in politics." Yet now, on the threshold of his own political career, he did not plead merely for the selfish interest of the party, but for "a glory which it will itself be glad to see merged and identified with the glory of the nation."

George Harvey heard Wilson's speech at Elizabeth and was carried away by its eloquence. In January of 1910, surveying the politics of the nation from his New York office, the publisher had sensed that the Republican party and its conservative Congress were riding toward disaster; and he thought the time auspicious for launching Wilson on a political career. He conferred twice with his old friend James Smith, Jr.

Enchanted at the prospect of promoting a promising candidate for the presidency in 1912, Smith agreed to swing the party regulars of New Jersey into line behind Wilson, provided Harvey could give assurance that his candidate would accept nomination for the governorship. But when the publisher spent a night with Wilson at Princeton and sounded out his man, he found him preoccupied by university affairs and determined not to seek the honor. However, when Harvey asked whether the nomination would be accepted if it came "on a silver platter" and without any pledge, Wilson said he would regard it his duty "to give the matter very serious consideration." Temporarily, this response satisfied Smith.

On April 16, Wilson delivered the speech at Pittsburgh that so clearly displayed his potentiality as a political campaigner. Three days afterward he wrote to his old friend Dabney: "I find myself very much disinclined to go into politics, but I must say that it is getting a little difficult to keep out of them in the present situation of affairs—not so much the present situation in the university as the present movement of opinion among my friends in this part of the country." A year earlier Wilson had felt that the forming of a third party in 1912 was inevitable, and he thought that he might be its presidential candidate. But now he did not "despair of seeing the Democratic party drawn back to the definite and conservative principles which it once represented."

By the middle of June, Smith found that a majority of his men demanded assurance that Wilson would play the game. Would he, if elected, act like a "Presbyterian priest"? Smith wanted a positive statement to aid him in lining up his forces for the election. And so a former student of Wilson's was persuaded to write a letter saying that Smith had no desire that the candidate commit himself in any way as to principles, measures, or men, but did wish to be satisfied that, if Wilson was elected, he "would not set about fighting and breaking down the existing Democratic organization" and replacing it with one of his own. To this letter Wilson replied on June 23 that he would not do so, that in fact he would not antagonize the Smith organization so long as it worked "with thorough heartiness for such policies as would re-establish the reputation of the state" and so long as he was left "absolutely free in the matter of measures and men."

Though Smith himself was satisfied with this, he found some of the party men leaning away from Wilson and inclined to look for a more "regular" candidate. Finally convinced that he must secure a guarantee that his man would accept nomination for the governorship if it was offered to him, Smith telephoned to Harvey for help.

With the pay-off of his efforts to build up Wilson now in sight, the publisher went into action. He tried to arrange a powwow on the evening of Sunday, June 26. Smith would be there, and Colonel Watterson —"Marse Henry," editor-politician of Louisville. But Wilson did not find it convenient to come, for there was no Sunday train from Lyme, Connecticut, where he was summering again at the Old Griswold Place.

In the summer of 1910, the talk *en famille* at Old Lyme became more serious. The family spoke often of political prospects, as they chatted privately in the big square bedrooms of the boardinghouse, and Wilson and his wife talked for hours about duty and service and about the hardships of a public career. She was fearful. "Politics" was a word that grated on sensitive academic ears: smoke-filled rooms, deals, front-page publicity seemed to threaten the idyllic domesticity of the family. She quoted Mr. Dooley to her husband: "If anny Dimmicrat has a stiddy job he'd better shtick to it." And yet good government was a cause dear to Ellen Wilson, and she knew that her man had never lost his youthful ardor to lead men in righteous political action.

It was during this time of vacillation that an agent of Harvey's presented himself at the door of the Griswold house. He had been commissioned to bring the reluctant candidate to the conference that had been arranged with Smith and Watterson.

Wilson showed no surprise and offered no resistance. He packed his bag, and by taxi and train was whisked to the publisher's home at Deal Beach, New Jersey, arriving just in time for dinner. In the evening the three promoters revealed their ambition to make him president of the United States. If he would accept nomination for the governorship, the party leaders of New Jersey would give that to him by acclamation. They had been urged to do so by representative politicians of the Middle West with whom Smith had talked and who already looked with favor on Wilson as a presidential candidate. They gave him a week in which to make a final decision.

Returning to Old Lyme the next day, June 27, he found the family agog for news. Teasingly, he walked calmly across the room, sat down on a trunk, took a rubber tee from his pocket, deliberately placed it on the floor, found a golf ball and demonstrated the use of the new gadget, and then put it back in his pocket.

Finally he told them. He had been offered the nomination in New Jersey, without pledges; and Smith, whose motives he mistrusted much, would not be a candidate when it came time for the next legislature to choose a United States senator.[12] A little wistfully, the paterfamilias added: "Colonel Watterson says it will inevitably lead to the Presidency."

Before committing himself finally, Wilson consulted his strongest supporters among the Princeton trustees, confessing to them that he felt like a man in a maze, that acceptance of the New Jersey nomination might look like a mere case of personal ambition. He was not, he insisted, allowing the prospect of the presidency of the nation to form his opinion as to his duty in the matter of the governorship. His friends absolved him of further responsibility to Princeton, urged him to follow his own inclination, and promised support if he chose to enter politics.

Early in July, therefore, he gave his consent to Harvey and Smith. His keen boyish zest for political eminence had been dulled by the wear and tear of executive experience, and yet the old longings still ran in his blood. Moreover, after preaching to Princeton students on the duty of the educated man to undertake just such service as this, Wilson did not see how he could stand aside. Yet he confessed to "a sneaking hope that the thing may not, after all, come off." [13]

The boom began early in July. One of Harvey's staff went to Old Lyme to write a news story that would "humanize" the candidate.

[12] E. W. McAdoo, 109. Smith later said that no statement was made that justified this conclusion by Wilson. (*See* pp. 171 n., 176.)

[13] W.W. to Huston Thompson, July 14, 1910. Wilson wrote to Villard on Aug. 23, 1910: "I consented to let my name be considered for the nomination in New Jersey with many misgivings, and only because I felt that I had no choice in the matter, if I would practice what I have preached all my life." Villard Papers (Houghton Library, Harvard College).

Smith's newpapers, and also leading "New Idea" journals in New Jersey, began to promote Wilson's candidacy; and a Hearst paper was screaming, much to the distress of the candidate: "Wall St. to put up W. Wilson for President." [14]

On July 12, Harvey invited influential politicians and a corporation attorney to meet Wilson at luncheon at the Lawyers' Club in New York; but he had to beg his guest of honor to come, and to assure him that notorious bosses would not be present. The politicians listened impassively when Wilson declared that he would not accept the nomination unless it came unanimously, that he was definitely not seeking office. When Smith, thinking it essential that he have the support of the liquor interest, bade a lieutenant to sound out the candidate on this issue, Wilson did not mince words. "I am not a prohibitionist," he declared. "I believe that the question is outside of politics. I believe in home rule, and that the issue should be settled by local option in each community." When reminded that Smith and the party had been fighting against local option for years, he said: "Well, that is my attitude and my conviction. I cannot change it." Later he gave the same reply to the Anti-Saloon League, and it coincided with what he had written some twenty years before: "The state ought not to supervise private morals."

Three days after the conference at the Lawyers' Club, in a letter to New Jersey newspapers, Wilson announced publicly that, though he would not campaign for the nomination, he would deem it his duty to accept it should it prove to be true that he was the choice of "a decided majority of the thoughtful Democrats of the State." Most of the local press welcomed this statement as an omen for better government for New Jersey.

Thinking that he had "reached" Wilson, Smith went into action in earnest. Forming an alliance with Boss Robert Davis of Jersey City and Hudson County, he lined up about two-thirds of the votes that would be needed to nominate his man in the party convention in September; and then, one by one, he induced the leaders of other local organizations to board the "band wagon."

The progressives in the party protested. Otto Wittpenn, who as mayor of Jersey City had been fighting Davis's machine, carried his case directly to Wilson at Old Lyme. Did the professor not know, he asked, what was notorious—that the Smith-Davis organization stopped at

---

[14] New York *Journal*, July 8, 1910. This was not the first time the Wilsons had been embarrassed by the Hearst press. The divorced wife of Cousin Wilson Woodrow had written trashy stories for a Hearst magazine under the name of "Mrs. Wilson Woodrow."

nothing, that their men stuffed ballot boxes, hired "repeaters" at the polls, levied blackmail, and took orders from the corporations? The delegates of Wilson's own county turned against him and pledged support to another man. Progressive newspapers proclaimed that the president of Princeton was allowing himself "to be used as a cat's paw, to serve the purposes of the bosses," that he was the tool of corporation financiers, "window-dressing" for a discredited machine.

Soon Wilson was under a barrage of embarrassing questions. Would he have courage to practice the principles that he had been preaching so glibly? the insurgents were asking. Face to face, now, with political realities and still lacking in *savoir-faire*, Wilson turned to Harvey for advice and received sound professional counsel. Every two or three days—sometimes oftener—he was in communication with his mentor, who wrote him little undated notes of reassurance, reporting that he and Smith had made "a fairly satisfactory understanding with Wittpenn," that all reports were good, that "the situation is well in hand; there are no breaches in the walls." The candidate must put on a bold front and say nothing definite about current issues, and must realize that it was necessary to have opposition in order to forestall allegations that the campaign was being railroaded through by bosses.

For a while Wilson avoided commitments, while suspicion grew that progressive newspapers were right in charging that he was "afloat on a bad hull." He fumed over a cartoon that depicted him as a weary horse dragging a cart in which a tiny Harvey was conducting a huge Smith to a United States senatorship. Charges of hypocrisy were fired at him, and his silence was held to be proof of his opposition to progressive ideas. But Harvey, warning the candidate that inevitably he would be "berated somewhat on account of the friends made" and that the liberal New York *World* doubtless would be "after" him, wrote seductively: "The talk about the Interests is wholly ignorable up to date . . . I should duck. Your position now is perfect." They had only to stand pat, the impresario insisted, and no one would dare asperse the president of Princeton.

For weeks Wilson followed Harvey's advice and refused to let his ideas be drawn out. To grant interviews to journalists, he informed James Kerney of Trenton, would be to give an impression that he was seeking nomination. However, when academic utterances made previously by Wilson against certain activities of labor unions were circulated out of context—particularly a speech on "Unprofitable Servants" in which he had excoriated abuses of labor's power along with the moral failings of businessmen—even Smith and his henchmen could not check the growing antagonism among workmen. A letter written on August 18 by Edgar R. Williamson, editor of the *American Labor Standard*, informed Wilson that the state federation had just condemned him as a foe of organized labor. Asked for his views, the candidate composed a two-page statement on his typewriter. Declaring that he had always been "the warm friend of organized labor" and that his criticisms had been made in a friendly spirit, he asserted that it was absolutely necessary that laborers form unions in order to secure justice from organized capital. Harvey told Wilson that the labor letter was "precisely timed and wholly effective."

In August and September the tide ran toward the amateur campaigner. Conviction grew that he was the ablest among the candidates. In the primaries of September 13, Smith and Davis easily carried their key counties for Wilson; and it seemed clear that when the nominating convention met on the 15th it would choose the president of Princeton. Wilson himself was so confident that he had already drafted a speech of acceptance that Harvey had outlined.

On the morning of convention day the candidate played golf at Princeton, ignorant of the rough-and-tumble in Trenton, where Harvey and Smith were toiling mightily to hold the lines against ferocious but disorganized attacks by independent leaders. The two archpromoters had been working all night, from their stale-aired rooms in the Trenton House, to cast their nets around wobbling delegates; but despite all their persuasiveness and the confident blarney of the men who heeled for them—Planked-Shad Thompson, Jim Nugent, and the rest—sharp words cut at the name of the candidate when it was put in nomination on the floor of the convention.

Judge John W. Wescott of Camden County, elder statesman of the progressives, shouted against "bargain and sale and double cross," against dictation by a "financial machine"; but Thompson merely reminded the convention that two-thirds of the delegates from Wescott's own county were already committed to Wilson. Antagonistic delegates from Wilson's Mercer County objected to the listing of the candidate as a resident of Princeton; but forty Princeton men, seated on the stage under the leadership of Smith's son, broke into a football cheer. Progressives howled and stamped and shook their fists; but the men of the machine sat tight and kept their eyes on their leaders. The bosses, the marching clubs, the bands had done their work well. If there was not an answer for every question, there was at least a long drink and a confident handshake. It was Wilson on the first ballot, with a few more votes than necessary. "Tommie" Wilson had been set on the road to high office by the very sort of convention that he had damned thirty years earlier as "his country's curse."

Judge Wescott bolted from the hall in disgust. As the other delegates were about to leave—the progressives among them morose and resentful—the secretary of the convention announced: "We have just received word that Mr. Wilson, the candidate for the governorship, *and the next President of the United States*, has received word of his nomination, has left Princeton, and is now on his way to the Convention."

Actually, Harvey had commissioned an agent to have Wilson in Trenton even before the nomination was made. The candidate was brought by automobile from Princeton and was kept in a hotel room in ignorance of the moil and barter that were giving him his opportunity. He was summoned to the hall for a well-timed entrance on the stage so expertly set. In contrast with the bosses, who wore frock coats and silk hats, he was dressed in the clothes in which he had been playing golf—a soft felt hat and a gray sack suit, a knitted golf jacket showing under his coat.

He was escorted by police through a mob that milled and cheered outside the stage door of the opera house. "God! Look at that jaw!" a ward heeler was heard to exclaim. There was nothing of the pallid academician in this man as he strode onto the platform. His weathered skin was flushed from the excitement of the occasion and the summer of outdoor living.

Joseph Patrick Tumulty of Jersey City, a sincere progressive who had worked for reform in the state legislature,[15] moved sullenly forward

[15] Like Woodrow Wilson, Tumulty had a grandfather who had immigrated from Ireland; and like Wilson, Tumulty loved parades, orations, and fights in a righteous cause. He had cut his teeth in the gerrymandered slum area of Jersey City that was called the Horseshoe, where in boyhood he had heard the affairs of the nation discussed in his father's grocery store. At the age of seventeen he made his debut as a political orator; and when Bryan paraded at Jersey City in 1896 he shot off firecrackers and orated on what he thought the great moral issue of the campaign—"the attempt of eastern financial interests to dominate the government of the United States."

Tumulty thought that the most effective way to work for reform was through the Democratic organization. In order to be elected to the Assembly, he had accepted the support of Davis and his minions and as an assemblyman had voted for many a "boodle" bill, knowing that in return the county boss would leave him free to work with the New Idea men for progressive laws for the state. His legislative leadership was so marked that in 1910, at the age of thirty-one, he was endorsed by his party to be speaker of the Assembly; but he felt that he must return to the practice of law to provide for his growing family. Tumulty and his progressive friends hoped that a Democrat true to their ideals might be nominated for governor. *See* John M. Blum, "Tumulty and the Wilson Era," a dissertation submitted to Harvard University, and the book based on this study, *Joe Tumulty and the Wilson Era* (hereinafter referred to as Blum, *Tumulty*).

to get a "close-up" of the man whom he thought the bosses had foisted
on the party. But now he was astounded by the words and the manner
of the candidate. Ignoring the bosses, proclaiming that the nomination
had come to him "absolutely unsolicited," Wilson pledged himself to
serve the people of the state with singleness of purpose if he was
elected. Did you ever desire, he asked the delegates, to do right because
it is right and without thought of doing it for your own interest? "At
that period your hopes are unselfish. This in particular is a day of unselfish purpose for Democracy . . ."

The little men in that crowded hall were swept up above their petty
interests and given a vision. Now it was not Princeton, but the Democratic party, that was committed to serve the state and the nation in
righteousness. Their candidate was sharing his dearest ideals, openly
and intimately, with winning smiles and with such phrasing as they
had never heard before on a political platform. "Government is not a
warfare of interest," he warned. "We shall not gain our ends by heat
and bitterness." In tones that almost sang, he came to an overwhelming
climax:

The future is not for parties "playing politics" but for measures conceived
in the largest spirit, pushed by parties whose leaders are statesmen not demagogues, who love, not their offices but their duty and their opportunity for
service. We are witnessing a renaissance of public spirit, a reawakening of
sober public opinion, a revival of the power of the people, the beginning of
an age of thoughful reconstruction that makes our thought hark back to
the great age in which democracy was set up in America. With the new age
we shall show a new spirit . . .

"Go on, go on," they yelled, thanking God that a leader had come
among them. A peroration to the flag brought tears, and it was over.
The crowd stood in their seats and cheered madly. Joe Tumulty's allegiance was won: throwing his arms around a friend, he predicted
that Jim Smith might find that in Wilson he had a political "lemon."
Delegates swarmed forward and tried to lift the candidate to their
shoulders. Finally, protecting policemen took him to an automobile.
Even then ebullient Democrats mobbed the running-board to shake
hands with their new-found messiah.

The prophet was getting through to the people without intervention
of trustees or bosses. Wilson told Stockton Axson that the people
accepted him because he could find moving words to express the feelings that were in their hearts, groping for release. The secret of his
power was the secret that had made his forebears great preachers.

With her husband plunged into a political campaign, Ellen Wilson foresaw new and ominous intrusions into the privacy of the family. "Sugar Jim" Smith, bringing his warriors to Prospect for a powwow, was so charmed by the house and garden that he asked why anyone could be "damn fool enough to give up this for the heartaches of politics." President Lowell of Harvard wrote: "Are not the seas of university management boisterous enough that you must seek the storms of politics?" And in reply Wilson confessed that he was still uncertain whether he had done the right thing or not. "I shall start out upon the new career as bravely as possible," he promised; and, characteristically, he took courage from preaching boldness to boys of the student Christian association who packed a college hall. "Don't go about seeking to associate only with good people," he advised them. "Endure hardness . . . The man who is working is the man who goes out and joins battle." From a current magazine he clipped a new poem, "If," by Rudyard Kipling: "If you can dream—and not make dreams your master . . . If you can talk with crowds and keep your virtue." Later he had a copy of "If" framed; and it remained with him until the day of his death.

What the candidate dreaded most, perhaps, was news reporters. Some he came to trust; but all his life he suspected the press of a lack of veracity and good taste. He had particularly resented sensational reporting of his speeches that represented them as attacks on wealth. Thinking now that he would avoid misquotation by releasing only written statements, he drafted an imaginary "interview"; but when one of Hearst's men bluntly asked him why he had allowed himself "to be nominated by the interests," the candidate forgot his academic preparations and blurted out, hotly: "It is a humiliating and absurd thing to say that I am the Wall Street candidate for governor of New Jersey." Not a fast reader, Wilson himself kept up with only one daily newspaper, the New York *Evening Post*; but his wife read the important journals of New Jersey and New York and gave him hundreds of clippings. After scanning them, he recorded ideas in a vest-pocket notebook.

Once Wilson began to campaign actively for election, a majority of the board of trustees decided that he could no longer serve as president of Princeton. There had been rumors that his enemies had been trying to get rid of him by promoting his political candidacy, and Wilson had been apprised of this possibility.[16] Relying on the carte blanche that his

[16] On July 18, 1910, Z. C. Felt, a Princeton classmate, wrote to Wilson thus: "Last spring one of your bitterest opponents unfolded to me quite at length the plans they hoped to carry into effect to get you out of Princeton. And one of these was to convince you that it was *your duty* to accept the nomination."

friends among the trustees had given to him, Wilson wished to devote three days a week to lecturing and to remain president at least until the election in November. However, a delegation was sent to tell him that he must withdraw from the presidency, and a resolution was prepared formally calling on him to resign, to be passed in case the informal suggestion was refused. He reluctantly accepted the inevitable, and on October 20 he read a letter of resignation to the trustees and left the room while they stood in silence.[17]

When Wilson discovered the actual feeling toward him on the part of what he called "the Pyne party," mortification would have broken him had it not been for the continuing confidence of certain friends. Deep within him as life itself were the bonds that had been forged with individuals whom he had come to love and respect—the "Witherspoon gang," Cleveland Dodge and the other loyal trustees, his preceptors and protégés, Henry B. Fine and the little band of university men. Princeton was the promised land to which in his last years he was to yearn to return. Lying at the gate of death he said to one of his old boys: "If they cut me open afterward, they'll find engraved on my heart—PRINCETON!"[18]

The rejected prophet lacked courage to admit to strangers that he had failed as the chief executive of a privately endowed corporation.[19] Yet the truth is that he had slipped from his platform of principle and been drawn into a feud with a powerful antagonist. He had weakened

[17] See Link, op. cit., p. 90. In wishing to retain his office until the election, Wilson probably was influenced by the plea sent by Henry B. Fine in a letter of July 10: "The only request which we, your Princeton friends, can in fairness make is that you do not retire from the presidency of Princeton until actually elected Governor of New Jersey." His election would be "very probable" but not "certain," Fine went on, and "Princeton should have the benefit of the difference between the certainty and the probability."

Accepting Wilson's forced resignation on Oct. 20, 1910, the trustees requested him to continue in his professorship of jurisprudence and politics as long as possible, and conferred on him the degree of Doctor of Laws. John A. Stewart, the senior trustee, was made president pro tem. Both the trustees and his students presented elaborate testimonials upon Wilson's departure. He refused to continue his teaching, however, and declined persistent offers by the university to continue his salary for a few months, taking nothing after Oct. 20, the effective date of his resignation, and moving from Prospect to the Princeton Inn within a few weeks.

Left without income, except for about $2,000 a year from investments and royalties from his books, Wilson applied to the Carnegie Foundation for a pension. Cf. pp. 212–13 below.

Wilson paid the personal expenses of the New Jersey campaign out of his own small funds. Later, when he discovered how expensive campaigning could be, he was forced to accept financial donations from friends who he thought could be depended on not to press him for political favors.

[18] Roland Morris to Francis C. MacDonald to the writer.

[19] For example, replying to a request of Oct. 31, 1912, from a Princeton admirer, Henry D. Pierce of the Class of 1868, for information about the Princeton controversy, Wilson wrote that there was at no time "the least likelihood" of his being forced out of the Princeton presidency. Such a statement as this gave support to the contention of West and his friends that Wilson was an unconscionable liar.

his position by suggesting an irrational but well-intentioned compromise on the location of the graduate college. His rectitude had kept him from wooing men as friends when his conscience told him that he wanted them only as patrons. His scorn of pettifogging had made him less than careful of the letter of truth. His conviction of the rightness of his cause had made him contemptuous, rather than sympathetic, toward contrary opinions and had chilled the feelings of both trustees and alumni who did not understand their president.

Nevertheless, in spite of his failure to hold the support of the entire constituency, Princeton had flourished under his leadership. New impulses had taken root that were to flower gloriously for decades afterward. Undergraduate scholarship had improved; and under the impetus of the new faculty committee on the graduate school, the number and intellectual quality of graduate students had grown. Moreover, the university had become richer in equipment, in annual gifts, and in endowment.

Woodrow Wilson would engage in shindies aplenty in future years; he would have to contend with men who, unlike Cleveland and Pyne, were ruled by self-interest; and he would have to bear malicious personal attacks that even Andrew West was to brand as false. But for the most part the hostility and its animus would be as obvious as gross. Never in subsequent struggles in the political arena, he said later, did he meet an antagonist as crafty as Andrew Fleming West.

CHAPTER X

FALL OF AN OLD REGIME

THE NOMINATION at Trenton put Woodrow Wilson on the front page. It was unprecedented for a man so renowned as a scholar to venture to give active political leadership. To what extent would he be able to make his ideals effective? everyone wondered. Did he understand them, the plain people, and their wants and needs in the autumn of 1910? Was he indeed the messiah to lead them through the economic wilderness without bloodshed?

Wilson himself, leaving the work to which he had given the best twenty years of his life and staking his family's livelihood on his ability to serve the people of New Jersey, wondered. "Am I equal to this big work when I failed in a much smaller one?" he asked an old friend a little wistfully. Then, reassuring himself, he said: "Yes, I believe I am, for now I shall be speaking to the American people, not to an academic group rooted in tradition and fearful of progress."

For several weeks he and the people sounded each other out, and reached only tentative conclusions. Folks were quick to see that they were being offered leadership of a caliber that was strange to them. They caught the awe that Smith had reflected from the floor of the nominating convention when he said: "It is not to be assumed that such as I should be acquainted with such as he, but it is clear from all I have heard that he will make a superlative governor."

The candidate, for his part, stepped lightly and uncertainly through the first weeks of the campaign. Meeting the Democratic leaders with great warmth and charm, he dodged state issues by taking refuge in discussion of national policies and academic generalities. He was keeping up his guard, not trusting all men to accept his virtuous intent as guarantee of his wisdom.

In council with party men it was decided that the candidate should woo the hearts of his new constituents by the eloquence of set speeches rather than the give-and-take of interviews. Twenty-seven addresses were scheduled. He was nervous about these public appearances, at first, begging his wife to stay away for fear that he would disgrace her by some deviation from perfection; and when his daughters went to hear him, they hid behind the curtains of a box so that he would not see them and become embarrassed. He had had little experience in addressing political audiences, and feared that he might not give the satisfaction that they demanded; and he did not write texts in advance, "in cold blood."

In his first speech to the electorate, at Jersey City, he was obviously ill at ease, lugged in irrelevant anecdotes, rambled a bit. Then he made a frank confession: "I never before appeared before an audience and asked for anything, and now I find myself in the novel position of asking you to vote for me for governor of New Jersey." That broke down the barriers; and at the end of his talk he drew prolonged cheers by stepping to the front of the platform and saying ingenuously: "And so, gentlemen, I have made my first political plea. I feel that I am before a great jury. I don't want the judge to butt in. I am content to leave the decision in your hands." They stopped him there, with applause that came from their hearts. They saw no haughty intellectual in this candid, friendly Scotch-Irishman. The crowds were bigger than expected; and even the newsmen were so affected that they sometimes neglected their work.

He did not harangue, though he occasionally indulged in a peroration —"those boys are strong for perorations," he sensed. For the most part he used simple words and short sentences. But one night, after a New York editor had taken exception to his diction, he began to speak waggishly in ornate and stilted phrases. Then suddenly he laughed, thrust his hands in his pockets, walked forward, and lifted the frowns from the faces in front of him by saying, "Confidentially, ladies and gentlemen, that's the way the New York ——— thinks I should talk to you, but I prefer a more informal way of speaking."

His powers of mimicry and repartee were brought into play. The Republican party, he told one audience, was like the mule on a Mississippi River steamboat that ate the destination tag that was tied to its collar. "Cap'n," shouted a Negro deckhand. "Dat mule done et up whar he gwine to!"

Yet his humor was not displayed at the expense of sincerity. Listeners were convinced that he was that very rare specimen: a completely frank candidate for office. He seemed to be thinking out loud in their presence, to be sharing himself with them most intimately. In the audiences that to prissy academic folk seemed "roughneck" Wilson saw genuine individuals who were moved by normal human impulses. He idealized men who knew their business and worked hard. In talking face to face with the people of New Jersey, Wilson felt the thrill that had come to him at the Cooper Union in New York six years before. He had testified then that the most penetrating questions ever addressed to him "came from some of the men who were the least well-dressed in the audience, came from the plain fellows, came from the fellows whose muscle was daily up against the whole struggle of life. They asked questions which went to the heart of the business and put me on my mettle."

Wilson's first campaign speeches were lectures in political science, each growing logically out of the preceding. Advocating the specific and immediate reforms—such as administrative reorganization, fairer taxation and regulation of corporations, and an effective corrupt practices act—he carefully held himself within the limits that were set by the party platform that he had helped George Harvey to draft. He was observing and evaluating the program being put forward by the progressives of both parties, remembering that a cautious regard for popular feeling made the difference between the parliamentary statesman and the wild-eyed reformer.

He took the campaign rather casually in the early days. In order to hold him to his speaking schedule, James Nugent, the party chairman and a man for whom Wilson had little respect, had to threaten to take the candidate's place in any meeting that Wilson missed. In late September, Democratic headquarters sent Joseph Tumulty to West Hoboken to hold an audience until the candidate could get there; and the young progressive performed his mission so brilliantly that Wilson made him his comrade and understudy on speaking trips and began to call him "my dear boy." Tumulty found the man unaffected and affable, able to restore his energy between speeches by taking catnaps in their automobile, willing to drive long distances in order to get home at night. But Tumulty still suspected his chief of being a wolf in sheep's clothing, playing "the old game of thimblerig" at the bidding of the bosses. Asked for his honest opinion of the first campaign speech, he told Wilson that it was most disappointing.

Other progressives begged the Democratic candidate to declare that he would not allow any corporations or bosses or machines to rule the state; and Wilson took this advice, feeling himself not yet expert in electioneering strategy. In his first speech in Smith's home city of Newark he urged that the state intervene to prevent men from "taking joy rides in corporations." Explaining the party platform in terms that all could understand, he stirred thunderous applause.

Before the address, Smith had sent an agent to Wilson to ask him to speak out against local liquor option in order to please the majority of the Newark audience. The candidate had refused, and escaped heckling on the issue by riveting the attention of his hearers on more vital topics. The persistence of Smith in trying to change what he knew to be Wilson's convictions on local option reawakened the suspicions of the prophet. He asked one of Sugar Jim's agents what the bosses really were up to; and when he was reminded that these men had nominated him and could elect or defeat him, Wilson replied: "I went in without pledges, asked or given, and it is the people, not the bosses, who will elect me if I am elected, and to whom I shall be responsible."

"If you are elected," the agent predicted, "you are going to hear a lot from Jim Smith."

In the treacherous footing at Princeton he had slipped from the code of his grandfather—"principles, not men"—but now it was commanding every move. He won converts from the progressive wing of the Republican party by asserting that he was being attacked personally, as a "professor," rather than on grounds of principle. Tumulty would have him slug it out with the Republicans and ridicule the political record of their candidate, but Wilson insisted on dealing mainly with the principles that were to prevail in the future.

A few days later, however, at Trenton, using a phrase that had been put in his mouth by an editor of that city, Wilson bluntly told the people that he would not, like his Republican opponent, be merely a "constitutional governor," but would truly represent all-of-them. He threatened that, if the legislators did not pass the laws that the people demanded, he would "take every important subject of debate in the legislature out on the stump and discuss it with the people." Then his lips compressed and his eyes seemed to narrow, as his deeper feelings surged up and he challenged: "If you don't want that kind of governor, don't elect me." He went on: "If you give me your votes, I will be under bonds to you—not to the gentlemen who were generous enough to nominate me."

It was no ordinary political campaign, he told them. There was more sincerity; people had come out to the meetings in unprecedented numbers, as if something was to be accomplished. Bearing down on the importance of close contact between government and public opinion, the candidate challenged his hearers to play out their role. "You have got into the game," he told them, "but are you going to stay there?"

In his October speeches, his blood started by the spur of competition, Wilson was projecting himself headlong into liberal thinking. He spoke of "the splendid program of the progressives—to put things forward—by justice, by fairness, by a concern for all interests, until men shall think in terms of the common weal and not in the terms of special interests or partisan advantage." Moreover, he got down to cases, argued that the price of gas could be cut in half by efficient regulation of the Public Service Corporation, explained just why New Jersey's election laws were "so loose and evil." He came to think of himself as representing "the reorganized Democratic party." Finally, he made the extravagant claim that he was and always had been an insurgent. "I am accused of being a radical," he said. "If to seek to go to the root is to be a radical, a radical I am."

He would not pander to labor unions any more than to corporations or to the liquor interests, in spite of their great voting strength. Warning laborers that the Republicans would not carry out their glib promises to the workingmen, he urged them to think of the best interests of "the people." And who were "the people"?

Do capitalists constitute the people? Certainly not. Do the merchants constitute the people? Certainly not. When you speak of the people are you thinking of levels? Are you thinking of those who are poor, are you thinking of those who are well-to-do . . . are you thinking of those who are very rich? The interesting thing is that the people consist of all these classes put together; it does not consist of any one, it does not consist of any two of them, or of any combination, except the combination that constitutes the whole.

As he warmed to the battle, the candidate tended more and more to stand apart. He became cockily assertive as he carried the political thought of the state, including that of the Republican candidate, far to the left. As a Trenton newspaper pointed out, he was "uniting the insurgent forces of New Jersey." The contest became one of personalities and character, with both candidates appealing to the fervor of the people for reform. The questions became: Which candidate would the people believe to be more sincere? Which would be strong enough to rule the reactionaries in his party? Which would lead the legislature and not merely follow it?

A chance to bind the confidence of the independent voters was provided by George L. Record, who publicly accepted a challenge to public debate that Wilson had flung out impulsively to "any politician in the state." However, the Democratic leaders saw only danger in such an event, fearing that Record might ask questions about the party machine that could not be dodged gracefully. After a conference with Wilson, Chairman Nugent wrote a public letter offering to arrange "joint meetings" if Record would appear as the accredited Republican spokesman. Actually, everyone knew that this could never be; and so Record met Nugent's parry with scorn. "The great Dr. Wilson," he taunted, "who is to lift the politics of New Jersey to a new and higher plane, at the first test has gone down to the Jim Nugent plane and commences to dodge and pettifog."

This, and the urging of progressive friends, goaded Wilson to direct action. Ignoring his party organization, he wrote a letter to Record saying that they would have to deal with each other as individuals rather than as party men. His speaking program, he explained, kept him from arrranging a debate. Yet he realized that he must not seem to try to dodge Record's challenge if he was to win the votes of the "New Idea Republicans." And so he suggested that Record's questions be propounded in a public letter to which a reply could be made for publication. In this way he ran no risk of being confounded by sharp cross-examination; moreover, intermediaries were working to prevent any trickery in Record's queries.

Wilson's suggestion was taken, and the nineteen questions that were drafted and published in the newspapers covered every important issue in detail. The problems raised were those that had been turning over in Wilson's mind for weeks. Intuition told him that they were in the minds of the voters, too; and both pastoral responsibility and political expediency required that he reply. By meeting the challenge both fearlessly and intelligently, he proved not only that he had been "born a politician," but that he was developing the stature of statesmanship. After days of stumbling and groping in a strange political wilderness—a land in which he had previously roamed only as a critic, never as a responsible leader—the intensely moral mind slowly settled on what it could regard as God's business in government. At last Woodrow Wilson felt "qualified to speak." When he sat down on October 24 to write his reply to Record, his words were exclusively and intimately his own.

Asked whether he favored election reforms, a corrupt practices act, and certain measures that would regulate public utilities more effectively, Wilson answered affirmatively; but on one issue—that of the nomination of candidates for office by direct primary elections—he no longer expressed doubts that he had held a few weeks before. Inconsistencies in his views on an issue from time to time never embarrassed him, so long as he was true to his basic principle of reasoned change. In a campaign speech he reminded the people: "We are not in the same America we were ten years ago. The standpat program is always wrong." And on another occasion he said: "I'll agree not to change my

mind if someone with power to do so will guarantee that if I go to bed
at night I will get up in the morning and see the world in the same
way."

It was in replying to the last five questions that Wilson wrote an
important page in American political history. Record condemned the
government of the state as a conspiracy among bosses of the two parties
and the public service corporations—"an evil that has destroyed representative government . . . and in its place set up a government of
privilege." In return for certain privileges, he alleged, the party leaders
were awarded favors by the corporation managers in "the form of
either direct money payments, or heavy contributions for campaign
expenses, or opportunity for safe and profitable business ventures, according to the standard of morality of the particular boss or leader."
Did Wilson agree with this statement? the Progressive leader asked.

"Of course," the candidate replied, the existence of the evil was
"notorious."

How would Wilson abolish it, if elected?

By the reforms agreed upon, and "by the election to office of men
who will refuse to submit to it and bend all their energies to break it
up, and by pitiless publicity."

Tapping what he thought would be the most sensitive nerve of all,
the inquisitor named names. Wherein, he asked, did the relation of
the corporation interests to the Republican bosses differ from the relation of the same interests to "such Democratic leaders as Smith, Nugent,
and Davis?"

The answer came straight to the mark: The Republican bosses "differ
from the others in this, that they are in control of the government of
the State, while the others are not and cannot be if the present Democratic ticket is elected." Wilson went even further in order to drive
misgivings from the minds of progressive voters. Attacking a doubt
that was implied in several of Record's questions, he wrote:

If elected I shall not, either in the matter of appointments to office or assent
to legislation, or in shaping any part of the policy of my administration, submit to the dictation of any person or persons, special interest or organization.
I will always welcome advice and suggestions from any citizen, whether boss,
leader, organization man or plain citizen, and I shall constantly seek the advice of influential and disinterested men, representative of their communities
and disconnected from political "organizations" entirely; but all suggestions
and all advice will be considered on their merits, and no additional weight
will be given to any man's advice or suggestion because of his exercising, or

supposing that he exercises, some sort of political influence or control. I should deem myself forever disgraced should I in even the slightest degree cooperate in any such system or any such transactions as you describe in your characterization of the "boss" system. I regard myself as pledged to the regeneration of the Democratic party which I have forecast above.

To Record's last query, asking whether Wilson would require candidates for the legislature "to pledge themselves in writing prior to the election in favor of such of the foregoing reforms" as he personally favored, Wilson replied: "I will not. Because I think it would be most unbecoming in me to do so. That is the function of the voters in the several counties."

Wilson's reply was published in a flyer and circulated. Record was dumfounded. Independent progressives and restless Republicans came into the Democratic camp in thousands. Joseph Tumulty told the candidate that the New Jersey democracy—meaning the progressive wing of it—gladly accepted his "virile leadership." Smith, with the election only weeks away, could only swallow the sword that had been aimed at him and hoped that it was made of rubber. "A great campaign play," the bosses told each other, whistling to keep up courage.

Actually, however, the sword became stiffer and sharper as the candidate made a final whirlwind tour of northern Jersey in a week of slush and snow. Perhaps, he said, the bosses had picked out the wrong man after all. And with mordant threats he mixed discussion of specific reforms.

In a final speech, at Newark, Wilson served notice that if elected he would consider himself chosen to lead his party, to conduct the government of the state in the interest of the people only, using party and party coherents for that service. "What I seriously object to," he said, "is any government conducted upon the basis of private understanding with anybody." There was nothing self-conscious or stylistic about his expression now. He no longer strained for effect, but showed the confidence and competence of one who had learned how. After this address an admirer climbed the platform, slapped the back of the speaker, and shouted: "Doc, you're a winner!" Smith, emotionally stirred by the man from whom he both hoped and feared much, turned to Tumulty with tears welling, and said hoarsely: "a great man . . . destined for great things."

Victory on election day was an anticlimax, but the plurality surpassed expectations. It was almost fifty thousand, in a state that the Republican presidential candidate had carried by some eighty thousand votes two years before. The counties of Smith and Davis gave Wilson large majorities, and even his own recalcitrant Mercer County finally supported the ex-president of Princeton.[1]

At ten o'clock on election night it became clear to Wilson that the people of New Jersey had chosen him to lead them. Soon the blare of bands rose above the hubbub inside Prospect, and fireworks and waving torches could be seen from the windows. He stepped out and looked upon the largest parade ever seen in Princeton. For hours the family sat up, talking it over, wondering how they would keep the air of their home breathable. Students and townspeople swarmed over the lawn to pay tribute with yells and cheering. Deeply moved, their hero said very simply: "It is my ambition to be the governor of all the people of the state, and render to them the best services I am capable of rendering."

New Jersey editors did not let the Governor-elect forget that his victory was but the culmination of the surge of protest that had started with the New Idea revolt; and realizing his debt to progressive pioneers, Wilson took pains to respond appreciatively to a letter of congratulation from Record. He made light of his triumph by explaining to his intimates that he had been "kicked upstairs" into public service; but his friends exulted in the new honor as evidence of the sure grinding of the mills of the gods. Fred Yates, the English painter, who had been visiting at Prospect during the campaign and had found the atmosphere of the Wilson home remarkably unrestrained and "breathable," remarked: "Yes, it's the same old story—the biggest are always the simplest. Dear W.W. is in a fight . . . There is only one danger . . . whether he can stand against the intriguers—whether he is not by nature an autocrat . . . He is a fighter—and I believe he loves the fight —I believe he has only one eye for anything and that is Truth. Jesus died for that—and Socrates—single-eyed— How few men . . ."

Very soon, however, the rosy afterglow of the election was overcast by the cloud of another battle. James Smith, Jr., unctuous and ready to be rewarded for services rendered, paid a visit to Prospect. He said that his health, to which rumor had attributed his apparent lack of interest in the forthcoming election of a United States senator by the state Assembly, was remarkably better. Now that a Democratic majority had come unexpectedly into control of the legislature, senatorial elec-

---

[1] John Blum has pointed out that a raise of 20 per cent in commuters' fares shortly before the election played a part in Wilson's capture of a larger share of the suburban vote than ever went to him again. *See* Blum, *Tumulty,* p. 24.

tion was no longer so unessential a matter to Smith as Wilson had been led to believe in July.[2]

There had been rumors, already, that Smith had been lining up support among the incoming legislators by the use of promises of patronage that he had no right to dispense. And when the plausible boss sat down in Prospect, where hundreds of lectures on political morality had been composed, and indicated his desire to go to the Senate, Wilson's composure was severely taxed. His sense of professional honesty was outraged. He had received letters from reliable witnesses that confirmed his suspicion that Smith had betrayed a political trust.[3] If he supported Smith's aspirations to the Senate, Wilson would become an accomplice in deceiving the voters; for Smith's name had not been entered in the primary election by which, under a new law sponsored by the progressives, the people had indicated whom they would like to have their legislature choose for the Senate.

The candidate who had won the preference of the few people who had bothered to vote in the primary was one James E. Martine, a Bryan Democrat whose progressive ideas were more enthusiastic than rational but who had the support of journals in Newark and Jersey City.

Wilson was in a dilemma as difficult as any that had faced him in the university. He could pay a personal debt and lose the confidence of progressive voters by supporting Smith, whom he thought able but dishonest. He could uphold a primary law that he thought good in principle, and accept Martine, the well-intentioned but incompetent candi-

[2] Smith had never publicly renounced his ambition to return to the Senate. He had told Harvey that he would be willing to make a public disavowal if ever that should become necessary in order to relieve Wilson of the disrepute that might result from accusations that his campaign for the governorship was in reality only a means of furthering Smith's personal ambition. That was a gesture of magnanimity that Smith could well afford to make, so slight was the chance that there would be a Democratic legislature at Trenton to elect him. Harvey had informed Wilson of Smith's offer, yet had refused to accept it immediately for fear of alienating Smith's henchmen, whose support had been needed to nominate Wilson at Trenton. While allowing their ingenuous candidate for the governorship to think that Smith had no plan to run for the Senate, the master tacticians calculatingly had built up the power of Sugar Jim by letting the minions think that he might become a senator and a source of federal patronage that would be worth following. And at the same time, from the other side of his mouth, Smith was time and again reassuring the progressive, editor James Kerney, that he would not run for the Senate. The assurances given to Kerney must have reached Wilson, sooner or later, and must have affirmed the impression of Smith's disinterestedness that Wilson had reported to his family after returning from the July conference at Deal. (*See* pp. 153 and 176.)

[3] Wilson was warned against Smith by John Moody in a letter of Nov. 29, 1910, telling of Moody's experience in soliciting campaign funds from Smith in 1903: "He apparently assumed that as I was a Wall Street man, I was naturally interested in politics 'for revenue only' and he was very frank . . . He told me in so many words that for many years he had been the dispenser of money received from the Pennsylvania Railroad and other corporations to influence legislation in the State of New Jersey. He explained that any men we might send to the legislature should surely 'behave themselves.'" John Moody to the writer, confirmed by a letter, Nov. 19, 1955.

date whom the Democratic voters had endorsed. He could urge the party to find a compromise candidate. He could stand aside and point out that he was under no legal obligation in the matter.

As usual, he made no immediate decision. Striving desperately to veil the moral indignation that Smith had aroused, Wilson suggested to him, when he called at Prospect, that by entering the senatorial race at this point Smith "would confirm all the ugliest suspicions of the campaign." Even if one assumed that the vote for Martine had been so small that it was inconclusive, he argued, the only way to give dignity to the new primary law was to take the outcome of it seriously. He did not flay this infidel, as he had Andrew West, by telling him grimly that it was necessary that he "be digested in the processes" of good government. Rather he pleaded with Smith, and told him that if he was not satisfied to have Martine represent the party he could suggest a compromise candidate who would represent no special interests, but the opinion of the entire state.

Smith, however, saw through the Governor's tactful subterfuge. Choosing a "compromise" candidate, after all, would invalidate the primary election just as thoroughly as if Smith himself were chosen. For all of his valiant efforts at diplomacy, Wilson's personal revulsion was obvious to his caller. There was academic reprobation in the air; and Smith went away feeling, as he told Harvey later, that back of the polite words "there seemed to be something arbitrary and autocratic." The boss's pride was hurt. ". . . by God," he told Harvey, "I guess I'll let him beat me!" Finally, in mid-November, he declared publicly that if his friends thought he should make the fight he would enter the race and would win it.

Another shindy was brewing. First Wilson listened to cautious counselors who advised him not to take sides. Then with his wife he sought guidance in prayer. Mindful of his pledge to the people to give leadership to the legislature, Wilson asked himself the question attributed to an Irishman whom he liked to tell about—a man who, entering a saloon and seeing a tangle of writhing, bleeding bodies on the floor, said: "Tell me now, is this a private fight or can I get into it?" Independent editors and other citizens had been importuning him to enter the fray. Judge Wescott warned that, if Smith ran and was elected, Dr. Wilson's "usefulness in American regeneration" would end.

Wilson had no stomach for governing a boss-ridden state, any more than he had for presiding over a university that could be directed by absentee wealth. If the party bosses were not going to leave him "absolutely free in the matter of measures and men," if they would not "work with thorough heartiness for such policies as would re-establish the reputation of the State," he felt no obligation to honor his part of the pre-election covenant—his promise not to replace the Smith organization.

Wilson sent influential go-betweens to try to dissuade Smith. Colonel Watterson of the Louisville *Courier-Journal* tried his hand at it, and failed. Cleveland Dodge brought pressure to bear indirectly and reported: "It is evident that Smith proposes to go to the Senate. I hear from a reliable source that all the Democratic Assemblymen but six are under such financial obligations to him that he owns them absolutely."

Wilson made use, also, of the good offices of his canny publisher in New York. To George Harvey he sent a letter that was composed obviously for the eyes of Smith. Again his distrust was masked by the promptings of gratitude and diplomacy. He wrote to Harvey on November 15:

I am very anxious about the question of the senatorship. If not handled right it will destroy every fortunate impression of the campaign and open my administration with a split party. I have learned to have a very high opinion of Senator Smith. I have very little doubt, that if he were sent to the Senate he would acquit himself with honour and do a great deal to correct the impressions of his former term. But his election would be intolerable to the very people who elected me and gave us a majority in the legislature . . . It was no Democratic victory. It was a victory of the "progressives" of both parties, who are determined to leave no one under either of the political organizations that have controlled the two parties of the State . . . It is grossly unjust that they should regard Senator Smith as the impersonation of all that they hate and fear; but they do, and there is an end of the matter. If he should become a candidate, I would have to fight him; and there is nothing I would more sincerely deplore. It would offend every instinct in me, except the instinct as to what was right and necessary from the point of view of public service. I have had to do similar things in the University. By the same token, ridiculous though it undoubtedly is, I think we shall have to stand by Mr. Martine . . .

Woodrow Wilson had closed the door: he had decided in favor of honesty and incompetence, against ability and what he knew, in spite of the conciliatory phrases written to Harvey, to be deceit. The letter went on:

I have stripped my whole thought and my whole resolution naked for you to see just as it is. Senator Smith can make himself the biggest man in the

State by a dignified refusal to let his name be considered. I hope, as I hope for the rejuvenation of our party, that he may see it and proceed to do so.

It is a national as well as a State question. If the independent Republicans who in this state voted for me are not to be attracted to us they will surely turn again in desperation to Mr. Roosevelt, and the chance of a generation will be lost to the Democracy: the chance to draw all the liberal elements of the country to it, through new leaders, the chance that Mr. Roosevelt missed in his folly, and to constitute the ruling party of the country for the next generation.

Gently and tactfully as the letter frustrated his ambition, Smith, nevertheless, was infuriated. By the end of November his forces had united with those of Robert Davis, and Wilson paid a surprise visit to the law office of Joseph Tumulty, Davis's friend, to ask practical advice. That astute young politician saw the intellect of the Governor-elect at work, weighing all the arguments that had come already from conservative friends, asking for the ideas of the progressives, listening avidly, with the conviction growing that in the longer, larger view both right and destiny compelled acceptance of progressive counsel.

Tumulty took Wilson to Davis's home. The plump, merry little man was dying of cancer in the house from which he had ruled Hudson County for decades. With a dramatic gesture that appealed to Irish hearts, Wilson went to the bedside of the boss and warned of the effect on the fortunes of the Democratic party if it went back on the principle of direct election that it had been advocating. Seeing a larger vision than the little men of New Jersey, Wilson was convinced that, unless there was a "new deal," the party would be put out of credit for the rest of their lives. But Davis, a man who boasted that he had never broken a promise, could only reply that he had given his pledge to Smith and that the Pope himself could not make him retract it. Suggesting a deal, Davis said that, if Wilson would keep his hands off, the bosses would support his whole legislative program. But Wilson did not trust this proposal, knowing that the prestige that would accrue to Smith from election to the Senate would undermine the Governor's influence over the legislature. In the end Davis took no strong measure to bind his men to Smith. To drive the wedge more deeply, however, Tumulty suggested that Wilson talk personally with the wavering Hudson County assemblymen. And so the delegates were invited to Prospect, and Wilson argued with them for Martine and for the popular election of senators. Only in this way, he said, could the party keep faith with the voters.

The Governor-elect was confident enough, now, to force the issue;

and Villard of the New York *Evening Post* was advising him that "from a personal point of view" he could do nothing better than to make a public declaration against Smith's candidacy. Before going to this extreme, however, Wilson called on the boss at Newark and begged him to preserve party unity by living up to the precampaign intentions that Wilson understood he had avowed. At the same time he served notice that, unless Smith withdrew by the evening of the second day, he would feel compelled to make a public announcement in favor of Martine and to oppose Smith "with every honourable means" at his command. When the boss asked whether the patronage would be used against him, Wilson replied: "No, I should not regard that as an honourable means. Besides, that will not be necessary."

Smith, who had sacrificed much for the cause of the party through the lean years and in the recent campaign, felt that he deserved better. Furthermore, Sugar Jim said, he wanted to redeem his name as a senator, for the sake of his children. It was a moving human appeal, and Wilson had genuine sympathy for the motive. But two days after the conference, having heard nothing further from the boss, Wilson wrote: "Ex-Senator Smith proves to be the tough customer he is reputed to be, and there is nothing for it but to fight him openly and to a finish. It is a hard necessity . . ." Refraining from any attack on the vulnerable political morality of his opponent, Wilson explained publicly that he felt morally bound, as elected "spokesman and adviser of the people," to tell the legislature what he deemed their duty to be in electing a senator. The preference that the people had expressed for Martine was to him conclusive, he said; and it was his opinion that it should guide the legislators.

Half an hour after releasing this public endorsement of Martine, Wilson received a letter from Smith asking for a delay of a few days. But the words could not be recalled.

Smith was surprised, hurt, then hotly indignant. He hammered upon Wilson's statement with all the arguments that his shrewd political sense could adduce. The assault on him, he said, was dictatorial, heartless, unfair. It was an "unwarranted attempt" to coerce the legislature on a matter that both state and federal constitutions had placed outside the province of the Governor, "a gratuitous attack upon one who had befriended him," and a grab at party leadership by a man who knew nothing of the toilsome grubbing for votes that built up a party and who had done nothing for the Democratic organization until he himself stood to benefit personally from its operations.

It was to be a duel on a frontier scale, fought out in Wilson's favorite medium, the free air of open publicity. One contestant inevitably would be killed, politically; the other would be supreme in New Jersey politics. And if Wilson won, the victory would take him far along the road to the Presidency.

Smith's Irish was up and he resolved to go down fighting. On December 14 he publicly announced his candidacy and his platform, in what was very nearly a vacuum of articulate sentiment.

In a powwow of progressive leaders, it was decided that the Governor-elect should stump for Martine as many times as seemed necessary. But more effective were Wilson's personal appeals to the individual assemblymen. In letters and in interviews, he revealed the full strength of his mind and heart. Even the delegates from Smith's own county came to listen to the prophet and went away impressed. "He is a great man," one of the them acknowledged, "and he talked to us as a father would."

They were veteran politicians, these men, of the sort whom Lincoln had described as "a set of men . . . who, to say the most of them, are, taken as a mass, at least one long step removed from honest men." Wilson could not meet them as a fellow frontiersman on the flat land of politics, could not add, as Lincoln had: "I say this with the greater freedom because, being a politician myself, none can regard it as personal." The Governor-elect of New Jersey never had been on the level of the ground, and below, with "the boys." He had to depend rather on the grace of his Presbyterian God to keep him humble, to make his heart beat in rhythm with the hearts of the little men from the Jersey counties. He talked as a preacher giving pastoral advice, offering no *quid pro quo,* asking the delegates merely to seek the truth and follow the dictates of conscience.

He gave these men a forthright account of his understanding of the senatorial controversy. In this, and in a statement that he released for publication, he was careless about the letter of fact. Once again, in the excitement of controversy, preoccupation with the larger issues blurred his view of the laws of evidence. When he alleged publicly that Smith had promised him, personally, not to run for the Senate, Smith challenged his truthfulness; and neither contestant wished to bring George Harvey into the dispute as a witness to what had actually been said in the conference at Deal in July of 1910.

In the heat of battle Wilson came to realize his need for an adviser who was instinctively expert in political tactics. In his safari into the political jungle Wilson wanted a guide who had grown up in its savagery. Moreover, if Smith, a Roman Catholic, should appeal to religious prejudices, it would be well for the Governor-elect to have politically enlightened men of that faith around him. And so Joseph Tumulty, who for some time had been urging Wilson to overcome his reluctance to attack Smith personally, was invited to serve as private secretary. The smart, sentimental young Irishman accepted the invitation from the man whom he had already begun to revere, and thus began a long stewardship that was to be filled to overflowing with both laughter and tears. Tumulty's bright blue eyes, yellow curls, and cherubic cheeks cheered Wilson, and his practical jokes served often to lift "the Governor" out of somber moods.

Tumulty managed the campaign of Martine; and at the beginning of 1911 it appeared almost certain that they would win. But the pace of the attack did not slacken. Smith was to be thoroughly drenched in what Wilson called "the cold bath of public opinion."

On January 5 the Governor-elect faced the first of a series of uproarious crowds. Introduced by Tumulty at Jersey City as "a great man with a great soul," he gave free rein to his caustic tongue as he damned the Smith-Nugent machine as "a wart" on the body politic and part of a domineering alliance of rascals of both parties who worked for corporate interests. The bosses had been "thrashed" at the recent election, he said, and they were "going to stay thrashed." Turning theatrically to Martine, who was sitting on the stage, Wilson begged him never, under any circumstances, to withdraw. Accepting a tactical suggestion from editor James Kerney, he spiked whispered rumors that he was anti-Catholic by citing Tumulty and others as "a group of men who illustrate in their lives and conduct not only public morality but the teachings of the great church of which they are members." Men sometimes forget, he said, "that religious principle is the one solid and remaining foundation. Find a man whose conscience is buttressed by that intimate principle and you will find a man into whose hands you can safely trust your affairs." His own heart went into the passage, he declared afterward.

In the speech at Jersey City the prophet called down the curse of war on the Philistines, and wavering minds were scorned as cowardly. It was camp-meeting evangelism, complete with everything but trumpet and choir of angels. Who was to be on the Lord's side, and therefore on the side of his true prophet? Such a harangue would have made the Princeton man of letters shudder ten years before. No college president could have put on such a performance and retained the intellectual respect of his associates. Free rein was given, now, to the spirit of extravagance that had made "Tommie" Wilson love a Pee-rade. The speech was egotistical, blatant, harsh, inaccurate—and effective!

Smith struck back immediately. Tripping up Wilson on a point of fact, he protested that his opponent talked of principle to some and of his powers to others. Referring to the diplomatic overture that Wilson had made to him privately—that a compromise candidate be named for the Senate in spite of the primary vote for Martine—Smith complained: "In private he laughs at the primary law and scowls at its 'preference.' In public he treats both as holy."[4] But this politician, who usually had been able to find human weakness through which he could work his will, was helpless before the fervor of the stampeding prophet. The people saw before them two men with contrasting records, essentially different philosophies. They already knew which man they could trust to act for the welfare of all-of-them. And great was their joy when they found that their prophet could talk their language as well as think their thoughts about such things as justice, responsibility, liberty, God.

In his last speech against Smith, Wilson let himself go as he had before the Princeton alumni at Pittsburgh. Elevating the immediate issue, he illuminated it with the fire of exalted prophecy, tracing great figures in the sky just above the horizon of his audience:

Gentlemen, what is it that we are fighting for? Does not your blood jump quicker in your veins when you think that this is part of the age-long struggle for human liberty? What do men feel curtails and destroys their liberty? Matters in which they have no voice . . . Whenever things go to cover, then men stand up and know and say that liberty is in jeopardy, and so every time a fight of this sort occurs, we are simply setting up the standard again. One can almost see the field of battle. On the one hand a fort that looks strong but that is made of pasteboard. Behind it stand men apparently armed with deadly weapons, but having only play-things in their hands. And off cowering in the distance for a little while is the great mass of fearful, free men. Presently they take heart: they look up; they begin to move slowly. You can see the dust of the plain gather. . . . And they go on, and, as in the Bible stories, the first shout of victorious and irresistible free men causes the stronghold to collapse.

In mid-January the legislature convened, and Wilson and Tumulty kept up pressure on the members until the final vote was taken. Davis had died, and Tumulty, wielding the state patronage, had little trouble

---

[4] Trenton, *True American*, Jan. 7, 1911, in Link, *op. cit.*, p. 231. Again, as in the irrational proposal to William Cooper Procter (*see* pp. 124–25 and 126 n.), a generous effort to compromise boomeranged to damage Wilson's case.

in making the party bosses in his native county see that Smith's cause was lost. Wilson was learning from his campaign-hardened secretary how to fight the devil with fire. Working all night, they put backbone into wobbly assemblymen. With Tumulty at his elbow, Wilson could now play the game of electioneering with the shrewdest. On January 25, in spite of a noisy Smith demonstration of the sort that had helped to nominate Wilson for the governorship, the legislature elected Martine by a large majority.

The victor recapitulated the battle in simple terms: "They did not believe that I meant what I said, and I did believe that they meant what they said." To the journalists, however, the controversy was a sensational drama. "Cloistered Professor Vanquishes the Big Boss!" one of them wrote: "this long-haired bookworm of a professor who had just laid his spectacles on his dictionary, came down to the Trenton State House and 'licked the gang to a frazzle.'" Only a part of the people could appreciate the message of the prophet, but all of them could love and respect a good fighter. The legislators of New Jersey now looked to the Governor as the source of patronage and an oracle of political wisdom. He was succeeding in his new milieu as extravagantly as he had triumphed in his first years as president of Princeton.

On January 17, 1911, eight days before Smith's defeat in the legislature, Wilson was inaugurated at Trenton. The ceremonies were pompous. Four prancing horses drew the landau of the Governor-elect and his predecessor from the State House to the Opera House. State troops in fancy dress marched to the beat of three bass drums. In a hall decorated with flags, evergreens, and Southern smilax, Wilson took the oath of office with his hand on the Bible, received the official seal, and, after the crowd had wildly cheered the playing of "Hail to the Chief" and seventeen guns had saluted, he was presented by the president of the Senate to the members of the legislature.

The Governor stood forth from those behind him as a man from another world. By the poise of his figure, the richness of his voice, the rugged force of his countenance, he commanded the hall to its farthest corners, more than ever a "noticeable man." For him the occasion had all the seriousness of a communion service. Under the awe of a new responsibility he departed from his custom of speaking from notes and suiting his words to the temper of the audience. This address was written out in advance, on the basis of advice from public men whom he trusted, and after long deliberation. He wished to confine himself to matters that had been prominent in the campaign and to enter office with as simple a manifesto as possible. "We have never seen a day," he said, "when duty was more plain, the task to be performed more obvious, the way in which to accomplish it more easy to determine . . ." Asserting the need for the specific reforms that had been set forth in the platform and in his open letter to Record, he developed, parenthetically but at some length, a vote-catching argument that Harvey had suggested.[5] Taking facts and figures from his adviser, Wilson accused food dealers of northern New Jersey of holding large supplies of meat and eggs in cold storage in order to keep prices high and urged the legislature to push through "some effective law of inspection and limitation."

Toward the end of his address he dwelt briefly and bluntly on economy, and committed himself to "familiar business principles so thoroughly understood and so intelligently practiced by Americans, but so seldom applied to their governments." He spoke, too, of his duty to conserve the natural resources of the state. In conclusion, he charged the legislators to serve the people, the whole people, to make their interest a constant study, and he held out to them "the satisfaction of furthering large ends, large purposes, of being an intimate part of that slow but constant and ever hopeful force of liberty and of enlightenment that is lifting mankind from age to age to new levels of progress and achievement . . ."

The speech was brief, businesslike, utterly serious. Those who knew the consistency of Woodrow Wilson's character could predict with certainty that he would press on for action, confident that the welfare of both self and party was secure only as long as the larger interests of the people were served. The scion of the preaching Woodrows and Wilsons at last had a congregation almost large enough to satisfy his zeal. He could shout joyfully, with St. Paul: "For a great door and effectual is opened unto me, *and* there are many adversaries."

[5] To keep Wilson before the nation as a progressive who must be reckoned with in the next presidential election, Harvey proposed the attack on the cold-storage interests as one that would not be too distasteful to his conservative friends in New York and yet would give evidence of Wilson's determination to put his state in such good order that the intervention of federal reformers would not be necessary. Such a proposal would be "a master-stroke at the psychological moment," Harvey assured Wilson in a letter written on Dec. 21, 1911.

CHAPTER XI

"Prime Minister" of New Jersey

As he settled into the routine of office at Trenton, Woodrow Wilson was deeply moved, he said, by his "new responsibilities as representative and champion of the common people against those who have been preying upon them." He took delight in his congregation of all sorts and conditions of men, and he felt very close to them. He was finding politics "the very stuff of life, its motives . . . interlaced with the whole fibre of experience, private and public, its relations . . . intensely human, and generally intimately personal." In a speech in November he had remarked that "a man's fortune is interesting only when it is lifted upon a great tide." Discovering that the current of popular feeling was running strongly with him, Woodrow Wilson thrived in body and spirit.

To his family the Governor-elect was still the knight in glistening armor, and for his sake they put up with danger and discomfort. Their hearts fluttered when at the inaugural ball two officers forbade guests to carry muffs or handbags, for fear of concealed weapons. Moving into a small suite in the Princeton Inn, eating in a public dining room, the Wilsons felt cramped financially as well as materially. In the absence of housekeeping duties, however, Ellen Wilson could concentrate her talents on her husband's business. She learned the tactics of politics quickly. Tumulty loved her as he had loved the mother whom he had lost. "She's a better politician than you are, Governor," he said to his chief.

One day, pestered by a fanatical idealist, Wilson remarked: "There should be a sign on the desk of every reformer: 'DON'T BE A DAMN FOOL!'" He must call a tune that his people could be persuaded to follow. And so, in aiming his program for reform legislation, the Governor restrained impulse with cold reason and concentrated on the measures most needed to give the people a healthful sense of control over their government and with it a feeling of responsibility. Realizing that the Democrats who sat in the legislature [1] would press for the passage of

[1] In the new Assembly the Democrats had a majority of 42 to 18, but at least ten of the party's assemblymen were henchmen of the fallen bosses. In the Senate the Republicans held a majority of 12 to 9, though in the Democratic minority Wilson was able to find four able spokesmen.

a certain number of petty laws, the Governor decided to throw all his own energy into the enacting of four bills that would redeem the pre-election pledges of the party by assuring (1) the expression of the will of the people through direct nomination of candidates for office, (2) the honest conduct of elections, (3) the just compensation of injured workmen, and (4) the fair regulation of public utility corporations. The day before his inauguration he invited New Jersey politicians and newspapermen to lunch with Record in New York; and he and the Republican progressive tried to imbue the men with zeal for the four measures.

Wilson had not been in office three weeks before he acted to give effect to concepts of direct democracy that appealed to the progressives of the nation.[2] He moved first for legislation that would compel respect for preferences expressed by the people in primary elections.

Soon after taking office the Governor arranged to have Record's primary and election bill introduced in the legislature, so that Smith's deceit could not be repeated and slates could no longer be rigged in secret and put over on the people. The sponsor of the proposed measure was a former student at Princeton named Geran; but behind him, campaigning among the legislators with every legitimate wile that Tumulty could devise, was Woodrow Wilson. To the Governor the battle for the Geran Bill was the senatorial contest all over again—the same forces arrayed against him and the same sort of fight needed for victory. He explained the measure in public meetings and issued this challenge: "Let no man oppose this thing unless he is willing to oppose it in public and for reasons." Sweeping aside the charges of dictatorship that Smith's newspaper leveled against him, he said: "I am not trying to run the Legislature . . . I know a majority of the members of that Legislature pretty well and I respect them thoroughly, and let me tell you that those men are going to act upon their consciences and cannot be run by anybody."

---

[2] In his inaugural speech, Wilson recommended that New Jersey's preferential primaries should be extended to every elective office, and he commended progressive laws of the state of Oregon as models.

Wilson had recently had a stimulating talk with William S. U'Ren, a progressive leader in Oregon, about the use of the initiative and referendum to force the will of the people on their representatives. In *The State,* many years before, Wilson had described these devices historically and had felt that, theoretically, they were unsound. But, though he continued to oppose the recall of judges, he had become convinced that in Oregon the initiative and referendum had proved their worth, in practice, as useful tools for an emergency. Moreover, his growing faith in direct primaries had been strengthened by testimony given to him by U'Ren. Oregon might also be a guide, he said in his inaugural, in framing new laws for the control of corrupt practices at the polls.

Having started a popular backfire, the Governor went to work on the legislators. He talked with the assemblymen individually and in groups. In a full Democratic caucus, on March 6, in which opponents hoped to kill the Geran Bill in secret, the Governor again showed that he could mix with the rank and file and talk their language. For more than half of a four-hour meeting he held the floor, answering questions, bringing to bear his academic knowledge of electoral practices in other times and other lands. When one of the party men complained that the Geran Bill would wreck the organization that had elected the Governor, Wilson insisted that the reform would strengthen the party by aligning it more exactly with the wishes of the people. The Governor had gone to the caucus without sanction of precedent, and a man of the Old Guard challenged his right to be present. There were hints, even, of impeachment. Did the Governor not respect the old American shibboleth of separation of powers? What constitutional rights had the executive to interfere in the drafting of legislation?

In the first place, Wilson replied, he conceived that the voters had made him leader of his party: they had elected him on that specific issue. Secondly, he read a passage from the constitution of the state: "The governor shall communicate by message to the legislature at the opening of each session, and at such other times as he may deem necessary, the condition of the state, and recommend such measures as he may deem expedient." He explained that he would have preferred to introduce the electoral reform bill to the legislature personally, but had used the good offices of Assemblyman Geran out of deference to regular legislative procedure. In the third place, it was in keeping with parliamentary tradition that the leader of a party should openly and personally direct the making of policy. How else could he be responsible?

"You can turn aside from the measure if you choose," he said solemnly; "you can decline to follow me; you can deprive me of office and turn away from me, but you cannot deprive me of power so long as I steadfastly stand for what I believe to be the interests and legitimate demands of the people themselves. I beg you to remember, in this which promises to be an historic conference, you are settling the question of the power or impotence, the distinction or the ignominy, of the party to which the people with singular generosity have offered the conduct of their affairs."

Woodrow Wilson was now practicing ideals of citizenship that he had been preaching for decades. He was now trying to make "free men" of politicians who had never fully sensed the glory of Greek and Anglo-

Saxon democracy. In the legislative caucus even the most hardened of the party hacks felt that they were listening to a major prophet whose appeal was to conscience rather than to self-interest. They came out of the room awed and chastened. The fight for the Geran Bill was as good as won, and it had been won by the power of the Word.

But James Nugent, who was still state chairman of the party, did not give up without trying all the stock tricks of legislative manipulation. Lurking in the offices and lobbies of the State House, he used threats and sarcasm to combat the zeal of the prophet. When the Governor politely asked the boss to keep off the floor of the legislature, of which he was not a member, Nugent went away in a huff. But Wilson took care to do nothing to give gratuitous offense; and to a reporter who rashly wrote that the Governor had "threatened to use fisticuffs" against Nugent, Wilson administered what the young newsman described as "the worst ten minutes a reporter ever had."

When assemblymen pressed for amendments to the Geran Bill, Wilson was not entirely unyielding. However, efforts by the opposition to kill the measure by shunting it to an inappropriate committee and by introducing a substitute bill were scotched. Finally, when Nugent came sullenly to the Governor's office and hinted that Wilson had used the state patronage to buy the votes of legislators, the Governor buttoned up his coat in the way that he had when ready for action, rose to his full height, swept his arm toward the door, and delivered a scorching "Good afternoon, Mr. Nugent!" Cartoonists made the most of the incident, depicting Nugent licking his wounds with Smith. "It was a most unpleasant incident, which I did not at all enjoy," Wilson confided to Mary Allen Peck; "but apparently it did a lot of good . . . I cannot help feeling a bit vulgar . . . I feel debased to the level of the men whom I feel obliged to snub. But it all comes in the day's work."

On March 21, after Record had swung vital Republican votes in favor of the Geran Bill, the Assembly passed the amended measure by a narrow margin; but difficulty was foreseen in securing its approval by the Republican-controlled Senate. Tumulty sensed that the situation called for more than logical and spiritual persuasion. His scouts among the legislators had reported that, though the lawmakers found their governor open and frank in conference, they felt that they did not really know him intimately. Wilson had made a formal talk at a dinner given to him by the senators and thought of them as "good and honest men, for the most part," though he did not then know how he would get the necessary votes from them. There were so many "personal equations" to solve that it seemed to him "a fascinating, as well as nerve-racking business."

Tumulty knew that some of the equations could be solved better by conviviality than by logic, and so he arranged an opportunity for Wilson to turn the warmth of his personality on the senators at a supper in the Trenton Country Club. Over fried chicken and waffles Wilson found the lawmakers "as jolly as boys." After exchanges of repartee a Republican senator, Walter Edge, persuaded the Governor to prance with him in a turkey trot. "This at least seems gained," Wilson wrote afterward. "I am on easy and delightful terms with all the senators. They know me for something else than 'an ambitious dictator.' " The Governor was neither a "Presbyterian priest" nor a doctrinaire professor, the legislators saw, but only a fellow who had never had chance enough to play. After the romp at the country club, Wilson felt that Republicans resorted to his office for counsel almost as freely as Democrats, and that he had "established relations almost of affection" with several.

In the Senate's deliberations on the Geran Bill, Record again entered the battle, revising the politically inspired amendments of the Assembly in order to give the measure consistency. Defending the bill in committee, he warned his fellow Republicans that they would oppose the measure at the risk of giving the Governor good ammunition to use against them when they stood for re-election in the fall. That was no empty threat; every legislator knew what Wilson might do to him in an election campaign, in full view of the people. There was such a thing as the fear of God.

The Senate adopted the Geran Bill unanimously, and the Assembly accepted the act with Record's revisions.[3] On the day of passage, the Governor was speaking in Indiana as the guest of Governor Thomas Riley Marshall, a man whom Wilson found likable. When a telegram announcing the Senate's vote came to the auditorium at Indianapolis, the toastmaster read it and the crowd cheered. Woodrow Wilson had taken another long step toward national leadership.

Once the channel of reform had been dredged and the Geran Bill launched, the floating of other measures of good government was easier. The need for electoral reform had been highlighted in the election of

[3] The Geran Law required that all elected officials and delegates to national conventions be nominated in direct party primaries. District election officials were to be chosen after examination by the Civil Service Commission and the courts were to supervise the choice of local election officials. In large cities, voters in general elections had to register in person; and provisions were made for the mailing of sample ballots and the use of an official ballot in place of a party ballot. See Laws of New Jersey, 1911, Chapter 183, pp. 276–325.

1910, when dummy voters, repeaters, and bought votes had been detected and officeholders had been lubricating the party machine with the oil of corruption. Even before the Geran Bill had become law, Record was lobbying in the Senate for a corrupt practices measure that he had drafted and that Wilson thought drastic enough to be effective. In April his bill passed both houses by unanimous votes. By its provisions, candidates for office in New Jersey had to file statements of expenditures and of personal contributions. It became illegal to hire "watchers" at the polls, to accept campaign gifts from corporations or majority stockholders, to register falsely, to stuff ballot boxes, to bet on election results. A violator of the law must forfeit his office as well as suffer other penalties.

By the time the bill providing for the regulation of public utilities came to a vote,[4] Assembly and Senate were vying with each other to have the honor of sponsoring the measure. The bill that the legislature passed—the Osborne-Egan Act—was one of the most thorough of its kind in regulating "public utilities," among which it included purveyors of transportation, communications, and domestic conveniences. A commission of three, to be appointed by the Governor with the consent of the Senate, was empowered to appraise corporation property, fix and enforce rates, and set standards of service; and the orders of the commission were to be subject to review by the Supreme Court of the state.

In achieving the enactment of his fourth bill—a measure for the compensation of disabled workmen—the Governor's powers of persuasion were taxed. The state law in this field was of the sort that Wilson described as a coat outgrown ("If you button it over the belly," he said, "it will split up the back!"). A laborer could secure recompense for injury only by bringing suit and establishing negligence on the part of his employer. The preceding governor had appointed a commission to

[4] In his inaugural Wilson had tried to clear the murky view of those who were frightened by the rapid concentration of economic power in corporate bodies. "Corporations," he said, "are no longer hobgoblins which have sprung at us out of some mysterious ambush, . . . but merely organizations . . . which have proved very useful but which for the time being slipped out of the control of the very law that gave them leave to be and that can make or unmake them at pleasure. We have now set ourselves to control them, soberly but effectively, and to bring them thoroughly within the regulation of the law." The abuse of the privilege of incorporation must be prevented, he declared. "In order to do this it will be necessary to regulate and restrict the issue of securities, to enforce regulations with regard to bona fide capital, examining very rigorously the basis of capitalization, and to prescribe methods by which the public shall be safeguarded against fraud, deception, extortion, and every abuse of its confidence . . . The matter is most obvious when we turn to what we have come to designate public service, or public utility, corporations." The Public Utilities Commission, which thus far had hardly more than powers of inquiry and advice, must be given complete regulative powers.

investigate this matter, and Republican Walter E. Edge, chairman of this body, reported to Wilson that a bill was ready for introduction into the Senate. Explaining that compulsory compensation would not be approved by the courts, Edge told the Governor that the commission had thought it best to make the plan one for optional adoption by agreement of workmen and employers. Doubtless thinking the statement as insincere as it was plausible, Wilson's impatience with legalism cropped out and he said petulantly: "I have no patience with either the Constitution or the Supreme Court." He urged Edge to accept a bill for *compulsory* benefits that a labor leader was trying to push through the Assembly. But Edge refused; and fearing a stalemate between the two houses, Wilson persuaded the assemblymen to accept the bill as it was rather than risk adjournment without action. Thus, by leading legislators to compromise, Wilson made it possible for a new compensation law [5] to take effect and completed his four-bill program for the legislature substantially as he had envisioned it.

Other reforms rode through the legislature: advances in school legislation, in the inspection of food storage and of factories, and in regulation of hours and conditions of labor for women and children. The Governor gave moral support to these measures, and nothing more was needed to assure their enactment.

Wilson was more active, however, in supporting a bill that would authorize a commission form of government for cities in which the henchmen of Smith and Nugent had taken cover.[6] His interest in this bill became keener when he was advised that this type of government was appealing to voters on his political horizon, in the Western states. In championing this measure the Governor again met resistance from entrenched interests in the municipalities, for local reform threatened the last defenses of the bosses. Nugent conspired with the Republican leader in the Assembly to secure the adoption of a crippling amendment;

[5] The Edge Act defined a schedule of benefit payments that was to take effect when employer and employee accepted them, abolished provisions of the common law behind which employers had sought immunity, and defined "willful negligence." See Walter E. Edge, *A Jerseyman's Journal*, pp. 73–75.

[6] Municipal reform was a cause that had long been close to Wilson's heart. True to form, and doubtless influenced by James Bryce's censure of the politics of American cities, Wilson had lectured at the Johns Hopkins on the superiority of the government of English cities. He had advocated making a few men responsible for municipal functions in America, integrating municipal agencies, and divorcing the judicial from other functions. Moreover, he called for universal suffrage in the election of city councils. Asserting that a city was "not an economic corporation but a humane economic society," Wilson thought it unsafe to "look to the selfish interest of leading classes alone to advance the interests of the city." See Henry W. Bragdon, "Woodrow Wilson Addresses the Citizens of Baltimore, 1896," *The Maryland Historical Magazine*, XXXVII, No. 2 (June, 1942).

and after the Democratic leader of the Senate also had capitulated to undercover influences, the progressives had to accept the Walsh-Leavitt Bill, with the emasculating provision only slightly revised. Less than half the cities of the state voted to adopt commission government.

During the session of 1911 the Governor vetoed only a few bills—usually to prevent wasteful expenditures of public money or effort or to protect the right of localities to rule themselves. In all cases his vetoes were sustained. His appointments met with the approval of the legislators; and the progressives were particularly pleased when he insisted that corporation lawyers should not be made prosecuting attorneys and when he appointed the first Jew ever to sit in the Supreme Court of the state—a man who had helped young Joe Tumulty to plead charity cases in the Jersey City criminal court, who had served individual clients against corporations, and who soon justified his appointment by finding a legal formula that made it possible to break the grip of racketeers who held the people of Atlantic City in fief. Men who were known to the Governor personally as exceptionally able and honest were brought by him into the service of the state.[7] He often asked questions about the character of men who were recommended to him; but he was too busy with larger affairs and too little interested in building a personal machine to give attention to the filling of minor offices. "The question of appointments drives me nearly distracted," he confessed, "it is so nearly impossible to get true information or disinterested advice about persons—and so many persons are trying to impose upon me. I shall get used to it, but am not yet, and it goes hard." Usually he solved the problem by telling Tumulty and other advisers to "make out a list"; and the aide used the prerogative of patronage so shrewdly that he gave substance to the charge with which Nugent had angered Wilson. When faced by demands that his appointees be removed, Wilson would endure much criticism before consenting. His Covenanting sense of loyalty could not be shaken easily; and once he had worked with a man and found him satisfactory he hated to break the relationship.

At the end of the legislative session of 1911, Wilson could justly rejoice in his debut as a responsible prime minister. He had made expert use of the prestige that had come to him from the battle with Smith.

[7] Notably Professor Winthrop M. Daniels, as a member of the Public Utilities Commission, and Calvin N. Kendall, an "outsider" to the local politicians, as head of the state's schools. Record, the Republican progressive who for years had given much time to public service without compensation, was at last recognized by appointment to the State Board of Railroad Assessors, though for a time Wilson hesitated to take this action. He had been attacked by Smith newspapers for surrendering his leadership to Record, and perhaps feared that the appointment of one who had so greatly aided his election might be regarded as a *quid pro quo*.

His zeal for civic virtue and pure democracy had cut across both party and sectarian lines. To be sure, he had not been able to realize a dream of revising the state constitution along parliamentary lines, and he had failed to persuade the Republican Senate to approve an amendment of the federal Contitution authorizing income taxes, though the Assembly ratified the measure unanimously. Nevertheless, conceding that there were still reforms to be achieved, he could point to the fulfillment by the legislature of every campaign pledge. Elated, he wrote boastfully to Mary Allen Peck: "The result was as complete a victory as has ever been won, I venture to say, in the history of the country . . . I came to the office . . . when opinion was ripe on all these matters, . . . and by merely standing fast, and by never losing sight of the business for an hour, but keeping up all sorts of (legitimate) pressure *all the time*, kept the mighty forces from being diverted or blocked at any point. The strain has been immense, but the reward is great . . . I am quietly and deeply happy that I should have been of just the kind of service I wished to be to those who elected and trusted me."

Wilson's faith in the inarticulate power of the plain people had been justified. It had become an article of religion, an understanding delicate and mystic. Yet his ardor for the good fight was not satisfied. He conceived that he was keeping himself "in training" for another bout with "the forces of greed" and prayed God for strength enough "to tip the balance in the unequal and tremendous struggle."

There were clear indications now that the prophet's voice was penetrating to ears outside New Jersey. Editors measured his achievement, the *New York Times* found it "really very great" and the Washington *Post* saw in him "a national rather than a purely local figure." However, before he won the right to serve the nation, more shots were fired in a running feud with the bosses of New Jersey's discredited Democratic machine.

James Nugent had clung to his chairmanship of the Democratic State Committee. But by the middle of 1911 his control of that body had weakened; and at a party at which liquor flowed, he shocked fellow Democrats by proposing a toast to the Governor, "an ingrate and a liar." Seeing his hold slipping, he brought strong-arm supporters into a meeting of his committee. Nevertheless, the committeemen, urged on by Tumulty, voted him out of office and replaced him with a chairman who cooperated with the Wilson forces.

Nugent's fall was only one result of the reorganization that Wilson and Tumulty effected during the summer and autumn of 1911. Actually, Grover Cleveland's prediction was coming true: the Democratic party was being made over in the image of its strongest man, the Governor of New Jersey.

Wilson was speaking now more like an avenging prophet than a servant of the people. In September, when the first primary election under the new Geran Law was to be held, he cracked the party whip repeatedly. He made a scorching attack on fraudulent voting in Essex County, but this bailiwick of Smith was the only one in which Wilson Democrats were not victorious. In Hudson County, Tumulty made enough concessions to carry the vote, and when the elected delegates met in convention they approved the Governor's policies; but when they tried to endorse Wilson for the Presidency of the nation, he opposed such a motion as inconsistent with the spirit of the new election laws of the people of New Jersey.

The next test came in the legislative election in November, and it drove him to work as hard as he had labored in the primary. His strategy was to widen the rift already made between the progressives and the regulars of the opposing party. Ridiculing the Republican machine, he called its platform "one of these old-fashioned, smooth-bore, brass-mounted affairs, that goes off like a blunderbuss . . . it has the same promises put in such phrases that they can be read backward or forward and mean the same thing; just the kind of thing you have been familiar with and never did know the meaning of." Pouring volley of sarcasm after fusillade of censure, he shamed the voters. At Atlantic City, in particular, he tried to inject the stuff of manhood into a citizenry that had been cowed by a boss who was under indictment for election frauds. "As I have stood here tonight and looked into your faces I have wondered how it feels to live under a reign of terror. How does it feel? How does your self-respect fare in the circumstance? You are my fellow-countrymen; you are men like myself . . . I have come to challenge you to self-consciousness. Have you been asleep?" He could not enforce the law, he admitted, but he could speak the truth in public. "Any gentleman who is a candidate to have his name gibbeted knows how to apply."

By and large, Wilson's speeches in this campaign lacked positive challenge to definite, constructive action. Perhaps from carelessness and overconfidence, perhaps from preoccupation with national politics, he failed to grip the imagination of the voters as securely as before. In Essex County the weak Smith-Nugent delegates, with little support from either their bosses or Wilson, were defeated by Republicans; and though in the rest of New Jersey the Democrats ran slightly ahead of their majorities of the preceding year and captured a plurality of the state vote, control of both houses of the legislature went to the Republicans.

Canny George Harvey, from his New York office, had foreseen the setback; and before the election he had sent his man Inglis to arrange a council of war. The publisher had hoped that the Governor might be persuaded to put up an umbrella against defeat by asserting before the election that the bosses of Essex County were about to try to undermine him.

Inglis caught up with the campaigning Governor in a New Jersey town and found him no longer the uncertain aspirant who had gone meekly from his summer boardinghouse to dine with the politicians at Deal in 1910. On that occasion, more than a year before, Inglis had seen a homely smile on the broad and powerful mouth, the eyes gleaming in kindness, a man "neither lacking dignity nor over-loaded with it, most companionable—in short, neighbor Wilson," lean and stringy-muscled, a Western rather than a Southern man. Now in New Jersey, however, Harvey's aide found a hardened campaigner on the warpath, a leader who walked with "stateliness" at the head of an entourage, a man with only seven hours for sleep between an evening speech and an early-morning departure for another engagement. Distantly cordial, Wilson offered his hand with a downward thrust[8] and said that he was too busy that week to give even ten minutes to his original sponsor. If Harvey would telephone his secretary, Wilson said, he might make an appointment for a few weeks later. Inglis returned to his chief with this report; and Harvey put the best face possible on the situation by analyzing the New Jersey election returns in such a way as to show that, outside of Essex County, Wilson had gained.

The legislative skies that had been so rosy were now overcast, and the Governor entered upon a six-month period that Tumulty called the "dark days." Wilson could no longer expect to dictate to the legislature. In his first message to the body in 1912 he sought not to drive but to help, to cooperate in every program that was for the common benefit. He proposed a thoroughgoing reorganization of the state's administrative agencies and the tax structure, and additional legislation in the fields of labor and public health. The Republican majorities, however,

---

[8] To protect his sensitive right hand from overzealous pumping, Wilson made it a practice to seize the other man's hand first, gingerly and from above. The effect, to William Allen White, was that of seizing "a ten-cent mackerel" and contributed to that journalist's impression of Wilson as "a cold fish." Wm. A. White, *Autobiography*, p. 479.

had no desire to pass laws that might pave Wilson's path to the Presidency of the nation; and the Governor in early 1912 was showing more interest in future prospects than in present problems. Even in his appointments he was tending more and more to favor his political allies, to strengthen the bonds of the Wilson Democrats in the state against the knives that were still wielded by Smith and Nugent. It was obvious that, if he was to win nomination to the Presidency at the Democratic National Convention, he must command the vote of New Jersey's delegation.

However, he provoked bitter enmity by vetoing fifty-seven measures—about one-tenth of those adopted by the legislature of 1912. Many of the bills were trivial and wasteful; some were attempts to emasculate the reform laws passed in 1911. Many of the veto messages were attacked by Republicans, who asserted that the measures did not get proper study because of Wilson's absence, campaigning for the Presidency. The Governor, however, brushed aside this accusation, which had some grounding in truth, as a "partisan attack" that did not take into account the physical impossibility of studying scores of bills within a few days.[9] By the end of the session the implacable streak in his nature was asserting itself and he was attributing personal maliciousness to politicians who differed with him because of loyalty to the opposing party. Woodrow Wilson found it hard to make sport of political principle: when his ideal won out, he was frankly elated, as by the great hymns of the church; and when one of his causes was buried by partisan opposition, he stood at the grave and mourned moodily.

"I am a person, I am afraid, who observes no sort of moderation in anything," Wilson once wrote of himself. It was true of his loves and his hates, of his work and his play, and especially of his dreams. After his election as governor he had been warned against self-intoxication by H. S. Pritchett, his colleague on the board of the Carnegie Foundation. "You are enough of an orator to be carried along by the sweep of your own speech," Pritchett had written. "It is a fine quality and the source of great power. It has however the danger that it betrays its

---

[9] Though Wilson left New Jersey many times in order to further his professional candidacy, his absences were so well timed that he was able to say, after the legislative session of 1912: ". . . the statement that I have by my frequent absences from the State in any degree neglected my duties as Governor, is absolutely false. No important matter of business has been allowed to fall in arrears in my office . . . I have been absent from the State only two of the session days of the legislature." See Link, *Wilson: The Road to the White House*, p. 305. He was resentful when the Senate of the state, giving the Governor the traditional dinner near the end of the session, arranged a menu in the form of a railroad timetable that poked fun at Wilson's travels.

possessor into saying things on his feet which go further than his cool judgment would permit. If you can keep a sharp eye on this it will save you from difficult situations."

By his very intemperateness, in Princeton and the state, Wilson had swept his constituency into immediate and constructive reforms. Then the momentum had been lost, mean-spirited men had undermined him, and the prophet, envisioning new mountains to climb, out on the horizon, had turned away in scorn from souls of little faith.

The spirit of the Governor rose above his stifling surroundings in Trenton, as he performed the routine duties of his office day after day. In a heavily paneled room with a tiny fireplace, a bronze Washington, rows of lawbooks, and portraits of past governors gazing solemnly from the walls, Wilson sat down each morning first to care for his correspondence and then to consider the problems of state in the order of their importance. Never a pen or a paper was out of order on his desk; and pressure of time did not fluster him. He tried a dictaphone, but his voice sounded so uncanny that he reverted to his old custom of typing many notes for himself. Sometimes he dictated more than a hundred letters in a morning, many of them at the behest of Tumulty or others well versed in political protocol. When his work permitted, he would tell jokes to whoever was at hand or stroll into the waiting room through the door that always stood open and chat with the citizens whom he found there. The Governor was trying conscientiously to be the practicing Democrat, though it went sorely against his instincts. His spirit flung itself about within him, he said, like a "wild bird in a cage." To relieve his restlessness he would turn in his swivel chair and look through the window on the muddy Delaware and the tides of traffic moving up and down State Street. Afternoons were consumed by tedious conferences and public hearings, and it was not until evening that he could be alone to concentrate on putting his ideas meticulously in order.

Even in the summer there was little privacy for a public man. At the stuffy executive cottage at Sea Girt on the Jersey coast, where as a concession to popular prudery a naked Narcissus had to be removed from the front hall, the Governor spent part of his Sundays perched on a horse—wearing a high hat and frock coat—while troops marched by on the adjoining parade ground. Or he would sit on the piazza confronting the breech of a gun, a row of military officers, and an official chaplain.

Here and there people began to trade on his name. Clubs and fraternal orders competed for his presence at their functions; photographers delighted to catch him with a hot dog in his mouth; and when he failed to attend the field day of the Woodrow Wilson Club of Trenton, the gate receipts slumped and in petulance the club changed its name. Sometimes, when his emotions were worn by inescapable appearances at state institutions, his wit stiffened his nerve: he said that, in the home for epileptics, three were driven to fits by his speech.

Wilson's daughters were now away from home much of the time, pursuing their interests in music, painting, and social work; and in the autumn of 1911, moving from the cramped quarters in the Princeton Inn, the family shared a house in Cleveland Lane with Lucy and Mary Smith. A half-timbered dwelling, with bay windows and fireplaces, and a studio and a garden that enchanted Ellen Wilson, it evoked memories of the old, carefree days in the beloved home on Library Place. But when he looked at the Hibben house next door or walked about the town, Wilson thought he detected hostility from those whom he had loved and sought to serve. He felt a lump in his throat and could have wept from disappointment and pity. Nevertheless, in his new home he hoped to find contentment. Commuting to this haven from his office at Trenton, the Governor delighted in the comradeship of relatives and guests. Vivacious Lucy Smith and her sister chatted and read with Ellen Wilson and conspired with the girls to relieve their father and mother of anxieties. Mary Allen Peck paid a visit and smoked cigarettes so charmingly that the Wilsons could not take offense, but she seemed to the Wilson girls overfastidious about clothes and too boastful of her gentlemen friends.

The face of Woodrow Wilson, which had flexed in comic grimaces in earlier years, had now set in a rigid "official" mask; yet smile lines suggested the old jesting spirit that was still alive, and it often shone out. Once when a Negro butler announced pompously, "Dinner is now being served in the dining room," Wilson caught the arm of his daughter Nell and swayed through the hall in imitation of a passenger on a railroad train. On occasion his eyes could still twinkle. Introduced at a meeting as "a plain man and learned statesman," he repeated a favorite limerick:

> "For beauty, I am not a star;
> There are others handsomer, far;
> But my face—I don't mind it,
> For I am behind it;
> 'Tis the people in front that I jar."

Often he conjured up "the night and sweet radiant spaces, the familiar houses and scenes of dear Bermuda." He wrote almost every Sunday to Mary Allen Peck, who personified that idyllic spot and whom he idealized as a paragon of misunderstood virtue. "Sometimes," he confided to her, ". . . my whole life seems to me rooted in dreams—and I do not want the roots of it to dry up. I lived a dream life (almost too exclusively, perhaps) when I was a lad and even now my thought goes back for refreshment to those days when all the world seemed to me a place of heroic adventure, in which one's heart must keep its own counsel while one's hands worked at big things."

The Governor of New Jersey found escape both near and far, in nature human and inanimate. He invited witty people to joke with him at luncheon in a Trenton restaurant, where he took a side table and was embarrassed by special attention from the waiters. With Tumulty and favorite journalists he walked for miles in the park and along the river. Sometimes he sought relief in losing his identity in a crowd, on the street, or at an athletic contest.

Of all the pleasures to which Wilson's passionate dreaming led him, none was greater than that of turning to "the friend with whom you never have to consider a phrase or a thought—with whom you can *let yourself go!*" The ideal of perfect friendship—a relationship that was "all largess," with nothing given from a sense of duty—was not one that he could give up, even after the disillusionment that he had suffered at Princeton.

The wound of that experience was still sore and open.

Wilson and his friends tried to bring about the election of Fine to the presidency of the university. The choice of Hibben, he thought, ought to be prevented at all hazards because no one else would so lay the dear university at the mercy of the "reactionary forces." To the ex-president the campus was now a blighted spot, inhabited by depressed scholars. The legality of the golf links as a site for the graduate college was approved by the chancellor of the state, Pyne and Procter made additional gifts, and ground was broken for Andrew West's enterprise. Early in 1912, Hibben was chosen as the administrator most likely to draw together the West and Fine factions. "The worst has happened at the University," Wilson lamented. West remained dean of the grandiose new graduate college, and Wilson felt that Hibben never would be strong enough to achieve greatness for Princeton.

As governor of the state, Wilson was also president ex officio of the board of trustees of the university, and protocol demanded that he attend the inauguration of Hibben in May of 1912. But the prophet could not so prostitute his intellect. "If I say what is in my heart and mind the dinner would end in a riot," he told a friend. "If I get up and indulge in the usual platitudes, the words would stick in my throat." He felt like a "runaway," he said, and "ungenerous," and staying away was hard for a man who took pride in the grim performance of duty. Not trusting his emotions, he arranged to be out of the state on the day of the inauguration. Reasoning it out, he concluded: "Perhaps it is better to love men in the mass than to love them individually!"

During the governorship, Wilson's intimates were women of wit and fine understanding. In repartee and persiflage with these ladies he found emotional release without fear of tragic conflict between friendship and public duty, without risk that what he called the "sensitive chain" of complete understanding might snap under the tension that a Covenanter's conscience placed on it. Had Woodrow Wilson always lavished his unreasoning passion for friendship on none but women, he might have been spared much suffering.

It seemed that his love would never be given again to any man as it had been poured out to Hibben. His associates in the business of government were not men whom he could take to his heart. Tumulty he liked, Record he respected for his clear intellect and devotion to the cause of good government. But these men lacked the grace of soul and the mellowness of philosophy in which a harried executive could find sanctuary.

And then, in the autumn of 1911, Woodrow Wilson met Edward Mandell House.

From the beginning the men were drawn toward each other. Like Wilson himself, House had been possessed in his youth by a passion to take part in great affairs. He had entered Cornell University but had not been graduated, for he had slighted his studies and had spent much time with friends at Washington just to be near the center of things. Like Wilson, he could recollect the horror of Civil War and Reconstruction in the South. Young Edward had thrived on mischief and on boyish games that were played with firearms, and twice he had almost killed playmates. When only twelve years old, he had fallen on his head from a swing and his health had been impaired permanently. Never strong enough himself to carry the ball in the political game, and lacking powers of oratory, he had shown genius in managing other players from the bench; and in applying New England capital to the development of a railroad in Texas, he had held the confidence of financiers and had become an expert in public relations. In a society in which a single discordant word might provoke a volley of bullets, the gentle-spoken, trouble-scenting little man had kept on friendly terms with hot-blooded frontiersmen without using the six-shooter that he sometimes carried. Governor Hogg, whose campaign for political reform had been furthered by House in 1892, had made his adviser a "colonel" on his staff; and, much to the distress of its recipient, the title had stuck.

For almost twenty years, from his hospitable porch on the hill at Austin, Colonel House had manipulated political candidacies without making enemies and had gained a reputation for sagacity. He read widely and observed keenly. His touch upon the affairs of the state was sensitive, devious, deft, and at times bold.

In 1910 the Colonel sensed the political opportunity of the hour for his party and was seeking a national leader to whom he might render the same service that he had given freely to governors of Texas. He was seeking, specifically, an Eastern man who would be acceptable to William Jennings Bryan of Nebraska, without whose approval, House felt, no Democrat could hope to be nominated for the Presidency. Like Wilson, he had given up Bryan on the currency question as "not susceptible to argument"; yet in a practical, reasonable way, the Colonel's own convictions on many matters of public policy were as progressive as those of Nebraska's "Great Commoner." He took pride in asserting that in municipal reform Texas led the way; and he was proud of progressive measures that Governor Hogg had advocated, such as laws regulating securities and the railroads. He had worked for reforms, not for Texas alone but in the hope that they might be taken up by the country at large.

By the summer of 1911, even before he met Wilson, Colonel House had fixed his mind on the Governor of New Jersey, not as the man "best fitted" to be president but as "the best man who can be nominated and elected." In the fall there were exchanges of letters between the men; and House, through Thomas W. Gregory, urged the Governor to accept an invitation to speak in Texas.[10] Moreover, ascertaining that

---

[10] Cf. 211 below. Thomas W. Gregory was a lawyer at Austin who had served the state of Texas as special counsel in prosecuting corporations for violating antitrust laws. Thomas B. Love, commissioner of insurance and banking in Texas, already had been working for Wilson and had promised that an invitation would be given to visit that state in the fall of 1911. Love to W.W., Dec. 1, 1910. Love told Ray Stannard Baker that Texas would have supported Wilson even if House had never existed and claimed that he had given more money to the cause than had House.

House's support of Wilson in Texas was less obvious than Love's for a reason that is ex-

Wilson had voted for the Democratic candidate in the last three presidential elections, he assured Texans, through Senator Culberson, of the party regularity of the Governor. The effectiveness of Wilson's address in Texas strengthened the colonel's interest in him as a presidential candidate. Then, on November 24, House's judgment was put to the test of a personal interview.

When Wilson went alone to New York to meet the Texan, who had been commended to him by George Harvey, he found a short, slight gentleman dressed in good taste, a man who walked with a firm, easy step and whose words seemed as unobtrusive and as well groomed as his gray mustache. Only a few months before, Wilson had written to Mary Allen Peck that, now that he was in politics, he was careful of *everybody*. But in an hour's talk, and in subsequent visits, House's friendliness broke down the monitoring caution. The Texan's soft speech and eager listening drew out the Scotch-Irish heart from under its shield of formality. Here was a counselor more soothing and respectful than Harvey—the high-strung, calculating Yankee. Moreover, the Texas colonel had an instinctive understanding of the Old South and at the same time shared the aspirations of the West. And the man's record of friendly service showed that he wanted nothing for himself but the delight of serving.

For his part House, physically handicapped but still ambitious to be in the thick of affairs, saw in Wilson a man with power to put wise counsel into action, a voice through which an adviser could speak effectively to the nation and to history. The colonel was captivated by a warmth of heart and strength of intellect such as he had never seen in the politicians of his own state. The day after the meeting he wrote to his wife's brother-in-law, President Sidney Mezes of the University of Texas: "We had a perfectly bully time. He came alone, so that we had an opportunity to try one another out. He is not the biggest man I have ever met, but he is one of the pleasantest and I would rather play with him than any prospective candidate I have seen. From what I had heard, I was afraid that he had to have his hats made to order;

---

plained in an entry in House's diary, Oct. 6, 1921. "Texas headquarters would have closed," the Colonel wrote, "if I had not sent Gregory to Cato Sells, who was the nominal manager, to tell him that he, Gregory, would guarantee Sells the expenses. My name was not mentioned because I feared they would be extravagant if they knew I was the real sponsor." Diary of Edward M. House, House Collection, Yale University Library, hereafter referred to as House Diary. Regarding House's work in Texas, Gregory said to Ray Stannard Baker on May 29, 1928: "I have never seen such a revolt against the duly constituted officials and machinery of a political party."

but I saw not the slightest evidence of it . . . Never before have I found both the man and the opportunity."

Within the next week they dined together alone, and they were soon exchanging confidences. Wilson felt the stimulus that always came to him from what he called "the laying of minds alongside each other." Encouraging each other to talk frankly, they found that, while their natures were complementary, their thoughts ran in agreement on most of the issues of the day.

Although ill that winter, House worked intensely in Texas while at the same time exerting his influence—always quiet, persistent, unofficial —upon national leaders of the party. He had a way of insinuating ideas into the minds of dull men so that they took pride in them as their own. He was wise enough never bluntly to oppose Wilson on a matter of principle or policy: when he differed he kept silent or else argued so subtly that Wilson could not take offense. When, for example, he presumed to advise his friend on tariff policy—a subject on which the Governor spoke with the pride of competence—he used as his mouth-piece a man whom Wilson might respect as a professional.[11]

The Wilsons quickly perceived House's peculiar gifts for confidential service—his capacity for objective and analytical thought, his discretion and disinterestedness, his tact and persuasiveness in contacts with politicians with whom a presidential candidate had to deal.

[11] David F. Houston, formerly president of the University of Texas, was placed next to Wilson at a dinner party, after House had reviewed Houston's academic theories on the tariff with the purpose of making them more comprehensible to the general public. Wilson's views on the tariff probably were little changed, though the occasion may have influenced him to give an important speech on the subject to the National Democratic Club a month later. But, at House's dinner, Houston was completely won by Wilson. The next day he wrote: "Wilson is the straightest-thinking man in public life, and can say what he thinks better than any other man . . . I am for him. Wilson is clean, courageous, and disinterested." And of House he wrote: "He has a vision. I should like to make him Dictator for a while . . ." Dr. D. F. Houston to Dr. S. E. Mezes, Dec. 11, 1911, in Charles Seymour, *The Intimate Papers of Colonel House*, I, 48. Hereinafter this four-volume work is referred to as *House Papers*.

CHAPTER XII

Candidate for the Presidency

By the spring of 1911 the Governor, through the brilliance of his campaign against Smith and his leadership of the New Jersey legislature, had made himself a popular American hero. On the national scene, in 1910, the Democrats won the House of Representatives for the first time since 1892 and secured the governorships in several states that were normally Republican. But in all the country no effort was more vital than Wilson's. He had done more than anyone, the New York *World* asserted, "to raise the political, moral, and intellectual level of the campaign"; and Theodore Roosevelt's *Outlook* acknowledged that Wilson, as the leader of the progressive movement in New Jersey, deserved to be elected. Wilson-for-President clubs had sprung up spontaneously. Encouragement and pledges of support had come in innumerable letters and telegrams from personal friends, educators, journalists, former students at Princeton, idealistic strangers. Colonel Harvey, perceiving the set of the journalistic tide, had written to his candidate late in 1910: "The pebble chucked into the pool has produced, not ripples, but waves."

As in the case of the New Jersey governorship, Wilson was a reluctant candidate for the Presidency. He protested that he was incorrigibly simple in his tastes, that while he would love to have a hand upon the affairs of the world, he shrank from the harness and trappings of high office. Tactically, it was still too early for a "boom"; moreover, a series of diplomatic crises around the Mediterranean had inflated his doubt of his adequacy. Wilson thought he would know better where he stood in the estimation of the people after a few public appearances in various states. Feeling a bit like a race horse, he allowed the National Democratic Club to size him up at Philadelphia and gave them a speech that led Judge Wescott, now fully converted, to write to Tumulty: "I pronounce it greater than the immortal efforts of Demosthenes . . . this personalized force has a great destiny."

In March of 1911, Wilson invaded Georgia to address the Southern Commercial Congress on "The Citizen and the State." Dejectedly, almost shamefacedly, he told himself that his only reason for going to Atlanta was because it was "politic." His conscience was in revolt. He feared even that he would not speak well, so self-interested was his motive. Old Judge Hillyer, who had licensed him to practice law back in 1882, introduced him as "a man who is going to be President of the United States," and the orator appealed to the South to "take its place in the councils of the nation." The audience of eight thousand responded with an ovation that Wilson thought better than those given to the other speakers—Theodore Roosevelt and President Taft. He was enheartened, and before leaving Atlanta he made tentative plans for a campaign in his behalf in Georgia.

A few weeks later he spoke at Norfolk with the feeling that the South was still essentially conservative. His conscience told him that, now conceiving himself a "radical" who would go to the roots of good government, he should speak out to prevent his boyhood neighbors from voting for him under the misapprehension that he was a standpat favorite son. Pleading for free speech and for exposure of corruption in government and in business, he pleased the agrarian progressives of the South as much as he alarmed the reactionaries who were hoping to deliver the delegates of the region to Governor Harmon of Ohio. And yet conservatives saw that, if they could not make Western Democrats accept Harmon, Wilson offered an alternative more safe and sane than Bryan.

It was apparent, in 1911, that to receive the presidential nomination a candidate must win the approval, if not the active support, of Bryan. Three times, in lean years, that peerless orator had carried the party's standard unsuccessfully in the presidential race; but of the 1912 campaign he said to his wife when she urged him to run again: "This may be the year for a Democrat to win. The other boys have been making their plans. I would not step in now."

Like Wilson, the Great Commoner was the son of both the frontier and the South, a zealous Presbyterian who led his family in morning prayers and could orate in Biblical figures. He was Scotch-Irish, too, with more of the Irish than ran in Wilson's blood. He thought untidily, his letters were scrawled to the very edges of the paper, and his oratory appealed chiefly to the emotions. From the age of twenty he had been a political campaigner, but never a responsible administrator. He could rouse a Western audience and hold its devotion to a cause as no American had done since Patrick Henry; but in the science of government he was, by Princeton standards, ignorant. He terrified responsible men in the large cities—"the enemy's country." They thought him a fanatic, bent on denuding every man who wore a clean shirt. In his presidential campaigns he had shaken confidence in New York by threatening to avenge from the White House what he considered to be wrongs committed by "the money power."

In Wilson, Bryan saw a new power in the East to be reckoned with. He rejoiced in the fight to democratize Princeton and sent a congratulatory telegram after the New Jersey elections. He could not quite forgive the Princeton professor for opposing the crusade for free silver in 1896, but approved his attitude toward legislation in 1911. The Nebraskan had sounded the depth of the progressivism of the new aspirant by sending him a copy of the Democratic platform of 1908 and asking for comments on its planks. Receiving a general endorsement, he went further, and asked the Governor to urge New Jersey's legislature to approve the adoption of the income tax amendment to the federal Constitution. When Wilson acted promptly on this suggestion, Bryan was more fully persuaded that the Governor's progressivism was no superficial gloss.[1]

Two years before this, Wilson had thought of Bryan—"The Great Inevitable"—as "the most charming and lovable of men personally, but foolish and dangerous in his theoretical beliefs"; and he had refused to speak from the same platform with the Nebraskan, explaining that what he would be obliged to say would introduce "a most inharmonious note." Yet, though thinking of Bryan's remedies for the country's economic maladies as mere nostrums, he could not, he said, quarrel with a large part of his diagnosis.

In the spring of 1911 the two great prophets of the party were preaching each his own gospel, but developing all the while a deeper respect for the voice and spirit of the other. It was Ellen Wilson who set the stage for the harmonizing of their tongues. Hearing that Bryan was to speak at the Princeton Theological Seminary on March 12, she telegraphed her husband to hurry home from Atlanta and arranged an intimate dinner at the Princeton Inn. There the two giants—the veteran campaigner and the aspirant—sat down for the first time together and capped each other's stories and confirmed each other in pastoral faith

---

[1] There were indications, as early as 1910, that Bryan might approve Wilson as a presidential candidate. Thomas B. Love, who had been trying to ascertain the attitude of Bryan, reported to Wilson that a mutual friend had told him that Bryan felt that Wilson was "covering himself with glory" in the fight against Smith. Love to W.W., Dec. 19, 1910. Another correspondent called Wilson's attention to a statement by Bryan in the current number of his journal, the *Commoner,* to the effect that Wilson was one of the four Democrats qualified as presidential timber. R. W. Jennings to W.W., Dec. 30, 1910.

in the great American congregation. Bryan's concept of Wilson as a cold scholar was challenged, though not eradicated, by the Governor's wit and spirits. Discussion of controversial issues was avoided, and the pleasantness of the occasion stirred Tumulty to tell Mrs. Wilson that she had as good as nominated her husband for the Presidency. And when Bryan spoke that evening at Alexander Hall, Wilson found him "a truly captivating man."

Three weeks later Bryan shared a platform with the Governor at a local Democratic rally and for the first time heard Wilson talk. Each spoke of the other as a preacher welcoming a visiting brother to a pulpit. Wilson testified: "Mr. Bryan has borne the heat and burden of a long day . . . it is because he has cried America awake that some other men have been able to translate into action the doctrines that he has so diligently preached." And the Great Commoner responded with what Wilson's promoters most wanted to hear: "Our hopes in the West are raised by Governor Wilson's record." [2]

If Wilson wanted the nomination he would have to convince Bryan's people of the sincerity of his concern for their welfare and, moreover, he would have to do this without alienating all the conservatives of the East and the South. The force of this necessity already had impressed three promoters—Walter Hines Page; [3] Walter McCorkle, who had just been chosen president of the Southern Society in New York; and William F. McCombs, a New York lawyer who had studied under Wilson at Princeton and idolized his former teacher as "a red-blooded man . . . a fighting man . . . the young man's man."

These three Southerners convinced Wilson that, in order to get the necessary support of Western delegates to the Democratic convention in 1912, he would have to talk to the people of the West. Among them,

[2] Trenton *True American*, April 6, 1911. Several weeks later Bryan gave further evidence of his deepening respect for the younger prophet, writing to Speaker Champ Clark: "Wilson is making friends because he *fights*. His fight against Smith was heroic . . . The people like a fighter . . . The right wins in the end . . ." Bryan to Champ Clark, May 30, 1911, in *The Memoirs of William Jennings Bryan*, p. 336. Bryan was disappointed by Clark's lack of aggressiveness and, later, by his inability to control his managers.

Bryan had doubts about Wilson's fitness as an executive. Visiting George Harvey, the Nebraskan warned against too exclusive commitment to Wilson, whom he still thought "an autocrat by training." The Great Commoner predicted: "If he should be elected president, everybody else would have to be a servant. Neither you nor I nor anybody else having self-respect could serve a full term in his cabinet. And when he got through there wouldn't be any Democratic party left. There might be a Wilson party, but the old Democracy would be gone." Bryan, however, gave Harvey the impression that either Clark or Wilson would be an acceptable candidate.

[3] In February of 1911, Wilson had sent McCorkle and other inexperienced impressarios to Page for "hard headed advice." Page, then editing *World's Work*, sent one of his journalists to "write up" the Governor of New Jersey. Wilson himself had no flair or enthusiasm for writing promotional articles.

they raised $3,000 and hired a publicity agent to arrange a speaking trip to the Pacific coast.

At the beginning of May, Wilson set out with his agent to meet the people of the Western states and to speak to representative organizations of businessmen. With them went a journalist representing the Baltimore *Sun*. While other candidates, such as Congressman Underwood and Speaker Champ Clark, worked down from Congress through party leaders, the prophet set forth with his two comrades into the grass roots, lugging a huge suitcase with his own hand. Never before had he been west of Denver; and he was intensely curious about what he saw and heard along the way. He rode in an open section so that he could meet his fellow travelers, and he shaved and rubbed elbows in the washroom. He would get off at stations and walk and take breathing exercises; and on a cold morning he delighted his comrades by dancing a hornpipe. Something in his blood was thrilled by the enterprise of the Westerners. These were the men of whom Turner had written and from whose stock Wilson's American heroes had sprung. He felt at home in their country, spoke of the West as the most genuinely American part of the nation.

To get good space in the newspapers, his agent wanted to give out advance copies of speeches. Wilson protested, however, that it was not his custom to write out his addresses in full and that the whole game of publicity repelled him. Finally, he was induced to prepare tentative drafts a week in advance, but usually he departed from them when he faced audiences and took their pulse and temperature. Only when his manager insistently reminded him that he was a national figure did he consent to talk with reporters who were not satisfied with the mere text of his speeches.

In his first address, delivered at Kansas City, Missouri, to a gathering in which Republicans predominated, Wilson set the keynote for his tour. He described his mission as the awakening of his congregation to the welfare of the whole nation, the conditioning of their spirits to the weather of progressive adjustment. Things do not stand still, he said, they go forward or backward. Sound politics demanded reasoned change in everything except the very principle of change. His remarks so frightened party leaders in the East that they later omitted the text of this speech from their campaign publicity. For example, the popular initiative and referendum and the recall of administrative officials, which Bryan and Theodore Roosevelt already had endorsed, were boldly recommended now by Wilson, not as a substitute for legislative action but rather as a means of taking government out of the hands of machines and restoring it to the people. Americans of both parties, he asserted at Kansas City, had been cheated by their own political machinery in the field of industrial action, and the liberty of individuals was being hampered and impaired. Though speaking in nonpartisan terms, he did not fail to assert that "the Democratic party is more in sympathy with the new tendencies." A demagogue without conscience, he warned, "could put this whole country into a flame"; as for himself, he was advocating "fundamentally conservative processes." What was needed, he declared, was an "alignment of all men free and willing to think, and to act without fear upon their thought."

Wilson's straight talk was refreshing to his Western audiences. Here was a man of learning who understood their problems and spoke their language. His prescriptions for reform fell as "cooling good sense," one editorial writer said, on the demagogue-ridden people of the West. And the candidate, for his part, rejoiced in the feeling that they liked him and accepted him as genuine.

On May 7, by lucky chance, the prophet had an opportunity to touch a chord in the Westerner on which Bryan knew so well how to play. Expecting to speak to a small Presbyterian congregation at Denver in celebration of the tercentenary of the King James version of the Bible, Wilson found that the meeting had been moved to the municipal auditorium, where the governor of Colorado would introduce him. Having only an hour in which to prepare an address worthy of the occasion, he felt utterly abashed when he confronted an audience of twelve thousand, with only a few notes in hand.

In the emergency he fell back on what was bred most deeply within him—the Presbyterian concept of man's relation to God. He wished to talk of the Bible, he declared, as "the people's book of revelation . . . a book which reveals men unto themselves, not as creatures in bondage, not as men under human authority, not as those bidden to take counsel and command of any human source. It reveals every man to himself as a distinct moral agent, responsible not to men, not even to those men whom he has put over him in authority, but responsible through his own conscience to his Lord and Maker. Whenever a man sees this vision he stands up a free man, whatever may be the government under which he lives, if he sees beyond the circumstances of his own life."

Calling the Bible the " 'Magna Carta' of the human soul," he went on: "Nothing makes America great except her thoughts, except her ideals, except her acceptance of those standards of judgment which are written large upon these pages of revelation . . . Parties are reformed and governments are corrected by the impulses coming out of the hearts of those who never exercised authority and never organized parties." Those impulses were the sources of strength, he said, in "that untiring and unending process of reform from which no man can refrain and get peace." He challenged every man and woman in the audience to baptize his soul in daily perusal of Holy Scripture.

The Christian soldiers of progressivism, their thoughts marching onward in step with the prophet's, saw in his leadership the coming of the Lord. One of the great forensic triumphs of his life and the culmination of the wooing of the Word by generations of Woodrows, the Denver speech was taken down by a stenographer and circulated during the next year to more than a million readers. Better perhaps than any other utterance, it revealed to the people the moral mainsprings of the candidate's character.

After two more speeches, Wilson was the hero of the city. On the day on which telephone communication was opened with New York, Denver reported: "The town is wild over Woodrow Wilson and is booming him for President."

The prophet had arrived on a local train and walked to his hotel carrying his own bag. Leaving on a day coach, he had a frugal lunch of fruit at the railroad station. But thenceforth the trip was a Roman triumph. At San Francisco, alumni of Princeton, Yale, and Harvard sponsored a dinner for which invitations went out on the stationery of a street railway company that had a finger on the city's politics. Hiram Johnson, the progressive governor, stayed away; and Wilson was advised not to identify himself with "the interests" by attending. Characteristically, he was made only the more eager to attend. He pricked the consciences of the businessmen and made them like it.

Visiting Portland next, Wilson won Oregon for good and all. At a dinner at the University Club he let loose a diatribe on clubmen, and then challenged his hosts to invest their "capital of heart and mind" in the service of the world. They thought him a great man because he dared to criticize the social obtuseness of those who posed as the elect and all-powerful of their state. "Wilsonism is today one of the largest facts in American life," a local journal proclaimed. "It is popular leadership with a safety valve. It is popular government with a balance wheel. It is statesmanship without demagogy . . ." Talking with U'Ren, the reformer who had convinced the theorizing Princeton professor of the value of the initiative and referendum, Wilson studied the "Oregon system" of direct government and heartily congratulated the citizens for "breaking the machine." At the same time he pleased his more conservative adherents in the East by remarking, to a New York reporter, that the system was not necessarily applicable to states where different conditions prevailed.

Wilson carried his scholarly point of view into Minnesota, where he spoke in the twin cities and received the state's military salute. Here the approval of leading Bryan Democrats came to the candidate; and he further identified himself with the cause of the Great Commoner by praising that leader at Lincoln, Nebraska—Bryan's home town. The orator himself was away on a speaking trip in New Jersey, but he sent a cordial telegram. His wife entertained Wilson, his brother contributed to the campaign fund, and the candidate responded with a gorgeous flight of eloquence that brought the audience to its feet and marked the speaker as a fellow crusader of their hero. But visiting the home of the Great Commoner, where a hodgepodge of political trophies was strewn about the room, Wilson thought the place resembled "a cross-section of Mr. Bryan's mind."

Wilson sensed at first hand the spirit of revolt that was agitating the West. The Socialist mayor of a town in Nebraska—a railroad laborer clad in jumpers—boarded the train and explained that he had been elected by a vote that was 20 per cent Socialist and 80 per cent protest. This seemed to sum up the feeling of the country. "Taft will be renominated by the Republicans," Wilson said. "Unless the Democrats nominate someone whom the people can accept as expressing this protest, there will be a radical third party formed and the result may be little short of a revolution."

Was the prophet now ready to consider himself a candidate for the Presidency? He asked himself the question many times. Away from his dear ones, traveling in a man's world, his conscience was gradually possessed by his own words. His sense of commitment to the congregations that he had addressed had grown until, on the long train ride across the Northwest, he said to his associates: "I do want to be president and I will tell you why: I want this country to have a president who will do certain things. There are men who could do these things better than I can. Of that I am sure; but the question is, *would they do them*? . . . I am sure that I will at least try to the utmost to do them."

But there were moments, too, when his thoughts withdrew into the inner temple of the scholar, into the Valley of the Doones. As a man—

a husband and father—he did not want to be president. "It means giving up nearly everything that one holds dear," he said. "The Presidency becomes a barrier between a man and his wife, between a man and his children. He is no longer his own master—he is a slave on the job. He may indulge no longer in the luxury of free action or even free speech."

En route to Washington he visited old Columbia, where as a boy he had watched his elders wage a brave battle for political order. Talking with the widow of his adored Uncle James Woodrow, he was overcome again by the foreboding that had once struck him on a beach in Bermuda.

"Now, Tommie," said his aunt, to whom "politics" was a career unworthy of a Woodrow, "what's all this talk about your running for the Presidency?"

"Aunt Felie," he replied, "I can only tell you this. If I am nominated, I'll be elected; and if I'm elected, I won't come out of the White House alive." [4]

Though at that time Wilson made no public statement of his intentions, it was generally understood when he returned to the East that he was a candidate in the fullest sense. He had identified himself, in the minds of millions of Western voters, with the cause of popular government; and he had shown himself a sincere "progressive" rather than a "radical." He had stimulated a gestation of opinion at the grass roots. Some of the political leaders, even, had come to think that the Wilson band wagon now had enough momentum to assure them of a good ride. There was a movement in Indiana toward the Governor of New Jersey; a senator from Oklahoma announced his support; and an informal poll of a group of Democrats in the House of Representatives showed four-fifths for Wilson. And so the pioneering solo flight into the West had cultivated ground from which in good time wonderful fruit was to sprout.

Turning north from Columbia, Wilson conferred with Josephus Daniels at Raleigh.[5] He reached Washington on June 4, 1911, having made thirty-three speeches in nine states. He was welcomed by Page and McCombs and Tumulty, who were enheartened by the response

[4] James Woodrow, who heard the conversation, to the writer, June, 1949; also Woodrow to Lewis, Sept. 9, 1950, Lewis Papers (Princeton University Library).

[5] Daniels had been for years a loyal Bryan Democrat, but shortly before Wilson's visit to Raleigh in 1911 he had met George Harvey at a shooting party. Harvey had taken the opportunity to plead for Wilson and, sizing up Daniels as a man who could be influenced by flattery, he had directed that a page of *Harper's Weekly* be given to celebration of an anniversary of Daniels's editorship of the Raleigh *News and Observer*.

of the people in the West and were now impatient to organize a national campaign.

But still Wilson hung back. First he wanted to talk with other potential candidates, especially with Congressmen Champ Clark of Missouri and Oscar Underwood of Alabama. The latter's handling of tariff legislation had led Wilson to hope that he might retire from the race in favor of the Alabaman; but after a conference he felt forced to conclude that Underwood was not emotionally committed to the fundamentals of democracy. And when Clark called on him, Wilson did not change his opinion that the Missourian was "a sort of elephantine smart Aleck." There seemed to be no escape from the conclusion that, if the American people were to be led along paths of reason and justice, Wilson could not indulge his desire to direct the drama off stage. He would have to face the music himself. Finally, he yielded to his promoters to the extent of allowing them to answer the heavy mail that now was coming to him. Fearing to create an impression of having "descended into the arena," he consented merely to the opening of a "bureau of information." [6]

During the summer the little group of managers was joined by another Southerner—a descendant of men of the Tennessee hills who believed in Judgment Day and of dueling planter-generals who had fought Indians with Andrew Jackson. One of seven children of a university professor, William Gibbs McAdoo had made his own way as a lawyer at Chattanooga until a street railway that he was promoting fell into bankruptcy. Taking his family to New York in 1892, in debt and without influence, he had learned the ways of corporate finance. It became clear to him that the center of gravity in the field of statecraft had shifted from the political to the economic plane. Hoping both to make money and to serve society, he undertook to promote the building of tunnels under the Hudson River. On the one hand, he held the confidence of financiers; at the same time, he developed and man-

---

[6] W.W. to Page, June 7, 1911. Wilson gave these instructions to Stockbridge: "I am not to be put forward as a candidate for the Presidency. No man is big enough to seek that high office. I should not refuse it if it were offered to me, but only if the offer came from the people themselves; no man is big enough to refuse that. You must not ask anyone to say a word or print a line in my behalf. Confine your activities to answering requests for information." Frank P. Stockbridge, "How W.W. Won his Nomination," *Current History*, July, 1924.

Rooms were rented at 42 Broadway and Stockbridge's name was put on the door. The bureau collected news clippings, which by August came in at the rate of 20,000 a week, and printed and distributed cuttings from the best of them. Meanwhile McCombs devoted himself to soliciting funds. By December he had collected about $35,000, half of which was contributed by Cleveland Dodge; but at the same time he was dispensing money rapidly, and at the end of 1911 the balance on hand was less than a hundred dollars.

aged property under the motto: "The public be pleased." His tunnel building had caught the imagination of the nation and brought congratulations from President Taft.

Going down to Princeton to see a sick son, McAdoo had been introduced to the president of the university. Wilson had liked the cut of the man's jib, his sincere concept of practical public service, his capacity for getting things done. When McAdoo asked, in the fall of 1910, whether his position as president of a traction company would prevent him from giving entirely disinterested aid to the crusade for good government, Wilson had congratulated him on his achievements and assured him that his help would be welcome. Wilson commended him to Page as "very sagacious and wide-awake." McAdoo lunched weekly with McCombs; and occasionally they were joined by Page and by Villard of the New York *Evening Post*, leaders of pro-Wilson sentiment among intellectuals.

As Wilson came to depend more and more on McAdoo's judgment, McCombs grew insanely jealous. Cynical suspicions worked upon his nerves. Lamed in boyhood, he was incapacitated by illness for days at a time. He flew into rages and was secretive about his plans. But the Governor was showing himself large enough to keep both "Macs" working for the cause. Already he had told Page that he did not need a man of "large calibre" to run his campaign.

With McCombs and others attending to the business of political promotion, Wilson continued to seek out the hearts of the voters. While enemies in the East began to whisper that Woodrow Wilson was a "dangerous" man and McCombs was urging him not to encourage such talk by advocating anything "new," Bryan was demanding answers to questions that were designed to commit him to the progressive cause. Letters from the West were urging Wilson to respond unequivocally.

The line of the candidate's strategy took direction gradually in addresses made in the summer and autumn of 1911. Addressing the Pennsylvania Federation of Democratic Clubs, he identified his party —"the party of the present and the future, the party of young men"— with his whole program of progressive reform: the return of the machinery of political control to the voters; serving the people through such agencies as postal savings banks and parcel post, revision of the tariff, conservation of national resources, and regulation of corporations. Finally, he made a general assault on "the money monopoly."

The leaders of the Pennsylvania Democracy recognized this as the best sort of electioneering talk, and the honor of recognition as the genuine Wilson organization was sought by both factions of the party in the state—the conservatives, dominated by national committeeman Guffey; and the progressives, led by such young men as Vance McCormick, A. Mitchell Palmer, and Roland S. Morris. Wilson immediately recognized the progressives as the party leaders in Pennsylvania.

In October the candidate visited two other states in which there were strong progressive sympathies in the Democratic party. Speaking at Madison, Wisconsin, he fell in with the reform movement that had already started under LaFollette's leadership. Then, going to Texas to make three addresses in one day, Wilson was introduced at the state fair grounds at Dallas by Senator Culberson, one of the ex-governors of Texas whom Colonel House had served. Speaking of the states as "the political laboratories of a free people"—a concept dear to House— Wilson pleaded for "a just, well-considered, moderately executed readjustment of our present economic difficulties." A Wilson-for-President movement already had gathered some momentum in Texas; and the candidate's appearance in October facilitated the work of organization that House was later to carry through so brilliantly.[7]

Support from Pennsylvania, Wisconsin, and Texas was to prove vital to Wilson's nomination. Moreover, the candidate made friends among the governors of other states who convened in September at Sea Girt. By the end of 1911, as the campaign for the Presidency was to swing from an informal movement into an avowed candidacy, Wilson's strength had become so conspicuous that he was marked by his enemies as a man to be beaten at all costs.[8]

Wilson's extravagant attacks on "the money monopoly" did not pass unnoticed by New York financiers. To responsible men who had less faith than he in the wisdom and restraint of the people, many of his remarks had seemed incendiary and demagogic. Personally, he had cut himself free of a fiduciary obligation by resigning in July from the board of the Mutual Life Insurance Company of New York, on which he had served since 1909. Moreover, he had impulsively denounced a

[7] When House began his work in the winter, Joseph W. Bailey, the conservative junior senator who opposed Wilson, controlled most of the votes of the Texas State Executive Committee. Asked how he achieved the miracle of the election of a solid Wilson delegation to the Democratic Convention in 1912 was achieved, the Colonel said: "We just picked the right people. That was all. We didn't use any brass bands." *See* A. D. Howden Smith, *Mr. House of Texas*, p. 48.

[8] Franklin K. Lane, a political observer who at that time never had met Wilson, pointed out that "on the Democratic side all of the forces have united to destroy Wilson, who is the strongest man in the West. The bosses are all against him." Lane to John Crawford Burns, Dec. 13, 1911, in *The Letters of Franklin K. Lane*, pp. 84–85.

plan for a centralized banking system simply because it had been proposed by Nelson Aldrich, a New York financier and senator who had
recently sponsored a Republican tariff bill that Wilson thought iniqui-
tous.

Wilson was forgetting Pritchett's warning against the effect of intemperate political talk upon his own judgment. Challenged by the *New
York Times* and others, he was compelled to admit that he had erred
in attacking the Aldrich plan; and an apologetic letter that he wrote
was circulated widely among financial men by Colonel House, who
had expressed the opinion that the Aldrich proposal seemed "a long
way in advance of the money trust" that dominated the credit of the
nation. He wished that Wilson, instead of shilly-shallying over ground
that had been made very slippery by memories of Bryan's unsound
monetary policies, would concentrate on one safe cause, such as reform
of the tariff. Clark and Underwood already had taken the initiative in
advocating this. Finally, in January of 1912, several weeks after House
had used David F. Houston as a mouthpiece to insinuate relevant suggestions in Wilson's ear, the candidate spoke out against Republican
tariff making. The theory of protection, he asserted in New York, had
been thrust on the government by business interests who went to Washington and said: "If you don't give us these things, who is going to pay
the campaign expenses next year?" He proposed to take tariffs out of
politics by imposing them for revenue only.

This change in the direction of his attack, however, hardly relieved
the nervous spasms into which Wilson's association with Bryan and his
criticisms of "the money power" had thrown certain financiers. Friends
and patrons of Harvey were pressing him to turn against the Governor,
and the publisher expressed himself as ready to do so if he became
convinced that Wilson was "a dangerous man." Men whom the prophet
had damned in New Jersey found willing allies among New York
journalists—notably Edward P. Mitchell, editor of the New York *Sun*,
and William Randolph Hearst.

The *Sun* got wind of the fact that the candidate had applied for a
pension from the Carnegie Foundation, on the executive committee
of which he had himself served. Wilson's case was first discussed by
the Carnegie trustees at a time when he had refused to take salary
from Princeton and had not been elected governor.[9] He was therefore

[9] On Nov. 1, 1910, Wilson addressed a letter of resignation to the board of trustees of the
Carnegie Foundation. On the 16th, Secretary Thwing wrote to notify him that the foundation
accepted the resignation with assurance of the "great respect and regard of its members." H. S.
Pritchett to W.W., Nov. 3, 1910, C. F. Thwing to W.W., Nov. 16, 1910. Wilson's claim for
a pension was discussed informally by trustees early in November; but Pritchett, president of
the board, wrote to Wilson on Nov. 3: "I will not bring up the matter of the pension until I

without income, except from his writings and from small investments. His formal application was encouraged by President Pritchett of the foundation, he resigned from the board before making it, and after he went on the payroll of the state he acquiesced in the board's refusal, which was based upon a change of policy.

Disregarding these considerations, biased editors and newsmen slanted the story for political effect. The great champion of the poor was himself a two-timing moneygrubber, they insinuated. The New York *American* went so far as to accuse him of willingness to accept largess "steeped in the human blood of Carnegie's workers." Induced to issue a rebuttal, Wilson did not take pains, in his rage of scorn, to make it either complete or entirely accurate.

And then there were assaults on his personality: the old cry of "autocrat" and "schoolmaster," accusations of political disloyalty and ingratitude. It was crafty George Harvey who fixed these arrows in the back of his quondam puppet. Colonel House inadvertently suggested the trap; and Wilson was betrayed into it by his natural candor. When *Harper's Weekly* displayed a Wilson-for-President slogan, Western Democrats suspected that New York money was supporting Wilson. To allay this suspicion, House tried to arrange through Martin (an associate of Harvey) to have *Harper's Weekly* "mildly criticize Wilson."

This advice reached Harvey at the very time when the editor was being pressed by New York friends to renounce Wilson as a second Bryan and when it was obvious that young amateurs had taken over the promotion of Wilson's candidacy without consultation with Harvey, who called himself "the original Wilson man." Yet the publisher could not, without himself losing prestige, suddenly desert the man whom he had long sponsored. If there was to be a break, the responsibility for it must be thrown upon Wilson.

Harvey's opportunity came at a political conference with the Governor at the Manhattan Club in New York, on December 7. They met

---

get your letter in regard to it, which, I take it, might better wait until after the election and after our annual meeting. In sending it give me the details of your twenty-five years of service . . . It is not necessary for me to tell you that the executive committee will consider any such suggestion in the most friendly spirit."

On Dec. 29 [1910?], Pritchett wrote: "A Mr. D. G. Slattery who claimed to be a newspaperman called at my office today and asked the details concerning the matter of a retiring allowance for you. I declined any talk with him and merely send you this line because I suspect he was trying to work up a story in the interest of those who are fighting you. Where he got such information as he seemed to have I do not know. I think he is a Trenton man. Yrs. faithfully." As Slattery was leaving, Pritchett reported, he asked whether Pritchett was "friendly" to Wilson, and got an unequivocal reply.

Wilson himself later felt that he had fully earned the pension and was "arbitrarily and unjustly refused it." W. W. to Tumulty, June 23, 1914, Swem transcription. *See also* E. A. W. to Dabney, Feb. 9, 1911.

before a log fire in the room of "Marse Henry" Watterson, the Louisville editor who alone among Harvey's original group of Wilson supporters had remained loyal. The night before, Colonel Watterson had arranged for Wilson to meet Frederick Penfield, who gave generously to the campaign fund; but the candidate had vetoed a suggestion by Watterson that money be accepted from the reactionary Thomas F. Ryan. Though unconvinced, Watterson had acquiesced. As the three men were leaving the room at the Manhattan Club after an hour or two of cordial conversation, Harvey urged Wilson to say frankly whether there was "anything left of that cheap talk . . . about my advocating you on behalf of 'the interests'?" The Governor, hurriedly putting on his coat and intent on keeping an appointment with his wife, said that he was sorry this question was raised, that actually some of his advisers had told him that such talk was indeed "having a serious effect in the West."

Declaring that he feared Wilson might feel that way, Harvey remarked: "Then I will simply sing low." Watterson agreed that this would be wise, and the men discussed ways of convincing the public of *Harper's* independence of Wall Street.

Wilson sensed no undercurrent. He did not imagine that Harvey could be piqued at a frank statement on a matter of political business, particularly when the remark was solicited by the publisher himself. Soon after the conference at the Manhattan Club, however, the Wilson-for-President slogan disappeared from *Harper's Weekly*. Stockton Axson scented trouble; and though astounded by his brother-in-law's reaction, Wilson nevertheless took the precaution of writing this protesting note to Harvey:

Personal

My Dear Colonel   21 Dec. 1911

Every day I am confirmed in the judgment that my mind is a one-track road, and can run only one train of thought at a time! A long time after that interview with you and Marse Henry at the Manhattan Club it came over me that when (at the close of the interview) you asked me that question about the *Weekly*, I answered it simply as a matter of fact, and of business, and said never a word of my sincere gratitude to you for all your generous support, or of my hope that it might be continued. Forgive me, and forget my manners!

Faithfully yours,

WOODROW WILSON

Two weeks later Harvey answered in a long letter, signed "Very truly yours," in which Wilson thought he saw evidence of a wound still open. So he wrote again in apology. And this time Harvey replied in six lines, saying that he had uttered no word of criticism and concluding with the statement: "I *have* to print a word of explanation to the *Weekly's* readers, but it will be the briefest possible."

Harvey saw that, coming from Marse Henry—an elder statesman of the party—the story of the Manhattan Club conference would strike the public far more forcefully than if it were told by the injured party himself. Therefore, keeping Wilson's apology to himself, the publisher importuned Watterson to take the initiative in revealing all that he knew. Marse Henry confided his story to at least two Democratic editors in the South. Soon rumors were circulating.

Through a letter written to her cousin in Louisville on January 12, Ellen Wilson succeeded in getting the whole story of the Manhattan Club affair before Watterson. Marse Henry's cocksureness was jolted by this evidence of the duplicity of his New York confederate. Knowing that Harvey already had drafted a statement for publication, in explanation of the removal of Wilson's name from *Harper's Weekly*, the Kentuckian telegraphed to ask that the release be held. But it was too late. Harvey had thrown his stiletto on January 16, giving to the press the statement that he had prepared.

Telling only a part of the true story, neglecting to explain that Harvey had himself raised the question that led to the break, the release announced that at Wilson's suggestion *Harper's Weekly* would cease to advocate his nomination. The implication was that Wilson was a shameless ingrate. The Hearst press, and others who were ready to believe anything evil about the Governor of New Jersey, had a day of unrestrained joy. "He who abandons a friend will abandon a principle," warned one Hearst editor, "and what a man does to an individual he will do to a people."

The truth came out the next day in a statement from Watterson. Marse Henry revealed that the Governor had not been discourteous to Harvey, but merely had given a frank answer to a direct question. However, reflecting his own pique at the rebuff that had been given to his offer to get money from Ryan, Watterson complained that the candidate's manner was "autocratic, if not tyrannous," that he did not make common cause with his political associates.

The air was cleared, but not in the way that Harvey anticipated. House could now recommend Wilson to Bryan as a candidate unembarrassed by support from "Wall Street," and spokesmen for the Governor had the ammunition they needed for a counterattack. "Ingratitude is one of the rarest virtues of public life," the New York *World* proclaimed. " 'Gratitude' is responsible for many of our worst political abuses. Upon 'gratitude' . . . is founded the power of every ignorant and unscrupulous boss; in 'gratitude' is rooted the system of spoils, of logrolling, of lobbying."

Bryan rejoiced with the fervor of a preacher welcoming a lost sheep and a week later he was sanctifying the break with Harvey as a "shining illustration that Mr. Wilson is the best modern example of Saul of Tarsus." The affair ended with Watterson's [10] railing at both Wilson and Harvey in a forlorn effort to smooth his own ruffled plumage, and with both principals keeping a grim silence. "I feel as though I had been walking through mud," Wilson said to his old friend Hiram Woods. "I just do not understand Harvey." His feelings were hurt by the break with this man for whom he had enough affection to write, a little more than a year before: "I have admired very deeply your disinterested part and your true friendship . . ." Once again Woodrow Wilson had been grievously disappointed by a friend to whom he had mistakenly ascribed blind loyalty.

And so George Harvey went over into the camp of Champ Clark, a candidate nominally progressive but more amenable to the traditions of political barter. As a result Wilson was without the shrewd advice that had been so vital to his election in New Jersey. House was busy in Texas, organizing a prenomination campaign; and McCombs and McAdoo were proving to be more valuable as executives than as policy makers. The Governor now had only his wife and Tumulty to advise him in meeting day-by-day problems. Neither was experienced in national politics, though both were learning rapidly.

Wilson was a target for just the sort of mudthrowing that had made the prospect of holding high office so distasteful to him. He was in mortal conflict with skillful manipulators of public opinion. Indeed, the Carnegie pension "exposure" was still being talked about and Harvey's implied aspersions were unrefuted when a third attempt was

---

10 As Joseph F. Wall has observed in his *Henry Watterson, Reconstructed Rebel*, pp. 269–81, Watterson was offended when the New York *Sun* quoted Wilson as saying: "The statement that Colonel Watterson was requested to assist in raising money in my behalf is absolutely without foundation." This seemed poor thanks for the zeal that Watterson had shown in helping to get a contribution from Penfield and in suggesting an appeal to Ryan. According to Arthur Krock, Watterson's influence was decisive in giving Champ Clark the endorsement of Kentucky for the Democratic nomination for the Presidency.

made by hostile journalists to put an end to the presidential candidacy of Woodrow Wilson.

This effort was aimed at bringing about an irreparable break between Wilson and Bryan. On January 7, 1912, a day before the Governor was to join the Great Commoner in Washington to address the Jackson Day dinner of the Democratic party, the conservative editor of the New York *Sun* published a five-year-old letter in which the president of Princeton had written: "Would that we could do something, at once dignified and effective, to knock Mr. Bryan, once for all, into a cocked hat!"

The recipient of that letter, a railroad president named Adrian H. Joline, later had opposed Wilson's plans at Princeton;[11] and then Wilson's feelings toward both Bryan and Joline had changed. The *Sun*'s stroke of malevolence threatened to undo all the wooing of the Great Commoner that had been arranged by Ellen Wilson and House.[12] How would Bryan react?

The question was answered on January 8, 1912, when Democrats gathered for the Jackson Day dinner that marked the beginning of the drive for votes in the June nominating convention. En route to Washington, Bryan stopped to visit Josephus Daniels, who did his utmost to assuage the irritation that was caused by the publication of the Joline letter, and by the time he reached the capital the *Sun*, rather than Wilson, was the main target of the Nebraskan's anger.

As for Wilson, he was content to stand on the truth and make no apologies that might seem to put him on the defensive. He was not ashamed, he said, of what had been an honest statement when it was written, although he was now of another opinion. "Don't be nervous about this," he advised his family before he left for Washington. "It is

[11] Wilson's "cocked-hat" letter of April 29, 1907, applauded a speech that Joline had delivered before his board of directors on April 4, 1907, bitterly attacking Bryan's proposal for government ownership of railroads as "the cry of the envious against the well-to-do—the old story." Within two or three years Wilson had turned against this reactionary, and after his election to the Presidency he said to a colleague who mentioned Joline: "If I wrote what I think of that man, it would have to be on asbestos." Luther P. Eisenhart, "The Far-Seeing Wilson," in William S. Myers (ed.), *Woodrow Wilson: Some Princeton Memories*, p. 67.

[12] The Bryans had lived next door to the Colonel one winter in the nineties, and House had found Mrs. Bryan very amenable to advice and suggestion, but Bryan himself wildly impracticable. During 1911, using his intimate insight into the mental processes of the Bryan family, House had begun to "nurse Bryan" in order to bring him around to his own way of thinking. He had faithfully informed the Nebraskan of threats by Underwood and Clark to his leadership of the party, and had played on Bryan's prejudices by sending all evidence that he could collect of the antipathy of "Wall Street" to Wilson and of its preference for Clark. On Nov. 11 the Colonel wrote to the Governor: "I have been with Mr. Bryan a good part of the morning and I am pleased to tell you that I think you will have his support . . . My main effort was in alienating him from Champ Clark and I believe I was successful."

only small men who allow such things to affect them and Mr. Bryan is not a small man."

When he came home from the Jackson Day dinner he told his loved ones all about it. Sitting before an open fire in the studio of the house on Cleveland Lane, deliberately taking off his glasses and balancing them on his thumb while he rubbed his eyes, he made them see the love feast with Bryan into which the Washington dinner had developed. They saw the Great Commoner enter, late, walk to the table where the presidential candidates and the entire Democratic National Committee were seated, turn first to greet Clark and then to put his arm around Wilson's shoulder. They could hear the rowdy friends of James Nugent who, when Wilson started to speak, hissed and heckled but were shouted down with cries of "Shame!" They could imagine the two great prophets rising to embrace each other in warm phrases.

Of the man whom he had once damned as a demagogic office seeker, Wilson said in all sincerity: "I for my part, never want to forget this: That while we have differed with Mr. Bryan upon this occasion and upon that in regard to the specific things to be done, he has gone serenely on pointing out to a more and more convinced people what it was that was the matter . . ." And then, with a burst of healing eloquence: "Let us apologize to each other that we ever suspected or antagonized one another; let us join hands once more all around the great circle of community of counsel and of interest which will show us at the last to have been indeed the friends of our country and the friends of mankind."

After Wilson's peroration, the ovation was tremendous. Bryan put a hand on the speaker's shoulder, murmuring "Splendid! Splendid!" Rising to respond, he declared himself ready to give more valiant service to the man who would bear the standard of the party than he could ever render to himself. Was the Nebraskan at last ready to abdicate leadership of the Democracy? his people wondered.

Wilson had now, at the beginning of the critical year 1912, been under heavy fire on a national battleground. He was learning to control his righteous ire and to fight back with the weapons magnanimity, tact, and silence. "All these things," he said of the malicious attacks upon him, "in the long run, discredit only those who do them, but for a while they are very trying."

There were still other machinations that Wilson's Celtic imagination ascribed to persecutors on "Wall Street": the threat of publication of a letter alleged to have been written by Grover Cleveland to Henry Van

Dyke of Princeton, impugning Wilson's self-control and intellectual integrity;[13] the financing of a great "trust" designed to divide political spoils among Harmon, Underwood, and Clark "with a division of territory quite after the manner of the industrial combinations."

Far more embarrassing than the canards of the conservatives were the efforts of pseudo progressives to prove Wilson an archreactionary. Hearst and other publicists for Champ Clark and Underwood were prominent in this campaign. Their evidence, taken largely from Wilson's *History of the American People*, was actually in print and in circulation.[14] In the last volume of the *History,* a henchman of Clark's claimed to have found quotations to show that the author "had a profound contempt for the Farmer's Alliance, the Populists, greenbackers, bi-metalists, trades unionists, small office seekers, Italians, Poles, Hungarians, pensioners, strikers, armies of unemployeed."

Late in Feburary, Hearst began to devote front pages to abuse of the Governor, denouncing him as a Tory, a Judas, "a perfect jackrabbit of politics." Wilson had firmly rejected suggestions from the journalist's agents that, like other candidates, the Governor should write a letter welcoming Hearst back into the party. "God knows," he said, "I want the Democratic presidential nomination and I am going to do everything legitimately to get it, but if I am to grovel at Hearst's feet, I will never have it." When Wilson publicly commended the appointment of his Princeton classmate, Chancellor Pitney of New Jersey, to the United States Supreme Court, he subjected himself to criticism from labor organizations against which the conservative judge had made decisions; but when Hearst tried to exploit this situation and attacked Wilson's views on labor, the executive committee of the New Jersey Federation of Labor circulated an endorsement of their governor.

Among one group of voters, however, the attacks of the Hearst press did irreparable damage. Passages from the *History* were quoted to make foreign-born voters fear that, if he became president, Wilson would act to restrict immigration. The foreign-language press took alarm and openly denounced the candidate. Though he wooed Polish

[13] A statement written by Tertius Van Dyke, son and biographer of Henry Van Dyke, to Edith Gittings Reid, dated Jan. 21, 1949, which was shown to the writer by Mrs. Reid, effectively disposes of the likelihood that such a letter existed. There was, however, a damaging letter from Cleveland to Prentiss Bailey, editor of the Ithaca *Observer*. See p. 115.

[14] When a new edition of Wilson's *History* was published, Mrs. Wilson wrote to Harvey to express the hope that the "limelight" of publicity would make the new edition sell enormously, explaining that the appeals to aid this and that were already legion and it was very inconvenient for a public man to be penniless. *Harper's* sent agents into New Jersey towns after Wilson's public appearances and promoted the sale of the *History*. See James Kerney, *The Political Education of Woodrow Wilson*, p. 126.

and Italian editors contritely and even swallowed his professional pride
to the extent of asking his publishers if he might revise certain passages, and though he established the fact that he had protested against
the restriction of immigration in 1906, Wilson lost the confidence of
many foreign-born voters.

Wilson's letters to intimates give glimpses of the pain that human
perversity caused this man who wished above everything to love and
be loved, to win and hold the confidence of the American congregation.
To Edith Gittings Reid, for example, he wrote: ". . . the world grows
sometimes to seem so brutal, so naked of beauty, so devoid of chivalrous
sentiment and all sense of fair play, that one's own spirit hardens and
is in danger of losing its fineness. I fight on, in the spirit of Kipling's
'If,' but that is oftentimes a very arid air." As he felt his candidacy
growing in strength he thought himself the more put upon by men who
were determined to destroy his character by fair means or foul. He told
his daughters that there were some people who could not be trusted.
His moods oscillated between neurotic suspicion and childlike faith,
and sometimes his family noticed an ominous twitching in his right
eye.

Wilson had been annoyed, in 1911, by persistent rumors that the
Princeton trustees would reveal the inside story of his controversies, and
he had suggested to his friends on the board that they might join with
him in meeting the situation publicly; but he was advised that probably
nothing would be done openly that might involve the university in
political controversy and enhance Wilson's position as a prophet of
democracy. Privately, however, his enemies worked with his political
opponents to undermine him. On February 9, President Taft wrote
to West that Wilson was "getting what his shifty dishonest nature
deserves." [15]

Occasionally Wilson responded directly and hotly to the abuse of
adversaries. Sometimes he steadied his nerves by quoting from Kipling:
"If you can wait and not be tired by waiting, or being lied about, don't
deal in lies." Often he forced himself to reply to attacks obliquely, by
dwelling on the debasing effect of mudthrowing upon the personnel of
government. "Misrepresentation," he complained to sympathetic Mayor
Gaynor of New York, "is the penalty which men in public life must
expect in the course of their effort to render service . . . These things

---

[15] West Papers (Princeton University Library). The Wilsons suspected that "the fine
Italian hand" of Dean West reached President Nicholas Murray Butler, of Columbia, whose
influence in Republican councils was great. E.A.W. to Nancy Toy, Sept. 23, 1912.

should be borne with fortitude, if not indifference, in order that our duty may be rendered without regard to our personal feeling."

The embattled candidate perhaps found his greatest comfort in the words of Peter Finley Dunne, whose column he liked to read to his family in extravagant brogue. "I don't know," said Mr. Dooley, "what'll happen to th' professor next. If I was him I wudden't walk on th' sidewalk; I'd always be home before sunset, I'd be careful what I et an' dhrank, an' if I saw a friend fr'm Princeton comin' tow'ds me with a pleasant smile on his face an' givin' me th' high sign iv our secret s'ciety, I'd run."

CHAPTER XIII

CHOICE OF THE DEMOCRACY

AT PHILADELPHIA, ON FEBRUARY 2, 1912, Wilson spoke to hundreds of periodical publishers on the same platform with Senator Robert M. LaFollette of Wisconsin. The audience was largely one of Republican reactionaries, and remarkably sensitive to public opinion. They saw revolutionary omens in the political skies, in this most critical year of American politics since 1860. Large strikes had charged the air with electricity of high potential. Socialist Eugene Debs had a vociferous following. At last it seemed clear that the voices of revolt were loud and articulate enough to influence political action.

LaFollette, a powerful orator, went to Philadelphia commanding Wilson's respect as "a very high minded champion of progressive ideas." Bitterly insurgent, he had for years been fighting special privilege and corruption, had made himself the very soul of grass-roots progressivism in the Republican party. But to prove that he was of presidential stature, he would have to capture the intellectual liberals of the East. And that he failed to do. Weakened by an attack of ptomaine poisoning, his nerve shaken by the deflation of his presidential boom by what he regarded as a betrayal by Roosevelt, he was in no condition to match oratory with Woodrow Wilson at the gathering of sophisticated publishers. Usually a temperate man, on this occasion he drank a stimulant to fortify his weakened vitality, and the effect was tragic. He spoke twice too long, became lost in repetition, ranted against newspapermen.

Wilson's briefer talk was urbane and charming even in its criticism of his hosts the publishers: "I used to be afraid that they would not publish what I offered them, but now I am afraid they will"—deftly discriminating in its definitions and prescriptions: "Progressivism means not getting caught standing still when everything else is moving . . . we are not steering by forms of government, we are steering by principles of government." In contrast, LaFollette's uncouth, humorless denunciation seemed as grim as a Puritan sermon. From the back of the hall men shouted "Sit down!" The audience melted away, LaFollette's star faded, and a few days later Theodore Roosevelt, with protestations of self-sacrifice, whooped, "My hat is in the ring!"

If the election of a Democratic president had already seemed a probability, it now appeared to be almost a certainty. But in spite of the rift in the Republican party Wilson continued his appeals to the voters. Late in February he went into progressive strongholds; and at Des Moines, addressing insurgent Republicans as well as Democrats, he inveighed against monopoly and special interests, called the United States Senate "a seat of privilege," and explained that the only difference between himself and the followers of LaFollette was over the tariff. "You speak of the tariff with a certain air of piety and I don't," he said. Closing his winter campaigning at Brooklyn, he asserted that the people were to be "absolutely trusted" in choosing their leaders and that those chosen would be responsible for the working out of a *modus vivendi*, before the "seething millions" of America turned upon themselves and the social melting pot grew "hotter and hotter." In general, however, in the speeches delivered in the East during the winter, the candidate held himself to inoffensive generalities and by sheer eloquence commanded the respect of his audiences.

In planning the campaign for the votes of the delegates, McCombs decided not to compete in states in which native sons were candidates. By a hands-off policy he hoped to win goodwill that would result in second-choice support for his man. Therefore, no fight was made for Wilson when Missouri, the first of the states to instruct its delegates to Baltimore, held its primary election on February 11. The vote of the machines of Kansas City and St. Louis ran heavily toward Congressman Clark, a strict party man. Distinguished and pleasing in manner, he did not have the magnetism of the nation's great progressive personalities. His progressivism lacked intellectual base and moral compulsion, but had proved to be a winning card; and agrarians felt that they knew him better than Wilson.

In the Midwestern primaries that followed shortly after that of Missouri, Wilson was entered by his managers and had the better of the voting. The tide turned, however, in April. In Illinois the Hearst press, the local progressive leaders, and a swarm of able speakers joined forces to draw out a 3-to-1 vote for Clark. His prospects grew even brighter when Bryan's Nebraska delegation was instructed in favor of the Missourian; and several other states fell in line.

Wilson, now on the defensive, took off his cloak of academic diffidence and got into the fight with both fists. The campaign was becoming a game to be won, if win he could by fair means. In a little pocket notebook he wrote a list of all the states, the number of their delegates to the convention, and the names of the Democratic leaders with whom McCombs hoped to do business. Most of those sought out were progressives; but in at least two states conservatives were wooed, and in Illinois Boss Roger Sullivan was regarded as the best hope.

McCombs was frankly spurring his candidate to efforts that would pay off in votes. "Now I must rush out again in search of delegates . . ." Wilson wrote on April 1, "shy birds more difficult to find in genuine species than the snark itself!" Sometimes his zeal was more fervent than wise, from the point of view of hardened politicians. Going to Illinois and making a score of speeches in two days, for example, he failed to redeem a cause already lost and thus drew national attention to a defeat that was inevitable in that state. But he had the pleasure of speaking his mind about Hearst—"a character assassin." And he sowed grass-roots sentiment that was to blossom at the nominating convention.

Again, in mid-April, the Governor took the warpath in an effort to stem a flood of conservatism on which Southern Democrats were drifting toward Congressman Underwood of Alabama. Actually this candidate had been born of a Unionist family in Kentucky, had gone south as a commercial lawyer, and had become substantial, respected—and limited—by the sort of milieu that had repelled Wilson at Atlanta. Hoping that his own more genuine Southern background would appeal to the people of that section, Wilson made a four-day tour of Georgia, taking along his wife and W. G. McAdoo, both descendants of old Georgia families. The Wilsons were received warmly by friends and relatives and visited the manse at Savannah where they had been married; and the journals welcomed "Tommie" as a native son. But conservative state organizations raised the bogies of Bryanism, Oregonism, and mob rule, endorsed Underwood's distinguished record in Congress, and presented him as the "safe and sane candidate." Underwood won the primaries in Georgia, Florida, Mississippi, and Virginia. Wilson succeeded in winning only a working majority of the delegates from South Carolina and a fourth of those from Tennessee.

By the middle of May, McCombs was thrown into gloom. The candidate was even less effective in attracting funds to his campaign chest than he had been in gathering millions for Princeton. The Wilson headquarters was almost bankrupt, and all but a few loyal henchmen had fallen away. At the end of the month Colonel House doubted their man could win. Working on Bryan's sympathies in April, at breakfast in a New York hotel, he was ably seconded by Mrs. Bryan; but the Great Commoner had gone no further than declaring that either Clark or Wilson was acceptable, and House suspected that the Nebraskan still hoped to capture the nomination for himself. In May the Colonel was urging Wilson to declare that he would accept only a single term in the Presidency, hoping thus to mollify competitors who would not want to wait eight years to replace him. A few weeks later he tried to make common cause with the Bryans by writing Mrs. Bryan that the purpose of the interests opposing Wilson was to prevent the nomination of either Wilson or Bryan.

To remain in the running for the Presidency, the Governor had to continue to command the support of New Jersey. In the winter the Republican legislature had passed a bill that could embarrass the Governor whether he signed it or vetoed it. This measure required railroads to abolish grade crossings at a rate that to some men seemed confiscatory. It posed a delicate decision for Wilson: Tumulty was urging him to sign the measure, as evidence of his faithfulness to progressive ideals, while McAdoo was advising him that this legislation was unfair to the railroads and had been drawn for the purpose of putting the Governor in a political trap. Wilson challenged the good faith of the legislators by vetoing the bill and commenting that, if they really believed in the measure, the lawmakers could pass it over his veto. They did not do so.

When the Smith-Nugent forces, aided by a smart young lieutenant named Frank Hague, tried to send uninstructed, anti-Wilson delegates to Baltimore, the Governor appealed directly to the voters of New Jersey through a statement in the press. Speaking out against what was being done "very quietly and very secretly" by Smith, "who knows no other way of acting in politics," he did not mince words. "Do you wish to slip back into the slough of old despair and disgrace?" he asked the citizens.

The response was heartening. The forces of James Smith and James Nugent—now known as "the Jim-Jims"—elected only four delegates, all from Essex County, out of the twenty-eight who were to represent New Jersey at Baltimore. On the same day, May 28, Texas definitely committed its forty delegates to Wilson; and very soon Utah, the Dakotas, North Carolina, and Minnesota were in line.

But by all mathematical reckoning the Governor's chances of nomination were still slim. A vote of two-thirds of the delegates was needed; and Wilson fell just short of controlling a vetoing bloc of one-third.

Yet House's hope had revived. On June 7 he communicated his optimism to Wilson, counseling cautious inactivity on the part of the candidate. Plans for organizing the supporting delegates were "already under way," the Colonel wrote. Taking House's advice, of which he confessed that he stood in need, Wilson resigned himself to silence.

A week later, having moved with his family to Sea Girt for the summer, he wrote to Mary Allen Peck: "The day is gray and drizzly; the sea makes a dismal voice across the bleak camp ground in front of us; we have had to light a fire in the huge fireplace to keep our spirits (and our temperature) up; but here we are a home group with that within us that can defy the depressing influences of the weather. What we now look forward to with not a little dread are the possibilities of the next fortnight in politics. I was saying at breakfast this morning, 'Two weeks from to-day we shall either have this sweet Sunday calm again, or an army of reporters camped on the lawn and an all-day reception.' 'Which would you rather have?' Nell asked. 'Need you ask?' I exclaimed; and that is the way I feel . . . I am well (I do not count a teasing sick headache!) and underneath, deep down, my soul is quiet."

Amidst his duties at Trenton and Sea Girt, the candidate kept an eye open toward the Republican convention at Chicago. There, in mid-June, Theodore Roosevelt commanded at the same time the fealty of genuine progressives, the support of certain leaders of finance and industry, and the votes of what at first seemed to be a majority of the delegates—only to have his men denied seats or won away by bosses of the party who had resolved to renominate President Taft. Wilson let it be known to his friends that, if the Democrats named a candidate as conservative as Taft, they might expect Woodrow Wilson to bolt, as Roosevelt was threatening to do.

Meanwhile the impresarios of the Democracy were indefatigable in discussion of tactics for their convention; and sometimes the Governor joined his managers in talk of plans for high-pressuring recalcitrant delegates and for packing the galleries with strong-lunged undergraduates. The nomination was to be made at Baltimore, a city preferred by the Wilson managers because popular sentiment in the region favored their candidate and might be expected to influence a close contest. Toward the end of the month a Wilson headquarters was set up in the Emerson Hotel, whence a private wire ran to the candidate's room at Sea Girt. Zealous Wilson delegates from Texas and Pennsylvania planned a relentless campaign to win individual "converts" from other delegations. All was ready for the great trial of strength.

McCombs, who had been working without respite all through the spring, had gone into conference with House for several days in June. The manager's nerves were so worn that the Colonel doubted his ability to carry the fight through the convention; and House had coached the worried man, realizing that McCombs was inexperienced in such matters.[1]

On June 25 the Colonel sailed for Europe, explaining to Wilson that he was physically unequal to taking part in the convention, and assuring the Governor that he had done his best to prepare both McCombs and the Texans to anticipate every contingency. "It leaves an empty feeling in my heart . . ." Wilson replied, "but it would be selfish to ask you to stay."

Meanwhile, out at Chicago, where the surge of progressive sentiment was undermining the solidarity of the Republican party, another devoted Wilson man had executed a self-imposed mission. William G. McAdoo, convinced that Bryan held the key to victory at Baltimore, had determined to woo the Great Commoner. Going to the Republican convention, where Bryan was accredited as a reporter, he had found his man in shirt sleeves in a crowded hotel corridor and tried to make him see that Wilson was the only genuine progressive in the Democratic race. But Bryan gave his pat answer: as a member of the Nebraska delegation he was bound to vote as he was instructed—for Clark. The Nebraskan was curious to know the intentions of Tammany. He asked McAdoo, who was a member of the New York delegation, and was told that Boss Charles Murphy was planning to switch New York's vote from Harmon to Clark as soon as such a move would give the nomination to Clark.

"Humph!" Bryan exclaimed; ". . . after I have complied with my instructions, in good faith, I shall feel free to take such course in the convention as my conscience shall dictate. Moreover if, during the course of the convention, anything should develop to convince me that Clark cannot or ought not to be nominated, I shall support Governor Wilson."[2] McAdoo went straight to Baltimore, well satisfied, though some in the inner councils of the party suspected that no candidate would

---

[1] *House Papers*, I, 63, and House-McCombs correspondence in the House Collection. When McCombs claimed 800 delegates for Wilson, for example, House commended the exaggeration but warned against specifying the states from which they would come, since that would make it easy to refute the claim. Leaders of the Texas delegation had been present at the House-McCombs conference, and tactics had been worked out for organized proselyting by their men among delegates who had been instructed to vote for other candidates. It was hoped that thus they might block a two-thirds vote for Clark.

[2] William G. McAdoo, *Crowded Years*, pp. 135–36.

completely satisfy the Great Commoner except William Jennings Bryan, that he hoped to survive after his rivals had killed one another off.

Utterly devoted to the progressive cause, and anticipating that the standpatters in his own party would use the same tactics that had been successful in the Republican convention, Bryan began to set backfires against the Clark-Tammany threat. When the committee on arrangements proposed to give the temporary chairmanship of the convention to Alton B. Parker, the favorite of the New York delegation, the Great Commoner protested that it would be suicidal to have a reactionary for chairman. Moreover, Bryan telegraphed to Wilson, Clark, and several favorite sons to challenge them to support his protest against Parker. Thus, even before the convention met, Wilson was asked to choose between progressive principles and the votes of Tammany.

The Governor called his family around him and listened to their advice, his manner whimsically questioning. The voice that he trusted as loyal above all others said firmly: "There must be no hedging." Smiling, he agreed. Once he had said of his Ellen: "Neither the powers above nor below can shake her when a principle is involved." Sitting on the edge of a bed, he jotted on a pad this reply to Bryan: "You are quite right . . . The Baltimore convention is to be a convention of progressives—of men who are progressive in principle and by conviction. It must, if it is not to be put in a wrong light before the country, express its convictions in its organization and in its choice of the men who are to speak for it . . . No one will doubt where my sympathies lie . . ."

Wilson was the only candidate who dared to respond to Bryan's challenge so forthrightly. Tumulty and McAdoo were delighted when they learned what he had done; but McCombs, who had advised Wilson to straddle and hedge like the other candidates, was frantic. "The Governor can't afford to have a row," he wailed. But McAdoo, who a year before had urged that Wilson must scotch the accusation that he was "dangerous," now sensed the political magic that lay in a fight on high principles. And so he responded: "The Governor can't afford to have anything but a row. The bigger the row the better for us."

The first session of the nominating convention assembled on the afternoon of June 25. In Baltimore's armory, gay with flags and packed to the rafters, the name of Parker was proposed as temporary chairman. Immediately Bryan was on his feet. Wearing a dowdy sack suit, with low collar and black bow tie, his thin mouth set grimly and his black brows frowning beneath a pointed, bald dome, he held up his right hand for quiet. And then through his thick jowls his voice boomed to the corners of the hall. "The Democratic party is true to the people," he shouted. "You cannot frighten it with your Ryans nor buy it with your Belmonts." The sentence brought delegates to their feet, waving and yelling.

A few moments later Bryan was nominated for the temporary chairmanship, and a Texan took the opportunity to trumpet the issue plainly to the convention: ". . . the fight is on and Bryan is on one side and Wall Street is on the other." The Wilson delegates voted for Bryan; but when Clark's men cast 228 of their votes against them, Parker was chosen, 579 to 508.[3]

When a majority of the committee on rules tried to force each state delegation to vote as a unit—a measure that Wilson already had condemned as a violation of the principle of direct primaries—Mayor Newton D. Baker of Cleveland and other pro-Wilson delegates fought the move on the floor of the convention. In the course of the struggle that followed, an Ohioan happened to mention the name of the Governor of New Jersey, and instantly the bands and flag wavers that had been prepared by McCombs's "chief of enthusiasm" went into action. The hall was in pandemonium for a half hour. The unit-voting rule was beaten and nineteen Ohio delegates who had been instructed for Wilson by the voters of their district were allowed to vote for him.

Bryan relentlessly pressed his crusade by forcing through a motion that put the convention on record as "opposed to the nomination of any candidate for President who is the representative of or under obligation to J. Pierpont Morgan, Thomas F. Ryan, August Belmont, or any other member of the privilege-hunting and favor-seeking class." Wilson's eyes sparkled when news of this move by Bryan reached him. "The old lion is at his best," the Governor said to his family.

Bryan's anti-Wall Street resolution was approved by a vote of more than 4 to 1; and finally, on the night of June 27, the formal nominations began. The naming of Clark by James Reed of Missouri set off a demonstration that lasted for an hour and five minutes. It was after three o'clock in the morning when Judge Wescott, chairman of the New Jersey delegation, rose and presented his candidate. The judge had come to adore Wilson as the first man in history to identify statesmanship with Christianity. Quoting from the speech at Pittsburgh in

[3] Parker was not made permanent chairman. The progressives combined to elect Ollie M. James, a friend of Bryan and a supporter of Clark, and a man who, in the view of the Wilson managers, would have been more troublesome at large on the floor of the convention than in the presiding chair.

which Wilson had bared his soul and denounced the Philistines of Princeton and the nation, Wescott went on to say: "He has been in political life less than two years. He has had no organization of the usual sort; only a practical ideal, the re-establishment of equal opportunity. The logic of events points to him . . . Every crisis evolves its master. Time and circumstance have evolved the immortal Governor of New Jersey." Wilson's cohorts outdid the demonstration for Clark by ten minutes—parading, flaunting banners, yelling, whistling, and tooting horns in a jamboree that expressed the college spirit of many of the participants.

Daylight was creeping in at the end of the hall when blind Senator Gore of Oklahoma rose to second the nomination. The first ballot was not taken until seven o'clock. It gave Clark 440½ votes and Wilson 324.

The changes on the next eight ballots were so slight that, when Tumulty reported the results to the Governor, Wilson said that he was reminded of two men who were walking and stopped three times to ask the distance to their destination and each time got the same answer: "Well," exclaimed one of them at last, "thank God, we're holding our own."

On the tenth ballot, however, came the break that had been feared by the Wilson men. Boss Murphy of Tammany shifted the ninety votes of New York to Clark. The partisans of the Missourian celebrated for more than an hour, hoping to stampede the convention. Clark now had 556 votes, a majority of the total. For sixty-eight years every Democratic candidate who had reached that point had gone on to win two-thirds of the votes and the nomination. Clark, in the speaker's office at Washington, prepared a telegram of acceptance.

McCombs's nerve broke completely after the all-night session that culminated in the tenth ballot. The next morning he telephoned to Sea Girt, just as Wilson was coming down to breakfast, to suggest that the delegates pledged to him be released. But just as he was about to give this advice McAdoo thrust him aside and seized the phone and said: "McCombs is going to tell you to withdraw. No one else believes you should." [4]

Though Wilson did not withdraw, he did not expect the nomination now. He was both disappointed and relieved. He anticipated the prospect of a trip to the English Lakes with his wife. His sense of humor

[4] Louis Brownlow, who was present, to the writer, and in a lecture at the University of Chicago, March 2, 1956.

came to his rescue too. Finding an advertisement of coffins in his mail, he quipped: "This company is certainly prompt in its service." All through the balloting he had remained serene—playing golf, reading aloud with his wife, walking along the shore, taking automobile rides with friends, telling stories to reporters who worked in a tent on the lawn.

All was not lost, however. The Wilson men had expected Tammany to shift to Clark still earlier in the balloting and had been prepared to stand firm against an attempted stampede. When the results of three ballots following the tenth showed little change, it was apparent that the Clark men had played their best card to no avail. When they departed so far from progressive gospel as to add Murphy and Tammany to their company, it was too much for the Democracy of the West to stomach. Bryan and other Nebraskans were in a mood to revolt against their instructions.

As the thirteenth ballot was being taken, Wilson sensed the trend of feeling and took the offensive, giving McCombs a message for delivery to Bryan. In it the Governor criticized the effort of the New York delegation to control the convention, declaring it "the imperative duty of each candidate . . . to see to it that his own independence" was "beyond question." "I can see no other way to do this," he said, "than to declare that he will not accept a nomination if it cannot be secured without the aid of that delegation. For myself, I have no hesitation in making that declaration. The freedom of the party and its candidate and the security of the government against private control constitute the supreme consideration."

When Bryan received this manifesto of Wilson's independence, he was already preparing to transfer his vote from Clark to Wilson. Finally, the opportunity came to explain his position on the floor of the convention. On the fourteenth ballot Senator Hitchcock of Nebraska, following a policy that McCombs had urged, demanded that his state's delegation be polled publicly. Since Clark had shown himself willing to accept the nomination from the hands of Murphy, Bryan explained that he felt bound by the spirit of his instructions to withhold his vote from Clark so long as New York supported him. Making himself heard through an uproar of yells, catcalls, and hisses, Bryan cast his vote for Wilson with the proviso that it would be withdrawn if New York should give its allegiance to that candidate.

The polling of the Nebraska men had only a slight effect on the totals; but Bryan's shift, topping a ground swell of popular opinion that was being expressed in the liberal press and in the polling of state delegations loosed a moral force that was titanic. A torrent of telegrams assured the Great Commoner that the people were with him. "Wait till you hear from the folks back home," the Wilson slogan advised.

Clark men now were on the defensive, raging at Bryan as "a money-grabbing, selfish, office-seeking, favor-hunting, publicity-loving marplot" who was deliberately throwing the convention into a deadlock so that he himself might be nominated. By this accusation any aspirations that Bryan may have had were effectively blocked.[5]

Meanwhile Bryan's move was embarrassing McCombs in his efforts to persuade the New York men that Clark could not win and that they should vote for Wilson. McCombs went so far as to ask the Governor whether he might assure conservatives that, if Wilson was elected, Byran would not be made secretary of state. Early in the campaign, however, Wilson had laid down the law: there was to be no commitment that would bind him in administering the government, no bargaining for votes. Politely, he said "no" to McCombs; and, to allay rumors that trading in public offices was being done in his name, he asserted to the Baltimore *Sun* that "not a single vote can be or will be obtained by means of a promise."

At Sea Girt the Governor still maintained his air of insouciance. While his daughters sat up late, eager for news, the candidate retired early and slept soundly, sometimes for as much as twelve hours. At meals, talk of politics was forbidden and the paterfamilias entertained his ladies on lighter subjects. All through the day newsmen ran in and out without knocking; and Tumulty paced up and down, watch in hand, eyes popping at each tidbit of news, denouncing all opponents as "damned crooks." The Governor amused himself by reading in his

---

[5] Actually, the Great Commoner had confirmed the impossibility that Clark could be nominated, but without committing himself irrevocably to Wilson. He openly suggested that the progressives might well compromise on another candidate; and he said to scouts of Roger Sullivan of Illinois that, if the convention should feel that it must nominate him, the party leaders would find it easier to deal with him than with Wilson. Though he told his wife that he would accept his fourth nomination only in the event of a hopeless deadlock and if he could unite the party, the stage was undeniably set, whether by accident or design, for a display of any pro-Bryan sentiment that might have been latent among the delegates.

Though Bryan's wife and brother have denied that the Great Commoner wanted the nomination for himself and Josephus Daniels believed that if that was his desire he would have played his cards differently, Carter Glass, John W. Davis, and other party men thought that Bryan intended to prolong the contest and eventually receive the nomination. In his autobiography, Cordell Hull wrote: "It was not generally known, but the truth is that Bryan felt that he was entitled to the nomination. I learned that very definitely later." *See* Wayne C. Williams, *William Jennings Bryan*, p. 331; Josephus Daniels, *The Wilson Era: Years of Peace,* pp. 64–65; and John W. Davis MS, Oral History Project, p. 117, Columbia University.

secretary's face the nature of each report from Baltimore and teased him by humming the Clark campaign song.

Gradually the delegates at the convention fell away from Clark and the work done by Wilson's managers in lining up second choices bore fruit. By the end of the day on which Bryan announced his shift, Wilson had gained more than eighty votes. Last-ditch efforts were made by the bosses, during the lull in balloting that was enforced by the Sabbath, to tempt some of the ablest of the Wilson supporters to desert. But something of their leader's Covenanting spirit seemed to bind his men; and this loyalty was strengthened by Sunday headlines of the pro-Wilson press. To the *World,* the nomination of Wilson was "a matter of Democratic life and death."

The first important break in the ranks of the boss-dominated states came when the votes of Indiana's favorite son, Thomas R. Marshall, were delivered to Wilson. One by one, men who worshiped success deserted their candidates and scurried under the winning colors, as McCombs hinted at the political perdition awaiting obstructing minorities; but not until the thirtieth ballot, when Iowa transferred fourteen of her votes, did Wilson's total exceed that of Clark. At that moment a band struck up "Glory, Glory, Hallelujah!" and Wilson men joined in a chant of triumph. When the newsmen at Sea Girt, with eyes sparkling, hunted out the candidate and shouted "You've passed him, governor!" he responded to their request for "a statement" by remarking casually: "You might say that Governor Wilson received the news that Champ Clark had dropped to second place in a riot of silence."

Then the crescendo stopped, and Wilson lost a vote. His managers were fearful that Bryan again would be the standard-bearer. Determined to prevent a debacle, they accentuated their wooing of Roger Sullivan, whom they had helped to seat his Illinois delegates against Hearst's opposition and who had promised to aid Wilson's cause whenever his nomination became likely. On the forty-third ballot, Sullivan delivered the fifty-eight votes of his state.

However, even when Virginia at last endorsed her native son, Wilson's nomination was still blocked by hundreds of delegates who were loyal to Clark and Underwood; and there were rumors that Sullivan was prepared to swing Illinois back to Clark if Wilson could not soon command the necessary two-thirds of the votes. Finally, fervent pleading by Congressman Burleson resulted in the release of the Underwood delegates, many of whom already had been committed to Wilson as their second choice as a result of effective canvassing by the Texans.

On the forty-sixth ballot Wilson was given a nominating vote of 990. The action was made unanimous and, at 3:30 on the afternoon of July 2, Woodrow Wilson was declared the Democratic nominee for the Presidency of the United States.

Hearing the news, Tumulty rushed to the porch at Sea Girt and waved wildly toward a clump of trees. He had a brass band hidden there; and now it emerged, playing "Hail, the Conquering Hero Comes!" Slyly, the Governor asked what instructions had been given to the musicians in case of defeat. "I can't effervesce in the face of responsibility," he said to his family in explanation of his calmness; but, for the first time in his life, Woodrow Wilson let himself go to the extent of commissioning an aide to buy a box of cigars. The nomination seemed to him a sort of political miracle.

The vice-presidential nomination went to Governor Thomas R. Marshall of Indiana, who was a protégé of Tom Taggart, the first of the state bosses to desert Clark for Wilson. Thinking Marshall an agreeable fellow but a man of small caliber, Wilson would have preferred Underwood. When the Alabaman refused, however, the presidential candidate let the managers have their way.

The party platform, which in this convention was of far less importance than the nominee, bore the imprint of Byran. Neglected by the convention until the last moment, it was read perfunctorily by a hoarse clerk and adopted without discussion.[6]

Through all the muddy performance at Baltimore, Woodrow Wilson had managed to keep his exacting conscience clear. His position was the same as it had been after the nomination in New Jersey. He was the nominee because the people wanted him; because the people wanted him, the bosses thought that he could salvage their derelict hulk of a party. He rejoiced in writing to his nephew, George Howe, "The nomination has been won in such a way as to leave me absolutely free of private obligations." Only as Princeton served the nation had he thought its existence justified; only as the Democratic party served the United States could Woodrow Wilson act as its sponsor.

[6] The platform promised to transmute the progressive sentiment of the country into law, to prosecute trusts and regulate business. It proposed constitutional amendments providing for an income tax and the direct election of senators. To please the American Federation of Labor, jury trials were advocated in cases of criminal contempt of court and labor organizations were declared to be not properly subject to antitrust laws. The establishment of a central banking system of the sort proposed by Republican Senator Aldrich was opposed. Moreover, the party's platform committed their presidential candidate to the principle of a single term of office, a pledge with which Wilson differed.

CHAPTER XIV

WINNING THE PRESIDENCY

THE SPOTLIGHT THAT FELL on Woodrow Wilson at Sea Girt, in July of 1912, was garish, relentless, and worldly. He squirmed in rebellion as political impresarios, news reporters, brass bands, photographers, and autograph hunters swarmed over the lawn, up on the porch, and even into the house. Outside of his bedroom the Governor had no privacy. Some ten thousand letters came in—more than half from people who said that they had *prayed* for the nomination of Wilson. He was awed by the trust of the masses and frightened by the pathetic faith of individuals in the omnipotence of their ruler.

Soon he was protesting: ". . . the more these new things crowd upon me the more I seem to be dependent for peace and joy upon those I love. The more public my life becomes the more I seem driven in upon my own inner life and all its intimate companionships." Most of all he rested on the devotion of Ellen Wilson, who was absolutely sure that all this great faith in him would never be disappointed. But he still demanded the refreshment that came in letters from Bermuda, messages trifling and humorous that he could share with his family. "The life I am leading now can't keep up," he wrote to Mary Allen Peck ". . . Not a moment am I left free to do what I would. I thought last night that I should go crazy with the strain and confusion of it." Coming out dripping from a hot room in which he had been sealed up to make phonograph records for the coming campaign, he exclaimed: "If any man ever tries to get me to run for president again, I'll break his neck!" [1]

Democrats from many states descended on Sea Girt to see the new chief. On the Fourth of July thirty-five members of the National Committee, some of them still sulking over the nomination of an amateur, came to listen and went away enthusiastic. The loyalty of Tammany and of Underwood and his followers was pledged. McCombs was welcomed with thanks for a hard job well done; but this man, who for months had simmered between the fire of Wilson's righteousness and the caldrons of the party bosses, was in no physical condition to

[1] Robert W. Woolley to the writer.

235

manage a presidential campaign. Many Democrats disliked him and preferred to work under McAdoo. More and more, however, Wilson was showing loyalty of strong fiber. Once he became accustomed to work with a man he hesitated to change for any but the most compelling reasons. And in this case his inclination was supported by expediency, for advisers warned him that to cast aside his campaign manager would be to stir up new charges of ingratitude. Therefore Wilson decided that McCombs should be made chairman of the National Committee, insisting at the same time that McAdoo be vice-chairman.

Soon, however, the feud between the two men became so bitter that Wilson felt that he must go to New York to restore order. Finally, on August 12, McCombs was prostrated with neurasthenia and taken to the Adirondacks and McAdoo became the acting director of the campaign. "It's hard on you, my dear fellow, but you're handling it magnificently," Wilson said to his new manager, with a hand on his shoulder; and McAdoo's energy for selfless service was quickened. From this point on, McCombs was a liability and, moreover, one that had to be carried indulgently and cheerfully.[2] As much as possible, however, Wilson held himself aloof from the details of organization, fearful of making a *faux pas* that might damage the favorable position that he held in the presidential race. More and more, during the autumn campaign, he came to depend on House. "Your advice is as necessary as it is acceptable," he wrote to the Colonel in September. "Here's hoping soon to have you at my elbow."

[2] "Never fear," Wilson wrote to House on September 11, "I shall not be so foolish as to accept McCombs's resignation." From the Adirondacks, McCombs went to Boston to confer with House and won the sympathy of the colonel by talk of perfidy on the part of McAdoo. McCombs asked House to see Wilson in his behalf. (*See* House Diary, Oct. 6, 1921, Yale University Library.) On Wilson's advice, the "wisdom" of which House confessed that he "afterward learned," the colonel investigated the row and found that his sympathy for McCombs was not justified, that "McAdoo was scarcely to blame at all." But Wilson was very careful to avoid criticizing McCombs even to such a close friend as Cleveland Dodge, writing, "He is really very unwell, poor heroic chap." The break with Harvey had taught Wilson that he must avoid even the appearance of ingratitude. But to his young cousin, Fitz William Woodrow, Wilson said apropos McCombs: "Don't ever get so ambitious that you forget you're playing on a team." F. W. Woodrow to the writer, April 12, 1948.

Though McCombs returned to campaign headquarters, his malady continued to express itself in unreasonable irritation, alcoholism, secretiveness, and insane jealousy of McAdoo, who had been receiving newspaper publicity. McAdoo wanted "to fire the whole headquarters crowd," and McCombs would have dismissed McAdoo had Wilson permitted it. The fact that McAdoo had raised less money than McCombs elevated the former in Wilson's esteem, for the Governor suspected, despite emphatic denials, that McCombs had made unethical promises to contributors. "McCombs is in conference most of the time with old-style politicians," House recorded in his diary late in October. "The whole character of the callers has changed since he took charge, and for the worse."

To compose his acceptance speech in tranquillity, Wilson confessed playfully, he ran away early in July from the buzz and glare of Sea Girt, put himself "in retreat" at the home of a friend, and then escaped by sea for six days on Dodge's yacht, carrying under his arm a copy of the party platform and an editorial from the *World* entitled "Planks to be Broken." For relaxation, he could not hear enough of recordings of the Scottish songs of Harry Lauder; and on his return to dry land he entertained reporters with this limerick:

> "I wish that my room had a floor;
> I don't care so much for a door;
> But this walking around
> Without touching the ground
> Is getting to be a damned bore."

When he came back to Sea Girt the candidate thought and prayed over the new responsibility before him. The address of acceptance that he had written was no hodgepodge of "expert" advice or "ghosted" phrasing, but a clear, straightforward exposition of the political philosophy of Woodrow Wilson himself. He was doing his best to belie the picture of a successful presidential candidate that his own yeasty pen had drawn some thirty years before, in *Congressional Government*.[3]

On notification day, August 7, great crowds gave to Sea Girt an air of fiesta. Standing on the porch, responding to the speech of notification, the prophet held out his hand for silence. He conceived that he spoke to "an awakened nation, impatient of partisan make-believe." The country, he believed, stood "confronted with an occasion for constructive statesmanship such as has not arisen since the great days in which her government was set up. Plainly, it is a new age. The tonic of such a time is very exhilarating. It requires self-restraint not to attempt too much, and yet it would be cowardly to attempt too little. The path of duty soberly and bravely trod is the way to service and distinction . . ."

It was a challenge to the restless spirit of a people still growing, as well as to intellects that had matured in wisdom. The voice that already had mastered great congregations in New Jersey was now appealing for the confidence of a people more heterogeneous. The prophetic art that he had cultivated so long and so well, generalities that healed wounds made by the barbs of factional argument, phrases that lifted thought

---

[3] ". . . he should wear a clean and irreproachable insignificance," young Wilson had written, ". . . the shoals of candidacy can be passed only by a light boat which carries little freight and can be turned readily about to suit the intricacies of the passage." *Congressional Government*, pp. 42–43.

above the spite of politics and arrayed it in the robes of statesmanship
—these touched his oratory with the sanction of divinity. Though he
thought the occasion too solemn for extemporaneous speech, he occasionally turned from his script and spoke familiarly. "I feel that I could
be a great deal more interesting," he said, "if I didn't have to read this
speech."

Running quickly over those provisions of the Democratic platform
that he approved, Wilson directed attention to the character and ideals
of the man who must be chosen to effect proposed reforms rather than
to analysis of the reforms themselves. Then, so that his people might
know him through and through, he set forth the ideals of representative
government that were dear to him.

At the end of his address he appealed to all classes and interests to
respect the common good. "We represent the desire to set up an unen-
tangled government," he asserted, "a government that cannot be used
for private purposes, either in the field of business or in the field of
politics . . . It is a great conception, but I am free to serve it, as you
also are. I could not have accepted a nomination which left me bound
to any man or group of men. No man can be just who is not free . . .
Should I be entrusted with the great office of President, I would seek
counsel wherever it could be had upon free terms."

Wilson gave evidence that he was thinking deeply and constructively
on the problems that the progressives of both parties were agitating.
He placed his greatest emphasis on the *bête noire* that he had fought
persistently for thirty years. "Trade is reciprocal," he said; "we cannot
sell unless we also buy." He left no doubt that he would seek to lower
tariffs. He proclaimed: "The tariff was once a bulwark; now it is a
dam." And then, parenthetically, "you can spell the word either way."

With the attitude of one trying to understand and not to blame, he
admitted that "up to a certain point (and only up to a certain point)
great combinations effect great economies in administration, and increase efficiency by simplifying and perfecting organization," that "the
organization of business upon a great scale of cooperation is, up to a
certain point, itself normal and inevitable." But his instinct for equality
of opportunity was too strong to permit him to let the case for trusts
rest on its economic justifications. "Big business is not dangerous because
it is big," he went on, "but because its bigness is an unwholesome
inflation created by privileges and exemptions which it ought not to
enjoy." He prophesied a restoration of "the laws of competition and of
unhampered opportunity, under which men of every sort are set free

and encouraged to enrich the nation," and asserted that the general terms of the federal antitrust law had apparently proved ineffectual.

Moreover, laws must be devised, he said, to prevent associations of capitalists in great financial centers that gave rise to suspicion of a "'money trust,' a concentration of the control of credit which may at any time become infinitely dangerous to free enterprise." Admitting that he did not know enough about banking to be dogmatic, he gave notice that "no mere bankers' plan" for reform would do.

There were other major issues that were challenging the government to act in the common interest. ". . . we have not yet found the rule of right in adjusting the interest of labour and capital," he reminded his people. No law that safeguards "the working people of America—the backbone of the Nation—can properly be regarded as class legislation or as anything but as a measure taken in the interest of the whole people . . ."

In dealing with the issues of the day [4] the prophet was not yet prepared to say that he had found a solution. He was now merely attempting to educate the people in his philosophy of reasoned adjustments of law in the public interest. Standpatters were reassured by the moderateness of his position. Here was a man who was aware of social evils and was temperate in his conception of remedies. In asserting that prices had climbed faster than wages, he had struck a note that rang sweetly in the ears of a people who were awakening to their needs as "consumers." Editors hailed the honesty, ability, and sanity of the speaker. The speech of acceptance became the keynote of Wilson's campaign. He ingeniously presented the same arguments again and again, freshly organized and phrased.

Wilson's tone was the more reassuring to thoughtful Americans in contrast with Bull Moose trumpeting. "After the earthquake a still small voice," the New York *Evening Post* commented. Just the day before the acceptance speech at Sea Girt, Theodore Roosevelt was nominated at Chicago by a convention of progressives who had rallied to that leader to form a third party. It was a constituency of diverse interests and opinions, drawn together by devotion to one of the most compelling

---

[4] As trustees for the Filipinos, Wilson asserted, "America was to set up the rule of justice and of right" in the Philippine Islands. He advocated a parcel post service, and provision for the health of the people. In conservation of the nation's resources, he said that "use and development must go hand in hand. The policy we adopt must be progressive, not negative, merely, as if we did not know what to do. With regard to the development of greater and more numerous waterways and the building up of a merchant marine, we must follow great constructive lines and not fall back upon the cheap device of bounties and subsidies . . . Such expenditures are no largess on the part of the Government; they are national investments."

personalities in American history. Social workers, random reformers, suffragettes, politicians with grievances, and an associate of J. P. Morgan —they were all there to cheer "Teddy." Their hero felt, he said, like a bull moose; and in accepting the nomination of the new party, he bellowed like one. His "Confession of Faith" struck his hearers like an evangelical challenge. It was a two-fisted, straight-from-the-shoulder appeal for a square deal for all the people, from a magnetic personality who in eight years in the Presidency had talked loudly about the curbing of trusts and had achieved little except conservation of certain natural resources.

Two of the great leaders in the early marches of the Western progressives already had fallen in step behind Wilson. At Baltimore, William Jennings Byran had surrendered the party standard to him. Though Senator LaFollette had remained nominally in the Progressive party after the split at Chicago, he thought Roosevelt's desire for a third term egotistical, his record as president opportunistic and unduly co-operative with undesirable corporate monopolies; and privately he expressed the hope that Wilson would "make no mistakes that would result in Roosevelt's election." Moreover, other Republican progressives were swinging toward the Democratic candidate, seeing the issue of the campaign as "Wall Street vs. Wilson."

The die-hard followers of Roosevelt, however, gave voice to the same criticisms of Wilson that George L. Record had raised at first in New Jersey. The educator might be a true progressive, they admitted; but was he not in reality just respectable window-dressing for a shop that was incorrigibly boss-ridden? Pleading fervently for paternalistic laws that would regulate trusts and set fair wages and working hours for women and children, Roosevelt declaimed fanatically about "establishing righteousness," cursed the Democrats, damned their platform as "vicious" and a model of "dangerous insincerity and bad faith," and nominated their candidate for the "Ananias Club." His staff had analyzed Wilson's record and speeches minutely, and hoped that the Democratic candidate, whom they recognized as their strongest foe, would be goaded into intemperate retorts.

Wilson, for his part, remarked that anyone arguing with the Bull Moose must be prepared to "adjourn his manners" and contradict categorical statements. He had protested against Roosevelt's "insane temper of egotism"; but later he exclaimed, "Yet what a glorious egotist he is!" There was a thrill for Wilson in the prospect of battling such a manly adversary. It made the game worth playing.

However much the Princeton scholar might disdain the intellect of his adversary, Wilson did not underestimate the physical and emotional force that he would have to overcome through appeals to reason. He counted President Taft out of the running. "The people will have none of him," Wilson thought. But of Roosevelt he wrote, late in August: ". . . just what will happen, as between Roosevelt and me, with party lines utterly confused and broken, is all guesswork. It depends upon what people are thinking and purposing whose opinions do not get into the newspapers—and I am by no means confident. He appeals to their imagination; I do not. He is a real, vivid person, whom they have seen and shouted themselves hoarse over and voted for, millions strong; I am a vague, conjectural personality, more made up of opinions and academic prepossessions than of human traits and red corpuscles. We shall see what will happen!"

Actually, Roosevelt's tricks of oratory were wearing thin. He fought by the law of the African jungle in which he loved to hunt, and often evoked sympathy for the object of his attack. The common touch that he had once exercised so masterfully had grown unpleasantly prickly with vituperation and braggadocio. "He has promised too often the millennium," Wilson observed. Moreover, Roosevelt's record as president had exposed him to accusations of opportune action at the expense of devotion to principle. He had definitely aligned himself with imperialists and advocates of a big navy, and thus forfeited the confidence of idealistic workers for world peace. But perhaps most damaging of all, he was challenging the American tradition that so far had forbidden more than eight years in the Presidency for any man.

In contrast, Wilson had made few enemies among progressives and his leadership in New Jersey had endeared him to Americans who put more faith in achievement than in words. More than forty thousand Republicans joined the Wilson Progressive Republican League and idealistic college men turned to the Democratic candidate in droves. Moreover, the chief financial support of the campaign came from new blood. Wilson stood strictly on his policy of accepting no contributions from men whose names had become politically bankrupt. At his direction, his financial managers were the first in an American presidential campaign to control expenditures under a budget. Wilson encouraged them to make "dollar drives" for "the people's candidate" and, enlisting the support of newspapers and banks in organizing such appeals, they took in almost a third of a total income of $1,110,952 in sums under $100. On the other hand, more than a third was contributed by forty wealthy givers—men from whom Wilson felt that gifts could be accepted without incurring embarrassing obligations. Enterprising men of proved intellect, drawn to an inspiring leader, were supplanting hacks, bosses, and demagogues in the inner councils of the party.[5]

Slipping away from Sea Girt occasionally in the late summer—but not always eluding his "keepers," as he called the newsmen—the Governor would spend a weekend in covert in New York, reveling in a gay show at the Hippodrome or in Isadora Duncan's dancing, and then sleeping around the clock at his club. He had come to find relaxation, too, in sources as diverse as detective stories and a translation of Chinese philosophy. To his lady friends he would quote respectfully from an Oriental sage. In spite of his resources for diversion, however, Wilson could not forget his aging arteries. He was a confirmed valetudinarian and still felt that the strain of the Presidency would take his life.

The candidate consented to deliver three speeches in New Jersey in August, but they were more polished and pleasant than moving. His thought floundered for a while in the gulf between his faith in local government and his recognition of the need for a strong executive, between his expressed fear that "government regulation will enslave us" and the rational conclusion that only by regulation could the power of monopoly be curbed. He was fearful that he might seem to be dividing the nation into "classes" and to be appealing to one against another. This was one thing, he said, that he prayed God he might never do.

Some critics found it hard to distinguish between the progressivism of Roosevelt and that of Wilson.[6] The Democratic candidate had criti-

[5] In New Jersey, Sugar Jim Smith tried to run again for the United States Senate and Wilson scourged him out of politics. William Hughes was nominated by a vote of almost two to one.

In New York, Wilson publicly called for a progressive candidate for governor and used his influence against the nomination of Dix by Tammany; but House, who was equally anti-Tammany but who had learned by experience "to work with the best material at hand," persuaded Wilson to compromise and to let a "bossless convention" nominate another Tammany brave.

[6] The appeal of Roosevelt, the New Yorker, was largely to urban voters and industrial workers. Having wandered far from his earlier conviction that individuals must work out their own destiny, Roosevelt seemed now to be leaning toward the sort of state socialism that had been introduced in Germany. The committee on resolutions of the Progressive party had approved a platform plank that would put teeth in the Sherman Antitrust Law. But George W. Perkins, Morgan partner and financial godfather of the party—a man who had lost the confidence of the people when Charles Evans Hughes had charged him with questionable business practices—had vetoed the antitrust proposal. And giving the dubious excuse that he feared the Sherman Law might be weakened, Roosevelt had concurred. He seemed willing to accept trusts, under safeguards to be imposed by government; and his supporters argued that there was no danger in having the people's affairs administered by a government that they themselves controlled. See George E. Mowry, *Theodore Roosevelt and the Progressive Movement*, pp. 270–71, and Richard Hofstadter, *The Age of Reform*, pp. 222–48.

cized Roosevelt's administration for its "passion for regulative legislation"; and in his speech of acceptance he had promised to restore "the laws of competition and of unhampered opportunity." But he was not well enough versed in the intricacies of trust regulation to combat his rival convincingly. A virile, disinterested intellect was needed to crystallize the virtuous impulses and tentative thoughts that were being generated by the prophet's will to serve.

In the fall of 1912 the counsel that Wilson needed was found in the mind of Louis Dembitz Brandeis. This brilliant lawyer belonged to a Hebrew family that for four generations had known the bitterness of war, revolution, and oppression. In his practice of corporation law, and in preparing lectures on business law for college students, Brandeis's sensitive mind perceived differences between legal justice and moral law. The strike of steelworkers at Homestead, the pitched battle of organized laborers with a private army of organized capital, set him thinking beyond the letter of the common law and in terms of the common welfare. He resolved to allow himself the luxury of helping to solve public problems, without compensation.

Brandeis thought of himself as a conservative, a conservator of the Constitution by the exercise of eternal vigilance against socialism, on the one hand, and unproductive, inefficient private monopoly of economic power, at the other extreme. He pleaded for the regulation of competition voluntarily, as far as possible, through cooperation within each industry; but by law when necessary in order to preserve equality of opportunity. In pursuit of these ideals he had subjected himself to the stern discipline that was required to walk the precarious tightrope of individual enterprise over the widening economic chasm. Nevertheless, when he pleaded in the public interest he was accused of inconsistency with arguments that he had previously put forth in behalf of private clients. Like Woodrow Wilson, he became a center of violent controversy. In Boston he was hated alike by the Irish bosses of the Democratic party and by reactionary bankers and lawyers.

Brandeis was wooed by Roosevelt's party, but thought of T.R. as a trumpeter of progressive impulses who had outlived his usefulness and of Wilson as "a man of substance" who could effectively put theory into action. A week after the Baltimore convention, Brandeis strongly endorsed Wilson. Early in August the two exchanged letters, and late in the month the lawyer was summoned to Sea Girt. The men talked for hours, mainly on the problem of curbing monoplies. "It seems to me," Brandeis wrote afterward, "that he has the qualities for an ideal

President—strong, simple, and truthful, able, open-minded, eager to learn and deliberate." And Wilson saw in the people's attorney a soul that shared his aspirations and a scintillating intellect.

In talks with Brandeis and in reading articles that the lawyer had written, Wilson found the technical advice that he needed on the problem of monopoly. On the issue that was foremost in the minds of sincere progressives, he could now attack the program of Roosevelt.

Beginning on Labor Day, the prophet spoke with new assurance, explaining the difference between the "New Freedom," as the Wilsonian program came to be called, and the "New Nationalism" of Roosevelt. Addressing ten thousand laborers at Buffalo, Wilson bitterly attacked Roosevelt's policy of retaining a protective tariff and legalizing monopolies under government supervision. The great monopolies were likened by Wilson to "so many cars of juggernauts" and he did not "look forward with pleasure to the time when the juggernauts are licensed and driven by commissioners of the United States." Regulation of trusts by "a self-appointed. divinity" or a "board of experts," he asserted, gave to the "wage slaves" no choice but that of involuntary servitude. "If you want a great struggle for liberty that will cost you blood," Wilson told the workers, "adopt the Roosevelt regulation programme, put yourself at the disposal of a Providence resident at Washington, and then see what will come of it . . ." He appealed to the common sense that he believed to reside in every responsible adult.

To seek specific ways of regulating competition without bringing government monopoly, Wilson went again to Brandeis. He was given a large dossier of papers on which he drew freely; and the advice of the counselor was given a bitter-sweet flavoring that made it no less palatable to Wilson. "I have no doubt," Brandeis wrote, "that your definite declaration on the lines indicated in this letter will make some enemies, as well as friends, but I assume that you have considered that matter adequately." Both the record and the philosophy of this legal genius were congenial, and he thanked Brandeis cordially.

In September the candidate set out on the first of two swings through the West. He was given an old, wooden private car that was attached to a slow train, and its frequent stopping made him talk from the rear platform more often than he wished. But in all his speeches on this trip he managed to set forth his ideas in ways so varied that even his traveling companions were not bored. Nine newsmen traveled with him, and clamored for advance drafts of his speeches; but after devoting two days to dictating addresses, he exclaimed: "By thunder, I've made my last speech to a stenographer!" He liked to talk, he said, right out of his mind as it was working at the time. Even when scripts were prepared, he did not follow them but used a few notes instead; and so, to protect him against misquotation, a recorder was employed to set down every word as he spoke it. He was grimly amused when told that his views on national politics, which seemed to him of more than passing importance, could compete with stories on the World Series only by prior reservation of newspaper space. He chatted with reporters who accompanied him, joked with them about their fortunes at poker, and amused them with anecdotes from his notebook collections. He was always solicitous for their comfort. Once, after a day of speech-making, he said, "I'm going to recuperate by having some fun with you boys"; and he sat up and swapped stories until nearly two o'clock. They marveled at his coolness under fire, his perspective. "It seems as if I can see myself and the campaign from a distance," he once remarked.

In South Dakota he gave voice to Brandeis's contention that Roosevelt's proposal to legalize trusts had originated in the minds of the president of the United States Steel Corporation and George W. Perkins. Conceding that "for all I know" it might be an honest proposal, Wilson argued that the effect of government sanction of this monopoly would be "to save the United States Steel Corporation from the necessity of doing its business better than its competitors." It was not mere bigness to which he was objecting—he knew that many voters worshiped big-ness—but monopoly, which Americans hated because it crushed such competition as helped to maintain economic efficiency and industrial freedom. Yet he still distrusted federal regulation of trusts. "The history of liberty is the history of the limitation of governmental power," he said on September 15 to the New York Press Club. And Roosevelt took this vivid assertion out of context and declared that to limit the power of the people's government was in effect to deny the citizens the right to check monopoly. Nevertheless, Wilson persisted in his argument, conferring with Brandeis again at the end of September and declaring to a New England audience: "I don't know enough to take care of the people of the United States."

In the speeches in the West, Wilson was slow to make contact with the mind of Main Street. When he made an obvious effort to lower the tone of his remarks, the effect was not happy; "let Roosevelt tell it to the Marines," he suggested awkwardly in one descent into the ver-nacular. His exalted concept of the office for which he was now a candidate made the gulf between him and his audiences wider than it had been in the New Jersey electioneering. His ingenuity was taxed to find ways of winning votes without offense to his concept of the dignity of the Presidency.

At Scranton, Pennsylvania, on August 23, he spoke in a hall with bad acoustics to an audience already wearied by other speakers. Appealing to the underdog—"the man who is knocking and fighting at the closed doors of opportunity" —he identified his personal revolt with the cause of all who were fighting monopoly. "I do feel proud of this," he said; "that no law, no rule of blood, no privilege of money, picked me out to be a candidate even . . . it is a fine system where some remote, severe, academic schoolmaster may become President of the United States." Then he went on to declare that, whether elected or not, he would find some way to keep on fighting. His audience cheered wildly.

Toward the end of September he went to New England, where the labor question had been dramatized by a violent strike at Lawrence. There he fitted his talks carefully to the biases of his audiences, assuring the people of the insurance center of Hartford that "the ancient traditions of a people are its ballast," telling the factory workers of Fall River that "we ought to hold a brief for the legal right of labor to organize," making a slashing attack at Bridgeport on "the money trust," but mollifying Boston investors by assuring them that he was not "fighting the trusts" but was "trying to put them upon an equality with everybody else." He was trying to reassure all of his congregation, to let every soul know that its prayer was heard by a leader who was both sympathetic and just. He waved gaily and threw out campaign buttons to crowds that gathered to catch a glimpse of him. Addressing admirers perched on boxcars in a railroad yard at Willimantic, he saluted them as "fellow-citizens and gentlemen in the pit, and ladies and gentlemen in the boxes," his literary mind not asking, apparently, how many of the boxcar sitters knew what "the pit" was.

Though he could not accept all the invitations to speak that came to him from local Democratic leaders, the oratorical artist in him was made supremely happy by the frequency of his bookings. In a flush of satisfaction over the feeling that he was winning because the people understood him, he gained seven and one-half pounds in two months. But the pace was grueling. Twice he narrowly escaped serious injury: once when a freight car sideswiped his Pullman, broke the windows and tore away the brass rail on the rear platform; again, when a rut in the road threw him against the top of the automobile in which he was riding and stitches had to be taken in his scalp. Outdoor speeches were always an ordeal for him, and after an attempt to make a huge audience hear without an amplifier, he complained that his voice "went wheezy and had no volume or resonance in it."

At times the whisperings of malevolent foes made him sick at heart. In December of 1911, New York newspapers had reported that Mary Allen Peck entered a libel for divorce against her husband, from whom she had been long estranged; and in 1912 she won her suit and reverted to the name of her first husband, Hulbert. The tongues of gossip had wagged damagingly, perverting facts that none of the principals tried to conceal from their true friends. To acquaintances in Bermuda the lady had often read letters from her dear friend at Princeton, and sometimes she lent them; and Wilson read her replies to the circle of family and friends in the house on Cleveland Lane. Shocked by the publicity given to her suit for divorce and by the malice of rumormongers, Mary Allen Hulbert told him that she raged inwardly, and sometimes laughed—it seemed so absurd. When an undertone of grief crept into her gay letters, Wilson responded with chivalrous loyalty, told her how much it meant to have a true friend, urged her to release her spirit by confiding in him without restraint, comforted her with the reminder that the divorce proceedings could reveal nothing to be ashamed of. Again, recklessly projecting his own ideals into the character of another, he created a beautiful figment of virtue set free. Her inner resources were unparalleled, he assured her, and she would emerge from her ordeal finer than ever. He confessed that his pastoral pride was touched by his success in drawing out the sweetness of her nature.

Political foes gleefully misunderstood. In April of 1912, Wilson's valise was stolen at Chicago; and apparently suspecting an attempt to find incriminating letters, he said very gravely to his family circle: "No letter of mine, nothing I have ever written, could hurt my reputation if published." But scurrilous minds, and politicians who pandered to such, continued to whisper; and the aspersions were the more insidious because they were confined to conversational sewers. Theodore Roosevelt himself had written similar letters to "Dear Maria"—Mrs. Bellamy Storer; but he delivered the unkindest slur of all against his Democratic rival. "It wouldn't work," he squeaked. "You can't cast a man as Romeo who looks and acts so much like an apothecary's clerk."

Toward the end of September the rumor reached Wilson that a scandal was being fabricated against him. When some of his political

associates questioned him, he solemnly assured McAdoo that he had
never written a word to any woman that he would not read to his wife.
House understood, and explained: "We Southerners like to write mush
notes." When the canard ran to the effect that Thomas Peck had insinuated certain things to a certain judge, Wilson suspected the integrity of
the magistrate and of another who was in a position to give evidence,
criticized a judge whom he thought ungallant to his friend, wanted to
break the neck of one of her persecutors.[7]

Sometimes it seemed hardly worth while to fight on in a world so
sordid. Halfway through the campaign, Wilson protested to Mary Peck
—now Mary Hulbert—that "there would be no bearing its tremendous
burdens if there were not the element of large duty and serviceableness
in it. There *are* great issues, the greatest imaginable, issues of life and
death, as it seems to me, so far as the sound political life of the country
is concerned; and I therefore keep heart and strength." The blood of
his pioneering ancestors was still stirring in the migrating mind. Like
a frontiersman, he would clear away the dead timber in the political
wilderness, would plow and harrow and plant seed that season and
climate demanded, would tend good old roots and try to make them
blossom more gloriously.

Millions of hearts were touched by the message of the prophet as
he campaigned through the West in October. At the baseball park at
Indianapolis the throng was so large that all could not hear; and when
a cry of "louder" arose, a man near the platform yelled: "Never mind,
Woody old boy. If they can't hear, we'll tell them about it tomorrow."[8]
The candidate's eyes glistened as he swept the crowd toward him. "To
my mind," he said, "it is a choice between Tweedledum and Tweedledee
to choose between the leader of one branch of the Republican party and
the leader of the other branch of the Republican party." Asserting that
Roosevelt was not a genuine progressive, he asked his hearers whether
they could see "any breach anywhere in the Democratic ranks."

The *Star* reported that the speech at Indianapolis was Wilson's "first
real campaign punch," and afterward the candidate said to a newsman:
"Did you hear? They called me 'Woody'!" He seemed to the journalist

[7] The unpleasantness of the Peck divorce is suggested by an item in the gossip column of
Town Topics of June 24, 1909: "Pittsfield, Mass., is now devouring with great glee the contents of the little notes which Thomas D. Peck has been sending out to tradespeople carrying
information that he has made Mrs. Peck a liberal allowance and that hereafter she will pay
all bills which she may contract . . ."

It seemed to Mary Peck that the very walls of her home reeked with suspicion, jealousy,
and melancholy. Mary Allen Hulbert to R. S. Baker, July 28, 1928.

[8] John W. Davidson, Jr., *A Crossroads of Freedom*, p. 318.

a jolly fellow who embraced throngs with the same thrill that comes in a first dance with a beautiful girl.

In Nebraska the candidate's throat was filled with dust and in ten talks his voice was worn to a hoarse whisper; but Bryan was ably supplementing his efforts, averaging ten speeches a day for seven weeks, imploring his loyal Nebraskans to do twice as much for Wilson as they ever did for Bryan and telling newsmen that Wilson was an expert campaigner and knew how to adapt himself to crowds. Resting on the Sabbath, as was his custom, the candidate stayed at Bryan's home at Lincoln; and the prophets went together to a Presbyterian service, the Great Commoner serving communion. A journalist begged him to pose for a picture with Bryan, shaking hands. The Nebraskan held out his, willingly; but Wilson said, "No, I'll not pose. It's too artificial."

At Denver, where they had not forgotten his great speech on the English Bible, Wilson paraded the streets between thousands of enthusiasts.[9] At St. Louis he encountered bagpipers, bands, tooting horns, and torches flaming in a procession four miles long. Men rioted to force their way into the packed Coliseum. At Chicago scores of thousands stood outdoors in a cold rain to cheer the candidate: offices were closed, streets festooned with streamers. In these cities, and at Cleveland, Wilson responded as well as his failing voice would permit. Stopping at Springfield, Illinois, he asserted that Roosevelt was "a very erratic comet now sweeping across the horizon," that the Democratic party was now more faithful than its opponent to the principles of Abraham Lincoln. Fatiguing as it was to throat and nerves, the Western trip helped the prophet to share the idealism of his people. His spirits were lifted, his resolution strengthened. Having spoken more than thirty times in ten days, he rested at home in mid-October.

While Wilson's fervor had deepened, Roosevelt's tactics were becoming more and more hysterical. The Bull Moose was using all his talent for showmanship. Climbing into the cab of a railroad engine, he ran it down the track, much to the discomfort of the passengers. When wounded in the chest by a fanatic at Milwaukee, he persisted in filling a speaking engagement at the risk of death. Wilson sent a message of personal sympathy. Colonel House, who liked to say that "the best politics is to do the right thing," went against the opinion of the campaign committee in urging their candidate to make the chivalrous

---

[9] In this visit to Denver, Wilson became specific in naming conditions that in his view led to monopoly and should be controlled by law: viz., collusion in fixing high prices, pre-emption of raw material, espionage, cutthroat competition, restrictive contracts.

gesture of canceling his speaking engagements until Roosevelt recovered; and Wilson saw the political effectiveness of such a move as well as its fairness. "Teddy will have apoplexy when he hears of this," he chuckled. He did, however, fill engagements already made, directing his fire against Taft and the conservatives rather than against the wounded leader of the Progressives. When Roosevelt, resuming his campaign, advocated antitrust laws so definite that judgments would not be exercised by any man or men, Wilson did not make capital of this shift toward his own position.

In Delaware the Democratic prophet paid tribute to La Follette, who was now wholeheartedly behind Wilson, and at Pittsburgh he harked back again to the American Dream, maintaining that it had been kept alive by the Democrats through a period of repression by monopolies. "The Democratic party," he asserted, "has stood steadfast in a deep-rooted faith . . . a faith as old as human liberty. It is . . . the only faith that has ever made the intolerable burden of life possible to bear, namely, the faith that every man ought to have the interest of every other man at his heart. The faith that would set up a government in the world where the average man, the plain man, the common man, the ignorant man, the unaccomplished man, the poor man had a voice equal to the voice of anybody else in the settlement of the common affairs, an ideal never before realized in the history of the world."

The shooting of Roosevelt was a reminder that every presidential candidate lived under the shadow of violent death. After an anonymous Italian had threatened to "shoot Wilson the same as Roosevelt was shot," Ellen Wilson did not sleep well until her husband was placed by Colonel House under the guard of Captain Bill McDonald of the Texas Rangers—a crack shot who was said to be able to hit a mosquito's eye at fifty paces. During the closing weeks of the campaign this guardian dogged the steps of the candidate, kept his eyes open, his mouth shut, and his finger on the trigger of his "artillery." When dense crowds hemmed in the candidate, Captain Bill lowered his shoulders and plowed a way through.

Even a bodyguard, however, could not protect Wilson from the heckling of special pleaders and fanatics who revived many canards that had proved effective among certain groups of voters. But Wilson had learned to laugh at the charges. "If all these fabrications could be brought together," he wrote to McAdoo on October 23, "they would leave a very flat taste in the mouth, for they would entirely neutralize one another and prove that I was nothing and everything. I am a normal man, following my own natural course of thought, playing no favorites, and trying to treat every creed and class with impartiality and respect." Through the campaign he had held himself accountable to history. Someday, he told one audience, a quiet jury would sit in a room, surrounded by books and documents, and judge him. "I think of the anticipated verdict of another generation," he said, "and I know that the only measure and standard by which a man can rise or fall is the standard of absolute integrity; that he can deceive nobody but himself and his own generation for a little space."

He had revealed himself to the people as he was—compassionate pastor, philosopher, historian, and orator, a man of intellect who could be depended on to act in the national interest. On October 26 he published a recapitulation of his campaign arguments: The nation must be free in order to be strong; and monopolies, protective tariffs, and political graft were the greatest obstacles to freedom. "Bosses cannot exist without business alliances," he said. "With them politics is hardly distinguishable from business."

By the last week of the campaign it seemed obvious that Wilson would be the winner. Gambling odds were 5 to 1 in his favor, and his final public addresses were saluted with all the ardor that crowds can bestow on a man crowned with success and riding to power. On October 31 the campaign came to its climax in New York City. The night before, the Bull Moosers had given Roosevelt an ovation that lasted forty-five minutes. To outdo them, the Democracy yelled and whistled for more than an hour. Even Bryan at the height of his power had evoked no outburst like this. After sixteen lean years, the wolves of the party smelled red meat. Overwhelmed and bewildered, gazing at Ellen Wilson as if to restore his equilibrium, the candidate forgot what he had planned to say, gave a rambling summary of the issues, and confidently put the case in the hands of "the jury." The Progressives had been inspired personally by their leader. "Follow, follow," they had sung, "we will follow Roosevelt; anywhere he leads we will follow him." But the enthusiasm of the Democrats, Wilson told his New York audience, thrilled him because it was a demonstration for a cause and not for a man. "What the Democratic party proposes to do," he told the people, "is to go into power and do the things that the Republican party has been talking about doing for sixteen years." He issued a national appeal for support for the Democratic candidates for the Congress; and the last few days of the campaign found him pleading before the voters of New Jersey for the party ticket. Then he retreated to the sequestered house on Cleveland Lane, to sleep soundly and await the verdict of the nation.

At ten o'clock on election day, November 5, the Democratic candidate walked down familiar Princeton streets to the polls in the firehouse. Refusing a preferred place in the line of voters, he cast his ballot. In the afternoon McAdoo and Josephus Daniels, for whom the Governor had developed "a real affection," joined the family, and the men took a long walk to the historic sites of the town. In a university building Wilson showed them the framed diploma of James Madison, the only Princeton man ever elected to the Presidency.

After supper the family circle gathered for a reading from Browning. As favorable returns came in, Wilson's face turned grave. At ten o'clock a message came to Ellen Wilson. Placing her hand lightly on the shoulder of her husband, she said: "My dear, I want to be the first to congratulate you." He took her hand and they stood in silence, but her serene face seemed to say: "I believed he could and he has." A half hour later McCombs confirmed the news and reported that the election of a Democratic Congress seemed assured also.

The covenant was now sealed; and Woodrow Wilson accepted the mandate of the people as solemnly as he had regarded his profession of faith, in adolescence, in the humble chapel of the Columbia Theological Seminary. But now there was no time for meditation. The college bell was pealing. More than a thousand students, waving flags and torches, were cheering in his yard, singing "Old Nassau." He went to the front door, stood on an old, broken rocking chair that his friends held firm. The light of a red flare fell on his face. When the boys saw him, they whooped jubilantly. The jaunty front that he had put on in the campaign wilted now. Tears filled his eyes, and for a few minutes he was silent. Then, with such emotion as he had felt when he bade farewell to his university congregation, he said: "Gentlemen, I am sincerely glad to see you . . . There is so much to reconstruct, and reconstruction must be undertaken so justly and by slow process of common counsel, that a generation or two must work out the result to be achieved . . . I summon you for the rest of your lives to work to set this government forward by processes of justice, equity, and fairness. I myself have no feeling of triumph tonight. I have a feeling of solemn responsibility."

As they swarmed up to him, Wilson shook hands with each briskly, thanked them "for caring so much." To his best friends, regardless of rank, he said heartily, "Go on inside." [10] Intimates went to the dining

[10] Mrs. George McLean Harper and F. C. MacDonald, who were present, to the writer.

room to enjoy Ellen Wilson's hospitality, and soon the house was seething with people and buzzing with talk. The President-elect escaped to bed as quickly as he could; and on the morrow, which President Hibben had declared a university holiday, Wilson went out to watch football practice.

When the final tally was made, it showed Wilson commanding 435 electoral votes, against 88 for Roosevelt and 8 for Taft. His popular vote was only a plurality and was less than that of Byran in the election of 1908. Like Jefferson and Lincoln, Woodrow Wilson had profited by a split in the opposing party. The victory was not of the Democracy, but rather a triumph of the spirit of the times and of a man's sincere sharing of that spirit. The validity of Edmund Burke's philosophy of representative government was being proved on the American scene. The needs of the people were to be served by reasoned change in the laws. There would not be another revolution now, or another civil war.

CHAPTER XV

TIME TO THINK

THE VERY DAY after the election, full consciousness of the weight of his mantle fell upon the prophet. Still as intellect-conscious as when he had first boasted to his father that he had a mind, Wilson felt that the issues of the campaign had been vague and nothing of importance had been settled. The prophecy of Henry Adams had been fulfilled: the progressives had voted for "anybody sooner than Taft"; the conservatives had "let in anybody sooner than Theodore." This political shindy had not satisfied a man who aspired to debate great issues in parliamentary dignity.

To his family he remarked: "One is considered queer in America if one requires time for concentrated thought." And yet he said boldly to the people: ". . . the time has come now to do a lot of thinking." Wilson now considered himself free to let his mind work at its natural pace and depth, at whatever cost in popularity.

However, some fifteen thousand messages came in and challenged his desire to meditate. Many of them were more concerned with preferment of the writers than with congratulation of the recipient. McCombs brought a list of Democrats "entitled to immediate and generous consideration" and reminded Wilson that party men wished to have their say about appointments. But the President-elect replied icily: "I must have a chance to think."

To cut himself loose from such stifling concerns, Wilson escaped to Bermuda. There—in a cottage [1] "free to the wind, open to the sun"— he relaxed and played with those dearest to him. He was getting "many kinks" out of his head, he wrote to McCombs. He wore old clothes, did the family marketing by bicycle, and brought food home in a basket hung on the handlebars. Sometimes the Wilsons would picnic on a beach, and he would display the treasures of scenery that he had discovered in previous visits. Then coming home for tea they would criticize canvases that Ellen Wilson had painted; and at supper, sitting

---

[1] With his wife and two younger daughters Wilson occupied the home of Mary Allen Hulbert, who was in New York. Margaret Wilson stayed at New York to continue her singing lessons.

by candlelight on a porch above lapping waters, they tried to see into the future. Wilson had just been plagued by neuritis and was often attacked by sickening headaches; and for several days after reaching Bermuda he suffered from indigestion. His wife watched over him anxiously, controlled his diet, stood behind his chair and massaged the back of his neck. In spite of the flushes of good health that had always come to him when he had dropped administrative cares and vacationed out of doors or indulged in the give-and-take of electioneering, Wilson had not been able to escape the invalidism that had been fixed on him six years before.

Even in the island haven his privacy was invaded. The Bermudians let him alone; but the soldierly governor general, who lived in a guarded palace and ruled some twenty thousand souls with Old World pomp, bowed to the civilian leader of a hundred million Americans by rapping at the kitchen door of his cottage. However, Wilson was so annoyed by curious tourists that he decided to forsake his bicycle for a carriage and to follow the local custom of "hanging out the basket" to signify that he was not at home and callers might leave their cards.

Trailed by news hawks who sought world-shaking import in every move, he indulged an impulse to tease them.[2] "Gentleman," the President-elect said to them one day, "you have interrupted me in the preparation of an important state paper." And then, as they apologized and backed away, he grinned and explained that he was drawing up a "domestic formula" for Mrs. Wilson to follow in entertaining the governor general at tea. At other times he would greet journalists with a look that led the unwary to hope for great revelations but was interpreted by veterans to mean that he had just made a discovery of colossal unimportance. Once he confided that by looking sideways at the waves on the South Shore, he and his daughters had tested and proved the theory that if one looks at a thing with head on one side, or upside down, the result is a compressed and comprehensive view of the beauties of the object. Ellen Wilson entertained journalists so delightfully that they were diverted from their quest. But let a reporter overstep a line of decorum that Wilson defined, and his wrath would rise quickly.

[2] At least once during the election campaign Wilson had delighted in deflating importunate and self-important newsmen. He took joy in his ability to manipulate words so that he could lead reporters to delude themselves. Colonel House called it "grazing the truth." Once two young cubs who had naïvely fallen into a trap set for them tried to rebuke Wilson by giving him a cold shoulder, and he had laughed uproariously and said to them, "Oh, come off your perch." See C. W. Thompson, *Presidents I've Known*, pp. 297–303. It was the feeling of this correspondent that Wilson had no desire to be mean or tricky, but was playing a game with words, as he had played in boyhood with his father.

One day, as he was courteously asking cameramen not to photograph the ladies of his family, a cad aimed his lens at Jessie Wilson. The cheeks of the outraged father flamed, he clenched his fists and started toward the man; and then, remembering himself, he shouted: "You're no gentlemen! I want to give you the worst thrashing you've ever had in your life; and what's more, I'm perfectly able to do it!" However, the intrusions that fame had brought upon him did not break the spell of the island. It was still, to him, a fairyland where make-believe was real, a place in which it was almost impossible to do anything but play, where one could lie abed in the afternoon and savor Kipling's *Rewards and Fairies*. Only by closing the blinds and turning on the electric lights, he said, could he recall the United States and its business.

After a few days of rest the President-elect devoted himself to answering messages from those whom he esteemed. He assured his classmate Hiram Woods that he wished him never in any circumstances to drop the old epithets of intimacy. Replying to Dean Fine's congratulations, he wrote of "the old days in Princeton, days of strain and pain . . . days when men were bound together by something more than ordinary affection," a feeling that "seemed to have iron put into it by the influences of strong conviction." He wrote affectionately to his nephew, George Howe, and invited him to visit at the White House. The President-elect yearned to be the same "Tommie" Wilson, the same Uncle Woodrow, unaffected by pride of position.

In the clear calm of life on Bermuda, Woodrow and Ellen Wilson meditated upon what would face them in Washington. He contemplated "plunging into the maelstrom" with many grave thoughts. "But having sought the opportunity, I must face it and meet it with the best that is in me," he wrote to George Howe.

In his island retreat the President-elect read a novel entitled *Philip Dru, Administrator,*[3] which Colonel House had written and given to him just before he left New York. Hoping to give wide circulation to his ideas for progressive federal legislation, the Colonel, in a vague and experimental way, had tried to express them through a fictional hero who forcibly seized the government of his state and became a beneficent dictator. In that position he established a league of nations that was based on Anglo-Saxon solidarity. Moreover, he destroyed trusts by abolishing protective tariffs and worked out a progressive income tax and a banking system that presaged the Federal Reserve. Believing that

[3] House's book, published in 1912, was dictated hurriedly, lacked literary merit, and did not circulate widely. House intimated that his hero was "all that he himself would like to be but was not." *See* Alexander L. and Juliette L. George, *W. W. and Colonel House*, p. 131.

"labor is no longer to be classed as an inert commodity to be bought and sold by the law of supply and demand," House's hero worked out a plan for social security.

Returning from Bermuda with idealistic fervor refreshed, Wilson gloried in using the prestige of a president-elect to strike out for what he conceived to be the interest of the people of New Jersey. During the Governor's absence, Tumulty had had to fight—figuratively and literally —to prevent the election of a Nugent-Hague man as speaker of the Assembly. Wilson returned in time, however, to oppose State Controller Edwards for the office of state treasurer. But he could not overcome the opposition of the bosses to proposals for revising the constitution of the state and transferring the power of drawing juries from the sheriffs to a governor's commission.[4]

Wilson's last months as governor, like his closing years as president of Princeton, were marked by impetuousness as the aspirations of his spirit broke through the restraint of administrative responsibility. He seemed determined to assert that he was a free individual, that his pledge of emancipation from control by all pressure groups was not just political talk. Speaking briefly at Trenton, he told the party men that only progressives would be chosen by him to guard the interests of the people. Goaded by assertions of Roosevelt's managers that New Jersey was the mother of trusts and that the Governor had failed to alter the laws, Wilson had the chancellor draw up remedial legislation and espoused it in his annual message, on January 14, Seven bills[5] were drafted to curb price fixing and other acts of collusion in restraint of trade. Applying Wilson's doctrine that "guilt is personal," this legislation provided for the fine and imprisonment of guilty directors of corporations. The measures were forced through the legislature by the Governor in February. The "Seven Sisters Acts" gave warning of what might soon be expected on a national scale if offending trusts did not put their houses in order of their own free will. Sincere progressives could not forget that, in two years under Woodrow Wilson, New Jersey had made greater strides toward good government than under any other governor.

[4] Wilson left the White House in the spring of 1913 to take the stump in New Jersey in behalf of these reforms. Finally, the legislature passed a compromise measure for jury reform that was declared unconstitutional by the courts.

[5] George Record, who had drafted the earlier reform bills and was not consulted about the "Seven Sisters Acts," felt that they were "stupid laws." Record to R. S. Baker, April 6, 1926. The effect of the laws, which followed interpretations of the antitrust laws by the United States Supreme Court, was to make corporations seek refuge in Delaware. The legislature began to amend them in 1915 and repealed them in 1920.

Now that he was no longer dependent on newsmen for favorable interpretation to the voters, the President-elect made less effort to conceal his scorn and irritation at their tactics. Nothing vexed Wilson more than self-appointed oracles who ventured to speak for him, unless it was opponents who strove to embarrass him by quoting his past words against his present beliefs. When a reporter pestered him for news of his choices for the Cabinet, he exploded with "Damn it, man, can't you take me as you find me?" and in the next breath he begged pardon for "blowing up."

In Bermuda he remarked, offhand, that it would be better if the inauguration could be held later than March 4 and was amazed when this personal whim was cabled to New York. Good copy became scarce, as the door closed on Wilson's policy of "pitiless publicity"; and in the absence of fact, reporters indulged in speculations that angered the Governor. In the last days at Trenton, there descended a cold front that presaged chilly press conferences in the White House.

Colonel House's apartment in New York was one of the few havens in which Wilson felt secure enough to express himself freely. A year after he met the Colonel, Wilson had had enough doubts about his friend to ask Captain Bill McDonald whether House had always been successful in his Texas campaigns and what sort of men he had chosen. But now Wilson knew that he could trust both the information and the judgment of the "Little Wizard" in New York. House could see so much more than other men and report it so much better, always getting the right point! The hand of the Colonel was constantly on the shaping of the President's Cabinet.

More than once the Wilsons ran up to New York for a night with the Houses and went to the theater with them. The President-elect was embarrassed by the applause of the audience. The colonel prompted him to bow; and after complying he spoke to his host, whose father was English born and who had gone to school in England, of the sense of fair play that prevented theatergoers at London from staring at royalty. Returning to House's rooms, the men would munch sandwiches and chat as Southern gentlemen.

The Colonel was impressed by his friend's essential gallantry. The talk drifted to the subject of war; and Wilson, though he thought it economically "ruinous," asserted that there was no more glorious way to die than in battle. "White lies" were discussed: Wilson thought them justified when the honor of a woman was concerned and also when the welfare of a people was at stake. But when House dissented mildly and suggested silence as a better means of defending secrets of public policy, Wilson agreed. Princeton affairs were reviewed without bitterness, and the President-elect expressed a yearning for ten million dollars to buy the university and make it what he thought it should be. On another evening he spoke to House of a college friend who harrowed him by complaints of huge responsibility and almost certain failure. As for himself, he confessed, he would lose his reason if ever he gave way to his apprehensions. House reassured him, saying that he would find strength in serving his fellow men without regard to self-interest. This had never been done by any other American leader, the Colonel suggested. "No," Wilson replied, "not since Jefferson." This fellow Virginian, the idol of Grandfather James Wilson, had grown in the esteem of the President-elect, who now wrote of Hamilton exactly what he had said of Jefferson years before: he was "a great man but not in my judgment a great American."

Woodrow Wilson could be depended on to pattern his policies on those of no other President. It seemed to him that the thought of a leader, like democracy itself, must be "a stage of development" if it was to be politically valid. He had once explained that, like all great men of affairs, Thomas Jefferson "took leave to be inconsistent and do what circumstances required, approaching the perfection of theory by the tedious indirections of imperfect practice." Only a few basic principles of government were rigidly fixed: as to the details of their application to social and industrial conditions in the year 1913, Wilson's mind was still open to advice from those who sincerely shared his fundamental purposes.

The President-elect of the nation had serious business afoot. He must be "Prime Minister," he thought, "as much concerned with the guidance of legislation as with the just and orderly execution of the law." When young Franklin D. Roosevelt came to Trenton to call and when Wilson began to summon congressmen to confer on federal legislation for the special session of Congress that he promised to convoke in April, it became evident that the national government was soon to feel the full force of the reforming will that had not spent itself at Princeton or in New Jersey. He found the national politicians self-centered and given to laboring the obvious, was as impatient with them as with badgering newsmen.

In Woodrow Wilson the protests of Greenbackers and Populists, of agrarians and laborers, had a spokesman who was solicitous for their economic freedom. Impulses that had agitated American society for decades were now mellowed, rationalized, and blessed in the person of the new President. Was his mind sufficiently free from the formalism of the Old South and the bonds of scholasticism to inject the moving blood of immigrants and frontiersmen into the hardening veins of a government that was leaning toward plutocracy and a statism that threatened the freedom of individuals? Would his own aging arteries bear the strain? Was he now completely master of his impetuous righteousness, his pride, his high temper?

Woodrow Wilson knew his failings as well as his responsibilities, in the winter of 1913. Twenty years before, in writing of Abraham Lincoln, he had conceived the burden of the Presidency as "too great to harden and perfect any sinew but that which was already tough and firmly knit." Characteristically, as he now faced up to the great challenge himself, Wilson found strength in ideas that in the eyes of little men of the hour were illusory but in the longer view of the prophets of mankind were eternal. In 1911 he said: "I have found more true politics in the poets of the English-speaking race than I have ever found in all the formal treatises on political science."

On the morning of March 3 came the hour for leaving Princeton. The trustees of the university had extended formal congratulations but they had planned no farewell for the prophet whom they declined to follow.

His people, however, let the President know how they felt. The boys added a verse to their faculty song:

> Here's to Woodrow Wilson who
> Cleaned up Taft and Teddy, too.
> So once in a hundred years we nip
> The Pres-i-dential championship.

And one night a crowd of three thousand villagers paraded to the house on Cleveland Lane, led by the president of the bank and the president of the Woodrow Wilson Club of Princeton. Bearing a loving cup to their hero, they clamored for a speech; and Wilson responded earnestly, as a citizen to his neighbors.

The man who sometimes had held himself aloof in pulpits of executive responsibility became again the youth who had reveled in singing glees, in ball games, burlesque shows, Coney Island, and Dwight Moody evangelism. He spoke tenderly of neighborliness and community fellowship. "If there is one thing a man loves better than another," he said, "it is being known by his fellow-citizens."

It would be a "very poor President," Wilson asserted, who lost consciousness of his home ties. He had always believed, he said, "that the real rootages of patriotism were local, that they resided in one's consciousness of an intimate touch with persons who were watching him with a knowledge of his character.

"You have got to know people in order to love them. You have got to feel as they do in order to have sympathy with them. And any man would be a very poor public servant who did not regard himself as a part of the public. No man can imagine how other people are thinking. He can know only by what is going on in his own head, and if that head is not connected by every thread of suggestion with the heads of people about him, he cannot think as they think.

"The real trials of life are the connections you break . . . I have never been inside the White House, and I shall feel very strange when I get inside of it. I shall think of this little house behind me and remember how much more familiar it is to me than that is likely to be . . . One cannot be neighbors to the whole United States. I shall miss my neighbors."

He would miss his college boys, too, and they did not forget him. Hiring a special train to Washington, they crowded into the coaches, cheering and shouting. They took the Wilson luggage to the station, and many tagged along with a band as the Wilsons, rebelling against the cavalcade of autos awaiting them at their door, walked the half mile to the train, past the home on Library Place that they had built twenty-one years before, and within view of Witherspoon Hall, where "Tommie" Wilson had discovered his mental powers. Stepping confidently, the President-elect swung his cane and doffed his tall hat and his Ellen smiled serenely. Old friends stopped them to say goodbye; and to one of them, a Presbyterian minister, the President-elect replied: "Had you not better pray for me?" Entering a parlor car at the end of the train that had been reserved for his party, Wilson heard the Princeton locomotive cheer—sharp, solid, and clear—and waving from the back platform, he joined in singing "Old Nassau" as the train gathered speed.

The singing was choked in some throats, and the Wilsons looked very wistful as the towers of the university sank into the horizon. The break with Princeton was complete; never again did Wilson spend a night in the village that had been his home for twenty-two years.

CHAPTER XVI

AT HOME IN THE WHITE HOUSE

DURING WILSON'S FIRST HOURS in Washington, Princeton associations were perpetuated. On the evening of his arrival a cheering mob of undergraduates escorted him to the Willard Hotel, where eight hundred alumni honored him at dinner and heard him say: "As I stand here upon the eve of attempting a great task, I rejoice that there are so many men in the United States who know me and understand me and to whom I do not have to explain everything . . . I thank God that it is so, and thank you profoundly for this evidence of it." The next day Princeton colleagues came to lunch at the White House, and in the evening he shared his exalted hopes for his country with the old boys of the Class of '79.

He had asked that he be allowed to take office without any extravagance that might overtax his physique or his pocketbook. As it was, he had to borrow a large sum—for the first time in his life—in order to finance the move to Washington and to outfit himself and his family. Ellen Wilson bought suitable jewels and dresses for her daughters, and a handsome gown for herself—not because she cared for clothes, she explained, but to do justice to Woodrow's inauguration. Her husband insisted on giving her a diamond pendant that became known, *en famille*, as "the crown jewel." But he decided that—for the first time since the inauguration of Princeton's other American president, James Madison—there would be no inaugural ball. He disliked making himself and his family the center of social and commercial aggrandizement. It was bad enough that his wife had come home from a shopping expedition complaining that she had felt, under the gaze of vulgar eyes, like an animal in a zoo. The ladies of the family wished to carry themselves with the easy grace that had marked them in the South as "quality," and though their man found it difficult to take himself seriously as a political figurehead, and danced around his Ellen in the privacy of their hotel room chanting "we're going to the White House today," [1] nevertheless, he assumed in public the dignity that he thought befitting the

---

[1] Alice Wilson McElroy to the writer, April 30, 1950.

Presidency. This citizen who had been accustomed to dress casually and to polish his own shoes and who had never owned a vehicle grander than a bicycle was unchanged beneath his tall hat and immaculate clothes when he stepped into the two-horse victoria that was to take him to his new home.

Inside the White House he was greeted by retiring President Taft. Together they faced a battery of cameras on the south porch, toeing a line that was made by face powder from the vanity box of a woman photographer. It was suggested that a view be taken that required the men to look away from the cameras; but Wilson remarked that they would much prefer to look toward the lady. Anxious faces broke into smiles, and the incoming President was off on the right foot in his first ordeal of publicity in the White House.

From the south porch the men went to a four-horse landau, and soon trumpets sounded and they were moving toward the Capitol. The air was balmy with promise of spring, buds were bursting, and the sky was overcast as they passed through the swampy lowlands and the motley stores and residences that bordered Pennsylvania Avenue. For the moment Wilson was diverted by the traditional pageantry of the day. The elite Essex Troop from his own New Jersey preceded him, and crowds kept cheers in the air until the procession reached the Capitol.

When the party appeared on the steps above the rostrum, tens of thousands of expectant faces turned upward and roared a welcome. William Howard Taft, ruddy and jovial, moved ponderously to his seat, while Woodrow Wilson, spare and alert and very solemn, showed signs of strain as he came face to face with the responsibility that he feared and the opportunity that he coveted. In front of the stand a large area had been kept vacant by cordons of cadets and midshipmen. Perceiving this, and seeing seas of eager faces beyond the pale, the President-elect motioned to a guard and said: "Let the people come forward!" Thus, in a phrase that became a watchword, Wilson's pastoral instinct asserted itself.

And come forward the crowds did, so that they might the better hear this prophet accept the charge that was administered by Chief Justice White. Wilson had asked that his wife's little Bible be used for this occasion, as it had been when he took his oath as governor of New Jersey; and when it was opened at random for the touch of his lips, it happened that a ray of sunlight broke through the overcast and fell upon the words of the 119th Psalm:

And take not the word of truth utterly out of my mouth; for I have hoped
in thy judgments.
So shall I keep thy law continually for ever and ever.
And I will walk at liberty: for I seek thy precepts.
I will speak of thy testimonies also before kings, and will not be ashamed.

When the twenty-eighth President of the United States stepped forward to deliver his inaugural address, the anticipation of his people
reached a climax. Would he talk to them now in the vein of his pre-
election speeches? Would he follow through and redeem his pledges?
Only two people knew. He had composed his message in the recesses
of the Princeton library, and had shared its text with his dearest confidants. One of these, Edward M. House, who disliked crowds and remained quietly in his club that morning, had read the address and
characterized it as "*off the beaten track* and full of spirituality." The
other intimate was present, however. During the ceremony she slipped
inconspicuously from her place on the rostrum and, going to a spot
directly beneath, gazed up with maidenly rapture at the noticeable man
whom she had served and guided for thirty years. For this was a great
day of fulfillment for Ellen Axson Wilson, as for her brilliant husband.
He had confessed to her, the very last thing before they were swept apart
by the people, that without her he never would be where he was.

His voice was strong and clear, but not oratorical, as he explained
the real significance of the most portentous time of change that the
United States had experienced since the Civil War. The occasion, his
scholarly perspective revealed to him, meant much more than the mere
triumph of a political faction.

"The success of a party," he asserted, "means little except when the
nation is using that party for a large and definite purpose. No one can
mistake the purpose for which the nation now seeks to use the Democratic party . . ." Americans had a new insight into their national life
and found it great in material wealth, in moral force, and in its system
of government. But evil had come with the good, corroding fine gold.
"With riches has come inexcusable waste. We have squandered a great
part of what we might have used . . . We have been proud of our
industrial achievements, but we have not hitherto stopped thoughtfully
enough to count the human cost . . .

"We have come now to the sober second thought," the prophet went
on. "The scales of heedlessness have fallen from our eyes. We have
made up our minds to square every process of our national life again
with the standards we so proudly set up at the beginning and have always carried at our hearts. Our work is a work of restoration."

And then, after enumerating some of the measures that he proposed to take, he came to a climax of challenge:

The nation has been deeply stirred. . . . The feelings with which we face this new age of right and opportunity sweep across our heartstrings like some air out of God's own presence, where justice and mercy are reconciled and the judge and the brother are one. . . .

This is not a day of triumph; it is a day of dedication. Here muster, not the forces of party, but the forces of humanity. Men's hearts wait upon us; men's lives hang in the balance; men's hopes call upon us to say what we will do. Who shall live up to the great trust? Who dares fail to try? I summon all honest men, all patriotic, all forward-looking men, to my side. God helping me, I will not fail them, if they will but counsel and sustain me!

It was one of the briefest inaugural addresses in the history of the nation, and one of the most moving.

The ceremony concluded, the incoming servants of the Democracy swarmed to the White House. When the President reached the mansion he found more than a hundred there—family, friends, and members of his Cabinet with their wives. The guests were all very polite, very deferential to the great man of the hour, and his face flushed with embarrassment when they kowtowed to him and called him "Mr. President." He was impatient, though, to go out front, where bands would be playing and men parading.

A little after three o'clock Wilson laid his plate aside and took his place on the reviewing stand as commander in chief of the armed forces, looking every inch the part. Again, as at the Capitol, he took thought for the people milling about below him. Noticing a lame woman who moved with difficulty through the pressing throng, he leaned over anxiously, intent upon helping her; and when someone went to her side his face brightened in a smile. In the exhilaration of cheers, music, and sunshine on glittering uniforms, Woodrow Wilson was happy and radiant, as on the holidays at Princeton when he used to say to his daughter: "Now let's find a band, Nellie." His family marked a change —a greater buoyancy in his walk, a gleam in his changeable gray-blue eyes. There was a chiseled keenness in the strong, deep-lined face that he had described as "that of a horse." God had made him ugly, a friend said, "but Woodrow has made himself handsome."

When it was over, he was reminded that he was no longer free to celebrate at will; for the police and secret service men closed around him and escorted him back into the White House. Once there, he thanked the Inaugural Committee and went quickly to join his family. But they could not yet be alone. Dozens of relatives had come to celebrate the investiture of the Wilsons. The clan were in high spirits as they ran hither and yon, exploring every cranny of the old mansion, exclaiming at their discoveries, impressing on the staff, with free-and-easy ways and drawling speech, the fact that, for the first time in forty years, the President was Southern bred.

Woodrow Wilson entered the jamboree with tolerant good humor, and joined with his kin in singing "Now Thank We All Our God." Finally, going to his room toward midnight, he rang for his trunk. Not knowing which bell to push, he tried several; and soon a doorkeeper appeared and found him prepared to sleep in underwear. The missing trunk was not delivered until one in the morning; and so at the end of his first arduous day in the capital, the President of the United States crept into the big carved bed of Abraham Lincoln without benefit of nightclothes.

The next morning he surprised a maid in the hall with a cheery "Good morning!" At breakfast he was in rare form, relating little incidents of the day before that had struck his funny bone, amusing the relatives and guests. He had his usual fare—two raw eggs in grape juice, and porridge and coffee. Exactly at nine he left for his office to prepare for the first meeting with his Cabinet.

The composition of the Cabinet was a secret that Wilson had shared only with his family and Colonel House. Immediately after election he had begun to worry about selecting men. He had found himself face to face with the constitutional question that he had analyzed in writing of Cleveland's administration twenty years before. Should the President take the Constitution literally, choose "a purely administrative cabinet," and himself dictate policy to it? Or should the party be held responsible for the character and motives of the men that it supplies to guide the President? The tendency had been in the direction of the latter system until Cleveland had included several independent citizens in his second Cabinet.

In 1893, Wilson himself had inclined toward party responsibility, feeling that efficiency in administration could not be attained unless the Cabinet served to link the President with his men in Congress. Yet when the problem became his own in the winter of 1913 he was moved, by academic impulses that had become ingrained, to appoint the ablest servants of his purposes regardless of party influences; and he let it be known that those who applied for jobs were least likely to be appointed. He told House that he wanted *practical* idealists of constructive ability —men who were honest, brave, efficient, and imaginative. However, much as he desired an official family that would be able and devoted to his higher purposes, he could not ignore political considerations.[2]

Even before the election House had begun to look for good men for Cabinet posts, so that he would be ready with counsel if consulted; and candidates for office, sensing this and flattered by the skill with which he played up to their egos, had made House a target of their pleas for recognition. Democratic politicians had sat so long in the seats of minority and opposition that their inexperience in leadership was equaled only by their long-starved appetite for perquisites. After the triumph at the polls the pressures increased, and the Colonel served as a buffer against them. He tactfully fended off men of influence who wished to hold office or to give advice. His experience told him that such men could be venomous if their urge for recognition was not gratified; and as he entertained them and mollified their fears, he learned much from one about another.

As early as September of 1912 the Colonel thought that he had convinced Wilson that it would be best to take William Jennings Bryan into the Cabinet, rather than risk the embarrassment that might result if the orator should turn his great influence against the Administration. The Colonel urged in November that his friend invite Bryan into conference and consider offering him the portfolio of State; but Wilson was reluctant to make direct contact, for fear that Bryan would insist on discussing appointments and other matters on which they could not agree. He was aware that the Great Commoner might try to sweep into office the great train of henchmen who had followed him without reward through twenty years of famine. Though he respected the sincerity of Bryan's emotions and was convinced by a flood of messages that it would be political suicide to exclude him from the Cabinet, Wilson asked House three or four times whether the Colonel persisted in recommending that this politician be made secretary of state. Receiving an affirmative answer each time, he offered Bryan the portfolio on December 21. The Great Commoner feared that his unwillingness to have liquor at his table might be embarrassing; but getting Wilson's

[2] Of the candidates for the Cabinet chosen tentatively by Wilson and House in November, the Colonel noted that five had voted for Taft and some had not voted the Democratic ticket for sixteen years. He spoke to Ellen Wilson about this and she replied: "But you would not keep them out of the Cabinet on that account?" No, the Colonel trimmed, but he would not include too many who were not rock-ribbed Democrats. He foresaw that, twenty years in the future, "no one would know how the different departments of the government had been run and . . . the President's fame would rest entirely upon the big constructive measures he was able to get through Congress; and in order to get them through he had to be on more or less good terms with that body." It seemed to House that this was one of the most important things to be considered and that Wilson's future reputation would rest almost wholly upon it.

assurance that he could suit himself in this matter, he tentatively consented to serve.

Distressed by a tendency of journalists to picture Bryan as an arbiter of policy and appointments, Wilson had several earnest talks with House in January. Inviting the Colonel to dinner at the Princeton Inn, the Wilsons questioned him on many matters of policy and etiquette that were plaguing them. On this occasion House was asked to choose for himself any of the Cabinet seats except that to be filled by Bryan. The Texan, however, did not wish to tie himself down to a responsibility that might overtax his strength. He still coveted the role of a "free lance" with a roving commission to serve. The day after their talk at Princeton he wrote to his friend: "As an ex-officio member . . . I can do my share of work and get a little of the reflected glory."[3]

In the disinterested spirit that he insisted on displaying, the colonel continued to act as conciliator and intermediary. In dealing with the rivalry of McAdoo and McCombs for the Treasury portfolio, however, House's talent was severely taxed. For some time Wilson had looked with favor upon William G. McAdoo, hero of the Baltimore Convention. Unlike his rival, William F. McCombs, who had asserted that if his erratic services as campaign manager were not rewarded with the Treasury post he would accept nothing,[4] McAdoo had put forward no impor-

---

[3] *House Papers,* I, 100–101; and House Diary, Jan. 8, 1913. Charles Seymour has suggested that House must have been influenced, at least subconsciously, by another consideration that had been impressed upon him by his experience in serving the governors of Texas. "He believed," Seymour wrote, "that in essential matters he and Wilson would agree in principle, but they might conceivably disagree as to method. If he were in an official position such disagreement would compel his resignation, unless he were to be placed in the unpleasant position of carrying out a line of action which he disapproved. So long as he remained in a private capacity, he could give what advice he chose; and if the President did not follow it, House could shrug his shoulders and turn his attention to other matters in which Wilson might accept his guidance. 'Had I gone into the Cabinet,' House once said, 'I could not have lasted eight weeks.' Outside of the Cabinet he lasted for eight years."

When House finally assumed official responsibility as an associate of Wilson at the Paris Peace Conference, the position actually did prove to be an "unpleasant" one for the colonel. (*See* Vol. II of this work.)

[4] McCombs complained that the President was ungratefully trying to banish him "to St. Helena." The neurotic invalid was with the President-elect for an hour late in December, and when he went Wilson felt weak and ill, as if he had been sucked by a vampire.

Colonel House tried to finesse by advising McCombs not to resign from the chairmanship of the National Committee, and trusting to his contrary nature to impel him to do the opposite. McCombs persisted in holding on, however, and threatened to do what he could to obstruct the administration if he was not treated better. Though Wilson refused to compromise by offering a Cabinet post to the man with a private understanding that it would be declined, he finally gave McCombs a public statement that both saved the man's face and protected Wilson himself against charges of ingratitude.

On May 2, House arranged a meeting between McCombs and McAdoo at the Vanderbilt Hotel and the latter reported afterward to the Colonel that the two "Macs" had "buried the hatchet" under six drinks. Told of this, Wilson exclaimed: "What children!"

tunate claim to recompense for his loyalty. In fact he sometimes gave the impression that, like House, he would prefer to be independent. On February 1, despite strenuous efforts by his rivals to block his appointment, he was called to the room of the President-elect at the University Club in New York and asked whether he would do Wilson the honor of serving as secretary of the Treasury. Flattered by the offer and the courteous way in which it was tendered, McAdoo expressed appreciation; but doubting his fitness for the position, he protested that he was neither banker nor financier. It was being gossiped about that he was too much the promoter to cope with technical problems of finance and that, on the other hand, his close associations with New York bankers might brand him as an agent of Wall Street.

Wilson reassured him, however. "I don't want a banker or a financier," he declared. "The Treasury is not a bank. Its activities are varied and extensive. What I need is a man of all-round ability who has had wide business experience. I know you have the necessary qualifications . . . We must enact a new tariff bill and a new currency or banking measure to fufill our platform pledges. The Treasury will have to play an important part in this legislation." Denying that he was trying merely to pay off a political obligation to McAdoo, the President-elect went on: "The responsibilities of the Presidency are great and I cannot perform them alone. If I can't have the assistance of those in whom I have confidence, what am I to do?" [5]

Having squared himself with his chief's principles, the man of enterprise who had once himself been bankrupt agreed to undertake the arduous task of financing the "New Freedom." McAdoo's political acumen won the respect of Colonel House and immediately showed itself in a magazine article interpreting the capacities and the manly compassion that he saw in his chief: "The Kind of Man Woodrow Wilson is," he entitled it.

When the President went into the Cabinet room on the morning after inauguration, he found Bryan on his right and McAdoo on his left. Beyond them sat three men who had served him well at Baltimore and

---

Bitterly disappointed because the President-elect had appointed only one of the thirteen men recommended by him for high offices, McCombs felt that his talents had been exploited by a sort of hypnotic power in Wilson, who had then treated him "like a red-headed stepchild." McCombs went to Paris in the summer of 1913, suffered an appendectomy, got married, and, appalled by the high cost of embassy life, decided once and for all in August to refuse the ambassadorship at Paris which Wilson had offered. But he remained chairman of the Democratic National Committee until 1916. Until his death, in 1921, he bitterly reviled Woodrow Wilson.

[5] W. G. McAdoo, *op. cit.*, p. 178.

were to stand by until his work as president was over: Josephus Daniels, Albert S. Burleson, and William B. Wilson. Daniels, the genial North Carolina editor who had been a disciple of Bryan and a member of the party's National Committee for sixteen years, had been considered for the office of postmaster general; but when House suggested that that office required a more aggressive man and one better known in Congress, Wilson offered Daniels the Navy.[6]

Congressman Burleson of Texas was appointed postmaster general. Wilson had wanted "one thorough-going politician" in his Cabinet— someone who had the confidence and esteem of legislators; but his first thought had been to keep Burleson in Congress, where he had sat in seven Houses of Representatives, and to use his influence there among the party men. But Burleson had worked for Wilson at Baltimore, and when the Colonel argued that to ignore the man would suggest ingratitude, Wilson and Burleson came to an understanding. The practical politician said: "I will be loyal to your administration and sympathetic with your policies. When I reach the point where I cannot give you my undivided loyalty, I will tender my resignation. When I talk to you, I will always tell you my candid views." And to this the idealist replied: "Burleson, that is just the kind of man I want."

William B. Wilson, unrelated and personally unknown to the President-elect, had been made secretary of labor after his sponsor, Senator Hughes of New Jersey, had declined the post. This Wilson had come from Scotland at the age of eight, had begun work a year later in Pennsylvania coal mines, had helped to organize the United Mine Workers of America, and had served as its secretary-treasurer for eight years. W. B. Wilson had once been imprisoned for defying an injunc-

---

[6] The appointment of Daniels was strongly urged upon Tumulty and Wilson by Thomas J. Pence of Raleigh, who had worked with Daniels on campaign publicity. Many Democrats felt that Daniels lacked executive ability and was ignorant of the Navy's problems.

Wishing to choose an assistant secretary of the navy from upper New York State, Wilson asked Herbert Bayard Swope of the *World* for suggestions and was told that Frank I. Cobb favored young Franklin D. Roosevelt. Secretary Daniels, who had been attracted by Roosevelt's enthusiasm for Wilson as a spectator at Baltimore and by his fight for liberal causes in the New York Senate, recommended the New Yorker to Wilson, who said, "Capital!" Daniels told the President that it had been suggested to him that every Roosevelt wanted to direct everything and that this one would try to become secretary of the navy. When Daniels asserted that any man who feared supplanting by his assistant thereby confessed that he didn't think himself big enough for his job, Wilson concurred. Roosevelt accepted the office on March 9 and told Daniels that McAdoo had asked if he would like to go into the Treasury but the Navy post would please him most since he loved ships and had studied naval affairs. Herbert Bayard Swope's review of Frank Freidel's *Roosevelt* in the *New York Times Book Review*, Nov. 9, 1952; Letter, Swope to A. M. Schlesinger, Jr., Dec. 6, 1954, in the possession of the latter; *F.D.R.: His Personal Letters, 1928–45*, p. 1121; Daniels, *The Wilson Era: Years of Peace*, p. 124; Daniels Diary (Library of Congress), March 6, 1913.

tion, but had a reputation for integrity, fairness, and devotion to the cause of industrial peace. Elected to the House of Representatives, he had played a part in developing the Bureau of Mines and had helped to draft the bill creating a separate Department of Labor; and it seemed fitting that he should become its first secretary.[7] Moreover, President Samuel Gompers of the American Federation of Labor had gone to Trenton to urge this appointment.

In addition to these stanch henchmen—Daniels, Burleson, and W. B. Wilson—there was another who was destined to serve the President-elect to the very end. David F. Houston was of all the Cabinet the closest to his chief in intellectual capacity, experience, and philosophy. He had attended South Carolina College when Uncle James Woodrow taught there and had seen Woodrow Wilson for a few moments in the revered professor's house. Houston had studied history and economics at the Harvard Graduate School, specializing in government and finance, and had served on the faculty and as president at the University of Texas. He had observed local politics keenly and had conceived a deep respect and admiration for Edward M. House; and when he had dined with Wilson and discussed the tariff, he had found the Governor to be "the straightest thinking man in public life." Believing himself better fitted for the portfolio of Agriculture than for the Treasury, which House once suggested to him, Houston was recommended to Wilson by both House and Walter Hines Page. He agreed to take the secretaryship of Agriculture with the understanding that he might retire at the end of two years, but became so devoted to his work and his chief that he remained in the Cabinet for eight.

House felt that he had found a liberal candidate for the Department of Justice in the person of James C. McReynolds. This man—a Democrat whom Theodore Roosevelt had made assistant attorney general—had acquired a reputation for radicalism as a result of his insistence on invoking criminal provisions of the antitrust law against tobacco and coal operators. In the view of McReynolds, who was actually the most conservative and consistent of legalists, his duty was to enforce the law, whatever its purport; and he had dramatized his prosecution of corporate interests by resigning when Taft's attorney general had made a settlement that seemed to nullify his efforts. The Colonel arranged a casual meeting between Wilson and McReynolds in mid-February, and

[7] The secretaryship of Commerce and Labor—an office established by an act of 1903—had not pleased either management or labor. An act creating separate departments of Commerce and Labor was signed by Taft barely in time for Wilson to appoint secretaries before Inauguration Day.

the President-elect was so well impressed that he appointed the man.

The Interior Department had worried the incoming President, for the problems of conservation were charged with political dynamite. During Taft's administration the national resources had been handled in a way that led to allegations of corruption and privilege; and progressives were wondering whether Wilson could find a man who would be able to resist private interests and state politicians that wished to exploit government lands. Here again Colonel House led Wilson to a promising candidate. Franklin K. Lane, born on Prince Edward Island, educated in California, and seasoned in many a battle for progressive principles, had been appointed by Theodore Roosevelt to the Interstate Commerce Commission. Now chairman of that body, he told House that he was content to remain in his position. The more Lane protested his unfitness for the Cabinet, however, the greater had been the inclination of Wilson and House to find a place for him. They were impressed by a thoughtful letter that he wrote to recommend a fellow Californian for the Interior portfolio, and he had a reputation as a speaker of charm. Asked by the President to sound out the candidate, House had brought his persuasive powers to bear and had secured Lane's consent to serve in any capacity that Wilson thought best—even the Interior Department, which he considered the most prickly of Cabinet seats. They planned to give him the War portfolio at first; but when Newton D. Baker refused to leave his reform commitments as mayor of Cleveland to join the Cabinet [8] and when party leaders vetoed Walter Hines Page as secretary of the interior, Wilson turned to Lane and appointed him at the last moment.

This left the War portfolio vacant. Various names were discussed; and Hugh C. Wallace, who later became ambassador to France, was given an invitation and declined. Finally Tumulty, who had been urging that at least one New Jersey man should sit in the Cabinet, looked through the Lawyers' Directory and ran across the name of Lindley M. Garrison,

[8] Wilson grieved over Baker's decision. This former student (at the Johns Hopkins) had worked effectively in the progressive movement in Ohio and had supported Wilson energetically at Baltimore, but had felt obliged to stay at Cleveland and try to carry out certain reforms that he had promised before his election. Declining Wilson's offer, he said that he considered the misgovernment of large cities the greatest disgrace to American citizenship. After Baker had gone out of the room, House—according to his Diary—"braced the Governor up again and told him not to mind Baker's refusal and that we could arrange without him." In March of 1916, Baker became secretary of war.

Party leaders had objected to Page because, as a Southerner, he was unacceptable in a post that controlled the distribution of Civil War pensions and, as an associate in a publishing business that operated an open shop, he might be a target of labor.

vice-chancellor of the state's highest court, whom he remembered as a judge of high repute. Thereupon Wilson invited Garrison to his office, sized him up quickly, and persuaded him that he owed it to his country to give up his secure position and risk the hazards of Cabinet life.

Likewise the secretaryship of Commerce, which had just been separated from that of Labor, had not been filled until the last moment. Wilson had intended to appoint Louis D. Brandeis, who had more support from progressives than any other candidate for the Cabinet. But a rumor of this possibility had created a panic of protest among businessmen, some of whom had supported Wilson; and five days before the inauguration opposition had grown so strong that the President had to cast about for another man.[9] It was finally settled on February 28 that the Commerce Department would be administered by William C. Redfield of New York, a manufacturing executive and a congressman whom Wilson had at first intended to make postmaster general. The President-elect was impressed by a tariff speech by Redfield that had been sent to him by Villard.

The casualness of Wilson's efforts in completing the choice of a Cabinet had been in contrast with the enthusiasm that he had shown for this responsibility just after the election. The Democratic party was destitute of seasoned officials and there were deficiencies in the group brought together. The South, represented by five of the ten men, was given unwarranted recognition, especially in view of the fact that much of Wilson's strength had come from the West. Moreover, most of the Cabinet were devoid of experience in the matters they were to deal with, and many of them were deplorably weak in political prestige. They

---

[9] After the election Wilson had been urged to make Brandeis attorney general and had given much thought to this possibility, but House dissuaded him from putting this controversial figure in the Department of Justice. When it was objected that Brandeis was a Jew, Wilson retorted: "And a fine one!" On Jan. 3, 1913, the President-elect wrote to his friend Tedcastle regarding Brandeis: "Of course I know how some of the best men in Boston hate him, but I think I know the reason for that feeling, and I want to get outside that circle." On Jan. 27, 1913, he wrote to Bryan, who favored having a Jew in the Cabinet but apparently distrusted Brandeis: "I think that Brandeis has been very grossly aspersed but of course I am looking into the matter very carefully and shall do nothing to bring the administration into question in any way."

Assured by the journalist Norman Hapgood, who had led him to Brandeis, that the charges against the man's integrity were groundless or distorted, Wilson made it plain that he would listen to objections based on political expediency but that, if more allegations were made against Brandeis's character, he would appoint the man forthwith. McCombs, Governor Foss of Massachusetts, and others induced Redfield to say that he would not serve in the Commerce Department under Brandeis; and then, on Feb. 27, they gave to Wilson a long list of opponents, including many congressmen. When financiers of the stature of Henry L. Higginson and Cleveland Dodge joined in the protest and House added a word of caution, Wilson yielded in order to preserve party harmony.

were, as Wilson himself had put it in writing of Cleveland's advisers, "without Washington credentials." Only Bryan had a large and compact following in the party, though Burleson had influence in the House, W. B. Wilson had prestige among labor organizations, and McAdoo had made rapid progress toward political leadership. Obviously it would require heroic efforts for the Administration, which had come into office on a minority vote of the American people, to generate power to enact the legislation to which its leader was committed.

When the President greeted the gentlemen of the Cabinet on the morning of March 5, he looked very trim and fit. Taking the chair at the head of the long table, he talked with an assurance that was in contrast with the nervousness of Redfield, who incessantly brushed back his reddish whiskers with finger and thumb, and with the ebullience of Daniels, who had entered the room exclaiming: "Isn't it great? Isn't it wonderful?" Burleson, who affected sideburns and the dress and manner of an uncouth politician and went about with a black umbrella hung on his arm, sat with a priestly dignity that led Wilson to call him "The Cardinal." Lane was bald, plump, and sociable. The others were decorously expectant. W. B. Wilson, the self-made man, seemed shy in this imposing company; and Garrison the jurist was ill at ease in his sudden plunge into a strange environment.

After a brief pause Wilson said, quite simply: "Gentlemen, I thought we had better come together and talk about getting started on our way." Then he and Bryan told a few stories.

When the Cabinet came together again the next day, they underwent an ordeal by photography. Finally the President, wearying under the steady fire, said that they had had enough; and after the photographers left he told of a spiritual convert who vowed to control himself, but, presiding at a religious meeting in which a controversy reached a climax in the throwing of eggs at himself, finally drew his revolver and shouted: "This damn Job business is going to last just two seconds longer!"

There were three meetings of the Cabinet during that first week; and the secretaries who had not known their chief intimately saw clearly now that the caricature of the cold and bookish Wilson was based on myths. He proved to them that he was not what Bryan once had pictured him to be: an incorrigible schoolmaster under whom no self-respecting man could serve and who would leave nothing of the Democratic party when he was through with it. He conducted the sessions like the experienced moderator that he was. First he presented matters on which he wanted "common counsel"; and after getting the opinions of the men, he then called on them one by one, in rotation, to present questions from their respective departments that required general consideration. There were sometimes sharp differences of opinion; and after listening well, Wilson would try to arrive at the sense of the meeting and to state it succinctly. He did not force through policies that did not commend themselves to the understanding of the body; and he drew upon his fund of stories to shut off discussions that grew fatuous or dangerously controversial. His courtesy kept the spirit constructive and friendly.

Moreover, he soon made it clear that they must have no secrets from each other. When Bryan whispered something to him and the others were obviously embarrassed, he said to them: "Mr. Bryan was just telling me," and then repeated the remarks. He feared that it might be inferred that the secretary of state and he had secrets from their colleagues. "I do this in the beginning," he explained, "because I recall the severe criticism in Gideon Welles's *Diary* because, as he said, Secretary Seward would upon occasion lead Lincoln into a corner and they would talk in an undertone for minutes while the other members of the Cabinet sat as if they had no part in the important matters that Seward was communicating in the President's ear. There will be no secrets between this President and the secretary of state and our colleagues at the Cabinet table." [10]

The qualities of leadership that had charmed men of the Princeton faculty and the New Jersey legislature were captivating the little band of public servants at Washington. They believed in one another and in their chief and were exhilarated by a feeling that they were achieving great things. They soon found their leader willing to delegate to them the management of their departments, ready with counsel when they sought it, and reluctant to interfere except when questions of foreign policy or Congressional leadership were at stake.

In the meetings of the Cabinet the President made quick estimates of

[10] Daniels, *The Wilson Era: Years of Peace*, pp. 140–41. After only a week in service Franklin K. Lane wrote to Walter Hines Page: "The President is the most charming man imaginable to work with . . . There has been a particularly active set of liars engaged in giving the country the impression that Woodrow Wilson was what we call out West 'a cold nose.' He is the most sympathetic, cordial, and considerate presiding officer that can be imagined. And he sees so clearly. He has no fog in his brain. As you perhaps know, I didn't want to go into the Cabinet, but I am delighted that I was given the opportunity and accepted it, because of the personal relationship; and I think all the Cabinet feel the way I do." Lane, *Letters*, p. 133. More than a year later Lane testified to House that at no time had the President hurt the feelings of any member of his Cabinet. House Diary, April 29, 1914. Houston thought Wilson "amazingly considerate . . . even more amazingly patient and tolerant." David F. Houston, *Eight Years with Wilson's Cabinet*, I, 88–89. On the other hand, Vice-President Marshall, invited by Wilson to attend Cabinet meetings, came to only one and felt that he would not be listened to. D. C. Roper, *Fifty Years of Public Life*, p. 287.

his men. On Saturday the 8th he talked them over with the Colonel, whom he invited to the White House to chat with him at nine in the morning. Dressed in a sack suit of gray, wearing a gray tie, Wilson chatted with his confidant for more than an hour and described the behavior of each of the secretaries at their first meeting. Houston had had a good deal to say and Burleson had been so garrulous that, if he kept it up, he would have to be suppressed. Redfield had shown the best mind for analysis, but Lane could analyze and at the same time use a lively imagination. McReynolds had talked seldom, but always to the point. Bryan had been the most surprising of the group. He had shown a restraint and a reasonableness that had endeared him to his chief, who soon was referring to his secretary of state *en famille* as "my elder son." [11]

Wilson gave himself conscientiously to the routine duties of an incoming president. He showed appreciation of traditional etiquette. On the afternoon of his first day in office he received 1,123 guests: the entire Democratic National Committee, legislators with constituents, officials, editors, and ambassadors. One of these, Lord Bryce, he met with genuine delight as an esteemed fellow scholar. He made contact, too, with the office staff that was taken over from Taft's regime and that now was to be directed by Joseph Tumulty.

For a time he had doubted that Tumulty, who was only thirty-three, could fill a position as exacting as that at the White House; and he was not unimpressed by hundreds of letters warning him against the dangers implicit in his secretary's Catholicism. But much as he liked Tumulty and appreciated his devotion,[12] he felt that a collectorship of revenue would be a more appropriate position for him than secretary to the President, and Wilson had hoped to persuade someone of the caliber of Newton D. Baker to serve him at Washington. House and McAdoo, however, had felt that Tumulty's "political instinct" would be an essential asset. Bryan had spoken in favor of including a Catholic

---

[11] Marjorie Brown King to the writer. When he became secretary of state, Bryan retired from the active staff of the *Commoner*. With Wilson's consent, he arranged to supplement his salary by lecturing to Chautauqua audiences. However, when leaving for one of his speaking trips the secretary of State notified the President that he was subject to recall to Washington at any moment. "It would be as unfair to me as to yourself," Bryan wrote, "to allow a pecuniary consideration to have a feather's weight if the public good is at stake."

[12] Wilson had named Tumulty clerk of the Supreme Court of New Jersey in the spring of 1912, though he had continued to serve the Governor as secretary without salary. When forming the Cabinet, Wilson and House looked for an eligible Catholic of Cabinet timbre and found none available. House Diary, July 7, 1914. House recalled later that, since his own experience had been confined to gubernatorial secretaries, he had accepted Tumulty at McAdoo's estimate. House Diary, May 24, 1916.

in the official family; journalists to whom Tumulty had endeared himself by joining in their pranks now stood by their jolly accomplice;
and when Ellen Wilson added her endorsement of the young man to
whom she had become a second mother, Wilson's conscientious doubts
had been overcome. Casually, one day in February, he had asked his
secretary if he would like to continue in his position, and the young man
had gone out and exploded to a friendly reporter: "Charlie, I've got
it!"

The presence of Tumulty brought practical jokes and merriment
into the office in the West Wing of the White House. Moreover, it
brought assurance that the routine of public business would go on
much as it had in the governorship, and it gave Woodrow Wilson the
comfort that he always derived from familiar associations.

Tumulty sat in the next room of the West Wing, free to enter the
President's office at any time, and strove to stem the torrent of callers
and correspondents. He digested incoming letters for his chief, and
amused Wilson by deftly culling grains of sense from verbose documents from Very Important People.[13] Every day Tumulty gave editorials to his chief, who read only a few of the friendly papers. The
youthful secretary was a political weather vane and helped in the process that Wilson was wont to refer to, mystically, as "sitting quietly and
listening with the inner ear." The President attributed to him an extraordinary appreciation of how a thing would "get over the footlights"
and thought him his most valuable audience. Many of Wilson's speeches
and state papers went to Tumulty for criticism that proved effective.
Moreover, the President's secretary took initiative and showed genius
in carrying out his chief's promise of "pitiless publicity" for affairs of
state.

Soon after taking office Wilson institutionalized press relations by
establishing regular conferences. All his life he had been devoted to the
ideal of a free press. He hoped that press conferences might give his
people the reassurance that the British derived from question periods
in Parliament. Facing about a hundred correspondents at the White
House, he replied extemporaneously with the understanding that he
would not be quoted directly. He was sometimes stricken with self-
consciousness when he remembered that the whole nation was listening

[13] The President, wishing to avoid waste of time and to guard himself against being influenced by personalities, preferred succinct memoranda to oral reports. He indicated approval
by an initialed "Okeh." Franklin D. Roosevelt once said that he learned a trick from Woodrow
Wilson, who had told him: "If you want your memorandum read, put it on one page." Louis
Brownlow, *The President and the Presidency*, p. 62.

for his words. At times his social instincts got the better of his reserve and he volunteered confidential remarks without making it clear that they were "off the record"; and when these were printed he felt that the reporters had been unappreciative of his frankness. His feelings hurt, he would turn cold and seem intellectually arrogant.

Sometimes he lectured the newsmen on his philosophy of journalism and invited criticism. Suggesting in his first conference on March 15 that the men "go into partnership" with him, he appealed to them to bring in a "precious freight of opinion" from the nation and then join him in making "true gold" to send out from Washington. He could share the objective view of able journalists toward the Presidency, but sometimes found it hard to understand when newsmen criticized him in good faith. He lacked time and energy to cultivate the friendship of individual journalists, except for a few who had won his confidence and respect. Indeed, he had learned at Trenton that by granting personal interviews to certain newsmen he might sow jealousy in the hearts of others.

During the first months in the Presidency, Wilson maintained spasmodic contact with the Washington correspondents. Six weeks after inauguration he enjoyed the traditional dinner of the Gridiron Club, where, he said, he received his "first public discipline as President, responsible to all who look on." Describing the occasion to Mary Hulbert, he wrote: "It was very amusing and very instructive, in a way, and I was treated with singular sympathy and consideration, as if they really liked and admired me, and were a wee bit in awe of me! Fancy! Can you imagine it? I was a good deal moved, and very much stimulated." Unfortunately he disappointed the journalists by failing to rise to their gibes with repartee, in the manner of Taft and Roosevelt.

Though Wilson at first held news conferences twice a week, he came to regard them as ordeals and was glad to avoid them whenever he could plead overwork or a critical need for national security. Tumulty supplemented the formal conferences with blarney and merriment—sometimes at the President's expense—and handled the journalists with a warmth that won affection for himself and loyalty to administration policies. He often worked discreetly to persuade his chief to send personal words of appreciation to deserving newsmen.[14]

---

[14] The press conferences were given up in the summer of 1915.

For an analysis of Tumulty's work and methods, *see* Blum, *Tumulty*, pp. 62 ff. The secretary made few mistakes in public relations, but his dealings with members of the Cabinet and others close to his chief were marred by self-assertion and jealousy. House kept the President alert to his secretary's fits of temperament; but the President continued to be fond of the young man in spite of his shortcomings.

The President could depend as surely on Tumulty's jovial, friendly propagation of the Word among the public oracles as upon House's handling of more sophisticated personages. He came to lean on others, also, in lesser matters. The clerical staff, which found itself handling a far greater volume of correspondence than during Taft's regime, soon came to respect not only the tidiness of the new chief's flat-top desk but the orderliness of his mind and the sureness and consistency of his rulings. It seemed as if they could see the shutter of memory open and close in his brain, as he recalled details of a case that was still open or disregarded them in a case in which he was satisfied that he had been all around the clock and reached a reasoned conclusion. They were to find him meticulously punctual, never willing to dodge a difficult assignment by working on an easier one, and masterful in handling the stream of callers who had appointments each morning. Still regarding Kipling's "If" as a model of conduct, he seemed determined "to fill the unforgiving minute with sixty seconds worth of distance run."

In the choosing of minor officials, Wilson soon found that he could not delegate authority without abnegating principles that were dear. Along the road to the Presidency he himself had incurred few political debts, and he dared to hope that he could choose men with the same freedom that he had enjoyed at Princeton and in New Jersey. He wished to refuse to bargain with campaign contributors or with members of Congress. He had taken so conscientious a view of his appointive power that he was oppressed by it. Sometimes, when the dictate of duty crossed personal inclination, he protected his own feelings by a brusqueness that seemed callous to those who did not understand the torment that he suffered. He confessed that he was often torn between the sacred duties of friendship and those of office, that sometimes it seemed as if he must choose between losing a friend and betraying his public trust.

His conscience had told him, at first, that he should pass upon the fitness of every appointee, even the thousands of postmasters; but after his election, so many supplicating letters had come to him that by March 5 he was ready to announce publicly that minor appointments would be made only through the heads of executive departments. "Gentlemen," he said to the Cabinet, "I shall have to ask you to sift the applicants for me and to make your recommendations. I think I owe this to the people." Nevertheless, he recorded in a notebook the major offices to be filled, kept an "eligible list" of about sixty names, set down the principal federal posts, with their salaries, and then figured up how much money each state would receive through offices held by its sons.[15]

Wilson insisted that his men observe certain basic principles that he had set forth in *Constitutional Government*. When Burleson said in Cabinet meeting that he would not present the name of anyone who had fought the President's candidacy, Wilson took issue with him quickly. He thrilled public servants like Houston by saying, straight from the shoulder: "It makes no difference whether a man stood for me or not. All I want is a man who is fit for the place, a man who stands for clean government and progressive policies."

At first the President stood resolutely against the use of patronage to build political power for congressmen. Facing Burleson one day over a pile of documents having to do with appointments, he had it out with his postmaster general. "Now, Burleson," he began, "I want to say to you that my administration is going to be a progressive administration. I am not going to advise with reactionary or standpat senators or representatives in making these appointments. I am going to appoint forward-looking men and I am going to satisfy myself that they are honest and capable."

Foreseeing ruin for the administration if the prophet persisted in this course, Burleson decided to be faithful to his pledge of entire frankness. Fixing his cold gray eyes on Wilson, firming his chin, and orating as if he were addressing an audience, he said that he proposed to appoint honest and capable men,[16] but that he must consult the legislators from the localities concerned. When the President bristled at this and alluded to his fights with reactionary Democrats in New Jersey, the postmaster general argued that they must avoid the sort of rows that Cleveland had had with Congress if they were to swing the party to a progressive program. "They are mostly good men," said this ex-congressman of his former colleagues. "If they are turned down, they will hate you and will not vote for anything you want. It is human nature. On the other hand, if you work with them, and they recommend unsuitable men for the offices, I will keep on asking for other suggestions, until I get

---

[15] Houston, *op. cit.*, I, 41. Joseph Wilson, a political reporter in Tennessee, had, at his brother's suggestion, kept a file on the politicians of that state. Wilson had this file at the White House and used it. "If I had such a record for every one of the states," he said to Louis Brownlow, "my political position would be impregnable." Brownlow Lecture at the University of Chicago, Feb. 21, 1956.

[16] Actually, Burleson was an advocate of the merit system and did much to extend its application to postmasterships. However, he went along with the dominant conservative machine in several Southern states, to the sorrow of progressives whom Wilson would have liked to favor.

good ones. In the end we shall secure as able men as we would in any other way, and we will keep the leaders of the party with us."

Wilson promised to ponder the matter, and a week later sent for the postmaster general to resume their discussion. Taking up a specific case—an appointment recommended by a Tennessee congressman—he told Burleson of hot protests against the candidate. Leaning back and throwing up his arms he said: "Burleson, I can't appoint a man like that!"

But the practical politician persisted. He reviewed all the factors in the case under consideration, all the typical ins and outs of small-town politics and the power of deeprooted party tradition. It was difficult to withstand Burleson's bull-like determination—"you have got to give him what he wants or 'kill him,' " a colleague wrote of him. When the postmaster general finished, the President consented to make the appointment. Wilson's sympathy for the better type of politician grew, and soon he was telling his Cabinet: "Poor Burleson has the hardest sledding of all." Yet the President always kept his eye open for rare men—"genuine progressives" who were free from "privileged interests." Seeking a comptroller of the currency a few months after inauguration, he wrote to his friend Thomas D. Jones: "What I want is a man of rising reputation and career and yet not a man who would use the place as a stepping stone to something better in a business way. Men who have made use of the place have invariably commended themselves, in one way or another, to the bankers with whom they were dealing." Wilson had the satisfaction of bringing to Washington a few Princeton colleagues and former students for whose integrity he could vouch.

To get experts for a Commission on Industrial Relations, Wilson went to Brandeis; and he had not been in the White House for a month before he asked House to take general charge of the whole matter of major political appointments. Nevertheless, Wilson himself never could escape worry over appointments. "The matter of patronage," he confessed to a friend six months after inauguration, "is a thorny path which daily makes me wish I had never been born."

Wilson was not willing at first that patronage should be a Democratic monopoly. Republican legislators were asked whether they objected to candidates proposed for appointment in their districts. "I feel it my constitutional duty . . . to make independent inquiries wherever possible . . ." the President wrote to a Democratic congressman two months after inauguration, "but I shall hope in every possible instance to comply with the recommendations and wishes of my colleagues in the House." Soon he was using his obligations to the Congress as a counterweight against Bryan's importunities in behalf of incompetent friends.

Though Wilson soon accepted the fact that a President cannot make all appointments conform to his own desires, he continued to insist that he must not favor his family in any way. It was arranged by Tumulty that a young Woodrow cousin should have a clerkship in the office of Attorney General McReynolds; but when told of it the President laid down the law: relatives could not accept jobs from men whom he had appointed, though he had no objection to their taking positions from officials who had been chosen by Taft.[17] When his own, and only, brother was recommended for office, it pained him to have to write thus:

April 22, 1913

My dear, dear brother:

I never in my life had anything quite so hard to do as this that I must do about the Nashville Post Office. Knowing as I do that a better man could not possibly be found for the place, and sure though I am that it would meet with the general approval of the citizens of Nashville, I yet feel that it would be a very serious mistake both for you and for me if I were to appoint you to the Postmastership there. I cannot tell you how I have worried about this or how much I have had to struggle against affection and temptation, but I am clear in the conviction that in the long run, if not now, you will agree with me that I am deciding rightly.

I can't write any more just now, because I feel too deeply.

With deepest love, I remain

Your affectionate brother,

WOODROW WILSON

Five days before the inauguration he confessed to House that he had almost lost the serene faith in friendship that had sustained him so often. Sooner or later self-interest seemed to crop out in even the best of comrades. He became especially distrustful of new friends, and of gifts that flooded in from many states. He refused to accept a keg of whisky from Andrew Carnegie, but feared to give offense to the philanthropist by sending it back. Finally, after a horned toad had arrived

[17] This rule was applied also in the case of another cousin, who had been offered second choice of McAdoo's appointments. When asked for advice, Wilson said that it was McAdoo's business, but he would prefer that the offer be declined. It was. Fitz William Woodrow to the writer, and James Woodrow to the writer, June 14, 1949.

from Texas, he remarked that he didn't want so much as a potato given to him, and large gifts were returned.

But hard as his conscience was set against family and personal friends in matters of public business, the President delighted in indulging them once he had left the executive offices in the West Wing and gone "home" to the White House. He liked to gather around him those on whose disinterestedness he knew that he could depend. All those welcomed into the inner circle were relatives or loyal friends, so that Wilson, who seldom talked shop at meals, could sit with them afterward and open his mind with confidence that he would not be betrayed.

All was so jolly and novel during the first week in the new home that it was hard for the Wilsons to understand what Taft meant when he said to the President-elect on Inauguration Day: "I'm glad to be going —this is the loneliest place in the world." Woodrow Wilson loved the swift pace of family life about him. He insisted that his wife and daughters preserve the candor and integrity of their own personalities, follow their own inclinations, and engage in no social activities with ulterior political motives. He wanted no weaving spiders in his household. Margaret's devotion to singing and Jessie's work for good causes gave him joy; and he shared in the ecstasy of Nellie as she lost her shyness in the bustle of the new life and gave play to frivolous girlish impulses. The normality of their doings helped him to escape unhealthful moods. His new office demanded dignity, but he could not put it on without being conscious of acting and, therefore, a little ashamed of himself. He liked to think of himself as standing next to the chair of State, not sitting on it. "The old kink is still in me," he explained to Mary Allen Hulbert. "Everything is persistently *impersonal*. I am administering a great office—no doubt the greatest in the world—but I do not seem to be identified with it . . . This impersonality of my life is a very odd thing . . . but at least prevents me from becoming a fool and thinking myself *it*!"

He kept his spirit young and humble by playing tag and rooster fighting with daughter Nellie in the White House corridors. Sometimes he would spend an evening at billiards. Adhering to the habits of earlier years, he punctually followed a daily schedule. Rising early, he sharpened his razor on a heavy leather strop and fancied that he could predict the weather by the sound. He retired at a discreet hour, as he had all his life; and when owls hooting in the magnolias awakened him, he would go to the window and hoot back, and then at breakfast boast that he had "hooted the hooters away." He refused to join the fashionable Chevy Chase Club, for fear that he might be buttonholed by lobbyists, and he best found relaxation at vaudeville shows, where he could himself become one of "the people" to whom he was devoting himself. He discouraged the playing of the national anthem and the rising of the audience when he entered. He often laughed aloud at slapstick antics and endeared himself to the actors as a sympathetic, uncritical patron, a man who went to the theater for fun and wanted no tragedies or problem plays. Sometimes he would send Tumulty to scout a show in advance; and once, taking Mrs. Wilson and the secretary of War to a performance that Tumulty had approved, he said afterward that he should have taken Secretary Daniels because it was a "naval display."

Even in the White House, Wilson could persist in practicing the manners of a gentleman in his own home. Servants who had seen Theodore Roosevelt set the pace in going through doorways with a cheerleader's flourish were impressed by the insistence of Wilson that others precede him. He had a sixth sense for the feelings of guests who had to rise from their chairs when the President did, and he quickly made them forget the elegance of their surroundings. His family continued to marvel at his deft use of humor to break social strains and at his attentiveness to his own kin even when entertaining distinguished guests at table.

Under her new responsibilities Ellen Wilson was unchanged. "Ike" Hoover, the head usher, admired her genius in "coseying up" the big mansion. Familiar rugs and furniture were transported from Princeton, with the piano and favorite books. Moreover, she soon saved enough from annual appropriations so that she could redecorate some of the rooms and divide attic spaces into small guest chambers. Soon the family regarded the White House as "home," and visiting relatives remarked that Ellen's homes, no matter where they were, always had the same feeling.

The President loved to operate the little electric elevator in the White House, with its panels of mirrors, and his favorite apartments were the dining room and the Blue Room. Next to the Oval Room, where the immediate family spent their evenings, was his own study. In this sanctum he could be alone with his choicest books and with the old, familiar typewriter and its noisy clack—"it and I have gone through many thoughts together, and many emotions," he had written on it a month before taking office. His desk here, unlike the official one in the West Wing, was always piled high with documents.

Though he plunged like a bridegroom into the events of Inauguration Day, his strength was overtaxed in that first week by the ordeal of speeches and handshakings, family reunions and Cabinet meetings, problems of personnel and of etiquette. He still had the knack of relaxing in a nap whenever there were idle moments, but no opportunity came during the first exciting days in the White House. He had been giving himself constantly, and by the end of the week he was exhausted and his digestion failed him.

Fortunately there was a physician at hand. Annie Howe, the President's sister, had fallen on the stairs in the White House on Inauguration Day and gashed her forehead, and Dr. Cary Grayson had been called to attend her. This young medical officer of the Navy had served Taft, and in introducing him to Wilson the ex-President said: "Here is an excellent fellow that I hope you will get to know. I regret to say that he is a Democrat and a Virginian, but that's a matter that can't be helped."

On Sunday morning, March 9, Dr. Grayson attended the President and began his study of a case that was to absorb him for eight years. He found that Wilson was accustomed to taking a good deal of medicine and to have his stomach pumped out now and then, that he suffered occasional twinges from his old enemy, neuritis. Grayson learned, too, that the sight of one eye was still defective as a result of the attack of arteriosclerosis suffered in 1906, and that Dr. S. Weir Mitchell of Philadelphia doubted that the President could stand the strain of his new duties. Here was a mortal with symptoms of chronic invalidism, undertaking the arduous life of an office that, Wilson himself once said, requires "the constitution of an athlete, the patience of a mother, the endurance of the early Christian." [18]

On March 25, Wilson told his Cabinet that he would have to limit his indulgence in social affairs. Remarking that social life seemed to be the serious business of the greater part of Washington, he explained:

[18] Ruth Cranston, *The Story of W.W.*, p. 114. Grayson treated Wilson's neuritis by baking and massage, and doing away with medicines, put him on a diet of orange juice and raw eggs. Downing the first egg, the President said: "I feel as if I were swallowing a newborn babe." Dr. Grayson probably was less inclined than modern physicians would have been to associate the President's occasional digestive upsets with the progress of arteriosclerosis. On March 9 he ordered his patient to stay in bed, but Wilson protested that he would set a bad example to his people if he did not go to church, and he went. Dr. Taylor, his minister at the Central Congregational Church, recollects that Wilson appreciated "the quietness and great courtesy of the congregation." Dr. Taylor also records that the President inquired about pew rents and regular sittings and discussed gifts to current expense and benevolence, that Wilson stayed after one Sunday service for a business meeting, and that he sent flowers every Saturday, never on Sunday. James H. Taylor, *W.W., in Church*.

"While I am not ill, my health is not exceptionally good, and I have signed a protocol of peace with my doctor. I must be good."

On his first Sunday in the White House, Woodrow Wilson was serene in the knowledge that the launching of his administration had been auspicious. He did not, however, let his spirits run with the lavish optimism that had been his undoing at Princeton. He knew now that there were men who could not be trusted and enemies awaiting a chance to strike. "Remember," he cautioned Nellie one day when she exulted over his success, "the pack is always waiting near at hand to tear one to pieces. Popularity is the most evanescent thing in the world, and the most unimportant."

CHAPTER XVII

Revolution in a Democracy

ONCE HE HAD MADE himself and his kin at home in the White House and had put himself on friendly terms with his official family, Woodrow Wilson lost little time in undertaking to satisfy the expectations that had shone from the faces of the multitude at the inaugural ceremony. The Presidency, of which he had written so perceptively, was now his own office, to be made consequential or paltry in the history of his age. All depended on his will and the scope of his powers. The president had it "in his choice," Wilson had written in 1907, to be the political leader of the nation: "Let him once win the admiration and confidence of the country, and no other single force can withstand him, no combination of forces will easily overthrow him. His office is anything he has the sagacity and force to make it."

To achieve the leadership that he had described, Wilson could be expected to deny his mind the "literary" indulgence of regarding principles as "unities." [1] As a political leader, his ear "must ring with the voices of the people" and he must check his prophetic impulses and "serve the slow-paced daily need." To keep aloft in the gusty air of spiritual controversy, from which he had fallen disastrously at Princeton, he would now have to convince a national constituency that every venture was conceived for the common interest and without regard to his own welfare. If his office was to have prestige and power, Woodrow Wilson would have to keep himself personally humble.

The President-elect was singularly free from affiliation with any selfish interest. He could justly claim—though he was too modest to do so—that his own livelihood had come from honest intellectual toil and a touch of native genius. He liked to feel that those who had financed and promoted his election had done it not for him, personally, or for material reward, but rather out of devotion to ideals that they shared with him.

[1] Wilson had written in "Leaders of Men" in 1890: "Principles, as statesmen conceive them, are threads to the labyrinth of circumstances. . . . Throw the conceiving mind, habituated to contemplating wholes, into the arena of politics, and it seems to itself to be standing upon shifting sands, where no sure foothold and no upright posture are possible." Motter (ed.), *Leaders of Men*, p. 46.

Wilson came to the White House with faith that he was predestined to give effective expression to the progressive impulses that had been agitating American society with growing insistence for twenty years. He believed that the discontent of masses of citizens must be met by constructive law lest it erupt in violence. Theodore Roosevelt had dramatized the cause of equal opportunity for the plain people, and Taft had dallied with it; but it devolved on Wilson to put trained and sympathetic minds to work upon social maladjustments that had accompanied the growth of economic colossi. Obviously the ever-shifting line between the "necessary" and the "optional" functions of government—the line that he had defined a quarter century before in *The State*—would have to be plotted and drawn anew, under the breadth and majesty of the Constitution.

While resting in Bermuda after the election and reading *Philip Dru, Administrator*—the novel in which House set forth his philosophy and program of reform—Wilson had written a preface for a book that was to bring together significant sayings from his campaign speeches.[2] In this work, entitled *The New Freedom*, he wished "to express the new spirit of our politics and to set forth, in large terms which may stick in the imagination, what it is that must be done if we are to restore our politics to their full spiritual vigor again." In the view of this prophet, the natural foe to freedom was an irresponsible governing group who might use political power to serve selfish ends. Whether it was a military autocracy, a proletarian bureaucracy, or a plutocracy, the outcome would be the same. There would be tyranny and not freedom. With all the fierce tenacity of his blood, Woodrow Wilson was clinging to his overpowering purpose—the preservation of the liberty of the individual. Lecturing on constitutional law in 1907, he had said, "Liberty fixed in unalterable law would be no liberty at all. Government is a part of life, and, with life, it must change, alike in its objects and its practices; only this principle must remain unaltered—this principle of liberty, that there must be the freest right and opportunity of adjustment." This dynamic purpose was to be the gyroscopic stabilizer of his ship of state.

Coming back from his island meditations full of crusading vigor and with the direction of his thinking set, Wilson had determined to keep alive the sense of accountability that he had preached during the cam-

---

[2] *The New Freedom* was first published in monthly installments in *World's Work*, January–July, 1913. This book was too much clouded by the dust of political battle to be taken seriously by students of the government. Many dismissed it as "a maze of words" and regretted that there were few specifications for translating the words into deeds.

paign. Having won the election, he was free to speak his heart and conscience without fear that any man would accuse him of soliciting votes; and his tongue was loosed by the exposure in a Congressional investigation of methods by which bankers controlled vast industrial enterprises.[3] Unprepared as he was to present any reasoned, consistent plan for economic reform, he had given way to his feelings in tirades that shook the confidence of businessmen who were committed to special interests.

At a dinner of the Southern Society of New York, whose leaders had promoted his candidacy, the prophet had loosed the indignation that had been festering in him ever since his frustration at Princeton. His tense, resonant voice had asserted, as the hall became quiet and people sat forward in their chairs: "Business cannot be disturbed unless the minds of those who conduct it are disturbed." To Wilson a panic—like hell—was merely "a state of mind," because, he said, "when a panic occurs there is just as much wealth in the country the day after the panic as the day before." Sometimes, he explained, "panics are said to occur because certain gentlemen want to create the impression that the wrong thing is going to be done." To any man living who dared to precipitate a panic in that way, Wilson promised "a gibbet . . . as high as Haman's." And then he had added: "But that is only figuratively speaking. What I will do will be to direct the attention of the people to him, and I think that they will cut him to the quick."

In the view of progressives, here was a new sort of political leader —a man who dared to say the same thing after election day that he had said in the campaign. Four other addresses of similar tone had followed. Two were delivered at Staunton, Virginia, at a celebration of the prophet's fifty-sixth birthday. He slept in the old manse, in the room in which he was born; and speaking in the church in which his father had served a Presbyterian congregation, he warned businessmen that "they must render a service or get nothing," that in the future "the men who serve will be the men who profit." After quips that were reminiscent of his father's humor, he grew grim with reminders that the Presidency was "an office in which a man must put on his war paint," that there were "men who will have to be mastered in order that they shall be made the instruments of justice and mercy."[4]

---

[3] See p. 301.

[4] Josephus Daniels, in *The Wilson Era: Years of Peace* (pp. 521–23), has pointed out that these words were directed particularly against the Democratic machine in Virginia and Senator Martin, its boss. A friend of Thomas F. Ryan, Martin had regretted Wilson's nomination at Baltimore and had had a ferocious argument with Wilson when both were guests at the home of President Alderman of the University of Virginia.

To the minds of financiers whose thinking grew out of experience rather than theorizing, such talk was frightening. Consternation seized Wall Street and stock averages slid off 10 per cent.

At that juncture Colonel House, who immediately after the election had persuaded Wilson to say a few words to soothe the nerves of financiers, had stepped into the breach. Wilson could not have had a better advocate than the polite, well-groomed Texan who had a reputation for integrity in handling other people's money. Attending a dinner in New York at which five billions of capital were represented, House used all his conversational art to convince the diners that Woodrow Wilson would sign no demagogic laws and was not a despoiler of legitimate investment, but rather a leader intent on establishing conditions under which men of good character could do business with decency and security. The financial uncertainty of the day was caused by their own fears, he said boldly, and not by the President-elect. Three months before, when votes were sought, House had advised McCombs how to make political capital out of the opposition of these very financiers; but now that the election was over, the Colonel counseled conciliation.

Wilson himself had realized that he should coax as well as threaten in order to enlist businessmen in the progressive cause. Having driven his mind "all the way around the clock," he had become specific and had presented four points of policy that reflected advice received from Brandeis and House. Admitting his own inexperience in commerce, Wilson said at Chicago, in January of 1913: "I must take counsel with the men who do understand business, and I dare not take counsel with them unless they intend the same things that I intend . . . There is no bright prospect otherwise."

In the offices that he had filled before coming to the Presidency, Wilson had achieved initial success by concentrating upon just a few reforms that were both urgent and practical. "It will not do," the college professor had said fifteen years earlier, "to incarnate too many ideas at a time if you are to be universally understood and numerously followed." To give effect to his program the President would have first to agree with the Congress upon a few vital measures and then to per-

---

In an article entitled "Freemen Need No Guardians," Wilson alleged that "the masters of the government of the United States are the combined capitalists and manufacturers of the United States," that "the government of the United States at present is a foster-child of the special interests. It is not allowed to have a will of its own. It is told at every move, 'Don't do that: you will interfere with our prosperity.' And when we ask, 'Where is our prosperity lodged?' a certain group of gentlemen say, 'With us.' "

suade committeemen to accept the provisions that competent experts wished to write into law. Fortunately, the way had been smoothed, in the House of Representatives, by a wave of progressive bills that had been put through by a Democratic majority only to meet doom in the Senate or on the desk of President Taft.

In his inaugural address Wilson had itemized the matters that most obviously called for legislative action.

A tariff which cuts us off from our proper part in the commerce of the world, violates the just principles of taxation, and makes the Government a facile instrument in the hands of private interests; a banking and currency system based upon the necessity of the Government to sell its bonds fifty years ago and perfectly adapted to concentrating cash and restricting credits; an industrial system which, take it on all sides, financial as well as administrative, holds capital in leading strings, restricts the liberties and limits the opportunities of labor, and exploits without renewing or conserving the natural resources of the country; a body of agricultural activities never yet given the efficiency of great business undertakings or served as it should be through the instrumentality of science taken directly to the farm, or afforded the facilities of credit best suited to its practical needs; watercourses undeveloped, waste places unreclaimed, forests untended, fast disappearing without plan or prospect of renewal, unregarded waste heaps at every mine.

Not only must the economy of these things be studied, he said, but means must be perfected by which government might serve humanity by safeguarding the health and the civic rights of the citizens. And all these matters must be considered, he insisted, without forgetting "the old-fashioned, never-to-be-neglected, fundamental safeguarding of property and of individual right." This was "the high enterprise of the new day" to which he dedicated his administration. "We shall restore, not destroy," he promised. ". . . Justice and only justice, shall always be our motto."

A few days after the inauguration, White House spokesmen announced that the new President would help to construct important legislation.[5] Ten days later they added that he would go frequently to the Capitol to confer with party leaders. And less than a month after he had taken office Wilson read to his Cabinet a message for the legislators that called for action on the tariff. He would begin with this issue, he explained, because the party was united on it.

[5] Some of Wilson's advisers felt that reform legislation should be deferred. However, when Houston raised objections to immediate action, House explained that bills could be passed most expeditiously before all the patronage was distributed.

When a Cabinet member recommended caution in lowering tariff rates, in view of uncertainty in business, Wilson replied that others had given that advice and that he was reminded of a cartoon of himself in a Western newspaper. He explained: "It pictures a great beast of a man standing over me saying: 'What do you mean by meaning what you said?' I must say now what I said before election."

Thirty years before, as a lawyer at Atlanta, Wilson had spoken before congressmen against protection; and in the long interval since, neither study nor experience had altered his view that the only justification for duties on imports was the need for revenue. He had denounced the Payne-Aldrich Law of the Taft regime as "merely a method of granting favours." He proposed no change so sharp or sudden that it might dislocate the economy, but wished to withdraw protection "steadily and upon a fixed programme upon which every man of business can base his definite forecasts and systematic plans." Reduction of duties had been a dominant issue in his campaign for the Presidency.

Once in office, however, Wilson knew that it would not be easy to redeem his pledge of tariff reform, in spite of the fact that many citizens attributed a sharp increase in the cost of living during the preceding decade to the high duties of Republican regimes. Cleveland's ship of state had foundered twice on the reef of tariff protection, and Taft had failed to effect the changes that his party's progressive faction had demanded. Consequently, Wilson resolved to dramatize the issue with a direct challenge to the legislators by his strongest weapon—the spoken word. He decided that he would speak before a special session of the Congress on April 8. It would be a long step toward the ideal of parliamentary responsibility that he had championed since youth.

When he told his Cabinet that he was thinking of taking this direct way of establishing a ministerial relation with the Congress, the men had qualms. To avoid offending the legislators, they decided to go to hear their chief individually instead of in a body; and Bryan, fearing that Speaker Champ Clark would be angered, decided to stay away. No president since the elder Adams had been so bold as to appear on the legislative rostrum. Jefferson had rejected the procedure as too reminiscent of addresses from the throne. Succeeding chief executives had transmitted their ideas by scripts that had grown voluminous. Droned by a clerk, they had lost point and bored those whom they were intended to exhort. And now, when an orator-president threatened to break tradition of more than a hundred years' standing and revert to a still earlier custom, there were fiery speeches from Democratic senators to whom the doctrine of "separation of powers" was sacred. Jealous of executive encroachment on their vested rights, senators were so obstructive that Vice-President Marshall, presiding over the Senate and fearing that formal action might result in a rebuff, declared the question to be one of high privilege for which unanimous consent was not necessary.

There was no doubt of the success of the President's bold venture in so far as it arrested unprecedented attention on the part of the legislators and the voters of the nation. Spick-and-span in a Prince Albert coat, Wilson left a Cabinet meeting to go to the hill soon after noon on April 8. He found the corridors of the Capitol thronged with men and women clamoring for admission. The members of Congress and hundreds of spectators had crowded into the House chamber, and when the President entered all rose to applaud. Yet there was embarrassment in the air, nervousness among the legislators, and sullen looks here and there. Wilson himself was a trifle pale and tense as he walked briskly to his place, for he was aware that the ice on which he trod was thin. After his old rival, Speaker Champ Clark, had mumbled an introduction, the invader from the White House stood quiet for just a moment with a trace of a smile on his lips, quaking inwardly. Then he launched into a disarming introduction that he had drafted with meticulous fondling of words.

He was glad, he said, to have this opportunity to verify the impression that the President was "a human being trying to cooperate with other human beings in a common service" and not "a mere department of the Government hailing Congress from some isolated island of jealous power, sending messages, not speaking naturally with his own voice." After this pleasant experience, he assured the legislators, he would feel quite normal in dealing with them.

The latent opposition thawed as he went on to win the confidence of his audience. Explaining that he had called Congress into extraordinary session so that the duty laid upon the majority party at the election might be performed and so that businessmen might not have to be kept too long in suspense as to fiscal changes to come, he said: "Only new principles of action will save us from a final hard crystallization of monopoly and a complete loss of the influences that quicken enterprise and keep independent energy alive. It is plain what those principles must be. We must abolish everything that bears even the semblance of privilege or of any kind of artificial advantage, and put our businessmen and producers under the stimulation of a constant necessity to be efficient, economical, and enterprising, masters of competitive supre-

macy, better workers and merchants than any in the world. Aside from
the duties laid upon articles which we do not, and probably can not,
produce, therefore, and the duties laid upon luxuries and merely for
the sake of the revenues they yield, the object of the tariff duties henceforth laid must be effective competition, the whetting of American
wits by contest with the wits of the rest of the world." They must not
move "with reckless haste," and should seek "a more free and wholesome development, not revolution or upset or confusion."

In ten minutes he had covered his subject and was through. After
a moment of silence the applause overwhelmed him. Delighted by the
success of his bold stroke of statesmanship, he laughed gaily when Ellen
Wilson told him, during their ride home, that it was the sort of thing
that Roosevelt would have enjoyed doing, had he thought of it. "Yes,"
he responded, "I think I put one over on Teddy."

The day after his address to the Congress, enheartened by editorial
approval of his venture, Wilson took the novel step of going to the
President's room at the Capitol and conferring with a committee of
the Senate. In 1897 he had written that Cleveland was disliked by
Congress because he was an "outsider." By cultivating close relations
with legislators he hoped to avoid similar embarrassment. He asked for
an album of photographs of the members of Congress and spent hours
in studying their faces. He set apart three hours each week to welcome
calls from them, and when he was unable to receive unannounced
visitors from the Hill, Tumulty did his best to assuage their disappointment. Freshman congressmen found him a sympathetic listener, for he
made them feel that he, like themselves, had much to learn about a
new job.

Woodrow Wilson's appearances in the Capitol in defiance of tradition were a symbol to his people of his creed. By taking initiative he
put upon private lobbies the burden of proving that their proposals
were in the public interest, and he discouraged logrolling among the
legislators. Moreover, he had ready for the congressmen a definite
schedule of revised tariffs that was the result of long study and that was
based on Democratic bills that Taft had vetoed. For months past Wilson
had conferred and corresponded with Chairman Oscar W. Underwood
of the Ways and Means Committee, an opponent for the nomination
at Baltimore who had now become a willing collaborator; and the
party's caucus had decided to gather into an omnibus bill the various
proposals of reform with which Democrats and Republican insurgents
had been inconclusively waging guerrilla warfare in 1911 and 1912.

Wilson had taken a hand in the setting of rates on sugar and wool that were lower than the party men dared to propose. Early in April he engaged in what he regarded as "a death grapple" with the sugar lobbyists and gave them an ultimatum: if they did not accept a drastic reduction in the duty on raw sugar for a trial period of three years,[6] he would insist on free sugar immediately.

When it became apparent that the reductions in tariffs would leave the government impoverished, it was decided to take advantage of the Income Tax Amendment, which had just been ratified by the states. Welcoming the opportunity to shift some of the burden of taxation from the poor to the rich, though with no intention of using the new tax to distribute wealth, Congressman Cordell Hull drafted a provision that the President studied with keen interest. Wilson explained that he wished to exempt everyone receiving less than $3,000 a year from making a report. He would burden as few as possible with "the obligations involved in the administration of what will at best be an unpopular law." [7]

The tariff bill that Underwood's committee reported favorably to the House on April 22 provoked debate that at times became acrimonious. The President and his lieutenants, however, stood solidly together. When opponents insinuated in the press that Underwood's prestige was being enhanced and might eclipse Wilson's, the President commented: "If Mr. Underwood or anybody else can displace me by the work they do in the service of the country, they are fully entitled to do so, and I have no jealousy in the matter. But I do not believe, for my own part, that there is any such thought or purpose." Under skillful leadership the tariff bill, with the income-tax provision, passed the House on May 8 with a majority of 281 to 139.

The outcome was not surprising, for more than a third of the 290 Democratic members of the new Congress had been elected for the first time under Woodrow Wilson's banner and therefore looked naturally to the President for direction. Furthermore, the old war horses, once they were assured that Wilson and Burleson would consult them on matters of patronage and would not supplant them with progressives in the committee chairmanships, were willing to cooperate

[6] Wilson set the trial period at three years in the hope that sugar would be on the free list before the end of his term of office. Daniels Diary, April 4, 1913.

[7] W.W. to Underwood, April 16, 1913. A corporation excise tax had been included in the Payne-Aldrich tariff to get revenue, and Hull persuaded the House to extend this to individuals. *See* Cordell Hull, *The Memoirs of Cordell Hull*, I, 70 ff. A "graduated income tax" was one of the measures advocated by Colonel House's fictitious administrator, Philip Dru.

with the leader who had brought the Democrats back to power. Realizing that the party's welfare depended on the success of the Administration, the legislators were eager to help their chief make good. Moreover, there was a disposition to act promptly, since the party, which had been voted into office by a minority of the ballots cast, could count on ascendancy only until the next Congressional election, a mere year and a half away.

The history of tariff legislation, however, gave warning that the Underwood Bill would not go through the Senate without controversy and change. Though Nelson Aldrich was gone from the Republican ranks, stalwarts were left who were competent to make the most of all the devices of obstruction. Moreover, the Democratic majority in the Senate was too small to be conclusive without unanimity, and it was certain that senators from states that raised sugar and wool would be under intense pressure from constituents who would be hurt by the new rates.

While the tariff bill was in the House, Wilson had worked—often at the instance of Congressional leaders—to bolster the morale of key men by conference or letter. He failed, however, to assure harmonious party action by immediately effecting a caucus of Democratic senators; and as soon as the Underwood Bill was put before the Senate, the air reeked with the sort of propaganda that the President had hoped to circumvent. When it was reported in the press that he sought a compromise, he said to newsmen: "When you get a chance just say that I am not the kind that considers compromises when I once take my position." Politicians and lawyers who were retained to represent business interests that would suffer under the proposed rates besieged the Capitol and asked to be heard before the Finance Committee. However, when the Administration argued that the issues already had been made clear through endless discussion, the Democrats stood together to defeat the obstructionists on the floor of the Senate by five votes.

This rebuff merely intensified the activity of interests that in the past had virtually dictated the rates that were to apply to their several products. Their pestiferous agents infested hotels, clubs, and even private homes. It seemed to Wilson that "a brick couldn't be thrown without hitting one of them." Senators were wooed by threats and entreaties, by editorials, pamphlets, and resolutions, and by a mass of personal messages. The President was alarmed; for if he failed in this venture he could expect to achieve little in other directions. When congressmen urged him to issue a blast that would put the lobbyists immediately on the defensive, he gave a bold statement to the press without consulting his Cabinet. Published on May 26, it read: "Washington has seldom seen so numerous, so industrous, or so insidious a lobby . . . It is of serious interest to the country that the people at large should have no lobby and be voiceless in these matters, while great bodies of astute men seek to create an artificial opinion and to overcome the interests of the public for their private profit . . . Only public opinion can check and destroy it." Thus did the prophet turn his well-known spotlight of "pitiless publicity" upon the "invisible government" at Washington.

This aggressive stroke in the public interest provoked resentment. Was there improper lobbying, the *New York Times* asked editorially, or were protected producers simply taking legitimate steps to present their cases to the Congress? Republican legislators complained that the President was aspersing their integrity, and they retaliated by insinuating that Wilson used questionable means to control the voting of his Democrats. Determined to make the President prove his imputation that senators were improperly influenced by "insidious" lobbies, the opposition proposed that a committee of five be appointed to investigate the matter. This move worked to Wilson's advantage, however, when Senator LaFollette made a suggestion that turned the investigation into a series of hearings in which, for the first time in American history, his colleagues had to bare their private economic interests to public scrutiny. Democrats who felt responsible to high-tariff constituencies could not withstand this ordeal by publicity, especially when it was supplemented by personal pressure from the White House.

The President hesitated to invite interviews, and explained his reluctance to Senator Hitchcock thus: "I shrink more than I think many persons realize from seeming to try to press my own views upon men who have an equal reponsibility with myself." Ellen Wilson, however, persuaded him to invite influential legislators to dinner; and after ironing out wrinkles in the tariff program with them, the President said to Grayson: "You see what a wise wife I have!" Realizing that on so vital an issue he must be aggressive, he received many delegations of senators and conferred with them often in his room at the Capitol. His argument followed the pattern used with the New Jersey legislators. "Here are the facts; here are the principles; here are our obligations as Democrats." What were they going to do about it? If they failed to share his feeling of the inevitability of a certain course of action, his smiles gave way to grim challenge. If they did not agree with him, they would still have to follow, for the responsibility had been put upon

him by the people. If they wished to debate the matter with him before
the people, that was their privilege. But to most legislators it was not
a privilege to be lightly exercised. To a group of seven legislators from
west of the Mississippi, who warned that the proposed bill so offended
sugar producers that, if enacted, it would prevent their re-election,
the President replied that if the party were to repudiate its tariff pledge
it would not matter whether or not it had any senators from the West
because it would "be kicked out of office by the American people."

Wilson had a special telephone put in so that he might keep in touch
with the Capitol constantly; and from the piles of commendatory messages that came to him from the people he forwarded to wavering
senators those from members of their own constituencies. Sparks from
his waving torch had set off rockets at the grass roots that were scorching the representatives of the people. Even hostile newspapers were
marveling at the consistency of the philosophy of the new President
and at his "matchless political strategy."

Finally, on June 20, Wilson succeeded in bringing together a caucus
of Democratic senators—the first, remarked the *New York Times*,
that anyone could remember. At the end of a fortnight of hot discussion, free sugar and free wool were approved and it was understood that
the bill would be a party undertaking that all Democrats were committed to support.

When the measure was formally laid before the Senate on July 11
by Simmons of North Carolina, whom Wilson had been persuaded not
to punish for voting for the Republican tariff bill in 1909, it was clear
that the President was winning the battle on which he had staked his
program. The Republicans prolonged debate; and the President failed
to convince the Louisiana senators that, having dutifully spoken in
caucus of their constituents' objection to free sugar, they were bound
by party loyalty to abide by the decision of the majority.[8] Yet after an
attack by radicals of both parties on the proposed income-tax schedules
forced a compromise that raised both the exemption and the rates for
the higher brackets, the tariff bill was passed. It went through on
September 9 by a vote of 44 to 37. A few days later the President had
a gay letter from Walter Hines Page, who had gone to London as
ambassador: "I have been telling Bagehot's successor in the editorship

---

[8] On July 15, Wilson wrote to Senator Thornton of Louisiana thus: "No party can ever
for any length of time control the Government or serve the people which cannot command the
allegiance of its own minority. I feel that there are times, after every argument has been given
full consideration and men of equal public conscience have conferred together, when those who
are overruled should accept the principle of party government . . ."

of the *Economist* that the passing of commercial supremacy to the United States will be dated in the economic histories from the tariff act of 1913."

After conferees from the Senate and the House had ironed out differences, the final measure, known as the Underwood-Simmons Bill, went to the White House for signature. Fifty loyal Democrats were at the executive offices on October 3 to celebrate the triumph. They clapped as their hero approached the desk where the act lay, ready for his signature, and he responded with deep feeling: "I have had the accomplishment of something like this at heart since I was a boy," he said, and then—appropriately enough in view of the loyal influence that Cabinet officers had wielded among the party's legislators—"I know men standing around me can say the same thing."

The act had been put through after what some men regarded as the most significant tariff battle in American history. It established the principle that the income tax was to supplement import duties as a major source of federal revenue, and one whose relative incidence on citizens of varying wealth could be precisely adjusted. Moreover, the new law effected a reduction in duties that to reactionaries seemed revolutionary.[9] The Underwood-Simmons Act had been honestly drafted, and as it underwent changes in the Senate the President had kept a vigilant eye on its wording and on at least one occasion had detected a "joker." He had made sure that this law would not, like the Payne-Aldrich Tariff Law, harbor devices that concealed exhorbitant rates from the eye of the casual reader.

By bold, aggressive tactics the new President had come through his first major offensive against reactionary forces and had established mastery of his party's legislators. The man of promise had become a man of achievement.

[9] In the new act the average *ad valorem* rate of the Payne-Aldrich tariff of 1909 had been brought down from over 40 per cent to about 25. In addition to putting raw wool and other staples on the free list, the new measure removed or reduced duties on goods that America supplied in great quantity to the world market, such as agricultural machinery and other manufactures. Altogether, tariffs were lowered on more than 900 items.

CHAPTER XVIII

BANKING AND CURRENCY REFORM

EXHILARATING AS WILSON'S triumph was, he did not gloat long over it, for there was still more difficult business afoot. In the same breath with which he congratulated his associates upon the passage of the tariff act, the President said: "There is every reason to believe that currency reform will be carried through with equal energy, directness, and loyalty to the general interest." This was the second step that he had proposed —to set the business of the country free.

Woodrow Wilson had come into the Presidency less expert in the technique of banking than in that of tariff making, but his grounding in the philosophy of credit was both broad and deep. At the Johns Hopkins he had read almost every treatise on the monetary history and experience of the United States and had mastered Bagehot's *Lombard Street*. His interest in the subject had quickened as a result of the Panic of 1893 and popular agitation for free silver, and in 1897 he had asserted that nothing but currency reform could touch the cause of discontent. He had ascribed the Panic of 1907, which had obstructed his quadrangle plan, in part to the nation's banking practice. Standing under a giant rubber tree in a Bermuda street, he had said to a friend: "I would reform the banking laws; they are a disgrace to our great country." [1]

The Panic of 1907 had stimulated bankers, under the leadership of Republican Senator Aldrich, to try to substitute a centralized banking system for the inelastic and unscientific credit structure that had collapsed three times since the Civil War. A National Monetary Commission studied the banking systems of the world and reported to Congress, in 1911 and 1912, a plan that was drawn up largely by Paul M. Warburg of Kuhn, Loeb & Company and endorsed by the American Bankers' Association. A great central institution was proposed, with fifteen regional branches that were to be controlled by member banks.

This proposal, and a Republican act of 1908 that had increased the reserve of currency, did not satisfy progressives, who dreaded the "money power" with which the name of Aldrich—a protectionist—was

[1] Mrs. Borden Harriman to the writer, Feb. 22, 1951.

indelibly associated. They feared a revival of the national bank that Andrew Jackson had destroyed. Wilson, however, saw both the economic advantages of the sort of scheme that Aldrich proposed and the danger of its exploitation by selfish interests. His essential problem was to give to the nation the technical safeguards against panic that the Republicans had worked out and, at the same time, to reassure his progressive Democratic colleagues by providing a controlling personnel in whose altruism the public would have confidence. This was by far the greatest challenge to his leadership that Woodrow Wilson had yet faced. Clearly envisioning the evil to be overcome and the goal to be attained, he knew that only by a concert of trained and selfless minds could a sound path be plotted.

Between election and inauguration, Wilson felt the full force of a new explosion of antitrust sentiment. During that period Congressman Pujo's Committee on Banking and Currency, which had been instructed by the House of Representatives to investigate the extent and significance of money monopolies, held spectacular hearings to which famous private bankers were summoned. There was an airing of the legal devices by which a few financiers, keeping clear of the Sherman Antitrust Act, were able to exert control over vast industrial empires. J. Pierpont Morgan, who had participated in drastic action to check the Panic of 1907, was forced to testify; and he and his associates, unskilled in public relations and unable to make clear the respects in which their interests coincided with those of the nation, left an impression of callousness to the common welfare. The Pujo Committee handed in a report of its investigation just four days before Wilson took office, the press played it up sensationally, and progressives looked the more eagerly to the new Administration for quick and decisive relief.

Fortunately, the Congressional probe of the trusts had a more constructive aspect than that which was luridly publicized. While one subcommittee was making sensational disclosures, another, directed by Representative Carter Glass and advised by an expert, H. Parker Willis, had taken in hand the report of the National Monetary Commission and was formulating a substitute for the Aldrich plan. Two days after the election Glass had written to Wilson, whom he had met and come to admire during the campaign, to report that a tentative bill had been drafted and that he wished advice from the President-elect, since the matter would require stern executive leadership in the next Congress. Impressed by the earnestness of this letter, Wilson replied: "The question of the revision of the currency is one of such capital importance that I wish to devote the utmost serious and immediate attention to it." Making good his intention, the President had studied the matter during his vacation in Bermuda. He invited reports from Professor Royal Meeker of Princeton, with whom he had discussed the possibility of giving flexibility to the gold content of the dollar; moreover, he had letters of advice from House, who as a banker and cotton planter in Texas had learned to distrust money monopolies and an inelastic currency.[2]

At first Wilson agreed with Bryan in distrusting the centralized nature of the Aldrich plan, and shared Glass's inclination toward a system of disconnected regional banks; and when House questioned the wisdom of this, the President referred him to the plank in the party's platform opposing "the so-called Aldrich plan or the establishment of a central bank."[3] The President was eager for more knowledge, more time to reflect, as he approached this massive legislative problem, which he described to House as "the most fundamental question of all."

Returning to Princeton from Bermuda in December, the President-elect had been ready to act. Though bitterly cold weather and Christmas festivities combined to put him to bed, he propped himself up with pillows and received Glass and Willis on December 26. Icicles hung outside the frosted windows as discussion began upon the most momentous economic legislation of twentieth-century America. Balancing his spectacles on his thumb, Wilson listened to the proposal of his advisers. Soon his eyes brightened and he said that they were "on the right track." He showed willingness to oppose banking interests on a principle that seemed economically sound; and then he made several suggestions. One of his proposals was to be a bone of contention for months to come. He recommended that supervision of the new system be entrusted, not to a board of bankers, as the Aldrich plan had contemplated, nor to the comptroller of the currency, as Glass proposed, but rather to an altruistic Federal Reserve Board that would stand at Washington as a "capstone" of the structure. He wished this body to exercise only supervisory powers and not the commercial functions

[2] On March 21, 1913, Meeker sent to Wilson a list of five questions that had been sent to twenty-four leading economists, with a summary of their replies.

[3] Baker has suggested (IV, 142 n.) that House's effort to justify a centralized system without dishonoring the platform may have resulted from the Colonel's being misled by the Democratic Textbook for 1912, which printed the plank in question so that it read, erroneously: "the so-called Aldrich plan *for* the establishment of a central bank." This would have permitted House to argue in good faith that the platform did not forbid any central bank, but simply one of the type proposed by Aldrich.

that had led to disaster in the past. He was for "plenty of centralization," he said, "but not too much." [4]

Glass had been impressed by the President-elect's insistence upon action and by his deference to expert advice. Red-haired and wiry, the Virginian had a peppery temperament that expressed itself forcefully in his newspaper and in the House of Representatives, where he had served ten years. Like Wilson, he had revolted against a state political machine; and when House came to offer him state patronage in return for his support for sound banking legislation, the Virginian's sense of propriety had been outraged. Glass had been bombarded by thousands of messages from citizens in all walks of life demanding reform legislation. Like Wilson, he had kept an open mind and listened to disinterested, scholarly advice. Though at first Glass looked askance at the President-elect's suggestion of a "capstone" board of control, he and Willis, after committee hearings at which bankers and businessmen advocated a system highly centralized and privately controlled, had drafted a bill that embodied Wilson's idea and had taken it to him at Trenton on January 30. The President-elect covenanted to support Glass when he learned that reactionaries were opposing the choice of the Virginian as chairman of the Currency Committee in the new House of Representatives. He told House and McAdoo that suggestions on banking legislation should be put before Glass.

On March 28, reading to his Cabinet the special message on the tariff that he was to give to the Congress in person, Wilson alluded to the reform of the banking and currency laws as a matter that "should press close upon the heels of the tariff changes, if not accompany them." He explained that he wanted action on currency legislation during the current session of Congress despite the desire of some Democratic legislators to concentrate on tariff reform for the present. Wilson felt that the prospect of salutary currency legislation would reassure those who feared that after tariff reductions there would not be enough money to do the increasing business of the nation.[5]

The details of the currency bill were so well guarded that serious controversy within the party had been avoided until the inauguration was over. However, the essence of the plan leaked into circulation and through news stories it reached the Cabinet members and also Robert

[4] Carter Glass, *An Adventure in Constructive Finance*, pp. 81–82; H. P. Willis, *The Federal Reserve System*, pp. 141 ff.

[5] Daniels Diary, Mar. 28, 1913. The party was committed to this course, Wilson reminded his men, even though the Administration might sign its own death warrant at the polls; in any event, it would be realized someday that they were serving the real interests of the people.

L. Owen, a friend of Bryan's who was chairman of the Senate Finance Committee. The senator wondered why he had not been consulted. Himself president of a bank in Oklahoma, Owen was drafting a currency bill that differed from Glass's measure in two important particulars: it would put control of the new system firmly in the hands of a board of public officials appointed by the President rather than a body in which bankers would be represented; and currency issues were to be the responsibility of the government rather than of the reserve banks.

When Bryan told the President that he shared the views of Senator Owen, Wilson was distressed. He saw the approach of the inevitable crisis that he had dreaded. The time was coming to deal with the agrarians. Although Wilson already had told Glass of his sympathy with progressive demands for control of the banking system by a board on which public appointees would predominate, he had not reached a conclusion regarding responsibility for the issue of currency. Colonel House, influenced by the views of financiers with whom he maintained contact—especially Paul Warburg, Aldrich's collaborator—had been warning the President against any concession to unsound sentiment. On the other hand, Wilson had to satisfy the agrarian progressives in order to hold his party together.

The thinking of the plainsmen was so foggy, in the view of the economists who were advising Glass, that it seemed best to solicit their political support by wooing Bryan himself. The conversion of the Great Commoner to a measure that was based essentially on spadework sponsored by Senator Aldrich, a Republican conservative, called for masterful leadership.

House set the stage for agreement by preliminary talks with both Bryan and Wilson; and on May 19 the President had it out with the colleague whose political support he needed in order to put Owen and the Senate behind a sound currency act. The President had been assiduous, since his inauguration, in reciprocating the goodwill that Bryan had shown. When he read the Glass Bill to the Great Commoner, therefore, Bryan responded in good spirit, offering to resign if his views embarrassed his chief and agreeing not to make his objections public. However, his criticisms of the draft were definite and apparently ineradicable. He was not willing to give private bankers control of the issue of currency. Moreover, he suggested that banking reform should not be brought up in Congress until the tariff bill had been passed and signed.

Having assured Bryan that he would be given another chance to review the bill, Wilson then asked Tumulty to try his hand at mollifying the veteran crusader by expressing the President's high regard for him. Accordingly, Tumulty called at the home of the secretary of state; and there, beaming with boyish pride, Bryan showed the emissary a picture that Wilson had autographed for him and spoke with deep feeling of his admiration for the President. Tumulty was able to allay Bryan's suspicions that Wall Street men were influencing the drafting of the measure; and when he returned to the White House he took with him the text of the Democratic platform and called to the President's attention certain passages on currency reform that Bryan had read to him. "I am convinced that there is a great deal in what Mr. Bryan says," Wilson commented noncommittally, and he permitted Tumulty to place Bryan's views before Glass and to suggest that the latter confer with McAdoo and Senator Owen in an effort to reach an understanding. Obviously it would take more pleading, and perhaps some concessions, to make the banking bill palatable to the secretary of state and his following in Congress.

Fortunately, the President had a secretary of the treasury who was both dynamic and tactful. Wilson discussed currency reform with McAdoo shortly after the inauguration, and the men found themselves in agreement on the vital points. McAdoo kept in touch with both conservative and progressive sentiment, and bankers gave him technical advice in conferences that he arranged at New York. It seemed to Wilson that his secretary of the treasury might aid in the education of their colleague, Bryan, and he asked McAdoo to undertake this.

Wooing the goodwill of the secretary of state without losing patience at his ignorance of fiscal realities, McAdoo appealed to Bryan's sense of responsibility as a member of the government. He made the Great Commoner see that, if the United States was to be responsible for the issue of currency under the Federal Reserve plan, as Bryan and Senator Owen wished, the notes must be secured by solid assets such as those of the member banks. Thus in the end the Great Commoner, softened by the blandishments of Wilson, House, and Tumulty, succumbed to McAdoo's patient accommodation of argument to Bryan's power of comprehension.

Meanwhile Colonel House was assiduous in catalyzing the meeting of minds. He dined with Owen and eased him back into sound channels when the senator broke loose with Bryanesque ideas; and he suggested that the currency measure be called "the Glass-Owen bill," hoping thus to flatter the senator and induce him to work harmoniously with Congressman Glass. Dining with prominent bankers whom he respected, the Colonel assured them of the soundness of the Administration's intentions. When they showed eagerness to participate in writing the new banking legislation, he reminded them gently that progressives were insisting that the President take no advice from financiers who had large private interests. Through the Colonel, Wilson could keep in touch with the thinking of financiers with whom he could not talk directly without forfeiting the confidence of agrarian progressives. But when House wanted to work with McAdoo and Glass to "whip into shape" a conservative measure that could be handed to Senator Owen, Wilson did not respond. House was a dear fellow and invaluable as an intelligence agent; but sometimes the friendly Colonel seemed to give his heart too freely to the last great man with whom he had dined and chatted, whether it was conservative Paul Warburg or trust-busting Samuel Untermyer. Wilson did not think it wise to prescribe to the Senate any bill prepared by House, McAdoo, and Glass. Desiring to avoid the appearance of dictating legislation, he preferred that Senator Owen, like Congressman Glass, should take the initiative and come to him for counsel.

Making himself available at all times to his lieutenants and putting his persuasive eloquence and the prestige of his office at their disposal, Wilson shrank from direct contact with strong prejudices, whether of the right or the left. As the ideas of bankers, economists, and politicians funneled in upon him, he tried to understand the reasoning of all but was aware of the bias of each.

In the last analysis, if his vision was to amount to more than a fancy, he must depend on the staff of his ship of state, who would float or sink together on the sea of history. He had to do business with Glass and Owen, who were the initiators of action in Congress, and with McAdoo, who was responsible for the credit of the government. But before sitting down with these men to make a final bill that would fully reconcile the Glass version with a draft that Owen sent to the White House late in May, Wilson turned once more to Louis D. Brandeis.

Denied a seat in the Cabinet, the "people's lawyer" lunched often with other liberal attorneys and publicists at the Willard Hotel in an informal group that called itself "the doughtnut Cabinet." Brandeis had been called to the White House to give advice at least twice since the inauguration, and he conceived that his role was to promote a harmonious council of progressives within the Administration. The attorney had perceived, in his studies of insurance and railroad corporations, how control had been concentrated in the hands of a few financiers who sometimes used their positions to increase their own economic power rather than to serve the public. After conferring with Wilson on June 11, he wrote on the 14th to the President thus:

The power to issue currency should be vested exclusively in government officials, even when the currency is issued against commercial paper. The American people will not be content to have the discretion necessarily involved vested in a Board composed wholly or in part of bankers, for their judgment may be biased by private interest or affiliation. The function of the bankers should be limited strictly to that of an advisory council. . . . Nothing would go so far in establishing confidence among businessmen as the assurance that the government will control the currency issues . . ." [6]

With this support from Brandeis, the President was convinced that he had been right in suggesting to Glass, months before, that the new banking system should be supervised by an altruistic public board rather than by representatives of member banks. Moreover, he was inclined now to reject House's final advice against government guarantee of currency and to support Bryan and Owen in this matter provided that the notes be based on the assets of the reserve banks. He was impressed also by Brandeis's proposal of an advisory board of bankers, thinking that this would help to ensure cooperative participation by those who would be responsible for the technical operation of the new system.

On June 18, Wilson called McAdoo, Glass, and Owen to the White House and told them that the Federal Reserve Board would be made up of Treasury officials and men appointed by the President, and that the currency would be guaranteed by the government, though issued by the member banks against commercial assets and a gold reserve. On the next day the text of the measure was published officially.

Glass rebelled against control of the reserve system by a government board, for he dreaded the possibility of political interference with sound banking. Wilson and McAdoo insisted, however, upon regulation in the public interest; and when McAdoo's fertile mind put forward a suggestion that appealed to Glass as a compromise, the congressman agreed to a "capstone" board of seven men, of whom two or three would be ex officio. [7]

[6] Alpheus Thomas Mason, *Brandeis*, pp. 398–99.

[7] Later it was decided that five of the seven-man board would be appointed by the President. Though Glass acted upon his chief's decision in the matter of government control, he was not convinced. Afterward he wrote a letter reiterating his views, and later he brought a

Having won Glass's reluctant acquiescence in this matter, the President had less difficulty in persuading the congressman to accept government guarantee of currency. At first, however, Glass enumerated the many kinds of security already provided for the notes to be issued and argued that an additional safeguard would be mere pretense.

"Exactly so, Glass," Wilson replied with a twitching of his left eye that bespoke his earnestness. "Every word you say is true: the government liability *is* a mere thought. And so, if we can hold to the substance of the thing and give the other fellow the shadow, why not do it, if thereby we can save the bill?"

While yielding to agrarian sentiment for government control of currency issue, Wilson would retain the solid substance of bank assets behind the notes. To make sure that his position was understood by Glass's committee, who had been consulted very little during the drafting of the bill and who had not organized until early June, he invited the members to the White House on June 20. It seemed to Glass that "the intimate touch of a tactician" was needed, and this the President tried to supply. One of the men asked rudely why they were there, since the text of the bill already had been settled. Taking offense at this imputation of dictatorship, Wilson was tempted to invite the questioner to leave the room; instead, he went on to answer queries courteously, parry objections with gentle reasoning, and command the respect of these politicians for himself, for Glass, and for their cause.

Finally, on June 26, Glass and Owen submitted identical bills to the House and the Senate, embodying Wilson's final decision. It was understood that, having chosen the ground with care, the Administration would stand and fight upon it no matter how hot the Washington summer or how heavy the fire of the enemy. When Wilson told Bryan of the compromise decisions, the Great Commoner assured him that the legislation would be acceptable to progressives and that he would release a statement to that effect.

The President himself brought the currency battle into the public

---

delegation of bankers to the White House to help him convince the President that he was wrong. Though two of the financiers assailed Wilson forthrightly and bitterly, the President listened so courteously that Glass was shamed and began to wish that he had not brought the men. When they were through, Wilson turned toward two caustic attackers and asked mildly: "Will one of you gentlemen tell me in what civilized country of the earth there are important government boards of control on which private interests are represented?" Getting no answer, he went on: "Which of you gentlemen thinks the railroads should select members of the Interstate Commerce Commission?" Carter Glass, *An Adventure in Constructive Finance*, p. 116. Thus the bankers were silenced and Glass was convinced. It was an interview that Wilson took a grim pleasure in recounting on occasions when the primacy of the public interest was challenged.

arena and fired the first shot at one o'clock on June 23, a few hours after Bryan had made known his endorsement of the program. The tariff bill had been passed by the House but was still in the Senate when Wilson went before the Congress for a second time to accelerate the momentum that he had gained by his unprecedented leadership. Cautious advisers had suggested that, if the wounds made in the tariff fight were irritated during the hot weather, it might be fatal to party harmony; but the President was so consumed by his cause that he could not free his mind of it for an hour. "Everybody must be seen," he confided to Mary Hulbert the day before going to the Capitol. "Every right means must be used to direct the thought and purpose of those who, outside of Washington, are to criticize it and form public opinion about it. It is not like the tariff, about which opinion has been definitely forming long years through. To form a single plan and a single intention about it seems at times a task so various and so elusive that it is hard to keep one's heart from failing." But he assured himself that his heart was not in the habit of failing.

He presented his banking program to a joint session of the Congress in a talk that was over in ten minutes. The principles were clear: there must be a currency "readily, elastically responsive to sound credit," a mobilization of reserves for legitimate uses, a ban upon concentration of resources for speculative purposes, and controls vested in the government, "so that the banks may be the instruments, not the masters, of business and of individual enterprise and initiative." Thus once more Woodrow Wilson singled out a great cause and dramatized it as a crusade for virtue in which he would march shoulder to shoulder with loyal comrades of the faith.

Having demanded that the Congress sit through the summer and legislate on the tariff and the currency, he could not himself escape from Washington. In the spring he had discussed vacation plans with his family, and falling in love with pictures of Harlakenden, an estate at Cornish in the hills of New Hampshire, they had rented it. Wilson hoped at least to escort his family to Harlakenden or to spend the Fourth of July there. The slow progreess of legislation, however, made him put off their departure for days. Finally Mrs. Wilson and the girls were persuaded to start out. The President could go with them only as far as the railroad station. When he left, his wife wept and lay in her berth and refused food. But once settled in the hill colony of artists and men of letters she took up her painting and lived from mail to mail, craving news of her husband. And as for him, it set his apprehensive mind at ease to read newspaper accounts of his Ellen's tea parties and to think of his dear ones amidst artists and literary folk. Such an idyllic environment was "just where they belonged," he thought.

July 2 was set as the date for announcement of the betrothal of his second daughter to Francis B. Sayre, whom the President had received, at first, with his usual stiffness toward suitors of his daughters, but whom he had come to regard as "almost good enough for Jessie." Wilson could not attend the engagement party because of an invitation to speak at Gettysburg on the Fourth, and he wrote on June 29 to break the bad news to his Ellen:

My darling sweetheart,

I can hardly keep back the tears as I write this morning. It is a bitter, bitter thing that I cannot come to my dear ones; but the duty is clear, and that ought to suffice. I cannot choose as an individual what I shall do; I must choose always as a President, ready to guard at every turn and in every way possible the success of what I have to do for the people. Apparently the little things count quite as much as the big in this strange business of leading opinion and securing action; and I must not kick against the pricks . . . The President is a superior kind of slave, and must content himself with the reflection that the *kind* is superior!

Explaining that he had declined the invitation to speak at Gettysburg with others of the same sort, but that Congressman Palmer had heard talk in Congress that had made the occasion seem of great importance, he went on:

It is no ordinary celebration. It is the half-century celebration of the turning battle of the war. Both blue and gray are to be there. It is to celebrate the end of all strife between the sections. Fifty years ago, almost, also on the Fourth of July, Mr. Lincoln was there (in the midst of business of the most serious and pressing kind, and at great personal cost and sacrifice to himself). If the President should refuse to go this time and should, instead, merely take a vacation for his own refreshment and pleasure, it would be hotly resented by a very large part of the public. It would be suggested that he is a Southerner and out of sympathy with the occasion. In short, it would be more than a passing mistake; it would amount to a serious blunder. And so I surrendered—the more readily because all this would have been so serious a misapprehension of my own real attitude. Nothing, while I am President, must be suffered to make an impression which will subtract by one iota the force I need to do the work assigned me. I can do this without any real risk to my health, and shall lose, not what I need but only what I want (ah, how much!).

My glimpse of Harlakenden is only postponed, my sweet one, and I shall study to get a little pleasure and frequent refreshment here . . . I shall thrive, *if only I surrender my will to the inequitable.*[8]

How shall I tell you what my heart is full of? It is literally full to overflowing with yearning love for you, my incomparable darling, and for the sweet little daughters whom I love with so deep a passion, and admire as much as I love! I dare not pour it out today. I am too lonely. I must think quietly and not with rebellion. The big house is still: I must copy its stately peace, and try to be worthy of the trust of those whom I try to serve and who make [*sic*] happy by their wonderful love!

Your own

Woodrow [9]

The address at Gettysburg was the only one that Wilson delivered during the summer, and he made several short trips to Harlakenden; but even when there he was bound to the White House by wire and his conscience was haunted by responsibility. However, among the creative spirits at Cornish he could confide his ambitions for America to sympathetic ears. He told a poet that he wanted to encourage a renaissance of his people that would express itself socially and artistically as well as politically, but that first he must construct solid economic piers for society.

Washington was unusually sultry that summer. The White House lawn yellowed under the sun and the President found little coolness in a marquee that had been set up on it. Nevertheless, he had spirit enough to write, and enjoyed keeping bachelor quarters with Dr. Grayson and Tumulty—"lovely fellows, both of them, and good company all the while," he thought them. Tactful and entertaining, the physician became the President's comrade day in and day out and cared for him with a solicitude that seemed to him motherly. Wilson had shrunk from personal relations with the men at Washington with whom he did business, dreading intimacies that might stir jealousies or expose him to pressures for unmerited favors. But Grayson's comradeship seemed legitimate, for no one could criticize a president for having his doctor constantly at his side. With the physician as opponent, and always using the same caddy, he played golf several afternoons each week because it took him outdoors and because it helped him "to keep alive and spend and be spent." After four or five holes he found that he

---

[8] This theme recurs in a letter written on the same day to Mary Hulbert in which Wilson said: "The most I can hope is, that by the end of the session I shall have learned not to tug at my chain and lacerate—my feelings! It's fine discipline, but it comes late in life! I learn hard. I am not so pliable as I once was."

[9] Unpublished letter, given to the writer by Eleanor W. McAdoo.

could forget the office and concentrate on the little ball. Then his
game would improve, his spirits rise, and he would jest, swing his arms,
and sometimes hum a merry tune. At the clubhouse he would permit
no special attention, and he refused invitations to play through those
ahead of him who had equal standing on the course. "My right eye
is like a horse's," he explained to fellow golfers one day. "I can see
straight out with it but not sideways. As a result I cannot take a full
swing because my nose gets in the way and cuts off my view of the
ball." [10] His score for eighteen holes usually exceeded a hundred.

He continued to draw refreshment from gallant correspondence. In
refined, intelligent womanhood he could find some of the spiritual
values that he missed in the public men with whom he had to do business. A lovely lady remained in his view a soul to be exalted and cared
for. He maintained his friendship with Mary Allen Hulbert and
wrote to her regularly on Sunday afternoons, confiding the thoughts
that came to him as he moved like a ghost through the echoing rooms
and corridors of the White House during the summer. He found
being President a solitary business, for he seemed to be the only one
whose duty it was to look out for the welfare of the whole country, to
study the pattern of affairs as a whole, and to live "all the while in his
thoughts with the people of the whole country." With his household
devoid of women, he found it hard not to fall in love with actresses
in the stock company whose performances he attended twice a week.
"Fortunately," he wrote, "I have a special gift for relaxation and for
being amused. But even then it is lonely, very lonely." He confessed
roguishly that he had "a private eye out for all the fun available and
for every escape not regarded as scandalous—especially seeking to see
all that is amusing in the frailties of fellow politicians."

Of his life on summer Sabbaths—the days on which he experienced a
"delightful renewal" of his normal thoughts and feelings—he wrote:
"I do not get out of bed on Sundays until about ten o'clock, just in time
to get a little breakfast and get to church; and after my letters are
written in the afternoon the doctor and I go off for a little drive in the
motor—unless, as this afternoon, a thunder storm comes up out of
mere exasperation that there should have been so sultry a day. It seems
to come up after such a day exactly as if in a bad humor, to drive the
maddening airs away, chasing them with its great angry breath and

[10] David Lawrence, *The True Story of W.W.*, p. 129. House sometimes accompanied the
golfers around the course, though he did not play. He wrote in his diary on April 14, 1914: "It
was evident to me that Grayson was not playing as well as he could, though I do not think
that the President noticed it."

growling the while like a wild beast in the chase." He attended what he described as "a dear old-fashioned church such as I used to go to when I was a boy, amidst a congregation of simple and genuine people to whom it is a matter of utter indifference whether there is a season or not . . ." Feeling stale and dull one Sunday, he went to this unpretentious church in a white linen suit and created what he described as a "mild sensation." But, he went on blithely, "that of course is what every public man wishes to do, at church or anywhere else, and it did not in the least interfere with my own state of mind during the service." Actually, he explained, the people of the church were too genuine and self-respecting to violate the privacy of the Wilsons or to make capital of them; but the secret service men were a constant trial. "What fun it will be some day to escape from arrest!" he wrote.

Sometimes official life brought compensations, as when the lord provost of Glasgow, a cultivated and gifted Scot, turned an official call into a delightful conversation. When his wife and daughter surprised him pleasantly by running down from Cornish late in August, he wrote to Mary Hulbert: "It is beyond measure refreshing to see them and unbosom myself to them." But it made him uneasy to have them remain in the "debilitating atmosphere" of the city.

All through the torrid summer a legislative battle over the currency bill raged. Even before June 23, when the President had put his program before the Congress, a spate of billingsgate rose from Western Democrats in the House who saw an opportunity to make political capital by flaying "Wall Street." Congressman Henry of Texas, chairman of the Committee on Rules, organized a campaign of heckling, proposed a handout of unsecured currency to subsidize agriculture, commerce, and industry; and to give strength to his insurrection against Glass's leadership he tried to conjure with the name of Bryan. He even went so far as to arraign the President as a political martinet.

The radical agrarians, with some support from Brandeis and Untermyer, mustered enough power to demand an amendment prohibiting interlocking among bank directorates; and when after futile efforts to dissuade them Wilson conceded this, they introduced provisions for the discounting of short-term agricultural paper. The Eastern press scoffed at what it called "cotton currency" and "corn-tassel currency"; but Bryan thought the proposal reasonable and urged Wilson not to oppose it, and the congressmen of the South and West forced an amendment through the committee. Though Wilson had tried all his resources of flattery, courtesy, and reason, he was not able to overcome impulses rooted in decades of polemics.

Finally when Glass, buffeted by the agrarians beyond endurance, came to his chief and offered to resign, Wilson was moved to profanity. "Damn it!" he said to his hard-pressed lieutenant, "don't resign, old fellow. Outvote them!"

The loyal Democrats on the committee did just that, and no vital provision of the bill was amended. To be sure, the dissenters carried their opposition into the party caucus that met on August 11; but the ground was cut from under them when Glass read decisive words that Bryan had written to him:

> You are authorized to speak for me and say that I appreciate so profoundly the service rendered by the President to the people in the stand he has taken on the fundamental principles involved in currency reform, that I am with him in all the details. If my opinion has influence with anyone called upon to act on this measure, I am willing to assume full responsibility for what I do when I advise him to stand by the President and assist in securing the passage of the bill at the earliest possible moment . . .

At hearing this the caucus submerged the obstructionists under cheers of derision and it was voted to support the Glass Bill with the amendment for agricultural credit and a few lesser changes. The measure finally was approved on September 18 by the House, 287 to 85.

The major battle, however, was still to come. Bankers saw behind government regulation the bugaboo of political influence and feared that the business mechanism they understood so well would be thrown out of adjustment. Some chattered of "confiscation"; and while one warned of "alarming inflationary features," another predicted "disastrous constriction of commercial credits." Thus the bill that had been carefully calculated to stabilize business was assailed as a disturber of stability.

Even enlightened bankers who had interviewed Wilson and Glass still protested the regulative provisions on which the President and Bryan insisted. Propaganda was organized, and journals devoted columns to attacks on the Glass Bill. A conference of bankers at Chicago issued a manifesto that seemed to Wilson and his friends to be an attempt to intimidate other financiers and threaten the government; and the President responded by telling newsmen that he wanted no suggestions from hostile interests. Certain editors took the view of protesting bankers and pictured Wilson as a master bending Congress to his indomitable will. "That is, of course, silly . . ." Wilson wrote in protest to Mary Hulbert. "I do not know how to wield a big stick, but I do know how to put my mind at the service of others for the accomplishment of a common purpose. They are using me; I am not driving them . . . And what a pleasure it is, what a deep human pleasure, to work with strong men, who do their own thinking and know how to put things in shape! Why a man should wish to be the whole show and surround himself with weak men, I cannot imagine! How dull it would be! . . . That is not power. Power consists in one's capacity to link his will with the purpose of others, to lead by reason and a gift for cooperation. It is a multiple of combined brains."

He wrote this in the flush of the victory won in the House of Representatives three days before. However, a week later he had to face the fact that certain Democratic senators were not disposed to work with him in the smooth way that he idealized. There were suggestions in hostile journals, also, that delay and reconsideration were desirable. Wilson, however, saw in these ideas a familiar device of obstructionism; and he feared that, while senators procrastinated, uneasiness among bankers might provoke a financial crisis.[11] He thought he detected a conspiracy "to poison the public mind against the currency bill." He therefore called the party's senatorial steering committee to the White House and discouraged adjournment for more than three days at any one time. Doubting that he could deal with the upper house in the ideal role of a statesman among peers, he was willing to use the lash if it became necessary. "Why *should* public men, Senators of the United States, have to be led and stimulated to what all the country knows to be their duty!" he complained to Mary Hulbert. "To whom are they listening? Certainly not to the voice of the people, when they quibble and twist and hesitate. They have strangely blunted perceptions, and exaggerate themselves in the most extraordinary degree. Therefore it *is* a struggle and must be accepted as such. A man of my temperament and my limitations will certainly wear himself out in it; but that is small matter; the danger is that he may lose his patience and suffer the weakness of exasperation. It is against these that I have constantly to guard myself."

[11] On October 11, Wilson wrote to his friend Senator Williams: "Things are going on in the banking world which are evidently based upon a desire to make the members of the two houses uneasy in the presence of the bankers' power, and it is possible that with expanding business and contracting credits a panic may be brought on while we wait. There is absolutely no excuse for the fall in the market value of the two-per-cents. It is being brought about by those who misunderstand or misrepresent, or have not read the bill."

His imagination delighted in exalting his correspondent in Bermuda as *Democracy personified*. He would resort to her, he wrote, as the high priestess of Democracy; and he asked how the picture looked to her from her island shrine. "It is more important to me to know how it looks outside of Washington than how it looks inside," he explained. "The men who think *in Washington* only cannot think for the country. It is a place of illusions. The disease is that men think of themselves and not of their tasks of service, and are more concerned with what will happen to them than what will happen to the country. I am not complaining or scolding or holding myself superior; I am only analyzing, as a man will on Sunday, when the work pauses and he looks before and after. My eye is no better than theirs; it is only fresher, and was a thoughtful spectator of these very things before it got on the inside and tried to see straight there."

In August he wrote to Edith Reid: "Hard as it is to nurse Congress along and stand ready to play a part of guidance in anything that turns up, great or small, it is all part of something infinitely great and worth while, and I am content to labor at it to the finish . . . So far things go very well, and my leadership is most loyally and graciously accepted, even by men of whom I did not expect it. I hope that this is in part because they perceive that I am pursuing no private and selfish purposes of my own. How could a man do that with such responsibilities resting upon him! It is no credit to be sobered and moralized by a task like this . . ."

Woodrow Wilson did not allow himself to forget that he was "nursing" Congress and not driving it. It hurt him to read reports that he had characterized dissenting senators of his party as "rebels and no Democrats," and he protested in a letter to the Washington *Post*: "Of course I never said any such thing. It is contrary both to my thought and character, and I must ask that you give a very prominent place in your issue of tomorrow to this denial."

Confident that, under his leadership, political motives could not corrupt the Federal Reserve System, Wilson felt that the New York bankers were "too much in the atmosphere of the thing" to see the situation whole. Roland Morris, one of his Princeton boys, reported to him that many financiers were embittered; but the President was not moved to reconsider the currency bill. Fixing his eyes intently on the man, he said: "Morris, I have seen those men. They came down here with a long brief. The essence of their case was that nothing whatever should be done. They asserted that the time was inopportune. I told them that so far as their principal contention was concerned the case was decided. It was *res adjudicata*. Something was going to be done. I told them I would be glad to have them suggest changes or criticisms to help me in making a better law. They went home and afterwards sent down a long brief which I considered carefully. I found that in its essence it was only a repetition of their former contention, really an argument to do nothing. What is the use of my seeing them again? I will not see them again. You can tell them exactly the reason why I will not see them again."

The bankers intensified their protests in the autumn. Paul Warburg wrote House that he was mortified by the "suicidal stubbornness" with which sound suggestions had been swept aside. Early in October the acting president of the American Bankers' Association denounced the Federal Reserve plan as "an invasion of the liberty of the citizens" and "unjust and un-American," and on the 23rd President Vanderlip of the National City Bank of New York proposed an alternate plan. But Wilson said promptly and emphatically that he would not have the national banking system dictated by any bankers.

McAdoo noted that the President's jaw was setting hard on the currency issue and feared the effect of his schoolmastering habits. Banking reform had become a cause so sacred to Wilson that he was prepared to build fires under the senators by direct appeals to the people. He had not forgotten what he had said in an academic lecture: the president had "no means of compelling Congress except through public opinion." Wilson's nerves were fraying badly. Difficulties with Mexico were irritating him and he suffered a week of illness that he laughed off as "a little spell of indigestion . . . due, undoubtedly, to my being worn out and unable to run both my stomach and the government."

Nevertheless, he managed to get off a note to his "precious sister," Annie Howe. "What a delight it was to get your letter," he wrote. "I am going to steal time enough to answer it on my own typewriter, as in the old days. I have to *steal* it . . . It is as if the office swallowed up the individual life, whether you would or not, and used every nerve in you, leaving you only the time you were in bed, in the deep oblivion of utter fatigue . . . There have been times, of course, when I have felt terribly fagged, and almost down and out, but I have come out of them at once all fit again. I am beginning to think that I am rather a tough customer, after all, physically, if not otherwise!"

The prophet's confidence in his cause was justified by the returns from local elections in November. Moreover, it was clear that many bankers, especially those outside New York, preferred the Glass-Owen bill to an extension of the status quo, in spite of their distrust of government supervision; and on October 24 the national Chamber of Commerce approved the measure, 306 to 17. Finally, the President felt that he was strong enough to compel party unity by summoning a caucus of Democratic senators. He defended this action against a vigorous protest from Hitchcock of Nebraska. Explaining that he harbored "no jealousy of differences of opinion," he wrote thus to the senator on November 11: "In all these matters I feel that successful action depends upon the yielding of individual views in order that we may get a measure which will meet the well-known principles of the party and enable us, by *common* counsel, to arrive at what I may call a corporate result—corporate in the sense of being the result of a comparison of views among colleagues who are equally obliged to agree upon a measure which will afford the country relief."

Though unable to control all the party men, the caucus voted unanimously to forgo holidays unless the currency bill was passed before Christmas. On November 22 the measure was reported out of committee. Debate followed party lines for the most part; but Hitchcock introduced an alternate draft that commanded Republican support. The Administration's version of the bill was attacked vehemently by Elihu Root, who saw in it "financial heresy" that would put the nation "in pawn." It would induce dreams of prosperity, he alleged, but actually would bring inflation and a vanishing gold supply. Using the political jargon with which Republicans had fought populist demagoguery for decades, Root held the floor for three hours and was answered by Democratic spokesmen with argument equally vigorous and unscientific. Amendments were beaten off; and finally the opponents, unable to vote down the Administration bloc, tried to delay decision by proposing to the exhausted Senate that it recess until after the holidays. Wilson, however, stood by the verdict of the caucus and let it be known that he would sanction no respite. The bill was brought to a vote on December 19 and passed, 54 to 34, with every Democrat present in favor, and also six Senators of other parties.

The differences between the acts of the two Houses were reconciled speedily; and on December 22, at five in the morning, the conference committee reached agreement. When the Senate delayed a few hours before accepting the final version, Wilson, who had been kept in bed for days by a bronchial cold and a relapse, lost patience for a moment and spoke of the Upper House as a lot of old women, one of them so feminine that it was immodest of him to wear trousers. But on the 23rd the Federal Reserve Act was on the President's desk for signature.

This law, over which Congress had labored for nine months, set up a central structure that would serve the nation's bankers by pooling reserves to meet the danger of credit stringency, providing an elastic currency, and supplying a national clearing system. Moreover, it gave the federal government adequate banking facilities; and by provisions for changes in rates, open-market operations, and examination of banks, it made it possible for a public board to prevent the sort of panic that had been disastrous more than once.

But in extending federal control over the nation's banks, the Federal Reserve Act had a significance still more far-reaching. The momentum that began with tariff and income-tax legislation was developing a force that was to carry the responsibility of civil servants into still other fields that previously had been left to private enterprise.

Wilson's pioneering spirit quickened at contemplation of what had been wrought on the legislative frontier. "There have been currents and countercurrents," he said on the day of signing the Glass-Owen Act, "but the stream has moved forward." In securing effective action on the tariff and on banking and currency, the prophet had realized the two visions of reform that had most allured him through the years when he had been only an outside influence in politics.

It was a radiant group that gathered at the executive offices to watch the signing of one of the most significant pieces of legislation of the twentieth century. Woodrow Wilson came in smiling, started to sit down at his desk, then hesitated and looked around the circle of friends for Carter Glass, who was standing at the end of the room. As the taciturn Virginian came forward, the President shook his hand warmly and invited him to stand with Senator Owen beside his desk. Sitting down, he signed the Federal Reserve Act with four gold pens, remarking, "I'm drawing on the gold reserve." Then he told his comrades of his appreciation of their steadfastness, and in letters to McAdoo, Owen, and Glass he repeated his praise of their efforts. But these lieutenants knew that the enactment of the law was due most of all to the guidance of their chief.

Wilson realized that too much trust must not be placed in the letter of any law, that the success of this one depended largely on the character and ability of the seven men who would sit on the Federal Reserve Board. While Tumulty was importuning the Chief to make appointments immediately, McAdoo was cautioning him to act deliberately.

Asked to take a hand in the matter, House gave to the President, on the day before the act was signed, some names that he had brought together on twenty-four hours' notice.

Wilson, however, wished time to meditate on appointments so vital. He had no sympathy for McAdoo's feeling that a board should be chosen that could be counted on to work in harmony with the secretary of the treasury. "McAdoo thinks we are forming a social club," he complained to House,[12] agreeing with his friend that they must not risk offending the secretary of the treasury by letting him know the extent of their discussions of his department. The President wanted board members who were removed as far as possible from politics and obviously beyond the influence of either Treasury or White House; and it was not until August of 1914 that he found five appointees who were satisfactory to himself and to the Congress.[13]

The President nominated Thomas D. Jones, who with his brother had defended Wilson's position at Princeton. This close friend, however, was a director of the International Harvester Company, then under indictment as an illegal combination. When senators from agrarian states feared to approve Jones, the President tried to defend his friend by explaining, in a public letter to the Senate Banking Committee, that Jones had become a director of the harvester company with a view to reforming its practices. When the candidate came before the senators, however, he bluntly asserted his approval of his corporation's acts. Wilson gave up and wrote to his friend thus: "I cannot say when I have had a disappointment which cut me more keenly than this . . . I am facing this outcome of the matter with the keenest personal sorrow." This defeat, in July of 1914, was the first that Wilson suffered in Congress.

It was a strenuous year, all in all, that Woodrow Wilson put behind

[12] Later McAdoo reported to Wilson that the members of the Federal Reserve Board were disgruntled because the State Department's expert in protocol ruled that the social precedence of the new body among the government commissions must be determined by the date of its creation. "I can do nothing about it, I am not a social arbiter," was the President's disdainful reply. And then, when McAdoo pressed him for a decision, he said with a broad smile: "Well, they might come right after the fire department." W. G. McAdoo, *op. cit.*, pp. 287–88.

[13] After dinner on Jan. 21, 1914, the Colonel commented that the success of the Federal Reserve System would depend largely on the character of the men who administered it; and Wilson replied: "My dear friend, do not frighten me any more than I am now." Remarking that the judgment of men was with him largely a matter of instinct, the President reacted decisively against a candidate who had been promoting his own name. He had not wanted a banker as treasurer of New Jersey or as secretary of the treasury, and he did not wish the new board to be controlled by bankers. Nor did he want to appoint as many as three members from the Treasury staff. House Diary, April 28, 1914. "I wonder if you have been able to get on the track of any really big, available, suitable businessman for the Federal Reserve Board," Wilson wrote to House on Feb. 16, 1914.

him when he signed the Federal Reserve Act and prepared for a Christmas holiday. But it was one of his great years, comparable to periods of spectacular success at Princeton and at Trenton and to the lofty summit of achievement on which he was to stand at Paris early in 1919. Like an architect who builds for an epoch rather than for a day, he had laid for twentieth-century America, in the tariff and banking acts, two piers strong enough to bear the stresses of an economy of freedom and opportunity.

Political opponents as well as loyal partisans applauded the achievement of the new President. Even the Republican New York *Tribune* praised him: "President Wilson has brought his party out of the wilderness of Bryanism. It has been a great exhibition of leadership." Progressive journals were appreciative; and William Howard Taft wrote generously in the *Saturday Evening Post*: "Never before, in its recent history certainly, has the Democratic party exercised such self-control. It is due to the circumstances and to Mr. Wilson's masterful personality and attitude . . ." And the New York *World* wrote of "a year of achievement for which there have been few, if any, parallels in American history."

Such opinions did not make Wilson complacent, but served rather to stimulate his pioneering impulses. When he signed the Federal Reserve Act he proclaimed that it was but "the first in a series of constructive measures." As at Princeton and Trenton, where his first years in office had been his most successful, there was to be no change in the direction of his enterprise, and confidence in himself and his cause was to tip the balance dangerously against his inclination to meditate.

CHAPTER XIX

CLARIFYING THE ANTITRUST LAWS

AT TIMES, DURING his first months in the Presidency, it had seemed to Woodrow Wilson that the American people whom he loved would kill him. Illness put him to bed for a few days in December and convinced him that he must have rest. His family had returned from New Hampshire in October. In November, however, daughter Jessie was married, and the loss cut deeply. After the ceremony Ellen Wilson was heard to say to a friend: "I know; it was a wedding, not a funeral, but you must forgive us—this is the first break in the family."

When Wilson was ill, in December, Colonel House went to his bedside and told him jokes and discouraged discussion of public affairs that might be exhausting; and afterward he recorded complacently in his diary that the President had been offended because he stayed overnight with McAdoo instead of at the White House. After a vacation trip to Europe,[1] House had returned in the autumn to his role as the President's confidant. He had found that he could aid the Administration by frequent visits with Cabinet members; and he cultivated rapport particularly with Bryan, McAdoo, and Houston, for these officials were the ones whom the President heeded most frequently in general matters. When the genial Colonel came smiling into the departmental offices, passing on words of praise that the President had spoken to him in private or dropping a hint of suggestion, the secretaries were as attentive as if they were facing the Chief himself. House was able to sound out the Cabinet members on their opinions of each other as well as of the President. Both Wilson and his men confided to him things that they would not say to one another, and without betraying confidences the Colonel prevented or alleviated frictions. Moreover, he kept informed about local situations that the President had no time to follow.[2]

[1] Explaining that he was going abroad to conserve his strength so that he might serve the President the better, House had written in May: "My faith in you is as great as my love for you—more than that I cannot say." He could not go to Washington in the summer, he explained in a letter written on Aug. 6 to Dr. Grayson, because he had suffered a heat stroke some years before and had been forced to avoid hot weather as he would the plague.

[2] The Administration had not been in office two months before *Collier's* had printed an

Realizing the value of these voluntary services, one day when House persuaded him to break an agreement with a senator that might violate the Constitution, Wilson told the Colonel to "scold" him frankly whenever he contemplated doing anything that might be wrong. Declaring that "he did not know how he could carry on without this friend," he thanked him again and again, addressed him in letters as "my dear friend," signed himself "affectionally yours," told him that, with one or two exceptions, he was the most efficient man he had ever known. The Colonel helped to solve the problem that Cleveland had once described to Wilson as one of the President's hardest: how to get the truth unwarped by flattery or self-interest. Wilson knew that this friend would not press matters of business upon him when he was too worn to discuss them; and House seemed always ready to respond with cheer for despondent moods, caution for moods of elation and overconfidence.

On the night before the signing of the currency act the Colonel stayed at the White House and was charmed by the unpretentious living of the first family. The adviser had noted that the President listened to advice from others when it was tactfully given, but that it was seldom invited; and the Colonel sympathized with Cabinet members who regretted that their business was discussed by the President with House more often than with themselves. Hoping to encourage his friend to keep his mind open, the Colonel congratulated him on never having reached "the 'know-it-all' attitude"; and he kept his tongue in his cheek when Wilson replied that his long university training had helped him to derive new and helpful ideas from conferences.[3]

article on "The President's Silent Partner." Wilson read the article, and his love for the Colonel was not diminished. But House wrote to his brother-in-law: "I do not know how much of this kind of thing W.W. can stand. The last edition of *Harper's Weekly* spoke of me as 'Assistant President House.' I think it is time for me to go to Europe or take to the woods." House to Mezes, April 24, 1913, *House Papers*, I, 150.

"The President has been so generous and kind to me in all my relations with him," the Colonel wrote in his diary on June 12. "that I cannot feel anything excepting the closest comradeship for him, and I express myself to him in a way that I seldom do to any other friend in the world."

[3] House Diary, Dec. 22, 1913. Four months later House was recording the same opinions, fortified by testimony from members of the Cabinet. When Wilson referred to Hamilton as "easily the ablest" of the fathers of the nation, the Colonel suggested that Washington's ability to use Hamilton was a measure of the greatness of the first President. "I told him," House wrote, "that all the really big men I had known had taken advice from others, while the little men refused to take it . . . He agreed to this. At another time in our conversation, he remarked that he always sought advice. I almost laughed at this statement." House Diary, April 15, 1914, in *House Papers*, I, 126.

Wilson's increasing reluctance to take his Cabinet into his confidence resulted in part from leaks of information that Wilson and other officials attributed to Secretary Lane's inclination to chat with newsmen and foreign diplomats after Cabinet meetings. W.W. to Redfield, Feb. 11, 1923, Redfield Papers.

While they were talking, Ellen Wilson came in and laid the family's financial problems before the Colonel, whom she trusted implicitly. The President remarked that he had not been able to supplement his salary by writing, because what he wanted to write would have little market.[4] Since inauguration they had paid their debts, given $5,000 to relatives, and saved about $2,000 a month. House offered to make a list of securities that a president could properly buy; and urging his friend to concentrate his thought on ways of leaving an impress of usefulness on the history of his times, he agreed with Mrs. Wilson that they would correspond on financial problems without bothering her husband.

It was nearly midnight when finally they left the study. Speaking of his satisfaction in talking without having to calculate either the substance or the effect of his words, Wilson accompanied his guest to his chamber and with affectionate solicitude all but tucked him in bed. This gentle, compassionate counselor who never oversold himself or his ideas had so won the confidence of the President's family that Helen Bones said one day to Mrs. House: "When Cousin Woodrow and the Colonel are together the family feels the country is safe, and nothing can happen." And at the same time the Colonel was recording in his diary: "There is not a piece of legislation he has advocated, a policy, or an important appointment that he has not discussed with me frankly, fully and frequently." No one but Jack Hibben ever had made himself so valuable to the Wilsons as friend and adviser. "What I like about Colonel House," the President said one day to a journalist, "is that he holds things at arm's length—objectively. He seems to be able to penetrate a proposition and get to its essence quickly." Sometimes he referred to the Colonel as his "eyes and ears."[5]

On the evening of December 23—the day of the signing of the Federal Reserve Act—the Wilsons set out by train for Pass Christian, a sleepy village on the coast of Mississippi, where they settled into the meandering life of the Old South. "This proves to be just the place we wanted," Wilson wrote to House from his retreat on December 27. "I have, myself, a greater sense of relief than I have had in many a long day." Living in a house built before the Civil War, they enjoyed the Negro servants and the gentle neighbors.

It was particularly comforting at this time for Wilson to live in a

[4] A year later Wilson told his family that someone wanted to serialize his *History of the American People* in the daily papers. Asked by a daughter whether there was "any money in it," he replied: "Oh yes—but that's the reason why I don't want to do it while I am the President."

[5] Lawrence, *op. cit.*, pp. 68, 71.

normal Southern community, for at Washington he had been under extreme pressure from progressive Negroes and their Yankee partisans. The Wilsons respected good colored folk but had little sympathy with aggressive ones. At Princeton they had been unwilling to force the issue of a Negro's right of admission to the university. It seemed to the President that segregation of the races kept embarrassing problems from arising and he did not comply with repeated pleas from champions of Negro rights whose support he had sought in the election campaign.[6] Urged to appoint a national commission to study problems of race relations, Wilson had explained in the summer of 1913 that such a move would rouse resentment among Southerners in Congress and thus put his vital legislative program in jeopardy.

Wilson condoned segregation of races in government bureaus as a policy "distinctly to the advantage of the colored people themselves" and one that made them the more safe in their possession of office and the less likely to be discriminated against. He was moved by the sentiment that had possessed Ellen Wilson when, stepping by mistake into a Jim Crow railway car, she had sensed a feeling on the part of its colored occupants that their rights had been violated by her intrusion. In reply to protests against segregation that came from Villard, the grandson of Garrison the abolitionist, the President wrote: "I hope and, I may say, I believe that by the slow pressure of argument and persuasion the situation may be changed and a great many things done eventually which now seem impossible. But they cannot be done, either now or at any future time, if a bitter agitation is inaugurated and carried to its natural ends. I appeal to you most earnestly to aid in holding things at a just and cool equipoise until I can discover whether it is possible to work out anything or not."

He had fended off protests from Southern legislators against the advancement of able Negroes in federal services. Moreover, he had no sympathy with extremists in his party who discharged and demoted colored workers without justification; and after the protests of Northern reformers were echoed by many progressive leaders, at least one federal department, the Treasury, began quietly to modify the policy of segregation. Though he had grown up in the South, he had never absorbed its extreme views. He spoke of himself as "a recent immigrant."

---

[6] In the 1912 campaign Wilson went no further than to promise "justice executed with liberality and good feeling" and "absolute fair dealing," and to make it clear that he would appoint no man to office because he was colored and also that he would appoint colored men on their merits. These generalities had convinced many champions of the Negroes that he was more to be trusted than his opponents.

The President had been equally patient and moderate in dealing with another social movement of which he had been made embarrassingly aware during his first winter in office. The day before his inauguration militant suffragettes had taken part in a parade in the capital. Before Wilson's departure for Pass Christian, lobbyists for woman suffrage had invaded the executive offices and presented their cause forcefully; and when the President's annual message to Congress had failed to mention the issue, they accused him of "dodging." The spokesman for a delegation of a hundred agitating women asked him point-blank: "Have we anyone to present our case to Congress?" He tried to turn the query by saying, with a laugh, that he had found the suffragists well able to speak for themselves; but when they pinned him down, the muscles of his face twitched for an instant and he gave them a blunt "no."

Under pressure from his daughters, Wilson had to some degree overcome the aversion to emancipated womanhood that had been bred in him and strengthened by his experience as a teacher at Bryn Mawr; but he was not yet convinced that suffrage was one of those compelling causes of which he had written in *Leaders of Men*—a "permanent purpose of the public mind of which a statesman must take account to keep himself in office," rather than a mere "breeze of the day" to which a demagogue might trim his sails. However, when he was reminded by a militant woman that she had been led to believe before his election that he would support the movement, and was accused of having "gunned for votes," his sensitive conscience was pierced and his face flushed. He explained that he had spoken then as an individual, but must now represent a party whose platform had not endorsed suffrage and whose Southern members were opposed to it. He was, he said, "tied to a conviction" that suffrage qualifications should be controlled by the states.

Actually, the force of public opinion was not yet strong enough to overcome the personal feelings of Woodrow and Ellen Wilson. Moreover, the President's understanding of feminine psychology cautioned him against giving the ballot to women. It seemed to him that they thought too directly to be enfranchised *en bloc*. They might refuse to recognize obstacles and to circumvent them wisely. "A woman will not do that," he said to a friend. "If she cannot do directly and immediately what seems to her logical, she won't play." [7] Once, asked for his

---

[7] Lawrence, *op. cit.*, p. 136. To Oliver P. Newman, Wilson said "We cannot enfranchise the women all at once. It would be very dangerous. Woman's mind is too logical . . . In politics, in governmental affairs, and in life you cannot go in a straight and logical line."

views on woman suffrage, he told of a deacon who escorted two ladies down a slippery hill and, when they began to lose traction, clung to a post and shouted as they gathered speed: "It grieves me sadly, ladies, but I can accompany you no further."

Wilson the man of thought realized that the issues of race equality and woman suffrage involved slow changes in the social mores of his people. He knew that he could not act upon them with constructive decisiveness, as in the case of economic maladies that obviously demanded remedy. In taking this view he disappointed ardent reformers.

The most baffling issue before Wilson, however, as he enjoyed Southern life at Pass Christian at the end of 1913, was the problem of trust regulation. He pondered much on the question and worked on a statement for the Congress. This was a matter that touched sensitive property rights and involved many frictional crossings of political and economic views. There was little unanimity of opinion as to what should be done—only vague sentiment that action should be taken to end abuses of economic and financial power. It was more difficult to bring practical politicians into agreement on antitrust laws than it had been to get assent to specific reforms of the tariff and the banking system. There were differences of opinion in the Cabinet, and Wilson's powers were taxed as he tried to keep his men functioning as a team in spite of them.[8]

Of all the Cabinet members, McReynolds had perhaps the most perplexing task, for it devolved upon him to prosecute corporations for breaches of law in a field where there were vague statutes and little precedent. The attorney general was determined to apply Wilson's policy of preserving conditions favorable to competition, and he intended to prosecute suits already pending in the courts against certain

---

At times Wilson's patience with importunate women gave way. Once, receiving a letter from a suffrage state warning that the women of the state would vote against him unless he did thus and so, the President replied that he thanked them and sincerely hoped that they would.

"Suffrage for women," Wilson said to Nancy Toy, "will make absolutely no change in politics—it is the home that will be disastrously affected. Somebody has to make the home, and who is going to do it if the women don't?" Toy Diary, Jan. 6, 1915. Wilson later gave vital support to the suffrage amendment.

[8] A month after inauguration the President had directed Burleson's thinking toward the possibility of government ownership of telegraph lines; but when the postmaster general proposed taking over private property at the value of the physical plant and operating it at a profit to the Post Office Department, Wilson thought that the time was not ripe for such a radical move and Burleson, who had to dispel rumors by issuing a public denial, felt that he had been made a "goat." House Diary, Dec. 22, and 23, 1913. Talking with Burleson on Oct. 30, House had considered the proposal for government ownership "a doubtful expedient" and had spoken of the wide ownership of the stock of the American Telephone and Telegraph Company.

large corporations. In this purpose he was supported not only by the President but by House, who was disturbed particularly by the restraint upon fair competition that was imposed by interlocking directorates. However, when Henry Clay Frick of the United States Steel Corporation, which had been reproved by the Pujo Committee, went to the Colonel confidentially and asked him to arrange a settlement of the government's suit out of court, both House and Wilson thought it politic to refer the matter to McReynolds, with no recommendation except that this corporation should enjoy exactly the same consideration as any other and should be allowed to propose a settlement.[9]

Brought face to face with the vast problem of government regulation of big business, Wilson and House were glad to evade responsibility for specific action. The President was perplexed because he owned nine shares of preferred stock of the United States Steel Corporation. He feared that if he sold them he might seem to be trying to escape the consequences of the government's suit, and if he held on he might be criticized if the outcome of the litigation favored the corporation.[10]

Woodrow Wilson had not been in office many weeks before he had become embarrassingly aware of the intertwining of problems of labor interest with those of trust regulation. For some years the American Federation of Labor had been struggling to have certain of its tactics, particularly the secondary boycott, exempted from prosecution under the Sherman Antitrust Law; and to further this purpose Democratic legislators had attached to the Sundry Civil Appropriation bill of 1913 a rider that prohibited the use of any of the appropriated funds for the prosecution of labor unions. Though Taft had vetoed this provision and had denounced it as "class legislation of the most vicious sort," Wilson had intimated soon after his inauguration that he would not oppose the measure if the Congress sent it to him. Samuel Gompers had put his arguments before Wilson in a long letter, and the President

[9] Left free to use his own judgment, McReynolds complained that the President seldom discussed policies with him. House Diary, Mar. 29 and May 7, 1914. The attorney general thought that the settlement proposed by the steel men would not restore fair competition in the industry and therefore he refused to accept it. *Ibid.*, Mar. 22, 24, 26, Sept. 30, 1913. House and Houston thought that certain interests were hoping to break down the attorney general and thus attack Wilson. Houston to Page, June 30, 1913, and House to Page, July 27, 1913. Page Papers (Houghton Library, Harvard University).

[10] House suggested that Wilson solve his dilemma by selling the stock and appointing a special counsel to handle the suit for the government, and the President made a note of the suggestion in shorthand. The Colonel had his own perplexities. Only three weeks after the inauguration he wrote in his diary: "It is a difficult task to steer oneself steadily in the uncertain seas where politics and finance meet. Hereafter, I shall refuse to have anything to do with the financial end of it, and confine myself to advising the Administration."

had replied cordially to this labor leader who had supported him in the election campaign. He was impressed by the insistence of Gompers that unions of workingmen were based on certain human considerations that forbade their classification with combinations of dealers in commodities.

When the appropriation bill reached Wilson's desk with the rider included, however, conservatives in his Cabinet and outside pressed him to reject it. It was an embarrassing dilemma, for he was unwilling to jeopardize the operations of the government by blocking the appropriation of funds in general. Finally, on June 23, he carried through his intention of signing the measure, but at the same time he announced that he would have vetoed the rider if it had come to him separately, that he considered it merely an emphatic expression of Congressional opinion, and that the Justice Department would find resources to prosecute any group that broke the antitrust law.[11]

Though the flurry of agitation over the labor rider on the Sundry Civil bill had impressed upon Wilson the sensitivity of the unions to any legislation governing corporations, it was but a passing diversion in the long search for legal remedies against abuses of economic power. For years Woodrow Wilson had been observing the problem, and in speeches and essays he had traced its general outline. He had not been blind to the commendable efficiency of large units in some industries; but where monopolies were inevitable or desirable, he insisted, with Brandeis, that they should be owned, not merely regulated, by the state. Private monopoly was anathema.[12] "A trust," Wilson wrote in *The New Freedom*, "does not bring efficiency to the aid of business; *it buys efficiency out of business.* I am for big business, and I am against the trusts."

Wilson's Republican predecessors had been concerned chiefly with the

[11] Wilson gave warmer approval to another labor measure that had been vetoed by Taft— a bill to regulate conditions of maritime labor that had been originated by President Andrew Furuseth of the Seamen's Union and sponsored in Congress by Senator LaFollette and by William B. Wilson, now secretary of labor. The State Department opposed action on this measure, which would unilaterally abrogate treaties with other maritime powers providing for the arrest of foreign seamen who deserted while their ships were in American ports. But the President finally signed the Seamen's Bill on March 4, 1915, after eloquent pleading by Furuseth had won over Secretary Bryan and LaFollette had promised that the State Department would be given time to adjust international agreements.

[12] After inauguration Wilson had stood on the plank of his party's platform: "A private monopoly is indefensible and intolerable. We therefore favor the vigorous enforcement of the criminal as well as the civil law against trusts and trust officials, and demand the enactment of such additional legislation as may be necessary to make it impossible for a private monopoly to exist in the United States." Moreover, he affirmed the party's demand for "the prevention of holding companies, of interlocking directorates, of stock-watering, of discrimination in price, and the control by any one corporation of so large a proportion of any industry as to make it a menace to competitive conditions."

immediate manifestations of economic maladies. By the Sherman Act and the creation of an Interstate Commerce Commission an effort had been made to protect small business from the power of firms that had grown large and monopolistic. But, eager to preserve the efficiencies resulting from large operating units, they had given little thought to nurturing the inventive and organizing genius that had made corporations great and that might guide new and still more efficient businesses to greatness.

Wilson had perceived that, if America was to continue to grow in strength, there must be freedom for the working of a process of natural selection that would eliminate inefficient enterprises and allow more worthy ones to prosper: for example, smart inventors and manufacturers, making a start perhaps in private cellars and attics, must have access to capital that would make them financially able to distribute their improved goods and processes. It was not enough merely to protect the financially weak from unscrupulous practices by those who had grown strong: all individuals and corporations must be guaranteed freedom to compete on equal terms in contributing to the nation's wealth and comfort. Otherwise, Wilson feared, enterprise might wither, and American industry might fall under the curse of the prophet Habbakuk: "Behold, it is laid over with gold and silver, and there is no breath at all in the midst of it."

During the 1912 campaign, when he had sought advice from Brandeis in order to combat Roosevelt's New Nationalism, Wilson had received proposals for clarifying the almost defunct Sherman Antitrust Act of 1890, facilitating its enforcement in the courts, and creating a fact-finding body to aid in making the provisions effective. After taking office the President had summoned Representative Stanley, chairman of a legislative committee that had probed the United States Steel Corporation, and listened intently for two hours while the congressman talked of disclosures of corporate wrongdoing. At the same time Wilson maintained contact with the "doughnut Cabinet." Moreover, the President studied magazine articles by Brandeis that were published in a book entitled *Other People's Money* and kept in touch with investigations by the Justice and Commerce Departments that attempted to determine whether certain corporations were violating the antitrust law and to what extent they controlled their industries.

Finally, in December of 1913, when passage of the Federal Reserve bill was certain, Wilson talked seriously with his Cabinet of pressing for new legislation that would supplement the inconclusive Sherman

Act. Attorney General McReynolds and others, however, thought the old law sufficient if it were enforced properly, and they feared that Congress would specifically exempt labor and farm organizations from a new act, and thus again put the President in the awkward position in which the Sundry Civil bill had placed him. It seemed to Houston that industrial activity had been chilled by the tariff and currency measures, that if the Administration made haste slowly it might reach its goal more surely.[13] Bryan, however, was urging that the party carry out its pledge to fight monopoly and Brandeis was advising that "the fearless course is the wise one."

As opinion in the Cabinet divided on the issue of monopoly, Wilson showed his stature as a leader of men. "I wonder that he does not explode sometimes," wrote Secretary Houston, his colleague of academic training, "when he has to listen to a lot of ill-considered, confused, and irrelevant advice. How refreshing his clear, concise, and well-expressed views!"

Sitting down before his typewriter at idyllic Pass Christian, his mind filled with the counsel of Cabinet colleagues, legislators,[14] and experts,

[13] In November the Cabinet had been reluctant to press the criminal action against officials of the New Haven Railroad that House's friend, Thomas Gregory, had been retained to direct. Brandeis had studied the situation thoroughly and had become convinced that the railroad, which had passed a dividend in December of 1913 for the first time in forty years, suffered both from excessive size and from monopolistic practices; and in 1914, he prodded both the Interstate Commerce Commission and the Justice Department to act.

Despite protests from the presidents of Yale and Harvard, Wilson bore down upon the officials of the railroad in July of 1914, when industrial depression was turning sentiment against progressive measures and peace in Europe hung in the balance. He studied reports of proceedings by the Justice Department and asserted, in a letter carefully drafted, that the directors of the railroad had failed, upon slight pretext, "to carry out an agreement deliberately and solemnly entered into and which was manifestly in the common interest." [The agreement referred to was made by officials of the railroad and the Justice Department on Jan. 10, 1914.] Wilson directed that a proceeding in equity be filed seeking dissolution of "the unlawful monopoly of transportation facilities in New England now sought to be maintained by the New York, New Haven, and Hartford Railroad Company; and that the criminal aspects of the case be laid before the grand jury." W.W. to the attorney general, July 9, 1914. When the Justice Department carried out the President's order, the railroad officials accepted the government's terms. See Mason, *Brandeis*, pp. 199–213.

[14] Beginning in November, Wilson had sought the views of party leaders in Congress; and when he went to Pass Christian, he had their recommendations as well as an elaborate report from Joseph E. Davies, whom he had appointed commissioner of corporations in the Commerce Department. (Unable to offer William F. McCombs any post that he would accept, Wilson had explained to Davies, who had been in charge of the Western headquarters in the election campaign, that he must appoint *some* campaign manager to *something* as a defense against charges of ingratitude to those who had served him. Davies to the writer, March 7, 1951.)

The Bureau of Corporations, created in 1903 in the new Department of Commerce and Labor, had, with President Roosevelt's support, investigated corporate practices and issued shocking reports. After talking with Davies, House commended to Wilson a proposal made by this adviser for an industrial commission that would build up a body of rule and procedure for relations between government and industry that would be similar to the work done in the field of transportation by the Interstate Commerce Commission. "It would largely take the

Wilson was ready to frame a program for legislation on the third of the economic ills that he had enumerated in his inaugural address: "an industrial system which, take it on all sides, financial as well as administrative, holds capital in leading strings, restricts the liberties and limits the opportunities of labor, and exploits without renewing or conserving the natural resources of the country."

At this juncture news came from New York that was given sensational play in the press. J. Pierpont Morgan and other financial magnates announced that, deferring to a change in public sentiment, they were withdrawing from the directorates of many corporations in which they held interests. "It may be," Morgan conceded, "that we shall be in a better position to serve such properties and their security holders if we are not directors." Though at first acclaimed as a "surrender of the Money Trust," the move was suspected by some observers to be mere "gallery play," and the *New York Times* pointed out that the withdrawals were so arranged as to leave the bankers with one member on most of the boards with which they had been affiliated.

Wilson was pleased by this symptom of the hold of his New Freedom on public opinion. Yet he was not convinced, and telegraphed to ask Tumulty and House for their interpretations of the news story. His secretary replied that the resignations were "an act of good faith on the part of 'big business' "; and the Colonel characterized the move, somewhat naïvely, as "an indication that big business is preparing to surrender unconditionally" and advised his friend to congratulate the country on the spirit that leading citizens were displaying. House was tiptoeing more cautiously than ever around the pitfalls that beset an advocate of antitrust legislation. He wished his friends to understand that he was "not unfriendly" to big business but dreaded the political uproar that would ensue if he were quoted publicly as "friendly" to the interests.

The President's mind ran parallel to House's thinking in the message that he was preparing for the Congress. To be sure, he persisted in dramatizing the situation as a fight in which "the masters of business

---

wind out of T.R.'s sails," the Colonel wrote, "and would not run counter to your views upon this subject . . ." Wilson replied that he had already given careful attention to the report of Davies. House to W.W., Dec. 31, 1913, and W.W. to House, Jan. 3, 1914.

Davies's proposal was contrary to the legalistic view of the attorney general. Noting that there was friction between these men, Wilson spoke of it to Davies one day, saying: "You don't like McReynolds and he doesn't like you. More causes have been lost through personal friction than for any other reason." Davies was moved to attempt to make peace. Joseph E. Davies to the writer.

on the great scale" had "begun to yield their preference and purpose, perhaps their judgment also, in honorable surrender." Going on, however, he became more generous and conciliatory. Government and business, he wrote, were ready "to meet each other halfway in a common effort to square business methods with both public opinion and the law." He aspired to be the spokesman of "the best informed men of the business world." Though the message lacked oratorical flourish, it closed with a typical challenge: "Until these things are done, conscientious business men the country over will be unsatisfied."

Sitting in the driver's seat when he returned to Washington in January of 1914, the President decided to deliver his message promptly in order to obtain laws that would facilitate an alliance between legitimate business and the public interest. There were final conferences in which the document drafted at Pass Christian was read and the support of legislative leaders was pledged. Then, according to Wilson himself, he gave his text the "doctoring" that he was accustomed to administer after using all the brains that he had and all that he could "borrow." On January 20 he made his fifth appearance within a year before a joint session of the Congress and read the message. It gave notice that he would like to "prevent such interlockings of the *personnel* of directorates of great corporations . . . as in effect result in making those who borrow and those who lend practically one and the same, those who sell and those who buy but the same persons trading with one another under different names and in different combinations, and those who affect to compete in fact partners and masters of the whole field of particular kinds of business." The President then went on to apply this principle to the specific case of the railroads, where the evils of interlocking directorates had seemed especially flagrant. The Interstate Commerce Commission, he said, should be given power to regulate the financing of railroads, as a step toward the separation of the business of production from that of transportation.

To meet these objectives, three bills that were based on the disclosures of the Congressional investigation of the steel industry were combined in an omnibus measure known as the Clayton bill. Studying the text and keeping in touch with Congressional leaders, Wilson guided the legislation through both houses of the Congress. "I think it is wise that we take only one step at a time," he cautioned Underwood.

The new antitrust bill contained a provision on farm and labor organizations that was so significant that he later referred to it as a "primer of human liberty." It declared:

The labor of a human being is not a commodity or article of commerce. Nothing contained in the anti-trust laws shall be construed to forbid the existence and operation of labor, agricultural, or horticultural organizations, instituted for the purposes of mutual help and not having capital stock or conducted for profit, or to forbid or restrain individual members of such organizations from lawfully carrying out the legitimate objects thereof, nor shall such organizations or the members thereof be held or construed to be illegal combinations or conspiracies in restraint of trade under the anti-trust laws.

This pronouncement fell short of demands made upon the President and the Congressional committees by labor leaders who wished to exempt their unions entirely from the scope of the new law. Despite a threat from union spokesmen that they would join the Republicans in defeating the entire antitrust program, Wilson refused to concede more than an amendment providing for jury trials in cases of criminal contempt and limiting the issue of injunctions. He approved the clause permitting labor and farm organizations to pursue "legitimate objectives" with immunity from prosecution, but at the same time he declared that under these provisions labor was not authorized to make war by methods already condemned by the courts. Thus he adhered to the compromise position that he had taken in dealing with the embarrassing Sundry Civil bill. As a result, Samuel Gompers of the American Federation of Labor, who had never ceased to insist that the principle of labor's immunity from antitrust action be written into substantive law, acclaimed the provisions of the Clayton Act as labor's "Magna Charta," while, on the other hand, the counsel of the American Anti-Boycott Association was satisfied and noted that actually the new bill made few changes in existing laws regarding the use of injunctions and contempt proceedings.

The Clayton Act was passed by Congress and signed by the President on October 15, 1914. Personal guilt clauses were omitted; and though the law prohibited price discrimination and certain practices that tended to create monopoly, it seemed to at least one progressive senator that it lacked teeth "to masticate milk toast."

Before the Clayton Act was ready for the President's signature, another bill was passed that set up machinery to facilitate application of the principles of the measure without involved processes of law. This supplementary antitrust legislation, which proved to be more constructive and far-reaching than the Clayton Act, was written in response to a proposal in Wilson's message to Congress in January of 1914. During the first months of the year the sag in industrial activity that had appeared in 1913 had grown worse and had been aggravated by a constriction of credit in Europe, where war clouds were hovering. The volume of business dropped, failures abounded, and opportunities for employment shrank. Accordingly, the Administration came to be moved less by the punitive zeal with which Wilson had denounced monopolies in his preinauguration speeches and more by a desire to help business-men of good faith to operate their monopolies in the public interest. Realizing that businessmen lived in fear of being jailed for violation of a law against "restraint of trade" that they could not understand, Wilson said to the Congress: "Nothing hampers business like uncertainty. Nothing daunts or discourages it like the necessity to take chances, to run the risk of falling under the condemnation of the law before it can make sure just what the law is." One remedy was to make very plain, by statute, exactly what practices were forbidden and what the penalties were; but the President felt that businessmen would not be satisfied merely to have the menace of legal action made clear.

Enterprising Americans who believed, like Wilson, in common coun-sel, had faith that there was a better, more constructive remedy. The President sensed this and recommended to Congress that such citizens be given "the definite guidance and information which can be supplied by an administrative body, an interstate trade commission." Wilson once had dreaded that such a commission might become a tool of monopolies, and he made it clear now that the proposed commission would not be expected "to make terms with monopoly or in any sort to assume con-trol of business, as if the Government made itself responsible." It would serve rather as an instrument of information and publicity and a clear-inghouse for facts, and as an instrumentality for doing justice to business where the processes of the courts or the natural forces of correction outside the courts were inadequate.

To create a federal trade commission, a bill was drawn by congress-men that supplanted Davies's Bureau of Corporations by a body with five members. For months the President listened to the arguments of progressive and conservative spokesmen as to the powers to be entrusted to the new commission. Southern agrarians and disciples of Bryan wished to provide for strict regulation of stock exchanges, a confisca-tory tax on the largest corporations, and complete destruction of those interlocking relationships that allowed businessmen to act on both sides of a transaction. On the other hand, the national Chamber of Commerce, embracing the ideal of "self-regulation" by business, wanted only friendly advice from a federal commission.

Finally, in an effort to achieve legislation that would be both effective and practical, Wilson went again to Brandeis for counsel. And on this occasion, as before, the tribune of the people had a solution ready. Brandeis, who wished to elevate "business" to the level of a profession in which all would have equal access to essential knowledge and all would practice uniform methods of accounting, had drafted a bill for a commission that would have plenary authority to issue cease and desist orders against monopolists, but not to punish offenders.

Calling Brandeis to the White House on June 10, Wilson told him that his bill, which already had been introduced in Congress, would be the foundation of the Administration's antitrust program; and three days later the measure appeared as an amendment of the Federal Trade Commission bill when it was reported out of committee in the Senate. Despite ardent efforts by Wilson and his advisers to overcome the opposition of conservative Democrats, provisions were added that would protect corporations against cease and desist orders by guaranteeing review in the courts. With this safeguard, the bill was passed, and signed on September 26, 1914.[15]

Thus the second of the remedies that the President had sought in his January message to Congress was enacted.[16] During 1914, Woodrow Wilson had veered far from the emphasis on personal guilt that had marked the impractical "Seven Sisters" acts of New Jersey, and toward acceptance of responsibility by the government in accordance with progressive policies. The Presbyterian moralist had yielded to the compelling logic of Brandeis, the social scientist who blamed current evils on the nature of the economic system. Wilson's concept of the "necessary functions" of the federal government had broadened.

In 1914, however, with foreign problems claiming an increasing quota of his time, Wilson found it impossible to satisfy all the champions

[15] The appointment of suitable men to the new body presented problems no less difficult than those faced in choosing the Federal Reserve Board. Joseph E. Davies was the logical choice for the chairmanship. House's diary records that on Nov. 5, 1914, he and the President went to Wilson's study after dinner and agreed on the commission's personnel "within the hour." Appointments were not made, however, until Feb. 22, 1915. George Rublee—an appointee who had the confidence of Brandeis—was prevented from serving when Senator Gallinger, minority leader, blocked his appointment on personal grounds. Brandeis felt that Wilson's appointments to this body were unfortunate and that its administration was "stupid."

Although in the autumn of 1913, before the recession of business and the outbreak of war in Europe, the President had advocated "real dissolution" of offensive trusts, and though he had to give the commission restraining powers, he later hoped and expected that it would not be necessary to use them extensively. He thought of the body as a counselor and friend of business rather than a policeman.

[16] The third specific recommendation of the address on trust regulation, advocating control by the Interstate Commerce Commission of the issue of new securities by the railroads, was the subject of a bill drawn by Brandeis and Representative Rayburn, which passed the House but became the first casualty of the New Freedom program after war broke out in Europe.

of sundry reforms. Speaking to the National Press Club at a house-warming in their new quarters, he cried out on March 20: "God knows there are enough things in this world that need to be corrected." Before the journalists he talked as a writer among his fellows. Protesting against the popular impression that he was a "thinking machine" that turned "like a cold searchlight" on national problems, he confessed that actually, inside, he sometimes felt like "a fire from a far from extinct volcano." He gave vent to his sentimental affinity for crowds. "A crowd picked up off the street is just a jolly lot," he said,—a job lot of real human beings, pulsating with life, with all kinds of passions and desires." It refreshed him to mingle with them, in his imagination, or to "get a rattling good detective story, get after some imaginary offender, and chase him all over"; in such "blessed intervals" he could forget that he was a monumental robot that had to shake hands of all sorts, even those belonging to "that class that devotes itself to 'expense regardless of pleasure.'" He confessed that he had thought often of buying an assortment of beards, rouge, and coloring. "If I could disguise myself and not get caught," he said, "I would go out, be a free American citizen once more and have a jolly time." [17]

In the same talk to the journalists Wilson gave voice to his sense of humility in the face of the expectations of the voters who had charged him to administer a part of their government: "When I think of the number of men who are looking to me as the representative of a party, with the hope for all varieties of salvage from the things they are struggling in the midst of, it makes me tremble. It makes me tremble not only with a sense of my inadequacy and weakness, but as if I were shaken by the very things that are shaking them and, if I seem circumspect, it is because I am so diligently trying not to make any colossal blunders. If you just calculate the number of blunders a fellow can make in twenty-four hours if he is not careful and if he does not listen more than he talks, you would see something of the feeling that I have." Two months later, under pressure that seemed to him "unconscionable," Wilson told a journalist that he felt like displaying in his office a sign that was once put up on the organ loft of a country church to defend the organist: "Don't shoot: he is doing his damnedest."

However, during the first months in office the President had not been so busy that he ignored heads of evil that had been sprouting from the

[17] One day Wilson actually made good his escape from the Presidency. Stuffing an old felt hat inside his coat, he eluded the secret service men and walked out the door of the White House, forbidding the doorkeeper to give him away. They found him later in a five-and-ten-cent store, buying penny candy for a gang of dirty-faced children.

hydra at which he had struck during his governorship in New Jersey. Going back to his own state to stimulate the passage of his jury-reform bill in a special session of the legislature that was called by Acting Governor Fielder, Wilson had flayed the bosses as of old. "There was a time," the President said at Newark, "when only two things would move those who defied the sovereignty of the people: fire and fodder. I am going to put the fire beneath them. Fodder has gone out of fashion." Though this foray gave heart to Jersey progressives and contributed to the election of Fielder as governor, it led doubters to ask whether the President had not diverted too much energy from his own job.

Wilson could count now on the continuing hatred of the New Jersey bosses as well as upon that of Tammany, which he defied by two successive appointments of collectors of the port who were outside the New York wigwam. Moreover, Senator O'Gorman of New York was hurt because he was not consulted and also because the President had not thanked him personally for support in the election or for a laudatory magazine article. Democratic senators of the old regime were complaining of the entertainment offered at the White House: one grievance, O'Gorman told Colonel House, was that at a conference with the President no drink but water was offered, and nothing to smoke. Sometimes, too, Wilson spoke unkindly to his intimates about legislators with whom he disagreed, and his critical attitude was magnified by political adversaries who felt, like Senator Lodge, that the President had won the plaudits of superficial people by exercising despotic power over Congress to a degree hitherto unknown.

Moreover, during his first year in office Wilson had made enemies among special interests that could be expected to denounce his efforts for the common good. Strong individuals who had made the most of the equality of opportunity in the United States were wondering whether private enterprise would be allowed sufficient reward to make it worth while. There were irresponsible whisperings of socialism, confiscation of wealth, and dictatorial trespass on legislative functions. Merchants and industrialists resented the tax placed on large incomes, and Washington storekeepers had not forgotten the loss incurred because of the President's insistence on a simple inauguration. The Administration was in disfavor with men whose advice had not been asked about the tariff and currency acts, as well as with some who had been consulted and not heeded. In a speech delivered at the Republican Convention of New York State on August 18, 1914, Senator Root recapitulated the complaints of Eastern businessmen, asserting that the new tariff had dampened industry without lowering the cost of living, the Federal Reserve Act had frightened venture capital, the income tax had discriminated against the East, and the Federal Trade Commission was merely one more dangerous step toward bureaucracy. Moreover, Root made the sort of allegation that had transformed the academic dispute at Princeton into class warfare: he declared that Wilson's policy was based on jealousy and ill-will toward successful businessmen.

Sensing the antipathy of conservatives, realizing that he was being blamed for a recession of commerce in the spring of 1914, Wilson made a speech in June that was intended to allay uneasiness. Insisting that signs of a revival of trade were more evident each day, he spoke of the criticism of business methods that had been rising for ten years. After ten years of apprehensive guessing, he asserted, businessmen now had a definite program of constructive correction. He promised that the antitrust laws would give opportunity for "rest, recuperation, and successful adjustment."

It was not only the materialists who had to be mollified, however. Ardent reformers likewise were disgruntled and had lost heart because Wilson's achievement had fallen short of their dreams. To be sure, he had insisted to his party men upon "the absolute necessity of a carefully considered and wisely balanced budget." [18] But he had disappointed militant suffragists, importunate champions of the Negro, the promoters of many other causes. Though at first giving support to proposals for conservation of natural resources, he had to conclude early in 1914 that they were beyond a possibility of legislative approval, save for an act that safeguarded valuable Alaskan resources. In May of 1913, fearful of "artificial disturbances," perhaps a strike of capital, he had suggested that Congress authorize a program of public works to stimulate business and afford employment; but nothing had come of this. The President had assented, under pressure from agrarians, to the inclusion in the Federal Reserve Act of a provision for agricultural credit and had approved a proposal of the Rural Credits Commission for a system of land banks that would be privately controlled, under federal

[18] Letter, W.W. to Tillman, read aloud at a Democratic caucus on Mar. 15, 1913. The letter predicted: "This business of building up the expenses of our Nation, piece by piece, will certainly lead us to error and perhaps embarrassment." In April of 1913, Brandeis and others conferred with Wilson on economy and efficiency in government and Brandeis urged, as a first step toward getting more value for expenditures, that a budget be adopted and administered by a legislative or legislative-executive committee. *See* Mason, *Brandeis,* p. 397. The budget bill constructed during Wilson's administration was not passed until 1921. (*See* volume II.)

charter. In his first annual message to Congress, in December of 1913, he commended the report of the commission to the attention of the legislators; but when, in the spring of 1914, a bill was introduced that would require the government to finance and operate the new land banks, Wilson shrank from the prospect of subsidy.[19]

Perceiving that misapprehension of his purposes was shaking the confidence on which commerce depended, Wilson welcomed delegations of bankers and businessmen to the White House and received such leaders as J. P. Morgan and Henry Ford. Moreover, he approved an announcement by McReynolds inviting corporations that had doubted the legality of their structure to go to the Justice Department for friendly advice.

Often in facing the struggles between capital and labor he drew on his inmost resources in order to keep his mind open and fearless. When coal operators and miners in Colorado came to a break over the issue of the "closed shop" and state authorities failed to prevent bloodshed, the President reluctantly supplied federal troops to suppress violence and at the same time he tried to persuade the operators to accept the mediation of the Department of Labor. He worked to set up an intermediary that would command the respect of each faction, until finally state agencies came to his aid and the ugly strike was settled, in March of 1916. His faith in the lawfulness of responsible labor leaders won respect; and when William B. Wilson was accused of partiality, the President went to the defense of his secretary of labor, declaring that he had "never known a more careful or judicial mind."

It was only in cleaving to purposes that he ascribed to God that Woodrow Wilson could find stability in the maelstrom of pressures that whirled about him in the year 1914. Though he was happy and comfortable in the White House, that residence was not the haven that his own house at Princeton had been. He no longer felt at home anywhere, and this was unsettling. The President might have taken deep comfort, however, had his ever-restless soul been willing to stake its immortality on the service that he had already given to his people. For under his leadership most of the great measures that House had planned for his

---

19 "I have a very deep conviction," the President wrote to a caucus of House Democrats, "that it is unwise and unjustifiable to extend the credit of the Government to a single class of the community." This conviction, he went on, was clear and permanent and had come to him as if "out of fire." W.W. to Glass, May 12, 1914.

Angered by Wilson's letter, the agrarians declined the sort of banking bill that was offered and there was no legislation until 1916, when the President changed his position under different political conditions. (*See* Volume II.)

fictional Philip Dru and that Wilson had espoused had become law or were on the way to enactment. In parrying the pressures of self-interested lobbies—bankers, industrialists, farmers, laborers—Wilson had fought valiantly for the exalted concept of public interest that he had set forth when he had written in *The New Freedom* of "a time when the systematic life of this country will be sustained, or at least supplemented, at every point by governmental activity." Within the short space of nineteen months his administration had gone far toward writing into statute the grass-roots tide of protest that had carried him into the Presidency. The stirrings of unrest that had agitated both political parties had at last been codified under the Constitution by a leader who was sentient, inspiring, and masterful.

Theodore Roosevelt had found no adequate force within the Republican party that would follow him to Armageddon; but Wilson had marshaled the support of Democrats who in many cases had more enthusiasm for political success than for the ideals that their leader pursued. Ruling elders of the party whose eyes centered on the next election had proved to be receptive to his doctrine of national salvation and more constant in their support than the independents and the progressives. With their aid he had fulfilled a large part of the charge that he conceived that his Presbyterian God had laid upon them.

However, Wilson the historian shrank from attempting to evaluate the legislation that had been enacted during his first two years as president. Addressing the Sixty-third Congress, on December 8, 1914, he ventured to predict that that body would long be remembered for its constructive labors. "But no doubt," he added, "we stand too near the work that has been done and are ourselves too much part of it to play the part of historians toward it."

CHAPTER XX

Moral Frontiers Abroad

ALTHOUGH THE PRESIDENT concentrated in 1913 on domestic reforms that had long challenged him, the affairs of the State Department pressed upon him with a force that he could not ignore.

The country that Woodrow Wilson undertook to lead occupied a peculiar place among the nations of the world. The American vision of manifest destiny shone brightly in the minds of its citizens. The genius of inventive pioneers, exploiting the riches of a pristine land, had amassed fabulous wealth. An ideology of enterprise had grown up and was now burgeoning beyond the boundaries of the United States.

The outward thrust, having little of the force of economic necessity behind it, had not followed the grim course of imperialism that had been made familiar in the nineteenth century by overcrowded nations of Europe.

Nevertheless, venturesome missionaries and traders had caused problems in diplomacy. In penetrating areas of political vacuum they had become entangled not only with rivals from European powers but with native caciques and the local prejudices on which they thrived. Soon the United States found itself assuming responsibility for political development in the Philippines, the Caribbean region, and elsewhere. During Taft's administration, American financiers had made efforts to deal with weak foreign economies by the methods that had led to monopolies in domestic industry. Critical issues of diplomacy had arisen that made the American people listen anxiously for a statement of foreign policy from their new leader. An editorial in the *New York Times* observed that current foreign problems were of a gravity unknown since 1865.

Woodrow Wilson had said nothing about external affairs in his inaugural address, and very little during the campaign. One could not be certain, as in the case of domestic legislation, what his direction would be. Before leaving Princeton for the capital he said to a colleague: "It would be the irony of fate if my administration had to deal chiefly with foreign affairs." Until he went to Bermuda in December of 1912 he did not fully comprehend the specific foreign problems facing the nation, nor had he evolved a policy for meeting them.

If during the past decade they had read Wilson's words on foreign affairs, however, his people could feel assured that he had sensed the world-wide political currents of his age and appreciated the opportunities and responsibilities of his office. As early as 1900, Wilson had perceived the major trends of the times. He had been aware then that the enterprise of Americans abroad had given great potential to the foreign policy of their government.[1] He accepted the end of isolation as not only the inevitable result of a "wholesome and natural impulse" to trade and profit but as an opportunity and a challenge to America to champion pure democracy in a world that had reacted against its eccentric manifestations in France and in South America. It seemed to Wilson that the end of isolation had been hastened by the closing of the American frontier, which had fixed in individuals a habit "of acting under an odd mixture of selfish and altruistic motives." Himself a grandson of immigrants, he sensed the restlessness of men who were beginning to feel crowded, even in America, by the forces that their ancestors had fled when they left Europe. At the turn of the century Woodrow Wilson had extended to the whole world his prophecy of "a time of change."

With this affirmation of the mission of the United States in the twentieth century, however, had gone a warning. Wilson declared that the ideals of democracy could not be realized fully at home if Americans allowed them to be discredited among the peoples who had yet to see liberty under just laws. The preservation of her own democracy, as well as the responsibility for weaker brethren, compelled the United States to break out of her traditional isolation.

Wilson had shown little confidence in the effectiveness of "international law," in which he had given a course at Princeton, and compared it with those social laws that a man does not break for fear of ruining his career. He had placed more faith in the combining of great powers

---

[1] The United States, Wilson prophesied in his *History of the American People*, was ready to become a creditor nation, and "might command the economic fortunes of the world." Writing a preface in 1900 for a new edition of *Congressional Government*, he had observed that after the Spanish-American War the Chief Executive had "greatly increased power and opportunity for constructive statesmanship"; and he suggested that the President might "substitute statesmanship for government by mass meeting." Pointing out that the Chief Executive could initiate negotiations with foreign powers and complete them without disclosing the steps of his dealings and asserting that the President, after heeding expert counsel, should exert a will and definite choice of his own, Wilson had foreseen that the President of the United States "must always, henceforth, be one of the great powers of the world."

Even before President McKinley announced that isolation was no longer possible or desirable, Wilson had declared that George Washington, in warning against foreign entanglements, merely had bidden his people to set their own house in order and wait until they were big enough to stand competition of foreign countries and go abroad in the world.

in understandings based on popular feeling; and he had been groping his way toward a political order such as mankind had not seen—a world in which democracy would prevail under an imperial guarantee.

Nations and their leaders, Wilson believed, were subject to the political morality that was natural in individual men. When a leader made a decision for a whole people he did so "at the risk of the integrity of his own soul." Legal rights, particularly in a field so ill-charted as that of international law, were secondary to ethics and the dictates of dedicated consciences. To a friend whom he met at Edinburgh in 1908 Wilson had remarked that nations were beginning to feel their way toward the consciousness that they were under the same moral order as individuals. "They have not got far yet," he remarked, "and very few would think it practical, but I suppose we will come to it some day."

To Wilson, as to Burke, a nation was "a moral essence." The moralizing of this American had a proselyting force that was lacking in the philosophy of his British hero. America came into the world in 1776, Wilson once said, with "a spirit and a mission" that was inherited from the Bill of Rights; and she had grown as if by predestination. As apostles of liberty and self-government, Americans had special responsibilities. Repeatedly proclaiming a sense of duty that was extralegal, the prophet had declared: "I will not cry 'peace' so long as there is sin and wrong in the world. . . . America was born to exemplify that devotion to the elements of righteousness which are derived from the revelations of Holy Scripture." Mere national patriotism, he had told his Princeton boys, was a narrow and provincial feeling. It was America's destiny to show other nations "a fortunate way to happiness," to "go to the ends of the earth carrying conscience and the principles that make for good conduct."

Wilson's intellect told him that every people should be free to work out their own political system; and at Princeton he had told a colleague that the Russian peasants enjoyed relative freedom, provided that they knew nothing better. But at the same time the evangelistic impulses in his blood told him that those who lacked the qualities needed to achieve political stability should be tutored by the more mature nations. They were not to be free to escape this schooling, which was to be administered by persuasion if possible, by force if necessary. He observed that before the American Revolution even the Ango-Saxons had had to learn to govern themselves in a peace-group that was ruled absolutely by a king; and Wilson felt that duty had compelled the United States to resort to the crude expedient of force against Filipino rebels who could be "moralized" only in that way. But the bond of conscience also required America to desist from exploitation and to allow the people of the Philippines to govern themselves as soon as they could be made ready.

Second only to his concern for international morality, during his academic years, had been Wilson's confidence in the political equilibrium of Anglo-Saxon peoples. He had not lost the kin-feeling for England that had taken root in him during his boyhood years in the South and had been nourished by travel in Britain, by youthful worship of British statesmen, and by studies at the Johns Hopkins into the origin of democracy among the German tribes and its transmission through Anglo-Saxons.[2]

In the years of his presidency at Princeton, Wilson had come to place less dependence on British precedent; and as his own spirit was hurt by frustration his religious zeal surged into his pronouncements on foreign affairs. In 1907, before the battle for the college quadrangles had been lost, he seemed to accept economic imperialism: "concessions obtained by financiers," he had written, "must be safeguarded by ministers of state, even if the sovereignty of unwilling nations be outraged in the process." By the spring of 1910, however, a few days after his prophetic fire had been released at Pittsburgh, Wilson was talking about a "day of reckoning" in international competition for trade. Henceforth there was to be "a new ideal of endeavour"—the public interest of "a world drawn together into one community." In the autumn of 1910, Wilson had asserted that the manifest destiny of America was not to rule the world by physical force or to accumulate a "mere mass of wealth," but to "do the thinking of the world."[3] The United States seemed to Wilson the ideal leader as she was swinging out of her isolation and joining the family of nations.

[2] Criticizing Cleveland's lack of diplomacy in the dispute with England over the Venezuela boundary, Wilson had written: ". . . only our kinsmen overseas would have yielded anything or sought peace by concession, after such words had been spoken." "Mr. Cleveland as President," March, 1897. In presenting John Hay for an honorary degree at Princeton in 1900 he had referred to that statesman as one who had "confirmed our happy alliance of sentiment and purpose with Great Britain." *Princeton University Bulletin*, XII (1900), 12. In 1901 he had conceived of the establishing of better government in the Far East as a joint responsibility of America and England, who could "moderate" the impact of Western standards on the Far East "in the interests of liberty." "Democracy and Efficiency," *Atlantic Monthly*, March, 1901.

[3] In December of 1911, Wilson's outreaching spirit was applied to an immediate issue: he spoke warmly in favor of reciprocity with Canada and regretted that the United States had neglected opportunities for trade with neighbors both to the north and to the south. By 1912, Wilson had lost his earlier hope that the Far East might provide a new field of expansion for the United States.

Thus had Wilson's thought run, spasmodically and often superficially, upon the affairs of the nations and the role of the United States in the contemporary world. Once the supreme responsibility had been fixed upon him, however, the President-elect determined to fail neither in understanding of specific foreign problems nor in judicious decision. In Bermuda, Woodrow and Ellen Wilson had applied their long-standing habit of joint study to the details of current issues. They pored over letters and reports on their country's relations with Mexico. Far Eastern affairs claimed much of their thought. They asked well-informed men for light on the Philippine situation and the character of the Filipinos. The President-elect gave consideration, too, to China and Japan, assuring Sun Yat-sen of his strong sympathy. Russia's treatment of the Jews, of which Wilson had made political capital in a New York speech in 1911,[4] was still a sore subject; the treaty that since 1832 had governed the relations of the United States with Russia was to expire in a few weeks, and Wilson asked for advice from the American envoy at Moscow so that he might thoroughly understand the matter.

The incoming President could ill afford to leave the appointment of diplomatic representatives to the whim of his secretary of state. Before inauguration he had thought it necessary to warn Bryan against appointing foreign-born citizens to posts in their native lands, as a sop to hyphenated Democrats. However, he had shared the secretary's concern for the encouragement of missionary enterprise in China and Japan; for his own Grandfather Woodrow had been a missionary and at one time his daughter Margaret aspired to be one. He had tried, without avail, to send to Peking first Charles W. Eliot of Harvard and then John R. Mott of the Y.M.C.A., whom he thought of as "a robust Christian." He had been usuccessful, too, in efforts to send Eliot to London and Henry B. Fine of Princeton to Berlin.[5]

---

[4] On Dec. 6, 1911, Wilson spoke in Carnegie Hall at a meeting protesting discrimination against American Jews by the Russian government. "The plain fact of the matter is," he said, "that for some fifty years we have observed the obligations of our treaty with Russia and she has not. That can go on no longer. So soon as Russia understands that it can go on no longer . . . the air will clear." The Congress and President Taft were impressed by the lobbying that resulted from the Carnegie Hall meeting, and the treaty with Russia was abrogated.

[5] The President-elect told House that he had offered Eliot the ministry at Peking in "such a complimentary way" that Eliot had intimated that he would accept if Mrs. Eliot assented. The offer eventually was refused, however, and also a later tender of the London embassy. When House told Bryan of the intention to send Eliot to China, the evangelistic secretary of state objected that Eliot as a Unitarian did not believe in the divinity of Christ and would be the worst possible representative in China, where a new civilization was being built upon the Christian movement! House Diary, Jan. 31, 1913.

In inviting Fine to go to Berlin, Wilson offered a subsidy that was to be provided by Cleveland Dodge. Ellen Wilson reinforced her husband's plea by writing to Fine's sister: "We have

Before the inauguration Wilson had been reluctant to discuss diplomatic appointments with his secretary of state, for he had foreseen
that he could not in good conscience accept all the "deserving Democrats" whom the Great Commoner wished to reward and he did not
know in what spirit his veto would be received; but once they were in
office and had established cordial personal relations, Wilson and Bryan
conferred and corresponded at great length. The President kept a
record of their decisions in his own hand. In a loose-leaf notebook he
jotted responsibilities that he denoted as "immediate" (for example:
"learn law and decide on policy regarding consular service"). He drew
up long lists of positions to be filled, and the names of leading candidates
and their sponsors. As in the case of domestic appointments, he recorded
political considerations, such as the state in which each candidate lived
and the proportion of patronage it already enjoyed. During his first
six months in office, more than half the chiefs of missions were replaced
by men approved by the President. Though insisting that consular
promotions be governed by rule, Wilson wished to choose personally the
ambassadors who were to represent him in dealings with other heads of
state.[6]

It was difficult, he found, to select men who could afford the expense
of diplomatic life and who were at the same time free from corporate
interests. Asked what was causing delay in making appointments, he
replied: "Lack of good men." Having failed to draft Eliot and Richard
Olney to fill the vacant ambassadorship at London, he turned to his
magnetic friend, Walter Hines Page. Another man of letters, Thomas
Nelson Page of Virginia, was sent to Rome. The ambassador to France

---

no complicated relations with Germany . . . It would be a splendid 'vindication,' like the
Presidency for Woodrow—and just think how furious it will make West and the others!"
Letter, Ellen Wilson to May Margaret Fine, Mar. 18, 1913. Fine, however, wished to devote
himself to teaching and to purge the air at Princeton of the poison lingering from the Wilson-
West feud. Moreover, he feared that in an official position at Berlin he might not see eye to
eye with Wilson and might have to resign. Philena Fine Locke to the writer, Oct. 15, 1955.
Refusal by his steadfast Princeton colleague made Wilson "feel blue." ("I do not know any
man I would more like to honor than Harry," he wrote to Dodge on March 30.) He had
better success, however, in persuading Professor Edward Capps to serve at Athens and in
inducing Professor Henry Van Dyke to go to The Hague.

[6] On Sept. 17, 1913, Wilson explained his policy regarding foreign service appointments
thus, in a letter to President Charles W. Eliot: "We are following the merit system in the consular service more strictly even than either of the preceding administrations and shall continue
to do so . . . In the matter of the diplomatic service . . . we find that those who have been
occupying the legations and embassies have been habituated to a point of view which is very
different, indeed, from the point of view of the present administration. They have had the
material interests of individuals in the United States very much more in mind than the moral
and public considerations which it seems to us ought to control. They have been so bred in
a different school that we have found, in several instances, that it was difficult for them to
comprehend our point of view and purpose."

was William B. Sharp, an Ohio manufacturer who had contributed liberally to party coffers; and Henry Morgenthau, another financial supporter, was sent to Turkey. The Russian embassy, which House had thought of as a safe repository for Bryan, was not filled for months, then given to a wealthy Californian who lacked qualifications for the post. Mayor Brand Whitlock of Toledo was chosen for Belgium, after Newton D. Baker wrote tactfully to Tumulty to praise the Administration and to express his reluctance to commend Whitlock to the President directly for fear of seeming to press his personal judgment too far. This was the sort of approach that Wilson seldom resisted; but he reacted against the importunities of friends of James W. Gerard of New York. He had appointed several men from that city already; and, although Gerard had contributed lavishly to the Democratic campaign fund, he had supported Champ Clark for the nomination. Finally, however, after this Tammany man had persuaded House and Senator Hughes of New Jersey to promote his name, Wilson reluctantly appointed Gerard to the foreign post that was to prove most critical of all—the ambassadorship at Berlin.

The President was disappointed because he had had to give so many of the foreign posts to inexperienced men of wealth who coveted them. He did not instruct each of the ambassadors, but left personal contacts largely to House, whom he had consulted repeatedly in choosing them. In the case of Page, he merely asked the Colonel to ascertain whether the editor would accept the post at London, and Page, calling at the White House for parting instructions, was disappointed because Wilson had nothing to say except that he wanted to have a friend at London on whose judgment he could rely. Seeing a prospect of indulging an ambition to play a part in international politics, House was assiduous in winning the confidence of the appointees. He reminded Page to pay his respects to Bryan, and accompanied him to the State Department, anxious that these officials comprehend each other. He put himself on intimate terms, also, with Gerard. In his outreaching mind there was taking shape a grand vision, a design for an understanding among the United States, Britain, and Germany that would clarify the Monroe Doctrine and would give Germany opportunity to develop trade outlets of which Britain would not be intolerant. Gerard was sent to Berlin by way of London, with a note to Page suggesting that a time might come when the American ambassadors to Britain and Germany should work together.

Well aware of Bryan's shortcomings, Wilson took the precaution of placing a distinguished jurist, John Bassett Moore, in the State Department as counselor, with power to sign documents for the secretary. Furthermore, the President soon applied his own mind to foreign affairs. Calling the Senate Foreign Relations Committee to the White House in the spring of 1913, he spent an evening in giving them a panoramic view of the specific problems facing the nation. He proposed that the several issues be dealt with under a policy that required understanding, patience, and scrupulous respect for obligations.

The time that Wilson devoted to the current problems of the State Department in the spring of 1913, after essential appointments were made, was claimed largely by controversies in the Far East and in Latin America. It was to these areas that the President most often turned the globe that he sometimes fingered in a corner of his study.

Before he had been in the White House for a week, New York bankers called on the secretary of state to ask whether they would be expected to participate in a six-nation consortium that was negotiating a loan to the Chinese government. Four New York banking houses had joined the international group in 1911 at the suggestion of Taft's administration, which wished to assure maintenance of an "open door" to all legitimate foreign interests in China. Though superficially a kindly provision of credit for a people going through political revolution, the proposed loan called for international supervision of the salt tax. The American minister at Peking, reporting opposition by Chinese patriots, was apprehensive of awkward entanglements and of wounds to China's pride and violations of her sovereignty in case the terms of the agreement could not be met in the future.

Bryan, whose impulse to help in the rebirth of the Chinese nation was at least as strong as that of his Republican predecessors, learned from New York financiers the terms on which they would be willing to go on with their negotiations. First, they desired for themselves a monopoly of America's share in the loan; secondly, the present combination expected to have the privilege of handling future loans; and thirdly, the national groups participating looked to their respective governments to use whatever measures might be needed, even a display of force, to make China carry out the terms of the contract. The secretary of state was urged to accept these conditions by men in his department who had served Taft and who argued for the sort of self-interested intervention that had come to be known as "dollar diplomacy."

When the secretary of state brought the matter before the Cabinet, Wilson was already convinced that the United States could help China in some better way. Nevertheless, he wished to hear the counsel of his Cabinet. On March 18 there was a long discussion of the matter. Bryan objected pointedly to the consortium, remarking that it gave a monopoly of American interest to four banking houses in New York and that, moreover, it granted a financial monopoly in China to an international group that would be free to violate that nation's sovereignty and to involve the United States government in a joint debt-collecting action that might be repugnant to American principles. McAdoo remarked that American bankers should not be asked to subscribe to the loan or to take a hand in managing China's economy. In the view of Lane it was as absurd to try to apportion China's debt as it would be to divide her territory: to him it seemed better for individual Americans to invest in China at their own risk, or even for the government to underwrite Chinese bonds rather than to license private bankers to take part in a scheme that had dangerous international ramifications. Essential to any settlement, Lane perceived, was preservation of China's self-respect. But Redfield reminded his colleagues of the realities of the financial market. Other nations, he warned, might make the loan if Americans did not, and then the United States might lose out in commercial competition.

As each man spoke from his own point of view or that of his department, it was evident that all were moved by a sentiment that was strong among the people. Every voice echoed the popular fallacy of the day: namely, that the millions of China, victimized by various manifestations of Asiatic despotism, were groping toward a Christian democracy patterned upon the Republic of the United States, and that it was the manifest duty of good Americans to aid them.

After listening patiently, the President told the men of his own conviction that better instruments to aid China could be found than the proposed loan. He read to them a statement of policy that he had drafted, naming certain nations and criticizing them severely. The text seemed amateurish to the Cabinet and they urged that he tone it down. Remarking that he seemed to be "a member of an anti-acid society," Wilson made changes; but in the afternoon he released the document, and it was still outspoken enough to arrest attention. Asserting that participation in the consortium would be "obnoxious to the principles upon which the government of our people rests," he promised that his administration would use all fair means to promote the trade of its citizens with China, but always through the Open Door—"the only door we care to enter." He pointed out that the conditions of the proposed loan seemed "to touch very nearly the administrative independence of China itself." [9]

The next day the New York financiers withdrew from the consortium, and they refused a request from Bryan that they extend the loan already made. Irresponsible journals, dramatizing the message from the White House, headlined their stories with such phrases as "a knockout for Wall Street."

Wilson promptly learned, however, that his sudden intrusion into affairs of state made enemies among diplomats both at home and abroad. Huntington Wilson, an assistant secretary of state who had urged dollar diplomacy on Bryan and had commended the Chinese loan to the President as an indispensable instrument of American policy, read the statement from the White House and reacted violently.[10] He sent off a letter of resignation by bearer to the White House; and the next day Woodrow Wilson, after consulting House, dictated a frigid acceptance and advised Bryan, who was out of town, that his assistant had been separated from the Department of State.

Moreover, the President's independent statement aroused suspicion among the governments of other nations whose bankers were participating in the loan to China and whom the American government had failed to apprise of its intentions through the usual diplomatic channels. Count Von Bernstorff, German ambassador, cited the act as an illustration of the fact that "the only consistency of the diplomacy of the United States lies in its surprises." Sophisticated chancelleries in Europe found it difficult to ascribe Wilson's profession to a pure missionary urge to help China; the German undersecretary for foreign affairs, for example, suspected with some reason that the New York bankers would

---

[9] *Papers Relating to the Foreign Relations of the United States* (hereinafter referred to as *F.R.*), *1913*, pp. 170–71. Wilson said to the Cabinet: "If we had entered into the loan with other powers we would have got nothing but mere influence in China and lost the proud position which America secured when Secretary Hay stood for the Open Door in China after the Boxer uprising." Wilson is reported to have declared, further, that the position of the United States would be stronger if she stood aloof and said to Russia: "What are your designs in Manchuria?" And to Japan, England, Germany, or any other nation: "What are your designs?" Wilson was assured by Mr. Rea, Sun Yat-sen's financial representative, that China could get private loans from American capital; and Secretary Redfield reported that an American manufacturer had just sent six modern engines to China.

[10] When Huntington Wilson gave his views to the President, the latter's face froze and the assistant secretary left with an impression of agile intelligence and overweening arrogance, and with his own views on the consortium hardened by opposition that he thought doctrinaire. H. Wilson, *Memoirs of an ex-Diplomat*, p. 249. In the view of loyal Democrats, however, Huntington Wilson, by rebuking a new president when he himself already had been notified that he was to remain in the State Department only a few weeks, "made an exhibition of himself."

be glad to be released from the consortium, and it was alleged that Wilson was yielding to their inclination in a way calculated to win Chinese friendship. Furthermore, the Japanese ambassador, eager to learn the "full mind" of the President, went to the White House to protest that Japan had been asked by the Taft administration to join in the loan.

At the next meeting of his Cabinet, Wilson acknowledged that in his preoccupation with American public opinion he had erred in giving his statement to the press before conveying it to the diplomats. "It seems," he said with a laugh, "that the United States has invited Japan to dinner and then absented itself when dinner was served, and Japan does not understand it." Though his precipitancy had offended conservatives and legalists and had added to the number of his personal enemies, his swift stroke for obvious fair play, following full and free discussion in the Cabinet, had bound his official family and many altruistic citizens more closely to him. Leaving the meeting at which the issue was discussed, Bryan exclaimed warmly: "I love his audacity and his courage." Moreover, the President had impressed upon emancipated Chinese minds the sincerity of American friendship—an impression that he deepened on May 2 by acting, against the advice of State Department experts and independently of other powers, to recognize the government of Yüan Shih-kai.[11]

Wilson was less fortunate during the first months of his presidency, however, in resolving a crisis that affected another Far Eastern nation and involved also a problem in American constitutional law. A critical issue had been raised when Democratic politicians in California tried to satisfy the prejudice of their voters against permitting Japanese colonists to own land in their state.[12]

[11] Though members of the Cabinet expressed doubt that the Chinese Republic was stable enough to merit recognition, and Bryan reported that there had been an assassination that might have had a political motive, it seemed clear to Wilson that the people had elected representatives to a parliament. Therefore, he decided upon recognition. He did not wish to make this action contingent upon that of any other nation, but directed Bryan to tell foreign ambassadors of his intention and express the hope that their governments might do likewise. Only Brazil and Mexico responded as the President hoped. When Bryan reported that the Russian envoy intimated that, since his government intended to follow United States policy in Mexico, the United States should reciprocate in China, Wilson and his advisers did not accept this proposal because conditions in Mexico and China seemed to them dissimilar.

Early in April Bryan had a talk with the Chinese minister, at the risk of giving offense by seeming to patronize. The secretary of state urged that the Chinese officials and their people be impressed with the importance of conducting themselves in such a way as to win the respect of other nations.

[12] The question of Japanese immigration was not a new one. It had annoyed Theodore Roosevelt, who had spoke softly through a diplomatic gentlemen's agreement and, at the same time, in order to serve notice that immigration was essentially a domestic concern, had shaken a "big stick" in Japan's face by sending battleships across the Pacific.

On the day after the inauguration, Ambassador Chinda called on the new President to seek his help in allaying resentment in Japan against the affront that the Californians proposed, and thus Wilson was forced immediately to deal with the matter. The President was not unsympathetic toward the feelings of his fellow citizens on the Pacific coast. During his election campaign he had confessed to James D. Phelan, a party leader in San Francisco, that he favored the exclusion of unassimilable foreigners; and in April of 1913 he reassured the same man of his understanding of California's problem and of his hope that any legislation passed might be "so modulated and managed" that it would give as little offense as possible to the pride of Japan. He suggested a compromise formula to Governor Hiram Johnson. When news came of a huge mass meeting in Tokyo that advocated dispatch of Japan's powerful fleet to California and when missionaries denounced the proposed legislation, Wilson and Bryan addressed a cautioning message to Johnson. The President was by no means sure that the federal government had legal power to override the constitutional rights of a state in such a matter, for it was a point never determined by the courts. Nevertheless, on April 22 he went so far as to appeal publicly to the California legislature to act in a conciliatory way rather than make invidious discriminations that would "draw in question the treaty obligations of the United States." [13] And on the same day the Cabinet discussed the matter and Bryan was asked to go to Sacramento to try to moderate the jingoism of the politicians. Wilson thought that the voice of the Great Commoner, speaking for the nation's security, would be heeded by the Western radicals.

The legislators on the Pacific coast, however, did not yield to persuasion. Though the California Assembly passed a bill that set a ban on landownership in tactful terms and included an assurance that the measure was in accord with the provisions of the nation's treaty with Japan, the state's Senate insisted on defining the interdict as one against persons not "eligible to citizenship" [14]—a phrase that provoked Japanese resentment. And despite Bryan's attempt to persuade the governor to veto it, the Alien Land Bill became California law on May 19.

[13] Telegram, W.W. to H. Johnson *et al.*, April 22, 1913. Japan contended that the California measure would violate an American-Japanese treaty of 1911. Wilson suggested to the Californians on April 22 that the measure *might* violate the treaty. His papers preceding this date did not raise the question of legality. *See* Harley Notter, *The Origins of the Foreign Policy of W.W.*, p. 236 and footnote. Counselor Moore of the State Department gave an opinion that the law could be set aside by federal courts.

[14] On May 13, Bryan told the Cabinet that the Californians refused to apply the ban to *all* foreigners "eligible to citizenship" for fear of discouraging French and German investors in California.

For a few days war clouds hovered over Washington. Ambassador Chinda delivered a protest in which the California law was called obnoxious, discriminatory, unfair, unfriendly, and in violation of a treaty.

Though Wilson deplored the decision of the Californians to put politics above statesmanship, he thought the Japanese statement unfair. It seemed to him that all treaty rights were safeguarded in the text of the California law and, moreover, that Japan was as free as the United States to air her grievances in a court of law. Agreeing that Japan's protest should be held in confidence, in order to avoid public excitement, the President authorized Bryan to tell Chinda informally that the language used was objectionable. Characteristically, he charged his secretary of state to heed the manner and expression of the Japanese spokesman in order better to appraise the intent of his nation.

At last, in the middle of May, the behavior of Chinda and activities of Wilson's own Joint Army-Navy Board brought the President to realize fully that the threat of war was serious. Admiral Fiske and General Leonard Wood, comrade-in-arms of Theodore Roosevelt, won the Joint Board and the assistant secretary of the navy, Franklin D. Roosevelt, to a policy of preparedness in the Pacific. The board decided that naval vessels should be ordered at once to reinforce Manila, Honolulu, and the Panama Canal. Stating that war was "not only possible, but even probable," the Joint Board warned against leaving the United States as unprepared as China and Russia had been when Japan attacked them suddenly.

When Wilson learned of this through press reports he was amazed that his subordinates should have acted on so vital a matter without consulting their commander in chief, and, worse yet, that they should have allowed their decision to leak out to newsmen. It seemed to him, and to Secretary of the Navy Daniels, that an effort was being made to force his hand. He feared that irresponsible news reports might lead the Japanese people to think that the United States expected war.

When he brought the matter before his Cabinet on May 16, Secretary of War Garrison intimated that that body's views on military affairs were not particularly valuable, especially when compared with those of the Joint Board. At this Bryan flared up and with flushing face bellowed that army and navy officers could not be trusted to decide what should be done in time of peace, that the problem was not how to wage war but how to keep out of war, that if ships were moved about in the Pacific it would be an incitement to hostilities. The debate was so heated, and the matter so critical, that at the end of the meeting Wilson asked the secretaries of war and the navy to come to the White House for further discussion. Sitting in the garden that afternoon, the three men talked for a long time. Garrison insisted on approval of the action of the Joint Board. He pleaded that the United States was well within her rights in moving her own ships as she pleased, and he stressed the responsibility of the Administration for national defense.

Wilson, though realizing that he would be criticized for unpreparedness if war came, decided to take the risk of ordering that the vessels remain where they were. He saw strong logic in the argument of the secretary of the navy that any movement of armed force that was not large enough to make victory certain might be provocative, and hence worse than inactivity. "We must not have war except in an honorable way," he said to Daniels, "and I fear the Joint Board made a mistake." [15]

On the same day on which the indiscretion of the Joint Board was discussed, the Cabinet considered a reply to Chinda that the President had drafted. Afterward Wilson rewrote it, in conference with Bryan; and on May 20, upon the signing of the Alien Land Act in California, the secretary of state gave it to the Japanese envoy. The note took issue with many of the arguments advanced in Japan's protest; but Bryan softened the effect by assuring Chinda orally that the federal government would do its best to prevent financial damage to Japanese in California and to induce Congress to compensate them for any losses incurred—also that the Administration would use its good offices to advance court hearings of Japanese citizens who had grievances. These oral assurances, Bryan told Chinda, were to be forwarded to Tokyo only if the Japanese government found itself seriously embar-

[15] Daniels Diary, May 16, 1916. Admiral Fiske was disappointed when he learned of the decision. Undeterred, however, he came to Daniels the next morning and asked that Wilson be requested to approve a recommendation by the Joint Board that naval vessels on the coast of California be sent at once to Hawaii. The President was "greatly put out," Daniels recorded in his diary, when he heard of this and of newspaper stories about differences between his views and those of his military advisers. It seemed to Wilson that the board had no right to discuss such a matter after the Cabinet had given its decision. "I wish you would say to them," Wilson declared, "that if this should occur again, there will be no General or Joint Boards. They will be abolished." Thereupon Daniels, about to leave the city, sent word to Fiske that the board should meet no more until he could talk to the admiral. Wilson ordered the board not to meet again without his permission, which he did not give until Oct. 16, 1915, when Daniels suggested that the body prepare to give advice on preparedness for the possibility of war in Europe. Daniels Diary, May 16, 17, 1913.

Another rebuke to indiscreet officers was delivered when Wilson demanded that a reprimand be given to members of the Military Order of the Carabao who had served in the Philippines. At a dinner on Dec. 11, 1914, at which Cabinet members were present, these men had ridiculed the Administration's Philippine policy and Bryan's addiction to grape juice. They had sung a song with the refrain: "Damn, damn, damn the insurrectos." If their officers did not hold their loyalty above all "silly effervescences of childish wit," Wilson wrote to Secretaries Daniels and Garrison on Dec. 22, 1913, what about their profession did they hold sacred?

rassed by jingoes. After this talk Bryan was able to say, at a garden party at the White House: "There will be no war. I have seen the Japanese Ambassador, and I am letting the old man down easy."

Unlike the problem of the Chinese loan, the issue with Japan was too incendiary to permit Wilson to use his favorite strategy of pitiless publicity. Instead, by taking decisive executive action, he had caused a relaxation of jingoistic tension. Negotiations for a mutual treaty on landownership went on for months through diplomatic channels, but Wilson and Bryan were unable to find an opportunity for getting favorable action from Congress. And so the wound to Japanese pride, which aggravated the hurt inflicted when Wilson had spoken out on the Chinese loan without consulting Japanese diplomats, was allowed to remain open and to fester.

In the spring of 1913, then, in crises involving China and Japan, Woodrow Wilson learned much about the realities of diplomacy. The sensitivity of national feelings and the need for constant vigilance had been brought home to him as it had never been by his academic studies.

Even more worrisome than the Far Eastern problems, however, were issues that arose from regions to the south. There was chronic conflict in Latin America between economic and political forces. At one of its first sessions, Wilson's Cabinet discussed policy in the Caribbean area. Their Republican predecessors had kept a strong hand upon native governments in that region and their policy had stemmed from enlightened self-interest and a desire to improve the living conditions of the inhabitants rather than from motives of political evangelism. At the same time, the Democratic minority in Congress had resisted economic and military pressures upon Latin America; and when the new Administration took office, native politicians hoped for a softening of policy on the part of the "Colossus of the North."

During his first days in the White House, Woodrow Wilson undertook to come to grips with the Latin-American situation that he had inherited. Fearing that irresponsible caciques, possibly with support from foreign interests, might take advantage of the change at Washington and instigate revolutions, the President decided to let it be known at once that the United States would recognize no government that was set up to line the pockets of either native dictators or foreign exploiters. On March 11, therefore, indicating to his Cabinet that he would take a personal hand in dealing with major international problems, he read a text that he himself had drafted. Secretary Bryan smiled approvingly; but other members of the Cabinet feared that the statement proposed by the President might seem superfluous and amateurish, and that such nations as Argentina and Chile would be insulted if they were included among countries in need of admonition. Finally, after a few changes, it was decided to release the statement through the press the next day.

Asking cooperation among the peoples of the Americas and their leaders, Wilson's plea set forth the fundamentals of Anglo-Saxon democracy and gave notice that the United States would "lend its influence of every kind" to the realization of his democratic ideals. "We can have no sympathy," he warned, "with those who seek to seize the power of government to advance their own personal interests or ambitions."

While denouncing leaders who violated private rights and constitutional processes, Wilson at the same time disclaimed selfish motives on the part of his own people. "The United States has nothing to seek in Central and South America," he asserted, "except the lasting interests of the peoples of the two continents, the security of governments intended for the people and for no special group or interest, and the development of personal and trade relationships . . . which shall redound to the profit and advantage of both and interfere with the rights and liberties of neither."

In this message appeared a tendency that presaged a major theme of Wilsonian foreign policy: distinction between peoples and their governments. Moreover, the President alluded to an abiding truth: there could be no lasting or stable peace among such governments as existed in certain Latin-American countries, for "mutual respect" was "the indispensable foundation of friendship between states, as between individuals." Wilson's first pronouncement on foreign policy projected into the politics of the hemisphere, and by implication into world affairs, the intellectual and moral criteria of his earlier years; and it was made clear to neighboring peoples that henceforth their governments would be judged by the United States not for their subservience to special interests but for their responsiveness to the common good.

CHAPTER XXI

Philistines in Mexico

Though the president's first paper on foreign affairs was couched in general terms, it pronounced a curse upon a conspirator who had violently seized control of Mexico. This adventurer, General Victoriano Huerta, had revolted against his chief, President Madero, who in 1911 had promised to liberate his people from the semifeudal system under which Mexico had been ruled by old Porfirio Diaz for a generation.

Madero was besieged in Mexico City on February 9, 1913, by troops commanded by Felix Diaz, a nephew of the former ruler; and after resigning and accepting Huerta's promise of safe-conduct out of the country, Madero was shot dead on the 23rd while being taken from prison to a penitentiary by an armed escort. Huerta's junta claimed that the prisoner was attempting to escape, and Henry Lane Wilson, the ambassador of the United States at Mexico City, voiced the satisfaction of the foreign colony in the restoration of order after days of violence. Many Americans, however, were not satisfied by the official explanation of Madero's death, which seemed to them merely a Latin euphemism for murder. It was taken for granted that Huerta was, to say the least, not ignorant of the plot; and there were allegations that the ambassador could have saved Madero's life.

The shooting of Madero filled Woodrow Wilson with indignation so deep that it seemed impossible for him to deal with the usurper. Among the White House family, Huerta's name could not be mentioned without a grimace and a scorching adjective, and Mrs. Wilson equated the rascal with all that was vile. "I will not recognize a government of butchers," the President said to a friend. Fearing that similar brutality might appear in other Latin-American countries, he proclaimed through the press on March 11: "We can have no sympathy with those who seek to seize the power of government to advance their own personal interest or ambition."

Alarming reports of violence came from American consuls in Mexico, and news that a follower of Madero—Venustiano Carranza of Coahuila Province—had proclaimed himself provisional president. All this made Wilson dubious of Huerta's assertion that he had pacified the country and would arrange constitutional elections. He distrusted reports favorable to the new government that came from Ambassador Wilson, who was actively nurturing the new regime, asserting its stability, and condoning its methods as traditional in Mexico and conducive to the sort of order that Porfirio Diaz had maintained.

It became clear that this new President of the United States was going to ignore the long-established policy under which his nation had given *de facto* recognition to new governments without too close scrutiny of the means by which they gained power. American mining and banking interests that hoped for restoration of the stable conditions of the Diaz regime brought pressure upon Wilson. Thinking him unrealistic and self-righteous, they approached him through House, who forwarded their proposals to the President with the comment that the situation had reached a point at which it seemed desirable that the United States take a hand. One interest advocated forcible intervention by the United States. Another complained that British citizens had been given an advantage through provisional recognition of Huerta by London, and urged that Washington recognize the dictator after exacting suitable constitutional guarantees both from him and from Carranza. A third proposal came from a New York banker who was anxious about redemption of a loan that was coming due in June. This man warned that, without recognition, payment would be difficult and as a result the regime at Mexico City might collapse financially and the United States might have to intervene.

Responding to these propositions, and to a statement from Counselor Moore of the State Department pleading for *de facto* recognition and warning against the assumption that the United States had a right to pass judgment on the legitimacy of another nation's government, Wilson at first was inclined to follow the advice of the businessmen, and the more so because one of them was vouched for by his dear friend Cleveland Dodge. But after hours of study and meditation with Ellen Wilson and with his Cabinet, he said: "I have to pause and remind myself that I am President of the United States and not of a small group of Americans with vested interests in Mexico." Great principles of constitutional government were at stake, and it was essential that they be regarded as primary.

Convinced that Huerta, once recognized, could not be controlled except by force, Wilson felt that he should go no further than to agree to leave Henry Lane Wilson in the embassy at Mexico City and to announce publicly that the United States would deal through him with the new regime "on the basis of its existence." Only time would tell whether

Huerta would make good on a promise that he had made to arrange an election. The President felt that he could afford to wait for any step that might advance the Mexican people toward the democratic order that he envisioned for them; for without constitutional government in Mexico and improvement of the lot of its masses, he despaired of enduring peace in North America.

Feeling a need of information more reliable than that coming from Ambassador Wilson, the President took a step that was to become characteristic of his diplomacy. On April 19, with Bryan's acquiescence, Wilson addressed a confidential letter to William Bayard Hale, his campaign biographer. "I am writing to ask," he said, "if you would be willing to undertake a tour of the Central and South American states, ostensibly on your own hook, in order that officially and through the eyes of an independent observer we might find out just what is going on down there." Hale, who had little background for an understanding of Mexican affairs, accepted the mission and soon was reporting that only a constitutional election could avert a crisis that would require forcible intervention by the United States.

That eventuality was regarded with dread by Wilson, the historian who had set down the Mexican War of 1848 as an inexcusable aggression on the part of a nation that had shown itself "disposed to snatch everything" from a weak neighbor; and moreover, armed interference in Mexico appealed no more to Wilson's common sense than to his historical judgment. "When two drunks are in a brawl across the street," he said to Stockton Axson one day, "law-abiding citizens don't cross over and mix in." Though he discussed the possibility of war realistically with House, it seemed to the President impossible to reach the individual culprits who were at the root of the trouble by attempting to fight the whole country of Mexico.

The Cabinet, too, feared military involvement; and on May 23 members spoke in favor of recognizing Huerta, arguing that the chief cause of the crisis was rivalry of British and American mining interests, that Europeans would support any dictator who preserved order, and that the United States would have to recognize him eventually.[1] Finally,

---

[1] In the Cabinet discussion of May 23, Houston warned that by accepting the usurper the United States would restore his credit; and Daniels declared that any deal with a foreign power that deprived the Mexican people of their mineral resources would be "immoral." When Secretary of War Garrison read an editorial that supported his insistence on recognition of Huerta as the only alternative to intervention, the President broke into the discussion. "That reminds me," he said, "of a statement made by Carlyle, who said that every man regarded an editorial in a newspaper as very wise and able if it voiced the opinion which he himself held." Daniels Diary and Daniels, *The Wilson Era: Years of Peace*, pp. 181–82; Houston, *op. cit.*, I, 69.

it was agreed that Bryan should ask the English and French ambassadors whether their governments were sponsoring loans to Mexico, and should warn that a credit guaranteed by a pledge of customs duties could not be enforced.

Meanwhile interested citizens of the United States grew impatient at their government's policy of watchful waiting. Accustomed to act aggressively, and eager above all to get political stability, the businessmen brought forward another proposal on May 26. This time they did not urge recognition, but rather a fair election, to be achieved by the mediation of the United States between Huerta's provisional government and Carranza's Constitutionalists.

These investors were representative of a group of citizens whom the President was irritating by tariff and currency reforms, and he had no desire to provoke other controversies with them. Finally the Administration broke its silence with a declaration that, if Huerta would assure a free election soon, refrain from being a candidate himself, and guarantee "absolute amnesty," the United States would try to reconcile the contending factions under one government. After a conference with Bryan and with Garrison, who had prepared the Army for intervention, this statement of policy was sent confidentially on June 14 to Ambassador Wilson.

That diplomat, however, was more active in pressing the State Department for recognition than in urging constitutional guarantees upon Huerta. He saw that the sending of an unofficial agent to an unrecognized government caused confusion among Mexicans, as well as resentment; and he understood how deeply Mexican pride was hurt by any hint of patronizing.

But the President trusted Hale's conscience and the objectivity of his view. He was impressed by his envoy's report that the ambassador was damning the Administration at Washington as "a pack of vicious fools"; and when he learned that Huerta had been invited to dine at the embassy, he was so shocked that he suggested to Bryan that Henry Lane Wilson be recalled. This was done in July, "for consultation." After an interview at the White House in which the Wilsons utterly failed to sympathize with each other's purposes, the ambassador's resignation was accepted and the embassy at Mexico City came under the direction of Secretary Nelson O'Shaughnessy, whom Hale had commended as a "perfectly honest man."

The aversion that Wilson had at first felt toward Huerta crystallized in hard, implacable denunciation. He was ready to feud with a usurper whose hand was strengthened by loans from other nations and by the assignment to Mexico City of an English envoy who was thought to be anti-American and sympathetic to oil interests that were vital to the British Navy.[2] The dictator was able to turn Wilson's innocent offenses to national pride to his own advantage and to command the support of Mexican jingoes by defying the "Colossus of the North." The unscrupulous mestizo was a tough antagonist. He was said to be able to clear his brain by heavy drinking, and Indian blood gave him a tenacity that matched that of the Scot in the White House. On August 2 he announced that he would neither resign nor permit foreigners to interfere in a matter involving his honor and that of his nation. And the next day Wilson accepted the challenge, writing to Mary Hulbert that he must consider "how that murderous Castro is to be choked off and kept in cold storage."

At this point the influence of the dean of Wilson's personal agents was felt. Colonel House, who had gone to Europe in May, talked frankly about Mexico with Sir Edward Grey, British foreign secretary. The Texan found in this unassuming philosopher a friend in whom he took delight. When he lunched at Sir Edward's home on July 3, the foreign secretary asked about the President's intentions toward Mexico. The Colonel replied, with more assurance than was justified by Wilson's inmost inclinations, that it was immaterial which Mexican faction held power, as long as order was maintained. This was the traditional English attitude and therefore pleasing to Sir Edward,[3] who responded, a month later, by instructing his minister at Mexico City to say to Huerta informally that refusal to receive an envoy from the United States would be a grave mistake and would put Mexico in the wrong. France also urged conciliation; and Germany, whose views were utterly materialistic, grudgingly cooperated.

At this juncture the President sent a second special envoy to Mexico

[2] Sir Lionel Carden, whose recall from a previous post in Cuba had been sought, unsuccessfully, by Secretary of State Knox. Wilson was led by undocumented reports to believe that Garden was the tool of Lord Cowdray and British oil interests. *See* p. 367 n. and Link, *W.W., The New Freedom,* p. 371 ff.

[3] A few days after the Colonel left England, Sir Edward Grey told Ambassador Page that House was a man whom he was glad to know and whom he hoped to see whenever the Texan visited London. Here was a fellow more practical than the ebullient Page, who provoked laughter from Sir Edward by advocacy of an "idealistic" intervention in Mexico that would "shoot men into self-government." Burton J. Hendrick, *The Life and Letters of Walter Hines Page,* I, 188. Hereinafter this work is referred to as *Page Letters.*

Page generously wrote to House about Sir Edward's remarks; and when House showed Page's letter to McAdoo, the latter insisted upon taking it to the President so that Wilson would fully appreciate the value of the Colonel's services. As soon as House returned to the United States, he asked McAdoo to tell the President of his talk with Britain's foreign secretary. House Diary, July 20, 1913.

City. John Lind of Minnesota, a political friend of Bryan who was without experience in diplomacy or in Mexican culture, was commissioned as "advisor to the American Embassy," and bidden to reassert the altruistic and paternalistic motives of the United States and to offer to mediate on terms that would end Huerta's dictatorship and bring peace.

Huerta's government scornfully rejected the suggestion of mediation that Lind brought. On August 16, in a letter filled with innuendo and sarcasm, the Mexicans asserted that they could not consider "for one moment" the conditions that Wilson had sent to them, and accused the Americans of trying to bribe them by offering a loan.

Lind was handicapped not only by the coolness of O'Shaughnessy and the foreign colony at Mexico City but by a feeling on the part of Mexicans that there was a serious division of opinion within the United States that might be exploited profitably. When the President's agent reported this to Washington and suggested that a strong statement of policy to Congress might be helpful, Wilson acted to uphold the hand of his envoy. The prophet in the White House was now in the sort of position in which he took delight. He was challenged to compete with a strong but wicked Philistine in a contest for public confidence, and he responded with a righteous thrill. In one of his Sunday letters to Mary Hulbert he referred to himself as a "President trying to handle an impossible President of Mexico," and two weeks later, in August, he wrote: "Our friend Huerta is a diverting brute! . . . He is seldom sober and always impossible, and yet what an indomitable fighter for his own hand!"

Wilson's ardor for moral triumph was heightened by the fact that Republican senators had been nourishing Mexican hopes for a division of opinion at Washington. Protests were being received from constituents, and there was a demand for a Congressional inquiry. On July 19, for example, Senator Albert B. Fall, who was sympathetic to the Doheny oil interests in Mexico, introduced a resolution calling on his government to give full protection to its citizens abroad and to their property. Among the prominent Republicans in the Senate only Elihu Root, whose experience as secretary of state had given him a deep comprehension of the forces at work in Mexico, gave general approval to Wilson's policy. Seizing upon this support from a political opponent, the President wrote to Root to express his "deep gratification." Furthermore, he conferred with the Foreign Relations Committee of the Senate and told them frankly what he was trying to do.

Dispatches from his personal agents in Mexico came so voluminously in August that Wilson found it difficult to settle upon a text for the message to Congress that Lind had suggested. But, finally, on the 27th he was ready to address the legislators. He asserted that all the Americas were waiting upon the development of Mexico, where the benefits of peace could be enjoyed only through "genuine freedom" and "a just and ordered government founded upon law." Present circumstances did not "promise even the foundations of such a peace"; and therefore he had volunteered the good offices of the United States through John Lind. His overture had been rejected by the authorities at Mexico City because they could not comprehend the altruistic spirit behind the offer, and also because they did not believe that the President spoke for the people of the United States. It would be futile for his government to thrust its services upon the Mexicans, Wilson declared. "So long as the misunderstanding continues we can only await the time of their awakening to a realization of the actual facts . . . We can afford to exercise the self-restraint of a really great nation which realizes its own strength and scorns to misuse it."

He urged that all Americans should be asked to leave the country immediately and Mexican authorities should be held strictly accountable for the safety of any who chose to remain. Furthermore, using authority granted to him by Congress, he would forbid the export of war materials to any part of Mexico. In conclusion, he asserted that all the world expected the United States to act in this crisis in her "immemorial relation" of "nearest friend and intimate adviser." Sending word indirectly to the rebels in the North of Mexico that they could not stand aloof from a constitutional election if they wished to retain his sympathy, he hoped that moral pressure might prevail and a new era might thus begin in Latin America.[3a]

For six weeks after Wilson's declaration before the Congress the Mexican horizon was comparatively tranquil. In the month of October, however, another storm broke. By the 7th it became clear that Huerta had no intention of arranging the constitutional election that Wilson understood to have been promised. On October 10 the dictator dissolved the Chamber and imprisoned a hundred and twelve deputies; and the United States was begged by the families of the proscribed men to save them from death. A farcical election was held on the 26th; but after it Huerta declared that, since so few had voted, his hand-picked Chamber would be seated and he would remain provisional president.

Wilson's moral sense was shocked again, the more so because he had

[3a] McAdoo, *The Priceless Gift*, p. 308.

allowed himself to believe undocumented reports that Huerta had promised not to be a candidate in the election. He bade O'Shaughnessy accuse the provincial government of "an act of bad faith toward the United States." Huerta not only had violated constitutional guarantees, the President said, but he had destroyed all possibility of a free and fair election.[4]

At the same time the President was indignant at Sir Lionel Carden, who, by formally presenting his diplomatic credentials to Huerta the very day after the imprisonment of the Mexican deputies, seemed to give the sanction of London to the dictatorship. Thinking that the British people would overthrow their government if they knew of an alliance of English oil interests with Huerta, Wilson tapped out on his typewriter one of the most incendiary notes that the machine ever produced. Accusing European powers of upholding Huerta and thwarting the efforts of the United States to establish constitutional government in Mexico, he asked the State Department to draft a circular note "as strong and direct as the courtesies and proprieties of pacific diplomacy permit." Bryan then worked with him on a message that reproached non-American nations for allowing their citizens to support Huerta in return for economic concessions. In his angry mood of frustration the prophet was ready to extend the Monroe Doctrine to preclude financial intervention by Europeans in the Americas. On October 27 his indignation stirred him to proclaim [5] "A New Latin-American Policy" and to inveigh against "concessions" in Latin America to foreign capitalists. He was willing to take strong measures even at the risk of provoking a coalition of European powers against the United States.

However, the impetuous President was dissuaded from folly by diplomats at home and abroad. Though he paid little heed to the advice of career men in the State Department, whom he thought wrapped up in legalisms and corrupted by experience in dollar diplomacy, he heeded John Bassett Moore, the scholarly jurist whom he had made counselor of the department as a steadying influence upon William Jennings Bryan. When Bryan requested Moore to polish the sharp note that he and Wilson had drafted and asked that a clause invoking the Monroe

[4] Huerta informed the diplomatic corps on Oct. 23 that if he were elected, his election would be null and void, for it was prohibited by the constitution and he had given his word not to be a candidate. His secret instructions to election officials on Oct. 22, however, spoke in a contrary vein. Notter, *op. cit.,* p. 265. On Nov. 8 the dictator notified the foreign powers that he would remain in office until he had pacified Mexico. On the same day the President gave notice that his fight to depose Huerta would go on.

[5] In an address at Mobile, Ala., before the Southern Commercial Congress. (*See* pp. 80–81.)

Doctrine be added, the counselor volunteered a professional opinion that made the President's position untenable.[6]

Like Wilson, Sir Edward Grey was disturbed by the sudden turn for the worse in Mexican affairs. With civil strife still unchecked, it seemed vital to come to an understanding that would preserve American goodwill and at the same time assure protection of British interests. The situation was "very grim," he told Page. To relieve the tension, the English diplomat sent abroad his engaging secretary, Sir William Tyrrell, as a temporary substitute for Sir Cecil Spring Rice, who had succeeded Lord Bryce as British ambassador at Washington and was ill at his summer home in New Hampshire.

When Sir William arrived at the capital, early in November, public feeling had been somewhat soothed by inspired press reports from London that there was no intention to thwart American policy in Mexico. Tyrrell called on the American secretary of state and found him unbelievably *gauche*. Haranguing the English visitor on the wickedness of the Empire, Bryan charged that British oilmen in Mexico were the "paymasters" of their nation's Cabinet. Fortunately the envoy from London had a sense of humor that enabled him to turn the insult aside lightly.

House, responding to a plea from Page[7] that Sir William Tyrrell

[6] Moore to W.W., Oct. 28. 1913. The United States, Moore pointed out, had never presumed to regulate European recognition of Latin-American nations or foreign investment in the Western Hemisphere. It was Moore's view that any such interference would be resented by other American peoples just as much as it would have been objected to by the United States in the days when they had needed capital. Moreover, the counselor reminded his chief that foreign loans had served, in all the Americas, to develop industrial and financial strength and, thus, political stability and independence. Such a note as the President proposed would anger Europeans and defeat his purposes; and it seemed particularly unwise to irritate Britain at the moment in view of other issues that were under discussion with that government.

Bryan, fearing that European loans to Latin America would lead to violations of the Monroe Doctrine, proposed that the United States government make nonprofit loans; but Wilson feared that this would "strike the whole country . . . as a novel and radical proposal." Wilson to Bryan, Mar. 20, 1914.

[7] Page—a sensitive, charming gentleman who was galled by the restrictions of official intercourse—had maintained friendly contact with Sir Edward and had reported faithfully to the State Department despite chilly silences from that organization. He found that he could reach Wilson most surely and sympathetically through House. In frank epistles that he often marked "good to burn" the ambassador confided his troubles to the Colonel.

In response to Page's laments, House wrote comforting replies, explaining the handicaps under which the State Department had been placed by inexperience and by Congressional restrictions on funds, assuring the ambassador that Wilson had enjoyed his remarks about Bryan and his artistic descriptions of life at London. When House was about to burn one of Page's letters, after reading it to the President, Wilson asked him to wait until he was sure that he had its content well in mind and then repeated the text almost verbatim before the Colonel dropped it in the grate. House Diary, Dec. 12, 1913. Though amused, he took his Ambassador's complaints to heart and replied: "We must certainly manage to keep our foreign representatives properly informed. The real trouble is to conduct genuinely confidential corre-

should "get the President's ideas about Mexico, good and firm and hard," took it upon himself to prepare the minds of both the President and the British visitor for an intimate talk. He persuaded Ellen Wilson to go to the theater with Tyrrell, though her husband could not join them. The President was unnerved by his quandary. As he lay awake he prayed that it would not be necessary to use force.[8]

With the President's authorization, the Colonel lunched with Tyrrell the next day and prepared the envoy's mind for an interview with Wilson at the White House. Nevertheless, the men were a trifle embarrassed when they confronted each other, the prophet wearing a gray sack suit and the Old World diplomat, an impeccable cutaway. Soon, however, each was speaking with confidence in the understanding of the other. The President outlined his policy toward Mexico; and Tyrrell agreed that Huerta by his highhanded action had forfeited British recognition. The visitor denied, however, that British commercial interests had formed the alliance with Huerta that the President suspected but could not prove. Moreover, he asserted that Carden was not antagonistic to the United States but was merely doing his duty.[9] It seemed

---

spondence except through private letters, but surely the thing can be changed and it will be if I can manage it." *Page Letters,* I, 212, 222.

In October, when the Mexican situation became critical, Page reported that he had explained the President's position to Grey, who had shown appreciation and increasing respect for Wilson's ideas, but seemed to be under financial pressure that was irksome." Page to secretary of State, Oct. 21, 1913.

[8] W.W. to Mary A. Hulbert, Nov. 2, 1913. In his extremity during these days Wilson talked for more than an hour with Chairman Bacon of the Senate Foreign Relations Committee, hoping to find help in this senator's long experience. He was vexed because there had been a leak of a dispatch sent by Bryan to Mexico City, stating that the United States would insist on forcing Huerta's abdication. When newspapers published this message, it became impossible for the dictator to resign without appearing to surrender to foreigners. This was a bad jolt, coming just at a time when Huerta seemed responsive to a final effort by Wilson's agents to persuade him to retire. House Diary, Nov. 5, 1913.

[9] House Diary, Nov. 13, 1913.

Ambassador Page was not able to adduce proof of his suspicions of Carden, and the President could not help him. On Jan. 6, 1914, Wilson wrote to Page: "I do not think you realize how hard we worked to get from either Lind or O'Shaughnessy definite items of speech or conduct which we could furnish you. It simply was not obtainable. Everything that we got was at second or third hand. That he was working against us was too plain for denial, and yet he seems to have done it in a very astute way which nobody could take direct hold of . . ." *Page Letters,* I, 221.

"Whatever British interests were doing in Mexico was entirely unknown to me," Grey wrote later in his autobiography. Since the British government could not interfere in Mexico without violating the Monroe Doctrine and the United States had thus far declined to assume responsibility, it seemed to the foreign secretary only fair that British interests should make any terms possible with whoever at Mexico City had power to protect or destroy them. Sir Edward Grey, *Twenty-five Years, 1892–1916,* p. 100.

Page asserted, in a letter of Mar. 19, 1914, to Wilson, that the British oilmen were "not dishonest, by their standard," but that their standard "permitted their taking the earth, if nobody got in the way."

to Sir William that rumors of British involvement with Huerta's cause had sprung from mischievous attempts to stimulate intervention.

The statesmen reached an understanding, not only on the Mexican issue but also about the revision of discriminatory Panama Canal tolls and the larger question of curbing armaments and the power of finance over world politics. Sir William was pleased by the President's sympathetic reception and afterward told House, with whom he arranged to perpetuate their informal contact, that never before had he talked so frankly about matters of such import. "If some of the veteran diplomats could have heard us," he confided, "they would have fallen in a faint." The Wilson-Tyrrell conversation and talks between Page and Grey brought about a change of sentiment at London.[10]

On the second day of the new year, while Wilson was vacationing at Pass Christian, he went far out into the Gulf to confer with John Lind aboard a cruiser that had brought that envoy from Mexico. Lind confirmed disturbing rumors that had reached the President earlier. Returning ashore to his family, Wilson told them that Huerta, made desperate by threats to his life and by lack of funds and a paralysis of government in central Mexico, was ready to declare war against the United States in a rash effort to unite all Mexicans under his leadership. He was said to await only the arrival of two shiploads of munitions from Germany.

It was difficult, Wilson explained, to piece out the truth from reports that came to him from men who had various points of view. He said that he was growing crosseyed, watching so many people in so many directions at the same time. "I listen carefully to what everyone says," he remarked, "and then piece together the parts that fit. Parts of truth

---

[10] Sir Lionel Carden, setting a precedent for European diplomats in Mexico, advised Huerta to abdicate. Furthermore, Sir Edward Grey gave the President a free hand to remove the dictator and pacify the country as best he might. Wilson was jubilant over the change in London's attitude, and congratulated Page on the way in which he was "pounding elementary doctrine" into the British statesmen.

One of Page's confidential letters (undated and marked "good to burn") informed House that he had notified the State Department of a rumor of Sir Lionel's impending transfer, that the message had leaked out, to Page's humiliation, that the Foreign Office had had to deny the report, and that the same sort of thing had happened twice before. Page to House, Jan. 8, 1914. Page blamed the State Department for the leak, but some of the Cabinet members suspected that Secretary Lane was responsible. The matter was discussed in Cabinet meeting on Dec. 19, and thereafter Wilson gave his official family even less insight into his thoughts on foreign policy and kept copies of important letters in a personal file, under lock.

Meanwhile, Ambassador Spring Rice had been complaining to his good friend, Sir Edward Grey, about Wilson's intransigence. Though the President was "extremely friendly," the envoy reported that it was quite out of the question to change his Mexican policy by talking to him. "There is nothing to do with this hardened saint," Spring Rice wrote on Feb. 7, 1914. And as for the secretary of state, talking with Mr. Bryan was "like writing on ice." Stephen Gwynn (ed.), *Letters and Friendships of Sir Cecil Spring Rice*, II, 202.

always match." He seemed to be putting his trust in infinite patience and absolute firmness; but his family noted that he was deeply troubled. Armed conflict with Mexico was to him a horrible prospect, and he turned more avidly than ever to comic relief. He communed at this time with no serious poets—only with humorists; and he tried, rather feebly, to rally his spirits with laughter over the dictum of Mr. Dooley's Hennessy: "Sure, with Mexico so contagious, we'll be takin' it soon whether we want it or not."

Wilson reluctantly reached the conclusion that force must be used to dislodge Huerta, but he hoped that it would not have to be the force of the United States. He continued to withstand European pleas for military action and to resist demands for armed intervention that were put forth by panicky Americans in Mexico and were taken up in the United States by certain Republicans and by jingoistic journals.

The President's mind had been turning toward Carranza as the best instrument for forcing Huerta from power and uniting the country. The name of the Northern faction—"the Constitutionalists"—charmed him. Wilson soon found, however, that Carranza's native pride was as sensitive as Huerta's when it came to accepting American advice on political matters. But Carranza did desire to be allowed to import arms, for he had been paying more for munitions than Huerta, who controlled seaports through which they could be brought from Europe.

Should the United States abandon its neutrality to the extent of permitting Carranza to get weapons that were denied to Huerta? On the evening of January 21, Colonel House found his friend "terribly worried" over the problem. Wilson said that the Constitutionalists, like Huerta's junta, were not beyond suspicion of receiving funds from oil interests—in this case American; but he felt that he could truthfully defend himself against any charge that he was favoring any such influence. Though Wilson foresaw that even if Huerta was eliminated the Constitutionalists still would make war on his successor, he concluded finally that Carranza's faction held out the only hope for avoiding intervention and yet doing away with feudal conditions that lingered in Mexico.

When Carranza sent an envoy to Washington to discuss the matter, the President called upon another special agent to help him to keep negotiations confidential. Evening after evening he received William Phillips [11] in his study and mulled over reports of conversations that

[11] Phillips, a young Republican who had been an assistant secretary of state under Roosevelt and who was commended to Wilson by Page, was asked to leave his post as secretary of the Harvard Corporation and go to Washington for a secret assignment, with the understanding that if he was successful he would become third assistant secretary of state.

Phillips had held during the day with Carranza's envoy, who brought assurance of the interest of his faction in land reform. After the President had puzzled for a while and thought out his course, he would go to his typewriter and tap out instructions for the next day, brief and to the point. He instructed Phillips to keep Bryan informed, but wanted the State Department to assume no part in the dealings. Because of leaks, he did not trust the ordinary channels of diplomacy; nor did he hazard discussion of his intentions with his Cabinet. He was taking the responsibility entirely on his own shoulders, where his conscience told him that it belonged in a matter affecting the peace of the continent, perhaps that of the world.

Finally, on February 3, after getting the general assent of the Senate Foreign Relations Committee, the President revoked the embargo on arms shipments. Though this act did not openly discriminate between the Mexican factions, its practical effect was to notify the world that Wilson put his trust in Carranza's leadership.

Huerta raged against outside interference, rallied conservative patriots to his support, and seemed to be entrenching his regime more strongly than ever. Early in March, after a British citizen had been killed by Constitutionalist forces under General Villa and Sir Edward Grey's policy was challenged in Parliament, Wilson was importuned to appoint a commission of distinguished jurists to deal with the Mexican problem —a proposal toward which both Huerta and Carranza seemed favorably disposed. But he had been "around the clock" and had shut his mind against any compromise with the political immorality that Huerta represented. He had publicly arrogated to the United States the duty of ousting the dictator, and it was unthinkable that he should default upon this responsibility. Huerta must go. But he still hoped to avoid the forcible intervention with which Lind had threatened Huerta if the usurper remained in office after an election.

In the spring, however, a chain of events forced the President's hand. Troops of the Mexican factions came face to face at Tampico with warships of the United States that were standing by to protect foreign oil installations. A paymaster and sailors from the USS *Dolphin* landed a whaleboat without permission in an area that was under martial law and were arrested by a Mexican colonel. They were promptly released and the Huertista commanding officer made a personal apology to Admiral Mayo. But the admiral, unsatisfied, sent an ultimatum that demanded a formal apology, punishment of the offending colonel, and the firing of a twenty-one-gun salute to the American flag. Huerta immediately responded with an expression of regret and assurance that the offending colonel would be punished if found guilty; but he asked at the same time that Mayo's ultimatum be withdrawn.

Thus the thing happened that Wilson had been dreading for months and had been praying to avert. The 14th of April was a harrowing day. The Cabinet discussed the crisis and were almost united in determination to follow up the ultimatum, when the time limit expired without Mexican action. The President was distressed by the admiral's boldness, but he had been convinced by other apparent insults [12] to his country that failure to support the ultimatum would enhearten Huerta and weaken the position of the United States. Later in the day he sent a sharp message to notify Huerta that he expected "prompt acceptance" of Mayo's terms. Suffering under moral responsibility that he had assumed, he besought his colleagues to ask God for peace if they believed in the efficacy of prayer. But he also took steps to keep his powder dry. He dispatched more warships to Tampico, though the Navy warned that such a concentration of power might lead to war. It was a "psychological moment" for a display of force, he said afterward, for the Constitutionalists seemed at last to have an open road to Mexico City.

In the crisis the President felt impelled to consult the Congress. On the 15th, therefore, he informed legislative committeemen of the steps already taken and agreed with them that, though he had power to order occupation of a foreign port to protect American lives and property without Congressional action, it would be best to ask for authorization.

When the President returned to Washington on April 20 from a weekend at White Sulphur Springs, where his wife was ill, it seemed clear that Huerta, though making concessions that satisfied Secretaries Bryan and Daniels, would not yield unconditionally to the American demand.[13] Meeting in the morning with his Cabinet, some of whom had been up half the night planning for a blockade and possible warfare, Wilson outlined an address that he proposed to deliver before the Congress that day.

Early in the afternoon he read his message to members of the Con-

[12] Two incidents that Wilson seized upon to buttress his position and that now seem insignificant are related in Baker, IV, 317, and in *P.P.*, III, 100. In one case the Mexican authorities were exonerated after an investigation by Admiral Fletcher. *F. R., 1914*, p. 465.

[13] It amused Huerta that Mayo's exaction should be made upon a government whose existence had not been recognized, and he sardonically agreed to give the requested salute if the Yankees would return it volley for volley. This proposal was viewed at Washington as a trick to get recognition and hence was rejected, though Mayo was willing to return a Mexican salute in the manner prescribed by naval custom.

gressional committees. It had been released to the press, and it was too late to change it; but at the conference Senator Lodge took exception to many aspects of it. The statement seemed to him weak and unsatisfactory—in reality a declaration of war against an individual. When Lodge told the President that under international law he could not, without a war blockade, carry out his intention of intercepting a cargo of German arms destined for Huerta, Wilson explained that he would seize the weapons at the customhouse at Veracruz after they were landed. The President had not given up hope of a solution that would be both peaceful and effective.

At three o'clock Wilson entered the Capitol to read his message as he had drafted it. There was an air of martial expectancy in the chamber. The galleries applauded, in violation of the rules, and the "rebel yell" of Civil War days arose from Democratic benches. The Cabinet sat in chairs flanking their chief, Bryan looking white and worn and fingering his chin nervously.

In the address Wilson detailed the several incidents of the past few days that had made him feel that the United States had been singled out for insult. "The manifest danger of such a situation," he warned, "was that such offenses might grow from bad to worse until something happened of so gross and intolerable a sort as to lead directly and inevitably to armed conflict." He was forced to sustain Admiral Mayo, he explained, in order to make Huerta understand that there must be no more incidents. War with the people of Mexico was not in question, he asserted emphatically. He was now trying to do, in dealing with a nation, what he had advocated doing in regulating corporations—fix the guilt on an individual and punish him. "If armed conflict should unhappily come . . ." he declared, "we should be fighting only General Huerta and those who adhere to him and give him their support, and our object would be only to restore to the people of the distracted Republic the opportunity to set up again their own laws and their own government." With no thought of selfish aggrandizement, he asked authority to use the armed forces of his nation not against the people of Mexico but "in such ways and to such an extent as may be necessary to obtain from General Huerta and his adherents the fullest recognition of the rights and dignity of the United States."

His audience found it difficult to comprehend this untraditional venture in diplomacy, and to many the incidents cited seemed trivial and inconclusive. The Congress could scarcely refuse to support the Administration in a matter in which national prestige had been made an issue; and yet it was not until two days later, after Wilson had made a trip to the Capitol to urge haste upon the Democratic leaders, that the Senate finally passed a resolution justifying the President in using the armed forces of the nation.

Wilson was thrown into a black mood by the attitude of the Senate. During the evening after his address he told his family that the reaction had not been very favorable; and then, with grim sadness, he said: "People seem to want war with Mexico, but they shan't have it if I can prevent it." [14] His military and naval chiefs conferred with him to perfect plans for sending Marines ashore at Veracruz when the German arms arrived; and Woodrow Wilson went to bed more conscious than ever of the threat of war.

At about three in the morning he was awakened by the telephone. It was Bryan calling, to transmit a report that one of the expected shiploads of munitions was destined to reach Veracruz in seven hours. Daniels was on the wire also, and joined the secretary of state in recommending that the Navy be ordered to intervene. The President felt that he must act immediately, under his own powers and without the advice of Congress, else Huerta would get guns that might be turned on Americans. When Daniels recommended that warships at Veracruz be directed to seize the customhouse, Wilson assented, while Tumulty, listening in on the conversation, marked the cruel irony of a situation that forced three lovers of peace to sanction an act of war.

The President expected no serious opposition to this illegal act of force. When news came that heroic Mexican naval cadets had given their lives in opposing the landing and that American bluejackets had been sniped at and nineteen had been killed, Wilson suffered as if a son of his own had been lost. He looked ill, his skin pale as parchment, as he faced newsmen to answer their queries. All day he was abnormally quiet and went methodically about his business, and finally he said to Tumulty: "I cannot get it off my heart. It had to be done. It was right. Nothing else was possible, but I cannot forget that it was I who had to order those young men to their deaths."

For four days the President was in a quandary and his spirit vacillated from stubborn optimism to dread that Huerta, cornered and at bay, would "stake everything on a dramatic exit." The dictator sent all available troops toward Veracruz, and American consulates were

[14] Asked by newsmen whether it was possible to deal with a *de facto* regime by using the Navy without declaring war, Wilson replied: "Why, certainly. It has been done many times." He cited the naval action at Greytown, Nicaragua (in 1854) as an example. Swem notes, Princeton University Library.

attacked and their officials imprisoned. Moreover, Carranza's tone became so menacing that the American embargo on arms was reimposed and more troops were sent to the border. Furthermore, there were diplomatic complications with Germany.[15] But worst of all the results of the futile landing at Veracruz, jingoism in the United States threatened to get out of control: the debate in the Senate had shown that the opposition wanted full-scale intervention on grounds that would stigmatize the United States in the eyes of the world as an imperialistic nation and would fan the antagonism that was now flaming in Latin America. Faced by all these consequences of his canny effort to intercept the German shipment by seizing the customhouse at Veracruz, Wilson realized that the path to war was very slippery indeed. He paced the south grounds of the White House, hour after hour, up and down, up and down, deep in speculation. "We have been in a blind alley so long," he wrote to a Princeton trustee who had befriended him, "that I am longing for an exit."

In his extremity, the prophet's God did not forsake him. On April 25, as Wilson was acting to check army plans for further operations in Mexico, Providence came to his rescue through the agency of three diplomats from South America. The envoys of Argentina, Brazil, and Chile offered their services as mediators. Wilson and House had discussed such a solution three months before, and the President seized upon it now on the very day of its proposal.

Immediately the air was cleared, not only at Washington but all through the hemisphere. By consenting to mediation the President gave proof of the just intent that he had been proclaiming. Moreover Huerta, as eager as Wilson to escape from the dilemma without loss of countenance, accepted the plan of the ABC powers; and on May 20 the commission went into session at Niagara Falls. Woodrow Wilson now had a judicious body before which to plead his cause, and during May and June he made the most of the unfolding opportunity for leadership of opinion by addressing a series of notes to the mediators. No solution would be acceptable to the United States, he warned, unless it provided for "the elimination of General Huerta" and "the immediate setting up in Mexico of a single provisional government acceptable to all parties." Moreover, the new government must satisfy "the just claims of the people of Mexico to life, liberty, and independent self-support."

---

[15] The State Department was forced to concede that the Navy had no right to order the arms-bearing German vessel to remain at Vera Cruz, with its cargo still aboard, and toward the end of May the ship unloaded its munitions at Puerto Mexico, a port through which arms passed to Huerta all through the spring.

At the same time the prophet exerted leadership through the press. On April 27, only a few hours after Huerta's acceptance of mediation, Wilson told Samuel G. Blythe, a journalist, that the mere removal of the dictator would not suffice. Sitting back in his desk chair with eyes half closed, the President put the current plight of Mexico in historical perspective while his auditor, accustomed to the muddied, platitudinous speech of politicians, listened with awe to the flow of language and was charmed by both words and gestures. Now and then the scholar lightened his phrasing with slang. ("We must hump ourselves," he said.) As he talked, his fingers laced and interlaced, not moving far or violently but conjuring up the image of a musician who accompanies his voice with the piano. Once they closed into a fist that banged the desk and set a paper knife rattling against a tray. As the prophet grew tense, cords stood out on his neck, his eyes narrowed, his lips parted, and he said: "My ideal is an orderly and righteous government in Mexico; but my passion is for the submerged eighty-five per cent of the people of that Republic who are now struggling toward liberty."

The President explained that revolutions in that nation had grown out of the passion of peasants for a fair share of the land. It was his conviction that landless people always furnished the inflammable material for revolt. The prospect of policing Mexico, and then retiring when order was restored, did not appeal to him. He saw that revolution would follow revolution until the Mexican people themselves solved fundamental political problems. "They say the Mexicans are not fitted for self-government," he said, moving his long white fingers in a gesture of contempt. "To this I reply that, when properly directed, there is no people not fitted for self-government." Minister and schoolmaster that he was, he proposed to help Mexicans to compose their differences, start them on the road to prosperity, and leave them to work out their own destiny; but at the same time he would watch them narrowly and insist that they accept help when they needed it. They would be "free" only so far as they showed themselves deserving of freedom.

Always the motive of the United States must be that of a good neighbor—not only human but humane. Though Mexico, like any self-respecting nation, would be expected to compensate individual foreigners who suffered damages, the United States must demand no indemnities in terms of territory or money, in the manner of the nineteenth-century empires. Moreover, Wilson promised with stern visage: "There shall be no individual exploitation of Mexico if I can stop it." Thus the prophet drew from circumstances that he could not immediately control, a

CHAPTER XXII

A Foreign Policy Takes Shape

As woodrow wilson dealt with the diplomatic crises that arose during his first year in office he did not lose sight of a fixed star on which the aspiration of idealists was beginning to center. Save for its brief hostilities with Spain, the United States had been at peace for almost a hundred years with the other great powers of the world: its people had grown physically strong, economically wealthy, and strategically secure against the fears and menaces that were rife on other continents. Out of their fortuitous isolation had grown a conviction that peace was normal and virtuous, war unnecessary and wicked. Failing properly to relate their political felicity to the geographic and economic conditions that made it possible, some Americans felt that they could dispense the blessings of peace to the world, along with democracy and Christianity.

During Wilson's academic years, his nation's desire to propagate peace had worked toward two goals: arbitration and disarmament. Unfortunately, proposals for curtailing the armed forces of the nations had not progressed beyond pious talk. Though the standing armies of the democracies were small, the empires of Central and Eastern Europe commanded vast forces; and moreover, the huge navies of Western Europe were being challenged by the growing fleets of Germany, Japan, and the United States.

Arbitration of disputes, however, was a process long familiar to the people of the United States, where a Supreme Court had acted for more than a century as arbiter of interstate differences. The American nation had applauded Theodore Roosevelt when he had mediated to end the Russo-Japanese War: and Americans had participated willingly in setting up a panel of judges at The Hague to serve nations that wished to submit their differences to law instead of a trial of arms. There was, however, no cosmic force to compel the submission of disputes to this judicial body, nor was there power to enforce its decisions. If peoples were sufficiently scared they would still demand the protection of armament: and if they became mad enough they would fight. In the Old World imperial ambitions and ancient grudges had created national psychoses that were unresponsive to ecumenical considerations.

As a university president Wilson had shown interest in conciliation among peoples through international agreements. In his inaugural address at Princeton, in 1902, he pointed proudly to the fact that his own country's greatest victories had been those of peace and humanity. He never escaped the grip that the horrors of the Reconstruction had fixed upon him in his adolescent years in old Columbia. Though not a pacifist, he joined the American Peace Society in 1908. His intellect told him that modern war was a brutal and clumsy way of getting at justice. Sometimes it struck him as silly. Riding from Princeton to take part in a celebration at the Bordentown Military Academy, he quoted this jingle to a young lady in his party:

> War is rude and impolite
> And quite upsets a nation.
> It causes weeks and months of strife
> And years of conversation.[1]

Wilson gave consideration to both disarmament and arbitration as means to peace. Though he said little or nothing in public about disarmament, he talked with Sir William Tyrrell of the necessity of curbing armaments and the power of financiers in politics. "It is the greatest fight we all have on today," he said, "and every good citizen should enlist." Moreover, he had spoken and written in favor of arbitration and, as we have seen, he accepted it eagerly in the crisis with Mexico.

Immediate problems had crowded upon the President so importunately after his inauguration at Washington, and he was so intent on his program of domestic reform, that the matter of world peace received little of his time. He was always conscious that it could not be bought, decreed, or even legislated if its roots did not lie deep in public opinion. He was sympathetic, however, to all sincere efforts to stimulate a love for peace and a will to maintain it; and when his associates took initiative in that direction, he gave his encouragement and blessing.

William Jennings Bryan had been obsessed since 1905 by a passion for a guarantee of the world's peace by international treaties. Before agreeing to serve as secretary of state he had secured Wilson's approval of such a program, and the two Presbyterians directed their energies toward the development of a kind of pact that promised to be more effective than those already in force.

The new type of treaty was designed to prevent friction between

[1] B. M. Green (Princeton, 1907) to Lewis, Lewis Papers (Princeton University Library).

nations, and not merely to compel arbitration of disputes that already had reached a dangerous temperature. Moreover, unlike the conventional treaties of arbitration,[2] it applied to all controversies that were not adjusted through diplomacy. Wilson and Bryan had not been in office two months before they were exchanging notes regarding drafts of the new instruments. After the secretary of state had discussed the matter with the Senate's Foreign Relations Committee and had found the members cooperative, it was put before the foreign diplomats at Washington. The plan, as outlined by Bryan and Counselor Moore, called for investigation of disputes by an international commission composed of two representatives of each of the interested parties, and a fifth commissioner whom they might select. Because the treaties provided that the signers would not resort to war until a year had been allowed for investigation and report, the measures came to be known as "cooling-off treaties."

Explaining the purpose of these pacts to his Cabinet, Wilson said that he was reminded of Major Bingham's school at Asheville, where the headmaster called in boys who had been fighting and said: "Any boy may fight another boy if he feels he has a grievance, but before doing so he must come to me and state his grievance and the fight must be supervised under the Queensberry rules." The result, the President explained, was that there was no fighting. When it was suggested that other countries might not be willing to submit to supervision of disputes, Wilson explained: "Let them say so. It will put them to their trumps to give a reason for not talking over the matter." [3]

Promoted by Bryan in a stirring speech on May 9, the "Treaties for the Advancement of the General Peace" were concluded with twenty-one nations, including several major powers, and they took effect during 1913 and 1914. Proud of the achievement, Wilson boasted to Congress in his first annual address that "so far the United States has stood at the front of such negotiations."

During the early months of his administration, while the Bryan treaties were being negotiated and specific threats to peace were being warded off, Wilson came to see that he should assert his leadership constructively in world affairs. In dealing with the crises in relations with China, Japan, and Mexico, the President had learned that the Christian goodwill that his secretary of state exuded was not adequate

---

[2] Elihu Root's treaties of limited arbitration were renewed with some twenty-four nations in 1914.

[3] Daniels Diary, April 8, 1913. Wilson's brother attended the Bingham school.

to maintain peace. Nor was he content merely to rest upon traditional pillars of American diplomacy, such as the Monroe Doctrine in the Americas and the Open Door policy in the Far East. The opening of the Panama Canal gave to the President of the United States a responsibility unknown to James Monroe—that of protecting one of the main trade arteries of the world—and the nation's Caribbean policy had to take account of this fact.

In the autumn of 1913, after Huerta had repudiated his promise to hold a constitutional election, Wilson's sense of responsibility for political order led him to prescribe Presbyterian morality for the salvation of all mankind. The occasion was a meeting of the Southern Congress at Mobile, Alabama, where delegates from Latin America convened with their North American friends. Just before going to the Gulf city Wilson took part in the dedication of Congress Hall at Philadelphia and exhorted his audience to "look abroad at the horizon" and take into their lungs "the great air of freedom which has blown through this country and stolen across the seas and blessed people everywhere." Going on to Mobile by train with Josephus Daniels, he thought aloud about what he would say and asked for criticism. He intended at first to talk on rural credits. On the morning of his appearance, breakfasting at Mobile's Battle House on broiled squab and blanket pompano à la Daniels, he still had written no text for his speech.[4]

When he faced the Southern businessmen, who had been confused by his policy toward Mexico and who sought a restoration of business-as-usual, the prophet spoke out from his heart and asked for a "spiritual union" between the continents of the Western Hemisphere. "Interest does not tie nations together," he proclaimed. "It sometimes separates them. But sympathy and understanding does unite them . . ." Charging that states in Latin America had been exploited by foreign capital, he warned his fellow citizens: "We must show ourselves friends by comprehending their interest whether it squares with our own interest or not."

Then the prophet went on to set forth a still larger concept—"the development of constitutional liberty in the world." As a professor he had written of liberty as a principle to be won by self-discipline; but when he himself had suffered under the restraints that economic forces exert upon liberty he had become less interested in personal austerity and more concerned with the control of restraining influences everywhere. Now he said:

[4] Daniels, *The Wilson Era: Years of Peace*, p. 183; and Leon F. Sensabaugh, "Some Aspects of the Mobile Meeting of the Southern Commercial Congress," *Alabama Review*, July, 1953.

Human rights, national integrity, and opportunity as against material interests—that, ladies and gentlemen, is the issue which we now have to face. I want to take this occasion to say that the United States will never again seek one additional foot of territory by conquest. She will devote herself to showing that she knows how to make honorable and fruitful use of the territory she has, and she must regard it as one of the duties of friendship to see that from no quarter are material interests made superior to human liberty and national opportunity.

Conceiving of the diplomatic questions of the day as "shot through with the principles of life," he concluded with a burst of prophecy:

I am fain to believe that in spite of all the things that we wish to correct, the nineteenth century that now lies behind us has brought us a long stage toward the time when, slowly ascending the tedious climb that leads to the final uplands, we shall get our ultimate view of the duties of mankind. We have breasted a considerable part of that climb and shall presently—it may be in a generation or two—come out upon these great heights where there shines unobstructed the light of the justice of God.[5]

In glorifying the concepts of righteousness that had taken shape on campuses and in churches of the United States, Wilson met resistance from men who worshiped other gods in other ways. He encountered Philistines both at home and abroad. At Berlin his gospel was dismissed as "colossal arrogance." Having predicted that the modern age was to be ruled by morality, Wilson was inevitably faced by the question: "Whose morality?" The concern that he showed for good government in other nations of the hemisphere was pastoral; but if implemented by men of less exalted spirit, it could easily become imperialistic.

This possibility was raised in 1913 by events in other Latin-American countries than Mexico. Wilson was being embarrassed by fellow citizens who were promoting their own fortunes in ways that often brought economic benefits to the natives but at the same time curtailed their political liberty. The President had a private report from a consul in Honduras, for instance, that told of the exertion of political pressure

[5] Speaking at Mobile immediately after his chief, Secretary Daniels commended the vision that had been revealed. Here, he said, was "another Monroe," blazing the way for American solidarity and equal sovereignty of all countries, great and small.

A few weeks after the speech at Mobile, Wilson said to Congress in his first annual message: "There is only one possible standard by which to determine controversies between the United States and other nations, and that is compounded of these two elements: Our own honor and our obligations to the peace of the world. A test so compounded ought easily be made to govern both the establishment of new treaty obligations and the interpretation of those already assumed." In the long run, he insisted, a nation was made formidable not by force of arms but rather by a sense of righteousness that appealed to all humanity, and an unselfish passion to extend to others the blessings of its own society.

in that country by a Yankee corporation that wanted economic concessions; and he acted to curb what he regarded as illicit use of material
power.[6]

Moreover, there were other awkward situations to the southward of
which Wilson had little firsthand knowledge and which he could not
investigate thoroughly. Yankees with interests in Nicaragua were urging
ratification of a treaty that would yield an option on a canal route and
would assure them of financial power in that country and give them a
right to intervene in its politics in order to enforce their standards of
civic order. Bryan himself refused to withdraw the Marines and expose
the country to chaos and, finding no escape from the inevitability of
dollar diplomacy, approved the financial arrangement of New York
bankers. "We cannot escape the responsibilities of our position," he
wrote to Wilson on June 12, 1914.[7]

Furthermore, in the Dominican Republic, where insurrection and
Yankee intervention had become chronic, a "deserving Democrat"
whom Bryan had appointed minister proved to be a partisan of a
financial interest and supported a native cacique against widespread
popular opposition; and a henchman of William F. McCombs showed
incompetence as a receiver of customs duties. Wilson tried to enforce
his ideals by sending commissioners to watch an election in December
of 1913. Moreover, he dispatched a financial expert, who gave Washington such a discouraging report that the President lamented to Bryan:
"What a perplexing question of duty Santo Domingo offers us": and
a week later: "I am ashamed of myself that I have not been able to
think out a satisfactory solution."

Finally he appointed a commission and instructed it to attempt to
disband guerrilla forces and reconstruct political authority by supervising an election. Balloting was arranged and minorities were sternly

[6] The secret message from Honduras, sent by Consul General David J. D. Myers and
delivered to Wilson at Pass Christian by a young friend, Benjamin King, reported that an
American corporation had engineered a revolution that had overthrown a Honduran President
who had refused to grant certain concessions. Moreover, it was alleged that when the new
president also declined to do the company's bidding, the Yankees had decided to bring the
people to terms by refusing to buy their products. Few exports had moved for six months and as
a result conditions were very serious. When he learned of this, Wilson assured King that the
offending corporation would hear from him. Within a month after delivering his message to
the President, King had a letter from Myers stating that exports were flowing freely again
and that all was well. Letters, King to writer, Dec. 10, 1948, and Jan., 1955.

[7] "The proposed Nicaraguan treaty has my entire approval," Wilson wrote to Bryan on
June 19, 1913. By the end of 1915 Nicaragua was regarded in the State Department as a
"sphere of influence." On Aug. 5, 1914, the Bryan-Chamorro Treaty was signed, making
Nicaragua a protectorate of the United States; and on Feb. 18, 1916, the United States Senate,
fearful of German designs on Central America, approved it.

warned that they must abide by the outcome. Subsequently, however, it became necessary to send another special investigator [8] and to reappoint Taft's minister to supplant Bryan's appointee. Eventually, when fighting began in 1916, the Administration had to conclude that the only way to ensure peace was by exerting military control.

Moreover, when a revolution broke out in Haiti, early in 1914, American bankers proposed a plan for seizing the customhouses in that land, constructing a naval base, and taking as much responsibility for the government as seemed practical—a proposal not unacceptable to Bryan, who was alarmed by reports of German intrigues against the new Haitian regime. Though Wilson confessed to a "sneaking sympathy" for Haitian officials who resigned in protest, he talked with his Cabinet about applying commission rule, feeling it to be "necessary for Haiti's salvation." A year later a bloody revolt made it necessary to send bluejackets, and Haiti became a protectorate.

Thus in several instances Wilson's administration was pressed by interested individuals and by civic disorders to take political responsibility in regions to the south. It became embarrassing for the prophet to stand as the champion of liberty. This altruist who once had asserted that "free men need no trustees" was now in danger of incurring the onus of trusteeship. But in the cause of constitutional government he was as ready to bear the reproaches of jingoistic politicians in Latin America as he was to prevent ruthless exploitation of their peoples by foreign interests. As long as his conscience told him that he was acting unselfishly he could approve the use of force in Latin America.

However, the loftiness of his principles was poor consolation to proud Latins who resented Yankee meddling and the protectorates that resulted. The conclusion of the Bryan-Chamorro Treaty, for example, angered Nicaragua's neighbors, and they accused the United States of "flagrant" violation of international law and arraigned Nicaragua before the Central American Court of Justice.

To overcome the distrust and resentment of Latin Americans, an assertion of positive policy for the hemisphere was needed in the year 1914. Moreover, a bold move toward international reconciliation would contrast favorably with the ungloving of mailed fists in Europe. An idealistic project to preserve peace in the Americas was suggested to the President from several sources; and in the summer the possibilities of

---

[8] When this investigator, James D. Phelan, gave publicity to the shortcomings of the appointees sponsored by Bryan and Tumulty, Wilson was mortified and was disappointed in his secretary. Blum, *Tumulty*, pp. 113–15.

concerted action had been impressed upon him when the ABC powers had rescued him from his impasse with Huerta by proposing mediation.

Wilson responded with enthusiasm, therefore, when Colonel House urged upon him, on December 6, a Pan-American pact that would serve as a model for the European nations when they finished the war in which they were then deadlocked. Sensing a feeling among Latin Americans that the Monroe Doctrine was a one-sided understanding that the United States had imposed by *force majeur,* the Colonel envisaged an arrangement of mutual responsibility and mutual benefit. He hoped that, instead of merely resigning themselves to what they regarded as an offensive protectorate under the United States, the Latin peoples might come to give enthusiastic allegiance to a partnership and a pooling of interests. This ideal had been in the air since the time of Bolívar.

The wording of the pact that House envisaged was of little concern to the Colonel, provided that it was undertaken in a sincere spirit. Realizing that the President's creative impulse could be gratified by verbal expression, he asked his friend to draft a statement of their purposes. Thus encouraged, Wilson took a pencil and wrote words that were to have epochal significance in the history of the world:

1st. Mutual guarantees of political independence under republican form of government and mutual guarantees of territorial integrity.

2nd. Mutual agreement that the Government of each of the contracting parties acquire complete control within its jurisdiction of the manufacture and sale of munitions of war.

The President asked whether House had anything else in mind, and the Colonel replied that the two clauses seemed sufficient, taken in conjunction with the Bryan treaties of arbitration. Typing what he had written, Wilson gave the slip of paper to House to show to the ambassadors of Argentina, Brazil, and Chile, through whom it was planned to open negotiations. The President told House that in talking with the envoys he could be most emphatic in stating that the United States would not tolerate aggression upon other republics.

The Colonel began immediately to ingratiate himself with the ambassadors, and he returned to the President within a week bearing pledges of support from the emissaries of Argentina and Brazil. Wilson congratulated him, but wondered whether they might not be moving too fast for the Committee on Foreign Relations to follow. They decided to take up the matter with the senators immediately after Christmas, and the Colonel advised his friend to avoid making any appointments that might antagonize legislators whose support for the pact might be needed.

At the end of the year House still had no response from Chile, whose diplomats were embarrassed by a boundary dispute pending with Peru. Wilson continued to discuss the project with House; and he ascertained in a talk with Chairman Stone that the Committee on Foreign Relations would interpose no obstacles. He was anxious that news of the proposed pact should not leak out through unfriendly politicians, and accepted the suggestion of Argentina's envoy that terms should be agreed on in secret by the four initiating powers before the smaller republics were consulted.

Finally a reply came from Chile that, though ambiguous, was "favorable in principle." Reporting this to Wilson, House wrote on January 21: "Everything now seems in shape for you to go ahead. I believe the country will receive this policy with enthusiasm and it will make your Administration notable, even had you done but little else . . ."

A few days later House sailed for Europe, and in his absence neither Wilson nor Bryan took initiative to overcome Chile's aloofness. However, after the Colonel's return in June of 1915 the President talked more than once with him about reviving their plan for a Pan-American pact. The President typed out a new draft that set down four propositions; [9] and in an address to the Pan-American Scientific Congress on January 6, 1916, Wilson publicly announced the gist of his proposals. The nations of America had been uncertain, he confessed, as to what the United States would do with her power. "That doubt must be removed," he declared. "And latterly there has been a very frank interchange of views between the authorities in Washington and those who represented the other States of this hemisphere, an interchange . . . charming and hopeful." Detailing his four proposals, he then went on to invoke divine blessing on them:

They are going to lead the way to something that America has prayed for for many a generation. For they are based, in the first place, so far as the stronger states are concerned, upon the handsome principle of self-restraint

[9] Retaining as its first article the guarantee of "territorial integrity" and "political independence," the new proposal would commit the contracting parties (2) to try to reach amicable settlement of pending boundary disputes, either by direct negotiation or by arbitration; (3) to submit all unsettled questions to investigation by a permanent commission for one year, and then, if still undecided, to arbitration, "provided the question in dispute does not affect the honor, independence, or vital interests of the nations concerned or the interests of third parties"; and (4) to prevent forcible intervention and to embargo the shipment of arms in case of insurrections. For the text of the four articles, see *House Papers*, I, 233–34. Limitation of the private manufacture of arms, which had been included in Wilson's first draft, was now considered impractical because of the need that the United States government felt for a reliable supply of arms in case of involvement in the European war.

and respect for the rights of everybody. They are based upon the principles of absolute political equality among the States, equality of right, not equality of indulgence. They are based, in short, upon the solid eternal foundations of justice and humanity. No man can turn away from these things without turning away from the hope of the world . . .

Chile, however, remained unconvinced of the disinterestedness of the United States despite efforts by Colonel House at London to convert the Chilean ambassador there and to invoke the sanction of British opinion. Nevertheless, the President's enthusiasm for the project grew as he apotheosized it, and he was willing even to proceed independently of Chile; but without that nation's cooperation Argentina and Brazil were reluctant to go ahead. The atmosphere was clouded by the dispatch of a punitive expedition from the United States into Mexico, and the prospect of an American pact for peace faded. In the excitement of the 1916 election it was forgotten. When the United States found itself involved in war in 1917, the ideal that Wilson had failed to make effective in the Western Hemisphere was buried, only to be disinterred in 1918 and applied to the whole world.[10]

The proposal of a peace pact for the Americas aggravated the perplexity into which Latin-American diplomats were thrown by apparent contradictions between the protestations and the deeds of the "Colossus of the North." Intervention by force at Veracruz and in Nicaragua, Haiti, and the Dominican Republic, even though not without benefit to some of the inhabitants. comported little with Wilson's policy of watchful waiting and mediation and his concept of a Pan-American pact against aggression to be drawn up among equals. Latin Americans were at a loss to interpret the policy of a president who talked of liberty and constitutional processes while his fellow citizens wielded economic and military power.[11]

[10] In the spring of 1916, Wilson and House discussed the Pan-American pact several times and assigned to Ambassador Fletcher (who had served in Chile and was appointed to Mexico) the task of getting Chile's cooperation. When Wilson learned that Chile was demanding recognition of certain boundary claims as the price of consent, he refused to sanction any concession at the expense of weaker nations. Chile. for her part, suspected that the United States was interested chiefly in securing a share of Chilean minerals and in circumventing Japanese infiltration. It was House's hope that Britain might become a party to the envisioned pact in behalf of her American possessions, and the Colonel undertook to effect a change of phraseology that would make it possible for a monarchy to join an association of American "Republics." House Diary, May 13, 1916, and other entries. But British opinion, overruling Grey's desire to cooperate, feared to offend Japan by reassuring Chile, encouraging Canadian participation, or joining the pact in behalf of British Guiana and Honduras. *House Papers*, I, 222–31.

[11] The duality was nothing new in the history of the foreign relations of the United States. Wilson himself had perceived it in his professorial years. In 1901, writing on "Democracy and Efficiency," he had alluded to a "double temper" of the American people that had manifested

Realizing that the enterprising spirit of his people was natural, ineradicable, and precious if directed into virtuous channels, Wilson persisted in trying to guide it toward the accumulation of moral rather than material capital. He dared to undertake what only a great leader of men can achieve—to give to eternal political ideals a luster that would make them outshine, in the eyes of his people, the glitter of canals, roads, armaments, and financial profits.

The prophet's determination to make his nation stand before the world as the champion of international honor and justice led him, in the year 1914, to act decisively on two issues that grew out of the opening of the Panama Canal. These were questions that the President saw in black and white and he was willing to battle with advocates of dollar diplomacy to get a moral settlement.

In 1904, Wilson had questioned the justice of the coup by which Theodore Roosevelt had wrested the Panama Canal Zone from Colombia on terms unsatisfactory to that nation. To a student he had said: "Probably you have been taught that international law has no penal code. If it had, this would be described as petty larceny." [12] When the Colombian minister opened this old sore, the President was sympathetic. Declining to arbitrate the matter, the Administration undertook direct negotiations and showed a sincere desire to work out reasonable terms. Finally, in the spring of 1914, an agreement was reached by the diplomats. It provided that Colombia would have free use of the canal and an indemnity of $25,000,000—more than Wilson had offered at first and half of what Colombia had demanded. Further. the United States was to express "sincere regret that anything should have occurred to interrupt or to mar the relations of cordial friendship that had so long subsisted between the two nations."

When the compromise was submitted to the Senate on June 16, 1914, it drew the fire of Theodore Roosevelt, who looked upon it as a condemnation of his own work. He publicly damned the indemnity as "belated blackmail" and asserted that the Wilson administration had forfeited all right to the respect of the people of the United States.

The President, noting that the proposed agreement with Colombia was acclaimed more warmly by Latin Americans than by the people of the United States, explained publicly that ratification of the pact

---

itself in the days of Thomas Jefferson. "We have become confirmed," he had written, ". . . in the habit of acting under an odd mixture of selfish and altruistic motives." In 1911 he said: "We have a great ardour for gain, but we have a deep passion for the rights of man."

[12] Letter, Hugh MacNair Kahler to the writer, Nov. 10, 1955.

would give prestige to his country throughout Spanish America. "This nation can afford to be just," he declared; "even more, it can afford to be generous in the settling of disputes, especially when by its generosity it can increase the friendliness of the many millions in Central and South America with whom our relations become daily more intimate." But Wilson did not get the support in the Congress that he had hoped to enlist; and the Republican following of Roosevelt blocked ratification by the Senate.[13] However, all through his presidency his sponsorship of a compromise settlement of Colombia's claims commanded goodwill from the peoples to the south.

The other Panama Canal issue that challenged Wilson's sense of honor was that of tolls. In the Panama Act of August, 1912, the coast-to-coast ships of the United States had been exempted from canal charges. However, the British Foreign Office argued, quite correctly, that this measure violated the Hay-Pauncefote Treaty, which had been concluded between Britain and the United States in 1901. London proposed that the matter be submitted to arbitration, and just after the inauguration Ambassador Bryce pressed Bryan for immediate action.

President Taft and Secretary of State Knox had been willing to have the tolls issue studied, perhaps even arbitrated, by a commission. Furthermore, Wilson heard arguments for repeal from Elihu Root and from Joseph H. Choate, who had had a part in negotiating the Hay-Pauncefote Treaty. Before he entered the Presidency, Wilson had made up his mind that canal tolls should be paid by American ships as well as by those of other countries. He did not mention his decision in his inaugural address and did not reveal it to British statesmen. On April 15, 1913, however, he told his Cabinet that he was inclined to favor rescinding the exemption provision immediately. The nation's treaty of arbitration with Britain was to expire in June, he said, and it was doubtful that London would be willing to renew it until there was an adjustment of the tolls question.[14]

---

[13] When Wilson pressed the matter again in 1917, as a security measure in time of war, he was rebuffed. His statesmanlike long-range view was not accepted until the month after he left the White House, when Colombia was granted the indemnity but not the word of regret. See Richard L. Lael, *Struggle for Ratification: Wilson, Lodge, and the Thomson-Urrutia Treaty*, in *Diplomatic History*, vol. 2, no. 1 (winter 1978), pp. 81–102.

[14] To hasten action on renewal of the Root arbitration treaty of 1908, which Wilson thought "of the most vital importance" (W.W. to Bryan, June 13, 1913), Wilson talked personally with senators who feared that the pact might be an instrument for forcing the United States to yield on the matter of canal tolls. On July 3, 1913, Page and House explained to Grey why there was delay in repealing the objectionable tolls law. As a result the British statesman, perceiving that any semblance of pressure on his part would make it more difficult for Wilson to persuade the Congress to act, attempted to soothe the indignation of his own people. His patience was rewarded when, in November of 1913, the President explained to Sir William Tyrrell that he proposed to settle the controversy in conformity with the British view, which he considered the right one.

However, there was opposition from Anglophobes in the Senate, and Wilson wished to avoid unnecessary tiffs with party men while the tariff and currency bills were before them. Therefore, it was not until the very end of 1913, when the Federal Reserve Act had been signed and the new session of Congress began, that the tolls problem was formally introduced by Chairman Adamson of the House's Committee on Interstate and Foreign Commerce, with whom Wilson had discussed suspending the tolls exemption for a two-year period. Urged by Page to act before the British Parliament convened, the President decided to invite the Senate Committee on Foreign Relations to the White House. On January 26, in a three-hour conference that reviewed critical foreign issues, Wilson said that free use of the canal by American coastwise vessels was clearly a violation of the Hay-Pauncefote Treaty and should be stopped either by repealing the exemption clause of the Panama Act or by suspending its operation. A few days later Wilson wrote a letter for publication in which he denounced the tolls exemption not only as a breach of treaty but as an unfair benefit to a monopoly.

Finally, on March 5, 1914, he stated his position formally in a five-minute speech before the Congress. He did this without consulting his Cabinet, with whom the tolls issue had not been discussed for almost a year, and he based his case on world opinion rather than upon legalistic interpretations. He said: "I ask this of you in support of the foreign policy of the administration. I shall not know how to deal with other matters of even greater delicacy and nearer consequence if you do not grant it to me in ungrudging measure." [15]

The position that Wilson took warmed the hearts of Britain's noblest statesmen. Page was ecstatic, and in his ebullience he followed too closely the parting advice that the President had given him—"go, and be yourself." Making a public speech that reflected the remarks Wilson had made at Mobile, the ambassador said that Americans would "prefer" that European powers acquire no more territory on their continent.

Unluckily, Page's generous words were misinterpreted by the Anglophobe press in the United States to mean that the United States would not forbid European aggression in the Western Hemisphere. Malevolent fury stirred in Irish-Americans and German-Americans. Learning of

[15] On March 26, 1914, Wilson interpreted this cryptic sentence to newsmen as a reference to the reputation for good faith that would be needed in entering into new treaties. Giving credence to this motive as a partial explanation, Notter comments: "There would be no justification, however, for concluding that Wilson had not in mind also at this time the justice—and possibly the necessity—of giving support to the British argument against the toll clause in exchange for their support of his Mexican policy." Notter, op. cit., pp. 286–87. When this interpretation was made by Republicans, Wilson called it a prevarication.

this, the ambassador quickly apologized to Wilson and offered to resign if he could thus gain a single vote for the cause in Congress; but the President, acknowledging that his friend had erred in touching even lightly upon a subject so explosive, loyally assured Page of his confidence and admiration. Contemptuous of those who were making trouble, Wilson wrote to his conscience-stricken ambassador: "We shall try to cool the excited persons on this side of the water, and I think nothing further will come of it." [16]

Page's indiscreet speech forced Wilson to fight all the harder to counteract the jingoism of hyphenated Americans and certain legislators who depended on their votes. On March 26, in a vigorous news interview, full of hard sense and homely anecdote, the President denied that the British government had been "exercising pressure" upon him; and to Democrats who thought themselves bound by the party platform he pointed out that actually there was in it two contradictory planks: one favoring free use of the canal; and another denouncing subsidies. Free tolls were in his view a subsidy. He welcomed support from Republican senators—the intellectual vigor of Root and the quiet voice of McCumber—and he took pains to acknowledge Lodge's "generous comprehension," first by letter and later by a telephone call. [17]

Wilson's heart was now thoroughly committed to battle and he put his weight behind a bill providing for outright repeal. He told Tumulty, who warned him of the reaction of Irish voters, that if Congress failed to support his position he would resign from office and go to the people and ask whether the United States was to stand before the world as a nation that violated its contracts as a matter of convenience and expedi-

[16] W.W. to Page, April 2, 1914. Page was writing to House that his expenses at London exceeded his means and that unless help was provided he must resign before the end of 1914. Page to House, undated, and *ibid.*, Jan. 30, 1914, House Collection. By summer the ambassador's distress became so acute that Wilson wrote his friend Cleveland Dodge that Page, who had "furnished him more light on difficult matters" than all other informants and advisers put together, needed an annual grant of $25,000 from a source that would not put him under obligations. Dodge agreed to provide the whole sum himself and to tell no one but his wife, and he thanked his friend for this "new mark of . . . confidence."
"Friendship such as yours," Wilson responded, "coming by fresh proof to me here in the midst of business at every turn of which it is necessary, in common caution, to scrutinize motives and reckon with what may be covertly involved, is like God's pure air to a man stifled and breathing hard to keep his lungs going." W.W. to Dodge, July 12, and 19, 1914; Dodge to W.W., July 13, 1914.
[17] Garraty, *Henry Cabot Lodge*, pp. 299–300. *Page Letters*, I, 257. As the battle of tolls repeal reached its height, Wilson was deprived of the services of Counselor John Bassett Moore of the State Department who, tired of working with Bryan appointees whom he thought incompetent (House Diary, Jan. 26, 1914), resigned on Mar. 4, 1914. He was succeeded on March 27 by Robert Lansing, a New York lawyer who was recommended by Elihu Root. House's Diary (Nov. 7, 1914) records that Wilson spoke of Lansing as more satisfactory than Moore.

ency. Bryan, who had been unconvinced until he felt the force of the President's appeal to righteousness, now supported him with an editorial in the *Commoner*; Burleson sat at the telephone and kept the wire to the Capitol hot with exhortations to legislators who looked to him for patronage; and Tumulty worked upon younger congressmen who were most responsive to the President's leadership. Despite the fiery opposition of Champ Clark and Underwood and the Irish-Americans, the House voted for repeal by a margin of 247 to 162. The Senate finally ended several weeks of oratorical fireworks by appoving the measure 50 to 35; and Wilson signed it on June 15, 1914.

With the tolls issue settled and Huerta shorn of power, Wilson was rid of two immediate problems that had been disturbing the relations of the United States with European powers. Sir Edward Grey, his patience vindicated, proclaimed in Parliament that Wilson's motive all along had been not an impulse to drive a bargain with Britain but rather a conviction that governments must never flinch from interpreting treaty rights in a strictly fair spirit. On March 11, London had approved the extension of the Anglo-American arbitration treaty of 1908; and on September 15 the two nations signed a Bryan pact.

The repeal of tolls exemption, however, was not so popular a triumph in the United States as those of the New Freedom had been. In bringing about repeal, the President had repudiated a plank in the party platform and had had to explain that a pre-election promise regarding foreign affairs is no more than "half a promise," and subject to foreign elements beyond control.

Wilson himself felt that the risk he had run in incurring the hostility of equivocating politicians was justified by the majesty of moral triumph. "If everything else in connection with this administration is forgotten," he said one day *en famille*, "the action in regard to Panama will be remembered because it is a long step forward in putting the relationships of nations and the dealings of one nation with another on a par with the dealings of honorable men, one with another."

By the summer of 1914, by force of necessity and the President's sense of personal accountability, foreign relations had replaced domestic reforms as the center of the President's interest. Wilson had come through the ordeal of foreign crises with his fundamental political faith unshaken. Holding his direction steadfastly toward morality and moderation, he had clung to his belief that the popular opinion of his hemisphere would respond to the ideals that he honored and that he had set forth publicly. Though he knew now, better than ever before, the strength of native pride and suspicion, he still imagined that among Latin-American peoples there existed a latent sense of political responsibility akin to that of his own people. Through conferences that would appeal to their common humanity, he saw hope of reaching solutions of hemispheric problems that would have effective sanction.

Woodrow Wilson's native faith had vaulted to embrace a hemisphere as nimbly as it had risen to take in a university, a state, and then a nation. Would its evangelistic power, feeding upon communion with congregations of increasing size, be strong enough to sanctify a new order in an entire world that, in the summer of 1914, seemed to be falling rapidly into political bankruptcy?

CHAPTER XXIII

In the Valley of the Shadow

As the prophet reached out to embrace the peoples of the Western Hemisphere and make them a family of nations, the breaking up of his own idyllic household was piercing his heart.

Woodrow Wilson always had enjoyed sanctuary in a sympathetic home. His affection for his dear ones was childlike, his concern for their welfare almost motherly. He expected obedience from them, but exacted it courteously: one day when a daughter wished to go riding in the park with friends whom he thought undesirable, he asked, "M'dear, can't you find a better way to occupy your time?" [1] Often the Wilsons planned their engagements so that the clan could be together, alone, on birthdays and other special occasions; and once the President canceled a weekend trip on the *Mayflower* in order to give moral support to daughter Margaret, who would otherwise have to stay alone at the White House and prepare for a speaking engagement about which she was nervous. His second daughter, Jessie, had been married less than five months when his secretary of the Treasury came to him to ask the hand of his youngest, his spirited, lovable Nellie; and after this conversation McAdoo wrote confidentially to House: "Miss Eleanor and I are engaged! 'The Governor' has consented and I am supremely happy." [2]

It was difficult for Woodrow Wilson to accept the departure of his little playmate—the girl for whom he had toiled on an American History so that she might have a pony. "I shall be poor without her," he wrote to Mary Hulbert, "she and I have been such ideal chums! It's hard, very hard, not to be selfish and rebel,—or repine! But her happiness is of much more importance than mine,—I mean to me." At the wedding, as he walked down the corridor to the Blue Room, prepared to give her away, he was relieved by a chance to chuckle to himself when

[1] Mrs. Katharine Woodrow Kirkland to the writer.

[2] McAdoo to House, Mar. 3, 1914, House Collection. According to Edith Galt Wilson, Woodrow Wilson was opposed to the betrothal because of the difference in ages. E. B. Wilson to R. S. Baker, Jan. 4. 1926. This marriage posed problems of decorum. Foreseeing that the President might be embarrassed by the presence of a relative in his Cabinet, McAdoo offered to resign; but Wilson assured him that, since he had been appointed solely on grounds of merit, he must not think of leaving. The President was careful to preserve impartiality in Cabinet meetings and fairness in all other relations. House Diary, April 15, 28, 29, 1914.

the train of her wedding dress overturned and she whispered desperately to tell an attendant to right it; but when the wedding party went out to the porch to see the bride off, the President had no spirit for the occasion. He remained inside; and Colonel House, who stayed with him, jotted in his diary that night: "I think he loves her better than any member of his household."

At the same time Wilson was worried about the health of one whom he had loved longer than Nellie; and furthermore, one on whom he depended more implicitly than on any other living soul. It was the wisdom of Ellen Wilson that had made the White House the home that he needed. She cultivated family piety of the Roman sort, a devotion that was to her something in the blood that drew relatives together whether they found each other queer or not.

The responsibilities of her role sometimes had seemed more than she could bear. On Inauguration Day her courage had failed for a moment, and rebelling against the noise and confusion of notoriety, she had covered her face with her hands and wept. She had played her part pluckily, however. Delegating responsibility wisely, she made even the large functions beautiful and unpretentious.

Many times she visited back alleys in which Negroes lived in squalor, often taking congressmen with her. She talked to the people, helping them with food and money, and gently insisted that legislative action be taken. Finding no rest rooms in public buildings, she had them installed for the workers. Day after day she came home worn and pale, changed her dress, and went to the Red Room to receive guests with her sweet, calm smile. Energetic philanthropists perceived her sensitivity and exploited it for their favorite causes with tales of woe. "I wonder how anyone who reaches middle age can bear it," she said one day to a cousin, "if she cannot feel, on looking back, that whatever mistakes she may have made she has on the whole lived for others and not for herself."

Amidst all her duties, domestic and civic, she never failed her husband. Though never interfering in an embarrassing way, she proved herself one of his soundest advisers on matters of public policy; and because her devotion was unquestionable, her motives pure, and her wisdom proven, he listened to her counsel as to that of no man. Questions that perplexed him sorely, like relations with Mexico, she studied with him. She tempered his moral fervor with sweet reason and fostered his understanding with House, Tumulty, and the Cabinet. She even protected his ears from petty gossip that might arouse prejudice against men who were valuable to him.

Early in 1914, as the weakness of disease stole over her, Ellen Wilson had less heart than ever for political strife, and she joined Tumulty in an effort to persuade the President not to risk a split in the party by insisting on repeal of the Panama tolls exemption. But she still encouraged her husband in carrying on the badinage with other ladies from which he derived refreshment. Though for his sake she invited Mary Hulbert to visit the White House, she did not enjoy the artful nonsense of this guest; and she delegated to Helen Bones—who thought her Cousin Woodrow something of a goose to be so easily titillated— the duty of protecting the President from malicious gossip by chaperoning his rides with his playmate.[3]

On the first day of March Ellen Wilson fell on the floor of her bedroom, aggravating a kidney ailment that had bothered her for a long time. The shock and soreness kept her in bed for more than two weeks. By sheer will she gathered her forces, and at Eleanor's wedding on May 7 she seemed her old self; but soon nervous indigestion was plaguing her constantly and it seemed impossible to get enough food or rest. She insisted that she must diet but the President spent hours at her bedside, coaxing: "Please do eat just a little of this. You will soon get well, darling, if you'll try hard to eat something. Now please take this bite, dear."

Lying on her sofa, very white, she refused to let callers talk about her condition. She spoke with tender pride of her husband, who was still her "noticeable man," in need of her ministration, and only incidentally President of the United States. One day she wrote indignant notes, which were never sent, to senators who were attacking his policies. The White House gardens were a joy to her, particularly one that she had planned herself. On fair afternoons she sat among her flowers and watched them bloom while her strength faded. "It will be so lovely, Charley," she said one day to the gardener who was carrying out her plans, "but I'll never live to see it finished."[4]

Late in May Dr. Grayson was alarmed by her symptoms and called specialists. The case was one of Bright's disease and it was hopeless. There were rallies, but they were temporary. Gradually her husband came to realize the truth, though his physician, who had learned that there were indications of a hardening of the President's arteries, strove to protect him from the ravages of worry.

Snatching moments from his engagements to take tea with the family

[3] Several letters, Helen W. Bones to the writer; also R. W. Woolley's account of conversations with Stockton Axson; Elizabeth Jaffray's book, *Secrets of the White House*, p. 35, and her articles in *Cosmopolitan*, January and February, 1927.

[4] Charles Hemlock and Margaret Norris, "Flowers for First Ladies," the *Saturday Evening Post*, Nov. 28, 1931. And Helen Bones to Margaret Callaway Axson, June 25, 1914, letter in possession of the latter.

circle, Wilson kept his eyes upon his Ellen's face, and before leaving the room he would hold her close for a moment. Relatives who had never heard an irate word pass between them were impressed more than ever by the blend of love and respect in his voice when he spoke her name; and they felt that no man and wife could be more truly one. His walk was no longer buoyant, and deep lines furrowed his gaunt face. Anxiety hung heavy upon him, and he said that he felt like a man suffering from malaria.

As the summer's heat mounted, Ellen Wilson would not seek coolness and quiet at Harlakenden, for separation from her Woodrow appalled her more than hot weather. She urged him to escape to the golf course, but he would not. Instead he sat very quiet outside her room, trying to put his mind on public business, but now and then giving up and tip-toeing over to lean against her door to listen. Sometimes he would get up in the night to comfort her and would sit by her bed and do his work until early morning.

Toward the end of the month Dr. Grayson moved into a room next to hers, where he could be on duty day and night. When he told Wilson that his daughters should be close at hand, the President at last accepted the truth. In the wilting heat the White House seemed drained of life. "Cousin" Lucy Smith, whom Ellen Wilson had asked to come with her sister Mary to cheer Woodrow, was stricken with appendicitis and rushed to a hospital. Little Helen Bones, the President's playfellow since Eleanor had left the household, was ill, delirious with fever. Wilson was unresponsive to efforts of others to console him. "I carry lead at my heart all the time," he wrote to Mary Hulbert on August 2. "I am held in Washington by the most serious duties any President has had to perform since Lincoln."

During the months of Ellen Wilson's decline, the confidential messages that dropped upon the President's desk had revealed a menace of war abroad. For a year Page's letters had told of Europe's diplomatic dilemma. "There's no future in Europe's vision—no long look ahead . . . ." the ambassador reported. "The Great Powers are—mere threats to one another, content to check, one the other! There can come no help to the progress of the world from this sort of action: no step forward." Page had dared to dream that the President himself might go abroad and stand beside the King of England and let the world take a good look at them. "Nothing else would give such a friendly turn to the whole world as the President's coming here," Page had written to House on August 25, 1913. "The old Earth would sit up and rub its eyes and take notice to whom it belongs. This visit might prevent an

English-German war and an American-Japanese war, by this mere show of friendliness. It would be one of the greatest occasions of our time. Even at my little speeches, they 'whoop it up'! What would they do over the President's!"

Wilson had been tempted by the appeal and appreciated the reasons for it; but he had felt that he must decline. "The case against the President's leaving the country," he wrote, "particularly now that he is expected to exercise a constant leadership in all parts of the business of the government, is very strong and I am afraid overwhelming. It might be the beginning of a practice of visiting foreign countries which would lead Presidents rather far afield." [5]

Early in 1914, Wilson's popularity in England had risen, and the ambassador reported that his stock was "at a high premium." Thinking it more than ever desirable that the President's moral influence be exerted to keep peace in Europe, House developed a grand plan. Since the main obstacles to international reconciliation seemed to lie in Berlin, the persuasive Colonel proposed to beard the Junkers in their den and make them see the folly of their opposition to arbitration and disarmament. The Colonel perceived that a reconciliation of the naval interests of Britain and Germany might impair the power of the United States on the high seas; but he was willing to run this risk in the interest of peace, for he felt that the outbreak of a European war would end the long period of isolation in which the extraordinary prosperity of the United States had been incubated. Moreover, taking up a constructive suggestion that Page had made and that would put the principles of Wilson's Mobile speech in play, House aspired to commit the rulers of England and Germany to an understanding on other matters that threatened the world's peace.[6]

On December 12, 1913, the Colonel had found Wilson ready to

[5] *Page Letters*, I, 271, 275–76. The President's decision may well have been based, at least in part, on a fear of seeming to commit the United States to alliance with Britain.

[6] He was especially eager to set up international machinery for developing backward lands in the interest of their inhabitants.

The Colonel discussed this far-reaching and ultimately fruitful proposal with Sir Edward Grey and others on June 24. They approved the plan in general, but said that it must be initiated by the President, because of the Monroe Doctrine.

After further discussions with British diplomats, House reported to Wilson on July 4: "It was the general consensus of opinion that a great deal of friction in the future would be obviated if some such understanding could be brought about in this direction, and that it would do as much as any one thing to insure international amity." *House Papers*, I, 266. Moreover, Sir Edward Grey was deeply interested in the idea and pledged his government's cooperation. Further discussions at London were planned, but the outbreak of war caused the shelving of the proposal. However, House and Wilson did not forget it. The Colonel discussed it in a talk with Wilson on Aug. 30, 1914; and the principles of the development of countries under a trusteeship blossomed forth in the mandatory system of the League of Nations. It seemed to the Colonel that had such a plan been in force, with the powers meeting at regular intervals, World War I probably would not have occurred.

facilitate disarmament by seeking legislation that would permit him to cut his nation's battleship budget if the Europeans should agree on a naval holiday. And so House set out to learn all that he could about German psychology and the character of the Kaiser. In May of 1914, with Page's encouragement and with an informal note of credence from Wilson, he went to Berlin. Before the end of the month he reported to the President that jingoism had "run stark mad," that unless someone acting for the American President could intervene effectively, there would be "an awful cataclysm." Soon afterward House wrote that he had been granted a private conversation with Wilhelm II, that he had let it be known that the President of the United States had courage as resolute and a will as inflexible as Bismarck himself, and that it was arranged that the Colonel was to keep the Kaiser informed after the Foreign Office at London was sounded.[7]

Wilson joyfully welcomed the reports of his enterprising diplomatic spokesman. "Your letter gives me a thrill of deep pleasure," he responded on June 16. "You have, I hope and believe, begun a great thing and I rejoice with all my heart. You are doing it, too, in just the right way with your characteristic tact and quietness and I wish you Godspeed in what follows. I could not have done the thing nearly so well." It was "a great source of strength and relief" to have an understanding friend to interpret his purposes to European statesmen.[8] In replying to House the President rarely commented on specific policies and procedures: he was content, as in his relations with others to whom he had given his whole heart, to bless any arrangement that satisfied their common will to serve. House's aggressive venture stirred the frontier spirit in Wilson, and he hoped that his friend was finding it exhilarating.

While the diplomats of Europe dallied and the Kaiser raced in his yacht at Kiel, a fateful spark was struck in the Balkans. On June 28 the heir apparent to the throne of Austria-Hungary was murdered at Sarajevo, and the German government, believing that Russia would not intervene forcibly, sanctioned any punitive measures against Serbia that Vienna might decide upon. When House wrote to the Kaiser on July 7 to report that the British government desired to reach an understanding

---

[7] *House Papers,* I, 249; and House to Wilson, June 3 and 11, 1914. Wilhelm II concurred in the view that an agent of the American President might act more effectively to avert war than a European, and he seemed pleased that House was undertaking the task; but, being obsessed by distrust of Japan and Russia, he demanded a navy large enough for defense against the combined fleets of France and Russia. Moreover, he objected to treaties of arbitration for the reason that he conceived Germany's defense to rest upon a degree of preparedness for war that would bring a quick victory.

[8] W.W. to House, June 16 and 22, 1914, House Collection. The Colonel's ego was so flattered by the President's "thrill of deep pleasure" that he quoted part of the letter of June 16 to his son-in-law, Gordon Auchincloss.

that would lay the foundation of permanent peace and security,[9] it was too late to get a response. Wilhelm II had gone on a Scandinavian cruise, and the ignited fuse was burning rapidly toward the heap of fears and hates that had been piled up for a decade by powers that had been combining and arming for war.

At the end of July new problems piled suddenly upon the United States government. Ocean liners were held in ports and tens of thousands of travelers were clamoring for funds and for transatlantic passage. Domestic business, already shaken by prolonged strikes and by uncertainties aroused by the New Freedom, was further dislocated by dread of an armed conflict that, some thought, might put an end to modern civilization in Europe. When Austria-Hungary declared war on Serbia, on July 28, financial markets became panicky. On July 31 the New York Stock Exchange was closed. What the European governments had been preparing for they were now to have—war on a vaster scale than the world had ever experienced. Wilson was amazed that in the twentieth century mankind could be so stupid. Learning of Austria's declaration of war, he said to his family at luncheon: "Incredible—it's incredible."

Preoccupied as he had been by antimonopoly legislation and by Latin-American affairs, the President had given no deep thought to the European problems of which House had written informally. He had expressed fear [10] that the spark in the Balkans would set off a general explosion, but his envoys in Europe, save House, were writing that there was no great danger. He was as surprised by the outbreak of hostilities, and almost as grieved, as he had been by the Mexican resistance that had cost the lives of his boys at Veracruz. What was to happen? his daughters asked him. Would the whole world be involved?

He stared as if dazed, covered his eyes, and replied: "I can think of

---

[9] Actually, though Grey was sympathetic to House's ideas, British politicians feared that diplomatic talks with Germany might disturb the nation's defensive *entente* with France and Russia. Moreover, party feelings were strong in England, the Cabinet was preoccupied with a crisis in Ireland, and suffragettes were threatening to dynamite the Houses of Parliament.

[10] To Louis Brownlow on July 1, 1914. Brownlow lecture at University of Chicago, Mar. 2, 1956.

On July 3, Colonel House had written to inform Wilson that Sir Edward Grey wished him to convey the ideas of the British government to the Kaiser and to try to arrange a meeting at Kiel, "so there may be no go-between or misunderstanding." The Colonel's letter concluded: "So you see things are moving in the right direction as rapidly as we could hope." Though Sir Edward Grey sent word to House on July 20 that the Austro-Serbian crisis was giving him grave concern, the Colonel, sailing for Boston the next day, did not communicate Sir Edward's feelings to the President until July 31, after House had landed in the United States and war between Austria-Hungary and Serbia had begun; and even in his letter of that date the Colonel suggested that a general conflict might be averted as a result of the improvement in British-German relations that he fancied he had brought about. Wilson was without warning of immediate disaster from his trusted agent until he was informed by a House letter of Aug. 1 that Germany, realizing that her best chance of victory lay in striking fast and hard, might take precipitate action in what she conceived to be self-defense. See *House Papers*, I, 271–81.

nothing—nothing, when my dear one is suffering. Don't tell your mother anything about it." Ellen Wilson never knew of the blotting out of the vision of human concord that she had shared with her husband.

In the first week of August declarations of war were exchanged and German forces violated the Belgian border, striking quickly for victory, as House had warned they would. Ellen Wilson sank rapidly, and on the 6th Dr. E. P. Davis, one of "Tommie" Wilson's Princeton classmates, had to tell the family that the end was only hours away.

After luncheon the President went upstairs with his daughters. He sat on the edge of the bed, clasping his Ellen's hand, looking beseechingly at Dr. Grayson for a sign of encouragement. A murmur came from the serene face on the pillow as the physician bent over it: "Promise me that you will take good care of my husband." Then the breathing grew fainter. The daughters, kneeling, saw on their mother's face a smile that they thought divine. Downstairs the chimes of a clock struck softly, five times. The President asked: "Is it all over?" The doctor nodded, and Woodrow Wilson's head fell forward. "When you die, I shall die," he had once written to her.[11] Walking to a window and looking out, he cried: "Oh, my God, what am I to do?"

Mostly he kept his grief in his Scottish innerliness, not daring to give it any escape for fear that it would burst all controls. They heard him say, as he pulled himself together, "I must not give way." He sat in a chair for endless hours, day and night, in lonely vigil beside a sofa on which the lifeless figure lay, its shoulders draped by a white silk shawl that he himself had thrown over them. Fighting valiantly for self-mastery, he came in to the services in the East Room only when the guests had been seated. The family did not feel that their emotions could endure funeral music, and there was no sound but the rustling of palm leaves near the open windows, and the voice of the minister: "Let not your heart be troubled: Ye believe in God, believe also in me." Afterward the President sent for his pastor and, head bowed and shaking with grief, thanked him. Later in the day, driving to the station to take a train for Rome, Georgia, he went quietly through the less-frequented streets.

At the destination, while several cousins of Ellen Wilson placed the casket in the hearse, the President stood very erect and fixed his eyes upon it as if seeking to penetrate it. He remained there beside it, alone, until the time came to go to the service at Rome's Presbyterian church, where he first had been attracted by the radiance of Miss Ellie Lou.

[11] Letter of W.W. to E.A.W. read to the writer by Eleanor Wilson McAdoo.

After the pastor spoke briefly and two of her favorite hymns were sung, the mourners were driven in carriages to the Axson lot in the cemetery on Myrtle Hill.

Beneath a great oak overlooking the Etowah River, Woodrow Wilson stood over the grave. Tombs of Confederate soldiers were round about —reminders of the scourge that was threatening again, after a half century, to afflict the United States. A canopy protected the gathering from rain that was beginning to fall; but soon there was a rush of wind and the flowers were scattered. The President stood unmoved by anything but the emotional storm within. For several minutes after the casket had been lowered he remained beside the grave and his eyes glistened. He assured himself that the separation was, after all, only temporary, for their love was immortal. He told Colonel Brown—the cousin who had charge of the funeral arrangements—that he wished to have space made for his own burial by the side of his beloved, and it was arranged to broaden the terrace.[12]

To mark her grave he ordered a stone of rare Italian marble, on which a woman's profile was to be carved by Ellen Wilson's favorite sculptor. He insisted that the little monument should be simple and fitting, in harmony with the headstones of her relatives. To the inscription he gave as much care as he had bestowed on that for the grave of the other immortal soul to whom he acknowledged eternal gratitude —his father. Finally he chose lines of William Wordsworth:

> A traveller between life and death;
> The reason firm, the temperate will,
> Endurance, foresight, strength, and skill;
> A perfect woman, nobly planned,
> To warn, to comfort, and command
> And yet a spirit still, and bright
> With something of angelic light.

He went back to Washington more lonely than he had ever been. He must face not only his own anxious people, but a whole war-ridden world, alone. The only human being who knew him perfectly, the only one who could rest him, was gone. The personality that had given him

---

[12] Mrs. Hallie Alexander Rounseville and Wade Hoyt, who was a pallbearer, to the writer. The writer was told by Mrs. Rounseville, who was president of the Ellen Axson Wilson Memorial Circle of Rome ladies who undertook to beautify and care for the grave, that Mrs. Wilson's tomb was made waterproof so that the body could be moved in case the President was not buried at Rome. A clipping dated Aug. 12, 1914, from a newspaper that cannot be identified, reports that the grave was completely covered by concrete and steel. Clipping in possession of Margaret Callaway (Mrs. B. Palmer) Axson.

courage to enter public life was no longer present to sustain him. No gentle hand met his groping one. No longer, before falling asleep and after awakening, would he have a partner to whom he could safely confess everything and from whom he could get oracular advice.

Dr. Grayson and the ladies of his family looked out for his bodily and mental health. Daughter Margaret became head of the household and Helen Bones came out of her delirious fever to hear McAdoo say: "You must care for him now." This little cousin worked with devotion and understanding to alleviate the loss, seeking to rally the President with levity, mixing a mild toddy for him now and again, and occasionally teasing him to sip port after eating foods that the doctor prescribed. The Smiths stayed on at the White House, too, and within the little circle of adoring ladies who vied with each other to please the great man, Wilson bravely kept up his custom of good talk and readings of poetry. He indulged his relatives in many ways. He took some of them through the White House from top to bottom. Though he often had paced the main corridors alone, hands behind back, this was his first complete tour of his dwelling.

But among the friends and relatives there was no guardian angel for his soul, no one who could say "Oh, Woodrow, you don't mean that!" Sometimes he stole away to the Corcoran Art Gallery to look at pictures of which Ellen Wilson had been fond. He carried out her commitments to charities, insisting that a fund sponsored by her for the education of mountain youth should be administered in a nonsectarian spirit. When instances of injustice or misfortune to individuals came to the President's notice, in the months of mourning, he seemed to respond as she would have wished. Even in death his Ellen was an angel of charity and conciliation. Old friends who had been estranged were moved by her passing to write to him in genuine sympathy. And he replied warmly.[13]

Finally, on August 17, he summoned courage to reply to a letter of sympathy received from House: "My dear, dear Friend: . . . I have acknowledged many letters of condolence but I am writing today for the first time to those whose friendship is dearest to me because there is something deeper in that and it is harder to get one's self-possession in doing it. I do not know of any letter which touched me more deeply

[13] One of those who sent a letter of condolence was "Marse Henry" Watterson. Another was Jennie Hibben, who wrote from St. Moritz: "All the years of sad estrangement grow dim and we remember only the days when we were young and happy . . . Jack and Beth join me . . . Ever yours." To this Wilson replied on Sept. 18: "I sincerely and warmly thank you . . . In these days when the darkness has settled about me thoughts of those old days at Princeton 'when we were young and happy' flash in upon me with peculiar brightness, despite the sadness that inevitably follows them." Scoon Papers (Princeton University Library).

than yours did . . . May God show me the way! Affectionately yours."

In his bereavement Wilson grasped and relished every recollection that his memory could supply, as well as those offered by friends and relatives. Yet, shaken as he was, he was finding in himself, in the summer of 1914, a toughness that surprised him. When the heat in Washington reached 100 degrees in the shade, Grayson tried to make him board the *Mayflower* and cruise to Beverly to visit House. But he would not hear of it. Wilson still thought that the Presidency would kill him; but somehow the catastrophe did not come off. He went at his work grimly, hoping to find release from his grief there. Though he refused to grant nonessential interviews, he insisted on seeing full copies of the reports from his diplomats abroad. He found little light upon the causes and significance of the war in the dispatches that came daily from chancelleries beset by panicky American tourists; but he plodded through them and through the mass of messages and articles that piled up on his desk, in the hope of broadening his understanding of his responsibility.

During the first week of August, while his dear one lay prostrate, Woodrow Wilson had met the impact of world war as his own conscience dictated. His first impulse had been to minister to his own country. Controlling his own feelings superbly, he had left his wife's chamber on August 3 to address newsmen in another room of the White House. Warning them against rousing public hysteria, assuring them that the government was meeting the emergency in finance and trade, he said: "I want to have the pride of feeling that America, if nobody else, has her self-possession and stands ready with calmness of thought and steadiness of purpose to help the rest of the world. And we can do it and reap a great permanent glory out of doing it, provided we all cooperate to see that nobody loses his head."

Formal proclamations of neutrality were issued, but this conventional step did not satisfy the President's desire to lead his people in serving mankind. If his nation was to work effectively for peace, he foresaw, mere legality of action would not be enough. He must cultivate a national attitude that by its justness would win the respect of all belligerents. He was glad, therefore, to meet the wishes of Bryan, and at the same time carry out the will of the Senate, by sending an offer of mediation to the rulers of the belligerent powers. After a long session with his Cabinet on August 4—the day of Germany's violation of Belgium's "territorial integrity"—Wilson had gone to his wife's bedside and composed this message:

As official head of one of the powers signatory to The Hague Convention, I feel it to be my privilege and my duty under article three of that Convention to say to you in a spirit of most earnest friendship that I should welcome an opportunity to act in the interest of European peace, either now or at any other time that might be thought more suitable, as an occasion to serve you and all concerned in a way that would afford me lasting cause for gratitude and happiness.[14]

Unfortunately, the offer of mediation did no immediate good except to establish the intent of the United States, for each warring government replied with a justification of its position. The President's desk was bombarded by partisan views of war guilt and by pleas for American participation in the fighting. Wilson was sickened by the contentious frenzy of hyphenated Americans and of self-appointed dispensers of "justice." In his determination to preserve neutrality in thought and action he shied even from a suggestion made by House and Olney. These men thought that the press should be allowed to state, "on high authority," what the Colonel and Page had done to reconcile England and Germany; but the President sensed that such a revelation might place the United States government in the position of an accuser of Germany.

Wilson's scholarly training demanded that he keep his mind open to hard fact and wait as long as necessary to understand exactly how the war originated; and the very superficiality of his knowledge of the causes of conflict made it the easier for him to take a detached point of view. Reading an article by Professor Albert Bushnell Hart, whose criticism had helped him to produce his own best work in history, he was struck by the iniquity of the whole diplomatic web that had caught the statesmen of Europe in its meshes and held them from reaching a peaceful solution.[15] Between Germany and Russia he saw little choice. If the Central Allies won, German militarism would be supreme; if the Entente won, czarist tyranny would dominate the Continent. He had written appreciatively of Bismarck and had studied German law and

---

[14] Wilson's offer was dispatched in spite of a cable sent by Page the day before, advising that it was the ambassador's "very definite opinion," and that of the British Foreign Office, that there was "not the slightest chance of any result if our good offices be offered at any continental capital." *F. R. Suppl., 1914*, p. 37.

[15] Acknowledging Hart's article, Wilson wrote on Aug. 4 to Charles R. Crane, who sent it: "The more I read about the conflict across the seas, the more open it seems to me to utter condemnation."

More than two years later Wilson's mind was still open in regard to responsibility for the war. But on June 14, 1917, after the United States became a belligerent, he said: "The war was begun by the military masters of Germany, who proved to be also the masters of Austria-Hungary." For Wilson's subsequent views of war guilt, *see* Notter, *op. cit.*, pp. 316–17, footnotes.

politics; but as a devotee of the Virginia Bill of Rights he rejected the Hegelian concept that citizens find fufillment only as members of the state and that the ruler is responsible for the people but not to them. On the other hand, he regretted that the fortunes of Great Britain, most liberal of the European powers, should be allied with those of Russia, a most absolute monarchy.

Woodrow Wilson loved the British people, indeed was bound to them by blood and breeding. The war had been going on scarcely a month when Sir Cecil Spring Rice—Britain's ambassador and himself a writer of verse—drew tears from him by alluding to the sonnets written by Wordsworth at the time of the Napoleonic Wars. After the President remarked that he had these verses in his mind all the time, Spring Rice replied: "You and Grey are fed on the same food and I think you understand." Through the ambassador, Wilson sent his warmest greeting to Sir Edward. He said to Spring Rice, "Everything that I love most in the world is at stake," and he confessed a fear that he would be forced to take such measures of defense as would be "fatal to our form of Government and American ideals." He spoke of the long trial of the Civil War, and said with deep emotion that he was sure that Britain would show its powers of endurance for a high cause. Realizing that a dispute with Britain would be a calamity, he promised to do all that he could to maintain absolute neutrality.

Nevertheless, guarding his official conscience fiercely against his personal feelings for England's countryside, her poets and parliamentarians, Wilson held himself now to the ideal that he once ascribed to General Lee: "conscious self-subordination to principles which lay outside of his personal life." When war's first shock to public opinion was followed by an epidemic of apprehension and jingoism, he drew desperately on the resources that his wife had left within him. On the long trip back to Washington from her grave, as the train sped through country that had been bloodied in Wilson's youth by battles and their grisly aftermath, the President remained for an entire day alone on the observation platform. "I want to think," he explained to Dr. Grayson. He searched the depths of his soul for thoughts and feelings that would be shared by his people.

Unable longer to consult Ellen Wilson, he sought the comfort of baring his mind to her brother and her sister. "I must depend upon you very much more than I ever did before now," he wrote to Stockton Axson on September 14, 1914, begging him to make a long visit to the White House. He felt the need of a comrade with whom to share his thoughts, especially a man who could join him in communion with the immortal spirit that had departed. Sitting on the White House porch with his brother-in-law in the summer dusk, he said: "I cannot help thinking that perhaps she was taken so that she might be spared the spectacle of some awful calamity." He spoke with pleasure of a personal letter that Sir Edward Grey had found time to dispatch to him despite the crisis. This statesman, he said, had lost his wife but had an interest in birds and in fly-fishing—a deliverance he did not know. When he talked of "release" and return to private life, Axson reminded him of his great scholarly design—the *Philosophy of Politics* that he had envisioned in his academic years; but he had only this to say: "I thought of it once as a great book; I can put all I know now into a very small one." Later in the autumn, walking in the White House garden with the young sister-in-law whose idol he had always been, he said in the saddest tone that she had ever heard: "If I hadn't gone into politics, she would probably be alive now. The strain of it killed her."

Realizing that his own welfare lay in fixing his thoughts on his public duty—"I believe that this is good 'doctor' sense," he wrote House—Wilson thought long and deeply about the plight of mankind. One day, communing with Axson, he gave voice to ideas so startling that his brother-in-law recorded the conversation. "It is perfectly obvious," he said, "that this war will vitally change the relationship of nations. Four things will be essential to the re-establishment in the world after peace is made." The first condition—one that Wilson already had set forth in public—required that no nation should ever be permitted to acquire an inch of land by conquest. Other propositions, which seem to have grown out of his experience in Latin-American affairs, were that the rights of large and small nations must be recognized as equal, and that war munitions must be made under public control rather than by citizens who might manipulate their manufacture for profit. Most significant of the prophecies revealed to Axson, however, was the fourth and last: "There must be an association of the nations, all bound together for the protection of the integrity of each, so that any one nation breaking from this bond will bring upon herself war; that is to say, punishment, automatically." [16]

[16] Wilson was perhaps influenced by a letter from Charles W. Eliot, dated Aug. 14, 1914, that he showed to the Cabinet. The educator suggested that the United States enter into an alliance to rebuke and punish offending nations. A policing power, Eliot thought, might ultimately supplant the balancing of alliances as a guarantee of peace; and in the creation of an international force the peoples of Europe might form a federal relationship and the cost of armament might be cut.

Wilson's faith in the principles underlying Bryan's treaties of arbitration was strengthened by the sudden outburst of war in Europe. On Aug. 13, 1914, Wilson wrote thus to Senator

It had taken the shock of bloodshed in Europe, coming at a time when his emotions had been set free by worship of Ellen Wilson's sacrificial spirit, to drive him to put into his own political creed a tenet that his fellow countrymen were still far from accepting. He had been merely plodding along early in the summer, his senses almost deadened by the discipline that he imposed as he grieved for his sick wife. But in August his thought vaulted beyond the day's task and reached out for practical ways of applying the ideals of service that he had been preaching. There was a spiritual impulse behind his thinking, now. It might be strong enough to hold him in the direction that he felt to be right, no matter if it led to persecution and even to martyrdom. He had found his great Cause, as he had in every pastoral charge of his career. It was to be not "Princeton in the nation's service," now, but the United States at the service of all mankind.

But he was face to face with a war; and his people, as horrified as he, and even terrified, needed assurance and guidance. He did not fail them. On August 19, in a proclamation to the Congress, he revealed a vision that could hold them steady: "We must be impartial in thought as well as in action, must put a curb upon our sentiments as well as upon every transaction that might be construed as a preference of one party to the struggle before another. My thought is of America. I am speaking, I feel sure, the earnest wish and purpose of every thoughtful American that this great country of ours, which is, of course, the first in our thoughts and in our hearts, should show herself in this time of peculiar trial a Nation fit beyond others to exhibit the fine poise of undisturbed judgment, the dignity of self-control, the efficiency of dispassionate action; a Nation that neither sits in judgment upon others nor is disturbed in her own counsels and which keeps herself fit and free to do what is honest and disinterested and truly serviceable for the peace of the world."

In this appeal the President met his people on the level of their immediate thinking. Everyone was asking how the European war would affect life in the United States. The answer that he gave was neither profound nor soothing, but it was challenging. He told his fellow countrymen that everything depended on their own behavior. Thus, characteristically, he sought for his people not the security of the ostrich but the more valid protection that he had often found in a cloak of aggressive righteousness.

William J. Stone, whose Committee on Foreign Relations were then considering twenty of the "cooling-off" treaties: "Action on our part would make the deepest possible impression upon the world and I covet and pray for it on that account."

CHAPTER XXIV

CARRYING ON ALONE

THE AMERICAN people were as astonished as their President by the outbreak of fighting in Europe. Hating no other nation, innocent of any thought of making war, and defended from attack by the Atlantic Ocean, they could not understand such lusts and fears as those that possessed the Old World.

Once hostilities had begun, however, and the quilt of innocence that had covered the minds of Americans was torn apart, prejudices surged up that had lain more or less dormant. Old bias against imperial Britain, fanned by citizens of Irish and German blood, began to glow again. The Hohenzollerns, who by commercial and naval aggressiveness had made themselves hobgoblins in the American Dream, now took on the menace of ogres.

The press of the nation gave vent immediately to emotional pressures that had been building up. Editors reflected feelings of affection for France, sympathy for the gallant underdogs—Belgium and Serbia—distrust of colossal Russia, and resentment toward a Kaiser who was reported once to have said to his troops: "Be terrible as Attila's Huns."

Contemplating the eddying of opinion in the first dark days of August, Wilson was swayed neither by journalists nor by politicians. Six months before war broke out, the President had given warning, in a press conference, that newspapers could do "a vast deal of damage" by printing speculations on foreign affairs. He was confident that he intuitively understood the temper of the American people better than editors and publishers who had criticized his New Freedom and scorned his Mexican policy of watchful waiting.

Financial magnates looked to the White House for reassurance; and Wilson was not displeased to feel that he could be of service to men who had thought him an impractical college president. When the impact of the war made the custodians of private capital shrink into their shells, he felt that he must safeguard his program of reform. The Clayton Bill was not yet enacted, and the President was by no means sure how this and the income tax and the Federal Reserve Act would work out in practice. These measures were not thoroughly set, he said to Daniels one day. "Big Business will be in the saddle. More than that—Free Speech and the other rights will be endangered. War is autocratic."

The most critical emergency at the war's beginning was met immediately by steps taken by McAdoo after consultation with the President. Early in September Wilson replied to a fearsome letter from J. P. Morgan. Telling the banker that some features of pending antitrust measures might be changed, Wilson replied: "I am sincerely sorry that you should be so blue about the situation. I believe that being blue is just the wrong thing, if you will permit me to say so."

While Morgan's letter was under consideration, Wilson heard a plea from six railroad presidents for support of their credit in the emergency brought about by the war. They had already petitioned the Interstate Commerce Commission for increases in rates, and they hoped that the President would say a good word for them. Meeting their request to the extent of writing a public letter to one of them, he showed broad sympathy and understanding.[1]

One of the calamities brought by war—the plight of the cotton planters who were prevented from disposing immediately of one of the largest crops in history—struck home with peculiar force to a statesman bred in the South. Rejecting price-fixing proposals as "unwise and dangerous," he promised that the government would give all the help possible "within the limits of economic law and safe finance." Before the end of October the British government was persuaded to rule that cotton was not contraband subject to seizure on the high seas. Moreover, McAdoo—"dear Mac" was bearing the brunt of the economic emergency so conscientiously that his nerves were worn bare and Wilson was "quite anxious about him"—cooperated with House and private bankers to raise a fund to help farmers to hold their crops until the demand stimulated by war conditions could make itself felt.[2]

[1] When it was suggested to him by Henry L. Higginson that he make recommendations to the Interstate Commerce Commission, Wilson drew back. How far was it proper for him to go, he wondered, in putting his personal convictions before the commissioners? "They are as jealous of executive suggestion as the Supreme Court would be," he reminded the Boston banker, "and I dare say with justification." He sent Higginson's letter, nevertheless, to Commissioner Winthrop M. Daniels, for he knew that this old Princeton colleague would understand. He hoped that Higginson's views, which he himself thought "in the main true," might impress the commissioners.

The commissioners asserted their independence by rejecting the plea and then, reconsidering the matter several weeks later on their own initiative, authorizing an increase in rates.

[2] Though Wilson had disliked subsidies that might make citizens less self-reliant, he concluded, after discussing the matter with House and getting a legal ruling from the attorney

Toward the end of 1914, when the twelve regional Federal Reserve Systems were opened, a measure of confidence came back and on December 12 the New York Stock Exchange was reopened. Early in 1915 the nation's banks returned about three-fourths of the currency that McAdoo had distributed in August as an emergency measure.

However, another crisis precipitated by the war—that in shipping—was a matter so entangled with the legal filaments of neutrality policy that it became a subject of bitter controversy and long legislative debate.

On July 31, even before it was certain that the European conflict would involve Britain, Wilson postponed his usual Cabinet meeting, called in two leaders of the Senate and two of the House and said to them: "Our bountiful crops are ready to harvest. Unless they can be carried to the foreign markets they will waste in the warehouses, if they do not rot in the fields." He asked for legislation that would provide ships to carry American commerce "to all ports of the world." A bill was introduced that made foreign-built vessels eligible for purchase and immediate registry under the American flag. The Congress passed the measure immediately, and on August 18 the President signed it.[3]

---

general, that the cotton pool stood in a class by itself and would not set a dangerous precedent. Before raising the cotton pool from private sources, McAdoo, building upon a Treasury-financed scheme that he had used to rescue cotton planters from a minor depression in the autumn of 1913, had acted in August, 1914, to issue emergency currency and to deposit government funds in Southern banks for loans to cotton and tobacco planters.

In the autmun of 1913 Wilson had congratulated the Treasury officials on their bold, prompt action, and he wrote in the New York *Commercial*, on Sept. 29: "The country has seen . . . McAdoo handle the money situation more successfully and with greater skill than the bankers have ever done . . . In the past secretaries of the Treasury have not put out Treasury funds before the harm was done, and then they devoted the money to checking panics in Wall Street, while the business of the country came to a standstill . . . Deep down in the mind of the public rests the suspicion that the banks have not been wise in the past and that government control in the open is something not to be feared."

In the autumn of 1914 Wilson confessed that the cotton crisis gave him "the greatest concern." Though the emergency fund was never applied effectively, a rise in the price of cotton somewhat alleviated the distress of the producers. On Aug. 20, 1915, the British government revised their ruling and declared cotton to be contraband. *See* Vol. II.

[3] Diplomats of the Allies protested against the Ship Registry Act. Their governments feared that Germany might receive, in payment for ships that were of no use in her war effort, credits that would buy essential munitions. Moreover, there was suspicion that contraband cargoes might be shipped to German ports in the interned German vessels, under the safe-conduct of the American flag.

The solicitor of the State Department, however, maintained that the transfer of ships to a neutral flag was legal even after the commencement of hostilities, if made in good faith; and Wilson, accepting this, wrote to Senator Saulsbury on Aug. 15 to explain that "the whole question comes down to the proof of *bona fides* in the transaction." The United States, he admitted, could not object to the seizure at sea of any ships that were not acquired in good faith. "I think," he wrote, "the whole thing can be divested of its risks by a wise and prudent administration of the law." On the legality of the Ship Registry Act, *see* Link, *W.W. and the Progressive Era*, p. 150.

Though Congress promptly followed up passage of the Ship Registry Act by approving a measure providing government funds for insuring merchant vessels, it was still obvious to Wilson, at the beginning of September, that private capital was too timid to make adequate plans for supplying the tonnage that was demanded by the nation's foreign trade. The nation as a whole could take the financial risk better than private owners, he thought.

Secretary McAdoo was concerned, too. Convinced that a few shippers were enjoying "an orgy of profiteering" while government-subsidized insurance relieved them of risk, he resolved to provide more vessels and lower rates. Conceiving a plan for a government-owned merchant marine, he drafted legislation providing for both the building and the buying of ships; and taking it to the President, he remarked that thus they could serve trade with Latin America that would not be exposed to the risks of war.

Wilson perceived immediately that the measure would be denounced by reactionaries as "socialistic" and took a day to meditate before giving his answer. Was the operation of shipping a "necessary function" that the government must perform in an emergency? This was not a revolutionary idea, for Roosevelt's administration had purchased the Panama steamship line and the government still operated it. The need for action on a larger scale now seemed dire, private enterprise hopelessly inadequate, and his son-in-law's vision compelling. The President handed the drafted bill back to the secretary of the treasury and said, smiling:

"We'll certainly have to fight for it, won't we?"

"We certainly shall," McAdoo replied.

"Well, then, let's fight."

Wilson called legislators to the White House on the day after he had signed the inadequate Ship Registry Act, and on August 24 McAdoo's new measure was presented in the House.

An immediate blast of protest came from businessmen and Republican politicians. Wilson was irritated again by lobbyists who infested Washington, but he announced through newsmen that if private capital would provide the facilities needed by exporters, which so far they had shown no intention of doing, the government might not carry out its shipping program. Otherwise, he said, much as he disliked to have

---

The qualms of shipowners were not diminished by a warning from Counselor Lansing of the State Department that every purchaser of a German vessel would have to satisfy the British government of his *bona fides* and that it was "too much to hope" that the belligerents would respect such transactions.

his administration enter into this business, he not only intended to press the legislation forward, but expected it to be enacted within two or three weeks. Journalists reported that the well-known jaw was setting hard.

By the end of September, however, the opposition had become so strenuous and persistent, and the Republicans were using it so tellingly, that Wilson's advisers wanted him to postpone legislation until the November election was over. There was resentment in the Cabinet because so important a measure had not been discussed there. Houston was opposed to it; and Secretary of Commerce Redfield, who bore the brunt of protests from shipping interests, complained that he could not understand its purpose. There was a feeling that the President already had asked so much of the legislators that their patience was at the breaking point. On September 29, therefore, when Wilson conferred with McAdoo, Tumulty, Burleson, and House, it was decided to let the legislators adjourn as soon as possible. And so the Sixty-third Congress, that had met continuously for more than a year and a half at Wilson's insistence and had enacted most of the reforms of the New Freedom, came to an end on October 24, two days after passing a bill voting higher taxes to meet a deficiency that was caused chiefly by shrinking import duties.[4]

With the fight for the shipping bill suspended, and the Clayton and Trade Commission Acts passed, the President was comparatively free to give attention to the forthcoming election, in which, under the Seventeenth Amendment, senators would have to face direct primaries and popular election.

The President was always under pressure, from one adviser or another, to make public statements in support of certain candidates and causes. This was particularly true in the months before elections. During October of 1914 he attended to the needs of his Congressional adherents. The President took a more indulgent attitude toward the bosses and wheel-horses of the party than he had shown earlier in his political career. "My head is with the progressives in the Democratic party," he told Tumulty, "but my heart, because of the way they stood by me, is with the so-called Old Guard in the Senate." The secretary— making the most of the days when the Governor seemed to be in an

---

[4] Appealing for additional revenue from internal taxation, Wilson said to Congress on Oct. 4: ". . . we ought not to borrow. We ought to resort to taxation, however we may regret putting additional burdens on our people . . . The country is able to pay any just and reasonable taxes without distress. . . . The people . . . know and understand, and they will be intolerant only of those who dodge responsibility or are not frank with them."

"Irish" mood—persuaded his chief to endorse two New Jersey congressmen whose tenure was in jeopardy and to appoint a lieutenant of despised James Nugent to the bench of the District of Columbia. Even the Tammany candidates in New York State received Wilson's blessing as a concession to the need for party harmony. The President was disturbed by conflict between two slates in the Democratic primary in that state—one supported by McAdoo, Mayor Mitchel, and Collector Dudley Field Malone, the other by Tammany and Tumulty. The rivalry was an irritating incident in a running feud that was developing between the President's secretary and his son-in-law, each of whom wished to command "the Governor's" entire confidence in political matters. Wilson did his best to requite the fealty of each of these lieutenants without giving offense to the other.[5]

On October 20 the President sent to Congressman Underwood a public letter that made it clear that if he seemed too indulgent toward some machine men, it was only because of his gratitude for past support in Congress and his hope of committing the party to liberal measures in the future. To strengthen the bond with progressive sentiment that had proved decisive in 1912, he expressed pride in reforms already put through and looked to the horizon of the future, beyond the emergency brought by war. He said that he was still contemplating strokes "to set business free." [6] In speeches before the American Bar Association and the Pittsburgh Y.M.C.A. he made appeals to the moral forces of the nation.

Woodrow Wilson seemed to be bringing to a focus, in the autumn of 1914, all of his talents for leadership. It was almost as if his whole life had become a testimonial to virtues of Ellen Wilson that he had always esteemed but never felt so poignantly. He had become truly a pastor to those near him. When jealousy between Tumulty and McAdoo became flagrant, he was constrained to remind his agitated secretary, in fatherly reproof, of "the green-eyed monster." He had grown fond of his son-in-law, with whom he shared a passion for detective stories, and he depended much on "dear Mac's" executive

[5] McAdoo, by his persistent interest in political appointments, seemed to show personal ambition. Colonel House took it upon himself to remonstrate with McAdoo, advising him that the surest path to the Presidency lay in doing his own job superlatively well, and not in interferences that would be interpreted as an attempt to build a machine for himself.

McAdoo took this advice "in an admirable spirit," the Colonel recorded, and was showing himself to be "one of the greatest Secretaries of the Treasury." House Diary, July 8 and Sept. 30, 1914.

[6] On Sept. 7, 1914, Wilson told Ray Stannard Baker that he had nearly reached the end of his economic program, but still hoped to develop a policy of "conservation for use." Baker, *American Chronicle*, p. 277.

genius. Yet it gave him indigestion when McAdoo talked business at meals. He told House that he would rather die than risk hurting the feelings of Nellie's husband; and so the tactful Colonel agreed to tell McAdoo that Dr. Grayson had asked him—House—to refrain from talking shop with the President at the table.[7]

The President encouraged his Cabinet to take part in the campaign. As he mended rifts and forged strong ties with political comrades, he rejoiced in a feeling that he was approved of and trusted by the party and the country.[8] But the satisfaction was only "for the moment," he told himself. There was still the old haunting dread of a turn in the tide, a premonition that someday he might find himself driven by conscience to do something that would make him intensely unpopular. He professed little interest in his own tenure in an office that had brought him "no personal blessing, but only irreparable loss and desperate suffering." He confessed to House that if he could feel that he was not obligated to stand for re-election in 1916 a great load would be lifted from him. He feared that the people would expect him to continue his pace of reform, and that it would be impossible.

As the President's prestige grew and both conservatives and progressives of his party fell in line behind him, the Republicans failed to mend the rift that had opened in 1912. Their leaders had endorsed Wilson's proclamation of neutrality at the outbreak of war; but now Root and Lodge and other regulars, with no aid from Taft, attacked the new tariff law and asserted that even in the war emergency there would be no need for increased taxes if only the President would practice the economy that he preached. At the same time Roosevelt aired intemperate views in print and on the platform, and thus dug a political grave for himself and his party.

On November 3 the President went with his people to the polls. His home town was still Princeton, where he had rented a room in a lodging house in order to keep his name on the rolls. A few old friends stood on the platform to greet him when he left the train,

[7] House Diary, Sept. 26, 1914. The same disinclination to risk any misunderstanding that might cause ill-feeling within the clan and hurt his daughter was apparent several weeks later, when Wilson urged House to discuss the prickly question of New York State politics with McAdoo. The Colonel thought it the President's duty to go to the bottom of this matter himself. House Diary, Nov. 6, 1914. On Jan. 3, 1915, Wilson asked Nancy Toy, a visitor at the White House, whether she thought that McAdoo could be elected to the Presidency if nominated.

[8] W.W. to Mary Hulbert, Sept. 20, 1914. Wilson's view was corroborated in the *New York Times* on Oct. 12: "Mr. Cleveland never, even in his first administration, had the grasp of it [the party] that Mr. Wilson has. The resemblances come down to the fact that his will is as iron as Cleveland's, though the iron hand is hidden in a velvet glove that Cleveland never wore. The fundamental difference is in the measure of success."

dressed as in the old days in a gray suit of rough texture, but wearing a black tie and a band of black on his sleeve. While they chatted, President Hibben suddenly appeared, a little breathless, and explained that he had been told by a student that the President of the United States was asking for him. Wilson thought that poor Jack Hibben was the victim of a cruel hoax. But he did not relent, and looking straight at the eager figure, he said only one word: "No." His manner was courteous, but his inflection of the single syllable seemed to ask why this man should imagine that the President of the United States might ask for such as he.[9]

Early returns suggested to Wilson that the electorate in the East, like the Princeton community, had surrendered to reactionary forces. When reports came in from the West, however, the President was enheartened. He got "solid satisfaction," he confessed, out of gains in the fields where he himself had once pioneered alone.

When the popular vote was checked, it was clear that the Democrats had suffered the slump that usually strikes the party in office at midterm. Though the voting power in the Senate did not change, the majority in the House was reduced from seventy-three to twenty-five. Progressives had drifted back into the Republican fold in large numbers.

The President was disconsolate because the nation as a whole showed so little appreciation of his labors. He wondered whether it was worth while to drive Congress as hard as he had driven it. House tried to comfort his friend by reminding him that he had not suffered defeat, himself; but for the present Wilson found the best solace for his ego in the vale of self-oblivion in which he had taken refuge since his bereavement. "My individual life has gone utterly to pieces," he wrote to Mary Hulbert five days after the election. "I do not care a fig for anything that affects me." The satisfaction that comes from service could not make him whole. There was no companionship in consorting with the policies of a state or the fortunes of a nation!

---

[9] Margaret Axson Elliott, *My Aunt Louisa and W.W.*, p. 268. Still unable to face up to his failure at Princeton, Wilson attended his thirty-fifth reunion in June of 1914, but refused an invitation to lead the Pee-rade with Hibben. In explanation of his attitude he wrote on May 21 to Robert Bridges: "I want everybody to forget for the day that I am anything except a member of the class of '79." After it was over, he admitted to Cleveland Dodge that being present cost him a good deal of pain. Returning to Washington, Wilson told Tumulty on June 23 that it should be made clear that he had not been forced out of the presidency at Princeton. "They would not have dared try it," he wrote, "but they were very glad to get rid of me because they were desperately fighting my attempt to change the social organization of the university." House noted that in their intimate talks they often drifted to the subject of Princeton, and on such occasions Wilson showed "how deeply the iron entered his soul."

He kept on functioning, he confessed, by holding himself to a daily routine. "On Sunday," he explained to Mary Hulbert, "all faculties seek rest and are in a sort of coma and I am no good. . . . I seem to be tough against all sorts of strain and all sorts of deep suffering. I have a vast deal to be thankful for, and I shall, I hope, never yield to the weakness of being sorry for myself." He did not impose the pall of an official period of mourning. He made his associates feel that they should carry on as usual, and even the concerts on the White House grounds went on.

When he sought refuge and relaxation in his automobile, and drove over routes that he named and numbered to suit his fancy, Helen Bones sat silent by his side as he dozed or put together the pieces of a puzzle of statecraft. When Grayson fell sick and was given a vacation to recuperate, she accompanied her cousin Woodrow around the golf course. "A perfect companion," he thought her, "because glad to think of me and what is best for me and not anxious to talk and to have her own way, bless her heart for the unselfishness! But I hate to think how dull it must be for her, and I chide myself for accepting such sacrifices." His "darling Nell" managed to run in on her father every day; and on Thanksgiving he went to Williamstown to visit the Sayres, who were soon to present him with his first grandson. When they came to the White House for the advent, the President stood outside the door of their chamber, eavesdropping, and when he imagined he heard two new voices, he whispered excitedly "Twins!"

But for all his fondness for his girls, he made it clear that his obligations to the American people superseded his parental love. At table, once, his daughters told him of a state governor who pardoned a son. They asked him, in jest, whether he could pardon them if they were convicted of a crime, and he grew very serious and replied, solemnly: "God help me, I don't believe I could."

Tumulty found, to his sorrow, that White House automobiles enjoyed no immunity from the laws to which other citizens were subject; and Wilson, relishing his secretary's discomfiture, had a habit of asking his family at dinner: "Well, who's been pinched today?" [10]

---

[10] Louis Brownlow to the writer, March 14, 1951. Appointing Democrats to the District Commission to fix party responsibility, Wilson said that, though he did not expect publicly to intervene, he wanted the commissioners to consult him about matters that in their judgment required his advice. He asked them to boil down their propositions, present them fairly, and tell him frankly what they thought he should do. "If you will do that and try to keep it all on one page and send it to me in mid-morning, I will try to do my part before it is night. . . . If you don't let me know exactly what you think, but try to pass the buck to me entirely, you may never get an answer, and certainly you wouldn't deserve one." Only once did Com-

It was not so easy now for Wilson to command the gay weekend mood in which he had been wont to write to Mary Hulbert; yet he was loyal to this old friend. Up until this time she had prided herself upon asking no favors for herself or her son.[10a] But now, when she confessed that her small fortune had been lost, he tried to suggest ways in which both mother and son might find profitable employment, and wrote letters to his friends in their behalf. She reaffirmed her confidence in her friend's gentleness and nobility; and each of these congenial spirits drew strength from the understanding and faith of the other.

As he wrote less to his "high priestess of democracy," he renewed an old correspondence with charming Nancy Toy—daughter of a Virginia clergyman and wife of an aged professor of Romance languages at Harvard University. Visiting the White House in January of 1915, Mrs. Toy joined appreciatively in the family evenings and the talk of poets and historians, of religion and philosophy. Wilson enjoyed the independence of mind that he found in her letters and assured her that she did "a real service" in informing him of what was being said by the critical people about her at Cambridge. It was not only the privilege but the duty of a loyal friend to tell him that he had made mistakes, he insisted. Nancy Toy pleased him immensely by giving him a great horn spoon for Christmas. "I am Scots very deep down in me," he wrote in thanking her, "and porridge in a great horn spoon seems to me like a thing of (minor) religion."

But Wilson did not find in Nancy Toy the intimate comradeship that his Scottish soul still craved. This lady, for one thing, felt that she could live a life worth while without depending on a personal God. When she advanced this view, he took up the challenge, declaring: "*My* life would not be worth living if it were not for the driving power of religion, for *faith,* pure and simple. I have seen all my life the arguments against it without ever having been moved by them . . . never for a moment have I had one doubt about my religious beliefs. There are people who *believe* only so far as they *understand*—that seems to me presumptuous and sets their understanding as the standard of the universe . . . I am sorry for such people."

In the President's loneliness, Edward M. House perhaps gave more comfort than anyone else to his friend's uneasy spirit. He felt that he

---

missioner Brownlow fail to get an answer before nightfall, and then Wilson apologized, two days later, that he had to communicate with Paris. Brownlow MS, *A Passion for Anonymity.*

[10a] On a typed copy of a letter that Wilson wrote to her on Dec. 8, 1913, Mrs. Peck wrote: "I never asked him anything for myself or my son." Copy in possession of Allen Hulbert.

could "unload his mind" to House; and when his friend took some of his rash impulses too seriously, he was mildly amused. The Colonel tried to supply the serene wisdom that Wilson always had found in his Ellen, and to give the President, in digestible doses, the criticism that he expected from loyal friends. Going to Harlakenden late in August for a weekend visit, accompanied by his devoted son-in-law, Gordon Auchincloss, House was met at the door by the President and shown to the room that had been Mrs. Wilson's and that was next his own, with a common bathroom between. They were in a wing of the house and quite by themselves. Descending a little staircase, they went down to a study where they sat and talked of the affairs of the world —the disappointing past and the dim future.

Wilson confessed he was heartsick over the narrow margin by which they had failed to prevent disaster in Europe. He condemned the philosophy of the German leaders as essentially selfish and lacking in spirituality; and of the Kaiser's idea of building a military machine as a means of preserving peace, he said in scorn: "What a foolish thing it was to create a powder magazine and risk someone's dropping a spark into it!" If Germany won, the President predicted, his own ambition for better international ethics would be frustrated and the United States would become a military nation. At one time their thought leaped to the distant future, and they speculated on the distribution of power in centuries to come. Wilson suggested that eventually there might be but two great nations in the world: Russia and the United States. House, however, thought there would be three: China, dominating Asia; Russia, Europe and a part of Asia; and the United States, dominating the Western world and perhaps the English-speaking colonies.

As the friends sat on the terrace and watched the afternoon sun throw the shadow of Vermont hills upon the broad valley of the Connecticut, the President began to talk of Ellen Wilson as if she were still a living presence. He showed photographs of her and read poems that she had written. Tears came as he said that he felt like a machine run down and dreaded the next two and a half years.

With an effort he shook off his gloomy thoughts, however, and tried to give the Colonel a good time. He joked about his ancestry, saying that he belonged to two clans that had been the worst lot of freebooters in Scotland. In the evening they played pool—"equally badly," House thought. The next morning the President rose very early so that he could finish shaving before his guest would wish to use the bathroom, and the Colonel's heart was touched by this little courtesy on the part of one so great. House—irrespressible flatterer though he himself was—felt flattered at being taken into the family so intimately. In his diary he recorded his host's attentions, and noted that Dr. Grayson filled his ear with mischievous, petty gossip of the White House that had not been reported to the President.

The ruling elder continued to whisper in Wilson's ear when appointments were to be made. He continued to protest that his motives were pure friendship and a desire to serve. When McReynolds was elevated to the Supreme Court, House recommended as attorney general his loyal Texas friend, Thomas W. Gregory. Furthermore, he persuaded Gregory to accept the post if it were offered and advised his protégé how to conduct himself.[11] Gregory was well prepared to serve, therefore, when the President, feeling that this man might reinforce the liaison with congressmen that Burleson and McAdoo had been maintaining, appointed him.

The President's dependence on his Cabinet seemed to be increased by his bereavement. On January 29 he invited the group for the first time to meet in the White House instead of in the executive office.

Another change in the Cabinet seemed likely. McAdoo was offered the presidency of the Metropolitan Life Insurance Company; and having been told by Grayson that the President had a tendency toward arteriosclerosis that was being aggravated by continual mental strain, he had inferred that Wilson would not run for a second term. This seemed to clear his own path to the Presidency, and so he confessed his ambition to friendly Colonel House and asked whether he would damage his prospect if he accepted the offer of the insurance company.

The Colonel was in a dilemma. McAdoo had shown himself a man of intemperate feeling and he did not work smoothly with Tumulty, with the Cabinet, or with the Federal Reserve Board. House felt that it would be best for all concerned that he be allowed to resign; but he knew that the very idea of a change would distress Wilson, and when he conferred with the President on October 29 he found him upset because McAdoo had come to the White House and suggested resigning. Wilson recalled that it had been said that the business interests intended to break up his Cabinet either by forcing men out or

[11] House Diary, Aug. 10 and 30, 1914. Gregory must never get into tenuous argument, the Colonel warned, but must state his position briefly and, above all, never repeat. When he found that their minds were in agreement, he must never waste the President's time by giving reasons for his opinion. Gregory was "very receptive," House noted. A letter from Gregory to House, Aug. 26, 1914, breathes devotion and gratitude. House Collection.

buying them out; and now he suspected that the latter course was being followed. When the Colonel argued that it was unlikely that McAdoo could ever become president if he remained in the Cabinet, Wilson replied that connection with an insurance company surely would destroy his son-in-law's chances. A day or two later House revealed that McAdoo, still carrying on the feud with Tumulty that had grown out of New York politics, was denouncing the President's secretary as too subservient to business interests. At this exposure of petty criticism by a member of his family in whom he had placed great trust, Wilson's face flushed and then turned gray. "Has McAdoo gone crazy?" he asked.

The President passed a wretched night after this discussion. The next evening House avoided controversial subjects, and they talked of philosophy and political theory. Wilson made merry with limericks, and they were off to bed early. When the President returned House's visit a week later, in New York, they walked down to Herald Square one evening, stopping here and there to listen to curbstone harangues. When they were recognized, they ducked into a hotel, went up in an elevator, came down on the other side of the building, and went out without detection. Wilson enjoyed the game of hide-and-seek hugely, said he would give anything if only he could get lost in a crowd, and was delighted when the Colonel suggested whiskers as a disguise. The President spoke again of his loneliness, and confessed that he had wished, as they walked, that someone would kill him. But though feeling unfit to do the work before him, he said that he had himself so well disciplined that he well knew that, unless someone did kill him, he would go on to the end, doing the best he could.

They talked little of public business during this visit, though they gave a few minutes to consideration of a plan for Belgian relief for which there was strong popular demand. But after drafting his annual message, the President asked the Colonel to come to the White House to go over it with him; and after its delivery he wrote: "Well, the broadside has been fired and I hope sincerely that it will have the desired effect in quieting those who are seriously in danger of making trouble for the country. You will see that I added one or two little passages after reading it to you." [12]

12 The Colonel's few suggestions were mainly in regard to foreign affairs. One of the dangerous citizens, House felt, was Bryan. After talking with the secretary of state on Nov. 8, the Colonel wrote in his diary: "He did not believe there was the slightest danger to this country from foreign invasion, even if the Germans were successful. He thought *after war was declared* there would be plenty of time to make the preparations necessary. He talked as inno-

The next time they met, the President was disturbed because Congress had rejected some of his nominations. He sought advice as to future tactics. House was ready with the answer: keep sending in other names of high quality as fast as suggestions were rejected, for thus the people could be made to perceive the obstructive spirit of their legislators. Two weeks later Wilson was inclined to let it be known that, if the senators would not accept his leadership, he would not be a candidate for re-election; but the Colonel advised him not to do it.

Both as comrade and as adviser, then, through the trying autumn of 1914, the Colonel comforted the sorrowing widower. No one was more selflessly devoted to his interest; no one could keep him so well informed about the feelings of his official family. The Colonel seemed to know all and to understand all. On Christmas Day, Woodrow Wilson gave expression to the gratitude that had been surging up within him. He wished he could see brought into House's life, he wired, some happiness and blessing equal to those brought into his by the Colonel's wonderful friendship.

At the beginning of the New Year, Wilson bore his cross with less protest. In February—six months after Ellen Wilson's death—a social party was given in the White House. The Cabinet and their families were invited to see moving pictures and partake of refreshments. The President was friendly and amazingly frank with the few chosen guests; but the old buoyancy of talk and manner were missing and Nancy Toy wondered whether in his formality she saw evidence of—in John Hay's words about Roosevelt—"the kingly shadow falling upon him."

However, the program that Wilson presented to the Congress on December 8, 1914, was mild and reasonable, and his manner was neither dictatorial nor importunate. Prolonging the keynote of service to mankind that he had already sounded so long and so loud, he called for action by the Senate on the Alexander Bill safeguarding the welfare of American seamen, on a measure providing for the development of the national domain under conserving safeguards, and on another bill that would grant more self-government to the Philippines.

---

cently as my little grandchild, Jane Tucker. He spoke with great feeling, and I fear he may give trouble."

When Bryan suggested a national primary law, House told Wilson that in practice, in Texas, such a measure had limited political candidacy to very rich men. "I advised the President to let Bryan direct the primary bill and get tangled in it as a fly in molasses," House recorded. "I told him not to help out, but to encourage him to go on, and I opined that the measure would be killed by the fact that Bryan was its sponsor. He seemed to like this."

He wished to make provision, too, for the survey and charting of the nation's coasts. He was not yet ready, he said, to make definite recommendations in the important field of rural credit—a matter that had been cared for to some degree by the Federal Reserve Act; but on the subject of governmental economy he delivered a little homily worthy of Poor Richard. Beyond the development of the National Guard and the training of citizens in the use of arms and the rudiments of military life, he felt that the time had not yet come "to turn America into a military camp" in anticipation of conflict, as some of his more rabid opponents advocated.

As for the emergency shipping bill, which had passed neither house of Congress, Wilson was emphatic. He was reluctant to try to drive this legislation through immediately, but he had covenanted on the measure with McAdoo, and House had pointed out that if the government was to act at all, it should do so while the need was acute and the necessary votes could be commanded in the present Congress.

But financiers raised questions. If the government were to conduct such businesses as shipping, and operate at a deficit as they were accustomed to do in state monopolies, the sources of taxes with which to meet such deficits would be reduced and the nation's economy would spiral downward to bankruptcy. Moreover, opponents of the shipping bill alarmed peace-loving citizens by citing the risk of war that would result if German vessels were operated by the American government in waters patrolled by the Allies. Cannily tying the issue to the President's Mexican policy, which had resulted in unnecessary fighting at Veracruz, Lodge addressed the Senate with great force on January 6, and on the 7th there was a clear breach between Wilson and the Congress on a bill to limit immigration.[13] At last it seemed as if the Republicans were making headway against the administration and the great advantage that its leader derived from the critical nature of the times.

Picking up their gauntlet on January 8, 1915, Wilson fought back. He had lost none of his sensitiveness to unjust criticism; in fact the wear of bereavement upon his emotions made him slug furiously at his tormentors. Speaking at Indianapolis on Jackson Day, he became

[13] This measure, supported by organized labor and passed by the Congress, was vetoed by Wilson on Jan. 28. He felt that he lacked a popular mandate, and he did not wish to exclude political refugees or demand a literacy test of "those to whom the opportunities of elementary education have been denied, without regard to their character, their purposes, or their natural capacity." Doubtless Wilson recalled the damaging attacks of the foreign-language press, during 1912, on anti-immigration statements in his *History of the American People*. The veto stood until 1917, when a similar immigration measure was passed over a presidential veto.

incoherent and came close to Jackson's summit of intellectual arrogance.

This outburst delivered Wilson from the morose thoughts that had afflicted him in his isolation at the White House from the people whom he loved and wished to serve. "It was good to get my blood moving in a speech again," he confessed. His audience was roused to loud cheers, and applauded wildly when they sensed in one of his remarks a hint that he would stand for re-election in 1916. Many friendly critics, however, regretted the excesses to which he had allowed his tongue to run. Actually, after his blood had cooled, the President confessed to "a palpable lapse of taste . . . produced by the psychology of the stump." He admitted that there was no excuse for it.

"But there is a real fight on," he insisted to Nancy Toy; ". . . the influences that have so long dominated legislation and administration here are making their last and most desperate stand to regain control." Criticism, if it was fair, he regarded as "the necessary tonic and test of men in public life." But he conceived that he was fighting against a formidable covert lobby. He wrote: "I think you cannot know to what lengths men like Root and Lodge are going, who I once thought had consciences but now know have none. We must not suffer ourselves to forget or twist the truth as they do, or use their insincere and contemptible methods of fighting; but we must hit them and hit them straight in the face, and not mind if the blood comes. It is a blunt business, and lacks a certain kind of refinement, but so does all war; and this is a war to save the country from some of the worst influences that ever debauched it. Please do not read the speeches in which I use a bludgeon. I do not like to offend your taste; but I cannot fight rottenness with rose water."

Wilson was not surprised when adversaries in the Senate filibustered against the shipping bill for thirty-seven hours. He attributed their position less to a desire to avoid involvement in a European war than to a fear of government encroachment on private property. When seven Democratic senators joined the opposition and the filibuster continued, with a Republican talking for thirteen hours and cots set up in the cloakrooms so that the talkers might snatch rest, Wilson was incensed. The sense of fealty that had compelled him to support his party's legislators at the polls was outraged by the defection of the seven.

As usual, opposition that he thought selfish hardened Wilson's mind against the arguments of sincere doubters. Charles W. Eliot, who was

alarmed by the possibility that the government would involve the
nation in war by using the interned German ships on transatlantic
routes, warned the President that he was in danger of antagonizing
"the great mass of the business men of the country," disrupting the
Democratic party, and making a Republican victory in 1916 probable.
But in reply the President bespoke trust for his administration, which,
he said, was "very keenly alive" to the difficulties that it might
encounter.[14]

Hoping that if he could drive the shipping bill through the House
the Senate might follow, the President cracked the party whip; on
February 16 the bill was passed by a vote of 215 to 121; and the next
day Wilson wrote to Congressman Adamson: "You certainly are a
fine soldier and I am your sincere admirer."

Dr. Grayson noted the grimness of his chief, and wrote to House
that he feared that "Thomas" (the doctor had fallen in with the
Colonel's use of code names) was taking the controversy "too hard
personally." For two years the President had oscillated between periods
in which he drove Congress harder than it had ever been driven before
and times when he hesitated to risk insulting the legislators by ex-
pounding what he conceived to be their duty. Now he gave the
appearance of a martinet who wanted only results, and no excuses.
House had gone to Europe, McAdoo underwent an operation, and
there was no First Lady to encourage him to make converts by persuasion. After talking with one legislator for an hour, he felt that he had
"made about as much impression on him as on his chair." It seemed
to him that there were too many "freaks" among the Democrats on
the Hill, too many radicals, too many who held to their own little pet
ideas. If only he could be a "mere figurehead," like the King of England, and his party could be led by a member of Congress! As it was
now, no one heard what he said to the legislators individually, while
the whole nation knew what was said at the Capitol. He had been
thinking of writing another book on the subject that he had treated in
his first essays on government; he would call it "Statesmanship," and
it would stress the personal element in politics.

As Wilson shrank from fighting the shipping battle with time-
honored tactics of American politics, his Republican opponents continued their appeal to popular fears and suspicions. When the loyal

---

[14] Eliot questioned whether "can you not trust *me*?" is ever a satisfactory answer to the
allegation that a man or party possesses "illegitimate and dangerous powers." *See* Baker, V,
130–32.

Democrats in the Senate refused to consider amendments to the bill
and used patronage to control votes, Lodge portrayed Wilson as an
overbearing egotist and dictator, and persuaded himself that he was
justified in this instance in using the filibuster, though he considered
it an unethical procedure. "I never expected to hate anyone in politics
with the hatred I feel towards Wilson," the senator wrote to Theodore
Roosevelt. "I was opposed to our good friend Grover Cleveland, but
never in any such way as this." [15]

With the support of the Republican leadership and the acquiescence
of dissenting Democrats, the filibustering in the Senate went on.
Wilson stubbornly refrained from making a frank statement of his
plans for the German ships; and when one that had been purchased by
an American citizen—the *Dacia*—was seized by a French cruiser on
February 27, the potential danger was dramatized before all the world.
The Congress adjourned on March 4 without any action by the Senate
on the shipping bill. Wilson and McAdoo, however, did not give up
the battle: a modified form of the measure was introduced early in
1916 and, the shortage of shipping having become obviously critical,
the new bill was passed. But the prices that the government had to
pay for ships were more than three times those that had prevailed in
1915.

The stormy session of Congress, in the winter of 1915, revealed that
the flaw in character that had led to Wilson's defeat at Princeton still
remained, more dangerous than ever. Shrinking into personal isolation,
indulging in dreams of the ideal government and giving way to intolerance of the hard realities of politics, he had lost touch with seven
important Democratic senators. His fury at them was so great that he
wrote out a damning indictment that, fortunately, he was persuaded
not to release. His friends wondered whether he had indeed cured
himself, as he boasted in a talk to the Presbytery of Potomac, of the
"very risky habit of always saying exactly what he thought"—a trait
that he said he had "in part inherited" from his father. [16]

---

[15] Garraty, *Lodge,* pp. 31?–14. This biographer observes that Lodge's hatred of the President
was the more dangerous l ?ause the senator honestly thought himself a scholarly and unprejudiced observer who, ir :he war crisis, was trying to forget politics.
[16] James T. Taylor, *Wo drow Wilson in Church,* p. 18.

CHAPTER XXV

A Lonely Man Finds a Comrade

Woodrow Wilson had never in his life been so lonely as in the early months of 1915. He was still mourning his Ellen and had not acted to carry out her injunction that he marry again. Fortunately, however, Ellen Wilson had taken the precaution of enlisting the help of Dr. Grayson. On the day before her death she had charged the doctor to remind the President—later, when he would listen—that it was her wish that he find another wife.

Grayson's opportunity came in the spring of 1915. Driving down Connecticut Avenue with the President, he bowed to a handsome woman who was wearing a red rose. Wilson asked: "Who was that beautiful lady?" He was told she was Edith Bolling Galt.

One of eleven children of a Virginia judge and the granddaughter of a physician, Edith Galt had been brought up in genteel poverty, under strict discipline, and with little formal education. Sixteen years younger than Wilson, she was the widow of a prosperous jeweler, whose store in Washington she supervised after her husband's death in 1908. It happened that a close friend of hers was being courted by Dr. Grayson and the doctor had won Mrs. Galt's support of his wooing.

Grayson noted the warmth of the President's interest in the lady and undertook to encourage it. He perceived an opportunity to discharge the duty that Ellen Wilson had laid upon him. Moreover, he saw in Edith Galt an ideal companion for Helen Bones, who had been ill, lacked intimate friends in Washington, and found her life in the White House confining.

When Grayson first asked Mrs. Galt to take Miss Bones for a walk he was rebuffed. The widow said that she was not "a society person" and desired no relation with official Washington. However, the doctor took Helen Bones to Mrs. Galt's residence in a White House car and they persuaded her to join them for a ride in Rock Creek Park. The ladies became friends and there were more outings, and after them tea by the fire in the Galt home. Helen Bones, faithful to the wish of the first Mrs. Wilson that her husband marry again, told of the unfailing sweetness of "Cousin Woodrow" to his relatives. Although the President seemed to Mrs. Galt very remote, her imagination was fired by the picture of a lonely man, bearing hs personal bereavement without complaint and dedicating himself to the responsibilities of his great office.

In March, after one of their walks, Miss Bones persuaded her new friend to have tea at the White House. When they went upstairs and emerged from the elevator, they came face to face with the President and Dr. Grayson, just back from the golf course. "I think you might invite us for tea," Grayson said. Edith Galt, happy that she was wearing an attractive hat and a suit tailored in Paris, noted that the golfers' attire was decidedly not smart. After changing, they joined the ladies before the fire in the sitting room for tea and an hour of good talk. But Mrs. Galt declined an invitation to remain for dinner.

On April 7 she dined at the White House, after Helen Bones had arranged that the President accompany them on one of their rides. He sat on the front seat, next to the chauffeur, and said hardly a word; but after dinner he charmed them with a reading of three English poems. Then he fell to talking about his boyhood and his dear father. Edith Galt felt her heart in tune with his because of her reverence for her own father. His warmth of heart that evening won her, she later recorded, as "a real friend." Their rides together, with Helen Bones present, became frequent. In the White House car in the cool, fragrant evenings of April their understanding deepened. He no longer awed her as the President of the United States. They shared enthusiasms for the Old South and for the fine qualities of life and its humors. He confided in her about the perplexities of his office with confidence that she would show the absolute loyalty that he demanded of all those close to him. After their tête-à-têtes his mind seemed cleared and sharpened. This lady of soft and musical voice was both vivid and lovely, the kind of person he would have raved about to his Ellen as a rare find.

Despite the limitations of his high office, Wilson's courtship became as spirited, in this his fifty-ninth year, as it had been when in his youth he had first set eyes upon Ellen Axson. He wrote his first note to Edith Galt on April 28 and gave her a book of essays by Hamerton. (He had given Miss Ellie Lou a similar work by this author at the beginning of his first courtship.) Two days later she was invited with Grayson's sweetheart to dine at the White House. On May 4 she came again for dinner. He arranged to be left alone with her on the south portico in the evening; and there he told her that he loved her and direly needed companionship.

Startled, she protested that he had been widowed less than a year, and also that he did not really know her. If it had to be yes or no, she said, it would have to be no. Though he warned of the gossip that might embarrass them and explained that this hazard would prevent his calling frequently at her home, she thanked him for his frankness and agreed that they continue their friendly talks during rides and at the White House. The next morning he looked so disconsolate that Helen Bones reproached Mrs. Galt. Her answer was that she did want the friendship to go on, but feared she might be enthralled by the glamor of the presidency rather than by true love. She rode with him in the May evenings, and he cleared his mind by telling her of his efforts to keep the nation out of war and to find a secretary of state in whom he could have confidence.

They plunged into a correspondence that was to go on for five months, deepening the channels of emotion as it flowed. They confessed that their thoughts turned to each other at bedtime, and often kept them awake. Lamenting his pitiful inability to satisfy her and to win her, he resolved to be patient without end. Every power in him was happily free, he wrote, when she was near. He needed her as a boy needs a sweetheart, or a man a helpmate. If only she could understand the boy's heart and simple mind that lay under the veneer of the public man! Would she not stretch out her arms and give him a chance to make her happy? He felt sure that she could love him for his own sake if she would shut out the circumstances of the world; but he would take her on a basis of friendship if that was necessary.

Vital papers of state were shown to her. When she praised a speech or a diplomatic note he attributed whatever merit it had to her inspiration. Sometimes he chuckled at her counsel, as when she advised that it might not be safe to confer alone with the German ambassador, Count von Bernstorff. Wilson explained that the envoy came not to murder him, but to help him to bring the crass German government to its senses, and that actually he had come to like the man. But he did not demur when she denounced William Jennings Bryan as a deserter or characterized him as an "awful creature" who, she hoped, would "expire of an overdose of peace or grapejuice." When Bryan resigned, however, the President confessed that he was "touched to the quick." He told her that when he invited Bryan to the White House for a peaceful farewell he could not do it with genuine cordiality, but consented on the best political advice in order to avert any reaction against himself on the ground of unfairness to the Great Commoner.

Reading and rereading his letters, she responded by quoting verse, and wrote: "I pledge all that is best in me—to help, to sustain, to comfort"—and "into the space that separates us I send my spirit to seek yours. . . ." But at first she asked for time to accept the unbelievable fact that he loved her. She promised to welcome his love if it could quicken what had long been dead in her. "If I am dead (as I believe) you will not blame me for seeking to live—even if it means pain in your own tender heart—when my pulses refuse to beat in unison with yours."

When the President went to New York in the yacht *Mayflower* to review the Atlantic fleet he took her along. They rode out heavy weather together and her presence made him feel that the ship was his home. Back in the White House, he bought orchids for her, and the head usher's little boy delivered them inconspicuously on his bicycle. When Wilson gave her a ring she assured him that although she took off her rings at night, this one would stay on.

In a letter written near the end of May he celebrated their self-discipline. He conceived that their love was one of patrician gallantry, and above self-indulgence. Only the thought of his knightly duty to her enabled him to keep himself in hand, and it was so hard! However, that very night, according to his confession in a letter written afterwards, he was thrilled by her parting kiss. The next letter alluded to a little unconscious trill that he detected in her voice. The next one, dashed off in pencil, implored her to find out whether or not she really loved him. To this she replied: "You are master of my heart but *you* must conquer!"

This crescendo was briefly interrupted by a misunderstanding. Helen Bones warned her Cousin Woodrow that his lady's feelings had been hurt by something he had said about "quicksand" (perhaps in description of her love at this moment). This threw him into a spasm of grief that led him to write of many, many hours of deep depression and exquisite suffering that brought on a kind of illness, an illness he could not explain and for which the doctor had no remedy. Yes, he would try to make himself master of her life, depending on a higher power.

She came to dinner that night, and when they parted it seemed to her—"radiantly happy," she said—that they had a better understanding than ever. To him it was the happiest of their trysts. Another chapter in their romance had begun.

Two days later he wrote of holding her in his arms and kissing her, she whispering that she could not be happy away from him. He confessed to homesickness for her after the delights of the evenings, and she wrote that she was happy because he felt that "home" was where she was. He wrote that every time he saw her he fell in love all over again. One night she had a headache and he eased it by laying on hands. On June 20 he recalled in a letter that when he had held her the previous night she was passionately awakened and shaken by the consciousness of it all. The love in which he held her close, he said, was a sort of worship, full of reverence for the sacred things that were being laid open to him.

After the sinking of the *Lusitania* on May 7, as American relations with Germany came to a crisis, it was more important than ever that the people of the United States should feel that their President was devoting all his energies to his duties. The man in the street could not be expected to accept Wilson's feeling that he could be a more effective public servant while carrying on an affair with a lovely and sympathetic woman. Despite the measures that were taken to protect the President's secret, gossip ran beyond control. There was dismay among the servants and men of the executive staff who had sweet memories of Ellen Axson Wilson and recalled that she had been dead less than a year. Grayson became alarmed, and began to wonder what the friendship that he had encouraged might portend for the nation. He wrote to House, when the Colonel returned from Europe in June, that there was much to tell him—something very confidential that was worrying him a lot. He wanted the Colonel's advice badly, he said.[1]

On June 24 Wilson bared his soul to House, saying that the Colonel was the only person in the world with whom he could discuss everything. What would House think of his marrying again? . . . Did he believe it would lessen the President's influence with the American people? . . . And when did he think it could be done? He needed companionship, he explained, and his "dear dead wife" would be the first to approve if she could know, for she had talked to him about it.

It seemed to the Colonel, who had just felt the passions of Europe at first hand, that as a symbol of national good will Woodrow Wilson was at that moment the greatest asset of the world. Convinced that the President's physical welfare would be served by marriage, he encouraged his friend; but he suggested that the wedding would be more acceptable to the people of the country if it were postponed until the

---

[1] Grayson to House, June 21, 1915. *See also* I. H. Hoover, *Forty-Two Years in the White House*, p. 64. Dr. Grayson had been dismayed by a gossipy story printed in *Town Topics* of Feb. 15, 1915, to the effect that rumor linked the President's name with those of Mary Hulbert and Mrs. Borden Harriman, who had just lost her husband. Such rumors, Grayson told House in a letter of Feb. 15, made him "feel like sending for Captain Bill [McDonald] and shooting."

following spring. Noting that Wilson was mentally exhausted after they had talked all morning about affairs abroad and politics at home, the Colonel advised him to have a long vacation and offered to take upon his own back any burdens that seemed too heavy.

This talk took place at Harlakenden, just after Wilson arrived at this vacation haven in Cornish, New Hampshire. Mrs. Galt, ostensibly on a visit to the President's daughters, had preceded him two days before in the company of Helen Bones, since it would not do for newsmen to see and photograph the glamorous widow traveling in Wilson's party. Some of the family accompanied them when they went out in the car in the afternoons. After dinner the lovers walked hand in hand in the moonlight. Then, sitting in the living room with the young relatives for readings of history in the making, the President revealed official papers and explained their significance. Sometimes they read from his own *History of the American People,* and he told them that it was harder to make history than to write it.

Late in July, Wilson had to go back to Washington for a week to confer with Secretary Lansing about the third *Lusitania* note. It was hard for her to let him go, and the day after his departure she wrote: "I would not go near the sofa—it was too full of memories." He found time to write to her daily, assuring her that she was the perfect play-mate and companion of his mind, that he had been invigorated by the three weeks under the same roof with her, and that the promise of the first chapter of their romance had been confirmed and fulfilled.

He returned to Harlakenden for another week of dalliance. On the last night before a long separation she capitulated, on the porch and "on the big davenport in the living room" (according to a letter that she wrote three week later). There was no doubt now but that she would marry him. She was not yet ready, however, to marry the President of the United States. Perhaps later, when he was out of office . . .

In order to throw gossips off the trail, they arranged to be apart all of August while she traveled about with friends. Solitary in the White House, he wrote daily letters that ran to great length, sometimes as much as twenty pages of his handsome script, and he took pride in the regularity with which he got them off when he went down to breakfast. In these effusions he idealized his passion as he had in woo-ing Ellen Axson, to whom he had once commended a "chivalrous, al-most worshipful regard for woman" as "the truest badge of nobility in man." He glorified their last evening together as a night in heaven, and their last week as the fourth chapter of their romance, so rounded out with sweet experiences of what they meant to each other, and ending in a happiness so full of every element of perfect love that no doubt or fear or question could touch it with so much as a shadow. Once she had unlocked the door, he wrote, she had loved royally and without limit, so that all the sweet things he had imagined had come true.

In these lonely evening hours in which they had become accustomed to draw the curtains and shut out the world he indulged in fantasies, kissing her portrait as if it were her very self. When he awakened, he told her, a delicious consciousness filled his heart. Everything she did was done with the rich greatness of royalty. He yearned almost beyond endurance to fondle her and stay by her. She could love as it would transport any man to be loved. In one epistle that ran to forty pages he declared that nothing made him so happy as a sense of union with her. And he felt as free as he was happy.

Her scrawled responses were on a lesser scale. They sometimes harked back to the nights together at Cornish. "How I do long for my love nest at Harlakenden," she wrote, "and find myself listening for a dear footstep in the hall, or the sound of a vibrant tone that finds its echo in my heart." A week after their last tryst she wondered whether he was "thinking of this time last Saturday night and of our happiness together." And a few days later she wrote, an hour before midnight: "I have come to look forward to this time with you every night . . . as the happiest part of the day," and "I hope you get to bed early and will dream that I am with you and holding you safe in my arms while, with very tender fingers, I press down your tired lids and bid you sleep while I keep watch beside you." And then, on August 19: "Oh how I want you this minute!"

In some letters she wrote as if he were a little boy; in others she addressed him as "my sovereign Lord" and "His Excellency Woodrow Rex" whose "most loyal subject" she was. She told him of reading one of his letters through three times without stopping. She wanted it to go on and on. "It brought you so vividly to me and I could feel your dear heart beating against mine as I held you close. . . ."

"The clock is striking midnight and I must go to bed," she wrote on August 16. "I have on my wrapper and am by the window—I also have on one pair of the lovely white silk stockings [he had sent her these, which were a gift to the President from a Belgian lady], and . . . they make me feel so very rich—I never had such a luxury before as twelve pair at once . . . —and they look so pretty on—that I think that is one of the reasons I sat up to write tonight—instead of getting in bed as

I usually do. A fond and very tender kiss my precious Woodrow, be-fore we put out the light—and I feel your dear arms fold round me."

And two days later: "Yes, dear heart, it is a bargain—we will cheat separation of its victory by putting more in our letters than even our lips can say—Really this is easier than it would seem—when we recall how little we do *say* when we are together—we *mostly know* each other's thoughts through the windows of the soul—instead of speech."

She signed her letters "yours now and always" and "always your own," and longed for wisdom so that she might be a staff for him to lean on. She offered "keen sympathy and comprehension," and wrote: "You will lay your hand on mine, and with the other turn the pages of history." He thought this sentence felicitous and congratulated her on it.

During their separation in August he frequently mailed to her what they called "the big envelope," enclosing copies of state papers. But near the end of the month he concluded that this practice was too risky and he abandoned it, sending only what he called "flimsies." To some of these he pinned slips on which he penciled frank opinions. He con-fided that he could discuss measures of preparedness with General Hugh Scott, the chief of staff, with assurance that they would be en-tirely understood and intelligently obeyed, whereas Secretary of War Garrison was a self-opinionated politician who would not listen.

On August 19 the *Arabic* was torpedoed, and Colonel House wrote to suggest several courses that might be followed in dealing with the German government. The President complained to his lady that House did not advise but put it up to the President. She ventured, apologeti-cally, to observe that although she knew House was "true," his appear-ance and letters did not suggest strength. After the Colonel had advised that their wedding be put off she had gone so far as to write that he seemed to her "a weak vessel." Wilson stoutly defended his most inti-mate counselor. Nevertheless the seed sown here did not perish. Four years later at the Paris Peace Conference, when House showed symp-toms of conceit, the criticism was finally to be accepted by the then ailing President.

In August the lovers communicated by mail and telephone without breaches in the system of security they contrived. Their letters did not go through White House channels. "Ike" Hoover, the head usher, mailed the President's in public post boxes; hers were addressed to Margaret Wilson. During the last week of August, however, Edith Galt became anxious about the future. When Wilson suggested that Margaret call on Mrs. Galt as soon as she returned to Washington, she questioned the wisdom of this. "It breaks my heart to say this," she wrote. ". . . I do want you so—and want to keep you with every fiber of my being—but don't you think people would know, and make gossip of it? I have racked my brain to think of some other way to make it safe to see you—but so far nothing comes." And on the next day she reminded him of the caution they owed "to that awful tyrant, the World." Telling of reports from her friends of gossip rampant in Washington, she wrote: "We have ourselves in hand, and I can go on—If we relax—we probably couldn't."

One of his letters invited her to come to the White House for dinner when she came home. She asked just how he proposed to arrange it. "Yes, my precious One," she wrote, "I do understand that we will have to stand gossip and try to be callous to it, and I do not mean to make your burden heavier by useless heed to such stuff, but I thought right now, when the country thinks you are giving every thought to the complications of the Government, it might be particularly bad to have you discussed. But I know you would not suggest anything that would not be dignified, so I live in the radiance of the thought that we will be together."

"My precious weary Pilot," she went on. "I will come and hold those dear strong hands that steer the ship of state in both my own, and kiss the tired eyes that have strained so to see the right course through the blackness ahead, and try to shut out the tumult that is raging around you on every side by whispering in your listening ears these tender words: 'I love you, my precious Woodrow, and I will stand by though the waters dash over the ship, and carry out your orders.'"

When she returned to her home at the beginning of September she found it decorated with flowers from the White House. A note invited her to dinner with the Wilson family. Afterwards the lovers went riding, with Helen Bones beside them. To Edith Galt her lover's eyes seemed pools of suffering. He now appeared to be even more wonderful than she remembered him, as he told her of the growing danger of war. It had been so long since he had held her hands in his, he said, that he found it hard to govern himself. Confessing that during the past day and a half they had been foolish, he nevertheless went so far as to say: "I have no right to ask you to help me by sharing this load that is almost breaking my back, for I know your nature and you might do it out of sheer pity."

At this she hugged him and replied: "Well, if you won't ask me,

I will volunteer, and be ready to be mustered in as soon as can be."

He protested that he needed her now. If the waiting continued much longer it was likely to become intolerable, he said. He aspired to give her *each day* just the sort of love she wanted on that day. He told his daughters immediately of the betrothal. They were delighted and no longer felt that, as they had informed Edith Galt, she was contributing to their father's depression. The only question now was the timing of a public announcement that would put an end to the threat of unpleasant publicity.

Meanwhile the politicians of the party had taken alarm. The people liked to cast their President in the mold of Abraham Lincoln—a remote, lonely patriarch, worn by personal sorrow and bowed by the grief of warring mankind. What would the citizens think if they learned that, only a year after the death of his first wife, he was behaving like a lovesick youth? The Democratic chiefs feared they might lose the election in 1916.

Told of the concern of the party men, Wilson asked McAdoo to discuss the matter with House and Lansing. Grayson, too, continued to fear the sequel of the events that he had started. Feeling that the President was using House's approval as an excuse for absorption in his lady, the doctor went to Beverly at the end of July to confer with the Colonel. Some of what was said to House was so disturbing that he did not care to confide it even to his secret diary. He did record, however, that the President seemed "wholly absorbed in this love affair" and was "neglecting practically everything else." House regretted the timing of the romance. Nevertheless he accepted Grayson's opinion that unless Wilson married, and quickly, he would go into a decline. House, thinking he had never seen a man more dependent on the companionship of a woman, regretted that this great leader should be attacked for doing what a private citizen could do without provoking criticism.

On September 10 Grayson wrote, using code names for the people mentioned, to warn House that Wilson was going to ask for advice on "an extremely delicate matter." The President wanted to know what the Colonel would think if the engagement should be announced in the autumn. Tumulty had told the doctor that it would be a fatal mistake, politically. But Wilson was impatient, and said: "If the people do not trust me, now is the time to find out."

At this juncture Wilson's friends meddled in a way that threw the President into a painful dilemma. Grayson whispered to McAdoo that the Chief had sent a large check to Mary Hulbert; and McAdoo, suspicious and wishing to ferret out the truth, invented a ruse that would, he hoped, make the President confess any wrong of which he might be guilty.[2] He often lunched alone with his father-in-law during the autumn; and one day he fabricated a tale about an anonymous letter mailed from Los Angeles, where Mrs. Hulbert now lived. This fictitious letter, McAdoo said, asserted that that lady was displaying improper notes from the President and tongues were wagging on the Pacific coast.

Having no sin to confess, Wilson's conscience was untroubled. But having confidence in McAdoo's word, and a comprehension of the depths to which political enemies could go, he did not entirely disbelieve the cruel story of the anonymous letter. He could not understand, though, how anyone who seemed as virtuous as his good friend Mary Hulbert could stoop so low. He was resolved to permit no blackmail. But he could not bring himself to expose Edith Galt's name to political scuttlebutt.

He called Grayson to his desk and began to write a note to release his beloved from her pledge. Setting his jaw and turning white to the lips, he took up a pen; but his hand shook and he could set down nothing. Finally he said to the doctor: "I cannot bring myself to write this; you go, Grayson, and tell her everything and say my only alternative is to release her from any promise."

The doctor performed his mission faithfully, and his manner conveyed to Edith Galt the intensity of his chief's suffering. She was hurt deeply, as if by an "awful earthquake" that "caused doubt about the *certainty* of anything." After a sleepless night she came to a decision before dawn. "I am not afraid of any gossip or threat, with your love as my shield," she assured her beloved. "This is my pledge, dearest one, I will stand by you—not for duty, not for pity, not for honour—but for love—trusting, protecting, comprehending love." This pledge released Wilson's pent-up tears, ending his misery and taking the strain off his heart. He would treasure this promise, he said, with the one she had written on the porch at Harlakenden. Mortified that he had not made her happy, he asked that he might go to her rather than she to him.

"Of course you can come to me," she wrote the next day, cautioning

[2] Edith Wilson testifies in *My Memoir* (p. 78) that House confessed to her, years later, that he and McAdoo had planned the ruse regarding Mrs. Hulbert together. "When I asked McAdoo about it," Mrs. Wilson wrote, "he said that it was entirely 'the Colonel's idea.'" In his diary House attributes the idea to McAdoo and calls it "cruel." See Arthur S. Link, *Woodrow Wilson*, Vol. IV, p. 5n.

him to bring Grayson as protection against public gossip. They spent that evening and the next together. She hesitated to reveal her wound for fear of hurting him. An hour after he left, however, she confessed in a letter that it was the "earthquake" that had made her doubt "the permanent fixedness of happiness." She begged him to bring her out of the shadows and help her to trust. "It is so easy to yield to love," she wrote. ". . . But I must not. We must both try to sleep and get back to normal—and think only that this earthquake has left our love untouched. . . . You have promised to get another man's point of view and I have promised to let things go on as before."

A few days later, on September 22, Colonel House came to Washington in response to word from Grayson that the "California situation" had become "embarrassing." No friend or associate of the lonely man had yet dared to risk incurring displeasure by giving the advice that they thought essential to his political welfare. He would confide only in House. When he and the Colonel were alone, he confessed that, though his relations with Mary Hulbert had been entirely platonic, he had been indiscreet in writing to her more emotionally than was prudent.[3] Learning that her son had lost money in the fruit business in California, he had sent a check for $7,500 to buy two mortgages on real estate. ("I am so glad, from the bottom of my heart, to have been able to help a little," he wrote to Mrs. Hulbert on November 10, 1915, "though it was no more than any friend would have done and involved no sacrifice of any kind.") Now he was told that Mrs. Hulbert had allowed his letters to become known to unfriendly gossips. If anyone intended to blackmail him, he told House, he was ready to let every letter he ever wrote be published.

In a note written to his lady after this conversation Wilson reaffirmed his faith in his friend as a counselor who could be depended on for cold-blooded judgment—a man of quiet, serene, benign strength. She had begged him to let House help in every way possible, at the same time reminding him that they both were "strong enough to do the right thing—no matter what it cost." She talked with House herself,

[3] The quotations that appear in this book from the letters to Mary Allen Hulbert have been chosen with the intention of presenting a truly representative sample of this lively correspondence. Wilson was too gallant ever to write to Mrs. Hulbert of the suspicions that McAdoo had aroused, and he wrote on Oct. 4, 1915, to tell this lady that he wanted her to be one of the first to know of the "blessing" that had come to him. Almost all of Wilson's letters to Mrs. Hulbert may now be seen in the Wilson Collection in the Library of Congress. A very few, containing scathing remarks about prominent men, were destroyed to end the possibility of their theft by political enemies. The writer confirmed his information about the relationship of Woodrow Wilson with Mrs. Peck and about their correspondence in a talk with Allen Hulbert on Sept. 17, 1964.

and wrote: "He is just as nice and fine as you pictured him—and his admiration for you is sufficient to establish my faith in his judgment and intelligent perceptions. . . . You will tell me honestly if he *liked* me." This brought a prompt response from her lover, to the effect that he had never seen House so enthusiastic, that the Colonel's face actually glowed as he said the engagement was most fortunate for the President and the country.

The Colonel, perceiving immediately that he could not tell his friend the whole truth without exposing offenses by Grayson and McAdoo that might never be forgiven, could merely give reassurance in general. Asked to decide when the betrothal should be announced, he was moved by the pathos of his friend's loneliness. It seemed to him that scandalous gossip should be checked by announcing the engagement. Moreover, he found Edith Galt truly charming and inspiriting. His ego was touched by her lively interest in him and her revelation that the President spoke of him as a man of lucid mind, almost like a business clearing-house.

After giving thought to the problem for a few days, House pronounced the verdict that his friend wanted. "I do not believe there is anything to be gained by delaying the announcement of your engagement," he wrote to Wilson on October 1. The President forwarded the letter to his lady.

By this time the shock of the "earthquake" had passed, after Wilson had given assurance that he understood the lady's struggle as well as if it had taken place in his own heart. He promised to guide her to a place of peace and certainty. Their plans would settle themselves. They would do the natural thing, which would prove to be the wise and dignified thing. In a letter of September 29 he recalled a warm embrace by the fire. Nevertheless, when she said good-night her exquisite beauty seemed to be not for him. She was still shivering at the prospect of publicity, though she had consented to an announcement of the engagement in the first week of October. Her lover passed a wakeful night, and at four in the morning composed a dialogue between Woodrow Wilson and the Imp Anxiety. The next day she apologized for what she described as her "sulking" when he proposed to consult old friends about their plan for the announcement. Confessing that she was "cross and half-sick," she challenged him to keep her in harness and to guide without her knowing it.

Their emotions rose to a crest in evenings spent together and in a continuing exchange of daily notes. On the fourth, exactly five months since he had first proposed, he wrote of love beyond expression, of his eagerness to whisper it in his darling's lips as he held her close. He had never felt more buoyant, he went on, than after an evening when her radiance made her love exquisitely real to him. Their devotion had grown inevitably, like a great tide, and the tasks of the day now looked pleasant and easy.

The President was not too absorbed in his love, however, to fail to rejoice when he received assurances from Bernstorff that seemed to him perfectly satisfactory. He informed his lady that Germany had come to terms. "I hope the German conquest is only the happy beginning of good fortune," she replied. "I loved you more last night than ever. I am so proud of you, my precious Woodrow, and so proud that the world will know you through big situations such as this, for only in big things can you find your true interpretation."

Wilson wrote radiantly to Mary Hulbert and to friends who had been close to his Ellen.[4] He typed an announcement of his engagement and, after showing it to Mrs. Galt, gave it to Tumulty. The secretary released it with a pledge of Wilson's support to woman suffrage in New Jersey, hoping thus to minimize the adverse reaction of feminine voters.

Woodrow Wilson could go and come with Edith Galt openly now. He entertained her family at the White House and began to introduce her to his friends. He was as eager to embrace his old cronies in his new happiness as he had once been to share Ellen Axson with Heath Dabney. He wrote to his Princeton classmate "Cow" Woods: "I will have to have the old gang over here sometime to make sure that Mrs. Galt gets authentic information about my past. I hope when the time comes you will all be easy on me." The Class of '79 was invited to dinner at the White House and elected the new First Lady an honorary member.

He made it clear that everything was to be shared in this marriage, as in his first: family, friends, and the secrets of state. When he had no time to visit his lady he would sometimes convey, by telephone or by messenger, an idea of the problems that preoccupied him. But all day on Sundays, after church, he was with her; and on other evenings he stayed late at night at her house and then walked home briskly in the crisp autumn air, taking the curbs with a dance step and whistling a

---

[4] Wilson was so considerate of the feelings of the White House servants who had loved Ellen Wilson that he was relieved when one to whom he confided his secret answered: "I am both glad and sorry. I believe if Mrs. Wilson could know, she would approve."

popular tune. Then he would be up early in the morning ready for golf. Dour secret service guards grinned at his boyish antics. It astounded them that a mortal of fifty-eight could be so agile, as he walked through Rock Creek Park holding hands with his lady and leaping over obstacles. The servants saw a change in his disposition. He took more interest in the affairs of the household and in his own appearance, was more considerate and understanding.

It seemed to House, who was conferring already with party leaders about tactics for the presidential election that was to come, that the President was so engrossed by his fiancée that he was neglecting public business. He appeared to be "dodging trouble" and, in the flush of self-confidence that came from success in courting, to be making indiscreet remarks about members of the Cabinet, the Senate, and the press.[5]

The Colonel was somewhat reassured when the lovers visited him in New York near the end of November and the President read his draft of an annual message to Congress that showed a masterful grasp of the issues of the day. Nevertheless, House was so concerned about Edith Galt's lack of experience for the duties facing her that he ventured to warn against people who would try to influence her husband through her. The Colonel suggested that she follow his own method of filing the names and causes of special pleaders, and explained that when he took his notes out of the file several weeks later, the problems usually had solved themselves without any worry to the President. She promised to do this, and the Colonel then advised her to think aloud with her husband at all times and to let him be her only confidant.

They fixed December 18 as their wedding day. Rather than undergo the publicity of a White House function, they invited their relatives

[5] Wilson appears to have been no less dependent upon House's friendly counsel, and perhaps more so, after becoming acquainted with Edith Galt. When, at the end of August, the *New York Herald* printed a story about a "break between the comrades over the question of recognizing Carranza," Wilson angrily banned all representatives of that paper from the White House, pending an apology and disavowal, and demanded the discharge of the offending reporter. To reassure the Colonel, the President wrote on Aug. 31: "Of course you have known how to interpret the silly, malicious lies that the papers have recently been publishing about a disagreement between you and me, but I cannot deny myself the pleasure of sending you just a line of deep affection to tell you how they have distressed me." Moreover, to show the public that there was no breach, Wilson insisted that House take a front seat in the presidential box when they went to the theater together on Sept. 24, 1915.

A few weeks later House was wondering whether the President was not indiscreet in showing the Colonel's letters to Lansing. "While Lansing does not show the slightest trace of jealousy," House wrote in his diary on Nov. 28, "I am wondering how much of that kind of thing he will be able to stand." Early in 1916 the Colonel, learning from Polk that Lansing showed pique at House's activities, cautioned the President to be careful. Wilson, who in the summer of 1915 had shown consideration for the *amour propre* of the secretary of state, now replied, bluntly, that Lansing must understand that the President himself was conducting foreign affairs and would do it in the way he thought best.

and the Cabinet to Edith Galt's little home for the ceremony. They made a game of their getaway, sitting behind drawn shades while their limousine outsped pursuing newsmen, and boarding a special train at Alexandria. Early the next morning, when they awakened at Hot Springs, Virginia, the bridegroom put on a frock coat and gray morning trousers, thrust his hands in his pockets, and danced a jig while he whistled a popular tune. The mountains were cloaked with snow, and in the crisp air they explored back roads by automobile and on foot. Woodrow Wilson was "exceedingly, perfectly happy," he wrote to Margaret Elliott the day after Christmas. "Edith is a very wonderful person, really and truly." At the same time Helen Bones was writing to Cousin Harriet Woodrow Wells, who had been Wilson's first love: "Perhaps few who don't know Cousin Woodrow can guess how truly he still loves Cousin Ellen, though he also truly loves this other sweet wife of his."

Edith Galt Wilson offered resources that he needed. At the White House they breakfasted alone before an open fire, following the homely custom of keeping dishes warm by setting them on the hearth. Then she would go with him to the study and blot his signatures on the stacks of routine papers that awaited him. Soon he depended on her to code and decode secret messages and to help him clear "The Drawer" of red-tabbed, urgent documents, some of which he burned as soon as he read them. She would linger sometimes for the delight of hearing his fluent, lucid dictation. Going off for a while to attend to her own duties, she would watch from her window for a signal that he was ready to go to the executive offices. Then she would join him and they would stroll together for a few moments outdoors—in Ellen Wilson's rose garden if the weather was fair. Reaching the office door, he would look at his watch, kiss her, and follow her with his eyes as she walked back to the house. When she turned and waved, he looked at his watch again, and if there was a minute left before eleven o'clock, he walked quickly to meet her in one more embrace.

Her humor and radiance stimulated his love of fun. She rode with him occasionally, and they went golfing together often. He told her stories in dialect, as he was accustomed to do when playing with his other comrades of the links, Dr. Grayson and Colonel Brown; and he drew her laughter with impersonations that spared no one, not even Grayson. In the evenings she read aloud with him, and played the piano and sang to him, or joined him in parlor games or in clownish revelry.

In public, however, they were a portrait of grace and dignity. The President's bride was a handsome foil for the "Tommie" Wilson who loved parades, the noticeable man who wore formal dress elegantly and looked every inch a statesman. Her social gifts relieved him of much of the strain that state functions imposed.

On January 7, dressed in a white gown with "angel sleeves," she made a dramatic debut as First Lady, greeting more than three thousand guests at a ball given in honor of the Wilsons at the Pan American Union. Responding to the beauty of massed orchids mirrored in a pool, the court uniforms of the diplomats, and the scarlet-coated Marine Band, Edith Wilson herself added an exotic touch—a large fan like those used in ceremonies in the Far East, fabricated of gray feathers mounted on a handle of mosaic. And the morning after this venture into society she was ready, spick and trim in traveling attire, to accompany her husband on an arduous speaking tour.

The wistful widower who had dragged himself through the preceding winter by burying his mind in routine was now a bridegroom fit to fight wildcats. Political life had become again the adventure that it had been when he first took high office in New Jersey. His daily work seemed to him "interesting and inspiring," full of "electrical thrills."

Book Two

WORLD PROPHET

CHAPTER I

The War Strikes Home

DURING THE MONTHS in which he mourned Ellen Wilson and wooed Edith Galt, the war in Europe haunted the President as "a nightmare" to which he could see no finish.

His first and most immediate responsibility—that of defending neutral rights against the pressures of the belligerents—put him in the position of an arbiter who was challenged to make judgments without benefit of either reliable evidence or a binding code of law. Such precedents as existed had grown out of international conferences at The Hague, the American Civil War, and the Congress of Paris that met in the year of Wilson's birth. But these antecedents seemed vague or definitely obsolete.[1] The President confessed that he saw no shore lights to a channel in which he might sail safely.

His own people were bombarding him with denunciation of atrocities said to have been committed by the contending armies. Lurid stories were given jingoistic play in the press of the United States, and taken up by citizens whose European ancestry made them susceptible to emotional reaction. But the President did not act hastily. When a niece spoke of one of the horrible tales that were in circulation, he said sternly: "The facts are bad enough. Don't repeat such a story."[2] Second thought, he found, often shaded the blacks and whites of morality into grays. It was cruel torture that his will inflicted on his heart; but the very same scholarly sensibility that was wounded deeply by the burning of the Louvain library by Germans restrained him from delivering verdicts on the basis of incomplete and partisan testimony. It would be unwise, premature, and unneutral, he said, for any single nation, no matter how remote, to form a final judgment.

He felt that war could be kept at ocean's length only by hard thinking, not by wishing. Keeping his eye intently on all vital dispatches of the State Department, he took foreign affairs upon his own conscience

---

[1] Counselor Robert Lansing, preparing to answer possible questions from Congress about the attitude of the State Department toward violations of The Hague Conventions, drew up for the President, on Nov. 23, 1914, three reasons for inaction: (1) that evidence was purely *ex parte* and impartial investigation was impracticable; (2) that a neutral government was not bound to interfere in the actions of belligerents which did not affect its own citizens; (3) that The Hague Conventions did not bind the parties to joint action in enforcing their observance. Wilson's comment on these observations was "sound and wise."

[2] Alice Wilson McElroy to the writer, April 30, 1950.

more closely than ever. He intended to uphold neutrality as rigidly as he had once kept classroom discipline—by immediate action against disturbances and deviations.

It was soon apparent that the Entente looked to the United States for large supplies of munitions, and Germany would need food, copper, and cotton. Wilson must deal, therefore, with commercial impulses that were as great a threat to neutrality as the emotions of moralists.

Before long, it became clear that the credit balances outstanding in America would not be sufficient to pay for the volume of goods needed by the hard-pressed belligerents, and Americans were tempted to stake money on the outcome of the fighting.

At the very outbreak of the war, Bryan had frowned on a proposal of French financiers for getting credits in the United States. Feeling that money was "the worst of contrabands" because it commanded all other things, the secretary of state argued that dollars committed to the service of a belligerent were no more entitled to protection by the nation of their origin than were citizens who enlisted in a foreign army. Moved by this argument during the days when he was distraught by bereavement, Wilson ruled that loans by American bankers to any foreign government that was at war were "inconsistent with the true spirit of neutrality." For a time New York bankers curbed their anxiety to aid France.

Early in October, however, officials of the National City Bank of New York sought a definition of government policy. They proposed to Counselor Robert Lansing of the State Department, who as a New York lawyer had learned to talk the language of the financiers, that to make it possible for foreign buyers to purchase from the United States rather than elsewhere American bankers should grant short-term credits to European governments, both belligerent and neutral, under certain conditions.

Adopting the views of the financiers as his own, Lansing took their statement to the President. Bryan was out of town, and Wilson's confidence in the counselor was sufficient to make it seem unnecessary to consult other advisers. The arrangement set forth by Lansing would neither draw gold from the American people nor result in the commitment of the savings of individual citizens to the financing of foreign war. It seemed to Wilson merely a means of facilitating trade by a system of credits that would avoid the clumsy and impracticable method of cash payments. Also, it offered hope of lifting the nation's foreign trade from the doldrums into which it had fallen. On October 30 the National City Bank announced that arrangements were being completed for a special credit to the French government, setting a precedent for a subsequent series of accommodations to the Allies that reached a total value of $1,900,000,000.

Not only credits, but munitions of war as well, were allowed to flow freely to belligerents. Wilson confirmed as "absolutely right" the contention of those who asserted that it would be unneutral to resort to a ban that might in practice hurt one belligerent more than another. Moreover, he told House that it would be "foolish" to check the trade in munitions because this would discourage American preparedness for the possibility of war. It would be neither practical nor constitutional, he explained, for him to do more than "exercise influence." Thus the way was left open for economic interest to complicate the problem of maintaining political neutrality.

Each armed camp was ready to strain any point of law and usage to check commerce that was suspected of aiding the enemy. To interrupt shipments that might conceivably strengthen their opponents, the British Navy was willing to adopt any measures short of provoking the United States to shut off the flow of supplies essential to the war machinery of the Allies. The Foreign Office was on very insecure ground but held its footing adroitly. Replying evasively to an American attempt to commit all belligerents to the code set forth in 1909 in the Declaration of London,[3] the British government extended its list of commodities that were to be subject to seizure at sea until even foodstuffs were included as "conditional contraband." Furthermore, British Orders in Council proclaimed that conditional contraband was liable to capture even if shipped to a neutral port, unless the shipper could prove that there was no intent that it should reach the enemy.

Britain's interferences with cargoes were obnoxious to Yankees who felt that under the Declaration of London no one had a right to meddle with shipments of staple commodities to the Germans, or with any kind of cargo consigned to European neutrals. American shippers, outraged particularly by Britain's assertion of a right to seize vessels on suspicion and take them into port for search, charged that British interests intended to kill American commercial competition.

[3] The Declaration of London, drafted at an international conference that closed on Feb. 26, 1909, divided marine shipments in time of war into absolute contraband (military goods), conditional contraband (commodities useful to civilians as well as to the military and destined for a belligerent port), and noncontraband (goods not essential for war, such as cotton, rubber, and metallic ores). Though passed by the House of Commons, the Declaration was not approved by the House of Lords and therefore never became binding on Britain.

With Wilson's approval, the State Department urged the belligerents to accept the Declaration of London immediately after the outbreak of war. Germany and Austria acceded, but only on condition that Britain also agreed. Since Britain stipulated conditions that she thought essential to efficient conduct of her naval operations, the understanding never became an instrument of international law. The American government hoped nevertheless that it might serve as a basis of practice; but it was soon apparent that new techniques of warfare were outmoding the Declaration's classifications of contraband.

Wilson did not take British departures from the Declaration of London lightly. The new Orders in Council offended him, and he instructed the State Department to prepare a "vigorous protest—one with teeth in it." The note that was drafted was dispatched on September 26. It directed Page to tell Sir Edward Grey of the "grave concern" of the American government and to suggest that public discussion of Britain's announced policy might "awaken memories of controversies which it is the earnest desire of the United States to forget or to pass over in silence." (Explaining to House that present circumstances and those of the War of 1812 ran parallel, he deplored Madison's folly and said: "I only hope I shall be wiser.")[4]

Meanwhile Page, on his own responsibility, was diluting the force of his government's representations. When pressed by Lansing to make representations to Sir Edward Grey that seemed disingenuous, the ambassador protested frankly and heatedly to his friend in the White House. They were "getting into deep water uselessly," Page complained to Wilson, and the argument seemed "academic" to one close to the life-and-death struggle for the existence of "English-speaking civilization." To ask Sir Edward Grey to accept a code of neutrality that Parliament had rejected even in time of peace, Page explained, was to weaken the foreign secretary's defense of the rights of neutral commerce against the attacks of the Admiralty.[5]

Energetic, magnetic, and wholly charming, Page was a powerful force in guiding public opinion both abroad and at home. Thinking that his envoy was overworked and overwrought, and unduly prejudiced by his immediate environment, the President acted to strengthen Page's loyalty in a way that would not wound his generous heart. Not wishing to reprove him directly, Wilson left it to House to steady and guide him. And then, on the 28th, he wrote, himself, to comfort Page:

[4] Foreseeing that the tone of this dispatch would offend Page and Sir Edward Grey, the Colonel persuaded Wilson that before official action was taken the matter should be explored further in private talks. House conferred with Ambassador Spring Rice, showed him a copy of the offending note, and observed that the British envoy was thoroughly alarmed and felt that one paragraph amounted almost to a declaration of war, and that once the message became public, both nations would be committed to positions that it would be difficult to reconcile and embarrassing to abandon. They prevented official presentation of the stern note and substituted a more tactful statement of the case of the United States.

[5] To make sure that his plaint would be heard sympathetically at the White House, Page sent a message secretly, through his son, to the Colonel: "God deliver us, or can you deliver us, from library lawyers. They often lose chestnuts while they argue about burns. See our friend and come here immediately if the case be not already settled. Of utmost importance . . ." House immediately sent the ambassador's feverish communication to the White House with a cooling statement: "I hardly know to what he refers, but perhaps you do. It may be the Declaration of London matter . . . Page is evidently disturbed."

House received another message from Page, dated Oct. 22, which warned that the ambassador had reached the end of his patience. "The Foreign Office doubts our wisdom and prudence since Lansing came into action," the ambassador reported. "If Lansing again brings up the Declaration of London—after four flat and reasonable rejections—I shall resign."

"You need not doubt, my dear friend, that we comprehend and look into the murky darkness of the whole thing with the same thoughts that you have, though, of course, on this side of the water our own life is, at any rate, still free, and I fancy we can manage a little more perspective than it is conceivable should be obtainable from any point of view on your side of the water. I have been distressed to have to maintain our recent debate with Sir Edward Grey, but it was absolutely necessary . . . if we are to remain neutral and to afford Europe the legitimate assistance possible in such circumstances. . . ." This letter was "not a sermon," Wilson assured Page, but "a message of friendship and sympathy and of sincere appreciation" for the ambassador's vivid letters.[6]

The diplomats were constantly embarrassed by the Admiralty's insistence on detaining, in British ports, American goods that were destined apparently for neutral cities but sometimes, actually, for Germany. Legislators, chambers of commerce, and trade associations badgered the State Department and demanded relief from interferences with cargoes and mails. Americans who sympathized with Germany contended that their government was not being strictly impartial in its protests. Tumulty frankly told his chief that he was being criticized for "letting up on Great Britain"; but looking his secretary squarely in the eye, Wilson replied: "I have gone to the very limit in pressing our claims upon England . . . War with England would result in a German triumph. No matter what may happen to me personally in the next election, I will not take any action to embarrass England when she is fighting for her life and the life of the world."

Unfortunately, salt was rubbed in the wounds when, near the end of October, the British added such commodities as petroleum and rubber to their list of absolute contraband. Moreover, retaliating against alleged planting of mines in the North Sea by Germany, they announced that they themselves would mine certain zones; and at the beginning of November they proclaimed the North Sea a military area into which neutral ships would go at their own risk except in accord with directions from the Admiralty. Protest rose to so high a pitch that

[6] W.W. to Page, Oct 28, 1914, Page Papers. Meanwhile Lansing, doubtless influenced by the softening that the flinty contentions of the State Department's lawyers had undergone at the White House, had sent the correspondence on the controversy to the President with a letter of capitulation. "In view of the rigid attitude of the British government," he wrote on Oct. 20, "further attempts to obtain an agreement on the Declaration of London would be useless." Accepting this position, Wilson approved a dispatch that was sent to Page on Oct. 22, bidding him inform his British friends of the concession, and asserting at the same time that the United States would insist upon "the existing rules of international law and the treaties of the United States." The ambassador responded by reporting that within twenty-four hours of the change in American policy every detained ship and cargo but one were released by the British authorities; and he and Sir Edward soon made progress in devising a "working arrangement."

Wilson was forced to take notice. It was now apparent that he must go to the length of issuing a public protest against the vexations that Page had not been able to end by private talks.

Bryan brought a draft of a formal note of remonstrance to the President's desk; but Wilson perceived that it was "in an entirely rough and unliterary form, threatening too." Deleting passages that might give offense, he handed the draft to the secretary of state and suggested that it be rewritten. A few days later, however, Bryan returned with the same text, without changes except those that his chief had indicated. But Wilson swallowed his disappointment and said nothing—"What was there to say?" he remarked in telling a friend of the incident.[7] After he polished the phrasing, the message was cabled to Page on December 26.

This public protest served to demonstrate to neutral shippers that action was being taken to protect their rights. Sir Edward Grey's reply was conciliatory; and the President was content to rest upon the "substantial agreement" on principles that was reached. He felt that it was not worth-while to debate details and he was not unaware that some of the neutral rights now claimed by Americans had been denied by their own government to British traders during the Civil War. Furthermore, he knew that some shippers had made dishonest manifestoes and had concealed contraband goods.

Unfortunately, however, Wilson did not escape detailed litigation with the Foreign Office. Early in January a citizen of the United States named Edward N. Breitung, acting for the German government, availed himself of the American Ship Purchase Act and bought an interned freighter, the *Dacia*, from the Hamburg-American Line with the intention of making shipments to Germany under the American flag. The British government quickly got wind of this transaction. ("Their spy system—'intelligence bureau,' they called it—discovers absolutely everything," Page informed Wilson.) Perceiving that, if the plan was carried out without challenge, it would set a precedent that would perhaps break the blockade, the Foreign Office warned the State

[7] Going over a dispatch written at the State Department at this time, Wilson threw down his pencil and exclaimed: "It's not right to impose such a task upon me." Asked whether he wished another term in the Presidency, Wilson said: "I wish with all my heart that it wouldn't be necessary. I should be much happier doing anything else. If I run again for the Presidency, it will be only to keep Bryan out. I feel like a pig when I sit in my chair and look at him and think, I mustn't let *him* be President; he would be ruinous to the country, ruinous to his own reputation . . . he's the worst judge of character I ever knew, a spoilsman to the core and a determined enemy to civil service reform." House's diary records that when Bryan telephoned to Wilson to discuss patronage and the best means of putting an independent senator "in the hole," the President was amused by the absurdity of the secretary of state's concern with so petty a matter when the world was on fire. When he hung up the receiver he uttered a forceful "damn." Wilson seldom swore, but there were two irritants that could drive him to it—Bryan, and a refractory golf ball.

Department that the ship would be seized if she sailed for a German port.

When the *Dacia* set out on the Atlantic, therefore, the diplomats were thrown into dismay. To be sure, the immediate dilemma was solved when, thanks to a canny suggestion by Page, the French Navy seized and purchased the ship and its cargo. But the President was convinced that the storm aroused was no passing cyclone when he received from Sir Edward Grey a protest so severe that it was designated for his eyes only and those of House.

Woodrow Wilson could say hardly anything now without being accused of favoring one warring alliance or the other. After hours of meditation he sent off to Page, on January 23, one of the longest telegrams that he ever wrote, explaining that the registration of the *Dacia* was no indulgence of German interests, but an affirmation of the constitutional rights of American citizens of German blood. "The great majority of our people," he insisted, "are sensitive about nothing more than about their legitimate trade."

Page was instructed to transmit this message to Sir Edward when a favorable opportunity came and to assure him that the government of the United States would adhere conscientiously to its course of neutrality. The ambassador, however, tucked the note in a pigeonhole and left it there.

There seemed to be only one way to escape the tentacles of controversy that were violating the veil of neutrality, and that was to stop the fight by finding a formula that would satisfy the contending powers. Woodrow Wilson therefore urged his ruling elder to explore the path of mediation.

Colonel House already had put himself on a friendly footing with the foreign offices and with the ambassadors at Washington as well as those at Berlin and at London, and he was ambitious that his great friend should win world-wide renown as a peacemaker. His political instinct told him that discussions might be carried on in private that, if made public or official, would run afoul of jingoism. During the first week of the war House prophesied that Germany was "riding for a fall." He saw that, if a political vacuum developed in Central Europe, it would be exploited fully by Czarist Russia—a view in which Wilson concurred and which he asked House to put before Sir Edward Grey as an argument for immediate peace talks.

Dining with the ambassador of Austria-Hungary, Count Dumba, and listening very well, the Colonel elicited information that Wilson thought "little less than amazing" and "immensely useful as a cross light." The envoy admitted that Germany, dreading that a long war might bring famine, would be ready to consider overtures for peace if only she could first win a decisive victory in France. And at the same time Wilson learned that Ambassador Bernstorff had just told German-American friends that in his opinion Berlin would accept an offer of mediation.

Unfortunately, Bernstorff's informal overture was not guarded so closely as Dumba's frank remark; and when it was reported in the press it lost whatever weight it might have had. For, while neither warring camp could afford to deny that it would cease fighting on what it considered "reasonable terms," yet neither was willing to appear to sue for peace for fear that the world would interpret this as a confession of weakness. Spring Rice hinted that a direct challenge to mediation might be considered by Britain to be an "unfriendly act." Wilson was forced to conclude, therefore, that there was little hope of fashioning a peace out of nothing more substantial than American good will.

Yet he told House that there would be "no harm" in going on with his negotiations; and the Colonel continued the tentative talks. The President agreed that House should keep the secret negotiations in his own hands and concurred in the Colonel's recommendation that "all outside efforts" be discouraged. He was unresponsive to Bryan's plea that the United States, as the leading exponent of Christianity and the foremost advocate of universal peace, should try to fix responsibility for continuing the war and, assuming leadership of world opinion, should urge the warring nations to confer.[8] Bryan's ideals were shared by Wilson and the Colonel; but the President preferred the methods of House. He knew that the Colonel could accomplish more than any official because he could talk and be talked to without commitment.

The envoys of the Central Powers, believing that their fatherlands should consolidate their gains and avoid possible destruction, continued to speak of peace, and Bernstorff fostered House's ambitions. Moreover, the Colonel had an encouraging note from Undersecretary Zimmermann of the Foreign Office at Berlin, intimating that Germany would be glad to listen to any overture that House might elicit from the enemy. This presented an opening, the Colonel suggested to Wilson on December 27: it would be easy now, he thought, to test the reliability of Bernstorff.

[8] Supporting a suggestion by Wilson that munitions be manufactured by a government monopoly, Bryan proposed reduction of armaments, an agreement among nations to respect present boundaries, and compulsory investigation of disputes before hostilities began. His argument was given force by a threat of South American neutrals to act on their own account if the United States did not lead—a challenge in which Wilson saw "dynamite" and which was first parried at a session of the Pan American Union by reference to a commission headed by Bryan, and then met by the proposal of a Pan-American Pact. *See* Vol. I, p. 384 ff.

During January the Colonel made two visits to the White House. On the first of these it was decided that he should prepare to sail for Europe at the end of the month. The friends confessed that their neutrality no longer commanded the respect necessary to keep them out of war and enable them to serve as peacemakers. Wilson was so sure that the Texan wizard would know what to do to restore American prestige that he did not attempt to bind his hands by instructions.

Instead he strengthened the personal bond between them by taking the Colonel into the bosom of the family, reading to him from essays on contemporary great men from the pen of the English liberal, A. G. Gardiner, and diverting him by the sort of high jinks that the clan was accustomed to enjoy when they were alone. McAdoo, sharing in the hilarity, pranced up the marble stairway with legs bowed; and out-doing him, the President followed, not only bowlegged but pigeon-toed. Cousin John Wilson said it made his legs ache, they all laughed immoderately, and the President was for a few moments the playboy who did not care whether or not school kept.

The sedulous Colonel recorded every detail in his diary for posterity, and did not fail to note that he was urged to remain another day at the White House, that the President said to him: "You are the only one in the world to whom I can open my mind freely, and it does me good to say even foolish things and get them out of my system."

On January 24 the friends had their last evening together before the Colonel sailed. The President approved what his agent intended to say to the Germans and to Sir Edward Grey, with whom Wilson instructed House to be entirely frank; and when the Colonel asked whether, if a peace conference could be arranged and the President were asked to preside, he would go to Europe, Wilson replied that the American people would desire that he do so. The next day, after House conversed with members of the Cabinet to see whether there were domestic matters that needed his attention before his departure, the friends practiced the use of a secret code that they had worked out; and the Colonel, for the first time, agreed to accept a credit for expenses that Wilson insisted he should have.

When the hour of parting came, they rode to the station and the President walked along the platform to the train, refusing to leave until the agent who carried the best hope for peace disappeared into a car.

The Colonel went first to London. There he took care to explain that he was en route to Berlin, but not as a tool of German diplomats who wished to embarrass Britain by a peace challenge. On February 15 he received from Wilson a report, sent by Ambassador Gerard, that an immediate and tactful proposal to Berlin might yield results. "If peace does not come immediately," the President warned, "a new and protracted phase of war will commence." However, when House told Sir Edward Grey of Gerard's suggestion of haste, the foreign secretary thought it absurd.

Wilson wondered whether the Colonel, like Page, was not falling too deeply under the spell of the English leaders. He suspected that the British were deliberately delaying until they might be in a position to drive a better bargain at the peace table.[9]

When Sir Edward was finally persuaded that the time had come for House to go, the Colonel made his way via Paris into Germany, arriving at Berlin on March 20. It was more than a month since Gerard had reported that the possibility of successful peace talks was "a matter of hours." Now Germany was committed to submarine warfare and hopeful that this would bring Britain to her knees; and it was the turn of the statesmen at Berlin to discourage immediate talk of peace. Only when the Colonel explained what benefits Germany might expect from an international understanding—and particularly when he outlined conditions for freedom of the seas—did Zimmermann show interest.

Sorrowfully, the enterprising Texan had to conclude that his second mission to Europe was as barren of immediate results as the first had been. "The trouble with Germany," he concluded in a letter to Wilson on April 11, "is that it is antiquated in some of its ideas. They started upon the rule of force at a time when the most advanced nations were going in the opposite direction." And in other letters he reported that some way must be thought out "to let the Governments down easy with their people." The Colonel detected in each of the belligerent camps the feeling that it would be worth-while to hold on for a few months longer in the hope that better terms could be gained.

House's work in Europe, however, was of value both to the cause of peace and to his friend's leadership in that cause. He made friendly contacts not only with statesmen and diplomats, but with other leaders of opinion who shared the ideals of international cooperation that Wilson and the Colonel had been urging upon Pan-American diplomats. The Colonel had impressed hardheaded Europeans by his argument for giving the sanction of law to usages that were at the mercy of national whims. However, he saw that the best-laid plans for peace

---

[9] The Colonel did not deny this possibility; but he had to inform the President that, if he left for Germany immediately, British statesmen would cease to consider Wilson as a mediator. House feared that his friend in the White House could not understand the popular psychoses that were bedeviling the diplomats: the hatred of the United States that existed at Berlin, and the suspicions at London.

might be scuttled by the intransigence of France concerning her eastern frontier, that of the British Empire regarding the right of blockade and the annexation of German colonies, and that of Germany vis-à-vis Belgium.

Thus it became apparent to Wilson that European governments, by and large, were as shortsighted as in the days when his ancestors had sought freedom in the New World. He again rejected a plea from fervent William Jennings Bryan for a public appeal to the belligerents. "I wish I could see it as you do," Wilson confessed to his secretary of state on April 28. "But in view of what House writes me I cannot. It is known to every government concerned that we believe the war should be ended and that we speak for all neutral nations in that wish . . . They are at present most appreciative and cordial,—ready to accept help when they can accept it. We know their minds and we know their difficulties. They are dependent upon their own public opinion (even Germany) and we know what that opinion is. To insist now would be futile and probably would be offensive. We would lose such influence as we have for peace . . . God knows I have searched my mind and my conscience both to get the best, the nearest approach to wisdom, there is in them."

And so the possibility of a cessation of hostilities through American mediation evaporated, if indeed it had existed; and even while House was abroad Woodrow Wilson was forced to wrestle, catch-as-catch-can, with a series of sinister challenges to the peace and security of his own people.

When the President had warned House that "a new and protracted phase of war" would commence if peace was not made immediately, he was responding to a challenge that Berlin had just issued to neutrals. Noting that the Allies had been able to follow the dictate of what they called "imperative necessity" without provoking the United States to war,[10] the German government decided that it too would take a step

[10] Wilson listened patiently to arguments that the United States was unjust in feeding Allied guns while permitting Britain to stop a flow of foodstuffs to German civilians. He wrote to Page early in 1915: "The protests made by German-Americans and by a portion of the Irish-Americans, while entirely without justification, are not unnatural. It is difficult for people to think logically when their sympathies are aroused." No one knew how difficult better than he, for he had constantly to guard himself against the tugging of his own personal ties with Great Britain. Nevertheless, the dismal picture of food shortages that was painted by German propagandists was not wholly convincing. He was not disposed to alter the legalistic policy that was based on neutral rights. It did not seem to devolve upon him to compensate Germany for the disadvantages that resulted from her geographical position and inferior naval power.

Ambassador Gerard, who was packing up to be prepared for a diplomatic break, reported that America was the object of a "veritable campaign of hate" in Berlin and that Zimmermann had warned that "in case of trouble" a half-million trained German-Americans would join with Irish-Americans and start a revolution in the United States. This, and subversive activ-

that was beyond the purview of nineteenth-century law. On February 4 it proclaimed that the waters surrounding the British Isles would be considered a war zone in which enemy merchant vessels would be destroyed without any guaranty of safety to crews and passengers; and it added that, in view of the misuse of neutral flags by the British government, ships of noncombatants that entered the forbidden zone would risk torpedoing through mistakes in identity. Though her submarines were ordered to avoid violence to neutral ships in so far as they were recognizable, Germany would give no guaranty against errors.

Already the Germans had offended American opinion by making air raids that killed civilians; and now they proposed an invasion of humane rights on the sea that seemed more reprehensible than the interferences of the British Navy. Yet when Lansing drafted a bitter note of protest to Berlin, the President gave to it the same judicious treatment that he and House had administered to the first drafts of earlier complaints to London. He agreed with the counselor in holding the German government to "strict accountability" for any act that caused the destruction of an American merchant ship or the death of United States citizens. But he added to the text an explanation that the United States was holding all belligerents responsible "for any untoward effects upon American shipping which the principles of international law do not justify," and that representations were being made to London regarding the unwarranted use of the American flag for the protection of British ships.

When Germany responded with an appeal for equalization of her trading position with that of Britain, Wilson sent identical notes to Great Britain and Germany, suggesting that the belligerents reach agreement on the proper use of mines, submarines, and neutral flags, and provide at the same time for the entry of food into Germany under American supervision.

This proposal was rebuffed quickly, however. The Germans demanded imports of raw materials in addition to food, as compensation for giving up their submarine warfare. On the other hand, the British and French let it be known that they were thinking not of relaxing their blockade of Germany, but of making it total; and on March 11 an Order in Council directed that the British Navy intercept and search all neutral ships presumed to be carrying commodities of any kind to or from Germany.

Another note went from Washington to London, protesting against

---

ities by professional German propagandists in New York, made the President even less inclined to cut off the flow of munitions to Britain, or to take other stern measures to reinforce his protests to London.

this severe measure. But two days before, Germany's first overt atrocity against the United States was committed. Several British merchantmen had been sunk previously, but on March 28 the *Falaba* went down with a citizen of the United States aboard.

The American press printed stories of the sinking that lacked extenuating facts and damned the act as "barbarism run mad," a "triumph of horror," "an atrocity against which the civilized world should protest with one voice." The fire of righteous indignation blazed through the land. Counselor Robert Lansing, like Wilson responsive to Presbyterian moral law, allowed emotion to ruffle his legalistic patience. He agreed with the journalists in thinking Germany's act "indefensible both legally and morally." Convinced that certain German officials thought it advantageous to their country to provoke war with the United States, he wished to instruct Ambassador Gerard to protest promptly and vigorously and to demand that Germany disavow the "wanton act" and punish the officer responsible for it.

William Jennings Bryan, however, was bound to question any public policy that threatened the peace of his people. He tempered Lansing's fiery denunciations with a series of questions. Was there not some force in the argument of contributory negligence? he asked. Was there, after all, some inconsistency in the position of a government that had warned its citizens to flee trouble in Mexico but failed to discourage travel on ships liable to torpedoing? Could the American people be asked to risk war in behalf of an individual whose action might be considered reckless? The secretary of state wrote repeatedly to keep his doubts before the President, and suggested that the victim of the *Falaba* sinking was not "differently situated from those who by remaining in a belligerent country assume the risk of injury."

Wilson himself was inclined to temporize. He thought it best to "compound policy with legal right in wise proportion." Professing the "greatest anxiety" about the case, he expressed to Bryan a desire for further details and for an opportunity to give his thoughts "time to settle" before taking action. He raised, too, a very pertinent and vital question: in view of the fact that the British government had advised merchantmen to arm themselves against submarines and ram them whenever possible, was the German commander who sank the *Falaba* perhaps justified in assuming that this ship was an armed adversary that could not safely be visited and searched? The peculiar vulnerability of submarines to ramming and small-gun fire was a factor not yet taken into account by international law.

Many courses were considered, and notes were drafted and not sent. Wishing to uphold the right of his people to trade and travel in peace, and at the same time fearful of giving offense unnecessarily to any belligerent, Wilson shrank from decisive action and took refuge in spiritual prophecy. Convinced that the root of the evil was in the human soul, he said to Southern Methodists on March 25: "Wars will never have any ending until men cease to hate one another, cease to be jealous of one another, get that feeling of reality in the brotherhood of man-kind which is the only bond that can make us think justly of one another and act righteously before God himself."

Persisting on his exalted plane of aspiration, Wilson spoke prophetically to members of the Associated Press. "My interest in the neutrality of the United States," he declared, "is not the petty desire to keep out of trouble . . . I am interested in neutrality because there is something so much greater to do than fight; there is a distinction waiting for this Nation that no nation has ever yet got. That is the distinction of absolute self-control and self-mastery." He was no more ready than Bryan to risk war because of the death of one American citizen; nor would he allow himself to be drawn into a controversy over the manner in which it had happened.

As the President pondered over the phraseology of a note of protest that Lansing had drafted at his suggestion, news came of violence done to two American vessels by Germany. One was attacked by a seaplane; the other was torpedoed by a submarine and three lives were lost.

Lansing was now ready to go to the limit in moral fulmination. He was the more outraged because on May 1, under a newspaper advertisement of the sailing of the Cunard liner *Lusitania,* appeared a notice from the German embassy that concluded with this warning: "Travellers sailing in the war zone on ships of Great Britain or her allies do so at their own risk." The counselor considered the release of such an announcement, without approval by the State Department, to be not only "highly improper" but even "insolent." But Bryan, in forwarding Lansing's ideas to the President, continued to question the right of individual travelers to involve their country in war and accepted the German warning as evidence of a friendly desire to avoid trouble.

Wilson could not escape the force of Lansing's contention. And yet he listened carefully to Bryan, for he was impressed by the sincerity of the man's convictions and by the vitality of the popular roots from which they stemmed. After a long talk with the secretary of state on May 4, Wilson hoped to satisfy public opinion and at the same time avoid war by making a strong protest to Germany, and then, if it were ineffective, deferring his claims until the end of the war.

On May 7 occurred the calamity that Wilson had dreaded—a deed that turned American sentiment against Germany with a violence that could never be overcome. Soon after the close of the Cabinet meeting on that day, and before he could start on his afternoon automobile ride, the President was handed a terse cablegram reporting that the *Lusitania* had been sunk by a submarine. One hundred and twenty-eight Americans were lost, among them thirty-seven women and twenty-one children. The ship was unarmed and was unprotected by a convoy, carried no troops, but had thousands of cases of ammunition in her hold.

When news of the disaster reached Wall Street, stock prices fell abruptly. In the view of the American press the act was palpably a slaughter of innocents, a barbarity without precedent in modern times. The mail sacks coming to the executive offices bulged with protests and resolutions from the citizens. Would the President hold Germany to the "strict accountability" that he had proclaimed?

Woodrow Wilson was stunned. He did not trust himself to express his thoughts, but left the White House quickly and walked a long way, alone, until his wrath was under control. Later he accepted Dr. Grayson's prescription of golf as usual.

When Tumulty tried to give "the Governor" a lurid account of the tragedy, Wilson silenced him, explaining that if he gave too much heed to heart-rending news stories he would "see red in everything" and could not act justly. He was not afraid to lead the nation to fight, he said, but he must not do it hastily or prematurely. If he went to the Congress the next day and asked for a declaration of war, he would be supported; but when the casualty lists came and people read them, might they not wonder why their President had rushed into war with Germany after he had been so indulgent of Great Britain, why he did not first exhaust every possibility of peaceful settlement? When he moved against Germany—and he now felt that he might eventually be forced to move—he wanted his people to be united and enthusiastic for a crusade. Moreover, he was governed by a sense of trusteeship not only to his own people, but to the whole civilized world. He foresaw that if the United States, the only mighty nation still standing aloof, were to join in the fight, civilization might be bankrupt in every respect.

He left his desk on the evening of May 10 to fulfill a promise to speak at Philadelphia to several thousand citizens who had just been naturalized. These immigrants before him were men whom Congress wished to exclude unless they could prove themselves literate; but by an executive veto Wilson had redeemed a political pledge and had kept the door open to the educational opportunities that his nation offered.

He began nervously, rocking back and forth on his heels, and his hands plucked at his lapels and his pockets. ". . . A man who thinks of himself as belonging to a particular national group in America has not yet become an American," he said, "and the man who goes among you to trade upon your nationality is no worthy son to live under the Stars and Stripes. . . . America was created to unite mankind by those passions which lift and not by the passions which separate and debase . . ."

Then he made one of his rare platform errors. He used a sentence against which Tumulty had warned him: "There is such a thing as a man being too proud to fight." And he went on to say: "There is such a thing as a nation being so right that it does not need to convince others by force that it is right."

The speech at Philadelphia was acclaimed by peace-loving citizens, and particularly by the press of the South and West. But political opponents and partisans of Britain cited the words "too proud to fight" as evidence of poltroonery. On the day after his *faux pas* the President, wishing that he had either avoided the offensive phrase or developed it more fully, let it be known that his address was not a declaration of policy in regard to the *Lusitania* case. It was merely an expression of "a personal attitude," he explained in his news conference.

Tumulty had never seen "the Governor" more serious than when he sat down alone to write a note of protest to Berlin. This was a charge too solemn to be delegated to another conscience.

By the time Wilson was ready to bring his draft before the Cabinet, on the morning of May 11, he had received an expression of regret from Bernstorff for the loss of American lives; and a dispatch from Berlin gave assurance that submarine attacks on neutral ships were contrary to orders and that regrets and compensation for mistakes would be tendered when justified.

Accepting the German assurances, repeating the argument of his February note of protest against the submarine blockade, and enumerating the grievances of his people, Wilson did not break diplomatic relations or deliver an ultimatum with a time limit, as bellicose citizens thought that he should. Rather he asserted that his government confidently expected that Germany would disavow the acts of which the United States complained, that she would "make reparation as far as reparation is possible for injuries which are without measure," and that she would take immediate steps to prevent the recurrence of "anything so obviously subversive of the principles of warfare for which the Imperial German Government have in the past so wisely and so firmly contended."

After the Cabinet deliberated for three hours, and Lansing and Bryan made suggestions that were accepted, Wilson was finally ready to release the protest. Bryan, however, wrote twice to the President of his qualms. "With a heavy heart," and in order to give direction to public opinion, he agreed that they should immediately send the note prepared. But he wanted to issue a supplementary statement that would call attention to the fact that Germany had conditionally endorsed the principle of the Bryan "cooling-off" treaties and consequently that there would be a year's time for investigation of the current dispute.

Wilson concluded that it might be wise, when the note of protest was released from the State Department, to give out at the same time from his office an interpretive "tip" such as Bryan had proposed. He even went so far as to compose a draft of such a statement and send it to the secretary of state.

However, Lansing and Tumulty saw dire perils in this scheme. Lansing warned that his own position was "becoming difficult," which might have been taken as an intimation that he would resign if the "tip" were released; and Secretary of War Garrison also opposed any qualification of the note. Tumulty was thoroughly alarmed, feeling that if Bryan's scheme were carried out, Wilson would be accused by his own people of double-dealing and Germany would infer that the United States would not fight for her rights. In what he described afterward as "the worst half hour of my life," Tumulty persuaded the President to reverse his decision, though Wilson at first insisted that Bryan could be trusted as a judge of public opinion.[11]

The *Lusitania* note was effective both at home and in Britain, and restored to a degree whatever prestige the President had lost by use of the phrase "too proud to fight." By and large, the public men of the nation stood behind him, and the press exulted.

Wilson acknowledged the response to his leadership in a letter to Nancy Toy: "I am deeply touched and rewarded above my desert by the extraordinary and generous support the whole country has given me. . . ." But with his gratitude he felt a "sense of overwhelming responsibility" and he was haunted again by the oft-recurring dread that someday he might have to sacrifice popularity, if his conscience should lead one way and the will of the people another.

When the reply from Berlin disputed the contention that the *Lusitania* had been unarmed, and claimed that the liner was in fact an auxiliary cruiser of the British Navy, the press of America immediately lashed out at the tone of this response. After making a Memorial Day address at Arlington, Wilson went to work at once on the drafting of

[11] For further information about the abortive supplement to the first *Lusitania* note and Lodge's use of the incident in the 1916 election campaign, *see* Blum, *Tumulty*, p. 97 and n.; Garraty, *Lodge*, pp. 329–32; Baker, V, 340–41 and n.; and p. 63n. below.

a second protest. He labored late into the evening; and the next morning, after a news conference in which he calmly refused to discuss the German reply, he met his Cabinet and read his draft to them.

Bryan came late to the meeting, and sat back in his chair and let his eyelids droop. He seemed to be straining to control himself; but when his colleagues turned down his suggestion of a counterprotest to London, he charged that they were not neutral.

Wilson resented this. His eyes turned to steel as he said: "Mr. Bryan, you are not warranted in making such an assertion. We all doubtless have our opinions in this matter, but there are none of us who can justly be accused of being unfair."

When the dissenter asked heatedly whether they were prepared to bend the knee to England, members of the Cabinet buttressed their chief's position by explaining that exports of cotton and foodstuffs to Europe had not been stopped, but had increased during the past months. But William Jennings Bryan was not a man to be convinced by economic statistics. At the end of the session he told the President that he could not bring himself to sign the second note, that it was unfair for him to remain in the Cabinet. He was convinced now that he was being asked to give to Germany the power to plunge his people into war. And so he denounced the proposed protest as a reversal of established policy. During the days that followed he persisted in bringing his arguments to bear upon the President. Wilson continued to listen respectfully, but had less and less sympathy for the Great Commoner's efforts to cooperate with Ambassador Bernstorff in giving the German Foreign Office "a way out."

The day after the grueling session of the Cabinet, he received Bernstorff. Though willing to negotiate, the President was determined not to give any hint of compromise. But he made it clear that, if Germany would voluntarily give up her inhumane tactics, he would try again to persuade the British to relax their blockade.

Two days later, on June 4, when he met his Cabinet again, the discussion was confused and tiresome. Wilson gave evidence that his patience was sorely tried and he seemed too weary to give leadership. He had no heart, either, to argue with Bryan. It had always been difficult for him to beg a man whom he respected to change a decision that was arrived at prayerfully.

The next day McAdoo came to his father-in-law to report that Bryan, haggard and nervous from lack of sleep, had confided that he proposed to resign and that he wanted to do it in a way that would embarrass the Administration as little as possible. He had just received support for his position from Democratic leaders in Congress, and hoped that their letters and the threat of his own resignation might move the President.

McAdoo had sought the aid of Mrs. Bryan. From her he had learned that, while the President wrote the most important notes and directly consulted the counselor of the State Department, while House negotiated with ambassadors who got no satisfaction from the secretary of state, Bryan had felt neglected and had tired of playing the role of a figurehead.

Wilson was not surprised. Actually, he had been embarrassed by Bryan's ineptness for some months and had been careful not to reveal the extent of his dependence on House, fearing that the secretary of state's feelings would be hurt. The President had intimated to the Colonel, near the end of 1914, that if his "elder son" ever wished to leave his office because of a disagreement on policy, it might be wise to let him go. And now, when he spoke to Edith Galt of the disaffection of Bryan—a man whom Ellen Wilson had worked to bind in loyalty to the Chief—Mrs. Galt begged him to accept a resignation if it were offered, "and thank God for the chance." But the crisis with Germany was so acute that the President feared the effect on the opinion of the world, and especially that of Germany, if Bryan were to step out immediately.

The Great Commoner came to the White House for one last effort at conversion, and the Presbyterian prophets confronted each other for the last time with their most persuasive arguments. Wilson said again that Bryan's fears were exaggerated, that his resignation would complicate the perils that did exist. Asking for a glass of water, the Great Commoner raised it to his lips with a hand so unsteady that it spilled. "Colonel House has been Secretary of State, not I," Bryan said, "and I have never had your full confidence. I know you are busy, and I will not detain you longer." They rose and clasped hands, and each said a "God bless you." [12] The secretary of state went home and wrote out a courteous but formal letter of resignation. On June 8 the President received it and announced its import to his Cabinet. Bryan came to the meeting and, taking his colleagues to lunch afterward, evoked their pity. Though Wilson did not attend this party, he contributed a felicitous letter to the send-off of the dissenting brother.

That evening, as newsboys were crying the resignation of the secretary of state, Wilson gave his attention to the note that Bryan would

[12] As recorded by W. C. Williams in *William Jennings Bryan*, p. 387; House Diary, June 24, 1915. During the summer of 1915 Bryan called at the White House; but he and, particularly, Mrs. Bryan were so hurt by the coolness of their reception that the Great Commoner vowed never to darken the doors of the mansion again while Wilson was there. House Diary, Sept. 14, 1915.

not sign. It was released on June 9 over the signature of Robert Lansing, secretary of state *ad interim*. Its tone indicated that the nation's policy was to be dictated neither by jingoes nor by those who sought peace at any price. Public opinion, except that tinged by German sympathies, back the President as solidly as had the Cabinet.

In this message Wilson showed his genius for extracting from a legalistic dispute those elements that could give it historic significance for humanity. He served notice to the world that the United States would expect the new weapons of the age to be used with the same regard for fair play and civilian rights that the usages of civilization had stipulated in nineteenth-century warfare. Brushing aside the assertions about the status of the *Lusitania* that Germany had made and that he did not accept, Wilson asserted that he was setting forth principles that lifted the case "out of the class of ordinary subjects of diplomatic discussion or of international controversy." There was an intimation that an ultimatum might follow if Germany did not give certain assurances.

This note reached Berlin at a time when there was a controversy between the naval authorities and the Foreign Office. Finally the Emperor was persuaded that submarine commanders should spare all large passenger ships and that no vessel should be attacked unless it was positively identified as hostile. Orders to this effect were given during the first week of June, but they were kept secret for fear that the world might interpret them as a sign of German weakness.[13]

When Germany's reply to the second *Lusitania* note arrived on July 8 it was analyzed by Lansing, who had become secretary of state. A quiet, philosophic gentleman, Lansing was to be—in the words of Secretary Houston—merely "the President's Private Secretary for Foreign Affairs." Wilson explained to his new appointee that experience and training were far more vital than political background, especially under present conditions; and, moreover, Lansing seemed to him young enough to adapt his thinking to changing conditions.

The President was not satisfied by Berlin's reply to the second *Lusitania* note. The imperial government still held that its duty "to protect and save the lives of German subjects" took precedence of its obligation to "the interests of neutrals." The old plaints against the British blockade and the "starvation" of Germans were repeated. The note explained that Germany would not allow American citizens to protect British

[13] Ambassador Gerard, who found the Kaiser "rabid" on the subject of shipments of American arms to the Allies, transmitted to Lansing, on June 24, a German suggestion that the Admiralty might be persuaded to agree to offer security to merchant vessels carrying passengers if the President would favor a guaranty that such ships would not carry arms and ammunition; but Wilson replied that this was "entirely unwise, or, at the least, impossible of acceptance."

vessels by their presence as passengers, but it offered to cooperate in safe-guarding American ships under certain conditions.

Wilson warned Gerard that the question was entirely one of principle and would not admit of compromise. Lansing advised that it was "well nigh impossible" to avoid war and at the same time force Germany to yield; and public sentiment plainly was growing more hostile to Germany. Yet Wilson persisted in hoping that firmness might bring peace. He felt that the Germans were modifying their methods, but should be made to feel that they must continue in their new way unless they deliberately wanted to provoke war.

At the same time Gerard, at Berlin, was finding it difficult to present a bold front to German officials who made light of America's will and power to fight. "They feel that our 'New Freedom' is against their ideas and ideals," he wrote on July 20, "and they hate President Wilson because he embodies peace and learning rather than caste and war."

With the aid of Lansing, the President drafted a third *Lusitania* note that was calculated to put an end to the correspondence that critics had begun to ridicule for its length and inconclusiveness. Calling the most recent communication from Berlin "very unsatisfactory," Wilson pointed out that the German government regarded itself as in large degree exempt from observing principles to which it subscribed. In conclusion, he warned that his government would feel impelled to insist very solemnly on the scrupulous observance of neutral rights; and he served notice that further sinkings in contravention of those rights "must be regarded, when they affect American citizens, as deliberately unfriendly."

The third *Lusitania* note, sent off to Berlin on July 21, was, if not an ultimatum, at least the last word of the United States on the subject. If the message left any doubt about the finality of the American position, Lansing removed it with blunt remarks to Ambassador Bernstorff. The secretary of state warned that war could not be avoided if American lives were lost in another torpedoing of a merchant ship.

Just before this, Wilson had urged House to work with Bernstorff and "to make him feel not only that some way should be found, but that some way *must* be found," that his government owed it to itself and the rest of the world to help find it. Persuaded by House that Wilson did not want war and was not swayed by pro-British opinion, Bernstorff reported this to his Foreign Office, at the same time giving assurance that if Germany met America's demands Wilson would then prosecute his case against England strenuously.

But at this very time McAdoo, having been instructed by the President to put the Secret Service on the trail of violators of neutrality, and hoping to frighten foreign spies and propagandists operating in the United States, revealed hostile activities on the part of Germans at New York. Wilson himself was sure that his country was "honeycombed with German intrigue and infested with German spies." When the telephone wires of the German and Austro-Hungarian embassies were tapped and conversations were found to contain unflattering references to high officials, Wilson found it hard to cling to the measure of faith that he still retained in the good will of Germany.

Gerard reported that Wilson's latest *Lusitania* note was received with hostility by the German press and by a government now dominated by the party of frightfulness. On the other hand, immoderate persecution of American citizens of German blood made it difficult for Bernstorff to feel that the United States was impartial.

On August 19 occurred the inevitable accident for which diplomats were waiting. The *Arabic,* a British merchantman bound for New York and therefore carrying no contraband, was sunk without warning by a submarine. Two Americans were lost. This seemed to be the overt act that the third *Lusitania* note had warned against; and it was regarded by Bernstorff and the American press as cause for at least a diplomatic break.

At this juncture there was a turn toward moderation in German policy. The American government was informed at last of the orders issued secretly at Berlin in June against ruthless sinkings; public assurance was given that just compensation would be forthcoming; and the State Department was urged to refrain from drastic steps until particulars of the *Arabic* case could be ascertained.

Again Wilson was the target of contending voices. He looked askance at the "extraordinary stuff" that was coming in dispatches from his somewhat bumptious ambassador at Berlin.[14] At the same time he suspected that Berlin's apparent yielding was merely a sparring for time; and he informed House that he trusted neither the accuracy nor the sincerity of Bernstorff. Finally, he told Lansing that they must demand satisfaction at once.

[14] Wilson's irritation at the tactlessness of Gerard mounted after the sinking of the *Arabic*. When his ambassador suggested that the President retaliate against Bernstorff for indignities suffered by Gerard at Berlin, Wilson wrote on a slip: "Ordinarily an ambassador ought to be backed up as a matter of course, but—this ass? It is hard to take it seriously." On another dispatch from Gerard regarding German politics, Wilson jotted: "Who can fathom this? I wish they would hand this idiot his passports!" His comment on still another message was a large black exclamation mark.

At the same time the President was dissatisfied with Page's attitude. On Sept. 10, 1915, almost a year since the ambassador at London had sent his protest about "library lawyers" who allowed chestnuts to burn, Wilson pinned this handwritten comment to a dispatch from Page: "I wish Page could feel a little more strongly that we are acting upon our own convictions and not upon English opinion. Of course they want us to pull their chestnuts out of the fire."

On his own responsibility the secretary of state delivered an oral ultimatum to Bernstorff on August 27, telling the ambassador that the time for debating the question of submarine warfare had passed, that unless the German government frankly declared that there would be no more surprise attacks on vessels carrying passengers, and lived up to that declaration, the United States would certainly declare war. Lansing had not told the President of his intention to say this; for he wished to be able, if his bluff was called, to withdraw gracefully from his threat by revealing that the President had not sanctioned it.

Fortified by Bernstorff's reports of the severity of the crisis at Washington, the German Foreign Office was able to persuade the Kaiser to overrule the Admiralty and stop the tactics to which the United States objected. Moreover, under pressure from Lansing, Bernstorff exceeded his orders. On September 1 he gave this assurance to the secretary of state in writing: "Liners will not be sunk by our submarines without warning and without safety to the lives of non-combatants, provided that the liners do not try to escape or offer resistance . . ."

Still Wilson was not satisfied. Feeling that the German government was deliberately moving with exasperating slowness, Wilson let Bernstorff know that he would not be content with anything less than an explicit disavowal of the attack on the *Arabic*. "Shall we ever get out of the labyrinth made for us by all this German 'frightfulness'?" he asked House. And on September 17 he wrote: "The country is undoubtedly back of me in the whole matter, and I feel myself under bonds to it to show patience to the utmost. My chief puzzle is to determine when patience ceases to be a virtue."

Meanwhile the circumstances of the sinking of the *Arabic* were established by the German government. Willing to concede that their submarine commander had acted "unfortunately not in accordance with instructions," they agreed to reprove him and indemnify the United States. Their pride, however, held them back from a frank admission of responsibility.

Lansing and Wilson agreed that the statement from Berlin was inadequate and were inclined to send Bernstorff home. But the secretary of state again raised the bludgeon of war over the envoy's head; and Bernstorff, convinced that only by a precise disavowal could a break be avoided, took it upon himself again to stretch his authority in the interest of peace. The Kaiser's orders to submarine commanders, he wrote to the State Department on October 5, had been "made so stringent that the recurrence of incidents similar to the Arabic case is considered out of the question. . . . The Imperial Government regrets and disavows this act . . ." Though there was still no disavowal of the sinking of the *Lusitania,* Woodrow Wilson had fought his long battle with the German Admiralty to a state of suspension.

By the end of 1915 Woodrow Wilson knew that a world at war had no comfortable place for a self-respecting neutral. The greater his restraint toward one contender, the greater the indignation shown by the other. The Germans repeatedly had tried to divert attention from their own offenses by pointing a finger at Britain's maritime policy; and while the *Lusitania* notes were being exchanged, the mood of the British public had been resentful of the President's patience.

It was plain by the end of 1915 that Wilson's notes of protest to Germany and the remonstrances to Britain were inconclusive in enforcing neutral rights. And the longer American complaints went unsatisfied the less seriously the belligerents took them. They could see that the United States was becoming for the first time a creditor nation, that the rewards of peace were sufficient to restrain America from taking part in European quarrels after keeping clear of them for a century.

During his honeymoon at Hot Springs, in the first week of 1916, Woodrow Wilson took time to think deeply, and with long perspective. Called back suddenly to Washington by the torpedoing of the British liner *Persia,* he found Tumulty panicky.

"I have made up my mind," the President said to his secretary, "that I am more interested in the opinion that the country will have of me ten years from now than the opinion it may be willing to express today. Of course, I understand that the country wants action, and I intend to stand by the record I have made in all these cases, and take whatever action may be necessary, but I will not be rushed into war, no matter if every last Congressman stands up on his hind legs and calls me a coward. . . . I believe that the sober-minded people of this country will applaud any efforts I may make without the loss of our honour to keep this country out of war."

His tough-fibered patience had endured the arrogance and espionage of Prussians, the gibes of English and French nationalists and their American friends, the quibbles of legalists, the pious protestations of pacifists, the indiscretions of ambassadors, and, what was perhaps most trying of all, the indignant surges of his own blood. But the succession of crises pressed him hard to reconcile himself to the necessity of preparing his people for war, both morally and materially, in case it should be forced upon him.

CHAPTER II

THE PROPHET HEARS THE VOICE OF THE LORD

DURING THE YEAR 1915 it became clear that in the twentieth century America might not be able to remain a hemisphere unto itself. The hope that economic depletion would end the fighting faded; and a policy of legalistic neutrality, lacking a firm base in international law, was invalidated when each of the warring camps reverted to the law of necessity. Diplomats found no recourse in history on which they could depend to stop the martial madness. The President perceived that, if the United States were publicly to start a neutral movement for peace and fail in it, her influence in the future would be nil.

Yet it was in 1915 that the vision of a world order of which he had caught a glimpse in earlier years gradually became fixed in his mind as a necessity for the salvation of mankind. With Europe destroying itself, he embraced the cause of international organization as an essential article of his faith.

Colonel House wished to keep alive the President's impulse to build a new world. If Wilson were ever to get out of the "labyrinth" that he conceived to have been created by "German frightfulness," it seemed to the Colonel that he could do so only by taking initiative. After his return from London in June of 1915, House received strong support from Sir Edward Grey. The foreign secretary wished to bring the United States into the war, but realized that any public expression of his desire would militate against its fulfillment. He ventured, however, to appeal to America to lead in making peace. "The pearl of great price," Grey wrote to House on August 10, ". . . would be some League of Nations that could be relied on to insist that disputes between any two nations must be settled by the arbitration, mediation, or conference of others. International law has hitherto had no sanction. The lesson of this war is that the Powers must bind themselves to give it a sanction. If that can be secured, freedom of the seas and many other things will become easy. . . ."[1]

[1] Charles Seymour has pointed out (*American Diplomacy during the World War*, p. 174 n.) that Grey's proposal reflected ideas from letters that the latter had received from Theodore Roosevelt. Moreover, British Liberals and Laborites, impressed by the domestic reforms that had been achieved under Wilson's leadership, looked to him to further the postwar objectives to which they were pledged and toward which imperialists at London were unsympathetic. Believing that a punitive peace would be unwise, and that by saying so they might stimulate

On September 22 the foreign secretary wrote again, to ask the Colonel how far the United States would go to get security against aggressive war. "Would the President," he queried, "propose that there should be a League of Nations binding themselves to side against any power which broke a treaty; which broke certain rules of warfare on sea or land . . . ; or which refused, in case of dispute, to adopt some other method of settlement than that of war? Only in some such agreement do I see a prospect of diminishing militarism and navalism in future, so that no nation will build up armies or navies for aggressive purposes. I cannot say which Government would be prepared to accept such a proposal, but I am sure that the Government of the United States is the only Government that could make it with effect . . ."

Wilson was receptive when House put a bold plan before him. The Colonel's idea was to ask the British first whether it would be agreeable to them if the United States demanded that hostilities cease; and then, if they gave the assent that was to be expected, House would go to Berlin and present the American demand without saying that he had discussed the matter first at London. He would even try to delude the Germans into believing that the British would reject the plan, hoping thus to make it the more tempting to Germany. If the Central Powers turned him down, House had it in mind to break diplomatic relations and marshal the force of all neutrals against them.

Such a scheme involved the hazard of eventual involvement in the fight; but if that came to pass, at least the United States would stand in a moral position that would command the respect of the world. Consequently it seemed better to take the risk than to let human nature take its course, and to slip into war on terms that had been familiar to mankind ever since its progenitors fought in trees and caves.

Wilson suggested, therefore, that the Colonel put his plan in writing for Grey; and House discussed with him a draft of a letter that explained that the United States stood ready to intervene and "demand that peace parleys begin upon the broad basis of the elimination of militarism and navalism." Furthermore, it suggested that when Grey

liberal opinion in Germany, Ramsay MacDonald and other leaders had organized a Union of Democratic Control a few days after the war's outbreak, with these principles:

1. No transfer of territory without consent of the populace.
2. No treaty-making without consent of Parliament.
3. Guarantee of peace by a concert, rather than a balance, of powers.
4. Drastic reduction and national control of armaments.

On May 2, 1916, a fifth point was added: Economic warfare should not go on after military operations ceased. By 1918 the U.D.C. had some 650,000 members.

In April of 1915 English intellectuals formed a League of Nations Society. *See* Lawrence W. Martin, "Anglo-American Liberalism and the Wilson Peace Program of 1918," a dissertation at the Yale University Library, 1955.

thought the hour propitious, House might go to London, and then on to Berlin, to notify Germany that, if she insisted on continuing the fight, "it would be necessary" for the United States to join the Allies and force the issue.

A vital word was inserted by the President, so that the clause read: "it would *probably* be necessary." He was not willing, he explained to House the next day, "to make it inevitable that the United States would be a party to forcing terms on Germany," for the exact circumstances of a future crisis seemed impossible to determine. In general, though, he thought the Colonel's draft altogether right. "I pray to God it may bring results," he wrote.[2]

On October 19 House sent off the letter to Grey; and during the next few weeks he devoted himself to furthering the project. He listened patiently to the chimerical pleas of American pacifists and cultivated the sympathy of journalists for the cause of peace, assuring them that no one was more eager than the President to serve that cause, no one more competent to decide what steps could be taken with hope of success.

The British foreign secretary, in his first reply to House's exploratory letter, merely asked whether the scheme proposed was to be considered in conjunction with Grey's own suggestion of a League of Nations. The President agreed that they should tell the foreign secretary that they found "the necessary programme" for the future in Grey's suggestion of a League of Nations. Thus was Woodrow Wilson committed, as early as November of 1915, to the greatest cause of the twentieth century. It was the beginning of the end of American isolation.

Meanwhile, Wilson had become alarmed by the prospect of a break with Germany. In September of 1915 House found his friend thinking more of preventing a German victory than of building a new world order. Wilson confessed that he had never been sure that the United States ought not to enter the war and, if it became evident that Germany would win, the obligation of America to act would be the greater. While the *Lusitania* case was still unsettled, violations of American law by Germans with diplomatic immunity made it seem necessary to send the attachés von Papen and Boy-Ed home to Berlin. On August 19 the *Arabic* was sunk, with loss of American lives. In

[2] House discussed his grand scheme with Lansing in the President's study while Wilson was out calling on Edith Galt. He won the approval of the secretary of state, who despite the sharpness of his legal protests to London was personally partial to the Allies. The Colonel wrote gleefully in his diary: "I now have the matter in my own hands. The President's only questions were when and how."

October Nurse Cavell faced German executioners with her immortal cry: "Patriotism is not enough"; and her martyrdom impressed American hearts once more with the frightfulness of Prussian militarism. In November sentiment in the United States was further aroused by the torpedoing of the Italian liner *Ancona,* with the loss of a score of American lives. Moreover, Lansing had become more aggressive and agreed with Tumulty that there should be more "punch" in the American policy.[3]

As the righteous wrath of Americans had turned against those whom they glibly called "Huns" and a hue and cry against German sympathizers had risen, the pacifists also had become still more alarmed and importunate. Twenty thousand telegrams urging a peace movement reached the White House in one day, and delegates paraded in to see the President. Henry Ford came to tell Wilson of an impractical plan of dramatizing the cause of conciliation by a "peace ship," only to find the Chief Executive in a prophetic mood, ready to make war in order to put an end to wars.

The conflict within Wilson's soul was becoming unbearable. His desire to enforce justice wrestled with his determination not to allow his people to use the barbaric instrument of war as a means of enforcement. By mid-December, just before his wedding, he was ready to spur the Colonel to undertake the mission that they had planned in October but for which, in the view of House and Grey, the time was not yet ripe.

Since Wilson thought it futile for the Colonel to go to Berlin unless he was invited,[4] House put the President's views before Bernstorff; and within a week word came from the German government that they would like to have the Colonel go directly to their capital to discuss general terms of military and naval disarmament.

When House asked for written instructions for his mission, the President at first told him that he needed none. "You know what is in my mind and how to interpret it . . ." Wilson wrote. "Your own letters exactly echo my own views and purposes." But he decided to make the Colonel a "special agent" in order to forestall possible Congressional criticism of him as a man acting for the government without authority.

---

[3] The secretary of state feared that Spain, which had been asking Cuba whether Latin-American countries would approve mediation by its king, would wrest leadership of peace sentiment from Wilson. Informed of this, the President advised Lansing to avoid direct comment and to tell the Cuban minister that the United States hoped that all the Americas would work in union.

[4] Conversing with Lansing and House, the President went to his safe and took out a message from Gerard that reported an interview with the Kaiser in which the German ruler had threatened "to attend to America when this war was over" and had spoken slightingly of Wilson as one ineligible to mediate because of his attitude toward Germany. On Oct. 1 Gerard had written to House: "Germany seems to be winning this war . . ."

In a note written during his honeymoon the President outlined his ideas very succinctly. The United States, he wrote, was to have nothing to do with local settlements. Lansing had given warning of complicated questions of boundary and indemnity that would have to be settled after the war; but Wilson wanted House to concern himself only with international undertakings essential to future peace. "The only guarantees that any rational man could accept," the President wrote on December 24, "are (a) military and naval disarmament and (b) a league of nations to secure each nation against aggression and maintain absolute freedom of the seas. If either party to the present war will let us say to the other that they are willing to discuss peace on such terms, it will clearly be our duty to use our utmost moral force to oblige the other to parley, and I do not see how they could stand in the opinion of the world if they refused."

Armed with this psychological weapon, the Colonel sailed for Europe on his third quest for the Grail of peace. He reached London on January 6 and reported to Wilson that the foreign secretary favored "freedom of the seas" provided the Germans granted "freedom of the land," and that Grey stipulated also that the United States should join in a general covenant of guarantee. They were to talk again soon, the Colonel said, and it would help if Wilson would cable some assurance of his willingness "to cooperate in a policy of seeking to bring about and maintain permanent peace among civilized nations."

This appeal elicited from the President a message promising to do exactly what his agent suggested. It was not enough, however, to sway the British statesmen from their will to fight until German militarism was crushed beyond hope of revival. The government at London was unmoved when House warned that Russia might be knocked out of the war and Germany might acquire a military position from which she could dictate terms far less palatable than those that could be secured through President Wilson. The British leaders felt that they must await the outcome of promising plans for spring campaigns on the battlefield.[5] House was discouraged by the attitude of the British statesmen.

[5] As for Page, the Colonel found him deeper than ever in sympathy with his English friends, critical now of the President as well as of the State Department, and opposed to any negotiations that might prevent the smashing of Germany. The "fatal moral weakness" of House's scheme, Page thought, was that the United States should "plunge into war, not on the merits of the cause, but by a carefully sprung trick." The ambassador had taken no effective steps to explain in London that "the freedom of the seas" was not a subversive slogan invented by German propagandists, but rather an ideal conceived at Washington. Page recorded in his diary that people were laughing at "the empty House" and were offended by his vanity for Wilson's "prestige." British opinion thought that, if the United States truly wished to help to kill the root of war, she could best do so by acquiescing in the blockade by which German militarism could be strangled.

Circumstances at Washington, however, were pushing the President in the opposite direction. On Jan. 12 he cabled to House that an adjustment of controversies with Germany was in prospect and that, if it came, American opinion and the Senate would demand that London

"I was never more impressed by their slowness and lack of initiative," he wrote to Wilson on February 9.

Going to Berlin, he learned that the naval officials were still at odds with the Foreign Office over submarine policy. The contention within the government was much the same as that at London. At each capital the men of the Admiralty felt that the protests of the United States had pulled the teeth of their blockade.

The President's agent left Germany convinced that, if the Foreign Office were forced to admit that deeds of German submarines were illegal, the Admiralty would gain supremacy and would force a break with Washington. On January 30 House cabled this conclusion to the President. Four days later he wrote that he doubted whether the German people would rise against their rulers, as many Americans hoped.

Believing more firmly than ever that the fighting had reached a stalemate and that the United States was the only nation able to break the deadlock, House worked at Paris to cultivate appreciation of this fact. But the statesmen of France were responsible to a public that put faith in military dominance and abhorred any gesture that smacked of pacifism. They feared that moves toward conciliation would be regarded by the world as signs of weakness. Sickened by the incompetent statesmanship that he had observed in Europe, House was more than ever convinced, as he wrote Wilson, that the President's opportunity was "the greatest, perhaps, that has ever come to any man." [6]

Returning to London, House hastened to resume conversations with Sir Edward Grey—the statesman who had given him the best hope of a humane peace in which the United States could play a leading part. After assuring Grey of the ability of the enemy to fight on, House thought that he had persuaded the foreign secretary [7]—at least for the

---

concede as much as Berlin to neutral rights. Page sensed in this message, when House showed it to him, "a certain fierce, blue-bellied Presbyterian tone." The Colonel informed Wilson that, if the United States pressed its case too strongly, it might force the resignation of Sir Edward Grey and thus lose its best friend.

[6] "In each government I have visited," the Colonel reported, "I have found stubbornness, determination, selfishness, cant. One continually hears self-glorification . . ." Observing the Kaiser playing at war as if it were the prerogative of royalty and never doubting that God was on his side, and noting the befuddlement of Chancellor Bethmann, House observed in disgust: "In such hands are the destinies of the people placed."

[7] "One of the Colonel's defects," comments Charles Seymour, "was that he was so irresistible in his quiet manner that he persuaded many persons out of their real beliefs."

Regarding House's persuasiveness in this instance, the *New Statesman* commented on March 13, 1926: "Sir Edward Grey seems to have been a better diplomat than most of us knew, for all talk of intervention was at that moment sheer nonsense, but Colonel House was allowed to suppose that he had made a deep impression and had even carried his point." Grey was not converted permanently—if at all—to a view that Wilson expressed to House; that is, that the war would last longer if the United States were a belligerent rather than a neutral. See E. H. Buehrig, *W.W. and the Balance of Power*, pp. 222–28.

moment—that rather than make the submarine issue a *casus belli* it would be best for the President to demand that all belligerents sanction the calling of a peace conference. Grey explained that every window in his house would be broken by mobs if it were known that he was discussing peace; but with a courage that the Colonel thought admirable, the foreign minister consented that the American proposal should be considered with his colleagues at a dinner to be given by Lord Reading.

On this occasion, after hearing his hosts cheerfully divide up the territory of Turkey, the Colonel observed the President's injunction against involvement in selfish war aims and went only so far as to commit Wilson to attend a European peace conference if one should be called at The Hague. When the gathering broke up, at midnight, it was with agreement that Grey and House should draft a memorandum setting forth a presidential offer of mediation that would be discussed with France, if Wilson approved it. There were conflicting opinions in the British Cabinet that made a decision as to timing difficult. Certain ministers doubted the nation's ability to withstand many more months of economic attrition. On the other hand, the men at Reading's dinner felt, and made House admit, that if the Allies could gain military victories, Germany would then be the more likely to accept mediation. Finally, it was decided that the choice of an opportune moment for the making of the American offer should rest with the Allies.

The memorandum resulting from this conference was taken to the President by House, whose name had now become a symbol in twentieth-century diplomacy.[8] Returning to Washington on March 6, the Colonel went riding with the Wilsons and gave them a full account of his stewardship. Before the ruling elder left the White House the President put a hand on his shoulder and said: "It would be hard to imagine a more difficult task than the one placed in your hands, but you have accomplished it in a way beyond my expectations." The next day Wilson typed a telegram for Sir Edward Grey, approving the memorandum that House had brought, in so far as he could speak for the

[8] During his visits to London, House discovered that English radicals against whom Spring Rice had warned him as "copperheads," were sane and able men who held views similar to his own and were potential allies in efforts to convert the British government to the new diplomacy. Moreover, influential journalists with whom the Colonel had cultivated friendships now came to him freely for information and guidance. His handling of newsmen elicited the admiration of Lloyd George—himself a master of the art. Fancying his talent in this regard, the Colonel wanted the President to appreciate it and suggested, after dinner at the White House on March 29, that Wilson read an article by A. G. Gardiner in the London *News*. The President responded with the appreciation that was called for. "I seem to see," he said with a smile, "something of the Colonel's fine Italian hand in this article." However, when Mark Sullivan wrote, in *Collier's*, "there are a good many thoughtful folk who think that the best thing about President Wilson is Colonel House," the Colonel recorded in his diary that this was the sort of thing that he feared most.

future action of the United States. To make doubly sure that it would be understood that he could not act without Senate approval, and also to make the memorandum completely consistent, he added one word— "probably." [9] House signed the message that the President had written and sent if off to Grey. Thus Woodrow Wilson was committed secretly to throw the moral force of his nation on the side of those statesmen who would accept a peace that would strike neutral opinion as humane and just.

On March 10, citing a Wilson victory over the pacifists in Congress [10] as evidence of his mastery of affairs at Washington, House wrote to Grey thus: "It is now squarely up to you to make the next move." Leaders of belligerent nations, however, could not accept the challenge if they would. They were now the victims of those popular passions that they had allowed to run unchecked and had even fanned, in their desperation. The French were fighting for their lives at Verdun, and the British did not dare to suggest anything that might weaken their resistance. Therefore, London failed to respond to reminders from the White House that Wilson's offer might at any time be withdrawn, and the United States revert to a policy of prosecuting its own interests, including that of unrestricted commerce on the seas.

On March 24 the French steamer *Sussex* was torpedoed, with loss of lives, and several Americans were wounded. Wilson's diplomatic battle with Berlin broke out anew, and for a time it seemed that his patience was strained to the breaking point.

Lansing, venting his wrath against the person of Bernstorff, wanted to send a protest to Germany that would be virtually an ultimatum. House thought a rupture inevitable and, looking forward to a peace conference at which Wilson, reinforced by technical experts and persuasive lobbyists, would represent his country alone and would preside, argued that this prospect justified a strong stand at the risk of war.

[9] With this change the "Memorandum of Sir Edward Grey" read, in part: "Colonel House told me that President Wilson was ready, on hearing from France and England that the moment was opportune, to propose that a Conference should be summoned to put an end to the war. Should the Allies accept the proposal, and should Germany refuse it, the United States would probably enter the war against Germany. Colonel House expressed the opinion that, if such a conference met, it would secure peace on terms not unfavorable to the Allies; and, if it failed to secure peace, the United States would *probably* leave the conference as a belligerent on the side of the Allies, if Germany was unreasonable. Colonel House expressed an opinion decidedly favorable to the restoration of Belgium, the transfer of Alsace and Lorraine to France, and the acquisition by Russia of an outlet to the sea, though he thought that the loss of territory incurred by Germany in one place would have to be compensated to her by concessions in other places outside Europe. If the Allies delayed accepting the offer of President Wilson, and if, later on, the course of the war was so unfavorable to them that the intervention of the United States would not be effective, the United States would probably disinterest themselves in Europe and look to their own protection in their own way."

[10] *See* pp. 47–49.

The President asked the Colonel to tell Bernstorff that they were at the breaking point and the United States would surely go to war unless a decisive change were made in Germany's submarine policy.[11] The dilemma upset his digestion and made him seem intractable. For weeks he had not been able to go to bed free from fear that he might be awakened by news that would mean war for his people. Dr. Grayson reported to House that the President was giving his entourage, from the secretary of state down, an unhappy time and was showing intolerance of any who dared to give advice that countered his convictions. Nevertheless, the Colonel ventured to speak his mind. On April 11, when he went to the White House to volunteer counsel on the note that Wilson had drafted to deal with the *Sussex* case, the President's voice seemed weak. But when the Colonel and Mrs. Wilson argued that the text needed strengthening, he held to his views. He said that he was not inclined to consult the Cabinet, for he did not want their ideas; and, moreover, he feared that the document would leak out through them and appear in the afternoon papers. He did decide finally, however, to present it to his colleagues—as an argument that ran in his own mind rather than as a note about to be sent. Mainly he trusted his intuition and his God, though he made a few concessions to pleas of Lansing and House for strengthening of his message.[12]

The note went off to Berlin on April 18, and the next day the President went before the Congress and reviewed the situation. He looked forward with unaffected reluctance, he said, to the possibility of a diplomatic break; but, he went on, "we owe it to a due regard for our own rights as a nation, to a sense of duty as a representative of the rights of neutrals the world over, and to a just conception of the rights of mankind to take this stand now with the utmost solemnity and firmness." On May 3, the day before the German reply arrived, he surprised House in a private talk by the virulence of his feeling against German leaders.

---

[11] Informed by both House and Lansing that the situation was very grave, Bernstorff pressed his government for concessions that might placate American opinion. But all that was vouchsafed by the officials at Berlin, who were incensed at Washington's failure to force Britain to moderate her blockade and who seemed utterly unable to control the submarine commanders, was a note that asserted that the *Sussex* was not torpedoed but rather the victim of a floating mine.

Wilson had been convinced by a study of affidavits that a German submarine sank the *Sussex*. He saw both falsehood and clumsiness in the message from Berlin, and the American press thought it filled with ludicrous evasions.

[12] The draft that was finally sent gave Germany a chance to avoid a break by disavowing the tactics used by her submarines. It served notice that "unless the Imperial German Government should now immediately declare and effect an abandonment of its present methods of warfare against passenger and freight-carrying vessels, the Government of the United States can have no choice but to sever diplomatic relations." Since no time limit was fixed, the note was not an ultimatum; and three days later the President indicated, in a letter to House, that it would be right to discuss with the Germans any plan that they suggested, provided that submarine warfare was stopped entirely during the talks.

He considered them responsible for the war and thought they should be punished personally, like erring directors of corporations.

Realizing that there were only two alternatives, the German Foreign Office on May 4 gave the pledge that was demanded. No more merchant ships would be torpedoed without warning and without regard to loss of lives, unless they offered resistance or tried to escape. But Germany made a reservation. Attacking America's plea for humanity by accusing her of acquiescence in the starvation of Germany, she reserved "complete liberty of decision" in case the United States did not succeed in inducing the Allies to lift their blockade.

Learning of the substance of the German message during a Cabinet meeting the President discussed it immediately with his men. He perceived that at last Germany had accepted his main contention. He therefore acted immediately to seize upon this vital concession, stating at the same time that he could not "for a moment entertain, much less discuss," the German reservation.[13]

Thus Woodrow Wilson again demonstrated the great truth that he had taught—that it took more courage to keep out of a fight than to mix in. As he wrestled with chauvinistic forces, like Antaeus, he sought strength from contact with the solid ground on which his people lived. The birth of his first granddaughter brought him joy, and on Easter Monday he was cheered by the traditional egg rolling on the lawn of the White House. Even more avid than usual for escape and anonymity, he said, "I seriously think of renting a pair of whiskers . . . because I am sorry to find out that the cut of my jib is unmistakable and that I must sail under false colors if I am going to sail incognito." He took weekend voyages down the Potomac and up the James for a few hours, substituting history for politics under the spell of infinite calm that he had always found in the sites along these rivers. He liked to study charts and explore back waters, to pass the time with fisherfolk and buy their catch for his luncheon.

Even on vacations, however, his trusty typewriter was taken along, and a packet of papers to study. He digested editorials in influential journals, and predicted that it was going to be "increasingly difficult to keep off the insistent demand" that he act. "It is much better," he wrote, "that we should initiate the final movement [for peace] than that the Pope should."

---

13 "Responsibility in such matters is single, not joint; absolute, not relative," the President wrote in his best academic manner in a paragraph that he added to a legalistic text drafted by Lansing.

On May 8, the day on which this final message on the *Sussex* case was sent to Berlin, the air was further cleared by an admission from the Foreign Office of liability for the attack upon the vessel and an offer of indemnification.

The Colonel thought it a bit too early to force mediation; but it seemed to him none too soon for the President to demand some action looking toward permanent peace. The nominating conventions were only a month away, and the canny Texan wanted Wilson to announce a strong, positive policy before the Republicans could steal his thunder. He found the President keen for this strategy.

House cast about for an occasion on which Wilson could publicly assert America's determination to lead in the making of a just and enduring peace. It occurred to him that the First National Assembly of the League to Enforce Peace, to be held in Washington on May 26 and 27, gave opportunity for an epochal declaration; and so he arranged that William Howard Taft, president of the League, should urge Wilson to make the main speech on that occasion.

Though in the midst of the *Sussex* crisis the President had declined an invitation to speak at the League's meeting, he reconsidered when Germany met his demands with its pledge of May 4. For a week or so he pondered, feeling his way to a momentous decision. On May 12 he opened his mind completely to Ray Stannard Baker, a man of letters whose instincts and discretion he trusted. Baker saw the rise and fall of the prophet's intellectual passions expressed in his eyes. Wilson's face seemed "singularly living." He pounced deftly upon things half-said, to consume them and add them to his own view, and thus carry along his auditor and make him feel that their minds had met and been enriched by the experience. The first need of a leader, he told Baker, was enthusiasm. He must have a definite program and a direction in which he could believe strongly, and then must stir people to respond, either emotionally or intellectually. He was seeking, more than anything else, a program for action by America to help to bring about peace. Speaking confidently of his plan for a Pan-American Pact, he expressed hope that such an idea might be applied to the rest of the world. He cautioned Baker to breathe no word of this, and asked whether he should tentatively outline his ideas at this time before the League to Enforce Peace; and the journalist replied that, though the hour had not come for calling a peace conference, the President could help to prepare opinion by making guarded statements in his coming speech.

Thinking aloud at a meeting of the National Press Club on May 15, the President sent up a trial balloon. Speaking of the strain that he was under in trying to interpret the spirit of his country, he confessed that he had only the most imperfect means of knowing what his people were thinking about. He particularly needed, he said, the support of "men who will divest themselves of party passion and of personal preference and will try to think in terms of America." Such citizens, he de-

clared, "will take the right leadership if they believe that the leader is
also a man who thinks first of America." As for himself, he was convinced that his land could not afford to withdraw from responsibility
toward the European war and, when it had passed, "have the reckon-
ings." Like his elders who had left their cloisters in South Carolina to
wrestle with the chaos of Reconstruction, Woodrow Wilson felt that
moral men could not ignore the threat of anarchy in Europe. If the
United States was to have the part that he coveted for her—that of leader
in the peacemaking—her President thought it necessary that she should
"act more or less from the point of view of the rest of the world."

At one point his words became sinister and Cromwellian: "If I cannot
retain my moral influence over a man except by occasionally knocking
him down, if that is the only basis upon which he will respect me, then
for the sake of his soul I have got occasionally to knock him down . . .
If a man will not listen to you quietly in a seat, sit on his neck and
make him listen." This point of view had seemed ridiculous to Lord
Grey, when Page had advocated the shooting of Mexicans into political
morality. Fortunately for the repute of the United States in European
diplomatic circles, these brash sentences were not reported to the public.

The day after his frank talk to the Press Club, Wilson's yearning for
positive action had become so strong that he wrote to House: "It seems
to me that we should get down to hard pan." The situation had altered
since the Colonel's visit to Europe, he observed. Indeed, it had reached
a decisive "turning point." The bettering of relations with Germany by
the *Sussex* pledge had concentrated attention on "the altogether indefensible course" that Great Britain was pursuing. Wilson's eye was
still fixed upon a league of nations—Lord Grey's "pearl of great price."

The prophet's zeal was now fully aroused, and he decided to reveal the
American vision to all the world. "To do nothing is now, for us, impossible," he wrote to House on May 16. Two days later he accepted the
second invitation of the League to Enforce Peace, and on the same day
he informed House that the speech in prospect might be the most important he would ever be called to make. He asked the Colonel to give
him the benefit of his insight into the minds of the leaders of the Allies.
He studied parliamentary addresses and winnowed editorial wisdom
from American journals that he respected. Clippings and shorthand
notes were kept in a folder that no one was allowed to touch.

The final text put forth the principles that the President had advocated already in his enunciation of Latin-American policy at Mobile in
1913. But, going further now, the President of the United States became
the first chief of state of his era to commit his people to support a
permanent international organization to enforce these principles. His

pronouncement on this occasion was the most significant of its kind since James Monroe set forth his doctrine.

On May 27, in the new Willard Hotel, facing some two thousand influential members of the League to Enforce Peace, the American prophet embarked publicly on his crusade for humanity. The occasion was the climax of a two-day session at which peace policy had been discussed and almost a half million dollars raised. Though the leadership of the organization was largely Republican, the meeting gave promise of a nonpartisan approach to the great problem of collective security. William Howard Taft and A. Lawrence Lowell sat on the platform; and Henry Cabot Lodge spoke before Wilson and deferred to the intellects of the League to the extent of recognizing the necessity for putting force behind international peace. "The difficulties cannot be overcome unless we try to overcome them," the senator said. Asserting that the founding fathers would not have discouraged an alliance that could diminish war and encourage peace, Lodge spoke of the aspirations of his audience as "beautiful and good and beneficent to humanity," and he quoted Matthew Arnold:

> Charge once more, then, and be dumb!
> Let the victors, when they come,
> When the forts of folly fall,
> Find your body by the wall.

At this time, however, Lodge's faith in the practicality of a League to Enforce Peace was already waning, particularly as he contemplated its effect upon American sovereignty. He suggested to his audience that they might not achieve their end and the outcome might be disappointing. He was willing to accept the benefits of an association of nations, but wary of the sacrifices that would make it effective. The learned man from Boston lacked the greatness of soul and the unshakable faith that were needed to force constructive action in this crisis in human history.[14]

If mankind was to be saved from the ravages of international an-

[14] A year earlier, at Union College, Lodge had spoken more confidently of international action for peace. A letter from Theodore Roosevelt to Lodge commended the Union College speech as "admirable." Moreover, Roosevelt, in a speech delivered upon receiving the Nobel Peace Prize in 1912, had declared that it would be "a master stroke" for the great powers to form a league that would use force, if necessary, to prevent breaches of world peace. And in a magazine article entitled "Utopia or Hell" he had proposed "a world league bound by a solemn covenant" to "act with the combined military strength of all of them against any recalcitrant nation." But on June 7, 1916, he wrote to Arthur Lee: "Wilson and Taft are now bleating for leagues to enforce peace." Morison (ed.), *Letters*, VIII, 1056. In 1912 the Republican Congress had passed a resolution calling for arbitration and disarmament and even for constituting the combined navies of the world an international police force for the preservation of peace.

archy, it would require the perspective of Olympus and the faith of the Apostles. A prophet who had been bred on Scripture and had regenerated institutions by the power of spiritual truth scarcely could fail to respond to this supreme call. Woodrow Wilson was ready to lead his people over the edge of a world that was, politically speaking, still thought to be flat. He was as eager as ever to explore new dimensions of government. When the critical, poetasting senator sat down, after telling the audience that the supreme vision of the age might fail, Wilson rose and proclaimed that it must prevail.

He played masterfully upon the creative impulses that he felt throbbing in the hearts of his national congregation. Beginning with assertions of inescapable fact, he spoke of the profound effect of the European war on American liberties and property, and the resulting conviction that the prevention of war had become a primary concern to Americans, as to Europeans. Pointing out that the current war would not have begun if there had been a period of open discussion of its causes, he concluded that peace must henceforth depend upon "a new and more wholesome diplomacy." He reasserted a familiar doctrine of Anglo-Saxon liberalism: nations should follow the same high code of honor that is demanded of individuals. Moreover, they must agree on the things that are fundamental to their common interests and concur on a way of acting in concert against any threat to those essentials.

We believe these fundamental things: First, that every people has a right to choose the sovereignty under which they shall live. . . . Second, that the small states of the world have a right to enjoy the same respect for their sovereignty and for their territorial integrity that great and powerful nations expect and insist upon. And, third, that the world has a right to be free from every disturbance of its peace that has its origin in aggression and disregard of the rights of peoples and nations.

So sincerely do we believe in these things that I am sure that I speak the mind and wish of the people of America when I say that the United States is willing to become a partner in any feasible association of nations formed in order to realize these objects and make them secure against violation.

There is nothing that the United States wants for itself that any other nation has. We are willing, on the contrary, to limit ourselves along with them to a prescribed course of duty and respect for the rights of others which will check any selfish passion of our own, as it will check any aggressive impulse of theirs.

If it should ever be our privilege to suggest or initiate a movement for peace among the nations now at war, I am sure that the people of the United States would wish their Government to move along these lines: First, such a settlement with regard to their own immediate interests as the belligerents may agree upon. We have nothing material of any kind to ask for ourselves, and are quite aware that we are in no sense or degree parties to the present quarrel. Our interest is only in peace and its future guarantees. Second, an universal association of the nations to maintain the inviolate security of the highway of the seas for the common and unhindered use of all the nations of the world, and to prevent any war begun either contrary to treaty covenants or without warning and full submission of the causes to the opinion of the world—a virtual guarantee of territorial integrity and political independence.

But I did not come here, let me repeat, to discuss a programme. I came only to avow a creed and give expression to the confidence I feel that the world is even now upon the eve of a great consummation, when some common force will be brought into existence which shall safeguard right as the first and most fundamental interest of all peoples and all governments, when coercion shall be summoned . . . to the service of a common order, a common justice, and a common peace. God grant that the dawn of that day of frank dealing and of settled peace, concord, and cooperation may be near at hand!

The response of Wilson's countrymen to this challenge was warm enough to convince him that he was moving in the right direction, and by the end of May his course was so firmly set that it never would be altered. To be sure, many contemporary observers failed to grasp the epochal portent of this speech, and Secretary Lansing questioned from a sickbed the wisdom of subjecting the nation's independence of action to the will of powers outside the Western Hemisphere. But the *Independent* called the address a "declaration of interdependence," to be set beside the nation's Declaration of Independence.

The pioneering prophet had found another Great Cause—greater than "Princeton in the Nation's Service," greater even than "The New Freedom." On Memorial Day he declared: "America is roused, roused to a self-consciousness such as she has not had in a generation." Addressing himself to critics who were still under the spell of the injunction of the founding fathers against "entangling alliances," he said: "I shall never myself consent to an entangling alliance, but I would gladly assent to a disentangling alliance—an alliance which would disentangle the peoples of the world from those combinations in which they seek their own separate and private interests and unite the people of the world to preserve the peace of the world upon a basis of common right and justice. There is liberty there, not limitation. There is freedom, not entanglement."

Unfortunately, Philistines in Europe fell upon a few phrases in the speech of May 27 that were infelicitous, and by harping on them obscured the great central purpose of the President. Nationalistic editors at London were apprehensive of a league that would try to make the seas secure "for the common and unhindered use of all nations" and the publicists of the Allies thought Wilson unsympathetic because he said of the war: "with its causes and its objects we are not concerned." It seemed as if he were placing France and England on a moral level with Germany. Page reported that the British people were "skittish about the President" because he seemed to speak only to "the gallery filled with peace cranks." Wilson learned, moreover, that by asserting the right of small peoples to self-determination he had angered the rulers of Austria-Hungary and had raised embarrassing questions about the status of minorities in the British Empire. Furthermore, France's ambassador hinted to House that the United States might find herself without sympathizers in a future war with aggressors unless she took the side of the Allies in their hour of trial. At the same time reports of an economic conference held at Paris suggested that the Allies intended to encroach on the commerce of neutrals and set up industrial monopolies if Germany were vanquished.

The prophet was exasperated by these rebuffs. Wilson had committed his emotions so completely that he would never be satisfied, from this day forth, until he realized his aspiration for American leadership in organizing the world for a peace based on reason. He knew that a longing for such a peace lay deep in the hearts of the French and British peoples. His stern sense of mission projected jagged edges in a note written to House on June 22: "The letters and the glimpses of opinion [official opinion] from the other side of the water are not encouraging, to say the least, and indicate a constant narrowing, instead of a broad and comprehending view of the situation. They are in danger of forgetting the rest of the world, and of waking up some surprising morning to discover that it has a positive right to be heard about the peace of the world. I conclude that it will be up to us to judge for ourselves when the time has arrived for us to make an imperative suggestion."

And then, as if conscious of the inconsistency of this hint of compulsion with his policy of free self-determination, he added a qualification: "I mean a suggestion which they will have no choice but to heed, because the opinion of the non-official world and the desire of all peoples will be behind it." And if they were not behind it? Infatuated by the new concept of manifest destiny that the elders among his people were shaping, the prophet did not raise this question.

CHAPTER III

KEEPING HIS POWDER DRY

WITH AN ELECTION in prospect, Woodrow Wilson realized that 1916 was "a year of political accounting" and that Americans were good accountants. If his own stewardship could not stand the glare of pitiless publicity, it seemed to him that it ought to be terminated. "I hope that every public man will get what is coming to him," he said to a New York audience on January 27. He intended to re-establish the rapport with his people that he had enjoyed in his first year in the Presidency.

Wilson's firm mastery of the party men had relaxed during his pre-occupation, in 1915, with foreign affairs and with the winning of Edith Galt. Indeed, he had suffered a legislative defeat when his shipping bill was filibustered to death in the Senate. And when the Congress met again in December the members reflected misgivings that had become rife among their constituents. At one extreme, Bryan's friends wished to reduce the risk of war by refusing passports to citizens intending to sail on belligerent ships; and at the other end of the arc of opinion, jingoes proposed measures that would promote war with Mexico or a break with Britain or Germany.

Many citizens feared that the United States would be attacked if Germany triumphed. The people—particularly those in the East—had been thoroughly frightened by the propaganda of organizations promoting preparedness, as well as by books and moving pictures that dramatized the force of Prussian militarism. Experts of the Army and Navy had been warning the public for many months that they lacked means to defend the nation. Theodore Roosevelt bellowed about the President's incapacity to face the world that he had to live in. And Franklin D. Roosevelt and Secretary of War Garrison gave comfort to those who championed preparedness.

The President, however, felt that the dogs of war, no less than the pacifists, must be held firmly in leash. Many citizens, he sensed, mistrusted the motives of professional soldiers who advocated expansion of their own business. Likewise many suspected sinister self-interest behind journalistic clamor for purchase of war materials. Yet early in 1915, under the pressure of public agitation, the President had signed a bill increasing the Navy. Furthermore, he had talked with Garrison about a plan for a military system that would have many of the features of the Swiss and would provide what was known as a "continental army." His interest in defense was stimulated by the defiant attitude of Germany in the *Lusitania* case and the embarrassment that American diplomats suffered in Europe because of the scorn of the belligerents for the inability of the United States to put military force behind her diplomatic notes.

On July 21 the President had asked Daniels and Garrison to draw up a preparedness program; and ten days later he had begun to prepare the doubting minds of Congressional leaders—Republican as well as Democratic—for nonpartisan discussions that might lead to "a single judgment in the matter and a single programme of action."

By November Wilson had final recommendations from Daniels and Garrison. He was ready to fulfill what he conceived to be the duty of going before the people and, at the same time, to satisfy those Democratic politicians who had been urging him to seize leadership of the growing sentiment for preparedness. It went against the grain to do this. He intended to prepare "not for war but for defense," he explained, and it was made clear to the generals of the Army—and particularly to Leonard Wood—that they were to refrain from any talk or acts that might be construed as "political." The President conceived that self-defense did not require the building of a military machine, for it seemed to him that even if Germany won, she would not be able to menace America for some years. He thought that labor leaders would balk and that his people expected him to lead in extending pacific idealism to the world rather than to expose America to such fears and jealousies as had followed military buildups in Europe. He had just had a letter from Oswald Garrison Villard that denounced the preparedness program as "a waste of the nation's resources" and "anti-moral, anti-social, and anti-democratic."

Wilson ventured to plot a path between the extremists by speaking at a dinner at the Manhattan Club in New York on November 4. He was glum and silent during the meal, and when he rose to speak his face was solemn, his voice strained. It seemed to an observer that he was "taking his medicine without licking the spoon." With war ablaze in the world, he asked, how far were Americans prepared to go to maintain themselves against any interference with their national action and development? Asserting again that there was no question of the willful use of force against any nation or any people, he declared: "We feel justified in preparing ourselves to vindicate our right to independent and unmolested action by making the force that is in us ready for assertion." The speech elicited only perfunctory applause, extremists on all sides being irritated by its moderation.

A fortnight before the date set for his marriage the President was immersed in contemplation of his third annual address to Congress. Delivering it on December 7, he talked first about Pan-Americanism and asserted that his nation's purpose was to make a common cause of national independence and political liberty. Then he said: "If our citizens are ever to fight effectively upon a sudden summons, they must know how modern fighting is done, and what to do when the summons comes to render themselves immediately available and immediately effective. . . . They must be fitted to play the great role in the world, and particularly in this hemisphere, which they are qualified by principle and by chastened ambition to play." With these ideals in the forefront, the President went on to recommend "essential first steps" that seemed to him "for the present sufficient." [1]

A gentle persuasiveness shone from the soul of the bridegroom as he pleaded with his men—"the sweetness of conscious strength," Secretary Redfield called it. The President was convinced, however, that he must use weapons more eloquent than courtesy. The essential responsibility of a real leader, he perceived, was to proclaim the preparedness program as a gospel, out in the West where many of his Congressional opponents had their roots and where vast rural areas were slumbering in ostrichlike isolation from the perils of the world. He could not permit vital divisions in the party as he led it toward the verdict of the voters. He must hammer home the truths that gave unity, eschew particulars that provoked debate. And so the prophet went forth, at the end of January, to tell his people that they must keep their powder dry and to lead them to a Lord whom they could trust—a God of peace and good will, but one jealous of his honor and his character. This was the only time during his first term that he appealed to the people in order to whip the Congress.

In twelve addresses, at New York and in the Middle West, he gave voice to the growing apprehension of danger from abroad. "All the rest of the world is on fire, and our own house is not fireproof," he said. He confessed that he had been awakened to many things that he had not realized a year earlier. "I cannot tell twenty-four hours at a time," he remarked, "whether there is going to be trouble or not. And whether there is or not does not depend upon what I say, or upon what any man in the United States does or says. It depends upon what foreign govern-

---

[1] Wilson proposed an increase in the tiny regular Army, and a supplementing force of 400,000 disciplined citizens who would volunteer for three short annual training periods and for service at call at any time during the ensuing three years. He then commended the five-year building program prepared by the Navy Department and went on to demand revival of the campaign for strengthening the merchant fleet that had been defeated by filibuster in the last Congress. As a part of his program for security, moreover, he asked for sedition laws adequate for the prosecution of "creatures of passion, disloyalty, and anarchy."

ments do; what the commanders of ships at sea do; what those in charge of submarines do; what those who are conducting blockades do."

The prophet told off fanatical critics on both sides. There were actually men in America who were preaching war, he declared. On the other hand, some of those who counseled peace went much further than he could go or his people could follow. America could not pay the price of losing her character, her self-respect. She must maintain the right of her citizens to travel unmolested, and to buy and sell in the markets of the world. He brought his people face to face with the dismal realities of the European scene. Modern wars were not won by mere numbers, or by sheer enthusiasm and patriotism. "They are won by the scientific application of irresistible force." In view of these considerations, it seemed "almost ridiculous" to state how little the administration was asking. The President had hardly troops enough to patrol the Mexican border. He was not seeking an army to command, but a trained citizenship. He did not aspire to be the "ruler on horseback" of which Americans were so deeply suspicious, but wanted rather to command the confidence and support of fellow citizens.

Near the end of his tour he invited his people to apply their "hard business sense" to the proposition, dismissing as "preposterous" the popular suspicion that agitation for preparedness had come chiefly from profiteers. But much of the President's philosophical argument went over their heads, and they could not be sure, from his veiled statements, just how imminent war with Germany was. The people found it hard to believe that this compassionate man could become the tool of irresponsible militarism. There was one phrase, however, that gave them pause: at St. Louis he spoke carelessly of a navy that would be "incomparably the greatest in the world." Opponents cited this as evidence of megalomania.[2] War-shy Democratic legislators perceived contradictions in the President's speeches and were perturbed at their ominous hints of fighting to come; and it became clear that the secretary of war was still unable to negotiate effectively with congressmen for a compromise plan of military training for civilians.

On February 4, the day on which Wilson returned to Washington full of cheer and confident that he carried with him the good will of an awakening majority of his people, the Senate passed the Clarke Amendment, which provided for Philippine independence in two years under

---

[2] When Wilson was told of the criticism, he confessed to the fault attributed to Gladstone—"intoxication by the eloquence of his own verbosity." The printed version of the St. Louis speech was changed to read "incomparably the most adequate navy in the world"; but when he returned to Washington and the Cabinet asked him whether he had been correctly quoted, he said: "Yes, and it is one thing that I said in my swing around the circuit that I actually believe." Daniels, *Years of War*, p. 41.

certain conditions. Garrison's ire was aroused by this. Believing that the Filipinos were not ready to rule and defend themselves, fearing that Japan would seize and exploit them, the secretary of war protested against the action of the Senate. "I cannot accept it or acquiesce in its acceptance," he wrote to the President.[3] If the War Department could not have its way immediately in this matter and in its plan for a strong standing army, he was through. He decided, for the fifth time, to resign.

This time the President did not try to dissuade him. As early as the summer of 1915 he had decided to let Garrison go. He wrote a gracious letter accepting the resignation, with "very warm appreciation" of distinguished service. Thus the departure of the militant Garrison followed that of the ultrapacific Bryan.

Fortunately the Middle West, the very region that had been most suspicious of Garrison's military program, raised up a man who could carry out its essentials. Mayor Newton D. Baker of Cleveland, whom Wilson had hoped to bring into his Cabinet in 1913, had risen higher in the President's esteem when he declined that honor in order to finish the job of reform to which the people of his city had committed him.[4] Now his second term as mayor had ended and he was looking forward to private practice of law.

"Would you accept the secretaryship of War?" Wilson telegraphed to him on March 5, 1916. "Earnestly hope that you can see your way to do so. It would greatly strengthen my hand."

Receiving a tentative acceptance, the President announced the appointment forthwith. When the appointee came to the White House three days later and explained that his association with peace societies made it inappropriate for him to serve in the War Department, Wilson merely asked: "Are you ready to take the oath?" At last he had found the perfect servant, a man who would feed his mind with the pith of fact and logic, never waste his time, and always accept the Chief's

[3] Wilson, for his part, had been opposed to the acquisition of the Philippines by the United States after the Spanish-American War; and when he became president he thought of these islands as a trust that must never be appropriated by the trustees. He had suggested that the Filipinos be given assurance of independence, to be conferred as soon as they were ready for self-government. The question of timing was difficult, however. Feeling that the hour for cutting the islands loose had not yet come, he had decided to move toward independence a step at a time. His first act was to give native citizens a majority in the governing commission, and he had done this in the hope that the Filipino leaders would prove their political capacity.

In the summer of 1914, Chairman Jones of the House Committee of Insular Affairs introduced a bill providing for independence as soon as a stable government should be established. On Nov. 4, 1915 Wilson told House that he thought it necessary to go through with the Jones Bill. On Feb. 4, 1916, the Senate passed the measure with the Clarke Amendment. Though the House passed the Jones Bill in 1914, it defeated the amendment in 1916.

[4] After the 1914 election Baker had written to Secretary Redfield about his city's vote, asserting that Cleveland was "the brightest spot" in the "general back-sliding . . ." and that there was no area in the nation where the President's policies were so keenly appreciated and so devotedly followed. Wilson had been delighted by this letter when it was shown to him.

decision on matters of general policy and strive to carry it out loyally and effectively.

Because of statements that he had made recently against preparedness, his slight stature, his glasses—he had been rejected as a volunteer for the Spanish-American War because of bad eyesight—Baker was nick-named "Violet" by journalists in Washington. But they came to respect his ability and devotion. When they asked him whether it was true that he was a pacifist, his reply was: "So much so that I would fight for peace."

Avowing innocence of "obsessions or prejudices," Baker appreciated the value of political confidences better than his predecessor had. He established cordial relations with the legislators with whom the department had been at loggerheads. Moreover, he tactfully prevented the President from interfering unwisely with the work of the War College.

The day before Baker took office, Congressman Hay introduced a National Defense Bill in the House with the President's approval. This measure, which conceded more responsibility to the National Guard than Garrison would permit and more than Wilson himself desired, was passed on March 23 with only two contrary votes. Though the pacifism of rural progressives had not been overcome by the President's speaking tour, the enthusiasm of his city audiences had its effect on congressmen. Moreover, the need for troops had been highlighted when two outrages by Francisco Villa resulted in the death of thirty-five American citizens and the subsequent crossing of the Mexican border, on March 15, by a punitive expedition under General John J. Pershing.[5] In the same month further impetus was given to the drive for preparedness by the

[5] Though overshadowed by the European war, the Mexican situation had continued to plague the President after Huerta's retirement and the submission of the matter to Latin-American arbitration in the summer of 1914. In the autumn of that year, Wilson and Bryan persisted in their efforts to reconcile the contending factions and at the same time to protect American rights without using force. By Nov. 23 the administration felt that the situation was stable enough so that troops could be withdrawn from Veracruz. But in 1915 civil war continued. On Oct. 19 Carranza's government was recognized.

By January of 1916 the situation had become so chaotic that Wilson wrote to Cleveland Dodge that his heart was "pretty sad" about it. On the 11th Villa, whom Wilson and Bryan had made the mistake of supporting because of his amenability to Yankee advice and his pretensions of land reform, went berserk in northern Mexico and seized and massacred sixteen citizens of the United States. Moreover, on Mar. 9 the bandit general crossed the border and raided Columbus, New Mexico, burning towns and killing nineteen persons. Thereupon, popular demand for military action became irresistible; and after negotiating a diplomatic agreement with President Carranza that sanctioned temporary police action, the President sent a punitive expedition into Mexico on March 15, 1916, under Pershing. The decision caused mental anguish. The night before it was made Wilson walked out alone and paced the portico pensively, fearful of falling into war in the manner of President Polk. In a message to the press Wilson explained that the "single object" of the intervention was to stop Villa's forays by capturing him, "in entirely friendly aid of the constituted authorities in Mexico and with scrupulous respect for the sovereignty of the Republic." Inevitably there were clashes with Carranza's troops in which blood was shed and by May there was serious danger of full-scale war. See pp. 50 and 61.

outbreak of a rash of German submarine outrages, particularly by the torpedoing of the French steamer *Sussex*.

Advocates of a large regular army made the most of these immediate threats to the nation's safety. It seemed to them that Wilson had capitulated to the National Guard lobby as a political expedient. His policy frightened Republicans, who conceived that their party had saved the Union, won the Spanish-American War, and projected their country to material eminence in the world. They feared that the United States would fade from the first rank of the nations. Moderates now attacked Wilson openly. Democratic Senator Chamberlain and his Military Affairs Committee persuaded the Senate to adopt a bill, on April 18, that would almost double the Regular Army approved by the House, "federalize" the National Guard, and establish a "continental army"—a volunteer reserve force of a quarter million men. Thus the President was challenged to mediate between the two houses of Congress to get a reasonable measure of protection for the nation.

Wilson's position was the more difficult because, after his return from the Middle West, he had been engaged in a battle within his own party over the question of the status of armed liners. This issue had come to the front again with the torpedoing in early January of the British ship *Persia*, with appalling loss of passengers, including an American consul. To remove the provocation of armaments, which Germany cited as justification for such acts, Wilson and Lansing had urged the Allies not to arm their merchantmen. But when Germany gave warning on February 8 that armed vessels would be dealt with as ships of war, the State Department had been forced to give up its hope of persuading the Allies to let their vessels go unarmed. The statesmen at London felt that by removing armament they would merely make their ships easier prey.

When American diplomats abroad were notified that merchant shipping had a right to defensive armament and that the killing of American passengers would be regarded as "a breach of international law and the formal assurances given by the German government," Congressional leaders, unaware of the ill-fated effort that had been made to placate Germany, began to suspect that the Administration wanted to maneuver the nation into war. Their fear increased when the President, asked on February 21 by three legislative leaders what would happen if Americans traveling on an armed ship were drowned as a result of a submarine attack, told them that he would hold Germany strictly accountable. He asserted that the Allies, though unwise, were within their rights in arming their merchantmen. Furthermore, he made it clear that he did not wish to forbid Americans to travel on armed ships.

Replying to a warning of Congressional opposition, Wilson wrote on February 24 to Chairman Stone of the Senate's Committee on Foreign Relations: "I cannot consent to any abridgement of the rights of American citizens in any respect . . . Once accept a single abatement of right and many other humiliations would certainly follow, and the whole fine fabric of international law might crumble under our hands piece by piece. What we are contending for in this matter is of the very essence of the things that have made America a sovereign nation. She cannot yield them without conceding her own impotency as a nation and making virtual surrender of her independent position among the nations of the world."

Early on the morning of the 25th influential congressmen called at the White House and Speaker Champ Clark, whom many Democrats hoped to nominate for the Presidency in 1916, told Wilson that two-thirds of his colleagues were ready to approve a resolution offered by McLemore of Texas, warning Americans against traveling on armed ships of belligerents. But the President stood firmly on what he had written to Stone.

Fortunately Wilson was physically in good fighting trim and fortified politically by the sentiment that he had built on his speaking trip. The excess of energy that he had brought back from his honeymoon vacation at the first of the year had been lavished in talks with congressmen of both parties and letters to publicists. On January 20 he had seen Senator Lodge, thanked him for advice, and agreed with him in opposing an embargo and deploring investigation of pending foreign negotiations by Congressional committees. He tried to hold the ruling elders to the patriotic, nonpartisan creed that he preached to the national congregation. But the task strained his patience when revolt was seething. His temper flared up on February 25 and he told a visitor what he really thought about Congress: "It is with such a ——— outfit as that that I am supposed to act and achieve nationally for America!"

Legislators who feared to offend pacifistic and hyphenated constituents were shamed by the prophetic lash. They began to shift ground and talk of delaying a vote on the McLemore resolution and a similar one introduced by Gore in the Senate. But Wilson, advised by Cabinet members that his scepter as leader of the party would pass to Bryan if he did not demand a showdown, insisted that his position be made crystal clear in the eyes of the world, and immediately. He took the unprecedented step of writing to the ranking member of the House Committee on Rules. Asking for a prompt vote on the Gore and McLemore resolutions, he wrote: "The report that there are divided counsels in Congress in regard to the foreign policy of the Government is being made industrious use of in foreign capitals. I believe that report to be false, but so long as it is anywhere credited it cannot fail to do the greatest harm and expose the country to the most serious risks."

This brought the legislators quickly to balloting on the question of tabling the controversial resolutions. In both chambers the President's supporters, responding to the popular feeling that Wilson had evoked, won an impressive victory. Senator Lodge and other Republicans took a nonpartisan position behind the President.

After this rift in the party, Wilson found it difficult to get the leaders to unite on a compromise between the plans for preparedness that were approved by the House and the Senate. He had to plead time and again for cooperation in the interest of national unity, asking for an act that would provide the large number of units that the Senate desired but would keep them at the skeleton size that the House recommended; and he requested "unmistakable authority" to fill up the ranks at any time that the public safety might require it.

Early in June the National Defense Act became law.[6] Moderate progressives and pacifists felt that it provided reasonable protection for the nation, but the act fell far short of the ambitions of ardent military men. There were mass meetings and parades under the slogan "America First," and those who dissented were stigmatized as "subversives" and became objects of derivision.

The President gave repute to the clamor by issuing a Flag Day proclamation calling for rededication to the nation, "one and inseparable." He himself joined in a huge parade at Washington and, to the dismay of the secret service guards, led the procession carrying a small flag over his shoulder. He came through the ordeal unharmed, though

[6] A compromise, this measure authorized a federal army of nearly a quarter million and, dropping the plan of the military experts for a continental reserve force, it provided that the National Guard be increased to nearly a half million within five years and integrated into the federal defense structure. Moreover, the War Department was empowered to conduct summer training camps for volunteers and to build and operate a nitrate plant. In the new act there was a clause authorizing the President to draft, in time of war and after authorization by Congress, enough militia to keep the Army's reserve battalions up to battle strength—a provision that came to be variously interpreted but paved the way for the acceptance of conscription a year later.

The National Defense Act was but the first of several measures to enable the nation to defend its rights in an anarchic world. To secure adequate appropriations for naval construction, the President found it necessary again to mediate between the houses of Congress. Moved by fear of the navies of Germany and Japan and, more immediately, by a desire to be independent of Britain, Wilson persuaded an antipreparedness block in the House to go along with the larger program voted by the Senate, after it was altered by provisions for reorganization of the service and for the erection of a government armor-plate factory that would check profiteering. The naval appropriation bill was signed by the President on Aug. 29, along with a measure making allotments for the Army and creating a Council of National Defense for the coordination of industries and resources for national security. In August of 1916, also, the long running battle to strengthen the nation's shipping came to an end, with the Senate following party lines to adopt a bill that laid the foundation for a twentieth-century merchant marine.

a week later a similar demonstration at San Francisco was broken up by a death-dealing bomb.

On June 18, when Villa was still at large, Carranza was accusing Washington of bad faith in keeping Pershing's punitive expedition in Mexico, and the War College was drawing up plans for full-scale invasion, Wilson took advantage of the National Defense Act to call out about a hundred thousand National Guardsmen to protect the Mexican border. And yet at the same time he used his eloquence to warn his people against chauvinism.

The conscience of the prophet was not satisfied by the discharge of obvious duties that were forced upon him by threats from abroad. Amid the controversies stirred by his program for preparedness, and to hold the loyalty of progressives who distrusted that program and thought it inspired by influences militaristic and venal, he carried forward the cause of the New Freedom.

The most telling impetus given to the progressive movement by the emergency of 1916 was in the field of taxation. Unprecedented appropriations for the armed services made it necessary, in this election year, to issue bonds or to levy higher taxes. Conservative legislators wished to raise new funds by inflating the public debt; but Wilson made it clear that he regarded borrowing as a shortsighted policy.

The Congress, with uneasy eyes on the 1916 election, began to debate a plan advanced by McAdoo for additional excises and a schedule of income taxes that bore heavily upon citizens of moderate and low incomes. The Ways and Means Committee of the House was overwhelmed by protests from labor leaders and from Eastern progressives; and Democratic congressmen gave notice that they would not support McAdoo's plan even if a party caucus commanded them. They insisted that funds for preparedness should be taken from large incomes, inheritances, and the profits of arms-makers.

Immediately there were countercharges that irresponsible demagogues were trying to "soak the rich"; but for the first time Wilson's administration lost control of the rebellious Ways and Means Committee, and the House approved imposts more revolutionary than any sponsored by the President.[7] Though the leveling effect of the legislation went far beyond Wilson's intention, he signed the bill.

Moreover, in this election year, he consented to a measure designed to

[7] The new measure did not lower exemptions, but raised the surtax above the limit imposed by the law of 1913, levied a tax on large estates, repealed excises of the emergency law of 1914, and placed a tax on the gross receipts of manufacturers showing a net profit of 10 per cent and over. Moreover, under the influence of such men as Robert M. LaFollette and George W. Norris, the Senate increased several of the rates and placed a levy on corporation capital, surplus, and undivided profits.

mitigate the problems of agricultural credit. Up to this time, provisions for the peculiar needs of the farmer had lagged and Wilson himself had given very little study to this matter. The President had commended to the Congress a proposal for a system of land banks that would be privately controlled under federal charter; but he had been unwilling that the government supply the funds that would be necessary to subsidize this "single class of the community."

In January of 1916, with the secretary of the Rural Credits Association stating publicly that the Democratic party could command the support of Midwestern farmers by providing special credits, Wilson listened sympathetically to Secretary Houston and Congressman Lever. He not only agreed that the government would buy the minimum of farm bonds that these men specified, but doubled their figure. The Administration put its full power behind a rural credits bill, and Congress passed it almost unanimously. As Wilson had feared, it was denounced by conservatives as "class legislation"; and agrarian radicals felt that it was inadequate. But the President signed it, on July 17. Like the Federal Reserve, the new system was to be regulated by a board appointed by the President. Wilson was able to say to his people that never before in their lifetime was credit so available to individuals. Farmers responded. Many Republicans shifted their allegiance; and the Nonpartisan League, mushrooming in the Middle West, became Wilson's partisans.

The imminence of an election also gave impetus to legislation that had long been urged by independent advocates of better working conditions. On February 2 the House passed a bill forbidding interstate commerce in goods produced by children under fourteen; but Wilson, feeling that such a measure invaded the police power of the states and hence was unconstitutional, made no effort for months to overcome the apathy that the Senate showed. In mid-July, however, he was warned that progressives were restive and considered this bill a test of the sincerity of his progressivism; and on the 18th he went to the Capitol to tell Democratic senators that the fortunes of the party demanded that they let the measure come to a vote. As a result, Southerners who like himself were jealous of states' rights yielded; and the opposition of the National Association of Manufacturers, who regarded the law as a forerunner of less justifiable interferences with industry, was overcome. The President signed this humanitarian act on September 1 [8] with great satisfaction, and he gave further comfort to advocates of labor by approving a model compensation bill for federal employees.

[8] The Child Labor Act of 1916 was declared unconstitutional two years later and thus Wilson's first opinion of the measure was sustained.

Meanwhile Wilson had been committed by his party to stand for re-election. Prominent Democrats were depending on him to keep them politically solvent, and he had said to his bride that he would respond if his people called him. But he had made it clear at a Gridiron dinner, on February 26, that he had no personal craving for a second term.[9]

In the early months of 1916, the leaders had lost their easy confidence in the re-election of the Chief. Wilson's New Freedom was still regarded by financiers with suspicion. Ambassador Morgenthau, undertaking the task of raising a campaign fund and finding wealthy New Yorkers cool and Tammany bitter, got no comfort from the President's entourage. Not one of the high officials with whom he talked thought that Wilson could be re-elected. Even House was dubious; for the minority triumph in 1912, when the opposition was split, could not be repeated unless the President made a strong appeal to independent voters.

Entertaining the National Committee at the White House, the President said: "The facilities of publicity are not on our side. We have to do something very dramatic and very striking to be talked about at all . . . It is absolutely necessary that the impression we make on the country should be one of momentum . . . We are not partisans of men, we are partisans of ideas." He touched upon ideas as delicately as if they were explosive.

As the day of the nominating convention drew near, he became absorbed in planning for it. He dramatized his intention when, going to the circus and passing a show ring, he pretended to throw his hat in. He took into his own hands the shaping of the party's platform, adding a plank advocating woman suffrage and, conscious that independent voters would swing the coming election, stressing the progressive legislation that had been enacted.

Urged by House to seize leadership of peace sentiment before the

[9] A month before entering the Presidency, asked for his opinion of a Congressional resolution that would prohibit a second term, Wilson had argued that to impose a constitutional ban against a second term would be to suggest that the people could not be trusted to choose wisely at the polls. "Four years is too long a term," Wilson had written to A. Mitchell Palmer on Feb. 3, 1913, "for a President who is not the true spokesman of the people, who is imposed upon and does not lead. It is too short a term for a President who is doing or attempting a great work of reform, and who has not had time to finish it. . . . I am not speaking for my own re-election; I am speaking to redeem my promise that I would say what I really think on every public question and take my chances in the court of public opinion." There was no doubt, in 1915, that Wilson's party was depending on his leadership for another victory at the polls, in spite of a Bryan-inspired plank in its 1912 platform that had favored limitation of each president to a single term.

Newton D. Baker, surprised at finding the President more of a party man than he himself was, remarked upon it, and Wilson replied: "But not stronger than you will be. You will discover that in a government like ours, progress is possible only through parties, and parties are possible only when men are willing to concede minor matters for great policies." N. D. Baker to Frederick Palmer, Jan. 5 and July 18, 1931.

Republicans, whose convention would precede the Democratic, could pre-empt this channel of appeal to the voters, the President wrote the great vision of the twentieth century into the party's platform. He asserted that the circumstances of the past two years had revealed necessities of international action that no former generation could have foreseen. Repeating three fundamental principles that he set forth on May 27, in his address to the League to Enforce Peace, he wrote:

The time has come when it is the duty of the United States to join with the other nations of the world in any feasible association that will effectively serve those principles, to maintain inviolate the complete security of the highway of the seas for the common and unhindered use of all nations, and to prevent any war begun either contrary to treaty covenants or without warning and frank submission of the provocation and causes to the opinion of mankind.

The platform committee of the party, reviewing this far-reaching statement, disapproved the last proposition. They accepted the rest, along with statements of other foreign policies of the Administration—respect for human and political rights above material interests, Pan-American concord, and nonintervention in Mexico.[10]

It was the intention of the President that his Indians should vent their war whoops in a patriotic demonstration to which no voter could take exception. He conceived that, while he paraded in Washington with a flag upon his shoulder, the nominating convention would celebrate Flag Day at St. Louis, subordinating the traditional strains of "Dixie" to "The Star-Spangled Banner." He telegraphed to the convention to urge adoption of a strong plank on Americanism that he had written.

The President's plank was accepted unanimously; but when the hubbub on the floor of the convention hall subsided and Martin H. Glynn, former governor of New York, rose to deliver a keynote speech that had been approved in part by Wilson and House, the delegates responded with no more than due respect to patriotic hyperbole. However, when the speaker came to what he called "the paramount issue"—the avoidance of war—pulses beat faster. Democrats felt that, because of Germany's disavowal of ruthless submarine tactics early in May, the party could claim credit for saving the nation from armed conflict.

Glynn quickly detected the note that made the sweetest music in the ears of the party men. When he cited cases in which the nation had not gone to war though her rights were violated, his audience roared for

---

[10] Wilson was not confident enough of his Mexican policy to wish to have it stated in detail, but the platform committee overruled him.

more. And so he alluded to instances in the administrations of five presidents, and after each he repeated a line that became a slogan: "But we didn't go to war."

Leaders who had hoped to unite the party under Wilson's program of Americanism were aghast at the demonstration of pacifist feelings. A slip of paper was passed to Glynn, to suggest that Democrats were willing to fight if necessary. But his Celtic spirits were roused, and he went on to strengthen the bond that was being woven. "Do Republicans realize," he said, "that when they arraign the policy of the President of the United States today, they arraign the policy of Harrison, of Blaine, of Lincoln, and of Grant?" There was no staying the tide of sentiment.

The next day Senator Ollie James, the permanent chairman, attributed the people's blessings to their chief. "Four years ago they sneeringly called Woodrow Wilson the school teacher. . . . Today . . . the confines of his schoolroom circle the world. His subject is the protection of American life and American rights under international law, the saving of neutral life, the freedom of the seas. . . ."

When he finished, every delegate was on his feet, cheering spontaneously in a bedlam that lasted for twenty-one minutes. They called for William Jennings Bryan, who was moved to tears by the apotheosis of peace; and the Great Commoner soon added his tribute. A few hours later Woodrow Wilson was nominated by acclamation.

The President was far from happy over the inclination of the party men to make political capital out of his avoidance of war. When the Resolutions Committee drafted a platform plank that commended "the splendid diplomatic victories of our great President, who has preserved the vital interests of our Government and its citizens, and kept us out of war," [11] and the last five words were picked out of context, used as a slogan, and flaunted on billboards, Wilson feared that his people were gloating over their blessings and forgetting their duty to prepare to defend their way of life by arms if it became necessary.

Though he gave eloquent notice that he was standing for the Presidency as a free moral agent, not responsible to any faction or party, Wilson's interest in a Democratic victory mounted during the summer. A series of speeches—three were given on a single July day—and conferences held almost daily with party leaders were imposed upon a docket of executive duties that in itself was staggering. Finding even the summer days too short, the President said that he would "steal up

[11] *Democratic Textbook,* 1916, p. 25. For comment on the origin of the controversial phrase "kept us out of war," *see* Baker, VI, 257 n. Robert W. Woolley, director of publicity, was careful in all campaign releases to use the wording: "With honor he has kept us out of war." It is Mr. Woolley's recollection that this wording was approved by both Wilson and Vance McCormick. R. W. Woolley to the writer, Dec. 6, 1955.

on them in the dark," and he and Edith Wilson made a practice of breakfasting at five or six o'clock.

House and Vance McCormick—new chairman of the National Committee—busied themselves in rebuilding party machinery. Funds were scraped together, and the managers allotted these and the party's speakers to a few states that were critical. They felt that the best hope for victory lay in running the President as if he were a candidate for justice of the peace. On July 25 House wrote cockily to the Chief: "I feel satisfied that we will have the only efficient organization that has ever been constructed in a Democratic national campaign." Noting that "the skein was getting tangled," Wilson decided to concentrate discussion of party policy in the hands of McCormick, who came to his study regularly on Monday evenings. "He brings the suggestions to me," Wilson wrote on Aug. 8, "and I know by experience what confusion will result if we do not coordinate and use a single channel."

Realizing the importance of capturing the independent vote, the Republican Old Guard felt that their best hope for victory lay in nominating Charles Evans Hughes, who had won popular acclaim by disclosures of questionable practices on the part of New York utilities and insurance companies. Hughes, who since 1910 had been a justice of the United States Supreme Court, was nominated easily and stood on a platform that differed from that of Wilson chiefly in its planks on Mexico, the Philippines, and the tariff.

Wilson respected this opponent as one who would have to be met with sound argument, and he discouraged politicians who wished to condemn Hughes publicly for "dragging the Supreme Court into the mire of politics." Members of the President's family were friendly to Hughes, but Wilson was disappointed when he received from his opponent a note of resignation so curt that he was advised not to dignify it by acknowledging it. Insisting, however, that the President of the United States must always do "the gentlemanly thing," he replied to Hughes's single sentence with two that were scarcely more gracious.

The son of a clergyman, Hughes had none of the love of polemics that was in the Wilson blood. His speeches were without color and warmth. His progressive pronouncements lacked the confirmation that the public found in the President's record. Independent journals in the East that welcomed his nomination were discouraged when he spoke to Western audiences in a way that left them cold. Roosevelt, struck by the similarity of background and aims, spoke of Hughes as "the whiskered Wilson."

Noting the feebleness of Hughes's campaign, Wilson was the more disposed to refrain from making speeches. On August 19 he wrote to

B. M. Baruch: "I am inclined to follow the course suggested by a friend of mine who says that he always has followed the rule never to murder a man who is committing suicide, and clearly this misguided gentleman is committing suicide slowly but surely." He was content, he said, to let the Republican nominee "blow himself off." He was more concerned about being worthy of re-election than about asserting his own claims for votes.

Immediately after his nomination, in July, he made a determined effort to commit representatives of special interests to a national covenant. To government workers, to labor leaders, to businessmen, his message was essentially the same: service to one's fellows above service to self.

In the summer of 1916 he was forced to act to protect the public against the consequences of a serious strike. The railroad brotherhoods demanded shorter hours without loss of pay and with time-and-a-half for overtime work. The United States Board of Mediation failed to settle the matter by arbitration; a strike was approved almost unanimously by the workers; and the Clayton Act made it impossible to prevent it by court injunction. Perceiving the seriousness of the threat, Wilson invited the spokesmen of management and labor to the White House on August 13. He reminded them that a strike would bring hardships to the public, perhaps even starvation, and that it would impede the preparedness program. He appealed for compromise in the national interest. But when both sides were unmoved, he resolved to end the impasse by imposing a settlement that seemed to him fair, and depending on public sentiment to enforce it.

Wilson went before the Congress on August 29, after the railroad presidents had finally refused to accept his verdict and the unions had called a strike for the midnight before Labor Day. The atmosphere in the Capitol was tense as the President proposed six measures that would facilitate the settlement of similar controversies in the future. Calling attention to the demands of national defense, the lawgiver made one last plea for judiciousness: "We should make all arbitral awards judgments by record of a court of law in order that their interpretation and enforcement may lie, not with one of the parties to the arbitration, but with an impartial and authoritative tribunal."

For a few days the outcome hung in the balance, while the President, fearing that he had failed, called 15,000 men from the Mexican border to preserve order in case of a strike. However, the Congress responded to his leadership and passed the Adamson Act on September 3, the day before the walkout was to begin. This measure decreed an eight-hour day and set up a commission to study the problem, and Wilson redeemed a promise to the executives by urging the Interstate Commerce Commission to grant the increases in freight rates that would be necessary. The Adamson Act became a model law governing labor relations.[12]

In his sympathy for farmers and laborers the President did not lose sight of the importance of healthy growth in industry. He threw his weight behind the Webb Bill, which would amend the antitrust laws to permit American manufacturers to combine in selling goods abroad. In order to give his people confidence that economic facts were considered in the fixing of tariffs, he overcame his earlier aversion to commissions, from which he feared that special interests might get favors more easily than from Congress. Yielding to the opinion of members of his Cabinet and to an overwhelming vote by the nation's Chambers of Commerce, he persuaded the Congress to provide a tariff commission. He responded to a plea from McAdoo for prompt appointment of commissioners as a means of nullifying the tariff platform of the Republicans, and sought "nonpartisan" rather than "bipartisan" members. Professor Taussig of Harvard, a low-tariff economist, was named chairman, and soon the new body won the admiration of both the President and his people.

Wilson's impulse toward another progressive goal was less productive of obvious gains. Personally, he was deeply interested in plans for conserving the natural resources of the nation. There were diverse opinions among senators, however, as to how his ideals could best be realized; and none of the measures proposed seemed to Wilson acceptable. Not until June of 1920 did the President have an opportunity to

[12] Wilson's enterprising spirit was responsible not only for the passage of the model Adamson Act, but also for its acceptance by a single vote in the Supreme Court on March 19, 1917; for he had the temerity to appoint a justice who was a champion of liberal interpretation of the law. On Jan. 28, 1916, after asking McAdoo whether Congress would approve the nominee and getting assurance that it would after a stiff fight, he had sent to the Capitol the name of Louis D. Brandeis, whom Attorney General Gregory endorsed as "the greatest lawyer in the United States." (This choice was in keeping with Wilson's long-standing concept of the nation's courts as not "strait jackets," but "instruments of the nation's growth." In his academic days he had likened the Supreme Court to "a constitutional convention in continuous session.")

Wilson was not insensitive to the political returns that would accrue in this election year from the honoring of a progressive such as Brandeis. He could afford to risk offending Southern conservatives who were congenital Democrats and would support the party ticket in any event.

When a storm of protest rose from private interests that Brandeis had tried to bring within federal regulation, Wilson sent an eloquent personal plea to the Senate's Committee on the Judiciary. He had not depended on "endorsements," he said, but named Brandeis only because he knew him to be singularly qualified by learning, by gifts, and by character. When the Senate acted favorably, Wilson could honestly say: "I am indeed relieved and delighted. I never signed any commission with such satisfaction."

On July 14, 1916, Wilson made his third and last appointment to the Supreme Court, that of John H. Clarke. "I dare say you are surprised by the nomination of Clarke . . ." he wrote to House on July 23, 1916. "He is a close friend of Newton Baker's and Gregory (whom I love and trust more than ever) picked him out."

sign a water-power bill; but on August 25, 1916, he approved an act establishing a National Park Service.[13]

Thus, before beginning to campaign for re-election, Wilson had made further progress toward the objectives of his New Freedom. By exerting both the power of persuasion and the persuasion of power, he had achieved results during his first term that could justly be compared with the first administration of his parliamentary hero, William E. Gladstone.

August of 1916 was a harrowing month. At the end, after the President had sat up part of a night working on his railroad labor message to Congress and had been called at six in the morning to face a full docket of appointments, his eyes were bloodshot, his face drawn and haggard. Finally, when the danger of a railroad strike was averted at the beginning of September, he was induced to go to his own state of New Jersey for the formal notification of his nomination. He consented to leave his desk only because it semed unfitting to use the White House for a purpose so partisan.

The Wilsons rented Shadow Lawn, an estate near Asbury Park. Its pretentious and ornate interior was offensive—it looked "like a gambling hell," the President thought—but he and his family enjoyed the privacy of the grounds and an out-of-doors dining room.

On September 2 hundreds of party men came for luncheon and performed the rite of notification. Independent voters listened attentively when Wilson, disclaiming any desire to "boast," declared: "The Republican party is just the party that *cannot* meet the new conditions of a new age." Not content merely to review his accomplishment, the prophet looked toward the future. Apologizing for lack of progress in developing natural resources, he called on advocates of conservation and capitalists "to get together in a spirit of genuine accommodation

[13] One phase of the conservation movement was so controversial and so complicated by technicalities that Wilson did not venture to discuss it openly with his people. The question of the leasing of the public oil reserves provoked a sharp division of opinion within the Cabinet. Franklin K. Lane wished to use his prerogative as secretary of the interior in ruling on the claims of private interests for patents to oil lands in the midst of California territory that had been set apart for the Navy by Taft's administration. Secretary Daniels, however, protested against Lane's leasing policy, feeling that the latter's California friends were being favored and that the Navy would be forced to pay exorbitant prices for oil. When Daniels explained his views to the President, Wilson asked him to put them before the Cabinet, so that Lane also could be heard and the attorney general could make a ruling. After the pros and cons had been frankly stated in the official family, the President was not willing to make a final decision.

Early in 1916 the problem was intensified by the drive for preparedness. Wilson therefore pleaded for enactment of a General Leasing Bill that had been worked out by Lane with experts in oil production and conservation. The legislators, however, took no conclusive action; and Wilson, hesitating, asked Lane to sign no leases until they could have another conference. Time and again he refused to sign documents that the secretary sent to him.

and agreement . . ." He asked for "justice to the labourer, not only by paying a living wage but also by making all the conditions that surround labor what they ought to be." He proposed coordination of the railway systems for national use and "their better adaptation as a whole to the life and trade and defense of the Nation." Recalling the measures taken to facilitate foreign trade, he proclaimed an end of "the day of Little Americanism with its narrow horizons."

In defense of his Mexican policy he said: "Test is now being made of us whether we be sincere lovers of popular liberty or not and are indeed to be trusted to respect national sovereignty among our weaker neighbours . . . Upon the outcome of that test (its outcome in their minds, not in ours) depends every relationship of the United States with Latin America, whether in politics or in commerce and enterprise." This was the great issue, he declared, and it was "a barren and provincial statesmanship" that lost sight of it.

In his survey of past and future, Wilson did not say whether or not he would continue to keep his people out of war, for he did not know. But he said: "If you elect my opponent, you elect a war." And he declared that, though property rights could be vindicated by claims for damages at the war's end, loss of human life and direct violations of sovereignty could not be brooked without resistance. The prophet was chiefly interested in something more fundamental and far-reaching —the prevention of a recurrence of the present catastrophe.

When the President returned to Washington, where the Congress was ending its session, the pressure of work became so intense that Dr. Grayson warned him that he must take time out for golf.

In mid-September, as he was laboring to clear his desk of an accumulation of papers, news of his sister's death reached him. He journeyed to old Columbia for the funeral, and visited once more the church of his father, the grave for which he had written the loving inscription, the house that his mother had designed, and the Woodrow relatives who shared memories of beloved Uncle James.

Returning from sleepy Columbia to the arena of political combat, Wilson found that the Republicans, desperate for an issue that would give vitality to their campaign, had seized upon the Adamson Law, on which his signature was hardly dry. Hughes challenged it as an abandonment of principle. As governor of New York he himself had signed a bill prescribing an eight-hour day for certain railway workers, but he asserted that Wilson had surrendered to dictation without adequate study of the facts and without resort to arbitration. Conservative sentiment joined exultantly in this criticism, and it seemed in September that the vote of the North and the East might go so solidly to Hughes that he would be elected.

the vote of the North and the East might go so solidly to Hughes that he would be elected.

When House and McCormick told the President of the wrath of employers, Wilson felt that at last he must take the warpath. Warming up to battle, he talked about "Labor and Capital" from a platform on the estate at Shadow Lawn. He spoke of the distress that had come to him when he spoke frankly with managers and employees of the railways. The nation could not compel citizens to work, he held, but the government could say to organizations: "You must not interrupt the national life without consulting us."

As in earlier campaigns, the President became combative in the face of unfair criticism. People who disliked him were repeating charges that he failed to pat public officials on the back, was not a good mixer, and was neglectful of the newsmen, to whom he no longer granted regular conferences. Wilson was accustomed to these reproaches; but he suffered when enemies descended to new depths of scurrility and pandered to the shallow minds of voters who had taken a personal dislike to him. Some said that Wilson was a megalomaniac whose object was to outdo Lincoln and sit at a table with czars and princes. It was bruited, by word of mouth, that he had left the tomb of Ellen Wilson unmarked and that corn was growing on it: actually, war conditions had delayed the shipment of a headstone of Carrara marble, and during the prolonged illness of an old friend who had taken care of the grave on Myrtle Hill, corn had sprouted from manure that had been put on the roses. It was gossiped that a pregnant young lady had demanded to see the President at the executive offices and had walked out with a check in her hand; actually, kindly Woodrow Wilson had been generous to a relative who was about to bear a child and lacked security.[14] Then, too, the old canards about Mary Hulbert and the letters were revived. Colonel House countered this by explaining, "We Southerners like to write mush notes." But the Colonel could reach only a few. Others close to the President were so outraged by the imputations that they refused to discuss them, and thus the roots of scandal spread in the shadow of secrecy. Wilson himself felt helpless. To deny the insinuations publicly would be merely to give them greater currency among the prurient. The more abusive the attacks the more impenetrable was his silence.

He suggested an antidote for poisonous gossip, however, in a letter to the Reverend Sylvester W. Beach, who had been his pastor at Prince-

[14] These sentences are based upon statements made to the writer by Mrs. Hallie Alexander Rounseville and Mrs. Will Harbin of Rome, Ga., and by Woodrow cousins of Woodrow Wilson: Helen Woodrow Bones, Katharine Woodrow Kirkland, James Woodrow, and Fitz-William McMaster Woodrow.

ton: "I do not know how to deal with the fiendish lies that are being invented and circulated about my personal character other than to invite those who repeat them to consult anybody who has known me for any length of time . . ." The campaign managers persuaded Stockton Axson to come immediately to Washington and write an article on "The Private Life of Woodrow Wilson." It was edited by Colonel House,[15] published in the Sunday supplement of the *New York Times,* and printed for distribution far and wide.

Easier to counter were the criticisms of policy offered in public by Republicans. Hughes continued to point to errors of the past rather than appealing to progressive hopes for the future. He pointed particularly to the inconclusiveness of Wilson's Mexican policy, even though it had resulted in negotiations by a Joint High Commission that gave hope of settlement.[16] The President, annoyed by criticism that seemed to him pettifogging, told newsmen that his opponent, while closeted in the Supreme Court, had lost touch with the spirit of the people.

Wilson was given an opportunity to show his independence when an importunate telegram came from the Irish president of an anti-British organization that had German support. The President read it calmly and penciled a reply on the same sheet, to be sent off at once. It said: "I would feel deeply mortified to have you or anybody like you vote for me. Since you have access to many disloyal Americans and I have not I will ask you to convey this message to them."

To a delegation that waited upon him, he said: "Politics must be left out because, don't you see, to put it plainly, that is a form of blackmail. I would resent it from one set of men as from another. You can vote as

[15] "I edited Dr. Axson's article on the President, cutting out what the newspaper boys term 'sob stuff.' It was too intimate and I was afraid the President would not like it." House Diary, Sept. 30, 1916. Mrs. Malcolm Forbes of Boston endowed the printing of a million copies for free distribution.

[16] Relations with Mexico had so deteriorated that House suggested to the President in mid-June that war was "inevitable." On the 20th Lansing gave notice that United States troops would not be withdrawn, and warned that Mexican attacks on them would "lead to the gravest consequences." Only a few hours after this stern note reached Mexico City, a skirmish near Carrizal resulted in the killing of twelve soldiers of the United States and the capture of twenty-three by Mexican troops.

Wilson demanded the immediate release of the prisoners, while at the same time insisting that he was not willing to determine for the Mexican people—unless they asked him—what the form and personnel of their government should be. He countered agitation for intervention that was coming from jingoes and investors by a fervent plea for tolerance. "The easiest thing is to strike," he said to the Press Club of New York on June 20. "The brutal thing is the impulsive thing . . . Do you think the glory of America would be enhanced by a war of conquest in Mexico?"

On July 4, Carranza suggested negotiations, and a Joint High Commission, with three members from each nation, met from Sept. 6, 1916, into January of 1917. Grievances of the United States and Mexico were discussed, and thus partisan attacks on Wilson lost force and Carranza was given an opportunity to hold elections.

you please. It matters little to me provided I am sure that I am doing the right thing at the right time." Sometimes, by sheer indifference to political consequences, he achieved effects that politicians strove for in vain. When most natural, he seemed most forceful.

Yet he was too canny to say anything to deflate Democratic orations that won voters by asserting that he had kept them out of war with honor and implying that he would continue to do so. It was obvious, too, that in catering to special interests of farmers, laborers, and industrialists he had used the national resources to benefit organized minorities. His devotion to a classless society and the common good had yielded to the exigencies of an election in which many citizens would cast ballots not as disinterested individuals but as members of groups seeking favored treatment. An impression of opportunism grew out of his recital of things done "for business," "for agriculture," and "for labor." There were sundry measures that he labeled "for general service," but "for mankind" only the premature child labor law. The necessity of rallying all factions and interests for defense against foreign aggression had made it the more difficult to resist pleas for special consideration.

The campaign theme that most clearly set apart Wilson the statesman from the politicians of the day was one that, though it was suggested by many, he was making peculiarly his own. In the last weeks of the campaign, he summoned his people repeatedly to sublimate their thought in a vision of united service to the cause of world peace. He said at Omaha: "For the next decade, at any rate—after that it will be a matter of our own choice whether it continues or not— . . . we have got to serve the world. That alters every commercial question, it alters every political question, it alters every question of domestic development."

The Wilsons jumped through the hoops of political publicity at Omaha. The President reviewed a pageant and his wife was introduced to Indian participants as a descendant of Pocahontas. They even went to a swine show, and afterward jested with newsmen about the size of the prize swine. Edith Wilson was proving herself a durable campaigner and took pains to write personal notes of appreciation to those who were kind to them. Her husband was proud of her. In one rear platform appearance he said: "I want you to see Mrs. Wilson. She is much better worth looking at than I am."

Liberal spokesmen and journals rallied to the President during October. Though the betting ran 20 to 17 in favor of Hughes, Wilson thought in the middle of the month that the outcome of the election was incalculable because of the large independent vote that would be cast.[17] In the closing days of the campaign he was not at all certain that his speeches were hitting the mark. Responding to House's urging he made a final assault, on November 2, on New York City, the metropolis that seemed to him "rotten to the core" and deserving to be wiped off the map.

The Colonel put on a good show at Madison Square Garden, intent that the meeting should be the greatest in the history of New York and should result in Wilson's carrying the state. Sheriff Alfred E. Smith led a parade of 30,000 of the faithful. The Garden was packed to the roof, and a crowd of 25,000 milled around outside and made it impossible for the Wilsons to approach the door. Going to the other end of the building, the President and his party crept up a fire escape, entered a window, and made their appearance on the platform. When he rose to speak, he was blasted for a half hour by brassy music and roars of the warriors. But for all its enthusiasm, the affair did not swing New York State away from Hughes.

In his last campaign speech, delivered at Shadow Lawn on November 4, Wilson made a personal confession, wistful and very humble: "To me has fallen the unspeakable good fortune of happening to be the spokesman of the American people at this critical and fateful time. . . . I cannot be sure that I judge right, but I am sure that my heart speaks the same thing that they wish their hearts to speak. It is only in this impulse, in this sympathetic connection which I am sure that I have with them, that I am worthy to speak for them at all."

The next day he acted to square his position with the gospel that he had been preaching. It seemed to him that if he was to be truly the servant of the people he should resign immediately if they voted against him. Thus he could give his country, in this instance, one benefit of the

---

[17] Wilson was plagued by a charge put forward by Henry Cabot Lodge, to the effect that after sending a *Lusitania* note to Berlin, the President had added a postscript that suggested that the Germans should not take his protest too seriously. Wilson had indeed considered tempering the first *Lusitania* note by releasing a qualifying statement to the press and had been dissuaded from that course by advisers; but he asserted that Lodge's statement was "untrue," that "no postscript or amendment" was secretly sent to Berlin. *Cf.* p. 17 above. This adroit denial satisfied citizens who were pestering Wilson for the truth; and Lodge, still incredulous, had to accept it.

On Dec. 29, 1916, Wilson declined to attend a church anniversary celebration when it was announced that Lodge was to be one of the speakers. He explained that the senator's conduct during the campaign made it impossible "with self-respect to join in any exercise in which he takes part." One of Wilson's favorite stories was about Colonel Pettigrew, a Southern lawyer who lost a civil suit and was called a cheat and a liar by his client but did not take offense until he was denounced as a Federalist. Asked why this accusation enraged him, he replied: "Damn him. It was the only true thing he said." There was just enough truth in Lodge's accusation to draw blood.

parliamentary system that he had long advocated. Discussing the idea with House and Burleson, he worked out a plan that would be both constitutional and effective. He wanted to put himself on record before the election, so that if he was defeated he could resign with no appearance of petulance or pique. But he did not attempt to make political capital of this decision by publicizing it, as some of his colleagues wished him to do. Two days before the election he set forth his intention in a letter that he addressed to Secretary Lansing, put in a wax-sealed envelope, and marked "most confidential."

Pointing out that if he were defeated he would be without authority to speak for the nation during his remaining months in office, he asserted that it would be his duty to relieve the country of the perils of such a situation. If he could gain the consent of the vice-president, he would ask Lansing's permission to invite Hughes to become secretary of state, and would then join the vice-president in resigning, thus opening to Hughes the immediate succession to the Presidency.

Having thus set his conscience at rest, Woodrow Wilson waited patiently at Shadow Lawn for the outcome of a campaign that had been waged by both candidates with a dignity unusual in American politics. The President's hope for victory was strong, and he made a little speech to his wife, outlining a program for his second term. When she spoke of a day to come when they could live their own lives, he said: "What a delightful pessimist you are! One must never court defeat. If it comes, accept it like a soldier; but don't anticipate it, for that destroys your fighting spirit."

He applied himself to his work, pausing once to telephone to the executive office nearby to ask for the early returns. At dinner he listed the states that seemed reasonably sure to support him, but they gave him only 217 of the 266 electoral votes that were needed. In the evening he threw himself wholeheartedly into a game of twenty questions with the family.

Finally bad news penetrated his seclusion: Hughes had won almost all the Northeastern states and his election had been conceded by New York newspapers. Over the phone Tumulty's voice sounded so dismal that Wilson chuckled and said: "Well, it begins to look as if we have been badly licked. . . . The only thing I am sorry for, and that cuts me to the quick, is that the people apparently misunderstood us. But I have no regrets. We have tried to do our duty." His chief concern seemed to be that his wife might not be so happy as he in retirement. Oppressed by the gloom of those around him, he took a glass of milk, went to bed, and slept soundly.

It was not until Friday morning that the Wilsons were sure that they would serve another term in the White House.[18] Hughes did not send his congratulations until November 22, when at last the official count of California ballots was virtually complete. By that time the electoral vote was 277 to 254 in Wilson's favor. His popular vote exceeded that of Hughes by more than a half-million, though it was a little less than half of the total.

While Wilson succeeded in his quest for the confidence of his people, serious rifts opened in his official family. In the spring of 1916 Dr. Grayson had whispered to House that Tumulty was responsible for most of the President's misfortunes and that the secretary was even trying to discredit the Colonel. Then, too, there were complaints from Protestant citizens against communicating with the President through a Catholic secretary.

Appreciative of his secretary's good intentions and abilities and reluctant, as always, to dispense with a man to whom he had grown accustomed, Wilson resisted for months the voices raised against Tumulty. He did not wish to risk dissension in the ranks until the election was over. In November, however, he yielded, and told his secretary, with concern for his financial welfare, that he would appoint him to the Board of General Appraisers if he would resign.

Tumulty was brokenhearted. He wanted neither money nor glory, but only the privilege of continuing to serve a great man. He told four intimate friends what had transpired. One of them was David Lawrence, the journalist, who had known Wilson since Princeton days. Lawrence's indignation was so great that he ventured to intrude upon the Presbyterian in the White House on a Sabbath afternoon. He told Wilson bluntly that the release of Tumulty would be the worst case of ingratitude ever known in politics and that the press would not stand for it. Woodrow Wilson had learned in the case of George Harvey, to his sorrow, what damage could be done to political repute by allegations of ingratitude; and he decided not to compel his faithful secretary to take another position. The President also stood firm against superficial—and often ill-founded—criticism of Secretary Daniels. He would not accept suggestions from House and Edith Wilson that these men be dismissed.

In addition to Tumulty and Daniels, McAdoo was giving concern to

[18] Wilson's deep satisfaction in the victory was revealed when he congratulated George Creel, a campaign speaker, on winning bets. When Creel remarked that he had supposed Presbyterians frowned on wagers, Wilson replied with a laugh: "Yes, but in this case it has the sanctification of a good cause. Spoiling the Egyptians has biblical approval." Creel, *Rebel at Large*, p. 156.

the President; and this was the more painful because in dealing with him Wilson was touching upon one of his dearest loves—that for his daughter Nellie. To House, in August of 1916, McAdoo seemed piqued because the President did not take him more closely into his confidence, and as ambitious as ever to occupy the White House. In fact there were indications at the end of 1916 that there might be contention among Cabinet members for the succession four years hence.[19]

But despite the jealousies and ambitions that were gnawing at the hearts of men close to him, the Chief still commanded their fealty. Moreover, during 1916 he had enlisted new associates who were serving with the undivided loyalty that would be required in surmounting the tasks ahead.

[19] Jesting about the competition for succession, House wrote to Wilson thus on Dec. 5: "Burleson . . . is grooming Josephus Daniels for the place with prohibition and woman suffrage to be the issues. With Lansing, McAdoo, Baker, and Burleson with their lightning-rods erect and with Crane grooming Houston and Bryan grooming Josephus, you have a Cabinet with a single-hearted purpose. Lane and [W. B.] Wilson were unfortunately born in British possessions."

CHAPTER IV

Caught in the Web of War

In the election year of 1916, while Wilson satisfied the yearnings of idealists by his vision of American leadership toward an international order, he wasᶜ careful to refrain from public comment on issues that might involve the nation in war overnight. Indeed, he did his best to quiet diplomatic controversy and to hold himself aloof from it. Nevertheless, he could not escape for a moment from the pressures from London and Berlin.

Britain's will to fight to a finish was impressed upon him by Walter Hines Page, who was called home to get what Wilson called "a bath of American opinion." Twice in August the President invited his old friend to a family luncheon at the White House. The talk was light and jocular; but Page got an inkling of the sternness of his chief's concept of neutrality when one of the Wilson girls asked, in all seriousness, whether she was unneutral in speaking of her admiration for the French. Unable to inject a word of business into the conversation, the ambassador was told to go off for a rest and come back for a serious discussion after the President had relieved his mind of the railroad labor crisis. Page left the White House distressed by what he called the "college professor's habit" of aloofness. He thought that Wilson was proving a vast failure as a leader.

Wilson wished to give Page time to feel the strength of anti-British sentiment at Washington before undertaking to argue with him. But finally he received a direct plea from the ambassador that he could not ignore. Inviting his friend to Shadow Lawn, Wilson devoted a morning to a thorough airing of the differences of view that had been developing for two years. The ambassador argued the British case fervently, and gave the President certain ideas that Grey had asked him to convey when the foreign secretary had bidden him farewell in July.

Wilson replied bluntly that when the war began he had been heartily in sympathy with the Allies, but that now he saw no one who was not vexed by Britain's acts. "Tell those gentlemen for me," he charged Page, that damage to any American citizen was in effect damage to himself, personally. When Page spoke of Germany's desire for an armistice and intimated that Britain would not grant it and would indeed be offended if the President fell in with any such scheme, Wilson replied that he would have nothing to do with promoting a military armistice; but he added, "If they propose an armistice looking toward peace—yes, I shall be glad."

The men parted friends, Page putting his hand on the President's shoulder and Wilson's eyes filling with tears. The ambassador thought him the loneliest man he had ever seen and quite out of touch with the pro-British sentiment that the popular envoy met as he went about in the South and the Northeast. And once again Wilson had to torture his heart by shutting it against the heresies of a friend whom he wanted to love. They never met again. When Page sent a note of resignation, in November, Wilson questioned its sincerity and could not bring himself to accept it at once. Soon thereafter American involvement in the war became so imminent that Page could not leave his post immediately without a consciousness of disloyalty; and the President, failing to persuade House or Cleveland Dodge to serve at London, concluded that he could find no wartime envoy more effective than Page.[1]

Wilson gave close attention to the dossier of reports that Page left with him on September 23, and the next day he read them to House in the Colonel's apartment. His friend suggested that the greatest irritant to English pride was the rapid expansion of the American Navy; but Wilson, who had just approved the largest naval appropriation ever passed by Congress, was not inclined to remove this source of friction.

Meanwhile sentiment at London turned still more emphatically against Wilson and the pacifism that was associated with his name. To be sure, there was agitation for peace among British radicals; and Wilson, kept informed of this by letters that House forwarded to him from British leaders as well as from W. H. Buckler, a special agent at the London embassy, was pleased by what he called "a strong drift of opinion towards reasoned calculation." Yet despite the appalling attrition of the warfare, and in spite of the failure of their armies to win the conclusive victories that were hoped for, the British people, by and large, were still not ready to take the reasonable, long-range view that House had commended to them. Laborers had lost patience with the American President, and men in the trenches referred to shells that failed to explode as "Wilsons." David Lloyd George, soon to succeed Asquith as

---

[1] On Nov. 14, House told Wilson of Page's opinion of the President—an able man, like Jefferson, who would not fight in any circumstances. The Colonel observed that his friend was "not pleased" but did not resent this. When the President calmly discussed possible remedies and declared that no man should stand in the way, House said that the whole staff of the London embassy should be removed. A few months earlier, House had passed along to Wilson the opinion that the embassy was "a nest of disloyalty to the President." Wilson told House on Jan. 12, 1917, that he was determined to accept Page's resignation, though fearful that the ambassador would come home disgruntled and write embarrassing articles for the *World's Work*. But when, on March 5, Mrs. Wilson asked House to take the London post, the President said that he had written Page that he would make no change for the moment.

prime minister, put himself *en rapport* with this sentiment. On September 28 he publicly challenged what he characterized as "a defeatist spirit working from foreign quarters to bring about an inconclusive peace."

When House told the President of the ugliness of the feeling at London, Wilson replied on October 10: "These are indeed deep waters. . . . I can only say that if our friendly relations with England should be imperilled . . . it would be only another illustration of how difficult it is to be friends with Great Britain without doing whatever she wants us to do." Moreover, his discouragement deepened a few days later when London sent unsatisfactory replies to a protest that he had made on July 26 against seizure of mails and the blacklisting of American firms that had dealt with the enemy.

Though annoyed by the British to the point of assigning them motives scarcely higher than those of Germany, Wilson could see no advantage in making war upon the Allies. Moreover, reports from Berlin suggested that, while England had closed the door to efforts to make peace, the German Foreign Office was being hard pressed by the Admiralty, as well as by desperation among the people, to sanction a renewal of offenses that Wilson already had designated as a cause for war.

Toward the end of October, Wilson received this memorandum, sent by the Kaiser to Ambassador Gerard:

Your Excellency hinted to his Majesty in your last conversation at Charleville in April that President Wilson possibly would try towards the end of the summer to offer his good services to the belligerents for the promotion of peace. The German Government has no information as to whether the President adheres to this idea and as to the eventual date at which this step would take place. Meanwhile the constellation of war has taken such a form that the German Government foresees the time at which it will be forced to regain the freedom of action that it has reserved to itself in the note of May 4th last and thus the President's steps may be jeopardized. The German Government thinks it its duty to communicate this fact to Your Excellency in case you should find that the date of the intended action of the President should be far advanced towards the end of this year.

"The German memorandum," House warned the President in forwarding this message on October 20, "is clearly a threat to resume submarine warfare, their idea being to force you before election to act, knowing that if you are defeated nothing can be done by anyone for months to come. They do not want to take the chance."

House's diagnosis made the President even more reluctant to act before the election. Nevertheless, Wilson received Gerard at Shadow

Lawn on October 24. Both he and his wife asked penetrating questions. Their ambassador told them bluntly that the United States faced war unless it made peace, that to gain the respect of German officials who did not understand the ideal of peaceful coexistence America must make a show of strength. There was nothing to suggest that the German government would listen to terms that the Allies would accept, or even the general principles that the President had laid down in his address of May 27 to the League to Enforce Peace and had repeated in his campaign speeches. And doubtless the German militarists were not endeared to Wilson's heart when Gerard said that they believed their atrocities might frighten Americans out of going to war. Nevertheless, when a cake presented by a German-American was served at luncheon, the Wilsons ate freely of it while their envoy abstained.[2]

The grim alternative mentioned in the Kaiser's memorandum became more menacing when submarine activity was stepped up. Three ships with Americans aboard had been sunk in September; on October 12 it was reported from Berlin that naval officers had petitioned the Kaiser for immediate resumption of submarine warfare; citizens of the United States were killed when the British merchantman *Marina* was sunk without warning on October 28; and ten days later the liner *Arabia* met the same fate.

Hesitating to take any step that might affect the voting of his people, Wilson tried to make light of the *Marina* disaster in talking with House and McCormick on November 2. "I do not believe," he said, "the American people would wish to go to war no matter how many lives were lost at sea." He and House had been doing all that they could, he thought, to persuade both warring alliances to take a long-range view of peacemaking. His essential duty, as he saw it, was to maintain faith with a people who rejoiced because he had kept them out of war and at the same time to rescue humanity from the scourge of international conflict. It seemed clearer than ever that security could be attained only by stopping the war and arranging a concert of nations to keep peace. "The minute the campaign is over," he wrote on November 4, "I shall be obliged to prepare some of the most interesting papers I have yet had to prepare."

Finally the voters made what Wilson called their "fundamental, final choice with regard to our foreign relationships." He had his mandate,

---

[2] When Gerard returned to Berlin, on Dec. 21, he told Joseph Grew that the President had given him two injunctions: he must "jolly the Germans" and must support the American stand against attacks on armed merchant ships without warning. Gerard also reported that, when he had agreed, Wilson banged his desk and said: "I don't want you merely to support my view; I want you to *agree* with it." Grew, *Turbulent Era*, I, 300–301.

and he could at last act boldly. The burden of responsibility was "heavier than ever," he confessed to his old friend Edith Reid. "If we can escape entering the war and bring about a rational peace, it is something worth living and dying for, and I believe the country feels that way or it would not have re-elected me."

The prophet found it hard to command time to concentrate on his ultimate objective, in the midst of pressures that had built up during the campaign. Faithful warriors of the party wanted to shake his hand, to congratulate him, and to keep their own interests before him. Executive decisions delayed by the election must be made in both domestic and foreign affairs. But on November 13 he demanded time to think, and penciled a note to Tumulty instructing him to say to everyone that he was engrossed with "business of the most pressing sort."

The next day he told House that he wanted to address to all belligerents a demand that the fighting cease. Unless he did so, he argued, the United States would inevitably drift into war with Germany on the submarine issue. It seemed to him that Berlin already had violated the pledge given on May 4 after the sinking of the *Sussex*; and if the United States was to maintain her position she would have to break diplomatic relations, unless he could move Britain to discuss peace.

The Colonel felt sure that the Allies would be offended by any venture of this sort and would interpret it as an effort to "pull Germany's chestnuts out of the fire." When his opinion was asked, he gave it with more directness than he was accustomed to use.

The President, in his zeal for a great purpose, seemed unable to understand that his friend, sincerely sharing in the enthusiasm, could not agree with the method that he had set his heart on using. He did not sleep well that night; and the next morning the Colonel noted his host's distress and was remorseful because he knew that he had caused it. But neither man yielded his opinion. Wilson told the Colonel that he would compose a first draft of an appeal and that then they could go over the matter with more intelligence. After House left, he felt so wretched that he went back to bed. He ate little lunch, and slept all afternoon; but after supper his spirits revived and he and Edith Wilson had one of their delightful evenings of companionship. For a fortnight he was not well, and Dr. Grayson made him give up the Army-Navy football game. His wife helped him to keep up with the torrent of papers, and after supper, too fagged to converse or play games, they would sit in the firelight and listen to opera music played by an electric piano.

But all the while he kept his mind on the great state paper that he had conceived. In a bulky folder he collected documents that revealed public opinion on questions of war and peace, at home and abroad. There were clippings from journals, tissues of diplomatic dispatches, quotations from speeches of foreign statesmen, reports from House of confidential talks with Bernstorff and with English observers. He set down his ideas first in shorthand, then in typing on small sheets. Brackets and parentheses were inserted, and shorthand notes in the margins.

Meanwhile House, closer than the President to the thinking of those liberals in Britain who held out the best hope for international concord, was eager to save his friend from giving unnecessary offense to London opinion. On the whole, the people of the United States seemed ready to accept the view of House that, if they were to have a war, it had best be with Germany. Americans who had at first condoned some manifestations of German frightfulness or had balanced it against suffering inflicted by the armed forces of the Entente, were inclined by an accumulation of misdemeanors to condemn the morality of the Central Powers. Furthermore, blood ties with Britain were stronger than those with other belligerents, and Americans had warm memories of French aid during their Revolution. To be sure, they were out of sympathy with Russian despotism, but the menace of czarism was far more remote than that of the Hohenzollerns. American youths were so partial to the cause of the Allies that they were enlisting in the British and French armies and auxiliary services.

It was not only ties of morality, blood, and historical sentiment that tugged the American people toward the Allies. During the war years their economic resources had been to a large extent pooled with those of England and France; and as a result of the need of the Allies for funds for the purchase of war goods in America, the extension of credit was reaching alarming proportions. Wilson thought that it would be most unwise to risk a loan to certain German cities, and he was skeptical also about a plan of the house of Morgan for accepting renewable notes of the British and French treasuries. The Federal Reserve Board, responding to his wishes, announced publicly that it did not regard it "in the interest of the country" that they invest in foreign notes of this character, that American banks must stand ready to meet domestic requirements that could not be foreseen, and that the British should arrange to get credit by pledging the collateral that remained in their hands or by stimulating trade "in other directions."

This warning was a jolt to Americans who were riding the crest of a wave of wartime prosperity. There was danger, on the one hand, that the nation's abnormal export trade would suddenly be curtailed; and, on the other, that the Allies, not allowed to purchase with treasury notes, would be forced to sustain the war commerce by pledging so much gold and collateral to the United States that inflation and instability would result. New York bankers were frightened, and the prices of foreign bonds dropped. Wall Street threatened to accept the proposed treasury notes anyway; but the British grudgingly decided not to provoke a crisis by issuing them.[3]

On November 24 Colonel House, having informed Bernstorff that the next submarine crisis could result only in a diplomatic breach, reported to the President that Germany was willing to evacuate Belgium and France under certain conditions. House already had sent intimations of support from British radicals for an American peace move at this juncture. Wilson felt that the moment was near, if not already at hand, for him to act. He wrote, therefore, to inform House that he hoped to make his peace note "the strongest and most convincing thing" that he had ever penned. Four days later he reported that he had finished his labor and had recovered partly from a severe cold. "I think things are thickening," his letter to the Colonel said, "and we should choose our course at once, if we have data enough to form a judgment on . . . I hope that I had a clear head for the draft."

Visiting the White House on November 27, House perceived that Wilson's text contained moralizing that might offend the Allies. He persuaded his friend to delete certain clauses and induced him to insert a specific renunciation of any desire to demand or force peace through his mediation. The Colonel advised also that the President delay release of his manifesto until public opinion in France and England was prepared to receive it favorably.

Appreciating the force of the Colonel's remarks, Wilson repeated a proposal that he had made before: he insisted that House go abroad in advance of his appeal for peace and, like a minor prophet, prepare the way. The Colonel, preferring "Hades for the moment" to such a mission, thought of many reasons why it was best for him to remain at home. He feared, for one thing, that his appearance at London would precipitate Page's resignation,[4] an eventuality that he viewed with more concern than the President. But, fearing that his friend might think

---

[3] Actually, Wilson feared that his people would think that the nation already had been partial to Britain in extending credit. When he was informed, on Dec. 6, that the comptroller of the currency was about to divulge the amounts invested by national banks in foreign securities, he questioned the wisdom of this, fearful of "the indirect effect the publication might have on some of our foreign relations."

[4] That House had reason for this apprehension is suggested by a draft of a letter to Wilson found among Page's papers, saying that House's visits had been "a mistake" that had provoked endless gossip about Page's position and about the intentions of the United States, and that the mistake should not be repeated. By advice of Irwin Laughlin, first secretary of the embassy, Page's letter was not sent. The Ambassador had written in his diary, after House's last visit to London: "He cannot come again or—I go." But Page realized that he must not appear to be moved by personal pique.

him giving way to selfish considerations, the Colonel asked Lansing to exert his influence to dissuade Wilson. Four days later he recorded in his diary, with relief, that he had learned from Counselor Polk that the President would not insist further.

On December 3 Wilson pressed ahead on his peace note. "One of the reasons why early action is necessary," he confessed to House, "is W.J.B." He had learned that Bryan was intent on going abroad "to fix the whole matter up himself" and would publicly oppose Wilson if the President showed any inclination to break relations with Germany.

The President's obligations to Congress diverted his thought for a day or two. He gave his annual address in the Capitol on December 4, calmly ignoring the flaunting of a yellow banner from a balcony by suffragettes. On the 8th he wrote to House: "Members of Congress have been sucking the life out of me, about appointments and other matters affecting the destiny of the world, and I have been prevented from perfecting the document."

While the President was polishing his masterpiece, the Foreign Office tired of waiting for Wilson to act and made a gesture of peace of its own. If this failed, Germany was to unleash its submarines in January. On December 12 the chancellor announced to the Reichstag those items of German policy that would bear the scrutiny of mankind. The imperial government, he said, was ready to act with its enemies to end the war. He informed Washington that he hoped that Germany's "formal and solemn offer" would "coincide with the wishes of the President of the United States"; and Wilson was asked to forward the overture to the capitals of the enemy.

Though complying with the German request, the President held to his resolve to go ahead on the single track to which his conscience had guided him. American liberals saw that it was too late, that Wilson was "fishing behind the net." But he released his paper to the State Department on December 18. It was delivered to the press and to all belligerent governments, and its text became known to the world on the 20th.

The manifesto that the President had finally arrived at, after many more changes than he was accustomed to make in his papers of state, stands as a landmark in the diplomacy of the century. The Colonel immediately recognized its immortality. "There are some sentences in it," House wrote in his diary, "that will live as long as human history." The message proclaimed:

Each side desires to make the rights and privileges of weak peoples and small States as secure against aggression or denial in the future as the rights and privileges of the great and powerful States now at war. Each wishes itself to be made secure in the future, along with all other nations and peoples, against the recurrence of wars like this and against aggression or selfish interference of any kind. Each would be jealous of the formation of any more rival leagues to preserve an unbalance of power amidst multiplying suspicions; but each is ready to consider the formation of a league of nations to insure peace and justice throughout the world.

To be effective, a move for peace at this juncture would have to satisfy the lusts of the creature man, as well as his aspirations. Before the final step in international organization could be taken, Wilson recognized that it was necessary to fix terms of peace that would guarantee to every belligerent its independence, territorial integrity, and political and commercial freedom. And so the President's appeal went on in a more practical vein. His own government did not wish to propose terms: he was not even offering to mediate; but he did feel "altogether justified," in view of the interest of his people in arrangements for the peace of the world, in "suggesting an immediate opportunity for a comparison of views as to the terms which must precede those ultimate arrangements." Though statesmen had set forth their war aims in general terms, none had "avowed the precise objects which would, if attained, satisfy them and their people that the war had been fought out." An interchange of views on this matter, he suggested, would clear the way at least for conference and make the permanent concord of the nations a hope of the immediate future, a concert of nations immediately practicable.

On December 18, the day on which this manifesto was given to the State Department, the President reverted to his old custom of calling a press conference. Fearing that his statement might be thought an endorsement of the German overture of the 12th, he made it clear that he merely had acted as a messenger in forwarding Germany's proposal.[5] He refused flatly to be drawn out on the significance of his own appeal, and insisted that anyone who spread false rumors regarding his intentions would be guilty of a very serious crime.

Unfortunately the secretary of state admitted to newsmen on December 21 that the nation was "drawing near the verge of war" and that the release of Wilson's statement indicated the possibility of her being forced in.[6] Thus Lansing raised British hopes, and German fears, that the

---

[5] Advised by Page that the German peace move was merely an offer "to buy a pig in a poke," the Allies indignantly rebuffed it on Dec. 30, 1916.

[6] Contemporary notes and manuscript of Arthur Sweetser, who was present. Also Sweetser to the writer. At his press conference on the morning of the 20th Lansing merely said that in the afternoon a note would be released that did not suggest peace and was not connected with the German proposal of the 12th. The secretary asked that the content be kept secret until the hour set for release—3:30 P.M. However, the tenor of the note was revealed by indiscreet newsmen and was reported by the Dow-Jones ticker at 2:05 P.M. The news aggra-

United States would join the Allies. This, coming after the long struggle of the President to draft a manifesto that would be genuinely conciliatory, vexed him greatly. It seemed to him that the secretary of state was not in sympathy with his purpose to keep out of war.

He summoned the offender to the White House on the afternoon of the 21st and once again stretched his patience to save an indiscreet servant. Though Lansing was impenitent, and argued that his remarks revealed nothing but the stark truth, Wilson did not force him to make a public retraction. He merely instructed Lansing to say that he had been misinterpreted.

Six days after he released his manifesto Wilson, the champion of "pitiless publicity," showed that he now fully understood the importance of deepest secrecy in discussions of a matter so delicate as the making of peace. On December 23 he instructed Lansing to suggest to the belligerents that they reply to his message "in strict confidence; it being understood that the Government of the United States may in its turn convey it in like confidence to the governments of the other group of belligerents, in order that it may in that way be ascertained without publicity whether there is any present ground or basis to hope for negotiations or conferences of any kind."

However, on January 12, when the British replied unfavorably to Wilson's appeal and made it clear that they intended to destroy German militarism and to exact huge indemnities, their reply did not take the private channels that Wilson suggested. British leaders, believing that they fought for principles that Americans were too timid to champion in battle, had been infuriated when Wilson stated in his appeal that the objects of European statesmen on both sides of the conflict were "virtually the same."

Germany's formal reply to Wilson also was made public. It repeated the suggestion of direct negotiations that had been made from Berlin on the 12th and made it clear that the Germans intended to use conquered lands as bargaining pawns over the peace table. A complete rebuff, it raised Wilson's temper so high that he almost demanded Bernstorff's resignation.

Baffled by the wilderness in which he could find no path to an honorable peace, Wilson found release in holiday festivities at the White House. On Christmas Eve, after walking over to the Treasury Building

---

vated a slump in security prices that had followed the German peace overture of the 12th. Men close to the administration were suspected of using inside information to speculate profitably; but in an investigation conducted by the Rules Committee of the House of Representatives they were exonerated. *See* Blum, "The 'Leak' Investigation of 1917," *American Historical Review,* LIV, No. 3 (April, 1949).

to hear children sing carols to the Prince of Peace, the family trimmed a tree in the oval room. The next morning they gathered around it, with a crackling fire on the hearth; and after a day of receiving callers, twenty-two relatives gathered for dinner and took part in charades, using the hall upstairs for a stage. For a moment Woodrow Wilson and his three daughters lived again in the rapture of the early years at Princeton. Three days after Christmas his sixtieth birthday was celebrated.

It was a time when Wilson needed the warmth of human sympathy as never before. For, though Democratic congressmen applauded his peace note, Bryan telegraphed congratulations, and the *New Republic* asserted that at last the liberals had "a leadership expressive of American idealism," General Leonard Wood proclaimed to advocates of preparedness that there was no leadership at Washington and partisans of the Allies were vociferous in condemnation of the President. On the day after Christmas, Wilson vented his annoyance in a letter to sympathetic Secretary Baker: "I wish every day that there were more mere Americans in this country. Almost all our fellow citizens this side of the Mississippi seem to think in terms set by the thinking or prepossessions of one side or the other across the water." On January 2 he wrote in discouragement: "Neither side in the war is pleased by anything I write unless it can be construed as favorable in feeling to them."

Yet Wilson continued to breast the tide that was floating his nation into the maelstrom. He refused to take part in plans for the relief of peoples persecuted by the Central Powers, though his friend Cleveland Dodge was one of the sponsors; for he felt that this would be unneutral. The Colonel repeated a warning that he had given often before, telling his friend, on January 4, that the nation should not be so totally unprepared in the event of war. But the lonely prophet replied: "There will be no war. This country does not intend to become involved in this war. We are the only one of the great white nations that is free from war today, and it would be a crime against civilization for us to go in." It seemed to House that Wilson was carefully avoiding any conference of advisers in which he might be outvoted overwhelmingly.

The President's manifesto of December 18 was the object of a furious debate in the Senate. The conservatives were as alarmed as Princeton's trustees had been by Wilson's soaring aspirations. His Republican adversaries were not slow to criticize Wilson's advocacy of a league of nations "to insure peace and justice throughout the world" and his commitment of the people of the United States as "ready to lend their every resource, whether of men or money or substance, to such a combination, so proposed and organized." A characteristic bellow came from Roosevelt; and Lodge attacked the President publicly and privately.[7] Other senators, resentful that the Chief Executive had taken so momentous a step without consulting them, raised doubts.

When Hitchcock of Nebraska submitted a resolution endorsing Wilson's action, a debate began that was to last for three years and to be recognized as one of the most portentous in the history of the century. Borah of Idaho argued that Wilson's proposal, committing American armed forces to protect the integrity of every little country, would plunge the nation into the storm center of European politics, and that the advice of the founding fathers would be renounced and the Monroe Doctrine destroyed. Weakening under the force of nationalistic oratory and tradition, Hitchcock accepted a substitute for his resolution. Only that part of Wilson's note was endorsed that requested terms of peace from the belligerents; and even on this basis seventeen senators were opposed and thirty-one abstained from voting.

Nevertheless, the prophet was so confident of the receptiveness of the plain people of the world that he resolved to speak to them over the heads of their rulers. On January 11 the Colonel came again to the White House. A week before, the friends had outlined an American plan to make the world secure from future wars and had decided that it should be revealed in a speech before the Senate. Now Wilson, closing the door of his study, read his first draft. House recognized that this, like the peace note of December 18, was a noble document that was imperishable. When he emerged from the room, after a talk of an hour or more in which the President agreed to strike out a word and a phrase that might give offense, the Colonel was glowing with praise. A few days later Wilson wrote to inform House that he had shown his masterpiece to the secretary of state and also Chairman Stone of the Senate Foreign Relations Committee, and that the latter seemed slightly stunned. The secret was shared only with these three advisers, and Edith Wilson.

On January 22, after an early round of golf in Virginia, Woodrow Wilson went before the Senate. Believing that he spoke for "liberals and friends of humanity in every nation," he stood as pastor to the whole human race, with compassion for all peoples and condemnation

---

[7] On Jan. 9, 1917, Lodge wrote to his cousin, John T. Morse, Jr.: "He [Wilson] has been working in combination with Germany, not that he sympathizes with Germany but because Bernstorff is willing to make deals, and also, I fear, has some sort of hold on him arising from other sources. Wilson thinks only of himself. The motives of his note were, I think, two: one, which you point out, to get into the position of peacemaker and be the saviour of civilization; and, the other, intense fear that if the war continued the Germans would press the submarine warfare so as to create a situation here which he might find difficult. I am inclined to think that in the back of his mind lurks the desire for a third term, and if he was not hopelessly cowardly at heart our damage would be greater than it is." Morse Papers.

for none. Reviewing the discouraging replies to his December request for the peace terms of the belligerents, he asserted optimistically that the world was "that much nearer a definite discussion of the peace which shall end the present war." When the settlement did come, he said, it must be followed by "some definite concert of power which will make it virtually impossible that any such catastrophe should ever overwhelm us again." This was taken for granted by "every lover of mankind, every sane and thoughtful man."

He then probed more deeply into the causes of war than many of the hot-minded patriots of the several nations could follow. He said:

The question upon which the whole future peace and policy of the world depends is this: Is the present war a struggle for a just and secure peace, or only for a new balance of power? If it be only a struggle for a new balance of power, who will guarantee, who can guarantee the stable equilibrium of the new arrangement? Only a tranquil Europe can be a stable Europe. There must be, not a balance of power, but a community of power: not organized rivalries, but an organized common peace.

. . . first of all . . . it must be a peace without victory. It is not pleasant to say this. I beg that I may be permitted to put my own interpretation upon it and that it may be understood that no other interpretion was in my thought. I am seeking only to face realities and to face them without soft concealments. Victory would mean peace forced upon the loser, a victor's terms imposed upon the vanquished. It would be accepted in humiliation, under duress, at an intolerable sacrifice, and would leave a sting, a resentment, a bitter memory upon which terms of peace would rest, not permanently, but only as upon quicksand. Only a peace between equals can last. Only a peace the very principle of which is equality and a common participation in a common benefit. The right state of mind, the right feeling between nations, is as necessary for a lasting peace as is the just settlement of vexed questions of territory or of racial and national allegiance.

The equality of nations upon which peace must be founded if it is to last must be an equality of rights; the guarantees exchanged must neither recognize nor imply a difference between big nations and small, between those that are powerful and those that are weak. Right must be based upon the common strength, not upon the individual strength, of the nations upon whose concert peace will depend . . . Mankind is looking now for freedom of life, not for equipoises of power . . . the nations should with one accord adopt the doctrine of President Monroe as the doctrine of the world . . .

Summarizing the three conditions that he had stated in earlier messages and explained fully in this one, he declared:

I am proposing government by the consent of the governed; that freedom of the seas which in international conference after conference representatives of the United States have urged with the eloquence of those who are the convinced disciples of liberty; and that moderation of armaments which makes of armies and navies a power for order merely, not an instrument of aggression or of selfish violence.

These are American principles, American policies. We could stand for no others. And they are also the principles and policies of forward-looking men and women everywhere, of every modern nation, of every enlightened community. They are the principles of mankind and must prevail.

Thus was the great manifesto of Anglo-Saxon liberalism delivered. It was cabled in advance to the European capitals. Humanitarian critics in both the United States and England rallied to the crusading leader. Never was Wilson's genius displayed more brilliantly. He had reflected the feeling of the peoples of the world, had given expression to thoughts pent up and perplexing. Eighty-nine Socialists in the French Chamber of Deputies characterized the speech as "the charter of the civilized universe." Even the Czar's Foreign Office commended Wilson's "broad humanitarian principles."

However, minor prophets in America found much to criticize in the President's broad commitment. The dissent was ominous, and the President did not miss its import. He wrote about it to Cleveland Dodge: "I must admit that I have been a little low in my mind the last forty-eight hours because of the absolute lack of any power to see what I am driving at which has been exhibited by the men who are looked upon as the leading Republican members of the Senate. After all, it is upon the Senate that I depend for the kind of support which will make acts possible, and there are sometimes hours of discouragement connected with trying to lift things into a better air. But discouragement is weakness and I do not succumb to it long. I firmly believe that I have said the right thing, and I have an invincible confidence in the prevalence of the right if it is fearlessly set forth."

At the same time Wilson, having kept his speech free from any specific plan for world organization that opponents might attack effectively, resolved to avoid any act that would give the Senate cause for irritation. Replying to a suggestion from Edward Bok that a part of his past writing on the Presidency be printed at this juncture, he wrote: "My feeling is that I better not seem to be talking too much just now about the functions of the Presidency. Those functions have their irritating sides to some of my colleagues in the Senate in particular, and I can do as much without talking about it."

As for the warring chieftains of Europe, they regarded the American President as wolves might look upon an interloper who would take away their meat after a kill. The idea of "government by consent of the governed" was not acceptable in empires that, like Austria-Hungary and Turkey, were honeycombed with unwilling subjects; nor could the Allies conceive of a lasting "peace without victory" [8] over German militarism.

Wilson had expected no enthusiasm from London for his appeal. Writing to House on January 24, he expressed interest primarily in discovering what was in the minds of the German officials. "If Germany wants peace," he wrote, "she can get it soon, *if she will but confide in me and let me have a chance.*" Under the sort of world order that the American President envisoned, Germany could afford to moderate the demands that had made it impossible that her enemies would negotiate with her.

Feeling that he had put himself in a position to help without favor to either side, Wilson asked the Colonel to see Bernstorff again, secretly, and to tell him that there was "a terrible likelihood" that relations between the United States and Germany might come to the breaking point. He added a personal word to enhearten the faithful agent who was so eager to have a hand in any deal that might bring peace and glorify the name of Woodrow Wilson. "God bless you for the encouragement and support you so constantly give me. I feel very lonely sometimes, and sometimes very low in my mind, in spite of myself."

The Colonel's response was prompt and cooperative. He found the ambassador discouraging, however. Though Bernstorff was restrained by his instructions from revealing Berlin's decision to unleash its submarines at the end of the month (a decision that the ambassador had learned on January 19), he confided to House that the situation was getting out of hand.

In desperate last-minute appeals Bernstorff warned his government of the inevitable effect of their new policy on relations with Washington, and begged for delay. But already twenty-one submarines had set out on their deadly missions under the new instructions and the Admiralty was intoxicated by the prospect of success. [9]

---

[8] The phrase "peace without victory," taken from context by critics unfriendly to Wilson and used to denote the sense of the speech, was perhaps suggested to the President by an editorial in the *New Republic* that developed an argument different from that of Wilson's address. *See* Baker, VI, 425. Wilson later explained to the French ambassador that "a scientific peace" would be a better term to describe his ideal.

[9] The German General Staff had promised that their large fleet of submarines would paralyze Great Britain before the United States could exert enough force to succor the Allies; and the Crown Council, meeting at Spa on Jan. 9, decided to unleash the sea dogs upon neutral and defenseless prey on Feb. 1 and meanwhile to keep the world in ignorance of their design.

Though in mid-January Bernstorff, acting on instructions, signified Germany's willingness to sign the Bryan treaty of arbitration, to enter a league of nations, and to approve a Wilsonian program for a peace conference, he qualified his statement when the President, burdened with the ultimate responsibility and more suspicious than House of Berlin's protestations, asked for

Wilson's inclination to exert economic pressure upon the Allies was increasing and the British treasury was close to bankruptcy. The President was still eager to cooperate with Berlin to end the fighting, and convinced that the opposing alliances were almost equally responsible for its perpetuation. Nevertheless, in spite of these considerations working in their favor, the Germans gave Wilson the only provocation that could have induced him to throw the power of the United States on the side of the Allies. On the last day of January they notified the American government of the withdrawal of their pledge of May 4, 1916. Henceforth all merchant ships that were met in certain zones around France, Italy, and the British Isles, whether belonging to neutrals or to belligerents, would be sunk—except for one ship that would be permitted to sail from America to Falmouth weekly, under strict regulations.

On the afternoon of January 31 Tumulty brought in a news bulletin announcing the German threat. Wilson read it and reread it. He was amazed at first, then incredulous. Color left his face as he took in the full meaning. His lips tightened and his jaw locked. Then he said with quiet grimness: "The break that we have tried so hard to prevent now seems inevitable." At eight in the evening he received official documents that Bernstorff had been holding in secret for twelve days and that he had just given to Lansing. Reaching for the telephone, Wilson called his secretary of state to the White House. He was ready now to break diplomatic relations with Berlin; but he was not so inclined as Lansing to go to war. His indignation at British policy had not abated. He said that, if he concluded that it was best for the world for the United States to remain at peace in the circumstances, he would be willing to bear the abuse of critics, which seemed negligible unless it impaired his usefulness. He must have more time to think: but he directed the secretary of state to draw up formal papers for a breach.

When Lansing brought them to the White House the next morning, Wilson was in conference with Colonel House, whom the crisis moved to hasten to Washington and give to the President certain hypothetical peace terms that Bernstorff had presented confidentially at the last moment. Wilson read the curious document aloud; and when he came

assurance regarding Germany's conduct while arbitration was in progress. "I do not want to walk into a trap and give them immunity for the next year," the President wrote to House on Jan. 17. His caution seemed justified when Bernstorff answered his queries by repeating an earlier proposal, that the general peace conference would take place only after the belligerents had bartered for peace in the time-honored European tradition. On Jan. 24 the President wrote to House: "What Bernstorff said to you the other day as trimmed and qualified by what he wrote afterward amounts to nothing." Wilson's confidence in House's judgment doubtless was shaken by the fact that Bernstorff's proposal, which proved to be so disappointing, had been naïvely commended to him by the Colonel on Jan. 12 as "the most important communication since the war began."

to a sentence that begged him to continue his efforts to bring about peace, the irony became cutting. In the light of the grim official announcement from Berlin, the protestations seemed shallow, almost mocking. When a cable came from Gerard with news that Zimmermann wanted the President to keep silent for two months to give the submarines time to bring England to her knees, it seemed clear that the Germans hoped to stall the United States until they would be in a position to disregard her.[10] While talking peace, they had been plotting a kind of war that would respect neither neutral nor humane rights.

The President's disillusionment was as intense as his hopes had been extravagant. He felt, he said, as if the world had reversed the direction of its rotation and he could not get his balance. He spoke of Germany as "a madman that should be curbed." When House asked whether it seemed fair to ask the Allies to do the curbing alone, he winced, but nevertheless held to his determination to keep clear of hostilities if he could.

They waited listlessly through the morning for Lansing's arrival. House could not lift his friend's spirits. Wilson paced the floor and nervously fingered his books. His wife suggested a game of golf, but the Colonel doubted that the President should do anything that might seem to his people like fiddling during a holocaust. At last Wilson suggested pool, and they were finishing their second game when the secretary of state was announced. It was agreed that Bernstorff be given his passports at once, in the faint hope that the Germans might be brought to their senses before the commission of an overt act that would make war unavoidable.

On the next day the President consulted his Cabinet and received the reactions that he expected. Reflecting the anxiety of the whole nation, the men rose to their feet when their chief entered the conference room. Wilson read aloud the offensive German declaration and called it an "astounding surprise." The faces around him showed sardonic wrath; and in the discussion that followed their voices were low. In so solemn a moment they hesitated to give advice, and the President drew it out with questions. "Shall I break off diplomatic relations with Germany?" he asked, repeating what he had said before about his willingness to bear imputations of weakness, even of cowardice, in order to keep the white race strong.

10 The chief of the Admiralty staff was less eager than the German diplomats to immobilize the United States. On Dec. 22, 1916, Holtzendorff wrote to Hindenburg thus: "By entering into the war the United States Government will give up by a single move the sources of that commercial prosperity which has given it the towering political prominence which it now occupies. It stands face to face with the Japanese peril; it can neither inflict material damage upon us, nor can it be of material benefit to our enemies . . ." *Official German Documents*, II, 1269–70.

Most of the men answered his query with an impulsive affirmative. McAdoo's blood boiled at what he regarded as an attempt to order the United States off the Atlantic. If the nation meekly accepted Germany's colossal insult, said Houston, she would not be worth saving if she were attacked. Which side would the President like to be the winner, one of the men asked; and Wilson maintained that he still believed in a "peace without victory." Both sides had been callous to the rights of neutrals, he said, though Germany had been brutal in taking life and England only in taking property. Lansing asserted that all nations must have liberal governments before peace could be permanent, and that democracies were never aggressive or unjust; and Wilson, saying "I am not so sure of that," argued that probably a draw would bring a more just settlement than a victory. Still another official mentioned the possibility of a combination of Germany, Japan, and Russia, and at this point the President observed that "the Russian peasant might save the world this misfortune."

After two hours with the Cabinet he went to the Hill. "I wonder what you are thinking I should do?" he said to the several legislators who gathered about him. One suggested addressing a note of remonstrance, but at that he drew himself erect and declared sternly: "Let us be done with diplomatic notes. The hour to act has come."

Returning to the quiet of his own chamber, he faced up to the decision forced upon him. The charge that Presbyterianism set upon its leaders oppressed him. His brother, realizing the strain that the family conscience put upon him, sent a "God be with you," and he thanked Josie for this "from the bottom of a very troubled heart."

His conclusion was not to declare war, but to go before the Congress and announce a break with the rulers of Germany, in the hope that they would be jolted into sanity. Thus, once more, he would put upon Berlin the responsibility for final decision for war or peace. He labored until midnight to compose an appropriate address, and the next day, after conferring with Lansing, he addressed the legislators at two o'clock. Three minutes before, Bernstorff had been given his passports.

The people came by the thousands, overflowing from the corridors of the Capitol into the streets. Those who could hear applauded when, after reviewing the diplomatic correspondence with Berlin that had followed the *Sussex* incident, the President announced that the United States must now take the measure that it had declared it would take to meet unrestricted submarine warfare: that is, sever relations with Germany. He followed this with an appeal to the better nature of the Germans. Drawing the distinction between people and government that he was later to exploit adroitly, he asserted:

We are the sincere friends of the German people and earnestly desire to remain at peace with the Government which speaks for them. We shall not believe that they are hostile to us unless and until we are obliged to believe it; and we purpose nothing more than the reasonable defense of the undoubted rights of our people. We wish to serve no selfish ends. We seek merely to stand true alike in thought and in action to the immemorial principles of our people which I sought to express in my address to the Senate only two weeks ago,—seek merely to vindicate our right to liberty and justice and an unmolested life. These are the bases of peace, not war. God grant that we may not be challenged to defend them by acts of wilful injustice on the part of the Government of Germany!

CHAPTER V

Leading a United People into Conflict

THE PRESIDENT HARDLY had finished speaking before he could sense that his people were uniting in support of him. The Senate passed a resolution of approval with only five contrary votes. Immediately American life began to move with a martial tempo. Ten thousand men were withdrawn from Mexico and the mustering out of National Guardsmen was delayed. Youths lined up to enlist while the War College began work on a plan for conscription. Warships were ordered to be prepared for action and the Congress was asked for a huge naval appropriation. Executive offices at Washington were closed to the public, and soldiers appeared to guard areas that might be targets of sabotage. A Shipping Board that the President had nominated to carry out the Shipping Act of 1916 was beginning to function; and men chosen to form a Council of National Defense were organizing for action. Even Christian ministers were preaching a gospel of hate that made the President wonder whether they were "going crazy."

Wilson did his best to check the trend of opinion that he had been forced to accelerate by breaking with Germany. In his message to Congress he had neither damned German "barbarism," as some advisers wished, nor had he appealed to his people to prepare for inevitable war. He continued to complain to his advisers of Britain's maritime policy. He cautioned the War Department against any extraordinary activity that would give Berlin reason to believe that the United States was expecting hostilities.

Wilson was alarmed by the virulence of popular feelings. He was embarrassed when advocates of preparedness tried to stampede him into a headlong rush to arms. Industrial and financial magnates besieged Washington with offers of cooperation in which Wilson thought that he saw patriotic motive not untainted by hope for profit. Realizing that dictatorship could feed upon national emergency, he feared for democratic processes and shied away from agitation by conservative Republicans for a coalition government that might become totalitarian. "It is the *Junkerthum* trying to creep in under cover of the patriotic feeling of the moment," he wrote to House. "They will not get in. They have now no examples of happy or successful coalitions to point to. The nominal coalition in England is nothing but a Tory cabinet such as they are eager to get a foothold for here. I know them too well, and will hit them straight between the eyes, if necessary, with plain words."

His diplomatic resources were not yet exhausted. There was a glimmer of hope in the possibility of collective action with other nations. In informing neutral governments of his decision to break with Germany, Wilson had suggested that they could contribute to the making of peace by taking similar action. Receiving a favorable report from the Swiss minister, he was encouraged to set down four "Bases of Peace," rephrasing the essential principles that he had already proposed as a foundation for a league of nations, and adding a prohibition against "any joint economic effort to throttle the industrial life of any nation." On February 10, however, the Swiss envoy forwarded a German proposal that any point might be negotiated except one that might break her blockade of England. Obviously talks on this basis would get nowhere. Moreover, only one other neutral, China, responded favorably. By February 12 Wilson had given up hope of effective joint action.

Austria-Hungary now remained the only agency that might help to thwart the will of her ally. Regarded by American opinion as a luckless pawn of Germany, that nation echoed the provocative German declaration of submarine warfare, while at the same time she sent an envoy, Count Tarnowski, to replace Dumba, who had made himself *non grata* at Washington. Moreover, the minister of foreign affairs at Vienna explicitly notified the United States of his nation's desire to maintain friendly relations.

Seizing this twig of olive, Wilson directed Page to discuss the matter with British statesmen. But the divergence in the aims of the two great English-speaking nations was too great to permit joint action. The State Department undertook to negotiate with Vienna and received a conclusive refusal to enter into discussions without Germany's participation. Tarnowski was not received, Ambassador Penfield was recalled to Washington, and on Easter Sunday, April 8, Chargé Joseph C. Grew was given his passports.

While the negotiations with Vienna were in process, Wilson acted vigorously to meet the emergencies that had been created by the break with Germany. He did not want Berlin to be goaded to a quick declaration of war by fear of growing military power in America; yet neither did he want the Germans to underestimate the force that the United States could muster if driven to it. On February 5 he told the secretaries of war and the navy that the diplomatic breach took the nation so close to war that they must prepare for anything. "Each of you must surround himself with the ablest men you have," he said, asking them whether their advisers were all worthy of being retained. "Get and keep the best" was his last word to them.

When sailings of American ships were canceled as a result of the menace of German submarines, and cargoes piled up on the docks, outraged citizens implored their government to give protection. Their pleas were ardently supported by members of the Cabinet, and Secretary Baker explained that unless American vessels were armed they would be kept off the seas by the German threat. After discussion, the President accepted the contention of the Navy that the supplying of convoys would merely double the risk. He allowed his officials to tell inquiring shipowners that they might take any measures against unlawful acts; but he resisted Lansing's contention that guns and gunners should be furnished to merchant vessels by the government. He felt that this should not be done without the approval of Congress. And about the interned German ships Wilson was most punctilious: he would seize neither the vessels nor the crews who had disabled them. On February 15 he said at a Cabinet dinner that he was not in sympathy with a high degree of preparedness, for by the end of the war European nations would be destitute of manpower and wealth and would not menace America.

Finally, on February 23, the Cabinet pierced the academic shell behind which Wilson had sought detachment as his mind went "around the clock." Although Germany's threat had so far proved worse than her performance and American shippers had recovered somewhat from their fright, sailings had been cut almost in half during the month of February. McAdoo, whose confidence in his own executive ability had led him to propose to House that he take the Navy portfolio and let Houston replace him in the Treasury, argued that the President should act immediately, Congress or no Congress. He and Lane were so aggressive that Wilson turned on them bitterly, letting them know that he thought them guilty of fomenting hatred and jingoism. When he reproached the group for appealing to the code duello, and for urging him to unseemly and dictatorial action, they were inclined to revolt. Yet for all their impatience, they knew their Chief well enough to contain themselves a little longer. It seemed to Houston that the President agreed with what they said but, awed by his responsibility, was determined to make them prove their points beyond any doubt. And Lane, who thought Wilson "slower than a glacier," reminded his impetuous brethren that, though in the past they had had to press the Chief hard to bring him to the point of action, he had always responded in the end, when convinced that something had to be done.

To Wilson's family his equanimity was amazing.[1] Nevertheless his indignation had flared when he learned that Gerard was being detained at Berlin, apparently as a hostage to bring pressure on Washington to make concessions to German vessels in American ports. But on February 25 a far greater strain was placed upon his patience. On this day he received evidence that German intrigue was threatening the territorial integrity of the United States. The President learned that Zimmermann, now foreign secretary at Berlin, had instructed his minister at Mexico City to tempt the Mexican government to join with Germany if she should become involved in war with the United States. Offering "the lost territory of Texas, New Mexico, and Arizona," Zimmermann had suggested also that Mexico seek the cooperation of Japan.

This revelation was the more shocking to the President because Zimmermann's message had been transmitted by the American Department of State, under an arrangement that had been made by House with Bernstorff in order to facilitate communications with Berlin that might promote the cause of mediation and peace.[2] Intercepted by British agents, the text was sent to the President through Page. Wilson was flabbergasted at this evidence of German plotting at the very time when he had been earnestly trying to reach an understanding through Bernstorff.

The President checked his first impulse to make the Zimmermann message public, for he realized that the reaction of his people might force him to go to war immediately. He had it sent to Mexico City— "to give Carranza a chance to say what he will about it," he explained. However, he was impelled at last to take the action that his Cabinet had been urging and that he had warned the Congress, in his speech of February 3, it might be necessary for him to take. Going again to the Capitol to address a joint session, he read a message to hushed expectant legislators. Because the term of the Congress was about to expire and time would be required for its successor to assemble and organize, he wanted assurance of an authority that he thought his under the Constitution and that he might be forced to exercise.

"There may be no recourse," he warned, "but to *armed* neutrality, which we shall know how to maintain and for which there is abundant American precedent." He asked authorization to supply merchant ships with defensive arms, should that become necessary, and with the means

[1] Letter shown to the writer by Margaret Flinn (Mrs. George) Howe.

[2] As early as Jan. 24 Wilson had written to House of his suspicion of the use to which Bernstorff might be putting his privilege. Informing the Colonel that the German ambassador had sent a long message to his government and that he did not know its content, the President wrote: "By the way, if we are to continue to send messages for him, we should know that he is working in this cause [that of peace] and should in each case receive his official assurance . . ."

of using them, "and to employ any other instrumentalities or methods that may be necessary and adequate to protect our ships and our people in their legitimate and peaceful pursuits on the seas." He asked also for a grant of sufficient credit, including insurance against war risks.

But certain legislators did not go along with the prophet. Senator LaFollette, sitting with hands folded across his breast, saw in the President's request merely a long step toward war. And at the opposite pole of opinion, but equally resistant, was Henry Cabot Lodge, regarding the speaker critically, with hands clasped just under his chin. He could agree with Wilson's specific request for authority to arm merchant ships; but when the President came to his second point, and asked for power "to employ any other instrumentalities or methods that may be necessary and adequate," Lodge unclasped his fingers and tapped their tips together tentatively. LaFollette, despairing of keeping the peace, threw up both hands.

The President reviewed damages inflicted by German submarines since the breaking of relations, and told the legislators that an "overt act" had not yet occurred; but even as he was speaking, news came to the State Department of the sinking of the Cunard liner *Laconia,* with the loss of two American passengers. This atrocity, which occurred on the 25th, shared the front pages with the President's address on the 27th; and the American people now had dramatic, convincing proof that Germany intended to take the law into her own hands, as she had threatened.[3]

Wilson already had drafted the ship-arming bill that he wanted, and it was introduced in the House. The President consulted his politically minded advisers, McAdoo and Burleson, to decide on the best way of using the Zimmermann telegram to influence Congress to act favorably. He approved a canny suggestion from the State Department that they allow the document to be published as one that had leaked out rather than as an official release, for thus they might avoid exciting suspicion of their real motive. When questioned in the Senate about the authenticity of the document, Wilson affirmed it; and on March 4 Zimmermann himself acknowledged that it was genuine. The impact of the revelation and of the reaction of citizens stampeded the House to pass an armed-ship bill on March 1 by the overwhelming vote of 403 to 14.

In the Senate, the Republicans marshaled their forces to defer action and thus force the President to call a special session of the Congress.

[3] After the Cabinet meeting of the 27th it was made known "semiofficially" that the sinking of the *Laconia* was the dreaded "overt act." For a discussion of this event, and also of the Zimmermann message, *see* S. R. Spencer, Jr., *Decision for War.* When a newsman asked Wilson to define "overt act," the President said that he could not, but would know one if he saw one.

(Plans already had been laid at a party caucus for obstructive tactics that would prevent the passage of essential legislation before March 4, the date set for adjournment.) The filibuster that finally developed, however, was led by fanatical devotees of peace from both parties. "Gumshoe Bill" Stone of Missouri, who as chairman of the Foreign Relations Committee had had to lay the armed-ship bill before the Senate, joined with LaFollette and ten others in continuous talk that prevented action on the measure. Wilson's disappointment vented itself in rage against Stone. He was through with this man. "I'll not even shake hands with him again," he told Tumulty.[4]

It rankled Wilson that a few stubborn men could so effectively controvert the will of the people, and he was incensed because they did not accept his protestations of peaceful intent. He denounced them bitterly to House, and when the Colonel begged him to release something in the newspapers the next morning, he said that he would try. Shutting himself in his study almost all afternoon, he prepared a blast; and discussing it after dinner with McAdoo, Burleson, and Tumulty, he let it go. On Monday, March 5—the day of the formal inauguration ceremonies—the Jovian thunderbolt fell: "A little group of willful men, representing no opinion but their own, have rendered the great Government of the United States helpless and contemptible."

A vast exaggeration, but a timely and effective one! It rallied his people to protect and defend him as the symbol of patriotism. When he rode to the Capitol for the inauguration ceremony on March 5 he was hedged about by force and vigilance. Threatening letters had come to the White House in greater volume than ever, and the President's family were alarmed for his safety.

Giving only a brief paragraph of his second inaugural speech to the record of his first term, the President said: "Perhaps no equal period in our history has been so fruitful of important reforms in our economic

[4] Brahany Diary, March 4, 1917, in the possession of Thomas W. Brahany.

The Republican regulars, once they were sure that a special session would have to be summoned, were ready to express the sympathy that they felt for the President's policy. Senator Hitchcock of the Foreign Relations Committee, who had taken over promotion of the bill from the dissenting Stone, was able to get seventy-five senators to sign a manifesto of approval. Emboldened by this, the President, who had consulted the Congress merely out of courtesy and a desire for a show of unanimity, proceeded to act on the authority that the attorney general assured him was his under the Constitution. Supported by a press that denounced the filibuster with such phrases as "dastardly moral treason" and assured by legalists that the arming of merchantmen would not contravene the piracy law of 1819, the President, confined to his room by a cold, discussed the matter with naval advisers. He bade his wife tell Daniels that the Navy was to arm ships; and on March 9 he gave instructions that any officer who failed to keep these orders secret should be court-martialed. On March 12, Lansing released the news that the government would provide armed guards for American merchantmen sailing in war zones. Thus the United States came a long step closer to open hostilities. Wilson would be able to engage in war without exposing defenseless American vessels at sea.

and industrial life or so full of significant changes in the spirit and purpose of our political action. . . . It is a record of singular variety and singular distinction. But I shall not attempt to review it. It speaks for itself and will be of increasing influence as the years go by." He claimed no credit for person or party.

Reviewing the effect of the war on national life, he came to the immediate present. "We stand firm in armed neutrality," he declared, "since it seems that in no other way can we demonstrate what it is we insist upon and cannot forego." But it was of the future that he spoke most eloquently. "We are provincials no longer," he said. "The tragical events of the thirty months of vital turmoil through which we have just passed have made us citizens of the world. There can be no turning back. Our own fortunes as a nation are involved, whether we would have it so or not."

After the ceremony the President returned to the White House to greet two or three hundred guests at a buffet luncheon, and afterward he stood in the biting air to review the traditional parade. In the evening the family and Colonel House went upstairs to the oval sitting room to look out upon the fireworks. The Wilsons took seats by a side window, curtained off, and the President held his wife's hand and leaned with his face against hers. They asked the Colonel to join them; and House, rising to the occasion, spoke of his joy that it was they, and not the Hughes family, who were there. He was achieving the great ambition of his life. Not only had he captivated the heart of a great man, but he had won the confidence of his hero's wife. She confided to him that McAdoo irritated the President and seemed to her thoroughly selfish; and she asked House what chance such a man would have for the next nomination for the Presidency.

The excitement of inauguration day, coming after the strain of the battle for the armed-ship bill, was too much for the President's endurance. Dr. Grayson put his patient to bed, and for a fortnight he was almost constantly in his own room, seeing few visitors and, with his wife's help, writing only essential letters. Nevertheless, in his illness Wilson discussed the disposition of the fleet with Franklin D. Roosevelt and House, and the Colonel noted that he was "pushing Daniels to an activity that did not seem possible." Propped up in bed, the President tried to find diversion in consulting the ouija board, but the spirit of Admiral Nelson presented itself and discussed submarine warfare.

The first weeks of his second term brought no slackening of the tensions that were racking Wilson's soul. With the backing of labor interests that feared the competition of immigrants, Congress re-enacted the Burnett Bill, which restricted immigration by means of a literacy test and discriminated against Orientals. Wilson repeated the veto that he had imposed two years earlier, but now the measure was passed over his opposition. Organized labor consolidated the victory that it had won in September of 1916. Railroad managers were testing the constitutionality of the Adamson Law, and the impatient brotherhoods issued a general strike order on March 15. The President appealed to both sides to seek a settlement "in this time of national peril." Finally, on March 16, it was decided in Cabinet meeting that Secretaries Lane and Wilson should go at once to confer at New York with representatives of labor and management. A settlement was negotiated and a tie-up averted.

Meanwhile, the Czar of Russia abdicated on March 15 and a constitutional government was established; and thus the Allies were relieved of an association that had embarrassed them in appealing for American sympathy. Woodrow Wilson was in a serious mood as he read an official report of the upheaval from his ambassador at Petrograd, David R. Francis, who naïvely pictured the revolution as the "practical realization" of the American principle of government by consent of the governed and argued that it was desirable from every point of view that the United States be the first to recognize the new regime.

Wilson was now to pay dearly for the tendency that he and House had shown to give more weight to political expediency than to efficiency, in choosing envoys to Russia. The President was too learned to accept unquestioningly the views of Francis, a former governor of Missouri. In his academic years Wilson had thought and written much about revolutions, particularly those of his own nation and of France. At Princeton he had scorned revolution as a "puerile doctrine," socially expensive and yet apparently necessary in eighteenth-century France as a path to freedom. Talking with a young colleague, one evening, about "liberty" as it applied to Russian peasants, he suggested that they were like birds in a cage—not conscious of their confinement and therefore free. In an undergraduate essay he had written: "The most despotic of governments under the control of wise statesmen is preferable to the freest ruled by demagogues."

It was clear, however, that the generous impulses of Wilson's people, like those of their genial ambassador, were stirred by the overthrow of a despotic regime. Americans wished the new government well and, in their ignorance of the true nature of the political processes at work in Russia, even ventured to hope that a democratized government might fight German autocracy with a zeal that the czarist armies lacked. Few Americans realized that at that very time Leon Trotsky, a political exile living on New York's East Side, was proclaiming that the revolution reflected a hunger for peace among the masses of Russia.

Colonel House, inspired by the Russian Revolution to see "more hope for democracy and human liberty than ever before," wrote thus to Wilson on March 17: "I want to urge that you recognize the new Russian government as soon as England and France do . . . you stand easily as the great liberal of modern times." Half-sick and despondent, Wilson put aside his intellectual doubts and made the United States the first nation to recognize the new Russian government.[5]

Meanwhile the offenses of the U-boats were increasing. Ships were being sunk at the rate of almost 600,000 tons a month. Even vessels carrying supplies for Belgian relief were sent down. American ships, which in February suffered little damage, were now being attacked; and on the 18th three were sunk without warning and with loss of American lives.

The press reacted violently to these outrages. Committees of Defense sprouted like the minutemen of 1776 all through the land. Yet peace sentiment was still strong at the grass roots. Many of the plain people were lethargic, or positively hostile to a declaration of war. But it was daily becoming clearer that Germany was making war on the American people, that to refuse the challenge now would be both shameful and dangerous. Responsible labor leaders pledged their loyalty in case of war; and a group of influential Socialists broke with the pacifistic policy of their national committee.

On March 19 the President was well enough to talk with the secretary of state about the three sinkings of American ships. The next day, having almost entirely regained his strength, he came face to face with his impetuous Cabinet. Walking through the swarm of newsmen, he entered the room smiling genially and shook hands with each official as if nothing exceptional was to take place. Recounting the measures taken to protect American ships, he asked questions that seemed to take it for granted that further action would be necessary. He asked whether he should summon Congress before April 16, the date he had already set, and what he should say to the legislators. He said he understood that the liberal element in the Prussian Diet was grumbling against its rulers, and he spoke of the warlike temper of his own people in the East and their apathy in the Midwest.

His deliberate manner sobered the men at the table. McAdoo spoke in a low, earnest voice, favoring an immediate call to the Congress and

---

[5] When the Russian Revolution was discussed by the Cabinet on March 23, Wilson, expressing pleasure at the speedy recognition of the new government, said: "It ought to be good, because it has a professor at the head." The next day the President told Daniels the story of the life of Foreign Minister Milyukov.

support for the ebbing credit of the Allies.[6] Baker spoke out for universal military training and the raising of a large army, believing that the people would demand it. The secretary of state thought war the best course, especially in view of the liberalizing of the Russian government, and he hoped that Wilson would publicly indict Prussian autocracy. Lansing spoke loud and vehemently; and the President asked him please to lower his voice so that no one in the corridor would hear.

As a whole, the Cabinet desired to clash with the Germans at once and with all the nation's power, though Daniels, the last to give in to martial sentiment, had tears in his eyes. Burleson, who wanted Congress to convene at the earliest moment, read telegrams typical of sheafs that were coming from the people, demanding war.

To this Wilson replied solemnly: "We are not governed by public opinion in our conclusion. I want to do right whether it is popular or not." He agreed that there would be added justification for entering the war if that act would strengthen the liberal forces in Russia and Germany; but he could not offer this motive as a reason for calling the Congress immediately, and he was not sure that he could influence the Russian people by yielding to a plea by Lansing for a public denunciation of German autocracy. The *casus belli* would have to be Germany's offenses and the obvious need of protecting American rights and safeguarding civilization against Prussian militarism.

After two and a half hours he felt that he had thoroughly canvassed the thought of the Cabinet. "Well, gentlemen," he said, "I think there is no doubt as to what your advice is. Thank you." He did not tell them what he would do, but he asked Lansing and Burleson to remain after the others went, and inquired how long it would take to prepare legislation by which Congress could declare war. More than a week, they replied. Encouraged by his question, Lansing ventured to ask whether the President would issue a call to Congress that afternoon. "Oh, I think I will sleep on it," Wilson replied.

He did not sleep well, however. In fact, he had been lying awake night after night, agitated by the doubts that he kept submerged under a cool exterior. The vital question, to him, was not the immediate cause

[6] Wilson gave no evidence that he was influenced by a desire to secure the credit of the Allies and help them to honor their commitments to American citizens. He made no reply to a plea from Page for support of British credit. The Federal Reserve Board had followed up its action of November, 1916, against accepting short-term notes from abroad by issuing a statement on March 8 that warned against unsound methods while encouraging foreign loans. There was no assurance that the Allies would not be bankrupt by the war and that by excessive loans and credits to them the United States herself would not, in the long run, suffer severe economic loss. In his speeches in 1916 Wilson had given expression to a hope that the surplus of economic strength that his nation was accumulating might be used "for the benefit of the world"; and he still hoped for a peace settlement that would make this possible. But economic interest was to him a consideration secondary to "the rights of humanity."

of war, but rather the larger problem that he had recognized as early as May, 1916, when he had said: "The danger of our time is nothing less than the unsettlement of the foundations of civilization." And so he asked himself: What would be the probable consequences to humanity if the United States entered the fight?

During the night of March 20 the prophet made his great decision. He was convinced that the hour that he had long dreaded had struck, that he could no longer "preserve both the honor and the peace of the United States." He issued a special proclamation the next morning, calling the new Congress to convene in special session on April 2.

Wilson and his colleagues acted henceforth as if they thought war inevitable. On the 23rd the Cabinet urged that the attorney general draft drastic security laws. On the 24th a plan for voluntary censorship was announced; and the President approved an increase in naval personnel and told Daniels that Marines should be placed aboard interned ships to prevent sabotage. House, to whom a member of the Council of National Defense had complained about inefficiencies, recommended that Daniels and Newton D. Baker be replaced,[7] and warned that the President would be held responsible by his people for their mistakes. But Wilson clung to these loyal, cooperative associates. Daniels's genius for public relations was compensating, in the view of many publicists, for the uncommunicativeness of Wilson and Baker. People liked his flamboyant speeches, filled with worn jokes, poetry, and biblical quotations. And he could be depended on to fight hard against graft and profiteering. Early in 1915, when the President had been told of derogatory gossip about Daniels, he had brought down his fist on a table and exclaimed: "His enemies are determined to ruin him. I can't be sure who they are, but when I do get them—God help them!"

Wilson pondered whether he should ask for a declaration of war or merely say that a state of war existed and that he needed means to carry it on. House advised the latter, fearing that an acrimonious debate might develop if the decision were left to the legislators. Mulling over this counsel, which coincided in the main with the sentiments of his Cabinet, Wilson jotted down the substance of an address; and House was as pleased as if he had written the memorandum himself.

[7] This recommendation by House reflected the feeling of Counselor Frank L. Polk of the State Department. House and Polk agreed that the Colonel's son-in-law, Gordon Auchincloss, should represent the department in New York in matters of security, finance, and trade.

For a while the Colonel wondered whether he himself should not take an official position on the President's staff in the event of war and organize, with Auchincloss, a confidential bureau. When he made this suggestion to Wilson twice in early February, the President replied: "I will with the deepest pleasure and alacrity place you wherever you are willing to be placed—as I am sure you know. But just what have you in mind?" To this confining question the tentative, roving mind of the ruling elder had no answer.

The President did not discuss the text of his address with the Cabinet when he met them on March 30. He feared that his work might be picked to pieces if he invited criticism of it. When the men raised the bogie of sabotage and recommended that protective measures already taken should be followed up, Wilson recounted absurd rumors that had come to him. Mentioning the fear of the White House staff of a German who tended the furnace, he said: "I'd rather the blamed place should be blown up rather than persecute inoffensive people." In this hour of crisis he deliberately tried to be casual and relaxed. At one point he stood up and did setting-up exercises, explaining that he had been sitting at a desk all morning and was stiff.

After two days of soul-searching, he felt the need of a confessor other than House; and so he sent for Frank I. Cobb, editor of the *World*, a man who was in sympathy with his policy. Entering the little study at one o'clock in the morning of April 2, Cobb had never seen him so worn down. Wilson confessed that he had not been so uncertain about anything in his life. He felt that he could honestly say that he had considered every loophole of escape and Germany had blocked each with a new outrage.

The consequences that he envisioned from American intervention were terrifying. The society that his people knew would be overturned. There would no longer be a preponderance of neutral nations and the whole world would be on a war basis. He predicted: "Once lead this people into war, and they'll forget there ever was such a thing as tolerance. To fight you must be brutal and ruthless, and the spirit of ruthless brutality will enter into the very fibre of our national life, infecting Congress, the courts, the policeman on the beat, the man in the street . . ." He thought the Constitution would not survive, that free speech and the right of assembly would go. Legal and moral restraints would be relaxed, industry would be demoralized, and profiteering run rampant. After the coming of peace it would require a generation to restore normal conditions. He said a nation couldn't put its strength into a war and keep its head level; it had never been done. "If there is any alternative," he cried out to Cobb, "for God's sake, let's take it."

On April 2 he was determined not to appear to be importunate; and House urged him to meet the convenience of the legislators. Learning that they would be ready for him at eight-thirty, he dined at six-thirty and talked of everything except the grave issue of the day. At eight-twenty the Wilsons left the White House, accompanied by Grayson and Tumulty. Heavily guarded, they drove through rain along the brilliant avenue, past thousands of citizens who waved little flags.

Edith Wilson left him in the room reserved for him at the Capitol.

He was alone for a few moments except for a secret service man—
Ellery Sedgwick, editor of the *Atlantic Monthly,* who had allowed himself to be sworn in so that he might enter the House chamber and hear
his hero deliver the decision that he had been advocating editorially for
two years. Unaware of the editor's observing eye the President walked
toward a large mirror. Sedgwick saw in the glass a face that was suffering the tortures of inferno. The features were twisted in spiritual agony,
the chin awry, the flesh deeply drawn and flushed. The President placed
his left elbow on a mantel and looked steadfastly at his distorted countenance. "A stroke!" the editor whispered to himself. But no; the tortured figure put his left hand to his brow to smooth the corrugations,
the right to his chin to set it straight and firm; and gradually the
features fell into a physiognomy as rigid as Calvin's. His "make-up"
completed, Woodrow Wilson was resolved to play out the tragedy that
had been forced upon him.

The President strode into the corridor and through the swinging
doors of the House chamber, ten minutes late. Champ Clark, re-elected
speaker, did his duty though he loathed both the occasion and the man.
"Gentlemen," he announced as the echo of his gavel died out, "the
President of the United States." The members of the Supreme Court
arose, and after them the other dignitaries who packed the room—legislators, Cabinet, and diplomatic corps. Woodrow Wilson was now, more
than ever, the symbol of security for the nation, and this feeling was
conveyed by the heartiness of the applause—the greatest ever given to
this President at the Capitol.

Wilson had never faced a more curious audience. No one, except
House and Edith Wilson, knew exactly what would be said. Waiting
for the clamor to die out, the President stood nervously on the rostrum,
fingering the cards on which his address was typed. Even from the
rear benches his face looked gaunt. As soon as the air was still, he rested
his arm on the green lectern and began to read in a voice that was at
first husky and low. But there was no gesture of voice or hand that
might rouse feeling in his audience; only an occasional raising of his
eyes. He dramatized the "absolute self-control and absolute self-mastery"
that he had bespoken for his nation.

His prophetic dignity made the cold indictment the more cutting.
Asserting that Germany had swept aside such international usages as
had been built up with great travail by humanity, that their submarine
policy was a menace to all mankind, he came to the essential that had
made his people ready to fight the Germans while they bore the insults
of the Allies. "Property can be paid for," he said; "the lives of peaceful
and innocent people cannot." Explaining why armed neutrality was

both impractical as a means of defense and ineffectual as a guarantee of peace, he made a ringing declaration: "There is one choice we cannot make, we are incapable of making; we will not choose the path of submission . . ."

At this point a tall figure rose in the audience. The secret service men fingered their guns; but it was Chief Justice White, an ex-Confederate soldier, raising his hands high and bringing them together with a clap. The galleries took the cue and roared their applause. They were obviously ready for what was to come, and the President came immediately to his grave pronouncement:

With a profound sense of the solemn and even tragical character of the step I am taking and of the grave responsibilities which it involves, but in unhesitating obedience to what I deem my constitutional duty, I advise that the Congress declare the recent course of the Imperial German Government to be in fact nothing less than war against the government and people of the United States; that it formally accept the status of belligerent which has thus been thrust upon it; and that it take immediate steps not only to put the country in a more thorough state of defense but also to exert all its power and employ all its resources to bring the Government of the German Empire to terms and end the war.

As for Austria-Hungary, a government that despite its adherence to German submarine tactics had not "actually engaged in warfare against citizens of the United States on the seas," Wilson took the liberty of postponing a discussion of relations. He spoke of the practical measures that must be taken immediately to prosecute the war in cooperation with the Western Allies. He made it clear that Americans were the sincere friends of the German people, and indeed had put up with the Berlin government through bitter months because of that friendship. Alluding to "the wonderful and heartening things" that had happened in Russia, he said: "The great, generous Russian people have been added in all their naïve majesty and might to the forces that are fighting for freedom in the world, for justice, and for peace. Here is a fit partner for a League of Honor."

He concluded with his great commitment of America to the service of humanity:

The world must be made safe for democracy. Its peace must be planted upon the tested foundations of political liberty. We have no selfish ends to serve. We desire no conquest, no dominion. We seek no indemnities for ourselves, no material compensation for the sacrifices we shall freely make. We are but one of the champions of the rights of mankind. We shall be satisfied when those rights have been made as secure as the faith and the freedom of nations can make them. . . . It is a distressing and oppressive duty, Gentlemen of the Congress, which I have performed in thus addressing you. There are, it may be, many months of fiery trial and sacrifice ahead of us. It is a fearful thing to lead this great peaceful people into war, into the most terrible and disastrous of all wars, civilization itself seeming to be in the balance. But the right is more precious than peace, and we shall fight for the things which we have always carried nearest our hearts,—for democracy, for the right of those who submit to authority to have a voice in their own Governments, for the rights and liberties of small nations, for a universal dominion of right by such a concert of free peoples as shall bring peace and safety to all nations and make the world itself at last free. To such a task we can dedicate our lives and our fortunes, everything that we are and everything that we have, with the pride of those who know that the day has come when America is privileged to spend her blood and her might for the principles that gave her birth and happiness and the peace which she has treasured. God helping her, she can do no other.

In thirty-two minutes he had finished speaking. For a few seconds there was stillness, save for the patter of rain on the glass roof, then a deafening roar in which Republicans and Democrats—Americans alike —gave voice to the feelings of a preponderance of the people. Henry Cabot Lodge, his face slightly puffed as a result of fisticuffs with a pacifist, shook the hand of the President warmly. At last the time had come for which Wilson had waited so patiently, the time when, as he explained later, his people were willing not merely to follow him, but to do so "with a whoop." In no previous crisis in American history had feeling been so unanimous.

War resolutions were quickly passed, with few dissenting votes. At one-eighteen on the afternoon of April 7 Wilson left his luncheon and with his wife stepped into the head usher's office. He was given the proclamation that formally declared the state of war that had "been thrust upon the United States." He read it with rigid jaw and grim countenance, then signed with a gold pen that he had given to Edith Wilson and that she asked him to use. The occasion was too solemn, he thought. to be witnessed by newsmen or photographed.

CHAPTER VI

CALL TO ARMS

A COUSIN, Fitz William McMaster Woodrow, accompanied Wilson from the Hill to the White House, and as they rode up in the elevator, the President said suddenly, with deep feeling: "Fitz, thank God for Abraham Lincoln."

"Why do you say that, Cousin Woodrow?" the astonished young man asked.

"I won't make the mistakes that he made" was the response.[1]

The circumstances of geography gave the President time to follow the rational process by which he was accustomed to attack new problems. The Atlantic Ocean, which had served so well to insulate the New World from the turbulence of the Old, made it impossible for the enemy to attack in force at once. The immediate need was to stiffen the morale of the Western Allies; and it seemed at first that this could be done best by providing ships and munitions, and the credits necessary, rather than by sending an American army to Europe.

Actually, there was no army to send. German military experts ranked the force of the United States on a level with those of tiny nations. Even had the President called up hundreds of thousands of volunteers, in the manner of "Father Abraham" a half-century before, there would not have been enough officers to train them. If he sent all of the little Regular Army abroad and it was decimated, as Britain's "First Hundred Thousand" had been in 1914, there would have been no training officers left. Americans must now do what Ambassador Gerard had told the Kaiser they would do: they must "invent something."

Given ample time to think, the President and his secretary of war applied themselves to building a foundation on which a large military machine might be erected if it should become necessary. While Wilson kept in mind the mistakes of Lincoln, Baker resolved to avoid such quarrels as Secretary of War Stanton had with Civil War generals. History taught that the fighting of a war demands unified control, that decentralization breeds delay, confusion, and error; and in the mechanized warfare of the twentieth century, good planning was more imperative than ever. Wilson realized that democracy could be saved

[1] F. W. McM. Woodrow to the writer, April 12, 1948. MS checked by Mr. Woodrow, May, 1956.

only if the people abdicated their power temporarily in favor of the experts.

At the beginning he used the soundest professional instrument available—the General Staff that had been created in 1903 as a result of the blunders of the Spanish-American War.[2] To the officers of this body was entrusted the shaping of military policy and its execution.

The problem of manpower, however, was one that could not be left entirely to military experts, for it affected a people who loathed the principle of conscription and whose grandfathers had rioted in protest against the Civil War draft. Many citizens felt that a knockout blow could be delivered if untrained volunteers rushed to France and communicated their enthusiasm to Allied armies that had become bogged in trench warfare. The President was besieged by petitions from Indian fighters, Texas Rangers, and Southern "Colonels" who had more zeal for vigilante raids than for subordination to military authority. Even close associates of Wilson were affected by a red-blooded urge to volunteer for combat, and he had to persuade them that they could serve best at their desks in Washington. The most embarrassing plea came from Colonel Theodore Roosevelt, who had served on his own terms in the Spanish-American War and wanted to do so again. Already he had rounded up some of his comrades of the "Rough Riders"; and even before the declaration of war he had offered to assemble a division and to put it into the trenches in France after six weeks of training. The enterprise would be financed from private sources, but the War Department would have to provide arms and supplies and some of the best officers.

The idea caught the imagination of the public; but Secretary Baker analyzed it carefully and immediately sent a courageous reply. Meeting with the Colonel face to face, Baker explained the technical difficulties. But Roosevelt sent another blast, and the secretary of war forwarded it to the President. On March 27 Wilson replied: "This is one of the most extraordinary documents I have ever read! Thank you for letting me undergo the discipline of temper involved in reading it in silence!"

When war was declared, Roosevelt determined to take his case directly to the White House. He called on April 10, and Wilson talked patiently with him, explaining that he had had for a long time the feelings that he had expressed in his war message, but had bided his time

[2] "In April, 1917, the General Staff consisted of fifty-one officers, only nineteen of whom were on duty at Washington. Of these, eight were occupied with routine business, leaving but eleven free for the real purpose for which the staff had been created—'the study of military problems, the preparation of plans for national defense, and utilization of the military forces in time of war.' " Seymour, *Woodrow Wilson and the World War*, p. 120. General Tasker H. Bliss supplanted General Scott, who was near retirement, as chief of staff.

until the people shared his sentiments. He said that he had been misunderstood by many people, and added that of course he did not refer to his guest as one of them.

It seemed to Roosevelt that this polite absolution was delivered "with obvious uncertainty." The Colonel was confident that he could still inspire youth, though he himself might "crack" after three months at the front; and he said that if his petition was granted and he went abroad to fight, he would promise not to come back. He suggested that, as good patriots, they let past hostilities be "as dust on a windy street."

Wilson was so charmed by the spirit of the petitioner that he almost gave way. For the moment he could forget that Roosevelt, now almost sixty years old, was blind in one eye and intermittently plagued by poisoning that had resulted from equatorial fever. The gallantry that had made Wilson speak of the battlefield as a glorious place to die responded to the exalted emotion of his rival. It would have been so easy and pleasant to give the old fellow his head. The President hated to burst the bubbles by asking penetrating questions. But to be true to his trust and his comrades he must.

Roosevelt failed to overcome the main obstacle—the President's fear that if he sanctioned a volunteer division, the Congress would be influenced against the essential principle of compulsory universal service. Nevertheless, the old warrior left with ardor undampened, slapped Tumulty on the back, and promised him a place in his division—it was not to be near headquarters, he later confided to a friend, for Wilson's secretary must be given no chance to act as a watchdog. Roosevelt had emotionally identified his own leadership with the salvation of the nation that he dearly loved. His mind was not disposed toward judicial review, nor his conscience toward shame. He continued to fulminate—constructively as long as there was a chance of realizing his martial dream, destructively when there was not.

If Wilson suspected political motives behind the fervor of Roosevelt, he made no allegations even to those closest to him. When he told his family that he could not release General Wood, Roosevelt's comrade-in-arms, from training duties in a Southern camp to which Wood had been assigned, they asked him why he did not give his people the reason for his decision. "In the first place, no one would believe me," he replied. "In the second place, they'd think they were getting under my skin. And in the third place, I'd see 'em in Hell first." [3]

[3] Letter, F. W. McM. Woodrow to the writer, May 6, 1956.

Roosevelt's argument was not ingenuous, according to an account that he himself wrote of his conversation with Wilson: "Of course, strictly for your private information, I had to choose my words rather carefully, in private and in public." T.R. to John C. O'Laughlin, April 13, 1917. *The Letters of T.R.,* VIII, 1173.

Asked for a press statement of his attitude toward Roosevelt's plea, Wilson wrote to Tumulty: ". . . I really think the best way to treat Mr. Roosevelt is to take no notice of him. That breaks his heart and is the best punishment that can be administered. After all, while what he says is outrageous in every particular, he does, I am afraid, keep within the law, for he is as careful as he is unscrupulous."

Finally, on May 17, Wilson's restraint gave way before an insult delivered in person by John M. Parker, one of Roosevelt's Rough Riders who came to the White House to plead for his comrade. "I feel I have the right to criticize," Parker said, "because you are my hired man, just as you are the hired man of the people." Moreover, he told Wilson to his face that the civilized world held "no more arbitrary ruler" than he.

In the position that he occupied, the President could not retaliate as man to man. Curbing his rage, he replied civilly but with complete frankness: "Sir, I am not playing politics . . . General Wood is needed here. Colonel Roosevelt is an admirable man and a patriotic citizen, but he is not a military leader . . . It is not I but the Republicans who have been playing politics and consciously embarrassing the Administration. I do not propose to have politics in any manner, shape, or form influence me in my judgment." [4]

Long before Roosevelt made his dramatic appeals, Wilson had been committed to a plan that would not only raise men for the armed forces

---

Roosevelt appealed to the British and French ambassadors for the intercession of their governments, and he sent them copies of voluminous arguments that he wrote to Secretary Baker. Encouraged by messages from thousands of sympathizers who felt that he was being martyred for his politics, Roosevelt proposed to influential legislators a device that he had suggested to Wilson—a rider to the draft bill that would provide for his division. But Baker, to whom General Bridges of the visiting British military mission had protested against the dispatch of amateur units from the United States, was adamant. On May 19th, the day after the choice of Pershing to command an expeditionary force was announced, Wilson telegraphed to Roosevelt that he could not permit him to raise a volunteer division; and on the same day he gave his reasons to the public. He had handled his adversary in the way that he had recommended to a new police commissioner of the District of Columbia. "When a man comes to you seeking special favors," he said, "be sure to control the conversation yourself and take high moral ground. Often he will be ashamed to mention his self-interested errand." Louis Brownlow to the writer.

Roosevelt thought of the Administration as "those Y.M.C.A. banditti at Washington," and in his office at the *Outlook* he was heard to squeak over the phone about the restraints put upon his freedom of action by "that skunk in the White House." Kerney, p. 248, and T. H. Watkins to Charles Seymour to the writer. Wilson was "an utterly selfish, utterly treacherous, utterly insincere hypocrite," Roosevelt wrote to William Allen White on May 28, 1917. *The Letters of T.R.,* VIII, 1198–99. Again and again, during the ensuing year, Roosevelt wrote to his friends in this vein, and in the columns of journals bitterly criticized the Administration's war policies.

Finally reacting against this persistent vilification, Wilson said almost two years later, at Paris, that if he had published his interchanges with Roosevelt, the latter probably would have denied what he said. The President asserted that Roosevelt's object was personal publicity, that he had admitted a lack of necessary qualifications and wanted to use the Army's best officers to make up for his own shortcomings. Edith Benham Helm's "Letters," *Cosmopolitan*, August, 1930.

[4] Hagedorn, *Wood*, II, 219–22. Actually, some of Wilson's advisers thought it would be politically expedient to send his Republican adversaries as close to the front line as possible.

but would bring home to every citizen his obligation to serve the nation in its hour of crisis. In the autumn of 1916 he had agreed to the publication of an opinion submitted by the chief of staff, General Hugh L. Scott, a son of an old Princeton family who had shown himself an able general and had served without political ambition or prejudice. The report of the staff held that the volunteer system, "in view of the highly organized, trained, and disciplined armies in Europe," should be abandoned, that "the only democratic method is for every man in his youth to become trained in order that he may render efficient service." The military experts had observed the failure of the people to volunteer for service in Mexico in large numbers; and the necessity for compulsion became even more evident when enlistments in the spring of 1917 fell far short of the need for soldiers. Moreover, it was noted that Britain's efforts at voluntary recruiting had been neither adequate nor just and had, after eighteen months, given away to a systematic plan of conscription.

Soon after the diplomatic breach with Germany, Secretary Baker had brought these considerations before the President and found him open-minded. Wilson's instincts revolted against the idea; but he was convinced that the War Department's plan offered a democratic way to meet a universal obligation. He said that he wanted to have a conscription bill ready so that, if he had to read a war message, he could refer to it.

The recommendation that the President made to the Congress on April 2 called for a half-million more men for the armed forces, as provided by the National Defense Act that he had sponsored in 1916. In his opinion, he said, they "should be chosen upon the principle of universal liability to service." The day after the declaration of war, the President insisted publicly that "the safety of the nation" required conscription, and he reassured zealous democrats by explaining that the system would be in force only for the duration of the conflict.

A bill was ready for the Congress. It provided that men of draft age should present themselves on registration day to local civil authorities, as if they were going to the polls to vote. Thus they would submit their lives to their neighbors, not to an autocrat at Washington. There would be civil appeal boards, and sitting above them would be the provost marshal general, then the secretary of war, and finally the President. The system would be called "selective service," not "conscription"—ever a harsh word to American ears.

The President gave wholehearted support to the measure, declaring that the Administration would not "yield an inch of any essential parts of the programme." Selective service bills were passed by the two chambers on April 28 over opposition that was bitter.[5] The system took effect smoothly under the direction of General Crowder. Thus Wilson's administration proved itself as ingenious in solving a critical problem of twentieth-century warfare as it had been in dealing with the new economic forces of the era.[6]

In the proclamation that Secretary Baker had asked him to issue to explain the new law to the public, Wilson again showed his genius in summoning his national congregation to service in the Lord's work. He made his people see a far wider vision than that of drafting privates. "In the sense in which we have been wont to think of armies," he wrote, "there are no armies in this struggle. There are entire nations armed . . . The whole nation must be a team in which each man shall play the part for which he is best fitted . . . It is in no sense a conscription of the unwilling; it is, rather, selection from a nation which has volunteered in mass."

He was not willing to yield to political agitation for the forming of a coalition war cabinet, like that adopted in Britain. He was held back not only by mistrust of the capacity of certain Republican leaders for nonpartisan thinking, but also by his preference for working with familiar associates whom he knew thoroughly. As members of the Cabinet filed into the regular meetings in the summer of 1917, all clad in white, the Chief had a personal word for each one. He would go around the table and give each a chance to speak, beginning one day with the first, the next time with the second, and so on. As in an old-time prayer meeting, there were no minutes, no votes, and no interruptions. Discussion of politics was barred, though sometimes the President asked Burleson to remain afterward to consider party matters. The President listened with an inner ear to the best advice he could find at home and abroad and tried to put himself and his authority at the disposal of those who would use his powers wisely. "The business now in hand,"

[5] Though Wilson's party held a clear majority in the Senate, it was able to organize the House only with the help of independent representatives. "This was a good thing from the standpoint of efficient leadership from the White House," William E. Dodd has pointed out. "It compelled the party in power to remain at its task and pay close attention to Mr. Wilson for whom there was little love in either house." *W.W. and His Work*, p. 221.

[6] The Selective Service Act was one of the greatest legislative achievements of the Wilson administration. It made it possible for all members of the National Guard to be taken into federal service, and for adequate forces to be raised by selective draft without using men who were essential to the normal functioning of civil life and war production. The act was accepted by the people in the spirit in which it was conceived; and on June 5 some ten million men between twenty-one and thirty, inclusive, peacefully registered with local civilian boards. Later the age limits were extended and still more manpower became available.

The President was sympathetic to those who resisted military service on principle. Forwarding to Tumulty a letter from Villard about the conscientious objectors, he clipped a note commending Villard's views as containing a great deal that was "interesting and sensible" and predicting that they would be received by Secretary Baker with as much sympathy as by himself.

he explained to his people, "is undramatic, practical, and of scientific definiteness and precision."

The Administration thought at first that the contribution of the United States should be chiefly in material. However, this view was changed by military missions that were sent to Washington by the Allies. When "Papa" Joffre, hero of the Battle of the Marne, paraded past cheering crowds in American cities, Wilson was impressed both by the man and by his plea for American aid. The marshal said that American troops should be seen in France at once, for moral effect,[7] and he promised that, if they knew the manual of arms and the rudiments of discipline, he could fit them for the front in five weeks. At the same time Balfour asked that men be sent immediately to the field of operations for training there; and his military adviser suggested that it would be best for American troops to cooperate with the British, rather than the French, because of their common language.

Adhering to a plan to send no large American army abroad until a million conscripts could be trained, Wilson and Baker made a concession to the pleas for a token force. On May 2 the President allowed Joffre to take it for granted that the troops that he wanted would be sent. On the 18th, the day on which Wilson signed the Selective Service Act, Baker announced that an expeditionary force of about one division would go to France as soon as practical, under the leadership of Major General John J. Pershing.

To select a commander for the first army that ever had gone from the New World to fight in the Old, the secretary of war had studied the records of all his senior generals. He resolved that he would choose the one who had shown himself most able and most devoted to duty, and then uphold his authority to the utmost. In the record of Pershing he found evidence of imagination, daring, and sound common sense. Moreover, this man had the rugged physique that would be essential. There was no hesitation, therefore, in selecting him in preference to five active major generals who outranked him.

Wilson was pleased by the choice. Pershing had handled the policing expedition in Mexico with restraint and fidelity. Moreover, he had shown himself an advocate of the principle of conscription. The President had read a letter from Pershing that interested him because of the light it threw on the man's loyalty to government policy, and he had suggested

[7] At this time the revolution in Russia had shaken the morale of the fighting men of Britain and France. British workers openly questioned the objectives for which their brethren had been conscripted to fight. At the same time French regiments, defeated in the Chemin des Dames and made restive by the emergence of "soldiers' councils" in Russia, were mutinous; and their leaders were fearful that the opposing German forces would be strengthened by troops released from the collapsing Eastern front.

to the secretary of war that they send this officer to France at once "to study the ground." When Pershing had been appointed and was about to sail, Wilson received him at the White House and said: "General, we are giving you some very difficult tasks these days."

When Pershing replied that he was "trained to expect this" and thanked the Commander in Chief for his appointment, Wilson said: "You were chosen entirely upon your record and I have every confidence that you will succeed." Thus was established a relationship of professional regard that was to withstand the strains of the hugest war in which the nation ever had been engaged.[8]

The President himself took little part in the shaping of military plans. Though he sometimes strolled over to the War Department and dropped in unannounced for a chat with Baker, he did not bother him about details and never overruled a decision made. Neither political expediency nor sentiment could induce Wilson to dispute disciplinary sentences. When Paderewski, Poland's patriot-pianist, proposed that a unit of Poles be organized within the American Army, Wilson felt that it would be unwise to do anything that might accentuate racial differences among his people.

Realizing that he was no military strategist, he still could follow the debates of the experts with keen attention. He spent his limited strength thriftily, disposing rapidly of minds that lacked balance and juice. "He knew a dry sponge on sight," Baker said of him. ". . . He sorted things out in the order of importance. Things never got lost in his mind, but lay there until it was time to act. . . . I deliberately thought a thing into its most compact form, and when he wanted details he asked for them."

It was soon clear that before the army could function on a large scale in France, the Navy had a challenging task to perform. Neither men nor supplies could be sent to the Western Allies in significant quantity if Germany's submarines were not checked. Their monthly toll had risen above a half-million tons and was still climbing. The Navy must gird itself to protect the transatlantic life line.

Wilson took a deeper interest in naval affairs than in those of the Army. He had once cherished an ambition to go to Annapolis, and ever since boyhood he had had a sentimental love for the sea and ships. Moreover, Secretary Daniels needed the stimulus of his mind, and his

---

[8] Sailing inconspicuously on the liner *Baltic* on May 28, Pershing took a few score of officers and men to London and Paris to pioneer the way. Soon after reaching France he advised Washington that the war must be won on the Western battlefront and that this required the use of a big American army as quickly as possible. With a large pool of manpower to draw upon, the General Staff already was making plans in this direction, developing a program for training junior officers and preparing to remedy a bad deficiency in guns.

support against the ridicule of critics. The secretary had made himself unpopular with industrial interests. After giving fair warning to American steel companies that made uniform bids, he had bought armor plate in England at lower prices; and he had attempted to reserve oil deposits for development by the government. Daniels had angered conservative naval officers by attempts to democratize the service. He had opened the door at Annapolis to qualified enlisted men and he had promoted able Captain Benson over the heads of admirals to be chief of naval operations. Furthermore, he had brought sophisticated ridicule on himself by prohibiting the use of alcoholic drinks in ships and installations of the Navy and by entertaining the French mission with nothing stronger than grape juice. Franklin D. Roosevelt's opinion of his superior had sunk so low that even House, who had urged the replacement of the secretary of the navy, was shocked.

Wilson had come to love Daniels for his geniality, his humor, his family life, and his long devotion to peace and to the public welfare. In basic matters they saw eye to eye. Contrary to the admirals who had wished to flaunt naval power in the Pacific, Wilson and Daniels had conceived that the proper function of the Navy was to defend American territory. The President now impressed upon the secretary the necessity of checking the undersea depredations of the enemy. He insisted that American enterprise find a defense against submarines that would be effective even if untraditional. Complaining that the Allies had not given enough attention to this and that they had not closed the English Channel with mines, he wrote to Daniels: "Can we not set this afoot at once and save all the time possible?"

After the declaration of war Wilson gave hearty approval to a message to Admiral Sims, who already had been sent abroad to make liaison with the British Navy, asking whether it was not practicable to blockade the German coast. Franklin D. Roosevelt had drafted a plan for a barrier of mines from Scotland to Norway and across the Straits of Dover, and Wilson had interested himself in this in 1916. However, Sims found no enthusiasm for the proposal in the tradition-bound British Admiralty and had to inform his chief that it was considered "wholly impractical."

When Page cabled that submarine warfare had created the most serious situation since the threat to Paris in the first month of the war, the President lost patience. Thinking that Sims, like Ambassador Page, was unduly awed by British prestige, he cabled very confidentially on July 4 to say that he expected Sims to send such advice as the admiral would give if handling an independent navy of his own. Observing that in the face of the emergency the Admiralty was "helpless to the point of panic," he asserted: "Every plan we suggest, they reject for some reason of prudence. In my view this is not a time for prudence but for boldness even at the cost of great losses." [9]

As early as February of 1917 the President had told his Cabinet that, in his view, merchant vessels should be gathered into groups and heavily protected by convoying warships. Though he suggested to the Cabinet that ships might dodge the enemy by constantly shifting their routes and ports of call, he thought the British policy of dispersion inadequate. The convoy system was tried out, and on May 20 the first group of ships arrived safely. Toward the end of June, Admiral Sims sent a series of messages to Washington to reinforce earlier pleas for destroyers, for convoying required the use of more small naval craft than the Allies could or would assign. Naval building plans were therefore revised. Franklin D. Roosevelt urged the use of small motorboats to patrol American harbors. Many private craft were purchased and armed, 110-foot submarine-chasers were built, and keels were laid for hundreds of destroyers.

The emphasis on small vessels would delay the construction of capital ships that had been authorized, and Colonel House feared that after the war the United States might find itself without adequate protection from battleships and cruisers. He raised the question with the British government and found them not unwilling to consider a postwar guaranty that would compensate the United States in some measure for unbalancing her naval strength by building destroyers.

Wilson was not impressed. He felt that his navy was already relatively strong in capital ships, and in this he was supported by British experts. Moreover, he observed that the submarine's success required that the traditional evaluation of capital ships be altered. He preferred to preserve America's freedom of action rather than bind her by naval treaties that might be as pregnant with future trouble as secret undertakings into which the Allies had entered under the stress of war. There

---

[9] In the summer of 1917 Admiral Mayo was ordered to England to tell the Admiralty of American plans for a mine barrier. The matter was considered at an Inter-Allied Naval Conference that met at London early in September, and finally the British gave their consent. On Oct. 29, Franklin D. Roosevelt wrote a letter to remind Wilson that the mine barrier had been approved by the naval authorities at Washington and London and definite orders should be given immediately for its execution. The next day Wilson replied that he was interesting himself in the plan. It was approved by him and by the Cabinet, but the project was not completed for a year.

In pressing his plan upon the President, Roosevelt had the aid of Winston Churchill, the American novelist. The President received Churchill on July 25, 1917; and on the next day Roosevelt, who admired Churchill's grasp of naval affairs, wrote to his wife Eleanor: "The more I think over the talk with the President the more I am encouraged to think that he has begun to catch on, but then it will take lots more of the Churchill type of attack" *F.D.R.: His Personal Letters*, II, 356–57.

seemed to be no way of binding the British short of a treaty, and that would have to go to the Senate, which did not seem to be in a mood to welcome such a measure. When he visited House at Magnolia in September, and the Colonel argued his point with more persistence than he was accustomed to risk, Wilson replied that he did not choose to discuss the question further. He approved the Navy's program for turning out light antisubmarine craft in quantity.

At Magnolia he told House of a talk that he had made on August 11 to the officers of the Atlantic fleet. He had refrained from making extemporaneous speeches on policy during the early months of the war because he felt that every word must be weighed carefully when the life of a nation was at stake, and he lacked time for this. But on the deck of the battleship *Pennsylvania,* which he boarded from the *Mayflower* in the course of a weekend cruise, he spoke to the naval officers as he might once have talked to Princeton's football team. Reminding them that they were all novices in the new methods of twentieth-century war, he spoke very confidentially, urging them to "throw tradition to the winds" and criticizing the British Admiralty for its sluggishness.

To pessimistic journalists who wrote of the wonderful efficiency of German arms, he said his reply was "Rats!" The United States was to him "the prize amateur nation of the world," Germany the prize professional. He asserted:

When it comes to doing new things and doing them well, I will back the amateur against the professional every time because the professional does it out of the book and the amateur does it with his eyes open upon a new world and with a new set of circumstances. He knows so little about it that he is fool enough to try the right thing. . . . Do the thing that is audacious to the utmost point of risk and daring, because that is exactly the thing that the other side does not understand, and you will win by the audacity of method when you cannot win by circumspection and prudence.

"Somebody has got to think this war out," he declared. "Somebody has got to think out the way not only to fight the submarine, but to do something different from what we are doing. We are hunting the hornets all over the farm and letting the nest alone." He invited "the youngest and most modest youngster in the service" to tell his superiors what they ought to do if he knew what it was. He was willing to sacrifice half the navies of the United States and Britain to crush the hornets' nest, he said, because if they could do that the war would be won.

In mobilizing the armed strength of the nation in other fields than that of naval operations, the President was confronted by problems on which the precedents of history gave little guidance.

Communications had become so complex, in the age of electricity, that the safeguarding of military secrets was an operation far more difficult than in previous wars. Remembering that Lincoln had felt it necessary to suppress newspapers and imprison citizens without due process of law, Wilson hoped that he would not have to go to this extreme. He was on guard against unnecessary offenses to the civil rights of American citizens. But the attorney general ordered the seizure of some two thousand enemy aliens whose loyalty to the United States was questionable; Wilson issued, on April 28, an order for government censorship of cables and of telephone and telegraph lines; and he approved the operation of all wireless stations by the Navy for the war's duration. He gave approval to an espionage bill that was before Congress, and he made it clear that he would not permit the measure to be used to stifle criticism of himself or his official acts.[10]

The espionage bill that the House passed included a provision for censorship of the press that aroused protests from newspapermen. Tumulty warned his chief that there was growing resentment against the very idea of censorship. Nevertheless, on May 23 Wilson told conferees from the Senate, which supported his position, that the measure was "an imperative necessity," that though most journals would observe "a patriotic reticence," something more than moral obligation must be imposed on any newspaper that printed information by which the enemy might profit.

The final act, which he signed on June 15, did not give the President all the powers that he sought. It did, however, set forth a new definition of crimes against the public interest in time of war. It empowered the government to regulate the export of goods.[11] Furthermore, the act

---

[10] Daniels Diary, April 6, 1917. One of the conflicts of departmental interests that made the President's burden the heavier broke out when the seizing of wireless stations was discussed. When Daniels made the proposition that the Navy take them, Burleson said: "I serve notice that when communication becomes governmental, it must be under the Post Office Department." The President asked: "Is that a threat or a prophecy?" And Daniels put in: "It is a bluff or a boast." Daniels, *Years of War*, p. 28.

When newspaper stories reported an indiscreetly frank speech about maritime losses made by Secretary Lane, who hoped to strengthen morale by making citizens feel that they were told the whole truth, Wilson showed his displeasure. He did not want American shippers to be thrown into a panic, or war insurance rates to go up, and he became more careful than ever to withhold confidential information from the Cabinet.

When Cabinet members took petty grievances to House, he did not annoy the President with them in these critical days. Nevertheless, he noted in his diary that Wilson was holding "a tighter rein" over his Cabinet and was impatient with the taking of initiative on their part, that the President was "as usual doing things too casually" and not getting enough information from all sides before acting.

[11] The constitutionality of the Espionage Act was upheld by the Supreme Court, but only for times when "a clear and present danger" existed.

Under the new act an Exports Council was created and Vance McCormick, as its agent, undertook to organize a Bureau of Export Licenses. When neutral nations were disturbed by this move, Wilson explained it in a public statement.

A Trading-with-the-Enemy Act, signed by the President on Oct. 6, gave Wilson sufficient

made it possible for postal officials to prevent the circulation of periodicals that some citizens thought seditious and others, merely critical. More stringent censorship laws were enacted within the year, and overzealous officials and juries of panicky citizens did not always draw the line wisely between prosecution and persecution. To one of the prominent liberals who protested against acts that they thought violations of civil freedom, Wilson replied: "I think that a time of war must be regarded as wholly exceptional and that it is legitimate to regard things which would in ordinary circumstances be innocent as very dangerous to the public welfare, but the line is manifestly exceedingly hard to draw and I cannot say that I have any confidence that I know how to draw it. I can only say that a line must be drawn and that we are trying, it may be clumsily but genuinely, to draw it without fear or favor or prejudice." [12]

On April 14 George Creel, a Western journalist who had crusaded for many a liberal cause, became chairman of a Committee on Public Information that the Congress had quickly authorized. His colleagues were the secretaries of war and navy, who were cooperative and permitted him to attach trained reporters to their departments, and also the secretary of state, who resented the intrusion of the journalist and hesitated to confide secrets of state to a man whose leanings he thought "socialistic." [13] Creel's work was as difficult as it was untraditional. He had to hunt down and kill untruths as well as dispense and nourish truth. Although not always diplomatic, he carried through his mission with

---

authority so that he appointed on Oct. 12 a Board of Censorship, an Alien Property Custodian, and a War Trade Board of which McCormick was chairman and which, in cooperation with other agencies, conserved ocean tonnage, encouraged the import of war necessities, and blacklisted firms that traded with the enemy.

[12] W.W. to Max Eastman, Sept. 18, 1917.
One instance in which the President himself "drew the line" is related by Norman Thomas in his record in the Columbia Oral History Project. Asked to read an article by Thomas in the *World Tomorrow* of August, 1918, entitled "Russia, the Acid Test," Wilson saw no cause to indict the author, who had been told by Burleson that he should be in Leavenworth Prison for life and who opposed armed intervention in Russia. However, Wilson said to Nevin Sayre, who showed him the article: "Go and tell Norman Thomas [once a student of Wilson's at Princeton] that there is such a thing as the indecent exposure of private opinions in public."

[13] Finally, on June 29, Wilson had to write to Lansing to ask him to cooperate with Creel in the release of all information. When Lansing wrote to the President, weeks later, to suggest that a few representative and trustworthy newsmen be organized into a council to advise Creel, Wilson replied that this proposal, which he had heard from other sources, was based upon a complex of misunderstandings and of jealousies. "The net result of my impressions," he wrote on Sept. 4, "is that it would be safest not to call them into systematic conference. They are a difficult lot to live with. They do not agree among themselves."
Creel noted: "Lansing, a dull, small man, made himself so unpleasant at the first meeting of the Committee that I never called another." Creel felt that the "persisted antagonism" of the State Department was due to jealousies and conflicts of authority between officials of the department and agents of the CPI in foreign capitals. Professional diplomatists were unsympathetic to propagandists who addressed peoples without reference to embassies and foreign offices.

industry, thrift, and loyalty to a chief who was genuinely fond of him. Mobilizing hundreds of patriotic speakers, issuing pamphlets and news stories, posters, moving pictures, and advertisements that were given free display, the news bureau stimulated enthusiasm among the people and awakened in American minds an appreciation of the causes and stakes of the war.

Professional newsmen muttered about "censorship" and "repression" and resented what seemed to many to be an arrogant assumption of their function. They asked that the President's press conferences be resumed; but Wilson was adamant when Creel urged this upon him. He wanted only essential and productive interviews. In the war emergency, personal approaches had given way to memoranda.

Requesting secrecy on certain vital matters, Creel announced that any censorship that might result would be purely voluntary. Nevertheless, the protests of the press, fed by indiscreet remarks by Creel himself and fanned by the chronic adversaries of the Administration, led to a request by the Congress for the young man's resignation. Wilson took up the cudgels for his appointee. But he could not prevent the House from cutting the funds of Creel's committee.

Like House and Newton D. Baker, Creel had won Wilson's loyalty by understanding the processes of his brain and coordinating his own work with them. Before every interview at the White House he drew up a pithy, well-organized brief. Ten seconds after shaking hands he plunged into it, and he followed it through logically. Creel found the President's mind the most receptive of those that he met in official circles. He noted that Wilson reached conclusions too carefully to give them up quickly and that he resented assertions not supported by fact; but once his facts were shaken, he surrendered.

Though the Congress balked at appropriating all funds that Creel requested, it acted with alacrity to provide the billions needed for military and naval operations. Before war was declared, the President had approved the expenditure of nearly three billions for the Army and a half-billion for the Navy; but when a distinguished economist suggested that the government would have to spend ten billions in 1917, there were smiles of incredulity. In the three preceding years the annual federal budget had not reached a level of one billion dollars, and yet only the new income tax law had enabled Secretary McAdoo to avoid deficit financing.

The task facing the Treasury seemed to McAdoo prodigious. After frequent conferences with the President, it was decided that the government should be empowered to lend up to three billion dollars to the Allies[14]; and to finance this operation and America's own mobilization, Treasury issues of five billions of bonds and two billions of short-term certificates were to be authorized. The President had said that "the industry of this generation should pay the bills of this generation." But he felt that to raise even half the cost of war by taxation would be excessive, and perhaps destructive of "the capital energy that keeps the wheels turning." In September the Congress completed its work on a war revenue bill that increased existing taxes sharply and levied many new excises. Approximately a third of the war costs were met by current taxation.

On May 14 the secretary of the treasury announced that a bond issue of two billions would be offered to the public, to be known as the Liberty Loan of 1917. McAdoo proved himself a master salesman and enlisted ardent help from volunteers. The loan was oversubscribed by more than a billion dollars. Save for taking up $10,000 of bonds from his own small income (after America entered the war he invested in nothing but government bonds), Wilson had little to do with the First Liberty Loan. Noting the excellent publicity that was given to the drive, and the predictions of success, he explained that he would "reserve his fire" for later issues of Liberty bonds. The total subscribed in five loans, running over a period of two years, was more than twenty-one billions.

The spending of the funds in the war chest was more troublesome than the raising of them. Control of costs was a consideration that grew upon the inherently thrifty President, as the average price of metals almost doubled within three months. He knew that he would have to deal with the same interests that had fought his banking, tariff, and antitrust programs. But now he could exert a stronger compulsion than before, for patriotism had become a matter of life and death. On April 16, appealing to citizens in all walks of life, he said: "The industrial forces of the country, men and women alike, will be a great national, a great international, Service Army." Middlemen would be expected "to forego unusual profits," merchants to adopt the motto: "small profits and quick service." In a Cabinet meeting, when copper prices were

[14] McAdoo has recorded (in *Crowded Years,* p. 376) that he reached the decision to lend to the Allies with great reluctance, reminding himself of the old adage: "To make an enemy of a friend, lend him money." Nevertheless, he argued before the Ways and Means Committee that to the extent that the United States sent dollars abroad, they would be able to save the lives of their young men.

On June 28, Page sent a message marked "Greatest Urgency" that informed the President that "the British agents in the United States now have enough money to keep the exchange up for only one day more," that unless America came to the rescue Great Britain would have to abandon the gold standard. And the chancellor of the exchequer reported that unless the government of the United States could fully meet British expenses in America "the entire financial fabric" would collapse in a matter of days.

under discussion, the President advocated a uniform rate for American and Allied purchases. He would offer a price that seemed fair, and then appeal to the country if it were declined. Once, at least, he suggested that the government take over plants of manufacturers who would not accept prices that seemed to the government reasonable. Thanking Daniels for a letter about "steel" prices, he said that he hardly knew how he should spell the word. Daniels, a stubborn bargainer, suggested that before merchants grew as rich as they had in England, the government should set fair prices for fuel, metals, and similar raw materials; and the President provided funds for a study of ways to do this. There were many opinions within the official family on this vexing question, and in June an altercation over the price of coal almost resulted in the resignation of Lane; but all agreed that prices should be high enough to maintain good production and low enough to prevent profiteering. Wilson insisted, too, that whatever his own government bought for its war effort should be available to the Allies at the same prices.

By summer the Administration's purchasing policy had taken shape sufficiently so that the President could explain it to his people. Announcing that the government was about to try to set fair prices on war supplies, he asserted on July 12: "We must make the prices to the public the same as the prices to the Government. Prices mean the same thing everywhere now; they mean the efficiency or the inefficiency of the Nation, whether it is the Government that pays them or not. They mean victory or defeat."

Military necessity threatened industrial freedom, and the Administration was forced toward a conservative position. As Wilson had foreseen, many of the monopolies that were being prosecuted by the Department of Justice were essential to the supplying of the armed forces. As a result, five or six pending cases were dropped for the duration of the war. The President and the attorney general agreed that they should relax pressure temporarily on certain corporations so that there would be no excuses for not contributing unreservedly to the prosecution of the war, and the chief justice confirmed this course as "patriotic and proper."

The prophet who had preached self-discipline in politics now applied his lesson to industry. "Beyond all question," he said, "the highest and best form of efficiency is the spontaneous cooperation of a free people." He told state defense officials that he conceived that his function was not to give advice, but to coordinate activity so that there would not be lost motion. He hoped to avoid duplication of work and to keep the state bodies constructively active in bringing the war program home to the people.

By and large, the men of his Cabinet were not figures whose knowledge of industry could impress industrial magnates. In August of 1916 Wilson had assigned six of them to a Council of National Defense that was charged with the coordination of industries and resources for the national security and welfare.[15] But actually the work was done by seven civilian advisers and experts who served with them. These men concentrated not only on recommending fair prices, but on conserving resources, controlling distribution, and stabilizing labor relations. Trained and competent executives served for a dollar a year to provide sinews of war with the least possible dislocation of civil life.

Soon, however, the volunteers were working at cross-purposes and without over-all direction. Moreover, it was difficult to persuade some corporations—often those without representation at Washington—to sacrifice competitive positions to the demands of the general welfare. On July 8 the Council of National Defense established a coordinating War Industries Board of seven members; but, though this body gradually established valid principles of industrial mobilization, it lacked power to enforce its rulings.

In no field was the need for firm control more obvious than in that of food production and distribution. The ravages of war had increased the dependence of Western Europe on imports, and, realizing that their people could not fight on empty stomachs, the leaders of the Allies looked to the New World for bread. Unfortunately, at that time the United States had little surplus wheat to send. Food prices rose sharply between March and July. It was estimated that Great Britain's grain supply would last but eight weeks. Recognizing the emergency, the President conferred with Secretary Houston and the Congressional committee on agriculture and declared that they must act promptly to impose controls. "It would be difficult to express in parliamentary language," he said, "what should be done with anyone who would speculate in food products in a situation like the present."

Fortune had provided a man of great stature to meet the emergency, Herbert Clark Hoover had won the respect of the humanitarians of the world by a ministry of mercy to the people of invaded Belgium; and his work had elicited sympathy, confidence, and financial support from the American people. He had proved himself a genius in choosing able subordinates and inspiring and organizing them, and a man of vision

---

[15] The six Cabinet members were the secretaries of war, navy, interior, agriculture, commerce, and labor. Serving under the chairmanship of Newton D. Baker, these executives worked through an Advisory Commission of seven civilian volunteers. Most of the civilian volunteers were Republicans. Earlier bodies that contributed to the work of the council were the Committee on Industrial Preparedness, the Naval Consulting Board, and the National Research Council.

and reliability. Page wrote to Wilson about him: "a simple, modest, energetic little man who began his career in California and will end it in Heaven; and he doesn't want anybody's thanks."

The President was inclined to have the food supply regulated in the same way in which other commodities were—by a coordinating board without any power but that of patriotic opinion. Wilson feared that a grant of extraordinary authority to a single man might offend the secretary of agriculture and give substance to news stories picturing Hoover as a "food dictator." And so it was as the unpaid chairman of a committee of the Council of National Defense that Hoover set up an office at Washington and chose volunteers. Continuing the flow of supplies to Belgian civilians, he endeavored at the same time to devise plans for squeezing, from a country that suffered crop failures in 1916 and 1917, enough surplus food to make up serious shortages in other friendly nations of Europe.

The ingenious engineer was not content to operate merely in an advisory capacity. He pointed out to the President that in Europe division of authority had bred friction, indecision, and delay. He suggested that the tradition of American business required a single responsible executive who would use boards only for advice and adjudication. To allay doubts that were being expressed in the Congress, Hoover thought that he might be given the title of "administrator"—a term that would connote coordination and executive leadership rather than dictatorship.

On May 19 Wilson made a public announcement that was intended to dispel the misgivings that had been reflected in the press and in the Congress. Drawing a distinction between the normal activities of the Department of Agriculture and the emergency needs of the war, he set forth the specific powers that he wanted to confer on Hoover: fixing of prices; full inquiry into stocks, costs, and practices; prevention of hoarding; requisitioning and licensing; and prohibition of waste. These powers were to be exercised only as long as the war lasted, and with the voluntary cooperation of the nation's women.

The Congress was slow to confer absolute power on any individual, even on a temporary and volunteer basis. Not until June did the House take up a bill proposed by Chairman Lever of its Committee on Agriculture, providing for "a governmental control of necessaries . . . which shall be exercised and administered by the President." This was a grant of power without precedent in American history, and immediately it was assailed by legislators who feared dictatorship. But Wilson insisted that the bill was one of the most imperative of the war measures, that its object was not so much to control food as to release it from the control of speculators and profiteers, and to protect the people against extortions. When the measure came to a vote, only five representatives dared oppose it.

The Senate, however, debated the Lever Bill for more than a month. Senator Reed called it "vicious and unconstitutional," and Hoover was attacked as a man more alien than American. The measure was encumbered with provisions for a food committee of three and for a joint Congressional committee on the conduct of the war. These embarrassments were approved by a majority of the Senate.

The President protested hotly against the proposed creation of what he called "an espionage committee." Pointing out that such a body had harassed Lincoln constantly and had made his task all but impossible, Wilson asserted that the idea was not only entirely foreign to the subject matter of the food bill, but impinged on the responsibility of the Administration. Abundant means of investigation already existed, he said, and though he was ready to "cooperate" in practical ways he could interpret such a measure only as arising from lack of confidence in the President. The objectionable Senate amendments were eliminated when the bill went to a conference; and on August 10 Wilson was able to sign the Lever Act, giving himself power to control foods, fuel, fertilizer, and the machinery and equipment to produce them. The President now could name Hoover as food administrator with the specific Congressional authorization that others of his dollar-a-year men lacked. Moreover, he appointed President Harry A. Garfield of Williams College to be fuel administrator. The Food Administration proceeded to set a price on wheat, to meet what Wilson regarded as "a very serious crisis," and later on other commodities. By the time Hoover was ready to try to stabilize the price of sugar and brought his plan to the President, a relation of such understanding had been established that Wilson merely initialed the paper set before him and, when asked whether the White House shouldn't have a duplicate copy, grinned and replied: "Would that get any more sugar?" By 1918, as a result of "Hooverizing," the United States was able to export approximately three times the usual quantities of sugar, as well as of meats and breadstuffs, and the President had learned to have great confidence in Hoover's "practical judgment."

Hoover called on patriots to observe meatless days and wheatless days, preached a "gospel of the clean dinner plate," and distributed stickers that every citizen could display in his window. The White House set an example to the nation by cooperating with this program. One of the red-white-and-blue stickers appeared in a window of the executive mansion, and out-of-season delicacies disappeared from the table. A war garden was planted and, later, sheep were brought to graze on the lawn and their wool was auctioned to benefit the Red Cross. The ladies of the household knitted interminably; and in the evening the President sometimes held their yarn on his hands while they rolled it into balls. Edith Wilson got out her sewing machine and made bandages.

When Wilson went riding and saw food stickers or Red Cross emblems [16] displayed in humble homes, his heart filled with gratitude to the citizens who were responding so nobly to his leadership. "I wish I could stop and know the people who live here," he would sometimes say to his wife, "for it is from them that I draw inspiration and strength."

Not such good fortune attended American efforts to supply Western Europe with a commodity that was needed as badly as food and munitions. The Allies were crying for ships. American men and supplies would be useless without vessels to transport them.

As soon as war had broken out in Europe, Wilson had seen that the United States must put an end to its dependence on the merchant tonnage of other nations; and after long legislative battles he had induced the Congress to pass a Shipping Act in September of 1916. Under this law the President appointed a Shipping Board of five men, with William Denman of San Francisco as chairman. The board set up an Emergency Fleet Corporation, which was to operate with businesslike efficiency and without the restrictive red tape that hampers government bureaus.[17] General Goethals of Panama Canal fame was made general manager. But Goethals and Denman failed to work in harmony. Finding the general critical and "a most difficult person to deal with," Wilson accepted his resignation and thought it best to ask Denman to withdraw also.

The President reached the conclusion that in creating shipping, as in meeting other challenges thrown at him by the emergency, it was best to depend on one man and to give him full authority. Edward N. Hurley, a loyal Democrat from Chicago who had headed the Federal Trade Commission and had been drafted into Red Cross work, was asked to direct both the Shipping Board, which remained as a policy-

---

[16] Wilson and House gave much thought to the promotion of the American Red Cross under Henry P. Davison. The President issued public appeals, contributed $500 himself, conferred with ex-President Taft, who remained chairman of the Executive Committee at Wilson's request, and took an interest in the operations of the organization in Russia and other countries of Europe. Stockton Axson became secretary of the American Red Cross in December, 1917.

[17] In June of 1917 an act of Congress gave the President authority to requisition, construct, or operate ships without limits except those imposed by the availability of funds. On July 11 Wilson delegated his powers to the Emergency Fleet Corporation. On July 27, Wilson at last satisfied a long-standing desire to bring Thomas D. Jones, who had supported him steadfastly in Princeton controversies, into the government. Jones was offered a seat on the Shipping Board and accepted.

making, regulative body, and the Emergency Fleet Corporation. When Hurley protested to Tumulty that he was not a shipbuilder and hence was unqualified for the position, he was told that the President had said: "You tell Hurley that this is personal." Regarding this as an order from the Commander in Chief, the appointee acceded.

At the end of June Wilson seized the interned enemy vessels that he had not allowed his Cabinet to take before a state of war existed but that he had directed Denman, at the end of April, "to put in repair." These were made ready to go to sea under the American flag. The government also contemplated the requisitioning of American ships abuilding; and on August 3 Hurley commandeered all large hulls that were under construction. On October 12 he took over the American steel cargo vessels and passenger liners of more than twenty-five hundred deadweight tons. Eventually the Emergency Fleet Corporation succeeded in increasing available tonnage about tenfold, and laid down two ships for every one sunk by submarines.

Thus Woodrow Wilson accepted and met the challenge of twentieth-century war. In the hour of crisis he proved himself quick to perceive essentials in new conditions and wise to choose men who could aid in defining policies and could be trusted to execute them with zeal and intelligence. He initiated little, but rather selected and coordinated. When finally the war Congress adjourned, on October 6, he commended it for the accomplishments of a remarkable session.

By persuasion, by legislation, and by applying the pressure of a public opinion that had reached crusading fervor, Wilson had led the ruggedest of individuals to defer to necessity and share in the common sacrifice of the nation. Using sometimes his own power as commander in chief, sometimes the emergency powers that the Congress granted, the war President took measures that resulted in socializing many of the processes of the nation's economic and intellectual life. But he did this without losing his respect for the institutions to which he had to do violence, and with a resolve to restore them to full vigor after the madness had passed. Having noticed a reluctance on the part of government departments to relinquish any powers granted them, he had avoided giving them any extraordinary powers that it might be difficult to withdraw after the war.

Though he reserved his own strength for essentials and could encompass a vast volume of work, there was not enough energy left in him to meet all the demands of duty. However, his efforts did not seem to him excessive when he measured them by the contribution of those who put their lives in jeopardy. Occasionally he issued little homilies to his soldier boys. He kept in close touch with Raymond Fosdick, a former student at Princeton who was chairman of a committee working to sustain morale in the training camps. Often, just before dinner, he called for his wife at a Red Cross canteen and shook hands with as many boys as time permitted. On Sundays, when his church was crowded, he insisted on sharing his pew with soldiers. He signed the membership pledge of the Pocket Testament League, committing himself "to read at least one chapter in the Bible each day"; and he kept his pledge faithfully, using a Bible bound in khaki. When a White House guard mentioned the fact that his son was one of the first to be drafted, the President grasped the man's hand and said in a muffled voice: "God grant he may come back to you!"

Realizing that violence might be done to fair labor standards in the drive of industry for better production, Wilson spoke on May 15 to the labor committee of the Council of National Defense. "I have been very much alarmed," he said, "at one or two things that have happened: at the apparent inclination of the legislature of one or two of our states to set aside even temporarily the laws which have safeguarded the standards of labor and life." Promising to exert his influence against any lowering of standards that generations of Americans had brought to their present level, he went on:

. . . we are fighting for democracy in a larger sense than can be expressed in any political terms. There are many forms of democratic government and we are not fighting for any particular form; but we are fighting for the essential part of it all, namely, that we are all equally interested in our social and political life and all have a right to a voice in the Government under which we live; and that when men and women are equally admitted to those rights we have the best safeguard of justice and of peace that the world affords. . . . We are just now feeling as we have never felt before our sense of comradeship. We shall feel it even more, because we have not yet made the sacrifices that we are going to make, we have not yet felt the terrible pressure of suffering and pain of war, and we are going presently to feel it, and I have every confidence that as its pressure comes upon us our spirits will not falter, but rise and be strengthened, and that in the last we shall have a national feeling and a national unity such as never gladdened our hearts before.

And so he brought his national congregation into the shadow of the Cross and consecrated the sacrifice that each would be required to make, whether it was the laying down of a life or merely the temporary abnegation of luxury and profits and the civil rights and privileges that a democracy could not afford in time of war.

CHAPTER VII

"We Are No Longer Provincials"

As he imparted spiritual strength to his American congregation, Woodrow Wilson did not neglect the sources from which his own morale stemmed. Cruising down the Potomac with a classmate, on a Sunday in June, he suggested that they sing a hymn that had been a favorite at Princeton in undergraduate days:

> When peace like a river attendeth my way,
> When sorrows like sea billows roll;
> Whatever my lot, thou hast taught me to say
> It is well, it is well, with my soul.

He found refuge and restoration, too, in the atmosphere of love and understanding that his family and close friends had created. To his intimates he was still a charming, humorous gentleman, considerate of each one of them. The traditional family evenings persisted, though now the President often had to step out of the firelit circle to talk on the telephone or sign papers in his study. A cousin of Ellen Wilson, visiting the White House in May, found him "strong and ruddy, the embodiment of calm and cheerfulness—the kind that you can *tie* to."

No wish of his wife seemed too trifling for him to be attentive to it. When she was ill, he read to her. When she confessed that she could not ride a bicycle and therefore could not accompany him in the cycling tour of England that he dreamed of taking when released from public duty, he bought a bicycle and took her to the basement of the White House to give her lessons. When she fell off, they laughed hilariously.

He still went frequently to vaudeville and especially enjoyed tap dancing. It refreshed him, he said, to consort with people who "took on no more at their hearts than they could kick off at their heels." He liked to start a phonograph record after dinner and show how a jig step was done; and after official receptions that required hours of smirks and polite nothings, he would escape upstairs and rest the muscles of his face by exercising them as an actor might.

When the summer of 1917 scorched Washington, the President set the pace for his warring people by announcing that he would take no summer vacation. But he looked to the sea for relief. "Edith and I are on the *Mayflower*," he wrote to Jessie Sayre on July 21, "to get away from the madness (it is scarcely less) of Washington for a day or two, not to stop work (that *cannot* stop nowadays) . . . but to escape *people* and their intolerable excitements and demands." He was never sure that the next day would not bring him to the breaking point. Once he said to Creel, who noted that at times his face was gray as ashes: "I'm getting to be like Dickens's fat boy. I could go to sleep at an angle of ninety degrees."

Wilson spent two days with House at Magnolia and talked as intimately with this adviser as he had been wont to do. He had not seen House for more than three months, and newspapers were speculating again about a breach between the friends. In their conversation on the North Shore, Wilson made many confessions. When he found it hard to pick up a thread of conversation that the Colonel interrupted, he smiled plaintively and said: "You see I am getting tired. That is the way it indicates itself . . ." He spoke of the nervousness that still beset him before speaking in public. Describing himself as "a democrat like Jefferson, with aristocratic tastes," he explained that this was unfortunate because his mind led him where his tastes rebelled. He spoke more kindly of Lincoln than he had to his cousin at the war's beginning, said that though Lincoln's outlook was limited by his lack of education his judgment was equal to the situations confronting him.

A major reason for coming to see House was to discuss the short-comings of Lansing, whose resignation the President was thinking of requesting. Every time he wrote a note or released a statement, he said, the secretary of state, who seemed to consort too much with society folk and reactionaries, would dilute it by putting a conservative construction on it. To be sure, he would correct it when the President objected, but nevertheless confusion was bred and the effect of the original was almost nullified. It seemed to him that Lansing was not well, and was leading a life that would tax a strong man, dining out every night, returning home to work until two in the morning, and reaching his desk regularly at nine. Moreover, he was consuming cigarettes and black coffee immoderately. The President thought that Baker might be a more serviceable secretary of state, though he did not see how this official could be spared from the War Department.

House was not surprised, for Polk had told him only three weeks before that Wilson did not appreciate Lansing and felt that the secretary of state did not write clearly and that he had to do too much rewriting. The Colonel suggested to his friend that he have a frank talk with the secretary and persuade him to delegate news conferences to Counselor Polk. If a change must be made, Lansing might be sent to replace Page; and then, too, at the war's end they might make him a peace commissioner. Wilson agreed tentatively that the London post might be suitable, but said that if Lansing were made peace commissioner he would nullify American efforts by indiscreet utterances.

While the President concentrated on the vital business of raising men, money, and supplies for a military establishment that would make the United States secure in a war-racked world, House pursued his special interest in foreign relations. He had many misgivings about the President's allocation of time and energy. Unable to persuade Wilson to act on more than one thing at a time, the Colonel thought him too dependent on his own individual efforts. It seemed as if diplomatic relations with South America, Japan, and Europe were being allowed to take care of themselves.

Actually, Wilson and Lansing were paying close attention to affairs in Latin America and the Far East and, in many instances, to good effect.

Immediately after Ambassador Bernstorff had been given his passports, the President ordered Lansing, contrary to that cautious official's inclination,[1] to send identical notes to the other American republics, inviting them to follow the course of the United States. Eight declared war on Germany and six broke relations. Yet reports coming to the State Department indicated that Germans were intriguing in Latin America along the lines suggested in the Zimmermann telegram.

In the early months of 1917 Mexico, the Latin-American nation that had been most troublesome, was reaching political equilibrium. The United States withdrew her troops, a Mexican election chose a new Congress and elected Carranza to the presidency, and Washington granted recognition. To a man who suggested that a shortage of petroleum for military purposes might be relieved by seizing the Tampico oil fields, Wilson replied: "You say this oil in Mexico is necessary for us. When they invaded Belgium, the Germans said it was 'necessary' to get to France. Gentlemen," he concluded, "you will have to fight the war with what oil you have."[2]

The importance of the Panama Canal in time of war, and rumors of

[1] Wilson and Lansing differed not only in general policy but in a specific Latin-American crisis in February of 1917. Federico A. Tinoco, a military man, seized power in Costa Rica by a personal coup that lacked popular support. Wilson told Lansing that the case was similar to that of Huerta, that he would "never recognize Tinoco," and that he intended to put a stop to revolutions of this sort in Latin-American countries.

Lansing obeyed orders, but with reservations in his own mind. He felt that if the people of Costa Rica accepted the man who had forced himself upon them, it was not "proper" for the United States to interfere.

[2] Wilson's sensitivity to the neutral rights for which he himself had until recently been contending led him to object on July 28 to a recommendation that no licenses be issued by the Exports Council for the shipment of foodstuff to Denmark. He had stood up for the rights

German plotting in that area and in Cuba, made it seem necessary for
the United States to take emergency action. John Foster Dulles was sent
to Panama, and warships and Marines to Cuba, where violence broke
out in protest against a fraudulent presidential election. These republics
were only one day later than the United States in declaring war on
Germany. The proximity of Colombia to the canal made the friendship
of this nation vital, and Wilson expressed to the Senate the hope that
they might be moved to ratify the treaty that he had been at pains to
negotiate. But there was no action on this important measure until the
war was over, and Theodore Roosevelt dead.

No better success attended the efforts of Wilson and Lansing to
clarify diplomatic relations with the chief countries of the Far East. For
the better part of two decades, Americans had spasmodically challenged
Japanese imperialism in China; and their distrust had increased when
Japan declared war on Germany. Wilson, assured by both Britain and
Japan that the integrity of China would be respected, accepted the assurances publicly; and the Japanese promises, given orally to the American ambassador, were set down in a note to Tokyo so that the interest
of the United States in their fulfillment would be thoroughly understood.

However, in January of 1915 Japan secretly presented twenty-one demands to China that menaced American policy for that nation and
threatened to reduce the country to vassalage. Though the most offensive of the demands was withdrawn as a result of protests from London
and Washington, the substance of them had been forced upon the weak
Chinese government. The United States had refused to recognize the
conditions imposed, and reserved its right to discuss the matter in the
future. But Japan saw no moral obloquy in playing an imperialistic
game in which European rivals had taken the lead.

Wilson had regarded the course of Japan with anxiety but had seen
no way in which he could intervene effectively without stirring a hostility in that nation that would be directed against China immediately.

Standing upon the traditional American policy of an "open door" in
China for all nations, Wilson took a pastoral view of that distraught
country. At a meeting of the Potomac Presbytery, in April of 1915, he
pictured China as "cried awake by the voice of Christ," and a month
later he spoke to newsmen of his joy in China's adoption of "a form of

---

of neutrals in the past, and he was not going to forbid them to trade with Germany. On
Nov. 13, though willing to accept a policy of supplying Norway with only those goods
in which she was deficient, he would not insist that that nation cut off all exporting to
Germany. Such a policy, he pointed out, would be inconsistent with the rights on which the
United States always had insisted.

government which seems to us the best vehicle of progress, the republican." Allowing his proselyting impulse to leap ahead of actuality, he dared to hope that China might share with the United States "a common conception of liberty for the progress of mankind." International misunderstanding, he felt, was often the result of lack of personal contact. He put faith in the Christian missions to which his father's parishioners had sent their mites even during the dark days of the Civil War. When he bade farewell to an envoy to Siam, his last words were: "Remember to be good to my missionaries." [3]

Whether or not China made war on Germany was of secondary importance to an American government that was chiefly interested in the long-range stability of the Chinese people. However, reactionaries in China, moved by internal politics, the diplomacy of the Allies, and urging from Minister Reinsch that exceeded Washington's intentions, declared war on Germany and Austria on August 14, 1917. On the 21st the President, who was kept posted constantly by Lansing, wrote to a cousin who was a missionary in China: "You may be sure we are watching developments in China, so well as we can from this distance, with the greatest solicitude. I hope with all my heart that in the providence of God some permanent and beneficent result may be worked out."

Britain and France, however, paid no more than lip service to Wilson's aspirations for the Chinese people. Indeed, they secretly negotiated deals with Japan whereby her active participation in the war against German submarines was encouraged by recognition of her claims to Shantung and certain Pacific islands. The prospect for a free, unified China was further clouded by the vulnerability of Chinese minds to foreign propaganda as well as by the venality of self-seeking war lords.

Washington's relations with Toyko already were strained as a result of the restrictions that the Pacific states had imposed on Orientals in 1913. As they deferred to the peculiarities of American law in this matter, the Japanese government pressed vigorously for some indication of American approval of the expansionist policy that overpopulation had forced upon the country. Apprehensive that the encroachment on Shantung that had begun so promisingly for them in 1915 might be checked, and fearful that the military force abuilding in the United States might be used in the Far East, Tokyo sent a special ambassador to Washington to try to secure clarification of a policy that the Japanese mind found difficult to understand. Viscount Ishii arrived at the American capital in the summer of 1917.

Wilson did not reciprocate the Japanese fear of a martial foray across

[3] Letter, F. C. MacDonald to the writer, June 19, 1950.

the vast distance of the Pacific Ocean, though he once admitted, confidentially, that the possibility of an attack on the Philippines "presented a possibility which could not be overlooked." Welcoming Ishii's mission cordially, he made it clear to his guest that the United States regretted the spheres of foreign influence that threatened the open door in China.

The task of concluding an understanding was delegated to the secretary of state. In thirteen conversations that extended over several weeks, Lansing and Ishii thoroughly canvassed, first, the war efforts of their nations, and then their policies vis-à-vis China. Finally they outlined, in identical notes exchanged on November 2, what became known as the Lansing-Ishii Agreement.

Wilson followed each step of the negotiations carefully and conferred at least twice with Ishii. He was gratified by Japan's assent to an agreement that declared not only that she herself had no purpose to infringe in any way upon the integrity of China or the rights of other foreigners in China, but also that she was opposed to infringement by other powers. There is no indication that Wilson was greatly disturbed by the fact that the protocol in which this pledge was stated had to be kept secret, in deference to Japanese opinion. The principle of the open door seemed to be completely upheld and Japan's ambition to develop a "Monroe Doctrine" for the Far East denied.

However, the Lansing-Ishii Agreement proved to be a formula that did not represent a true meeting of minds. The studied ambiguity of the document made it susceptible to many interpretations. It was publicized by Japanese spokesmen in a way that suggested to Chinese that Tokyo had won a great diplomatic victory at their expense and that traditional American policy had been reversed. The Chinese Foreign Office, indignant that, after they had joined the United States in the war, their territory should be considered a "special interest" of Japan, asked embarrassing questions.[4] Disturbed by the Chinese reaction, Wilson wrote on his own typewriter to Lansing, on November 9: "There has not only been no change of policy but there has been a distinct gain for China, of course, and I hope that you will be kind enough to send Reinsch such a message as will serve to put the whole thing in the right light at Peking and throughout China."[5]

[4] The ink was hardly dry on the Lansing-Ishii Agreement before Japanese officials in Asia were claiming "paramount interests," instead of the "special interests" agreed upon. In a note written to Lansing on July 3, Wilson had made it explicit that "Japan's *political* influence over China" was "the thing we have *not* assented to in the sense she evidently has in mind."

[5] Actually, two days before, Lansing had sent to Reinsch a statement for the Chinese Foreign Office, pointing out that the Lansing-Ishii Agreement introduced "a principle of non-interference with the sovereignty and territorial integrity of China, which, generally applied, is essential to perpetual international peace, as has been so clearly declared by President Wilson."

China's need for credit became desperate during 1917, as American bankers continued to

At the same time the President made efforts to improve relations with Japan. On October 19 he received a trade commission that was introduced to him by Ambassador Sato; and he sent one of his old Princeton boys, Roland Morris, as envoy to Tokyo. Saying an affectionate farewell to Morris, he cautioned him against falling into Page's irritating habit of writing notes that were too discursive. Soon Morris was giving his chief valuable summaries of the opinion of the Japanese people and press. When the President was told that it was remarkable that an untrained diplomat could do so well, he retorted: "Untrained? Why, I trained him myself."

The services of Colonel House were not solicited in 1917 in the delicate negotiations with Latin America and Japan. But Wilson considered that Europe, the third area that House felt was being allowed "to take care of itself," was a province in which the Colonel could operate most effectively. He agreed with House that their essential responsibilities were coordination of war effort with the Western Allies and leadership in a peace offensive that would erode enemy morale and appeal to the basic political impulses of the peoples of the world.

House insisted that the first duty was the more urgent in the spring of 1917. Most vital, in his view, was better rapport with London. By virtue of the personal relationships that he had cultivated the Colonel was prepared to guard and strengthen the diplomatic life lines that spanned the Atlantic. Despairing of any constructive action toward peace on the part of Lloyd George's coalition cabinet, House found in Sir William Wiseman a kindred spirit who, invalided from the front and attached to the Washington embassy as chief of intelligence, worked faithfully to seek better cooperation between Washington and London, and an early peace that would give immunity from militarism.[6]

---

hesitate to accept risks without guarantees by the State Department, and all the resources of large European powers were devoted to the needs of war. Britain and France, fearing that Japanese capital might secure monopolies in China, urged Wilson to set aside his objections to the sort of consortium loan on which he had frowned in 1913. On Nov. 9, 1917, the President permitted Lansing to announce that the government was thinking of forming a new four-power consortium. On July 4, 1918, the President approved a plan for a China consortium that, in his view, would bring no monopoly or commitment that might embarrass the government. Wilson had at last come to the view that bankers might be enlisted as agents of diplomacy. After nearly three years of negotiations as to shares and spheres of operations, the participating powers finally signed a new consortium agreement in 1920. See Whitney Griswold, *Far Eastern Policy of the United States*, pp. 208 ff.

[6] Thinking Wiseman a reliable interpreter of British opinion, a resourceful diplomat, and a valuable liaison man, House arranged to have him introduced to the President in a way that would not arouse the jealousy of diplomatic functionaries. The meeting was brought about at a reception in the Pan American Building, late in the evening of June 26. Wilson found the young man so interesting that he talked with him until his entourage took him away, and Wiseman was invited to dine at the White House with the family. The President found him a sympathetic listener, more eager to get Wilson's ideas than to advance his own.

In the autumn of 1917 Wiseman occupied an apartment under that of Colonel House in

The Colonel and his British friends found the President at first fearful to offend a current of American thought that suspected that the United States had been lured into the war to fight the battles of England and France—a view as biased as that of British patriots who insisted that they were doing America's fighting for her. Wishing to appear independent, Wilson used the phrase "associated power" to indicate the position of his country and suggested that his people be led to think that the coordinating commissions that came from Europe in the spring of 1917 were merely symbols of unity. The President could not allow it to be thought that the United States was committed to fight for the glory of foreign empires; nor, while war raged, could he appear to differ with England and France.

Private talks of the realities of peacemaking went on in the friendly atmosphere that House was adept at creating. The President saw no harm in informal discussion of war aims with Balfour. He himself lunched with the distinguished Briton, with the secretary of state present, but felt that their talk was unsatisfactory—"Lansing has a wooden mind," he told House afterwards, "and continually blocked what I was trying to convey." He asked the Colonel to bring Balfour to a "family dinner," and first to sound out their guest about secret treaties in which Britain and France were said to have won allies by promising territorial rewards at the peace table. These agreements had been negotiated under the compulsion of necessity; and their spirit—distateful to Sir Edward Grey and other British Liberals—was inconsistent with the war aims that the Allies professed in public and contradictory to Wilson's ideals of peacemaking.

On April 30, after House had talked with Balfour and had ventured the opinion that the diplomacy represented by the secret treaties was "all bad," the two men came to the White House. The President was at his genial best. He had been resting most of the afternoon and seemed keyed up for the occasion. He talked of the value of a liberal education, protested against the binding of men's minds by material fact, and pleaded for flights into spiritual realms.

When they turned to business, House tried to guide the talk so that it would cover the points that he had discussed previously with each of

New York and kept in touch with the Foreign Office by special code. Through him and House, the President could communicate with the foreign secretary more swiftly and more secretly than through formal diplomatic channels.

On June 23, Wiseman visited House at Magnolia and they planned a trip to London on the part of Wiseman, so that he might talk with Lloyd George to make sure that no important Anglo-American negotiations would be attempted except through the House-Wiseman channel. By Aug. 10 the Colonel was able to advise Wilson that word had come from Wiseman, at London, that a plan had been worked out with the British government whereby the President would be kept "fully informed about what is going on in the Allied countries and armies."

the statesmen. The Colonel had told the President of the Treaty of London, under which Italy's ambitions in the Adriatic region would be satisfied and had urged both Wilson and Balfour to refrain from discussion of war aims for fear that they might provoke controversies that would obscure the prime necessity—the defeat of German military power. Nevertheless, House asked Balfour about a plan that they had formed to have copies of certain secret treaties sent to Wilson, and the foreign secretary indicated that this would be done.[7] After the conference Balfour, a philosopher, praised the President's idealism and political sagacity; and Wilson rejoiced in his visitor's responsiveness to his own ideas of a peace settlement. Quizzed by Senator Knox about his talks with Balfour, the President said that it had been thought best to make no definite commitments to the British statesman. "But of course he knew that we should never go back on them," he added, "and that binds us in honor."

Nevertheless, the skein of Anglo-American relations often became tangled in the critical year of 1917. For one thing, the British had crushed the Sinn Fein movement for Irish independence in 1916 and had executed the leaders, and there were fiery denunciations by Irish-Americans and protests on the floor of the United States Senate. Wilson followed a policy of avoiding action that would endanger Anglo-American war effort, while at the same time intimating that public opinion in the United States would never be satisfied until the aspirations of Irish nationalists were realized to some degree.

Another strain was imposed on transatlantic relations when Lloyd George decided to send his overimportunate backer, Lord Northcliffe, on a special diplomatic mission to Washington. Because Ambassador Spring Rice deemed this dynamic journalist "a bounder" and because Wilson thought both the idea of another mission and the choice of agent "most unusual," House and Wiseman considered it inadvisable for Northcliffe to come. But when he arrived they made the best of the situation.

With inexhaustible energy, Northcliffe worked to stimulate America's production of war supplies; and he reported directly to the British

[7] Copies of certain secret pacts were sent to the President by Balfour, with a confidential statement about them that the foreign secretary had made to the Imperial War Council. *See* E. L. Woodward and Rohan Butler (eds.), *Documents on British Foreign Policy*, 1st Series, V (1919), 1015–17. No indication has been found that Wilson answered Balfour's covering letter or referred to the texts at this time. It is probable that, agreeing with House's view that the treaties were a dangerous source of potential friction and feeling powerless to do anything about them until the war was over, he thought it of no use to spend any of his precious time in studying them.

"I was absolutely open in 1917 with President Wilson about the secret treaties," Balfour wrote to House on July 17, 1922. *See* House Papers, IV, 364–65. Certain omissions in the papers sent to the President by Balfour, notably the agreements concluded with Japan in February of 1917 regarding Shantung and the Pacific Islands, are noted in Baker, VII, 74–75.

War Cabinet on the importance of the United States to the success of Allied arms. Pointing out that Sir William Wiseman was the only Englishman who could talk intimately with Wilson and House at all times, Northcliffe cabled thus to Winston Churchill: "The Administration is entirely run by these two men. Wilson's power is absolute and House is a wise assistant. Both are pro-English." On June 16 the President received the visitor, and the next day he was informed by House that he had "charmed Northcliffe."

By September the British Cabinet had been so well advised by its experts in the United States that it realized that America's heart was in the war and that she must be treated as the most important ally, and frankly and fully informed about everything. However, political hazards that menaced the flow of credit to the Allies had not yet been entirely overcome. McAdoo was apprehensive, not only that the war aims of the Allies would be questioned by legislators who held the strings of the public purse, but that Bryan's faction would object to the assumption by the government of loans that private bankers had made to the Allies before the United States entered the war. Responsible to American taxpayers, the secretary of the treasury wished to be certain that their money was expended wisely by those to whom it was advanced; and he proposed to the Cabinet that inter-Allied bodies be created at Washington and in Europe to coordinate the requisitions of the various armies and navies and to rule on matters of priority.

While tactfully refraining from making any one Cabinet officer so privy to his counsel that the others might take offense,[8] Wilson gave his son-in-law his head in so far as he could do so without interfering with the functions of other departments. When the chief Allied powers finally consented, in August, to the creation of a purchasing commission at Washington, McAdoo urged that Bernard M. Baruch be made the chairman of the body, and the President tried to bring this about. Secretary Baker objected because people said that Baruch was a Wall Street speculator. Moreover, House was opposed. Nevertheless, the President appointed Baruch.

---

[8] It seemed to McAdoo that the President was too slow to make executive decisions on matters such as this, and remiss in facing differences of opinion and settling them. He confessed to Colonel House, early in May, that the pace at which he was driving himself had affected his heart, and he never felt so much "the need of a complete deflection of thought." He had not been in the White House for six months except at large functions, he said, and he would resign if the President did not remove restrictions with which he felt himself hedged in. On the other hand, to fellow members of the Cabinet he seemed more than ever a man ambitious to extend his power and dominion.

McAdoo thought it necessary for himself to see all State Department dispatches, be represented on the embargo board, and control the shipping board and the purchase and the transport of supplies, so that he would know how to apportion loans to the Allies. "If given all this," House wrote in his diary on Aug. 7, "he would become arbiter of both the United States and Europe."

This upstanding, forthright Southerner had been active in the 1916 election campaign, and Wilson had invited him to come with his parents to tea at Shadow Lawn. The Wilsons were fond of old Dr. Simon, who had served as a surgeon in the Civil War, and of his wife Miss Belle; and they observed with approval that young Bernard's world revolved around these revered elders. As the nation was drawn into war, the man's keen, purposeful mind seemed hungry for jobs to be done efficiently. He did not presume to offer unsolicited advice. Wilson called him "Dr. Facts" and learned to admire his reluctance to seek power or profit in public service and his comprehensive grasp of the problems of resources and production. At the same time Baruch's respect for the President's qualities of leadership and statesmanship grew into veneration.

Though Wilson acted to coordinate Allied purchasing at Washington, he did not appoint an American delegate when representatives of the Allies met at Paris and drafted a plan for cooperation. Fearing that it might be inferred that the United States was discussing "ultimate purposes" and peace terms with imperialists, he suggested that American participation should be deferred until she had a larger force in Europe and took over a portion of the battle front.

During the summer credits were sustained mainly by the personal intervention of Colonel House, who simultaneously urged Washington to save the Allies from bankruptcy and London and Paris to coordinate their purchasing. Moreover, with Wilson's approval, Wiseman was sent to London to insist on the creation of an inter-Allied council and also to urge that a financial expert of high official rank be sent to Washington. Northcliffe reported to Viscount Reading, lord chief justice, that American pride demanded that someone of his eminence come as a special envoy. And House added his word in a cable to the Foreign Office, explaining: "What is needed is someone who can dominate the situation and who would have the entire confidence of the President."

Reading presented himself at the White House on September 20. This distinguished envoy brought to the President a long confidential letter from Lloyd George. Suggesting that the attacks of the Allies should be directed at the associates of Germany, who seemed weak both politically and militarily, the prime minister's note advised Wilson that soon it would be necessary to make far-reaching decisions that might be vital. He urged that at future conferences of the Allies the United States contribute "independent minds, bringing fresh views, unbiased by previous methods and previous opinions." Moreover, the Foreign Office wrote, in response to an inquiry from Wilson as to what was expected from the United States in the way of embargoing shipments to neutrals, that the difficulties arising in the policy of blockade could be resolved only by a conference at London in which American representatives would take part.

Finally, on October 9, Wilson summoned House to Washington to discuss the vital question of coordination of war effort. He was at first inclined to put the Colonel in charge of this matter and to appoint an American commission to function in Europe. Talking to his Cabinet on October 12, he revealed his concept of America's role in the postwar world. He felt that she would be so wealthy that by her power to give or withhold credit she could impose her views upon Europe for the common welfare and the preservation of peace.

House was advising that Lloyd George's methods and purposes, unlike those of Grey and Balfour, were not always the highest. "I find myself not altogether trusting Lloyd George's plan . . ." the Colonel wrote to Wilson on September 18. "The English naturally want the road to Egypt blocked, and Lloyd George is not above using us to further this plan." When Wiseman suggested that there was danger of shifting the center of gravity of the war from Washington to London or Paris, the President drew back. Wilson wished to guard his policy of independence of action and to keep a firm hand on the situation.[9] Therefore, instead of taking the risk of putting an American commission at the disposal of the Allies for the duration of the war, he decided to send House abroad with representatives of the American war services who could discuss their technical problems in conferences with their opposite numbers in England and France. He felt that such a delicate task could be entrusted to no diplomat but the Colonel. He was confident that this friend would not betray him and would keep free from entanglements and antagonisms. Moreover, he knew that the sending of House would please Lloyd George.

After a talk with Reading, the Colonel accepted the charge. Soon the ruling elder, drawn out from backstage and given a mission more vital than any that he had undertaken before, was showing the same jealousy of responsibility that he had marked in Wilson and McAdoo and other strong executives. "I am glad I am going alone," he wrote in his diary

[9] "He told me distinctly," House recorded in his diary on Oct. 13, "that he preferred everything to go to him rather than to the State Department, and he would refer to the State Department what he thought necessary. Later I got him to agree, since I am going to Europe, for Mezes to keep in touch with Lansing, but the President added, 'and also with me.' I shall arrange this and shall endeavor to give Lansing a larger and larger part." (Page wrote in his diary, on Nov. 24: "In a very important sense, there is no State Department.")

Immediately after the country went to war, the President had all letters from House and from the State, War, and Navy Departments go to him unopened. Brahany Diary, April 14, 1917. On Sept. 3, House wrote in his diary that Wilson was "something of an autocrat by nature" and desired no interference from commissions going or coming. Charles Swem noted that, under war conditions, the Chief seemed obsessed by the need for secrecy.

on October 19, "for I can do better work when the responsibility is entirely on my shoulders."

The House mission arrived in Europe at the moment when the Italian front had been pierced, the Bolsheviki were seizing power by violence, and the French Cabinet was facing dissolution. Moreover, the position of the British coalition government was shaken by insistent demands for what a respected elder statesman, Lord Lansdowne, called a "covenanted peace" and by protests against subordinating British military policy to an over-all grand strategy. The Colonel applied his peculiar talents to the vital issue of unity. After he had been at London for four days he reported to Wilson that the lack of organization was driving him "around in circles," but that the Foreign Office offered him access to any of their confidential papers that he wished to see. On November 15 he telegraphed that the military situation was critical.

When the Italian front broke and French reserves were obliged to walk over the Alps to reinforce their ally, the lack of coordinated planning became scandalous. Lloyd George, whose war cabinet had demonstrated the value of unified direction at the summit, hastened to Rapallo to press for a unifying command of all Allied armies. A Supreme War Council was formed, to act politically through monthly conference of the chiefs of state at Versailles and militarily through a permanent professional staff.

Lloyd George, back at London, explained his views to House and asked that the United States send a representative. That very night the Colonel, who felt that the prime minister was indiscreet in making such a positive proposal without consulting Washington, cabled to the President thus: "France, England and Italy have agreed to form a Supreme War Council and believe that we should be represented in it because of the moral effect that it will have here . . . I would advise not having a representative on the civil end . . . but would strongly urge having General Bliss on the military end . . . It is important that an immediate decision be made as to this . . ."

Wilson replied promptly and vigorously. He wanted House to take "the whip hand." His message directed: "Please take the position that we not only accede to the plan for a single war council but insist on it, but I think it does not go far enough . . . The war council will, I assume, eventually take the place of such conferences as you went over to take part in and I hope that you will consider remaining to take part in at any rate the first deliberations and formulations of plans. Baker and I are agreed that Bliss should be our military member. I am happy the conference is to be postponed until the recalcitrant parliaments have settled to their senses . . ."

Wilson's decisive support saved Lloyd George's government and the Supreme War Council. On November 20 opposition in Parliament was finally overcome, and on that day and the next House had frank conversations on war aims with Lloyd George, Reading, and Balfour. Going on to Paris on the 22nd, House's mission engaged in informal talks with Georges Clemenceau, who had just formed a government in which he was minister of war as well as premier and who was summoning French resistance to a heroic pitch. With General Pétain they revised Lloyd George's plan, so that the Supreme War Council would have an executive officer who would be in effect a commander in chief. However, when the prime minister arrived on the scene he made it clear that because of the prevailing feeling in England he would have to go back to London if his plan was not accepted as he had conceived it. House and Clemenceau were persuaded that they must give up their scheme for military efficiency; and when the council met at Versailles on December 1, under the presidency of Clemenceau, it took on the aspect of an academic body for the study of vital military problems, rather than that of an executive agency.

Though the new council had a strong military committee on which General Bliss served effectively—albeit handicapped by lack of liaison with the State Department—House was disappointed and thought that the armies of the enemy had superior organization.[10] He was distressed, too, because the conference had not provided intelligent diplomatic leadership at a moment when the morale of the Allies was dangerously low. It had failed to frame a "world-appealing policy" that would satisfy liberals and radicals throughout Europe. House felt that faith was not being kept with those who were fighting and dying. Nevertheless, when compelled to address the second plenary session, on December 3, he confined his talk to harmless amenities. He would wait until he returned to Washington, he resolved, and then would urge the President to say what should be said about war aims.

In mid-December House came home and gave an account of his mission, and he spoke also of his impatience with the unregenerate ideology of the Allies.

---

[10] House used the fortnight at Paris to good purpose, sitting with Clemenceau, Bliss, and Pétain to determine how many American soldiers should go to France, and when, and how, and the possibility of brigading them with French troops for training. He sensed the grandeur of Clemenceau—the "Tiger of France"—and Pétain's lack of vision; and he impressed upon Pershing the necessity of making good, so that people would not say that the President should have sent Roosevelt and Wood. The United States would be judged for a century or more by the conduct of its army in France, the Colonel said. House thought that the progress made toward coordinating economic resources very great. "Heretofore," he wrote at Paris, "everything has been going pretty much at sixes and sevens. From now there will be less duplication of effort . . . This conference may therefore well be considered the turning point in the war even though the fortunes of the Allies have never seemed so low as now."

CHAPTER VIII

THE WAR OF IDEAS AND WORDS

IN DECEMBER OF 1917—the month in which Colonel House returned to Washington to report on his mission to coordinate American policy with that of the Allies—two of the enemies of Germany stopped fighting. On the 3rd leaders of the Russian Bolsheviki met German representatives at Brest-Litovsk to discuss peace, and twelve days later an armistice was signed. On the 6th Rumania agreed to a truce.

The Western Allies, stunned by the collapse of Russian resistance, could conceive of no way of establishing relations with the new rulers at Petrograd, who were denouncing them as imperialistic robbers and proclaiming a strange code of personal and political morality. In this crisis Woodrow Wilson, driven by the commitment that he had made to his people to win the war, ventured to act to prevent a complete collapse of resistance to Germany on the Eastern front.

American policy toward Russia after the Czar's downfall had been based on the unwarranted faith that Ambassador Francis had put in the provisional government and had maintained with undiplomatic partisanship. In recognizing the new regime, Wilson had felt that the only practical course was to cultivate relations with the faction that was amicably disposed toward the United States and, for the present at least, in the seat of power. He had been encouraged when Russia's leaders recognized the independence of Poland and suggested the repudiation of aggressive war aims. In May the provisional government had renounced the idea of making a separate peace and had sent a commission to Washington. The President expressed "the greatest sympathy" with the revolution and welcomed the new ambassador, Boris A. Bakhmeteff, with the remark that now the United States had a partner in the fight for democracy. Wilson had consented to send a commission under Elihu Root to Russia,[1] and had written a message of "friendship of the

---

[1] Fearing that Root, a New York lawyer, would be regarded with suspicion by the revolutionaries in Russia, Wilson appointed a representative of labor and a moderate Socialist to the commission. He was so unsure of the wisdom of the venture that when a friend of labor declined to join it, he treated the man with great respect. The purpose of the mission, he informed Ambassador Francis, was to show sympathy for the "adherence of Russia to the principle of democracy" and to consider "the best ways and means to bring about effective cooperation between the two governments in the prosecution of the war."

When the mission returned, in August, Wilson paid little attention to Root's report, which events of the subsequent months showed to be illusory.

American People for the People of Russia." The President warned the Russians against professions of liberality and justice on the part of the ruling classes of Germany.

While asserting the purity of American motives, Wilson refrained from opposing the lust for the Bosporus that kept Russian patriots fighting. Credits totaling $325,000,000 were extended to the provisional government at low interest; and Root bluntly advanced the formula "no fight, no loans." Commissions of Red Cross workers and railway engineers were sent. At Wilson's insistence, a secret Anglo-American effort was organized to counter German propaganda in Russia. But in the strange assortment of American adventurers who pioneered on the new social-political frontier, Wilson saw risks of confusion and frustration.[2] The ambassador found himself without power to regulate the movements of his compatriots or to coordinate their work with official policy. Wilson and House talked so sympathetically with some of them before their departure from America that they considered themselves the personal agents of the President. Observing only a small segment of Russia, often without benefit of knowledge of the language, these men exuded the good will that Americans bore toward "the Russian people"; but some failed to sense that the Russians, by and large, conceived of the war as a creation of czardom and were as weary of battle as of despotism. Though a sort of democracy was practiced locally, there was no prevailing concept of disciplined freedom on which a national republic could be built. In fact a bitter contest for political power was raging among revolutionary factions. Of these actualities Wilson drew from the Americans in Russia no deeper understanding than came from his bemused ambassador. Fortunately House was able to supply somewhat more reliable reports from British agents at Petrograd.

Liberal sentiment among democratic peoples everywhere had been quickened by the Russian Revolution. In Britain the influential Union of Democratic Control, which even before the downfall of the Czar had enthusiastically endorsed Wilson's demand for statements of peace terms, now urged him to persuade the belligerents to renounce their aggressive war aims. Europeans who were familiar with the progressive achievement of the American prophet in his own country had begun to look to him to free the Old World, not only from political despotism, but even from the sort of economic aggression that had provoked war.

---

[2] By November, Wilson was so bothered by disorganized and unofficial American efforts in Russia that he wrote to Charles Edward Russell, the Socialist member of Root's mission: ". . . all sorts of work in Russia now is rendered extremely difficult because no one channel connects with any other, apparently."

For a colorful and compassionate account of Americans in Russia in 1917, *see* George F. Kennan, *Russia Leaves the War*, pp. 32 ff.

Tribunes of the people in many lands were trying to organize an international gathering of laborites and socialists, to be held at Stockholm; and the Kaiser's government was depending on the German delegates to that conference to fight the Fatherland's ideological battle.[3]

In his concentration on the prime necessity of overthrowing the Junkers, Wilson could not ignore the challenges to the war aims of the Allies that were rising from the forces of unrest all through Europe. For weeks he hesitated, fearing to weaken the military effort of the Allies and contradict policies announced by their statesmen. But when House informed him that sincere liberals, both in England and in Russia, wanted him to define the aims of the Allies, the President decided to speak out.

The Flag Day celebration at the Washington Monument was the occasion chosen for his pronouncement. A downpour of rain and hail had driven most of the crowd to seek shelter; but thousands remained under dripping umbrellas to hear an impassioned challenge to battle for the right as God gave their leader to see the right.

The prophet singled out the enemy and laid a curse upon him. "The war was begun by the military masters of Germany, who proved also to be the masters of Austria-Hungary," he said. Hurling charge after charge against the Kaiser's government, he repeated the assertion that he had made in his war speech of April 2: that Americans were not the enemies of the German people, who were themselves "in the grip of the same sinister power that has now at last stretched its ugly talons out and drawn blood" from the United States. In words reminiscent of his attacks on the bosses of New Jersey, he called the hosts of the Lord to the fray. "The military masters under whom Germany is bleeding see very clearly to what point Fate has brought them. If they fall back or are forced back an inch, their power both abroad and at home will fall to pieces like a house of cards . . . deep fear has entered their hearts." Their only hope, he asserted, was to secure an immediate peace with immense advantages still in their hands. They were trying to deceive and make use of liberal Germans whom formerly they despised. "Let

[3] Warned by Lansing that a gathering of Socialists near to Petrograd might undermine the mission of conservative Elihu Root, Wilson agreed that the Stockholm conference was "likely to make a deal of mischief, especially in connection with affairs in Russia," and the State Department ruled against the issue of passports to American delegates who made what the President considered "almost treasonable utterances."

The decision against issuing passports to Stockholm was made in spite of the intention of the Socialist minority in the French Chamber to send a representative and Balfour's view that it was inadvisable to try to keep British Socialists away from the conference. Considerations influencing the American decision, which was made orally by Wilson, are suggested in a footnote on page 84 of Baker, VII.

The conference convened on Sept. 5–7, 1917, and issued a manifesto of which the last lines were: "Long live the international mass struggle against the war! Long live the Socialist peace!"

them once succeed," he warned, "and these men, now their tools, will be ground to powder beneath the weight of the great military empire they will have set up; the revolutionists in Russia will be cut off from all succor or cooperation in Western Europe and a counterrevolution fostered and supported; Germany herself will lose her chance of freedom; and all Europe will arm for the next, the final struggle."

Despite this eloquent denunciation of the enemy, popular suspicion of the war aims of the Allies persisted. The German chancellor alleged to newsmen, on July 29, that Western powers were greedy for conquest and had concluded imperialistic secret treaties.

Wilson knew that his people felt themselves to be arbitrators who wished to stand apart from the Allies, that they were determined to crush Prussian autocracy, and longed to arrive at a peace settlement that would make future wars impossible. He wished to know what his allies meant by "security against German aggression," an aim with which he sympathized in general. He hoped that House would help him to understand the feelings that moved all European nations—friends, enemies, and neutrals—so that he might shape his policies wisely and pitch his public utterances in harmonious tones. Wilson wanted the Colonel to take steps to prepare the American case for a peace conference "with full knowledge of the position of all the litigants." Discussing the idea with Lansing, he decided to give his ruling elder a free hand to form a research organization.

House, whose attention already had been drawn by his English correspondents to the importance of such a step, envisioned a peace conference at which the President would be the only representative of the United States and the serious problems would be settled by a few qualified experts. "If good fortune follows," he wrote in his diary on September 4, "he has a chance to leave a record in history second to no man that has yet lived." [4]

In midsummer the President received another challenge to make peace on an idealistic basis. On August 1, Pope Benedict XV, probably prompted by Cardinal Pacelli, who as nuncio to Bavaria had been in touch with war-weary German Catholics, appealed for an ending of conflict on a basis of restoration of occupied territory, disarmament, and international arbitration. Wilson at first felt that appreciation of the Pope's motive and purpose should be expressed, but objected that his

---

[4] House brought together a group of experts that came to be known as "The Inquiry." Dr. Sidney Mezes, Mrs. House's brother-in-law, was named director; Walter Lippmann, who as editor of the *New Republic* had been in touch with many influential British Liberals, served as secretary; Dr. Isaiah Bowman, director of the American Geographical Society at New York, became executive officer.

terms constituted no settlement, that to discuss them would be "a blind adventure." He called Lodge and other senators into conference and said that he was "adrift and troubled" and ready to listen to all views. He thought that he ought to say publicly that they could not negotiate until there was a government of good faith in Germany; but he feared that if he did this he would be accused of renouncing the principle that every people was entitled to determine its own form of government.

American diplomats in the capitals of the Allies reported that sentiment was more or less favorable to the Pope's proposal. While Lloyd George steered an erratic middle course, British radicals were insisting on a frank statement of Allied war aims and were disappointed that Wilson had not forced his European associates to speak out. House felt that the President might lose a great opportunity to lead the pacifist opinion of the world, and to strengthen whatever liberal sentiment might exist in Russia. He wrote to Wilson more than once about this, and his persistence was as effective as it was unusual.[5] The President drafted a reply to the Pope and asked House for a frank opinion of it.

"You have again written a declaration of human liberty," the Colonel responded. "I endorse every word of it. I am sure it is the wise, the statesmanlike and the right way to answer . . ." Suggesting only slight changes of words that might offend the Allies, House thought it advisable to get their cooperation by giving advance copies of the note to them. But the President felt that if the Allies were informed they would ask for changes that the writer could not make in good faith, and he would be embarrassed.

Wilson sent off his note on August 27. Reasserting the disinterestedness of the United States, but insisting that the intolerable wrongs done by "the furious and brutal power" of the Kaiser's government should be repaired, he wrote: "We cannot take the word of the present rulers of Germany as a guarantee of anything that is to endure, unless explicitly supported by such conclusive evidences of the will and purpose of the German people themselves as the other peoples of the world would be justified in accepting."

[5] The Colonel realized that he was dissenting from the advice of the State Department and all those who suspected that the Pope's offer was designed to save the Germans from the consequences of their brutality, but he was confident that his sources of European opinion were superior to those of the State Department.

Influenced by reports of British radical opinion that came from his agent in the London embassy, W. H. Buckler, the Colonel urged the President not to frighten the German people with threats of dismemberment and economic discrimination.

The British government was embarrassed by the resignation from the Cabinet of Labor leader Arthur Henderson, who wished to sponsor British representation at the Stockholm conference, and Ambassador Page ordered Buckler to cease reporting the views of such men to House without telling the Colonel why he stopped. But House arranged to continue to receive information from Buckler through the latter's half brother, Henry White. *See* Lawrence W. Martin thesis.

The declaration was applauded alike by Anglo-Saxon liberals and by certain journals in France and Italy; and Americans of German ancestry took heart in the prospect of rapport with liberal opinion in the Fatherland. In Germany, where Bethmann-Hollweg had been forced out of office and his successor had yielded to the determination of the military men to disregard a peace resolution passed by the Reichstag, Wilson's statement was dismissed as "a trick." Nevertheless, the document was an effective part of the long-range campaign that Wilson had undertaken, with House's encouragement, to make war relentlessly on the German government and at the same time woo the German people. The President's position as a leader in peacemaking was strengthened when the Allies did not respond to Benedict XV, and Germany, replying on September 21, failed to mention the restoration of Belgium.

Affairs in Russia, as well as in Germany, challenged Wilson toward the end of 1917 to make specific applications of the creed of peace that he had been proclaiming in generalities for a year. After the Bolshevik revolution, it was futile to think of wooing Russia further with loans and technical aid. The Treasury Department was inclined to continue to extend credit as long as Russia remained in the war, but Ambassador Francis advised against this, and House telegraphed from Paris: ". . . the Russian situation is considered at the moment hopeless. There is no responsible government within sight. I would advise making no more advances at present or permitting any further contracts for purchases . . ."

Of all the leaders of the nations at war with Germany, the American President was in the best position to try to convince the Russians that the success of their revolution was imperiled by Germany's designs. Compared with the peoples of the Allied nations, Americans were remote and uninfluenced by socialistic propaganda, by financial stakes in the old Russia, or by ambitions to exploit the new. Their President could talk with them confidently about their attitude toward the Bolsheviki in Russia as well as toward fellow travelers in America.

Six days after the Bolshevik coup at Petrograd, Wilson left Washington to address labor delegates at a convention at Buffalo. As he took the train he received a report that he had requested, describing adjustments that had been made in certain war labor disputes. To his audience he said, on November 12: "Nobody has a right to stop the processes of labor until all the methods of conciliation and settlement have been exhausted." Speaking of "a body of free men" that he imagined to exist in Russia and misinterpreting the minds of the German leaders, who actually were more interested in breaking Russian resistance and making material gains than in any ideological campaign, Wilson said that, though his heart was with the pacifists in Russia, his mind held them in contempt. Then, alluding to efforts that had been made by agitators to stir American laborers to class hatred and mob violence, he gave this counsel: "Let us show ourselves Americans by showing that we do not want to go off in separate camps or groups by ourselves, but that we want to cooperate with all other classes and all other groups in the common enterprise which is to release the spirits of the world from bondage . . . There are some organizations in this country whose object is anarchy and the destruction of law, but I would not meet their efforts by making myself partner in destroying the law . . . I would be too proud not to see them done justice, however wrong they are." [6]

The President waited cautiously, unwilling to shape American policy until he had a clearer picture of events in Russia. On the 13th he indicated that he had not lost faith in the outcome by any means. "Russia," he wrote to a friend, "like France in a past century, will no doubt have to go through deep waters but she will come out upon firm land on the other side, and her great people, for they are a great people, will in my opinion take their proper place in the world."

But he was not led to hope for a quick restoration of good relations by the tactics of Trotsky, who had installed himself as foreign minister. On November 21 this leader publicly renounced any desire for the Bosporus and proposed to the United States and the Allies that there be no delay in arranging an armistice on all fronts and opening peace negotiations. Expressing profound respect for "the people" of the United States, he did not mention their government; and on November 24 it was reported in the American press that he had told a newsman that, if Wilson's government did not support his peace policy, the American people would. Thus he loosed against the United States the same kind of subversive argument that Wilson was aiming at Germany.

Moreover, Trotsky published the secret treaties among the Allies and delivered a speech before Soviet delegates that ascribed sordid war aims

[6] Wilson applied this principle to the case of Tom Mooney, a California labor leader who was under sentence of death and whose plight was publicized in Russia as an example of capitalistic oppression. Accepting a suggestion from House, he asked Attorney General Gregory to have a thorough investigation made of the Mooney case. Later he acted on a report of a mediation commission—which he permitted to be made public for its "effect on the people as a whole in this country and the effect in connection with our foreign relations"—by suggesting to the governor of California that the execution of Mooney be postponed until a new trial could be held that would give full weight to important changes in evidence. "I urge this very respectfully indeed but very earnestly," he wrote, on Jan. 22, 1918, "because the case has assumed international importance." (On Jan. 19 it had been announced that the Bolsheviki were holding Ambassador Francis responsible for the lives of Mooney and others who were being prosecuted in the United States.) When Senator Poindexter attacked Mooney and the I.W.W. in the Senate, two months later, this letter was read aloud to the senators, with Wilson's permission.

to America and asserted that Wilson had entered the conflict at the insistence of "finance capitalists" in order to create a boom in war industry.

This was more than a man could take who had striven to the limit of his strength to keep his people out of war. Reading the Russian's vitriolic sentences to his Cabinet, Wilson said that he would make no direct answer for fear that it might imply recognition. Ambassador Francis was told that there was no reply, was left at Petrograd with no clear directive, and was threatened with violence by Trotsky.

Nevertheless, Trotsky's attack spurred Wilson to try to purify the purposes of the nations still fighting Germany. On December 1, replying to a cable in which House proposed a mild joint manifesto of war aims, the President commended his agent's efforts and suggested that it would be "unfortunate" if the Inter-Allied Conference discussed peace terms in a spirit antagonistic to his own program. The Colonel had to conclude that it would be useless to press American purposes upon what he set down as "the reactionary crowd" at the Paris conference. It was left to each nation to notify the Bolsheviki of its willingness to discuss war aims with any stable Russian government.

Alarmed because the Bolsheviki were regarded at Paris as outcasts, and also because American jingoes were advocating that Russia be treated as an enemy, fearing that the President might state his case "piecemeal" and fail to cover all the ground that talks with the Allies had shown to be essential, the Colonel cabled from Paris to ask his friend to make no statement on foreign relations until they could confer. But Wilson replied: "Sorry impossible to omit foreign affairs from address to Congress. Reticence on my part at this juncture would be misunderstood and resented and do much harm."

In his annual message on December 4—the day after armistice negotions between the Bolsheviki and Germany began at Brest-Litovsk—the President called for "very grave scrutiny" of the war's objectives and of ways to attain them. He warned that the peace settlement must not impose "such covenants of selfishness and compromise as were entered into at the Congress of Vienna." Efforts to win must not slacken, he said, "but it is worth while asking the question, When shall we consider the war won?" Peace could be discussed, he asserted, only "when the German people have spokesmen whose word we can believe and when those spokesmen are ready in the name of their people to accept the common judgment of the nations as to what shall henceforth be the bases of law and of covenant for the life of the world." He declared that "the masters of German intrigue" were using a crude formula—"no annexations, no contributions, no punitive indemnities"—to lead the people of Russia astray. He prescribed "truth" as "the only possible anti-dote," asserting that it could not be uttered too plainly or too often. And he avowed that, though America had become a combatant, her idealistic attitude toward a peace settlement had not changed.

"Let there be no misunderstanding," he declared. "Our present and immediate task is to win the war, and nothing shall turn us aside from it until it is accomplished . . . One very embarrassing obstacle that stands in our way is that we are at war with Germany but not with her allies." Characterizing Austria-Hungary as "simply the vassal of the German government," he recommended an immediate declaration of war against that nation, with whom relations had been broken eight months earlier.

At this the applause that had punctuated the President's speech be-came a great shout. Ladies waved handkerchiefs, Southerners pierced the bedlam with the yip-yip-yip of the rebel yell. Wilson stepped aside until the hubbub was over, and his countenance masked whatever emotion he felt. This address, which many thought his greatest presidential speech so far, was sent to all the world by wireless and gave him the largest audience that an American president ever had reached. Within three days of its delivery, a resolution for war with Austria-Hungary was passed and was signed by Wilson.

As the Bolsheviki carried on peace negotiations with Germany at Brest-Litovsk in December, Wilson continued to express good will toward them. But on the 21st, commenting on the plan of Trotsky for propaganda abroad, he said to his Cabinet: "The impudence of it!"

While he waited in indecision, Boris A. Bakhmeteff, the lingering envoy of the overthrown provisional government, helped him to settle one immediate problem. Unable to get an appointment with Lansing, the ambassador of the fallen regime persuaded George Creel to put in the President's ear the idea that, extending the doctrine that Wilson had applied to Germany, he differentiate between the Russian people and the misguided Bolshevik government. Accepting the suggestion, Wilson allowed Bakhmeteff to remain at Washington as the agent of "the Russian people." This envoy, who was aided by Colonel House in maintaining his titular position, induced the United States government not to cancel contracts that had been made under the provisional gov-ernment, and soon an official ban was placed on American trade with Bolshevik Russia.[7]

When an armistice was concluded at Brest-Litovsk, on December 15, the crisis in both arms and morale, already severe, threatened to become

[7] Boris A. Bakhmeteff's record in the Oral History Project, Columbia University.

extreme. Germany was free to transfer vast forces to the Western battle front, and now that the Bolsheviki had revealed secret treaties among the Allies and had denounced them,[8] the Germans could pose before the liberals of the world as a people no more imperialistic than their adversaries.

Colonel House reached Washington on the 17th, carrying discouraging reports about his efforts to persuade the Allies to announce liberal war aims. Wilson listened to him attentively. The next day the Colonel urged his friend to speak out. He found the President's mind receptive, and in a very few minutes Wilson decided that he might soon make an address that could prove to be a turning point in the psychological war. Before the Colonel left the White House, Wilson asked him to get a memorandum from The Inquiry on the various points that a peace conference should consider; and the President was persuaded that Wiseman should be allowed to check his draft for this address so that it would give no offense and would harmonize with British policy.

Wilson remarked that his first purpose in planning a statement on war aims was to persuade the Russian people that they would be trampled underfoot by a victorious Germany but could count on the Allies for a peace that would uphold democratic and liberal principles. At the same time he hoped to "knock the Kaiser off his perch" by feeding the suspicions of German Socialists that their government was waging a war of conquest rather than one of defense. And, thirdly, he wanted to stimulate the Allies to consent to a liberalization of their war aims.

Wilson had just had a report from Edgar Sisson, who had been dispatched to Russia in October to start an aggressive [9] publicity campaign.

---

[8] In January of 1918, Wiseman informed Balfour of the President's concern about the secret treaties, and especially the Treaty of London, concluded with Italy. According to the *New York Times* of Nov. 25, Dec. 1 and 2, 1917, Trotsky made public at that time the terms of the treaties negotiated by the Allies with the Czar's government as well as the terms of the Treaty of London. These pacts were published in full in the *Manchester Guardian* on Dec. 13, 1917, and in the New York *Evening Post* serially beginning Jan. 25, 1918. They were transmitted to the State Department by its representatives at Petrograd and Stockholm. *F.R., 1917,* Suppl. 2, I, 447, 493–507.

Boris A. Bakhmeteff recorded that in 1917, when he told Lansing that Russians were apprehensive about the secret treaties and suggested that, since the United States was financing the Allies she could ask them to clear the air, Lansing protested that it was better for him to be ignorant of the treaties, since he could not ask Europeans to wipe them out without danger of embarrassing the conduct of the war. Bakhmeteff's record.

Now that the terms of most of the secret treaties had been made public, Wilson could no longer afford to ignore them, as he had when the texts of most of them had been sent to him in May of 1917 by Balfour. Cf. p. 131n. above.

For an illuminating discussion of the "new diplomacy" that was developed by Wilson and the Russian leaders, see a dissertation by Arno Mayer entitled "The Politics of Allied War Aims," Yale University, 1954.

[9] "We want nothing for ourselves," the President wrote to Sisson in a personal note, "and this very unselfishness carries with it an obligation of open dealing. Wherever the fundamental principles of Russian freedom are at stake, we stand ready to render such aid as lies in our power, but I want this helpfulness based upon request and not upon offer. Guard particularly

Sisson promised that if the President would restate his warm aims and requisites for peace in "short almost placard paragraphs," such a declaration would be translated, fed into Germany in great quantities, and circulated in Russia. Wilson was amused at the prospect of such blatant propaganda. He told Creel, dryly, that he had never tried his hand at composing slogans or advertising copy. Nevertheless, the importunities of the publicists, coming simultaneously with similar pleas from other agents in Russia and with a blast from Trotsky assailing the Allies for refusal to talk peace or give their reasons, helped to induce the prophet to move swiftly from contemplation to action.

When Wilson and House buckled down to the drafting of a speech on war aims, during the first week of the year 1918, they considered particularly what they should say about Russia. The first half of the address was devoted to the significance of the peace parleys at Brest-Litovsk. Wilson asserted that the negotiations there had been broken off because the Russian representatives, lured to the peace table by German professions of liberalism, had discovered that the terms actually were to be dictated by "the military leaders who have no thought but to keep what they have got." Having made this charge, the address went on to ask whether the German delegates at Brest-Litovsk expressed "the spirit and intention of the liberal leaders and parties in Germany." Commending Russia's insistence on open peace negotiations—"in the true spirit of modern democracy"—and her challenge to adversaries to define their purposes,[10] Wilson's text asserted:

There is no good reason why that challenge should not be responded to ... with the utmost candor. We did not wait for it. Not once, but again and again, we have laid our whole thought and purpose before the world, not in general terms only, but each time with sufficient definition to make it clear

against any effect of officious intrusion or meddling, and try to express the disinterested friendship that is our sole impulse."

As a result of this note and an interview with the President that Creel arranged, Sisson felt that he was Wilson's "special representative in Russia." But he was given no specific instructions regarding his relations with other Americans in Russia and was introduced to Ambassador Francis by the State Department as representing only Creel. Sisson exceeded his instructions by sending to Creel a recommendation that Francis be recalled and informal contacts with Bolshevik officials be established. The State Department intercepted his message and Lansing conferred with Wilson, who telegraphed to Sisson thus: "President insists that you avoid political entanglements and personal matters." See Kennan, *op. cit.*, pp. 124–29. This was but one instance of the tangled relations that developed among Americans in Russia and that might have been prevented by adequate and precise instructions from Washington.

[10] In his wishful efforts to win Russia's military support, Wilson was able to overlook the undemocratic challenge that Trotsky had made on Dec. 29 in behalf of "the working class" and to accept unverified and false rumors to the effect that the negotiations at Brest-Litovsk had been broken off by Russian delegates who refused to be deceived.

Kennan (*op. cit.*, pp. 255–57) has cited respects in which Wilson's eloquent passages on Russia in the Fourteen Points Speech were "inaccurate and unrealistic."

what sort of definitive terms of settlement must necessarily spring out of them . . . There is no confusion of counsel among the adversaries of the Central Powers, no uncertainty of principle, no vagueness of detail. The only secrecy of counsel, the only lack of fearless frankness, the only failure to make definite statement of the objects of the war, lies with Germany and her Allies. The issues of life and death hang upon these definitions . . .

There is, moreover, a voice calling for these definitions of principle and of purpose which is, it seems to me, more thrilling and more compelling than any of the many moving voices with which the troubled air of the world is filled. It is the voice of the Russian people. They are prostrate and all but helpless, it would seem, before the grim power of Germany, which has hitherto known no relenting and no pity. Their power, apparently, is shattered. And yet their soul is not subservient. They will not yield either in principle or in action. Their conception of what is right, of what is humane and honorable for them to accept, has been stated with a frankness, a largeness of view, a generosity of spirit, and a universal human sympathy which must challenge the admiration of every friend of mankind; and they have refused to compound their ideals or desert others that they themselves may be safe. They call to us to say what it is that we desire, in what, if in anything, our purpose and our spirit differ from theirs; and I believe that the people of the United States would wish me to respond, with utter simplicity and frankness. Whether their present leaders believe it or not, it is our heartfelt desire and hope that some way may be opened whereby we may be privileged to assist the people of Russia to attain their utmost hope of liberty and ordered peace . . .

Denouncing "secret covenants entered into in the interest of particular governments and likely at some unlooked-for moment to upset the peace of the world," the argument moved to the first of fourteen specific aims:

open covenants of peace, openly arrived at, after which there shall be no private international understandings of any kind but diplomacy shall proceed always frankly and in the public view.

The second point—freedom of the seas—had been forecast by statements that the President had made earlier. He knew that this point would meet opposition in England, and yet House had found some approbation for it in the minds of influential British Liberals. Wilson realized, too, that there would be criticism—in this case in the Congress —of his third proposal, calling for "the removal, so far as possible, of all economic barriers and the establishment of an equality of trade conditions among all the nations . . ." The fourth point called for disarmament "to the lowest point consistent with domestic safety"—a proposal with which the Bolsheviki were to show little sympathy. The

fifth advocated "a free, open-minded, and absolutely impartial adjustment of all colonial claims," with due regard to the interests of the
inhabitants and the claims of other governments.

It was in the sixth point that Wilson came to grips with the colossal
problem that was the chief reason for his statement:

The evacuation of all Russian territory and such a settlement of all questions affecting Russia as will secure the best and freest cooperation of the
other nations of the world in obtaining for her an unhampered and unembarrassed opportunity for the independent determination of her own political
development and national policy and assure her of a sincere welcome into the
society of free nations under institutions of her own choosing; and, more
than a welcome, assistance also of every kind that she may need and may
herself desire. The treatment accorded Russia by her sister nations in the
months to come will be the acid test of their good will, of their comprehension of her needs as distinguished from their own interests, and of their
intelligent and unselfish sympathy.

In the points that followed, Wilson dealt with the specific problems
of national territories and sovereignties. The phrasing of a statement
about the future of Alsace-Lorraine perplexed him. In rewriting it he
evolved the general principle that he would use the word "must" when
there was no difference of opinion and "should" in setting down solutions of controversial questions. His final version read: "The wrong
done to France by Prussia in 1871 . . . should be righted."

Only in shaping a settlement of the problem of the disposition of
Austria-Hungary and the Balkans did he seek counsel beyond his circle
of American advisers. He sent House, against the latter's judgment, to
consult the head of the Serbian mission at Washington and was depressed when the Colonel returned with a report that Serbia insisted
there could be no lasting peace in Europe without a breakup of the
Austro-Hungarian Empire. He was aware that the freeing of subject
nationalities, though in some cases to be desired, might, if pushed to
an extreme, lead to the disruption of existing governments to an inde-
finable extent. Disregarding the Serbian view, he stated in Point Ten
merely that "the peoples of Austria-Hungary, whose place among the
nations we wish to see safeguarded and secured, should be accorded the
freest opportunity of autonomous development."

Wilson would have liked to limit his conditions of peace to thirteen,
his favorite number. The Fourteenth Point, however, was the most
significant of all, and the one that gave hope that the others might be
given practical application. Though he had not talked much in the
early months of the war about a "league of nations," he had not for-

gotten his oft-repeated commitment to the development of a world-wide political organism. A committee under Lord Bryce had drawn up a British plan for a League to Enforce Peace; and the American organization of that name was still active. Though he had endorsed its purposes, Wilson had been careful not to subscribe to its program, which he thought "very much too definite," or to any other program that might arouse jealousies or provoke differences of opinion. To a congressman who had come on August 3, 1917, to the White House to propose adapting the federal Constitution to the purposes of international organization, Wilson said that they must first win the war. "I quite agree with your general purposes," he went on, "but I fear that no accomplishment so great as our own Constitution can be hoped for. A most happy combination of historical conditions alone made that achievement possible. What I do hope to accomplish is to establish a structure containing the tendencies which will lead irresistibly to the great end we in common with all other rightly constituted persons desire. But there are going to be difficulties even with this modest desire. I have in mind the ridiculous importance which some persons assign to the official who will be charged with such conspicuous work —but, friends and enemies both will admit that my 'jaw' has proved adequate in past struggles!"

When finally he decided to draft a league-of-nations plank for his platform for world peace, he phrased it in this way:

A general association of nations must be formed under specific covenants for the purpose of affording mutual guarantees of political independence and territorial integrity to great and small states alike.

The timing of the release of the most far-reaching of all Woodrow Wilson's speeches gave anxiety to its author. He was eager to put out his manifesto before Lloyd George and Clemenceau could forestall him.[11] He typed a cable for the prime minister, stating the intention of speaking more specifically about war aims than he had before, and expressing the hope that no utterance was contemplated across the Atlantic that "would be likely to sound a different note or suggest claims inconsistent with" the objects of the United States.

---

[11] The Colonel was disturbed by this and also because Taft, asked by Balfour to go to England and accepting, talked it over with the President and then told newsmen what Wilson said: viz., that the United States did not desire closer relations with England, and there was great anti-British feeling in the country. Citing the Treaty of London as an instance of British self-interest, Wilson said that there were too many Englishmen carrying on propaganda in the United States and he had asked House to have some of them go home. He told Wiseman that, to be permanent, Anglo-American understanding must rest on a surer basis than artificial propaganda.

But suddenly, on January 5, as the President was discussing his own address with the Colonel, Lloyd George, who was as sensitive as Wilson to the trends of opinion in Russia and Germany and the response of British radicals to them, restated Britain's war aims in a speech to trade-union delegates at London. Balfour telegraphed to Wilson to explain that there had been no time to consult allies about this move, that the prime minister had been forced to speak out immediately to facilitate negotiations with the union men, that a further statement along the same lines would receive an equally warm welcome.[12]

When Wilson learned that Lloyd George had spoken without consulting him, both his morality and his pride were offended. Not only had the prime minister differed in principle by insisting that Germany pay reparations, but by proposing almost all of the President's Fourteen Points he seemed to have pirated the ideas that Wilson had set down with great pains. Wilson, the man of literary property, seemed to forget the biblical truth that his father had preached but had often overlooked—that no servant of the Lord had light of his own, but merely bore witness to the "heavenly light." The ambition to seize the pulpit of peace for himself and to give leadership to his own people in serving the world still burned strongly in the prophet in the White House. He was no more inclined than he had been at the age of thirty to be any man's follower in a matter on which he felt that he had qualified himself to speak.

For a moment he thought that it would be impossible for him to make the address that he had been preparing. However, House insisted that Lloyd George had cleared the air and made it the more necessary to act, that the prime minister had not himself written the speech that he had delivered, that it would be so smothered by Wilson's own effort that the President would be recognized as spokesman for all the enemies of Germany.

Taking heart, Wilson set to work again on his momentous utterance. He and House were most anxious about the reaction of their own people to their declaration of territorial aims for Europe. Wilson was not so much concerned about a criticism that he expected from the Germans: that since the Monroe Doctrine forbade interference by Europeans in the Americas, the Old World should insist that there be no intrusion from the New into their affairs. He was prepared to reply that he was willing to have the same principles applied to the Western Hemisphere that he prescribed for the whole world. He was wary of

[12] House doubted that the political necessity for a pronouncement by Lloyd George was as dire as Balfour suggested. A letter from Sir William Wiseman, written to House on March 20, 1933, expressed the opinion that Lloyd George's speech was probably made to forestall the Wilsonian pronouncement, of which the Colonel had warned the prime minister.

provoking argument and spoke to House of the wisdom of avoiding assertions that might stir controversy. But he insisted that by and large their proposals were just, and he showed no hesitation in adhering to them. On January 8 he proclaimed his gospel before the Congress.

Once the epochal speech was uttered, the whole world gave heed. Washington circles and American newspapers, even some that were usually in opposition, were laudatory. Even in the uttermost parts of the world the words of the prophet stirred a worshipful response in hearts that were yearning for the American gospel of which missionaries and traders were telling them. Human beings everywhere felt the magic of the tug on sensibilities that are deep in all men. Here was a creed that was free from the class bitterness that was associated with the Stockholm conference and from the institutional origin of the Pope's appeal. The doctrine of self-determination appealed to traditionalists in Europe as a line by which radical opposition could be short-circuited.

Sophisticated foreign observers, however, were more reserved in their reception of this bold projection of American philosophy into world affairs. The Western Allies readily applauded Wilson's strictures on German militarism; and liberals welcomed his statement of general principles of peacemaking. But conservatives thought his ideals almost utopian and questioned their validity as a practical basis for peace. Queries arose about his proposals for territorial settlements. It seemed to some nations that they themselves would receive too small a share of the spoils of war, that their enemies would get off too lightly. Not only did the Fourteen Points speech fail to persuade the governments of the Allies to renounce the terms of the secret treaties; but by creating suspicion among the peoples that they might not get what they were fighting for, it made it the more difficult for statesmen to maintain resistance to Germany at a high pitch.

In Russia, Wilson's words were given the wide circulation that had been promised. When Sisson took a translation of them to Lenin, the commissar grabbed it and sprinted for a telegraph office to send it to Trotsky at Brest-Litovsk. According to Sisson, Lenin thought the speech a tolerant one for a "class opponent" to write and accepted it as "a great step ahead" toward world-wide peace. Its prescriptions for territorial settlements were similar to his own. But he criticized the clause dealing with colonial claims and pointed out that Marxist ideals transcended the right of peoples to self-determination. He continued to ask that the United States give substance to her professed friendship by recognizing the Soviet government. As for Trotsky, he read Wilson's speech and continued to speak cynically of America's motives. Composed without regard to the effect in Russian translation, and ambiguous as to Wilson's view of Bolshevik power, the address left many questions unanswered. While the government press followed Lenin's thinking, *Pravda,* speaking for the party dictatorship, raved against Wilson, calling him "the representative of the American dictatorship, chastising its own workers and poor people with prisons, forced labor, and death sentences . . ." One propagandist referred to the address as a "very deliquescent program of political rascality." Whatever effect Wilson's speech, translated and displayed on hundreds of thousands of posters, may have had on the plain people of Russia, it doubtless dulled their hope for immediate peace. By contrast, it highlighted the pacific prospect that Trotsky was offering.

However, Wilson did not entirely lose faith in the Russian Revolution as a manifestation of democratic potential, not even when, on January 18, the Bolsheviki dissolved the elected Constituent Assembly and served notice that they would rule by decree.[13] At one time he considered establishing *de facto* relations with Petrograd as a practical step toward combating German intrigue. The changes taking place in Russia were so kaleidoscopic that all information and advice seemed futile; but his conscience kept his mind working on the dilemma. On February 6 he wrote to John Sharp Williams: ". . . I do not know that I have ever had a more tiresome struggle with quicksand than I am having in trying to do the right thing in respect of our dealings with Russia."

Trotsky pursued a policy of making neither war nor peace with Germany, and the German Army lost patience, ended the armistice, and dispersed the remaining fragments of Russian forces. Finally at the end of February, when German seizure of Petrograd seemed imminent and Lenin's regime was tottering, Ambassador Francis, despairing of maintaining resistance to the enemy, left the city with his staff and the Red Cross mission. When the Bolsheviki decreed the repudiation of Russia's state debts, France became implacably hostile to the new regime and Lansing and McAdoo thought recognition impossible.

In a last desperate effort to prevent ratification of the Brest-Litovsk treaty, the President sent a greeting on March 11 to the Congress of Soviets that was convoked at Moscow to supplant the prorogued Constituent Assembly. He expressed sympathy with their efforts to free themselves forever from autocracy, and the hope that this body might be persuaded not to approve the peace with Germany. But the applause

---

[13] As Kennan has observed (*op. cit.,* pp. 362–63), the dissolution of the Constituent Assembly, which was not featured in the American press, overweighted any inclination that the Allies may have had to recognize the Soviet government and turned them toward a policy of aiding anti-Bolshevik factions in Russia. On Jan. 21 Wilson wrote to Samuel Gompers thus regarding the Assembly: ". . . apparently the reckless Bolsheviki have already broken it up because they did not control it. It is distressing to see things so repeatedly go to pieces."

that greeted his overture was scattered and thin.[14] The Bolshevik leaders replied with rant, and expressed concern for "all peoples suffering from the horrors of imperialistic war." A happy time was not far distant, the Soviet note predicted, "when the laboring masses of all countries will throw off the yoke of capitalism and will establish a socialistic state of society which is alone capable of securing just and lasting peace, as well as the culture and well-being of all laboring people."[15]

In view of this brash rejection of his sympathy and the violent methods that the Bolsheviki had to use to hold their power, and when reports came from both Ambassador Francis and Sisson that seemed to prove that the leaders of the Bolsheviki were in German pay,[16] the President abandoned efforts to establish cordial relations between the great revolutionary peoples of the New World and those of the Old. His government perpetuated the fallacy that had embarrassed the provisional government and that precluded diplomatic understanding between Washington and the Bolsheviki. The State Department took the position that the United States persisted in regarding the Russian people as comrades-in-arms and in refusing to recognize that there was any government to speak for them.

Wilson was frustrated, then, in two of the purposes that had been foremost in his mind when he prepared his Fourteen Points speech. He did not persuade the self-constituted rulers of the Russian people to stand with the Allies against Germany; nor did he shake the determination of Britain and France to honor the agreements that had been set down in secret treaties.

However, he realized to some degree his intent of jarring the confidence of the peoples of Germany and Austria in their military masters. Wilson had hurled words of peace so effectively that officials at Berlin and Vienna felt it necessary to parry them. There was talk of revolt, and strikes broke out. On January 24 legislative committees at both

[14] DeWitt C. Poole's record in the Oral History Project, Columbia University. Poole, who gave Wilson's message to the chairman of the Soviet Congress, confirms the account printed in *F.R., 1919, Russia*, I, 395 and 399, except as to the volume of the applause. According to Lawrence Martin, Wilson's communication was "really intended to caution Japan." Martin thesis.

[15] According to Ambassador Francis, a Soviet minister boasted: "With these words we slapped President Wilson in the face." House thought this "a tough one to answer" and concluded that formal correspondence had best be discontinued.

After Wilson's greeting of March 11 had been sent, the State Department received from Francis a message that Trotsky had given to Raymond Robins of the Red Cross on March 5. Trotsky asked what aid the United States would give if the war against Germany were renewed and also asked what could be done to get British help through Murmansk and to prevent a Japanese landing in Siberia. On March 19 the State Department replied that Wilson's message of March 11 was an adequate answer. When the British also failed to give definite assurances, the Congress of Soviets ratified the Treaty of Brest-Litovsk, in mid-March.

[16] *See* p. 263 below.

capitals were told that the governments tentatively agreed with Wilson's general points, though differing from most of the territorial proposals. Chancellor Hertling criticized the tone of the speeches of Lloyd George and Wilson, but expressed sympathy with the concept of a league of nations. Count Czernin, Austria's minister of foreign affairs, showing more sincerity and warmth than his ally at Berlin, remarked that "Austria-Hungary and the United States of America are the two great powers among the two groups of enemy states whose interests least conflict."

Encouraged by the mere fact that his adversaries took public notice of his attack, by a report from House that it looked "as if things were at last beginning to crack in Germany," and by a resolution of British Laborites calling for a joint declaration of peace terms, the President was disturbed by the disinclination of the leaders of the Allies to follow him in a peace offensive. He resented suggestions from abroad that this was not his business and wished to try to make it plain that "each item of a general peace is everybody's business." His irritation was inflamed in the first week of February when the Supreme War Council, which had been constituted to deal with military affairs, stepped into the political field and declared that the enemy's responses to Wilson's speech offered no basis for peace. He protested strongly. "I am afraid of *any* expression of policy framed jointly at Paris," he wrote to Lansing. "There has been none yet that seemed to me even touched with wisdom."

Wilson determined to reply to Hertling and Czernin. When he discussed his plan on January 29 with House he seemed to be feeling his way, without confidence that he was on the right track; but the Colonel reassured him by praising the first draft.

Addressing a joint session of the Congress on February 11 he reviewed the proposals of Hertling and Czernin and condemned their method of peacemaking as that of the Congress of Vienna. "We cannot and will not return to that," he proclaimed. "What is at stake now is the peace of the world. What we are striving for is a new international order based upon broad and universal principles of right and justice— no mere peace of shreds and patches." He threw in an economic threat that he and House had discussed at some length: if the making of a settlement in Eastern Europe was none of the business of the Allies, perhaps tariff barriers in Western Europe were none of Germany's business! [17] He felt that German citizens would not be indifferent to the

---

[17] In January, Wilson told Wiseman that control of raw materials would be a weapon of enormous value to England and America at the peace conference and he was prepared to use it fully, if necessary, to bring the German militarists to reason.

threat of a tariff war after the shooting was over. Then, in conclusion, he presented four generalizations that he thought essential to a just peace:

First, that each part of the final settlement must be based upon the essential justice of that particular case and upon such adjustments as are most likely to bring a peace that will be permanent;

Second, that peoples and provinces are not to be bartered about from sovereignty to sovereignty as if they were mere chattels and pawns in a game, even the great game, now forever discredited, of the balance of power; but that

Third, every territorial settlement involved in this war must be made in the interest and for the benefit of the populations concerned, and not as a part of any mere adjustment or compromise of claims amongst rival states; and

Fourth, that all well-defined national aspirations shall be accorded the utmost satisfaction that can be accorded them without introducing new or perpetuating old elements of discord and antagonism that would be likely in time to break the peace of Europe and consequently of the world.

Although the address was well received, it did not stir enthusiasm to the pitch that had been reached on similar occasions before. It seemed to House that few members of Congress understood the President's intention to "build a fire back of Ludendorff" and that fewer still sympathized with Wilson's strategy. Returning to the White House, the prophet himself appeared to be "only scantily hopeful" that his effort would be considered an immediate success. But he was cheered when the Colonel waxed enthusiastic and brought glowing praise from Reading and Wiseman—"I would have given a year of my life to have made the last half of the President's speech," the British ambassador said. It was gratifying, too, that his four principles were adopted by an Inter-Allied Labor-Socialist Conference that met at London.

Slight as was the immediate effect of the manifestoes that Woodrow Wilson delivered in the first months of 1918, their historical significance was immense. The Allied governments were unwilling to accept Wilsonian "points" that impinged upon their special interests and therefore held back from quick adherence to his program. But it had become evident, during America's first year of war and Russia's months of freedom from czarism, that in Washington there was a formidable rival to the Soviet commissars for leadership in the new diplomacy of propaganda.

CHAPTER IX

"Force without Stint or Limit . . . Righteous and Triumphant"

The failure of Woodrow Wilson to maintain Russian resistance to Germany hardened his conviction that the immediate necessity was to smash his enemies in Central Europe.

The winter of 1917–18 was one of the coldest ever. On January 11 snow, sleet, and rain were falling as the President walked late one afternoon from the executive offices to the White House. "Well," he observed in a gloomy voice to his secret service guard, "this means stalled freight trains and more suffering because of lack of coal."

In this month in which he was concentrating on psychological warfare, the problem of mobilizing manpower and munitions of war became acute. During 1917 few of his people had dared openly to criticize his military program for fear of seeming unpatriotic; and save for outbursts of invective from the Roosevelt-Wood clique, the President had been relatively immune from obstruction by the Republicans and other factions.[1] When the Russian front collapsed, however, and the United States had hardly made its power felt in France, dissatisfaction that had been long seething erupted. A great wave of protest rolled up with the assembling of the Congress.

Sensing this, Wilson concluded that there must be a tightening of controls all along the line. In his annual address to the legislators, on December 4, he proposed an extension of measures already enacted to

[1] In August of 1917 General Leonard Wood, to whom Wilson had sent "a word of very warm and genuine congratulation" on his "admirable services" when Wood had left the post of chief of staff in 1914, was transferred to Camp Funston in Kansas. On Oct. 4 Pershing, in a letter to Secretary Baker, included Wood in a list of generals whom he considered "unavailable for overseas service." Wood was considered physically unfit because of a limp and an old injury to his skull.

However, Secretary Baker sent Wood abroad to study the training methods of the Allies. While overseas, the general embarrassed both Ambassador Page and Pershing by talking freely and indiscreetly in criticism of the President and America's war effort. Pershing wrote a "personal and very confidential memorandum" to Secretary Baker, on Feb. 24, 1918, saying that not only was Wood "seriously and permanently crippled," but was a "political general" who went about discrediting the Army and the Administration. Pershing ordered him home.

Democratic Senator Thomas tried to persuade Wilson to call Wood to the White House and hear his story, and the press asked whether the President could refuse to do this. But though this controversy hampered the efforts of the Administration to secure greater powers from the Congress, Wilson stood aside from it. On Jan. 30 he told House, who now had lost patience completely with Wood, that he had not known that the general had been sent abroad and that when he had asked Baker about it the secretary of war explained that it had seemed better to let Wood go than to have people feel that he was being martyred by being kept in the United States.

deal with enemy aliens. He said, too, that the government must be authorized to set price limits, for the law of supply and demand seemed to have been "replaced by the law of unrestricted selfishness." The Congress would be able to suggest other action, he declared, but he insisted that in the present session attention should be concentrated on the vigorous, rapid, and successful prosecution of the great task of winning the war.

On one recommendation that he made he was ready to act forthwith. It had become clear that the railroads of the country, handicapped by problems that were aggravated by the impact of war, were not able to move food and munitions expeditiously. In the autumn of 1917 their plight had disturbed Wilson more than any other domestic problem. He wished to avoid the responsibility of administering them if it was possible, shrank from adding this burden to those that were already overwhelming him. It was essential that he delegate the job to a man who would not bungle it. On a Sunday afternoon he said to Stockton Axson: "I know only one man who can handle the tangled, abortive situation—Mac—but unfortunately he is my son-in-law, and I can't reverse my position on nepotism." It seemed natural to turn to the secretary of the treasury because the problems of the railroads were largely financial. Canny advisers, perceiving that action was imperative, suggested that the President seek the advice of Brandeis. Wilson accepted this counsel, went to call on the justice, and was convinced that scruples should not interfere with the appointment of the man who seemed most suitable.

On December 26 the President issued a proclamation by which he took possession of the railroads, acting through the secretary of war. McAdoo was designated director general and took vigorous steps to accelerate the flow of war materials over the rails.

Another bold stroke for the general welfare was less pleasing to the American people. On the very day of the railroad proclamation, Fuel Administrator Garfield was testifying before a committee of the Senate that he would like to have the mines, as well as the railroads, operated by the government. Wilson did not endorse this idea; but when it became apparent that the fuel supplies were not adequate to meet the unprecedented needs of wartime industry as well as the heating requirements of civilians in a winter of abnormal cold, he conferred secretly with Garfield and the secretaries of war and navy. They told him that it would be necessary to limit civilian consumption of coal; there must be "heatless days," and closings of offices and factories for certain periods. Garfield thought that an executive order should go out immediately, before the press guessed their intention.

Wilson saw instantly that such a measure would raise a whirlwind of protest, and the storm was as furious as he expected. A Senate resolution requested that the order be suspended for five days until it could be investigated. Even Wilson's friends were shocked.

The President stood stanchly behind his administrator. On January 18—the same day on which he notified his people that they might have to tighten their belts further to conserve food—he explained to the nation that not only had he fully approved the fuel order, but that it was necessary, much as he regretted it. "It is extraordinary," he wrote to Baruch, "how some people wince and cry out when they are a little bit hurt." He expressed confidence that his people were willing to endure the same discipline that was involved in the actual fighting of the war. When Garfield telephoned to offer to supply fuel to country clubs at which the President played golf, Wilson asked Tumulty to say that he "would not for anything" have an exception of this sort made.

The President had no convincing rejoinder for the critics of his organization of the nation for war. Willing to discuss the criticisms with his confidants, he would not permit public replies. Asked to explain his policies, he said that he would not "exploit" them. He was determined not to forget the dignity and responsibility of his position, as he felt that Roosevelt had done. He feared that a brazen assertion of growing military power might be construed abroad as a note of defiance, calculated to operate as a rebuff of all peace offers.

Yet he was far from satisfied by the progress that was being made. Both politicians and businessmen worried him by their manipulations. He told his Cabinet that they should be cautious in guarding against a popular impression that rich men's sons were getting soft berths at Washington. And he said at a Gridiron dinner: "My troubles with the war are slight compared with the difficulties of satisfying my distinguished dollar-a-year associates . . . I am like an opera impresario, every member of whose troupe wants to be recognized and applauded as the prima donna." Sometimes it seemed as if everything that went well took care of itself, and only problems reached his desk.

The lid of patriotic restraint blew off completely in January of 1918. The Senate's Committee on Military Affairs, which for some time had been studying the munitions program, unanimously approved introduction of a bill providing for a director of munitions. The chairman, Democratic Senator Chamberlain, had commanded attention the month before when he spoke on the Senate floor of the lag that all knew to exist between production plans and actual output. Going to New York to address the National Security League on January 19, the senator declared that the military establishment of the nation had fallen down, that it had stopped functioning because of "inefficiency in every bureau and every department of the Government of the United States." As the speaker sat down, Theodore Roosevelt jumped to his feet and applauded loudly. Soon the old Rough Rider went to Washington to support a revival of the public demand for administrative reorganization that had risen spasmodically, in one form or another, ever since the beginning of hostilities.

The President's liberal friends, noting that the hotels of Washington were filled with businessmen from all parts of the country who were not getting what they wanted, insisted on attributing the attacks to political motives. They charged that Wilson was the target again of reactionary interests that feared government encroachment on their prerogatives, under the compulsion of national emergency. The President felt that he could not trust the Congress to act impersonally. On September 1 he had explained to Senator Williams that a supervising Congressional committee, if it was created, would introduce "very great added difficulty and burden," that fortunately the many consultative bodies that already existed were under his own authority, where he could hope to keep a coordinating eye on all at the same time.

Yet friendly newspapers suggested that there was some truth in the allegations of Chamberlain. House called on Baker to try to convince him that reorganization was desirable; and, though feeling that the criticism reflected political bias, the secretary was not unwilling to admit deficiencies in the Ordnance Department and to consider changes.

The President, however, was enraged by the immoderate onslaught and rose to defend the secretary of war. Ascertaining first that Chamberlain had been quoted accurately, Wilson publicly declared that the criticism was "an astonishing and unjustifiable distortion of the truth." As a matter of fact, he asserted, despite "delays and disappointments and miscarriage of plans" the War Department had "performed a task of unparalleled magnitude with extraordinary promptness and efficiency." His affection and admiration for Baker was such that he found it hard to restrain himself from more intemperate words.

Actually the attacks of January, coming while the President was wining prestige by his peace offensive, served to enlist support for the strengthening of controls that he wished to achieve as soon as popular opinion was ready. He could see that the criticism was advantageous in so far as it enabled the Administration to rebut reckless attacks. He felt the need of a law that would free his hands, rather than bind them in red tape wound up by political adversaries.

On January 24 he asked his associates to take up a remedial bill that

Secretary Baker had sent to him in a tentative draft. Burleson persuaded Senator Overman, known as a defender of states' rights, to introduce the measure in the Senate on February 6. It gave the President broad power to "coordinate and consolidate" the activities of the government, to win the war. The bill was worked over at White House conferences; after a month of vitriolic debate, in which the measure was denounced as a step toward absolute monarchy, it was passed by the Congress; and on May 20 Wilson signed it.[2] Authorized now to "make such redistribution of functions among executive agencies" as he thought necessary, he issued an executive order, on May 28, making the War Industries Board independent of the cumbersome Council of National Defense and delegating extraordinary powers to it. He had long been seeking a "superman" to direct this board—someone who could stand above tradition and special interests in making and carrying through decisions. In anticipation of the action of the Congress, and under the authority of a section of the National Defense Act, he had announced on March 5 that Baruch would head the board. The chairman was empowered to appoint committees at his own discretion and to control them absolutely, except the one that set prices. The price-fixing committee reported directly to the President and he passed upon its decisions.

Baruch already had won voluntary cuts in the prices of several metals; and Wilson directed him now "to guide and assist wherever the need . . . may be revealed" and to "act as the general eye of all supply departments, in the field of industry." This South Carolinian had shown a vast and detailed knowledge of the sources of strategic raw materials and the prevailing price scales; he knew the people who were in key positions; and he had a master plan, a vision of voluntary cooperation within industry to put the nation's need above profits. (As early as October of 1915 he had given the President an outline of a plan for industrial mobilization for defense.) But best of all, Baruch had a faith in the integrity of business that Wilson lacked. He did not share the President's feeling that industrialists would take advantage of the emergency raised by war to seize political power. Though Baruch, like the President, fancied lovely ladies—he had celebrated Wilson's sixty-first birthday by presenting a copy of Merrick's *Whispers*

---

[2] Of the Overman Act, Frederic L. Paxson has written (in *America at War,* pp. 224–25): "Few statutes have in so few words surrendered so much; and none has vested more discretion in the President. . . . The Overman Act authorized him to redistribute the functions of executive agencies as he saw fit; 'to utilize, co-ordinate, or consolidate any executive or administrative commissions, bureaus, agencies, offices, or officers now existing by law'; to create new agencies; to transfer, redistribute, or abolish the functions of others; and to utilize funds voted for any purpose for the accomplishment of that purpose by whatever means might to him seem good."

about Women—it was said of him that "his love of country exceeded that for any woman." Here was a man who seemed as gallant and patriotic as he was competent.

This lieutenant was both facile and persuasive in talk with everyone —colleagues, industrialists, and newsmen. Radiating love of work and achievement, and assuming sole responsibility while delegating authority, he got "jobs" done with dispatch and with the least friction possible.

Gradually the War Industries Board developed an authority over production and supplies that was almost as absolute as that of the War and Navy Departments over military affairs. "Let the manufacturer see the club behind your door," the President advised Baruch.

When his cooperation was sought, Woodrow Wilson directed the same close personal attention to Baruch's problems that he had been giving to those of Secretaries Baker and Daniels.[3] He formally notified all agencies and departments that the War Industries Board had become a separate administrative arm to act for him and under his direction. When Baruch and Baker had differences, and personal feelings were hurt, Wilson was able to mediate without losing the services of either man.

As the merciless grip of winter relaxed and the armies of Germany began to slog relentlessly forward into the mud of France, the President was convinced that it was no time for party considerations to govern appointments. His Council of National Defense was almost solidly Republican. Brushing aside protests that were based on political grounds, he allowed Baker to appoint Edward R. Stettinius, partner of J. P. Morgan & Company, to be surveyor general of army purchases. When aircraft production failed to match the rosy forecast that had been made by civilian promoters, and citizens in whom Wilson had confidence were insisting that the matter be probed, the President chose as investigator his rival of the 1916 campaign. Hughes's report, published October 31, 1918, found inefficiency, confusion, and minor violations of law.

When labor agitation slowed production that was essential to the war

[3] Grosvenor B. Clarkson, director of the Council of National Defense, wrote thus in *Industrial America in the World War*, p. 102: "The writer . . . interviewed some twoscore of the executives of the War Industries Board and the Council of National Defense, and . . . all of them, regardless of party affiliation, who had any personal contact with President Wilson, united in expressing appreciation of his quick grasp of the fundamentals of the most abtruse and technical problems that were laid before him. It is possibly true that the President did too long defer a determination of the problems of industrial centralization for war purposes; but, on the other hand, once he had decided his course and mapped it, in the lucid and comprehensive letter of authority to Mr. Baruch [March 4, 1918], the supporting decisions were always prompt and clear-cut."

effort, Wilson acted positively, but with regard for decent standards. To the president of a carpenters' union that was striking in the shipyards he wrote a tart note, ending with the question: "Will you cooperate or will you obstruct?"[4] Relying in many instances only upon his power as commander in chief, Wilson invoked administrative sanctions that projected the wartime power of the Presidency into new dimensions. Yet when a strict court-martial bill was proposed he denounced it as no better than Prussianism, and he warned against infringements of civil liberties that were based on "a suspicious attitude."

On Wednesdays he conferred regularly with his war council—men of action and achievement, lieutenants who could be given responsibility with the knowledge that they would accept it conscientiously, function within its limits, and soon report solid accomplishment. The value of his Cabinet had been impaired by personal ambitions and animosities and by indiscreet talking after meetings, so that the sessions of that body, on Tuesdays and Fridays, were devoted to storytelling and trivial matters. But in the war council the atmosphere was more nearly that of a corporate executive committee.

McAdoo was the only member of the Cabinet who sat regularly in the emergency body. To avoid hurting the feelings of the secretaries who were not invited, the President said little about the meetings of the new group and held them in his own study upstairs in the White House.[5] He would stand near the door and greet each man with a cheery, informal word. Before sitting down at his flat-top desk he took

[4] Daniels's diary reports discussions of labor problems in the Cabinet in July of 1917 during which Wilson concurred when Baker stated that union labor should be recognized and union wages paid everywhere. But when the President received a telegram from Hayward of the I.W.W., threatening strikes, he said indignantly: "What Hayward desires is to be a martyr. What shall I do?"

Secretary Baker pioneered in labor negotiations with unions. An adjustment commission was set up, and the procedure developed was extended to the Navy, with Daniels's approval. At Wilson's request, an attempt was made to extend this service to the shipbuilding industry; and when Hurley insisted on reviewing the decisions of the adjustment board, Wilson upheld the authority of the board. In the autumn of 1917, mediation of labor relations in other war industries was placed by the President in the hands of a commission headed by the secretary of labor, and the government did not enter into agreements.

On April 18, 1918, Wilson created a National War Labor Board "to promote and carry on mediation and adjustment in the field of production necessary for the effective conduct of the war" except "where there is by agreement or by Federal law a means of settlement which has not been invoked." Ex-President Taft was made a member of this board. In one particularly troublesome strike at Bridgeport, Conn., the President used what one observer has described as "improvised compulsion," issuing a threat of outlawry similar to the medieval threat of attainder. See Louis B. Wehle, Hidden Threads of History.

[5] Apparently the President's efforts to avoid hurt feelings were not altogether successful. Resentment was shown by Lane, Redfield, and others, according to testimony given by Vance McCormick to Ray Stannard Baker on July 15, 1928.

The men invited to the first meeting of the war council were McAdoo, Baruch, Hoover, Hurley, McCormick, and Garfield.

away a vase of flowers so that he might see the faces of his visitors. He offered cigars, asked whether the extra chairs brought in from outside were comfortable, and told a story or two. Then, getting down to business, he would listen intently as specific problems were presented for solution. He surprised his men by his grasp of practical affairs; and at least one, Hurley of the Shipping Board, felt that he had never met a business executive who was Wilson's equal.

The President felt it his duty not only to listen patiently, but to reach constructive decisions. His mind did not shirk. He would give his opinion, sometimes jotting it on a slip of paper and passing it to the man on whom the responsibility would rest. When they left the room, each man knew what his duty was and that his chief would back him to the limit as long as he did not stray from its path. They knew, too, that they were not expected to make suggestions about the work of a department other than their own, and that they should not speak in public unless the President requested it.

Wilson took comfort in the loyalty and ability of this inner council, as he became increasingly suspicious of men's motives. He came to suspect disaffection in places in which there was no proof that it existed. Going with House on February 24 to the unfinished National Cathedral, it seemed to him that the rector was about to preach about deficiencies in the War Department but had changed his mind when the President entered. Wilson noted that whenever legislators battled with him there was a backwash of scurrilous letters and gossip. The newspapers and their owners still drew his ire.

Colonel House, who had been warned by Frazier, at Paris, that "everybody is feeling the working-class volcano under his feet," thought his friend was outdoing him in leaning toward the left, despite Wilson's insistence that labor should not obstruct the war program. House found him impressed by a labor conference that met at Nottingham, England, and challenged statesmen to set forth their war aims so that the people would know for what they were suffering. Wilson, believing that the Democratic party never could serve liberal causes because of the influence of Southern reactionaries, said that a new party might be needed to pursue the ends that they had in view; but then, turning to his friend, he said pathetically: "That is a big program for a tired man to think of undertaking." The Colonel noted that his weariness was genuine. "He does not remember names so well," House recorded on February 27, "and he does not do the things we decide upon." And yet the President seemed to do more work in the eight-hour day that Dr. Grayson permitted than any other man of the Colonel's acquaintance.

There were no official functions at the White House now. Wilson enjoyed the theater more than once a week, sometimes going backstage afterward, and often humming over the tunes that he heard and retelling the jokes. He had fun in going to the circus and sharing a bag of peanuts; and he was still a rabid baseball fan. After a benefit game for the Red Cross, he greeted his problem-weighted fuel administrator breezily: "Hang it all, Garfield, I have just been to a ball game and I wish I could say three strikes and out to this job." His artistic sensibilities were still alive, too: visiting the office of a war official, he protested that he had no time to sit down, and then, attracted by a piece of sculpture, dropped into a chair and talked at length about beauty and art and its place in a world at war. Sometimes he allowed himself to think of retirement. When his fighting days were over, he confided to House, he would follow warm weather. He spoke of Bermuda as a "lotus land" where he would like to live out his days if only it belonged to the United States.

Inspecting an English tank one afternoon in April, he burned his right hand painfully on a hot exhaust pipe. He had to keep his arm in a sling, but treated the wound cavalierly and managed to play golf with one hand and to do his desk work—"Woodrow is becoming the greatest one-arm champion in the world," Edith Wilson wrote to the Colonel. The injury made him lean more than ever upon his wife's competence. Four days after the accident she reviewed a parade in his behalf. It was the first time that she stood in his place before the people.

At the Inter-Allied Conference in December it had been agreed that the United States would have about a million men in Europe in 1918, and another million ready to go. All through the winter British and French officials had been asking that American forces might be consolidated with theirs, by regiments and companies. They wished to fill up their ranks, and felt that the newcomers would be seasoned most quickly by serving in battle alongside European veterans.

In December, after House's return from abroad, Wilson had discussed the matter with the Colonel and drafted instructions to Pershing. Cautioning the general against any loss of identity of American units, the message explained that this political consideration was "secondary to the meeting of any critical situation by the most helpful use possible" of the expeditionary force.

Later he informed Baker that they must continue to trust Pershing's judgment, but should advise the general that "nothing except sudden and manifest emergency should be suffered to interfere with the building up of a great distinct American force at the front, active under its own flag and its own officers."[6] When he sat on March 1 with his Cabinet for what seemed to Secretary Lane to be "the first real talk on the war in weeks, yes, in months," he still refused to speak of his European associates as "allies."

Before the end of the month a military catastrophe gave the impetus needed to break the bonds of national tradition and to create the international high command for which House had striven at Paris at the end of 1917. On March 21 Ludendorff's armies attacked at a point that already had been pronounced vulnerable by an Executive War Board of the Supreme War Council but had not been made secure. Severance of the British and French armies seemed imminent. Unity of command was immediately imperative.

On March 27 Wilson was relieved to learn from Secretary Baker, who had gone abroad for a firsthand view of affairs, that the line of defense had been restored, that Pershing was temporarily placing all American resources at the disposal of the British and French commanders, and that the Allies had agreed that General Foch, acting under Clemenceau, should be coordinator of the armies on the Western front. On the 29th he cabled his congratulations. By this time he had before him a resolution for the use of American infantry that the Supreme War Council had adopted and that Secretary Baker endorsed.[7]

Calling in Hurley on March 30 to ask for a survey of cargo ships available for army use, Wilson spoke of his concern. He said: "Unless we send over every man possible to support the Allies in their present desperate condition, a situation may develop which would require us to pay for the entire cost of the war to the Central Powers." With pale face and drawn features he went on, calmly but firmly: "Hurley, we must go the limit." Though hesitant to commit himself until Secretary Baker returned from Europe, Wilson agreed that 120,000 troops would be sent in each of the subsequent months, subject only to the limits of

[6] Wilson felt that, if the American government bargained for British transports by placing its troops at the disposal of foreign commanders, his people would resent it and would suspect that their national military machine had broken down. But the President thought that the effect on the public would not be so bad if Pershing, as American commander in chief, decided after the men arrived in France that it was necessary to place some of them at the disposal of the British. Nevertheless, he made it very clear that he had not delegated to Pershing the right to interpret the will of the American people as that commander ventured to do. Sir William Wiseman to the writer, April 22, 1957.

[7] In March, Lloyd George tried to force the President's hand through a message that was made public. Wilson was indignant at this breach of diplomatic decorum and thought it cause for sending the British ambassador home; but House urged him not to complain, and Reading called at the White House to present the prime minister's pleas. Wilson heard his story and responded fervently: "Mr. Ambassador, you need say no more. I will do my damnedest." But when Reading persisted in pleading the British point of view, Wilson thought the ambassador too much the advocate. In June, Wilson's irritation was so great that he refused to see Reading.

shipping facilities. By the middle of April the flow of Americans across the Atlantic was increasing and Wilson confirmed Pershing's approval of Foch's position as commander in chief of the Allied armies.

Occasions arose that required the President to intervene to preserve the chain of command that Baker had forged. General March, who as chief of staff showed an extraordinary capacity to get things done, sometimes phrased dispatches in a manner that his associates thought "very curt." Pershing and other generals were irritated to the point of protesting to the secretary of war. Moreover, Leonard Wood, acting under House's advice, again sought an interview with the President.

Wilson felt that as commander in chief he must now listen judicially to the protest of so able an officer. He received Wood on May 28, and in a half-hour interview he heard his protestations of loyalty and his objections to a last-minute order that forbade his going abroad in command of a division that he had trained.[8] But the President did not retreat from the position that had been taken by Baker and March and Pershing. They talked for an hour. Wilson praised his visitor's ability as a training officer and agreed that the nation must accept a program of universal military service. He promised nothing.[9]

Wood went back to Fort Houston under a halo of martyrdom. His case was aired in the Congress by partisans and in the *New York Times*. Taft intimated that the hero was still being disciplined for talking too frankly to the Senate's Committee on Military Affairs about the Army's shortcomings. The President was forced to defend his position even to such a sympathetic critic as Richard Hooker of the Springfield *Republican*. "In the first place," Wilson wrote, "I am not sending him because

---

[8] Wood's departure for Europe in command of an American division that he had trained was prevented by a belated order from the War Department. In a letter written to Pershing on June 6, 1918, Secretary Baker explained that March had delayed the Wood transfer order for a few days. Baker later blamed himself for not realizing that Wood and his division were heading abroad until the division had entrained for New York. James W. Wadsworth MS, pp. 188 ff., Oral History Project, Columbia University.

[9] Actually the President, warned by House that frustrating Wood might be a costly political mistake, asked Baker casually whether any harm would be done by giving Wood a command in Europe apart from Pershing. On June 1, therefore, Baker cabled to Pershing that the Wood incident had led to considerable newspaper agitation and much speculation. While assuring the American commander that Wood would not be sent to France without his assent, the secretary remarked: "I am strongly inclined to think it would be wiser to let him go to Italy when our first contingent goes there."

Asked for his opinion of this idea, Pershing replied on June 10 that Wood was not only physically unqualified, but politically ambitious, unscrupulous, superficial in his military knowledge, and inclined toward the spectacular, that General Bliss felt that Wood's presence would disturb relations with the Allies. Suggesting that Wood might well be sent to Russia as a military representative or retained in the important role of training officer, Pershing urgently requested that the man not be sent to France or Italy in any capacity. "This is no place for political generals," the message said.

Near the end of the war Wilson, advising a cousin to obey military orders without complaint, confessed he was "sick and tired" of army officers who wanted to be shifted. F. W. McM. Woodrow to the writer.

General Pershing has said that he does not want him, and in the second place, General Pershing's disinclination to have General Wood sent over is only too well grounded. Wherever General Wood goes there is controversy and conflict of judgment. On this side of the water we can take care of that sort of thing, because the fighting is not being done here, but it would be fatal to let it go on anywhere near the front . . . He is a man of unusual ability but apparently absolutely unable to submit his judgment to those who are superior to him in command. I am sorry that his great ability cannot be made use of in France."

His own proper function, Wilson conceived, was to exert his influence on the home front and the psychological front rather than in the councils of battle. He reacted to the military crisis of the spring of 1918 in the same way in which the political leaders of the Allies had responded to earlier crises.

On April 6, in a speech opening the campaign for a Third Liberty Loan, he delivered his most caustic indictment of German militarism and accepted without cavil the gage of battle. The prophet wished, in a brief, striking talk, to leave the door of peace open but at the same time to burn the fear of his God into the hearts of his adversaries. Only one response to the obduracy of the Philistines seemed to him possible; this was, he said, "Force, Force, to the utmost, Force without stint or limit, the righteous and triumphant Force which shall make Right the law of the world, and cast every selfish dominion down in the dust."

In this, again, he reflected the mood of his people, as their soldiers were getting into battle and casualty lists grew longer. In the middle of May they let their prophet know that they were harkening to his word. Visiting the Houses at New York, the Wilsons went to see Fred Stone perform in *Jack O'Lantern*; and when the President was impersonated on the stage the audience went into a frenzy of applause. But the object of their enthusiasm was not elated. Forced to respond, he rose and said: "Ladies and gentlemen, you are laboring under a delusion. You think you see the President of the United States. You are mistaken. Really you see a tired man having a good time!"

The next day he was to review a Red Cross parade; but he insisted, against the protests of his family, on marching. Walking for two miles at the head of the procession, he laughed like a Princeton boy when the multitude hailed him. In the evening Cleveland Dodge introduced him to a throng at the Metropolitan Opera House, and he delivered a powerful appeal for national unity and international amity. He warned against peace talk by the enemy, deprecated it as a ruse to get a free hand in carrying out their purposes of "conquest and exploitation" in the East. "So far as I am concerned," he said, "I intend to stand by Russia as well as France." Wilson was surprised when this bold assertion, injected as an afterthought, brought his New York audience to their feet cheering.

Though he had been harsh toward German militarism, Wilson had not lost his scholarly perspective. "I would be ashamed to use knockdown and drag-out language," he said to a group of foreign correspondents two days later. "That is not the language of liberty." Quoting Burke, he went on: " 'A government which those living under it will guard' . . . is the only possible definition of a free government. . . . There isn't any one kind of government which we have the right to impose upon any nation. . . . I am not fighting for democracy except for the peoples that want democracy . . . the people have the right to make any kind of government they please."

In shaping a policy for restoring the shattered Eastern front, the President found himself dealing with forces remote and enigmatic. As early as January of 1918 British officials had suggested that Japan send troops to occupy the trans-Siberian Railway and the port of Vladivostok, where a small British contingent was already stationed. The War Cabinet at London hoped that the United States would send a small force to cooperate. Moreover, at the end of February Wilson received a report from the American engineering mission in Siberia to the effect that the German menace was "imminent and increasing" and Japan would go in whether America joined or not.

Balfour pressed the proposition upon House at the end of January as one that the British Cabinet regarded as "of great military importance" and "of immediate urgency." But the Colonel advised Wilson that it would be a great political mistake to let Japanese troops enter Siberia. It seemed to House, who discussed the matter with Ambassador Boris A. Bakhmeteff, that such a venture would rouse ill will among the Bolsheviki and stir up Slavic resentment throughout Europe "because of the race question if for nothing else." The State Department, too, regarding the Japanese as the prime promoters of an occupation of Siberia, thought that it would be unwise for the United States to take part.

After discussing the arguments pro and con with House, the President drafted, and then redrafted, a note for the Allied ambassadors. In the first version, of which the State Department gave the substance to the envoys, Wilson explained that it seemed unwise to join in a Siberian expedition, while at the same time giving assurance that he had no objection to such an enterprise on the part of Japan.[10]

After the treaty of Brest-Litovsk was signed and ratified, French and Italian statesmen demanded immediate action in Siberia; and the British government renewed pressure upon Wilson. Six times, in the early months of 1918, the United States government rejected proposals of the Allies for intervention, and it warned its officials repeatedly to stay aloof from Russia's internal affairs. But the moral indignation of the Western world was castigating the revolutionaries in a torrent of messages to the State Department. It was asserted that, if the flags of the Allies appeared in Russia, the people would rally to them and throw out the leaders who had collaborated with their German enemy.

For months the President resisted the pleas that came to him from many quarters.[11] The reconstruction of an Eastern front seemed to him impractical. He did some very lonely thinking about Russia. Refusing the offer of a summer place that would take him away from the sweltering heat of the capital, he told House that he had been "sweating blood" and that the puzzle seemed to go to pieces like quicksilver under his touch. He found it hard to fix a policy, in his desire to leave the Russian people free to work out their own salvation and his fear of driving the terror to still greater extremes, as the French Revolution had been driven by external pressure.

In the first week of July he reached a decision. On July 3 he learned

[10] In a redraft of this paper, after further caveats from House, Wilson wrote on March 5: "If it were undertaken the Government of the United States assumes that the most explicit assurances would be given that it was undertaken by Japan as an ally of Russia, in Russia's interest, and with the sole view of holding it safe against Germany and at the absolute disposal of the final peace conference . . . it is the judgment of the Government of the United States, uttered with the utmost respect, that even with such assurances given, they could . . . be discredited by those whose interest it was to discredit them; that a hot resentment would be generated in Russia itself, and that the whole action might play into the hands of the enemies of Russia, and particularly of the enemies of the Russian revolution, for which the Government of the United States entertains the greatest sympathy, in spite of all the unhappiness and misfortune which has for the time being sprung out of it."

[11] French officials were especially vehement. Noting that philosophic Lord Balfour had succeeded in his mission to Washington, they drafted Professor Henri Bergson to go to the White House and plead with the prophet whom he admired and from whom his praise drew tears. Ambassador Reading, citing an inquiry from Trotsky about the aid that the Allies now could offer, persistently urged that the United States send many divisions to help to re-establish the Eastern front against Germany. Boris A. Bakhmeteff, too, now recommended the creation of a "political beachhead" in Russia at which all anti-Bolshevik forces could gather. On May 2, Ambassador Francis telegraphed that the hour for intervention had come ("The longer we wait," he wired, "the stronger foothold Germany will secure"); and on June 5, Minister Reinsch wired from China that all American agents in that country agreed that the Allied action in Siberia was "absolutely demanded" to save the region from German control, and that joint action was desirable because of Russian distrust of Japan.

The President was moved also by deep sympathy for Masaryk, the crusading Czech statesman who had come to Washington on May 9 to plead the cause of the army of his compatriots that had migrated eastward into Siberia. On June 19, Masaryk called at the White House and found the President to be "the most intensely human man" he had ever met—a man "actually incandescent with feeling!" See Kennan, *The Decision to Intervene*.

that migrating Czech units had entered Vladivostok and that more British and Japanese forces had landed there. Simultaneously a message came from the Supreme War Council, reporting a unanimous feeling that military intervention in Siberia was essential to an Allied victory. They sought Wilson's approval "before it is too late."

Jotting on a pad of paper an outline of American policy, the President read his notes to his chief military and civil advisers on the 6th. Though he would not sanction the participation of American troops in Russia's civil strife, and argued that intervention would not help to win the war against Germany, he did consent to the dispatch of two policing expeditions: one to support a British venture at Murmansk; [12] another to aid— and control—a Japanese force at Vladivostok. In each case the intention was to prevent the Bolsheviki from seizing supplies shipped to czarist armies; and it was hoped too that the expeditions would re-establish rallying points for anti-German factions and especially for beleaguered Czech troops. The forces dispatched to Vladivostok had the additional mission of protecting American railway engineers.

In July Wilson's determination to maintain his faith in the Russian Revolution was undermined by shocks to his emotions from the brutality of the new regime. While dining at the home of Secretary Lane he learned of the murder of the Czar and the royal family; and he rose from the table and broke up the party, saying that a great menace to the world had taken shape and he was sure that all would share his feeling that it was no time for gaiety.

Wilson had been urged, both by Soviet leaders and by his associates at Washington, to embark on a constructive policy of economic relations with Russia. Offering to permit American participation in the de-

[12] In May of 1918 Wilson had been ready to share in "any practical military effort" in North Russia as a part of the war effort against Germany, but only if the venture had the approval of Foch and would proceed "on the sure sympathy of the Russian people . . ." The President had approved, in April, the dispatch of an American warship to Murmansk; and as of June 11, after Washington had been warned that Germans planned to capture Murmansk and operate their submarines from arctic ports, a hundred and fifty American Marines landed.

When Foch cabled to the President on June 27 that since no appreciable diminution of the forces to be sent to France would result, the sending of a few American troops to Russia would be justified, and when Bliss reported on July 12 that there would be "undercurrents of resentment" and a greater possibility of failure if the United States refused to participate in Russia, and that the nation should be represented by her "fair part," Wilson gave his decision reluctantly to the secretary of war. Baker suspected that "other considerations" than the winning of the war moved those on the Supreme War Council who favored the expedition, and he had his first serious disagreement with Wilson over this policy. "Baker," the President said, "I wholly agree with all you say from a military point of view, but we are fighting this war with Allies and I have felt obliged to refuse to do so many things they have asked me to do that I really feel obliged to fall in with their wishes here. I have, however, stipulated that the American contingent in both cases is to be small."

When Wilson noted, at the conference on the 6th, that General March opposed the expedition to Siberia, for military reasons and because of a fear of Japanese expansion, the President replied: "Well, we will have to take that chance." See March, *The Nation at War*, pp. 123 ff.

velopment of railroads, mines, waterways, and agricultural tracts, Lenin had sent an overture to Washington in May through Raymond Robins, an American Red Cross man who maintained a precarious contact with the leaders at Moscow. Wilson considered the proposal and wrote thus to Lansing on July 3: "The suggestions are certainly much more sensible than I thought the author of them capable of. I differ from them only in practical details." In an *aide-mémoire* written on his own typewriter and given to the ambassadors of the Allies on July 17, the President asserted that it was the hope and purpose of the United States to send an economic mission to Siberia at the earliest opportunity; but when the British government approved his general plan he showed no eagerness to proceed, and remarked that the mission that he had in mind would be concerned much more with relief and education than with economic development.[13]

In giving priority to military intervention and the restoration of order, Wilson insisted that the expeditions should not fall into the paths of nineteenth-century imperialism. His *aide-mémoire* explained that the United States, feeling that military intervention would "injure rather than help" Russia, would not "take part in such intervention or sanction it in principle." It yielded, however, to the Supreme Command in establishing a small force at Murmansk to guard military stores, and it stated there was "immediate necessity for helping the Czecho-Slovaks at Vladivostok." However, Wilson proposed "to ask all . . . to unite in assuring the people of Russia in the most public and solemn manner that none of the governments uniting in action either in Siberia or in northern Russia contemplates any interference of any kind with the political sovereignty of Russia, any intervention in her internal affairs, or any impairment of her territorial integrity either now or hereafter, but that each of the associated powers has the single object of affording such aid as shall be acceptable, and only such aid as shall be acceptable,

---

[13] Lansing had warned the President on June 13 that the American people were demanding a constructive policy, and had favored putting off Allied demands for military intervention until an economic commission could report on the situation. But Wilson had not acted.

When House raised the question several weeks later, the President replied that Secretary of Commerce Redfield had "messed the matter up." Wilson felt that an economic mission to Russia, to be successful, must be unofficial and financed by private funds; but Redfield had objected that under private sponsorship a mission would be open to suspicion as a profit-seeking enterprise.

Agreeing with Wilson's purposes toward Russia, House—like Secretary Baker and Brandeis —disapproved of the President's temporizing. House, hoping that Hoover might undertake a mission of relief and economic aid and take along Leonard Wood and hold him "in subjection," had discussed the matter with Hoover in June and with Wilson. Lansing and Baruch also suggested Hoover as head of an economic commission; but Wilson felt that he could not get along without his food administrator at that time.

Finally, on Oct. 10, 1918, Wilson approved the sending of an *aide-mémoire* to the Allies regarding American plans for economic aid to Russia. In the spring of 1919 this idea was brought forward again, with emphasis on relief. *See* p. 292n. below.

to the Russian people in their endeavor to regain control of their own affairs, their own territory and their own destiny." Thus, while failing to provide liaison with the Allied forces in Russia, Wilson by an ambiguous and straddling pronouncement made his nation vulnerable to the charge of unauthorized meddling in the affairs of Russia.

However, Wilson pressed Tokyo, in particular, for assurance that the expedition to Siberia would not be used for imperialistic purposes. The elusiveness of Japanese statesmen fretted him, and he sent an impatient message to Ambassador Morris, suggesting that, unless the Japanese limited their force to seven thousand men, he could not approve the expedition. Finally, after several parleys between diplomats, Counselor Polk informed the President on August 3 that, though the Japanese government still felt that more than the stipulated number would be needed to maintain order in Siberia, they would yield to the necessity for immediate action and the pleas of the United States, while reserving the question of sending additional forces until circumstances should arise that might make this necessary.[14] Taking this as the best assurance that could be gotten from Tokyo, the President prepared a statement for the press that followed the argument of his *aide-mémoire* of July 17.

Thus Wilson accepted the view that military victory was the first essential and that the United States should do her share in the fighting on the Western front and the policing of the borders of Russia. But he resisted temptations to seek aggrandizement for self or nation. Refusing to buy British bonds that would yield 6 per cent, he invested every penny that he could save in American Liberty Bonds at lower rates of interest. Some of his people hoped that their commercial position in China and Latin America might be improved by the war's outcome, but he convinced Sir William Wiseman that he did not share this feeling.

In the months when the fighting in France ebbed and flowed precariously, the prophet kept his concept of a just peace clear and vibrant. It was the more important that he do this because, as a war leader, he now found himself obliged by the necessity for victory to pursue stern policies that he had criticized when he had been neutral, measures such as a bill extending the age limits of the manpower draft, an amendment to the espionage act that gave the government absolute powers, and the adoption of British strictures on neutrals in regard to contraband and trading with the enemy.

[14] Polk reported his conversation with the Japanese ambassador to the President thus: "I asked him two or three times whether it was his understanding that the Japanese forces would be limited to ten or twelve thousand men, and he said that . . . he felt there was no question on that point." Polk reported that the ambassador said that Japan had no intention of sending more men than were needed to assist the Czechs.

On July 4, when the United States had more than a million men overseas and they were helping to turn back the crest of a German wave, he
reopened the moral battle that he had waged months earlier without
immediate gain. On this day on which his people celebrated their own
emancipation he reinforced the appeal to humanity that he had made
in his epochal addresses of January and February.

Often Woodrow Wilson required an impresario to cast him in a
compelling role. The spur for the Fourth-of-July address came from
George Creel. The Committee on Public Information decided to cele-
bate the holiday by asking every foreign-language group in the country
to take part in a pilgrimage to Mount Vernon, and Creel begged the
President to be the speaker of the occasion.

At first Wilson shrank from the idea as if it were grossly improper.
"At the grave of Washington on the Fourth of July!" he exclaimed.
"Why, my dear fellow, I would be crushed under a weight of presumption." It was a week before he surrendered, Creel tells us, but then he
entered into the affair with enthusiasm and invited the foreign-language
delegates to go downriver with him on the *Mayflower*. Waves of heat
were shimmering over the Potomac; and Wilson, noticing the discomfort of guests who wore dress clothes, insisted that everyone "peel off
the funeral wrappings." He set an example by taking off his own coat.
Happy and laughing, he looked upon this cosmopolitan gathering as a
living demonstration of the possibility of a league of nations.

The President's yacht anchored in midstream, the company went
ashore and climbed the slope, and the prophet took his place beside the
tomb. He said:

It is significant . . . that Washington and his associates . . . spoke and
acted, not for a class, but for a people. It has been left to us to see to it that it
shall be understood that they spoke and acted, not for a single people only,
but for all mankind. . . . These are the ends for which the associated peoples
of the world are fighting and which must be conceded them before there can
be peace:

I. The destruction of every arbitrary power anywhere that can separately,
secretly, and of its single choice disturb the peace of the world; or, if it
cannot presently be destroyed, at least its reduction to virtual impotence.

II. The settlement of every question, whether of territory, of sovereignty,
of economic arrangement, or of political relationship, upon the basis of the
free acceptance of that settlement by the people immediately concerned, and
not upon the basis of the material interest or advantage of any other nation
or people which may desire a different settlement for the sake of its own
exterior influence or mastery.

III. The consent of all nations to be governed in their conduct towards each other by the same principles of honor and of respect for the common law of civilized society that govern the individual citizens of all modern states in their relations with one another; to the end that all promises and covenants may be sacredly observed, no private plots or conspiracies hatched, no selfish injuries wrought with impunity, and a mutual trust established upon the handsome foundation of a mutual respect for right.

IV. The establishment of an organization of peace which shall make it certain that the combined power of free nations will check every invasion of right and serve to make peace and justice the more secure by affording a definite tribunal of opinion to which all must submit and by which every international readjustment that cannot be amicably agreed upon by the peoples directly concerned shall be sanctioned.

These great objects can be put into a single sentence. What we seek is the reign of law, based upon the consent of the governed and sustained by the organized opinion of mankind.

Again Anglo-Saxon liberals took heart. The American prophet could feel now that he stood pre-eminent before the peoples of the world as their champion in the human cause that he sensed to be the greatest of the century. The age was indeed writing its "political autobiography" through him.

But on the day after the speech at Mount Vernon a report from abroad revealed that Lloyd George had laughed at the proposed league and Clemenceau had sneered at it.

The prophet received this news with eyes unblinking and flashing. "Yes," he said, "I know that Europe is still governed by the same reactionary forces which controlled this country until a few years ago. But I am satisfied that if necessary I can reach the people of Europe over the heads of their rulers."

CHAPTER X

BUILDING FOR A WILSONIAN PEACE

IN THE SPRING OF 1918, while the warmaking agencies at Washington were being strengthened by centralization of authority, the President was embarrassed by the strong ego of a lieutenant very close to him. McAdoo, who wished to drive down the price that his railroads had to pay for coal, seemed to the fuel administration to be "butting in." Ill with tonsillitis and frustrated because his own conscience was overruled by his father-in-law's sense of right, he asked Colonel House whether he could hope to enforce his will by threatening to resign.

When the Colonel warned Wilson that McAdoo might resign over the issue of the price of coal, the President replied: "He may resign if he wants to, but I am determined that he shall not have his way because he is wrong in this instance." Complaining that his son-in-law had drawn up revenue bills and other important papers without consulting him, he felt that McAdoo had grown too arbitrary, that sooner or later their relationship must come to a crisis. "Son-in-law or no son-in-law," he declared, "if he wants to resign he can do so. The country will probably blame me, but I am ready to stand it." He feared that the people would think that he had turned McAdoo out because he himself was ambitious for a third term in the White House and regarded his son-in-law as a rival.

The Colonel, understanding and sympathizing with the complex emotions of kinship, public duty, and ambition that intertwined in the hearts of these Scots, brought about a reconciliation with the aid of Dr. Grayson. McAdoo satisfied his conscience by airing his views in an eleven-page letter to the President, without a suggestion of resignation. He then conferred with his father-in-law thrice during the next two days; and on May 24 the controversy over the coal price was settled and the railroads were required to pay the government rate.

House was active also in healing fissures in executive-legislative understanding. More cautious than ever about volunteering counsel that might be offensive, he never allowed himself to appear perturbed when his friend ignored him or differed with him, never complained if Wilson forgot to give him a share of credit for what they achieved together. In conversation with an English journalist, the Colonel confessed his method: "Never begin by arguing. Discover a common hate,

exploit it, get the President warmed up, and then start your business."
Fearing that a book published under the title *The Real Colonel House*
was too complimentary, he confessed to Wilson that he felt like soap
being advertised. His friend replied: "I have known in reading certain
passages that you would squirm. . . . We just have to grin and bear it."

If the President sensed that House was sometimes disingenuous, he
did not let this perception outweigh his appreciation of the Colonel's
good intentions and effectiveness. But it was not so easy as it had been
for the counselor to hold the confidence of the man through whom he
hoped to make his mark in history. Often Edith Wilson was present
when they met, and the tactics to which the President was responsive
were not equally appealing to her. Nevertheless, she sent House a confidential report on her husband's attitude toward McAdoo and assured
him that, though some people got on her nerves, it was always fun to
talk to someone as understanding as the Colonel. "Please remember we
need and want you always," she wrote to House on May 6.[1]

In mid-May the Wilsons and the Houses dined together at the
Waldorf Hotel, with no one else present but Dr. Grayson. It seemed to
the Colonel that the President talked most indiscreetly in the presence
of waiters. After the meal, when Wilson complained of acute indigestion, House urged him to get some rest by visiting at Magnolia during
the summer. The President promised to do this.

On August 14 the Wilsons arrived by special train at the North Shore
resort. The President showed a desire to be with his friend as much as
possible, and suggested that Mrs. Wilson chat with Mrs. House in the
evenings. Some of those present thought that his wife resented this
separation. She did not seem happy, either, when House ventured to
advise her that her husband did not delegate enough of his work, and
she protested that when it had been delegated it had not been done well.

Early in this summer of 1918 the enemies of Germany, striking back
from the verge of disaster, had been gaining on the battlefield. But at
last, under the impact of a threat to survival, the Western democracies
conferred upon capable men the authority that was required to check
the military machine of the Kaiser. Under Lloyd George and Clemenceau, divisive interests in Britain and France were channeled to the
common cause of victory. Ferdinand Foch directed the smashing of the

---

[1] Mrs. Wilson's own recollection of her feelings toward Colonel House at this time, as set
forth in *My Memoir*, pp. 155 and 237, does not agree with the documentary evidence. Either
her memory was faulty or, deferring to her husband, she did not reveal her true feeling to
House in 1918. In her book she testifies that as early as January of 1918 she thought the
Colonel a trimmer who changed his mind too quickly and that she questioned his ability as
an adviser.

last great German drive and took an initiative that he was never to relinquish. In the spearhead of his counterattack he used the fresh vigor of two American divisions. The United States had sent more than a million men across the Atlantic.[1a]

In August it seemed that the military situation had improved enough so that a peace conference was not too remote for serious contemplation. A month earlier Wilson had felt that at last the time had come to put on paper the ideas for organizing the world for peace that he had repeatedly presented in general terms; and now he had with him a constitution for a league of nations that House had drafted at his request and had called a "Covenant"—to appeal to his friend's Scottish nature.

The President could not forget what he had taught his students: that the political constitution that had best withstood the buffets of fortune had been one that grew out of custom—that of England. He thought that, if the executive council of a world league commended itself to the public opinion of the world, it would get authority as it needed it. He still held the view that he had set before House in a letter of March 22, 1918:

My own conviction, as you know, is that the administrative *constitution* of the league must *grow* and not be made; that we must *begin* with solemn covenants, covering mutual guarantees of political independence and territorial integrity (if the final territorial agreements of the peace conference are fair and satisfactory and *ought* to be perpetuated), but that the method of carrying those mutual pledges out should be left to develop of itself, case by case. Any attempt to begin by putting executive authority in the hands of any particular group of powers would be to sow a harvest of jealousy and distrust which would spring up at once and choke the whole thing. To take one thing, and only one, but quite sufficient in itself: the United States Senate would never ratify any treaty which put the force of the United States at the disposal of any such group or body. Why begin at the impossible end when there is a possible end and it is feasible to plant a system which will slowly ripen into fruition?[2]

[1a] For a summary of the effect of American participation in the war see André Kaspi, *Le Temps des Américains,* Paris, 1976, pp. 341–43.

[2] On Sept. 3, 1917, Lord Robert Cecil had written to House to suggest that able men in Britain and America begin to consider peace machinery for the postwar world. He had warned against the danger of setting up another "Holy Alliance," which at its beginning, he said, was actually a "League to Enforce Peace." House had taken this letter to Wilson, and the President had suggested that the scholars of The Inquiry follow Cecil's suggestion. He dreaded premature discussion of a league of nations constitution by reformers whom he characterized as "woolgatherers."

House consulted many oracles—foreign as well as American, Republican as well as Democratic. After preparing his draft of a covenant, he had checked it with plans drawn up by a French government committee under the chairmanship of Léon Bourgeois and also with a constitution drafted by a committee of British experts under Lord Phillimore. He adopted several articles from the latter. Notified by Cecil that the British government proposed to

When the friends conferred at Magnolia, Wilson took the Colonel aside one morning and criticized the draft covenant that House had prepared. To put the author of the document in good humor, he told of once writing a platform for the Indiana Democratic Convention and receiving this comment: "We put it through just as you wrote it except we cut your six pages down to three." In comparison, the treatment that he had given to the Colonel's masterpiece seemed gentle. He had merely eliminated five of the twenty-three articles and rephrased some of the remaining text. Provisions that he struck out called for an international court and the use of national courts by members of the league.

As the friends talked at the seaside they had before them a long, scholarly letter from Elihu Root, who agreed with House and disagreed with Wilson, in thinking that legal institutions should be set up to which members of an international league could be directed to submit their differences for "consideration." Root raised a perplexity that had beset the President already. To what extent would the people of the United States stand back of world government? Would they agree to go to war at the command of a supranational organization? "Nothing can be worse in international affairs than to make agreements and break them," Root cautioned. Yet, in revising the Colonel's draft of a covenant, Wilson boldly strengthened the sanctions against offending nations by providing for the use of military force in addition to economic measures that House had proposed.

He differed, too, with the Colonel's reluctance to give small states an equal share with the large in a league of nations. To fail to insist on such a policy would contradict all his protestations, Wilson asserted, deeply concerned. To this criticism House tactfully replied that he believed in his friend's ideal, but had practical reservations: the little nations, voting as a majority, might overrule the few large nations that would bear the burdens of policing the world.

Protecting his views cannily from both journalists and politicians who might exploit them for selfish purposes, Wilson treasured the draft that was discussed at Magnolia, and later took it to Paris and used it as the basis of the final Covenant of the League of Nations.

Carrying out the President's wishes, House and Wiseman drafted a message to London that explained Wilson's views in detail. Not only did they inform the British government of his desire to postpone discussion of the nature of the league that might be set up to preserve peace; but in a separate cable they reported the President's adverse reaction to

---

publish the Phillimore report but first would welcome American views, the Colonel had warned Wilson that Britain and France might seize postwar leadership from America by publicly making a proposal around which opinion would crystallize.

the ambition of British and French citizens to divide the spoils of war and monopolize postwar trade.[3]

Six days after this cable was sent the Colonel recorded in his diary: "Both Sir William and I scent trouble between our governments and it will take considerable vigiliance to ward it off. I think the main trouble comes from Lloyd George's inability to act in any but a thoroughly selfish way—a way, indeed, which approaches discourtesy . . . Both he and Clemenceau dislike the President and the President dislikes them. . . ." In September a letter from Lord Robert Cecil warned Wilson that the establishment of a league of nations would be opposed by the bureaucracies of Europe, who were past masters of threats and obstruction and resistance, by the militarists, of whom there were many outside Germany, and by people who thought that the Germans would join and make use of the league, "lulling us and others to sleep, and then falling on us when we have disarmed."

Old World statesmen were not ready to jettison the policy of preserving peace by balancing powers; for, after all, Europe had been free of major wars for almost half a century before the system had broken down in 1914. Traditionalists were skeptical of the prophet who was rising like a young Lochinvar in the West. To be sure, he had to be respected as leader of a nation that was swinging the military tide against Germany and that now possessed the most powerful economic force on earth. His words were glamorous and made hearts beat faster. But might not his prescription of a concert of powers take the world back to the war-breeding system of the Congress of Vienna? It was no easy task to achieve what Colonel House set down in his diary to be the prime essential to the creation of a league of nations—"get Great Britain and France committed first."

On August 14 the German General Staff confessed to their Kaiser that the Fatherland's hope of crushing victory must be abandoned; and with this prospect removed, the Austrians were theatening to sue for peace. Civilian morale in Germany drooped, so undermining the spirit

[3] The message, signed by Wiseman, said: "The President thinks we ought to adopt the line that we have no desire to deny Germany her fair share of the world's commerce, and that it is her own militarists who are ruining her trade by prolonging the war and obliging us to maintain a blockade. . . . For your own private information, I may tell you that the President will try to get Congress to give powers to the Executive to control American raw-material exports for a period of years after peace. While this would not be openly aimed at Germany, it would be a formidable weapon for the United States to bring to the Peace Conference."

While protesting against the British government's inclination to discriminate in favor of her own merchants—in a letter to Lansing on Aug. 29 he had asked that Britain be urged to reciprocate American policy of allowing the Allies to make purchases in the United States on the same terms as those applied to the American government and civilians—Wilson warned Hurley to make no plan for postwar shipping that might be taken to mean "that we, like the English, are planning to dominate everything and to oust everybody we can oust."

of the Army that by September 10 General Hindenburg thought the need for negotiation was "immediate."

Wilson continued to avoid argument that might threaten the unanimity of efforts to win the war. By the middle of the month, however, American troops were completing the pinching out of the St. Mihiel salient. Bulgars and Germans fled headlong north of Salonika. On the 16th an Austro-Hungarian note, reaching Washington through Swedish channels, proposed a "confidential non-binding conversation" on peace terms, to be held on neutral soil.

Wilson rejected the Austrian offer immediately and bluntly. "The United States," he declared, "will entertain no proposal for a conference upon a matter concerning which it has made its position and purpose so plain." His reply was approved heartily by the Congress. And his faith in democratic public opinion was stiffened when, on September 19, an inter-Allied labor conference unanimously endorsed his Fourteen Points as a basis for peace.

Further to strengthen the unity of his own people, and to sway the Allied governments to his kind of peace, he carefully wrote out a new pronouncement of his war aims. Calling House to Washington for a weekend visit, he said that he had decided to speak out publicly, rather than undertake secret negotiations with London as the Colonel had recommended.

The text of this address settled, the talk of the friends strayed to other subjects: world sentiment for an association of nations and the French concept of the ideal league, which Wilson now saw for the first time as House set it before him; a new stamp for imprinting "Woodrow Wilson" on the flyleaf of books, a device of which the President seemed as proud as he had once been of the ornate signatures that he had inscribed in the books of his boyhood. The Colonel found his friend pensive about his place in history, conscious that his fame depended largely on the result of the war.

The *éminence grise* put in a word for his own profession. When Wilson spoke of criticisms of George Washington, House repeated an opinion that he had expressed before, that Washington's greatness grew from his ability to know good advice from bad. This was a virtue that the Colonel did not attribute to the President. It seemed to House that in rejecting the Austrian peace overture, out of hand, the President had offended against the spirit of team play that he preached. The Colonel sometimes grew restive under his responsibilities, a little resentful of the exacting will of his master and of his secretiveness.

That evening at dinner the President was reminded again of his dependence on good counsel. Edith Wilson's sister told House of the compliments that she had heard paid to him. "You are a maker of men," she said to the Colonel.

The "made" man at the head of the table took the remark with a wry smile. "He ought to change his pattern," the President jested.

On September 27 Wilson went to New York to deliver the speech that he had prepared. On the train he explained to Tumulty that the time had come to proclaim America's opposition to a backsliding peace, a reversion to the old days of alliances, competing armaments, and land-grabbing. Reading his address at the Metropolitan Opera House before five thousand sellers of war bonds, he devoted only a few sentences to the finance drive and then went on to strike another strong blow for his peace aims.

Plainly the Allies could not "come to terms" with the Central Empires, he said; there could be no peace obtained by any kind of bargain or compromise with governments that were without honor and a standard of justice. His audience, fearful above all that America might be caught in a "peace-trap," understood this and applauded. But as the prophet lifted his thought from the jungle toward Heaven, the blood of the bond sellers responded less warmly. The price that must be paid for genuine peace, he insisted, was "impartial justice in every item of the settlement, no matter whose interest is crossed; and not only impartial justice, but also the satisfaction of the several peoples whose fortunes are dealt with."

Here Wilson's thinking ran into a fundamental dichotomy that was to rend him apart and prostrate him before the making of peace was achieved. Devotion to "justice" was nothing new among peacemakers. The delegates to the Congress of Vienna had professed it a century before. But nineteenth-century diplomats had been accustomed to accept the concepts of justice that grew out of their own nation's "sacred egoism" and special interests; and sitting down with the statesmen of other nations who took an equally practical view, they had tried to work out a reconciliation of purposes that they recognized to be conflicting.

At the end of this war, however, Wilson conceived that the United States had no selfish interests except those that she shared with all civilized nations—to prevent a recrudescence of chauvinistic despotism, trade wars, and other phenomena that might disturb the peace. Therefore, the prophet sensed a rare opportunity to build a great rainbow arch of what he called "impartial" justice far above the limited concepts of justice that were worshiped in the temples of the nations. He said: "No special or separate interest of any single nation or any group of nations can be made the basis of any part of the settlement which is not consistent with the common interest of all." National interests would be expendable for the good of all humanity. If only he could make the peoples see that all would be better off if each would sacrifice something! His sympathies forked out toward mankind where he found them, and at the same time to the exalted New Jerusalem to which he wished to lift them. He was expressing at once the palliative instincts of an Irish heart and the prophetic impulses of a Scottish soul.

A paralyzing fission was prevented by faith in an ideal plan of action. If he could set in motion a force that might in time lift all mankind to an estate a little below the angels, the motives that surged within him would be no longer irreconcilable. And so, after promising "impartial justice" and then "the satisfaction of the several peoples," he went on immediately to say: "[The] indispensable instrumentality is a League of Nations formed under Covenants that will be efficacious . . . And as I see it, the constitution of that League of Nations and the clear definition of its objects must be a part, is in a sense the most essential part, of the peace settlement itself." Within the league there were to be no "special covenants and understandings," economic or political; for such things, he was convinced, were "the prolific source in the modern world of the plans and passions that produce war."

Having put forth his platform for the peacemaking, Wilson then challenged the leaders of the Allies to "speak as they have occasion" as plainly as he had tried to speak. He invited them to criticize both his interpretation of the issues and the means that he recommended for settling them. He was giving them due notice of what they might expect from him at a peace conference.

After the address at the Opera House, still flushed with the fervor of his pleading, the President went to his hotel sitting room with the Colonel and speculated on the effect of the speech. The next day, returning to Washington in his private car and resting his mind by holding a skein of yarn for Edith Wilson to wind, he learned that the reactions of the American press were those of the five thousand who had heard him. Applauding his firmness toward the enemy and approving his general intent, they seemed to ignore his challenge to constructive peacemaking. To be sure, certain liberals at home and abroad endorsed the President's views: from England, Lord Grey cabled congratulations and Lord Robert Cecil called the speech "the finest description of our war aims yet uttered." But Clemenceau and Lloyd George were unconvinced.

Meanwhile events in Europe were speeding the approach of peacemaking. On the very day on which Wilson spoke out, General Bliss was writing to General Pershing: "It looks as if you are going to get the damned Germans out of France this year." Two days later Bulgaria, on whom the United States had never declared war, stopped fighting. The next day Allenby's British army took Damascus and Turkey was in an agony of collapse.

From Berlin, where already there had been efforts toward mediation by a neutral, the President's speech drew a positive response. On September 30 the Kaiser granted parliamentary government to his people; and on the same day General Ludendorff concluded that a proposal of peace should be sent forthwith to Washington through Switzerland, that the Army could not wait forty-eight hours longer for a move that would save it from disaster.

Prince Max of Baden, becoming chancellor on October 4 with an endorsement from the Reichstag, wished to delay. He sensed that the Army was trying to shift the onus for defeat to civilian shoulders. However, pressed by Hindenburg, he sent a note to Washington asking the President to take steps for the restoration of peace, to notify all belligerents of this request, and to invite them to send delegates to begin negotiations. Accepting the program laid down by the President, the Germans asked that further bloodshed be avoided by the immediate conclusion of a general armistice.

News of the coming of the German note reached Woodrow Wilson on Sunday, October 6. It was a day of uncommon quiet in Washington. While a lethal epidemic of influenza raged through the city and kept people from congregating in churches, dispatches from France reported the bitterest fighting in which Americans had taken part. As had been his habit since he had proclaimed the observance of "gasless Sundays," the President went riding in an old surrey with fringed top, drawn by a pair of bay horses and escorted by secret service men on bicycles. The German message dropped like a bomb into the doldrums in the capital.

The military leaders of the Allies, not daring to expect an end of hostilities before 1919, still were calling for men and munitions. Moreover, General March was insisting that shipments of troops proceed on schedule despite the urging of medical men that no more soldiers be sent to France until the influenza epidemic was checked. Pressed by March for assent to his plans at the very time when the enemy were asking for peace, the President turned in his chair and gazed through the window in a way that had become habitual. He found relief, as he made the life-and-death decisions that were required of him, in watching the antics of the birds and the squirrels outside. On this occasion, after a moment of relaxation, he sighed faintly and gave March a slow nod that might add hundreds of deaths by disease to America's lengthening casualty list.

Though Wilson was not ready to take the risk of curtailing military plans for a continuing war, he nevertheless took the German overture with the deepest seriousness. It was clear now that at last his gospel was penetrating the minds of the German people; and he did not feel it necessary to inquire too closely whether they were converted, or merely seeking a convenient sanctuary. He telephoned immediately to House and asked for advice. Responding with both a telegram and a letter, the Colonel recommended that the President make no direct reply to the German note. It seemed to House that the Allies should share the responsibility of replying to the enemy's overture.

The next day Wilson wrote a trial draft of a reply; and in the evening, going to his study as the clock was striking nine, he read from his script to House and Lansing.[4] The Colonel objected that the nation would think Wilson's tone too mild, that stronger guarantees were needed to assure acceptance of the President's terms by his own people, who had become "war-mad."

The President did not leave his study until after midnight; and the next morning he gave up his game of golf and again went into conference with the Colonel, each opening his mind to the point of view of the other. House reported opinions from European liberals that went along with the President's thought; and Wilson in turn read from bloodthirsty speeches that had just been delivered in the Senate. Their minds met finally on a version that satisfied neither, completely. Finally, suffering under the realization that thousands of lives hung upon their words, they allowed the text to be released as "not a reply, but an inquiry" into Germany's true intentions.

Would the Germans agree to base negotiations on the principles already set forth by the President? the message asked. Would they consent immediately to withdraw their forces everywhere from invaded territory? Was the chancellor speaking "merely for the constituted authorities of the Empire who have so far conducted the war"? The last of the three questions were an unheard-of intrusion into Germany's domestic politics and was resented as such.

In spite of the firm tone that House had injected into the note, the three queries did not satisfy the war-weathered premiers of the Allies. Conferring at Versailles on October 9, they addressed themselves to the President, recognizing the "elevated sentiments" that had inspired his reply to Germany but drawing his attention to the importance of basing conditions of armistice on the advice of the military men at Versailles.

[4] There is no evidence that Lansing played a part in shaping policy at this juncture. House's diary (Sept. 27, 1918) contains this note: "He [Wilson] remarked that Lansing was so stupid that he was constantly afraid that he would commit some serious blunder. I could not but confess that he was stupid. He seems less alert than when he first became secretary of state, and I wonder whether his health has not made this difference."

Lloyd George intimated that he would like a definition of the phrase "freedom of the seas"; and the President was asked to send a representative to Paris to explain the policy of the United States. Foch expressed to Pershing the fear that the President might get himself involved in a long correspondence and be duped.

Though there was no public display of pique by the Allied leaders, though the press by and large commended the President's note of inquiry, an undercurrent of feeling convinced American diplomats that French pride had been hurt by the addressing of the first German message directly to Washington. When a report of this reached the White House, however, it found Wilson perplexed over what General March denounced to him as the "astounding proceedings" of the premiers in suggesting conditions for an armistice. Realizing that immediate discussions with vindictive Allied generals might shake the confidence of the German people in his avowed purpose of making a just peace, Wilson resented any voice that might put the enemy in fear of extermination and give them the courage of despair.[5]

The peoples of Western Europe were appreciative of Wilson's efforts. Reports to the State Department told of peace demonstrations in Italian cities and strong sentiment for peace at Paris and among English laborers. It was a delicate game of psychological warfare that the President was playing, in his effort to bring peace before exhaustion exposed Europe to the virus of anarchy. The prophet again had "heaped all his winnings" on a single toss, against the advice of his most trusted counselor and without consulting his allies. He had risked a hard-won military ascendancy upon the promptings of his own intuitive sense of public opinion in Germany. Actually he thought his note of inquiry "dangerous," in view of the uncertainty of conditions in Central Europe.

Having placed his bet, Wilson could only let the wheel of German politics spin. Going to New York for Columbus Day, he marched for almost seventy blocks at the head of a parade, smiling broadly and doffing his tall hat frequently. He passed shop windows filled with paintings of German atrocities; and downtown, mounted police were carrying bedraggled effigies of the Kaiser.

Attending a benefit performance at the Metropolitan Opera House, in the evening, he learned that his number had come up. Word was brought that Germany had replied favorably to the three questions in his "inquiry." At his hotel that night he asked Tumulty to come to his

---

[5] On the evening of Oct. 10, Ambassador Jusserand delivered the premiers' note of Oct. 9 to the President and left the White House with the feeling that the misunderstanding had been cleared up. Later, however, House found that Wilson still failed to understand that the premiers were not attempting to dictate, as March had suggested, but only to propose a conference. Polk Diary, Oct. 11, 1918.

rooms and assured him that—as he was accustomed to say in considering the gravest problems of state—his mind was "open and to let" on the question of the next step toward peace. The ebullient Irishman gave him a sample of public feeling, vehemently denouncing traffic with "the Kaiser and his brood." It was two o'clock before the secretary had talked himself out; and the next day, traveling to Washington, the President had what he called another "dose of Tumulty." It was a medicine that helped him to keep his ear close to grass roots, to hear what was being said in the ward clubs and the country stores of the land. This was the primitive emotion that he was striving to channel from hate to constructive ends.

Never in all their association had Tumulty been more fearful that "the Governor" would disregard political realities in his zeal for ultimate truth. He found Wilson obsessed with determination to do the right thing, convinced that it would be foolish to go on to Berlin at a cost that he set at a million lives, confident that the notes from Germany set forth, by and large, the will of the people, regardless of the repute of the government that had written them. When Tumulty reminded him that he would disappoint his own people if he accepted less than unconditional surrender, Wilson recalled that John Jay had been burned in effigy and Hamilton stoned for defending Jay's treaty with Great Britain. "If I think it is right to accept the German note," Wilson insisted, "I shall do so regardless of consequences. As for myself, I can go down in a cyclone cellar and write poetry the rest of my days, if necessary."

Late on October 14th, the second note to Germany was made public. It bore down so hard upon the enemy that press comment was favorable and Senator Lodge expressed himself as "genuinely pleased." Before armistice terms could be discussed, the President wrote, atrocities must cease on land and sea, and the Allies and Americans must know with what sort of government they were dealing. Moreover, the military supremacy of the armies opposing Germany must be safeguarded absolutely. Bulletins went out from the White House emphasizing that there would be no letup in the military effort of the United States.

The prospect of peace was clear enough now so that it seemed time to try to reach an understanding with the Allied statesmen. General Bliss had reported that his English colleagues on the Supreme War Council had been advocating that the Allies agree on peace policies while they were still held together by military necessity.

From his friend House counsel came more soothingly. The Colonel had never seen "the Governor" more distraught than he was after breakfast on October 14. A maze of possibilities confronted him, Wilson said. If he went in at the right entrance, he would reach the heart of the matter, there would be no more note-writing, and the loss of human life would stop; but if he took a single false turn, he would have to begin all over again. Repeatedly he said that, if Germany was beaten, she would accept any terms; if she were not defeated, he did not wish to deal with her. He did not trust the sincerity of the German overtures, yet he felt that he must not give to the war-weary peoples of Europe any reason to feel that he was slamming a door against peace.

Giving the morning to the drafting of a tentative text, the President tried it out on his advisers in the afternoon. A senator reported that his colleagues were bewildered, and fearful that the President would commit the country to peace prematurely. Hurt by this lack of confidence, Wilson asked: "Do they think I am a damned fool?" He looked around at Lansing with the impish expression that he assumed when he made one of his occasional ventures in profanity; and the secretary of state was reminded of a little boy uttering his first "Gosh!" or a man learning to smoke with a cigarette holder.

Lansing spoke of expediency, suggesting that they keep in mind the coming Congressional elections. But Wilson and House already had heard too much from the pleaders for expediency; and the Colonel bristled a bit and asserted that they could not do their work "properly or worthily" if they thought of party politics.

Wilson therefore asked House to go to Europe at once, as the personal representative of the President for whom the Allied statesmen had asked. The Colonel had shied at the prospect of serving alongside the President as a delegate at the Peace Conference, as Wilson had suggested at Magnolia. He foresaw the risk that as equals in rank they might cease to be friends. But the place that was offered now was on the very summit of fame and alluring even to an ambition that, as the Colonel had himself confessed in 1916, was so great that it seemed futile to try to satisfy it. He had abjured officeholding because nothing short of the top position would satisfy him, and because he was not physically strong enough to fill such a post. Now he had the great chance of his lifetime—to go down in history as one of the illustrious statesmen of his century. And so he accepted the President's commission.

On the evening of the 14th, giving to his friend a letter of credence and a secret code-book, the President said as they parted: "I have not given you any instructions because I feel you will know what to do." There was no word of direction, advice, or discussion, no prescription of a program for peacemaking to be placed before the statesmen of the Allies.

The Colonel left for Paris on the 18th, and Wiseman went to London to serve his government as adviser on American affairs during the peacemaking. While they were on the high seas, the President fixed his mind on dealing with Austria-Hungary. A month earlier that empire had proposed discussion of a compromise peace and Wilson had replied tersely. In October the Hapsburg government tried again, suggesting this time that an armistice be concluded and peace negotiations begun on the basis of Wilson's principles.

This proposal had reached the White House on October 7. Ten days later it still lay on Wilson's desk, unanswered. Moreover, on October 14 he had a request from Turkey, against whom the United States had never declared war, asking that he take upon himself the task of re-establishing peace and invite all belligerents to appoint plenipotentiaries.[6] Wilson was intrigued by a vivid phrase from Senator John Sharp Williams, to whom he wrote on October 17: "Your idea about letting the populations of Germany, Austria-Hungary, and Turkey 'wobble on the gudgeon' has been in my own mind, and it has been partly for that reason that I have not replied to either the Austrian or the Turkish note yet. I shall presently have to do so, but the conditions of our dealing with Austria-Hungary have been radically altered by our recognition of the Czecho-Slovaks and our official encouragement of the national aspirations of the Jugo-Slavs."

For five months Thomas G. Masaryk, leader of the Czechoslovak nationalists, had been at Washington pleading the cause of the subject peoples of the Hapsburg Empire. This patriot-scholar had received recognition of his people as an Allied belligerent under the *de facto* government that he represented. Appealing to Wilson's political creed by quoting pertinent passages from one of the President's own books, Masaryk persuaded the President that the Hapsburgs were not merely the tools of the Hohenzollerns, but in their own right quite as wicked, and that protestations of reform that now came from Vienna under pressure of military collapse should be given little credence. In October this political adventurer drew up a Czechoslovak Declaration of Independence that was calculated to appeal to the pride that Americans took in their own Declaration.

No American felt more flattered than Woodrow Wilson at this emulation of a political gospel that he had honored all his life. When an

---

[6] Turkey accepted the principles of peace laid down by Wilson and asked an immediate armistice. The President intended to communicate this news to his allies and to urge them to hasten the collapse of Germany by making a separate peace with Turkey. But Lloyd George sent a hint that, since Turkey was about to collapse, it was necessary only to refer her to any Allied commander whom she might choose to approach. Word reached Washington on Oct. 22 that armistice discussions between Turkish and British representatives had been arranged, and on Oct. 30 an armistice was signed by Turkish delegates with a British general.

advance copy of the Czechoslovak document was given to him, he confessed to Masaryk that he was deeply moved, as would be seen when his reply to the Hapsburg Empire was published.

On October 19, the day after the publication of Masaryk's Declaration, Wilson sent off a message to Vienna that recalled that among the Fourteen Points was one that guaranteed to the peoples of the Hapsburg Empire "the freest opportunity for autonomous development." The President insisted that the liberated peoples, rather than an outside authority, should decide what the Hapsburg government must do to satisfy their aspirations. Wilson's verdict was received at Vienna as the death sentence of the old regime.

Meanwhile the German leaders were facing up to the clear and unpleasant choice that Wilson's second note put before them. Seeing no hope of stopping fresh armies that were advancing fast in Belgium and were poised to attack in Lorraine, the German ministers yielded to all of the President's conditions.

With the German capitulation in hand, Wilson was ready to take his Cabinet into his confidence. At their regular meeting on October 22 they found their chief plainly disturbed. For some weeks their sessions had been given over to storytelling and to trivial affairs. But now the President was all business, and said solemnly: "I do not know what to do. I must ask your advice. I may have made a mistake in not properly safeguarding what I said before. What do you think should be done?"

It was as if he had given to them a charge of pastoral responsibility. For a moment these ministers of state were as silent as praying elders. Then, one by one, they spoke. Their feelings ran with those of their fellow citizens; and they assured their leader that the people of the West, like the press of the East, were demanding drastic terms. It was agreed that armistice conditions should be dictated and not discussed, and that they be given only to a government that truly represented the German people. But when Secretary Lane declared that the Allies should not treat for peace "until Germany was across the Rhine," the President ventured to dissent.

Wilson felt that he must warn his men that threats to the world's future peace could now be expected from the Allies as well as from the enemy. The governments of Western Europe, the President explained, were "getting to a point where they were reaching out for more than they should have in justice." When it was objected that the publishing of peace notes without the consent of the Allies might seem to America's partners a form of coercion, Wilson replied that they needed to be coerced in the matter of peace aims and could attain their military objectives when they dictated armistice terms. He seemed fearful of bolshevism in Germany, but confident that a peace based on his Fourteen Points would do everything possible without crushing Germany and wiping her out—"everything except to gratify revenge."

After his war council was given a chance to make suggestions, the note went off to Germany almost as Wilson had drafted it. Copies of it and of the previous correspondence with Germany were transmitted to the Allies on the same day; and the President, having turned the negotions into the traditional channels, had only to await the outcome of events in Europe. Doubt crept into his mind. He clutched at words of moral support, uttered by men whom he trusted. To an old comrade who sent verses entitled "Fight and Hold Fast," he wrote: ". . . do you think, my dear fellow, that we are on the verge of yielding to the sort of hate which we are fighting in the Germans? I am beginning to be fearful lest we go too far to be in a mood to make an absolutely and rigorously impartial peace, and God knows the disposition to make a peace of that sort is growing less and less on the other side of the water." He was oppressed by a miasma of "unwholesome purposes" that seemed to be in the air at home and abroad.[7]

The first full breath of the acrid controversies of the Allies came to him in a cipher cable from House, who, reaching Paris on October 26, found the premiers inclined to shift responsibility for peace negotiations to the shoulders of the President, and at the same time frankly jealous of the role that he had assumed without consulting them. On the day of his arrival the Colonel received from Clemenceau, in deep secrecy, terms that Foch and his generals recommended for the Armistice. Taking the precious document to bed with him and posting a guard at the door, House tucked it under his pillow and the next day cabled its text to the President.

On the Sunday on which the armistice terms reached Wilson he already had before him a long report from Pershing that made seven recommendations about this matter. The coming of House perplexed the American military men. They were not sure that he had full authority to represent the President; nor did they have instruction regarding their own proper part in the deliberation on an armistice in the Supreme War Council.[8]

[7] Republican reaction is described by Alice Roosevelt Longworth in *Crowded Hours*, p. 273: "His note of the twenty-third we all at first professed to think good, but after a second reading we found flaws; we never failed to find them. We were ingenious in our criticisms—when it was not of content it was of presentation. 'Deliberately involved,' we would say ominously."

[8] Foch felt that the terms agreed upon were as severe as any that might have been imposed if Berlin were taken, and feared that if the conditions were hardened, Germany would not sign and would retreat to a strong position, and French opinion would be outraged by prolongation of the war. He complained to Clemenceau that it was "like going against granite" to get Pershing to accept advice.

General Bliss, who insisted that humane feeling required that an armistice be granted just

Encouraged by Wilson to take to House any consideration that might have been overlooked, Pershing handed to the Colonel, at their first meeting on October 30, a letter advocating a dictated peace and the winning of a complete victory through unconditional surrender.

House showed this paper to his colleagues, and they bristled. "Theatrical!" said Clemenceau. And Lloyd George: "Politics!" House let the general know that the statesmen favored granting an armistice, which they thought a political matter; and Wilson advised Secretary Baker not to send a proposed letter of reproof to Pershing, but to leave the matter in House's hands. Otherwise, he explained, the Colonel might be embarrassed.

In the meantime the President had under consideration a note from Austria-Hungary that claimed that all of the American conditions had been accepted and urged that Wilson take steps to bring about an armistice immediately. This appeal was laid before the Cabinet on October 29. The Hapsburg Empire, which the President had been content to let "wobble on the gudgeon," was breaking up so rapidly that Wilson hardly knew to whom he should reply. On the very next day Austria-Hungary made a military surrender to Italy. Terms were drafted at Versailles very swiftly—conditions so severe that Clemenceau remarked: "We have left the breeches of the Emperor, and nothing else." On November 3 Vienna accepted what was offered. Thus the matter was taken out of Wilson's hands and Austria-Hungary could come to the peace table without definite commitment to the President's principles.

At Berlin militarists now had lost the confidence of the civil government; Ludendorff had been dismissed; liberal amendments to the German constitution had been adopted by the Reichstag; and on October 27 the German government had reported to Washington that the people were in control of the nation, actually and constitutionally. Public opinion was responding to the threat in Wilson's last note that, if the United States must deal with "monarchical autocrats," it must demand not negotiations, but surrender. There were suggestions that the Kaiser resign. German leaders were telling their people that civil violence would play into the hands of vindictive Allied statesmen and make it difficult for Wilson to effect a humane peace.

Now that the time had come for each nation to demand its pound of flesh, Wilson and House thought it their duty to hold the Philistines to

---

as soon as complete victory was assured, felt that if complete disarmament and demobilization were accomplished, no other armistice terms would be necessary. He was not supported in this view by Pershing.

Cabling to Pershing on Oct. 27, the President approved all of his seven recommendations except those calling for occupation of Alsace-Lorraine, the east bank of the Rhine, and German submarine bases. This, he felt, would be an unjustified invasion of the enemy's land.

the law of the prophet. The President had pledged to "make the world safe for democracy"; and the United States could not afford to risk the danger of having to undertake another military crusade. This must be a peace that would breed no lust for revenge, a "peace without victory," one that would impose Wilsonian principles on the enemy without humiliating him. Woodrow Wilson had not forgotten the visitation of utter hopelessness that he had known as a boy in war-ravaged Columbia; House remembered post-Civil War days in Houston. The President might even have to become the advocate of the Germans "against American Prussianism," he said to Daniels. "We must never do the things that we condemn."

From the very beginning of his negotiations at Paris, House asked for endorsement of the President's principles. Wishing to offer a definite program to European statesmen who thought Wilson a visionary without capacity for decision, the Colonel seized upon the only specific statement of peace terms that the President had made—the Fourteen Points, which had been formulated as propaganda to influence public opinion in Germany and Russia rather than a scientific basis for peace. Men of The Inquiry who already were questioning the viability of some of Wilson's Points—particularly the doctrine of self-determination—were now asked by House to prepare an interpretive commentary of the American doctrine. They did so, and the Colonel set it before the leaders of the Allies and at the same time its text was cabled to the President. On the very next day Wilson replied. The document was "a satisfactory interpretation of the principles involved," he cabled, "though the details specified could be regarded only as suggestions, subject to further consideration at the Peace Conference." The next day the President made it clear to his agent that he considered Points I, II, III, and XIV to be "the essentially American terms in the programme."

One by one, the European premiers gave voice to their doubts and set forth national interests in the time-honored manner. Journalists at Paris and London sensed that the only definite policy of the Allies, individually and collectively, was to take control of peace negotiations out of the hands of President Wilson. The politicians, they reported, were showing "Junker tendencies," but the masses supported Wilson so overwhelmingly that the leaders dared not oppose him openly.

To the prophet in the White House, the fractious Europeans were like the Southern Secessionists whom he had set down as "legally right" but "historically wrong." They must be mastered and made to acknowledge the voice of the Lord as it spoke to free consciences that were consecrated to the common good. Philistines and Pharisees were always the same to a minister of a congregation, whether at Princeton, at Trenton, at Washington, or at Paris. They were heathen to be converted—by persuasion if possible; by force of public opinion if necessary.

Fortunately, in the greatest of all of Wilson's crusades for the common good he had an ideal ruling elder, a man loyal to gospel and yet one who knew how to fight Satan with his own wiles. Colonel House had learned the political language of the Allies and had found it not much different from that of his old friends in Texas. He made it his business, before going into conference at Versailles, to know exactly what each man was thinking and what he would say. Distilling the essential points into as few words as possible, he spoke scarcely above a whisper—"down where I come from," he explained, "if a man doesn't speak soft he may never speak again. . . ."

In so far as he could, House used persuasion and a frank appeal to national interests to achieve his ends. When the President cabled, menacingly, that, if the Allied statesmen intended to nullify his influence, the Colonel should "force the purpose boldly to the surface" and let him speak of it to all the world, House realized that if he read this intemperate message to his colleagues it might lead to serious trouble. He replied to his fervent friend thus: "I hope you will not insist upon my using your cable except as I may think best. If you will give me a free hand in dealing with these immediate negotiations, I can assure you that nothing will be done to embarrass you or to compromise any of your peace principles." Wilson replied on October 31 that he could not recede from his principles, but that he depended on House "to insist at the right time and in the right way."

And so the Colonel went about making personal friends, soothing suspicions, persuading Lloyd George that it was not America's intent to forbid naval blockade under certain conditions, explaining the strength of sentiment in the United States for revision of maritime law, arguing that reservations proposed by Italy impinged upon the Fourteen Points, enlisting the support of Lord Northcliffe's press for Wilson's principles, and encouraging Wiseman to stand up to Lloyd George when the Welshman tried to play a lone hand. Shrewdly this Texan statesman-elder sensed currents of jealousy and ambition that ran among the Allies. He appreciated the strength of what had been cabled to him by the President: "England cannot dispense with our friendship in the future and the other Allies cannot without our assistance get their rights as against England." House was alert also to the motives that prompted the tactics of the premiers. Reporting to the President that Lloyd George wished the United States to become trustee for German East Africa, the Colonel remarked that the British "would like to have us accept something so they might more freely take what they desire."

It soon became apparent, when House laid the Fourteen Points before the premiers for discussion, that diplomatic bargaining would not suffice to accomplish the President's purposes. Therefore, when Lloyd George opened the floodgates of reservation by attaching conditions to two of the Fourteen Points and Clemenceau was preparing to elaborate the objections of France, House decided that the time had come to make a stand, before Sonnino of Italy joined in a nullifying deluge and made the breach in the Wilsonian front irreparable. The Colonel resorted to a bluntness that he rarely exercised. He told his French friend that, if the Allies objected extensively to Wilsonian principles, he would advise the President to lay the facts before Congress and ask the American people whether they wished to fight on for such terms as the Allies were suggesting, or to make a separate peace with Germany.

The effect was magical. Delighted by House's reports of progress, the President cabled: "I am proud of the way you are handling things." [9]

The most perplexing difference of opinion, however—that between Britain and the United States regarding "freedom of the seas"—was still to be resolved. Because of Britain's alliance with Japan and the prospect that warships from the German Navy might be added to the British fleet, Americans feared that they would be at the mercy of an overwhelming naval force. A huge building program was under consideration in Congress, and the President authorized House to say that, if the Allies persisted in opposing "freedom of the seas" in principle, they could count upon the development of the strongest Navy that American resources permitted. Wilson felt that the problem of maritime blockade, so vexing during the years of America's neutrality, could be most satisfactorily solved by a league of nations that would eliminate all neutrals. He wished assurance against a repetition of the sort of blockade that the British had imposed in 1915. But to the average Englishman "freedom of the seas" meant an end to all blockades. Seeming not to realize that insular Britain was of all nations the most vulnerable to this form of attack, the English knew only that blockades of the Continent had helped them to win two great wars.

Seeing that the impasse could not be broken by threats and realizing that the British would not accept the President's position, nor the President the irrational attitude that had sprung from British pride and fears, House and Lloyd George finally faced realities and a formula for agree-

---

[9] Auchincloss, House's son-in-law and his secretary, wrote thus to Frank L. Polk on Nov. 19, 1918: "You have no idea how skillfully the Colonel conducted himself during the ten days of the negotiations . . . George and Clemenceau scrapped like wild cats at one meeting while we looked on and cheered inaudibly. . . . As usual the Colonel is the confidant of each of the Prime Ministers; each plays just as close to the Colonel as it suits his purpose at the time and go closer."

ment was found by Sir William Wiseman, who before leaving Washington had been told by Wilson that the latter had no desire to weaken British sea power and that the submarine had introduced a new element that must modify existing maritime law. At the Colonel's suggestion, the prime minister wrote a letter stating that the British were "quite willing to discuss the Freedom of the Seas in the light of the new conditions which have arisen in the course of the present war." Thus a basis was laid for the elimination of a bogie that had long haunted Anglo-American relations.

However, the naval terms did not please Admiral Benson, who felt that the German warships should be destroyed at once, and not added to the fleets of the victors. House relied implicitly on this officer. When the question was referred to Wilson, he felt that the naval terms proposed by the British were unduly severe. He struck out several conditions that appeared to cut German pride too deeply. It was enough, it was agreed, to require the enemy to surrender her submarines and submit most of her other vessels to internment. In leaving open the eventual disposition of these ships, the council handed down a thorny problem to the peace conference that was to come.

On another ground, also, seeds of future discord were allowed to fall and take root. Clemenceau insisted doggedly that his people would not accept armistice terms that did not specify "reparation for damages"; and to this the French minister of finance added a clause that reserved the right of the Allies to make financial claims in the future. Having concentrated his fire on getting recognition for Wilson's peace conditions, which covered the problem of reparations, House acceded to this demand, as a sop to French feelings.

The President did not challenge this French exception, nor did he resist the British reservation on "freedom of the seas." When House forwarded the conclusions of the council and outlined the action that the President was expected to take, Wilson proceeded accordingly. On November 5 he sent to the Germans the memoranda from Paris agreeing to accept his Fourteen Points as the basis for peace, with the two qualifications. At the same time the President wrote that Marshal Foch was authorized to receive German representatives and give them terms for an armistice. The next day the enemy delegates left Berlin, and on the 8th they were received by Foch on a train in the forest of Compiègne and given the actual military conditions. They had no defense, except to conjure up the specters of famine, anarchy, and bolshevism.

A mutiny of the German navy was spreading. Revolution broke out in Munich. On November 9 the abdication of the Kaiser was announced, red flags went up, and the next day a provisional government was proclaimed. The President's barrage of eloquence, beginning in May of 1916 and ending in September of 1918, had brought fighting to an end even before the armies of the enemy were completely broken; and not only the enemy but the Allies as well were committed to write such a peace as the world had never before known. The principles that the prophet had conceived first as a battle cry for his own people, and then as a softener of enemy morale, were now blithely accepted by Western liberals as omens of successful peacemaking. Germans depended on them for protection against vindictiveness; and Americans, by and large, were proud of them as something "made in America" that brought kudos to their President. Their shortcomings as a basis for a rational peace settlement were not yet generally apparent.

On the morning of November 7, responding to a false press report of the signing of the Armistice, throngs milled about in the streets of Washington. Bands blared and sirens cut loose. Nell McAdoo, crossing the street from the Treasury, was caught in a rush of dancing, singing citizens. Edith Wilson, loving the stir and good spirit of the people, begged the President to appear on the portico and, in the afternoon, to ride out into the streets. But he shook his head. "No," he said, "what a pity all this is going on, when it's not true." [10]

At breakfast on the 11th he got word of the end of hostilities. He telephoned right away to direct Lansing not to reveal the terms of the Armistice until he could address Congress. Then he took up a pencil and wrote out a little message to his people: "The armistice was signed this morning. Everything for which America fought has been accomplished. It will now be our fortunate duty to assist by example, by sober, friendly counsel and material aid in the establishment of just democracy throughout the world."

Going to the Capitol shortly after noon to address the Congress, he waited for a few moments in the anteroom of the House. There he spoke of his forebodings. The problems of policy that now confronted America, he said, were even more perplexing than those of the past. A tremendous duty rested upon the nation, he felt, to prevent chaos in the rest of the world. America had done well, militarily; and now she must prove herself, politically, to be worthy of the world's respect.

He spoke huskily at first. Reading the terms of the Armistice, he said: "The war thus comes to an end. . . . Armed imperialism such as the men conceived who were but yesterday the masters of Germany is at an end, its illicit ambitions engulfed in black disaster. Who will now seek to revive it?"

[10] E. W. McAdoo to the writer, March 12, 1952.

The representatives of the people could cheer this. But when their leader went on to preach and to teach, the House became quiet.

With a perspective that stemmed from his academic days, he analyzed the politics of Europe. The revolutions that had come to Russia and to Central Europe, he pointed out, seemed "to run from one fluid change to another, until thoughtful men are forced to ask themselves, With what Governments, and of what sort, are we about to deal in the making of covenants of peace? . . . When peace is made, upon whose promises and engagements besides our own is it to rest?" For their own best interest, he said, the victors would do well to help the vanquished to their feet and, if they chose the way of self-control and peaceful accommodation, put aid at their disposal in every way possible. "Hunger does not breed reform," he warned; "it breeds madness and all the ugly distempers that make an ordered life impossible."

For Woodrow Wilson it was a day of vindication rather than of triumph. His principles seemed to have conquered the legions of evil.

But once during the historic day he allowed himself to speak as the harassed, weary mortal that he was, beneath his cloak of ministerial responsibility. "Well," he said to Tumulty, "the war's over, and I feel like the Confederate soldier that General Gordon used to tell of, soliloquizing on a long, hard march: 'I love my country and I am fightin' for my country, but if this war ever ends, I'll be dad-burned if I ever love another country.' "

Radiantly happy in spite of weariness of mind and nerve, he reviewed a parade of war workers in the afternoon and in the evening he drove out with his wife to share the jubilation of his people. The whole Western world was rioting in joy. In New York, Paris, London, Rome, celebrations went on all day and all night, with gun salutes, snowstorms of paper, bells, sirens, searchlights, fireworks, and *Te Deums*. Crowds surged around the automobile of the Wilsons, overwhelming the secret service men and stopping their progress until soldiers locked arms and escorted the car back to the White House.

Too exhilarated for sleep, Wilson proposed going to a reception at the Italian embassy in honor of the King's birthday. There, on this day on which thrones were shaking in Central Europe, he drank the health of Victor Emmanuel.

When they returned to the White House they still were not ready for sleep. Kindling the fire in Edith Wilson's room, they sat on the big couch and talked far beyond midnight. Finally the President was ready for bed. But not until he had read a chapter of the Bible, and thus kept his covenant with the men who had done the fighting.

CHAPTER XI

PARTY BATTLES

THOUGH Wilson had refused to allow armistice negotiations to be influenced by considerations of domestic politics, he had not been unaware of the importance of retaining control of both houses in the Congressional election of 1918. He knew that, if the Republicans gained a majority in the Senate, Lodge would become chairman of the powerful Foreign Relations Committee and there might be subversion in his rear while he fought to represent America before the world as champion of an idealistic peace.

An opportunity had arisen for the Administration to strengthen itself at the polls. Suffragists were agitating for action by the Senate on a woman-suffrage amendment that already had been approved by the House. On September 16 the President told a delegation of them that he was heartily in sympathy and repeated an earlier pledge to help in every way possible; but militant women burned his words that afternoon in Lafayette Square, and he was periodically heckled until the suffragists won the right to vote.

Wilson had not forgotten that in the 1916 election he had carried most of the states where women had full suffrage. At the President's request, therefore, Secretary McAdoo had put in a hard week in the lobbies of the Senate, grubbing for votes; but he fell two short of the number required.

Fear of losing the chance to take the lead in the suffrage crusade drove McAdoo to call at the White House to talk business on a Sabbath morning, before church. The Senate would vote on the next day and no time could be lost in urging the President to go before the body and plead for the amendment.

On several occasions Wilson had been irritated because his son-in-law had presumed to invade his privacy to discuss matters that other officials would have reserved for more formal occasions. On this Sunday morning, however, Wilson listened patiently. But he hesitated to address the Senate, doubting that he could influence any votes. It was unprecedented for the President to address either house of Congress in behalf of any bill pending, and Wilson was afraid that senators would resent a breach of custom in a cause that had little relation to the war effort.

He still believed, however, what he had written in "Leaders of Men" thirty years before: that a President must "throw his bait" among the

majority and perform a minister's duty of translating the popular will
into law. He had often remarked that "a man who never changes his
mind is dead." Persuaded by his daughters to overcome his personal
distaste for emancipated women, he had become convinced that woman
suffrage was part of the "firm and progressive popular thought" that
a statesman must heed. And so on this Sunday afternoon he wrote a
message hastily; and on the next day, September 30, he appeared in the
Senate chamber and read it. As he expected, the air was chilly with
suspicion and resentment; but the frigidity merely stimulated his
powers. Speaking for only a quarter of an hour, he associated women's
voting so aggressively with the war and the peace that public opinion
was responsive, though none of the opposing Southerners was converted
then and there and the measure was not approved and submitted to the
states for ratification until June 4, 1919.

Woodrow Wilson needed all the votes that he could muster for his
Democrats as the Republicans laid plans to avenge their defeat of 1916,
perfecting their organization and raising the pitch of their criticism and
their protestations of devotion to the smashing of Germany. They had
offered nonpartisan cooperation in prosecuting the war; and they blazed
with indignation when Democratic leaders accused them of lack of
patriotism and even the President seemed to spurn their support. Theodore Roosevelt and George Harvey, meeting with Senator Beveridge at
Beverly Farms, arranged for the publication of a journal to be called
Harvey's Weekly, with a guaranteed circulation, and plotted a campaign to win the Presidency in 1920.[1]

Wilson was now staking the validity of his leadership on his exalted
concept of peacemaking. Though he thought it politically dangerous
for him to give "even so much as the appearance of an effort to pick
and prefer a candidate," he did not fail to act when his advisers told him

---

[1] William E. Dodd to Edith B. Wilson, May 29, 1921. This information was given to Dodd
on Nov. 12, 1918, at a dinner with Beveridge, to whom Dodd had given criticism on his biography of John Marshall. Beveridge also informed Dodd at that time that Roosevelt was to be the
Republican nominee for the Presidency in 1920 and he, Beveridge, the nominee for the Vice-
Presidency. Beveridge said, further, that Wilson was the ablest man they had ever had to do
with and must be destroyed.

According to a letter written by Dodd to Wilson on Nov. 19, 1918, Beveridge said that it
was planned to bring on serious industrial disturbances, even a financial panic. That, Beveridge
is alleged to have said, was "one thing that the President cannot escape the responsibility for if
it comes." Dodd wrote further: "He said in so many words that England was to be attacked
because she is making us take up this league of nations in her own interest. She must be
attacked because it would be snobbish submission to her lords if we kept close to her. I said
because the German and Irish votes were at stake? That was not denied or acknowledged. But
the real reason for the fight on the league of nations is the purpose of having a free hand in
Spanish America. He said no man who knows history will deny that we must some day annex
Mexico. Why then tie our hands in any league of nations? . . . He was not an extremist in
1916 and he says he has never spoken disrespectfully of you. Only now he must 'go down the
line with T.R.' "

that control of the Senate in the next Congress might hang upon the single vote of the senator to be elected from Michigan. He listened when Josephus Daniels reported that the only hope of electing a Democrat in Michigan lay in Henry Ford, and that the only man who could persuade the manufacturer to run was Woodrow Wilson, whom Ford admired heartily and had aided financially in the campaign of 1916. Advised by Daniels to apply the "selective draft" to this manufacturer who had shown himself a zealous advocate of peace, Wilson had asked his secretary of the navy to try his own hand at persuasion. "If you fail," the President said, "bring him over and I'll have a try at him."

Unable to persuade the manufacturer, Daniels had taken him to the White House, where the President came straight to the point. He would give anything to lay down his own job, he told Ford, but he could not expect to enjoy the quiet of private life until two great battles were won: that of the war and that of the peace. It was a challenge to the deepest consecration. The undemonstrative manufacturer was stirred and, returning to Michigan, he was nominated by the Democrats; but the Republicans raised a campaign fund of about a half-million dollars to support Truman Newberry, who had been Roosevelt's secretary of the navy.

As early as June, the President had asked Tumulty to work out a tactful plan for appealing to the country for a sympathetic Congress without arousing party rancor. In response his secretary had advised him to keep silent and to give the Republicans time to hoist themselves with a petard of rash allegations. When Wilson told the Colonel in September that he had decided to make an appeal in a speech or a letter, House indicated disapproval by saying nothing.

Undeterred by this, Wilson informed Vice-President Marshall that shortly before the election he would issue a call to his people for a Democratic Congress. "I have no doubt that they will give it to me," he said. "They have refused me nothing so far."

Finally, in mid-October, his conscience drove him to act in the direct way that was dearest to him. Resolving to lay his case frankly before his entire constituency, he concluded that he must risk a public appeal that to opponents doubtless would seem partisan and immodest. He explained that the Constitution made him "the greatest autocrat in the world." There were honorable precedents: Lincoln and McKinley had spoken out in time of crisis against divided councils and changing leadership.

So he drafted and redrafted an appeal to his people and discussed it with the party's chairman, Vance McCormick, and the temporary chairman, Homer Cummings. To them it was a life-and-death matter.

Conferring with the President, they found him disposed to accept their suggestions.

The final text of the message read: "Unity of command is as necessary now in civil action as it is upon the field of battle. If the control of the House and Senate should be taken away from the party now in power, an opposing majority could assume control of legislation and oblige all action to be taken amidst contest and obstruction. . . . Spokesmen of the Republican party are urging you to elect a Republican Congress in order to back up and support the President, but even if they should in this way impose upon some credulous voters on this side of the water, they would impose on no one on the other side." A Republican victory, he said with a frankness that he might come to rue, "would certainly be interpreted on the other side of the water as a repudiation of my leadership."

And in conclusion, to forestall criticism: "I need not tell you, my fellow-countrymen, that I am asking your support not for my own sake or for the sake of a political party, but for the sake of the Nation itself, in order that its inward unity of purpose may be evident to all the world. In ordinary times I would not feel at liberty to make such an appeal to you. . . . But these are not ordinary times . . . I submit my difficulties and my hopes to you."

The President did not show the appeal to his Cabinet before releasing it, but on the evening of October 24 he read it to Edith Wilson. "I would not send it out," she advised. "It is not a dignified thing to do."

"That is what I thought at first," was his reply, "but it is too late now. I have told them I would do it." He must do this for his loyal party men, as well as for the great cause that he was serving. Ringing for the head usher, he gave him the text for release.

The appeal was made public on October 25. It solidified party support behind some of the Democratic candidates; but, as certain advisers immediately sensed when they saw the message in cold print and as Wilson himself soon admitted, it opened him to a volley of blows from his archenemy.

Theodore Roosevelt fell upon the appeal with glee. Suffering from an ailment that was to carry him off within three months, the ex-President allowed his emotions to run riot. Deterred not at all by the fact that, without the existence of a war emergency, he himself in 1906 had written a letter [2] stressing the urgent need of keeping his Republican Congress in power, he called Wilson's appeal an insult to the patriotic honor of those Republicans who had supported the prosecution of the war. He telegraphed influential senators to urge that the Senate declare itself

[2] To James E. Watson, Aug. 18, 1906.

against adopting the Fourteen Points. "I am glad Wilson has come out in the open," he wrote to Lodge. "I fear Judas most when he can cloak his activities behind treacherous make-believe of nonpartisanship." It was the sort of message, he said, that could have been expected from a pro-German, unprincipled, cold-blooded, selfish, tricky, cowardly, unscrupulous, shameless, hypocritical, double-crossing President. Throwing away a paper that he had prepared for delivery at Carnegie Hall, Roosevelt sat down at his desk and drafted instead a denunciation of Wilson, his conduct of the war, and his peace proposals. Waving his manuscript in the packed auditorium, clicking his teeth, the old warrior charged that the President was placing support for himself above loyalty to the nation.[3]

Wilson's appeal united Taft and Roosevelt in a public statement to "all Americans who are Americans first," and some independents were goaded into the Republican party. "This is not the President's personal war," said opposition leaders in Congress who recalled that only five months earlier Wilson had proclaimed that politics was "adjourned." Torches of criticism that had seared Woodrow Wilson's good name so many times were rekindled. Already, in the year 1918, efforts had been made in Congress to pass emergency legislation that would give him a dictator's power; and his peace correspondence with Germany and his dependence on House to represent him at Paris had been held up by his foes as examples of personal, secretive diplomacy. And now this appeal for political support made it easy for his adversaries to stir dissension among legislators and journalists whose pride had been wounded because the prophet had ignored them.

While an epidemic of fatal influenza afflicted nearly a quarter of the people of the nation, killed a half-million, crippled the executive offices at Washington, and everywhere prevented the gathering of crowds to hear Democratic orators proclaim the achievements of their administration, newspapers printed Roosevelt's diatribes to good effect. Professional politicians dragged the campaign ever lower. At the end of October the restraints imposed by the Liberty Loan drive were gone, and there were protests against a pending revenue bill that would impose higher taxes to support the Administration's pay-as-you-go policy. Only an immediate announcement that Germany had surrendered unconditionally could have stampeded public sentiment toward the President.

[3] Letters from T.R. to S. P. Spencer, Oct. 15, 1918; A. Reaveley, Oct. 31, 1918; Senator Hinman, Nov. 6, 1918; and G. W. Maxcy, Nov. 4, 1918, Roosevelt Papers. Longworth, *Crowded Hours*, p. 274. Republican Chairman Will H. Hays, whose policy of nonpartisanship in foreign affairs was given luster by contrast with Wilson's effusion, spoke out indignantly: "A more ungracious, more unjust, more wanton, more mendacious accusation was never made by the most reckless stump orator, much less by a President of the United States, for partisan purposes." *New York Times*, Oct. 28, 1918.

But Woodrow Wilson was not a man to let this consideration influence his resolve to deal patiently with the enemy.

Election returns came in on November 5, the day on which the President was rejoicing with his Cabinet over the acceptance by the Supreme War Council of his Fourteen Points and the fixing of armistice terms that he felt would be accepted by Germany. He was confident of winning at home as well as abroad, and his advisers found him jocose and high-spirited. Asked whether he would resign if the vote went against the Democrats, he explained that the world's need for American leadership prevented this. "I cannot do it . . ." he said to William E. Dodd the historian. "It happens to be a case where, even if defeated by the people, I shall have to try to obtain the objects for which we went to war." [4]

And then the blow fell. Great blocks of German and Irish votes went against him; and the Republican electorate in the North was augmented by Negroes who had migrated for war work. Women voters in states that had enfranchised them, blaming Southern Democrats in the Senate for the blocking of the Suffrage Amendment, favored the Republican candidates. Added to the expected defection of farmers in the West who felt that the Democratic regime had supported the price of cotton better than that of wheat and the opposition of business interests that had been hurt by war restrictions and by the New Freedom, these forces gave the Republicans their innings. In Michigan, despite the delivery of labor support to Henry Ford by Gompers, Newberry won by about two thousand votes. When all the returns were in, the Republicans were in control of the upper chamber by a margin of one vote and of the House of Representatives by forty-five. The United States, for the aftermath of the greatest war that it had ever fought, was to have the sort of Congressional government that had prevailed after the Civil War and that Woodrow Wilson had criticized in his first book.

The President's appeal to the voters had stated plainly that defeat at the polls would be interpreted abroad as a "repudiation" of his leadership, and he knew that he now stood politically bankrupt in the eyes of the world. The last act of the tragedy of Woodrow Wilson had begun.

"You may be sure that the stubborn Scotch-Irish in me will be rendered no less stubborn and aggressive by the results of the election," he promised with a grimness reminiscent of his reaction to opposition to other great movements that he had championed.

There was no word of reproach for those who had helped to draft the fateful message. He would sink or swim with the loyal men of the party. But of those defeated Democratic congressmen who had been faithless

[4] Samuel F. Bemis, *The United States as a World Power*, p. 161.

he said to members of the National Committee: "Some of them got exactly what was coming to them and I haven't any bowels of compassion for them. They did not support the things they pretended to support. And the country knew they didn't." He believed what Tumulty and others told him, that his people simply did not understand the momentous problems of the peace. Someday he would have to tour the country to educate them. Assuring his daughter Jessie that he was very tired, but not too tired, and not at all dismayed or disheartened by the election, he wrote: "I think the Republicans will find the responsibility which they must now assume more onerous than joyful, and my expectation is that they will exercise it with some circumspection. I shall see to it that they are put in a position to realize their full responsibility, and the reckoning in 1920 may hold disappointing results for them."

Yet his conscience would not yield the categorical responsibility that he had assumed during the war—the personal obligation to make a peace that would be both durable and consistent with American concepts of justice. Weary and aging though he was, the prophet felt that he could effect another bloodless revolution. There was one more blow to be struck for rational political adjustment. In asking for an armistice the Germans had surrendered completely, in a military sense; but in committing both the Germans and the Allies to the Fourteen Points as a basis for peace, Wilson and House had deferred the political reckoning. His Americans had played a part in winning the fight by "inventing something." Now, by going to Paris himself, the President hoped to carry American political enterprise into the peace settlement. Once a neutral who wished to stand aside, he had turned belligerent in a world that would not respect American neutrality. As a belligerent, he had not only espoused such chauvinistic measures as had repelled him in the days of neutrality but, to shorten the conflict, had developed a new diplomacy of propaganda. Now, finding himself in a position to lead the world in reconciliation, he was to seek to prevent a recurrence of war by establishing those principles that he had proclaimed to soften the morale of the enemy. The greatest of his crusades against evil circumstances was yet to come.

Woodrow Wilson could not sit at his desk in the White House while lawyers and politicians, over in Europe, patched up an old fabric of diplomacy that he thought rotten. The Protestant pressures within him would not permit his taking sanctuary in a high pulpit in a hierarchical tabernacle. Wilson saw that there was still spiritual pioneering to be done, back at the hearths of Europe from which his own venturesome grandparents had set forth for the western frontier. Like the "saving remnant" of his ancestors in old Columbia after the Civil War, he could not hide out in a manse or a pulpit while civil chaos threatened the whole community. He knew what the historians of posterity would expect of him.

Six months earlier he had said emphatically to Stockton Axson that when peace came he would not go himself to the peace table, that House would be there to keep him informed; but as the lines of the diplomatic battle were drawn and the Colonel cabled his accounts of the pre-Armistice deliberations, Wilson felt that he must be present himself, to catch every word of the negotiations and the very tones in which they were spoken, and, most particularly, to look into the faces of the European leaders and see what purposes moved them. "I want to tell Lloyd George certain things I can't write to him," he said. Already he was spending almost half his time in decoding secret messages from Paris and answering them. A Scot who made it a principle never to give proxies could hardly be expected to delegate power in a matter in which he had committed himself so deeply and so personally. Ever since, as a lad, he had organized the Lightfoot Club in his father's hayloft, nothing had given him so much pleasure as to lead men in the drafting of laws and constitutions. Even had moral compulsions not forced him to go to Paris, his love for participation in great affairs hardly would have permitted him to stay away. On October 28 he had cabled to House: "I assume that you cannot honorably turn the present feverish meeting into a peace conference without me."

A few counselors, daring to stand in the way of the prophetic impulse that possessed the President, had advised him to keep his distance and from his pulpit at Washington, unsullied by the bartering of European interests, to proclaim the purity of America's purposes. When Lansing gave this advice, Wilson's face grew harsh and obstinate. ("He said nothing, but looked volumes," Lansing recorded in his diary.) Herbert Hoover ventured to give the same counsel; and Tumulty suggested that domestic affairs would suffer and that the rising Republican tide would swirl into the vacuum in the capital. Masaryk, just elected president of the infant Czechoslovak Republic, came to say farewell and begged his American benefactor not to go to Paris, or at least not to remain there after the opening of the Peace Conference.

Most of the Cabinet, however, felt that the President should go; and Secretary Lane was applauded when he told a conference of state governors that the success of the Peace Conference depended on Wilson's presence at the head of the American delegation. General Bliss wrote to Newton D. Baker: "I wish to God that the President could be here for a week. I hear in all quarters a longing for this. The people who want to get a rational solution out of this awful mess look to him alone.

. . . In this dark storm of angry passion that has been let loose in all quarters I doubt if anyone but he can let in the light of reason."

Ray Stannard Baker reported to the State Department a division of opinion in Europe: the people, seeing the triumph of their cause in Wilson, were clamoring for him; and the "ruling class," knowing that he would upset their plans for making a nineteenth-century peace, hoped that he would stay away. Liberals whose confidence Wilson had won both by his New Freedom and by his championship of farsighted war aims, were advocating that the President go to Paris, the *Manchester Guardian* describing him as "the only statesman of the first rank who has concerned himself seriously to think out any policy at all." [5] He was looked upon by the Germans as the one man who could be depended upon to insist on considerations of abstract justice.

It was on Colonel House that the President leaned most confidently in making plans for the Peace Conference. After the master stroke that had committed the Allies to base the peace treaty on the Fourteen Points, House had remained in Europe, preparing for the negotiations. His success in the Armistice parleys had so inflated his confidence that he would have liked to continue as America's chief delegate, with associates of his own choosing. Though he had felt at one time that Wilson should be the sole American spokesman in the peacemaking, he had advised the President, in the summer of 1918, not to go to Europe. He wished to deal in a friendly, firm way with the statesmen of the Allies, threatening politely when necessary and referring back to his chief for orders.[6] Finding Clemenceau of the opinion that it was neither desirable nor possible for the President of the United States to take part in the conference as an equal of European premiers—the Tiger felt that Ger-

[5] Lloyd George had said that the President must attend the Peace Conference but, like Clemenceau, he opposed Wilson's presence at the executive sessions. "Clemenceau and I can quarrel as equals and say anything we like," the prime minister explained to Cobb, "but we cannot talk that way to the President, and it is sometimes necessary to talk that way to achieve results." Frank Glass, an old schoolmate, cabled to Wilson that Balfour said: "Great Britain has no single leader able to grapple with Clemenceau." According to Glass, Balfour asked whether Wilson was a fighting man and, when assured that he was, pounded the table and said: "Then by all means the President should go to Versailles."

"Nearly everyone in the Department [of State] wished that he would not go," William Phillips wrote in *Ventures in Diplomacy*, p. 93. For a summary of advice given to the President on the question of going to Paris, *see* J. Daniels, *The Wilson Era, Years of War*, pp. 351–52.

[6] "I wish in my soul the President had appointed me as Chairman of the peace delegation with McAdoo and Hoover as my associates. . . . If I could have had these two men as my associates and only these, I would have been willing to guarantee results." House Diary, Dec. 3, 1918. In "Memories," a paper written by House in 1929, he confessed that at times, when his advice had been disregarded, he would have liked to be President instead of the President's adviser. "I did not approve of President Wilson going to Paris. . . . It was . . . the kind of work for which he was not best fitted and the strain of it was too much for him." House to George W. Watt, Oct. 16, 1934. A statement, House to Seymour, Jan. 15, 1938, records that the disagreement over Wilson's going to Paris was the first flat and vital difference of opinion between the friends.

many might use Wilson to escape just retribution—House passed this view along to Wilson three days after the Armistice, and explained that protocol required that Clemenceau be made president of the conference if it was held at Paris. Moreover, at the same time House cabled that though "everyone" wanted the President to come over for preliminary talks, Americans whose opinions were of value were practically unanimous in the belief that it would be unwise for Wilson to sit in the Peace Conference.

Having set his own heart on entering the lists, Wilson was cast down by this report. That he should go to Paris but not sit as a commissioner seemed a way of "pocketing" him. Objecting very strongly to letting protocol interfere with obtaining the results that he had set his heart on, projecting his own will into the minds of other men, he asserted without reason that it was "universally expected and generally desired" at Washington that he should attend the conference. He could only infer, he said, that the French and British leaders feared that at Paris he might lead the weaker nations against them. "I hope you will be very shy of their advice," he wrote House, "and give me your own independent judgment after reconsideration."

The Colonel had need of all his finesse. Actually, he thought Wilson not an effective negotiator *inter pares,* believing that he did not know when to yield and when to be firm. The President was not accustomed to debate. House was convinced that he himself could better attain the high purposes that were dear to both men; and yet he knew that he could not flatly advise Wilson to stay at Washington without seeming to put himself forward as the chief American delegate. This might break their understanding irreparably. And so he could only cable, inconclusively: "My judgment is that you should . . . determine upon your arrival what share it is wise for you to take in the proceedings . . . When you are here you will be in a position to assess the situation properly. It is impossible to do so from Washington."

Appearing unexpectedly at Lansing's house during a dinner party on the evening of November 18, Wilson said that he had decided to go abroad; and the next day he cabled to House that he would sail for France immediately after addressing the opening session of the new Congress.

When the decision was made public, partisan opponents renewed their charges of dictatorship and grandstand playing, and questioned the legality of his departure from his responsibilities at Washington. There was no possibility, now, of extending to the peacemaking the political truce that had attended the war effort. To be sure, there were many Republicans among the technical experts whom House had recruited to advise the President; and unity in the councils of peace was furthered when Taft judiciously warned his party that they would be held by the people to a strict accountability for the way in which they used their power. At the same time advising Wilson to consult the foreign committees of both houses about the treaty, Taft issued this admonition: "Should he consult no one but his closest personal and partisan advisers, he will run the risk of arousing the closest scrutiny of what he presents to the Senate and of awakening a popular approval of a critical attitude of that body toward a treaty." [7]

In June of 1918 Stockton Axson had talked with brother Woodrow about the opposition to the President's peace plans. Sitting on the veranda of the White House and chatting in the same intimate way in which they used to converse on the porch at Princeton when old Joseph Wilson was with them, Axson had urged the President to call all the war leaders together—Republicans as well as Democrats—and, addressing them as a family, to talk frankly about the great battle to come after the war was over. If only they might be given "a warm sense" of their leader's "personal nature!"

Edith Wilson had assented when her opinion was asked; but the President had listened with his eyes upon the floor. It was so like good old Stock, who could see possibilities of redemption in even the Republican sinners! "Well, it might be wise to do that," he remarked at length. "It may be that would be a step that would help to suppress party opposition." He never did it, though. His contempt of senators, Democratic as well as Republican, was too deep-seated to permit him to woo their good will.[8] He could not bring himself to make peace in the American

[7] Republican opposition took shape in mid-December, when the dying Roosevelt called Lodge and Root to his hospital bedside and mapped out a strategic plan for amending whatever settlement the President might bring back from Paris. These Republicans conjured up all the provisos that could be conceived by minds ruled by jealous and fearsome regard for their own country's interests and for their own party's position.

"I am insisting upon Nationalism as against Internationalism," Roosevelt had written to Senator Beveridge on Oct. 31. "I am for saying with a bland smile whatever Nationalism demands. I will then adopt with that extra consideration any wise and feasible plan for limiting the possible area and likelihood of future wars. Mine is merely a platonic expression, designed to let Taft and his followers get over without too much trouble, and also to prevent any accusation that we are ourselves merely Prussian militarists." *Letters of T.R.,* VIII, 1385. (Eventually Taft did "get over." *See* p. 345 below.) Roosevelt cautioned his disciples against any revelations of their true feelings to the public. The political situation, he assured Cabot Lodge, was so good that he must not "make the mistake of overplaying" their hand and "causing a reaction of sympathy." Lodge, who in August had become minority leader in the Senate, carefully followed this advice, never wholly rejecting the idea of a league, but exuding pessimism as to its practicality.

[8] When House asked Wilson whether Senator Gilbert M. Hitchcock knew that the President had tried to remove him from the chairmanship of the Committee on Foreign Relations, Wilson replied that he had told Senator Martin and others that he would not consult Hitchcock about anything because he would not trust him with any information. Pinning his friend down, the Colonel found that there was no other Democrat on the Committee on Foreign Relations whom Wilson would have preferred, that he considered them all "a rum lot."

family, in spite of House's urging that he cooperate closely with the
Senate's Committee on Foreign Relations. Though he once had advocated this course in academic lectures, he felt that it would be futile to
attempt to get cooperation from Lodge, whose leadership in the Senate
he anticipated, he said, "with genuine anxiety." He could only fall back
on an alternate method that he had mentioned in a lecture—the presentation of a *fait accompli* to the Senate for approval.

Associates at Washington who knew the President well took it for
granted that he would hold full responsibility for the peacemaking in
his own hands and be accountable for the outcome. Quoting Euripides
on the power of the people, Brandeis felt that the realization of progressive ideals at Paris was "an affair of the prophets and not of the priests."
James Kerney, a New Jersey friend, returned from a publicity mission
to Paris and, telling Wilson of the intrigue and cunning of European
politicians, found him aware of what was ahead. "The terrible thing
about war," the President said, "is that the young manhood of the world
is sacrificed to the stupidity of the politicians. It's my business to see
that that kind of thing is stopped."

The prophet's defiance was building up in reaction against the Philistines abroad. On November 20, two days after he had told Lansing of
his decision to go to Paris, he was in a crusading mood. Professor Rappard of Geneva, calling at the White House, found him more gay and
candid than he had been a year before.

Urged not to become *pratique,* Wilson replied: "I'm not going to
relax in the least. I'm going over to Europe because the Allied governments don't want me to." He hoped, he said, to keep the talks from
taking a vexatious course.

His visitor suggested that public opinion would endow him with a
power that would enable him to go over the heads of the Allied governments. "I know it," he responded, "and I know how jealous they are.
I'm stubborn but one has to be worldly wise." He had had their jealously
in mind, he said, when he had finally told the Germans that they must
address all the Western powers.

The Allies thought he wanted "to run it all," Wilson remarked.

"But you are, I hope," said Rappard.

"I hope so too," the President replied, "but it would be unwise to let
them feel it too obviously."

He talked intimately with this fellow professor, explaining that he
hoped to do at Paris what he had failed to accomplish in the Americas,
to make of the Monroe Doctrine "not a big-brother affair, but a real
partnership" for mutual protection. He wanted disarmament, but when
asked whether, in the absence of an international police, it would run

into mutual rivalries and suspicions, he answered: "I'm sure of it. France and Italy, for instance, have no use for each other. It will be a long rocky road." [9]

In choosing four American commissioners to guide and protect him along the precarious path ahead, Wilson held to a principle that he had observed through the war. He selected the men who promised to be the most helpful in doing the job. To be valuable to him, they must be men who, if they did not have his spiritual purpose in their hearts, at least would be faithful, patriotic servants of their chief. If one or two of the delegates were Republicans, that would be so much the better; but they must not be partisans who might betray his cause to Lodge. He could not appoint any senator, he explained, because in that case the man eventually would have to vote upon the treaty that he helped to negotiate. When House had recommended Taft and Root as peace delegates, Wilson responded that he considered them "impossible" and out of sympathy with his ideas. Considering Root "a hopeless reactionary" who had failed in his mission to Russia and who would "discourage every liberal element in the world," Wilson was not willing even to appoint him to the international court at The Hague, for he thought that, at seventy-three, his mind was narrowing and losing resiliency and he was "past his period of usefulness." On November 29, 1918, Wilson wrote to Richard Hooker of the Springfield *Republican* thus: "I . . . must say frankly that I would not dare take Mr. Taft. I have lost all confidence in his ability. And other prominent Republicans whom one would naturally choose are already committed to do everything possible to prevent the Peace Conference from acting upon the peace terms which they have already agreed to [in the pre-Armistice negotiations]. It is a distressing situation indeed, but one which they themselves have created."

When Masaryk suggested one day that it would be wise to take Republican advisers to Paris, Wilson confessed that he had no talent for compromising differences that might arise within the American delegation. "I tell you frankly," he said, "I am descended from Scottish Presbyterians and am therefore somewhat stubborn." He and House would speak for the United States. He would have to take the secretary of state, on whom he depended for legal advice but whom he thought "not big enough" to lead the delegation. He would like to take Newton D. Baker; but when he had spoken to House of this wish, the Colonel had advised against it, fearing jealousy on the part of other members of the Cabinet. The matter was settled when McAdoo resigned from office,

---

[9] Quotations from Rappard's journal printed in William E. Rappard, "W.W., La Suisse et Genève," in *Centenaire Woodrow Wilson: 1856–1956* (Geneva, 1956).

pleading poor health and financial necessity, and it became essential that Baker keep his hand on affairs at Washington while the President was at Paris. At the suggestion of the secretary of war, Wilson appointed General Tasker H. Bliss, who had won the confidence not only of his American colleagues but of the members of the Supreme War Council as well.

For the fifth place on the American Commission, the secretary of state was authorized to offer appointment to Justice Day of the Supreme Court, a Republican who had negotiated with Spain in 1898. Day consulted the chief justice and declined to serve, and Lansing then suggested Henry White. This veteran diplomat, whose daughter married a German, had been conspicuous for his judicial poise during the period of American neutrality, and he had served the President well by informing him of *gaucheries* of Ambassador Gerard at Berlin and by transmitting reports of British liberal opinion from his half brother, W. H. Buckler.[10] At Wilson's request Lansing sounded White's opinion of the Fourteen Points and, finding him sympathetic, appointed him.

Everyone liked Henry White. He was "above such trifles as war," Henry Adams wrote of him. Known as "the first professional American diplomatist," he could be depended on to grace the peace table with tact and fidelity. Theodore Roosevelt, who had called White "the most useful man in the entire diplomatic service," was moved to write to Lodge that he was "simply overjoyed," in spite of the fact that White was "not a Republican but an Independent." Root also was pleased.

To solve the most urgent problem of Europe, Wilson chose another agent who had proved his capacity to serve and who was more patriot and humanitarian than party man. He proposed that Herbert Hoover, who had been pleading for united, nonpartisan support for the President, be delegated to direct the relief and reconstruction of Europe. The war food administrator had served as chairman of the Allied Food Council and had just completed a survey of the world's food supplies and needs. "I have learned to value your judgment and have the greatest trust in all your moral reactions," Wilson wrote on November 4 to this tried and able servant of humanity. The President agreed that his food administrator should work with the Allies along the line of recommendations that had come from House, who was eager that an "International Relief Organization" be set up under Hoover, to serve needy peoples without interference by Allied blockade or by traders seeking profits.

Wilson made it clear to the men of his Shipping Board that they

---

[10] In writing to Wilson about Gerard on April 5, 1915, White had said: "I often wish that I could be of assistance to you in your heavy labors."

must give first consideration to Hoover's need for ships, rather than to any desire of businessmen to make good sales. Moreover, he instructed that surpluses of raw materials should be held for future use. The control of exports, he had told Wiseman three months before, would be a formidable weapon at the Peace Conference.

The war council was breaking up rapidly now, with McAdoo resigning and Hoover and Hurley going abroad. Indeed, it seemed that soon there might be little need in the United States for economic administrators of this type, for Wilson sensed a reaction in popular feeling toward governmental economic controls. On November 29 Baruch submitted his resignation and recommended that his War Industries Board be discontinued as of January 1, 1919. Members of the board's price-fixing committee soon resigned also, stating that "no new price regulations seem to be called for."

Wilson's political advisers were worried by the haste with which the transition was being made. Winter was coming on, and men were working on war contracts hundreds of miles from their homes. It was an impolitic hour to take away their jobs. But the prophet of peace had little time now to comfort politicians and extend controls over normal business. Though he approved a bill that had been designed by the Federal Trade Commission to regulate a favorite political target—the meat-packing industry—he drew back when urged to form a federal board to advise local public utilities.

The President and his advisers had learned much, since their first venture into economic legislation, about the headaches that come from conflicts of interests. The nation was now clamoring for a lower cost of living; and at the same time Herbert Hoover, though gradually removing controls over many commodities, was insisting on maintaining certain prices so that production would be stimulated and there would be surpluses with which to feed Europe. Moreover, while exporters demanded that world trade be allowed to flow freely, Hoover insisted that it was "positively necessary" to continue the embargo, or every foodstuff would be overdrawn and the American people faced with shortages.

In November the President had to face up to another conflict between efficiency and political expediency. With the authorization of Congress, he had announced in July that the telephone and telegraph systems of the country would function under Burleson's direction, as a war measure. Subsequently the postmaster general had learned that to assure continuous transmission of overseas messages without delays, the cables must be operated under the same authority as that governing the land wires. Moreover, it had been found necessary to keep a wire from France constantly available for the State Department, and another for the War

Department. On November 2, therefore, Wilson signed a proclamation that placed all marine cables under Burleson's direction. Putting the decree into effect ten days later, the postmaster general gave assurance that the news associations would be given every facility for handling press dispatches during the period of the Peace Conference.

Political advisers of the President sensed the danger that the public might confuse government control of the cables with censorship, which ended on November 15. However, when Wilson was advised to reconsider his decision, he wrote: "I have not the least fear that the misrepresentations . . . will do any harm. They are too contemptible to be worthy of notice, and it will presently become evident that what we did was done in the course of business . . ."

Only very rarely had the President suggested that government officials consider anything but efficiency in the management of the nation's business. Nevertheless, though he could do nothing for his family and little for old friends in the way of preferment,[11] he continued to give of himself to less fortunate relatives. When the daughter of his brother "Dode" planned to marry a clergyman, Uncle Woodrow insisted that the wedding be in the White House and acted as best man himself, his dress clothes wilting in the August heat as he rejoiced in the young couple's happiness. ("Do not be a chaplain," he said to the groom. "There are plenty of those. Be a missionary.")[12]

In mid-November, with daughter Margaret gone to France to entertain soldiers with her singing and the McAdoos soon to leave Washington, he felt bereft of his flesh and blood. Except for McAdoo, however, the men of the Cabinet stood by loyally. In the eyes of those closest to him, despite the errors that the politicians attributed to him, Woodrow Wilson was still a master among men and the hope of the party, the nation, and now even of the world. The philosophical House had left the White House in October with the feeling that never would he meet a more sympathetic mind. The dynamic McAdoo was to cherish afterward the years of their close association, to remember Wilson as a president with a deeper instinct for accomplishment than he had ever seen in any other man and a horror of fatuous ideas—"blank cartridges," Wilson called them. One day the President had stretched the mind of National Committeeman Cummings over a panorama of the world's affairs; and on another he had listened patiently while a Cabinet

11 In August he had asked that a family friend of long standing not be removed as postmaster at Rome, Ga., unless it was "absolutely necessary to the service to do so." And a little later he had requested the reappointment of a Princeton classmate as warden of Sing Sing Prison, but only if he deserved it. Herbert Hoover told the writer that in the course of his association with Woodrow Wilson, the President had asked only once that Hoover try to find a job for a friend, though the pressures were constant and strong.

12 Alice Wilson McElroy to the writer, April 30, 1950.

officer confessed his perplexities, and then, by a few deft questions, had helped the disciple to see his way to a solution. On one day he would seem all Scot, talking with "Dr. Facts" or make Hurley think him the keenest man of business that he had ever met, and on another he would give play to the Irish in his nature, swapping stories with his Cabinet, chuckling at Tumulty's absurdities and practical jokes. He had "recruited" Henry Ford. He had cajoled Carter Glass, who complained that his experience had been too much legislative and too little administrative to permit him to fill McAdoo's place in the Treasury Department. With twinkling eyes he said: "I rather think, Glass, that we'll be able to manage the job together."

On December 2, Woodrow Wilson delivered his parting charge to the elders in the Capitol, at a joint session of the Congress. Crowds milled about, outside and in; and in the chamber of the House, foreign diplomats joined the high functionaries of all branches of the American government.

The President began hoarsely and uncertainly, as in his address on Armistice Day. He spoke first of the victory and the sacrifices that had made it possible. Then he discussed economic readjustment and made it clear that the nation could not revert to prewar conditions. Finally he came to the great concern that possessed him. Speaking of the sacrifices made by America's fighting men, he said: "It is now my duty to play my full part in making good what they offered their life's blood to obtain. I can think of no call to service which could transcend this . . .

"I realize the magnitude and difficulty of the duty I am undertaking; I am poignantly aware of its grave responsibilities. I am the servant of the Nation. I can have no private thought or purpose of my own in performing such an errand. I go to give the best that is in me to the common settlements which I must now assist in arriving at in conference with the other working heads of the associated Goverments. I shall count upon your friendly countenance and encouragement. . . . I shall be happy in the thought that I am constantly in touch with the weighty matters of domestic policy with which we shall have to deal. I shall make my absence as brief as possible . . ."

Many of the senators sat sullen and stolid as Woodrow Wilson concluded his speech. He had not asked their advice, had not invited any of them to go to the Peace Conference. So far as most of them knew, he had done no careful planning of American policy. No one knew to what he might try to commit them. But the prophet found it easy to ignore the political reckoning that was being calculated by the priests of the national temple as moral impulse drove him toward the New Jerusalem to keep his personal covenant with the millions who had bled and died.

CHAPTER XII

THE NEW WORLD RETURNS TO REDEEM THE OLD

TWO DAYS AFTER his challenge to the Congress, Woodrow Wilson boarded the transport *George Washington*, the first President of the United States to sail for Europe while in office. He expected to be able to return within two months, though doubtful that the work of peacemaking would be entirely finished then.

The prospect of a sea voyage and a constructive role in the peacemaking made him relaxed and genial, and he talked freely and frankly with those near him. To a query about his health he replied: "Yes, I have a cold in my throat. Grayson says he will get rid of it for me by the time we get over there. I am going to have to do some plain talking when we get on the other side and I'll need my voice."

He said: "Upon the very first opportunity I have after meeting the premiers and finding out at first hand what sort of chaps they are, as well as letting them know what kind of fellow I am, I shall find out from them what their program is. I have just had a cable from Colonel House. Lloyd George and Clemenceau held a meeting the other day in London at which House was not able to be present, because an unusually robust germ had boarded him which he could not get rid of soon enough. House's cable was badly garbled, but I gather that these men have agreed on a definite program. Apparently they are determined to get everything out of Germany they can, now that she is helpless. They are evidently planning to take what they can get frankly as a matter of spoils, regardless of either the ethics or the practical aspect of the proceeding . . . If they insist upon this sort of program, I shall be compelled to withdraw my commissioners and return home and in due course take up the details of a separate peace. But, of course, I don't believe that that will come to pass. I think that, once we get together, they will learn that the American delegates have not come to bargain, but will stand firmly by the principles that we have set forth; and once they learn that that is our purpose I believe we shall come to an early agreement."

What would probably be the English program at the conference? he was asked.

"You know," he replied, "I was surprised at Colonel Roosevelt's statement that England won the war and should have anything she wants.[1]

[1] The irreconcilable ex-President had publicly denied Wilson's authority to speak for his countrymen, in view of the loss of Congress to the Republicans. He wrote: "Mr. Wilson and his

216

I don't believe our soldiers will be inclined to feel just that way about it. The question of who won the war is a relative one, but if they want to be specific about it, we have as good a claim as anyone else . . . England in agreeing to the Fourteen Principles written into the Armistice is in the parodoxical position of submitting to the principle of disarmament and simultaneously announcing through her spokesmen that she means to retain naval supremacy. I once said in fun, but with sufficient point, to M. Tardieu that, if England insisted upon maintaining naval dominance after the war, the United States could and would show her how to build a navy! If England holds to this course at the conference, it is tantamount to admitting that she does not desire permanent peace, and I will so tell Lloyd George. I'll do it with a smile, but it will carry its point. . . .

"Militarism is no different on sea than it is on land. The suggestion which has been made that the American and British navies act together as the sea patrol of the world is only another form of militaristic propaganda. No one power, no two powers, should be masters of the sea; the whole world must be in on it. It must be definitely set forth in the treaty that no one nation or group of nations can say what shall or shall not be done on the high seas. It should be left to a league of all the nations to declare a blockade or override international law for the purpose of retaliating upon a power which threatens the peace of the world. . . .

"The freedom of the seas is itself subject to a variable interpretation . . . This war has demonstrated that international law must be altered to meet the new conditions of marine warfare . . . By the arbitrary use of her blockade England very seriously infringed upon our rights as a neutral before we became a belligerent—and with no other excuse than necessity. I am frank to admit that if I had not been convinced that Germany was the scourge of the world I was ready then and there to have it out with Great Britain on that point.

"England will want the German colonies. Mr. Borden, the Canadian premier, has declared that Canada would be opposed to the mother country's acquiring any more colonies. He incidentally expressed the desire that the German colonies be turned over to the United States, if to anybody. Of course, we don't want them and wouldn't have them. . . .

Replying to a question as to his insistence upon a league of nations, he said:

Fourteen Points and his four supplementary points and his five complementary points and all his utterances every which way have ceased to have any shadow of right to be accepted as expressive of the will of the American people." "Of the terrible sacrifice which has enabled the Allies to win the victory, America has contributed just about two per cent." And so, Roosevelt asserted, the United States had no right to set herself above her allies in making the peace.

"I am going to insist that the league be brought out as part and parcel of the treaty itself. A league I believe will of necessity become an integral part of such a treaty as I trust we shall work out . . . The nucleus of the league will probably be Great Britain, France, Italy, the United States, and Japan. The other nations will enter to preserve their interests. Germany's present chaotic state will undoubtedly make it necessary to put her on probation until she can qualify in the estimation of the other powers for entrance. A similar policy will have to be followed in the case of the new states to be carved out of portions of the Austro-Hungarian Empire. . . .

"The principle of self-determination has given rise to an interesting problem to be worked out. As you know, German Austria has declared her desire to become affiliated with the original German Empire. Now, such an affiliation, if permitted, would mean that the new Germany would be the most powerful country on the Continent—and a great Roman Catholic power. I have no bias derogatory to the Roman Catholic Church, but I do not want to see that church or any church become a great political entity. The dangers are obvious. It is certainly a hard knot to unravel, if we are to apply the principle of self-determination literally, and I am just now thinking that it might be handled by requiring that Austria and Germany, although affiliated, act separately until they have proved themselves in the eyes of the world. . . . Poland is another knotty question. I am determined that the new Polish state should have an outlet to the sea . . . But all these things will have to be worked out carefully and deliberately." [2]

Aboard the *George Washington*, to aid in working out the settlements that the President outlined, were several hundred advisers and assistants, and cases of books, maps, and reports. Though a little distrustful of the enthusiasms of specialists, Wilson welcomed the counsel of The Inquiry—the body of competent scholars that House had assembled, at his request, more than a year before. He called these gentlemen to his cabin on December 10, as the vessel stood in toward the mist-shrouded Azores. Though he had taken it easy during his first days at sea—staying in his cabin until nearly noon and retiring early at night—he had been pondering further on the matters that he had discussed informally. As he recovered from his cold, he took up his burdens again, working even on Sunday; and on the 10th he gave the scholars his gospel—fervently, candidly, quite charmingly.

He committed them to a standard of justice that he hoped all the world would accept—the same sort of justice that the United States had

[2] These quotations are taken from the records of Charles Swem in the Princeton University Library.

championed in keeping an "open door" in China. It was his wish that by proving themselves "square" Americans would win the regard of the rest of the world and could act as trustworthy umpires. He gave the impression that he felt that absolute justice in specific cases would be actually unattainable. However, with an obtuseness to reality that he often showed when purposes that he held sacred were at stake, he remarked that the peoples of Europe were being betrayed by leaders who did not truly represent them and seemed to him "too weather-wise to see the weather." Unless the Peace Conference followed the will of the people rather than that of the European leaders, he predicted, there would soon be a breakup of the world that would be no mere war, but a cataclysm. The American people were to get the truth about the Peace Conference, for already he had arranged with some difficulty for the removal of British and French restrictions on political news. If they did not get the truth, he predicted, the peace treaty would not work; and if it did not work right, the world would "raise hell."

The new order, the prophet proclaimed, must be neither a repressive concert of great powers such as had emerged from the Congress of Vienna, nor the balancing of powers that had failed so dismally. His hope for both elasticity and security lay in the forming of a league of nations. Like the Monroe Doctrine, the international league would develop through experience. A council would be set up, and war-breeding issues referred to it and thereby given full publicity. When a nation was found guilty of evil designs against a neighbor, it might be cut off from trade and communication with the world. The President suggested that the German colonies become the property of the league, to be administered under trusteeship. The new organization would be given stability by assuming responsibility for material possessions, he foresaw.

In conclusion, the President said that, though he expected the experts to work through the other American commissioners, he wanted them to feel free to come straight to him with anything that affected a critical decision. "Tell me what's right and I'll fight for it," he covenanted with them. He spoke as a seeker of truth, an unassuming scholar among peers. His colleagues were charmed and went back to their quarters reassured of their opportunity to serve humanity and of their important role in a great historic event.[3]

Messages came to the *George Washington* that kept alive Wilson's

[3] The substance of Wilson's talk to the experts has been taken from contemporary notes made by Isaiah Bowman and printed in Miller's *The Drafting of the Covenant*, I, 41–44, from notes taken by Charles Seymour and read by him to the writer, from contemporary letters written by Raymond Fosdick, from the diary of George Louis Beer, at the Columbia University Library, and from James T. Shotwell's *At the Peace Negotiations*.

suspicions of the motives of the Allies. The Armenians sent a plea for succor; the Jews asked favors for Palestine; the Koreans, defense against Japan; the Swedes wanted the Aaland Islands; Vienna, the return of stolen pictures. Little Albania lamented that she had found no advocate in Europe to take her part. Along the Adriatic coast, Italians were squatting on coveted land. Everyone wanted something; no one seemed eager to help America to apply high principles to the peacemaking.

Approaching the dock to board the *George Washington* early on the morning of sailing, Raymond Fosdick had asked a laborer coming off the ferry how long he worked each day. The man had replied: "Fourteen hours"; and then, pointing to the *George Washington*, the workman had continued: "Do you see that boat? There's a man aboard her that is going to Europe to change all that!"

When Fosdick brought this story to the President, with a recommendation that a bill of industrial rights be written into the peace treaty, Wilson replied that it frightened him to think how much the people expected, that it did not seem possible to take up such questions at the Peace Conference, that he hoped an international conference of labor would press for these things.

Among the messages of good will sent to the *George Washington* was one that brought to Woodrow Wilson, over the years, the voice that often held him true to his trust, that had kept him obedient to the ideals of service that had ruled a little manse in Georgia. Stockton Axson, now serving as an official of the Red Cross, had written movingly to his brother-in-law: "I wonder if you fully understand how entirely you carry overseas with you the hearts, and hopes and dreams, and desires of millions of your fellow Americans. Your vision of the new world that should spring from the ashes of the old, is all that had made the war tolerable to many of us. That vision has removed the sting, has filled our imaginations, and has made the war not a tragedy, but a sacrament. For many of us your thoughts have been our daily thoughts, and we have tried to 'catch your great accents,' not in vainglory, but in a desire to assist even a little in driving the great truths home by reiteration. Nothing but a new world is worth the purchase price of the war, and the comfort of millions of us is that you have the vision to glimpse it and the power to realize it in action."

Reading these words, the prophet could hear again the voice of Ellen Axson Wilson. He found inspiring, also, an expression of confidence from the wife of William Phillips, assistant secretary of state. In reply he wrote:

It is not the people "in the game" whom I am seeking to serve, but the people not in the game and with whom political motives count for nothing except to excite suspicion. That you should judge me so encourages the hope that I am judging myself without self-deception, and makes the whole immense task easier. It transcends my comprehension, and the only thing I can hope to make sure of is my motive.

With the warmest regard,
Gratefully yours,
WOODROW WILSON

This is not dictated but written on my own typewriter.[4]

Out on the Atlantic, the Commander in Chief went often to the bridge of the ship, cloaked in a heavy coat with coonskin collar. Captain McCauley came to love him as a passenger who put on no "side" and contributed to the morale of the ship's company. To keep the spirit democratic, Wilson attended a Sunday service in the hall of the enlisted men and went below to the "Old Salt" theater that the troops attended. He liked to hear the boys sing war songs, and to join in. They sang "Old Nassau" for him, and eagerly accepted his invitation to shake his hand. When he walked on deck his quick, eager step matched that of his wife, who, vivacious and trimly dressed, held his attention with small talk. To those around him he seemed young for his sixty-three years.

Sometimes, though, he would stand alone at the rail, gazing over the bow, across the wintry sea—toward Europe. At such moments the hewn face seemed to be set against the political erosions of the era. Parting from Tumulty at New York, Wilson had predicted that his trip would be either "the greatest success or the supremest tragedy in all history." "I believe in a Divine Providence," he had said. "If I did not have faith, I should go crazy . . . it is my faith that no body of men . . . can defeat this great world enterprise."[5]

To the Scot who had thirteen letters in his own name and had often marked the close association of this number with his career, it was a good omen that the *George Washington* steamed into the harbor of Brest on Friday, the 13th of December. A thick mist was rising. From tiers of land batteries and the decks of warships salvos of welcome boomed as the presidential ship came on. Woodrow Wilson was on the

---

[4] William Phillips, *Adventures in Diplomacy*, p. 94.
[5] At the same time, Wilson had taken care to supplement prayer with vigilance. He would depend on Tumulty, he had told his secretary, for candid reports on the state of public opinion in America. "When you think I am putting my foot in it, please say so frankly," was his parting shot. And to Secretary Daniels he had written before sailing: "I know you and all my colleagues will keep your eyes skinned against anybody getting the better of us while I am on the other side of the water."

bridge, laughing and waving in appreciation of each tribute. The day was just cold enough to be invigorating.

In the outer harbor the great liner came to anchor just as the sun broke through. French and American dignitaries boarded her and went to the President's suite. There was a boisterous reunion of war heroes. John J. Pershing had come to meet the eye of the Commander in Chief whom he thought a good President to him; and Admiral Sims, seeing the general for the first time since the Armistice, hailed him with: "Hello, Jack, how the hell did you do it? I didn't know you had it in you." [6]

A side-wheeler ferried the President's party to the quay, where they were met by officials who wore sashes of tricolor. Words of mutual greeting were exchanged with Brest's Socialist mayor. And then, stepping on French soil with silk hat in hand, his face radiant, Wilson bowed right and left to acknowledge the cheers of peasants who were crowding close—women in quaint headdresses, fishermen standing with wooden shoes in the mud. Between lines of French soldiers, past generals in red hats and Bretons in vivid costumes, through streets thronged with children waving American flags, the President was conducted to a pavilion decorated with crimson silk. There he heard the mayor hail him as the apostle of liberty, come to release the people of Europe from their tortures. The trim, formally dressed gentleman from America looked grave as he listened to the extravagance of the greeter. He responded in the intimate, appealing way that he had when he reached out to pluck at men's heartstrings. But he laughed when he read a banner that saluted him as the founder of a league of nations. This, he said, was a bit premature.

Arriving at Paris at ten in the morning, the party left their rose-colored armchairs and stepped into the vestibule of the car. There were cheers, and Wilson responded with a thin, shy smile. Down on the platform was Raymond Poincaré, President of the Republic, correct and formal in morning coat, and beside him his lady. A few paces behind stood a squat man under a high hat, wearing a square-tailed dress coat of good broadcloth, very much in need of pressing. His long arms were folded across his breast and he was grinning impishly. "Now I am going to see him," he was mumbling. "This is where we first take each other's measure." Lunging forward to the side of the car, Georges Clemenceau, The Tiger of France, the soul of his nation's resistance, stretched his hand high toward the American about whom everyone was talking.

Stepping out into the pale sunshine, the Wilsons found themselves in

[6] Palmer, *Bliss, Peacemaker*, p. 358; Charles Seymour, who was present, to the writer.

a city gone mad. On both sides soldiers bordered the avenues, statuesque at present-arms, yielding only to let wheel chairs carry comrades to the edge of the line of march; and behind them stood myriads of people, waving flags and yelling. Parisians who for years had muttered *c'est la guerre* now shrieked *"Vive Wil-son! Vive l'Amérique! Vive la liberté!"* There were miles of them, some delirious in the contagion of excitement, some weeping for joy. They crowded the sidewalks and the buildings, even perched on creaking trees. From windows and roofs, flowers rained down on Edith Wilson's carriage. Planes zoomed and battle flags dipped.

The hero from the West stood up in his open victoria, bareheaded, his hands stretched out toward the people, on his flushed face a smile that was to the Parisians the dawn of a new day. *"Le grand Américain,"* they called him, *"le pur champion du droit et de la justice, le Christophe Colomb d'un nouveau monde."* The press gave him more space than they had devoted to visits of kings, the Socialist journals acclaiming him as their champion, the conservatives accepting him indulgently.

Suddenly the carriages turned, rolled between heavy doors through an ivy-draped wall, and swept around a drive to imposing steps. The Wilsons found themselves in the privacy of the Murat Palace, where the voices of the people penetrated only faintly. Here this American of simple tastes was to dwell for two months—his sensibilities chilled by the artificiality of the furnishings.

Buttoning himself tightly into an old-fashioned frock coat that his valet had providently brought along, Wilson was soon off for a formal luncheon in the palace of the French President. There he found a world remote from the men and women who had greeted him along the boulevards. In this salon of Old World diplomacy, after a feast of fine viands and choice wines, the first sniping shots in the warfare of the peace were fired in the toasts of the two Presidents.

The host, who had advocated a harsh reckoning with Germany, gave his guest a taste of bitter sentiments. "The French government will hand you documents," Poincaré promised, "in which you will yourself see how the German Command, with astounding cynicism, set forth its program of pillage and destruction. Whatever precautions we may take, nobody, alas! can assert that we shall save humanity forever from further wars!"

Wilson responded directly to the challenge in a speech that was translated. "From the first," he said, "the thought of the people of the United States turned toward something more than the mere winning of this war. It realized that . . . it must be won in such a way as to insure the future peace of the world . . ." Sympathizing with France's indignation against German wantonness, the American said: "I appreciate, as you do, sir, the necessity of such action in the final settlement of the issues of the war as will not only rebuke such acts of terror and spolia- tion, but make men everywhere aware that they cannot be ventured upon without the certainty of just punishment."

Labor leaders of Paris, hoping to use the American as a lever to pry concessions from Clemenceau, proposed a "manifestation" at the Troca- dero, where thousands of working women were to present a bas-relief to the American as the "incarnation of the hope of the future." When the French premier cannily referred this proposal to Wilson, the Presi- dent just as shrewdly told the workers that their own government should make the decision. When conditions were imposed that made the women abandon their plan, they went instead in a small group to the Murat Palace and gave their trophy to their hero.

Before the President had left America he had from House a timetable of projected events and a warning that the Allies were tending to delay discussions. Even when Wilson arrived at Paris, the French had not appointed their commissioners; and Lloyd George, who had been occu- pied in securing a mandate from his constituency in a national election, was waiting to see what would happen in Germany and was conferring with representatives of the Dominions. The Colonel, loyally accepting Wilson's decision to come to Paris, kept on working to create an atmos- phere of understanding. He assured the President that his suspicions of a reactionary conspiracy among European statesmen were groundless— a journalistic dream—that in reality all the powers were trying to work with the United States and not as a European bloc. Now, with Wilson on the scene, the Colonel considered that the second House mission had ended its duties and henceforth, though a peace commissioner of equal rank with the President, he would not take responsibility for making decisions, but would revert to his old role of informant, impresario, and friend. When Wilson told him that a league of nations would be the center of his program, that almost all the difficulties would vanish once the league was set up, the Colonel faithfully curbed his fears of anarchy in Central Europe and his own inclination to give priority to a military and economic settlement.

Impatient at the lagging of the peacemaking, Wilson was irritated by news that came by cable from Washington. Especially was he aroused by a message from Frank I. Cobb of the New York *World,* saying that that influential liberal had reached the opinion, in his talks with high officials at London and Paris, that Clemenceau and Lloyd George had been stacking the cards against the President. Wilson had depended on Cobb to direct the publicity policy of the American delegation at the conference. Consequently, when he arrived at Paris and found that House had allowed the editor to sail for home, the President expressed deep disappointment, even though the Colonel had established cordial relations with other journalists.[7] Moreover, Wilson was very angry when he heard of two appointments that had been made in the American secretariat by Lansing.

The President had not been at Paris long before Tumulty was cabling that news of the peacemaking was inadequate, that the President must cooperate more actively with the press. Specifically, he must visit hospitals, sit at the bedside of private soldiers, shake hands with the *poilus*, "put across" his wonderful smile, and always have reporters and photographers on the alert beforehand.

And so Wilson motored with his wife to the American hospital at Neuilly, where he went from cot to cot, missing not one of the eleven hundred patients, making a little speech, telling a private who gave his name as Thomas Wilson that he was glad to be the namesake of such a brave man. Later in the same day they went to a pathetic Christmas party in a shabby ward in a French hospital. On Christmas Eve they boarded a frigid train, to awake at Chaumont in a snowstorm and be driven with General Pershing to crude billets where green sprays and bits of red paper were the only reminders of the season. There was a review of troops that sloshed through deep mud, and then joking and storytelling over a turkey and pumpkin pie, and a drive to the general's château, where they sat before an open fire and steaming tea.

The President was disappointed because he had his Christmas dinner at an officers' mess rather than with the soldiers in their barracks. But out in the gray dampness he looked for a few moments into the faces of the men who had fought for him and for whom he now stood ready to fight. "You knew when you came over what you came over for," he said, "and you have done what it was appointed you to do. I know what you expect of me . . . It is difficult, very difficult, men, in a formal speech like this to show you my real heart . . . A thrill has gone through my heart . . . with almost every gun that was fired and every stroke that was struck in the gallant fighting that you have done . . . I feel a comradeship with you today which is delightful. . . ." The nearer he approached to the fields of death, the stronger he found the impulse of the people toward a league of nations.

During the days of waiting at Paris there were evenings when the President could sit quietly with his wife in a room dimly lit by a shaded

---

[7] Cobb, who had been urged by Auchincloss to print an editorial eulogistic of House, felt that the Colonel, wishing to keep the reins in his own hands, had kept essential information from Wilson. It seemed to Cobb that House had made an unnecessary capitulation to Lloyd George on the freedom of the seas in the pre-Armistice negotiations.

lamp and flickerings from an open fire. An old friend found them sitting up late. "Edith never wants to go to bed," Wilson explained, "but along about this time I begin to get drowsy. When we retire from the White House we are going into vaudeville as 'Dopey Dan and Midnight Mary.' " Spread before him was a sheet of paper, cross-ruled, and on it he was rating Bermuda, California, and five Eastern cities on the score of Freedom, Climate, Intellectual Advantages, Social Advantages, Recreation, and Amusements. Like millions of Americans, he was finding refuge from the tempestuous present in anticipation of a secure old age.

Forced to bow to the exigencies of both European and American politics, Wilson and House conceived ways in which their sacred cause could be furthered directly. The President said bluntly to journalists that he believed the formation of a league of nations to be indispensable to the maintenance of peace. The ideal could be kept alive in the headlines, he hoped, by personal conference with Clemenceau and Lloyd George and by public appeals to the Allied peoples.

When he asked House to be present at his first meeting with The Tiger, the Colonel was prepared to coach each of his friends for the occasion. During the pre-Armistice negotiations House had won the personal respect of Clemenceau and had secured from him a pledge to bring up no matter in the coming conference that he did not first discuss with Wilson.

The champion of French resistance, facing in his seventy-eighth year the greatest ordeal that he had met in a half-century of public life, came to the conference professionally skeptical but personally cordial. The skullcap that he wore perpetually was on his massive head. Gray gloves covered the diseased skin of his hands, giving a silky gloss to a squat body and a mind tense with the coiled springs of epigram. Half-concealed under heavy eyebrows and a brushy mustache, eyes and mouth did not betray the thoughts of this redoubtable pleader as he exchanged pleasantries. Having lived in the United States for four years—he had entered Richmond just after General Grant and had married a New York girl from whom he had been divorced—Clemenceau spoke the language of the Americans.

Wilson greeted him charmingly and showed himself the brilliant colleague whom House had been commending, not the intractable bigot that political enemies had been caricaturing. Afterward the Colonel gloated. "I have never seen an initial meeting a greater success," he wrote in his diary. "The President was perfect in the matter and manner of his conversation . . . neither said anything that was particularly misleading. They simply did not touch upon topics which would breed discussion. I saw to that in advance." House was coming to look upon the Peace Conference as his Grand Guignol.

The cordial interview fired Wilson's impatience to come to grips with the formidable Frenchman on the subject that was to him all-important —the league of nations. And so House was asked to set the stage for a more serious conversation. This time, arriving at the Murat Palace fifteen minutes before the French premier, the Colonel suggested to Wilson that Clemenceau could best be brought around to the league through mention of freedom of the seas, a topic on which American and French views might be expected to harmonize, in contrast with Britain's ideas. Again House's tactics were successful. The President talked at great length—and very well indeed. The Tiger began to see that the American could be counted on to be fair to France on questions on which Lloyd George had been opposing her; and soon he was hoping that Wilson would sit in the inner councils of peacemaking. Frankly doubting that a league would prove to be practical, Clemenceau nevertheless agreed that the experiment should be tried.

While committing their leader, the prophet from the West continued to woo the French people. At the Murat Palace the hours were filled with dinners, receptions, auto rides, calls from the great men of Europe. On a Sunday he went to the American Presbyterian Church, and then to Lafayette's tomb, insisting that he go himself with a wreath instead of commissioning a florist to deliver it. The next day an open carriage took him to the Hôtel de Ville to be acclaimed a citizen of Paris; and again there were crowds and troops in brilliant array, and a presentation of a gold pen with which to sign the peoples' peace, and toasts drunk in the best champagne.

The members of the French Academy—robed in yellow, blue, and scarlet—rose and cheered the American scholar when he appeared at a ceremony at which Marshal Joffre was made one of the Forty Immortals.[8] Invited to the Sorbonne to receive the degree of *Doctor Honoris Causa,* Woodrow Wilson felt himself back in the atmosphere that he most loved. Speaking without notes, as in all of his appearances at Paris, he extolled the university spirit for its intolerance of all things that put the human mind under restraint. He took the occasion to set forth his concept of a league of nations.

During these days of honeymoon with *La Belle France,* Wilson was disturbed by the tardiness of the British peace delegates. Northcliffe, whose cooperation House had been cultivating, noted the President's

---

[8] From Marshal Joffre's address on this occasion, Wilson jotted down this sentence: "Let her [France] never forget that the weak and the small cannot live free in the world if the strong and the great are not ever ready to place their strength and power at the disposal of right."

impatience and suggested to Balfour that Wilson be invited to visit England. As plans for the trip took shape, House thought it wise to use newspaper space that had been put at his disposal by Northcliffe. Accordingly, a report of an interview with the President was drafted by House's men, accepted by Wilson with slight changes, and published in the London *Times*. In this statement the President paid tribute to the British fleet and recognized "Britain's peculiar position as an Island Empire," but showed no sympathy for the imperialistic ambitions of some Englishmen.

The King was irritated because Wilson's arrival was set for Boxing Day—a bank holiday. Nevertheless, he and the Queen and the prime minister met the Wilsons on a crimson carpet at Charing Cross Station. The President's smile grew broadest when he greeted Lord Robert Cecil, English champion of a league of nations.

When Professor Woodrow Wilson had traveled in England some twenty years before, frequenting literary shrines and quiet, rural places, he had gone home feeling himself a better American for having been there. He still loved the traditions that had become familiar to him in his youthful studies of Gladstone and Bright; and yet he was amused by the fuss made over him as a statesman, and quite unawed. The next morning he exchanged familiar greetings with the servants—all except one, whose crust he could not pierce.

After a palace dinner His Majesty toasted the efficacy of American arms; but the President, standing in his black dress suit and flaunting no medals, responded by asserting the obligation of governments to obey "the great moral tide running in the hearts of men." He gave no brotherly pat on the back for a war well fought, no glorification of Anglo-Saxon victory in battle. He seemed to take England for granted. ("After all, in a certain sense, England is a success in the world," Walter Bagehot had written fifty years before.)

Lloyd George, sitting at the table, noted a coolness in the applause and remarked on it to Reading. Word was passed to the President; and the next day, speaking at the Guildhall, Wilson did lip service to the "prowess and achievements" of the British and the other Allies. Then the prophet went on to preach his gospel, hoping to align the dignitaries publicly with his own thinking. "There must now be," he proclaimed, "not a balance of power, not one powerful group of nations set off against another, but a single overwhelming group of nations who shall be the trustee of the peace of the world . . ." This was the "incomparably great object" that had brought him overseas, this "final political enterprise of humanity."

At luncheon in the Mansion House the next day, in a hall medieval in atmosphere, the lord bishop of London asked grace; and when wine was poured for toasts, it was tasted first by a functionary as a precaution against poison. After this demonstration of ancient ritual the American prophet assailed the fetters of old custom. It had seemed a normal thing for him to come to Europe, he said, because the necessity for intimate conferences took precedence over every other duty. "After all," he proclaimed, "breaking of precedents, though this may sound strange doctrine in England, is the most sensible thing to do. The harnessing of precedent is sometimes a very sad and harassing trammel." Determined not to be absorbed by British atmosphere, as he felt that Page and Sims had been, he preached an American gospel.

After the speechmaking there were complaints among the shipping interests that the American had not congratulated England on her incomparable fleet; and Lloyd George was far from satisfied by Wilson's preceptive attitude. It seemed to him poor taste, to say the least, for the American to preach on the ascendancy of right over might to men who for four years had been bleeding in support of his text.

In the Midlands, however, the President found auditors were congenial. Early on a rainy Sunday morning the King's train brought him into the town of Carlisle, near the Scottish border. The old kirk in which his grandfather had preached offered a restful contrast to the glitter of royalty. In deference to Thomas Woodrow's aversion to lay preaching, Wilson determined to remain silent, but less than an hour before the service the minister prevailed on him to change his mind. Invited to the pulpit, he preferred to stand in front of the communion rail. Harking back to his grandfather, he recalled "how much he required" and "the stern lessons of duty he gave." He could still hear that voice— flavored by a mild toddy and smoke from a clay pipe—asking, challenging: "Tommie, what is the chief end of man?" As he stood on boards that his mother's tiny feet had once trod, he was moved to recall her "sense of duty and dislike of ostentation." He spoke fervently of his twentieth century mission to the world: "I believe that as this war has drawn the nations temporarily together in a combination of physical force we shall now be drawn together in a combination of moral force that will be irresistible . . . It is from quiet places like this all over the world that the forces accumulate which presently will overbear any attempt to accomplish evil on a large scale."

Save for the compelling voice, there was no sound but the patter of rain on the roof. The bishop of Carlisle, closing the service, could hardly master his feelings to articulate the benediction: "God save you and guide you, sir!" The President was glad to step into the seclusion of the vestry to sign the book, for there he could get control of his emotion.

At Manchester the lord mayor hailed him as "foremost of all Americans who have ever visited England." He spoke twice, making the most of this chance to attack the old order and to steady the merry-go-round platform of Lloyd George. In the Free Trade Hall in which John Bright's voice once had thundered he said:

You know that heretofore the world has been governed, or at any rate an attempt has been made to govern it, by partnerships of interest, and they have broken down. Interest does not bind men together. Interest separates men, for the moment there is the slightest departure from the nice adjustment of interests, jealousies begin to spring up. There is only one thing that can bind people together and that is a common devotion to right. Ever since the history of liberty began men have talked about their rights, and it has taken several hundred years to make them perceive that the principal part of right is duty, and that unless a man performs his full duty he is entitled to no right.

Serving notice that the United States would "join no combination of power which is not the combination of us all," he ended with a devout wish that like his "very stern ancestors . . . who were known as the Covenanters," they might enter into a great league and covenant for all the world.

Here was the essence of Wilsonism—the same vague and generalized appeal to common counsel and dynamic morals that had transcended the interests of ingrown groups at Princeton and at Washington. It cut across national boundaries, soared above party concerns. It was working in the hearts of Europeans.

Going to the Midland Hotel for luncheon, he declared that it was not skill of hand, but elevation of spirit, that made worthy men; and stopping at the Royal Exchange, he reminded the traders that he knew something about their business, and hoped that they "would all make money out of it." They laughed when he added, with a sly wink: "I suspect that in the transactions at this place occasionally a little is lost." The bustling lord mayor found him comradely and jovial, as they sat on the captain's bridge on a tender in the ship canal and watched an American vessel unload cotton. The people of the Midlands discovered in their visitor a warmth and understanding that he had not revealed at London.

Wilson received assurance in England that not only the liberal citizens, but their leaders as well, were devoted to his ideal. Grey, Asquith, and the archbishop of Canterbury came to him to plead for a league of nations and found him utterly confident. He said proudly that his wife considered him the most obstinate man in America, and that nothing could induce him to yield. He told of an issue that had come before Lincoln's Cabinet: after a unanimous chorus of "noes," the President said "aye" and then "the ayes have it!" At this evidence of fanaticism Asquith's heart sank and filled with grave forebodings for the success of their ideal.[9]

Some British politicians with whom Wilson conferred gave more heed to the voters who had just re-elected them than to the American prophet who had been repudiated by his own electorate, by ex-President Roosevelt, and, in a speech in the Senate in mid-December that was intended chiefly to impress the Allies, by Henry Cabot Lodge. David Lloyd George, especially, seemed no man to take up a great cause and joust for it against all comers. He had a record of prewar liberalism, however, that matched that of the President. The "born politician" that Wilson fancied in himself could not but admire Lloyd George's adroitness, his accessibility to people with whom he did not agree. Wilson felt that if only he could trust the "little man" he could get along with him more easily than with the rather terrifying intellect of Foreign Secretary Balfour. If only he could set the veering Welsh weather vane steadfastly toward the league of nations!

The British leaders had been studying their man and as a result feared to cross the President unnecessarily. Both Lloyd George and Balfour inclined to agree that, once set up, a league could assist in working out specific settlements that seemed vital. The prime minister was relieved to get assurance that Wilson did not contemplate giving executive powers to a league, and to learn that the American's ideas resembled those of Lord Robert Cecil and General Smuts of South Africa.[10] But they disagreed on the question of indemnities; and when the President's

---

[9] Gilbert Murray in *The Listener*, LIV, No. 1388 (Oct. 6, 1955). Grey wrote on Dec. 30 to assure House that if a league took "practical form," the undercurrent of opposition would be "completely snowed under by an overwhelming mass of public opinion." But Grey feared that a treaty creating a league might be wrecked by the United States Senate. "We are afraid that for us to force the pace here might contribute to that result," he wrote.

[10] House had not felt well enough to accompany Wilson to England and in his place had sent his son-in-law, Gordon Auchincloss. By telephone, the Colonel had advised that the President bear down on the league of nations but keep off the dangerous topic of "freedom of the seas."

Auchincloss, attempting to set up Wilson-Lloyd George conferences in the way in which House had guided Wilson's meetings with Clemenceau, offended the President and his official "family" by his officiousness. The presence at Paris of the Colonel's daughter and son-in-law and the latter's law partner, David Hunter Miller, as well as that of Mrs. Mezes, Mrs. House's sister, put a severe strain on the President's respect for his beloved Colonel. (American delegates were expected to leave their wives at home.) Moreover, Dr. Mezes did not include among the experts taken to Paris the President's own son-in-law, Francis B. Sayre, who had canceled other plans in order to work in New York for The Inquiry.

It was suggested to the President by those near him that the Colonel had presumed on his friendship. Later, when it was proposed that Auchincloss serve as Wilson's secretary in council meetings, the President resented this, as an attempt to "keep track" of him on the part of House and the other commissioners. Irwin H. Hoover's notes, Library of Congress.

views were reported by Lloyd George to the Imperial War Cabinet, they were received with skepticism and partisan feeling.

Wilson returned to Paris on the last day of 1918, surprised at Lloyd George's acquiescence in a league and doubting the steadfastness of the Welshman's support. He put greater faith in a plan published by General Smuts, and hoped that the South African's influence in British councils might be strong enough to bring the great cause to fruition.

Talking with his fellow commissioners in House's rooms, Wilson said that his trip to England had cleared the air, that Britain was closer than France to the American point of view. This feeling was confirmed in discussion of a speech that Clemenceau had made in the French Chamber three days before, favoring the balancing of power through international alliances, accepting a league of nations only as a supplementary guarantee of French security, and referring to the *"noble candeur"* of the American President—a phrase that was interpreted to imply that Wilson was a well-intentioned simpleton.[11]

With House, the President went through stacks of papers from Washington. He unhesitatingly signed documents that the Colonel vouched for, but remarked that he would veto any legislation sponsored solely by the Republicans. Together the friends disposed of a vast accumulation of business in a few hours. House was in deep gloom. But the President, holding to his faith in "the people," seemed confident that they would drive their statesmen to base the peace on a durable foundation.

On the first day of the new year, he left Paris for Italy, where, his ambassador had reported, English propagandists had been undermining American prestige.

All forebodings, however, seemed at first unwarranted. The Wilsons were given a triumph worthy of the Caesars, as the royal coach drove them from end to end of Rome's Via Nationale and the multitudes waved flags and shouted *"Viva Wilson!"* To Edith Wilson it was a day of thrills. They visited the war hospital to which most of the rooms of the palace were still devoted and, lunching informally with Their Majesties at a villa outside the city, they saw the royal family at home—genuine, lovely, talented. She appraised every detail and loved it all, while her husband chafed and bridled at delays that made it impossible to get on with his mission.

[11] Clemenceau explained to House that he had not intended to give offense and had used the phrase to applaud Wilson's frankness and loyalty, while giving warning that both he and the President were in a difficult situation and must necessarily view it from different standpoints. Bonsal, *Suitors and Suppliants,* p. 211.

The vote in the Chamber approving Clemenceau's policy was about in the ratio of four to one.

Honored by a request that he be the first nonmember to address the Italian Chamber of Deputies from the floor, Wilson found that the Socialists had protested by withdrawing in a body. Undaunted, he asked for sympathy for the Balkan States that "must now be independent." It was a bold stroke, this plea for tolerance toward Yugoslav aspirations that ran head-on into Italy's territorial ambitions along the Adriatic. Again the prophet warned Old World politicians that a new concept of government was dawning.

Whether the President should visit the Pope was a problem without precedent. Protestant clergymen in America had warned against it; but Cardinal Gibbons had urged that the President call on "the highest moral authority left in the world" and Tumulty had reminded Wilson of the influence that His Holiness could throw behind a league of nations. And so the President agreed to visit the Vatican, but insisted on attending a Protestant reception on the same day.

Pope Benedict greeted him warmly in English, commending his efforts toward a league of nations. While these spiritual leaders talked, sitting in gilded chairs before an open window, a multitude of Italians stood in a piazza for hours, waiting for a speech by the American that had been advertised. However, when the time came for him to go out and address them, they had been dispersed by officials. Foreign Minister Sonnino explained that the authorities feared that the crowd might get out of hand, that it was unnecessary for the President to speak.

Wilson was angered. He was not used to being denied the right to preach to a congregation, wherever he found it. But he was not surprised. House had directed his attention to the failure of the Italian ministers to urge him to go to North Italy, where he might expect to find liberal support in the industrial cities.

On the way back to Paris, however, he made brief stops. Leaving the train at Genoa, he paid lip service to Christopher Columbus, and stood with bared head before Mazzini's monument, deeply moved, he said, by a spirit of "veneration" and "emulation." There were six brief speeches at Milan, where placards announced: "Italy demands only the frontiers marked out for her by God." When his voice was drowned by a band playing a Sousa march he waved his arms and led the music until the last bar. The next day he made five short talks on a rainy day in Turin, one of them at the university, where Wilson delighted the students by wearing one of their blue caps. More than a thousand mayors came from surrounding towns to shake his hand—some to bend and kiss it. Here, in North Italy, he had his chance to appeal directly to the people for a new world order, and they swarmed about him and cheered themselves hoarse.

When the train stopped at Modena, a messenger brought in a tele-gram. As he glanced at it, his companions saw in his face, first, surprise, then pity, and finally relief. His political archenemy would throw no more stilettos into his back, would never again declare him politically bankrupt and without honor in his own land. The Scottish fiber in him had somehow outlasted a rival who was his junior by two years. Theo-dore Roosevelt, his lusty antagonist, was dead.

Sitting quiet for a moment, he dictated a message to Roosevelt's widow. The news had "deeply grieved" him, he said, but on second thought he changed "grieved" to "shocked." It was equally decorous and more honest.[12]

Woodrow Wilson returned to Paris with a confidence that was all-possessing. It was easy, at this point, to convince himself that the people of Europe had been cheering for Wilson the peace giver rather than for a living symbol of their own victory or a guarantee of security for them-selves in the future. Moreover, he did not doubt that his Americans would repudiate the disciples of the fallen Republican leader, once he could go home and plead with them. However, his advisers were feeling the brute force of nationalistic ambitions. House had reported to the President in November that the whole world was vitally interested in America's plans for using her vast resources of credit and raw materials; and the Colonel had suggested that experts in these matters be brought to Paris. This had been done, and as the American specialists had wrestled with the immediate problems of reconstruction in a spirit of charity and forbearance, their apprehensions were being realized all too fully. Herbert Hoover, who had been made director general of relief and rehabilitation, was striving to give practical effect to the ideal of collective altruism. He worked day and night to break down economic barriers to a flow of food and fuel to Central Europe. Scores of thou-sands of civilians were stalked by famine; city populations were threat-ened by anarchy and by the unpredictable bolshevism that was seeping westward; more than a dozen little nations—many of them just liber-ated—were writing provisional constitutions, building armies, grabbing territories, setting up obstacles to trade. But, torn as the Continent was by political parturition, officials of the Allies were slow to yield to Hoover's appeals for civilian relief. As individuals, they thought idealis-tically; but as representatives of peoples who had been ruined and bled white, they naturally thought first of the welfare of their own constitu-

---

[12] Lloyd George reports that when he entered the President's room at Paris and expressed sorrow at Roosevelt's death, he was "aghast at the outburst of acrid detestation which flowed from Wilson's lips." Lloyd George, *Memoirs of the Peace Conference,* I, 147.

encies. They too expected succor from the United States—a nation that had gained much in credits and lost little in blood. Moreover, they were suspicious that Uncle Sam would use his bulging granaries to buy political influence in Central Europe. Wilson was shocked when Hoover denounced many of the Allies as "second-story workers" who thought Americans a foolish people, pliable to ingenious propaganda, and accepted the United States as a "golden-egged goose." [13]

When the President returned to Paris he learned of political machinations that aggravated his distrust of his allies. There were rumors that the French were holding back the rehabilitation of war-ravaged lands so they might exhibit them to him and make him "see red." Suspecting that there was some truth in this report, Wilson put off a French suggestion that he visit the devastated region, and explained to his staff that he already knew enough about the ravages of war: his own family's property had suffered when Sherman marched to the sea.

There was an even more ominous undercurrent in a secret meeting of the British delegation that was held early in January. Giving his colleagues a realistic picture of American politics, Lloyd George portrayed Wilson as a man whose political credit was insecure, whose drafts America might not honor, and yet a powerful leader whose thin skin must not be pricked by any reminder of the precariousness of his position.

[13] Hoover in the *Saturday Evening Post,* Nov. 1, 1941; and Hoover to the writer. Hoover's experience in economic relief led him to advise Wilson to give a league of nations no powers, but only the right to inquire and to state facts. The only solid foundation for a league was a spirit of cooperation, this enterprising executive felt, and such a spirit might be dampened by too legalistic a constitution.

Though Wilson thought him unduly pessimistic, Hoover did not despair of effective action. At a dinner party he told guests who were criticizing the President that he had seen Woodrow Wilson solve many difficult problems by sheer force of intellect.

CHAPTER XIII

MAKING A COVENANT FOR THE TWENTIETH CENTURY

WOODROW WILSON RETURNED to Paris on January 7 physically worn out. Dr. Grayson saw that before coming to grips with the premiers he must rest for a day or two. The physician himself, in an effort to shield his patient from strain, performed many of the duties of a staff officer, fending off importunate journalists and pleaders for divers causes.

In his struggle for a world political order Wilson would have to operate without the party machinery that he had used at Trenton and Washington. There would be no caucuses, no patronage, no party whips, no legislative committees to help to frame new measures. Even his most intimate and incisive weapon—The Word—would be blunted by translators. More than ever before, he was to need a well-disciplined, competent staff; but he had only his White House secretaries, who knew little about either the languages or the diplomacy of the Continent.

On the very day of his return from Italy, the President talked for a half hour over the private wire that ran directly from his study to the desk and bedside of Colonel House. The Colonel, established at the Hotel Crillon, was already performing many of the functions of diplomacy. Wilson was well pleased, he said, with his trip to Rome, and he listened eagerly to House's résumé of events at Paris during his absence. Late in the afternoon he met the American commissioners. He was received respectfully by the four appointees who were technically his equal in rank and who had been meeting together during his absence, unsure of their powers and responsibilities in relation to those of the diplomats, the military and naval staffs, and the special agents.

Lansing, to whom the President had paid little attention, was thinking of resigning. Sitting alone at his desk, hour after hour, the secretary of state recorded his dissents in a diary in a copybook hand.[1] He was

---

[1] Lansing's views were, in brief: "democracy was enough; no sanctions or legislative power were needed (by an international body); the peoples wanted justice and peace; expansion was legitimate against half-civilized people; rival territorial claims could be settled by diplomacy or court action." W. E. Rappard, *op. cit.*, p. 4.

Flatly opposing Wilson's positive plan for guaranteeing nations against aggression, Lansing complained in his diary that it was farcical to think that any foreign government would surrender a single right or aid any victim of aggression unless it appeared to be to its material advantage to do so. Moreover, he wrote in his diary that the right of self-determination—"government by consent of the governed"—was "simply loaded with dynamite" and "bound to be the basis of impossible demands on the Peace Congress and to create trouble in many lands." He felt that nations could be expected to do nothing more than sign a legalistic, negative

scornful of Wilson's deficiencies as an international lawyer and perturbed because the President had not even acknowledged a proposal for
guaranteeing security that he had taken pains to draft. He attributed
Wilson's rejection of his ideas to inordinate ambition to cut a heroic
figure in history.

Told by Henry White of Lansing's pique at the President's preference
for the counsel of House, Wilson said, "It never occurred to me," and
then, underestimating the Colonel's intelligence, "I am quite sure it
never did to House." Discussing the problem with Edith Wilson and
with the Colonel, he concluded that, as had been the case with Bryan,
this dissenting Presbyterian had better be in his bosom rather than on
his back. Not willing to risk shaking public confidence in his cause by
dismissing a servant unsympathetic to it, he patiently suffered Lansing's
repetitive dissents with courteous smiles and nods that were misinterpreted as signs of sympathy.

Like Lansing, General Bliss had strong views of his own. Gruff, very
shy of personal publicity, a man who always carried a Latin text in his
pocket, studied Oriental botany, and swore beautifully, Bliss craved
peace. He saw, perhaps more vividly than any of the military men at
Paris, the handwriting on the sky of the future. He was distressed by
the vagueness of the President's remarks on policy and by the casualness
of the meetings of the American Commission; and he put more emphasis than his chief on the necessity for disarmament.[2] Bliss was to
prove a valiant lieutenant, rarely volunteering advice, quickly supplying
information when it was called for. Wilson thought him "a real thinking man who takes the pains to think straight."

The President could depend, too, on the disciplined loyalty of Henry
White, a diplomat of fine old vintage with a bouquet of quality and
tradition, commanding both respect and affection as he limped into the
Crillon from his daily walk, his cheeks apple-red under thick white
hair, in one hand a proper cane and in the other a tall black hat with a

---

undertaking not to commit acts of aggression. Lansing criticized Wilson as "too deliberate" or
else "not just sure what he wants."

Lansing brought his misgivings to House and the Colonel did his best to excuse Wilson's
indifference toward the secretary of state by attributing it to ill-health and by telling white
lies. Lansing set down House's tactful approaches to the President as evidence of weakness.
Though the Colonel's method seemed to work, it was to him *infra dig*. "I must either keep
quiet or else speak frankly my views," he protested. And yet only a week before writing this
in his diary he had indulged, in talking with Wilson, in a diplomatic prevarication of his true
feeling about the positive guarantee that was so dear to the President.

[2] A letter from Baker to Bliss, dated Dec. 3, 1918, reported the invention of an aerial bomb
that could be produced in quantity and, carrying 200 pounds of high explosives, would deviate
less than one-eighth of 1 per cent at a range of 50 miles. It seemed to Bliss that such a weapon
would be a constant argument for a league of nations as well as for limiting armaments to
policing necessities.

broad band around it. Wilson became fond of the old gentleman. A master of French and of diplomatic protocol, gallant with the ladies, White did his best to create teamwork among his compatriots and liaison with Europeans. He hinted to Wilson that he be detailed to make the personal contacts that his experience had taught him were necessary. Not encouraged, he presumed no further, but sought the confidence and help of Edith Wilson. At first lukewarm toward the President's league ideal, he grew to appreciate Wilson's character and his purposes, and wrote appreciatively of them to his Republican friends at home— "affectionately" to "Dear Cabot." [3]

It was at the office of Colonel House—not at the President's residence —that the American commissioners first met formally with their chief. The Colonel soon excused himself from the meeting and went into another room to greet Clemenceau, just back from a soothing respite in the Vendée. In a heart-to-heart talk House pointed out that France no longer could count on Russia as an ally against Germany, nor could she be sure of the support of Britain and the United States except under a league of nations. "Wilson can force the league through," House asserted, because with all their "brag and bluster" the Senate would not dare to defeat a peace treaty and thereby continue alone at war.

The champion of France seemed to see it all clearly, and placing both hands on House's shoulders, he said: "You are right. I am for the League of Nations as you have it in mind and you may count upon me to work with you." [4]

[3] Before accepting a place on the peace commission, White had lunched with his friend Lodge and other Republicans of the Senate Foreign Relations Committee. Moreover, he had conferred with Root at the bedside of Roosevelt, and had taken notes on the ideas of these men on international organization. Just before sailing he had received from Lodge a long message, insisting that Germany be crushed, divided, and heavily loaded with indemnities, and warning that any attempt to weave a league of nations into the peace treaty would make the Senate's ratification of the treaty extremely doubtful.

Lodge asked that Henry White show this paper in strict confidence to Balfour and Clemenceau, hoping that it would help "in strengthening their position" at the expense of that of the President of the United States. White, however, disapproved his friend's views on Germany; and realizing that the senator's maneuver might subvert the President's dearest ideal, he kept the message discreetly to himself. White assured Lodge that Wilson was quite equal in argument and clearness of statement to the European statesmen. To William Phillips he wrote on Jan. 24: "The President is really a wonderful man . . . He has absolutely established the combination of President and prime minister to an extent that I should never have believed possible."

[4] Ever since the Armistice, Colonel House had been as busy in Wilson's interest as recurring disorders of his gall bladder had permitted. Under the carte blanche that the President had given to him, he had placed his large clerical staff at Wilson's disposal. He felt that the President was burdening himself needlessly by taking the care of documents on his own conscience and by getting along with the aid of only two permanent secretaries whom he had brought from Washington.

Journalists came to regard the Colonel as "the small knothole through which must pass many great events." Moreover, many of the pressures of cranks and promoters of sundry causes— exerted through hundreds of scouts and lobbyists—tried the unfathomable patience of the Texan. Then, too, spokesmen of nations large and small, born or reborn, flooded through House's hospitable door to whisper messages that they could not, or dared not, deliver to the

House then took Clemenceau into the room where the President was talking to the American commissioners. Immediately The Tiger leaped at Wilson with an old, sore question: When would the President go to see the devastated areas of France? Wilson put him off, and he did not like it. Nevertheless, he now agreed with the President's desire to begin the conferences at once, and seconded Wilson in urging Lloyd George to come to Paris.

Having given little thought to peace terms until the war was won, Clemenceau had hastened after the Armistice to have traditional procedures laid down for the peacemakers. His Foreign Office had drafted a precise and conventional plan: first, settlement of the war; secondly, organization of a society of nations; thirdly, study of territorial and political affairs and general international questions.

Wilson had been unimpressed by the exact, legalistic coldness of the proposition, when it had been sent to him by the State Department. It characterized his principles as "not sufficiently defined in their character to be taken as a basis for a concrete settlement of the war."

In the first week of January, when Wilson had expected that the Peace Conference would begin, there was still no agreement on a program. Indeed, the Anglo-Saxon leaders preferred to improvise a procedure from day to day rather than commit themselves to a plan dictated by Latin logic. As explosive fears and ambitions flew about in a vacuum of indecision, Wilson moved cautiously but persistently toward his Fourteenth Point, the league of nations that he thought vital to establishing many of the other points.

He thought that if he rightly interpreted the temper of the world's people, through the intuitive sense on which he prided himself, they would respond now, while the wounds of war were still open; but soon they might sink into a coma of complacency from which only a more terrible war could rouse them. To those who were near him he disclaimed credit for originating the idea of a league. "Along with thousands of my fellow countrymen," he once explained, "I got the idea twenty years ago, chiefly from Republican public men."

Wilson hoped that at least he might lay a durable foundation for a league before he had to return to the United States for the closing of Congress in February. But he made up his mind that, if the Allies made this impossible, he would surprise them by returning later to France.

President, remote in the Murat Palace. Bypassing the secretary of state, the British delegation kept liaison constantly with the Colonel through Sir William Wiseman.

House's position depended on holding the confidence that Wilson had extended to him as to no other man. He must make sure that he kept a finger on all vital pulses of opinion and action during the peacemaking. He must guard vigilantly against personal animosities and jealousies. His inmost thoughts were preserved for history in a diary to be opened thirty years later.

Moreover, he said that, if necessary, he could use financial pressure to bring them around.

Early in January he communicated his enthusiasm to his American colleagues; and they agreed with him in placing the league first among five topics to be proposed for discussion by the Supreme War Council.[5] In giving the American list to the premiers, he spoke of the folly of regarding it as a fixed agendum and suggested that each national delegation be asked to comment on it. He wished to avoid the appearance of dictating anything, but he insisted that all eyes be kept intent on the highest objectives. His own ideas about both the method of making peace and the terms were still in a formative stage, and he was as shy as ever about releasing the product of his political thinking until it was complete and ripe.

Still looking to the poets and philosophers for truth, he turned more readily to academic talk than he had under the pressures of the war. One night he spoke feelingly of the impossibility of peace on no moral foundation but hatred. The world's people wanted a just settlement, he thought, but the ruling classes did not. Justice did not require that the German people be punished, for they would suffer enough when the world shunned them for generations to come.

He spoke of the resentment of the people against their statesmen for delay in the parleys, a delay that some of the French newspapers had been unjustly attributing to him. It was so hard to get people together. Clemenceau had needed rest, but was now back. However, dear House was stricken severely by influenza. After the Colonel's fever subsided, the President went almost daily to his bedside to take counsel.[6]

Finally, the statesmen of Europe turned their thoughts in earnest toward the inevitable battle of peacemaking. Woodrow Wilson's sensibilities were shocked at the very first gathering of the Supreme Council on January 12. Giving up his Sabbath rest on that afternoon, he donned his frock coat and silk hat, tucked a large black portfolio under his arm, and motored with Dr. Grayson to the Quai d'Orsay. There he was met

[5] One topic on the agenda suggested by the American Commission—representation of the various nations at the conference—already had been discussed by the council. The other five were: league of nations; reparations; new states; territorial adjustments; colonial possessions.

[6] Colonel House shared his friend's political faith with a quiet sincerity that other Americans lacked. He did not forget that only the impulse of the people could give life to the league, that democratic spirit could be stirred by phrases that touched men's hearts, that the President had given his country mottoes that had sent men to their death with cheers. In his book, *Philip Dru,* he had envisioned a league of nations. The public of America and Europe demanded this, he felt, and he wrote in his diary that "the consensus of public opinion comes nearer being right than the opinions of the leaders of a country." The President's dependence on House's skill in negotiation was more complete than ever. When Wilson visited the Crillon, he passed swiftly by Lansing's office and went up to House's room. He was vexed if anyone but the Colonel took initiative.

with diplomatic flutter and bustle. The President found twenty-two men from the major powers sitting along three sides of a formal room—the premiers and foreign ministers in the forefront, and the secretaries, experts, and interpreters behind or to one side. Soon serious discussion was interrupted by retirement to a tea table, where all munched macaroons and brioches. It all reminded him of an old ladies' sewing circle: everyone talking and to no purpose.

Wilson had foreseen the ineffectiveness of such a group. He had said, while on the *George Washington*: "Twenty-five or thirty delegates in one room mulling and quarreling over the details of a treaty would be a criminal waste of time . . ." He favored a small council, composed of the premiers of England, France, and Italy, and himself, to meet secretly and prepare tentative proposals for presentation to a general gathering of delegates in the public view. It was obvious to him that the first of his Fourteen Points—"open covenants openly arrived at"—could not be applied literally to all the proceedings at Paris.

Wilson expected that arrangements for the first plenary session would be discussed at the meeting of January 12. Instead, with their military men present, the French insisted on taking up conditions for extending the Armistice agreement, which was to expire in five days. Perceiving what was in the wind, the President quickly summoned General Bliss to his side. Then, asking for a reading of the original terms, he made it clear that it would be unsportsmanlike to force more severe strictures upon Germany now if the military advisers had failed to think of them at the proper time. The question of renewing the Armistice was referred to General Bliss and the other military men. Nine days later, still resisting French pressure for further emasculation of Germany, Bliss wrote to his wife: "Peace seems to be worse than war."

Clemenceau retained the chair without challenge. He adroitly eliminated the military men from the Supreme War Council and transformed it into a Council of Ten in which the five major powers (Japan was the fifth) were to write the peace. The ministers of state who sat in this body were not, like the American President, secure in their positions for a definite term of years. They were doughty parliamentarians, accustomed to battle for their political lives; and they had magnetism that was hard to escape, when they turned the currents on.

The question of national representation came up, and Lloyd George stepped forward to plead for the British Dominions. Dressed in an unconventional gray suit and a bowler, the Welshman was accustomed to come to meetings a moment late, with a step that seemed to swagger a bit and greetings that were bluff and genial. When he claimed two peace delegates from each of the Dominions, Wilson took issue with him. Arguing that the question of representation was "largely one of sentiment and psychology," the prophet warned that if the empire were given so many delegates, it would appear that the large powers dominated the Peace Conference. To this the Welshman replied: "After all, they ran the war. Those who fought hardest should talk loudest."

The discussion turned then to the representation of small powers. Sitting bolt upright in his armchair, inclining his head at times toward his advisers, Wilson listened intently. Then, leaning forward and resting on the arms of his chair, he spoke like a college professor criticizing a thesis.

Everything affecting the world's peace was the world's business, he remarked. The dispatch of Serbian troops into little Montenegro distressed him, he said, for Montenegro had a handsome political history.

"Do you recognize the King?" quizzed Lloyd George.

"We do," Wilson replied.

"We pay for him," Balfour put in.

Clemenceau let himself go in a demand that small powers, though having moral rights equal to those of all, should not be allowed to share in decisions on matters that did not directly concern them. Wilson and Balfour had in mind some sort of preliminary conversations among the great powers, to be followed by consultation with the little countries when their interests were at stake. All were agreed, however, that enemy nations should not be represented until agreement had been reached among themselves.

They were trying each other out in this first session. The American scholar-prophet puzzled the others with his passion for academic justness, his desire to get the "sense of the meeting." British secretaries thought him very tiresome and "a quaint bird." It seemed so hard to bring him to a decision on details on which European negotiators were used to speaking quickly and firmly. When Clemenceau asked his opinion, he reviewed arguments that had been made on both sides of the case. And when The Tiger canvassed the other members of the council and came back to the President with "Well, what shall we do?" Wilson suggested referring the question to a committee of experts or asked whether anyone had prepared a resolution. Usually the British delegation had one ready and was quick to put it forward, though sometimes, if the President had expressed his own views, Clemenceau would ask him to draft a resolution. Then, writing in pencil and without revision, Wilson would phrase his thoughts with a clarity and conciseness that no colleague could match. They soon came to admire his control of his tongue, his utter fairness, his patient courtesy toward all shades of opinion, his eagerness that decisions, when finally made, be carried out.

The perfection of his discourse gave an air of finality to his words. Perhaps realizing this, and embarrassed by the thought that anyone should consider him an oracle, he sometimes interrupted the flow of language with a little nervous chuckle—a mannerism that his associates had noted seldom before. He wished to treat these able fellow statesmen as colleagues, bearing with their thought as long as possible, making no remark that would give offense, until his conscience was satisfied and a decision had to be made.

Face to face with what he called "conjectural journalism," Wilson saw that something must be done about relations with the American newsmen who swarmed about, standing in doorways, looking over shoulders, hungry for copy, many of them unfamiliar with the language and customs of Paris. There were five hundred of them, more or less. Some were more interested in the market value of sensational news than in aiding the President, and they looked forward with unholy glee to the "wig-pulling" that they expected when the great statesmen came to grips on the issue of the league of nations.

At Paris, Wilson's desire to avoid discrimination among newspapers or to influence their opinions obsessed him to the point of squeamishness. Realizing that he could not hope to talk with all the journalists, he decided to see none. But he gave the newsmen daily access to each of his colleagues on the American Commission; and he persuaded Ray Stannard Baker to direct the release of daily bulletins through an American Press Bureau. The President hoped that under this policy news might be handled with discretion, efficiency, and impartiality.

Wilson's disappointment over the lack of progress of the meeting on January 12 was slight, in comparison with the letdown that the public opinion of the world suffered when the people were given only an official four-line report of the session. The American journalists sent a formal protest to their President. Where, they asked, were the "open covenants openly arrived at"? Moreover, Tumulty cabled that the President should do anything—even bolt from the conference—rather than submit to a policy of secrecy.

In the absence of fact, rumors mushroomed overnight. Furthermore, facts somehow seeped into the French newspapers; and they seemed so well chosen, from France's point of view, that Wilson was moved to speak bitingly of "careful leakage." The French, however, explained that their journalists actually were at a disadvantage because they were censored and the Americans and British were not. Perhaps, if all could be restricted to one official communiqué a day . . . ? But Wilson felt that under such an arrangement he would lose the right to appeal directly to the idealism of humanity, over the heads of the national leaders.

Lloyd George said that the British press well understood that it was excluded from Cabinet meetings, and here at Paris the delegates were acting as a cabinet for the nations. He put in a compromise suggestion: that the public be educated in the danger of giving out information on negotiations before decisions were reached. And when Wilson proposed that such an explanation be made to all press representatives at Paris rather than directly to the public, his colleagues assented.

The journalists were brought together, but the national loyalties of the correspondents proved to be stronger than any common devotion to their profession. The American newsmen were not convinced of the good faith of these diplomats who promised frankness within the limits of discretion, and they continued to agitate. Tumulty cabled frantically to urge that Wilson talk personally with three correspondents representing the press associations. But the President replied that the rule of secrecy made it impossible to correct the imaginative accounts that were reaching America. Once, to be sure, he did address a group of newsmen; but after a reporter betrayed a confidence he had no stomach to try it again. And so he became the only important chief at Paris who refused to meet his nation's correspondents regularly and personally. Ray Stannard Baker implored him to use his magnetism on the journalists. When he urged the President to explain something to them, however, Wilson protested: "But I've already said that." It was true. He had said it in a speech; and he hated to repeat as much as he disliked to be told things twice.

The council gave their compromise explanation to the press, Baker went on issuing a daily bulletin to the American journalists, Dr. Grayson gave interviews and fended off the curious as best he could, American correspondents went listlessly to interview their commissioners, and the leaks continued. Bound by nothing but his own conscience and judgment, Wilson was free to adhere to the policy of Cabinet confidence or to use his favorite weapon in case of crisis—an appeal to the people.

When the Peace Conference met in plenary session, however, the press was invited and the people of the world were given fuller reports.[7] The first of six general assemblies met on January 18. To the Salle de la Paix came seventy-two delegates from twenty-six nations and four dominions. Most were dressed in sober black coats. At the end of the

---

[7] At first the policy of admitting the press to plenary sessions had been opposed by the Old World diplomats; but finally Wilson's view—buttressed by the demands of the press of America, England, Italy, and small nations—prevailed. Actually, the result was that vital discussions were excluded from the plenary sessions. The negotiating came to be done, the tentative decisions made, in "conversations" in small groups and behind closed doors, after study of masses of data supplied by expert advisers.

horseshoe sat the President of France, directly in front of a statue of Peace bearing the torch of Civilization.

After Poincaré had paid a gracious tribute to each country, Wilson stepped forward. Black and trim in his striped trousers, he wore a high collar, cravat with pink pin, and pince-nez. Playing the role ordained for him, he grasped the hand of the French President. Then he nominated Clemenceau as permanent chairman of the conference, lifting both the man and the occasion to the awesome heights on which he sensed that the hearts of mankind were placing them. He spoke appreciatively of the sufferings of France, of the historic importance of her capital in the making of peace.

Clemenceau rose from his great golden chair to respond to Wilson's declaration of confidence, and he pleaded for union among the peoples who had fought together. He spoke like one converted to the ideals of perpetual peace and a league of nations. Laying on the table the rules that had been prescribed for the conference by the council, he made it clear that the program of the President of the United States would be followed—the five-point procedure that Wilson had worked out with his American commissioners, placing the framing of a league Covenant first. Within two hours the meeting had adjourned without dissension and Wilson was free to indulge in philosophical talk with General Smuts, whose thoughts on the league he found agreeable and stimulating.

At the second general session, on January 25, The Tiger showed his claws and established a mastery over procedure that he was never to yield. Delegates from certain small nations protested against the council's ruling that they would be allowed representation in that body only when questions affecting their interests were to be discussed. The threat challenged Clemenceau's parliamentary skill. Rising slowly, he sprang into action and cuffed the irreverent cubs with a blow of eloquence. Then he snapped his jaw on an "adopté!"—thus clinching a point already set up by the caucus of major powers.

When his turn came to speak, Woodrow Wilson seized the occasion to give the people of the world another glimpse of his vision. From the eyes of the men of little faith—already in their speeches revealing the direction of their national interest—he swept the cobwebs of tradition. Taking them up to his high perspective, he made them see the largest issue of the day, the problem of human survival. He warned that mankind must break loose from worship of the juggernaut-nations that had been colliding with each other for generations. His own United States, he said, could not take part in guaranteeing European settlements "unless that guarantee involved the continuous superintendence of the peace of the world by the associated nations of the world."

A league of nations was essential, "a vital thing," with "a vital continuity." "It should be the eye of the nations to keep watch upon the common interest, an eye that does not slumber, an eye that is everywhere watchful and attentive." Science as well as armed men could be kept within the harness of civilization only by vigilant cooperation.

"I have only tried in what I have said," he explained, "to give you the fountains of the enthusiasm which is within us for this thing, for those fountains spring, it seems to me, from all the ancient wrongs and sympathies of mankind." Seizing his own pulse and holding up his hands, he came to a dramatic finale: "The very pulse of the world seems to beat to the surface in this enterprise."

Resolutions favoring the creating of a league of nations as part of the peace treaty were adopted by the delegates,[8] many of whom stepped forward to congratulate the speaker. The American had won the first skirmishes of his greatest battle. Elated, he jotted a sentence on a fragment of paper that he passed to House: "We have got them all very solemnly and satisfactorily committed." He had bound first his own commissioners, and then the delegates of the other powers, to the proposition that a league of nations was essential to the world's welfare and that it should be an integral, inseparable part of the treaty of peace.

The initial success stimulated the President to pursue his cause even more ardently. Throwing the full weight of his prestige into the fray, he decided to sit with the commission that was chosen to work out a constitution for a league of nations. As chairman of this body he must face up to problems that lay close to the nerves of national protagonists.

While avoiding commitments that might be attacked by enemies at Washington and Paris, Wilson had kept the problem constantly on his conscience since he and House had drafted their tentative Covenant at

---

[8] After informal talks in House's rooms at the Crillon, where Cecil and Smuts went to discuss the arguments that might best persuade the other statesmen to make the Covenant of a league an integral part of the treaty, Wilson had approved, with a few slight changes, a set of resolutions that had been drafted by the British. The resolutions, as presented to the plenary session on Jan. 25, were:

"1. It is essential to the maintenance of the world settlement, which the Associated Nations are now met to establish, that a League of Nations be created to promote international cooperation, to ensure the fulfillment of accepted international obligations, and to provide safeguards against war.

"2. This league should be created as an integral part of the general Treaty of Peace, and should be open to every civilized nation which can be relied on to promote its objects.

"3. The members of the league should periodically meet in international conference, and should have a permanent organization and secretariat to carry out the business of the League in the interval between the conferences."

Magnolia. In September he had felt that there must be a league of nations with force enough to bring any chauvinistic government to terms. If an economic boycott was not enough, the united forces of other nations must be called into use, and no country could withstand that. When he talked with Professor Rappard in November, after he had learned of House's difficulties in committing the Allies to his Fourteen Points, his opinion had changed somewhat. He felt that if an effort were made to set up an international police force, the question of command would break up the Peace Conference. Nor had he been ready to embrace a plan of Frederick J. Turner, the historian whose work on the American frontier he had admired and encouraged, for a world league with a legislature in which there might develop around the arc from left to right, international political parties that might hold the interests of groups and sections in equilibrium.

Immediately after reaching Paris, Wilson had talked with House about their tentative Covenant for a league that would operate through a council of diplomats at the capital of a small nation. He drafted new articles, and drew help from a pamphlet that was published by General Smuts on December 15. From this document, which like his own draft omitted plans for compulsory arbitration, he had taken a provision for a permanent council that would act as the executive committee of the league. He accepted much of Smuts' language on the matter of mandates and was captivated especially by that statesman's phrase: "Europe is being liquidated and the League of Nations must be heir to this great estate." [9]

On January 8, after House assured him that his second draft was a great improvement on the first, the President was ready to show the secret document to others. First taking his fellow commissioners into his confidence, he asked their advice. Already Lansing and his counselors had pressed their objection to the positive guarantee against aggression on which Wilson insisted. The secretary of state had been encouraged by Colonel House to put his ideas of a league of nations into a draft of a treaty; and the commissioners had approved a plan to have a tentative text prepared that would make use of the court at The Hague. On January 10, at a meeting of the American commissioners,

---

[9] Smuts' pamphlet, "The League of Nations—A Practical Suggestion," was given to Wilson by Lloyd George at London. It dealt with territories formerly belonging to Russia, Austria-Hungary, and Turkey. In the preface Smuts wrote: "To my mind the world is ripe for the greatest steps forward ever made in the government of men . . . If that advance is not made, this war will from the most essential point of view, have been fought in vain, and great calamities will follow."

The principle of trusteeship of undeveloped territories was not a new one. It had appealed to House as early as 1914 and was set forth in Wilson's Point Five. It was formulated, in the technical sense in which it was eventually used in the treaty, in a memorandum submitted to The Inquiry on Jan 1, 1918, by George Louis Beer. *See* House Papers, IV, 284.

Lansing mentioned a draft treaty that his experts had prepared and given to his colleagues so that they might reach an understanding.

"Who authorized them to do this?" Wilson asked sharply. "I don't want lawyers drafting this treaty." Why had they wasted their time on this, he wondered, when they knew that he himself was preparing a draft? In his fervor for immortal ideals he was forgetting the mortal men about him. (House could have answered the President's question but did not, preferring to confide later in private that he had encouraged the draft in order to keep the mind of the secretary of state harmlessly occupied.) The sharp challenge lodged in Lansing's mind and festered, until it loomed as an insult to him and to his profession. The next day, however—perhaps to compensate for his curtness—Wilson solicited and accepted advice from his commissioners.

In the daily meetings of the Council of Ten Woodrow Wilson found a more appreciative response than that from his own commissioners. This was a body larger and less familiar, and its members listened respectfully to the prophet from the New World, heeding him not merely because of his power and their fear that he would use it to bargain in their own manner, but because his moral and intellectual force impressed them. Balfour was astonished to see him "as good round a table as he was on paper." He was showing the qualities with which he had mastered his Cabinets in Washington—firmness, restraint, intelligence, eloquence.

For a few days he held his moral indignation in check, despite European attitudes that seemed sinful. Near the end of January, however, Wilson found himself engaged in combat with the British Empire over the disposal of Germany's colonies. Disregarding the approval that the council had just given to the President's plan to put the league of nations first and colonies last, Lloyd George began to plead that colonial problems be attacked at once. This, he argued, would be the best way to satisfy the public appetite for definite decisions promptly. When Wilson did not oppose this argument resolutely the council decided to ask that all powers having territorial claims should file them within ten days.

This gave Lloyd George an opening, and the next day he seized it with a flourish of drama. His claims had been ready for weeks. Now, after first committing Wilson and the others to agree that the German colonies should not be restored to Germany, he advocated a system of mandates that, he said, would not differ greatly from the colonial methods of the British Empire in the past. But the lands that had been captured by the Dominions were an exception, he explained. These territories were described as populated by uncivilized peoples who had suffered under German misgovernment; and therefore, the prime minister contended, they should be administered as part of their captors' territory rather than by an organization in Europe. Invited by Clemenceau to "bring the cannibals in," Lloyd George introduced the delegates of the Dominions, who presented their demands. And other nations revealed imperialistic ambitions.

Wilson said, frankly, the game was to use American principles as a cloak to cover selfish designs. Sitting forward in his chair, fixing his eye first on Lloyd George, then on Clemenceau, he told them what the world would say. He warned that such acts would make a league of nations impossible and would bring back the old system of competitive armaments, with accumulating debts.

Some institution, he asserted to the council on January 27, must be found to carry out the ideas that all had in mind, namely, the development of a country for the benefit of those already in it and those who would live there later. A league of nations could perform this function, laying down certain general principles and at the same time giving mandates to safeguard the interests of both the inhabitants and all members of the league who might wish to trade freely with them. As for the United States, he thought it her duty to accept mandates but felt that the nation would not do so, for the people would feel that they were acquiring territory under false pretenses. (A month later he characterized the attitude of his people on this question as "Pharisaical cleanliness.")

In general Lloyd George approved the principle of trusteeship, but there were the Dominions to consider. Hughes of Australia and Massey of New Zealand recognized the ideal but disputed its immediate application to the lands that they wished to annex.[10] The French, however, were more blunt: they considered that they had a right to the territories assigned to them in secret understandings made with England during the war. They were prevented from reading letters substantiating their claim only by Lloyd George's fear that Wilson's patience might be strained beyond endurance. As for the Japanese, their spokesmen reminded the gathering of their claim, under the secret understanding that had brought them into the war, to the German Pacific islands north of the equator.

At this Wilson rose and, urging trusteeship rather than annexation, told an appropriate story from Mr. Dooley. One of the American experts laughed aloud and Lloyd George smiled. Clutching at the one risible response, the President went out of his way, the next morning, to shake hands with the expert who had laughed. Obviously the

[10] Arthur Sweetser, assistant to Ray Stannard Baker, reported to Secretary Newton D. Baker on Feb. 4, 1919, that "it was only by strong pressure, when the President took along his stenographer to give a speech out to the world, that he [Hughes] was temporarily calmed."

colonial question was too hot to be handled even in the comparative insulation of the council. Anglo-Saxon statesmen therefore undertook to reach an agreement in private talks.

The next day Wilson exerted pressure upon Lloyd George in the council. He said that, since the principle of mandatories had been denied in the discussions of the past days, it looked as if their roads diverged. He begged that the intensity of his own feeling should not be ascribed to personal antagonism. Really, the league would be a laughing-stock without the attribute of trusteeship. They must agree genuinely on this ideal and leave its application to the league. If the principle were not accepted, the United States would have to believe that her sacrifices during the war had been in vain, and in that case her people would feel that they had to maintain a large army and navy. That, he reminded his colleagues, would be intolerable to the thought of Europe. Old Testament iron could be detected in the voice of the prophet.

Lloyd George, convinced that the President was adamant, seized upon a plan drafted by General Smuts as a solution; but before presenting it to Hughes and Massey, he asked Smuts to ascertain whether Wilson would approve. Though this lofty, lonely South African had caught the imagination of Wilson the literary historian, and though House had commended his plan as "a fair compromise," the President was not ready to accede to it. "I could agree to this," he wrote on the document, "if the interpretation were to come in practice from General Smuts. My difficulty is with the demands of men like Hughes and the certain difficulties with Japan. The latter loom large. A line of islands in her possession would be very dangerous to the United States."

In the council on January 30 Wilson said that he could not accept a convenient theory of Lloyd George's that the league had been established by the plenary session and therefore those who made the league could immediately hand out colonies on terms to suit the recipients. Actually, the Covenant was still an undefined instrument; and if vital questions like this were settled without reference to it, it might never command enough attention to be adequately defined. The building of the league must precede the assignment of mandates.

At that point the tempers of the premiers gave way. Lloyd George, who had worked hard to get agreement, almost yielded to despair. Patiently, Wilson tried to cheer him. He would accept the Smuts resolution as "a precursor of agreement," he said, and subject to reconsideration when the full scheme of the league was completed;[11] and in turn

---

[11] The Smuts resolution, defining three classes of mandates, was later adopted, almost intact, as Article XXII of the Covenant. Wilson agreed orally to France's demand that she be permitted to raise volunteer troops in territory mandated to her, but would not consent to an explicit statement to this effect.

Lloyd George agreed to urge his colleagues to hasten the drafting of the Covenant.

When Hughes and Massey argued [12] that their people could not be expected to invest in the Pacific islands without the security of permanent possession, Wilson asked whether these representatives of only six million people were prepared to defy the will of "the whole civilized world."

"That's about it," Hughes retorted doggedly, resenting the tone.

In this crisis General Botha—a solid, generous man from South Africa, full of sense and humor but weakened by a fatal disease—made a long, conciliatory appeal. Wilson, all pins and needles from too much sitting, got up and paced back and forth on the soft carpet, kicking his black shoes. Immediately afterward he told Lloyd George that Botha's speech was the most impressive to which he had ever listened.

In the afternoon session on the 30th the British representatives agreed that the Smuts compromise resolution be taken as "a provisional decision." The prophet achieved what to disciples of slower zeal had seemed impossible. The framing of the league Covenant would take precedence over a division of spoils.

Despite his distaste for the philosophy of the Council of Ten, the President dared not be absent from the daily meetings for fear that something would be put over on Lansing. He was infinitely bored, sometimes roused to righteous scorn, and at least once was moved to make peace between quarreling colleagues.

Against Clemenceau's campaign for material protection for France, the President was kept on guard by his advisers on military and economic affairs. Marshal Foch, whom Wilson thought as able as he was narrow, was developing a grandiose scheme for an anti-Bolshevik army in Central Europe to which the United States was expected to contribute troops and financial support. When this was reported to him, the President backed General Bliss in opposing it—only to have the scheme crop up again and again. "In my opinion," Wilson said once, "to try to stop a revolutionary movement by armies in line is to use a broom to stop a spring tide." [13]

---

[12] Hughes released, for publication in London, an account of the discussions of Jan. 28 that portrayed Wilson as a doctrinaire schoolmaster to whom the British government was kowtowing. Quivering with indignation at this when he came into the council on the 30th, the President threatened to resort to publicity himself. So far, he reminded his colleagues, he had played the game and had released no statement of his views. Nevertheless, he warned, he might be compelled against his wishes to make a full public exposure of the situation and to break off negotiations and go home. *Lord Riddell's Intimate Diary,* p. 18. That night he said, at home, grimly, that he felt sure there would be no leakages from *that* meeting.

[13] Paul Mantoux, "Le Président Wilson au Conseil des Quatres," in *Centenaire Woodrow Wilson: 1856–1956* (Geneva, 1956), p. 21.

When French economists proposed military restrictions on German industries, Wilson denounced the scheme as a "panic program." He had hoped to hold regular meetings with his economic experts, like those of his war council at Washington; but he was diverted by other affairs. Finally, on January 30, House called a conference of economic advisers with General Bliss and Admiral Benson and it was agreed to protest against a food blockade of Germany. On February 7, buttressed by a strong letter from Hoover, Wilson introduced the matter in the council and his European colleagues gave assent to the American program; but the blockade was not relaxed. "I am surrounded by intrigue here," the President lamented, "and the only way I can succeed is by working silently, saying nothing in public unless it becomes necessary to bring about an open contest."

Emancipated nationalities of Europe for whom Wilson had sought self-determination were now coveting territory and power, raising armies, and begging the United States for troops, money, and arms. In several instances they had seized disputed territories and peoples of other nationalities. Wilson said that he would not stand for aggressive annexations, that he would rather be stoned in the streets than give in. The council finally had to issue a warning that nations that tried to establish themselves by force in disputed territory would harm rather than help their cause before the Peace Conference.

Rumblings of militarism were heard from Germany, too. To meet the threat of a resurgent enemy and Western demands for quick demobilization, a special commission under Foch recommended that naval and military terms of peace be drawn immediately and imposed—a proposal that Wilson approved with the additional suggestion that the Armistice be renewed without change and made terminable on a few days' notice. Clemenceau dissented at first, fearing that this would bring premature demobilization, which would make the Germans "ferocious" and leave the Allies impotent to enforce hard terms of peace. However, when Balfour pointed out that German disarmament could keep pace with Allied demobilization, and the military experts promised to draft final terms very rapidly, The Tiger assented and the council took formal action.[14]

As the French statesmen became unnerved by signs of truculence in Germany and at the same time came to see in Wilson the main obstacle to the guarantees of immediate security on which they had set their

---

[14] There was concern that the Germans might not accept a renewal of the Armistice on this basis. However, on Feb. 16 they agreed. Neither French nor German public opinion was satisfied, and both blamed Wilson for the arrangement.

hearts, criticism and innuendo came from the press of Paris.[15] Public morale was afflicted by a depression that journalists called *La Malaise*.

Thinking that he was disliked because he insisted on sympathizing with small nations as well as with France, Wilson burned with resentment. After nine years in public life, he was not yet callous to criticism. His sensitive skin was pierced when the French press lampooned him as a comic and irritating busybody and suggested that the United States, which had come into the war at the last moment, would rob France of the fruits of victory and would set up a league of nations, only to go home and shirk responsibility for its functioning. He became doubly secretive and suspicious. On February 10 he asked Dr. Grayson to drop a hint to the American newsmen that they let it be known that if the Parisian press continued its obstructive tactics it might be necessary to remove the conference to a neutral country.

As the full scope of the purposes of the Allies was revealed, Wilson grew dour. By the end of January he was totally possessed by his work, giving to it sometimes as much as eighteen hours a day. Life was becoming very tedious, he wrote to Newton D. Baker, and "the difficulty of weaving all the strands into a single pattern" bewildered him.

When it was suggested that a whole day be devoted to prayer for the world, the prophet was cool to the idea. He felt that the business of the Peace Conference was lagging and must be pushed forward. He gloated a little, once, when his pride of authorship was gratified by the acceptance of some of his phrasing by colleagues. But when Edith Benham, his wife's secretary, spoke of him as a Messiah, he protested. Religious teaching had never found a practical solution for the world's troubles, he asserted. Presbyterianism, like patriotism, was not enough. His intellect told him that God revealed himself to man in many ways, that some of the worst wars had been incited by religion. The hope of the world lay in a *man*, he said, a Carlylean hero. Like the Scottish seer of whom he had written in "Leaders of Men," Woodrow Wilson would be "the apostle of a vague sort of lay religion—a religion with sanction but without hierarchy." The prophetic vision that had outspanned the Princeton campus, New Jersey, and Washington was now transcending heights of Western Christianity. Standing on Ben Nevis, he was aspir-

---

[15] A French editor gave to Wilson a copy of an order issued through the government's *Maison de la Presse,* instructing newspapers—

1. To emphasize news of opposition to Wilson by Republicans and others in America.
2. To emphasize disorder and anarchy in Russia, in order to provoke Allied intervention.
3. To publish articles demonstrating Germany's ability to pay a large indemnity.

Baker, *American Chronicle,* p. 387. On Feb. 12, taking a paper from his pocket, Wilson read this order to Professor Rappard and said that France's press was not free and her government was as bureaucratic as Prussia's. Rappard, *op. cit.,* p. 56.

ing to Everest. Scottish instinct was urging him to the stature of individuality that the race had always demanded of its great men. Then he could give the people of the world relief from international anarchy.

Yes, Edith Wilson assured him, he could do it. Henry White had told her that the President was "the greatest statesman of the age," and her faith in her husband's powers was as great as his own.

He went on to say, mystically, that he thought he sensed in the minds of the American people certain ideals for the world, latent and unsuspected by them but nevertheless of high potential. When he phrased the ideals and presented them to his congregation, he felt sure that they would say, as they had always said before: "Why, yes, that's true." He was asked how he detected these budding ideals, if not from the press, which he felt to be controlled by venal interests and out of touch with the pulses of the people. And he explained that his insight came from various sources, from saturating himself in American political history, from wooing the spirit that seemed to him essentially American. His mind, he said, pieced together all the fragments supplied by sense and intuition, fitting them into a mosaic. He said this all very simply and humbly, but with a confidence founded upon the rocks of ages.

He did not respond now so quickly to his wife's loving solicitude, her cheery smile, her mimicry and anecdotes. He begrudged even the time that it took to walk to the Quai d'Orsay, preferring to take no exercises. He delegated little, and within the limits of his strength refused nothing that he thought politically constructive. In the evening, after a bath and a change and a good dinner, he would go to a conference at the Crillon, or into his study to bend over his typewriter.

By giving up a Sunday's rest he mitigated one of the annoyances that the French press had inflicted upon him. He had said, petulantly, that if all France were a shell hole, it wouldn't change the peace settlement. But finally on January 26—the day after Lloyd George had dealt Wilson a backhanded blow by reminding the conference that *he* had seen the devastated areas of France—the President and Edith Wilson went to the battlefields near Château-Thierry, where they saw meadows and orchards stark and shell-holed, and the landscape marred by trenches, barbed wire, and burial mounds. At Rheims, where 120,000 had once dwelt, they found some 5,000 living in cellars among the debris, and snow falling through the roof of the riddled cathedral.

Going through Soissons, they noted that the town was virtually deserted; but returning unexpectedly a few minutes later, they perceived that the place was suddenly teeming with French troops who clamored for a word from the President. Where had these soldiers been when they first passed through the village? the Wilsons asked. Ordered to stay in their billets, the Americans were told, while the President's car was going by. "So that is what is going on," he thought. To a friend who had asked him weeks before whether he would visit the devastated areas, he had replied: "I don't want to get mad over here because I think there ought to be one person at the peace table who isn't mad." But he had yielded, finally, and now he was angry, not at the Germans, as he had feared, but at French officialdom.

The visit had been made too late to silence the voices of criticism that had been rising against the prophet. "It might help if I could get to the people," he said to Creel, "but I am being shut off completely . . . Every day the Republicans tell Lloyd George, Orlando, and Clemenceau that I do not and cannot speak for America, and that my one function is to act as their rubber stamp." [16]

Wilson was standing alone, with no man on whose sympathy and discretion he could depend entirely. Lansing had annoyed and embarrassed him,[17] and he missed House, who was suffering from gallstones.

Fortunately House's health permitted him to resume his role before the Commission on the League of Nations held its first meeting. From his sickbed, through intermediaries, the Colonel already had been discussing the Covenant with Lord Robert Cecil. "He agrees with our views more than he dares admit," House recorded. "I am to get Orlando in line and he is to get the French, and when this is done we will have a general meeting."

When the Colonel brought the Italian premier to the Murat Palace on the evening of January 30 to discuss a league of nations, the question of Italy's eastern boundaries was considered. After Orlando showed sympathy for the league and offered suggestions that the President accepted, Wilson reciprocated by saying impulsively that as far as he was concerned the Trentino was as good as ceded to Italy. When the talk was over, the American, who had seemed dog-tired and depressed at luncheon, was in high humor and generous in praise of the attitude

[16] Creel, *Rebel at Large,* p. 214.

[17] Lansing insisted, in a meeting of the American commissioners, on a resolution that would restore peace immediately and proclaim the general purpose of the league, leaving the details of the Covenant for later consideration. The President rejected the idea with a curtness that cut into Lansing's pride. The next day the blundering secretary went over his chief's head to repeat his proposal in a session of the Council of Ten, where the President could not oppose him frankly without weakening the American position before the world. When the council had received Lansing's views sympathetically, Wilson managed to conceal his annoyance and asked the secretary of state to put his ideas in the form of a resolution. Accordingly, a draft was sent to the President on Jan. 31, with little faith on Lansing's part that Wilson would "see the wisdom of it." The President did not acknowledge it, and the secretary of state found it hard to keep his temper. In his diary, Lansing recorded that Wilson was even a greater egotist than he had thought him to be.

House, constantly on guard against the jealousy of those over whom he was given precedence by his friend, persuaded the President to hold ensuing meetings of the American Commission in the rooms of Lansing and the others, instead of in the Colonel's suite.

of the charming Italian toward his great cause. In his elation, however, he sinned against his doctrine of self-determination. Agreeing to a commitment of the secret treaty of London that violated his Point IX, he delivered almost a quarter-million Germans in the Trentino to Italian rule, and thus sowed the seed of a grave crisis.

At House's suggestion, Wilson met the next day with Lord Robert Cecil and with Smuts, to whom the President had secretly dispatched Grayson with his latest draft of the Covenant.[18]

On February 2, the compromise text was explained to Wilson. But the President was not satisfied. Objecting that it lacked "warmth and color" to win the allegiance of the people of the world, he asked that his own draft be rewritten, with a few clauses taken from the joint version. This was done overnight, and Wilson awoke on February 3 fully intending to present this third American draft to the commission when it met in the afternoon.

House, however, foresaw friction. Wiseman warned him that Lord Robert had heard of the President's work on the new draft and was disturbed because this matter that he thought settled might be reopened. Telephoning to Wilson, House reminded him that Lord Robert was the Englishman who had the league most at heart and that they must maintain harmony with him. The Colonel managed to bring Wilson and Lord Robert together in his study fifteen minutes before the first session of the commission was to open. "The meeting bade fair to be stormy for the first seven or eight minutes," he recorded in his diary. "After that things went better and the President finally decided . . . to take the joint draft . . . and use it as a basis for discussion. After that everything went smoothly."

Woodrow Wilson had made a personal sacrifice that hurt; he had deferred to another in the drafting of the greatest creation of his life. From House's study he went into a salon in which the members of the Commission on the League of Nations were gathering, and he held their attention with a speech while an agent hurried to get a copy of the British-American draft of the Covenant to lay before them.

Between February 3 and 13 the Commission on the League met ten times,[19] often working late at night so that the Covenant might be com-

[18] Grayson was asked by Wilson on Jan. 18 to put his draft into Smuts' own hands. At the meeting with Smuts and Lord Robert on Jan. 31, apparently conscious of crosscurrents of feeling among his delegates, Wilson came back to a suggestion that he had made on the *George Washington*, remarking that it might be best for the nations to be represented in the league's assembly by their regular ambassadors. He had observed jealousy and contention about unimportant things, he said, when there were two representatives of a country in one place.

[19] The Commission on the League of Nations consisted at first of fifteen members—two from each of the major powers and five from small nations. Though Wilson felt that the proceedings would be unduly delayed by the enlargement of this commission, the little countries made such strong representations that four more delegates were chosen to speak for them.

pleted before February 14, the date set for the President's departure for home. In contrast with the meetings of the Council of Ten that Wilson attended in the mornings, the sessions of the League Commission were more delight than duty to a man whose lifelong hobby had been the study and the making of constitutions. He took a lively part in the discussions, opposing the keeping of minutes because he wanted to be free to shift his mental ground on this new political frontier. He explained that, like the body of men who had drawn up the Constitution of the United States, they should withhold their work from the public until it was finished. He desired complete fluidity of thought and frankness of expression.

Clemenceau, conceding that there must be a league created if for no other reason than to humor his American colleague, was bent upon making the new body of some practical value to France's security. And so Léon Bourgeois—the French spokesman on the commission and a man who had used the phrase "league of nations" as early as 1910—was instructed to advocate a strong military arm, with a general staff that would command an effective army, dictate its recruiting and training, and inspect the military establishments of the member nations.

Anglo-Saxon statesmen were traditionally apathetic to the principle put forward by Bourgeois. Conscript armies, which appealed to French democrats as protection against sneak attacks as well as against *coups d'état* by volunteer units, were anathema to peoples who were nurtured on tenets of individual self-restraint and freedom and whose territory was well enough protected by water barriers so that the threat of invasion had not driven them often to national regimentation.

When the British-American draft was presented, Bourgeois proposed amendments. Yielding to French objections to a general denunciation of conscription by the Covenant, Wilson consented that a clause on that point be eliminated. But this concession did not suffice. By February 11 the question became so acute that the commission met all day. The French spokesman threw Wilson's own words at him, reminding the President that he had once said that "force must be created, force so superior that no nation or combination of nations can challenge or resist it."

Wilson listened with an indulgent smile to the retranslation of his words and made a correction. At first not inclined to reply, he whispered with House and then spoke up. Courteously acknowledging the allusion to his own statement, he pointed out that it had been made "in the stress of desperate war." His attitude had not changed, he said. "The situation" was different, however. The construction of a unified military machine in time of peace merely would substitute international militarism for national. Moreover, coming down to hard reality, he pointed out that the Constitution of the United States made international control of its army and navy impossible. In fact, enemies of the league in the Senate were complaining that American troops might become liable to fight at any moment for the most remote causes.

With a despairing gesture the French delegate slumped back in his chair, to emerge later with a hint that France might not join a league of the kind that the Anglo-Saxons visualized. Bourgeois was building up bargaining power that Clemenceau would know well how to use later in his crusade for security for France. At one juncture the French gave notice that they would present reservations at a plenary session.

Wilson met the opposition with a fervent plea for mutual trust. In the meeting of February 11 he gave the French an expression of his own feeling of solidarity with them. "When the danger comes," Wilson said to Bourgeois, "we too will come, but you must trust us."

By the morning of February 13 all of the articles of the British-American draft of the Covenant had been passed tentatively and the commission was ready to begin a second reading, with Wilson in the chair. At one o'clock, however, when the President had to leave to attend a session of the Council of Ten, he was despondent because only six of the twenty-six articles had been agreed upon.

Into the breach at this critical juncture stepped Colonel House. Heretofore, in the meetings of the commission, he had expressed his thoughts only in discreet whispers to the President. But now the Colonel came into his own. Inviting Lord Robert Cecil to take the chair, he stiffened Lord Robert's backbone against a new French drive for an international general staff. Then by an understanding with the Japanese delegates, whose confidence he had won already, it was arranged tentatively to omit from the Covenant both a religious clause that Wilson had inserted and a guarantee of racial equality for which the Japanese had been clamoring and which Hughes of Australia had refused to accept even in a diluted form.

Lord Robert cut off fruitless discussion by calling for votes, and by seven o'clock House was able to tell Wilson over the telephone that the Covenant had been approved. Immensely relieved to learn that there would have to be no night session, as he had feared, the President gladly assented to the Colonel's sacrifice of his religious clause in the interest of harmony. Against Wilson's judgment, also, provisions for arbitration and for a world court were allowed to stand in the final draft.

Under the hand of Woodrow Wilson the League Commission had been driven harder than any other peacemaking body. He had both drawn out discussion when it was needed, and checked it when it ran too wide in speculation or too deep in technicalities. From the very first he had kept the delegates facing forward. As the days went by, the majesty of his faith in the reasonableness of free men sunned dark fears and cleansed sordid ambitions. The real sanction of the principles of the Covenant lay in public opinion, he said.

The public for whom he labored knew little of the details of the President's achievement, but Colonel House intended that it should not be forgotten. One day he recorded in his diary: "I have never known anyone to do such work so well." Resolving that the great feat of Wilson's commission be recorded for posterity, House arranged on the last day for a photograph of its members. But when flashlight pictures were proposed, Wilson objected. "Everybody looks as though he was laid out in a morgue," he said, "and besides the flashes hurt my eyes." When the Colonel insisted that history should not be cheated, the man who aspired to speak for a billion people stood shyly among the chattering statesmen and turned to his interpreter for support. "You mustn't leave me in this Tower of Babel," he said.

Under Wilson's presiding genius the Commission on the League not only had achieved agreement among the nations, but had done so with more consideration of the small powers than European peace conferences had been accustomed to show. Meeting in a milieu new to diplomacy, a salon of the Hotel Crillon, while the Council of Ten met in the gray, tradition-webbed Quai d'Orsay, "Wilson's commission" had taken in representatives of several countries that could not claim a seat in the council. And so the President regained some of the prestige that had been lost in the eyes of democratic peoples when he had failed to protest against Clemenceau's bullying of the small powers and when he favored only a minimum representation of little countries on the Executive Council of the League itself.[20]

On February 14—the greatest day in a life that had known many superlative occasions—the American President stood before the world as the victorious leader of a great and triumphant cause. He was to give a constitution to the twentieth-century world. When the hour came for him to present the Covenant to a plenary session—the hour for which Woodrow Wilson had been born into the world—he was recognized by

[20] In the second session of the Commission on the League, Wilson with Lord Robert Cecil's assent had said that, since the League was to guaranty the political independence and territorial integrity of large and small nations alike, he thought it no injustice to give the major powers five seats on the permanent council, and the small powers only two. The larger the membership, he pointed out, the slower would be the proceedings of the body. It was finally agreed that the small powers should have four seats in the League's council. "It is of course our purpose," Wilson said at the second session of the commission, "to call in the lesser powers and also the neutral powers as progress is made." Bonsal, *Unfinished Business*, p. 25.

the chairman. Conscious of his responsibility to the twelve hundred million mortals who were represented in the stately room, he read the document in even tones, without gestures, and then went on to speak of its significance. A ring of resolution came into his voice and his eyes shone when he declared: "A living thing is born, and we must see to it that the clothes we put upon it do not hamper it . . . I think I can say of this document that it is at one and the same time a practical and humane document. There is a pulse of sympathy in it. There is a compulsion of conscience throughout it. It is practical, and yet it is intended to purify, to rectify, to elevate. . . ."

For a moment it seemed as if the political morality of the world had been lifted into a new dimension by a major prophet. "Dear Governor," House jotted on a slip of paper, "your speech was as great as the occasion." The voice through which the Colonel hoped to secure a place in history had not failed him. Returning the chit, Wilson scribbled in the margin: "Bless your heart. Thank you from the bottom of my heart." [21] As the day outside faded into a misty dusk and the lights in the crystal chandeliers sparkled over the rococo scene in the Hall of Clocks, the listeners sensed that it was a great moment in history. Scores of newsmen, standing on chairs and tables, rose on tiptoes to see the President's face. When the calm, almost casual voice ceased, the hall was as silent as a church. Then, after Bourgeois and the Japanese presented the matters that they had reserved for the occasion and the draft of the Covenant was deposited with the secretariat of the conference, the delegates besieged the American to shake his hand and thank him for his leadership. Sophisticated statesmen walked out into a cold fog with warm confidence that the horrors of world war would not afflict humanity again.

Wilson smiled radiantly at the American soldiers who were saluting him as his car went through the gates of the Murat Palace. He got out and mounted the steps two at a time, in his elation that he was going home as a minister who had been true to his charge.

At the station in the evening all of official France was on hand to say *adieu.* From the gloomy drizzle in the streets the President walked from curb to train over a long red carpet, shaking hands punctiliously with diplomats who clicked heels and kissed Edith Wilson's hand.

Georges Clemenceau, leaving the railroad station, was asked how he liked the President. His reply was: "He is a nice fellow." And then, smiling at two Americans who were present, he added: "He may mean well, it is quite possible."

[21] According to Bonsal, House now felt that he had erred in feeling that the President should not come to Paris, for he saw that without Wilson's personal leadership the powers would have split into groups and would have made contradictory peace treaties that would have been worthless as guarantees against war. *See* Bonsal, *Unfinished Business,* p. 282.

CHAPTER XIV

The New World Grows Old

It was a weary but jubilant prophet who set sail for his native land on February 15, as the guns of Brest reverberated in the wintry air and French Marines stood at salute along the old city walls. In a period of six weeks he had fought the greatest battle of his life, had built the house of his Lord and put the ark of the Covenant into it, that nation might not lift up sword against nation.

Wireless messages came to him on the *George Washington* from Colonel House. Wilson had asked that no one should know of this, and his secret code was used. The news received was disconcerting. Orlando, who had returned to Rome, had not been able to persuade his government to join the Yugoslavs in accepting the President's offer to arbitrate their territorial disputes. Lloyd George had returned to London to deal with domestic problems, boasting that, while Wilson had only a bundle of assignats, he had come home with a pocket full of sovereigns in the shape of German colonies. And on February 19, Fate in the guise of a demented fanatic struck down the only member of the Big Four who remained at Paris. As Clemenceau drove in his automobile to meet with House and Balfour, seven shots were fired at him point-blank, one of them lodging behind his shoulder blade and forcing him to bed for several days.

Before leaving for Washington for the closing of Congress, the President had thrown his mantle upon the shoulders of the Colonel, confident that his "alter ego" could somehow hold the line of law and order against greed, apathy, and panicky fears that were possessing the minds of Europeans. As he bade his friend *au revoir*, he had fervently clasped his hand and put an arm around his shoulder. "Heavy work before you, House," he said. It was the last time the Colonel felt "the Governor's" embrace.

Though Lansing would be the official chief of the American delegation, Wilson asked House to take his seat in the Council of Ten and to act for him. "I do not wish the questions of territorial adjustments or those of reparations to be held up," he said. But when House asserted that he could "button up everything within four weeks," Wilson showed alarm. The Colonel noted the shadow crossing his friend's countenance and quickly reassured him. He would not attempt to make decisions, but would try merely to prepare the way for a final settlement when the President returned. Four things should be done, he said, to facilitate a preliminary peace with Germany.[1]

Asked if this agenda would suffice, Wilson agreed that it would; and then House, wishing that his friend would put specific instructions in writing but realizing that that was not his way, reminded Wilson that to get action it might be necessary to compromise on details, as the President himself had done and as House hoped that he would do again when he returned to Washington. But there would be no compromise of principle, the Colonel asserted: particularly, he was resolved there be no concession to France's demand for a Rhenish Republic, for that, the Colonel realized, would invalidate the fundamental doctrine of self-determination. With this unwritten understanding, the Colonel remained at Paris to try to get constructive action toward settlements.

One of the grisly problems that was unsolved when Wilson left Paris and that fell upon the Colonel's shoulders on February 14 was that of relations with Russia. American policy in this sphere was embarrassingly entwined with British and Japanese ambitions; and on the very day of his departure Wilson had clashed with Winston Churchill, who had come over from London to plead for more vigorous military intervention.

As we have seen, the President had reluctantly consented, as an inevitable part of the struggle with Germany, to join with his allies in sending troops into Siberia and northern Russia. He had hoped thus to aid in restoring law and order under a responsible native government to which economic aid might later be given, and he had carefully qualified his assent to military action in such a way as to guard against a recrudescence of nineteenth-century imperialism. However, not many weeks passed before the expeditions in Russia were acting in ways that placed the President's political principles in jeopardy.[2]

---

[1] House had in mind a *general* preliminary peace, not a settlement merely of military matters such as the Council of Ten already had decided on. His four points were:

1. A reduction of Germany's army and navy to a peace footing.
2. A delineation of the boundaries of Germany. This to include the cession of the colonies.
3. The amount of money to be paid for reparation and the length of time in which to pay it.
4. An agreement on the economic treatment of Germany.

[2] Through a confusion of orders at Washington, the troops sent to northern Russia failed to report to Ambassador Francis, and instead put themselves under the British commander in that area and soon were involved in an offensive against Soviet forces. Learning of this, Wilson ordered General March to place the troops under the orders of Francis. Francis, *Russia from the American Embassy*, p. 271, confirmed by Breckinridge Long to the writer.

During the autumn of 1918, moreover, the Japanese justified the misgivings that Wilson had held regarding their intentions. After the United States, through a misunderstanding, sent 8,500 men instead of the 7,000 agreed upon, Japan took advantage of this technical error and poured troops into Siberia by the tens of thousands.

Wilson had grounds for considering the Soviet government as an ally or as an enemy. He was not willing to consider them neutral, for that would imply recognition of the peace of Brest-Litovsk. The problem was further complicated when his diplomatic agents and those of the Allies were forced out of Russia and the terror sank into a mire of blood and billingsgate. Furthermore, on September 15, 1918, with Wilson's approval, Creel published certain controversial documents that were sent from Russia by his agent, Edgar Sisson. These papers purported to be facsimiles and copies of correspondence by which the German General Staff had secretly bought peace from the Council of People's Commissars.[3] House asked the President whether the release of these documents was not virtually a declaration of war on the Bolsheviki. Wilson admitted that it was.

The publication of the Sisson papers and the expedition to Siberia in collaboration with Japan—Russia's historic enemy—had evoked a blast of anti-American propaganda from Moscow. A scornful, taunting note, signed by Chicherin and dated October 24, had been addressed to the President of the United States, who was being classed by Soviet spokesmen with the "imperialist robbers" of the Allied nations. At about the time when Wilson read this provocative challenge, he learned that the leaders of the revolution were sending funds into Sweden and Switzerland to stir up unrest and that they hoped for a revolution of the proletariat in Germany and in Hungary. He feared that, with the Hohenzollerns out of the way, another absolute regime might be set up in Germany. His imagination even saw his own America menaced from within by the hammer and sickle. To allay fears at home, it was important to come to an understanding with Moscow.

All through the autumn of 1918 the President had waited vainly for the appearance of a reliable political core that could represent the Russian people. The use of force was provoking a need for more force. Yet when the Armistice with Germany was signed, the policy of intervention lost its main moral prop—the necessity of combating German influence in Russia. Consequently, Wilson had become more doubtful than ever of the wisdom of military action; and in his conference with Lloyd

[3] The Sisson documents, consisting of facsimiles and copies of secret correspondence that was alleged to have been passed between the German General Staff and the Council of People's Commissars, had been placed in Wilson's hands on May 9, 1918. Creel had the documents checked by two scholars—Dr. J. Franklin Jameson, director of the Department of Research of the Carnegie Institution, and Professor Samuel Harper of the University of Chicago—who consulted other experts and concluded that there was no reason to doubt the authenticity of the papers. They were published in newspaper installments on Sept. 15 and were made available in October in a government bulletin entitled "The German-Bolshevik Conspiracy." Their authenticity was challenged immediately by the British Foreign Office and by the Department of State. Lansing did not know of the papers in time to stop their publication.

George at London in December he had made it clear that he was very much opposed to armed intervention, indeed was inclined to withdraw American troops from North Russia, and was reconciled to the Siberian expedition only as a means of arresting Japanese aggression.

However, when the question of evacuation was raised at a meeting of the American peace commissioners in January, Wilson said that, since this matter would be one of the first considered at the Peace Conference, he wished to take no immediate independent action. He insisted that the Western powers should reach an immediate decision, and together go in effectively or get out of Russia. He felt that he knew too little about the Soviet government to make any public statement. "What I am at present keenly interested in," he wrote to Lansing on January 10, "is in finding the interior of their minds." What actually was the "chief end" of these rulers? What was their moral direction? If only he had firsthand knowledge!

A note addressed to him on December 24 by Maxim Litvinov had presented an opportunity to study the new regime more closely. The tone and substance of it impressed Wilson favorably. "The real thing with which to stop Bolshevism is food; . . . force will not stop it," he wrote to Lansing on January 10; and he urged haste in dispatching an agent to confer with Litvinov at Stockholm. Accordingly, W. H. Buckler was ordered to the Swedish capital and there on January 14 he received proposals that Wilson reported to the Council of Ten on January 21.[4]

The council had been discussing the Russian situation for several days, Lloyd George having introduced the subject with the assertion that it was "impossible to make peace for Europe without settling the Russian question." There was a certain latent force behind bolshevism, the President reminded the council, that attracted sympathy as much as its brutal aspects provoked disgust. Throughout the world there was an impulse of revolt against "large vested interests" that operated in both the economic and the political sphere.

[4] Litvinov told Buckler that the Russian people had been impressed by President Wilson's expression of friendship and sympathy for their revolution. But intervention in northern Russia had raised doubts of the sincerity of the President's belief in the right of a people to regulate its own affairs. And, moreover, Russians at Moscow resented the fact that Americans had been misled by such "forgeries" as the Sisson documents. Consequently, Litvinov said, the people of Russia were now asking whether the aim of the Western powers was peace or the total destruction of the Bolshevik government. He promised that if the fighting could be stopped, revolutionary propaganda, violence, and terror would cease. Realizing that for many years Russia would need to import technical advice and manufactured goods, his government was said to be ready to compromise on all points at issue, including that of assuming the czarist debt on practical terms to be worked out by experts. Skeptical of the power of an association of imperialistic nations to prevent war, Litvinov doubted that a league would materialize immediately. W. H. Buckler's manuscript recording a conversation with Litvinov at Stockholm, Jan. 14, 15, 16, 1919, House Collection.

Wilson was not at all sure that out of the Russian Revolution would grow a government that would give the guarantees to individual liberty that Americans demanded; but he felt that the old order, if it were restored, would be more disastrous than the present one. "We should be fighting against the current of the times if we tried to prevent Russia from finding her own path to freedom," he prophesied. He knew that the threat of foreign intervention had given to Bolshevik leaders a whip with which to lash their people into line.

Lloyd George, explaining that he had honored Britain's obligations to the remnants of Czarist armies that had fought on against the Germans after the peace of Brest-Litovsk, professed himself now ready to deal with the Soviets as the *de facto* government of Russia. He felt that Wilson would like to support him in this. These leaders, however, despaired of carrying with them either their fellow commissioners or electorates that had been thoroughly terrified by the violence that had been done in Russia to life, to property, and to religious faith. When Lloyd George proposed that all Russian factions be haled to Paris to state their cases, Clemenceau protested that his Chamber was unanimously opposed. He threatened to resign if they came.

Wilson acted to break the deadlock. Informed by a cable from Tumulty that Lloyd George's proposal produced a very unfavorable impression in the United States, the President suggested that the Russian factions come together at a place nearer to Moscow and be heard together, "all in one room" if possible. Wilson hoped that a reaction against extremism in Russia might be brought about.

At first Clemenceau would not consider such a proposal. Thinking the Bolsheviki not worthy of the notice of civilized peoples, he denounced the Litvinov overture that Wilson had read to the council. The Tiger's own preference had been to erect barriers to prevent the spread of bolshevism. But perceiving that the sense of the meeting was against him, he asked Wilson to draft a paper setting forth the views of the Allies, explaining that they had no wish to interfere in the internal affairs of Russia or to restore czardom, but wanted merely to hasten the creation of a dependable government. He urged that the manifesto be, above all, a humanitarian appeal.[5]

It was a great triumph for the prophet of the New World. Never before had an American taken the lead in a council of European powers on a matter that primarily concerned the Old World. Woodrow Wilson,

[5] Afterward in the antechamber, as he pulled on his big fur-lined coat, The Tiger was asked how the discussion had come out, and replied in one word, explosively, "Battu!" He was beaten, but he felt that Wilson's suggestion of an all-Russia conference had made it possible for him to yield gracefully. C. T. Thompson, *The Peace Conference Day by Day*, pp. 132–33.

having been "all the way round the clock," gave to the council a draft of an eloquent message of good will. He proposed that each Russian faction should cease military action and send delegates before February 15 to Prinkipo, a resort on the Sea of Marmara.

This invitation, however, elicited only curses from the most influential Russian conservatives at Paris, who knew that they could refuse without forfeiting French sympathy and aid. As for the Bolsheviki, they sent a belated acceptance of Wilson's invitation but failed to promise to stop the westward advance of their troops, which at the moment was rapid. Wilson thought their reply "studiously insulting." Behind a protestation of readiness to make concessions in economic and territorial matters he sensed an undertone that seemed to say: "We are dealing with perjured governments whose only interest is in striking a bargain, and if that is the price of European recognition and cooperation, we are ready to pay it."

Wilson was exasperated not only by the apparent disingenuousness of the Soviet leaders but by agitation among his conservative associates for military action. There was guerrilla fighting in North Russia, where the Allied expedition remained, icebound, and tried to protect a wobbly anti-Bolshevik government at Archangel.[6] Admiral Kolchak was mobilizing and terrorizing the peasants of Siberia by methods made familiar by the old regime. French generals, spurred on by the Russians at Paris and the conservative press, were training a Polish Army in France to act as nucleus of a force that was to include all the peoples that lived along the western fringe of Russia.

As Wilson was about to sail for America and Lloyd George prepared to return to London, the French militarists were reinforced in the councils at Paris by Winston Churchill, who had taken the opportunity to come from the War Office to put forth his views. On February 14 they collided with Wilson's. The President remarked that among all the uncertainties of the Russia situation it was quite clear to him that Allied troops in Russia were doing no sort of good, did not know for whom or for what they were fighting, and ought to be withdrawn. Churchill insisted, however, that withdrawal would lead to the destruction of all non-Bolshevik armies in Russia, numbering a half-million men: thus the "linchpin" would be pulled from "the whole machine" and Russia would be doomed to an interminable vista of violence and misery. To

---

[6] On Feb. 12, General Bliss reported to Wilson that the 5,100 American troops at Archangel would not be safe unless the railroad was kept open to Murmansk and the British headquarters. For security and to assure an easy withdrawal, Bliss approved a British request for two companies of American railroad troops, and Wilson assented. In the President's view, the United States was "irrevocably" committed to withdraw its troops as soon as the weather permitted, and this was the intention of the British also.

Wilson, withdrawal seemed inevitable. "Sooner or later we'll have to clear out," he predicted.[7]

But Churchill persisted. After Wilson's departure he proposed to the council at Paris that the Bolsheviki be given ten days in which to stop fighting or expose themselves to the consequences. He advocated that a staff be organized to consider military intervention on a larger scale and suggested that publicity be given to these measures. Colonel House, on whom both Wilson and Lloyd George[8] depended for resistance to Churchill, set aside his own views[9] and wirelessed a report of Churchill's proposals to the President.

Wilson replied immediately with a protest that checked the trend to which fear had driven the secondary men of the council. He would not favor any course, he said, that would not bring "the earliest practicable withdrawal of military forces." He made it clear that the United States was not at war with Russia and that it would be "fatal to be led further into the Russian chaos." He was relieved when, after sessions of the council in which House and Balfour argued with Churchill in words too acrimonious to be reported fully in the minutes, the Colonel cabled to him on February 23: "Churchill's proposal is dead."

As Wilson looked forward to the United States from his cabin on the *George Washington*, the prospect was more familiar and more pleasing. He was coming home to his own people. A generation of Americans that had produced vast wealth and escaped the ravages of war and famine were sharing their bounty with the people of impoverished lands that their ancestors had left. Now they were ready to prescribe a Chris-

[7] Wilson's feeling against military intervention had been reinforced by a cable sent by Secretary Baker on Feb. 12: "Public opinion at home has been restless about our troops in Russia on three grounds: (1) fear that the force is insufficient for our safety; (2) desire to have the soldiers all brought home; (3) fear that our forces may find themselves opposed to popular government and in alliance with reactionaries." Baker urged that the American forces be withdrawn "by the next boat."

[8] Wilson could not understand why Lloyd George had allowed Churchill to make these proposals, and the prime minister himself had been concerned about the independence of his young colleague. Willing to fulfill commitments already made to anti-German generals in Russia, but convinced that a full-scale war with the Bolsheviki would be "the direct road to bankruptcy and Bolshevism" in the British Isles, Lloyd George wired his views from London to Churchill at Paris and took the precaution of having his telegrams shown to Balfour and to House.

[9] House, who had been wondering "how to finesse the situation against the Bolsheviks," did not agree with Wilson's policy of trying to draw together the various factions. Russia, he thought, was "too big and homogeneous for the safety of the world." With Siberia separate and European Russia divided into three parts, however, he hoped that there would be no more danger than was posed by the British Empire. Balfour favored taking steps "to put the Bolsheviks in the wrong" in the eyes of those who held the view that bolshevism was democracy gone astray with large elements of good in it. DeWitt Poole reports: "High military leaders [of Britain and France] had definite plans for dividing Russia up, as they frankly told me in Paris in July, 1919. The top leadership did not." Poole MS, Oral Research History Project, Columbia University.

tian justice for all the world [10]—a *Pax Americana* that would confer
liberty even upon individuals who had not learned how to exercise it
and somehow would give to every people the right to self-determination
that the American colonies had asserted in 1776.

But there were doubters and scoffers in America, and the seeds of
opposition were sprouting. Philistines talked about their country's
sacrifices in terms of net gain and loss, invoked the constitutional right
of the Senate to make war and peace, spoke knowingly of the cussedness
of human nature. A creed of isolationism developed that cut across the
lines of political parties. A supreme preaching effort would be required
to arrest a backsliding of the American congregation.

The President was advised to land at Boston, where a well-financed
movement for the League of Nations was under way, with Taft, Lowell,
and ex-Senator Crane participating. It was thought that Lodge's own
state would give a welcome that would make the senator take notice
and would, moreover, impress European opinion. Fearful of the bad
impression that a Roman triumph would make upon Congress, Wilson
stipulated that the reception at Boston should be informal and extemporaneous and should not appear to be a personal tribute.

The *George Washington* took a southerly route, and several times the
President went to the top deck to cheer up soldiers who were conva-
lescing in the sun. One evening he went to see a hilarious minstrel show
that was put on by the male crew; and once the leading "lady" left the
stage, threw hairy arms around him and, nuzzling a rope wig against
the presidential brow, chucked him under the chin. To the prophet, this
was an insult to his high office. His face turned to ice. Franklin D.
Roosevelt was in the audience and never forgot that look.[11]

At the entrance to Boston harbor a freak current took the vessel off
its course. An island loomed up directly ahead, and the captain had to
reverse the engines at full speed, shaking the ship so that the passengers
were alarmed. Wilson came out on deck, with the precious Covenant
tucked securely in the breast pocket of his greatcoat. Just then a heavy
snow squall blew down on the ship and it was necessary to anchor until
the visibility improved. Noting the skill with which the emergency was
met, the President sent for Captain McCauley and congratulated him.

The next day—the 24th of February—Governor Calvin Coolidge

---

[10] The St. Louis *Globe-Democrat* commented on Feb. 15: "It [the Covenant] is born, and
no birth in history, save one, is of greater importance to mankind." On Feb. 25 the New York
Tribune remarked: "The discussion . . . must be lifted above the plane of personalities. To
do other than this is to degrade a theme almost as lofty as that contained in the *New Testament*." On March 29 the *Literary Digest* reported: "Not one member of the religious press, so
far as we have observed, opposes the League *in toto.*"

[11] F. D. Roosevelt to R. S. Baker, Oct. 3, 1939, Baker Papers, Princeton University Library.
Eleanor Roosevelt to the writer, March 8, 1954.

came on board and escorted the Wilsons ashore and through thronged streets. Stores and schools had declared a holiday, and thousands lined the route. At Mechanics Hall eight thousand Americans—a curious mixture of Irish Democrats and liberal intellectuals—waited more than an hour for their hero. Governor Coolidge welcomed the President with a speech in which he characterized the reception as "even more marked than that accorded General George Washington, more united than any that could have been given at any time during his life to Abraham Lincoln"; and Mayor Andrew Peters hailed the Covenant as a document that would go down in history with Magna Carta and the Declaration of Independence.

Wilson knew, as he faced this reception from his own folk, that his opponents in the Senate had read the Covenant and had opened fire on it. He had expected nothing better. Condemning "narrow, selfish, provincial purposes," he broadcast a warning: "I have fighting blood in me and it is sometimes a delight to let it have scope, but if it is challenged on this occasion it will be an indulgence." He declared: "Speaking with perfect frankness in the name of the people of the United States I have uttered as the objects of this great war ideals, and nothing but ideals, and the war has been won by that inspiration."

And then he brought home his great challenge. "We set this nation up to make men free and we did not confine our conception and purpose to America, and now we will make men free. If we did not do that, all the fame of America would be gone and all her power would be dissipated. . . . Think of the picture, think of the utter blackness that would fall on the world." Asserting that peace could not be maintained for a single generation unless guaranteed by the united forces of the civilized world, he declared: "Any man who thinks that America will take part in giving the world any such rebuff and disappointment as that does not know America. I invite him to test the sentiments of the Nation."

"I have tried in all soberness and honesty," he told his people, "to speak your thought." At this point, a journalist wrote, the applause "leaped to thunder before the words were fairly out of his mouth."

The acclaim of audience and press struck a chill into the soul of the venerable senator from Massachusetts, whose sense of honor had moved him to respect the President's request from Paris that the League Covenant be not discussed until it could be explained by Wilson to members of Congress. Lodge suggested to his Republican colleagues that the President had taken an unfair advantage. Wilson had asked him to say nothing and then had gone to his home town and made a speech. "Very characteristic," the senator asserted.

On the floor of the Senate, on December 21, 1918, Lodge had served notice that that body could reject a treaty of peace or debate and amend it *ad infinitum*. Five days after the League Covenant was published in American newspapers, the senator described the document as "not only loose, ill-drawn, full of questions about which the signatories will be disputing within a twelfth-month, but . . . a breeder of misunderstandings if not of war."

The lines of partisan battle already had been drawn indelibly when the President arrived at Washington on February 25. His train was very late, but he was told that a huge crowd had waited hours in the streets to welcome him. He said, almost choking up: "I thought I had been entirely deserted."

Before leaving Paris, Wilson had thought that it would suffice to explain the Covenant in an address to the Congress; but House had feared that this method might seem dictatorial and had suggested that the President win the confidence of the legislators and satisfy their pride by consulting their committees.

Wilson, however, had little faith in his ability to convert senators who were already emotionally committed—in some cases publicly—against him and all his works. He had cabled home in January to ask that the House of Representatives pass a pro-League resolution, and nothing had happened. He felt that he could expect even less of the Senate, that he would have first to educate the people, and through them influence their representatives. But there were hopeful omens of popular support. Many Republican journals approved the Covenant and few Democratic papers of importance opposed it. More than half of the governors and state legislatures had indicated their support.

The President had yielded to House's urging and at Paris had signed a message asking that a dinner be arranged for the Congressional committees on foreign policy. On the evening of February 26, Wilson welcomed thirty-four curious members of Congress to the White House. Senators Borah and Fall had refused to come. The others found the state dining room made festive for the first time in two years. Edith Wilson, beautiful and gay, sat next to Henry Cabot Lodge and reminded him—"innocently," her husband later explained—of the magnificent reception that Boston had given to them. After dinner the guests went to the East Room; and the host, sitting in the open end of a horseshoe of chairs, put himself at their disposal.

As he sat down and leaned back in his chair, something fell out of his pocket and bounced loudly on the floor. It was the horse chestnut that he had treasured since Princeton days, for good fortune and because he liked to run his sensitive fingers over its velvety surface. When a congressman retrieved it and handed it to him, he reddened and looked sheepish. "It's my good-luck buckeye," he explained with a smile. "I keep it in my pocket to ward off the rheumatism." The roar of laughter that followed seemed to unify the group.[12] They listened respectfully as he told them what he had done at Paris. Senator Knox, who had been Taft's secretary of state, sat at first in sullen silence and then opened fire with questions. For more than two hours Wilson gave his best to these men, noting their honest anxieties, freely and frankly answering their queries, pleading with them to accept the document. But no conversions were made, and the legislators had gathered new grist for the mill of argument in the press[13] and on the floor of the Senate. The gentleman from Massachusetts listened with a stony face; his crony, Senator Brandegee, hectored the witness; and the two went home feeling only as wise as they came, complaining to friends about the personal appearance of their hostess, the paucity of cigars, and the temperateness of the drinks.

Only two days later, in a long polished speech, Lodge put the burden of proof on the proponents of the Covenant and suggested the first of what was to be an interminable barrage of amendments—"bad amendments as well as good amendments," Wilson called them when he learned of the speech, which he thought had been provoked, perhaps, by his wife's remarks to Lodge at the dinner table.

Lodge warned of threats to Washington's sacred doctrine of isolation, to the Monroe Doctrine, and to the right of the United States to control immigration. Coming to Article X, which Wilson had shown to be closest to his heart, he called its guaranty against aggression "a very grave, a very perilous promise." His eloquence dramatized an imaginary crusade by armed Americans in Europe's political jungles. Working on fears that had been aroused by the economic unrest that had resulted from demobilization and the reconversion of industry, he urged that the United States be not drawn "by any glittering delusions, through specious devices of supra-national government, within the toils of international socialism and anarchy." He asked for "consideration,

---

[12] Connally, *My Name Is Tom Connally*, p. 96.

[13] At the conference Wilson told his guests that they were free to discuss the affair afterward with newsmen. On Feb. 28, the unfriendly New York *Sun* reported that the President had "stated with finality" that "the United States must surrender vital points of sovereignty; Chinese and Japanese exclusion goes out of American control into the hands of League control; Ireland is to be left to the mercies of England." Hitchcock, McCumber, Brandegee, Knox, and Lodge were cited as witnesses that Wilson actually made these statements. Hitchcock immediately denied every part of the charge; McCumber soon made it clear that he had no part in thus falsely interpreting the President's remarks; but the others kept silent.

time, and thought." Peace should come first, and disarmament; and
these things seemed to him to be delayed by discussion of the League of
Nations.[14] Declaring that his opinion of the commission that had
drafted the Covenant was not one of "veneration," Lodge said: "I do
not think their intellect or position in the world are so overpowering
that we cannot suggest amendments to this league."

Other senators joined the dissenting chorus. Going to Lodge's library
early one morning, Brandegee suggested that it be made clear that a
league of nations like that proposed could not win the approval of two-
thirds of the senators. Hastening together to the home of Senator Knox,
they drafted a resolution to that effect, and by the end of March 3 they
had the names of thirty-seven senators signed to their "round robin"—
enough to reject a treaty of peace. At two minutes after midnight,
Lodge rose and read the document from the floor, knowing that he was
out of order and depending on some Democrat to raise objections and
thus prevent the resolution from being voted down. He had calculated
well. Senator Swanson fell into the trap and objected; and so Lodge,
immediately recognizing the objection, read the names of the signers
into the *Record*. The resolution was circulated to the voters under government frank, the document was given to the press, and the whole
world soon knew that the Covenant had been repudiated by an effective
minority of the Senate of the United States.

At the same time the adversaries were asserting their will by another,
and more familiar, method. They tightened the purse strings, hoping
that the President would be compelled by impecuniousness to convoke
the Senate by May and thus allow them to use the floor and the *Record*
to publicize their criticisms of Woodrow Wilson. The Democrats
lacked the strong leadership that was needed to secure the funds that
Wilson and Hoover were requesting for European relief.[15]

At luncheon in the White House on the very day of Lodge's critical
speech in the Senate, Wilson reminded Democratic leaders of the great

[14] This argument was used effectively and repeatedly by Wilson's opponents both at
Washington and at Paris. Actually the framing of the Covenant, though leaving him time
enough to attend the sessions of the Council of Ten, had diverted much of Wilson's energy
from other urgent issues. On the other hand, however, the League had become a convenient
repository for problems that could not be solved quickly and that threatened to delay the
making of the treaty.

[15] Henry White had reinforced the plea for relief funds by cabling to Lodge to explain that
Germany would pay cash for whatever food she got; but the senator had replied, incoherently,
that there was a very strong feeling in America "against giving food or money to the
Germans." A relief bill had passed the House; but in the Senate Lodge had amended the
measure by excluding Germany, Austria, Bulgaria, and part of Turkey. At the urging of
Hoover, Wilson had cabled to Congressional leaders on Jan. 10, 1919, and later to Glass, to
urge the passage of the bill without amendment; but a conference report, accepting most of
the Senate version with Lodge's amendment, finally had become law.

purposes to which he had committed them. Flicking the lash of discipline, he suggested that all the men of the party had not been as "cordial" in support of their leader's program as they might have been.

He insisted that the real issue of the day was the League of Nations, that they must not even appear to make a mere party issue of anything so sacred. "Believe me, gentlemen," he pleaded, "the civilized world cannot afford to have us lose this fight. I tried to state in Boston what it would mean to the people of the world if the United States did not support this great ideal with cordiality, but I was not able to speak. . . . I tell you, frankly, I choked up; I could not do it. The thing reaches the depth of tragedy."

Responding to Lodge's warning against involvement of the United States in "international socialism and anarchy," he said: "The only thing that that ugly, poisonous thing called bolshevism feeds on is the doubt of the man in the street of the essential integrity of the people he is depending on to do his governing." According to his reading of the Virginia Bill of Rights, any people is "entitled to any kind of government it damn pleases. Sometimes it will have a very riotous form of government, but that is none of our business. And I find that that is accepted, even with regard to Russia."

He explained that, though there was no real foundation for a League of Nations but the good faith of the subscribing parties, the Covenant was "a workable beginning of a thing that the world insists on." Though not a guaranty of peace, it came "as near being a guaranty of peace as you can get." The League was "the only solid basis of masonry" in the peace treaty.

"Now, if you put that case before the people of the United States," the prophet challenged, "and show them that without the League of Nations it is not worth while completing the treaty we are making in Paris, then you have got an argument which even an unidealistic people would respond to, and ours is not an unidealistic people but the most idealistic people in the world."

As for the adversaries—"I would reserve the right in private to say in unparliamentary language what I think of them, but in public I would try to stick to parliamentary language." And then, before the men of his own faith, he castigated the Philistines with a vehemence that revealed the chaos of his nerves.

It was a "very cheering thought," he said, that on the 5th of March, 1921—only two years away—he would "begin to be an historian again" and in that role "have the privilege of writing about these gentlemen without any restraints of propriety." Confessing that, if his own experience was a standard, the President of the United States was "liable some day to burst by merely containing restrained gases," he asserted:

Anybody in the Senate or House can say any abusive thing he pleases about the President, but it shocks the propriety of the whole country if the President says what he thinks about them. . . . But when the lid is off, I am going to resume my study of the dictionary to find adequate terms in which to describe the fatuity of these gentlemen with their poor little minds that never get anywhere but run round in a circle and think they are going somewhere. . . . My hope is that we will all put on our war paint, not as Democrats but as Americans, get the true American pattern of war paint and a real hatchet and go out on the war path and get a collection of scalps that has never been excelled in the history of American warfare.[16]

More patently than ever, Woodrow Wilson was the mind and soul of the Democratic party. Here was the hardened leader, following the *Realpolitik* that had been defined by Wilson the scholar in 1890: "A party likes to be led by very absolute opinions; it chills it to hear it admitted that there is some reason on the other side."

Wilson's complete devotion to the cause of the League left no enthusiasm for constructive domestic measures that Tumulty was urging upon him; but he was willing to review legislation proposed by men of the Cabinet to take care of problems raised by demobilization and reconversion. When he arrived at Washington he had gone to his desk as quickly and quietly as possible, to attack accumulated papers and to see the stream of callers who awaited him. However, when he addressed a meeting of governors and mayors on matters of reconstruction, his talk was brief and general and strayed inevitably to Europe.

He found his official family worrying about new problems. There was a streak of dependability in this group that contrasted agreeably with the opportunism of the men in the improvised councils at Paris. Carter Glass, who thought of public office as "human slavery" but whose elevation to the treasury secretaryship had not lessened his devotion to his herd of Jersey cattle, had been cabling often to Paris to seek the cooperation that the President had promised when he had appointed the Virginian. Glass faced the immediate job of selling a large Victory Loan to the American people. Realizing that Congress expected him to collect foreign debts to the United States, he nevertheless saw that further advances must be made to supply food in European areas that were threatened by anarchy. But it went against the grain of his integrity

---

[16] From quotations in Tumulty, *op. cit.*, pp. 332–34 and 367–79, that have been checked with Swem's transcription of his stenographic record, at the Princeton University Library. Cf. Blum, *Tumulty*, p. 305, no. 42.

to lend money abroad so that the Food Administration could sell American products, such as pork, at prices artificially pegged. The conflict of views between the Treasury Department and the Food Administration presented a puzzle that was not solved for some time. Nor did Wilson find a quick solution for a difference of opinion about the price of steel rails.

The other secretaries, too, had problems for the lap of their returning leader. Newton D. Baker, who amid public pressures for demobilization had needed more than ever the relaxing influence exerted by his favorite pipe, had held for Wilson's consideration an executive order to abolish censorship—a move to which General March objected. Josephus Daniels was advocating a government monopoly of international radio.

Burleson, fisherman for Potomac bass and Democratic votes, had turned businessman; and in administering the nation's communications systems he was incurring the wrath that accrues to those who set rates, hold down wages, and give less than perfect service. Franklin K. Lane was still arguing about the nation's oil reserves. Then there were Redfield and W. B. Wilson—men without hobbies, zealous in good works —the former despondent because the Industrial Board was meeting opposition to its efforts to fix prices,[17] the latter trying to carry out the President's charge to the War Labor Board that it "should use all means within its power to stabilize conditions and to prevent industrial dislocation and strife."

There were the philosophers and raconteurs, too: David F. Houston, with a new stock of epitaphs from rural tombs; and Thomas R. Marshall, telling ripe yarns of Newt Plum, Hoosier justice of the peace. Attorney General Gregory was resigning and going to Paris; and to replace him Wilson had appointed A. Mitchell Palmer of Pennsylvania, the aggressive custodian of alien property who was urged upon the President as a man who would strengthen the sagging Northern wing of the Democratic party.[18]

[17] An Industrial Board was set up in February, 1919, to extend such control as that exerted by the War Industries Board through the months of transition to a peacetime economy. Lacking strong support from public opinion as well as legal powers and including no officials immediate responsible to the President, this board was ineffective. Of the agencies set up to meet the war emergency, the only one of importance to endure was McAdoo's War Finance Corporation, under Eugene Meyer.

[18] It seemed clear that the preponderance of Southern influence had contributed to the party's defeat in the November election; and yet Wilson had found it hard to work this problem out in the "cold blood" of political advantage. The appointment of Palmer was much against the judgment of Gregory, who felt that his assistant, Todd of Virginia, merited the position. "This disturbs me," Wilson confessed to Tumulty. "It also disturbs me that, beginning at the bottom of the ladder in the Department of Justice, Todd worked his way from the top and earned every step."

However, the President had followed the wishes of Baruch, McCormick, and other party men. The experienced Todd resigned, and Palmer was placed in a post which he appeared to exploit to make political capital for himself.

"Everything looks so delightful and homelike to me over here," Wilson wrote to an old colleague at Princeton, "that it goes harder than I can say to pull up again and leave, but evidently the chief work is on the other side, at any rate for the present." Too rushed to confer with his aides individually, Wilson told them that they must carry on without him for another three months. He expected that he would be back again in June.

On the night of March 3 Lodge presented his Machiavellian "round robin" resolution, and the next day the Senate closed its session in a Republican filibuster, without acting on a vital deficiency bill or on the return of the nation's railways to their owners. While the obstructive talk went on, Wilson sat in his room at the Capitol and talked cheerfully with Democratic senators, preparing to denounce the infidels publicly. "A group of men in the Senate," he charged in a message to the people, "have deliberately chosen to embarrass the administration of the Government, to imperil the financial interests of the railway systems of the country, and to make arbitrary use of the powers intended to be employed in the interest of the people." Democratic Senator Martin already had seen through the Republican plot to force a special session during the President's absence. He had served notice, on February 26, that Congress would not be called until Wilson's final return from abroad. And now the President himself affirmed this in his statement to the press.

Soon after noon on March 4, the day on which this assertion was printed, Wilson took a train for New York. His indignation at his adversaries was boiling up dangerously. At Philadelphia there was a sweet, short interlude, when he went to a hospital to visit daughter Jessie and a new-born grandson and namesake. The infant could not be coaxed to open its eyes, but its red mouth gaped persistently. Observing this phenomenon, the President remarked gravely: "I think from appearances that he will make a United States senator."

The mood of the prophet was black when he reached New York and went to the Metropolitan Opera House to speak to five thousand people. He walked on the stage arm in arm with William Howard Taft, to whom he had appealed for support against Republican opponents of the League and who hoped that the President would continue to insist on including the Covenant in the peace treaty. Returning from a crusading tour across the country and appearing against the advice of his physician, Taft spoke first and refuted objections to the Covenant so convincingly that for a moment Wilson wondered what was left for him to say.

When the band played "Over There," the President took his cue from it. "I will not come back," he pledged, "till it's over, over there. . . . I pray God in the interests of peace of the world that that may be soon." His voice hardened as he laid down a public challenge:

Every man at the Paris conference knows that the treaty of peace will be inoperative, as Mr. Taft has said, without this constant support and energy of a great organization such as is supplied by the League of Nations. And men who, when I first went over there, were skeptical of the possibility of forming a league of nations, admitted that if we could but form it, it would be an invaluable instrumentality through which to secure the operation of the various parts of the treaty; and when that treaty comes back, gentlemen on this side will find the Covenant not only in it, but so many threads of the treaty tied to the Covenant that you cannot dissect the Covenant from the treaty without destroying the whole vital structure. The structure of peace will not be vital without the League of Nations, and no man is going to bring back a cadaver with him.

Advocates of a league were filled with misgivings. By bluntly defying the bloc of senators who had signed the "round robin" resolution, the President had alienated many citizens. He had failed to educate those whose minds were open. Overtired, overwrought, suffering from a cold, the prophet had unleashed his emotions too rashly. There was an edge upon his tone and menace in his manner as he threatened the vengeance of a wrathful God on his sinful adversaries. In his voice were echoes of lost causes—the South fighting for its concept of the right, the president of Princeton alienating alumni. The next morning the Indianapolis *Star* suggested that the President of the United States might be "riding for a fall."

Backstage, after the speech, the President found Tumulty ready to bring in a delegation of Irish-Americans who wished to plead for home rule for Ireland. Their leader was Daniel F. Cohalan, a man who had a record of disloyalty during the war and was beyond the pale of Wilson's morality. The President took out his watch and very decisively ordered that Cohalan be taken out of the building by a secret service man.[19]

After the ejection of its leader, the delegation gave its petition to an austere, steely-eyed chief executive, who thought the Irish Question a domestic concern of the British Empire in which no outsider should interfere—except, perhaps, someday, the League of Nations.

The Wilsons sailed the next morning, the President plagued by an aching tooth, indigestion, and a feverish cold that kept him in bed for two days. His sublime faith in his liaison with his constituency was

[19] Myles McCahill, the secret service man, to the writer.

still unshaken. "The people of the United States," he informed House, "are undoubtedly in favor of the League of Nations by an overwhelming majority . . . but there are many forces, particularly those prejudiced against Great Britain, which are exercising a considerable influence against it, and you ought to have that constantly in mind. . . ." The prophet did not see the newspapers the morning after his parting speech at New York and little criticism reached him now. When it did penetrate his sensitive mind, he showed irritation if it was unfavorable.

For a sweet interval, while the *George Washington* took the shortest route back to Brest, the President could cast off the net that was enmeshing his mind and be a whole human being, undivided by fears and pressures. He had his friends in for luncheon, said grace in a low, reverent voice, and indulged in familiar give-and-take, limericks and puns, and stories of golf. One day he signed the Prohibition Amendment, with a wry observation about the "personal deprivation" that it might cause. Occasionally, coming in from the damp, chilly air, he would himself take a very little Scotch.

Sometimes he would think of the precarious transatlantic tightrope on which he was walking, with head winds from France pressing him toward a guarantee against aggression stronger than that given in Article X and blasts from the Senate pushing him toward a less binding commitment.

Before leaving Paris he had let it be known that not one word, not even a period, of the Covenant could be revised. When House had quoted Burke to him—"to govern is to compromise"—the President quickly had seen the application and had laughed and shaken his finger. "For once," he said, "I do not agree with you or with Burke, if you have quoted him correctly. I have found that you get nothing in this world that is worth while without fighting for it." He saw that to reopen discussion of the Covenant at the conference would be to give France a chance to reassert her self-centered demands for security.

Nevertheless, Wilson's visit to America led him to wonder whether he should not make an effort at Paris to resolve the major doubts that were besetting his own people. While crossing the ocean he studied notes that he had made at the Congressional conference at the White House. "No matter what I do, they will continue their attack," he said disconsolately. But he had an encouraging letter that had been written at his request by Senator Hitchcock. This Democrat, who would be supplanted by Lodge as chairman of the Foreign Relations Committee in the next Congress, reported that some signers of the "round robin" actually would vote for the Covenant if it was a part of the peace treaty, and still more would support it if certain specified changes were made.

Though Wilson had little hope of appeasing the more implacable of the senators, he saw a possibility of taking some action to reassure those who sincerely accepted the basic principles of the League. Even mild reservations, however, might require compensating concessions to France when discussion was reopened at Paris. If only House had been able to stand firm in his absence, he felt, perhaps he would not have to concede so much as to make of the peace merely another "Holy Alliance." But if the Colonel had yielded a little to France and he himself now had to concede more to the French in order to get the changes in the Covenant that his people wanted, the outlook would be black indeed.

On March 13 House came to Brest to welcome his friend, eager to give a full account of his stewardship during the month of their separation. Left at Paris to conduct negotiations without specific instructions, he had maintained a good understanding with the leaders of the Allies and had tried to hasten decisions that would conform in general with his chief's principles.

Left alone among Europeans to whom he had made himself agreeable, the enterprising Texan had seemed to his colleagues to revert to the boy who had untiringly swapped jackknives, the businessman who had traded in such a way as to let the other fellow profit enough so that he would come back to trade again. Bliss and White had thought House too sympathetic to his French friends. Moreover, the Colonel himself had questioned his own ability to keep a hand on all the nerve centers at the conference. "When I fell sick in January," House wrote in his diary on February 26, "I lost the thread of affairs and I am not sure that I have ever gotten fully back."

The moral atmosphere that Wilson had cultivated had not long survived the absence of his own voice; and the specific provisions of his Fourteen Points on such matters as boundaries and reparations were proving inadequate as a basis for settlements. Colonel House, realizing the strength of Republican opposition at Washington, saw that the solidarity of Clemenceau and Lloyd George in their own constituencies "put the finishing touches to a situation already bad." In his chief's absence, House had assumed as much responsibility as the European premiers took. By cable and wireless he had faithfully reported the major moves and the trend of the thinking, though the exchanges of cables with the President had not been clear because of difficulty with a new code.

In reply he had had a sweet personal message from Edith Wilson, but only a few business notes and cables from the President. Wilson's messages had taken few exceptions to the Colonel's diplomacy. In fact, in replying to a report that Marshal Foch was urging an immediate imposition of severe terms upon Germany—territorial and economic as well as military—the President reaffirmed his faith in his agent. "I know," he said, "I can trust you and our colleagues to withstand such a programme immovably . . . we should not risk being hurried into a solution arrived at solely from the French official viewpoint . . ."

Believing that delay could be favorable only to Germany and thinking that the Germans would be more easily reconciled to severe military terms if they knew the whole reckoning, House wished to open Germany to a flow of food and trade by a preliminary treaty, set the League in operation, and leave the most thorny issues to be handled when order and confidence returned to Europe. He had initiated discussion of territorial and economic terms, in accordance with the procedure that he had laid before the President on February 14. Undertaking discussion of a settlement for the west bank of the Rhine, he reported to Wilson that Clemenceau was "insistent" on the creation of a disarmed Rhenish Republic, and then on March 7, that in a conference with Lloyd George and Clemenceau, no tentative agreement was reached "because of Clemenceau's very unreasonable attitude."[20]

The President, fearful of a breach of the principle of self-determination, had warned House specifically against determining the geographical boundaries of Germany. Now, on March 10, the President wirelessed that he was a "little uneasy" and hoped that House would not consent, even provisionally, to separation of the Rhenish provinces from Germany under any arrangement, but would reserve the whole matter.

Charles Swem, to whom Wilson's message of March 10 was dictated, thought that the President put it mildly when he described himself as "a little uneasy." Actually, he seemed deeply concerned.[21] Doubtless the President remembered that at their parting in mid-February, House had pleaded repeatedly for conciliation of the Senate and had warned that

[20] On March 2, House had convoked a conference in the apartment of Vance McCormick, who was serving at Paris as an economic adviser. The Colonel recorded in his diary: "I had a long talk with Tardieu and we got nearer together on the question of the Rhenish Republic . . ." McCormick, however, left the meeting with the understanding that a definite agreement was reached for the creation of a Rhenish Republic—an arrangement that he later learned was absolutely contrary to Wilson's wishes. McCormick's diary records that an agreement was reached also on a plan for the Saar Basin and on the transfer of Danzig to Poland and Luxembourg to Belgium, with reservations. No message reporting this meeting to the President has been found. It is not recorded whether McCormick's version reached Wilson, but this is not unlikely. *See* McCormick's Diary, March 2, 1919; also McCormick's statement to Ray Stannard Baker, July 16, 1928, Baker Papers. Lloyd George's *Memoirs of the Peace Conference*, I, 188, records that House told him and Clemenceau, on March 7, that they might reach agreement on Tardieu's plan "provided the principle of self-determination was postponed until the whole of the terms of peace had been fulfilled."

[21] Charles Swem to the writer.

he might have to compromise with the Europeans on minor matters in order to safeguard American principles. Moreover, news dispatches had given the impression that the Colonel had consented to—unpardonable heresy—the separation of the Covenant from the treaty.[22]

When the *George Washington* put into the harbor at Brest on a rainy afternoon Wilson was pale and anxious. He had to be polite to Jusserand, who came out to welcome him in the name of France; and he did not see House until he disembarked at a landing stage late in the evening, in full moonlight. After inspecting a French guard of honor, he went with the Colonel to a train. Before they reached Paris they went over the situation on both sides of the Atlantic. Wilson spoke fatalistically of the enemy in the Senate. Complaining of the sullen spirit of Knox and Lodge at the White House party that the Colonel had promoted, he said: "Your dinner was a failure as far as getting together was concerned."

The Colonel reminded his friend that at least the dinner had served to give evidence that the President was willing to listen to advice. It seemed to House that Wilson had been unduly irritated because true friends of the League criticized his New York speech as too contentious.

On the train to Paris the President did not reproach the old friend who had served him so long and so well. To his wife, however, he confessed the depth of his disappointment. He would have to start all over again, he felt, to restore the Covenant to pre-eminence in the peace settlement. By listening sympathetically to French demands for guarantees beyond those expected under the League of Nations, House had conceded that the protection given by the Covenant might not be adequate; and now, to meet the views of critics in the United States, Wilson would have to ask for revisions that would make the Covenant even less satisfactory to France as a guarantee of security. He saw his lonely task complicated because it must now be clear to foreign statesmen that even his own fellow commissioners did not cleave entirely to his ultimate principles.

He faced up to the challenge like the Covenanter that he was. "Well," he said to Edith Wilson, as he threw back his head and the light of controversy came into his eyes, "thank God I can still fight, and I'll win . . . or never look these boys I sent over here in the face again. They lost battles—but won the war, bless them."

---

[22] Actually, House merely had discussed with his secretary the possbility of making such a separation, to appease the Senate. Auchincloss told David Hunter Miller of this conversation, and possibly gave an inkling of it to others who were less discreet than Miller.

CHAPTER XV

Revelation and Revolution

WHEN WOODROW WILSON left his train at the Gare des Invalides on March 14—just three months after his first triumphal entry into Paris— he was no longer regarded by the French as a savior to be feted. They had expected that by this time their *poilus* would be sent home and Germany would begin paying for its depredations. But now their press was telling them that these essentials had been sidetracked in favor of an untested formula—President Wilson's League of Nations. The people of Paris plodded to their daily tasks muttering "So Wilson is back!"

Work was to take precedence over everything now, in the mansion at 11 Place des Etats-Unis that was placed at the disposal of the Wilsons. Lloyd George was waiting to talk business. In the afternoon Clemenceau joined them for a three-hour conference. The Colonel had arranged that The Three meet secretly in his wife's sitting room; for he was determined to spur these men to make peace with Germany at the earliest moment possible, and wanted to keep a hand on proceedings. He and Wilson perceived that, working in secrecy, The Three could rub along without deep wounds to personal vanity or political prestige.

The American emerged smiling from the first conference. The premiers, however, were solemn. They could not but contrast the session with those that they had had with Colonel House during Wilson's absence. The Texan had proved himself a gentleman who never preached, listened well. In Clemenceau's view, the Colonel was "really first-class" as a negotiator, a man whom he could frankly disagree with and yet respect—"a good American, very nearly as good a Frenchman." Both crack pistol shots, each thought the other's argument as straight as his aim. They had come to love each other like brothers. In this affection House saw opportunity of converting The Tiger to the President's views, while Wilson, for his part, envisioned the possibility that his Colonel would be subverted.

Sitting in his wheel chair, the wounded Tiger had done some deep thinking. Resisting the efforts of nursing sisters to give him bitter doses and make him say his prayers, he had been reviewing the Covenant with all the caution that he had warned Wilson he would exercise.

Actually, the more he studied it the more inadequate it seemed as protection against the outnumbering hordes from Central Europe that had swarmed upon France, twice within a half-century.

Lloyd George was fretful, too. In England his coalition had lost two seats in a bye-election. Northcliffe's press was flailing him because he did not support French demands along the Rhine. Traders who once had hoped to profit by a prolonged blockade of Germany were now complaining that they could not do business until peace was made; and the British command in Germany reported that food shortages raised a specter of anarchy.[1] The prime minister wished to get from the United States a promise not to build in competition with Britain's navy. He hoped also for support for England's claim for the payment of the costs of the war by Germany.

During Wilson's absence the statesmen had become indifferent toward the Covenant to which the American prophet had committed them and which he had kept constantly before them while he was at Paris. Even Colonel House, lacking eloquence, and driven by fear of anarchy to negotiate a quick settlement of issues in dispute, had not exerted himself greatly to keep the American vision of a league in the foreground. In the presence of Arthur Sweetser, who was in charge of American publicity in the absence of Baker, House conferred many times with a few outstanding journalists. He talked convincingly of his own deft diplomacy, of his efforts to reach compromises in private talks of secretaries and experts. "It slows up the preliminary work very much to have the big men here now," he had told them on February 27, "so we are glad to have them out of the way." On March 5 he so far forgot himself as to say that Wilson could have made his path very much easier by using newsmen at Paris as House had urged. "I have

[1] Herbert Hoover, who had gone abroad after the Armistice eager to use American surpluses to feed the hungry of Europe, soon had found that the idealistic professions of individuals at London and Paris did not square with their actions as officials of electorates that were swayed by war hatred and economic necessity. Shipments had been delivered to Allies and to neutrals, but British officials had refused to break their blockade to let cargoes go into Germany. Moreover, Germany had failed to act on an agreement to turn over merchant ships before receiving food, and showed no desire to pay for shipments in gold—a possibility that French financiers were thought to be opposing so that their nation might get what gold there was as indemnity.

Frustrated by apathy and obstruction, Hoover was brought on the carpet by Lloyd George, who was inclined to brush him off as "that Salvation Army man." The prime minister, distressed by reports of famine in Germany, wanted to know why Hoover had not done his job. At this the American let him have the bitter truth. Lloyd George, feeling that tact was not one of Hoover's great qualities, asked him to give the council an expurgated version of his remarks. This was done, and a stormy and wordy session ensued.

When Wilson returned to Paris, the long-dammed flow of food to Central Europe was beginning. On April 28, when Hoover complained that he was not getting enough American ships to carry food, the President wrote to Henry M. Robinson to urge that "the strongest representations" be made to the Shipping Board "to divert to carrying food ships that might make large profits on commercial routes."

never known a man," the Colonel said, "who has such a faculty for doing the right thing in the hardest way. He always makes the most conceivable trouble for himself . . ."[2] At last the disciple's tact had broken under the strain. When Wilson returned to Paris it was being gossiped not only that Auchincloss was singing the praises of his father-in-law immoderately, but that House himself had "swelled up like a poisoned pup."

There were many at Paris who were deliberately blurring the vision presented by the prophet. Irresponsible Americans were saying that the Republican party was the real friend of Europe, that the British and French ought to get together and compel the President to do what they willed. European observers had noted the outspoken opposition of American senators. Foreign Minister Pichon was proclaiming that the Covenant would not be in the treaty of peace; the French press was accepting this as a fact; and at London *The Times* assumed it. An able correspondent welcomed Ray Stannard Baker back to Paris with "Well, your league is dead." Even Lord Robert Cecil admitted that it had been sidetracked.

Believing that publicity was "the lifeblood of democracy," Ray Stannard Baker again urged the President to improve his public relations, advising him that the essential thing was not to convince the people of the world that a league was needed, but to persuade them that the Covenant drawn was the best obtainable. This was what Wilson had failed to do in his messages to his people in America.

But, though he could not bring himself to try to influence opinion by heart-to-heart talks with individuals, Wilson saw that in order to win in what he called the "deadly grapple" of Past and Present he must act emphatically. On the very morning of his arrival at Paris, he picked up his telephone and called Baker. "I want you to say," he directed, "that we stand exactly where we stood on January 25 when the Peace Conference adopted the resolution making the Covenant an integral part of the general treaty of peace." Baker phrased the manifesto and put it out that afternoon. On the same day David Hunter Miller was directed to confer with Sir Maurice Hankey, secretary of the British delegation, about the form that the Covenant should take in the final treaty.

In this hour of supreme trial Woodrow Wilson needed all the resources of his ancestors. He must husband his energy for bouts with the premiers. But when little men came to him with tales of woe and hopes of loot—patriots who were not satisfied to plead the cause of their nations to any ear less authoritative than that of the great champion of

---

[2] Arthur Sweetser's notes of news conferences, in his possession.

self-determination himself—he satisfied his conscience by seeing them. He signed his name hundreds of times to polite acknowledgments and reassurances written for him in French. Sometimes he would receive more than a score of petitioners in a day: Armenians, Albanians, Lithuanians, Irish, Egyptians, Jews, a Greek priest who impressed Wilson deeply, and Galician peasants who had walked scores of miles to a railroad station so that they might ask the great American to attach their little mountain pocket to Poland. And then there were special pleaders to be seen, representing world-wide associations of interest: women, labor, the farmers, the Negroes. He did not arrange to be briefed on the pleas of these visitors before he heard them; nor would he delegate the interviews to his staff. When they told their stories, however, he held his sympathy in reserve, not wishing to promise more than he could fulfill, and lacking energy for give-and-take. Often the pleaders thought his face stony as they talked, heard his formal greeting and dismissal, and went away to add their testimony to the legend of the inaccessible, schoolmastering prophet.

Sometimes Wilson gave fellow delegates the feeling that he was beating them down. He was advised to make more use of the arts of traditional diplomacy; but with the world on fire, he felt that there was no time for social chitchat, for palaver with journalists, or for nursing hurt egos among Americans whose total loyalty he wished to take for granted. "I fear being misquoted," he told Baker, "and if I talk freely I do not know how to be discreet."

Seeing in him America's "best instrument" to give her ideals to the world, resolving to feed his mind with useful facts, Baker went each afternoon at six to 11 Place des Etats-Unis. Usually the President was still in the study where The Three had met, picking up documents and putting them away in a steel box. There, or across the hall in a drawing room that was always bright with flowers, Wilson would go over the events of the day with Baker and decide what should be made public. Sometimes Edith Wilson joined them, and by her questions helped to clarify their thinking.

Baker gave a daily bulletin to the newsmen and listened to their grievances. The American commissioners continued to grant some interviews, but now knew less than ever about the actual negotiations in the inner council. Some journalists found that it paid to go to House for news. Even the Colonel, however, began to have difficulty in keeping his finger on the pulse of events, as The Three continued to meet at the President's house in secrecy, sometimes admitting Orlando and occasionally calling in expert advisers.

Having restored the Covenant to a place of honor, Wilson hoped that it would not now be necessary to bring up the amendments that fellow Americans were suggesting. When House and Lord Robert Cecil went to him on March 16, to urge amendment and clarification of certain articles of the Covenant, Wilson resisted—"with his usual stubbornness," the Colonel jotted in his diary. Any change at this time, the President felt, would be interpreted at home as a yielding to the Senate and would damage the chances for ratification of the peace treaty.

On the same day the President had a cable from Tumulty reporting that polls showed a strong drift of opinion toward the League and that Taft was urging slight changes of language to reassure "conscientious Americans" in whom unjustified fears had been aroused. Wilson replied that he appreciated Taft's advice and would welcome suggestions that the former President had offered to send. These came from Tumulty in a cable of March 18. The President had sanctioned an effort by House to get from Lodge, through Henry White, some definite and constructive suggestions; but the senator, faithfully pursuing the policy that had been outlined with Roosevelt and suspecting that White's request had been inspired by the President, replied that nothing short of redrafting would get the Senate's approval of the Covenant.

On March 18 Wilson invited House and Lord Robert Cecil to dinner to discuss possible revisions, one by one. When his guests approved an amendment on its merits, the President willingly accepted it; but let them so much as suggest that it would be expedient to yield to the Senate on any point, and he bristled ominously. He could not find the letter [3] in which Hitchcock had enumerated revisions that would please the Senate, but did his best to recall the contents.

Two days after his dinner with House and Lord Robert Cecil, the President welcomed a score of delegates from thirteen neutral nations to a hearing before members of the League Commission. This was their

---

[3] The disappearance of this important letter and the fact that the President did not cable to Washington for a duplicate of it are striking instances of the lack of organization and enterprise in Wilson's office of which House's men complained. Hitchcock had written to the President, on March 4, that the following revisions were "likely to influence votes in the order given:

"First, a reservation to each high contracting party of its exclusive control over domestic subjects.

"Second, a reservation of the Monroe Doctrine.

"Third, some provision by which a member of the league can, on proper notice, withdraw from membership.

"Fourth, the settlement of the ambiguity in Article 15.

"Fifth, the insertion on the next to the last line of first paragraph of Article 8, after the word 'adopted,' of the words, 'by the several governments.'

"Sixth, the definite assurance that it is optional with a nation to accept or reject the burdens of a mandatory."

opportunity, he told them, to make their views known as the Articles of the Covenant were laid before them. He answered their questions patiently and lucidly, explaining that members of the League assumed three obligations for action toward an aggressor: they must break commercial relations, allow the military forces of the League to pass over their territory, and consider whether they would join in military or naval action. They might make, among themselves, such alliances as the Executive Council decided were genuinely defensive; but offensive pacts would be strictly forbidden. The neutrals were encouraged to suggest changes in the text, and Wilson thanked them for participating and assured them that their suggestions would be examined by the council with great care. He was now showing what he meant by "open covenants openly arrived at."

When the Commission on the League of Nations met on March 22 to re-examine the text of the Covenant, the French brought out arguments that already had been worn threadbare but were still useful as a means of barter. Nothing short of international inspection of armament and an international general staff would make the French feel secure under the League, Léon Bourgeois insisted. The President had to remind the commission that it was their principle to reject the concept of a superstate.

He went home wearied by the staleness of the talk. He knew what these men were going to say before they opened their mouths; and their arguments made him wonder whether France wanted to renew the war, annex some of Germany, and stir up bad feeling generally. Nevertheless, he tried to conciliate French opinion by visiting devastated villages on a Sunday and by going with Clemenceau and Lloyd George to make peace with Foch, who was sulking because his plan for using Poland as a military base against Russia had not been accepted.

At an evening session of the commission Wilson tried to soothe Bourgeois, who felt that his life's work was wiped out because the world court at The Hague was not to be carried on under the Covenant. Out of respect for the feelings of the French jurist, he restrained his tongue, but later he said to House and Cecil: "The talkfest at The Hague in 1899 . . . ended in fog overhead and in bog underfoot. The whole business was wishy-washy—though well meant, of course . . . Now we are met here for hard-and-fast agreements, for binding stipulations, for commitments, and it's my task to see that no nation or group of men holds out on us—those silly pawns in the murderous game of power politics!" [4]

Wilson studied proposals for amending the Covenant that had come

[4] Bonsal, *Unfinished Business*, p. 152.

from Lowell of Harvard,[5] and also Taft's constructive ideas. He found very useful, too, a poll of the world's newspapers that appeared in the Paris press.

On his typewriter he tapped out three amendments on a single sheet of paper.[6] That on the Monroe Doctrine, he told the commission at the meeting of March 24, would be introduced later. But two were presented to the commission that night. One of these, exempting from League action those disputes that might arise out of domestic matters, was approved in principle. The other provided for withdrawal of a nation from the League. Wilson sponsored this change with reluctance, having always been, he said, "an anti-secessionist." He told the commission that only moral compulsion could guarantee the historical continuity of the League. Yet the fact must be faced that his own nation might refuse to join the new body if definite provision was not made for withdrawal. For many public men, especially in the United States, sovereignty was "a sort of fetish." One had to make concessions to existing ideas in order to make new ideas viable. Some day, Wilson prophesied, "men will be as ardent partisans of humanity as they are today of national sovereignty." It was agreed, finally, that members of the League in good standing might withdraw on two years' notice.

By advocating this amendment to reassure the Senate, Wilson displeased Europeans who had counted on permanent American membership. The French, in particular, were distressed. If they must yield in this matter to American opinion, they hoped at least to get a concession in return. They had an amendment of their own to propose—a plan for an economic section in the League. But the President refused to barter. He warned that acceptance of the French proposal might result in "the flag following the dollar." Speaking of his own experience with commercial imperialists, he made it clear that there must be no economic exploitation by an international empire.

[5] The text of three amendments proposed by Lowell after his Boston debate with Lodge had been cabled to Lansing by the State Department on March 22. Moreover, Wilson had analyses of American press opinion and criticisms of the Covenant from William Phillips of the State Department, Dwight Morrow, and others, through Thomas W. Lamont. See Lamont, *Across World Frontiers*, pp. 186–91.

Furthermore, Polk cabled on the 20th that Charles Warren, assistant attorney general, had discussed the League with Root, and that they concluded that the paragraphs on the machinery of the new government were not clear enough. "Two or three friendly newspaper men have told me in the last few days," Polk reported, "that they feel the League is losing ground as no one seems to have authority here to explain the document or answer criticisms of Republican Senators. The opponents are carrying on a very active and cleverly planned campaign and something must be done . . . I find many friends of the President are becoming confused." A cable dated March 28, from Phillips to Lamont, concluded thus: "A very solid sentiment is appearing that it [the Covenant] should be amended in many vital particulars."

[6] For a discussion of the three amendments and a fourth, making the acceptance of colonial mandates optional, see Baker, *W.W. and World Settlement*, I, 329–31. The presentation of the amendment on the Monroe Doctrine is discussed on pp. 301–303 below.

Discussion in the commission's session of March 26 became heated; and as idealism ebbed and the conference gave the public no hint of progress toward peace, the spring mists of Paris thickened into thunder-clouds. Rumblings of popular protest assailed the delays, the secrecy, the lack of decisive action against bolshevism in Central Europe. President Wilson and his League were blamed for it all—especially by those who saw no profit in the Covenant.

Wilson thought he knew the source of delay. From many of his experts came the same complaints: "The French are holding us back; the French are talking us to death." He himself would spend an hour in arguing Clemenceau around to a certain position, only to find when the subject was reopened that The Tiger had yielded again to the promptings of his instincts. One had to deal with him as one would play with a trout, Wilson thought, jerking him up suddenly, then letting him run a little, and all the while watching to see that he did not get away.

When American newsmen asked permission to be candid, the President told them that he would not object if they were "indiscreet enough to tell the truth." But Wilson could not bring himself to break openly with his French colleague in the little World Cabinet, run home, and tell Europe to save itself as best it could. He had declared himself responsible to all humanity. Convinced that the cause of peace could not be served by the public row that the headline-hunters hoped for, he resolved to curb his tongue a little longer.

However, he felt that he could speak in a general way to revitalize public morale. On March 27 he struck boldly and positively at subversive thought by giving out a reassuring word on the progress of the Commission on the League of Nations. He explained that the commission had met at hours that did not interfere with other discussions. Moreover, the revised Covenant, "practically finished," was in the hands of a drafting committee and would "almost immediately" be given to the public.

At the very moment when the prophet of the Western world was concentrating his powers on the revision of the League Covenant, the ogre of revolution was casting its darkest shadow from the east. On March 24 the republican government of Hungary was upset by a Communist coup. Soviet propaganda, originally devised in desperation as a defense, was being shaped by the new Comintern into an offensive weapon that was sapping Allied morale on several fronts.

The Bolshevik government had been in existence now for more than a year and had maintained itself in central Russia—an area comprising hardly a fourth of the Czarist Empire—against the pressures of a fringe of militarists of the old regime who had more or less support from the Western powers. What if men lacking respect for civil liberties and for sanctity of contract should seize control of all of Central Europe? What if Asiatic despotism should supplant German absolutism?

This denouement had been made less probable by Wilson's pre-Armistice dealings with Germany. The German revolution at the time of the Armistice had been liberal in purpose, peacefully executed, and Western in ideology. The problem now, in the spring of 1919, was to guide revolutionary forces in Eastern Europe, and particularly those in Russia, into paths equally sane.

During Wilson's absence from Paris it had seemed wise to House and Lansing, as well as to Balfour and Lloyd George, that an unofficial effort be made to bring about the understanding with Moscow that official overtures had failed to establish. It had long been the custom of the British Foreign Office to send daring young bloods on diplomatic adventures to the ends of the earth, under a gentlemen's agreement that they would be heroes if they succeeded but disowned if they caused embarrassment to their government. It happened now that there was a young liberal in the American peace delegation who was willing to take a chance.

William C. Bullitt, who had been briefing the American commissioners on incoming intelligence, responded to the challenge. Taking along the liberal journalist Lincoln Steffens, Bullitt reached Moscow two days after the Third International Congress closed its sessions. Talking with Litvinov, Chicherin, and Lenin, he found them resentful of the world's low opinion of their honor, but confident that President Wilson, whose Fourteen Points they praised, would understand that a dull, inexperienced people were trying conscientiously, but at cost of great suffering to themselves, to find a better way to live for the common interest. The ruling party seemed strong, politically and morally; but lack of food made the people an easy prey of anarchy. Their armies had been winning, and they feared that their enemies would use a truce to rally their forces.

In Nicolai Lenin, Bullitt saw "a straight-forward man of the quickest intelligence and a certain serenity, humor, and broad-mindedness." By exerting his persuasiveness against the will of Trotsky and the generals, Lenin said, he was able to persuade the Central Executive Council to give Bullitt a reasonable proposal to take to the statesmen at Paris.

The young emissary arrived with Lenin's written message on the evening of March 25, and went directly to House's bedroom. The

Colonel saw hope, at last, for solving the most baffling problem of the peacemaking. He telephoned immediately to Wilson, but found the President suffering from a headache and unwilling to see Bullitt that night.

Lenin, suspicious of France's military intentions, had set a deadline at April 10. Preferring to take up the question with the President first but given no opportunity to do so, House advised Bullitt to talk with Lloyd George. The prime minister, who had given unofficial encouragement to Bullitt's venture, seemed favorably disposed toward Lenin's proposition. If Wilson would take the lead in opening negotiations, he would follow along, Lloyd George said, though he feared that the Northcliffe press would tear him limb from limb.

In the American delegation Bullitt found the same skepticism that prevailed among other conservatives at London and Paris. All the while, however, Colonel House persisted in working for agreement. Realizing that Wilson was the only statesman of sufficient stature to build a bridge over the chasm, the Colonel sent Ray Stannard Baker to the President with Lenin's proposal. At the same time other liberals among Wilson's advisers were prodding him to act.

The President, however, did not see the picture in black and white. He could not believe that Lenin's proposals had been made in simple good faith; and even had he honored them he would have been restrained from action by reports that came from Washington.[7] Clearly, Americans did not want to fight the Bolsheviki; nor would they permit their statesmen to treat with them. Wilson perceived that the political temperature was too high in the democracies for any rational rapprochement. Lloyd George, summoned home to face questions in Parliament about alleged secret dealings with the dreaded "Reds," was forced to belittle the Bullitt mission and throw responsibility for ignoring it upon the President. And Wilson, meeting Bullitt at the Crillon after receiving a letter from the young man that seemed "insulting," cut him coldly. The prospect of solving what Wilson had called "the acid test" of the peacemaking grew very dim when news came that Admiral Kolchak's army was gaining rapidly in Siberia, for the reac-

[7] Before Bullitt's return from Moscow, American journalists got wind of his mission and cabled the news home. This disclosure aggravated the "anti-red" hysteria that had been stirred up at Washington by lurid hearings that were conducted by a subcommittee of the Senate's Committee on the Judiciary.

On April 2, when Bullitt was reminding House that only eight days remained for accepting the Russian offer, Tumulty sent this message to Paris: "The proposed recognition of Lenin has caused consternation over here."

Undersecretary Polk, who was about to "wind the Russians up financially," read Bullitt's report and cabled: "I do not think I would be prepared to act on any report framed by Bullitt and Steffens after a three days' stay in Russia."

tionaries at Paris then believed that military action might eliminate the Soviet regime.[8]

While the time limit set by Lenin for action on his proposals was expiring, the President was worn down by British and French efforts to further their national interests by trading them against American suggestions for revision of the Covenant.[9] On March 24 Wilson began a series of intense sessions with Clemenceau and Lloyd George, in many of which they were joined by Orlando or Makino of Japan or both. At first there was no other man present but Paul Mantoux, the official interpreter. "I never saw him lose his calm," Mantoux has testified. "The relations of President Wilson with his associates were constantly the most courteous, whatever the difference of opinion might have been at certain moments and on certain points." Another interpreter noted that the President depended on reason and never tried to exploit his rank as the only chief of state among the peace commissioners.[10]

The Three argued over economic problems. British and French politicians had led their electorates to hope that the entire cost of the war would be wrung out of Germany. There were suspicions that certain

[8] When House came on March 27 to plead for action on Lenin's proposal, Wilson asked him to go to Hoover and to the Shipping Board to see whether ships and food could be sent to Russia. The next day Hoover brought to him a proposal for "a second Belgian Relief Commission for Russia," without political or economic advantage to the United States.

It seemed to the President that Hoover's plan made sense: it would convince liberals that Russia's problems were not being overlooked, and at the same time it would forestall the schemes of both militarists and economic exploiters. Consequently, a project was worked out for sending food that the Russians would pay for. Though the plan was safeguarded against perversion to political ends, it was regarded by French interests as tainted with American commercialism. But Colonel House adroitly won Clemenceau's assent.

When the proposal for relief reached Moscow in May, the Bolsheviki expressed willingness to talk about it and to pay for food; but they would not accept transportation controls that might hamper their military movements. Their reply was a propagandist blast against the ways of capitalism and the masking of political aggression by protestations of humanitarianism. The vituperation of the Bolsheviki and the countercharges of their French foes could not be reconciled by persistent efforts on the part of House and Hoover.

[9] Having agreed, on March 17, on military terms that set a time limit on the forcible control of Germany and vested eventual jurisdiction over this matter in the League, the council soon forgot its idea of concluding a quick preliminary peace. At one time Wilson gave Lansing reason to think that he wanted to include the Covenant in a preliminary agreement, with an understanding that everything included in the tentative pact would go into the final treaty. The secretary of state advised plainly that any document that changed the situation from war to peace had to be ratified by the Senate; and Wilson, who confessed that he felt compelled to free himself from "the servitude which many of the senators seek to impose," expressed surprise that he could not do it by this method.

[10] Paul Mantoux, "Le Président Wilson au Conseil des Quatre," *Centénaire Woodrow Wilson: 1856–1956* (Geneva, 1956); A. H. Frazier, ms., "Recollections of President Wilson at the Peace Conference," p. 9.

The principal conclusions of the treaty with Germany were reached by the inner council of heads of states. The foreign ministers met in a council of five, and occasionally the two groups combined to meet, as they had in January, in a council of ten, which had been made ineffective by leakage and by badgering from curious observers who asked whether this and that rumor was true. The Supreme War Council of military men and the Supreme Economic Council, which had been created on Feb. 8, continued to meet.

French militarists and industrialists sought to use their dominant position for economic exploitation of the people of Central Europe. When French peasants put in their claim for cows that the "Boches" had driven off, it was too much for Wilson's patience. Just how, he ventured to ask, could French farmers go into Germany and pick out their own cattle? It was difficult to separate France's pure passion for security from the lust that some of her citizens showed.

Bored by economic detail, as he had been all his life, Wilson felt at first that, since the United States claimed no share in reparations except a few ships, the settlement would have to be left to the political discretion of Clemenceau and Lloyd George. When he did join in the discussion, it was to suggest that the experts be cautioned against fixing a sum that would destroy Germany completely, keep her from accepting their proposals, or sow seeds of a war of revenge.

The political plight of Clemenceau and Lloyd George brought negotiations to a serious pass by the end of March; and the President came out of one of the intimate sessions to ask his advisers to try to meet the views of the premiers, else their ministries might fall. At the same time he reminded Lloyd George and Clemenceau that they must unite in submitting a definite bill to Germany.

A subcommittee of three experts was directed by the council to take up the question of defining "war costs," and Norman Davis, the American member, sought the advice of the President. Lloyd George was agitating for the inclusion of such indirect costs as soldiers' pensions and even separation allowances, under the heading of "war costs." (Was it fair, he asked, to repair damaged roofs in France at the expense of families that had lost a father?) Wilson's pre-Armistice agreement with Germany had made it clear that indirect costs were not to be assessed against the enemy, and the President deemed it unfair now to raise the reckoning against a prostrate debtor. Yet his experts told him that England would not get the share of reparations to which she thought herself entitled unless pensions were included among the damages. And in the suppliant position in which the Senate had placed him vis-à-vis revision of the Covenant, he must play ball with the prime minister.

In this quandary the President clutched at the sanctifying support of General Smuts. Wilson knew that this man wished to be fair to Germany; and so it was enough for him that Smuts had set down pensions as "damage to the civilian population." When the President's experts came to dissuade him and asserted that they could find no lawyer in the American delegation who could see logic in such a policy, Wilson's reply was: "Logic? I don't give a damn for logic! I am going to include pensions." And so the President sanctioned charging Germany with indirect war costs which a month before he had felt "bound in honor ' to forgo. Those on whom he depended to tell him "what was right" thought this unwise and unnecessary, but he yielded to British interest and to a humane argument. At the time it seemed that actually no added burden would be thrown on the Germans, who would not be able to pay even the direct costs of the war; but the French, who would get a smaller share of what was paid, were unhappy. On March 29, after a session in which he had suggested that in the peace terms it would be best to repeat their pre-Armistice views on reparations, Wilson confessed that he did not know whether the conference could go on. "M. Clemenceau called me pro-German and left the room," he said.

French demands for a secure frontier also came to a head late in March. On the 17th Clemenceau had given notice that he must ask that the part of Germany west of the Rhine be detached from the Reich and shaped under the League of Nations into an independent state. He would have the new republic policed by French troops. However, France would assent to a limitation upon her military control of the Rhineland—thirty years was suggested—provided that Britain and the United States would bind themselves to give military aid to France in case Germany should commit an act of aggression.

To Wilson it seemed clear that the policing of more than five million Germans by French forces was inconsistent with the Fourteen Points and menaced the future peace of the world. He explained to Clemenceau that he sought to avoid a formula that, by substituting action by an alliance of states for action by the League, might suggest that the League's guarantee was inadequate. Asked whether the suggested guarantee could not be written in the League Covenant, Wilson replied that it would not do to put provisions applying to a particular nation in a covenant of general principles. He was willing that certain nations have a mandate to act without delay in a case of aggression, while waiting for an expected action on the part of the Executive Council of the League. But to the French plan of military occupation of the Rhineland he was unsympathetic. For days neither he nor Clemenceau yielded an inch, as House and Tardieu scurried back and forth with counter proposals. The ice that overlay this question was so thin that the President dared not venture upon it in direct conversation with Clemenceau. In the Polish settlement, when two of the Fourteen Points had been in conflict, the principle of self-determination was sacrificed to economic considerations; but to give in again and put Germans under French rule would compound a precedent that it would be hard to overcome later. On the other hand, he could not afford to break with Clemenceau, for then he might have to deal with a more vengeful

French premier who would not share The Tiger's determination to maintain unity among the Allies and who would be intolerant of the League of Nations.

Driven to the end of his wits by French intransigence on the Rhenish question and by a plan for military action against Russia that was sprung upon him on March 28, Wilson gave way to his impatience when Clemenceau introduced another claim of his nation. France, the premier said, thought herself entitled to annex the Saar Valley up to her old frontier of 1814 and, by way of indemnity, to seize coal mines beyond that border.[11]

Wilson, brushing aside the historical arguments, reminded his colleagues that the question of annexation of the Saar was one that the French had not brought up in the pre-Armistice negotiations. Delivering a little sermon about their responsibility to peoples who believed in a "just" peace, he told Clemenceau that it was "painful" to oppose him, but protested that he could not do otherwise without failing in his duty. The most that he would concede was the working of the mines by the French for a limited period. Annexation or political control did not seem a wise solution. "The only principle that I recognize is that of the consent of the governed," Wilson declared. France would like to own the mines, Clemenceau responded, but not on conditions that would set up perpetual conflict with the Germans for the future.[12]

Believing that the world's salvation depended on their going on with their talking, Wilson drove himself to continue. He had a feeling, confessed to House, that no one liked him. The time that he had long dreaded seemed to have come, the crisis in which he would have to break with those around him to fulfill what he thought to be his duty to humanity. Usually patient and calm in his own home, the prophet was in an irritable rage after luncheon on April 2. The French were delaying proceedings intentionally, he told his family, and they were throwing the blame on him, hoping to break him down. Their attitude, he thought, was "damnable."

Ray Stannard Baker saw the President every day and, though he did not love him, had come to believe and trust in Wilson beyond any other mortal and set him down as "the only great man here." Baker tempted

[11] Here, again, two of Wilson's principles were brought into conflict. Self-determination forbade the political control of some 300,000 Germans in the Saar by the French. Yet the mines in France had been flooded by the invaders during the war, Point VIII promised reparation to France, and it seemed possible to give this in the Saar. The French statesmen not only insisted that as a practical matter they could not operate the mines under a German government, but they went so far as to adduce historical reasons to support their claim for outright annexation. Wilson opposed the historical argument of the French, explaining that Point VIII referred to the wrongs done in 1871, not 1815.

[12] Mantoux, *Délibérations*, I, 74, 89. For the Saar Settlement, *see* pp. 299–300 below.

him now, as he had done a week before, to tell the truth to the people. American delegates were hoping that the President would notify the premiers that if they did not reach agreement he would go home and let Congress decide what to do.

"If I were to do that," the President replied, "it would immediately break up the Peace Conference—we cannot risk it yet. But we've got to make peace on the principles laid down and accepted, or not make it at all." If a decision could not be reached by the middle of the next week, he said, he might have to make a positive break.

For three weeks Woodrow Wilson had been under a crossfire such as no other man at Paris had sustained. He worked harder than any other major figure at the conference. Everyone wondered—even the redoubtable Lloyd George—how he survived from day to day. After an eight-o'clock breakfast, he did in two hours what in normal times might be thought a day's work at his desk. Then a conference or two before the morning meeting of the inner council; guests at lunch and sometimes at dinner; sessions all afternoon—sometimes two at once in adjoining rooms, with the President going back and forth and carrying in his mind the threads of argument. In the evening a daily talk with Baker, then dinner—for which he no longer took time to dress—and afterwards another conference, or study of maps and reports to prepare for the business of the morrow. Yet this man was being represented to the people of the world as the cause of delay in making peace.

Under the relentless strain the President had grown gaunt. His face was haggard and the muscles twitched alarmingly around his left eye— the one that had been impaired in 1906.

When Wilson questioned the wisdom of their arguments, the French began to insinuate that he was losing his powers. On March 23 Clemenceau had sent agents to House to suggest that too much activity had dulled Wilson's mental processes. "He seems quite *vide*, and then nothing is done," these men complained to the Colonel. "Clemenceau thinks that the President . . . is spending too much time in social matters which are also exacting . . . Clemenceau thought that you might suggest to the President that he cut out his jaunts with Mrs. Wilson." Yes, indeed, he might, House had replied, but most certainly he would not!

On April 2 Wilson had thought the skies as dark as dark could be. But on the 3rd there arose a cloud of jet. The advisers on reparations came early in the day to report that Britain's appetite for indemnities had not been sated. The President felt that Lloyd George had very nearly put something over on him; and he approved a plan drafted by his men to scotch the scheme. Later in the day, however, the Americans came back to their chief in deeper gloom. They reported that the Allies "were acting like the Devil." Discussing reparations in the council on that day, the Europeans reminded House of "a lot of children telling each other what they expected to do when they 'grew up.'"

When the American experts went to Wilson with their discouraging report, late in the afternoon of April 3, they found him in bed, suffering from what seemed to be a bad cold. It had come upon him very suddenly. As the night wore on, his condition took a sinister turn. Violent fits of coughing seized him, and profuse diarrhea. His temperature rose to 103 degrees. Dr. Grayson, suspecting at first that the President's food had been poisoned, brought the spasms of coughing under control; but his chest was congested and obstruction in his breathing prevented the deep sleep that he needed for restoration. For three days, too weak to leave his bed, he lay resting fitfully.[13]

While Dr. Grayson tiptoed in and out and Edith Wilson stood by, the sick man was at a loss to know how to solve the dilemmas that faced him. He felt powerless to use his favorite weapon—appeal to the people—for disclosure of discord would benefit only Germany and the subversive forces of Eastern Europe. Moreover, he could not afford to antagonize his European associates until he had finished the labor that Americans had saddled on him—the revision of the Covenant.

In his weakness his roused conscience pricked and goaded him to action. Not for a moment, after the first dreadful, feverish night, did he give up his trust. Grayson could see that anxiety about the handling of affairs for which he was responsible did more harm than actual participation. Therefore, the physician accepted his decision that the council should meet in the next room, with House sitting in his place and bringing to his bedside a report of each move. The day before he was

[13] Dr. Grayson wrote to Tumulty on April 10: "That night was one of the worst through which I have ever passed." Present-day experts on arteriosclerosis, with greater knowledge of this insidious affliction, have questioned Grayson's diagnosis of the illness at Paris as influenza and have concluded that it was caused by a slight vascular occlusion incident to the progress of arteriosclerosis and brought on, as the attack in 1906 had been, by prolonged high pressure on brain and nerves. See Dr. Walter C. Alvarez, "Cerebral Arteriosclerosis," in *Geriatrics*, I (May–June, 1946), 189–216.

In *Personal Recollections of Woodrow Wilson*, p. 52, A. W. Patterson reports that two distinguished doctors gave the opinion that Wilson was suffering from arteriosclerosis when he went to Paris and that while he was there the effects became quite manifest. Among those at Paris who have suggested that Wilson suffered a "stroke" are Herbert Hoover and John W. Davis.

"I never knew the President to be in such a difficult frame of mind as he is now," Gilbert Close, his secretary, wrote to his wife on April 7. "Even while lying in bed he manifested peculiarities . . ." The record of Head Usher Ike Hoover reports: "When he got back on the job, his peculiar ideas were even more pronounced. He now became obsessed with the idea that every French employee about the place was a spy for the French government. Nothing we could say could disabuse his mind of this thought. About this time he also acquired the peculiar notion he was personally responsible for all the property in the furnished place he was occupying. . . . Coming from the President, whom we all knew so well, these were very funny things, and we could but surmise that something queer was happening in his mind. One thing was certain: he was never the same after this little spell of sickness." I. H. Hoover, *Forty-Two Years in the White House*, p. 98.

stricken the President had talked for almost an hour over the telephone with the Colonel, who was confined by a cold, and had asked the Texan to do something to break the impasse with the French over the Saar and the Rhineland.[14]

Once more, now, House could serve. He could apply his talent for negotiation in the way that had proved effective before the Armistice and that he had hoped to extend to the peacemaking. He could explore solutions, discuss them tentatively, and refer the results to his chief for a final ruling. He was now in a position to make good his boast to newsmen that "peace could be made in an hour." Taking the President's seat in the council, the Colonel said little. In one long session he spoke only thrice—once to remark that he did not share Wilson's distaste for permanent commissions to inspect military conditions in Germany. From his sickbed Wilson tentatively approved a formula that House persuaded Clemenceau to put in writing as a basis for settlement of reparations.

On the afternoon of Sunday, April 6, the President was well enough to receive his commissioners and to discuss American strategy. Neither he nor House had seen the others for days. He said to them: "Gentlemen, this is not a meeting of the Peace Commission. It is more a council of war." The Colonel left the session with the impression that, if nothing happened within the next few days, Wilson would say in the council that he would have to go home or open the conferences to the public.[15]

Already he had given notice that his patience was near the breaking point. While Edith Wilson sat beside his bed, trembling for fear of a relapse. he asked her to call Grayson, and when the doctor came in, he ordered that word be sent to Washington that the *George Washington* should be put in shape for his return trip as soon as he was well enough to go.

Tumulty cabled from Washington that this was looked upon as an act of impatience and petulance, and not accepted in good grace by either friends or foes. Wilson should place responsibility for a break where it belonged, his secretary thought. A withdrawal would be interpreted in the United States as a desertion. That was the attitude taken

[14] However, when the Colonel reported to Mrs. Wilson two meetings in which the Saar and the Rhineland had been discussed with Tardieu, Wilson was alarmed, as he had been during his absence in February. He asked his wife to telephone to House to tell him not to commit himself on these questions.

The Colonel had sensed the suffering of his friend, his loneliness and frustration as he was denied both support from American colleagues and acclaim from the people whom he strove to serve. House was still sure that in the long verdict of history his hero would win out. He put aside a quotation from Gladstone to give to the President for comfort: "Men ought not to suffer from disenchantment; they ought to know that ideals in politics are never realized."

[15] Sweetser's summary of House's news conference of April 6, 1919.

by the French press, which jeered at the President as a spoiled child, running home to mother; and Clemenceau, in private, likened him to "a cook who keeps her trunk ready in the hallway" and threatens to leave. But both officials and public got the point: the wrath of the prophet was rising.

When Wilson struggled back into harness and met the premiers, he found that negotiations were in the doldrums. House had tried to make the most of his own last days in a seat of influence, advising his British and French colleagues that they could get better terms from him immediately than from the President later. However, neither the Colonel's hint nor the summoning of the *George Washington* brought progress. French experts haggled over words and commas in the compromise on reparations, and Clemenceau showed his age. To display his displeasure, the Colonel had walked out of a meeting and reported to the President, who commended his action.

The prophet's soul was torn apart, as his mind made him face realities. When Ray Stannard Baker resumed his evening calls to see how he might give currency to the master's words, Wilson's eyes, protruding from hollowed sockets, peered out at him. His hair had whitened and his face was pale; and all the energy left in his haggard body seemed to be burning in those large luminous orbs. Tell the newsmen, he directed, to read again the Armistice agreements. He was unwilling to face up to the fact that his Fourteen Points, conceived originally as propaganda, were a confusing and inadequate basis for a realistic settlement. "The time has come to bring this thing to a head," he said. Negotiations with Clemenceau had become to him "one mass of tergiversations." Baker left the prophet's side utterly convinced that he had not been bluffing when he had asked that the coming of the *George Washington* be hastened. The statesmen at Paris felt the force of religious prophecy. Their people recognized it; and here and there crystals of common sense formed in the fog of military and financial hysteria. "Certainly things are speeding up," the Colonel jotted in his diary.

Asserting that it was a great mistake to sacrifice a sound, constructive economic plan to political expediency, Wilson nevertheless agreed that experts on reparations should perfect a scheme that would suit the statesmen of the Allies. He insisted, however, that the Reparations Commission that was proposed should exact no more than Germany could pay within one generation and should fix the sum as soon as possible after ratification of the treaty.

As for the Saar, Wilson set his jaw hard against its political separation from Germany. He would concede the mines to France, but not political control. He adopted a suggestion of the experts that for fifteen years sovereignty rest in a commission under the League of Nations and thereafter be determined by a plebiscite. He feared that they might be imposing too many duties on the infant League, that they might not find enough worthy men to perform them. When Lloyd George tried to reassure him by referring to the civil servants of the British Empire as an example of what could be done, he replied: "Your functionaries have one of the strongest motives that act on men; they serve their country. That motive doesn't exist yet for the League of Nations." [16]

On April 14, he accepted, with a wry face, a plan that the Colonel brought from Clemenceau for making France secure along the Rhine; and a week later the text of an Anglo-American guaranty of French security was settled.[17]

While compromising with the French statesmen in order that he might secure their support for amendments to the Covenant that Americans were demanding, Wilson had to deal also with Lloyd George's determination to exact a *quid pro quo*. On April 7, just as he was struggling back to his feet, he had a letter from Secretary Daniels reporting Lloyd George to be very earnest in saying that he would not give "a snap of his fingers" for the League of Nations if the United States kept on building warships.

With further revision of the League Covenant in prospect, the issue of naval power was too incendiary to be left smoldering or to be entrusted to the contentious wills of navy men. Wilson therefore turned once again to the resourceful Colonel. Cautioning Daniels against making remarks in public on naval policy that might inflame British opinion, House tried to pin down Lloyd George. He got from Lord Robert Cecil a written statement of the British position, and with Wilson's approval sent a reply invoking the spirit of the League of Nations as a preventive against naval rivalry, pledging America's devotion to that spirit, and asserting that the President had no idea of building a fleet in competition with Britain.

However, on April 10 Wilson had to go to an evening meeting of the League Commission not knowing whether efforts to amend the Covenant would have British support. Already, at a session of the commission on March 24, he had signified his intention of proposing an amendment that would recognize the Monroe Doctrine. He had himself studied suggestions by Taft and Senator Hitchcock for the amendments

[16] Mantoux, *Délibérations*, I, 228.
[17] The treaty of guaranty was approved by Wilson and Clemenceau on April 20 and presented to the council on the 22nd. It included this clause: "The present treaty will continue in force until, on the application of one of the parties to it, the Council of the League of Nations—acting, if need be, by a majority—agrees that the League itself affords sufficient protection." It was in consideration of the treaty of guaranty, with this provision included, that Clemenceau accepted the House-Tardieu formula for the Rhineland.

that he had persuaded the commission to accept in March; but now he turned over belated proposals from Elihu Root to his legal counselors.

The text that was cabled to Paris did not elucidate the reasons for the revisions that the elder statesman proposed; and David Hunter Miller, to whom it was submitted for legal analysis, found most of the suggestions impractical. When he showed Root's proposals to Lord Robert Cecil, the British statesman said that he would prefer no covenant at all to one that followed these suggestions.

Root feared that in the long run the positive guaranty in Article X would make of the League "an independent alliance for the preservation of the *status quo*." In that event it would be futile, mischievous, and contrary to the laws of change and growth; and to prevent this he advocated that after a limited time—say five years—members might withdraw from the provisions of Article X.

Woodrow Wilson shared Root's dread of concerted enforcement of a *status quo* against legitimate change, and in his early drafts of the Covenant had taken pains to guard against it. One day at Paris a newsman told him, at luncheon, that his opponents were saying that Article X might compel the United States to support an old regime against a popular uprising; and Wilson jumped up, poked his informant in the chest with his forefinger, and exclaimed: "My boy, if I thought that, by direction or remote implication, any clause or phrase forbade to any peoples the sacred right of revolution, I would tear up the Covenant with my own hands." He was advised by Miller that the political aspirations of the world's people would not be strait-jacketed by Article X so long as the Covenant provided for its own revision and so long as member nations, under the amendment that had been adopted in March, could withdraw on two years' notice.

With some of Root's suggestions already cared for, and with his legal adviser questioning the practicality of others, Wilson was not inclined to act on the advice of this Republican statesman who was remote from the negotiations at Paris.

On March 28 William Howard Taft, who ten days before had advised that the "Monroe Doctrine reservation alone would probably carry the treaty through the Senate," suggested that without such a reservation the treaty would *not* be accepted in the United States. Heeding this dire warning, Wilson sat down to ponder over the text of a reservation that Taft suggested. Penciling a few changes on the cablegram that had brought Taft's advice, Wilson typed out a clause to be added to Article X, providing that "nothing in this covenant shall be deemed to affect or deny" the application of the Monroe Doctrine in both its positive and its negative aspects, which were explicitly stated.

This proposal, defining the doctrine but not naming it, was submitted through Colonel House to the British, who brought back a shorter statement that named the Monroe Doctrine without defining it. Revising the brief British draft slightly, Wilson and his advisers arrived at this formula:

Nothing in this Covenant shall be deemed to affect the validity of international engagements, such as treaties of arbitration or regional understandings like the Monroe Doctrine, for securing the maintenance of peace.

The President could put this generalized statement before the League Commission without appearing to ask special consideration for his own nation; and at the same time he hoped to reassure sincere friends of the League in the United States.

On the evening of April 10 he went into a session of the commission to plead his cause in a convincing speech that lasted only ten minutes. He was greatly cheered when Lord Robert Cecil, whose nation's position had been in doubt because of the controversy over naval building, supported him by explaining that the Monroe Doctrine was intended merely "to quiet doubts and to calm misunderstandings." Standing up against the British reactionaries in the trying days of April, this great liberal had threatened to resign if he were not given more authority; and now he answered the questions of the French with quiet sincerity. At eleven o'clock he was ready to call it an evening; but House and Wilson, willing to give their last breath in support of this all-important amendment, insisted that the session continue as long as anyone wished to talk.

It was near midnight when there was a pause and the President rose and gave the occasion its setting in the spiritual history of the race. A century before, he said, when the world was in the grip of tyranny, England had suggested to the United States that they take a step to keep this evil from the American continent. And so principles had been laid down that from that day to this had proved an effective barrier against absolutism. The Monroe Doctrine was the forerunner of the League of Nations. Absolutism had been ended by a world war that the United States had entered in accordance with principles that she always had honored. Now a document was being written that extended the Monroe Doctrine logically to the whole world. Was the United States to be refused recognition of her leadership in this glorious cause? Was there to be denied her, Wilson asked, the small gift of a few words which, after all, only state the undoubted fact that her policy for the past hundred years had been devoted to principles of liberty and independence? Indeed, were they not assembled at Paris to consecrate and extend the horizon of this document as a perpetual charter for all the world?

Americans who heard it thought this the most moving speech of the Peace Conference. It left the secretaries breathless, gasping with surprise and admiration, their pencils quiet in their hands and hardly a word set down. Afterward the President confessed to his colleagues that his effort should not be regarded as *ex tempore*. "To me at least," he said with a chuckle, "it had a very familiar ring. I was, or professed to be, a teacher of American history for twenty years, and rarely a month passed that I did not preach what the Monroe Doctrine meant to me, and now we are offering it to the world."

On the morning after the eloquent appeal to the commission, Wilson had his usual meeting with the council. It was a lovely spring day, and in the afternoon, above the city's park-lined avenues, a daredevil aviator was looping backward and forward under a clear blue sky. But the President had no time to get out of doors. Instead he breathed the fragrant air through an open window while Dr. Grayson stood foot to foot with him and, clasping his hands, pulled him to and fro. "Indoor golf," said Wilson whimsically when Baker interrupted the exercise.

In the evening, at the end of a full day, the President plunged into another stormy session with the League of Nations Commission. The winds of controversy whirled for hours around two Japanese proposals that were finally put aside. Then the delegates got down to the point on which Woodrow Wilson's political solvency seemed to hang in precarious balance. They had left the long meeting of the night before with the understanding that the reservation on the Monroe Doctrine should be attached not to the critical Article X but rather to Article XX, which dealt with obligations inconsistent with the terms of the Covenant. But now the French wanted to pile a nullifying reservation upon the reservation already agreed on.

Wilson protested immediately. If the French were to oppose the American amendment publicly, he warned, the effect on opinion in his country would be most unfortunate. He rejected the French redraft, and also a watered-down version that was so devoid of meaning that it seemed to confirm gossip that House had picked up during the day. The Colonel's network of intelligence had brought news that Bourgeois had confessed to an American friend that actually the French had cared nothing about the amendment on the Monroe Doctrine: they regarded it simply as a good thing to trade against. Therefore, when the President seemed momentarily disposed to yield, House suggested that the French could "go to Hell seven thousand feet deep." Finally Wilson declared their amendment defeated, and they gave notice that they would be heard from again at the plenary session.

When at last the meeting broke up, Wilson relieved the tension by saying that his mind refused to function after midnight and that whatever took the place of his mind was wholly unreliable. But this man who had just been ill held his own with the strenuous statesmen; and the strain put upon him was more than compensated by the feeling that at last they had found a formula that would make it possible for him to convert his own people and for Clemenceau to put the Covenant through the French Chamber. The reaction from the United States was quick and reassuring. "Monroe clause eminently satisfactory," Taft cabled; and Senator Hitchcock: "Congratulation on great success . . . You have done more than seemed possible. Sentiment for League has been much strengthened, opposition evidently diminished if not defeated."

The Monroe Doctrine reservation, House confided to his American colleagues, was "in the bag." Moreover, the President himself had quietly slipped into Article V a clause of far-reaching significance. Under this provision, the rule of unanimity that Wilson had found convenient in presiding over discussions in the commission was to be applied to all meetings of the League's Council and Assembly "except where otherwise expressly provided" in the Covenant. Thus each nation represented in the council was to have power to block action by a veto.

The public meeting on the 28th proved to be anticlimactic. Wilson rose to give explanations of changes that had been made in the Covenant, many of them against his best judgment and to reassure legalists. There seemed to be no fire, no grace, no lift left in him—simply grim, plodding devotion to The Word as it had been written. When he closed with "I now move the adoption of the Covenant," the applause merely rippled up to him.

Clemenceau then gave the floor to Bourgeois, and closed his eyes and masked his parchmentlike face. Wilson slumped in his chair, Balfour gazed at the ceiling; and the French delegate haltingly read a speech that they had heard a dozen times. After about ten minutes Bourgeois stopped for breath and probed into a pile of notes. Suddenly The Tiger pounced. Rapping sharply with his gavel, he announced loudly: "As I hear no objections, I declare that the conference has considered and adopted the revised Covenant."

House pooh-poohed the possibility that the League would be disowned in the United States; for in revising the Covenant they had taken care of most of the suggestions of Taft, Hughes, and Root. Moreover, a bulletin from the League to Enforce Peace reported sixty-four senators ready to ratify the Covenant, twenty doubtful, and only twelve opposed.

One of the twelve avowed enemies, however, was Henry Cabot Lodge, the man who had expressly warned Wilson not to do the thing that was now irrevocably done—tie the treaty into the Covenant with an umbilical cord. Fearing that his Republican colleagues might express pleasure at the revision of the Covenant, Lodge immediately sealed their lips with a telegram asking that opinion be reserved. He professed a desire to examine the Covenant carefully and said, ominously: "It is obvious that it will require further amendments if it is to promote peace and not endanger certain rights of the United States which should never be placed in jeopardy."

It was as the prophet had foreseen. Concessions to the Philistines at Washington, won from Europe with deep agony of soul and body, had begotten only demands for further change. Would the Congress, as Wilson had predicted in his speech to a joint session late in 1917, "feel the full strength of the tides that run now in the hearts and consciences of free men everywhere?" Would its conclusions "run with those tides"?

General Smuts put these questions in Olympian focus as he strode away from the plenary session at which the Covenant was adopted. Not the greatest man born of woman could have saved the Allies from their folly, in his opinion. Only the manliness and dogged will of a Woodrow Wilson could have carried through the Covenant of the League of Nations. The statesmen of Europe had thrown to the persistent prophet, as an innocent little sop, one of the greatest creative documents of the human race.

Colonel House, walking beside Smuts as they left the plenary session, looked into the noble face and sought out the steely eyes under the straight brows. The South African shrugged his shoulders, and then spoke: "The peace treaty may fade into oblivion—and that would be, I sometimes think, a merciful dispensation of a kind Providence—but the Covenant will stand—as sure as fate. It must and shall succeed because there is no other way to salvage the future of civilization."

CHAPTER XVI

THE PEACE IS SIGNED

THE ARK OF THE COVENANT was now built and dedicated. Woodrow Wilson had put into it American planks that were offered by Republicans and had set aside foreign timbers that seemed unsound. But the Ark was still high and dry. Before the League could be launched on the waters of strife that were inundating the earth, the treaty to which it was anchored must be firmly established.

Even while he had been fighting for revision of the Covenant in sessions of the League Commission, Wilson had been meeting almost daily with the inner council to consider many questions for which his Fourteen Points provided no adequate solution. In these sessions he had stayed both the grasping hands of aggrandizement and the raised fists of retribution, and he had softened the impact of the treaty on Germany's economy.[1]

On the advice of his counselors, he was "fighting shy" of economic involvement in Europe and was striving to keep his nation's purposes pure; but he took the risk of consenting to American representation on the commission that was to supervise German reparations, explaining that that body would "undoubtedly need an umpire."

On April 2, the day before he fell sick, he had spoken out against punishment of the Kaiser or any individual for starting the war. Heretofore, he explained, the responsibility for international crimes had been solely collective. It would be unfair, and contrary to judicial tradition, to place the responsibility now on an individual. One could not act on a principle before it was acknowledged as law. "I wish to doom Germany to the execration of history," he explained, "and to do nothing that would permit it to be said that we have gone beyond our right, in a just cause." Lansing had reminded him of strong sentiment among his own people for punishment of German leaders, and he had replied that he did not care what the people thought. His own sense of justice seemed adequate authority.

[1] It was decided that before May 1, 1921, Germany should pay—in cash, commodities, and bonds—fifteen billion dollars, of which bonds could make up at least two-thirds. The total amount that she might be required to pay was estimated at between thirty-two and forty-four billions. The Reparations Commission of the Peace Conference was to continue to supervise the settlement and could recommend abatements or require the issue of more bonds up to Germany's capacity.

When Lloyd George and Clemenceau insisted that history would condemn them if they did not punish crimes without precedent—such as those of Germany's submarines—Wilson rebelled against this obvious appeal to his personal experience. "As for myself," he observed, "every time I read documents about atrocities, I saw red and took care not to reach a decision in those moments, but always to be in a position to judge and act according to reason. . . . You think me unfeeling, but I struggle constantly against emotion, and I am obliged to bring pressure on myself to keep my judgment steady."

Clemenceau would not accept this. "Nothing is done except with emotion," he insisted. "Was not Jesus Christ moved by passion the day that he chased the merchants from the Temple?" And Lloyd George tried another line of argument to which he thought the American peculiarly vulnerable: "If we want the League of Nations to have, in the future, the power that we desire for it, it ought to show from the beginning that it is able to punish crime."

But the fibers of the prophet's morality would not ravel. "I think as you do about the crimes committed," he said, "but I wish that we ourselves might act in such a way as to satisfy our consciences." [2] Finally he drew up a formula that his own conscience could approve and his colleagues signed it.

His morality intruded also—quietly but forcefully—into arguments among his colleagues about territorial claims in Asia Minor that were based on three secret pacts that had been made in 1916 and 1917.[3] House thought that he talked too much on matters in which the United States had no immediate interest; but the prophet had declared himself responsible for everything that had to do with the peace of the world, and so he delivered another little sermon.

Asking whether the secret treaties provided a plan that would work, he suggested that the people concerned be consulted. He made it clear that, for his part, he was quite disinterested, since the United States did not want anything in Turkey. To be sure, it had been put to him by T. E. Lawrence and Emir Feisal that he should approach his own people on the question of taking a mandate for an independent Syrian state. He intended to try to persuade them, and felt that his nation must take

[2] Mantoux, *Délibérations*, I, 122–24. Also Swem notes taken on the *George Washington*, December, 1918.

[3] These were probably in Wilson's mind on Dec. 1, 1917, when he referred in a cable to House to "plans for division of territory such as have been contemplated in Asia Minor." The text of one of the three treaties (the Sykes-Picot Agreement) had been sent to Wilson by Balfour on May 18, 1917. Frank L. Polk's diary records under Oct. 11, 1918, that Barclay, British chargé at Washington, said that there had been three secret treaties made during the war regarding the disposal of Turkey and that it was a question how binding they would be. "Mr. Barclay explained the whole situation to the President," Polk wrote.

the responsibilities, as well as the benefits, of the League of Nations. Nevertheless, there was great antipathy in the United States to the assumption of the duties of trusteeship. Even the Philippines were regarded as something hot in the hand that should be dropped.

Having raised these questions, Wilson proposed an American method of solution. He suggested that the fittest men that could be obtained should form an inter-Allied commission to go to Syria, extending their inquiries, if led to do so, beyond the confines of that region. The body should be made up of an equal number of French, British, Italian, and American representatives. In his desire for objectivity, he proposed to send not experts on the region under consideration, but men without contact with Syria, educational or military. He would send them with carte blanche to tell the facts as they found them. This would convince the world that the conference had tried to do all it could to find the most scientific basis for a settlement. To make peace quickly, it was necessary now only to tell Turkey that she was to have nothing. The question of mandates could be settled later, under the League.

His plan accepted, the President told Ray Stannard Baker that he wished to appoint "the two ablest Americans now in Europe" to the proposed commission. Charles R. Crane and President Henry Churchill King of Oberlin College were chosen.

By April 14 both the revision of the Covenant and the discussion of the specific settlements had progressed far enough so that The Four felt that they should issue a public statement inviting Germany to send delegates to Versailles to receive the treaty of peace. Wilson was asked to compose this paper.[4] It announced that there would be no interruption in the discussion of pending matters, and priority would be given to consideration of questions affecting Italy. This promise was necessary to gain Orlando's consent to the summoning of the Germans; for the premier feared that the conference might rush to a close without satisfying Italian claims.

In fixing the boundaries of Italy the council was faced by two commitments that were based on irreconcilable principles. The Fourteen Points had promised Serbia—now merged with neighbors in Yugoslavia—"free and secure access" to the Adriatic Sea and had decreed that Italy's boundaries be readjusted "along clearly recognizable lines of nationality." On the other hand, the secret Treaty of London, signed in

---

[4] In protest against the refusal of the council to award the left bank of the Rhine to France, Marshal Foch at first refused to deliver this message to the Germans. When Wilson heard of this defiance of civil authority, he remarked: "If I were Clemenceau, he'd never have a chance to refuse again. I would know what to do with him."

1915 by Britain and France to bring Italy into the war, recognized the right of the Italians to a frontier that would include many alien people. This pact did not grant them the port of Fiume, however. Reminding Orlando of that fact in a session of The Four on April 3, Wilson suggested that it be made a free city, without customs link with any neighboring state.

Meanwhile the people of Italy, conceiving that they had fought to "liberate" their compatriots in Fiume, agitated for annexation of the city. But Wilson saw nothing but megalomania in the rising popular clamor. Already he had conceded to Orlando what the Treaty of London had given in the Trentino.[5] Now the Italians seemed to want the moon, and the planets likewise.

Confronted by divergent advice from his counselors,[6] Wilson gave hours of his time to the problem. He determined to grant to Italy all that his concept of justice would allow. But at the same time he instructed Norman Davis to hold up an advance of fifty million dollars to Italy for a few days, "until the air clears—if it does." Italy was particularly vulnerable to closure of the "financial tap," House said to newsmen who might be counted on to pass the word around.[7]

Commencing on April 19—the day on which Sir Maurice Hankey began to sit regularly with the inner council and to keep formal records that minimized emotional tensions [8]—The Three argued for hours with

[5] The Treaty of London is one of the secret treaties mentioned on p. 131 above. In the winter of 1918, Sir William Wiseman told Balfour that Wilson would like to know his thought on the treaty. On his first day at Paris, Wilson had asked for a copy of this troublesome document. When House had remarked that there might be substance to the Italian claim, Wilson replied: "Then let them plant their case in the full sun of publicity. If there is anything in it, then it will grow into a great cause. If there is nothing in it, then it will wither away."

Though Wilson had been told that the Trentino region that was promised to Italy by the Treaty of London included some 240,000 people who spoke German, he had agreed on Jan. 30, in order to get Orlando's approval of the Covenant, to the transfer of the district to Italian sovereignty. (See p. 255 above.)

In May, 1919, Wilson explained to Charles Seymour that the giving away of the Tyrol was "based on insufficient study." On May 28, Wilson told Ray Stannard Baker that he regretted the decision on the Tyrol, that he had been ignorant of the situation when he made it. Asked whether he could not change it, he said: "I am afraid not: but those Tyrolese Germans are sturdy people—and I have no doubt that they will soon be able themselves to change it." R. S. Baker's Journal, May 28, 1919.

[6] Wilson's conclusions, both then and later, followed closely the recommendation of his specialists on the Adriatic region. Sometimes he felt that he was not closely enough in touch with the specialists; but some of them felt that he did not consult them sufficiently. Mezes, Miller, and other American delegates gave more weight to Italy's need for security and considerations of general policy and sought by talking with Italian delegates to reach ground for compromise.

[7] Wilson wrote to Norman Davis on April 15 regarding credits other than those to Italy: "I think that it is perfectly legitimate that we should ask ourselves before each of these credits is extended, whether our colleagues are cooperating with us in a way that is satisfactory."

[8] House implored the President not to continue to meet with the clever premiers with no one of his own staff at hand to make a record; but Wilson was content when Sir Maurice Hankey, able secretary of the British delegation, began in mid-April to keep a *procès-verbal*.

the Italian statesmen. Orlando pleaded long and passionately, invoking the principle of self-determination. Wilson could not resist the temptation to ask whether New York City was claimed because of its Italian population.

Lloyd George made an eloquent effort to mollify Orlando, recalling that Italy had carried out her part of the Treaty of London "in blood, treasure and sacrifice" and reaffirming Britain's intention to fulfill her bond. At this, Orlando began to gulp. Getting up from his chair, he walked to a window and stood there and shook with great sobs. Woodrow Wilson rose and went to him, took his hand, assured him that he had played his role well but that they were all responsible to consider every claim and to be just to everyone. Then the President led the premier back to his chair, feeling as if he were comforting a small boy and ought to take out his handkerchief and dry the tears. The Three assured Orlando of their affection for him; and he thought them all generous, even Wilson, who promised him everything except what was absolutely necessary to protect his position as premier. If they were fond of him now, he said, they perhaps would be fonder still in a week, when they might be confronted by the swashbuckling d'Annunzio.

Nevertheless, the President would not give Fiume to Italy; nor would he shift his boundary eastward in Istria. He was ready to crack the whip of public opinion over the heads of the Italian statesmen. On the morning of Easter Sunday, April 20, he typed a manifesto that he wanted Orlando to read to his parliament, and in the afternoon he sent a copy to Balfour. His colleagues counseled delay, and the President agreed not to publish immediately.

On the 23rd Lloyd George and Clemenceau, fearful that Wilson might provoke an irreparable breach with Italy, introduced a draft of a letter to Orlando that denied him Fiume, in accord with the Treaty of London. Thus a way was open to the President to get from under and shift the burden of opposing Italy to his allies. This would be smart diplomacy, but it would give sanction to Italian possession of islands and Dalmatian mainland that American experts assigned to Yugoslavia.

Wilson thought that the time had come to make a dramatic stand. He feared that if the Yugoslavs felt that injustice was done them, a path would be opened to Russian influence and the forming of a Slavic bloc hostile to Western Europe. He reminded the council that the Slavic people had behind them the immense reservoir of Asia's population—eight hundred million people whose attitude and destiny would be the great problem of the future.

To General Bliss, one of his Americans who had been pressing him to act, the President explained that, though his colleagues in the council thought it unwise for him to publish his manifesto, he was standing out for his "constitutional rights." In a tense session of The Three on April 22 he said: "Let me publish my paper. It could only clear the air." And Lloyd George replied: "Yes, like a tempest." [9]

Wilson insisted on releasing the document. Appearing in the press in the evening of April 23, it reminded the Italians that it had been agreed that the peacemaking was to rest on well-defined principles of right and justice. Wilson explained that under those ideals as well as under the Treaty of London, Fiume must go to Yugoslavia; but he assured Italy that adequate guarantees would be given, under international sanction, "of equal and equitable treatment of all racial or national minorities," and that the eastern coast of Italy would be made secure by the reduction of armaments and fortifications. America, he reminded, was linked in blood as well as in affection with the Italian people. "She trusts Italy, and in her trust believes that Italy will ask nothing of her that cannot be made unmistakably consistent with . . . sacred obligations."

The manifesto reverberated through the world and shook the apathy of public opinion toward a conference that seemed to have burrowed underground and disappeared from view. The conflict of the new diplomacy against the old had never been highlighted more dramatically. [10]

Orlando immediately struck back in justification of his position. He characterized the President's message as an ill-timed precipitation of a public crisis while diplomatic talks were still going on. Offended by

[9] Mantoux, *Délibérations,* I, 338. On May 2, Wilson recalled to Lloyd George and Clemenceau that it had been "agreed at first" that their letter would be published the day after his. *Ibid.*, I, 453. On this point Lord Hankey comments, after a review of the minutes and his personal contemporary notes: "If there was any understanding, which I do not think there was, it must have been reached informally outside of the formal conversations." Lord Hankey to the writer, Dec. 24, 1953.

The British excused themselves to Wilson for not publishing the Anglo-French letter by explaining that after reading the President's paper, Balfour had conferred with Clemenceau and they had agreed that they could add nothing to Wilson's splendid exposition of the case.

Wilson resented a statement by Poincaré that added to the impression that the United States was isolated. He was fearful that both House and Lloyd George would make efforts at reconciliation that would make him appear unreasonably hard. But House felt that the prime minister had given the Italians "hope where there is none." Moreover, he thought that his wife's brother-in-law, Sidney Mezes—the titular head of The Inquiry—had been too prone to compromise, that every time Mezes had dined with the Italians he was willing to give them another island.

[10] The powerful labor federation of Paris sent a delegation to Wilson to express their approval, and wired their views to their Italian brethren. Faithful Americans took courage from the manifesto. "I have never been so proud of you," Tumulty cabled on April 24. The President's stand was approved even by the Republicans, Polk reported. But Philistines made what capital they could of the message. Henry Cabot Lodge wrote to the Italians of Boston to assure them that, in his view, Fiume was as vital to Italy as New Orleans to the United States. The French and British press, though publishing Wilson's appeal, found it so foreign to the thought of the Old World that it was covered with a dust of ridicule and neglect. "Wild-west diplomacy," the London *Morning Post* asserted. "President Wilson has come among the allies like a rich uncle. They have accepted his manners out of respect of his means."

Wilson's implication that his people could submit to a will other than its own, he felt that his self-respect demanded withdrawal from Paris, the calling of his parliament, and the re-establishment of his authority.

Wilson not only did not oppose Orlando's departure; he encouraged it. At the meeting of the council that both attended on the 24th, the President protested that he had never thought of going behind Orlando's back. He had merely wanted the premier to know the American position. He stood ready to discuss any aspect of the question, to go over the ground a hundred times if necessary. He suggested that the premier tell his constituents the truth, say simply that Britain and France were bound by the Treaty of London and the United States by certain principles, and then ask his parliament: "Have I the authority to go back to Paris and settle as I can?"

Before starting for the railroad station, on the 24th, the Italian premier was given a copy of the letter that had been signed by Lloyd George and Clemenceau, confirming Wilson's views on Fiume. Orlando therefore went away informed that The Three stood together; but before departing he persuaded Lloyd George not to have the Anglo-French letter published.

Time and again Wilson pleaded with his colleagues to extricate him from his apparent isolation by publishing their letter. He argued that by bolting from the conference, Italy had broken the Treaty of London and therefore was no longer entitled to the rewards promised by that pact. They debated for days and while they talked news came that Italy had sent a warship to Smyrna, had thirty thousand men in the Balkans, and was terrorizing the inhabitants of islands that wished to join with Greece. On May 3 Wilson was notified by his embassy at Rome that anything might happen, that no Italian government could yield Fiume and hope to stand.

Clemenceau, zealously guarding the unanimity of The Three, seconded Wilson's plea for the publication of the Anglo-French letter. But Lloyd George held back cannily, protecting the frail thread by which he hoped to mend the breach. If they did not stir public feeling any more than it already had been roused by Wilson's manifesto, perhaps the Italian premier would return in a mood for compromise. On the contrary, if they published the letter, against Orlando's wishes, Italy might send another man who would be not only more imperialistic, but pro-German as well.

Lloyd George's clever argument prevailed. Wilson tried to catch him in a contradiction, but the prime minister's wits were too nimble. When Wilson threatened to withdraw, the Welshman let him know that the feeling was growing among Europeans, and especially in London, that they were being bullied by the United States.[11] If this sentiment were not handled with care, Lloyd George warned, it might put an end to the League of Nations. Again and again he came back to a formula for compromise. When his policy was justified by the return of Orlando, the Adriatic question was driven into the background—a menacing cloud that constantly shadowed deliberations on other dark issues.[12]

On the morning of April 21, when the debate with Italy was approaching a crisis and the council could hardly afford to risk alienating Japan, Viscount Chinda went to the President's house and insisted that Japan's secret treaties with Britain and France be fulfilled to the letter, in respect both to Shantung Province and to the Pacific islands. After years of galling inferiority the island empire had emerged from the war as the most powerful nation of the Far East, and her ego was demanding recognition.

Wilson already was almost as unpopular in Japan as he had become in Italy. He had made enemies by supporting the British Empire in a minority veto of a "race equality" amendment to the Covenant that Makino had pressed. Moreover, odium fell upon him because the United States had forbidden the immigration of Japanese and also had denied them an outlet in Siberia for their dense population.

As Wilson's prophetic ardor had been dampened by unresponsiveness and misunderstanding, his wisdom in diplomacy had grown. He had begun to show awareness that the United States, like other nations, could not afford to be completely disinterested, that she would do well to think realistically of security and diplomatic rapport. He did not wish to interfere with treaties, he said. The war had been undertaken partly in order to establish the sanctity of treaties. Nevertheless, there were

[11] Lloyd George was told that some of his men at Paris were "fed up with Wilson" and "tired of playing second fiddle"; and he noted that America, which disclaimed self-interest, was to get from Germany twice as much merchant shipping as she lost. Geddes was complaining to him that the Americans were doing their best to appropriate the trade of the world "while Wilson was doing the big bow-wow." "Well, that is what they always say about Great Britain," the prime minister reminded his men. "I am one of the few people who think Wilson honest. . . . Occasionally he has to deviate for political reasons." Riddell, *Lord Riddell's Intimate Diary,* April 23 and 27, 1919.

[12] *See* p. 372 below. The Adriatic question remained undecided through the remaining weeks of the Peace Conference. Wilson told House that his mind was open to possible solutions as long as they did not give Fiume to the Italians; and the American experts worked diligently for agreement between Italians and Yugoslavs. The Colonel, feeling that the President was bungling the negotiations, very nearly succeeded in arranging a compromise, but his efforts broke down when the Italians demanded eastern Istria and the Yugoslavs and the President refused this. On May 18, Wilson threatened to send word to the Italians that he would make no further concession whatever.

Meanwhile Italy's passions ran unchecked. On June 17, Ambassador Page reported from Rome to the State Department: "A leaning toward German reaffiliation grows more apparent." By the treaty concluded with Yugoslavia at Rapallo on Nov. 12, 1920, Fiume was made an independent city and Italy got more in Istria than she had asked of Wilson.

cases, he felt, where treaties ought not to have been entered into. There was a lot of combustible material in China, he remarked, and if flames were put to it the fire could not be quenched, for China had a population of four hundred million people. As for Japan, he said that he knew from experience that her statesmen were "very ingenious in interpreting treaties."

Makino declared that Japan wanted an "open door" in China, that there had been precedent for Japan's twenty-one demands in an era of imperialism. The Japanese were not bluffing, Wilson knew, and would go home unless given what he thought they should not have. He could not break the legal bonds by which Britain, France, and China were bound. Moreover—hardest reality of all—the Japanese were in possession in Shantung; and who was going to use force to drive them out? But he made an eloquent appeal to Chinda and Makino, in the presence of the Chinese delegates. He warned that the peace of the Far East depended on mutual confidence between the two nations. He invited the Japanese to share the spirit of "his missionaries," and to carry out *all* of their obligations to China.

To the Chinese delegates, who were handicapped by political strife at home and among themselves, Wilson explained patiently that he had urged the Japanese, without avail, to put the leased property in Shantung under an international trusteeship.

The Chinese spokesmen were expert at winning the friendship of the American delegates. They accused the Japanese of behaving badly since they had taken over the German rights and of using dire threats to force China to keep their one-sided agreement secret. At the same time clever Chinese publicists were skillfully stimulating anti-Japanese feeling outside the council; and in this they were aided by Japan's brutality in suppressing a revolt in Korea.

Again Woodrow Wilson's heart tugged against his head. He was bombarded by emotional appeals from his own people. Tumulty tempted him to make political capital of the issue by publishing another manifesto like that to the Italian people. American colleagues whose advice he sought could see only the moral black and white of the question. "We shall be sowing dragon's teeth," General Bliss warned. Lansing felt that the Japanese threat to withdraw from Paris was a bluff and their claim to rights in Shantung quite bogus.

The question seemed the most baffling that the President had met at Paris. He recognized, he explained to Lloyd George on April 22, an apparent contradiction between his attitude toward Japan and that toward Italy. It stemmed from the fact that China still existed, and Austria-Hungary did not. But actually another difference between the two cases was apparent to him; Italy had consented to the League Covenant, and Japan was withholding hers and trading on it. "As for Japan," Wilson said, "one must do what is necessary so that she will enter the League of Nations." [13]

On April 24 the Japanese presented a peremptory demand. The next day, when Wilson tried "to take the chains off China" by suggesting that all powers renounce their extraterritorial rights, Lloyd George objected. Wilson told his family afterward that sometimes the statesmen seemed no better than bandits.

On the 28th Ray Stannard Baker, after an evening of talk with Chinese statesmen and their American friends, went to the President to plead China's case. Wilson listened with an intensity that was disconcerting. Finally he said: "Baker, the difficulty is not with the facts of the controversy, but with the politics of it." The easy way would be to decide against the Japanese and go home. But there might be an alliance of Russia, Germany,[14] Italy, and Japan, and a new balance of power; and doubtless Japan would go more deeply into Shantung. What, then, would become of the great cause of collective security which, quite obviously now, included the security of the United States?

This question was put to the President by Colonel House, the only fellow commissioner who had a divided mind. At the urging of Lloyd George, House advised the President to accept a pledge of good behavior that the Japanese gave orally to Balfour.[15] But the conscience of Woodrow Wilson would not subside. Was there not some way out, it kept asking, some course that would be fair to Japan and China and true to the Covenant? In the council on the 29th he lectured the Japanese. Bearing down hard, he pressed them to make minor concessions.

In the evening, consulting no one, Wilson drew up a one-page statement about the settlement finally reached. He intended it for public use, but not as a quotation from him. Permitting the release of the substance of his decision, he asked Baker to explain his distressed thinking to the Chinese. To keep Japan within the League of Nations and to prevent a

---

[13] Mantoux, *Délibérations*, I, 336.

[14] During the war Wilson had been aware of rumors of Japanese-German negotiations, but he had never found any substantial foundation for them. However, his adviser, E. T. Williams, felt that the Japanese were negotiating with the Germans behind the scenes and feared that Japan might join Germany in an attempt to control Russia. Fifield, *op. cit.*, p. 221 n.

[15] On the 28th Lloyd George called House aside and asked him to put Wilson into a more amenable frame of mind toward Japan's claims. Balfour recorded for the council, in writing, conversations between himself and the Japanese in which they agreed to carry out the policy of the open door "in the spirit as in the letter" and to give back the leased territory to China, retaining only the economic rights held by Germany. Wilson explained to McCormick, on July 5, 1919, that this commitment was made to Balfour orally because the Japanese felt that to sign a statement of this sort would be to admit that their good faith had been questioned. Japan justified the confidence of the British statesmen by concluding a Sino-Japanese agreement in 1922 that resulted in more friendly relations and the return of Kiaochow to China.

separate alliance of that nation with the enemies of democracy, he was willing to risk denunciation by friends. Baker saw an heroic figure emerging. "He is the only Man here," he jotted in his journal.

"I find a general disposition," Wilson wrote in his statement for the public, "to look with favor upon the proposal that at an early date through the mediation of the League of Nations all extraordinary foreign rights in China and all spheres of influence should be abrogated by the common consent of all nations concerned."

It was the League that offered the best hope for eventual reconciliation with Russia, too. The menace of bolshevism was brought home to Wilson on May Day, when social disorders came almost to his own door. Wearing caps and little red boutonnières with sprigs of white lilies of the valley, workmen thronged the streets and shouted *"A bas Clemenceau,"* *"Vive Wilson."* His message to the Italian people had made him once again their hope for deliverance from the scourge of war.

But liberal journals were criticizing him for yielding to Japanese imperialism as vehemently as they had applauded his opposition to Italian ambitions; and young Chinese agitators were denouncing him as a traitor. "Somehow or other," House mused, "the President is always put in a false light." Though distressed when ladies of his household rode through the streets on May Day, Wilson shrugged off physical danger, and his bodyguards were as hard put to protect his person as was the Colonel to safeguard his prestige.

The May Day riots kept alive the fear that had been roused by the March coup of Communists in Hungary. The possibility of intervention in Russia was still being discussed by The Three, as the pendulum swung between war and peace in Eastern Europe. By April 20 Lloyd George had veered toward use of force; but the President told him point-blank that he had lost patience, that every time Russian conservatives had been given a subsidy they had "backed away from their objective." The President directed that Ambassador Morris go from Tokyo to Omsk and see Kolchak and find out what sort of man he was and what motives controlled him.

Unable to get a report from Morris, Wilson went along with the policy of the Allies; for it was clear that The Three must stand together and avoid giving substance to Lenin's charge that they represented "imperialist powers" that devour each other. Nevertheless, he continued to work to get foreign forces out of northern Russia. "The withdrawal of our troops should be in no way interrupted or delayed," he wrote to Bliss on June 10. All of the American units were evacuated by autumn. Thus Woodrow Wilson gave up hope of doing more for Russia than saving her from foreign invasion. The people should have economic aid without political interference, he told Hoover, but no foreign body could give help that the Bolsheviki would accept as disinterested. In the long run the world would be less distressed if the Russians solved their own political problems in their own way. "We cannot rescue Russia without having a united Europe," Wilson had said in February to his national committeemen at Washington. ". . . We may have to go home without composing these great territories [of Russia], but if we go home with a League of Nations, there will be some power to solve this most perplexing problem."

All rational paths seemed to lead in the end to the League. Problems of reparations, of boundaries, of colonies, of social revolution—all required a supranational code of justice evolving out of a parliament of mankind. It was not only the large nations that were offending against the common good. Even little Belgium—the very land in which martyred Nurse Cavell had proclaimed that "patriotism is not enough"—sought special favors. The pressures of national greed that assailed him would have seemed to Wilson to be crucifying human hopes for peace had not the Covenant been adopted by the plenary session on April 28 and given first place in the treaty that was to be presented to the Germans.

During the first week of May, many details had to be settled to make the treaty ready for presentation to the Germans. However, the Italian question took care of itself, temporarily. Orlando rejoined the council on the 7th, and the President said quite casually: "You will have the same chair as always." Wilson had yielded nothing, but, as Lloyd George had surmised, Italy could not afford to abstain from signing the treaty and forfeit her claims under the Treaty of London. The Belgians, too, after concessions to their demands, reluctantly agreed to sign. Only the Chinese were still standing aside.

As the clauses of the document were edited, Wilson was vigilant to scotch "jokers" that might creep into the official text. The Allies were suspected of tampering with the draft in order to bind the United States permanently to economic obligations in Europe.

Wilson was bedeviled also, during the first week of May, by responsibility under his pledge of "open" arrival at the covenant of peace. Lloyd George had been asserting stoutly that it would be foolish to let the small nations discuss, much less amend, the terms on which the council agreed. If the little fellows didn't like the treaty, they needn't sign, said the ministers of Britain and France. Prevailing against this view, however, Wilson effected the calling of a plenary session at the Quai d'Orsay on May 6, at which the terms of the treaty were read. It was a secret meeting, but at least the official spokesmen of the world's minorities were given a chance to comment.

Hours were spent, too, in setting up a plan for release of the huge document—the longest treaty ever framed. Clemenceau pointed out that if they did not give the entire text to the world, the Germans would; but Wilson supported Lloyd George's view that, since the document was not final, only a summary should be supplied to the press.

All of these perplexities took their toll. On May 3, when Baker went to the President for his news story, Wilson seemed "so beaten out that he could remember only with an effort what the council had done in the forenoon." A man due for a complete breakdown, he appeared to his associates; yet they knew it was no use to tell him to let go. More and more, he was demanding from those close to him an unquestioning loyalty that would build confidence in himself and his cause. Since his illness he had withdrawn further and further. Once, to be sure, Cary Grayson took him to Bernard Baruch's house at St. Cloud for luncheon. He was persuaded, too, to take an evening off and attend a musical show, and one day their afternoon drive took them past such idyllic fields as Millet had painted. But he preferred to stay at home with those whom he could trust, and pray over the great issues on which the peace of the twentieth century was poised. He had obtained a strongbox for his most vital papers, and held the secrets of state more closely than ever in his own head. Evenings, to rest his mind, he played cards, saying to the ladies: "I am afraid you will always think of me as an old man playing solitaire."

On May 7, the fourth anniversary of the sinking of the *Lusitania*, Wilson motored out to Versailles to meet the enemy whom he had been fighting but had never seen. He dreaded coming face to face with the men of Germany's new order, and had tried to think of some way of avoiding it. Their delegation, more than two hundred strong, included a manufacturer of poisoned gases; and it was headed by the foreign minister, Count Brockdorff-Rantzau—only recently a servant of the Kaiser's government.

The French had set the stage with traditional genius. This was their day of vengeance, just and sweet. Sunshine flooded the room in which the participants took their seats. Clemenceau sat grim-visaged at the center of the main table, Wilson at his right, Lloyd George at his left. At exactly three o'clock a functionary proclaimed: "Messieurs les Plénipotentiaires Allemandes!" Everyone stood in funereal silence as the Germans entered and stalked to the places set apart.

Clemenceau rifled a few sentences at them, stern, almost harsh. "It is neither the time nor the place for superfluous words," he said. The observations of the German delegates were to be submitted in writing within fifteen days.

The squat old Tiger stood up as he spoke. But Brockdorff-Rantzau—tall, spare, black-clad, his face deathly pale and perspiring—merely leaned forward in his big leather chair, reached for some papers, then, still seated, began to talk. His bad manners accentuated the prejudice that his audience bore against him and his kind. Admitting his country's helplessness, he said defiantly: "It is demanded of us that we shall confess ourselves to be the only ones guilty of the war. Such a confession in my mouth will be a lie." The last sentence sizzled with bitterness.

When he alluded to the Allied blockade of Germany and ascribed to it the death of "hundred of thousands of noncombatants," Lloyd George fidgeted and broke an ivory paper knife in his hands. Clemenceau's face turned red with suppressed anger; he tapped the table, then turned to his British colleague and whispered biting comments. Wilson, toying with a pencil with which he seemed about to make notes, joined in the conversation *sotto voce*. However, when the German referred to his principles as binding upon the parties to the peace and promised to examine the treaty with these ideals in mind, Wilson leaned forward on his desk, gazed intently at the count, and shifted a little in his chair. He felt his blood rushing to his head. He knew that to get a League of Nations he had sacrificed many of his ideals.

Walking out of the historic meeting he said: "What abominable manners! . . . The Germans are really a stupid people. They always do the wrong thing. They always did the wrong thing during the war—that's why I am here. They don't understand human nature. This is the most tactless speech I have ever heard. It will set the whole world against them."

The treaty that was presented to the Germans at Versailles on May 7 seemed to Wilson to fall far short of his ideal concept of justice. "If I were a German," he said, "I think I should never sign it." Yet he hoped fervently that they would sign, if for no other reason than that he could be free then to go home.

He had shrewdly analyzed the plight of the enemy. He knew that their delegates, who represented a very unstable government, would have to consider each of the terms to decide whether it could be accepted without their being unseated. If they should be turned out, a weaker ministry doubtless would replace them. Hence the problem was one of dynamics. One must deal with the action of forces in a body that was in unstable equilibrium.

The treaty would hit the German economy hard, not only by depriving the people of property and of opportunities abroad, but by compelling them to open their own country to the enterprise of foreigners. The fact must be faced that Germany could not pay reparations unless she had a balance of trade in her favor. It would be ineffective to fine her unless she could pay the fine. "We ought to see that Germany could put herself in a position where she could be punished," Wilson said to the council.

The privilege of protest was exercised almost immediately by the Germans. It seemed to their spokesmen as if they were being committed to economic slavery for as long a time as the conquerors might set. "President Wilson is a hypocrite," Chancellor Scheidemann declared, "and the Versailles Treaty is the vilest crime in history." Their very first note of protest insisted that the terms were intolerable, impractical, and unfaithful to the "peace of right" that had been agreed on before the Armistice.

But Wilson was not moved. He felt that a submissive public opinion lurked beneath the official complaints. At the behest of the council, he drafted a retort. Asserting that the treaty had been drawn with constant thought of his principles, he wrote: "The Council can admit no discussion of their right to insist upon the terms of the peace substantially as drafted. They can consider only such practical suggestions as the German plenipotentiaries may have to submit."

More irritating than the expected dissents of the enemy were the criticisms of American delegates. The President was set upon by liberals whose disappointment in the shortcomings of the peace terms he himself shared. Ray Stannard Baker was in a quandary, and tempted to "go to the hills and nurse . . . happy plans for the human race." But Wilson held him true, and Baker concluded that the alternative to accepting the treaty was anarchy. There were others, though, whom the prophet could not persuade. "Apparently he wants no help," one complained. "He never does," echoed another. Bullitt resigned on May 17. Several young liberals in the American delegation wrote letters of protest and offered to go home; and in June two of these resigned. Lansing and General Bliss, who had not forgiven the President for his decision on Shantung, were giving comfort to the dissenters.

Herbert Hoover felt that the economic consequences of the treaty alone would pull down all Europe. When Hoover denounced many of the treaty's articles in words that he later characterized as "over-vigorous," Wilson took personal offense, flashed back angrily, and did not again invite this able adviser into his inner councils. It seemed to Hoover that the President's mind had lost resiliency during his severe illness.

On May 22 word reached the President that Smuts and another British commissioner would not sign the treaty and that Lansing and Bliss were thinking of withholding their signatures.[16] The draft of the document, read as a whole for the first time by many of the delegates, seemed to suffer from lack of coordination between various parts that had been composed separately. There were inconsistencies, and certain terms made it difficult for other terms to be carried out.

The President himself, however, was less perturbed than his advisers by the shortcomings of the settlement. He had faith in the League as a means of rectifying maladjustments. Moreover, his own people had not objected to the treaty's terms and Tumulty had cabled that they would not approve any softness toward the enemy. Wilson seemed very conscious now of his position at home; the new Republican-dominated Congress began its sessions on May 19.

House, deriving comfort from John Morley's saying that the world's turmoil was not due to the realists but to "the tireless and often thoughtless activities of . . . *perfectabilitarians*," went to the President during May with pleas for concessions to Italian sentiment. He was as distressed by his friend's intransigence as was Wilson by the Colonel's importunities. House's friends among the journalists were embarrassing the Colonel again by immoderate praise. Wickham Steed wrote, in an editorial published April 6: "During their [Wilson and Lloyd George's] absence Colonel House, who has never found a difficulty in working with his colleagues because he is a selfless man with no personal axe to grind, brought matters rapidly forward. The delay that has occurred since the return of President Wilson and Lloyd George has been due chiefly to the upsetting of the good work done in their absence."

Mrs. Wilson read this and discussed it with Dr. Grayson, who suggested that it was typical of publicity inspired by the Colonel's staff. When she confronted House with it, he was embarrassed and anxious that Wilson should not see it.[17] Edith Wilson, who was not slow to

[16] This rumor reached Wilson through Hoover and McCormick. The President tried to hold Lansing's loyalty by writing to welcome him back from a trip to London: "We have missed you very much," he said. He did not believe that his Americans would refuse to sign and asked McCormick to sound out Lansing. The latter was found to be ready to sign but "a bit sore at not being consulted more." In the end, Smuts signed the treaty and protested publicly against its terms.

[17] On April 23, 1924, House recorded in his diary that, though the President had never expressed resentment, the Steed article "was one of the real grievances of the Wilsons." "I knew nothing of the article until it was published, and had as little to do with it as the man in the moon," the Colonel wrote. By printing stories of differences between Wilson and House, the press poured oil on the fire that Steed had helped to start. Auchincloss recorded in his diary on March 28, 1919, that the editorials in the *Daily Mail* since Jan. 1 often were "part and parcel" of his discussions with Wickham Steed.

apprise her husband of presidential ambitions that she saw or imagined in the hearts of his staff, had done nothing to check the suspicions that had been aroused by the Colonel's personal attachment to Clemenceau, his overplaying of the role of stage manager, his bestowal of favor on relatives lacking in tact, his advocacy of concessions to the Allies that he thought necessary to hasten the making of peace, to prevent anarchy, and to save the League of Nations, and his assumption of responsibility for saving the President from an isolation that threatened to shut out political realities and to separate Wilson from press and people.

Now she told her husband of House's reaction to the objectionable editorial. She had previously said to him: "If Colonel House had only stood firm while you were away, none of this would have to be done over. I think he is a perfect jellyfish." And the President had replied: "Well, God made jellyfish, so, as Shakespeare said about a man, therefore let him pass, and don't be too hard on House. It takes a pretty stiff spinal column to stand against the elements centered here." Now the President's first thought was for the feelings of the Colonel. "I would as soon doubt your loyalty as his," he said to his wife. "All this is another attempt to misrepresent things at home." [18]

After the episode of the Steed editorial, House did not go to the Wilson home except for business meetings at which others were present. Without personal intimacy he could no longer insinuate realistic political advice that the President did not care to hear. As the prophet went into the last days of his fight for the ideals that both held dear, he did not avail himself often of the help of the faithful ruling elder who had established Wilson's Points as the basis of the Armistice, who often had reconciled the views of his chief with those of Allied statesmen, who had removed many a hurdle in the path of the League Covenant, and whom European statesmen looked upon as America's most effective diplomatic negotiator.[19] Yet on May 6, when House thought of going home, Wilson told him that he must wait until the treaty was signed and that he was to represent the United States on the Mandates Commission of the League of Nations.

The President himself was cut off from further constructive work on

---

[18] E. B. Wilson, *My Memoir*, p. 252.

[19] The President's increasing dependence on his doctor after the April illness had resulted in Grayson's giving political advice and acting as an intermediary in political contacts, and behind Grayson was his friend Baruch. On May 19 the doctor cabled to Tumulty that he had advised the President to allow his message to the new Congress to be given out "in Washington alone," and that "Colonel House confers with newspapermen daily and gives out information of which we have no knowledge." Lunching with the Wilsons on June 5, Lansing heard Grayson say that the little man on the third floor of the Crillon—"the great little agreer"—was to blame for much of the trouble. House's critics referred to his organization, deprecatingly, as "upstairs." McCormick recorded in his diary on April 4: "Baruch . . . sore at the Colonel's crowd, which he thought too free in criticizing the President to outsiders."

the League, during May and June, by the cross fire of protest against the terms of the treaty. His allies, as well as the enemy and his own men, were rebelling against certain of the provisions. Word came to the President that aggressive Frenchmen were plotting a sham revolution and a coup that would give them political control of the Rhineland; and Wilson appealed effectively to Clemenceau to foil this scheme. It was more difficult to detect and defeat French machinations looking toward economic control of the left bank of the Rhine and the breaking up of Germany into small, weak states. His colleagues in the council sometimes seemed "madmen," possessed by fear of the Germans and pitiful self-commiseration.

Wilson had to sit with them, day after day, and witness frantic efforts to partition Turkey in a way that would satisfy the demands of secret treaties and popular greed. By the end of May, suffering from a severe headache, he was laughing contemptuously at the bartering of foreign peoples. The aging President was now almost perpetually on the defensive against the tides of attrition that threatened to overwhelm him. He conceived that he was engaged in a holding action. "No more changes in the Treaty will be considered," he said. "Here I am. Here I have dug in."

The main German reply came to Paris on May 29. It threw Lloyd George into a panic. Early in May the prime minister had urged coercion of Germany. Now he was thoroughly alarmed by rumors that the enemy was preparing to renew resistance, as well as by fears that a crisis in his Cabinet would be precipitated by allegations that the treaty strengthened France unduly at the expense of Germany. He felt that he must ask for an alleviation of certain terms.

Clemenceau, however, intended to stand firm against any betterment of Germany's position, no matter what the consequences. He would be overthrown in his Chamber if he yielded anything more, he said to the council on June 2.

Faced by this rift of opinion, Wilson studied the counterproposals of the German message. On June 3, moreover, he undertook to canvass the sentiment of the entire United States delegation in a way that he had heretofore neglected.[20] He had been warned that, if he did not do this, some of the experts would be disgruntled and might make trouble; and so he had arranged through Lansing to talk with his Americans in the office of the secretary of state.

He had become very proud of the men in The Inquiry: to journalists

---

[20] In May, Wilson had invited memoranda, from the American commissioners only, on questions remaining to be settled after the German and Austrian treaties were disposed of. He had carefully annotated the suggestions received.

he praised their efficiency and, above all, the "complete disinterested-ness" that made their views usually prevail. Frankly inviting their advice in regard to the German reply, he explained that the French and Italians were having similar meetings and he suggested interna-tional talks among the experts so that they might learn each other's minds "without the usual roundabout expressions of diplomacy." Wilson held constantly before his men the paramount necessities of the moment: they must make peace; they must maintain the alliance with Great Britain and France; and they must do these things without undue sacrifice of justice to expediency. The argument of expediency ought not to prevail, he said, lest they have to fight again for what had been won.[21]

In the last minutes of the two-hour conference, the President gave play to the emotion that he had kept in check in the meetings of the council. He was "a little tired" and "very sick" at heart, he said. Asked whether he was blaming the French, he replied: "Not so much as the British . . . From the unreasonable to the reasonable, from Winston Churchill to Eustace Percy, from the pert to the priggish, they are unanimous, if you please, in their funk. They ought to have been ra-tional to begin with and then they would not have funked at the end . . . it is not very gracious for me to remind them—though I have done so with as much grace as I could command . . . If we had written the treaty the way they wanted it the Germans would have gone home the minute they read it. Well, the Lord be with us." [22]

The next day Wilson suffered from a headache that he ascribed to bottled-up wrath at Lloyd George. "I have never seen him more pug-nacious or bellicose," Lansing noted. Everyone was getting on edge. There was no strong executive hand upon the President's work save his own. In his official household there was homesickness and grumbling, and contention between civil and military members. Only three of the President's "family" had not been changed by the atmosphere at Paris, Wilson thought—his wife, daughter Margaret, and "Ike" Hoover.

As the Austrian treaty took shape, the President again had to grapple with specific cases in which his principles were in conflict with the stark realities of Europe. There were some fourteen petty wars in prog-ress on the Continent, many of them abetted by resources that had been contributed by the United States for the purpose of reconstruction. Im-

[21] Apparently the premonition of another world war grew upon Wilson during his last month at Paris. According to Sir William Wiseman, he said to Philip Kerr, Lloyd George's secretary, on the night before his last departure from France: "This is all a great pity. We shall have to do the same thing over again in twenty-five years at three times the cost!" Sir William Wiseman to the writer, May, 1954, and April 22, 1957.

[22] R. S. Baker, *W.W. and World Settlement*, III, 503-4, amended by reference to the notes of Charles Seymour, who was present.

poverished by armament and undermined by disaffected minorities, the states that had succeeded to the territories of the Central Empires showed little genius for democratic government. Their concept of "justice" seemed to depend upon what they were able to seize and to hold. They responded willingly to the propositions of foreign agents who were distributing arms and busily developing future allies.

The prophet was disappointed in the people for whose liberation he had pleaded, and wrote to Henry White that he was going to see what could be done about it. Actually, however, hope had to be abandoned of any effective action short of eventual regulation of all armaments under the League of Nations.[23]

Under pressure to dispense with armament that they thought essential to national pride and safety, the small states were in no mood to applaud the terms that were drawn for a treaty with their neighbor Austria. They assembled on May 31 in secret plenary session and objected belligerently. It was argued that a clause safeguarding religious and political minorities would lead to undue interference in their internal affairs by the large powers, acting through the League of Nations. The debate began to get out of hand. Even Clemenceau's gavel was inadequate.

The President, however, stepped into the breach with a speech admirably conceived and perfectly expressed. In his conversations with British statesmen he had given the impression that he felt that their empire and the Anglo-Saxons would give the essential leadership and force to the League of Nations; but he had heretofore refrained from impolitic expression of this feeling. Now, he said, he wished to call attention to a fundamentally important fact: "the chief burden of the war fell upon the greater powers . . . therefore . . . in the last analysis the military and naval strength of the great powers will be the final guarantee of the peace of the world." In these circumstances, he asked, was it unreasonable or unjust for the great powers to say to their associates, as friends and not as dictators: "We cannot afford to guarantee territorial settlements which we do not believe to be right, and we cannot agree to leave elements of disturbances unremoved, which we believe will disturb the peace of the world"?

His assertion of the paramount interest of the world—that of peace for all men—soothed the ruffled politicians of the nascent states. Clemenceau was able to dismiss the gathering without untoward incidents.

Other small states than those of Eastern Europe gave anxiety to the

[23] When Lloyd George proposed that limits of armament be set for Austria and adjoining states, Wilson saw an opportunity to try again for a general application of one of his Fourteen Points—reduction of arms to "the lowest point consistent with domestic safety." However, he found his allies far more willing to apply his standards to others than to themselves.

President at this time. The aggressiveness of one, in particular, vexed him because of the political strength of its sympathizers in the United States. Late in February, more than five thousand partisans of a free Ireland had met at Philadelphia and sent a delegation of three men to France, headed by Frank P. Walsh, former cochairman of the War Labor Board.

Wilson was as embarrassed as his adversaries in the Senate had hoped. If he took action, he would offend British opinion by seeming to interfere in the very sort of domestic matter in which his American enemies would not brook interference by the League. On the other hand, if he sidestepped, liberals might accuse him of deserting his principle of self-determination and Republican partisans would tell the Irish voters that the President was letting them down. "My first impulse," he confessed later, "was to tell the Irish to go to hell, but feeling that this would not be the act of a statesman, I denied myself this personal satisfaction." Instead he received the delegation of three Irish-Americans.

He pointed out to Lloyd George that, unless some satisfaction were given to Ireland, her sympathizers would surely attack the peace settlement; and the prime minister, seeing a possibility of laying a ghost that had haunted Anglo-American relations for a century, received the three delegates, found them "very high-class men," and gave them a ride to Ireland on a destroyer. When they landed on the old sod, however, they felt the worse for their voyage and welcomed a few nips of usquebaugh. They broke into Fenian speeches, ranted of "atrocities" by Britain.

When the Irish-Americans returned to France from this lark, Wilson was not glad to see them. He had learned from Tumulty that the Senate had passed a concurrent resolution asking that the American commissioners get a hearing for the Irish delegates; and now he replied that their utterances while in Ireland gave the deepest offense to those with whom they were seeking to deal and had "rendered it impossible for the commission to serve them any further." The delegates returned to the United States in a mood to urge their fellows to make common cause with the enemies of Woodrow Wilson.

The President heard also from another large minority in his own land—the Jews. After a huge demonstration in New York against Polish pogroms, Rabbi Wise cabled to express uneasiness over the absence of an antirace-discrimination clause in the Covenant and asked for a reassuring message similar to one that Wilson had sent to Taft a few days earlier.[24] Moreover, Felix Frankfurter wrote on May 16 that he was

---

[24] "Please say to Mr. Taft," the President cabled to Tumulty on May 8, 1919, "that the necessity of protecting the Jews is fully appreciated here and that we are endeavoring to take substantially the action that he suggests."

plunged into gloom by Wilson's failure to champion the Balfour Declaration favoring the establishment of a national home for the Jewish people in Palestine.

On his nation's Memorial Day, Wilson rallied popular morale by an address at the American cemetery near the top of Mont Valérien. Beyond the flower-decked white crosses and the acacia groves stretched the panorama of the valley of the Seine. The great men of the world came subdued and reverent to the scene. Thousands of American troops, with many a scar and empty sleeve among them, listened pensively. Honest Scottish sentiments could flow freely here from the soul that had been stifled by months of haggling.

No one with a heart in his breast, no American, no lover of humanity, can stand in the presence of these graves without the most profound emotion. These men who lie here are men of a unique breed. Their like had not been seen since the far days of the Crusades. Never before have men crossed the seas to a foreign land to fight for a cause which they did not pretend was peculiarly their own, but knew was the cause of humanity and of mankind. . . . The League of Nations is the covenant of governments that these men shall not have died in vain . . . I look for the time when every man who now puts his counsel against the united service of mankind under the League of Nations will be just as ashamed of it as if he now regretted the union of the States . . . if this is not the final battle for right, there will be another that will be final.

Then Wilson made a personal profession of consecration. "I sent these lads over here to die. Shall I—can I—ever speak a word of counsel which is inconsistent with the assurances I gave them when they came over?" Only by summoning all his grit could he hold to the end the restraint that distinguished his effort. People were sobbing as he finished. He and Edith Wilson could not trust themselves to speak and drove home in silence. Told of the overwhelming impact of his words on both disciples and critics, the President responded humbly. "When I speak extemporaneously," he said, "I am as uncertain and nervous just after it is over as I usually am just before." To guide him, he had only a brief outline on two slips of paper.

Meanwhile, the terms of the treaty with Austria assumed final form in the Council of Foreign Ministers. On June 2 the document was delivered, at St. Germain, to delegates whose bearing was in contrast to the defiance of Brockdorff-Rantzau. They were given fifteen days to reply. Release of the text of this treaty did not relieve the anxieties that were felt about the economy of Central Europe. Austria did not sign until September 10, 1919.

With the signing of the peace still a matter of speculation, in the first week of June, social distempers broke out anew. Several thousand strikers paraded with red flags, and Foch and his generals were alarmed. In many ways this was the most critical moment of the entire conference. "I think if I could have a really good piece of news, I should fall dead," Wilson said. It seemed imperative that the statesmen quickly form a common front and move rapidly to agree on a response to the Germans.

But first Lloyd George's demands for revision had to be dealt with. To Wilson it seemed too late for major changes. He had covenanted with the French, and Clemenceau was learning to appreciate his dependability. Together the two advocates of consistency tried to hold the Welshman to the line that they had laid down. Lloyd George seemed to heed only expediency and to come to each meeting, like a chameleon, "bright with the color" of the last man he had talked with. One day the President thought the Welshman "very offensive." In fact, he told House, he took occasion to be ugly himself.

In the conference with his Americans, Wilson had decided to urge once more the fixing of a definite sum that Germany could pay. But to no avail. Clemenceau argued that Germany must be forced to sign the treaty as it stood; and Lloyd George feared to face his electorate with any set figure that the Germans would think possible. The Welshman was now at least definite on this point.[25]

Wilson felt that his colleagues erred in trying to make a treaty that would suit their parliaments. He was haunted by a mystical, irrational faith that there was, deep down, a fine, intelligent strain of public opinion that the leaders were failing to cultivate. But the President could not take issue with them at this juncture, publicly, without giving undue comfort to the Germans; and, moreover, their peoples were more deeply involved than the Americans. Consequently the reparations clauses remained to the end potential threats to the peace of Europe.

On other points raised by Lloyd George concessions were made by

---

[25] Helm Diary, June 9, 1919. One of Lloyd George's own economic advisers had quit. John Maynard Keynes, the ingenious juggler of words and credits whom the prime minister had called his "Puck of Economics," left Paris in disgust, covering his withdrawal with a brilliant sputter of criticism, asserting that Wilson, who had declined to accept Keynes's plan to have the United States guarantee German bonds, was "the greatest fraud on earth." Harrod, *Keynes,* p. 250.

Keynes's plan had been presented to Wilson in a letter from Lloyd George of April 23, 1919. Replying on May 5, Wilson had stated that Congress could not authorize a guarantee of bonds of European origin and that the Treasury wished to retire from the banking business and preferred that loans be made through private channels. "How," the President asked, "can anyone expect America to turn over to Germany in any considerable measure new working capital to take the place of that which the European nations have determined to take from her?" Any action that the United States might take, Wilson said, should be "along independent lines," though "in close and cordial cooperation with European governments."

the council. Wilson agreed to a plebiscite in Upper Silesia and promised Poland military protection during the voting and time enough to eliminate unfair German influences. Moreover, a compromise was reached on the terms of the occupation of the Rhineland, and two agreements on this matter were signed in June with Germany separately from the treaty. Furthermore, Wilson wrote into the treaty a weak statement looking toward the admission of Germany to the League "in the early future." So, very slowly, The Three progressed by a path that seemed to the prophet to "spiral" toward decisions.

By the 13th of June, Lloyd George's "funk" had passed and he again showed the agility that made General Bliss set him down as "a greased marble spinning on a glass table-top." The prime minister was ready to threaten reimposition of the blockade to supplement military measures that Foch was taking to make the enemy see the futility of resistance. Baruch had suggested preparation of "the fullest possible pressure of blockade upon Germany," to be applied in case of a German refusal to sign the treaty. But Wilson preferred military occupation to starvation, and grew angry when Lloyd George insinuated that the President's antipathy to a blockade reflected America's desire to sell surplus food at high prices.[26]

On June 16 Clemenceau, giving the last word of the Allies to the enemy, bore down hard. After the delivery of his manifesto, which gave Germany seven days to decide whether to sign or let the Armistice lapse, there was a lull in the work of the Peace Conference. The Wilsons took advantage of it to accept an invitation to visit Brussels that the Belgians had been extending for weeks.

Back at Paris, the President appeared refreshed and smiling, and wore a new straw hat jauntily. In the air around him, though, was a tenseness that had been created by sharp exchanges of notes with the enemy, and The Three met with their military men to prepare steps to be taken if the Germans failed to form a government that would capitulate promptly. The Cabinet at Weimar had lost its majority and resigned and a new government had not yet been formed.

Before seven on the morning of June 23, secretaries of the British and French delegations went to Wilson's residence to deliver a German note asking delay. Waking the armed detective who lay on the mat outside his suite, they were admitted to the President's chamber and taken by him into the bathroom. Perched on the tub, he read the dispatch. Its

---

[26] Baruch was urging that the economic settlement in general should be fair to American foreign trade and that where commercial credits were granted, they should be used in the country making the advance. It was obvious that the United States, the nation best able to grant credits, would be favored by such an arrangement. See Margaret L. Coit, *Mr. Baruch*, pp. 231, 234, 264, and sources cited.

substance was laid before the council later in the day, and the Allied statesmen, angered by news of the sinking of interned German warships by their crews,[27] refused to grant another extension of their time limit. Finally, late in the afternoon, a meeting of the council was interrupted by an announcement that the Germans would yield to overwhelming force and sign unconditionally.

For three days no German officials could be found who would bear the shame of putting their signatures on the treaty. Nevertheless, Paris was celebrating the signing as a *fait accompli*. The President's automobile, driving him to the Crillon through back streets to dodge trouble, was almost hemmed in by boisterous, yelling crowds. On the evening of June 26, Wilson was dragooned to the Elysée Palace to a dinner in honor of President Poincaré, whose attempts to interfere and to hold Clemenceau to narrow views had made him loathsome to the American prophet. The two chief executives exchanged decorous toasts; but during the evening, with Poincaré almost at his elbow, Wilson spoke of his boredom at stuffy dinners such as the one that he had just attended.

On the morning of June 27 two Germans arrived at Versailles, prepared to sign the treaty. That afternoon, looking forward to the final session on the morrow—the event that would release him at last to go home—the President shook off his fatigue and talked for a full hour with newsmen, answering questions and commenting openly on many phases of the conference and of his plans for the future. Making the best of the situation, the prophet asserted that the peace was closer to his principles than he "had any right to expect." As for the archaggressor of 1914—Germany—it was "a pretty tough peace" for her; but after all, she had done a great wrong. In conclusion he said to the journalists: "All things considered, I think a wonderful success has been achieved . . . It's a long job that I'm glad to see finished, and it is a good job." Lincoln Steffens, one of the correspondents present, recorded that the President was "humble, mater-of-fact and yet very positive, and, of course, informed," that if he talked to the public in the same vein, he would win his fight for ratification in the United States.

Only one knot was still unraveled: he had not been able to persuade the Chinese to sign without reservations, nor would the French permit them to make exceptions. As a result, the Chinese delegates drew away

---

[27] It seemed to Wilson that the sinking had relieved the council of an embarrassing request by France for many of the ships that the British and Americans were inclined to scrap. On June 24, Wilson discouraged the raising of the question of the renewal of the blockade of Germany. He was having trouble enough, he said, in keeping Clemenceau from renewing the war on account of the sinking of the ships and the burning of battle flags that the Germans were to have returned to France. Finally the council merely sent a note of protest against the sinkings.

in tears and a fifth of the world's people were excluded from the peace settlement.

Otherwise everything was ready, on the afternoon of the 28th, for the sealing of the pact that would order the twentieth-century world. The air was bright and clear and Woodrow Wilson's spirit rose in the gay atmosphere of fiesta. Early in the afternoon, with Edith Wilson, he called formally upon the Poincarés, and later in the day the French President returned the courtesy. Wilson bought for his wife a blue and gray bag that matched her gown, and a single crimson rosebud. It was the nearest that he could come to red, white, and blue, he said. He bought orchids for her, too, and put on his own frock coat and high hat for the pageant at Versailles.

The ceremony was an impressive staging of history in the spirit of Louis XIV. In the *Galeries des Glaces*, at a horseshoe table in the middle, hedged about by great mirrors on one side and by rows and rows of tabourets, under a scroll proclaiming *Le roi gouverne par lui-même*, sat the squat Tiger of France, his short legs scarcely touching the floor. He remembered the birth of the Hohenzollern Empire here, and now he was to witness its death.

Wilson and Lloyd George are among the last to come in. They take their seats to the right and the left of Clemenceau, who makes a sign to the ushers. "Ssh! Ssh!" The chatter ceases. The bustle of secretaries and autograph hunters subsides. A quilt of hush descends. Then a sharp order cuts, and the swords of the guards at the doorway click into their scabbards. *"Faites entrer les Allemands,"* in the voice of Clemenceau, distant and harsh. Isolated and pitiful, announced by bugles and escorted by ushers, more ghosts than men, come the two victims, erect under their high collars, their feet clacking on the parquet when they step between carpets—one of them tall and thin, the other short and peering through thick lenses like a lost owl. Recalling the discourtesy of Brockdorff-Rantzau, the statesmen of the Allies do not rise to greet them. The silence is complete. Until the Tiger raps out: *"Messieurs, la séance est ouverte."*

The Germans are escorted to the table where the big seal-bound volume lies. They are to sign first, for Clemenceau is taking no chances on a last-minute balk by the enemy, after the Allies have signed. Wilson and his Americans follow. Hands reach out to congratulate the President as he walks, smiling broadly, to the table where the treaty lies. His seal already has been affixed to the document by use of a signet ring bearing the shorthand characters for his name. Beside this imprint he signs "Woodrow" firmly, the full significance of the moment striking him and his hand almost failing as he completes "Wilson." In less than an hour all the signatures are affixed.

Outside, guns boom, airplanes dip low, and the fountains on the terrace spurt for the first time since the war began. The Three walk out together. Crowds burst through cordons of troops and swarm upon them, shouting *"Vive Clemenceau!" "Vive Wilson!" "Vive Lloyd George!"* For a moment the three top hats are lost sight of. The statesmen stand stanchly together, as they did when the peoples of the world pressed divisive arguments upon them and they resolved to preserve unanimity at all costs. They are swept along the terrace—still together, arms locked—and finally rescued by a platoon coming up on the double.

With Sonnino and Makino, they went to the foyer of *l'Opéra de la Cour* for a final session. Wilson insisted that the minutes of their intimate sessions should not be published—indeed, not even cited. He said that he would not have permitted a recording of their sessions, filled as they were with plain speaking and changes of opinion, had he thought the question of publication would be raised. It was agreed that the intimate records would not be released to anyone, save to their successors. Wilson would not concede even that his successors had a right to the documents.

At the station there was more enthusiasm for the departing American than had been manifest at his leave-taking in February. He was cheered by a crowd that included most of the notable men at Paris except the British. Clemenceau was on hand, more than an hour after his bedtime, to walk to the train with the prophet who had almost, but not quite, converted him. At the steps of the car they clasped hands. A little teary, The Tiger purred: "I feel as though I were losing one of the best friends I ever had." France had her redeemed territories, her reparations, her treaty of guarantee. And America had, for her taking, her League, her Monroe Doctrine of the whole world.

But would she take it?

The train moved out. The lights of the Old World capital grew dim. Woodrow Wilson stood with his wife at an open window, happy at last to be on the way home. "Well," he said, "it is finished, and, as no one is satisfied, it makes me hope we have made a just peace; but it is all on the lap of the gods."

CHAPTER XVII

CHALLENGE TO AMERICA

ON JUNE 29, AT BREST, Woodrow Wilson boarded the *George Washington* for the last time. The social turmoil of Europe had pursued him to the water's edge; a Socialist demonstration was surging in the old French seaport even as the President's train moved between lines of American soldiers and took him alongside a quay.

Descending a steep flight of stone steps, he was ferried out to his vessel. A flicker of cheer shone through his haggard face. Here was the America for which he had been yearning. Safe on the big ship, escorted by the Navy, he felt again the thrill of the constructive genius of his countrymen. At last he was home among his own people, sailing under his own flag. His mind fell back into a native vale, to thoughts familiar and comfortable.

Looking back over the months of contention with the shrewdest politicians in Europe, he could feel that—as he had once said of John Hay—he had "promoted that concert of nations which is the best security for the peace of the world." He had exalted political ideals before the peoples of the world as cogently as he had once expounded them in Princeton classrooms. He had awakened faith in the power of man's reason to lift him out of political jungles; and his very presence at the peace table had been construed as assurance of moderation. Vast strides had been taken toward codification of political usages that might end international anarchy. Many peoples had been liberated from repressive rule, had been ministered unto with a generosity unprecedented in human history, and had been given a chance to develop political responsibility and to join as equals in the family of nations. Moreover, states that governed alien peoples were to be held accountable to world opinion through mandates. Then, too, by provisions of plebiscites and by a labor charter, recognition had been given to the rights of minorities to resist exploitation, both political and economic. Under the new order, mankind would have a chance to think and talk before fighting, to balance the cost of war against that of compromise. Public registration of treaties would be required, and disarmament encouraged. Small nations would have a hearing before the world. Germany would be given a chance for redemption.

Most significant of all, the centuries-old dream of idealists had at last come true: a League of Nations had been created to serve as a forum for the voices of morality and intelligence. In this respect the treaty of

1919 had set up a milestone in the progress of the race. Even statesmen who were unenthusiastic about the League had found it a convenient catchall for problems that seemed insoluble and disruptive.

Yet Woodrow Wilson confessed disquietude because he had fallen so far short of the aspiration of idealists. He said to Baruch that some people seemed to expect of him what only God could perform. Actually, patriots in the free states still thought in nationalistic patterns, so that the world seemed to revolve around them, rather than they and their sister states round a world-wide logos. Statesmen of the Allies went home muttering that, though the peace was perhaps the best that could have been salvaged from the cross fire of purposes under which they had negotiated, it was after all a bad job. The document seemed too strong to some, too weak to others; too vague in certain respects, too specific in others. Many critics thought its economic clauses hopelessly contradictory, its territorial changes provocative of strife.

The bitter plaints did not spare the statesman whom Europeans held chiefly responsible for its terms, and many of the voices that had hailed the American prophet as a savior were now the most vociferous in condemning the obvious lag between his promises and the product. Moreover, the very covenanting zeal that ran in his blood and gave his challenge its force had led him to project his convictions with a fervor that repelled responsible men who felt the awful shadow of Presbyterian sin cast over them.

But Woodrow Wilson, out on the Atlantic and homeward bound, was in no mood to join the voices of disillusion and despair. He did not lose faith in the people. The cause was so sacred to him, so vital to humanity, so dependent, for success, upon unanimity of opinion among those who had worked with him at Paris! He could forgive the ignorant—those who knew not what they did: but he had only frigid scorn for the "perfectabilitarians"—the men of little faith. Disappointed though he was in many of the provisions of the treaty, he was ready to uphold the document to which he had sworn fealty, with trust that the League of Nations eventually would correct maladjustments and injustices. No one knew better than he on how precarious a base the treaty rested. And no one felt more keenly the necessity for protecting this fragile handiwork in the jungle-era to which European politics seemed to be reverting.

Great as was Wilson's contribution toward a cosmic political order, however, he and his economic advisers had not lifted the world's trade and industry out of the old channels that had led persistently to war. The President usually had followed the counsel of the businessmen who advised him. He himself had had little time to ponder deeply on the economic causes of war. He had been urged to try to set up world-wide controls of trade similar to those in force in the United States. But the President had not acknowledged this proposal. From the beginning of the Peace Conference he had relegated economic matters to a subordinate place until they had thrust themselves upon him in connection with the reparation settlement. Woodrow Wilson's first love was politics, not economics. Nevertheless, he saw that the processes of history were making isolation impossible for the United States—economically as well as politically. He had reminded the new Congress that "America has a great and honorable service to perform in bringing the commercial and industrial undertakings of the world back to their old scope and swing again, and putting a solid structure of credit under them." [1]

Many of Wilson's own people, however, were no more willing to pool their economic resources with Europe than to put their military power at the disposal of foreigners. As the stimulus of a war emergency expired, Americans had become as impatient of political control of their foreign trade as of regulation of interstate commerce. The President saw no way in which he could carry out his desire to have his country put "a solid structure of credit" under the world's trade and industry. With the disbanding of the Supreme Economic Council, the tenuous economic bonds that had held the victorious nations together through the stress of war would be ruptured. To relieve Europe's financial burden, there seemed to be no feasible course but to issue still more credits from the United States to fund the existing indebtedness of the Allied governments. [2]

[1] In his message to Congress, on May 19, Wilson had hedged his assertion of idealism by recommendation of a tariff that would protect American industries that were essential to military defense and that would enable the nation to retaliate effectively against any foreign legislation that might militate or discriminate against American interests.

[2] Wilson had permitted Hoover to notify the Supreme Economic Council, on June 27, that that body should cease to function after the ratification of the treaty "lest it should give the impression to the world of an economic block of the governments who have been aligned in war." In a session of the inner council, on his last day in Paris, Wilson explained his unwillingness to prolong the Supreme Economic Council. "I shall have to take up this question on my return to America," he said, "and if need be, I shall call for appropriate legislative measures. I have a mind to authorize the Supreme Economic Council to present a plan to us. I ask only that this plan be drawn in a way to avoid the criticisms that I have indicated." In the one important instance in which the United States was committed to joint economic action in Europe after the war—representation on the Reparations Commission—Wilson had made the same reservation that he had quietly worked into the Covenant. Under this safeguard the commission, like the Council of the League, must act unanimously; and thus the United States retained a power of veto against any issue of bonds that might upset the money market in New York.

On June 4 a committee of economists of the four Western powers had made a confidential report that was never seriously considered by the council, recommending that steps be taken to reorganize currencies, that international trade be re-established ultimately on private rather than government credit, but that governments should set up immediately a fund to supply raw materials and producer's goods for the new states of Europe.

So far as the United States was concerned, Wilson felt that the question of further interna-

On the *George Washington*, the President kept more to his cabin than during his earlier crossings. Now and then he called in advisers for conferences. He walked the deck each day, hating it and doing it only because his wife insisted.

He lunched with Baruch and McCormick, and almost every day he met them on deck and chatted about economic matters. These veterans of his little War Cabinet were devoted disciples who gave advice straight from the shoulder, respectfully and without the arts of salesmanship.[3] They saw no feet of clay in their leader, and their admiration for his wisdom had grown.

Uppermost in the President's mind was ratification of the peace treaty by Congress. Within the new political order, he hoped, economic adjustments could be worked out in peaceful cooperation. At Paris his hero, General Smuts, had challenged him directly. "*Can* you carry the treaty? *Can* you get your two-thirds majority?" the South African had asked. And Wilson had responded solemnly: "I absolutely can." Communing still with the poets and the seers, he was depending on his intuition, what he called his "independent mind," unprejudiced by fact and logic. With no security but good intentions, he had given his word to men whom he honored. He must now redeem his pledge.

He had been assured by messages from Washington that his political lieutenants were looking to him for leadership. "There is a great depression in our ranks here," Tumulty had reported on June 16, "but with a definite thing presented by you to the people in the League of Nations . . . our enemies will be left in a most pitiable plight."[4]

---

tional conference on economic matters must rest for decision with the officials of the permanent departments of the government at Washington.

Though he hesitated to use his economic power brazenly, for political advantage, Wilson had wielded it in emergencies of the peacemaking to enforce his concepts of justice. Under moral and spiritual pressures, the prophet had turned ruling elder, conscious of his power to withhold the beneficence of a welfare fund from unworthy brethren; and Hoover's men were exercising this power in distributing grants for relief. Thus the United States had been tightening to some extent the financial grip that Wilson had foreseen two years earlier. How much the President might have made of his economic power, had he been willing to make full use of the methods of Old World diplomacy, has been suggested by Herbert Hoover in his *Memoirs*, I, 451.

[3] Baruch had displayed genuine concern for the common good by willingness to share his personal fortune through taxation and charity, and he had shown devotion to Wilson by declining to serve as secretary of the treasury for fear that a taint of "Wall Street" might embarrass the President.

[4] The "great depression" in the party ranks to which Tumulty referred is described vividly in a letter from R. W. Woolley to House, dated June 17, 1919. "There isn't any Democratic Party in this country," Woolley wrote. "He is with you in Paris. You and I know what will happen when he returns. Meanwhile the pigmies are having a wonderful time. Every fellow with a grouch is romping over the landscape . . . Senator Hitchcock, who has put his grievances on ice for the time being, is doing his best to represent the Administration in the Senate, while other so-called Democratic leaders,—Senator Walsh of Montana excepted,—let everything go by default and the Republicans get away with pretty much all they undertake . . . Outside of officeholders—and a goodly number of them are none too loyal—the aggregation championing the Administration is fast assuming the aspects of Falstaff's army."

Political interest coincided with Woodrow Wilson's personal devotion to the cause of the League. But it was to be understood that his own political fortunes were to be subordinated to the great cause. From now on, the Covenant was to be The Word. During the transatlantic voyage, which was extended at Dr. Grayson's insistence to give the President a longer rest, Wilson worked hard on a message that would present the treaty to Congress. He read his draft to his associates and asked for advice. Baruch counseled aggressiveness. It seemed to him that the President should explain just what the League of Nations was and what it would do, that if Wilson delayed long in doing this he would find himself on the defensive. But the President heeded only his inner voices. He was obsessed by his dream of unity with the plain people, and by intuitive confidence that he expressed their latent aspirations. His doctrine and his motives seemed to him so transparent that souls of good faith would understand and sympathize. There were sincere isolationists, he knew, but he thought that his people would perceive that many of the criticisms of the League were captious. He had placed the same prophetic faith, once, in Princeton's alumni, and they had disappointed him grievously.

On the morning of July 8 the *George Washington* neared New York. Escorted by battleships, destroyers, and planes, saluted thunderously, she steamed majestically up the harbor. Sailors clad in white lined the deck. The sun was bright, the sea calm, and the ship's company happy and expectant.

The great city that had so often cold-shouldered the prophet now put on its best manners. He had first visited its canyons of wealth as Miss Ellie Lou's fiancé, ashamed of his plain clothes; and it was here that the Philistines had laughed and raged at him most irritatingly. But Manhattan now blared its recognition of the returning President. Members of his Cabinet and Governor Alfred E. Smith met him in the harbor, and Frank L. Polk, who had taken the new title of undersecretary of state. He was so glad to be home that even the docks of Hoboken looked pretty, he said with a twinkling eye. Citizens crowded the route across Twenty-third Street and up Fifth Avenue, to lavish cheers and tears upon their leader. Their enthusiasm drew him to his feet and kept him standing in his automobile.

But behind those who cheered and shook his hand in welcome there were men who blamed him for misfortunes personal and national. Politicians whom he had offended were spewing poison, souring public opinion, making it curdle around nodes of anti-League sentiment. George Harvey was spreading vitriol through his weekly journal. Neurotic William F. McCombs, ill in a suite at the Waldorf-Astoria, went to his window and leaned far out over the street to put a curse upon the prophet whom the crowds applauded.

The Covenanter entered the hotel and closed the door of his suite. His daughter Margaret, ecstatic with pride, threw her arms around him and rejoiced in the plaudits of the multitude. But he regarded her with a look that she knew she could never forget. "Wait till they turn," he said quietly, remembering the cooling of the peoples of Europe.

At midnight he reached the White House. The quiet dignity of the old mansion offered sanctuary. It was sweet to be home once more, sheltered from the summer heat and from distasteful persons, in the care of servants whom he knew as friends and trusted. There were flowers everywhere, the summer linen was on the chairs, and everything was spick and span, and simple. And there came a reminder that his old friends—the class of '79 at Princeton—still loved him. "The class drank your health in the usual liquid," one of them wrote. "I exhort you never again to miss a reunion. You really count on Great Occasions."

Two days later, dressed immaculately and carrying a bulky copy of the treaty, he went before the Senate to seek their approval of it. He had thought of calling a joint session of the Congress, but Tumulty had advised that this would be adding insult to the upper house.

He had written out his speech painstakingly; the occasion was so solemn that he did not trust himself to speak extemporaneously. As he stood before the Senate, his emotions threatened his forensic perfection. Now and again he stumbled over a word. Sometimes it seemed that he was not addressing the senators, but rather projecting his spirit to the galleries and to the people whom they represented. "Senators do not know what the people are thinking," he had remarked at Paris. "They are as far from the people, the great mass of the people, as I am from Mars."

He told the senators and the people above them that the forming of a League of Nations was no academic concern, but a matter of life and death to human civilization. Actually, what had once seemed a counsel of perfection had come to seem a plain counsel of necessity. The League was "not merely an instrument to adjust and remedy old wrongs under a new treaty of peace; it was the only hope for mankind . . . Dare we reject it and break the heart of the world?"

"America may be said to have just reached her majority as a world power," he asserted. Then, laying aside his manuscript, he gave these elders his charge. "The stage is set, the destiny disclosed . . . We cannot turn back. We can only go forward, with lifted eyes and freshened spirit, to follow the vision. It was of this that we dreamed at our birth. America shall in truth show the way. The light streams upon the path ahead, and nowhere else."

He did not need to ask, as in his sesquicentennial challenge to the men of Princeton: "Who shall lead us to this place?" It was obvious that the establishment of the League of Nations under American leadership was now the "chief end" of this Presbyterian. He could not rest except in pursuing this single track to a logical, ethical, destination. Putting on a mien of complete confidence, he said to newsmen on the day of his address at the Capitol: "The Senate is going to ratify the treaty."

Earlier in the year 1919, while the memory of the horror of war was fresh and poignant, many associations of citizens had been advocating a league of nations. The churches had declared themselves in favor, the women of the country were for it, the American Federation of Labor supported it, and the American Bar Association voted unanimously for participation by the United States. A poll of the press taken early in April had shown opinion leaning heavily toward ratification of the treaty.

Nevertheless, as the shock of carnage passed and the wounds of war healed, subversive emotions of race and religion had asserted themselves. Citizens of Italian blood responded warmly to a denunciation by Lodge of Wilson's stand on Fiume; Chinese intellectuals and their American friends could not forgive the Shantung settlement; communities on the West Coast dreaded that the League might forbid barriers against the immigration of Orientals.

Americans of older lineage were turned against the Covenant by impulses that they thought "patriotic." Some felt that the League would prove to be merely a device for the aggrandizement of the British Empire. Others feared that the United States would give more than she got, that her tariff laws might fall under control of the League, and above all, that the positive guarantee against aggression that appeared in Article X would involve the nation in war against its will.

Independent efforts had been made by anti-League zealots of both parties to organize those who preached "America First" into a League for the Preservation of American Independence. This association argued that an appeal to force as a means of preserving peace was "at best futile and at worst dangerous," that the United States should be assured "freedom to defend right, to refuse to fight, to mind our own business." [5] Conferring with irreconcilable senators at the Washington home of Lodge on the evening of April 28, the day the revised Covenant of the

[5] G. W. Pepper, *Philadelphia Lawyer*, pp. 124–29.

League was adopted, the leaders of this crusade had found Lodge "cautious and resourceful." Moreover, at subsequent sessions of Wilson-haters at the homes of Brandegee and Alice Roosevelt Longworth, plans were laid for spreading propaganda through mass meetings and the press.

While Wilson was still at Paris, Lodge had begun to marshal his forces in the Senate for relentless warfare. Observing that the Democratic party would stake its position in the 1920 election on Wilson's peace treaty and the League, Republican leaders saw that their own party—divided as it was by a vast range of personal views toward the Covenant—must be united on defensible ground if they were to retain the power given them by the previous Congressional election. Lodge discussed strategy with Senator Borah of Idaho, who thought the peace treaty a breeder of future wars and the League a bar to America's freedom of action. Lodge, according to his own record, explained to this archisolationist that any immediate attempt to defeat the treaty by a straight vote in the Senate would be hopeless, even if it were desirable, that there was only one thing to do and that was to proceed in the discussion of the treaty by way of amendment and reservation. The senator from Massachusetts felt that the public, unaware of dangerous implications of the Covenant to which their President would commit them, could best be enlightened by debate on specific ways of improving the instrument.

With a Republican majority of two in the Senate and thirty-nine in the House, Lodge was ready to draw the lines of battle. Making the most of his prerogative as chairman of the Foreign Relations Committee, he appointed new members on whom he could count[6]; and he looked for aid on the floor of the Senate from a few dissenting Democrats, especially Reed of Missouri.

Turning Wilson's own phrase against him, Lodge served notice that the peace treaty was not to be debated in closed session but was to be given "pitiless publicity." Already, on June 6, the Senate had passed a resolution calling on the secretary of state to give the tentative treaty to the Senate. And on June 9, Borah, too impulsive to await the constitutional process by which treaties are customarily submitted to Congress, got a copy from a newsman and had it read into the *Congressional Record*. Lodge and Borah stirred the jealousy of their colleagues by talk

[6] When Lodge appointed irreconcilable Hiram Johnson instead of moderate Frank B. Kellogg, several wavering Republicans were in a mood in which they might have been won by Democratic diplomacy. Dissertation of James E. Hewes, Jr., Yale University Library, pp. 223-26. The packing of the Foreign Relations Committee with senators opposing Wilson's League gave Lodge control of nine of the seventeen votes. His tactics were assailed by Taft publicly, and on the floor of the Senate by the Democratic minority leader, Hitchcock, who had charged that the purpose of the Republican was "to kill the League of Nations, if possible, and to kill it by indirection."

of a "leak" that had permitted "special interests" in New York to get the treaty while the august representatives of the American people were kept in darkness.

This was partisan, political nonsense, Wilson had perceived at once. The President had nothing to conceal, had curbed his own inclination to publish the tentative treaty merely out of a desire to cooperate with Lloyd George, who had hoped for changes before the final signing. When Senator Hitchcock put through a resolution calling for a full investigation of the alleged "leak" and the American press published the treaty, Wilson was relieved.

During the last month at Paris, Wilson had been plagued by other heckling moves in the Senate. Long debates spun out the campaign of delay and questioning on which the cabal was well embarked. Knox attacked Article X and tore the Covenant to shreds.[7] When Fall proposed that the war be ended by decree and a separate peace made with Germany, the President felt that the senators' assertion of their right to advise had gone too far. He then reminded the newsmen that the Senate was empowered by the Constitution only to advise and consent, or refuse to consent, to treaties brought before it by the executive. "If they go beyond that, and undertake to change the treaty," he warned, "then the executive can reject such action as exceeding the Senate's prerogative, and entering upon that of the executive."

The scholar who had written forty years before about the "treaty-marring power" of the Senate did not propose to be put upon. He had insisted to Lansing that the attacks were all part of a general plan to make as much mischief as possible. "The only way to handle them," he wrote at Paris, "is by making a direct frontal attack in reply. Article X is the king pin of the whole structure . . . without it, the Covenant would mean nothing. If the Senate will not accept that, it will have to reject the whole treaty. It is manifestly too late now to effect changes in the Covenant, and I hope that Polk will urge Hitchcock and all our friends to take a most militant and aggressive course, such as I mean to take the minute I get back."[8]

[7] Knox's name was scarcely less distasteful to Wilson than that of Lodge. Attending a baseball game on Labor Day, 1919, he turned to a friend and taking off his straw hat and pointing at the "Knox" label on the band, said: "Isn't that a hell of a name to wear near one's brain?" Louis Brownlow, *Lectures and Seminar at the University of Chicago in Celebration of the Centennial of W.W.,* p. 143.

[8] In his autobiography, *Across the Busy Years,* II, 201, Nicholas Murray Butler reports (without complete dating or documentation) that Ambassador Jusserand, having secured the assent of the British and French Foreign Offices to a set of reservations to which Butler had committed several wavering senators, took these reservations to Wilson at Paris and assured the President that if the Democrats in the Senate would support them, enough Republicans would join them to ratify the treaty. "To Jusserand's horror," Butler reports, "the President in a stern voice replied: 'Mr. Ambassador, I shall consent to nothing. The Senate must take its medicine!'"

He felt that he had acted on Republican proposals for reservations to the best of his judgment and ability. Yet, during his last month at Paris, the Republicans had continued to formulate reservations. The essence of their objections appeared in a public letter written on June 21 by Elihu Root to Lodge, who committed forty-seven of the forty-nine Republican senators to support the reservation on Article X that Root proposed, and all forty-nine in favor of two other reservations suggested by Root—one safeguarding the right of withdrawal from the League, the other asserting positively the two aspects of the Monroe Doctrine. The Republican elder statesman believed that his reservations could be included in a nation's instrument of ratification without requiring a reopening of negotiations with other signatories. He thought that the reservations could be approved effectively by silence on the part of the other contracting parties, that if there should be any doubt on this point it could be dispelled by asking the four largest signing powers to state their positions.[9]

Sensitive to the danger of reopening and again probing the festering matters that he had treated so painfully at the Peace Conference, Wilson was in no mood to act on Root's suggestion that the opinions of the four largest Allied governments be sounded. Never a man to probe deeply into legalism, the President, in the fatigued condition to which work and worry had reduced him, had no will to take steps that might seem obedient to an opposition that he had resolved to fight. His patience had worn thin at advice that had become repetitive and was, he suspected, insincere. He explained to newsmen, on the day of submitting the treaty to the Senate, that reservations "presented a grave difficulty in that every nation joining the League would have to assent to them, and while this slow process was going on the United States would

[9] Chandler P. Anderson, a lawyer who undertook to fabricate reservations for the Republicans, wrote to his friend Root on July 10 that, though he had little doubt that the other signatories would accept the United States on its own terms, strict legality required that each sign a *procès-verbal* definitely accepting the reservations.

The solicitor of the State Department advised the President that the United States had a right to deposit interpretive resolutions with the ratified treaty, but that these would not bind other governments unless adopted by them. In giving his opinion, the solicitor confessed that he found no authoritative statements concerning the effect of reservations on the obligations of the United States to the other signatories or theirs to the United States. The solicitor adduced further advice on this debatable point that had been given by Solicitor J. E. Clark of the State Department on Aug. 5, 1911. Clark wrote: "The uniform practice of the Executive is now and seems always to have been that where the Senate proposed an amendment to a treaty submitted to it by the President for its advice and consent, the President, upon receiving the treaty with such proposed amendment, renews negotiations with the other Power to learn whether or not such an amendment is acceptable to such Power. If the amendment is not acceptable, either an entirely new treaty must be negotiated or the treaty falls." On this opinion David Hunter Miller commented, on Sept. 13, 1919: "Submission to the various Powers . . . means, in most cases, submission to their legislatures . . ." *See* two memoranda forwarded from the solicitor to Adee of the State Department and printed in Miller Diary, XX, 494–501.

be at war with Germany." On the same day he told a newspaper publisher who had friends in both camps that he was "open-minded as to every proposition of reasonable interpretation," but would not "consent to any proposition that we scuttle."

This statesmanlike position, however, availed nothing. McAdoo wrote the next day to suggest that the noble address to Congress was "like casting pearls before swine, so far as the Senatorial cabal is concerned." To Senator Brandegee the speech was "soap bubbles of oratory and soufflé of phrases"; and to Senator Warren G. Harding it was "utterly lacking in ringing Americanism."

Having failed to make conversions from the pulpit in the Senate chamber, the prophet called a few of the wavering brethren to the White House and pleaded with them.[10] He talked for hours, patiently and persuasively, as he had talked so many times before with legislators who seemed to need educating. He refused to risk a controversy by discussing the merits of the reservations that they proposed. He chose rather to explain that to attach amendments to the treaty would be to jar the delicate balance into which conflicting national interests had been brought at Paris. It was distasteful, this business of begging men to do what seemed so patently their duty; but when Senator Hitchcock had said that it must be done, there had been no course but to comply.

Unfortunately, however, the press dramatized the talks at the White House. Senators sensed that the public was watching them, ready to interpret any yielding on their part as surrender or acknowledgment of sins for which they had received pastoral reproof. Thus their pride was stirred and they became the more receptive to partisan arguments that they should assert their right to a share in the authorship of the treaty.

"I am pondering very carefully," Wilson wrote to McAdoo on July 15, "the method of action best calculated to bring about the right results in these difficult days." And to Senator John Sharp Williams: "Your advice about using gentleness and tact in our present task . . . is good advice." Undersecretary Frank L. Polk, conferring with Wilson near the end of the month, found him changed and more conciliatory.

On the 18th Sir William Wiseman came for luncheon, and Wilson talked frankly with him. The President was eager to go before the people, he said, and explain the treaty to them; but the State Department had advised against it, fearing that wavering senators might construe the move as an appeal over their heads and take offense. He pre-

---

[10] On July 16, Wilson wrote as follows to Senators Capper, Colt, Jones, Kellogg, Kenyon, McCumber, McNary, and Nelson: "Matters of so grave a consequence are now under consideration that I would very much appreciate an opportunity to have a talk with you about the treaty and all that it involves."

ferred to try to win the legislators personally; in fact, he had talked
with three Republicans that very morning. If he were able to gain
enough votes in this way, he would not have to carry his case to the
people.

He confessed to Wiseman, most confidentially, that to hasten action
and to avoid foolish reservations that might lead the world to believe
that the United States gave only half its heart to the League, he might
have to approve "interpretations" of the language of certain articles of
the Covenant. After all, he had traded his ideals against selfish interests
at Paris, and if absolutely necessary, he would do the same at Washington; but he was resolved to drive a hard bargain in the name of humanity's common good, to concede nothing until it became inescapable. In
public he would maintain an adamant front as long as possible; for he
felt that any sign of weakness would be taken by the opposition as a
signal for inflated demands. Actually, there was only one criticism of
the Covenant that seemed to him to be very persistent outside of the
Senate chamber. That was the objection that the United States might
not be able to withdraw at will from the League.

It seemed to the British visitor that anxiety had gnawed deeply into
the President. His face was gray and drawn, and twitching as it had
after the illness at Paris. Heeding a warning from Edith Wilson, Wiseman sheered away from controversial topics that might excite his host.

The President did not go often now to the executive offices, but
instead made appointments at the White House. He would retire to his
chamber during the day from time to time. Immediately after lunching
with Wiseman he went downriver on the *Mayflower*, hoping to relax;
but even on his voyages on the Potomac he took his typewriter and
papers, and after dinner went below and worked late into the night,
while Edith Wilson sat on deck and entertained those in their party.

During the summer he spent an occasional evening at vaudeville. But
when a friend invited him to the theater, he wrote: "Not on your life!
I would not go to a serious play, no matter how fine, which dealt with
the critical matters now daily pressing upon my judgment as matters
of policy, for anything in the world. The weight of this weary unintelli-
gible world is great enough anyhow on those of us poor devils who have
to take some part in straightening things out, and when I go to the
theatre I must, for psychological reasons, see something that does not
extend the strain of the day. You will understand."

As the President's health failed, the ravening wolves of the Senate
raised the pitch of their cries. To Hiram Johnson the League seemed a
"gigantic War Trust." Wilson was smeared by Borah as "Britain's tool

—a dodger and a cheater," and by Penrose and Reed as a man who preached sacrifice but took extravagant presents from crowned heads. Moreover, these old warriors were joined by the voice of one who had thus far held aloof—William Howard Taft.

When Wilson had acted on his proposals at Paris, Taft had continued to give ardent support to the League. In June he had advised the President not to attack the Republican senators personally but to concentrate on pleading his cause, and Wilson had followed this counsel. When the President returned to Washington in July, however, he had given to Taft no recognition of his generous aid.[11] Under pressure from Chairman Hays, who was trying to draw all elements of the Republican party into unanimity, the ex-President finally heeded the call of the political pack. On July 21 he sent a draft of five interpretations and one "reservation" to Hitchcock. Stating that there was no objection to showing the letter to the President, Taft expressed the hope that Wilson would continue to confer with the mild reservationists and would make more converts among Republicans. Though he said emphatically that were he a senator he would vote for the treaty as it was, he suggested that it would be good statesmanship to recognize the personal and political exigencies of the day. Taft's temporizing proposals were released for publication on July 23 by Will Hays.

Root and Lodge had put forward objections that, Wilson felt, France and Britain might not accept. And now it seemed to him that Taft was muddying the rapidly fading vision of international understanding by suggesting that a time limit be placed on the efficacy of Article X. As Roosevelt had foreseen before his death, the Republican policy of giving lip service to a league of nations was paying out: it had indeed enabled Taft to "get over" from his independent position to the party line. If Wilson had "dug in" before he left Paris, he was now completely mired in emotional revulsion toward men whom he could think of only as devils. "I have been talking to some more senators about the treaty," he told Hurley on July 31, and then he added: "They are endeavoring to humiliate me." The sad tone of his voice suggested that he realized now that he had been thrown back into a defensive position.

The seed of doubt had been sowed so well that the public was begin-

---

[11] House had tried to foster the Wilson-Taft understanding by suggesting that David Hunter Miller, an expert on the Covenant, go to the United States in June to talk with Taft; but Wilson had not encouraged this.

Men in the State Department felt that Taft might have been held loyal to the Covenant as drawn if the President's pastoral ardor had been greater. "Taft would not have flopped," wrote William Phillips to Polk on July 26, "if the President had sent for him as soon as he had returned and patted him gently on the shoulder. How much easier it would make everything if the President would only put his arm on a few other shoulders."

ning to believe that reservations would do no harm and would be a wise safeguard of American rights. Lodge had reason to feel that, though the moderate men of his party might not support "amendments," he could get the majority vote that was needed to approve "reservations." The wily senator "had very much at heart," as he explained in a book six years later, the creation of "a situation where, if the acceptance of the treaty was defeated, the Democratic Party, and especially Mr. Wilson's friends, should be responsible for its defeat, and not the opponents of the treaty who were trying to pass it in a form safe for the United States." And so the articles that had been put together with such pain at Paris were hacked apart.

Debate raged back and forth on the floor of the Senate. The wolves nagged and snarled. Why did the President insist, they wanted to know, that the absurd language of Article XXI protected the Monroe Doctrine? Why was the British Empire given six votes in the League's Assembly, and four-fifths of the mandated territories? Soon it became clear to Wilson that no desire of his could command the votes of a majority of the Committee on Foreign Relations.

Rebuffed in one instance in which he had been led to expect cooperation—a request for the Committee's assent to American representation on the Reparations Commission—and incensed by the unfair attacks of his enemies, the President was in no mood to live up to an offer that he had made to the Senate on July 10. He had declared himself willing, then, to put all his information at the disposal of Lodge's committee at any time. But it was not until July 29 that, responding to a Lodge resolution, he formally transmitted to the Senate the treaty of guarantee with France that already had been published in full in the American press. And the protocol with Germany was not formally submitted until a day or two later. When the Senate went so far as to ask by what legal authority Wilson had acted at Paris and to demand the minutes that the members of the inner council had pledged not to reveal, the President drew back.[12]

Once more Woodrow Wilson was thrown into confusion as practical difficulties impinged upon his ideal. Asked for the successive drafts of the Covenant, for a full record of all discussion on the League, and for the text of an agreement on reparations signed by The Three, Wilson's faulty memory betrayed him, his moral indignation got the better of

[12] The spirit of the Committee on Foreign Relations did not encourage the President to cooperate. Having badgered him for the text of the treaty of guarantee, the senators lost interest once they had it, and pigeonholed it. As for the Treaty of Versailles, Lodge gave it a deliberate official "reading," intoning all 268 pages in his cultured accent, sometimes with several members of his committee as audience, often with only a clerk present, and, on the last day, in a roomful of empty chairs.

his reason, and he gave equivocal answers, as he had done under the cross-examination of Princeton trustees.[13]

The wolves took up other scents for a time. On July 31 Chandler P. Anderson, Root's protégé, had a revealing interview with the secretary of state. Lansing confessed his objections to the League, his preference for arbitration, but said as long as he was in office he could do nothing publicly in support of the opposition. Anderson sensed that he had considerable satisfaction because the result of their failure to follow his advice had gotten the Administration into its present difficulties.

Within a week the Foreign Relations Committee gave Lansing an opportunity to speak publicly. Getting little satisfaction from him, the committee questioned a series of witnesses in open hearings that extended from August into the autumn, hoping for evidence that might be turned against the President in press propaganda. Baruch, who was trying to make contact between the moderate senators in the two camps, was asked to testify on the economic clauses of the treaty. But Lodge, told of Baruch's efforts, said that no compromise was possible, that if the Democrats did not agree with the reservations that the Republicans had power to make, they ran the risk of having the whole Covenant thrown out of the treaty. Lodge was confident now that public feeling was growing rapidly against the Covenant.

In the Senate, on August 12, Lodge delivered a speech that was both learned and impassioned. From his knowledge of history he conjured up ill-fated efforts for an international concert of power. He criticized, one by one, the articles of the Covenant that seemed to him "most dangerous," showing how some of them, instead of preventing war, might induce it. He appealed again to George Washington's wisdom. "Let us beware how we palter with our independence," he warned. Alluding to "those who have tried to establish a monopoly of idealism" through "a murky Covenant," he proclaimed: "Our first ideal is our country, and we see her in the future, as in the past, giving service to all her people and to the world. Our ideal of the future is that she should continue to render that service of her own free will." It was one of the

---

[13] It was obvious that publication of the minutes of acrimonious debates in the councils at Paris would not aid the cause of peace. Moreover, Wilson could not honorably release the records of the Peace Conference without permission from the other participants, the more so because on his last day at Paris he had pledged his colleagues to secrecy and because he had already refused to permit Clemenceau to submit to his Chamber of Deputies the minutes of the League of Nations Commission.

In replying to the Senate's demand for drafts of the Covenant, Wilson at first intended to say that he had withheld certain papers, such as the minutes of the League of Nations Commission, because they were in the hands of colleagues at Paris. But when Lansing suggested that the Foreign Relations Committee might ask him to send for copies and that it would be better to tell the whole truth—namely, that it was the policy of the Peace Conference to hold the papers in confidence—Wilson wrote to Lodge accordingly.

great orations of American history: veteran Marines who sat in the gallery were carried away by its eloquence and applause reverberated for several minutes.

Woodrow Wilson, standing in the west wing of the White House with Stockton Axson, put his hands in his coat pockets, spread his feet, and brought them together precisely. "Stock," he declared, "if I said what I thought about those fellows in Congress, it would take a piece of asbestos two inches thick to hold it." [14]

On July 30 four Republican moderates had told him frankly that the treaty could be ratified quickly, but only with reservations, and that if he did not approve them now, the Senate would force them through eventually. Senator Kellogg assured him that thirty-seven Republicans would support the treaty with moderate reservations; but Wilson did not seize this opportunity. On August 1 Republican Senator Watson, to whom Lodge had revealed his basic, long-range strategy, had come to the White House and told the President that there was only one way by which the United States could be taken into the League, and that was by acceptance of the Lodge reservations.

"The *Lodge* reservations!" the prophet fairly snorted. "Never! Never! I'll never consent to adopt any policy with which that impossible name is so prominently identified." The black fury on which Lodge depended was mounting.[15] Wilson's temper flared up, too, when Lansing appealed to him to lose no time in reaching agreement with Republican moderates. He felt that such a course would raise the very questions in other nations that he had determined to avoid. He would have his America go into the League boldly, intent upon serving, not counting only the cost and the gain.[16]

Finally Lodge closed in upon the President himself. Two days after his oration, he gave notice that the Foreign Relations Committee would take advantage of Wilson's offer to confer with them in a public session. The President accepted the challenge immediately, setting August 19 as the date.

Somehow Woodrow Wilson managed to overcome his fervent indignation and to welcome the Foreign Relations Committee on the morning of August 19 with a display of courtesy that seemed to the head usher almost obsequious in its extravagance. This was the first time in history when this body had come to the White House to interrogate the Presi-

---

[14] James Woodrow, who was present, to the writer.

[15] Watson, *As I Knew Them*, pp. 201–2.

[16] Wilson's position at this juncture was weakened by an ill-considered statement given by Senator Hitchcock to the press after a conference at the White House on Aug. 15. Even mild reservations would be "tremendously embarrassing" to the President, Hitchcock said, and therefore it was necessary "to remove absolutely any probability of the dotting of an 'i' or the crossing of a 't.' "

dent. It was an occasion of great moment, the press sensed, when the big iron gates were unlocked and the senators began to arrive, some in limousines, some on foot, Senator Borah walking and carrying a copy of the treaty under his arm. Reporters waited at desks that Tumulty had arranged in the corridors, poised to transmit every word to the American people. It had been agreed that nothing said should be treated as confidential. The senators brought their own stenographer, and the President had his.

In the East Room, with Lodge and Knox sitting almost within arm's length, Wilson presented a strong case for prompt action. Reading a message that he had prepared after receiving reports from Cabinet members on the necessity for peace, he cited certain examples of American industries that were being hurt by the halt in foreign trade. The United States could not compete for the markets of Central Europe, he said, if they did not act presently. "Every element of normal life amongst us depends upon and awaits the ratification of the treaty of peace."

Nothing stood in the way, he asserted, except doubts about the meaning and implication of certain articles of the Covenant. "I must frankly say," he confessed, "that I am unable to understand why such doubts should be entertained." Nevertheless, he respected the sincerity of some of the doubters. Summarizing the objections that had been raised at his previous conference with the committee in February, he said: "On my return to Paris all these matters were taken up again by the Commission on the League of Nations and every suggestion of the United States was accepted." He then commented on each of the articles in question, concentrating on Article X. Explaining carefully that the United States would be doubly protected against dictation by the League Council under Article X—once through the clause that he himself had cannily inserted to give veto power to each member of the council in disputes to which it was not a party, and again through the constitutional right of Congress to exercise independent judgment on matters of peace and war—he set forth his own views on reservations very clearly:

There can be no reasonable objection, to . . . interpretations accompanying the act of ratification provided they do not form a part of the formal ratification itself. Most of the interpretations which have been suggested to me embody what seems to me the plain meaning of the instrument itself. But if such interpretations should constitute a part of the formal resolution of ratification, long delays would be the inevitable consequence, inasmuch as all the many governments concerned would have to accept, in effect, the language of the Senate as the language of the treaty before ratification would be complete. . . . If the United States were to qualify the document in any way, more-

over, I am confident from what I know of the many conferences and debates
which accompanied the formulation of the treaty that our example would
immediately be followed in many quarters, in some instances with very
serious reservations, and that the meaning and operative force of the treaty
would presently be clouded from one end of its clauses to the other.

After the President had read his formal message, his adversaries
aimed the darts that had proved most piercing. When the prosecutors
delved for weaknesses in his position on reparations, on mandatories,
on Shantung, they got nothing but the truth, so far as Wilson remembered it and could tell it without betraying diplomatic confidences. He
admitted frankly that the Shantung settlement had not pleased him [17]
—an admission that was used by his enemies to make him appear the
victim of Japanese blackmail.

Unable to prove that the Covenant would bind its members too
strongly, the adversaries then took the opposite course and criticized the
document as "a rope of sand and not an effective tribunal which would
result in promoting peace." Senator Warren G. Harding asked timidly
what permanent value there was in the Covenant if the United States
had veto power, what would happen if nations shrugged off their
obligations as "only moral."

"Why, senator, it is surprising that that question should be asked.
There would be a repudiation of good conscience," the prophet replied
in mild reproof. ". . . I should think that was one of the most serious
things that could possibly happen . . . a moral obligation is of course
superior to a legal obligation and, if I may say so, has a greater binding
force . . . In every moral obligation there is an element of judgment.
In a legal obligation there is no element of judgment." He conceded
that it would be quite as moral for the United States to determine its
own obligations as for the Council of the League to do so. Actually, it
seemed to him that generally his people would concur in the moral
judgment of the world; and without specific assurance of concerted
action by all the responsible governments of the world, he warned, "you
have reached the situation which produced the German war." By joining in a "concert of judgment," he insisted, the United States "steadied
the whole world."

[17] Wilson had made strenuous efforts to hold Japan to her promises. On July 25, Lansing
had told the Japanese chargé that, unless Japan published her promises regarding Shantung
within four days, the President himself would do so. A day later Wilson asked his secretary of
state to tell the chargé that negotiations with China on the basis of the treaties of 1915 and 1918
would not be tolerated.

The requested Japanese statement on Shantung was received by the State Department on
Aug. 1 and was forwarded by Lansing with a report that it was unsatisfactory and a recommendation that the President state his own version of the understanding at Paris. This Wilson
did; and Lansing released the statement to the press on Aug. 6.

Many observers felt that a "concert of judgment" was hard to attain and offered an unstable basis for peace. His adversaries were giving him, according to the New York *Tribune*, "probably the most searching inquiry ever directed, for a public record, at any President of the United States or any other head of a great power." Wilson had never been a strong witness under cross-examination; and now when they asked him specific questions about his knowledge of the European secret treaties, he made the mistake of trying to pluck answers from a nebula of vague memories.

Under the blunt questioning of William E. Borah, Wilson's sensitive mental processes broke down. When this opponent asked when the Administration had first learned of the secret agreements regarding Shantung, the President replied candidly: "I thought that Secretary Lansing had looked that up and told you . . . I heard of them only after reaching Paris."

Assuring the witness that Lansing had indeed agreed on this point, Borah asked about the secret agreements concerning Europe. Did these also first come to his knowledge at Paris?

"Yes," answered the President. Encouraged by the fact that his recollection as to Shantung had agreed with Lansing's record and had satisfied his doughty inquisitor, he ventured to depend further on his faulty memory.[18] "The whole series of understandings," he asserted, "was disclosed to me for the first time there."

Was the United States government informed before the Armistice of pacts like the Treaty of London? asked Hiram Johnson of California.

"No, sir." He had had no knowledge of the secret agreements, he declared, when he had proclaimed the Fourteen Points in January of 1918.

This testimony was incredible to senators who did not know Woodrow Wilson well, and it was amazing to the public. How could their president have been ignorant of vital international understandings that had been exposed by the Bolshevik government and published in newspapers? Wilson's lapse of memory now put him in a position as awkward as that into which he had fallen before the trustees of Princeton. Actually, he had had at least an awareness of the existence of many of the secret treaties before he went to Paris.[19]

[18] Apparently Wilson never came to realize the imperfection of his memory. In the autumn of 1920, filling out a self-evaluating questionnaire, he characterized his memory as "rather good."

[19] *See* pp. 130–31, 146, 307, 309, and Mary Reno Frear, "Did President Wilson Contradict Himself on the Secret Treaties?" *Current History*, June, 1929. Wilson's fragmentary and inaccurate recollections remained in his mind at least as late as Feb. 28, 1920, when he wrote to Polk: "They [the Allies] do not even attempt to justify the fact that they did not let even their associates, e.g., the United States, know anything about it [the Treaty of London], and that we discovered it, so to say, after we reached Paris."

But the inquisitors were not done with him yet. They read from the testimony that they had wrung from Lansing a few days before. The secretary of state had confessed that he had yielded at Paris, in deference to the President, his opinion that the Japanese would have joined the League even if the decision on Shantung had gone against them. Wilson's face reddened as if it had been slapped. But he responded suavely: "Well, my conclusion is different from his, sir." He had been "notified" at Paris to the contrary, he explained.

There was a volley of other queries to be parried; and finally Senator Fall tried twice to introduce a list of twenty questions. At this the President ventured at last to speak in self-defense. "I have no objection to sitting here all day," he said mildly. "Indeed, I have taken the liberty of having lunch prepared. But since your questions are written, perhaps you would leave them." The next day he wrote out replies to the queries, one by one.

A half hour after the usual lunch time, having sat continuously for three and a half hours, the conference was ready to break up. "You have been very considerate in putting your questions," Wilson said to them. "Will you gentlemen not come to lunch with me? It will be very delightful to have you." They went to the dining room, were well entertained, and emerged in good humor, declining to accept their host's offer to continue the quizzing into the afternoon.

And so the inquisition ended, and the committee recessed and subsequently adjourned. No votes were changed, but the pro-League minority was inspired by the patient elucidation to which they had listened. The independent press commended the tone and substance of Wilson's replies, an editorial in the *New York Times* declaring: ". . . the President has exhausted the resources of reasoning and exposition."

It seemed possible at this juncture that Lodge might overplay his hand. Root, impressed by accusations of obstructionism, cautioned the senator against overdoing the policy of reservation, and urged him to get into final form a proposition on which all Republicans could agree. There was no yielding, however, on the part of the enemy. Feeling that they had the President on the run, they nagged at his heels, making the most of Wilson's lapse of memory in regard to the secret treaties, asserting that under the Covenant the United States would have to guarantee the terms of pacts that her allies might conceal from her. A few days after the August conference at the White House, Brandegee was threatening to separate the League from the treaty. Knox invited the other irreconcilables to luncheon to lay plans for a speaking tour of the West to oppose ratification. Senators who wished only mild reservations swung to Borah's view that the reservations must be made a part of the treaty and be approved by other signatory nations.

On August 26 the Foreign Relations Committee adopted some fifty amendments that would keep Americans from membership on almost all of the international committees that were to carry out the treaty. At the end of the month, representatives of small nations who had not been invited to Paris or were dissatisfied with the treaty were given their "day in court"; and thus the divisive prejudices of hyphenated Americans were stimulated. Lodge read to his Republican brethren a list of British subjects who would hold influential positions in the League, citing this as evidence that the body would be a tool of the empire. Moreover, he wrote to the President to ask for the text of various collateral treaties and agreements that had been concluded in Europe. And he put through the Foreign Relations Committee, by a vote of 9 to 8, a motion that would reverse the decision of the Peace Conference on Shantung.

At the end of August Wilson wanted to rally his faltering Democrats, to get them to concentrate on a policy of keeping all reservations out of the formal act of ratification. On the President's behalf, Senator Pittman offered reservations similar to those proposed by Kellogg and other Republican moderates, but these were to be put in a separate instrument expressing America's understanding of the treaty. Forty-six Democrats were said to be ready to accept this proposal, but Lodge held the moderates of his party to the principle that reservations must be included in the resolution of ratification.

Though this effort failed, Wilson took one more step of great significance. Calling Hitchcock to him privately, the President gave him four interpretive reservations and told the Democratic leader to accept them if compelled to, to save the treaty. If Lodge knew that he was making this concession, he thought, that infidel would demand four times four reservations. Hence he swore Hitchcock to keep the authorship of his proposals secret. As a result other senators never knew whether they were "official," whether they might be used effectively as a rallying-point for true friends of the League.

The pattern of action that had brought about Woodrow Wilson's administrative failure at Princeton was taking shape again. He had once more allowed a difference of opinion to become a personal feud. The resources of political leadership that had served him so well when he had a Democratic Congress to whip, or a Peace Conference to master by moral prestige and economic power, were inadequate now. He was justifying House's estimate of him as a man with little talent for negotiating with adversaries whose power equaled his own. He had made it easy for sincere Republican advocates of the League to believe the charges of intransigence that his enemies were casting at him. By the end of August he regarded the Republican senators as a body of wicked men who wished to humiliate him and who could be driven to the Truth only by denunciation before their masters, the American people. In this state of mind, he was ready to court temporal failure as surely as when he had denounced Andrew West and appealed his case to the alumni of Princeton. He seldom laughed heartily now; but a note from Charles Hamlin of the Treasury amused him hugely. "Sometimes I wonder if Senator Lodge has any sense of humor," wrote this Massachusetts Democrat. "His frantic wailing about the danger of petty war and his willingness to reject the treaty and to plunge the nations into incessant strife reminds me of an ode of Martial:

> 'Poor Fannius who greatly feared to die
> Embraced the enemy he fain would fly.

> 'Strange contradiction, weary of strife
> He ceased to live for very love of live!

> 'With his own hand, he stops his vital breath:
> Madness extreme! To die for fear of death!' "

"It is most apposite. I shall be tempted to quote it to Mr. Lodge himself," was the response of the embattled President.

CHAPTER XVIII

Last Appeal to the People

While lodge's committee was working its will upon the treaty of peace, Woodrow Wilson persisted in thinking about consolidating and extending the New Freedom. On the 8th of August—the same day on which young Franklin D. Roosevelt proposed half-holidays for federal departments and better coordination of their labor policies—the President delivered before Congress a challenging message that he had drafted in shorthand. In this Wilson suggested that the food control act be extended to years of peace and that its provisions against hoarding be applied to other essential commodities. He asked, too, for licensing legislation that would "secure competitive selling and prevent unconscionable profits," and he favored the passage of laws to control the issue of securities. He advocated, once again, full publicity as a cure for profiteering and made a moral appeal to producers and merchants to deal fairly with the people.

Voices had been challenging the weary prophet to take the lead in further advances toward social ideals. George Record, who more than any other man had stimulated him toward progressivism in New Jersey, had written a strong letter to him on March 25: "As conditions are now, your political fortunes are at a low ebb, your prestige impaired, and your party demoralized." The one big reason for this, Record's argument went on, was that Wilson had "ignored the one great issue" that was slowly coming to the front—"the question of economic democracy, abolition of privilege, and securing to men the full fruits of their labor or service." These questions seemed as essential to Record as slavery had been in the middle of the nineteenth century. These were the issues that caused wars; and the League of Nations, valuable as it was, would assure peace only to the extent that economic justice was established in the nations that were parties to it.

Record had proposed a definite program that the President might lay before the Congress to divert public attention from the investigations that the Republican majority seemed sure to undertake into the war record of their opponents. Tumulty had encouraged Record to send his advice to Wilson while the President was at Paris; and on June 4, after American radicals had put bombs in the mails of prominent officials and an unsuccessful attempt had been made on the life of Attorney General

Palmer, Tumulty himself drew up a comprehensive program for economic action and challenged Wilson, as leader of the liberal forces of the world, "to speak the truth about the whole situation and to propose a remedy." It was not until August 15, however, that the President wrote to Record to say that he had read his letter with "genuine interest and appreciation," that he realized "the gravity and pressing importance" of the things that were urged.

To get essential appropriations, Wilson had been forced to do what he had hoped to avoid—call the new Republican-controlled Congress into special session on May 19. In his message to them he had suggested that transportation and communication revert to private agencies, with governmental regulation to assure coordination. He gave primary attention to issues that had been raised by the unrest of American labor.[1]

On the homeward voyage from Europe, Wilson had had time to ponder on the ever-present problem of adjusting the shifting line between the "necessary functions" and "optional functions" of government. With violent action on the extreme left and clamor for *laissez faire* on the right, he was unwilling to yield to either. Chatting with Baruch, he said that the time soon would be ripe to apply a well-planned program for government control of such necessities as water, electricity, and rail transportation—things which seemed almost as vital to the national life as air for the lungs. Under the stress of bad feeling between capital and labor, the President was inclined to bring more of the nation's economy under a strong hand that would protect the public interest against sabotage from left or right.

In August the President was forced to act in a crisis precipitated by a strike of railway workers. On the 7th he told Walker D. Hines, McAdoo's successor as director-general, that the men must return to their jobs before their demands could be considered. On August 25 he

---

[1] As a sop to laborers who were agitating so strenuously for alcoholic beverages that Tumulty feared that Wilson might find himself "whipped into action," the secretary persuaded the President to allow him to insert in the May message to Congress a paragraph recommending that provision be made for the sale of light wines and beer until July 1, when the Prohibition Amendment, which had become part of the Constitution on Jan. 16, 1919, took effect. The question of what liquor should be deemed intoxicating was finally settled when the Volstead Act was passed over the President's veto on Oct. 28, 1919. Wilson vetoed the Act because he felt that it invaded the police power of the states and, being impossible to enforce, would lead to nefarious practices. Baruch, "The Democracy of W.W.," an address at Brown University, Oct. 25, 1950.

Legislation in the field of labor was chiefly the function of the states, Wilson told Congress, and at best could "go only a very little way in commanding what should be done." For solutions he looked to "common counsel and voluntary cooperation of capitalist, manager, and workman." However, he believed that some federal legislation was practical. Referring to the achievement of the eight-hour day and the improvement of conditions of work, he expressed faith in the ability of Congress to find a way of preventing child labor and to help in coordinating existing agencies for arbitration and in setting up new sources of information and advice. Though the League would provide international agencies, he put his trust in national action to get immediate results.

addressed an appeal directly to the representatives of the railway shopmen, who had called a strike to take effect on September 2. He went
on to make it plain that he was in no mood to throw off the responsibility for economic justice that the federal government had been assuming under the compulsions of war. His pleas were effective. The leaders
of the shopmen postponed their strike, and inflationary increases in
wages were avoided.

Having called a truce in labor-management strife until settlements
could be made "by peaceful and effective common counsel," Wilson
hastened to act. At a meeting with his Cabinet September 2—the last
in which the aging leader was to bring his full powers to bear upon the
problems that his men put before him—a plan was discussed for airing
the vexing issues of industrial relations. In a Labor Day message, the
President already had announced that a conference would be called in
which "authoritative representatives of labor and of those who direct
labor will discuss fundamental means of bettering the whole relationship of capital and labor and putting the whole question of wages upon
another footing."

The call for an industrial conference went out on September 3. It
followed almost exactly the plan that had been proposed by Tumulty
on June 4. Wilson asked that the proposed gathering be attended by
fifteen representatives of labor, fifteen of management, and fifteen men
to uphold the public interest.

The meeting of these minds, Wilson prophesied, would result in the
devising of "methods by which we can speedily . . . obviate the waste-
fulness caused by the continued interruption of many of our important
industrial enterprises by strikes and lockouts." The delegates were
asked to gather in Washington on October 6.[2]

Lansing, who equated labor unrest with bolshevism, had been recommending blunderbuss tactics. He was alarmed when the President suggested that the tendency of labor to revolt against the economic order

[2] Before Oct. 6 arrived, the antipathy between labor and management was intensified by a
steel strike and by a threat of a walkout of miners of bituminous coal. On Oct. 19, Secretary
of the Interior Lane, representing the public at the Industrial Conference, notified the President
that constructive action was impossible. "The elements have come to an impasse." Lane informed
Wilson. "They cannot agree as to collective bargaining. The labor people say that unless we
can recognize this right we can get nowhere. The employers say that they are not yet ready
to give up dealing with their men as individuals. The public group is most liberal, siding
strongly in this matter with the labor group . . . some of the delegates are angry and pretty
nearly everyone disgusted . . . and so I turn to you for a word that will help."

By the time this plea reached him, the President's health had failed and he could give no
leadership. He was barely able, on Oct. 22, to send to the Industrial Conference a letter of
appeal that Lane had proposed. When this failed to bring about an understanding, Wilson,
leaning upon advice from representatives of the public, called together a new group of men
to continue the conference that, he hoped, would find a way of orderly negotiation within
industries. The second National Industrial Conference, however, came to an end without
fulfilling his hopes, although significant patterns of federal action were shaped.

sprang from an awakening consciousness of a right to share profits that was essentially just, that "industrial democracy" was fundamental to political democracy. There would be "violence and bloodshed," Lansing foresaw, "because the demands of labor will be beyond reason. Then the reformers who started the movement will too late attempt to check it . . . The President . . . will issue appeals but they will not be as effective as they were in the past."

A crisis that threatened law and order right at the President's gates gave point to Lansing's fears. Disturbed when the American Federation of Labor granted a charter to a policemen's union in the District of Columbia, Wilson advised the commissioners of the district to forbid affiliation with any national labor body. On Labor Day Wilson courageously appeared at a baseball game between the police and a Home Defense League and threw out the first ball; and the next day, with his approval, an ultimatum went out threatening the discharge of anyone who remained after September 7 in any organization affiliated with a labor union. A few weeks later, after the Boston police had struck, he reaffirmed his advice to the commissioners in the face of hostile senators.[3]

In the summer of 1919 messages from abroad reported disintegration and despair. The tensions of a state of war were wearing on the nerves of the peoples of the world and undermining the institutions that held them in political and economic balance. The emancipation that had been achieved in Central Europe would result only in chaos if the steadying hand of the League did not take hold soon.

He had an urgent cable from House who, working at London for the League, was embarrassed because senators were blocking the appoint-

[3] On Sept. 5 the District of Columbia police union secured an injunction against the commissioners. Wilson was attacked by Republican senators, who offered to back Commissioner Brownlow against the President. On Sept. 17 Brownlow received this wire from Wilson, who was then in California: "I am quite willing that you should tell the Senate Committee that my position in my conversation with you was exactly the same as I have expressed recently in my speeches here in the West, and, of course, I am as desirous as you are of dealing with the police force in the most just and generous way, but I think any association of the police force of the capital city, or any other great city, whose object is to bring pressure upon the public or the community, such as will endanger the public peace or embarrass the maintenance of good order, should in no case be countenanced or permitted." Eventually Congress raised the pay of the district police and forbade unionization.

Wilson held a Washington newspaper responsible for inciting riots on June 21 in order to embarrass the police commissioner. He hoped to see the owner indicted for this, and sent word to the district attorney to this effect. The President was determined that employers as well as labor organizations should not influence police action.

This issue was as black and white to Woodrow Wilson as to Governor Calvin Coolidge, who was making an equally strong—and more dramatic—stand against police unionization in Massachusetts. It was embarrassing to the prophet of world peace that there were threats of violence among his own flock. He was hurt, one evening at Keith's, to hear a stage joke that linked his name with an organization that had resorted to illegal use of force—the Industrial Workers of the World.

ment of Americans to commissions that had been set up under the treaty. The Colonel asked when the Senate might be expected to come to a vote. Would it help, he inquired, if the treaty were ratified soon by Britain, France, and Italy? And what about the meeting of the International Economic Council that was to convene on September 15?

On August 21 Wilson replied that he could not prophesy what would happen at Washington, that it would be a distinct advantage if the Allies would ratify the treaty as soon as possible. He asked Congress for funds to keep the American peace commission operating at Paris for another four months. He thought that the Council of the League ought not to organize until at least four powers and a majority of the minor nations had approved the treaty; otherwise the organization would lack moral authority and would resemble the Old World alliance that its opponents accused it of being.

All the domestic problems besetting the President were overshadowed by the categorical imperative of the moment. Above everything, international order must be restored. If the United States did not take the lead in adapting political forms to new conditions, she might have to defer to those who were more enterprising. It was imperative, Wilson felt, that his own people should not fulfill the cynical prophecy that had been made in the French press. They must not, after giving birth to the League of Nations, go home and shirk responsibility for its nurture.

It was inconceivable, to a mind disciplined by Presbyterianism, that responsible men could try to stop the process of inexorable universal law. And to a mind steeped in British tradition it was equally unbelievable that an Anglo-Saxon nation would not put aside considerations of party and, acting as a principal, ratify the Covenant to which its accredited agent had committed it.

At the end of August it seemed time to take direct action. He would "appeal to Caesar," he said. On the 25th, enraged by the effort of Lodge's committee to reverse the treaty's ruling on Shantung, he told Lansing that he would go to the people at once, that if the senators wanted war he'd "give them a bellyful." Instead of remaining at Washington and encouraging the compromise settlement to which Senators Kellogg and Pittman were close, he chose to risk everything on his power to sway his national congregation.

Wilson had long contemplated a speaking trip to educate his people.[4] He had been advised by the State Department that an appeal to the

[4] A letter written by Gilbert Close to his wife on March 22, 1919, records that the President was then thinking of making a trip to the Pacific coast very soon after he reached home. Tumulty had made out a tentative itinerary in June, an outline had been drawn up at Paris, in consultation with House on May 17, of what should be said in the speeches, and Wilson had spoken of his plans to newsmen just before leaving France.

country over the head of the Senate would offend and alienate senators who held moderate views about revising the Covenant. Lansing felt that industrial unrest made it unwise to go among the people. Moreover, some observers noted that most senators, having four to six years to serve, would not be swayed easily by sentiment stirred up among the voters. At the end of July he had deferred his trip until he could make more efforts to convert wavering legislators.

During August, voices came to the prophet from beyond the stuffy rooms of the capital. Leaders of his party who had toured the West had found the people eager for an oracle who would guide them to an honorable place in the world community. Moreover, House reported that there was "a noticeable sag" in popular interest in the League in Europe as well as in America and that the President's voice was eagerly awaited to remind the whole world how the new institution could serve it.

It was as inevitable that the prophet embark on this last educational crusade as it had been that his Uncle James Woodrow seize the challenge of his adversaries in order to educate his denomination in the truths of natural science. There was still a Woodrow down in old Columbia who understood this as none of the President's household could. "You have my deepest sympathy," wrote James Woodrow's daughter, "in your struggle with those wicked men in the Capitol. God grant you strength to stand firm, to refuse to consent to the slightest change, reservation, or interpretation of the Treaty . . . If you should yield finally and consent to the change of the obscurest jot or more obscure tittle a shout of triumph would go up from their ranks; for they would use their consent as a lever with which to overturn the whole beautiful fabric, and lay all the blame on you. Thank God, you see this more clearly than anyone else can, and I am sure He will give you strength to stand firm, and guard . . . your precious treasures." [5]

It was this niece of his proud little mother who had once reminded him of the Woodrow motto: *Audaci favet fortuna.* She was the historian of the clan, and now perhaps he could give her another great controversy to add to the annals. If only he could beat the enemy—"horse, foot, and dragoon"—as his father had vanquished the Kentucky theologians when he had "come down from the stilts of study." Maybe, after all, he could be worthy of his greatest heroes—his father and his Uncle James. To Tumulty he seemed an old man intent on dying with his face to the enemy. He said to a journalist who suggested that he was

[5] To W.W., Aug. 30, 1919. In acknowledgment of this advice from Marion Woodrow, Wilson wrote, on Sept. 11, 1919: "I want to express my deep appreciation of your generous attitude towards what I have been trying to do."

not well enough to undertake a speaking trip: "I don't care if I die the next minute after the treaty is ratified." He was not ready, yet, to pay the price that even moderate Republicans were asking. He would not allow reservations to be included in the resolution of ratification, and thus perhaps reopen the peace settlement to further attrition by Europeans. He would give his life, if necessary, to avoid this and to keep the faith that he had pledged in behalf of his country.

His Cabinet and his physician begged him not to toss his life away in what seemed to many a mad gesture. No doctor could be responsible for the outcome, Grayson warned.

Wilson listened attentively, then walked to a window and looked out pensively at the monument of George Washington. "I promised our soldiers," he said, "that it was a war to end wars; and if I do not do all in my power to put the treaty in effect, I will be a slacker and never able to look those boys in the eye. I must go." It was a last desperate resort. "If the treaty is not ratified by the Senate," he explained, "the war will have been fought in vain and the world will be thrown into chaos."

And so the prophet went forth to castigate his adversaries and preach in the clear, crisp air of the West. Perhaps there came back to him the lines that he and Miss Ellie Lou had quoted often:

> In front, the sun climbs slow, how slowly,
> But westward, look, the land is bright.

To meet the economic ills for which the timorous Lansing prescribed repression, the racial passions that had erupted in violence, the religious prejudices that were perverting the political thinking of citizens, he would boldly proclaim a living, cosmic gospel to which all Americans might constructively turn their emotions. Moreover, by regenerative preaching he might make whole again his own split self, might redeem his pledges and escape the political bankruptcy that had haunted him ever since the Congressional election of 1918. He could not forget that in 1912 his one-man evangelical crusade through the West had paid off in votes.

On September 3, then, after directing that all communications about the treaty from legislators should be forwarded to him in cipher, and after charging Senator Hitchcock to present four interpretive resolutions only if necessary—Wilson put on his straw hat, a blue coat, and white trousers, and went with his wife to the special train that was to take him west. He was in the high humor that always came to him under the stimulus of a campaign.

Every minute of the journey had been mapped out. One itinerary after another had been drawn up and discarded. All had provided for a few days of rest at the Grand Canyon; but when the President heard of this he would have none of it. It was to be a "business trip, pure and simple." He had brought along his indispensable typewriter but, he confessed to Tumulty as they boarded the train, he was "in a nice fix." He had not had time to prepare speeches and did not know when he would get time. "For the past weeks I have been suffering from daily headaches," he said, "but perhaps tonight's rest will make me fit for the work of tomorrow." He could but exist from one day to the next—hoping, praying, working late and early on his speeches, enduring the nagging headaches.

The next day, however, at Columbus—in Senator Harding's state of Ohio—he delivered an address that reassured those who wondered whether he still had his power to work magic with words. His heart was so full that he needed no script. He talked now as a teacher among friends. "I have for a long time chafed at the confinement of Washington," he confessed quite ingenuously. "I have for a long time wished to fulfill the purpose with which my heart was full when I returned to our beloved country, namely, to go out and report to my fellow countrymen concerning those affairs of the world which now need to be settled . . ."

Expressing astonishment at misinterpretations of the peace treaty, he explained its historical importance. The peacemakers had done a huge job, he insisted. So far as the scope of their authority permitted, they had rectified wrongs that had been a fertile source of wars. They had made advances in the history of the race that were of far more consequence than the temporary task of punishing Germany.

The next war, the prophet warned, would have to be paid for by American blood and American money. As the wealth and power of the United States grew, her interest in preventing war would exceed that of any other power. Hence it seemed inevitable that she be "trustee for the peace of the world." The people must decide whether they would be "ostriches or eagles," whether they would play their part in history "as members of the board of directors or as outside speculators." "It is acceptance of great world duties or scuttle now and come back afterwards," he prophesied.

To more than a thousand businessmen, at a Chamber of Commerce luncheon at St. Louis, he posed a practical question: "Who can say that our interests are separate from the interests of the rest of the world, commercially, industrially, financially?" But he did not like to argue on this level, he said, for "America was not founded to make money; it was founded to lead the world on the way to liberty."

In speech after speech, some from the rear platform of his car, some before vast assemblages, he proclaimed the contributions that had been made at Paris. He warmed to the challenge that his scholar's conscience had put upon him thirty years before. And yet, against the scholarly tradition that bade him keep pace with the latent thinking of his people and refrain from attempting, by what he had once called "the foolishness of preaching," to revolutionize the whole thought of a nation and of an epoch, against this monitoring force the prophetic impulses of his ancestors surged. The spiritual fires deep within him were fanned as he spoke to twelve thousand in St. Louis's Coliseum and was hailed as "Woodrow Wilson, Father of World Democracy." He challenged "some gentlemen" to show him how they would prove that, having gone into an enterprise, they were not "absolute, contemptible quitters" if they did not see the game through. He threatened that such men would be "gibbeted" in the annals of mankind. He remarked, too, that he sometimes wished that "both parties might be smothered in their own gas."

This "peacemaker" was talking like Andrew Johnson who, according to Wilson the historian, uttered "violent speeches which swelled the number of his radical opponents as rapidly as the leaders of the Congressional majority could have desired." By setting himself up in a righteous pulpit above the folks of the West, Wilson opened himself to suspicions of his motives. *Harvey's Weekly* portrayed him as a "whirling dervish" taking a "hippodroming excursion" at the expense of the taxpayers. It was whispered that he was beginning to campaign for a third term in the Presidency.

Thoughtful proponents of the League saw the danger and from Washington advised the President that he was stiffening the opposition, that he must not allow political controversy to divert him from direct, positive explanation of the peace treaty. Accepting the warning, Wilson typed on a single sheet a list of topics to be interpreted. As he progressed westward he spoke on matters that he had previously brushed aside as "hypothetical questions" in which the people were not interested. He dealt now more explicitly with the controversial clauses of the Covenant. Moreover, he paid heed to the special concerns of the various audiences.

As he went into the Northwest, where labor agitation had been violent, he departed from his main theme to speak of industrial conciliation and to hold up the example of "pitiful Russia." A "lovable people," he explained, had "come under the terror of the power of men whom nobody knows how to find . . ." The President paused for a moment in his pleas for the peace treaty and spoke out to strengthen the arm of the law in American cities. The principles that he held dearest, indeed his very faith in America's ability to give order to the world, were shaken by the Boston strike. The next day, in Idaho, he came back to this "intolerable crime against civilization."

The prophet was making converts in all walks of life. The constituencies of irreconcilable senators turned out to honor him in the stimulating air of the Northwest.

At Seattle, however, a sinister plot was hatching. There had been serious strikes in the city, and representatives of the I.W.W. had prepared to call on Wilson and petition for the release of political prisoners; but the city government announced that the radical leaders would not be allowed to "annoy" the President. The presidential party drove through dense crowds of citizens whose fanatical cheers drowned out the music of the bands. Then, suddenly, there were five long blocks of awesome silence and sidewalks packed with thousands of men in grimy overalls, the sleeves of their work-shirts rolled up above muscles that bulged from arms folded across their chests. Among these demonstrators were ex-soldiers wearing overseas caps and others displaying hatbands that read: "Release Political Prisoners!" With their women beside them, they stood still and silent. Not a sound, not a move. Not even a glance at the President, for they had been instructed to look past him. It seemed, suddenly, as if the light of the sun had gone out.

Woodrow Wilson had been standing in his automobile, bowing and smiling. Suddenly his face went white. His jaw sagged and the lines in his countenance deepened. He looked limp and hunched up, and the hand holding his tall hat hung at his side. But he remained standing in his swaying car, and after the five awful blocks had been passed and people began to cheer again he waved his hand and smiled wanly.

Here was a patent distemper in the body politic, to be faced with sympathy and courage. The next morning, though it was Sunday, Wilson requested a delegation of labor leaders to make the call upon him that the fearsome city fathers had forbidden. He received these outcasts while naval officers were kept waiting in the lobby of the hotel. He was determined that all citizens should have access to their president. He could not forget that he had said in a speech only a few days before: "Revolutions come from the long suppression of the human spirit. Revolutions come because men know that they have rights and that they are disregarded."

The labor delegates found him at his rooms in the afternoon, standing by a long, heavy table, holding on to its edge, looking very old. The hand that he gave to them felt dry. There were two ex-soldiers in the group and he could scarcely summon courage to meet their eyes. The leader of the delegation cleared his throat but could not get a word out, so he merely offered the petition to the President.

Wilson took it with a hand that shook until he steadied it by gripping the lapel of his coat. In a voice that sounded strained he said that he would read their plea immediately, that he had been displeased by the decision of the local authorities to keep them away from him and deny their right of petition.

The spokesman managed to mutter a few words. He had planned to refer to some of his comrades as "ex-soldiers and ex-sailors who have served in the war to make the world safe for democracy." But he had forgotten this line, and later he was glad that he had. The breaking man before him might not have been able to bear it. During the interview Wilson's eyes closed and he looked even more ghastly. His face twitched. When the men left, he followed them for a few steps, then stopped in the middle of the high-ceiling room, with bowed head.[6]

Only those close to him knew that in Montana the hot, dry air had brought on an asthmatic affliction. Headaches clamped down upon him and made the faces of his audiences blur and multiply. Tobacco smoke in halls in which he spoke made him suffer. Dr. Grayson sat up at night to spray his throat, fed him liquids and predigested foods. At Seattle, worn as he was, he spoke three times in one day. When he reviewed the Pacific fleet, his launch collided with another boat, listed badly, and shipped a little water. A secret service man leaped to his side; but the President dismissed the danger with a smile. That night he sat with Edith Wilson in a little roof garden of their hotel and gazed in awe at the lights of the Pacific fleet, stretching out to sight's end. When he retired he did not sleep, and the next day a headache beset him, so that when he tried to dictate he sat with his head resting on the back of a chair.

A day later, as the presidential party sought relaxation in motoring, one of the automobiles crashed and a popular newsman was killed and another injured. As soon as Wilson heard of this he went to the bedside of the surviving victim and arranged that he be given a drawing room on the party's train. Ever since leaving Washington he had shown concern for the comfort and morale of his comrades of the road, sharing the vicissitudes of travel with many a good story and never a complaint. But when the journalists urged him to speak flatteringly, in each city, of local units that had served conspicuously in the war, he would have none of it. When they spoke of the effectiveness of "sob stuff," the phrase sank into the Covenanter like a knife and there was a freezing silence. And when a newsman watched him composing on his typewriter, he remarked pointedly that he could do much better work when no one was looking on.

[6] Louis Adamic, "The 'Assassin' of Wilson," *American Mercury*, XXI (October 1930), 82.

Tumulty was standing by valiantly, working up little memoranda that would focus the Chief's efforts upon salient, nonpartisan arguments, and adducing quotations from Republican statesmen that acknowledged that the age of isolation was past and advocated the idea of a League of Nations. The ebullient secretary, who through the years had plagued the President with many a "dose" of advice, had so well mastered the trend of affairs, during Wilson's absence at Paris, that his political sense was rising toward the level of statesmanship.

At Portland, on September 15, journalists brought word that William Bullitt, whose plan for peace with Russia had not been accepted by Wilson at Paris, had given damaging testimony before the Committee on Foreign Relations. At a session at which no Democratic senators were present to check him, this frustrated young man had asserted that he had been urged to publish a report on his Moscow venture by Lloyd George and by some of the American commissioners, that "it was only Mr. Wilson" who stood in the way. The Senate committee had struck pay dirt. When the testimony was concluded, Lodge expressed his thanks warmly.

The *Nation,* for which Wilson had privately expressed "utter contempt," now reopened its fire on the President. The *New Republic* also took the "perfectabilitarian" view. In articles that were made a part of the Senate's record, the treaty was denounced as wicked and its acceptance by Americans as "a violation of faith." The ideal concept that Wilson had set forth in the first of the Fourteen Points and later had found impractical—"diplomacy shall proceed always frankly and in the public view"—was thrown back in his teeth.

The worst shock came, however, when Bullitt exposed the full measure of the infidelity of the secretary of state. He asserted that Lansing had said privately at Paris, on May 19, that the League was useless, that the great powers had simply arranged the world to suit themselves, that if only the senators could understand what the treaty meant and if the American people could really understand it, it would unquestionably be defeated.

At this exposure of his defection from the faith, the secretary of state took alarm and hastened to telegraph a palliating version of the May interview with Bullitt. Lansing resorted to pious denunciation of his accuser, whom he called "a disloyal young man who is seeking notoriety at the expense of all honorable men."

Ah, yes, Brutus was an "honorable man." The pastoral insight that had been able to perceive House's essential loyalty in spite of the Colonel's indiscretions saw clearly where the truth of this matter lay. Wilson had surmised that Lansing was undermining and upsetting morale.

And now here was verification of everything that he had suspected. "Think of it!" he exploded to Tumulty. "This from a man whom I raised from the level of a subordinate to the great office of secretary of state of the United States."

Woodrow Wilson went down into California, then, in a mood approaching despair; and yet there was hope in the increasing ardor of the people for his message. It sometimes seemed, as he gave four addresses in the bay cities within two days, that they would smother him with flowers, glut him with feasts, suffocate him with tobacco smoke, wear him down with their long parades and blaring bands, talk him to insanity in conferences and interviews, badger him to death with questions and protests directed against the British Empire and the Japanese. When he began to speak at the civic auditorium, his voice was drowned by heckling from little hostile groups, and at the end there was only a polite patter of palms; but another audience, composed of women, cheered him heartily. Coming to his rooms from the din of admirers who milled around him, he dropped into a chair and groaned: "They mean so well—but they are killing me!"

Yet in public he yielded not at all to weariness of the flesh, nor to inner voices of discouragement that were rending his soul. An ominous message from Washington reported that the "mild reservationists" had worked out a program of changes in the treaty that had Lodge's approval.[7] Nevertheless, the President said to a San Francisco audience: "I am arguing the matter only because I am a very patient man. I have not the slightest doubt as to what the result is going to be."

Popular excitement reached its highest pitch at San Diego, where Wilson spoke through an amplifier to an audience of fifty thousand in a stadium. The next day he talked at Los Angeles, and many of the effervescent, progressive people of the region were converted. The toll of the effort was so severe, however, that the President was in need more than ever of a restful Sabbath. On Sunday morning, taking a few hours from "business" for the first time on the trip, he drove out to a humble bungalow on an unfrequented street to call on a girlhood friend of Miss Ellie Lou—a woman whose lot in life had been hard and to whom Ellen Wilson had ministered until her own death. Joe Tumulty loved him that day for the purity and simplicity of his motives, though the secretary was vexed because the act of kindness was not capitalized by a "tip-off" to reporters and photographers.

[7] The day after the speech at San Francisco, Vance McCormick wired that the reservations on which the moderates were working with Lodge would make United States action under Article X or United States acceptance of a mandate dependent "in any particular case" upon action by Congress. Wilson wired to Lansing that McCormick's information should be conveyed to Senator Hitchcock with advice that the President would regard any such reservations "as a practical rejection of the Covenant."

Having performed this mission for Miss Ellie Lou, Woodrow Wilson returned to his hotel. He had asked his old friend Mary Allen Hulbert to lunch with him and to meet his second wife. Edith Wilson and Dr. Grayson received the guest warmly; and soon the President came in, animated at the prospect of a visit with one who had often brought him release from his cares. He looked less worn than Mary Hulbert had expected, and she commented on his appearance. "Oddly enough," he replied, "I do not feel well. I feel as if all those things which I have succeeded in escaping have fallen upon me." After luncheon they went into another room, where they were interrupted now and then by the calls of delegations whom the President felt he must see—"Converts, sir," Grayson whispered as he announced them.

From each interruption Wilson came back to chat with his old playmate. The material world had dealt as harshly with his vision of feminine charm as with his dreams of human security. The blooming, vivacious Mary Peck was still sweet-faced, but faded and careworn. She had been slightly lamed by an accident. To earn bread and butter, she and her son had tried their hands at many things: ranching, writing stories, selling books, movie acting. And all the while she had been persecuted by enemies of Woodrow Wilson who hoped to find immorality in her relationship with the President. They had shadowed her, insinuated, threatened, cajoled, ransacked her rooms. At his pastoral urging, every detail of her story came out. When she told him of traducers who had claimed to have support from members of his Cabinet, he murmured: "So-and-so did that? Why did So-and-so do that?" More dirt, more disloyalty!

He laughed over the ludicrous tales of their iniquity that gossips had been circulating for years. In his overwrought condition, however, he blamed himself for her plight. "God," he cried out at last, "to think that you should have suffered because of me!" As they were about to part he laid his hand on his wife's shoulder and said: "Isn't there something we can do?" Edith Wilson went out of the room for a moment, and they were alone. He repeated the practical question that he had asked his wife; but, chin up, Mary Hulbert replied that she would take care of herself, but perhaps he might help her son. As they paced slowly down the hall, she recited lines that were familiar to them:

> "With all my will, but much against my heart,
> We two now part."

From Los Angeles the prophet turned eastward. In the Sierras he suffered from gas fumes in the tunnels, the acrid smoke of forest fires, and sudden changes of altitude. Crossing the desert, he met suffocating heat and dust; and the nervous twitching in his face that had been so marked at Paris became continuous. At this juncture Congress was adding insult by introducing a resolution for an inquiry into an alleged "shower of gifts" received by the Wilsons in Europe.

Speaking in the tabernacle of the Mormons, at Salt Lake City, he read the reservation to Article X that had been proposed by "mild reservationists" and approved by Lodge. This, he asserted, would be a refusal on the part of the United States to carry the same responsibility that other League members assumed. Hence it would be a rejection of the treaty.

The auditorium was packed, and the air grew stale and oppressive. Edith Wilson gave him a handkerchief soaked in lavender salts, and somehow he got through an ordeal that lasted for two hours. Once he lost control of his nerves and replied tartly to a heckler. Tumulty told him afterward that in his speech he failed to land a "punch." He left the hall soaked with perspiration; and when he changed to dry clothes, they were soon wet through. The next day, at Cheyenne, he was too exhausted to deny that he was ill.

Yet he could not be persuaded to undergo a week's rest. There were still eight speeches left on the schedule, and he refused the continuing pleas of wife and doctor for a brief respite. "No," he said. "I have caught the imagination of the people." Sensing his wife's deep concern, he tried to cheer her. "This will soon be over, and when we get back to Washington I promise you I will take a holiday."

The sympathy and admiration of the newsmen on his train had increased almost to the point of veneration. Whether he would be able to complete the tour was a sporting question among them. But he assured them that he could finish. "My constitution may be exhausted," he jested, "but I ought to get along for a good while on my bylaws."

He reached Denver late at night and was greeted by a lady whom he had loved in idyllic days—his Cousin Harriet Woodrow, now Mrs. Welles. They chatted at his hotel until after midnight. He was up early, though, and at nine o'clock began a parade between lines of cheering school children to the state capitol, where he spoke outdoors to a huge gathering. Then on to the auditorium in which he had made his great address on the English Bible. Here the aging prophet faced a sympathetic audience, but had to contend with faulty acoustics.

He went on for an afternoon program at Pueblo, where in 1911 he had walked from the station to the hotel carrying his own bag. He wished now that he might be let alone as he had been then. He objected petulantly when told that he was expected to appear at the fair grounds before going to the city hall to speak; but since citizens had bought tickets with the understanding that they would see him, he agreed to compromise by riding in his car past the grandstand.

"This will have to be a short speech," he said in a new auditorium that he took a part in dedicating. And in an aside to the newsmen: "Aren't you fellows getting pretty sick of this?" But soon his spirit transcended the bonds of his protesting body, and the emotional taps that Tumulty had opened for him were allowed to run freely. He harked back to the moving scene at the cemetery outside Paris where he had spoken over the graves of American soldiers on Memorial Day. If only the opponents of the treaty could visit such a spot! Tears came into his own eyes, and his voice seemed to lose its sonority. "I wish," he said, "that they could feel the moral obligation that rests upon us not to go back on those boys, but to see the thing through . . . to the end and make good the redemption of the world. For nothing less depends upon this decision, nothing less than the liberation and salvation of the world." [8]

There was moisture even in the eyes of newsmen who had heard him many times. To Tumulty he seemed a great organist playing expertly upon a keyboard of emotions. Finally he came to his valedictory, the last words that he was ever to speak face to face with a large assemblage of his people. "Now that the mists of this great question have cleared away, I believe that men will see the truth, eye to eye and face to face. There is one thing that the American people always rise to and extend their hand to, and that is the truth of justice and of liberty and of peace. We have accepted that truth and we are going to be led by it, and it is going to lead us, and through us the world, out into pastures of quietness and peace such as the world never dreamed of before."

The hurrahs of the audience at Pueblo were still ringing in his ears when the racking pains that had pursued him for ten days settled upon his head. He had asked several times whether he could not get some exercise, and now Dr. Grayson prescribed a walk in the crisp mountain air. When the train stopped for a change of locomotives, the Wilsons strolled on a white, dusty road, stopping on a wooden bridge and looking pensively into the stream beneath. Urged by the doctor to exert himself, the ailing man ran until he was winded, and color came into his face.

---

[8] Wilson never fully exploited a line of argument that General Bliss had suggested to him before he left Paris: that in his speeches he dramatize the horrors of future wars. According to Bliss, Wilson believed that the next war, if it came, would be no worse than that just concluded, for he thought that noxious gases and other barbarities would be effectively outlawed. At Denver, however, Wilson alluded to this theme in a paragraph in which he said: "What the Germans used were toys compared to what would be used in the next war."

He returned to the train to eat some dinner, and remarked that his head bothered him less than it had for days. But late in the evening he knocked at his wife's door and said that he was in great distress.

She found him sitting on the edge of his bed, his tortured head resting on the back of a chair. Dr. Grayson was summoned but could do nothing to give relief. He observed a curious drooping at the left side of the President's mouth, and a trace of saliva trickled out. The patient's nervous controls were shattered. He could not recline comfortably on the pillows that were provided, felt that he must move about, got up and dressed. Then followed long hours of agony, and a harrowing vigil for Grayson like that of the April night at Paris. It was another acute episode in the relentless progress of arteriosclerosis.

At five in the morning, while he sat upright on a hard seat, the tortured head drooped and sleep came. His wife sat opposite; and his ghastly face told her that she now, alone, would have to bear responsibilities that she had shared with him. She felt that henceforth she must protect him from the public. Moreover, she must shield him from himself; she must never let him know how ill he really was.

Soon after seven he appeared, shaved and dressed but piteously sick. Immediately they began to urge him to end the speaking trip then and there. It might be fatal to continue, Grayson warned. His wife and doctor decided that it was their duty to be firm, no matter what anguish of soul their decision might cause. He accepted their verdict as a decree of fate and took up a cross that he was to bear for four years without a murmur of self-pity. But he was to feel, in future years, that it would have benefited his great cause if only he could have died that night.

When the train slowed down near Wichita, and Tumulty went out to tell a welcoming committee that the President was unable to meet them, Wilson realized the finality of the decision that had been made for him. He sent messages to his daughters so that they would not be unduly alarmed by press reports of his condition; and he dictated a statement to the people of Wichita, telling them of his regret at disappointing them.

With shades drawn against the stares of the curious, the train roared on to Washington. For two days and two uncomfortable nights the Wilsons sat in the confinement of their car, he sitting disconsolate and contemplating the ruins of his ambitions, brooding upon the disloyalty of Lansing and the others, she knitting and trying to divert him with small talk.

He mulled over reports from Europe that had been distressing him for several days. Racked by pain and unable to digest anything but liquids, he approved Polk's intention to send strong American naval reinforcements to the Adriatic as quickly as possible, as an expression of disapproval of Italian demands for more concessions.[9]

In his last mission to the American people, the spirit of the old Covenanter had defied the bounds of his mortality, had driven him through thirty-four addresses and scores of interviews, parades, and rear-platform talks within twenty-two days. Bands had waked him up and bands had played him to bed, and the crowds had been vociferous enough to encourage him to plan to extend his tour to New England. He had told the people what he thought they ought to know. He had given a picture of the whole Covenant of the League, to prevent the basing of a national decision on a line, a clause, or only on one or two of the twenty-six articles. He had preached a gospel of arbitration as opposed to armament, of playing-the-game against sulking-on-the-bench. He had explained the veto power that the Senate would hold against illegitimate drafts upon America's strength to settle controversies beyond the scope of her interests; and as for involvement in a dispute to which the United States was a party from the beginning, he reminded his people that in such a case they would be "in the scrap anyway." His life-long scorn of special privileges, unequal opportunities, and secret arrangements had been burned into the minds of his Western audiences.

Finally, he had delivered to his age the warning that was to establish his place securely among the major prophets of his century: "I can predict with absolute certainty that within another generation there will be another world war if the nations of the world do not concert the method by which to prevent it." And in that struggle, he prophesied, "not a few hundred thousand fine men from America will have to die, but as many millions as are necessary to accomplish the final freedom of the world."

However, the effect of his efforts upon the voting of the senators was insignificant, perhaps even negative. His eloquence had intensified the hatred of his enemies and roused resentment among some who, by a laying on of hands, might have been persuaded to accept the interpretative amendments that he had given secretly to Hitchcock. Against the venom of personal hate that had been spewed out against him, Wilson

[9] Frank Polk, now head of the American Commission at Paris, had been conferring with Lloyd George and Clemenceau about a solution of the Adriatic question, which had become acute once more in September when swashbuckling Italians squatted in Fiume. Polk had worked out a solution that the President had accepted. But Lloyd George and Clemenceau, who wanted quick ratification of the treaty by Italy because the League Council could not act on certain questions vital to France and Great Britain until the treaty was ratified by three powers, were now supporting an Italian demand for more concessions.

At news of this yielding, Wilson had grown indignant. It seemed to him that d'Annunzio was "behaving like an ass," that everyone was failing him—Lloyd George, Clemenceau, Orlando —all of them!

knew that he was helpless. "If I had nothing to do with the League of Nations it would go through . . ." he had confessed to Mary Hulbert.

The broken man returned to Washington on a Sunday morning. At the station his daughter Margaret ran down the platform to greet him. He insisted on walking to his automobile, and smiled and nodded to a group of soldiers who cheered him. For four days he made spasmodic efforts at a normal life. He saw movies in the White House, and went out motoring huddled in an overcoat. But the servants remarked that the President was not the same jaunty man whom they had known. He was more peaked and florid and he kept much to his own apartment.

He was encouraged by a report that Clemenceau, speaking in the Chamber of Deputies, had referred to him with respect and had urged the American Senate to ratify the Covenant. Moreover, on the second day after his return to Washington, Tumulty cheered the Chief with news that sentiment on Capitol Hill was improving.

On October 1, after evening movies and before retiring, the President felt well enough to read a chapter from the Bible as he had been wont to do during the war. His voice was strong. But after he wound his watch he forgot to take it to his bedroom, and this aberration worried him.

When he awoke in the morning his left hand had no feeling in it, and he had to ask for help in getting to the bathroom. He moved with spasms of pain. Edith Wilson, alarmed, went to the telephone to call Dr. Grayson. Returning, she found her husband on the floor. The voice that had commanded the thought of millions was barely able to whisper to ask for a drink of water. He stirred a little and his wife managed to slip a pillow under his head. His faithful doctor came hurrying, and together they lifted him to the big bed that once had been Abraham Lincoln's. There he lay, looking as if he were dead, while his family rallied to give him comfort and hope, and specialists came to consult. The verdict was that a thrombosis—a clot in a blood vessel—had impaired the control of the brain over a side of the body that already had been weakened by neuritis. The President's left arm and leg were helpless. Though there had been no lesion, there was danger of one. If the clot was not absorbed by nature, it might impair the heart's action and cause death.

CHAPTER XIX

Pulling Down the Temple

For days it was touch and go, and for weeks it seemed possible that a Wilson prophecy might be fulfilled straightway—the prediction that he had made eight years before, that if ever he entered the White House he would not come out alive.

The old mansion became a hospital, as a procession of doctors and nurses visited the sickroom, bringing medical apparatus of many kinds. Cary Grayson stayed constantly at his patient's side through six nights of vigil. After two weeks of precarious progress, a stricture of the bladder set back recovery. Consulting specialists recommended surgery; but the two old Virginians who knew him better—Dr. Grayson and Edith Wilson—felt that an operation would kill him and that nature could cure the abnormality if given a chance. Their faith in rest and quiet was justified, and with the aid of external treatment the crisis passed. For the next six months, however, the sick man was pitifully dependent, and his wife and daughter Margaret kept alternate watches over him.

Four years had gone by since this mortal had had an adequate vacation. Now he must pay the price for the pace at which he had driven himself through the years of crisis. His nerves were raw, and any excitement was torture to them. On the second day after the thrombosis he was able to take a little nourishment; after a week he even had some appetite, took an interest in pending affairs of state, and listened to his wife's reading.

The sick man himself never doubted that he would recover. He was eager to know nature's methods of healing and to cooperate as best he could. He was considerate of those near his bedside, tried to cheer them with jests. When a doctor tapped him he asked: "Why are you knocking? I am at home." And when they took a sample of his blood he said, "That's what the Senate has been trying to do to me." He seemed, to Grayson, as game a patient as the doctor had ever known.

His thought still burned clearly, but feebly as a flickering candle. By the end of October he was able to read papers that were brought to him when his powers rallied a little. Charles Swem, the brilliant young stenographer who had served him since the 1912 campaign and who was trusted to send off dictated statements without checking by the

President, came now to his bedside to take dictation—at first once a week, then more frequently. The invalid would start a letter; then, articulating more and more indistinctly and finally losing the thread of his thought, he would stare into space. Minutes later, reminded that he had been dictating, he would pick up the thread and go on as if there had been no lapse. When they brought a letter to him for signing, they put a pencil in his hand and steadied and pointed it so that he could scrawl out a poor imitation of his copper-plate signature. By November he was dictating as many as three or four letters a day with characteristic perfection.

The psychological ravages of arteriosclerosis were evident as his emotions swung in an arc that was wide and eccentric. There were vast expansions of charity, and contractions that shut his heart implacably against the sinners in the Senate. He wept too easily, and was no longer able to probe a subject deeply or to go "round the clock" in the judicial way that had once been habitual. This man who always had prided himself on earning his pay by being "first-rate" now was unable to grapple rationally with the problems raised by his own disability. His acute creative impulses remained and, thwarted by lack of strength, threw him into moods of frustration. He could not face up squarely to the fact that he, a great moral leader, was not doing his own job from day to day. He even made those around him promise not to reveal his condition to the public. Indeed, he connived with them to conceal his infirmities.

From the secluded sickroom little news of the President's condition seeped out to the people. To ensure absolute quiet, it was necessary to bar all casual visitors from the White House and its grounds. Those nearest to the invalid felt that it would be a betrayal of trust to reveal the truth about the prophet of Truth. To Edith Wilson the suffering man was first of all her husband and her hero; to Admiral Grayson he was a commander in chief whose orders must be obeyed, and also a patient whose health was of prime importance. It was clear to them that any effort to remove the incapacitated President from the White House would disturb his emotions to a degree that might be fatal. The passing weeks brought gradual improvement, and it seemed quite possible that he would again be able to perform the routine of office. The bulletins of Grayson and Tumulty were written in vague generalities and at every opportunity stressed the patient's progress.

This secretive policy had an unfortunate effect on public opinion. Once again—this time, mercifully, without his knowledge—Woodrow Wilson was the victim of a spate of rumors. It was gossiped that he had venereal disease, even that he was insane. Most cutting of the canards, however, was the insinuation that the President was not really ill, but merely sulking in his chamber because he had learned on the western trip that his people did not agree with him about the peace treaty. He himself had become a ruler whom "nobody knew how to find." Loyal friends noted the vicious gossip and wished that it might be stopped by a recital of the truth.

For a while the executive arm of the government seemed to share the paralysis of its chief. Letters sent to the sickroom for the President's signature did not come back; even emergency communications vanished. No pardons were signed, no proclamations issued, and bills were allowed to become law without the President's signature.

As the invalid's interest in affairs of state returned, Tumulty could refer important matters to him through Edith Wilson, who with Dr. Grayson worked out a policy intended to conserve both the strength of their patient and the interests of the nation. Problems for the President were to be presented in writing, and as succinctly as possible. The documents that came were to be screened by Edith Wilson, whose work on "The Drawer" during the last four years had given her insight into the processes of the executive office. The invalid was to be consulted only on those matters that seemed to his wife likely to interest him and unlikely to irritate him.

Under this regimen, the mind that Woodrow Wilson had "discovered" at college and that had been applied to the greatest problems of the age now worked feebly and without adequate knowledge. The failure of resiliency and sensibility that advisers had noted after the severe illness at Paris was now patent. His thoughts ran like a shrunken brook in autumn, clear as ever, but trickling only in the deepest channels. The "single tracks" had become deep ruts, and though he could still perceive their direction he could scarcely see over the sides.

All through October, Joe Tumulty parried questions about his chief's health, and officials of the government had no direct evidence of the President's competence except a few notes bearing a scraggly signature. The secretary, however, conceived it his duty to give an inkling of the truth to the vice-president and to members of the Cabinet of whose discretion he felt sure.

Most of these men acquiesced in the policy that had been laid down by the consulting doctors. However, Lansing felt that, if the work of the Administration was to go on at all, it might be necessary for Vice-President Marshall to act as chief executive. When it was learned that the Republican majority in the House of Representatives was proposing a resolution for an investigation of Wilson's condition with a view to enabling Vice-President Marshall to act for him, Grayson was informed that the Cabinet should be convened to block such a move. Consulting with Tumulty, therefore, the physician and the secretary of state arranged for a meeting on October 6, only four days after the thrombosis.

When the men assembled, Lansing quoted from the Constitution: "In case of the removal of the President from office, or of his death, resignation, or inability to discharge the powers and duties of the said office, the same shall devolve on the Vice-President." Tumulty, who was summoned to the meeting, repeated what he had told Lansing previously, that he would take no part in certifying to the President's disability. The Irish in him flared up, and other stanch supporters of Wilson were hardly able to suppress their indignation at Lansing's suggestion.

The Cabinet called in Grayson for advice, and he told them that Wilson's mind was clear, that he was suffering from nervous breakdown, indigestion, and a depleted system. The scales might tip either way, the doctor said, and excitement by matters of business would press them the wrong way; in fact, he reported, the President already had been irritated by a rumor that his associates were to convene without a call from him. "The President asked me what the Cabinet wanted with me and by what authority it was meeting," said Grayson, with a gleam in his eye that suggested the displeasure of the stricken, egocentric prophet. As for himself, the doctor would have no part in a verdict of disability.

Secretary Baker asked Grayson to say to the President that they had met primarily to extend sympathy, to get information about him, and to consider departmental business that had been held up since the last meeting, a month earlier. The doctor took this message to his patient and, with Wilson's knowledge, the Cabinet held other informal meetings through the autumn. They studied the critical labor problems of the coal mines and railroads, and maintained contact with their chief through Secretary Houston, Grayson, and Tumulty. There was no more serious talk within the official household of disability and retirement.

However, allegations of boudoir government were not easily countered. The adversaries in the Senate seized upon all rumors of disability and magnified them. Bills to oust the President were introduced. Some of Lansing's friends among the Republicans were remarking that only foreigners were allowed to call on the President of the United States. Foreign embassies, they complained, were better informed than his own people about Wilson's condition, through visits to the sickroom by Belgium's monarch and the Prince of Wales.

The members of the Committee on Foreign Relations took a particularly keen interest in the President's health; and it happened that in November a diplomatic crisis arose that provided an excuse for an inquisitorial expedition to his sickroom. When Senator Fall cast doubt on Wilson's ability to cope with a crisis in relations with Mexico that had arisen out of the alleged kidnaping of Consular Agent William O. Jenkins,[1] Hitchcock suggested that his colleague go himself to call at the White House and drew his own conclusions; and finally Fall and Hitchcock were delegated to do this.

By December 4, two days after Congress had heard the reading of an annual presidential message that had been composed by Charles Swem under the direction of Tumulty,[2] the curiosity of the legislators about Wilson's health could be withstood no longer.

Henry Cabot Lodge, who was now complaining to Root that "a regency of Tumulty and Barney Baruch . . . was not contemplated by the constitution," was instructed by his committee to telephone for an appointment. When he did so, on December 5, he was invited to send delegates to the White House that very afternoon.

Before receiving Fall and Hitchcock, the President was briefed by letters from Lansing and from Senator Pittman. The latter suggested that the jingoism of irresponsible senators could be stopped, and the interview cut short, if Wilson would merely ask for a copy of a report that Fall was to file with the Foreign Relations Committee, and promise to study the matter.

The President and those around him, however, set the stage for a more elaborate denouement. Propping him up with pillows, covering him with bedclothes to the chin, and allowing only his sound right arm to protrude, Dr. Grayson and Mrs. Wilson bade the senators enter the

---

[1] The Jenkins case was brought up by Lansing at a Cabinet meeting. Secretary Daniels suspected that there was some truth in the Mexican allegation that Jenkins was the tool of oil prospectors who wanted armed protection from the United States government. When it became clear that Lansing had no facts to disprove this suspicion, and the secretary of state remarked that the Mexican embassy at Washington spawned "red" propaganda and that by intervening in Mexico it might be possible to settle social problems in the United States, a majority of the Cabinet reacted strongly against such a policy. The Jenkins case must be settled on its legal merits, they insisted, regardless of the opinion of interested parties.

Lansing hoped to make use of the Jenkins affair to put an end to the violations of civic rights that American citizens had been suffering in Mexico. He went before Lodge's committee and urged delay. When Mexico replied equivocally to his note of protest, the secretary of state called on the Mexican ambassador and insulted him. Though Tumulty telephoned to urge that the policy toward Mexico be discussed with the President before the State Department went too far, Lansing held to his independent course. He sent another note to the Mexican government, this one so sharp that the editor of the *New York Times* found it hard to discover in history "a severer indictment of bad faith, a more scathing condemnation of unfriendly behavior."

[2] Tumulty collected reports from the Cabinet members and, tossing them on Swem's desk, said: "You know how the Chief writes. You can put them together." Swem to the writer. The draft of the message shows corrections in Mrs. Wilson's hand, presumably dictated by the President. A word was changed here and there (for example, a sarcastic reference to Russia as "a fine object lesson" was changed to "a painful object lesson"). A plea for ratification of the peace treaty was struck out, and also paragraphs contributed by the director-general of railways on problems that Wilson chose to cover in a message of Dec. 24. At the urging of advisers who feared that Republican legislation pending in Congress would take the initiative away from the President, and in the face of a plea from labor leaders that government ownership be extended for two years, Wilson proclaimed the return of the railroads to their owners on March 1, 1920.

sickroom. To guard against misquoting of her husband's words, Edith Wilson sat across from the visitors, ready with notebook and pencil to record the conversation.

Fall approached the bed with a smile that seemed to ooze oil. Woodrow Wilson seldom had been so moved to hit a man. For some time he had thought of this senator as a man who did not even try to tell the truth. He put all his strength, however, into a handshake. The senator presented his views on Mexico and promised to send a memorandum, and the President thanked him for his statement and commended its fullness. The caller noted that his host articulated clearly, though somewhat thickly, and that he could freely turn his head and move his right arm about. The talk was lively, and the sick man proved his wit still sharp by repeating his favorite remark of Mr. Dooley's Hennessy: "Sure, with Mexico so contagious, we'll be takin' it soon whether we want it or not."

Hardly had Fall presented his case for intervention and asserted that four-fifths of the Mexican people would welcome it, when Grayson came in to report the release from jail of Consular Agent Jenkins. Fall could hope only to escape from the sickroom quickly. But in his confusion he opened himself to one more body blow. "I hope you will consider me sincere," the senator said, unctuously leaning over the bed and pressing the sick man's hand between his own. "I have been praying for you, sir."

Again Wilson's temper threatened to get the better of him. Why did this unconscionable meddler want to queer him with the Almighty? he wondered. But he restricted himself to three words: "Which way, senator?"

At the next meeting of the Committee on Foreign Relations the question of the President's mental disability was laughed off and dropped; and soon a message came from Wilson reminding the committee that "the advice of the Senate is provided for only when sought by the Executive in regard to explicit agreements with foreign governments." The passage of such a meddling resolution as Fall had proposed, the President asserted, "would constitute a reversal of our constitutional practice which might lead to very grave confusion in the guidance of our foreign policy." Thus the immediate danger of armed intervention in Mexico was averted.

The ordeal took a toll on the President's limited energy. And yet it gave him confidence and cheer to know that he could still smite the Philistines. He was able to derive some pleasure from the festivities of a family Christmas and from a deluge of birthday greetings three days afterward. He was able to dress himself each morning and to sit up for several hours; and on the day after Christmas, bowed forward in a wheel chair, he was taken to the East Room of the White House to see a moving picture. A horse race was portrayed and it exhausted him, but the cinema became a regular diversion every morning except Sundays. Edith Wilson was constantly at his side; and when his head fell forward, she raised it and caressed it, oblivious of the presence of guests. At first the cinema was merely a means of killing time, but soon he became a "fan," with a weakness for western and detective films and an aversion to those that scoffed at marriage. Before the daily show they sometimes wheeled him through the downstairs rooms on a sightseeing excursion, with Grayson's infant son perched on the foot rest, or, wrapping him in blankets, out to the south portico to take the sun and talk with Tumulty through a window.

Very gradually, but persistently, the invalid gained a measure of control over his paralyzed arm and leg. He found that he could take a few steps—totteringly, at first, with someone supporting him on each side; then more confidently, leaning on a blackthorn stick. As the winter wore on, he found strength to hook his cane around a pillar of the portico and triumphantly swing his wheel chair about on the flagging.

At the same time the President was regaining some power of decision and action. During the winter Secretaries Lansing and Lane, who had dissented from the view of the majority of the Cabinet toward oil interests and intervention in Mexico, became embarrassingly aware of their chief's recovery.

The President's impulsive opinions on matters affecting Europe and the Far East yielded usually to the advice of Polk or Phillips or Long—men in the State Department whom he trusted; but anything that Secretary Lansing proposed was almost certain to meet rebuff at the White House. It seemed as if the Wilsons were acting with the intent of provoking Lansing to resign, so that they would be spared the unpleasantness of dismissing him. When the secretary pleaded with Mrs. Wilson for action on pressing matters of state, she informed him—curtly, it seemed to him—that the President did not like to be told a thing twice.

The breach between the President and the secretary of state was bringing the diplomacy of the nation to a standstill. European statesmen were refusing to accept messages from the State Department as authoritative, and awaited definitive verdicts from the sick President. Indecision and delay were nurturing seeds of dissension in the Balkans, in Asia Minor, and especially at Fiume. Italy, smarting under moral rebuke, tended toward the policy that was to bring her into World War

II as an ally of Germany. And Russia received no response to a public offer to negotiate a settlement of all questions making for hostilities.

It was impossible, even, for the State Department to establish normal relations with Britain. Pending the appointment of a permanent ambassador to succeed Lord Reading, Grey had come to Washington in September to deal with questions left unsettled at the Peace Conference. Disinclined to do business outside official channels, he waited patiently for Wilson's health to improve, marveling the while at the awkwardness of the government.

Unfortunately there was on Grey's staff an officer whom the Wilsons did not like. When they became aware of the presence of this undesirable, they wrote to Lansing to ask that the man be sent home. Grey, however, was as loyal as Wilson himself to men who served him well, and contended that it was unfair to condemn anyone unless charges were brought and proved. As a result the British statesman was not invited to the White House, not even to accompany the Prince of Wales.

After listening to Republican amenders of the League Covenant and sympathizing with their views, the envoy returned to England and sent to the London *Times* a letter intimating that in practice the Lodge reservations probably would prove to be harmless and that Britain would accept the conditional cooperation of the United States. This statement, which was supported almost unanimously by the press of Britain and France and was quoted in American journals, brought biting comment from Mrs. Wilson,[3] who thus introduced another obstacle to an understanding that might have resulted in the Senate's approval of the peace treaty.

A well-intentioned effort that Lansing made in Grey's behalf proved to be merely another plank in the coffin that the secretary of state had been building for himself for a year. At last, under the succession of insults that had come from the White House, the man sensed that the Wilsons not only distrusted him, but thoroughly disliked him. His thoughts again turned longingly toward retirement, as his chief had intended. Journalistic predictions of his resignation became more insistent.

Another and stronger nudge was required, however, to push the secretary of state to the point of action. Whether or not the President's own mind went "around the clock" on this question is uncertain.[4] But on

---

[3] Mrs. Wilson's written statement said: "It may be safely assumed that had Lord Grey ventured upon any such utterance while he was in Washington as an ambassador . . . his government would have been promptly asked to withdraw him."

[4] According to Mrs. Wilson's *My Memoir*, p. 301, the "precipitating incident" was "the last and almost the least" of many disloyalties on Lansing's part. When she asked her husband why he opened himself to allegations of meanness and injured vanity by resting his case on this single basis, he replied: "Well, if I am as big as you think me I can well afford to do a

February 7, 1920, he struck directly at Lansing by reminding him by letter that no one but the President had a right to summon the Cabinet, that only the President and Congress could legally ask for the views of the secretaries on public questions.

The edge of this letter was sharp enough to draw blood. The secretary of state thought the language "brutal and offensive" and the argument like that of "a spoiled child crying out in rage at an imaginary wrong." The absurd charge that Wilson cited put the secretary in a position to resign with honor. The President had delivered himself unwittingly into his hands, the obtuse secretary thought. "And of course I took advantage of his stupidity," Lansing recorded. When the resignation reached the White House, the President gladly accepted it, to take effect "at once."

In the opinion of the press and of his good friends, the President performed a necessary operation on the body politic, but used the bluntest of instruments. The egocentric prophet was showing himself hopelessly out of touch with political realities, and incapable of taking good advice even from those nearest and dearest to him. Lansing was now free to consort as much as he chose with his Republican friends and to tell all he knew and all he felt. He was received enthusiastically by Wilson's enemies and by those who had lost confidence in the President. Lodge assured him that his final note to Wilson was "extremely good." Two days later the secretary of state drafted a reply in pencil: "It is a satisfaction to receive your praise. The friendly good will which you have constantly shown me will always be one of the pleasantest memories of my public service."

The resignation of Lansing was but one of the withdrawals from the Cabinet early in 1920. In the opinion of Franklin K. Lane, who had spoken often in support of Lansing's views, the President seemed to have given way to petty impulses. Lane had sent to the White House certain leases of government oil lands, assuring Mrs. Wilson that they were legitimate. But when the agreements were put before the President, Wilson drew back. He suspected the motives of Lane, who wrote to Grayson on January 5 that he was contemplating resigning from the Cabinet in order to make money. Too ill to study the matter, Wilson thought it better to wait than to take a step that might be questioned.

When this word went back to the secretary of the interior through Edith Wilson, he was deeply hurt, and on February 5 he made the

generous thing. If not I must take the blame." Professing a liking for Mrs. Lansing and respect for her father, former Secretary of State John W. Foster, he explained: "The disloyalty is a personal act; the calling of meetings of the Cabinet is official insubordination; it is my duty to put a stop to that."

move that he had been considering for four months; he wrote to Wilson to offer his resignation, to take effect on March 1.

At about the same time another Cabinet seat became vacant when the governor of Virginia appointed Secretary Carter Glass to fill the unexpired term of Thomas S. Martin, the deceased Democratic leader in the Senate. Encouraged by the Virginians close to him, Wilson had come to depend much on the secretary of the treasury. Glass's resignation took effect on February 2, 1920, and on the next day he took his oath as a senator. Secretary Houston replaced him at the Treasury.

Colonel House noted, in December, that never in his political experience had he seen "such a desertion of the ship in times of stress." The infirm President no longer had genius for binding men to him. Emotional instability precluded rational transaction of the business of government. He gave reality to the character in which caluminators had cast him: the spoiled child who would have his own way at any cost, the vain preacher who pointed the only path to redemption, the proud author who refused to submit his masterpiece to revision, the dictatorial executive who would not take counsel from Congress, the politician who was not serving a great cause but using the cause to keep himself in office. People forgot the gallantry of the European and western trips as under the influence of arteriosclerosis the prophet revealed more and more the streak of pettifogging that ran in his Scottish ancestry. Shorn of his powers, he was an easy prey to the tortures that his adversaries were inflicting upon his soul. The people saw the President in the austere light in which he had put himself—an implacable opponent of any reservations that might require assent or provoke objections by other signatories of the treaty.

The counselor who had been most helpful in political crises of the past could not help now. Colonel House had remained in Europe and had tried to keep alive the prophet's vision of world democracy by giving substance to the League of Nations. The Colonel's appeal for concessions to British opinion confirmed the impression that had lodged in Wilson's mind and that was strengthened by those closest to him. House still seemed too sympathetic to foreign points of view, too much the good fellow. But the President did not reproach the Colonel, nor let anyone speak ill of his old friend. When the press again printed stories of a "break" between them, Wilson had been incensed. He wished to spare House's feelings, and he did not want the ending of this political partnership, like his separation from Hibben and Harvey, to provoke the charges of personal disloyalty that political foes would know so well how to exploit.

It had seemed unwise, however, to risk the return of the Colonel to

Washington, for doubtless he would seek compromise with the foes of the treaty and perhaps undermine the solid front that the prophet had resolved to present.

However, when it became apparent that the treaty might fail in the Senate if reservations were not accepted, the Colonel decided to take matters into his own hands and do what he could for the cause that his friend could no longer further effectively. On the 5th of October, two days after the French Chamber ratified the peace treaty, he embarked for home.

At this juncture the Colonel's health, which had been precarious, failed badly. An attack of renal colic grew worse as he neared the United States; and at New York he was taken from the ship on a stretcher. His vitality was so low that the doctors feared to perform an operation that was long overdue. His first impulse was to go to Washington to bare his heart to his friend. Immediately he sent off a letter to Senator Lodge, expressing his willingness to testify before the Committee on Foreign Relations as soon as his physician would permit.

Receiving a noncommittal reply from Lodge, the resourceful Colonel made a more devious effort. He asked Stephen Bonsal, Wilson's interpreter at Paris and a personal friend of Lodge, to go to the senator and tell him frankly that House could explain everything as soon as he was able to travel. The mediator quoted to Lodge what Smuts had said at Paris of his article dealing with mandates: "I warn you that if even a word is changed or perhaps even a comma, the whole edifice will collapse." Bonsal was able to report to House that there was some prospect of concessions by the senator; but if this information ever reached the President, it did not move him to seek compromise.[5]

Senator Lodge seemed to Wilson's friends to be determined to cut out what the President regarded as "the heart of the Covenant." On November 6 his majority in the Committee on Foreign Relations presented fourteen reservations to the Senate. The next day another reservation was added that was particularly offensive to Wilson—a change in the preamble of the Covenant that would require acceptance of all the reservations by at least three of the four major cosigners of the treaty.

[5] Bonsal recorded that Lodge wrote on a printed copy of the Covenant about forty words of altered phrasing and about fifty inserts that would make the treaty acceptable to him and, he felt sure, to the Senate, and that this document was mailed to House and that the Colonel mailed it to the White House.

This document is not in the Wilson Collection in the Library of Congress, and the only evidence of its existence is Bonsal's testimony in *Unfinished Business*, pp. 277 and 285–86, in his letters to Charles Seymour, May 27, 1944, and April 9, 1944, and in his conversations with Robert W. Woolley and James F. Reynolds. When Charles Seymour asked Colonel House and his secretary, Miss Denton, about this incident several years later, neither had a definite recollection of it. Charles Seymour to the writer, Dec. 8, 1953. There is no reference to the episode in House's diary.

On the same day on which this culminating indignity was proposed, Hitchcock was admitted to the President's bedside for their first consultation since the thrombosis. As acting minority leader in the Senate and a member of the Committee on Foreign Relations, Hitchcock had taken no effective initiative on the basis of the interpretive reservations that Wilson had left with him in August. He had been so accustomed to depend upon the White House for leadership that he was at a loss without it. He had, however, observed Republican tactics closely and he concluded, in mid-November, that Lodge's reservations were intended to defeat the treaty. The Democratic leader was willing to compromise with the mild reservationists on almost any revisions that would command enough votes to frustrate Lodge's intentions.[6]

When Hitchcock went to Wilson's chamber to suggest concession, he was shocked by the emaciation of the white-bearded figure that had been propped up in bed to receive him. With Edith Wilson and Grayson standing by to protect their patient, Hitchcock dared not attempt rational argument. He could merely convey the black truth: the Democrats could not raise even a bare majority for ratification without reservations, to say nothing of the two-thirds needed.

"Is it possible! Is it possible!" the tortured prophet groaned.

"Mr. President," Hitchcock ventured, "it might be wise to compromise . . ."

"Let Lodge compromise!" Wilson shot back.

"Well, of course, he must compromise also," the senator conceded, "but we might well hold out the olive branch."

"Let Lodge hold out the olive branch," the President retorted.

Hitchcock came again to the President's bedside on November 17, as the hour of voting drew near. In this second conference Wilson did not refuse all of Lodge's measures, but gave ground to meet the views of the mild reservationists. He threatened, however, to give the treaty a pocket veto if it were passed without a change in the reservation on Article X and if senators did not omit the preamble that required three of the major signatory powers to assent in writing to the American reservations. In Wilson's view, Article XII of the Covenant, which provided for compulsory arbitration, was a second line of defense to which he was unwilling to retreat. That method had been tried before, and found inadequate to preserve peace. Rather than assume the responsibility of vetoing the treaty, however, and thus play out the role that Lodge had

---

[6] On Nov. 13, Hitchcock prepared to introduce the four reservations that Wilson had given him secretly before setting out for the West, and a fifth that he had added himself. These interpretive reservations dealt with withdrawal from the League, Article X, domestic questions, the Monroe Doctrine, and the votes of the British Dominions in the Assembly. The reservation on Article X was almost identical with the one sponsored by moderate Republicans.

assigned to him, the President supported the plan of his men in the Senate to vote against ratification with Lodge reservations. "I would like," he said, "to have some of the senators go home to their constituents while the treaty is still pending." If there was a deadlock, he felt that public opinion would break it in his favor. He put faith still in the cheers that he had stirred in the West, in the tears that he had seen in the eyes of American mothers when he had talked of another war.

McAdoo advised concessions, and the prophet answered: "Mac, I am willing to compromise on anything but the Ten Commandments." Baruch went to the sickroom to press the Chief to yield: and the master, thinking this friend "true to the bone" for giving advice known to be unpalatable, said, "And Baruch too!" Finally, after a talk with Hitchcock, Mrs. Wilson came to her husband and asked whether for her sake he would not "accept these reservations and get this awful thing settled."

Turning his head on the pillow, he responded with a challenge to her fealty. "Little girl, don't desert me, that I cannot stand. Can't you see that I have no moral right to accept any change in a paper I have signed without giving to every other signatory, even the Germans, the right to do the same thing? It is not *I* that will not accept; it is the nation's honor that is at stake." His eyes were afire as he dramatized his cause— the grandest that he had ever fought for, the greatest of his century. "Better a thousand times to go down fighting than to dip your colors to dishonorable compromise," he told his wife.

His mind set, he dictated a letter to Hitchcock, adapting a text supplied by Hitchcock but replacing the word "defeat" by "nullification." The Senate Resolution, he wrote, did not "provide for ratification but rather for the nullification of the treaty." "I sincerely hope," he advised, "that the friends and supporters of the treaty will vote against the Lodge resolution of ratification. I understand that the door will probably then be open for a genuine resolution of ratification. I trust that all true friends of the treaty will refuse to support the Lodge reservations."

Wilson's letter was given to the newspapers and was read to the Democratic senators in caucus and later on the floor of the Senate. Reservationists who were fundamentally friendly to the League saw in the message an imputation of bad faith, and they resented it.

On November 19 a vote was taken. The party men stood, with four exceptions, against the revised treaty. Their ballots, added to those of thirteen Republican irreconcilables, were enough to block the two-thirds vote needed for ratification. Afterward, Republican moderates joined the irreconcilables to defeat a Democratic motion for approval of the treaty without reservations; and a similar alignment defeated a motion to consider the treaty with the President's interpretive reservations.[7] Then a resolution declaring the war with Germany at an end was introduced by Senator Knox and referred to the Committee on Foreign Relations.

Many of the Democratic leaders, favoring compromise, continued to try to work through House and Tumulty to put political realities of the day before the cloistered prophet. Indeed, their pressure was so insistent that House overcame his reluctance to impose advice on his friend. In November the Colonel was well enough to operate in his characteristic way. He established contact with Lord Grey and with Republican policy makers, and on November 24 he wrote to Mrs. Wilson to suggest that her husband's place in history was "in the balance," that otherwise he would not disturb the President while he was ill. At the same time House composed an accompanying letter to the President himself, recommending that the treaty be turned back to the Senate for action, for thus the Republicans could be saddled with responsibility for passing the measure in a form that would be acceptable to the other signatory nations. Three days later the Colonel pressed his argument home in another letter. There was no reply from the White House to either. It seemed to Edith Wilson that her husband's place in history was already assured.[8]

Margaret Wilson did her best to restore the old relationship. Going to New York, she talked with House about the things that had offended her father and found that the Colonel thought himself justified in what he had done out of concern for the League and his friend's political welfare. But when his explanations were brought back to the White House, Wilson gave a sigh of disappointment. In the old days, he said, when he conversed with House it seemed as if he were talking with himself. Now his clear concept of his friend was overlaid and blurred by a picture of a man different from the one that he had known. It would be awkward to bare his mind in the presence of a stranger. Unless he could talk without shyness, he would not really be talking with the friend that he remembered. And so it seemed best not to see the Colonel. Moreover, if House was the man Wilson thought him, he

[7] Hitchcock hoped that enough Republicans would support his motion to keep the matter before the Senate for possible compromise. He had proposed this course in a conference with Lodge, who said that he could not accept this procedure unless he knew in advance what compromise the Democrats could offer. Hitchcock reported this to Mrs. Wilson by letter on Nov. 18; but since no definite proposals for compromise came from the White House, Lodge blocked Hitchcock's motion for consideration of the treaty with interpretive reservations.

[8] Unlike letters written to Wilson by House in September of 1919, which were not opened until they reached the Library of Congress in 1952, the Colonel's letters of Nov. 24 and 27 were opened before they reached the Library. But it is not known whether Wilson ever knew of them. By Dec. 2 House himself had changed his mind, and thought that the treaty should not be returned to the Senate until sixty-six senators were committed to vote for it with reservations agreed on in advance.

too would be embarrassed by a meeting that would remind them both of the failure of their exalted mission. Maybe the fault was his own, he said. Perhaps he had expected too much in thinking that the good Colonel could stand against strong pressures. The President loved the Texan still, but considered him of a caliber too light to bear the cross that the prophet was prepared to carry to the grave, alone. And so Colonel House's independent effort to save the treaty came to naught; and this disciple, loyal to his friend and his great cause, and feeling that only illness prevented their continuing collaboration, grew bitter toward what he called "the shortsighted coterie" that surrounded the President.

On one point, the wisdom of throwing responsibility on the Republican senators—Wilson's mind ran along with that of House. The President had contemplated this strategy after the Congressional election of 1918 and now his thought harked back and seized on it again. When Lodge stated that nothing further could be done until the President withdrew the treaty from the Senate and resubmitted it, Wilson countered in mid-December with a public assertion that the Republican leaders who controlled the Senate's vote should continue to bear "the undivided responsibility."

A year earlier, after the adverse vote in the Congressional election, he had been sensitive about his political insolvency; and now he was on the brink of bankruptcy. His nerves could endure no more palaver with the Philistines in the Senate. He had said to them, directly and through Hitchcock, everything that he had to say. On some days he would sit glum and unresponsive to all ideas of constructive action, fearful that any move might be construed as a yielding to an enemy and an exposure of his feebleness. In his determination to die facing forward he was possessed by the very fear of seeming fearsome.

Yet in January of 1920 he explored two ways to bring the sinners to the truth. His first scheme was fantastic. Consulting the attorney general, he hoped to work out a plan whereby opposing senators would be challenged to resign and stand for re-election on the issue of the treaty; and if his opponents won, he himself was prepared to resign from the Presidency. His advisers, however, were able to persuade him that his plan was impractical under the election laws of the nation.

Balked in this venture, the prophet next resolved to use the occasion of Jackson Day to give the infidels a public flailing. On January 8 Chairman Homer Cummings read his message to Democrats who crowded into the dining rooms of two Washington hotels. It asserted that the United States had "enjoyed the spiritual leadership of the world until the Senate failed to ratify the treaty." The party men were reminded that they were still at war with Germany, that the old stage was "reset for a repetition of the old plot," complete with alliances, secret treaties, and intrigues. "Five of the leading belligerents," the message explained, "have accepted the treaty and formal ratifications will soon be exchanged. The question is whether this country will enter and enter whole-heartedly . . ." The President's impression that ratification was the wish of an "overwhelming majority of the people" had been "confirmed by the unmistakable evidences of public opinion" during his visit to seventeen of the states. If there was any doubt on this matter, he asserted, "the clear and single way out" was to submit it to the voters at the next election.

The President had commented on the iniquity of delay in making peace. So when he suggested postponing ratification for almost a year, until he and Lodge could submit their differences to the voters, it appeared that he was trying to give himself and his party a strong issue for the 1920 presidential campaign. Sincere friends of the League were forced to conclude that, in the three months that had passed since his last public utterance on the treaty, their President had shrunk deplorably in mental and moral stature. As in the 1918 election, it would be impossible to draw the issue so clearly that the popular vote could be regarded as a mandate; and, moreover, even if the Democrats won all the Senate seats that would be open in 1920, it still would be mathematically impossible for them to gain the two-thirds vote that was necessary for ratification.

Members of the Cabinet had recognized the folly of Wilson's tactics and had done their best to tone down the Jackson Day message. Experts on whom Wilson had depended at Paris signed an appeal of the League of Free Nations Association, urging acceptance of reservations necessary for ratification. Moreover, leaders in education and finance were giving similar advice. Pressures for concessions by both parties reached their peak soon after the opening of the new year.

The prophet in the White House, however, would admit no share of guilt for the failure of the treaty. In his view, it had been butchered to death by the Foreign Relations Committee. Feeling that public opinion would force one side or the other to capitulate, he resolved that it would not be his side.

In January this policy seemed to bear fruit: for toward the middle of this month, Republican mild reservationists, who on December 26 had served an "ultimatum" on Lodge demanding compromise, induced him to arrange a bipartisan conference, in which four Democrats and five Republicans were to meet informally to discuss revision of the fourteen reservations that the Senate had voted down in November. This move was welcomed by Senator Hitchcock, since proposals from

Republicans obviously would command fairer treatment from Lodge than would those from Democrats. Moreover, Hitchcock dared to hope that Wilson might accept a definite bipartisan suggestion for compromise even though he would not initiate or encourage such a proposal. Tumulty, in collaboration with members of the Cabinet, tried to persuade the President to sign and send to Hitchcock a letter accepting the core of Lodge's reservations but safeguarding the rights of the Executive. This proposal went to Edith Wilson on January 15—the day before the Council of the League convened at Paris at Wilson's call, but without a representative from the United States.

The Wilsons, however, felt that Lodge's profession of open-mindedness was not sincere. Hitchcock had reported on January 5 that this adversary was "a cold-blooded, calculating politician" who was merely dallying with and trifling with the moderate Republicans to keep them quiet.[9] It seemed to the Democratic leader that a "deadlock of opinion" existed that might be broken by careful negotiation and by winning recruits to the bloc of moderate Republicans. But there was no response from the sickroom to Tumulty's proposal.

On January 22 Hitchcock reported that the conferees were seriously considering a revision of Lodge's reservation for Article X. The new draft, which the senator enclosed with his letter, was sponsored by Democratic Senator Simmons. Replying in a letter dated January 26, Wilson expressed his views on Article X, clearly and frankly. To the substance of the Simmons reservation, he said, he adhered. He was bound to, having sworn to obey and maintain the Constitution of the United States. But he went on to say: "I think the form of it very unfortunate. Any reservation or resolution stating that 'the United States assumes no obligation under such and such an article unless or except' would, I am sure, chill our relationships with the nations with which we expect to be associated in the great enterprise of maintaining the world's peace. That association must in any case, my dear senator, involve very serious and far-reaching implications of honor and duty, which I am sure we shall never in fact be desirous of ignoring. It is the more important not to create the impression that we are trying to escape obligations."

[9] Hitchcock to Mrs. Wilson, Jan. 5, 1920, in Garraty, *Lodge,* p. 385. Hitchcock's diagnosis of Lodge's motive is confirmed by a note written by the senator to his friend Beveridge on Jan. 3, 1920, and printed in Garraty, *op. cit.,* p. 384. "It would have been a mistake," Lodge wrote, "for me to have taken the attitude . . . that we would not even consider modifications. We could not afford to say that . . ."

Insight into Lodge's thinking at this time is given by Alice Roosevelt Longworth in *Crowded Hours,* pp. 294–95. Her conclusion after talking with the senator on Sunday before Christmas, 1919, was: "In his heart he was really as opposed to it [the League] in any shape as any irreconcilable but his job was to see that the reservations were on and to deal with and harmonize the mild and strong reservationists to that end."

Realizing finally that negative criticism was not all that was called for in so serious a matter, he gladly reaffirmed his approval of the four interpretative reservations that he had given to Hitchcock in August and that the senator had returned to him at his request, with one addition, on January 5. Included among the five interpretations was one on Article X that reserved the rights of Congress without denying the obligation of the United States to exercise its conscience and judgment on each appeal from the League's council.

In forwarding the letter of January 26 to Hitchcock, Mrs. Wilson indicated that he might make it public at his discretion. The senator did not do so, however, until February 9, when the Senate again considered the treaty. It was already too late for the conciliatory note to be effective. For on January 23, after the bipartisan conference had agreed on many compromises and just as Lodge seemed to be leaning toward the views of the moderates of his party, he was summoned out of the session by his friend Brandegee and haled before a powwow of the irreconcilables that was meeting in Senator Johnson's office. The bitter-enders threatened the Republican leader with a public scalping if he bated a jot on Article X and drew from him a promise to stand firm on all but matters of phrasing. Consequently, the bipartisan conference was unable to reach agreement on Article X and two other clauses, and at the end of the month it finally broke up.

Early in February Wilson was plunged into a cloud of fatalism. Perceiving that dismal thoughts wore on his nerves when he was alone, Edith Wilson stayed at his side almost constantly and tried to divert and rest him. Late in each day a massage soothed his distress, and early in the evening he was enveloped by a comforter that had seldom failed him—sleep.

During February the morale of the Democratic senators, like that of the President, reached a low ebb. Realizing that they were fighting for a lost cause, they were disposed to abandon their struggle to soften the Lodge reservations. In fact, Hitchcock warned the President on February 24 that only another command from Wilson would hold his men in line.

From the President's chambers, however, came no guidance. The Lodge reservations, Wilson said dolefully to Ray Baker, represented "a dishonorable attempt, on the part of the leaders who do not speak for the people, to escape any real responsibility, so far as the United States is concerned, for world peace in future years." They were essentially partisan political devices, the President went on. "If I accept them, these senators will merely offer new ones, even more humiliating." And then, after a long pause: "These evil men intend to destroy the League."

The senators moved swiftly, once the treaty was called up for action in February.[10] On March 4 Lodge complained that the Democrats had not been satisfied with the compromises evolved. For the first time he confessed, with pious solemnity, that the treaty had "fallen by the way-side." Actually, either the Senate would pass the treaty as he had revised it, and he would get credit for establishing peace with security for his country, or else the Democrats would oppose the treaty and Wilson would be blamed for killing it and would be repudiated by the voters. Either denouement would be satisfactory to Henry Cabot Lodge. The Republican party would be drawn together and Woodrow Wilson discredited.

Wilson acted on his own initiative in a way that played into the hands of this archenemy. He snuffed out all lingering hope for ratification by the tone of a letter that he sent to Hitchcock on March 8. In this message his emotions surged militantly. Somehow he drew echoes of his pristine vigor from his shattered physique and showed himself once more the rough-and-tumble fighter of a political frontier, cudgeling scribes and pharisees with whacks of spiritual truth. He begged everyone "to consider the matter in the light of what it is possible to accomplish for humanity, rather than in the light of special national interests." Practically every so-called reservation—those still under discussion as well as those already accepted by a majority vote of the Senate—was denounced as "a rather sweeping nullification" of the terms of the treaty. Declaring that he could not understand the difference between "a nullifier" and "a mild nullifier," Wilson killed any impulse that might linger in the mild reservationists to break from Lodge's control. Even the efforts of his own men to establish interpretative reservations were dismissed as a work of "supererogation." Opponents were branded as men of little faith—secessionists, militarists, imperialists.

Thus the prophet, isolated in the White House, his mental diet carefully controlled, his body made comfortable by an ingenious chair-back for his bed, a wheel chair, and a fur muff for his feet, completed the process of alienating independent citizens that had begun with his appeal for a Democratic Congress in 1918. Partisans of the League who after the thrombosis had envisioned a martyr's halo above their stricken President now saw him as an egocentric zealot or a scheming politician. Yet even now Elihu Root was disturbed when Lodge, reacting against Wilson's glorification of Article X as "the essence of Americanism," added two phrases to his reservation that made it a still stronger negation of the gospel that the President preached. Root cau-

[10] On Feb. 9, the Senate voted to reconsider the treaty and referred it to the Committee on Foreign Relations. It was reported back the next day with the Lodge reservations, and debate was resumed on Feb. 16. By March 7 eight of the fourteen reservations had been passed again, either unchanged or revised as agreed in the bipartisan conference.

tioned the senators of his party against action that might be interpreted by the voters as nullification. But Lodge explained in reply that he had not acted with his eyes shut, that he was making sure that the treaty would not be killed by Republicans alone.

Fantastic as some of the reservations were, it was doubtful whether the Democratic senators could be held in line to deliver the negative votes that the President was requesting. The alternative was more clear-cut than ever, between a Republicanized treaty and no treaty at all. Now, fearing an extension of the state of war in which the nation still lived, independent journals of Democratic leanings were urging the party's senators to vote for ratification; and they were joined by the voices of two ex-secretaries of state, Bryan and Lansing.

The outcome was in doubt, therefore, when the Senate prepared to vote on March 19. Would the senators approve a resolution to ratify the treaty with the Lodge reservations included? The clerk began to call the roll. Of the first four Democrats to respond, three turned against Wilson and voted for the treaty. The next was venerable Senator Culberson, House's old comrade of Texas campaigns. A "yea" from him might have stampeded the party. Not sure what he should say, he looked perplexed and hesitated. But finally his habit of party loyalty prevailed and he uttered a "nay."

While twenty-one Democrats—mostly from the North and candidates for re-election that autumn—voted with the opposition, twenty-three others—all from the South—adhered to their losing cause as fatalistically and steadfastly as their grandfathers had clung to Robert E. Lee. This time, however, the diehards were standing not for secession but for a union far more challenging, more venturesome, than that championed by Abraham Lincoln.

There was a majority of the Senate in favor of the treaty—forty-nine to thirty-five—but not the two-thirds vote that was needed for ratification. Hoping that some of Wilson's men might come over, Lodge proposed unanimous consent for a motion to reconsider the matter; but Hitchcock, holding firm to the last, blocked this move.

Thus, after more than eight months of fruitless conference and oratory, Woodrow Wilson had pulled down the temple that the Philistines had set up in place of the Ark of the Covenant. Taking refuge in a pettifogging subterfuge, he indignantly denied a charge that he had refused to sign the treaty. But everyone knew that he had obstructed participation in world affairs by his nation in any spirit but that of the Covenant. Moreover, as Europeans pursued their centuries-old habit of doing diplomatic business by conference, Wilson was shying away; for now he felt that America's few ventures in international cooperation had not been successful.

He became, in the eyes of European statesmen, a man who would not practice what he preached. Germans felt that he had laid a peace trap for them by declaring Fourteen Points that had not been fully honored. French statesmen lamented America's crippling blow to the effectiveness of the League as a protection against aggressors. Georges Clemenceau, thinking that France would accept a version of the treaty that the Senate would ratify, regarded Wilson and Lodge as "two stubborn old mules kicking each other around." To Lloyd George it seemed that when the American Senate walked out of the League and slammed the door behind them, 50 per cent of its power and influence vanished.

The reproaches of Europe made Wilson's conscience cringe under the weight of the sin that he felt resting upon the nation and on himself as its responsible leader. His first impulse was to shift the burden of guilt to those senators who, he had convinced himself, had maliciously scuttled the peace.

Righteous fury possessed him when Congress passed Knox's joint resolution declaring the war at an end. Without consulting his men in the Senate, he vetoed the measure and wrung from his tortured nerves a brilliant arraignment of its inadequacy. It represented, he said, a shameful shirking of moral responsibility and a repudiation of pledges that the nation had made when it entered the war. "Nothing is said in this resolution," he pointed out very specifically, "about the freedom of navigation upon the seas, or the reduction of armaments, or the vindication of the rights of Belgium, or the rectification of wrongs done to France, or the release of the Christian populations of the Ottoman Empire from the intolerable subjugation which they have had for so many centuries to endure, or the establishment of an independent Polish state, or the continued maintenance of any kind of understanding among the great powers of the world which would be calculated to prevent in the future such outrages as Germany attempted, and in part consummated. We have now in effect declared that we do not care to take any further risks or to assume any further responsibilities with regard to the freedom of nations or the sacredness of international obligations or the safety of independent peoples."

The Knox resolution was not passed over this veto. The American nation, which had entered the war in order to end war became the last of the contestants to make peace.[11] Mankind's inexorable search for a cosmic political godhead was set back a quarter-century.

[11] The United States remained at war until July of 1921, when a resolution similar to Knox's was passed and signed by President Harding.

CHAPTER XX

LATTER DAYS

ON APRIL 14, 1920, for the first time in more than six months, Wilson was able to meet his Cabinet.[1] The members were ushered into the President's study and found him seated behind a desk at the end of the room. Each man was announced as he entered, so that the invalid would be sure to recognize him. His old friends almost wept as they looked at his drooping arm, saw his jaw sag to one side as he struggled to articulate, and heard him repeat himself in a voice curiously weak and strained. He tried to rally them with a volley of jokes and did his best to soothe wounded feelings that had been festering during his absence. Turning to the attorney general, who had alarmed the nation by ordering dramatic raids on New Year's Day and had been feuding with the secretary of labor over methods of handling subversive workers, he cautioned: "Palmer, do not let this country see red!"

His mind was clear about things that had happened before the thrombosis; but when the men began a discussion of new developments in the railroad situation,[2] he seemed unable to follow. The talk went on for an hour or so, while Dr. Grayson anxiously observed his patient's condition from the door; and when Mrs. Wilson came in and suggested that the session break up, the President explained that the meeting was an experiment and he could not stay long. It was so successful, however, that others followed. Before the spring was over, Wilson was able again to stimulate his men to work for the large objectives that had caught the imagination of his people in 1913 but now were thought secondary to immediate peace and prosperity.

Though unable to reach common ground with Republicans and Europeans, the President reasserted his influence over his party. For the

[1] On Feb. 10, 1920, Lansing had had the Cabinet notified that there would be no more meetings unless called by the President. From April 14 to Dec. 14 the Cabinet met with Wilson on many Tuesdays.

[2] The President had referred the matter of railroad regulation to Congress in December of 1918, without recommendations on his part; and when the Esch-Cummins Transportation Act came to his desk on Feb. 28, he signed it in spite of opposition from the brotherhoods and four members of his Cabinet. At the suggestion of Director General Hines, Wilson himself talked on Feb. 13 with a delegation of railway workers and asked them to cooperate with him by withdrawing their strike orders. The roads reverted to private ownership on March 1. Soon after the situation was discussed at the Cabinet meeting of April 14, a nine-man rail labor board was functioning in a way that was to make it a model of conciliation machinery.

senators who had stood with him in a losing cause he had no reproaches. "You did everything that it was possible to do," he assured Hitchcock four days after the final vote on the treaty; but he had only lashes for the deserters. He felt that he could confide in Bainbridge Colby, a progressive lawyer whom he had appointed to succeed Lansing because he would write and speak effectively.[3] He became impatient with the censorship that had been placed on his communications; and by August he was directing Secretaries Colby and Daniels to send messages directly to him, and not "through third persons." He explained that this would save "a great deal of time and roundabout traveling of papers."

As he became able once again to give spiritual backing to his ruling elders, they rallied even more closely to him in defense of executive prerogatives against Congressional encroachment.[4] With his little band of disciples once more functioning, Wilson continued to denounce and defy his adversaries in the Capitol.

Grayson did his utmost to persuade his patient to go away to a cool, quiet resort for the summer; but, although one such arrangement was made, it was canceled by Wilson. Even to attempt to motor into Maryland to join his old Princeton chums seemed to him "folly." He clung to the familiar, comfortable things that he and his wife had come to enjoy—the movies, the sunning on the south portico. He went often to vaudeville, refusing free tickets, and unaware that friends bought a block of seats adjacent to his box, to protect him against the fate of Lincoln. He refused to be photographed for the movies, saying that he would not make an exhibition of himself by displaying his affliction to the country.

Wearing a cape because he could not easily put his limp arm into an overcoat, he went automobiling when warm days came. They lifted him into the front seat where he was braced so that he would not slide down nor topple over. He took comfort, on his rides, in following regular routes and making roadside acquaintances. Little vignettes from

[3] To succeed Lane as secretary of the interior, Wilson appointed Judge John Barton Payne, chairman of the Shipping Board, after failing to persuade McCormick and H. M. Robinson to take this post. Lansing suggested to the opposition that Payne was untrustworthy and that Colby, whose lack of experience made him seem pathetic in the eyes of career men, would be embarrassed by his identification with oil interests that were still being pleaded before the department. J. W. Alexander, appointed to succeed Redfield as secretary of commerce, became the second Missourian in the Cabinet. These appointments reflect the sick President's inability to comprehend political and economic realities.

[4] Wilson leaned on Houston, now secretary of the treasury and still ready to "dig stumps" for his chief, for a veto of a faulty bill that provided a federal budget system of unified estimates and independent audit. This was a reform long overdue; but the Republicans inserted an objectionable clause that provided that the comptroller general—an officer appointed by the President —could be removed by a concurrent resolution of Congress.

In his annual message of Dec. 7, 1920, Wilson advocated a modified form of the budget bill and it was passed soon after Harding took office.

real life were balm to the nerves; and the invalid took comfort, too, in watching the sheep that grazed placidly on the White House lawn. But he was easily irritated by small matters. It grieved him that live trees had been felled in Rock Creek Park and that the wood had been allowed to go to waste.

In the spring of 1920, long-simmering problems of labor and industry were brought before the recuperating President for settlement. During his illness the men of his Cabinet had been debating delicate, incendiary issues of law. Now, when Palmer suggested the use of an injunction to suppress a strike in New York Harbor, the President turned to him quietly and said: "Every lawyer knows that is an abuse of the writ." Labor could never be forced back into the conditions under which it had worked before the war, Wilson thought. He wished to deal with labor through processes of discussion and arbitration. He appointed commissions to adjudicate disputes in the coal mines, insisted on enforcement of the verdicts, and sought to terminate the work of the commissions when miners and operators came to an agreement.

In June of 1920 two laws were passed to guide and aid the development of economic enterprises in ways that were compatible with the national interest. Under a merchant marine act, the Shipping Board was to sell the nation's wartime merchant vessels to private operators and to operate ships that it would not sell. And under a water-power act, a Federal Power Commission that included the secretaries of war, agriculture, and the interior was given authority over all navigable streams and all waterways on public lands—a responsibility that was to be lightly held for many years until economic emergency made it suddenly vital.

Wilson wrote letters to hasten ratification of the Woman Suffrage Amendment by the states; and he had opposed Volstead's National Prohibition Act, which Congress had passed over his veto. These moves had endeared him to large masses of voters. But at the same time he showed a courageous concern for the general welfare that made him unpopular with many groups. He backed Senator Glass and Secretary Baker in opposing raids on the Treasury by war veterans. He supported Secretary Houston in his contention that the government had no obligation to maintain the market price of its bonds in spite of the selling operations of thriftless or overextended citizens. Moreover, he offended starry-eyed voters by refusing even to listen to petitions for the pardon of Eugene Debs, the Socialist, whom he considered a "traitor."

At the beginning of 1920 the question of his role in the coming election was prominent in the mind of the convalescent President. On

January 8 he had released his Jackson Day plea for a "great and solemn referendum" on the League of Nations; and on February 29 the leaders of his party, dining at the Chevy Chase Club, had received a chit from him on which was written in his hand: "What part shall I play in politics this Fall?" The politicians had concluded that it would be unwise for their stricken leader to seek a third term; but their answer to the White House was equivocal. They could not bring themselves to tell their revered master that he was not the man that he had been.

William G. McAdoo, who had no desire to oppose his father-in-law, was in a strong position politically. New York's Democrats pledged their support to him. Though fellow executives had been offended because he seemed constantly to reach out for power and to encroach on their prerogatives, though he was vulnerable to insinuations that he was a nepotist—a "crown prince"—McAdoo appealed to the rank and file of the party as a strong man of action.

Wilson thought his son-in-law deficient in the qualities essential to a president of the United States. "The next President must be not only a man of action," he had remarked to Stockton Axson in 1918, "but he must also have great powers of reflection. Now nobody can do things better than Mac, but if Mac ever reflects, I never caught him at it." This being his measured opinion, Woodrow Wilson could not indulge his little daughter by giving professional endorsement to her husband. Actually, he felt that Newton D. Baker was best fitted for the Presidency and that Houston or Glass would make a good chief executive, but he doubted that these able servants had the fire and presence needed to win election.

As the spring wore on and the Senate worked its will with the treaty, the wretched prophet had no spiritual comfort but his faith in the verdict of the people at the polls. His wife and sycophantic friends encouraged him in this delusion. Mrs. Bainbridge Colby, lunching at the White House, noted the completeness of his dependence upon Edith Wilson, the lack of a vitality to stretch across the table and identify himself. Putting her hand over his and uttering a "darling," she seemed to speak for both.

In April, Wilson summoned energy to sound a keynote for the coming political battle. He wrote out a challenge to the voters and sent it to a national committeeman, Jouett Shouse.

Calling Homer Cummings of the National Committee to him on May 31, Wilson asked this lieutenant to represent him at the forthcoming Democratic convention at San Francisco.

Cummings found the Chief on the portico in his wheel chair, with his wife standing by. He appeared too weary to talk as much as of old, but when he spoke, it was with limpidity; and he hit the bull's-eye with every remark. The fingers of his left hand did not move, and he picked at them occasionally, as if they were numb or prickly.

They talked of a keynote speech that Cummings had prepared, and the President objected to an allusion to the possibility of defeat in the election. Furthermore, noting that the script referred to him as one who had been on the point of death, Wilson looked at his caller pathetically and said that that was not true. He still did not fully comprehend the seriousness of his affliction.

He recalled that past presidents, by seeking to choose their successors, frequently had provoked factional disputes that had split their parties. But he spoke a word of caution. "It is dangerous to stand still," he said. "The government must move, and be responsive to the needs and wishes of the people. Revolution is everywhere in the world and any body of men who think they could drive down stakes and pull the world up . . . are the most dangerous enemies that our country has."

Presenting a code book to Cummings for secret communications from San Francisco, he said: "This was Colonel House's code book. He won't need it any more." [5]

It was not in the tradition of the Woodrows and Wilsons to abdicate responsibility by leaving a pulpit; and their scion, weak as he was, still felt an urge to remain in the thick of the fight for the cause that he thought the greatest of his century. The impulse grew when an article in the New York *World* gave a rosy picture of his health and vigor and presented him as a man able to bear the strain of another term. This story, based on an interview that Tumulty had arranged with Louis Seibold, brought offers of financial support and made Wilson the favorite candidate of Wall Street betting.[6]

Just as the Seibold article appeared, McAdoo was telling his men that he wished to withdraw from the race and that he wanted his adherents to support Carter Glass. To Glass, however, who ascertained that McAdoo's managers had not accepted their candidate's disavowal as final, this was "amiable nonsense." Impressed by the obvious fact that

[5] Cummings Diary, May 31, 1920; and Cummings to the writer, Feb. 15, 1951. Like a John Bunyan, the President gave allegorical names to some of the Democratic candidates: "Bryan—Dove; Palmer—Pilgrim." And on the names of others, he could not resist punning: "Hoke Smith—Pokus; Glass—Crystal; Cox—Swain."

[6] Tumulty's plan had been to have the President give his views on the large issues of the day and deny any desire for renomination. However, to his distress, Mrs. Wilson let him know that nothing but exaltation of her husband would be countenanced. Seibold's article urged that the election be a solemn referendum, despite Republican efforts to becloud the issue of ratification of the treaty.

the party had no man big enough to follow Woodrow Wilson, Glass went to the White House to get final instructions.[7]

Sipping noonday tea on the portico with the senator, the President asked for an opinion of McAdoo's intentions.

"He says nowhere that he would not accept a nomination," Glass observed.

"No, he does not," Wilson responded with quick emphasis.

Discussing other candidates, the President remarked that the choice of Palmer would be "futile"; and when the name of the governor of Ohio was mentioned, the President broke in with: "Oh, you know Cox's nomination would be a joke!" The possibility of victory seemed to him to depend on the choice of his son-in-law or himself; and "dear Mac" lacked qualities that the Presidency demanded.

While the politicians were plying their trade, those who cared for Wilson undertook to save their patient from the consequences of his erring judgment. On Sunday, June 13, Dr. Grayson went to see Robert W. Woolley, who was to attend the San Francisco convention. The physician insisted that the President "just must not be nominated." Grayson said: "He still believes that it is possible to persuade the country to join the League without the Lodge reservations and he says that he would gladly resign when that has beeen accomplished. He couldn't survive the campaign. He is permanently incapacitated and gradually weakening mentally. At times by sheer grit he pulls himself together, keeps himself in good spirits for a week or ten days, transacts business through Tumulty, and even seems to improve. Then he slumps and turns so morose that it distresses me to be near him. We must take no chances at San Francisco." [8]

Woolley and Grayson agreed that Glass could be trusted to block any effort that might be made to prolong Wilson's suffering in public office; and the doctor put his case before Glass and got assurance that the convention would not nominate a man so disabled. But the old party

[7] Wilson had urged Glass to accept the chairmanship of the resolutions committee at the nominating convention, and had approved a platform that had been drafted by Glass for Virginia. "I have perfect confidence in Homer Cummings and Glass," Wilson wrote to Secretary Baker on June 11, 1920. Wilson asked Glass his opinion about the advisability of modifying the Volstead Act (he already had given to Cummings a platform plank that would permit the sale of light wines and beer), and the senator suggested that any effort in this direction would be interpreted as an attempt to modify the Prohibition Amendment in the interest of the brewers. "Maybe that is so," Wilson replied, dismissing the subject. Then he gave Glass an initialed paper advocating the assumption by the United States of a mandate for Armenia, and he asked the senator to get it into the platform. Glass Diary, June 1920, Glass Papers (Alderman Library, University of Virginia). "I have set my heart on seeing this Government accept the mandate for Armenia," Wilson had written on April 19 to Cleveland Dodge, who had missionary interests in that country.

[8] Woolley Papers, and Woolley to the writer.

regulars distrusted Secretary of State Colby, who had been made a delegate from the District of Columbia and whom Wilson favored for the permanent chairmanship of the convention.

Arriving at San Francisco, Glass found the city bowing down before pictures of Woodrow Wilson. Hucksters waved Wilson souvenirs in his face. The President's name flared in electric lights. Clubs paraded and yelled for the Chief. In the auditorium a huge American flag was lifted to reveal a portrait of Woodrow Wilson, and marching delegates stampeded in acclamation. Only the New York standard remained in its place—until a handsome young man leapt from his seat with a yell and, after a scuffle, seized the banner and carried it into the parade with the same precipitancy that he was to show as the next Democratic President of the United States.

The demonstration was one of admiration, however, rather than a stampede for a third term; for the nucleus of leaders who were loyal to their chief felt that they could best serve him by denying him the nomination.

When coded dispatches began to come from Cummings at San Francisco, Wilson showed them to no one. Sitting on the veranda, he deciphered them himself in his own shorthand. When Colby wired on July 2 that, "unless otherwise definitely instructed," he would move Wilson's nomination by acclamation, word was conveyed to Colby by telephone from the White House that his plan was not unacceptable to the President.

Wilson's friends at the convention were thrown into dismay by Colby's intention.[9] Called together by Cummings, they conferred for hours. They were indignant at Colby and told him that he was being cruel to their beloved chief. Glass, swearing that he would rather vote for Woodrow Wilson than for any other man alive, felt that his nomination would ruin both the man and his party; and the others agreed that the idea was fantastic. Therefore they forced Colby to explain in a telegram sent to the White House on July 4, that it was the belief of all their friends that the lines of existing candidacies were drawn very tight and that were Wilson's name put before the convention it

[9] Burleson, who at first had not considered renomination impossible, had been sounding out the delegates and had found nine-tenths of them in sympathy with Wilson and desirous of choosing him were it not for a fear that the stress of a campaign would kill him; and when he learned of the call to Colby, he wired the President that his friends were watching events closely and would act in his behalf if an opportune moment came. He was not given that opportunity, however; for Wilson, resenting the fact that Burleson had telephoned to the White House from San Francisco to try to get the President's support for McAdoo, directed Cummings to exclude the postmaster general from the inner councils at the convention. Wilson's wrath led him to consider dismissing Burleson, but Tumulty dissuaded him from thus chastising so loyal and devoted a servant. Burleson to W.W., June 3, 1920; W.W. to Cummings, June 4, 1920; Kerney, op. cit., pp. 456–57. Woolley and Swem to the writer.

would not command the votes sufficient to nominate and might draw a response that would be disappointing and injuriously affect the party's position in the coming campaign. Colby concluded his message with a request for a statement from Wilson to Cummings, that would ask for a course that the conferees might agree upon as "practicable and judicious." On the next day the President did as requested, using some of the very phrases that had been suggested to him.

When the ballots were cast at the convention, Woodrow Wilson was recognized on only one—by two complimentary votes. Governor James M. Cox of Ohio finally was nominated, and the vice-presidential nomination went to the young warrior who had flung out the banner of New York State—Franklin D. Roosevelt.

The decision of the party did not please its proud leader. He found it hard to understand the motives of his lieutenants, for no one had told him of the precariousness of his hold upon life. He felt, however, that Cummings and Glass were loyal to him and devoted to his cause, for these men had seen to it that the party platform advocated Wilson's treaty. Therefore he accepted their judgment.

The President was sympathetic when Cummings came to him and complained that by appointing a national chairman from Ohio, Cox was "yielding to pressure" and bringing ward politics into national affairs. "It is a terrible mistake," replied Wilson. "If Governor Cox ever gets to be President and continues that course of conduct, temporizing with situations, his administration will be a failure and will end in a guffaw very much like the administration of Mr. Taft." As for himself, he confessed: "I would rather be hated than be the object of derision." So long as he could convince himself that, in the view of his God and of human history, he was right, so long as he had disciples who would share his vision of politics as a crusade rather than a means of livelihood, he could sustain his self-respect against the attacks of those who derided him.

At the end of July his health was the best since the thrombosis. One day he swapped golf yarns with Cummings, and then, commenting on the election, asserted that Harding could be easily destroyed. Still able to turn an inspiriting phrase, he said: "We must fight with lightning and not with thunder."

The prophet was still too ill, however, to campaign actively. He showed no heart for the fray and gave little help.[10] He excused himself,

---

[10] Wilson wrote to Tumulty late in September: "No answers to Harding of any kind will proceed from the White House with my consent." Undated note reproduced in Tumulty, *op. cit.*, p. 497. "Of course I will help," Wilson replied to one of Tumulty's pleas. "I was under the impression that I was helping. But I will do it at my own time and in my own way." Facsimile in *ibid.*, p. 503.

in a letter to Edward Bok, by explaining that he had "no intention whatever of qualifying as a Mr. Butt-in-sky." And yet he continued to hope that his people would perceive, better than their shortsighted senators, the inevitability of a world order and the opportunity of the United States to lead in establishing it. He acceded to arrangements for a visit from Cox, and sent the nominee away inspired to crusade for the League of Nations.[11]

Henry Cabot Lodge, however, had made it clear to the Republican nominating convention that in his view Wilson was whipped and his League beaten. After a battle between the isolationists and the internationalists of the party, a compromise plank was adopted. An agile straddle was maintained by the Republican candidate, Warren G. Harding, who had endeared himself to reactionaries by saying at Boston in May: "America's present need is not heroics but healing; not nostrums but normalcy; not revolution but restoration . . . not surgery but serenity." The Republicans made the most of the offenses that the President had given to partisan interests in his concern for the common welfare.

The pattern of political failure that had been unfolding since November of 1918 was in full view. As Wilsonian ideals went into eclipse in that tragic autumn, few believers dared to move boldly against the tide.

In October, Wilson broke his own silence. On the third of the month he released a paper asserting that the election was to be a genuine national referendum. A week before election day he roused himself to make the first formal talk that he had delivered for more than a year. Sitting in his wheel chair, he addressed fifteen pro-League Republicans. "The Nation was never called upon to make a more solemn determination than it must now make," he insisted. "The whole future moral force of right in the world depends upon the United States rather than upon any other nation, and it would be pitiful, indeed, if, after so many great free peoples had entered the League, we should hold aloof. I suggest that the candidacy of every candidate for whatever office be tested by this question: 'Shall we, or shall we not, redeem the great moral obligation of the United States?' "

Right up until the votes were counted, the prophet did not lose faith. "You need not worry," he said to his Cabinet on election day. "The American people will not turn Cox down and elect Harding. A great

---

11 Cox and F. D. Roosevelt went to the White House and found the "old man" very weak, and wearing a shawl over his left shoulder. They spoke of the extreme heat of the day, but Wilson assured Cox that the White House would be a comfortable place to live. With tears welling up, Cox said: "We are going to be a million percent with you and with your administration, and that means the League of Nations." And the invalid replied in a voice scarcely audible: "I am very grateful." Going directly to Tumulty's office, the nominee sat down, asked for paper, and drafted a statement that made the League the paramount issue of his campaign. Cox, *Journey through the Years*, p. 24.

moral issue is involved. The people can and will see it. In the long run, they do the right thing." He would not listen when Houston and Daniels tried to prepare him for the defeat of Cox.

While many Democrats were too apathetic to go to the polls, a landslide of hostile votes completed the burial of their party that had begun two years earlier. The leader who prided himself on mutual understanding with his people now knew the whole devastating truth. It was not only his partisan adversaries who were blocking the purposes that he held sacred. The people themselves had failed him. The ministerial bonds that he had woven were broken, and he was isolated. Driving through the streets of Washington, he saw in the faces of staring bystanders not faith but mere curiosity. His eyes showed his anguish and he groaned: "If only I were not helpless." Sitting almost alone in the middle of the great ballroom of the White House, he watched a moving picture of his triumph in France: the *George Washington* sailing majestically into Brest, and he on the bridge, erect, radiant, waving his hat; the Arc de Triomphe and Napoleon's Tomb, and the Presidents of France and the United States riding through a sea of idolizing mortals. Woodrow Wilson took in the re-creation of his past glory, sitting in the darkness of the big room, his head bowed, motionless and silent. He was no longer a hero who rode on winged steeds and magic carpets, but an old man who shuffled along floors from which rugs were removed for fear that he might slip on them, a cripple who tried daily to climb three or four low steps—and failed.

Stockton Axson went to the White House expecting to find the President prostrated by disappointment. But when he saw him, on the portico, Wilson's color was good and his face serene, save for pathetic little spasms at the corner of his mouth, as if he were pressing back grief. The day had come that he had foreseen in the heyday of reform, when he had prophesied to Axson that, once his step slipped, the Philistines would run over his prostrate form like cattle over a fallen steer. Indomitable spirit still shone in his large eyes and animated his handshake and his wit. Stifling his disappointment at being denied the privilege of leading his people across the River Jordan, he spoke compassionately of a nation temporarily misled in "a period of very great trial." The people's search for what is right could be depended upon, ultimately, to find the truth; and that was more than he could say for "so-called intellectuals" who were activated by prejudices and selfishness.

The day after the election he was able to laugh and tell stories. He took comfort in an anecdote about a man who had lost a donkey and was heard to repeat "Thank the Lord! Thank the Lord!" Asked why he was showing gratitude, the man replied: "I thank the Lord that I was not on him because I would have been lost too."

Never before had loyal and generous friends meant so much to Woodrow Wilson. Now that he was going out of office, his true disciples could open their hearts to him without rousing suspicions of sycophancy. They deluged him with messages of consolation, and assurance that, because of the equivocal position of the Republicans on the League, the voters truly knew not what they did. Actually the election had proved to be not the great national referendum on League membership that the President had desired, but merely a vote for a change.

Wilson responded in good spirit and wrote to Cox in appreciation of the fight that he had waged. Perhaps he had gone too fast, had given the people more than they could digest in eight years. Possibly they would have to have an awakening more horrible than that given to them by World War I.

A week after the election, and a few days before the Assembly of the League of Nations held its first meeting at Geneva without the participation of the United States, Wilson seemed stronger; but he looked worried and expressed grave concern for the future of the nation and the world.

During his last weeks in office his concern was to further as many constructive measures as a hostile Congress would permit, and not to embarrass his successor. Immediately after the election, Wilson summoned up courage to come to grips with the ticklish problem of European debts to the United States. Lloyd George had written on August 5 to urge that the United States be represented at conferences on European affairs by men of real authority and that America take part if a conference could be arranged with Russia. Specifically, the prime minister pointed out that France would not consent to fixing a definite and reasonable reparations burden on Germany unless she in turn could be granted relief from her heavy indebtedness to Great Britain; and furthermore, Britain could not afford to remit any of France's debt "except as part and parcel of all-around settlement of inter-Allied indebtedness."

Consulting Secretary Houston and getting from him a draft of an answer, Wilson replied on November 3 at great length. "It is not easy to understand," he wrote, "why wars, which arouse such high aspirations and require such willing and great sacrifices, should be followed by a lowering of ideals . . . As to Russia, I cannot but feel that Bolshevism would have burned out long ago if let alone, and that no practicable and permanent settlement involving Russian territory and rights can be arrived at until the great Russian people can express themselves through a recognized government of their own choice. . . ."

The President pointed out that the United States Treasury had been authorized to arrange a long-term funding of the demand obligations of the British government and to grant a postponement of interest payments. No one had been empowered by Congress, however, to remit or cancel any part of the demand obligations of the Allied governments to the United States. It was "highly improbable," he wrote, that either Congress or popular opinion would permit this.

Nevertheless, the President was willing to draw on the surplus wealth of his people to aid the weak and needy of the world. On February 28, 1921, he sent to Glass an eloquent appeal for an appropriation of funds for relief. To prevent "moral and material chaos," he wanted to have a small part of the nation's exportable surplus of food made available on credit. He still wished that the United States might serve as elder brother to peoples needing guidance in democratic government, as she had served in the Philippines.

The President urged Colby to go to South America to create ties of friendship, and in December the secretary of state undertook this mission. Moreover, the question of the recognition of Mexico was discussed with the Cabinet often and again. It seemed to Wilson "a matter full of doubts and 'ifs.' " [12] Though his policy of patience and faith was soon to be vindicated by the growth of a stable, indigenous government, the *de facto* regime of Obregón was not yet willing to negotiate a treaty that the Senate would approve; and so in this matter, as in many others, Woodrow Wilson was not able to share in the fruition of good seed that he had sown.

In preserving the purity of motive of his administration in its last days, the prophet sometimes had to contend with men who, too honest to take illegitimate fees while in government offices, had left his Cabinet to represent special interests. Thomas Gregory, ex-attorney general, wrote to him in behalf of oil men; and McAdoo was persistent in advancing the interests of clients. But Wilson now drew the line more

---

[12] W.W. to Colby, June 26, 1920. Pressed on the one hand by American and British financial interests and, on the other by George Creel, who claimed to have won Obregón's confidence and who in turn pleaded for Mexican rights and sensibilities, Wilson hesitated to follow the recommendation of the State Department that the embargo on shipments of arms into Mexico be lifted, and explained his views to Norman Davis in a letter of Nov. 23:

"Men like Doheny and others who are deeply involved in the oil intrigues have shown more and more recently their somewhat desperate anxiety to have this embargo lifted . . . We cannot be too careful not to serve these predatory interests, because they intend the demoralization of our own policies and the control of Mexican politics."

"Never was he more the master of his mental processes," Creel wrote in *Rebel at Large*, p. 228, of his talk with Wilson about Mexico in October of 1920.

finely than ever between the men who served the common good for love of serving and those who served a private interest for gain. He was more particular than ever about appointments, and more partisan. He continued to resist people who wished to pay personal debts by persuading him to sign certain executive orders. ("They would make the Government an eleemosynary institution," he once said of such tempters.) [13] He investigated recommendations for appointments to make sure that the candidates were untainted by legalism or by association with a political enemy.

In his final charges to Congress, also, Woodrow Wilson held true to his principles of earlier years. In the last annual message, which he dictated to Swem, the President pointed out that the government's expenditures for 1920 were less than the receipts and were at about one-third the wartime level of 1919. He pleaded for economy, for simplification of the tax laws, for adequate care of sick and disabled veterans of the armed forces, and for a grant of independence to the peoples of the Philippines. In the last days he vetoed a measure that would further postpone the effective date of an important provision of the Clayton Antitrust Act; and he refused to sign an emergency tariff bill that would set up barriers against the payment of European debts by a flow of goods.

As the winter wore on and the annual message to Congress and other responsibilities of state were put behind him, his prayers for greater vigor seemed to be answered. Giving up the invalid's chair, he came down for luncheon every day. He still used a cane—his "third leg," he called it—and found it a convenient excuse for not shaking hands with Senator Lodge when that antagonist came with a committee to notify him formally that Congress was in session.

He was thrilled to be recognized as a peacemaker by the award to him of the Nobel Peace Prize; and when his fellow prophet, General Smuts, published an article on "Woodrow Wilson's Place in History" and attributed the failure at Paris to "humanity" rather than to any man, the President wrote to the South African of his deep gratification: "I know of no one I have met whose good opinion I value more than I value yours."

The emotional bonds with the true disciples became taut in the last weeks of their association. Baker and Houston, in particular, marveled at the working of the invalid's mind in the meetings of the Cabinet. Though his speech was sometimes slow, and his left side almost immobile, he seemed to them to have a depth of perception beyond that of any of the little band of public servants. "The President finished strong,"

[13] Swem MS, p. 162, in the Princeton University Library.

Baker reported on March 17, 1921. "At the last Cabinet meeting he still showed that he saw more clearly and decided more impersonally than any of us or indeed all of us." And yet, when the business of the last meeting was over, Woodrow Wilson broke down and sobbed.

It was suggested that Secretary Colby call the Cabinet together so that they could discuss a suitable tribute; but Colby declined, reminding them that one secretary of state had been "bounced" for taking such a liberty. They decided therefore to sign a letter of appreciation:

March 3, 1921.

Mr. President:

The final moments of the Cabinet on Tuesday found us quite unable to express the poignant feelings with which we realized that the hour of leave-taking and official dispersal had arrived.

Will you permit us to say to you now, and as simply as we can, how great a place you occupy in our honor, love, and esteem?

We have seen you in times of momentous crisis. We have seen your un-complaining toil under the heavy and unremitting burdens of the Presidency. We have had the inestimable privilege of sharing some of your labors. At all times you have been to us our ideal of a courageous, high-minded, modest gentleman, a patriotic public servant, an intense and passionate lover of your country.

You have displayed toward us a trust and confidence that has touched us all, supporting and defending us, when under partisan attack, with staunch and untiring loyalty, and placing at our command, always in the most considerate way, the wisdom of your counsel. History will acclaim your great qualities. We who have known you so intimately bear witness to them now.

We fervently wish you, dear Mr. President, long life and the happiness that you so richly deserve and have so abundantly earned.

On the morning after the final meeting of the Cabinet, Woodrow Wilson prepared to discharge the only public duty that lay between him and the freedom he had so long coveted. Putting on his cutaway and gray trousers, taking up his gloves and his high hat, he drank a stimulant to help him overcome his pain, grasped the blackthorn stick without which he could not walk, and went down to the Blue Room, where he exchanged courtesies with his successor. At the door of the White House he was helped into an automobile seat next to Harding and behind Senator Knox.

He had rejected suggestions that he use his infirmity as an excuse to escape the inauguration ceremonies. As the day had approached, his love of his country's institutions had triumphed over his distrust of his successor. When he had been urged to act in a way that would put Harding and the Republican party "in a hole" he had replied: "I do not wish to put Mr. Harding in a hole. The situation of the nation and the world is too serious . . . I should like to help Mr. Harding and I hope every good citizen will try to help him."

On Inauguration Day the presidential car moved slowly through crowds that disregarded the crumpled prophet and cheered the incarnation of "normalcy." At the Capitol, Harding mounted the long flight of steps in full view of the crowds, smiling and waving his hat, taking all the cheers. His crippled predecessor walked slowly to an elevator, his left shoulder drooping and his left arm hanging limp. When a friend extended a hand to him, Wilson was able to stand for a moment without other support. Reaching the President's room, he was relieved of his overcoat and sank into a chair. For just an instant he was nervous and fidgety; but grasping a pen firmly, he went about the business of signing bills passed during the last hours of Congress.

Finally, noting that the clock in the corner of the room was moving toward the hour of noon, he said, "Well, I think I had better scoot now." But before he could make good his escape he had one unpalatable duty to perform. A committee from the Houses of Congress appeared before him to give formal notice that their sessions were over. In the front row he recognized Henry Cabot Lodge—to him the personification of the forces of privilege and selfish interest that he had fought for two decades.

Woodrow Wilson's face froze in a way that suggested that he was struggling hard to control a demon within him. Looking his victorious archenemy straight in the eye, he said very clearly and frigidly: "I have no further communication. I would be glad if you would inform both houses and thank them for their courtesy—good morning, sir."

It was a distant "sir," uttered by one who seemed to be holding himself aloof from contamination.

After everyone but Wilson's immediate party had left the room, the old clock struck twelve and he ceased to be president. He struggled into his overcoat. Then, as the strains of "Hail to the Chief" came faintly from the inaugural ceremony, he walked to the elevator, his cane tapping the stone floor, his head downcast, his eyes steadfastly ahead.

He motored with Edith Wilson out Massachusetts Avenue to a house on S Street. When they passed the White House the prophet looked away and gazed inscrutably over the heads of strollers in Lafayette Park, self-control apparent in every gray feature. Told of this years later, one of his daughters remarked: "That was just like father; he never looked back."

CHAPTER XXI

RECONCILIATION

HAD WOODROW WILSON been a man to look back upon his eight years in the White House, he might well have regarded his achievements with some complacency. Entering the Presidency with the same mental vigor that he had applied to the problems of Princeton and the state of New Jersey, he had pioneered a path around the pitfalls of plutocracy and mob rule and had effectively led a groping people toward political salvation. He had laid down a basic pattern for solving, without violence, those social and economic problems of the age that grew out of new ways of life. He had honored the principle that men's labor was not to be regarded as a commodity, had given impetus to collective bargaining, and had established the supremacy of the public interest above the advantage of any special combination of labor or capital or industrial management. His Federal Reserve policy gave promise of meeting the danger of recurring panic, and his tariff measures had helped to wean the nation from the pap of privilege. His administration had laid a foundation for a "welfare state" by providing for the matching of federal funds with those of the states to equalize certain facilities through the nation; new taxes had been levied to make this possible.

Moreover, Wilson had met, with firmness and patience, the threats to democracy and peace that had risen from Central Europe. He had restrained jingoes from resorting to war to further selfish purposes and satisfy partisan emotions, and he had restrained his people from fighting until the justness of their cause was clear enough to raise moral indignation to a crusading pitch. And in the great culminating ordeal of making a righteous peace he had advocated consistency with the philosophy that had sustained the war effort. To him, democracy had never ceased to be "a stage of development." He had succeeded in rallying free minds in many lands to support his moral purposes for humanity, until evangelical overconfidence and the psychological ravages of arteriosclerosis combined, as they had at Princeton, to bring him to temporal failure.

As he rode toward his new home on Inauguration Day of 1921, however, Woodrow Wilson was not given to casting up credits in the ledger of criticism. Asked at the last Cabinet meeting what he would do in retirement, he replied: "I am going to try to teach ex-presidents how to behave." He hoped that now, for the first time since the old days at Princeton, he could enjoy a home that satisfied his Scottish instincts.

In his years of devotion to public duty he had not adequately provided for himself. While he was at Paris, it had been necessary to borrow money to pay his income tax; and he had been generous to the White House staff. Four months before leaving the Presidency of the nation, however, Wilson had given way to a yearning for a dream house. Consulting an architect about plans for building on a site overlooking the Potomac, he wrote: "There are a good many 'ifs' in the case, the chief 'if' being if I have money enough." [1]

For several weeks the invalid had diverted himself by studying the plans, his instinct for architecture still as keen as it had been at Princeton. He read architectural journals and clipped pictures of lovely doorways and windows; and he considered practical details as well, even those having to do with the convenience of the servants. It became apparent, however, that funds were not available for building. When his wife expressed interest in a house on S Street, however, Wilson bought it with financial help from ten loyal friends, and surprised her by presenting the deed to her. A little later he performed the old Scottish ceremony of giving her a key and a piece of sod from the grounds.

Arriving at their new house on the morning of March 4, the Wilsons found the street below their front door crowded with cheering friends. Inside, everything had been done to make the transition smooth. An elevator was ready to take him to his third-floor bedroom, and he found there a duplicate of the Lincoln bed on which he had slept at the White House, and his old mahogany desk with secret drawers. He leaned on his cane at the threshold to marvel at the familiarity of the furnishings. He did not linger there long, however, for hundreds of citizens thronged the street in anticipation of a word from him. Twice he went to a window to greet them, but he choked up and could only wave and point apologetically to his throat.

In the days that followed, letters came in stacks from Americans who felt that, now that the bars of officialdom were let down, they could communicate directly with their hero. Some wanted only to help and to cheer him, others claimed a share of his time or sympathy or money. Hundreds of ex-soldiers asked for autographs from their old commander in chief, and they got them though other petitioners did not.

Though tears came too easily, Wilson could still smile at himself. In

[1] W.W. to P. M. Day, Oct. 11, 1920. Though Washington ranked lowest among five cities that the Wilsons carefully rated as possible residences, they decided not to go away from their physician, even in the summer.

his correspondence, as in his conversation, there were glimpses of the old-time force and brilliance. But for the most part his expression was perfunctory, and at times it was embittered and soured by disease.

Most of all he needed mental work that would be systematic but not too arduous. Mrs. Wilson had hoped that this would be supplied by a law practice that had been arranged before he left the White House. Bainbridge Colby had agreed to be his partner; and luxurious offices were opened in New York and Washington. His temperament was as ill suited to commercial practice, however, as it had been in his youth. He could not and would not seek private business, and went to the office only once. When dazzling fees were offered by corporations that hoped to use the former President's name to influence government action in ways that many officials thought legitimate, Wilson would not allow his partner to accept them. At the end of a year, he saw that he was a liability to Colby and agreed to end the venture.

He received proposals, also, that he exploit his literary talents for profit. While in office he had refused to allow his *History of the American People* to be used by the moving pictures, and he had declined an offer of thousands of dollars for a revision of this work.[2] And now he still shrank from using his public fame to swell his personal income. He was cold to proposals that he write reviews, prefaces, a column, a biography of Edmund Burke, and a life of Jesus.

"What I have done and stood for is of record," he wrote to Norman Davis in explanation of his reluctance to justify his deeds in print, "and any consequent interpretation or explanation that I might make would not affect the event, and would not be a contribution to history. So far as I am concerned, I have done the best I know how. My conscience is clear and clean. I am confident that what I have fought for and stood for is for the benefit of this nation and of mankind. If this is so, I believe that it ultimately will prevail, and if it is not, I don't want it to prevail." He was particularly determined that he should write nothing like Jefferson's *Anas*, that he should refrain from derogatory personal remarks in public prints.

Actually, Wilson explained to an editor, he had literary plans of his own that he had quite set his heart upon. He wanted absolute freedom to do his writing at the time and in the form that he chose. The one work for which he still had real enthusiasm was the colossal "Philosophy of Politics" that he had projected at Princeton. Just before leaving the White House he had told his wife that he soon would have leisure

---

[2] The offer was "not acceptable to the people of the country," he wrote to his publisher on Oct. 1, 1918. Nor did it excite him to be told that an autobiography might be made to "yield half a million." "As to my personal memoirs," he wrote to an inquiring agent, " 'there ain't going to be none,' if I may use the vernacular."

to carry through this venture. But here again he overestimated his powers. He wrote a brief, beautiful dedication of the book to his wife—and that was all. Even when he had been well he had confessed that he wrote "with difficulty," that the effort took "everything" out of him.

Though Wilson gave no heed to a publisher's offer of $150,000 for a record of his work at Paris, he was so impressed by a little book entitled *What Wilson Did at Paris* that he encouraged Ray Stannard Baker, its author, to undertake a longer work on the Peace Conference. In 1918 he had written to Professor Corwin of Princeton: "I have always had the feeling that an official 'Remembrancer' never could do the same work that a historian could do at a later time." But now he put trunkfuls of papers at the disposal of Baker and invited him to work in the new house. For this work Wilson released the minutes of the inner council at Paris, which he had been insistent upon keeping secret even from his successors in office; and thus he made it the more difficult for his European colleagues to understand him.

Baker found him propped up in bed by a pile of pillows, looking inconceivably old and brittle, his skin thin and parchment-yellow, drawn over his cheekbones in such a way as to thrust his nose into prominence. His eyes burned like glowing coals amid ashes. Flashlights were on the stand near him, and a book of detective stories and some chocolate; and near the head of his bed was a Bible that he read every day. There was a dignity of reconciliation about him as he shared his knowledge. Scholarly habit restrained him from surrendering to Baker's ardor, but one day he characterized the project as "the biggest work any American writer ever attempted."

By summer he was able to help Baker by deciphering notes that he had written in shorthand on the margins of the documents of the Peace Conference. Wearing a purple velvet jacket and keeping his helpless hand curled down and hidden by his side, he showed a more wholesome color and his voice was stronger. He had been told by Dr. Mayo that he might again use his crippled limbs if he would take certain exercises, and he went at them persistently every day.[3]

Though his daughters and Stockton Axson came often to the house on S Street, and Miss Ellie Lou's painting of the Madonna hung in the front room of the new residence, the glowing domesticity of the old days could not be re-created.

Woodrow Wilson wanted to be himself. He refused honorary memberships in fraternal organizations in which he had no genuine interest. It was his old, tried friends that he wanted to see. From his intimates

[3] F. W. McM. Woodrow to Mrs. James Woodrow, Dec. 20, 1921, letter in the possession of Mrs. Katharine Woodrow Kirkland.

came gifts large and small; and his acknowledgment of a brace of partridges or a book was as warm and gracious as that of a case of bootleg whisky from a journalist or a Rolls-Royce that several men combined to present to him. Even strangers sent tokens of esteem of various and strange sorts.

Refusing to concede that there was such a thing as mental fatigue, he told his family that the more one used one's mind the more one *could* use it. But hard as he strove to master his misery with his mind, he found that mental exertion tired him easily. Most of his flagging mental strength was expended lightly—in playing games of solitaire of which he kept a running count, hearing readings of detective stories and the novels of Scott and Dickens, writing place cards for his wife's luncheons, enjoying vaudeville on Saturday nights at Keith's.

Off and on, however, the prophet brandished his old political torches. With Franklin D. Roosevelt he discussed plans for the use of a Woodrow Wilson Fund that friends were raising. He didn't want a "memorial," he said, because that would suggest that he was "a dead one." The development of the Woodrow Wilson Foundation, however, gave him satisfaction.

His worst fears seemed to be justified as his successor showed a willingness to put pleasure before duty. He denounced Harding to his friends as a miserable kind of politician and "a fool of a President," and his administration as stupid, faithless, and ill-principled—a dull regime that did not know "how to make anything happen." When a relative asked him what he thought of his successor, he made a noise far up his nose. He thanked God and took courage, he said, when the Democrats captured seventy-five seats in the House in the election of 1922.

Solicitous old friends kept in touch with him to prevent undignified utterances that might discredit the prophet and his party. Democracy had not yet been made an instrument of justice, the prophet told Homer Cummings. But of Karl Marx he said: "I know of no man who has more perverted the thinking of the world." Continuing to feel responsibility for the social and economic welfare of his people, Wilson wrote to Brandeis, Baruch, and others to solicit ideas for a party creed. He still feared revolution, and felt that the country looked to him for a constructive program that would avert violence.

Correlating the advice that he received, Wilson framed a platform. On April 9, 1922, he sent it to Brandeis—whom he still thought intellectually the most stimulating man that he knew—and a week later he invited the justice and several others to his home "to help round the matter out." He conceived that he was engaged, he wrote to Norman

Davis, "in concerting the measures and perfecting the means for emancipating the world by leadership on the part of this country and our party." During 1922 he was encouraged constantly to assume leadership in the next presidential campaign. On December 3 Carter Glass, reminded by Dr. Grayson that the excitement of a campaign would kill their friend, wrote in his diary: "Only the good sense of Mrs. Wilson saves the situation."

When Tumulty asked for a message that he might read at a Jefferson Day banquet in New York in April, 1922, the Chief replied that the time was not appropriate for the breaking of his silence. Nevertheless, Tumulty called at S Street and drew out some of Wilson's ideas without reference to the impending banquet; and the next day he gave out a brief statement over Wilson's name to the diners. A major address by James M. Cox followed, and the enthusiasm of the audience led the press to interpret the spurious message as an endorsement of Cox.

Actually Wilson thought the movement for Cox fatuous, even suicidal. Discovering Tumulty's equivocation, he flatly repudiated the words that his ex-secretary had put in his mouth, refusing a plea from Tumulty for mercy. He expected that his secretary would sulk for a few days, then come like a spanked child to ask forgiveness. But he did not come; and "the Governor," shortly before his death, gave to his devoted follower the solace of a recommendation for one of New Jersey's seats in the Senate.

In 1922, gaining in health, Wilson was stimulated by visits from men who had been his most intimate colleagues at Paris. Like himself, Clemenceau and Lloyd George had been thrust aside by their proud peoples after the crisis of war had passed; and the French leader had been pilloried for permitting the "autocratic Wilson" to bully him. When he came to the Wilson house, however, in December, the old Tiger was merry and genial. Scorning the elevator, he dashed upstairs to embrace the prophet whose gospel he had ridiculed at the Peace Conference. They forgave each other for their quarrels at Paris, tried to recapture the good moments of the past.

Lord Robert Cecil also was received at S Street, and it gave comfort to the old prophet to talk with this colleague, whom he regarded as the ablest Englishman of his acquaintance. They spoke of the ideals for humanity that were closest to his heart; and more than once he said, to encourage this idealist and the others who were keeping the faith alive through the dark days: "Remember we are winning: make no concessions." [4]

---

[4] Lord Cecil's speech to the Woodrow Wilson Foundation, Dec. 28, 1924; and Lord Cecil to the writer, Nov. 4, 1954.

Mercifully, there was no transatlantic radio to bring the voice of George Harvey, who, speaking as his country's ambassador at London less than three months after Wilson's retirement, asserted that the United States had gone to war solely to save itself and would never have anything to do with the League or its commissions, directly or indirectly, openly or furtively. Wilson was unaware that the German press was cursing his "poison fangs." He did not know that, because actual conditions had fallen far short of the hopes that he had encouraged, he was the most unpopular individual in the countries of Central Europe that he had saved from a peace of vengeance.

His faith in the inevitability of an association of nations never grew dim, and every step in that direction heartened him. A disarmament conference called by his successor cheered him somewhat. "The Conference seems to be doing some good at last," he wrote to Baruch, "though it is amazing to see the Republicans lead us into a group alliance after the European fashion."

He insisted that, had he not been stricken, he could have carried through the treaty. At times he derived comfort from the thought that American participation in the League should be complete to be effective, that if the nation had joined in 1920, it would have been only a personal victory for him and the misrepresentation of opponents would have prevented full allegiance on the part of the American people. Moreover, he philosophized, the aloofness of the United States had made Europeans more keenly aware of the need for a system of international cooperation. But philosophy was not enough. "If I had nothing but philosophy to comfort me, I should go mad," he said to Homer Cummings one day.

Once the boy Tommie Wilson had remarked that it was dreadful that Moses had not been permitted to enter the promised land; and his father's answer had been: "It was God's will and his work was done." Religion now gave secure refuge to the rejected American prophet. It taught him that statesmen were merely the very humblest instruments of a greater power. He thought that wells of popular thinking had been so poisoned that it might be thirty years before the people would see the truth; but he was sure that eventually it would be made clear to them, and when that day came it would be altogether right that they should enter an international organization. To hasten the day of revelation, he corresponded with private associations in England and the United States that were devoted to the cause of the League.

As the year 1923 wore on, it became clear to those about the old prophet that his days were numbered. To "Ike" Hoover, who was disconsolate because he had not been allowed to leave the White House and serve at the Wilson home, he said: "I am tired swimming up-stream." When Lloyd George called, he found him badly warped in body and spirit.

He received callers slumped in a high-backed chair by the fireplace, his head set a little toward one side, a shawl over his shoulders. His face and body seemed heavier, and his wisps of hair were brushed straight back over a scalp almost bald. He did not move his head. Only his eyes followed his visitors. Sometimes he sat with his hands in his lap; and then as he talked in a feeble voice he would swing his right hand back and forth and occasionally strike the arm of the chair to empha-size an idea. One moment he would be the welcoming host—"You must excuse me for not rising; I'm really quite lame." And then he would turn crusader and say: "I've got to get well, and then I'm going out to get a few scalps." [5]

Not content to have had the whole world for a classroom, his thoughts went back to Princeton, and the old longing came again to realize his dream of the ideal university. He confided his vision to Raymond Fos-dick. Higher education in the United States was at a crossroads, he said, and with strong progressive leadership might yet attain the standards of Oxford and Cambridge. He had made a start in Princeton, and now he wished to find an institution at which he might continue the refor-mation. In his view, beloved Princeton had been bought once, was probably "for sale again." "The sands are running fast," he said. "You must get your friends to provide me the opportunity." Tears rolled down his face as he begged for another chance to serve.

Begged by Mrs. Wilson to humor her husband, Fosdick discussed the matter with his colleagues of the General Education Board and they concluded that they had no power to appoint a president of any uni-versity. When he returned to S Street with this verdict, Wilson would not accept it as final.

There were other channels through which the failing prophet could leave a last testimony to posterity. His friends were reminding him that his people had not had a message from him for more than two years. Finally he brought his disordered thoughts to a focus. Neuritis pre-vented him from writing down his ideas, even on the typewriter; but as the sentences came to him, lying in bed, he rang for his wife and dic-tated them to her. Sometimes, at night, he could not sleep until he un-burdened himself of a thought. Bringing the sentences and paragraphs into a semblance of order, he gave the paper to an agent, but then refused to permit publication in a magazine that he thought not appro-priate. Actually, the article did not do justice to its author, and Edith

[5] F. L. Allen, *Only Yesterday*, p. 39; Wm. Phillips, *op. cit.*, p. 97.

Wilson gave him this critical verdict as they rode through the park with Professor Stockton Axson one afternoon.

"They kept after me to do this thing, and I did it," the invalid replied petulantly. "I have done all I can. I don't want these people bothering me any more."

When they reached home, Edith Wilson's fortitude gave way. Sobbing, she said to Axson: "I just want to help and I don't know how."

Asking for the script, Axson took out two or three paragraphs, made a transition, and gave the paper to Wilson with the remark that it was a challenge rather than an argument and should be allowed to stand.

"You see exactly the point," the invalid told his old comrade.

Sent to the *Atlantic Monthly*, the paper was published in August, 1923, under the title "The Road Away from Revolution." Warning against the sort of social system that had given rise to the Russian Revolution, Wilson wrote:

. . . We should not entertain a narrow or technical conception of justice. By justice the lawyer generally means the prompt, fair, and open application of impartial rules; but we call ours a Christian civilization, and a Christian conception of justice must be much higher . . .

The sum of the whole matter is this, that our civilization cannot survive materially unless it be redeemed spiritually. It can be saved only by becoming permeated with the spirit of Christ and being made free and happy by the practices which spring out of that spirit. Only thus can discontent be driven out and all the shadows lifted from the road ahead.

The prophet's people, ignorant of the pains that had gone into the composition of this article, welcomed it as a sign of recovery. But those who were closest to him knew better. He wrote to his Edith, visiting on Cape Cod: "I never before realized fully how completely my life is intertwined with yours." She returned in September and saw a change for the worse. Her dear one seemed to have slumped into an abyss of depression. To cheer him, Baruch's daughter Belle arranged that he speak over the radio. He agreed to do this, but the writing of a talk on "The High Significance of Armistice Day" was agony. Somehow his will wrenched a few paragraphs out of his ebbing reservoir of vitality, and on the evening of the appointed day he left his bedroom in dressing gown and slippers and went down to the library to confront a microphone.

It was too late now to employ the new invention to save the League, but the prophet did his best. Even though denied the direct intercourse with an audience that was the breath of life to him, he resolved to put his whole self into his effort. He insisted on standing up before the microphone, though one hand grasped his cane and he had trouble in handling the manuscript, which he was determined to hold himself. A blinding headache made the words blur, and his wife stood behind him with a copy of the script, ready to prompt him. When it was over he was sure that he had failed in his first public audition; and he went to bed depressed and spent a restless night.

The next morning, however, he learned that the public had heard him and had listened, that he had spoken to the largest audience ever reached at one time by a human voice. Buoyed by this news, he summoned his forces to make his way on swollen feet to the front porch, where an Armistice Day crowd of thousands had gathered. Casualties of the war—the armless, the legless, and the sightless—faced their crippled leader and drew his tears. His voice was husky and broken when it was his turn to speak. He was barely able to tell of his pride in being commander in chief "of the most ideal army that was ever thrown together," and to pass the laurels of victory to General Pershing.

Halting for breath, he whispered, "I can't go on." He started to hobble into the house, leaning on a servant, and the band broke into "How Firm a Foundation." Then, just inside the door, the old prophet turned and whispered to a Princeton disciple who put an ear close to his mouth: "Stop the band. I have something to say."

Struggling back to the steps, he began falteringly upon his last public challenge: "I am not one of those who have the least anxiety about the triumph of the principles I have stood for. I have seen fools resist Providence before, and I have seen their destruction, as will come upon these again, utter destruction and contempt." The fire came back to his eyes and the resonance to his voice as he concluded: "That we shall prevail is as sure as that God reigns."

The response to his Armistice Day efforts lifted the ego of the failing prophet. With the rise in his spirits his health improved. Wrapped in a blanket, he could sit out on an upper sun porch and chat with visitors. His mind was flashing brightly upon the hates and loves that were deeply ingrained. "His master's voice has spoken," he said of President Coolidge's message to Congress. He insisted that, in a desire to get their income taxes reduced, the Democrats must not surrender to the "pocketbook brigade."

He still fancied himself the leader who must set the moral tone of his party. When it was suggested to him late in 1923 that he might champion his ideals effectively by running for a New Jersey seat in the Senate, his thought seemed to veer rather toward a return to the Presidency. His intimates knew that he persisted in hoping that the nominating convention of 1924 might seek his leadership. In January he was collaborating with Newton D. Baker on a platform; and on the 16th he asked Chairman Cordell Hull to bring the members of the Democratic National Committee to call on him. His feeble body was crumpled in an armchair but his haggard face smiled recognition as he shook hands with each.

When the McAdoos visited, he asked his wife not to leave him alone with his son-in-law, for fear that he might be asked for an endorsement for the presidential nomination in 1924. He had thought of declaring publicly that McAdoo was not the man to lead the party, but memories of Miss Ellie Lou restrained him. He could not bear to wound the husband of their daughter Nell. It comforted him to have this girl of his at his bedside, to share recollections of the good days of family life—the picnics, and Ellen Wilson painting, or reading poetry under the pines. "I owe everything to your mother," he said tenderly one day.

He sensed that the end was not far distant; but he was still keen in mind. When a guest asked about his health, he quoted a predecessor in the Presidency: "John Quincy Adams is all right, but the house he lives in is dilapidated, and it looks as if he would soon have to move out." His thoughts ran back to 1914, and to the utter stupidity and waste of international war as a way of settling anything. "It must never happen again," he said. "There is a way of escape if only men will use it." Indignant at those who objected to the "idealism" of the League of Nations, he exclaimed: "The world is *run* by ideals. Only the fool thinks otherwise." The new organization was America's great contribution to the race, and already it had proved its worth, he said. It had handled various disputes, had established itself as a clearinghouse of information, and had worked for humanitarian causes. "They are learning teamwork at Geneva," he said. "If only they will give the seed a fair chance, and let it grow!" His guest went out haunted by a tear-stained face, an indomitable jaw, and a faintly whispered "God bless you!"

During this last month Wilson gave his blessing to a biographer— Ray Stannard Baker—and granted access to his papers. In discussing the work he stressed the importance of emphasizing principles and shrank from the idea of "making too much of a single man." He was solicitous chiefly for the immortality of his ideals. Mere men did not matter.

As his strength ebbed, the prophet drew nearer to the God of his youth. His father and uncle still commanded his veneration. However, the twentieth-century leader of the clan harbored none of the Presbyterian prejudices that his father had once denounced as asinine. He could jest about peculiarities of form and ritual: with an arm around his Episcopalian wife he loved to repeat a Negro's criticism of the Episcopalian service: "Dey spends too much time in de readin' ob de minutes ob de las' meetin'." Talking one day with Bishop Freeman, he said:

"The old enmities and antagonisms are rapidly disappearing, and we lay less emphasis upon denominational labels than we once did." He conceived that a national cathedral that the bishop was planning might become "the greatest spiritual force in the country."

His belief in the goodness of God and the essential nobility of man had weathered all his vicissitudes, and asserted itself as the end drew near. Sacred love and holy rage resigned themselves to the force by which they had been inspired. Listening to a reading of Thompson's *Hound of Heaven* on a Sunday evening, he took comfort in assurance of the omnipresence of God and the futility of human efforts at escape.

Toward the end of January, Edith Wilson was kept from his room for five days by a high fever, and he made his way to her door to express his devotion. But when Dr. Grayson went on vacation, his concern for himself got the better of him for just a moment. When his wife started to cancel the doctor's vacation, however, he caught himself and reasserted the creed that he had preached all his life. "No," he said to her, "that would be a selfish thing on my part. He is not well himself and needs the change." And then slowly: "It won't be very much longer, and I had hoped he would not desert me; but that I should not say, even to you."

He failed alarmingly on January 28, and they telegraphed Grayson to return. The physician took up a desperate bedside vigil that lasted for three days, while the street outside was closed to traffic, so that members of his national congregation could gather and pray for the departing spirit. They remained there through the winter days and chilly nights, some of them kneeling, while the tortured body suffered its last agonies.

On the last day of the month he was better, and they expected him to recover. But on Sunday, February 3, he moved his lips and whispered: "I am ready." His suffering ended, as church bells summoned the people to worship.

Five minutes after he had drawn his last breath, Dr. Grayson appeared on the steps before the crowd of mourners. He read a bulletin in a voice that trembled but did not break. Many could not hear him, but when he wiped tears from his face they understood. Soon reporters were racing down the street to telegraph the news and church services were interrupted by announcements of the prophet's passing. A little boy climbed the steps, rang the bell, and gave a red rose to the servant who answered. A young woman, humbly dressed, handed in a single white lily as her tribute to a force that defied death. A big black limousine rolled up, and President Coolidge left a card that testified to the respect of the nation. Old friends and colleagues flocked to the scene, and Grayson greeted them with downcast eyes.

Those who were invited came again three days later to the funeral service in the house on S Street, where Wilson's body lay in front of the fireplace in the drawing room; but two who had served him most intimately were not present. Tumulty plodded in the cortege on foot; and House, informed that no reservation had been made for him and thinking that it might be embarrassing if he were to go to Washington uninvited, stood in the rain in New York and heard the memorial service broadcast through a loud-speaker.

At the service in the house, the bishop of the cathedral intoned the last verses that the prophet had read from a book that he kept by his bed: "The eternal God is thy refuge, and underneath are the everlasting arms: and he shall thrust out the enemy from before thee; and shall say, Destroy them."

Feeling that the growth of the national cemetery at Arlington had offended the dignity of the estate of the Lees of Virginia, Wilson had asked not to be interred there. And they did not lay him to rest beside Ellen Wilson deep in the Old South, in the plot on Myrtle Hill that he had once asked to have prepared for him. Instead, they carried his body to an elevation above the capital city, and buried him in a crypt beneath a chapel small and exquisite. Above him, the walls of a National Cathedral were rising. Woodrow Wilson was to serve to support, even in death, the realization of sublime visions.

Great universities are acting on Woodrow Wilson's concept of preceptorial teaching and democratic living in residential colleges, citizens intent on good government pursue his ideals, timbers of law with which he bulwarked American society against eroding currents are still sound after dire stresses, and the nations of the world have come closer to his envisioned parliament of man.

Jan Christian Smuts thought that at Paris the people had failed their prophets. But Woodrow Wilson took a more compassionate view. The people were not ready, he said, and perhaps they were right in thinking that the hour had not come.

Yet he never doubted that it would come. On a fragment of paper, unsigned and undated, the biographer finds written in the firm, familiar hand this favorite verse from Habakkuk:

The vision is yet for an appointed time, but at the end it shall speak, and not lie: though it tarry, wait for it; because it will surely come, it will not tarry.

It is upon the validity of this faith that the measure of Woodrow Wilson's greatness depends.

A NOTE ON SOURCES

The research on which this work is based, extending over a period of ten years, has taken account of all important sources that have been opened up to the moment of going to press. The Wilson and Baker collections in the Library of Congress have been studied with care, and also the papers relating to Wilson in the libraries of Princeton, Yale, and other universities.

In general, sources familiar to earlier biographers have not been cited in the footnotes. But reference has been made to important fresh sources.

Particular attention has been given to the documents that have come to light since Baker published the last volume of his incomplete work in 1939. See pages xi–xii. New material has been found principally in the following repositories:

The Library of Congress. Some 18,000 pieces have been added to the Wilson Collection itself, and there have been many acquisitions of collateral papers. These, as well as the earlier accessions, have been described by Katharine E. Brand in the leading article in the *L. C. Quarterly Journal of Current Acquisitions* for February, 1956. In addition, certain papers of Edith Bolling Wilson have been acquired in 1957.

The Princeton University Library. Acquisitions pertaining to Wilson that have been made since 1945 have been described by their curator, Alexander P. Clark, in *The Princeton University Library Chronicle* (Spring, 1956), pp. 173–84. Attention has been given also to the earlier Wilson materials reviewed by Henry W. Bragdon in the *Chronicle* for November, 1945. The records of Charles L. Swem were used, and also transcripts from letters written at the Paris Peace Conference by Gilbert F. Close. Most of these important documents from Wilson's personal stenographer and secretary came to the Princeton library in the spring of 1957.

The Yale University Library. In the House Collection: the diary of Edward M. House, filling some 3,000 pages of typescript; also the correspondence of House, notably that with Wilson, Walter Hines Page, James W. Gerard, W. H. Buckler, and the principal political leaders of the United States and Europe; also the papers of Gordon Auchincloss, Sir William Wiseman, Frank L. Polk, William C. Bullitt, and George W. Watt.

The Harvard College Library. In the Houghton Library: Wilson's correspondence with Frederick J. Turner, and the papers of Joseph C. Grew, David F. Houston, Walter Hines Page, and Oswald Garrison Villard.

The Columbia University Library. Several manuscript records deposited in the Oral History Project by important men of the Wilson period.

The New Jersey State Library. Twelve boxes of Wilson's correspondence of the period of the New Jersey governorship.

Pertinent new material has been found also in the libraries of the University of Virginia, The Johns Hopkins University, The Massachusetts Historical Society, and The Woodrow Wilson Foundation, and in the Roosevelt Library at Hyde Park.

Certain letters of Wilson to Ellen Axson Wilson that are not otherwise available have been read or shown to the author by Eleanor Wilson McAdoo.

Many of the witnesses who have been interviewed by the author (*see* Acknowledgments, Vol. I) have contributed valuable documents. In some cases these papers are still in their own hands and have been examined with their generous permission. Notable examples are a manuscript by Arthur Hugh Frazier, entitled "Recollections of President Wilson at the Peace Conference"; letters written by Raymond B. Fosdick from the *George Washington* and from Paris in December of 1919; notes by Arthur Sweetser of news interviews at the Paris Peace Conference (February–March, 1919); the diary of Thomas W. Brahany, clerk in the executive offices, covering days in the months of March and April, 1917; the diary of Mrs. C. S. Hamlin, in the possession of Mrs. Hamlin; a manuscript by Benjamin Chambers, Princeton 1909, which was based on contemporary notes and is in the possession of Cleveland E. Dodge; and letters in the possession of Margaret Callaway Axson, Katharine Woodrow Kirkland, Philena Fine Locke, and Edith Gittings Reid.

Extensive collections of printed sources are available at the Princeton University Library and the Woodrow Wilson Foundation. They include many of the voluminous writings of Wilson himself, which have been catalogued by Laura S. Turnbull in *Woodrow Wilson Bibliography* (Princeton, 1948); and also the "Books in the Wilson Field" that are listed by Miss Brand on pages 144ff. of that volume.

Books and articles of the last decade that have contributed much to an understanding of certain aspects of Wilson are:

Em Bowles Alsop (ed.). *The Greatness of Woodrow Wilson.* N. Y., 1956.
Bernard M. Baruch. *Baruch, My Own Story.* New York, 1957.
Louis Brownlow. *A Passion for Politics,* Chicago, 1955.
———. *A Passion for Anonymity.* In press.
Edward H. Buehrig. *Woodrow Wilson and the Balance of Power.* Bloomington, Ind., 1955.
——— (ed.). *Woodrow Wilson's Foreign Policy in Today's Perspective.* Bloomington, Ind., 1957.
John M. Blum. *Joe Tumulty and the Wilson Era.* Boston, 1951.
Centenaire Woodrow Wilson. Geneva, 1956.
Margaret L. Coit. *Mr. Baruch.* Boston, 1957.

Jonathan Daniels. *The End of Innocence*. Philadelphia, 1954.

Josephus Daniels. *The Wilson Era* (2 vols.). New York, 1946.

John W. Davidson, Jr. *A Crossroads of Freedom*. New Haven, 1956.

Vincent L. Eaton. "Books and Memorabilia of Woodrow Wilson," *L. C. Quarterly Journal of Current Acquisitions,* November, 1946.

Russell H. Fifield. *Woodrow Wilson and the Far East*. New York, 1952.

Alexander L. George and Juliette L. George. *Woodrow Wilson and Colonel House*. New York, 1956.

John A. Garraty. *Henry Cabot Lodge, a Biography*. New York, 1953.

Louis L. Gerson. *Woodrow Wilson and the Rebirth of Poland*. New Haven, 1952.

Herbert Hoover. *Memoirs*. Vol. I. New York, 1951.

Edith Benham Helm. *The Captains and the Kings*. New York, 1954.

George F. Kennan. *Russia Leaves the War*. Princeton, 1956.

———. *The Decision to Intervene*. In press.

Lectures and Seminar at the University of Chicago January 30–February 3, 1956 in Celebration of the Centennial of Woodrow Wilson. Chicago, 1956.

McMillan Lewis. *Woodrow Wilson of Princeton*. Narberth, Pa., 1952.

Tien-yi Li. *Woodrow Wilson's China Policy, 1913–1917*. New York, 1952.

Arthur S. Link. *Wilson, The Road to the White House*. Princeton, 1947.

———. *Wilson, The New Freedom*. Princeton, 1956.

———. *Woodrow Wilson and the Progressive Era, 1910–1917*. N. Y.

Walter Lippmann. "Woodrow Wilson's Approach to Politics." *New Republic,* Dec. 5, 1955.

Paul Mantoux. *Les Délibérations du Conseil des Quatre*. 2 vols. Paris, 1955.

Alpheus T. Mason. *Brandeis, A Free Man's Life*. New York, 1946.

T. H. Vail Motter (ed.). *Leaders of Men* by Woodrow Wilson, with a preface. Princeton, 1952.

———. "Woodrow Wilson and the Power of Words," *The Princeton University Library Chronicle,* XVII, 3 (Spring, 1956), 163–72.

William S. Myers (ed.). *Woodrow Wilson, Some Princeton Memories*. Princeton, 1946.

George C. Osborn. "The Influence of Joseph Ruggles Wilson on His Son, Woodrow Wilson," *North Carolina Historical Review,* October, 1955.

Charles G. Osgood. "Woodrow Wilson," in *The Lives of Eighteen from Princeton*. Princeton, 1946.

Francis B. Sayre. *Glad Adventure*. New York, 1957.

The Virginia Quarterly Review, Wilson Centennial Number, Autumn, 1956.

Louis B. Wehle. *Hidden Threads of History*. New York, 1953.

Arthur Willert. *The Road to Safety*. New York, 1953.

The vast store of journalistic and monographic literature concerning Wilson and his times has been greatly enlarged by numerous articles and speeches that appeared in the centennial year of 1956. A collection of these is available in the library of the Woodrow Wilson Foundation.

An extensive Wilson bibliography may be found in pages 172–83 of *Great Lives Observed,* edited by John Braeman and published by Prentice-Hall in 1972.

The standard collection of Wilson's writings, including those used in this work, is *The Papers of Woodrow Wilson,* edited by Arthur S. Link, John W. Davidson, David Hurst, et al. and in process of publication in many volumes by the Princeton University Press.

INDEX

Adams, Charles Francis, I, 104n.
Adams, Herbert B., I, 42–43, 46, 48
Adamson, William C., I, 389, 424
Adamson Act, II, 56–57, 59, 93
Albert I, King of Belgium, II, 377
Alderman, Edwin A., I, 289n.
Aldrich, Nelson, I, 212, 300–301, 304
Alexander, J. W., II, 396n.
Alexander Bill, I, 421
Alien Land Act of California, I, 353, 355
American Anti-Boycott Association, I, 334
American Bankers' Association, I, 300, 317
American Bar Association, I, 413; II, 339
American Federation of Labor, I, 271, 328, 334; II, 339, 358
American Labor Standard, I, 156
American Peace Society, I, 378
Ancona, the, II, 28
Anderson, Chandler P., II, 342n., 347
Anti-Saloon League, I, 154
Arabic, the, I, 433; II, 22–23, 27
Archbishop of Canterbury, II, 230
Asquith, H. H., II, 68, 230–31
Auchincloss, Gordon, I, 398n., 418; II, 96n., 195n., 225n., 231n., 281n., 284, 321n.
Augusta Female Seminary, I, 2
Aurora, The, I, 4
Axson, Edward, I, 79, 81, 82, 94
Axson, Ellen Louise, I, 34–41. *See also* Ellen Axson Wilson
Axson, Margaret (Mrs. Edward G. Elliott) I, 75, 82, 148, 441
Axson, Rev. Samuel, I, 34–37, 38n., 39, 44
Axson, Stockton, I, 74, 78, 80, 81, 86, 94, 145, 158, 214, 360, 406; II, 61, 120n., 206, 209, 220, 348, 398, 404, 413, 418

Bacon, A. O., 367n.
Bagehot, Walter, I, 22, 38, 48, 54, 73, 76, 89n., 134, 138, 298, 300
Bailey, Joseph W., I, 211n.
Bailey, Prentiss, I, 115n., 219n.
Baker, Newton D., I, 229, 272, 276, 348; II, 45–46, 57n., 66n., 77, 87–88, 95–96, 101, 104n., 105–108, 114, 117n., 124, 132, 135, 157n., 160–62, 163n., 165, 167, 171n., 172n., 192, 206, 211–12, 237n., 249n., 253, 267n., 275, 377, 397–98, 407–408, 419
Baker, Ray Stannard, I, 150, 198n.; II, 35, 207, 243–44, 249n., 283–85, 291, 295–96, 299, 303, 308, 309n., 315–16, 318, 320, 413, 420

Bakhmeteff, Boris A., II, 137, 145, 146n., 169
Balfour, Arthur James, II, 107, 130–31, 134, 136, 139n., 146n., 150n., 151n., 169, 207n., 228, 231, 238n., 242, 248, 252, 261, 267n., 290, 309n., 310, 311n., 315
Balfour Declaration, II, 327
Barclay, Colville, II, 307n.
Baruch, Belle, II, 418
Baruch, Bernard M., II, 56, 132, 158, 161–62, 163n., 172n., 213, 215, 275n., 318, 322, 329, 334, 336, 336n., 347, 356, 378, 386, 414, 416
Baruch, Dr. & Mrs. Simon, II, 133
Beach, Rev. Sylvester W., II, 60
Beecher, Henry Ward, I, 51
Belmont, August, I, 229
Benson, William S., II, 196, 252
Bernstorff, Johann von, I, 351, 428, 439; II, 8, 16, 18, 21–23, 28, 32–33, 72–73, 76, 78n., 81–84, 89, 125
Bethmann-Hollweg, Theobald von, II, 30, 142
Beveridge, Albert J., II, 200, 209n.
Bliss, Tasker H., II, 102n., 135–36, 167n., 171n., 183, 187, 191n., 206, 212, 237, 241, 251, 252, 266n., 279, 310, 314, 316, 321, 329, 370n.
Blythe, Samuel G., I, 375
Bok, Edward, II, 80, 403
Bones, Helen Woodrow, I, 36n., 324, 395–96, 402, 416, 426–27, 428, 429, 431, 434, 441; II, 60n.
Bones, James, I, 10, 34, 36
Bones, Jessie (Mrs. Brower), I, 11, 34, 36
Bones, Marion Woodrow, I, 11, 36n.
Bonsal, Stephen, II, 260, 260n., 384
Borah, William E., II, 78, 270, 340, 344, 349, 351
Borden, Sir Robert, II, 217
Botha, Louis, II, 251
Bourgeois, Léon, II, 178n., 257–58, 260, 287, 303–304
Bowman, Dr. Isaiah, II, 140n.
Boy-Ed, Karl, II, 27
Bradford, Gamaliel, I, 43n.
Brandegee, Frank B., II, 270–72, 340, 343, 352, 391
Brandeis, Louis Dembitz, I, 243, 245, 273, 281, 290, 306–307, 313, 329–31, 336, 336n.; II, 57n., 158, 172n., 210, 414
Brest-Litovsk, Treaty of, II, 137, 144–45, 147, 153, 154n.

Bridges, Robert, I, 22, 32, 51, 52, 64, 132, 145, 415n.
Brockdorff-Rantzau, Ulrich, II, 318–19, 331
Brooke, Francis J., I, 13, 14
Brougham, H. B., I, 127
Brown, Colonel E. T., I, 441
Brownlow, Louis, I, 230n., 280n., 416–17n.; II, 358n.
Bryan, William Jennings, I, 130, 144, 146, 157n., 197, 201–205, 207, 210, 212, 215–18, 224–25, 228–29, 231–32, 232n., 234, 240, 249, 251, 253, 267–69, 274–76, 282, 292, 302, 304–305, 307–309, 313–14, 322, 329n., 331, 335, 346–56, 360–61, 363, 365, 366n., 368n., 370–73, 378–79, 382–83, 383n., 388, 391, 404, 420n., 428; II, 2, 6, 8, 11, 13–14, 16–19, 46n., 48, 54, 74, 77, 132, 393
Bryan, Mrs. William Jennings, I, 207, 225; II, 19
Bryan-Chamorro Treaty, I, 382n., 383
Bryce, James, I, 43n., 48, 65, 73, 187n., 276, 366, 388; II, 150
Bryn Mawr College, I, 45–50
Buckler, W. H., II, 68, 141n., 212, 264
Bullitt, William C., II, 290–91, 320, 366
Bureau of Corporations, I, 331n., 335
Burgess, John W., I, 53n.
Burleson, Albert S., I, 233, 270, 274, 276, 280, 327n., 391, 419; II, 64, 66n., 90–91, 95, 106, 112n., 113n., 161, 213, 275, 401n.
Burnett Bill, II, 93
Butler, Nicholas Murray, I, 141, 220

Capps, Edward, I, 347n.
Carden, Sir Lionel, I, 362n., 365, 367, 367n., 368n.
Carnegie, Andrew, I, 117, 118, 282
Carnegie Foundation for the Advancement of Teaching, I, 160n., 192, 212–13, 216
Carranza, Venustiano, I, 358–59, 369–70, 373; II, 46n., 50, 61n., 89, 125
Cavell, Edith, II, 28, 317
Cecil, Lord Robert, II, 178n., 180, 183, 228, 231, 246n., 256, 258, 284, 286–87, 300–302, 415
Chamberlain, George E., II, 47, 159–60
Chicherin, George V., II, 263, 290
Child Labor Act of 1916, II, 51n.
Chinda, Sutemi, I, 353–55; II, 313
Choate, Joseph H., I, 388
Churchill, Winston Spencer, II, 110n., 132, 262, 266–67, 324
Clark, Champ, I, 203n., 204, 209, 212, 216, 216n., 217n., 218–19, 223, 225, 227, 229–33, 292–93, 348, 391; II, 48, 98
Clark, John B., 134n., 149n.
Clarke, John H., II, 57, 342n.
Clarke Amendment, II, 44, 45n.

Clarkson, Grosvenor B., II, 162n.
Clayton Act, I, 333–34; II, 56, 407
Clemenceau, Georges, II, 136, 150, 175, 177, 180, 191n., 192, 195–96, 207–208, 216, 222, 224, 226–27, 232, 238n., 239–42, 245, 249, 251–52, 255, 257–58, 260–61, 265, 279–80, 282, 287, 289, 292, 292n., 293–96, 298–300, 304, 307, 308n., 310, 311n., 312, 318–19, 323, 325, 328–29, 331–32, 347n., 372n., 373, 394, 415
Cleveland, Grover, I, 58, 66, 67, 85, 93, 104, 105, 108, 109, 111, 115, 116, 117, 145n., 190, 218, 292, 294, 345n., 414n.
Close, Gilbert, II, 297n., 359n.
Cobb, Frank I., I, 270n.; II, 97, 207n., 224, 225n.
Cohalan, Daniel F., II, 277
Colby, Bainbridge, II, 396, 401–402, 406, 412, 418
Colby, Everett, I, 142
College of New Jersey, I, 18–23, 51–61. See also Princeton University.
Colorado coal strike, I, 340
Columbia Theological Seminary, I, 12, 59, 112
Commission on the League of Nations, II, 256–60, 287–89, 300–304, 349
Committee on Banking and Currency, I, 301
Committee on Public Information, II, 113, 174
Congress of Paris, II, 1
Coolidge, Calvin, II, 268, 358n., 419, 421
Corwin, Edward S., II, 413
Council of National Defense, II, 49n., 117–18, 122, 161–62
Council of Ten, II, 241, 248, 257–58, 264, 292n., 297
Cowdray, Lord, I, 362n.
Cox, James M., II, 400, 402, 405
Cram, Ralph Adams, I, 93, 119
Crane, Charles R., I, 405n.; II, 308, 310
Creel, George, II, 65n., 113–14, 145, 147, 174, 255, 263, 406n.
Crowder, Enoch H., II, 106
Culberson, Charles A., I, 198, 211; II, 393
Cummings, Homer S., II, 201, 214, 388, 398–99, 400n., 401–402, 414, 416
Czernin, Count Ottokar, II, 155

Dabney, Heath, I, 27, 28, 34, 38, 63, 67, 149n., 151
Dacia affair, I, 425; II, 6–7
Daniels, Josephus, I, 43n., 208, 217, 232n., 252, 270, 274, 284, 289n., 354–55, 355n., 360n., 371, 373, 380; II, 42, 65, 66n., 87, 91n., 92, 94n., 95–96, 108–109, 112n., 116, 163n., 193, 201, 221n., 275, 300, 396, 404
Daniels, Winthrop M., I, 70, 122, 188n., 409n.

d'Annunzio, Gabriele, II, 310, 372n.

Davidson, Henry P., II, 120n.

Davies, Joseph E., I, 331n., 332n., 335, 336n.

Davis, E. P., I, 400

Davis, John W., II, 297n.

Davis, Norman H., II, 293, 309, 406n., 412, 414–15

Davis, Robert, I, 154, 156, 157n., 168, 170, 174

Day, William R., II, 212

Debs, Eugene, I, 222; II, 397

Declaration of London, II, 3–4

Declaration of Paris, I, 1

Democratic party, in New Jersey, 1910, I, 142–45, 150–59, 162–92; election of 1912, I, 200–52; election of 1914, I, 412–15; election of 1916, II, 52–65; election of 1918, II, 199–205; election of 1920, II, 397–402; election of 1924, II, 415

Denman, William, II, 120–21

Derry, Professor, I, 9

Diaz, Félix, I, 358

Diaz, Porfirio, I, 358–60

Dodd, William E., II, 200n., 204

Dodge, Cleveland, I, 129, 160, 173, 209n., 236n., 237, 273n., 346n., 359, 390n., 415n.; II, 68, 77, 168, 400n.

Doheny, Edward L., I, 363; II, 406n.

"dollar diplomacy," I, 349, 381–83, 387

Duane, William, I, 4

Dulles, John Foster, II, 126

Dumba, Konstantin, II, 87

Dunne, Peter Finley, "Mr. Dooley," I, 221

Edge, Walter E., I, 185, 187

Edward, Prince of Wales, II, 377, 381

Edwards, Edward I., I, 257

Eliot, Charles W., I, 346, 346n., 406n., 423

Elliott, Margaret. See Axson, Margaret.

Ely, Richard T., I, 42n., 134

Emergency Fleet Corporation, II, 120–21

Esch-Cummins Transportation Act, II, 395

Espionage Act, II, 112n.

Exports Council, II, 112n., 125n.

Fagan, Mark M., I, 142

Falaba, the, II, 13

Fall, Albert B., I, 363; II, 270, 341, 352, 379

Federal Power Commission, II, 397

Federal Reserve Act, I, 300–21, 410

Federal Reserve Board, I, 302, 307, 319; II, 95n.

Federal Trade Commission, I, 335–36; II, 213

Feisal, Emir, II, 307

Fielder, James F., I, 338

Fine, Henry B., I, 66, 70, 88, 98, 105n., 110, 118n., 160, 195, 256, 346, 347n.

Fiske, Bradley A., I, 354, 355n.

Fitz-Randolph, Nathaniel, I, 101

Fletcher, Frank F., I, 371

Fletcher, Henry P., I, 386n.

Foch, Ferdinand, II, 166–67, 171n., 186, 191, 191n., 196, 251, 287, 328–29

Ford, Henry, I, 340; II, 201, 204, 215

Fosdick, Raymond, II, 121, 220, 417

Foss, Eugene, I, 273

Foster, John W., II, 382n.

Fourteen Points and supplementary principles, II, 147–56, 174–75, 191, 193, 199, 203, 205, 217, 241, 247, 279, 290, 295, 299, 306, 308, 322, 326n., 366

Francis, David R., II, 93, 137, 142, 143n., 144, 147n., 153–54, 262n.

Frankfurter, Felix, II, 326

Frazier, Arthur Hugh, II, 164

freedom of the seas, I, 1; II, 29, 53, 79, 148, 186, 195–96, 217, 225n., 227, 300

Freeman, James E., II, 420

Frick, Henry Clay, I, 328

Furuseth, Andrew, 329n.

Gallinger, Jacob H., 336n.

Galt, Edith Bolling (Mrs. Norman). See Wilson, Edith Bolling.

Gardiner, A. G., II, 9, 31n.

Garfield, Harry A., II, 119, 158–59, 163n., 165

Garrison, Lindley M., I, 272–74, 354–55, 360n., 361, 433; II, 17, 41–42, 45–46

Gaynor, William J., I, 220

General Education Board, II, 417

George V, King of England, II, 228

George Washington, the, II, 216–22, 241, 256n., 267–68, 278, 281, 298–99, 333, 336

Geran, Elmer H., I, 182–83

Gerard, James W., I, 348; II, 10, 11n., 13, 20n., 22, 28n., 69–70, 83, 89, 212

Gibbons, James, II, 233

Glass, Carter, I, 301–308, 313–14, 319; II, 215, 272n., 274, 383, 397–99, 401–402, 406, 414, 422

Glass, Frank P., II, 207n.

Glass-Owen Bill, I, 308–17

Glynn, Martin H., II, 53

Godwin, Parke, I, 6

Goethals, George W., II, 120

Gompers, Samuel, I, 271, 328, 334; II, 153n., 204

"good neighbor" policy, I, 375–76

Gore, Thomas P., I, 230; II, 48

Grayson, Cary T., I, 285, 297, 311–12, 395–96, 400, 402–403, 405, 414, 416, 419, 424, 426, 427, 430, 430n., 435–36, 441; II, 15, 59, 64, 71, 92, 97, 164, 176–77, 216, 236, 240, 244, 253, 256, 297, 303, 321, 322n., 337, 361, 365, 368, 370–71, 373–78, 380, 385, 395–96, 400, 414, 421

Gregory, Thomas W., I, 197, 419; II, 57n., 143n., 275, 406

Grew, Joseph C., II, 70n., 87
Grey, Viscount, I, 362, 362n., 366, 368, 370, 386n., 388n., 391, 397n., 398n., 399n., 405–406; II, 4–7, 9–10, 25–27, 29–32, 36, 67, 130, 134, 183, 230, 231n., 381, 387
Gridiron Club, I, 278
Guffey, Joseph M., I, 211

Hague, Frank, I, 225, 257
Hale, William Bayard, I, 360–61
Hamlin, Charles S., II, 354
Hankey, Sir Maurice, II, 284, 309
Hapgood, Norman, I, 273n.
Harding, Warren G., II, 343, 350, 362, 402–403, 408–409, 414
Harlakenden, I, 309, 396, 418, 431
Harmon, Judson, I, 201, 219, 227
Harper, George M., I, 70
Harper, Samuel, II, 263n.
Harper's Weekly, I, 144, 208n., 213–16, 322n.
Harriman, Mrs. Borden, I, 113n., 430n.
Hart, Albert Bushnell, I, 64, 404
Harvey, George, I, 65, 68, 143–44, 145, 151–57, 164, 172–73, 176, 180, 191, 198, 203n., 208n., 213–16, 219n.; II, 65, 200, 337, 416
Harvey's Weekly, II, 363
Hay, John, I, 345n., 351n.; II, 46
Hay-Pauncefote Treaty, I, 389
Hays, Will H., II, 203n., 345
Hayward, William D., II, 163n.
Hearst, William Randolph, I, 159, 212, 219, 224
Helm, Edith Benham, II, 253
Henderson, Arthur, II, 141n.
Henry, Robert L., I, 313
Hertling, Georg F., II, 155
Hibben, Jennie, I, 93, 98, 108, 112, 122, 403n.
Hibben, John G., I, 70, 81, 98, 108, 109, 110, 112, 114, 121, 194–96, 253, 415
Higginson, Henry L., I, 273n., 409n.
Hillyer, Judge George, I, 201
Hindenburg, Paul von, II, 181, 184
Hines, Walker D., II, 356, 395n.
Hitchcock, Gilbert M., I, 231, 297, 318; II, 78, 91n., 209n., 278, 286, 300, 304, 336n., 340n., 341, 343, 345, 348n., 353, 361, 367n., 372, 385–86, 388–93
Hogg, James S., I, 197
Hooker, Richard, II, 167, 211
Hoover, Herbert Clark, II, 117, 172n., 206, 207n., 212–13, 214n., 235, 252, 283n., 292n., 297n., 317, 320–21, 335n., 336n.
Hoover, Irwin H., I, 284, 430n., 433; II, 297n., 324, 348, 416
House, Edward Mandell, I, 196–99, 211–13, 215–17, 224–27, 242n., 249–50, 255n., 256, 258–59, 264, 266–73, 279, 281, 288, 290, 291n., 295n., 302–304, 306–307, 320, 322–24, 327, 328, 331n., 332, 340, 346n., 348, 351, 359–60, 362, 366–69, 374, 376n., 384–85, 388n., 390n., 393–94, 397–99, 400, 402–404, 414, 415n., 417–22, 424, 430–31, 433, 435, 436n., 437–38, 440; II, 7, 9–12, 21, 23, 25–32, 35–36, 52–53, 55, 60, 63–66, 68–74, 77, 81–83, 88–89, 91–94, 96–98, 109–11, 112n., 114, 124–25, 129–34, 136–42, 144–47, 149, 150n., 151n., 154n., 155–56, 164–65, 166n., 167–69, 172n., 176–81, 185, 188–89, 191–96, 206–208, 210–11, 214, 216, 218, 224–27, 231n., 232–34, 236, 239–40, 246, 248, 256–60, 262, 267, 270, 278–84, 286, 289–91, 292n., 295–300, 302–305, 309, 311n., 313n., 315–16, 321–22, 328, 358, 360, 366, 383, 387–88, 399, 422
Houston, David F., I, 199n., 212, 271, 275n., 276, 280, 291n., 322, 328n., 331, 360n., 412; II, 51, 66n., 84, 88, 117, 275, 377, 383, 396n., 397–98, 404–405, 407
Howe, George, I, 79, 234, 256
Howe, Mrs. George (Annie Wilson), I, 8n., 285, 317; II, 59.
Howe, Rev. Dr. George, I, 8n., 79
Huerta, Victoriano, I, 358–65, 367, 369–71, 373–75, 380, 391
Hughes, Charles Evans, I, 242n.; II, 55, 59, 61–65, 162, 304
Hughes, William, I, 242n., 270, 348
Hughes, William M., II, 249–51, 258
Hulbert, Mary Allen, I, 99, 113, 146, 184, 189, 194–95, 198, 226, 235, 247, 248, 254n., 278, 283, 309, 311n., 312–13, 315, 362–63, 393, 395–96, 415–17, 430n., 436–37, 439; II, 60, 368, 373
Hull, Cordell, I, 295; II, 420
Hurley, Edward N., II, 120–21, 163n., 164, 166, 180n., 213, 215, 345

"If," by Rudyard Kipling, I, 159, 220, 279
Industrial Conferences, II, 357
Industrial Workers of the World, II, 163, 358n., 364
Inglis, William O., I, 191
Inquiry, The, II, 140n., 146, 178n., 193, 218, 231n., 323–24
Inter-Allied Conference, Dec., 1917, II, 144
International Economic Council, II, 359
Interstate Commerce Commission, I, 330, 331n., 333, 336n., 409; II, 57
Ishii, Viscount, II, 127–28

James, Ollie, II, 54
Jameson, J. Franklin, I, 65n.; II, 263n.

Jenkins, William O., II, 378–79
Joffre, Joseph J. C., II, 107, 227
Johns Hopkins University, I, 35, 39–45, 53n.
Johnson, Hiram, I, 353; II, 340n., 344, 351, 391
Joline, Adrian H., I, 217
Jones, Thomas D., I, 281; II, 120n.
Jones Bill, II, 45n.
Jordan, David Starr, I, 129
Jusserand, J. J., II, 186n., 281, 341n.

Kellogg, Frank B., II, 340n., 348, 353, 359
Kendall, Calvin N., I, 188n.
Kennedy, Marion Wilson, I, 8n., 79
Kerney, James, I, 155, 171n., 177; II, 210
Kerr, Philip H. (Lord Lothian), I, 324n.
Keynes, John Maynard, II, 328n.
King, Benjamin, I, 382n.
King, Henry Churchill, II, 308
Klotz, Louis L., II, 196
Knox, Philander C., 362n., 388; II, 131, 271–72, 281, 341, 349, 352, 387, 394, 408
Knox Resolution, II, 394
Kolchak, Alexander V., II, 266, 291, 316
Krock, Arthur, I, 216n.

Laconia, the, II, 50
LaFollette, Robert M., I, 211, 222–23, 240, 250, 297, 329n.; II, 50n., 90–91
Lamont, Thomas W., II, 288n.
Lane, Franklin K., I, 211n., 272, 274, 275n., 276, 323, 350, 368n.; II, 66n., 88, 93, 112n., 116, 163n., 166, 171, 190, 206, 275, 357n., 380, 382, 396n.
Lansdowne, Lord, II, 135
Lansing, Robert, I, 390n., 431, 435, 440n., II, 2, 4, 5n., 12–14, 16–17, 20, 22–23, 29, 32–33, 39, 47, 61n., 66n., 74–76, 82–84, 88, 91n., 95, 113n., 124–25, 127–28, 129n., 130, 134n., 139n., 140, 146n., 153, 155, 172, 180n., 185, 188, 197, 206, 208, 210, 225, 236–37, 240n., 247–48, 251, 255, 261, 263n., 288n., 290, 314, 320–21, 323–24, 347–48, 350n., 351–53, 357, 358–61, 366, 371, 376–78, 380–82, 393, 395n., 396n.
Lansing, Mrs. Robert, II, 382n.
Lansing-Ishii Agreement, II, 128
Lawrence, David, II, 65
Lawrence, T. E., II, 307
League for the Preservation of American Independence, II, 339
League to Enforce Peace, II, 35–37, 150, 178n.
Lee, Robert E., I, 7
Lenin, II, 152–53, 172, 290–92, 316
Lever, A. F., II, 51, 118
Lever Act, II, 118–19

Liberty Loans, II, 115, 168, 274
Lind, John, I, 363–64, 367n., 368, 370
Lippmann, Walter, I, 40n.; II, 140n.
Litvinov, Maxim, II, 264–65, 290
Lloyd George, II, 31, 68, 130n., 131, 133–36, 141, 150–51, 155, 166n., 177, 180, 186, 192, 194–96, 206, 207n., 216, 224, 225n., 226, 229–32, 235, 239, 241–42, 244, 247n., 248–51, 254–55, 261, 264–67, 279–80, 282–83, 283n., 287, 290–93, 296, 300, 307, 310–19, 321, 323–24, 325n., 326, 328–29, 331–32, 372n., 394, 404, 415–16
Lodge, Henry Cabot, I, 23, 66, 338, 372, 390, 414, 422–23, 425; II, 37, 48–49, 63n., 90, 100, 141, 187, 209n., 210–11, 231, 238, 269–73, 276, 278, 281, 286, 305, 311n., 339–40, 342, 345–49, 350–54, 359, 366–67, 369, 378, 381, 384, 385–86, 388–93, 394, 403, 407, 409
Long, Breckinridge, II, 380
Longworth, Alice Roosevelt, II, 191n., 340, 390n.
Lotos Club dinner, I, 144
Love, Thomas B., I, 197n., 202n.
Lowell, A. Lawrence, I, 68, 114, 129, 159; II, 37, 268, 288
Ludendorff, Erich von, II, 166, 184, 192
Lusitania case, I, 430, 431; II, 14–24, 27, 42

Madero, Francisco, I, 358
Makino, Baron Shinken, II, 292, 313–14, 332
Malone, Dudley Field, I, 413
Manhattan Club conference, I, 213–16
Mantoux, Paul, II, 292
March, Peyton C., II, 167, 171n., 184, 186, 262n., 275
Mariana, the, II, 70
Marshall, Thomas Riley, I, 185, 233, 234, 293; II, 201, 275, 376
Martin, Edward S., I, 213
Martin, Thomas S., I, 289n.; II, 209n., 383
Martine, James E., I, 171–73, 175–79
Masaryk, Thomas G., II, 189–90, 206, 211
Massey, William F., II, 249–51
Max, Prince of Baden, II, 184
Mayo, Henry T., I, 370, 371, 371n., 372; II, 110n.
McAdoo, Eleanor Wilson, I, 393, 395, 416; II, 197, 420. See also Wilson, Eleanor.
McAdoo, William Gibbs, I, 209, 210, 216, 224–25, 227–28, 230, 236, 250, 252, 268–69, 270n., 274, 276, 282n., 303, 305–307, 316, 319–20, 322, 350, 362n., 393, 402, 409–11, 413, 419–20, 422, 424–25, 435–36; II, 9, 18, 21, 50, 57, 66, 84, 88, 90–92, 94, 114–15, 132, 134, 153, 158, 163, 176–77,

199, 207n., 211, 213–15, 343, 356, 386, 398–99, 400, 401n., 406, 420
McCombs, William F., I, 203, 208, 209n., 210, 216, 223, 224, 227–33, 235–36, 252, 254, 268, 269n., 273n., 290, 331n., 382; II, 337
McCorkle, Walter, I, 203
McCormick, Vance, I, 211; II, 55, 60, 70, 113n., 163n., 201, 275n., 280n., 321n., 322n., 336, 367n., 396n.
McCosh, James, I, 17, 35, 51, 58, 83, 91, 102
McCumber, Porter J., I, 390
McDonald, Captain Bill, I, 250, 258, 430n.
McElroy, Alice Wilson, II, 214n.
McLemore, Jeff, II, 48
McReynolds, James C., I, 271, 276, 282, 327, 331, 332n., 340, 419
Meeker, Royal, I, 302
Meyer, Eugene, II, 275n.
Mezes, Sidney, I, 198; II, 134n., 140n., 231n., 309n., 311n.
Miller, David Hunter, II, 231n., 281n., 284, 301, 309n., 342n., 345n.
Milyukov, Paul N., II, 94n.
Minor, John B., I, 24, 27
Mitchell, Edward P., I, 212
Mitchell, John Purroy, I, 376n., 413
Monroe Doctrine, I, 365, 380, 381, 384, 397n.; II, 79, 151, 210, 219, 271, 288, 301–304, 332, 342, 346
Moody, Dwight L., I, 51
Mooney, Tom, II, 143n.
Moore, John Bassett, I, 349, 353n., 359, 365, 379, 390n.
Morgan, J. Pierpont, I, 68, 109, 135, 229, 301, 332, 340, 409
Morgenthau, Henry, I, 348; II, 52
Morley, John, I, 117
Morris, Roland S., I, 211, 316; II, 129, 173; 316
Morrow, Dwight, II, 288n.
Mott, John R., I, 346
Murphy, Charles, I, 227, 230
Myers, David J., I, 382n.

National Association of Manufacturers, II, 51
National Defense Act, II, 49–50, 161
National Democratic Club of New York, I, 135
National Monetary Commission, I, 300–301
National Park Service, II, 58
National Security League, II, 159
Newberry, Truman, II, 201, 204
"new freedom, the," I, 244, 399, 412–13; II, 50–53, 355, 410
"new idea, the," I, 142–43, 154, 167, 170
New Jersey Commission on Uniform State Laws, I, 144

New Jersey Federation of Labor, I, 219
"new morality," I, 148
"new nationalism," I, 244
Nicholas II, Czar, II, 170
Nonpartisan League, II, 51
Norris, George, II, 50n.
Northcliffe, Lord, II, 131–33, 227–28, 283, 291
Nugent, James, I, 156, 164, 166–68, 184, 187, 189, 190, 192, 218, 225, 257, 413

Obregón, Álvaro, II, 406
O'Gorman, James A., I, 338
Olney, Richard, I, 347, 404
"Open Door" in China, the, I, 350, 351n., 380
Orlando, Vittorio E., II, 255, 261, 285, 292, 308–13, 317, 372n.
O'Shaughnessy, Nelson, I, 361, 363, 365, 367n.
Other People's Money, I, 330
Overman Act, II, 161n.
Overman, Lee S., II, 161
Owen, Robert L., I, 304–308, 319

Paderewski, Ignace Jan, II, 108
Page, Thomas Nelson, I, 347; II, 313n.
Page, Walter Hines, I, 32–33, 43n., 68, 70, 203, 208, 210, 271–72, 274n., 298, 347, 362n., 366, 367n., 368, 388n., 389, 397, 404; II, 4–7, 22n., 29n., 36, 67–68, 74, 75n., 87, 89, 95n., 109, 115n., 118, 124, 141n., 229 ↑
Palmer, A. Mitchell, I, 211, 310; II, 275, 356, 395, 397, 400
Panama Canal tolls, repeal of, I, 368, 388–91
Pan-American Pact, II, 35
Pan-American Union, I, 442
Papen, Franz von, II, 27
Paris, Congress of, I, 1
Paris Peace Conference, II, 216–67, 277–337
Parker, Alton B., I, 228–29
Parker, John M., II, 104
Patton, Francis L., I, 51, 57, 60, 66, 70, 84, 88, 105n., 110, 114n., 116n.
Payne, John Barton, II, 396n.
Payne-Aldrich Tariff, I, 292, 295n., 299, 299n.
Peck, Mary Allen. See Hulbert, Mary Allen.
Peck, Thomas D., I, 99, 248
Pence, Thomas J., I, 270n.
Penfield, Frederick, I, 214; II, 87
Penrose, Boise, II, 345
Perkins, George W., I, 242n., 245
Perry, Bliss, I, 70, 84
Pershing, John J., II, 46, 104n., 107–108, 165–68, 183, 186, 191, 191n., 192, 222, 225, 419
Persia, the, II, 24, 47
Peters, Andrew J., II, 269
Phelan, James D., I, 353, 383

Philip Dru, Administrator, I, 256, 288, 295n., 341
Phillimore, Lord, II, 178n.
Phillips, William, I, 369; II, 207n., 220, 238n., 288n., 345n., 380
Pichon, Stéphane, II, 284
Pitney, Mahlon, I, 219
Pittman, Key, II, 353, 359, 378
Poincaré, Raymond, II, 222–23, 245, 311n., 330–31
Poindexter, Miles, II, 143n.
Polk, Frank L., II, 74, 96n., 124, 173, 288n., 291n., 307n., 311n., 337, 341, 343, 371, 372n., 380
Poole, DeWitt, II, 267n.
Pope Benedict XV, II, 140, 142, 233
Princeton Theological Seminary, I, 18, 202
Princeton University, I, 17–22, 35, 41, 51–69, 84–98, 101–42, 159–61
Prinkipo Conference, II, 266
Pritchett, Henry S., I, 192, 213
Procter, William Cooper, I, 119, 120, 122, 123, 124, 125, 126, 127, 130, 141, 195
Progressive party, I, 239–40
Pujo Committee on Banking and Currency, I, 301, 328
Pyle, Howard, I, 66n.
Pyne, Moses Taylor, I, 111, 112n., 119, 120, 123, 124, 125, 126, 128, 141, 160, 195
Rappard, William E., II, 210, 247, 253n.
Rayburn, Sam, I, 336n.
Raymond, John M., 140n.
Reading, Viscount, II, 31, 133, 136, 156, 381
Record, George L., I, 142–43, 166–70, 182, 184–85, 188n., 196, 240, 257n.; II, 355–56
Redfield, William C., I, 273, 274, 276, 350, 351n., 412; II, 163n., 172n., 396n.
Reed, James, I, 229; II, 119, 340, 345
Reid, Edith Gittings, I, 39n., 219n., 220, 316; II, 71
Reinsch, Paul S., II, 127–28
Renick, Edward, I, 31, 47
Reparations Commission of the Paris Peace Conference, II, 306n., 335n., 346
Republican party, in New Jersey, 1910, I, 163, 165–68, 182, 184–85, 187, 189, 192; election of 1912, I, 222–23, 226; election of 1914, I, 414–15; election of 1916, II, 55, 61–65; election of 1918, II, 202–204; election of 1920, II, 403
Rhoads, Dr. James E., I, 45, 50n.
Robins, Raymond, II, 154n., 172
Robinson, Henry M., II, 283n., 396n.
Rogers, H. H., I, 100
Roosevelt, Franklin D., I, 259, 270n., 277n., 354; II, 41, 92, 109–10, 268, 355, 402, 403n., 414
Roosevelt, Theodore, I, 53n., 67, 147–48,

200–201, 204, 222–23, 226, 239–42, 245, 249–51, 253, 271–72, 278, 284, 288, 294, 331n., 341, 352n., 354, 378, 387–88, 414; II, 25n., 37n., 41, 55, 78, 102–104, 136n., 160, 200, 202, 209n., 216, 231, 234, 238n., 286
Root, Elihu, I, 318, 338, 363, 388, 390, 414, 423; II, 137–38, 139n., 179, 209n., 211, 238n., 288n., 301, 304, 342, 347, 352, 378, 392–93
Rublee, George, I, 336n.
Rural Credits Association, II, 51
Rural Credits Commission, I, 339
Russell, Charles Edward, II, 138n.
Ryan, Thomas F., I, 214–15, 229, 289n.

Sato, Aimaro, II, 129
Sayre, Francis B., I, 310, 416; II, 231n.
Sayre, Jessie Wilson (Mrs. Francis B.), I, 322, 393, 416; II, 123, 205, 276. *See also* Wilson, Jessie.
Scheidemann. Philipp, II, 320
Scott, Hugh L., I, 433; II, 102n., 105
Scudder, Horace, I, 49
Sedgwick, Ellery, II, 98
Seibold, Louis, II, 399
Selective Service Act, II, 106n., 107
Sells, Cato, I, 198n.
"separation of powers," the doctrine of, I, 293
"Seven Sisters Acts," I, 257
Seventeenth Amendment, I, 412
Seymour, Charles, I, 199n.; II, 309n.
Sharp, William B., I, 348
Sherman Anti-trust Act, I, 301, 328, 330
Shipping Act, II, 120
Ship Registry Act, I, 410n.
Shouse, Jouette, II, 398
Simmons, Furnifold M., I, 298; II, 390
Sims, William S., II, 109–10, 229
Sisson, Edgar, II, 146–47, 152, 154, 263
Sloane, William M., I, 52, 85
Smith, Alfred E., II, 63, 337
Smith, James, Jr., I, 143–44, 151–56, 158, 159, 162, 164, 165, 168–79, 184, 187, 190, 192, 225, 242n.
Smith, Lucy and Mary, I, 194, 396, 402
Smuts, Jan Christian, II, 231–32, 245, 246n., 247, 250, 256, 293, 305, 321, 336, 384, 407, 422
Sonnino, Baron Sidney, II, 195, 332
Southern Presbyterian Church, I, 7, 16n., 31, 44, 59
Southern Society of New York, I, 289
Spring Rice, Sir Cecil, I, 366, 368n., 405; II, 4n., 8, 31n., 131
Stanley, Augustus O., I, 330
Steed, Wickham, II, 321
Steffens, Lincoln, II, 290, 330

Stettinius, Edward R., II, 162
Stevens, Edwin A., I, 144, 145n.
Stewart, John A., I, 64n., 160
Stockbridge, Frank P., I, 209n.
Stockholm Conference, II, 139n.
Stone, William J., I, 385, 407n.; II, 48, 78, 91
Sullivan, Roger, I, 224, 232n., 233
Sundry Civil Appropriation Bill of 1913, I, 328–29, 331, 334
Sun Yat-sen, I, 351n.
Supreme Economic Council, II, 292n., 335
Supreme War Council, II, 135–36, 150, 166, 187, 191, 212, 240–41, 292n.
Sussex, the, II, 32–33, 34n., 35–36, 47, 84
Swann, Mrs. Josephine T., I, 117
Swanson, Claude A., II, 272
Sweetser, Arthur, II, 249n., 283
Swem, Charles, II, 280, 374, 378, 407
Swope, Herbert Bayard, I, 270n.

Taft, William Howard, I, 201, 210, 220, 226, 241, 250, 253, 263, 272, 276, 278, 282–83, 285, 288, 291–92, 294, 321, 328, 342, 346n., 388, 414; II, 35, 37, 120n., 150n., 163n., 167, 203, 211, 268, 286, 288, 300–301, 304, 340n., 345, 402
Taggart, Tom, I, 234
Talcott, Charles, I, 21, 47
Tammany Hall, I, 227, 231, 235, 242n., 338, 413
Tardieu, André, II, 280n., 298n.
Tariff commission, II, 57
Tarnowski, Count Adam, II, 87
Taussig, Frank W., II, 57
Taylor, James H., I, 285n.
The Hague Conventions, I, 377; II, 1
Thomas, Martha Carey, I, 45, 47
Thomas, Norman, II, 113n.
Thompson, William J., I, 69, 143, 156
Thwing, C. F., I, 212n.
Tillman, Benjamin R., I, 339n.
Tinoco, Federico A., II, 125n.
Todd, George Carroll, II, 275n.
Toy, Nancy, I, 417, 421; II, 17
Trading-with-the-Enemy Act, II, 112n.
Treaty of London, II, 308–12, 317
Trotsky, Leon, II, 93, 143–44, 146n., 152–53, 154n., 290
Tumulty, Joseph Patrick, I, 157, 158, 169, 174, 177–79, 181, 184, 188–91, 193, 195, 203, 208, 216, 225, 228, 230, 232, 234, 257, 270n., 272, 276–79, 282, 284, 294, 305, 311, 332, 348, 373, 376n., 383n., 390–91, 394–95, 412–13, 416, 435, 439; II, 15–17, 24, 28, 64–65, 71, 82, 91, 97, 103–104, 106n., 121, 159, 182, 186–87, 198, 201, 205–206, 215, 221, 225, 233, 244, 265,

274, 275n., 277, 286, 291n., 298, 311n., 314, 322n., 326, 336, 338, 348, 355–57, 359n., 360, 362, 366–67, 369–71, 373, 375–78, 380, 387, 390, 399, 401n., 402n., 403n., 414, 422
Turner, Frederick J., I, 64, 65n., 145, 204; II, 247
Twain, Mark, I, 68, 70, 100
Tyrrell, Sir William, I, 366–68, 377, 388n.

Underwood, Oscar W., I, 204, 209, 212, 217n., 219, 224, 233–35, 294–95, 333, 391, 413
Underwood-Simmons Act, I, 299
Union of Democratic Control, II, 137
U. S. Chamber of Commerce, I, 318
U. S. Shipping Board, II, 86, 120, 212, 292n., 397
University of Virginia, I, 24–28, 63
Untermyer, Samuel, I, 306, 313
U'Ren, William S., I, 182n., 206

Vanderlip, Frank A., I, 118, 317
Van Dyke, Henry, I, 105n., 109, 110, 111, 218–19, 347n.
Van Dyke, Paul, I, 128
Versailles, Treaty of, II, 319–21, 328–34, 336, 339–54, 384–94, 416
Victor Emmanuel III, King of Italy, II, 198
Villa, Francisco, I, 379; II, 46, 50
Villard, Oswald Garrison, I, 113n., 115n., 150, 175, 210, 273, 325; II, 42, 106n.

Wallace, Hugh C., I, 272
Walsh, Frank P., II, 326, 336n.
Warburg, Paul M., I, 300, 304, 306, 317
War Cabinet, II, 191
Ward, Humphry, I, 70
War Finance Corporation, II, 275n.
War Industries Board, II, 161–62, 213
Warren, Charles, II, 288n.
War Trade Board, II, 113n.
Washington, Booker T., I, 68
Watson, James, II, 348
Watterson, Henry, I, 152–53, 173, 214–16, 403n.
Webb, Beatrice, I, 83
Webb Bill, II, 57
Welles, Harriet Woodrow, I, 29, 441; II, 369
Wescott, John W., I, 156–57, 172, 200, 229–30
Wesleyan College, I, 50–52
West, Andrew F., I, 66, 84, 85, 86, 88, 98, 102, 104, 105, 107, 108, 109, 110, 116, 118, 120, 121, 122, 124, 125, 126, 128, 131, 140, 141, 160, 195, 220; II, 354
Western Herald and Gazette, I, 4
White, Edward D., I, 263; II, 99

White, Henry, II, 141n., 212, 237–38, 254, 272n., 279, 286

White, William Allen, I, 191n.

Wilhelm II (Emperor of Germany), I, 398, 398n., 399; II, 20n., 23, 28n., 30n., 69, 146, 184, 192, 196, 306

Williams, John Sharp, I, 315n.; II, 189

Williamson, Edgar R., I, 156

Williamson, Isabella, I, 5

Williamson, Marion, I, 5

Willis, H. Parker, I, 301–303

Wilson, Anne Adams, I, 4

Wilson, Edith Bolling, I, 426–42; II, 19, 33, 62, 64–65, 68n., 70–71, 78, 97–98, 100, 120, 122–23, 165, 177, 181, 183, 197–98, 202, 209, 223, 226, 232, 237–38, 254, 260, 270, 279, 281, 285, 296, 298, 318, 321, 327, 331–32, 344, 365, 368–69, 373–82, 385–87, 390–91, 393, 395, 398, 399n., 409, 412–14, 417–18, 420–21

Wilson, Eleanor, I, 75, 194, 226. *See also* McAdoo, Eleanor Wilson.

Wilson, Ellen Axson, I, 67, 70–76, 78, 80, 81, 82, 83, 88, 94, 95, 99, 122, 129, 152, 159, 181, 194, 202–203, 215–17, 224, 228, 235, 250–56, 262, 264, 277, 283–84, 294, 297, 309, 310, 322, 324–26, 346, 358–59, 367, 376n., 394–96, 400–402, 413, 418, 426, 431, 439, 439n.; II, 19, 220, 367–68, 413, 420, 422. *See also* Axson, Ellen Louise.

Wilson, Henry Lane, I, 358–61

Wilson, Huntington, I, 351

Wilson, James, I, 4, 19, 259, 282n.

Wilson, Jeanie, I, 3, 4, 35

Wilson, Jessie, I, 256, 283, 310, 322. *See also* Sayre, Jessie Wilson.

Wilson, John, II, 9

Wilson, Joseph R., I, 8n., 15, 18, 30n., 35, 36, 43n., 45, 280n., 282; II, 84, 209, 214, 360

Wilson, Dr. Joseph Ruggles, I, 2, 4, 7–16, 40n., 46, 49, 50, 58, 64, 67, 79–81, 94, 427

Wilson, Margaret, I, 254n., 283, 346, 393, 402, 433–34; II, 214, 324, 338, 373–74, 387

Wilson, Thomas Woodrow:
birth, I, 3; boyhood, I, 7; taught by his father, I, 8–10, 18; a student at Davidson College, I, 14, 15; political ambition, I, 16, 25, 41, 44, 47–49, 145–48, 151–53; an undergraduate at the College of New Jersey, Princeton, N.J., I, 17–23; influenced by English parliamentarians and "our kinship with England," I, 15, 19, 21–22, 25–26, 33, 44, 48; a leader in debating and oratory, I, 19, 22, 24–26, 54–55; his reading, I, 21–22, 24, 28, 43, 108; a law student at the University of Virginia, I, 23–28; studies law at home, I, 27; woos Harriet Woodrow, I, 29–31; passes bar examination, I, 28; practices law at Atlanta, I, 31–34; pleads before federal tariff commissioners, I, 32–33; studies at the Johns Hopkins University and becomes a Doctor of Philosophy, I, 35, 39, 40, 42–45; falls in love with Ellen Louise Axson, I, 34–41; married to Ellen Louise Axson at Savannah, June 24, 1885, I, 41; teaches girls at Bryn Mawr College, I, 45–50; aspires to write a "Philosophy of Politics," I, 49, 406; teaches at Wesleyan College, I, 50–52; a professor at Princeton, I, 52–60; president of Princeton University, I, 66–160; his writing habits and ambitions, I, 53–54, 67, 72–73, 77; II, 412–13; travels in Europe, I, 73, 81, 98, 117; lifts the academic standards, I, 86–92; leads in revising the course of study, I, 88–89; develops the preceptorial system, I, 89–92; as a solicitor of university funds, I, 90–91; interest in scientific education, I, 62, 93; makes plans for Princeton's landscape and architecture, I, 93; interest in intercollegiate athletics, I, 57, 95; relations with Princeton alumni, I, 95–97; visits Bermuda, I, 99–101, 113, 128, 288; efforts to replace the Princeton clubs with residential quadrangles, I, 102–115; his ideals for the instruction of graduate students, I, 116–19; his controversy with Dean West, I, 116–42; spends summers at Old Lyme, Conn., I, 120, 152; senses the challenge of an industrial age, I, 132–39; a potential political candidate for the Democratic party, I, 128, 142–56; appointed to the New Jersey Commission on Uniform State Laws, I, 144; drafts a conservative "credo," I, 146n.; attitude toward labor and capital in 1909, I, 148–50, 155–56; agrees to run for the governorship of New Jersey, I, 151–54; attitude toward liquor control, I, 154, 164–65; nominated for the governorship, I, 156–57; as political campaigner in 1910, I, 162–69; opposes the candidacy of James Smith, Jr., for the U.S. Senate, I, 171–79; invites Joseph P. Tumulty to serve as his secretary, I, 177; Governor of New Jersey, I, 179–99; secures reform legislation in N.J., I, 182–91; views on the initiative, referendum, and recall, I, 182n., 204–205, 207; campaigns for the presidential nomination, I, 192, 200–25; meets Edward M. House and exchanges confidences with him, I, 198–99; nominated for the Presidency at Baltimore, I, 226–34; Democratic candidate for the Presidency, I, 235–51; seeks counsel from Brandeis, I, 243–44; elected

to the Presidency, I, 251–53; President-
elect, I, 254–61; leaves Princeton for the
White House, I, 260–61; inaugurated as
28th President of the U. S., I, 262–66; his
amazement at the outbreak of war in
Europe, I, 399–400; travels to Rome, Ga.,
to attend Ellen Wilson's funeral, I, 400;
his marriage to Edith Bolling Galt, I, 426–
42; nominated for the Presidency, II, 52–
54; re-elected, II, 64–65; his War Cabinet, II, 163–64; appeals for a Democratic Congress, II, 201–203; attends the
Paris Peace Conference: first trip, II, 216–
67, second trip, 277–337; tours the West in
behalf of the Treaty of Versailles, II, 359–
73; stricken by a thrombosis, II, 373; an
invalid in the White House, II, 373–409;
awarded the Nobel Peace Prize, II, 407;
resides on S Street, II, 410–22; death, II,
421

ADDRESSES OF: oration on Bright at the University of Virginia, I, 25; "Leaders of
Men," I, 48–49; speech before the International Congress of Education, 1893, I, 60;
"Princeton in the Nation's Service," delivered at the Princeton Sesquicentennial,
I, 63; "Princeton for the Nation's Service,"
inaugural address, 1902, I, 68–69, 116,
378; speech to Princeton alumni in New
York, Dec., 1902, I, 90; to the western
alumni of Princeton at Cleveland, 1906, I,
97; baccalaureate, 1907, I, 114; at the Mc-
Cormick Theological Seminary at Chicago,
1909, I, 121; to Princeton alumni, 1910, I,
129–30; "That Pittsburgh Speech," I, 134–
39, 151; to the National Democratic Club
of New York, 1908, I, 135; to the American Bankers' Association in 1908 and 1910,
I, 135; to the Virginia Bar Association in
1897, I, 135; baccalaureate, 1910, I, 141;
"True Patriotism," I, 149; "Ideals of Public
Life," I, 149; "Law or Personal Power," I,
149; to a gathering of reformers, Jan.,
1910, I, 150; to Democrats at Elizabeth,
N. J., I, 150–51; "Unprofitable Servants," I,
155; accepting the Democratic nomination
for Governor of New Jersey, I, 156–58; at
the Cooper Union, I, 164; in the campaign
for the New Jersey governorship, I, 163–69;
against the senatorial candidacy of James
Smith, Jr., I, 177–78; inaugural address
at Trenton, N. J., I, 179–80, 186; to the
National Democratic Club, I, 200; to the
Southern Commercial Congress, on "The
Citizen and the State," I, 200–201; at
Norfolk, Va., 1911, I, 201; at Kansas City,
Mo., May, 1911, I, 204, 205; at Denver,
on the King James version of the Bible, I,
205–206; on the Pacific Coast, 1911, I,
207; to the Pennsylvania Federation of
Democratic Clubs, 1911, I, 210; in Texas,
1911, I, 211; at the Jackson Day dinner at
Washington, 1912, I, 217–18; to periodical
publishers at Philadelphia, 1912, I, 222;
at Des Moines, 1912, I, 223; at Brooklyn,
1912, I, 223; in acceptance of the nomination for the Presidency, 1912, I, 237–39;
to the New York Press Club, 1912, I, 245;
at Scranton, Pa., 1912, I, 246; in New
England, 1912, I, 246; at Indianapolis,
1912, I, 248; in the closing days of the
campaign of 1912, I, 249–51; farewell to
his neighbors at Princeton, I, 261; inaugural as 28th President of the U. S., I,
264–65, 290, 332; to the Southern Society of New York, 1912, I, 289; at Staunton, Va., in his father's church, 1912, I,
289; before Commercial Club of Chicago,
1913, I, 290; to the Congress, on regulation of trusts, I, 332, 336; to the National
Press Club, 1914, I, 337; to the Congress,
annual address, 1914, I, 341; on discrimination against American Jews in Russia,
1911, I, 346n.; to the Congress on Mexican
policy, I, 364, 372; to the Southern Commercial Congress at Mobile, I, 380–81, II,
36; to the Pan-American Scientific Congress, I, 385–86; to the Congress on repeal
of Panama Canal tolls exemption, I, 389;
"too proud to fight," at Philadelphia, May
10, 1915, II, 15; to the National Press Club,
May 15, 1916, II, 35–36; to the League to
Enforce Peace, May 27, 1916, II, 37–40; at
the Manhattan Club, N. Y., Nov. 4, 1915,
II, 42; third annual message to Congress,
Dec. 7, 1915, II, 43; speeches on preparedness, 1916, II, 43–44; speech accepting the presidential nomination, Sept.
2, 1916, II, 58–59; speeches of the 1916
campaign, II, 60–63; on "a scientific peace,"
Jan. 22, 1917, II, 78–80; speech to the Congress on arming merchant ships, Feb. 26,
1917, II, 89–90; second inaugural, March
5, 1917, II, 91–92; war message, April 2,
1917, II, 97–100; to the Atlantic fleet,
August 11, 1917, II, 111; at the Washington Monument, June 14, 1917, II, 139–40;
to the A.F. of L., Buffalo, N. Y., Nov. 12,
1917, II, 142–43; annual address to Congress, Dec. 4, 1917, II, 144–45, 157; Fourteen Points speech, Jan. 8, 1918, II, 146–
53; Third Liberty Loan, at Baltimore, Md.,
April 6, 1918, II, 168; at Mt. Vernon,
July 4, 1918, II, 174–75; Fourth Liberty
Loan, at New York, Sept. 27, 1918, II, 182;
to the Congress, Nov. 11, 1918, II, 197–98;
annual address to the Congress, Dec. 2,

1918, II, 215; response to Poincaré's welcome, Dec. 14, 1918, II, 222–24; greetings to the U. S. soldiers, Dec. 25, 1918, II, 225; at the University of Paris, Dec. 21, 1918, II, 227; at the Guildhall, London, Dec. 28, 1918, II, 228; at the Mansion House, London, Dec. 28, 1918, II, 229; at Carlisle, England, Dec. 29, 1918, II, 229; at Manchester, England, II, 230; to the Paris Peace Conference, Jan. 25, 1919, II, 245–46, Feb. 14, 1919, 259–60; at Boston, Feb. 24, 1919, II, 269; at New York, March 4, 1919, II, 276–77; to the Commission on the League of Nations, April 10, 1919, II, 302; at the Paris Peace Conference in behalf of the Covenant, April 28, 1919, II, 304; at Suresnes Cemetery, May 30, 1919, II, 327; in behalf of the Treaty of Versailles, in the West, Sept., 1919, II, 362–70; radio talk on "The High Significance of Armistice Day," Nov. 10, 1923, II, 418–19

CABINET OF: as President, I, 258, 266–76, 292, 303, 322–23, 330–31, 368n., 393n., 412–14, 418, 421; II, 19, 33, 44–46, 65–66, 83–84, 88, 94–97, 106, 110, 112, 116, 190, 192, 357, 376–77, 395

FOREIGN POLICY OF: American Commission to Negotiate Peace, II, 211–12, 236–38, 240, 359; arbitration, I, 374, 377–79, 397–99; II, 8–11, 17, 179, 287, 385; Armistice of 1918, the, and pre-Armistice Agreement, II, 184–98, 244, 252, 293, 295, 299, 320, 329; colonialism, II, 194, 217, 219, 240, 247–51, 307, 308; credits to belligerents, I, 412; II, 2–3, 72–73, 114–15, 132–34; diplomatic appointments, I, 346–48; II, 93; disarmament, I, 378, 398; II, 8n., 29, 210–11, 217, 236, 252, 325, 416; inter-Allied conferences, American participation in, II, 133–36; League of Nations, I, 49, 50; II, 25–27, 29, 36–40, 74–75, 77, 79, 149–50, 175, 178–80, 183, 218–19, 227–28, 231–32, 238–40, 245–46, 255–60, 269–73, 276–79, 281, 283–89, 300–306, 315–17, 325–27, 332–34, 336–55, 359, 362–63, 366, 383–87, 390–94, 403–404, 416, 420; mandates, see "colonialism"; mediation between belligerents, I, 404; II, 8–11, 26–40, 71–81, 87, 129–30; neutrality, I, 403–408; II, 1–24, 54, 62, 67, 76–77, 125–26, 133, 410; "new diplomacy, the," II, 129–31, 137–56, 186–87, 197, 207, 311; Panama Canal tolls exemption, repeal of, I, 388–91; Pan-American pact, I, 384–86; peacemaking, II, 190–91, 193, 198, 205–12, 215–337, 394, 410; presidential trips abroad, I, 397; II, 205–208; punishment of war criminals, II, 306–307; reciprocity in trade, I, 345n; II, 155,

335; relations with the Senate's Committee on Foreign Relations, I, 349, 363, 370, 372, 384–85, 388, 389, 390, 407; II, 48, 78, 91, 199, 209–10, 270, 278, 340, 346–54, 359, 366, 377–79, 384–87, 388–93, 405; relief and reconstruction in Europe, II, 212–13, 234–35, 252, 283, 292n., 324–25, 405–406; reparations for war damage, II, 196, 240, 283, 293–94, 299, 306, 328, 335, 343–45, 406; representation of nations at the Paris Peace Conference, II, 240–42, 256n., 259n.; secrecy in negotiations at Paris, II, 241–44, 256; secret treaties, II, 129–31, 146, 148, 249, 307–15, 323, 351–52; self-determination, II, 149, 152, 156, 174, 188–89, 193, 218, 240, 256, 268, 280, 284–85, 294–95, 310, 323; the "veto" in the League of Nations Council, II, 304; visions of world peace, I, 343–45, 406–407; II, 10–11, 25–40, 59, 62, 155–56, 174–75, 220, 223, 229–30, 254; war aims, II, 144–56, 174–75, 181–83; war trade, II, 3–7, 11n., 12

FOREIGN POLICY TOWARD: Armenia, II, 400n.; Austria-Hungary, II, 87, 99, 145, 149, 180–81, 189–90, 192, 218, 324–25, 327; British Empire, the, II, 248–51, 325; China, I, 346, 349–52; II, 126–29, 173, 219, 300, 314–16, 330–31; Colombia, I, 387–88; Czechoslovakia, II, 170–72, 189–90; Dominican Republic, the, I, 382–83; Far East, the, I, 345n., 346, 349; France, II, 107, 136, 149, 170, 179–80, 195–96, 223–25, 235, 239, 241, 243, 251, 254–255, 257–58, 262, 279–80, 287–89, 292–95, 299–300, 303–304, 323, 324, 394; Germany, I, 397–99, 418; II, 1, 7–24, 30, 32–34, 69–70, 72–76, 81–85, 88–90, 94, 98–100, 139–42, 184–87, 218, 224, 240–41, 252, 262, 299–300, 308, 318–20, 330; Great Britain, I, 345, 336–68, 388–91, 396–97, 404–405, 409–10, 418; II, 1–13, 25–32, 67–69, 72–76, 109–111, 129–36, 150–51, 171, 179–80, 194–96, 217, 228–32, 262–67, 292–94, 324, 329–30, 381, 406; Haiti, I, 383; Ireland, II, 131, 277, 326; Italy, II, 232–34, 255–56, 308–13, 372; Japan, I, 352–57; II, 126–29, 169–73, 250, 258, 264, 303, 313–16, 350; Latin America, I, 356–57, 380–81, 384–92; II, 53, 59, 125–26, 173, 406; Mexico, I, 346, 358–76; II, 46, 50, 53, 59, 61, 89, 125, 378–79, 406; Nicaragua, I, 381–82; Palestine, II, 326–27; Poland, II, 108, 218, 329; Russia, I, 344, 346; II, 93–94, 99, 137–40, 142–49, 152–54, 169–73, 251, 262–67, 289–92, 316–17, 363, 381, 405–406; Serbia and Yugoslavia, II, 149, 189, 242, 308–11; Syria, II, 307–308; Turkey, II, 189, 308

HEALTH OF: I, 27, 72, 81, 96, 98, 131, 194,

242, 246, 255, 283, 285, 311, 312, 315–16, 317–18, 322, 396, 416, 434; II, 33, 71, 73, 92, 98, 236, 296–97, 318, 323, 344, 362, 365–92, 398–99, 408–409, 410, 412–21

HIS POLICIES AS PRESIDENTIAL CANDIDATE AND PRESIDENT ON: agriculture, I, 291, 409, 422; II, 50–51, 62; appointments, I, 188, 254, 267, 279–82, 319–20; II, 57, 396, 407; arming merchant ships, II, 47–49; banking, I, 239, 289–91, 300–309, 313–21, 339–40; II, 50–51; classless society, a, I, 242; II, 62, 414; commission rule, I, 244; II, 57, 213; conservation, I, 239n., 272, 291, 339, 421; II, 57–58; executive offices, I, 276–79; foreign affairs, see Woodrow Wilson, foreign policy of; immigration, I, 219–20, 422; II, 92–93; industry, I, 327–41; II, 57, 60, 62, 116–17, 158–62, 176, 213, 355–58, 378n., 395, 397; labor, I, 239, 244, 246, 328, 334, 340; II, 51, 56–57, 59, 60, 62, 93, 122, 163–64, 355–58, 364–65, 395, 399, at the Paris Peace Conference, II, 220, 224, 311n., 316, 328; lobbying, I, 294, 296–97, 406–407, 423; party finance, I, 241–42; II, 52; Philippine independence, I, 239, 345–46, 355n., 421; II, 44–45; police strikes, II, 358, 363–64; political leadership, I, 250–51, 266, 280–82, 287, 321, 331–36, 412–14; II, 41, 52–53, 65–66, 200–204, 208–10, 336, 353, 388–409, 414–15, 419–20, at the Paris Peace Conference, II, 236, 240, 243, 245–46, 248–54, 259–60, 274; preparedness, I, 422; II, 41–49, 77, 86–88; Presidency, the, I, 287, 289; II, 52, 63–64, 121, 398–402, 410; press relations, I, 222, 233, 244–45, 255, 258, 277–78, 375; II, 113–14, 164, 169, 219, 348, 365, 369–79, at the Paris Peace Conference, II, 243–44, 253, 284, 289, 311n., 316, 318, 330; prohibition, II, 356n., 397; public works program, I, 339; race relations, I, 325, 327; relations with Congress, I, 291–99, 309, 313–18, 415, 421–25; II, 43, 46–51, 56–57, 89–91, 98, 105–106, 114, 118–19, 121, 159–61, 188, 199, 204, 215–17, 270–79, 305, 326, 335, 336, 338–54, 356, 359, 376–79, 386, 388–94, 396, 407, 409; shipping, I, 239n., 410–12, 422–25; II, 88, 212–13; Supreme Court, the, II, 57; tariff, I, 211, 238, 244, 251, 291–99; II, 57, 335, 407; taxation, I, 189, 202, 295, 412; II, 50, 115; transportation, see industry; trust and monopoly regulation, I, 238–39, 242–46, 249n., 251, 327–36; II, 213–14; warmaking, II, 96–97, 101–122, 131–36, 157–68, 184, 213–14; woman suffrage, I, 326–27; II, 199–200, 397

RELIGION OF: I, 10, 12, 13, 20, 15–16, 40–41, 50, 67, 87, 95, 114–15, 176, 177, 189, 205–206, 252, 285n., 312–13, 417; II, 1, 4, 97, 106, 122, 126–27, 182–83, 198, 221, 253, 334, 339, 373, 413, 416, 421–22

WORKS OF: essays at Princeton, I, 22; "Cabinet Government in the U. S." I, 22; essay on Gladstone, I, 25–26; article on convict labor, I, 32; "Committee or Cabinet Government," I, 32; Congressional Government, I, 41–43, 237, 343n.; "The Study of Administration," I, 47n.; review of Bryce's American Commonwealth, I, 48; An Old Master and Other Political Essays, I, 48n.; The State, I, 49–50, 149, 182n., 288; "A Calendar of Great Americans," I, 53; Mere Literature, I, 54n., 147; On Being Human, I, 54n.; "Of the Study of Politics," I, 60n.; Division and Reunion, I, 63; George Washington, I, 64; A History of the American People, I, 65, 143, 219, 324n., 343n., 431; II, 412; "A Wit and a Seer," I, 89n.; "What is a College For?" I, 121; Constitutional Government in the U.S., I, 147n., 280, 287–88; "Leaders of Men," I, 48–49, 326; II, 199, 253, 274; The New Freedom, I, 288; "Freemen Need No Guardians," I, 290n.; "Democracy and Efficiency," I, 386–87n.; "The Road away from Revolution," II, 417–18

Wilson, William B., I, 270, 274, 329n., 340; II, 66n., 93, 275
Wise, Stephen S., II, 326
Wiseman, Sir William, II, 129, 130n., 131–34, 146, 173, 179, 180n., 189, 194, 196, 213, 239n., 256, 309n., 324n., 343–44
Wittpenn, Otto, I, 154–55
Wood, Leonard, I, 354; II, 42, 77, 103–104, 136n., 157n., 167, 172n.
Woodrow, Fitz William McMaster, I, 236n., 282n.
Woodrow, James, I, 12, 35, 59, 80, 112, 114, 131; II, 360
Woodrow, Mrs. James, I, 208; II, 360n.
"Woodrow, Mrs. Wilson," I, 154n.
Woodrow, Thomas, I, 5, 30, 346
Woodrow, Thomas, Jr., I, 5, 13; II, 229
Woods, Hiram, I, 129, 216, 256, 439
Woolley, Robert W., II, 54n., 400
Wyman, Isaac C., I, 140

Yates, Mr. and Mrs. Fred, I, 99, 117, 170
Yuan Shih-kai, I, 352

Zimmermann, A., II, 8, 10, 11n., 83, 89
Zimmermann telegram, II, 89–90, 125